New coverage of ethics and global happenings digs deep into important media issues such as election fraud through social media, the #MeToo movement across the media industries, politics reviving interest in several classic novels, underrepresentation of female artists at the Grammys, augmented reality gaming and *Pokémon Go*, how China's dominant media corporations rival America's, news bias around the globe, and much more.

A brand-new extended case study has readers analyze Facebook data breaches and asks the question, "Can we trust Facebook with our personal data?" Engage in the critical process of media literacy through the book's five-step critical process.

Thoroughly updated facts and figures that reflect the new economic and social realities of the current media landscape.

The critical and cultural perspective and engaging media stories tie all of this material together, addressing the importance of convergence, the digital turn, history, and media literacy.

Media & Culture respects students' opinions while challenging them to take more responsibility and to be accountable for their media choices. This text is essential for professors who are truly committed to teaching students how to understand the media.

Drew Jacobs, *Camden County College*

The critical perspective has enlightened the perspective of all of us who study media, and Campbell has the power to infect students with his love of the subject.

Roger Desmond, *University of Hartford*

I love *Media & Culture*! I have used it since the first edition. *Media & Culture* integrates the history of a particular medium or media concept with the culture, economics, and technological advances of the time. But more than that, the authors are explicit in their philosophy that media and culture cannot be separated.

Deborah Larson, *Missouri State University*

The book comprehensively covers relevant material for an introductory mass communication text in an interactive and adaptive way for students in an online learning environment.

Lisa Heller Boragine, *Cape Cod Community College*

MEDIA & CULTURE
Mass Communication in a Digital Age

Twelfth Edition

Richard Campbell
Miami University

Christopher R. Martin
University of Northern Iowa

Bettina Fabos
University of Northern Iowa

bedford/st.martin's
Macmillan Learning
Boston | New York

"WE ARE NOT ALONE."
For my family—Reese, Chris, Caitlin, and Dianna

"YOU MAY SAY I'M A DREAMER, BUT I'M NOT THE ONLY ONE."
For our daughters—Olivia and Sabine

For Bedford/St. Martin's

Vice President, Editorial, Macmillan Learning Humanities: Edwin Hill
Senior Program Director for Communication and College Success: Erika Gutierrez
Senior Development Manager: Susan McLaughlin
Developmental Editor: Kate George
Senior Content Project Manager: Harold Chester
Senior Media Editor: Tom Kane
Media Project Manager: Sarah O'Connor Kepes
Senior Workflow Project Manager: Jennifer Wetzel
Marketing Manager: Amy Haines
Assistant Editor: Kimberly Roberts
Copy Editor: Jamie Thaman
Photo Researcher: Brittani Morgan, Lumina Datamatics, Inc.
Permissions Associate: Allison Ziebka
Permissions Editor: Angela Boehler
Permissions Manager: Kalina Ingham
Director of Design, Content Management: Diana Blume
Text Design: Maureen McCutcheon
Cover Design: William Boardman
Cover Image: Paul & Paveena Mckenzie/Getty Images
Composition: Lumina Datamatics, Inc.
Printing and Binding: Transcontinental Printing

Printed in Canada.

1   2   3   4   5   6   23   22   21   20   19   18

For information, write: Bedford/St. Martin's, 75 Arlington Street, Boston, MA 02116
    (617-399-4000)

ISBN 978-1-319-10285-2 (Paperback)
ISBN 978-1-319-10471-9 (Loose-leaf Edition)

Acknowledgments
Art acknowledgments and copyrights appear on the same page as the art selections they cover.

About the Authors

RICHARD CAMPBELL, founder and former chair of the Department of Media, Journalism and Film at Miami University, is the author of *"60 Minutes" and the News: A Mythology for Middle America* (1991) and coauthor of *Cracked Coverage: Television News, the Anti-Cocaine Crusade, and the Reagan Legacy* (1994). Campbell has written for numerous publications, including *Columbia Journalism Review, Journal of Communication*, and *Media Studies Journal*, and he is on the editorial boards of *Critical Studies in Mass Communication* and *Television Quarterly*. He also serves on the board of directors for Cincinnati Public Radio. He holds a Ph.D. from Northwestern University and has also taught at the University of Wisconsin–Milwaukee, Mount Mary College, the University of Michigan, and Middle Tennessee State University.

Dianna Campbell

CHRISTOPHER R. MARTIN is a professor of communication studies and digital journalism at the University of Northern Iowa and author of the forthcoming *The Invisible Worker: How the News Media Lost Sight of the American Working Class* (Cornell University Press) and *Framed! Labor and the Corporate Media* (Cornell University Press). He has written articles and reviews on journalism, televised sports, the Internet, and labor for several publications, including *Communication Research, Journal of Communication, Journal of Communication Inquiry, Labor Studies Journal, Culture, Sport, and Society*, and *Perspectives on Politics*. He is also on the editorial board of the *Journal of Communication Inquiry*. Martin holds a Ph.D. from the University of Michigan and has also taught at Miami University.

Bettina Fabos

BETTINA FABOS is a professor of visual communication and interactive digital studies at the University of Northern Iowa. She is the executive producer of the interactive web photo history *Proud and Torn: A Visual Memoir of Hungarian History* (proudandtorn.com); the cofounder of a public archive of Iowa family snapshots, Fortepan Iowa (fortepan.us); and a champion of the Creative Commons. Fabos has also written extensively about critical media literacy, Internet commercialization, the role of the Internet in education, and media representations of popular culture. Her work has been published in *Visual Communication Quarterly, Library Trends, Review of Educational Research*, and *Harvard Educational Review*. Fabos has also taught at Miami University and has a Ph.D. from the University of Iowa.

Christopher Martin

Brief Contents

1   Mass Communication: A Critical Approach   *3*

PART 1: DIGITAL MEDIA AND CONVERGENCE   32

2   The Internet, Digital Media, and Media Convergence   *35*
3   Digital Gaming and the Media Playground   *63*

PART 2: SOUNDS AND IMAGES   92

4   Sound Recording and Popular Music   *95*
5   Popular Radio and the Origins of Broadcasting   *127*
6   Television and Cable: The Power of Visual Culture   *161*
7   Movies and the Impact of Images   *199*

PART 3: WORDS AND PICTURES   232

8   Newspapers: The Rise and Decline of Modern Journalism   *235*
9   Magazines in the Age of Specialization   *271*
10   Books and the Power of Print   *299*

PART 4: THE BUSINESS OF MASS MEDIA   324

11   Advertising and Commercial Culture   *327*
12   Public Relations and Framing the Message   *361*
13   Media Economics and the Global Marketplace   *387*

PART 5: DEMOCRATIC EXPRESSION AND THE MASS MEDIA   420

14   The Culture of Journalism: Values, Ethics, and Democracy   *423*
15   Media Effects and Cultural Approaches to Research   *455*
16   Legal Controls and Freedom of Expression   *483*

EXTENDED CASE STUDY: Can We Trust Facebook with Our Personal Data?   *511*

Preface

This is an exciting and tumultuous time in the media. Developing an understanding of mass communication and becoming a critical consumer of the media is vitally important, especially now as the media are under siege and the lines between fact and fiction are being continuously blurred. *Media & Culture* reaches students where they are and puts the media industries into perspective both historically and culturally, helping students become more informed citizens who use critical thinking and media literacy skills in their daily lives, even as they are bombarded by information, in a variety of ways and via a variety of media.

While today's students have integrated digital media into their daily lives, they may not understand how the media evolved to this point; how technology converges text, audio, and visual media; and what all these developments mean. This is why we believe the critical and cultural perspectives at the core of *Media & Culture*'s approach are more important than ever. *Media & Culture* pulls back the curtain to show students how the media really work—from the roots and economics of each media industry to the implications of today's consolidated media ownership to how these industries have changed in our digital world. By looking at the full history of media through a critical lens, students will leave this course with a better understanding of the complex relationship between the mass media and our shared culture.

Throughout the twelfth edition, *Media & Culture* digs deeper than ever before into the worldwide reach and ethical implications of today's media by highlighting global issues, such as foreign interference in social media and the effect of international box-office revenue on decisions made by the domestic film industry, and ethical considerations, such as the fight against sexual harassment across the media industries and the coverage of recent mass shootings. *Media & Culture: Mass Communication in a Digital Age* is at the forefront of the ever-changing world of mass communication, addressing the most current issues of our time—including the proliferation of fake news, the #MeToo movement, the use and abuse of social media platforms, consumer privacy, and the role media plays in our democracy.

Media & Culture shares stories about the history of media, the digital revolution, and ongoing convergence—and the book itself practices convergence, too. The twelfth edition is available packaged with LaunchPad, combining print and digital media in an interactive e-book featuring dozens of video activities, a new video assessment program, our acclaimed LearningCurve adaptive quizzing, our interactive timeline, interactive Media Literacy Activities, and a new career unit for students interested in a future in media—along with quizzes, activities, and instructor resources.

Along with our exciting digital resources, those using LaunchPad in their courses will get even more through the twice-annual currency updates, which will appear at the base of the LaunchPad table of contents with new information and activities. Content updates for each of the book's chapters provide fresh new information about the latest developments that have occurred in the media since the publication of the latest print edition. The digital updates will also include a new interactive activity for each chapter, as well as a digital-only interactive Extended Case Study.

Of course, *Media & Culture* retains its well-loved and teachable organization, which supports instructors in their quest to provide students with a clear understanding of the historical and cultural contexts for each media industry. Our signature five-step critical process for studying the media has struck a chord with hundreds of instructors and thousands of students across the United States and North America. We continue to be enthusiastic about—and humbled by—the chance to work with the amazing community of teachers that has developed around *Media & Culture*. We hope the text enables students to become more knowledgeable media consumers and engaged, media-literate citizens who are ready to take a critical role in shaping our dynamic world.

The Twelfth Edition of *Media & Culture* Navigates Today's Hyperfast Media Landscape

Media & Culture has taken the digital turn, and the twelfth edition continues to keep pace with the technological, economic, and social effects of today's rapidly changing media landscape. Since the publication of the eleventh edition, we've seen more changes than ever: the ongoing issues of social media privacy and fraud, the fight against sexual harassment in the media industries, the change in meaning of the term *fake news*, and so on. The twelfth edition of *Media & Culture* covers all of this and more. It features the following:

- **Expanded global coverage throughout the book** allows students to see how media consumers all over the world are interacting with the media. An increase in international examples throughout and a Global Village box in each chapter will help students gain an appreciation and understanding of the global effects of the media.

- **Expanded ethics coverage** helps students develop their critical analysis skills through the examination of various ethical issues involving the media. Current events, such as the recent Cambridge Analytica data breach targeting Facebook users, are addressed both throughout the chapters and in a dedicated Examining Ethics box in each chapter and will help students as they hone their skills in questioning the ethical implications of these events.

- **Highlighting the importance of and challenges to media during this time of worldwide political upheaval** keeps this book current. Topics such as the use of social media in politics, media coverage of mass shootings, celebrities fighting back against sexual harassment in the media industries, and many more will allow students to examine current issues and analyze how they affect both media and our society.

- **Current media issues** are addressed, explored, and analyzed throughout each chapter. These issues include social media fraud in the 2016 election; fake news; sexual harassment in the music, film, and TV industries; and net neutrality.

- **For consistency, each chapter now contains one Media Literacy and the Critical Process box, one Global Village box, and one Examining Ethics box.**

- **Print and media converge with LaunchPad in brand-new ways.** LaunchPad for *Media & Culture* merges and converges the book with the web. Twice-a-year digital-only updates make this book and media platform more current than ever before. Our new Video Assessment Program—powered by GoReact—allows instructors and students to record, upload, embed, and critically analyze of-the-moment videos. A new interactive timeline helps students explore and understand the development of mass communication through the years. A variety of video activities, including a new activity for each chapter of the book, gets students critically thinking about media texts. A brand-new career unit helps students on the path toward exploring and realizing their future career goals. In addition, LaunchPad offers a wealth of study tools—including LearningCurve's adaptive quizzing, chapter quizzes, and other assessments, along with the e-book—and, for instructors, a complete set of supplements. For more ideas on how using LaunchPad can enhance your course, see the Instructor's Resource Manual. For a list of available clips and access information, see the inside back cover of the book or visit **launchpadworks.com**.

Media & Culture Provides a Critical, Cultural, Comprehensive, and Compelling Introduction to the Mass Media

- **A critical approach to media literacy.** *Media & Culture* introduces students to five stages of the critical-thinking and writing process—description, analysis, interpretation, evaluation, and engagement. The text uses these stages as a lens for examining the historical context and current processes that shape mass media as part of our culture. This framework informs the writing throughout, including the Media Literacy and the Critical Process features in every chapter. New online interactive Media Literacy Activities will give students even more practice to develop their media literacy and critical-thinking skills.

- **A cultural perspective.** The text focuses on the vital relationship between the mass media and our shared culture—how cultural trends influence the mass media and how specific historical developments, technical innovations, and key decision makers in the history of the media have affected the ways our democracy and society have evolved.

- **Comprehensive coverage.** The text supports the instructor in providing students with the nuts-and-bolts content they need to understand each media industry's history, organizational structure, economic models, and market statistics.

- **An exploration of media economics and democracy.** *Media & Culture* spotlights the significance and impact of multinational media systems throughout the text. It also invites students to explore the implications of the Telecommunications Act of 1996, net neutrality, and other media regulations. Additionally, each chapter ends with a discussion of the effects of particular mass media on the nature of democratic life.

- **Compelling storytelling.** Most mass media make use of storytelling to tap into our shared beliefs and values, and so does *Media & Culture*. Each chapter presents the events and issues surrounding media culture as intriguing and informative narratives rather than a series of unconnected facts and feats, mapping the accompanying—and often uneasy—changes in consumer culture and democratic society.

- **The most accessible book available.** Learning tools in every chapter help students find and remember the information they need to know. Bulleted lists at the beginning of every chapter give students a road map to key concepts, Media Literacy and the Critical Process boxes model the five-step process, and the Chapter Reviews help students study and review for quizzes and exams and set them up for success.

Digital and Print Formats

Whether it's print, digital, or a value option, choose the best format for you. For more information on these resources, please visit the online catalog at **macmillanlearning.com/mediaculture12e**.

- **LaunchPad for *Media & Culture* dramatically enhances teaching and learning.** LaunchPad combines the full e-book with video activities, Video Assessment Program, test bank, quizzes, interactive timeline, twice-a-year digital updates, instructor's resources, and LearningCurve adaptive quizzing. For access to all multimedia resources, package LaunchPad with the print version of *Media & Culture* or order LaunchPad on its own, **ISBN: 978-1-319-10468-9**.

- **The Loose-Leaf Edition of *Media & Culture*** features the print text in a convenient, budget-priced format, designed to fit into any three-ring binder. The loose-leaf version can also be packaged with LaunchPad for a small additional cost, **ISBN: 978-1-319-23307-5**.

- ***Media & Culture* is available as a print text.** To get the most out of the book, package LaunchPad with the text, **ISBN: 978-1-319-23239-9**.

- **E-books.** *Media & Culture* is available as an e-book for use on computers, tablets, and e-readers. See **macmillanlearning.com/ebooks** to learn more.

- **You want to give your students affordable rental, packaging, and e-book options.** So do we. Learn more at **store.macmillanlearning.com**.

- **Customize *Media & Culture* using Bedford Select for Communication.** Create the ideal textbook for your course with only the chapters you need. You can rearrange chapters, delete unnecessary chapters, and add your own original content to create just the book you're looking for. With Bedford Select, students pay only for material that will be assigned in the course, nothing more. For more information, visit **macmillanlearning.com/selectcomm**.

Student Resources

For more information on student resources or to learn about package options, please visit the online catalog at **macmillanlearning.com/mediaculture12e**.

LaunchPad for *Media & Culture*

At Bedford/St. Martin's, we are committed to providing online resources that meet the needs of instructors and students in powerful yet simple ways. We've taken what we've learned from both instructors and students to create a new generation of technology featuring LaunchPad. With its student-friendly approach, LaunchPad offers our trusted content—organized for easy assignability in a simple user interface. Access to LaunchPad can be packaged with *Media & Culture* at a significant discount or purchased separately.

- **Easy to Implement** Combining a curated collection of online resources—including video activities, LearningCurve, iClicker questions, quizzes, and assignments—with e-book content, LaunchPad's interactive units can be assigned as is or used as building blocks for your own learning units.
- **Video Assessment Program** Powered by GoReact, LaunchPad's video assessment tools help instructors bring the most current video into their courses and provides students with the space to practice their vitally important critical analysis skills. The program is simple to use, with superior commenting, recording, and rubric functionalities.
  - **Record, upload, embed, or live-stream videos** to share with the class and build assignments around.
  - **Multiple comment-delivery options** are available for providing rich feedback.
  - **Customizable visual markers** allow the user to pinpoint critical aspects of the video being discussed.
  - **Videos can be recorded** or submitted directly from mobile devices using the Macmillan Mobile Video IOS and Android apps.
- **Intuitive and Useful Analytics** The gradebook quickly and easily allows you to gauge performance for your whole class, for individual students, and for individual assignments, making class prep time as well as time spent with students more productive.
- **Fully Interactive E-Book** The LaunchPad e-book for *Media & Culture* comes with powerful study tools, multimedia content, and easy customization tools for instructors. Students can search, highlight, and bookmark, making studying easier and more efficient.

To learn more about LaunchPad for *Media & Culture* or to purchase access, go to **launchpadworks.com**. If your book came packaged with an access card to LaunchPad, follow the card's login instructions.

Media Career Guide: Preparing for Jobs in the 21st Century, Twelfth Edition

Practical, student-friendly, and revised to address recent trends in the job market, this guide includes a comprehensive directory of media jobs, practical tips, and career guidance for students who are considering a major in the media industries. *Media Career Guide* can be packaged at a significant discount with the print book.

New! *The Essential Guide to Visual Communication*

is a concise introduction to the evolution, theory, and principles of visual communication in contemporary society. This guide helps students develop the skills they need to become critical consumers of visual media by examining images through the lens of visual rhetoric. Students see how images influence and persuade audiences, and how iconic images can be repurposed to communicate particular messages. *The Essential Guide to Visual Communication* can be packaged at a significant discount with the print book.

Instructor Resources

For more information or to order or download the instructor's resources, please visit the online catalog at **macmillanlearning.com/mediaculture12e**. The Instructor's Resource Manual, test bank, lecture slides, and iClicker questions are also available on LaunchPad: **launchpadworks.com**.

Instructor's Resource Manual

Prepared by Bettina Fabos, *University of Northern Iowa*; Christopher R. Martin, *University of Northern Iowa*; Marilda Oviedo, *University of Iowa*; and Lewis Freeman, *Fordham University*

This downloadable manual improves on what has always been the best and most comprehensive instructor teaching tool available for introduction to mass communication courses. This extensive resource provides a range of teaching approaches, tips for facilitating in-class discussions, writing assignments, outlines, lecture topics, lecture spin-offs, critical-process exercises, classroom media resources, and an annotated list of more than two hundred video resources. The Instructor's Resource Manual has been streamlined to make it even easier to use. And with this edition, your resource manual has gone interactive with an assignable online media literacy activity. These activities, adapted from activities in the Instructor's Resource Manual and built into each LaunchPad unit, provide students with extra practice as they develop their media literacy skills.

Test Bank

Prepared by Christopher R. Martin, *University of Northern Iowa*; Bettina Fabos, *University of Northern Iowa*; and Marilda Oviedo, *University of Iowa*

Available formatted for Windows and Macintosh, the test bank includes multiple choice, true/false, fill-in-the-blank, and short and long essay questions for each chapter in *Media & Culture*.

Lecture Slides

Downloadable lecture slide presentations help guide your lecture and are available for each chapter in *Media & Culture*.

iClicker Questions

Downloadable iClicker question slides help keep your students engaged and help you make your class even more interactive.

ACKNOWLEDGMENTS

We are very grateful to everyone at Bedford/St. Martin's who supported this project through its many stages. We wish that every textbook author could have the kind of experience we had with the Macmillan humanities team: Edwin Hill, Vice President of Humanities; Erika Gutierrez, Senior Program Director for Communication and College Success; Jane Knetzger, Director of Content Development; and so many others. Over the years, we have also collaborated with superb and supportive editors: on the twelfth edition, Development Editor Kate George and Assistant Editor Kimberly Roberts. We particularly appreciate the tireless work of Harold Chester, Senior Content Project Manager, who kept the book on schedule while making sure we got the details right, and Jennifer Wetzel, Senior Content Workflow Manager. Media is such an important part of this project, and our LaunchPad and media resources could not have come to fruition without our fantastic media team: Tom Kane, Senior Media Editor; Sarah O'Connor Kepes, Media Project Manager and Digital Activities Specialist; and Audrey Webster, Media Editorial Assistant. Thanks also to Susan McLaughlin, our wonderful Senior Development Manager; Amy Haines and her fearless marketing team; and Billy Boardman for a fantastic cover design. We are especially grateful to our research assistant, Susan Coffin, who functioned as a one-person clipping service throughout the process. We are also grateful to Jimmie Reeves, our digital gaming expert, who contributed his great knowledge of this medium to the development of Chapter 3.

We also want to thank the many fine and thoughtful reviewers who contributed ideas to the twelfth edition of *Media & Culture*: Lisa Heller Boragine, *Cape Cod Community College*; Vic Costello, *Elon University*; Richard Craig, *San Jose State University*; Donald Diefenbach, *University of North Carolina–Asheville*; Sarah Dugas, *Houston Community College*; Christal Johnson, *Syracuse University*; Brad Kaye, *Colorado State University*; Abigail Koenig, *University of Houston–Downtown*; Julie Lellis, *Elon University*; Hsin-I Liu, *University of the Incarnate Word*; Rick Marks, *College of Southern Nevada*; Andrea McDonnell, *Emmanuel College*; Siho Nam, *University of North Florida*; William Price, *Georgia State University Perimeter College*; Stephen Swanson, *McLennan Community College*; Erin Wilgenbusch, *Iowa State University*.

For the eleventh edition: Amelia Arsenault, *Georgia State University*; John Chapin, *Pennsylvania State University*; Juliet Dee, *University of Delaware*; Joshua Dickhaus, *Bradley University*; Chandler W. Harriss, *University of Tennessee–Chattanooga*; Ben Lohman, *Orange Coast College*; Valerie J. Whitney, *Bethune-Cookman University*.

For the tenth edition: Mariam Alkazemi, *Virginia Commonwealth University*; Ronald Becker, *Miami University*; Tanya Biami, *Cochise College*; Dave Bostwick, *University of Arkansas*; David Bradford, *Barry University*; Alexis Carreiro, *Queens University of Charlotte*; David Cassady, *Pacific University*; John Chalfa, *Mercer University*; Jon Conlogue, *Westfield State University*; Don Diefenbach, *UNC Asheville*; Larry Hartsfield, *Fort Lewis College*; Phelps Hawkins, *Savannah State University*; Deborah Lev, *Centenary University*; Thomas Lindlof, *University of Kentucky*; Steve Liu, *University of the Incarnate Word*; Maureen Louis, *Cazenovia College*; Mary Lowney, *American International College*; Arnold Mackowiak, *Eastern Michigan University*; Bob Manis, *College of Southern Nevada*; Michael McCluskey, *Ohio State University*; Andrea McDonnell, *Emmanuel College*; Ryan Medders, *California Lutheran University*; Alicia Morris, *Virginia State University*; Lanie Steinwart, *Valparaiso University*; Stephen Swanson, *McLennan Community College*; Shauntae White, *North Carolina Central University*.

For the ninth edition: Glenda Alvarado, *University of South Carolina*; Lisa Burns, *Quinnipiac University*; Matthew Cecil, *South Dakota University*; John Dougan, *Middle Tennessee State University*; Lewis Freeman, *Fordham University*; K. Megan Hopper, *Illinois State University*; John Kerezy, *Cuyahoga Community College*; Marcia Ladendorff, *University of North Florida*; Julie Lellis, *Elon University*; Joy McDonald, *Hampton University*; Heather McIntosh, *Boston College*; Kenneth Nagelberg, *Delaware State University*; Eric Pierson, *University of San Diego*; Jennifer Tiernan, *South Dakota State University*; Erin Wilgenbusch, *Iowa State University*; Cindy Hing-Yuk Wong, *College of Staten Island*.

For the eighth edition: Frank A. Aycock, *Appalachian State University*; Carrie Buchanan, *John Carroll University*; Lisa M. Burns, *Quinnipiac University*; Rich Cameron, *Cerritos College*; Katherine Foss, *Middle Tennessee State University*; Myleea D. Hill, *Arkansas State University*; Sarah Alford Hock, *Santa Barbara City College*; Sharon R. Hollenback, *Syracuse University*; Drew Jacobs, *Camden County College*; Susan Katz, *University of Bridgeport*; John Kerezy, *Cuyahoga Community College*; Les Kozaczek, *Franklin Pierce University*; Deborah L. Larson, *Missouri State University*; Susan Charles Lewis, *Minnesota State University–Mankato*; Rick B. Marks, *College of Southern Nevada*; Donna R. Munde, *Mercer County Community College*; Wendy Nelson, *Palomar College*; Charles B. Scholz, *New Mexico State University*; Don W. Stacks, *University of Miami*; Carl Sessions Stepp, *University of Maryland*; David Strukel, *Hiram College*; Lisa Turowski, *Towson University*; Lisa M. Weidman, *Linfield College*.

For the seventh edition: Robert Blade, *Florida Community College*; Lisa Boragine, *Cape Cod Community College*; Joseph Clark, *University of Toledo*; Richard Craig, *San Jose State University*; Samuel Ebersole, *Colorado State University–Pueblo*; Brenda Edgerton-Webster, *Dubai Women's/Higher Colleges of Technology UAE*; Tim Edwards, *University of Arkansas at Little Rock*; Mara Einstein, *Queens College*; Lillie M. Fears, *Arkansas State University*; Connie Fletcher, *Loyola University*; Monica Flippin-Wynn, *University of Oklahoma*; Gil Fowler, *Arkansas State University*; Donald G. Godfrey, *Arizona State University*; Patricia Homes, *University of Southwestern Louisiana*; Daniel McDonald, *Ohio State University*; Connie McMahon, *Barry University*; Steve Miller, *Rutgers University*; Siho Nam, *University of North Florida*; David Nelson, *University of Colorado–Colorado Springs*; Zengjun Peng, *St. Cloud State University*; Deidre Pike, *Humboldt State University*; Neil Ralston, *Western Kentucky University*; Mike Reed, *Saddleback College*; David Roberts, *Missouri Valley College*; Donna Simmons, *California State University–Bakersfield*; Marc Skinner, *University of Idaho*; Michael Stamm, *University of Minnesota*; Bob Trumpbour, *Penn State University*; Kristin Watson, *Metro State University*; Jim Weaver, *Virginia Polytechnic and State University*; David Whitt, *Nebraska Wesleyan University*.

For the sixth edition: Boyd Dallos, *Lake Superior College*; Roger George, *Bellevue Community College*; Osvaldo Hirschmann, *Houston Community College*; Ed Kanis, *Butler University*; Dean A. Kruckeberg, *University of Northern Iowa*; Larry Leslie, *University of South Florida*; Lori Liggett, *Bowling Green State University*; Steve Miller, *Rutgers University*; Robert Pondillo, *Middle Tennessee State University*; David Silver, *University of San Francisco*; Chris White, *Sam Houston State University*; Marvin Williams, *Kingsborough Community College*.

For the fifth edition: Russell Barclay, *Quinnipiac University*; Kathy Battles, *Oakland University*; Kenton Bird, *University of Idaho*; Ed Bonza, *Kennesaw State University*; Larry L. Burris, *Middle Tennessee State University*; Ceilidh Charleson-Jennings, *Collin County Community College*; Raymond Eugene Costain, *University of Central Florida*; Richard Craig, *San Jose State University*; Dave Deeley, *Truman State University*; Janine Gerzanics, *West Valley College*; Beth Haller, *Towson University*; Donna Hemmila, *Diablo Valley College*; Sharon Hollenback, *Syracuse University*; Marshall D. Katzman, *Bergen Community College*; Kimberly Lauffer, *Ball State University*; Steve Miller, *Rutgers University*; Stu Minnis, *Virginia Wesleyan College*; Frank G. Perez, *University of Texas at El Paso*; Dave Perlmutter, *Louisiana State University–Baton Rouge*; Karen Pitcher, *University of Iowa*; Ronald C. Roat, *University of Southern Indiana*; Marshel Rossow, *Minnesota State University*; Roger Saathoff, *Texas Tech University*; Matthew Smith,

Wittenberg University; Marlane C. Steinwart, *Valparaiso University*.

For the fourth edition: Fay Y. Akindes, *University of Wisconsin–Parkside*; Robert Arnett, *Mississippi State University*; Charles Aust, *Kennesaw State University*; Russell Barclay, *Quinnipiac University*; Bryan Brown, *Southwest Missouri State University*; Peter W. Croisant, *Geneva College*; Mark Goodman, *Mississippi State University*; Donna Halper, *Emerson College*; Rebecca Self Hill, *University of Colorado*; John G. Hodgson, *Oklahoma State University*; Cynthia P. King, *American University*; Deborah L. Larson, *Southwest Missouri State University*; Charles Lewis, *Minnesota State University–Mankato*; Lila Lieberman, *Rutgers University*; Abbus Malek, *Howard University*; Anthony A. Olorunnisola, *Pennsylvania State University*; Norma Pecora, *Ohio University–Athens*; Elizabeth M. Perse, *University of Delaware*; Hoyt Purvis, *University of Arkansas*; Alison Rostankowski, *University of Wisconsin–Milwaukee*; Roger A. Soenksen, *James Madison University*; Hazel Warlaumont, *California State University–Fullerton*.

For the third edition: Gerald J. Baldasty, *University of Washington*; Steve M. Barkin, *University of Maryland*; Ernest L. Bereman, *Truman State University*; Daniel Bernadi, *University of Arizona*; Kimberly L. Bissell, *Southern Illinois University*; Audrey Boxmann, *Merrimack College*; Todd Chatman, *University of Illinois*; Ray Chavez, *University of Colorado*; Vic Costello, *Elon University*; Paul D'Angelo, *The College of New Jersey*; James Shanahan, *Indiana University*; Scott A. Webber, *University of Colorado*.

For the second edition: Susan B. Barnes, *Fordham University*; Margaret Bates, *City College of New York*; Steven Alan Carr, *Indiana University/Purdue University–Fort Wayne*; William G. Covington Jr., *Bridgewater State College*; Roger Desmond, *University of Hartford*; Jules d'Hemecourt, *Louisiana State University*; Cheryl Evans, *Northwestern Oklahoma State University*; Douglas Gomery, *University of Maryland*; Colin Gromatzky, *New Mexico State University*; John L. Hochheimer, *Ithaca College*; Sheena Malhotra, *California State University, Northridge*; Sharon R. Mazzarella, *Ithaca College*; David Marc McCoy, *Ashland University*; Beverly Merrick, *New Mexico State University*; John Pantalone, *University of Rhode Island*; John Durham Peters, *University of Iowa*; Lisa Pieraccini, *Oswego State College*; Susana Powell, *Borough of Manhattan Community College*; Felecia Jones Ross, *Ohio State University*; Enid Sefcovic, *Florida Atlantic University*; Keith Semmel, *University of the Cumberlands*; Augusta Simon, *Embry-Riddle Aeronautical University*; Clifford E. Wexler, *Columbia-Greene Community College*.

For the first edition: Paul Ashdown, *University of Tennessee*; Terry Bales, *Rancho Santiago College*; Russell Barclay,

Quinnipiac University; Thomas Bedell, *Iowa State University*; Fred Blevens, *Southwest Texas State University*; Stuart Bullion, *University of Maine*; William G. Covington Jr., *Bridgewater State College*; Robert Daves, *Minneapolis Star Tribune*; Charles Davis, *Georgia Southern University*; Thomas Donahue, *Virginia Commonwealth University*; Ralph R. Donald, *University of Tennessee–Martin*; John P. Ferre, *University of Louisville*; Donald Fishman, *Boston College*; Elizabeth Atwood Gailey, *University of Tennessee*; Bob Gassaway, *University of New Mexico*; Anthony Giffard, *University of Washington*; Zhou He, *San Jose State University*; Barry Hollander, *University of Georgia*; Sharon Hollenbeck, *Syracuse University*; Anita Howard, *Austin Community College*; James Hoyt, *University of Wisconsin–Madison*; Joli Jensen, *University of Tulsa*; Frank Kaplan, *University of Colorado*; William Knowles, *University of Montana*; Michael Leslie, *University of Florida*; Janice Long, *University of Cincinnati*; Kathleen Maticheck, *Normandale Community College*; Maclyn McClary, *Humboldt State University*; Robert McGaughey, *Murray State University*; Joseph McKerns, *Ohio State University*; Debra Merskin, *University of Oregon*; David Morrissey, *Colorado State University*; Michael Murray, *University of Missouri at St. Louis*; Susan Dawson O'Brien, *Rose State College*; Patricia Bowie Orman, *University of Southern Colorado*; Jim Patton, *University of Arizona*; John Pauly, *St. Louis University*; Ted Pease, *Utah State University*; Janice Peck, *University of Colorado*; Tina Pieraccini, *University of New Mexico*; Peter Pringle, *University of Tennessee*; Sondra Rubenstein, *Hofstra University*; Jim St. Clair, *Indiana University Southeast*; Jim Seguin, *Robert Morris College*; Donald Shaw, *University of North Carolina*; Martin D. Sommernes, *Northern Arizona State University*; Linda Steiner, *Rutgers University*; Jill Diane Swensen, *Ithaca College*; Sharon Taylor, *Delaware State University*; Hazel Warlaumont, *California State University–Fullerton*; Richard Whitaker, *Buffalo State College*; Lynn Zoch, *Radford University*.

Special thanks from Richard Campbell: I would also like to acknowledge the number of fine teachers at both the *University of Wisconsin–Milwaukee* and *Northwestern University* who helped shape the way I think about many of the issues raised in this book, and I am especially grateful to my former students at the *University of Wisconsin–Milwaukee*, *Mount Mary College*, the *University of Michigan*, and *Middle Tennessee State University*, and my current students at *Miami University*. Some of my students have contributed directly to this text, and thousands have endured my courses over the years—and made them better. My all-time favorite former students, Chris Martin and Bettina Fabos, are now coauthors, as well as the creators of our book's Instructor's Resource Manual and test bank. I am grateful for Chris's and Bettina's fine writing, research savvy, good stories, and tireless work amid their own teaching schedules and writing careers, all while raising two spirited daughters. I remain most grateful, though, to the people I most love: my grandson, Reese; my son, Chris; my daughter, Caitlin; and, most of all, my wife, Dianna, whose line editing, content ideas, daily conversations, shared interests, and ongoing support are the resources that make this project go better with each edition.

Special thanks from Christopher Martin and Bettina Fabos: We would also like to thank Richard Campbell, with whom it is always a delight working on this project. We also appreciate the great energy, creativity, and talent that everyone at Bedford/St. Martin's brings to the book. From edition to edition, we receive plenty of suggestions from *Media & Culture* users and reviewers and from our own journalism and media students. We would like to thank them for their input and for creating a community of sorts around the theme of critical perspectives on the media. Most of all, we'd like to thank our daughters, Olivia and Sabine, who bring us joy, laughter, and excellent media insights, as well as a sense of mission to better understand the world of media and culture in which they live.

Media & Culture, Twelfth Edition, connects to the learning outcomes of the National Communication Association (NCA)

The National Communication Association (NCA) has published learning outcomes for courses within the discipline. The following table shows how these learning outcomes are reflected in *Media & Culture,* Twelfth Edition.

Learning Outcome	Campbell, *Media & Culture*, 12th Edition
Employ communication theories, perspectives, principles, and concepts	**Chapter 1: Mass Communication: A Critical Approach** gives students a solid overview of mass communication. • The **"Culture and the Evolution of Mass Communication"** section provides a knowledge base of all the types of mass communication, from the oral and written eras to the print revolution, through the electronic era, and into the digital era. • **"The Development of Media and Their Role in Our Society"** section invites students to begin thinking about the relevance of mass communication in their own lives and plants the seeds of convergence and its effects on business and culture, and the importance of media stories as a part of their everyday lives. **Chapter 15: Media Effects and Cultural Approaches to Research** is directly focused on these learning outcomes and examines specific mass communication theories and both social scientific and cultural studies research perspectives. Industry-specific chapters throughout the book provide in-depth study and exploration of the types of mass communication: • **Chapter 2: The Internet, Digital Media, and Media Convergence** • **Chapter 3: Digital Gaming and the Media Playground** • **Chapter 4: Sound Recording and Popular Music** • **Chapter 5: Popular Radio and the Origins of Broadcasting** • **Chapter 6: Television and Cable: The Power of Visual Culture** • **Chapter 7: Movies and the Impact of Images** • **Chapter 8: Newspapers: The Rise and Decline of Modern Journalism** • **Chapter 9: Magazines in the Age of Specialization** • **Chapter 10: Books and the Power of Print** The history of mass media is threaded throughout the book. Book sections that specifically explore history include the following: • "Culture and the Evolution of Mass Communication" and "The Development of Media and Their Role in Our Society" in **Chapter 1** • "The Development of the Internet and the Web" in **Chapter 2** • "The Development of Digital Gaming" in **Chapter 3** • "The Development of Sound Recording" in **Chapter 4** • "Early Technology and the Development of Radio," "The Evolution of Radio," and "Radio Reinvents Itself" in **Chapter 5** • "The Origins and Development of Television" and "The Development of Cable" in **Chapter 6** • "Early Technology and the Evolution of Movies," "The Rise of the Hollywood Studio System," "The Studio System's Golden Age," and "The Transformation of the Studio System" in **Chapter 7** • "The Evolution of American Newspapers" in **Chapter 8** • "The Early History of Magazines" and "The Development of Modern American Magazines" in **Chapter 9** • "The History of Books, from Papyrus to Paperbacks" in **Chapter 10** • "Early Developments in American Advertising" in **Chapter 11** • "Early Developments in Public Relations" in **Chapter 12** • "Early Media Research Methods" in **Chapter 15** • "The Origins of Free Expression and a Free Press" in **Chapter 16** The **Interactive Digital Timeline**, available in the **LaunchPad**, allows students to explore the histories of mass media industries and examine how these histories interact with one another and with the history of our society in general. **LaunchPad video activities** in each chapter give students the opportunity to hear from industry professionals, make connections with film and TV clips, and explore current issues in media. **Part Opening Infographics** help students make connections between mass communication, their own lives, and the world around them.
Engage in communication inquiry	**Media Literacy and the Critical Process** boxes in each chapter provide real-life examples of how we interact with the media, and a step-by-step breakdown of the critical process helps students practice the art of critical thinking. The **LaunchPad** of each chapter provides an additional interactive and assignable Media Literacy Activity, which allows students to practice their skills as critical consumers of the media. Even more Media Literacy Activities in the **Instructor's Resource Manual** provide instructors with ideas for additional practice that they can use as classroom activities or as inspiration for assignments.

Learning Outcome	Campbell, *Media & Culture*, 12th Edition
Critically analyze messages	**Richard Campbell's** critical and cultural approach to the media, particularly his five-step **Media Literacy and the Critical Process** boxes, gets students describing, examining, analyzing, interpreting, evaluating, and engaging in topics in the media to actively build media literacy. **Media Literacy and the Critical Process** boxes in each chapter and the additional interactive and assignable Media Literacy Activities on the LaunchPad allow students to practice their skills as critical consumers of the media. Even more Media Literacy Activities in the **Instructor's Resource Manual** provide instructors with ideas for additional practice that they can use as classroom activities or as inspiration for assignments. The **Extended Case Study: Can We Trust Facebook with Our Personal Data?** is an extension of the activities that students have done throughout the semester and allows students to further develop their media literacy and critical-thinking skills by analyzing a contemporary media problem. Extended Case Studies from previous editions are also available in the **Instructor's Resource Manual**.
Demonstrate the ability to accomplish communicative goals (self-efficacy)	The ***Media Career Guide*** that accompanies the book helps students define and achieve their career goals in the communication fields of their choice. Additionally, the **Media Literacy and the Critical Process** boxes and activities allow students the space to practice and develop their skills as critical consumers of the media.
Apply ethical communication principles and practices	*Media & Culture* strives to help students understand contemporary issues and controversies. The **Examining Ethics** boxes and **Extended Case Study**, in particular, dig deep into exploring such issues and controversies. **Examining Ethics** boxes throughout the book discuss ethics issues across the media industries: • "Examining Ethics: Covering War and Displaying Images" in Chapter 1 • "Examining Ethics: Social Media Fraud and Elections" in Chapter 2 • "Examining Ethics: The Gender Problem in Digital Games" in Chapter 3 • "Examining Ethics: The Music Industry's Day of Reckoning" in Chapter 4 • "Examining Ethics: How Did Talk Radio Become So One-Sided?" in Chapter 5 • "Examining Ethics: #MeToo and TV Station Policy" in Chapter 6 • "Examining Ethics: Breaking through Hollywood's Race Barrier" in Chapter 7 • "Examining Ethics: Alternative Journalism: The Activism of Dorothy Day and I. F. Stone" in Chapter 8 • "Examining Ethics: The Evolution of Photojournalism" in Chapter 9 • "Examining Ethics: Contemporary Politics Revives Interest in Classic Novels" in Chapter 10 • "Examining Ethics: Do Alcohol Ads Encourage Binge Drinking?" in Chapter 11 • "Examining Ethics: Public Relations and 'Alternative Facts'" in Chapter 12 • "Examining Ethics: Are the Big Digital Companies Too Big?" in Chapter 13 • "Examining Ethics: WikiLeaks, Secret Documents, and Good Journalism" in Chapter 14 • "Examining Ethics: Our Masculinity Problem" in Chapter 15 • "Examining Ethics: Is 'Sexting' Pornography?" in Chapter 16 **Chapter 14: The Culture of Journalism: Values, Ethics, and Democracy** digs into the ethics issues and judgment calls that journalists face every day. The chapter also explores the values that journalists promise to uphold. **Chapter 15: Media Effects and Cultural Approaches to Research** provides an in-depth study of media effects on society, taking students through early media research methods, research on media effects, cultural approaches to media research, and media research and democracy. **Media Literacy and the Critical Process** boxes and interactive online activities help students hone their critical media skills.
Utilize communication to embrace difference	**Global Village** boxes throughout the book connect students with issues from all over the world: • "Designed in California, Assembled in China" in Chapter 2 • "Phones in Hand, the World Finds Pokémon (and Wizards)" in Chapter 3 • "Latin Pop Goes Mainstream" in Chapter 4 • "Radio Stories from Around the World" in Chapter 5 • "Telling and Selling Stories around the World" in Chapter 6 • "Beyond Hollywood: Asian Cinema" in Chapter 7 • "Newspaper Readership across the Globe" in Chapter 8 • "Cosmopolitan Style Travels the World" in Chapter 9 • "Buenos Aires, the World's Bookstore Capital" in Chapter 10 • "Smoking Up the Global Market" in Chapter 11 • "Public Relations and Bananas" in Chapter 12 • "China's Dominant Media Corporations Rival America's" in Chapter 13 • "News Bias around the Globe" in Chapter 14 • "International Media Research" in Chapter 15 • "The Challenges of Film Censorship in China" in Chapter 16

Learning Outcome	Campbell, *Media & Culture*, 12th Edition
Influence public discourse	The relationship among politics, democracy, and the media is a recurring theme in *Media & Culture*. Examples can be found throughout: • the **Chapter 1** opener, which discusses the media's coverage of mass shootings • "The Internet and Democracy" in **Chapter 2** • "Digital Gaming, Free Speech, and Democracy" in **Chapter 3** • "Sound Recording, Free Expression, and Democracy" in **Chapter 4** • "Radio and the Democracy of the Airwaves" in **Chapter 5** • "Television, Cable, and Democracy" in **Chapter 6** • "Popular Movies and Democracy" in **Chapter 7** • "Newspapers and Democracy" in **Chapter 8** • "Magazines in a Democratic Society" in **Chapter 9** • "Books and the Future of Democracy" in **Chapter 10** • "Advertising, Politics, and Democracy" in **Chapter 11** • "Public Relations and Democracy" in **Chapter 12** • "The Media Marketplace and Democracy" in **Chapter 13** • "Democracy and Reimagining Journalism's Role" in **Chapter 14** • "Media Research and Democracy" in **Chapter 15** • "The First Amendment and Democracy" in **Chapter 16** **Chapter 16: Legal Controls and Freedom of Expression** takes a close look at the First Amendment and how it relates to mass media. Finally, the last step of the critical process discussed throughout the text is **engagement**, which urges students to become involved in the public discourse of media questions of our day.

Contents

ABOUT THE AUTHORS   iii
BRIEF CONTENTS   iv
PREFACE   v

1 Mass Communication: A Critical Approach   3

Culture and the Evolution of Mass Communication   5

Oral and Written Eras in Communication   6

The Print Revolution   6

The Electronic Era   7

The Digital Era   8

The Linear Model of Mass Communication   8

A Cultural Model for Understanding Mass Communication   9

The Development of Media and Their Role in Our Society   10

The Evolution of Media: From Emergence to Convergence   10

Media Convergence   10

Stories: The Foundation of Media   13

Media Stories in Everyday Life   14

▶ Agenda Setting and Gatekeeping   14

Surveying the Cultural Landscape   15

Culture as a Skyscraper   15

▣ EXAMINING ETHICS   Covering War and Displaying Images   16

Culture as a Map   20

Cultural Values of the Modern Period   22

Shifting Values in Postmodern Culture   23

Critiquing Media and Culture   25

Media Literacy and the Critical Process   25

Benefits of a Critical Perspective   25

■ MEDIA LITERACY AND THE CRITICAL PROCESS   26

CHAPTER REVIEW   30

▶ LaunchPad   31

© Michael Nigro/Pacific Press via ZUMA Wire

▶   **For videos, review quizzing, and more, visit LaunchPad for *Media & Culture* at launchpadworks.com.**

 LaunchPad

Tuzemka/Shutterstock

2 The Internet, Digital Media, and Media Convergence 35

The Development of the Internet and the Web 37

    The Birth of the Internet 37

    The Net Widens 38

    The Commercialization of the Internet 39

Social Media and Democracy 41

    ◉ **EXAMINING ETHICS** Social Media Fraud and Elections 43

Convergence and Mobile Media 44

    Media Converges on Our PCs and TVs 44

    Mobile Devices Propel Convergence 44

    The Impact of Media Convergence and Mobile Media 45

    The Next Era: The Semantic Web 46

The Economics and Issues of the Internet 47

    Ownership: Controlling the Internet 47

    Targeted Advertising and Data Mining 50

    Security: The Challenge to Keep Personal Information Private 51

    ◉ **GLOBAL VILLAGE** Designed in California, Assembled in China 52

    ■ **MEDIA LITERACY AND THE CRITICAL PROCESS**
    Note to Self for Healthy Digital Consumption 54

    Appropriateness: What Should Be Online? 56

    Access: The Fight to Prevent a Digital Divide 56

    Net Neutrality: Maintaining an Open Internet 58

    ▶ Net Neutrality 58

    Alternative Voices 58

The Internet and Democracy 59

CHAPTER REVIEW 60

    ▶ LaunchPad 61

3 Digital Gaming and the Media Playground 63

The Development of Digital Gaming 65

Mechanical Gaming 65

The First Video Games 66

Arcades and Classic Games 67

Consoles and Advancing Graphics 67

Gaming on PCs 70

Portable Players 70

The Internet Transforms Gaming 70

MMORPGs, MOBAs, Virtual Worlds, and Social Gaming 71

Gaming Apps 72

The Media Playground 72

Video Game Genres 72

Communities of Play: Inside the Game 72

Communities of Play: Outside the Game 74

▣ **GLOBAL VILLAGE** Phones in Hand, the World Finds Pokémon (and Wizards) 76

Trends and Issues in Digital Gaming 78

Electronic Gaming and Media Culture 78

▶ **Video Games at the Movies** 78

Electronic Gaming and Advertising 78

Addiction and Other Concerns 79

▣ **EXAMINING ETHICS** The Gender Problem in Digital Games 80

Regulating Gaming 82

▮ **MEDIA LITERACY AND THE CRITICAL PROCESS** First-Person Shooter Games: Misogyny as Entertainment? 83

The Future of Gaming and Interactive Environments 84

The Business of Digital Gaming 84

The Ownership and Organization of Digital Gaming 85

The Structure of Digital Game Publishing 86

Selling Digital Games 87

Alternative Voices 88

Digital Gaming, Free Speech, and Democracy 89

CHAPTER REVIEW 90

▶ **LaunchPad** 91

AFP Contributor/Getty Images

Mark Ralston/Getty Images

4 Sound Recording and Popular Music 95

The Development of Sound Recording 97

From Cylinders to Disks: Sound Recording Becomes a Mass Medium 97

From Phonographs to CDs: Analog Goes Digital 99

Convergence: Sound Recording in the Internet Age 100

▶ **Recording Music Today** 100

The Rocky Relationship between Records and Radio 102

U.S. Popular Music and the Formation of Rock 102

The Rise of Pop Music 103

Rock and Roll Is Here to Stay 103

Rock Muddies the Waters 104

Battles in Rock and Roll 107

A Changing Industry: Reformations in Popular Music 109

The British Are Coming! 109

Motor City Music: Detroit Gives America Soul 110

Folk and Psychedelic Music Reflect the Times 110

■ **MEDIA LITERACY AND THE CRITICAL PROCESS** Music Preferences across Generations 112

Punk and Indie Respond to Mainstream Rock 113

Hip-Hop Redraws Musical Lines 114

The Reemergence of Pop 116

The Business of Sound Recording 116

Music Labels Influence the Industry 116

Making, Selling, and Profiting from Music 117

▣ **GLOBAL VILLAGE** Latin Pop Goes Mainstream 118

▶ **Alternative Strategies for Music Marketing** 119

▣ **EXAMINING ETHICS** The Music Industry's Day of Reckoning 120

Alternative Voices 122

Sound Recording, Free Expression, and Democracy 123

CHAPTER REVIEW 124

▶ **LaunchPad** 125

5 Popular Radio and the Origins of Broadcasting 127

Early Technology and the Development of Radio 129

Maxwell and Hertz Discover Radio Waves 130

Marconi and the Inventors of Wireless Telegraphy 130

Wireless Telephony: De Forest and Fessenden 131

Regulating a New Medium 133

The Evolution of Radio 134

Building the First Networks 135

Sarnoff and NBC: Building the "Blue" and "Red" Networks 136

Government Scrutiny Ends RCA-NBC Monopoly 137

CBS and Paley: Challenging NBC 137

Bringing Order to Chaos with the Radio Act of 1927 138

The Golden Age of Radio 139

Radio Reinvents Itself 142

Transistors Make Radio Portable 142

The FM Revolution and Edwin Armstrong 142

The Rise of Format and Top 40 Radio 143

Resisting the Top 40 144

The Sounds of Commercial Radio 145

Format Specialization 145

▣ **EXAMINING ETHICS** How Did Talk Radio Become So One-Sided? 146

Nonprofit Radio and NPR 148

New Radio Technologies Offer More Stations 149

▶ **Going Visual: Video, Radio, and the Web** 149

■ **MEDIA LITERACY AND THE CRITICAL PROCESS** Comparing Commercial and Noncommercial Radio 150

Radio and Convergence 151

▣ **GLOBAL VILLAGE** Radio Stories from around the World 152

▶ **Radio: Yesterday, Today, and Tomorrow** 154

The Economics of Broadcast Radio 154

Local and National Advertising 154

Manipulating Playlists with Payola 155

Radio Ownership: From Diversity to Consolidation 155

Alternative Voices 156

Radio and the Democracy of the Airwaves 157

CHAPTER REVIEW 158

▶ **LaunchPad** 159

Heather Kennedy/Getty Images

Netflix/Photofest

6 Television and Cable: The Power of Visual Culture 161

The Origins and Development of Television 163
Early Innovations in TV Technology 163
Electronic Technology: Zworykin and Farnsworth 164
Assigning Frequencies and Freezing TV Licenses 165
Controlling Content—TV Grows Up 165

The Development of Cable 168
CATV—Community Antenna Television 168
The Wires and Satellites behind Cable Television 168
Cable Threatens Broadcasting 169
Cable Services 169
GLOBAL VILLAGE Telling and Selling Stories around the World 170
DBS: Cable without Wires 171

Technology and Convergence Change Viewing Habits 172
▶ Television Networks Evolve 172
Home Video 172
The Third Screen: TV Converges with the Internet 172
Fourth Screens: Smartphones and Mobile Video 173

Major Programming Trends 173
EXAMINING ETHICS #MeToo and TV Station Policy 174
TV Entertainment: Our Comic Culture 175
TV Entertainment: Our Dramatic Culture 176
▶ Television Drama: Then and Now 177
TV Information: Our Daily News Culture 178
Reality TV and Other Enduring Genres 180
Public Television Struggles to Find Its Place 180
MEDIA LITERACY AND THE CRITICAL PROCESS TV and the State of Storytelling 181

Regulatory Challenges to Television and Cable 182
Government Regulations Temporarily Restrict Network Control 182
▶ What Makes Public Television Public? 183
Balancing Cable's Growth against Broadcasters' Interests 183
Franchising Frenzy 184
The Telecommunications Act of 1996 186

The Economics and Ownership of Television and Cable 187
Production 188
Distribution 189
Syndication Keeps Shows Going and Going . . . 189
Measuring Television Viewing 190
The Major Programming Corporations 192
Alternative Voices 194

Television, Cable, and Democracy 194
CHAPTER REVIEW 196
▶ LaunchPad 197

7 Movies and the Impact of Images *199*

Early Technology and the Evolution of Movies *201*
The Development of Film *201*
The Introduction of Narrative *204*
The Arrival of Nickelodeons *204*

The Rise of the Hollywood Studio System *204*
Production *205*
Distribution *206*
Exhibition *206*

The Studio System's Golden Age *208*
Hollywood Narrative and the Silent Era *208*
The Introduction of Sound *208*
The Development of the Hollywood Style *209*
Outside the Hollywood System *211*
■ **EXAMINING ETHICS** Breaking through Hollywood's Race Barrier *212*
■ **GLOBAL VILLAGE** Beyond Hollywood: Asian Cinema *216*

The Transformation of the Studio System *218*
The Hollywood Ten *218*
The Paramount Decision *219*
Moving to the Suburbs *219*
Television Changes Hollywood *220*
Hollywood Adapts to Home Entertainment *221*

The Economics of the Movie Business *221*
Production, Distribution, and Exhibition Today *222*
The Major Studio Players *224*
■ **MEDIA LITERACY AND THE CRITICAL PROCESS**
The Blockbuster Mentality *226*
Convergence: Movies Adjust to the Digital Turn *226*
Alternative Voices *227*

Popular Movies and Democracy *228*
▶ **More Than a Movie:** Social Issues and Film *229*

CHAPTER REVIEW *230*
▶ **LaunchPad** *231*

© Lucasfilm Ltd./Everett Collection

© Moviestore collection Ltd/Alamy Stock Photo

8 Newspapers: The Rise and Decline of Modern Journalism 235

The Evolution of American Newspapers 237

Colonial Newspapers and the Partisan Press 238

The Penny Press Era: Newspapers Become Mass Media 239

The Age of Yellow Journalism: Sensationalism and Investigation 240

Competing Models of Modern Print Journalism 242

"Objectivity" in Modern Journalism 242

Interpretive Journalism 244

Literary Forms of Journalism 245

Contemporary Journalism in the TV and Internet Age 246

▶ **Newspapers and the Internet: Convergence** 247

The Business and Ownership of Newspapers 247

Consensus versus Conflict: Newspapers Play Different Roles 248

■ **MEDIA LITERACY AND THE CRITICAL PROCESS**
Covering the News Media Business 249

Newspapers Target Specific Readers 251

Newspaper Operations 254

■ **EXAMINING ETHICS** Alternative Journalism: The Activism of Dorothy Day and I. F. Stone 256

Newspaper Ownership: Chains Lose Their Grip 257

Joint Operating Agreements Combat Declining Competition 258

Challenges Facing Newspapers Today 259

Readership Declines in the United States 259

Going Local: How Small and Campus Papers Retain Readers 259

▶ **Community Voices: Weekly Newspapers** 259

■ **GLOBAL VILLAGE** Newspaper Readership across the Globe 260

Convergence: Newspapers Struggle in the Move to Digital 261

New Models for Journalism 263

Alternative Voices 264

Newspapers and Democracy 265

CHAPTER REVIEW 268

▶ **LaunchPad** 269

9 Magazines in the Age of Specialization 271

The Early History of Magazines 273

The First Magazines 273

Magazines in Colonial America 274

U.S. Magazines in the Nineteenth Century 274

National, Women's, and Illustrated Magazines 275

The Development of Modern American Magazines 276

Social Reform and the Muckrakers 276

The Rise of General-Interest Magazines 277

The Fall of General-Interest Magazines 279

▣ **EXAMINING ETHICS** The Evolution of Photojournalism 280

Convergence: Magazines Confront the Digital Age 283

The Domination of Specialization 284

▶ **Magazine Specialization Today** 285

Men's and Women's Magazines 285

▣ **GLOBAL VILLAGE** Cosmopolitan Style Travels the World 286

Sports, Entertainment, and Leisure Magazines 286

Magazines for the Ages 288

Elite Magazines 288

■ **MEDIA LITERACY AND THE CRITICAL PROCESS** Uncovering American Beauty 289

Minority-Targeted Magazines 289

Supermarket Tabloids 290

The Organization and Economics of Magazines 291

Magazine Departments and Duties 291

▶ **Narrowcasting in Magazines** 291

Major Magazine Chains 294

Alternative Voices 294

Magazines in a Democratic Society 295

CHAPTER REVIEW 296

▶ **LaunchPad** 297

Daniel Zuchnik/Getty Images

Mandel Ngan/Getty Images

10 Books and the Power of Print *299*

The History of Books, from Papyrus to Paperbacks *301*

The Development of Manuscript Culture *302*

The Innovations of Block Printing and Movable Type *302*

The Gutenberg Revolution: The Invention of the Printing Press *303*

The Birth of Publishing in the United States *303*

Modern Publishing and the Book Industry *304*

The Formation of Publishing Houses *304*

Types of Books *305*

▣ **EXAMINING ETHICS** Contemporary Politics Revives Interest in Classic Novels *308*

Trends and Issues in Book Publishing *309*

▶ **Based On: Making Books into Movies** *309*

Influences of Television and Film *309*

Audio Books *310*

Convergence: Books in the Digital Age *310*

Preserving and Digitizing Books *311*

Censorship and Banned Books *312*

▣ **GLOBAL VILLAGE** Buenos Aires, the World's Bookstore Capital *313*

■ **MEDIA LITERACY AND THE CRITICAL PROCESS**
Banned Books and "Family Values" *314*

The Organization and Ownership of the Book Industry *314*

Ownership Patterns *315*

The Structure of Book Publishing *316*

Selling Books: Book Superstores and Independent Booksellers *318*

Selling Books Online *319*

Alternative Voices *320*

Books and the Future of Democracy *320*

CHAPTER REVIEW *322*

▶ **LaunchPad** *323*

11 Advertising and Commercial Culture 327

Early Developments in American Advertising 330

The First Advertising Agencies 330

Advertising in the 1800s 330

Promoting Social Change and Dictating Values 333

Early Ad Regulation 334

The Shape of U.S. Advertising Today 334

The Influence of Visual Design 334

Types of Advertising Agencies 335

The Structure of Ad Agencies 337

Trends in Online Advertising 340

▶ **Advertising in the Digital Age** 342

Persuasive Techniques in Contemporary Advertising 343

Conventional Persuasive Strategies 344

The Association Principle 345

Advertising as Myth and Story 345

Product Placement 346

▣ **EXAMINING ETHICS** Do Alcohol Ads Encourage Binge Drinking? 347

■ **MEDIA LITERACY AND THE CRITICAL PROCESS** The Branded You 348

Commercial Speech and Regulating Advertising 348

Critical Issues in Advertising 349

▶ **Advertising and Effects on Children** 350

▣ **GLOBAL VILLAGE** Smoking Up the Global Market 352

Watching Over Advertising 354

Alternative Voices 356

Advertising, Politics, and Democracy 356

Advertising's Role in Politics 357

The Future of Advertising 357

CHAPTER REVIEW 358

▶ **LaunchPad** 359

Kaling International/3 Arts Entertainment/Universal TV/Kobal/Shutterstock

Kirby Lee-USA TODAY Sports/Newscom

12 Public Relations and Framing the Message *361*

Early Developments in Public Relations *363*

P. T. Barnum and Buffalo Bill *364*

Big Business and Press Agents *364*

The Birth of Modern Public Relations *365*

The Practice of Public Relations *368*

Approaches to Organized Public Relations *368*

Performing Public Relations *369*

☐ **EXAMINING ETHICS** Public Relations and "Alternative Facts" *372*

☐ **GLOBAL VILLAGE** Public Relations and Bananas *374*

Public Relations Adapts to the Internet Age *376*

Public Relations during a Crisis *377*

Tensions between Public Relations and the Press *378*

Elements of Professional Friction *378*

▶ **Give and Take: Public Relations and Journalism** *378*

Shaping the Image of Public Relations *380*

Alternative Voices *380*

Public Relations and Democracy *381*

■ **MEDIA LITERACY AND THE CRITICAL PROCESS**
The Invisible Hand of PR *382*

CHAPTER REVIEW *384*

▶ **LaunchPad** *385*

13 Media Economics and the Global Marketplace 387

Analyzing the Media Economy 389
 The Structure of the Media Industry 390
 The Business of Media Organizations 390

The Transition to an Information Economy 391
 ▣ **EXAMINING ETHICS** Are the Big Digital Companies Too Big? 392
 From Regulation to Deregulation 393
 Media Powerhouses: Consolidation, Partnerships, and Mergers 394
 Business Tendencies in Media Industries 397
 Economics, Hegemony, and Storytelling 398

Specialization, Global Markets, and Convergence 400
 The Rise of Specialization and Synergy 401
 Disney: A Postmodern Media Conglomerate 401
 ▶ **Disney's Global Brand** 401
 Global Audiences Expand Media Markets 404
 The Internet and Convergence Change the Game 405
 ▪ **MEDIA LITERACY AND THE CRITICAL PROCESS**
  Cultural Imperialism and Movies 406

Social Issues in Media Economics 408
 The Limits of Antitrust Laws 408
 ▣ **GLOBAL VILLAGE** China's Dominant Media Corporations Rival America's 411
 ▶ **The Impact of Media Ownership** 412
 The Fallout from a Free Market 412
 Cultural Imperialism 413

The Media Marketplace and Democracy 415
 The Effects of Media Consolidation on Democracy 415
 The Media Reform Movement 416

CHAPTER REVIEW 418
 ▶ **LaunchPad** 419

Jim Wilson/The New York Times/Redux

14 The Culture of Journalism: Values, Ethics, and Democracy *423*

Modern Journalism in the Information Age *425*

What Is News? *425*

Values in American Journalism *427*

Ethics and the News Media *429*

▣ GLOBAL VILLAGE News Bias around the Globe *430*

Ethical Predicaments *431*

Resolving Ethical Problems *434*

Reporting Rituals and the Legacy of Print Journalism *435*

Focusing on the Present *435*

■ MEDIA LITERACY AND THE CRITICAL PROCESS
Telling Stories and Covering Disaster *436*

Relying on Experts . . . Usually Men *437*

Balancing Story Conflict *439*

Acting as Adversaries *439*

Journalism in the Age of TV and the Internet *440*

Differences between Print, TV, and Internet News *440*

Pundits, "Talking Heads," and Politics *442*

Convergence Enhances and Changes Journalism *442*

▶ The Contemporary Journalist: Pundit or Reporter? *442*

The Power of Visual Language *443*

Alternative Models: Public Journalism and "Fake News" *444*

The Rise and Decline of the Public Journalism Movement *444*

The Shifting Meanings of "Fake News" and the Rise of Satiric Journalism *446*

Democracy and Reimagining Journalism's Role *448*

Social Responsibility *448*

Deliberative Democracy *448*

▣ EXAMINING ETHICS WikiLeaks, Secret Documents, and Good Journalism *449*

A Lost Generation of Journalists *450*

CHAPTER REVIEW *452*

▶ LaunchPad *453*

15 Media Effects and Cultural Approaches to Research *455*

Early Media Research Methods *457*

    Propaganda Analysis *458*

    Public Opinion Research *458*

    Social Psychology Studies *459*

    Marketing Research *460*

Research on Media Effects *460*

    Early Theories of Media Effects *461*

    ▶ Media Effects Research *461*

    Conducting Media Effects Research *462*

    ■ MEDIA LITERACY AND THE CRITICAL PROCESS
    Wedding Media and the Meaning of the Perfect Wedding Day *465*

    Contemporary Media Effects Theories *466*

    Evaluating Research on Media Effects *469*

Cultural Approaches to Media Research *469*

    Early Developments in Cultural Studies Research *469*

    ▣ GLOBAL VILLAGE International Media Research *470*

    Conducting Cultural Studies Research *472*

    ▣ EXAMINING ETHICS Our Masculinity Problem *474*

    Cultural Studies' Theoretical Perspectives *475*

    Evaluating Cultural Studies Research *477*

Media Research and Democracy *478*

CHAPTER REVIEW *480*

    ▶ LaunchPad *481*

Netflix/Photofest

Alex Wong/Getty Images

16 Legal Controls and Freedom of Expression *483*

The Origins of Free Expression and a Free Press *485*

The First Amendment of the U.S. Constitution *486*

Censorship as Prior Restraint *487*

Unprotected Forms of Expression *489*

■ **MEDIA LITERACY AND THE CRITICAL PROCESS**
Who Knows the First Amendment? *490*

First Amendment versus Sixth Amendment *495*

Film and the First Amendment *497*

Social and Political Pressures on the Movies *497*

▣ **GLOBAL VILLAGE** The Challenges of Film Censorship in China *498*

Self-Regulation in the Movie Industry *499*

The MPAA Ratings System *500*

Expression in the Media: Print, Broadcast, and Online *501*

The FCC Regulates Broadcasting *501*

Dirty Words, Indecent Speech, and Hefty Fines *502*

Political Broadcasts and Equal Opportunity *504*

▶ **Bloggers and Legal Rights** *504*

The Demise of the Fairness Doctrine *505*

Communication Policy and the Internet *505*

▣ **EXAMINING ETHICS** Is "Sexting" Pornography? *506*

The First Amendment and Democracy *507*

CHAPTER REVIEW *508*

▶ **LaunchPad** *509*

EXTENDED CASE STUDY
Can We Trust Facebook with Our Personal Data? *511*

Step 1: Description *513*

Step 2: Analysis *514*

Step 3: Interpretation *515*

Step 4: Evaluation *516*

Step 5: Engagement *516*

NOTES *N-1*

GLOSSARY *G-1*

INDEX *I-1*

MEDIA & CULTURE

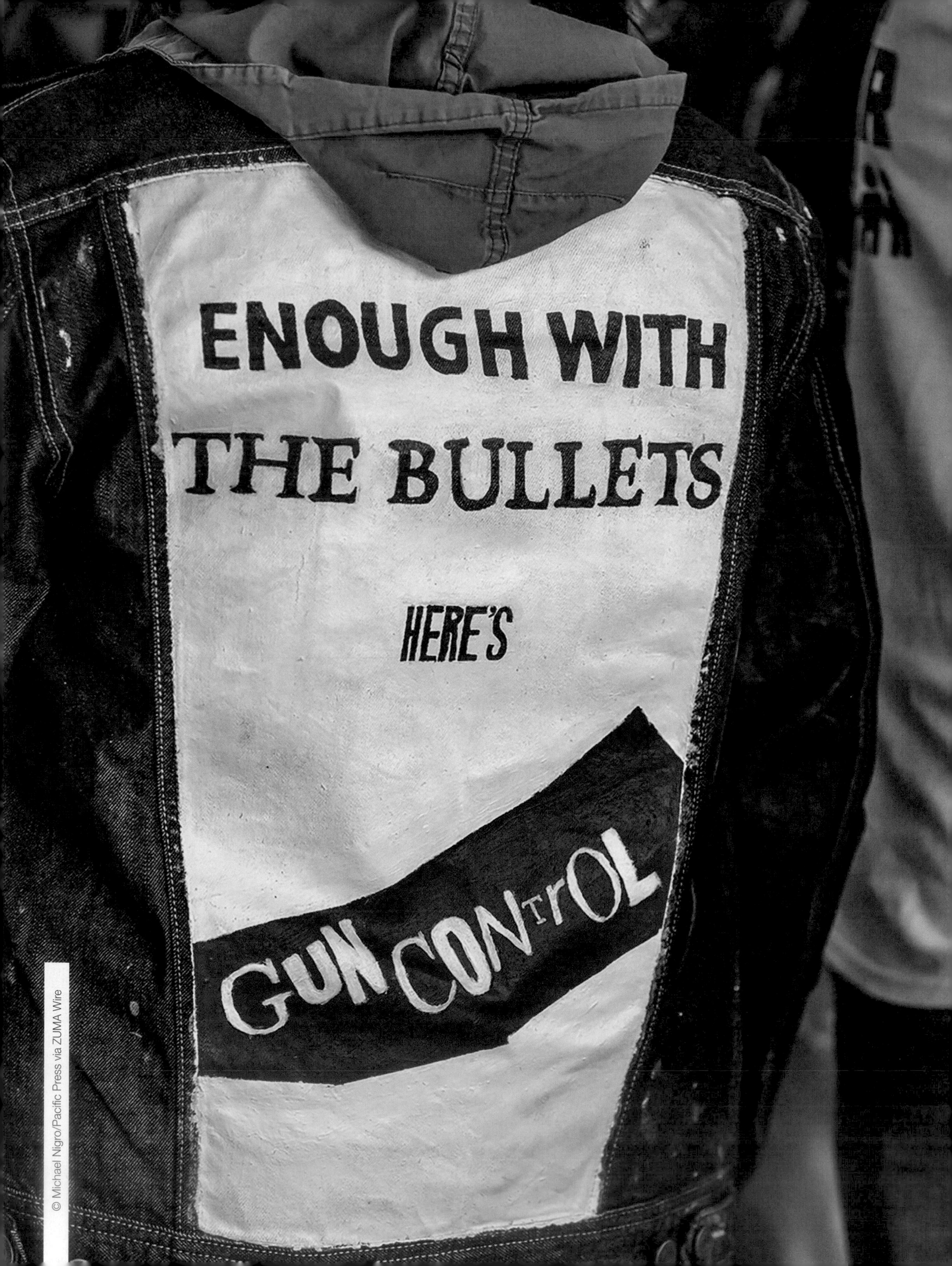
ENOUGH WITH
THE BULLETS
HERE'S
GUN CONTrOL

Mass Communication

A Critical Approach

AFTER THE 2018 school shooting at Marjory Stoneman Douglas High School in Parkland, Florida, where fourteen students and three staff members died, the *Washington Post* compiled a twenty-first-century list of U.S. school shootings: "Since 2000 . . . there have been more than 130 shootings at elementary, middle and high schools, and 58 others at colleges and universities."[1] But something happened after Parkland that did not happen after the murders of twenty schoolchildren and six adults at the Sandy Hook Elementary School in Newtown, Connecticut, in 2012, or the 2017 Las Vegas mass murder of fifty-eight concertgoers.

After the Parkland tragedy, young people took to social media and sustained an online debate over gun control and gun violence that lasted much longer than those following previous shooting tragedies, in which social media and TV

CULTURE AND THE EVOLUTION OF MASS COMMUNICATION
p. 5

THE DEVELOPMENT OF MEDIA AND THEIR ROLE IN OUR SOCIETY
p. 10

SURVEYING THE CULTURAL LANDSCAPE
p. 15

CRITIQUING MEDIA AND CULTURE
p. 25

◀ On March 24th, 2018, a demonstration led by student survivors of the Marjory Stoneman Douglas High School mass shooting gathered more than 1.2 million people to advocate for stricter gun control laws.

news reports usually died down after a couple of weeks. Take a look at the story leads from several newspapers from around the world after Parkland:

"Florida students have turned social media into a weapon for good. Teenagers' use of Twitter, Snapchat and Instagram is social media at its best—a cudgel against political discourse that desperately needs to change." —*Guardian*, 2/21/18

"A spontaneous show of anger from the survivors of the Friday school shooting has suddenly morphed into a national movement of young Americans calling for gun control." —*Australian*, 2/23/18

"Teenage survivors of the Parkland . . . shooting [have] amassed huge followings on social media in the weeks since the gunman attacked their school, assembling powerful social media tools in the national debate over guns and mass shooting." —*The Hill*, 3/3/18

The Hill reported at the time that one survivor of the shooting, senior Emma Gonzales, had more than 1.1 million followers on Twitter, compared to just 600,000 for the NRA (National Rifle Association), which exerts powerful sway over the nation's lawmakers.[2] In describing the social media storm after Parkland, the *Guardian* noted: "It took teenagers with smartphones and . . . confronted with injustice to jostle us out of that studied complacency."[3]

The question remains, however, whether the use of social media by young people can actually change laws and swing elections. Two months after the Parkland shooting, NPR and Marist pollsters offered this report: "While almost half of all registered voters (46 percent) say a candidate's position on gun policy will be a major factor in deciding whom to vote for, that number is down 13 points from February [when the Parkland shooting occurred]."[4]

In the end, Darrell West from the Brookings Institution noted in the months after Parkland that at the congressional level, efforts to pass reasonable gun control laws had "gone nowhere." However, West noted that if more young people turn out to vote in serious numbers on issues they care about—like gun control—they could determine an election that could change a law. "In 2010, when Republicans gained 63 seats in the U.S. House of Representatives and six in the U.S. Senate," West writes, "only 21 percent of young voters between the ages of 18 and 24 cast ballots. This was well below the 61 percent turnout for senior citizens and the overall total of 45 percent for the eligible population." According to West, "These turnout numbers were devastating for Democrats because young people are more liberal than the population as a whole and more likely to support meaningful action on gun violence."[5]

In a democracy, we depend on eligible voters to vote, and we rely on newspapers like the *New York Times*, the *Washington Post*, and the *Guardian* to provide information and analyses to help us make good decisions about our laws and leaders. And as Parkland demonstrated, we are seeing the power of social media to confront wrongdoing and organize a movement that might make things better. Despite their limitations, the media—from Twitter to the *Times*—serve as watchdogs, monitoring the social landscape and bringing problems to light. It is all of our jobs to point a critical lens back at the media and describe, analyze, and interpret news stories, political opinions, and social movements, arriving at informed judgments about the media's overall performance. This textbook offers a map to help us become more *media literate*, critiquing the variety of media that surround us, not as detached cynics or rabid partisans but as informed citizens with a stake in the outcome and with the power to effect change.

SO WHAT EXACTLY ARE THE RESPONSIBILITIES OF NEWSPAPERS AND MEDIA IN GENERAL? In an age of economic and social upheaval, how do we demand the highest standards from our media to describe and analyze complex events and issues? At their best, in all their various forms—from mainstream newspapers and radio talk shows to blogs—media try to help us understand the events that affect us. But at their worst, media's appetite for telling and selling stories leads them not only to document tragedy but also to misrepresent or exploit it. Many viewers and critics disapprove of how media, particularly TV and the Internet, hurtle from one event to another, often dwelling on trivial, celebrity-driven content.

In this book, we examine the history and business of mass media and discuss the media as a central force in shaping our culture and our democracy. We start by examining key concepts and introducing the critical process for investigating media industries and issues. In later chapters, we probe the history and structure of media's major institutions. In the process, we develop an informed and critical view of the influence these institutions have had on national and global life. The goal is to become media literate—to become critical consumers of mass media institutions and engaged participants who accept part of the responsibility for the shape and direction of media culture. In this chapter, we will:

- Address key ideas, including communication, culture, mass media, and mass communication
- Investigate important periods in communication history: the oral, written, print, electronic, and digital eras
- Examine the development of a mass medium from emergence to convergence
- Learn about how convergence has changed our relationship to media
- Look at the central role of storytelling in media and culture
- Discuss the skyscraper and map models for organizing and categorizing culture
- Trace important cultural values in both modern and postmodern societies
- Study media literacy and the five stages of the critical process: description, analysis, interpretation, evaluation, and engagement

As you read through this chapter, think about your early experiences with the media. Identify a favorite media product from your childhood—a song, book, TV show, or movie. Why was it so important to you? How much of an impact did your early taste in media have on your identity? How has your taste shifted over time? What do your current media preferences indicate about your identity now? Do your current tastes reveal anything about you? For more questions to help you think about the role of media in your life, see "Questioning the Media" in the Chapter Review.

LaunchPad
macmillan learning

launchpadworks.com

Visit LaunchPad for *Media & Culture* and use LearningCurve to review concepts from this chapter.

CULTURE AND THE EVOLUTION OF MASS COMMUNICATION

One way to understand the impact of media on our lives is to explore the cultural context in which media operate. Often, culture is narrowly associated with art—the unique forms of creative expression that give pleasure and set standards about what is true, good, and beautiful. Culture, however, can be viewed more broadly as the ways in which people live and represent themselves at particular historical times. This idea of culture encompasses fashion, sports, literature, architecture, education, religion, and science, as well as mass media. Although we can study discrete cultural products, such as novels or songs, from various historical periods, culture itself is always changing. It includes a society's art, beliefs, customs, games, technologies, traditions, and institutions. It also encompasses a society's modes of **communication**: the creation and use of symbol systems that convey information and meaning (e.g., languages, Morse code, motion pictures, and binary computer codes).

Culture is made up of both the products that a society fashions and, perhaps more importantly, the processes that forge those products and reflect a culture's diverse values. Thus, **culture** may be defined as the symbols of expression that individuals, groups, and societies use to make sense of daily life and to articulate their values. According to this definition, when we listen to music, read a book, watch television, or scan the Internet, we are not usually asking "Is this art?" but trying to identify or connect with something or someone. In other words, we are assigning meaning to the song, book, TV program, or website. Culture, therefore, is a process that delivers the values of a society through products or other meaning-making forms. For example, the American ideal of "rugged individualism"—depicting heroic characters overcoming villains or corruption—has been portrayed on television for decades through a tradition of detective stories and police procedurals, such as PBS's *Sherlock* and *Endeavor* and CBS's *Elementary* and various incarnations of *NCIS*.

Culture links individuals to their society by providing both shared and contested values, and the mass media help circulate those values. The **mass media** are the cultural industries—the channels of communication—that produce and distribute songs, novels, TV shows, newspapers, movies, video games, Internet services, and other cultural products to large numbers of people. The historical development of media and communication can be traced through several overlapping phases or eras in which newer forms of technology disrupted and modified older forms—a process that many critics and media professionals began calling *convergence* with the arrival of the Internet.

These eras, which all still operate to some degree, are oral, written, print, electronic, and digital. The first two refer to the communication of tribal or feudal communities and agricultural economies. The last three feature the development of **mass communication**: the process of designing cultural messages and stories and delivering them to large and diverse audiences through media channels as old and distinctive as the printed book and as new and converged as the Internet. Hastened by the growth of industry and modern technology, mass communication accompanied the shift of rural populations to urban settings and the rise of a consumer culture.

Oral and Written Eras in Communication

In most early societies, information and knowledge first circulated slowly through oral traditions passed on by poets, teachers, and tribal storytellers. As alphabets and the written word emerged, however, a manuscript—or written—culture began to develop and eventually overshadowed oral customs. Documented and transcribed by philosophers, monks, and stenographers, the manuscript culture served the ruling classes. Working people were generally illiterate, and the economic and educational gap between rulers and the ruled was vast. These eras of oral and written communication developed slowly over many centuries. Although exact time frames are disputed, historians generally consider these eras as part of Western civilization's premodern period, spanning the epoch from roughly 1000 BCE to the beginnings of the Industrial Revolution.

Early tensions between oral and written communication played out among ancient Greek philosophers and writers. Many philosophers who believed in the superiority of the oral tradition feared that the written word would threaten public discussion. In fact, Plato sought to banish poets, whom he saw as purveyors of ideas less rigorous than those generated in oral, face-to-face question-and-answer discussions. These debates foreshadowed similar discussions in our time in which we ask whether TV news, Twitter, or online comment sections cheapen public discussion and discourage face-to-face communication.

The Print Revolution

While paper and block printing developed in China around 100 CE and 1045, respectively, what we recognize as modern printing did not emerge until the middle of the fifteenth century. At that time in Germany, Johannes Gutenberg's invention of movable metallic type and the printing press ushered in the modern print era. Printing presses and publications spread rapidly across Europe in the late fifteenth and early sixteenth centuries. Early on, the size and expense of books limited their audience to the wealthy and powerful, but as printers reduced their size and cost, books became available and affordable to more people.

Books eventually became the first mass-marketed products in history because of the way the printing press combined three necessary elements. First, machine duplication replaced the tedious system in which scribes hand-copied texts. Second, duplication could occur rapidly, so large quantities of the same book could be reproduced easily. Third, the faster production of multiple copies brought down the cost of each unit, making books more affordable to less-affluent people.

Since mass-produced printed materials could spread information and ideas faster and farther than ever before, writers could use print to disseminate views counter to traditional civic doctrine and religious authority—views that paved the way for major social and cultural changes, such as the Protestant Reformation and the rise of modern nationalism, as people began to think of themselves as part of a country whose interests were broader than local or regional concerns. Whereas oral and written societies had favored decentralized local governments, the print era supported the ascent of more centralized nation-states.

Eventually, machine production became an essential factor in the mass production of other goods, which led to the Industrial Revolution, modern capitalism, and the consumer culture of the twentieth century. With the revolution in industry came the rise of the middle class and an elite business class of owners and managers who acquired the kind of influence formerly held only by nobility or clergy. Print media became key tools that commercial and political leaders used to distribute information and maintain social order.

As with the Internet today, however, it was difficult for a single business or political leader, certainly in a democratic society, to gain exclusive control over printing technology (although many leaders tried). Instead, the mass publication of pamphlets, magazines, and books in the United States helped democratize knowledge, and literacy rates rose among the working and middle classes. Industrialization required a more educated workforce, but printed literature and textbooks also encouraged compulsory education, thus promoting literacy and extending learning beyond the world of wealthy upper-class citizens.

Just as the printing press fostered nationalism, it also nourished the ideal of individualism. People came to rely less on their local community and their commercial, religious, and political leaders for guidance. By challenging insulated tribal life and rituals, the printing press "fostered the modern idea of individuality," disrupting "the medieval sense of community and integration."[6] By the mid-nineteenth century, the ideal of individualism affirmed the rise of commerce and increased resistance to government interference in the affairs of self-reliant entrepreneurs. The democratic impulse of individualism became a fundamental value in American society in the nineteenth and twentieth centuries.

The Electronic Era

In Europe and the United States, the impact of industry's rise was enormous: Factories replaced farms as the main centers of work and production. During the 1880s, roughly 80 percent of Americans lived on farms and in small towns; by the 1920s and 1930s, most had moved to urban areas, where new industries and economic opportunities beckoned. The city had overtaken the country as the focal point of national life.

The gradual transformation from an industrial, print-based society to one grounded in the Information Age began with the development of the telegraph in the 1840s. Featuring dot-dash electronic signals, the telegraph made four key contributions to communication. First, it separated communication from transportation, making media messages

Scala/Art Resource, NY

EARLY BOOKS
Before the invention of the printing press, books were copied by hand in a labor-intensive process. This beautifully illuminated page is from an Italian Bible made in the early fourteenth century.

instantancous—unencumbered by stagecoaches, ships, or the pony express.[7] Second, in combination with the rise of mass-marketed newspapers, the telegraph transformed "information into a commodity, a 'thing' that could be bought or sold irrespective of its uses or meaning."[8] By the time of the Civil War, news had become a valuable product. Third, the telegraph made it easier for military, business, and political leaders to coordinate commercial and military operations, especially after the installation of the transatlantic cable in the late 1860s. Fourth, the telegraph led to future technological developments, such as wireless telegraphy (later named radio), the fax machine, and the cell phone, which ironically resulted in the telegraph's demise: In 2006, Western Union telegraph offices sent their final messages.

The rise of film at the turn of the twentieth century and the development of radio in the 1920s were early signals of the electronic phase of the Information Age, but it really boomed in the 1950s and 1960s with the arrival of television and its dramatic influence on daily life. Then, with the coming of ever more communication gadgetry—personal computers, cable TV, DVDs, DVRs, direct broadcast satellites, cell phones, and smartphones—the Information Age passed into its digital phase, where old and new media began to converge, thus dramatically changing our relationship to media and culture.

The Digital Era

In **digital communication**, images, texts, and sounds are converted (encoded) into electronic signals—represented as varied combinations of binary numbers (ones and zeros)—that are then reassembled (decoded) as a precise reproduction of, say, a TV picture, a magazine article, a song, or a telephone voice. On the Internet, various images, texts, and sounds are digitally reproduced and transmitted globally.

New technologies, particularly cable television and the Internet, developed so quickly that traditional leaders in communication lost some of their control over information. For example, starting with the 1992 presidential campaign, the network news shows (ABC, CBS, and NBC) began to lose their audiences to cable channels and partisan radio talk shows. By the 2012 national elections, Facebook, Twitter, and other social media sites had become key players in news and politics, especially as information resources for younger generations who had grown up in an online and digital world.

Moreover, e-mail—a digital reinvention of oral culture—followed by Facebook, Twitter, Instagram, and Snapchat (among other social media), assumed many of the functions of the postal service and is outpacing attempts to control communication beyond national borders. Furthermore, many repressive and totalitarian regimes have had trouble controlling messages sent out over the borderless Internet. In the old snail mail days, it was easier for governments to monitor communication coming in and going out of a country.

In reinventing oral culture, *social media* have enabled people from all over the world to have ongoing online conversations, share stories and interests, and generate their own media content. This turn to digital media forms has fundamentally disrupted traditional media business models, the ways we engage with and consume media products, and the ways we organize our daily lives around various media choices.

The Linear Model of Mass Communication

The digital era also brought about a shift in the models that media researchers have used over the years to explain how media messages and meanings are constructed and communicated in everyday life. One older and outdated explanation of how media operate viewed mass communication as a linear process of producing and delivering messages to large audiences. According to this model, senders (authors, producers, and organizations) transmitted messages (programs, texts, images, sounds, and ads) through a mass media channel (newspapers, books, magazines, radio, television, or the Internet) to large groups of receivers (readers, viewers, and consumers). In the process, gatekeepers (news editors, executive producers, and other media managers) functioned as message filters. Media gatekeepers made decisions about what messages actually got produced for particular receivers. The process also allowed for feedback, in which citizens and consumers, if they chose, returned messages to senders or gatekeepers through phone calls, e-mail, web postings, talk shows, or letters to the editor.

But the problem with the linear model was that in reality, media messages—especially in the digital era—do not usually move smoothly from a sender at point A to a receiver at point Z. Words and images are more likely to spill into one another, crisscrossing in the daily media deluge of product ads, TV shows, news reports, social media, smartphone apps, and everyday conversation. Media messages and stories are encoded and sent in written and visual forms, but senders often have very little control over how their intended messages are decoded or whether the messages are ignored or misread by readers and viewers.

A Cultural Model for Understanding Mass Communication

A more contemporary approach to understanding media is through a cultural model. This concept recognizes that individuals bring diverse meanings to messages, given factors and differences such as gender, age, educational level, ethnicity, and occupation. In this more complex model of mass communication, audiences actively affirm, interpret, refashion, or reject the messages and stories that flow through various media channels. And audiences can assign completely opposite meanings to the same message. For example, when President Trump has referred to CNN or the *New York Times* as "fake news," his supporters have interpreted such language as a justified attack on elite out-of-touch news media, whereas his critics have viewed this kind of unsubstantiated generalization as an attack on the First Amendment and the news media's essential job to report on government leaders.

While the linear model may have shown how a message gets from a sender to a receiver, the cultural model suggests the complexity of this process and the lack of control that senders (such as media executives, moviemakers, writers, news editors, and ad agencies) often have over how audiences receive messages and interpret their intended meanings. Sometimes the producers of media messages seem to be the active creators of communication, with audiences serving merely as passive receptacles. But as the Trump example illustrates, research shows that consumers and citizens in general shape media messages to fit or support their own values and viewpoints. This phenomenon is known as **selective exposure**: People typically seek messages and produce meanings that correspond to their own cultural beliefs, values, and interests. For example, studies have shown that people with political leanings toward the left or the right seek out blogs or news outlets that reinforce those preexisting views.

In addition, a cultural approach to media focuses us on how meaning is produced rather than on how messages are transmitted. Under this model, a key point is understanding that meaning emerges at the tangled intersection of (1) the creator's vision, usually conveyed in story form; (2) the industry's control of production and distribution processes, or the telling and selling of stories; and (3) audiences' fragmented responses—that is, why we choose and enjoy particular stories (and not others), how we use and consume various media, and how we impose our own varied meanings on the array of media available.

The rise of the Internet and social media has also complicated the communication and meaning-making process. While there are still senders and receivers, the borderless, decentralized, and democratic nature of the Internet means that anyone can become a sender of media messages—whether it's by uploading a video mash-up to YouTube or by writing a blog post. The Internet has also largely eliminated the many gatekeepers. Although some governments try to control Internet servers, and some websites have restrictions on what can and cannot be posted, the Internet for the most part allows senders to transmit content without obtaining approval—or undergoing editing—from a gatekeeper. For example, some authors who are unable to find a traditional book publisher for their work turn to self-publishing on the Internet. And musicians who don't have deals with major record labels can promote, circulate, and sell their music online.

THE DEVELOPMENT OF MEDIA AND THEIR ROLE IN OUR SOCIETY

The mass media today constitute a wide variety of industries and merchandise. The word *media* is, after all, a Latin plural form of the singular noun *medium*, meaning an intervening substance through which something is conveyed or transmitted. Television, newspapers, music, movies, magazines, books, billboards, radio, broadcast satellites, and the Internet are all part of the media, and they are all quite capable of either producing worthy products or pandering to society's worst desires, prejudices, and stereotypes. Let's take a look at how mass media develop, how they work, and how they are interpreted in society and by individuals.

The Evolution of Media: From Emergence to Convergence

The development of most mass media is initiated not only by the diligence of inventors, such as Thomas Edison, but also by social, cultural, political, and economic circumstances. For instance, both telegraph and radio evolved as newly industrialized nations sought to expand their military and economic control and to transmit information more rapidly. The Internet is a contemporary response to new concerns: transporting messages and sharing information more rapidly for an increasingly mobile and interconnected global population.

Media innovations typically go through four stages. First is the *emergence*, or *novelty*, *stage*, in which inventors and technicians try to solve a particular problem, such as making pictures move, transmitting messages from ship to shore, or sending mail electronically. Second is the *entrepreneurial stage*, in which inventors and investors determine a practical and marketable use for the new device. For example, the Internet had its roots in the ideas of military leaders, who wanted a communication system that was decentralized and distributed widely enough to survive nuclear war or natural disasters.

The third phase in a medium's development involves a breakthrough to the *mass medium stage*. At this point, businesses figure out how to market the new device or medium as a consumer product. Although the Pentagon and government researchers helped develop early prototypes for the Internet, commercial interests and individual entrepreneurs extended the Internet's global reach and business potential.

Finally, the fourth and newest phase in a medium's evolution is the *convergence stage*. This is the stage in which older media are reconfigured in various forms into newer media. However, this does not necessarily mean that the older forms cease to exist. For example, you can still get the *New York Times* in print, but it's also now accessible on laptops and smartphones. During this stage, we see the merging of many different media forms onto online platforms, but we also see the fragmenting of large audiences into smaller niche markets. With new technologies allowing access to more media options than ever before, mass audiences are morphing into audience subsets that consume and chase particular products, lifestyles, politics, hobbies, and forms of entertainment.

Media Convergence

Developments in the electronic and digital eras enabled and ushered in this latest stage in the development of media—**convergence**—a term that media critics and analysts use when describing all the changes that have occurred over the past decade, and are still occurring, in media content and within media companies. The term actually has two meanings—one referring to technology and one to business—and describes changes that have a huge impact on how media companies are charting a course for the future.

The Dual Meanings of Media Convergence

The first meaning of media convergence involves the technological merging of content across different media channels—the magazine articles, radio programs, songs, TV shows, video games, and movies now available on the Internet through laptops, tablets, and smartphones.

Camerique/ClassicStock/Getty Images

Blend Images/Getty Images

Such technical convergence is not entirely new. For example, in the late 1920s, the Radio Corporation of America (RCA) purchased the Victor Talking Machine Company and introduced machines that could play both radio and recorded music, helping radio survive the eventual emergence of television with more music-based content. However, contemporary media convergence is much broader than the simple merging of older and newer forms. In fact, the eras of communication are themselves reinvented in this "age of convergence." Oral communication, for example, finds itself reconfigured in part in e-mail and social media. And print communication is re-formed in the thousands of newspapers now available online. Also, keep in mind the wonderful ironies of media convergence: The first major digital retailer, Amazon, made its name by selling the world's oldest mass medium—the book—on the world's newest mass medium—the Internet.

A second meaning of media convergence—sometimes called **cross platform** by media marketers—describes a business model that involves consolidating various media holdings, such as cable connections, phone services, television transmissions, and Internet access, under one corporate umbrella. The goal is not necessarily to offer consumers more choice in their media options but to better manage resources and maximize profits. For example, a company that owns TV stations, radio outlets, and newspapers in multiple markets—as well as in the same cities—can deploy a reporter or producer to create three or four versions of the same story for various media outlets. So rather than having each radio station, TV station, newspaper, and online news site generate diverse and independent stories about an important issue or a significant event, a media corporation employing the convergence model can use fewer employees to generate multiple versions of the same story.

Media Businesses in a Converged World

The ramifications of media convergence are best revealed in the business strategies of digital age companies like Amazon, Facebook, Apple, and especially Google—the most profitable company of the digital era so far. Google is the Internet's main organizer because it finds both "new" and "old" media content—like videos and newspapers—and aggregates that content for vast numbers of online consumers. Although Google does own YouTube, the company does not produce traditional media content but functions instead as a delivery or distribution site. Most consumers who find a news story or magazine article through a Google search pay nothing to the original media content provider or to Google. Instead, Google—as the distributor, or intermediary—makes most of its money by selling ads that accompany search results. But not all ads are created equal; as writer and journalism critic James Fallows points out, much of the company's money comes from shopping-related searches rather than from the information searches for which it is best known. In fact, Fallows writes that Google, which has certainly done its part in contributing to the decline of newspapers, still has a large stake in seeing newspapers succeed online.[9] Over the last few years, Google has attempted to help older news media make the transition into the converged world. Since they aren't in the content creation business, Google executives depend on news organizations to produce the quality information and news stories that healthy democracies need—and that Google can deliver.

Still, as the website Mashable reported late in 2017, "The internet is filled with too many fake news websites . . . and Google's taking another step to stop this garbage from misleading people. The tech giant is now blocking websites from showing up in search results on Google News when they mask their country of origin."[10] Here is Google's policy:

> Sites included in Google News must not misrepresent, misstate, or conceal information about their ownership or primary purpose, or engage in coordinated activity to mislead users. This includes, but isn't limited to, sites that misrepresent or conceal their country of origin or are directed at users in another country under false premises.

As Mashable noted at the time of the policy announcement: "The change may seem small, but it will have wide-ranging impact. By not including websites that mask their country of origin, Google is effectively burying fake news and reducing its chances of spreading."

Today's converged media world has broken down the old definitions of distinct media forms like newspapers and television—both now available online and across multiple platforms. And it favors players like Google, whose business model works in a world where customers expect to get their media in multiple places—and often for free. But the challenge ahead in the new, converged world is not only distinguishing legitimate sites from fake ones but also resolving who will pay for quality content and how that system will emerge. In the upcoming industry chapters, we take a closer look at how media convergence is affecting each industry in terms of both content production and business strategies.

Media Convergence and Cultural Change

The Internet and social media have led to significant changes in the ways we consume and engage with media culture. In the pre-Internet days (say, back in the late 1980s), most people would watch popular TV shows like *Dallas*, *Happy Days*, or *M.A.S.H.* at the time they originally aired. Such scheduling provided common media experiences at specific times within our culture. Although we still watch TV shows, we are increasingly likely to do so at our convenience through websites like Hulu, Amazon, and Netflix or through DVR/on-demand options. We are also increasingly making our media choices on the basis of Facebook, YouTube, or Twitter recommendations from friends. Or we upload our own media—from photos of last night's party to homemade videos of our hobbies, exploits, and pets—to share with friends instead of watching traditional network programs. While these options allow us to connect with friends or family and give us more choices, they also break down old rituals, like a family's gathering one evening a week to watch the comedy lineup on ABC or NBC. Instead, most media experiences find us chasing our individual interests online and on our smartphones. However, the upside in the digital age is that today, many families gather on weekends or during holidays to binge-watch TV series they've missed during the week.

The ability to access many different forms of media in one place is also changing the ways we engage with and consume media. In the past, we read newspapers in print, watched TV on our television sets, and played video games on a console. Today, we are able to do all these things on a computer, tablet, or smartphone, making it easy—and very tempting—to *multitask*. Media multitasking has led to growing media consumption, particularly for young people. A Kaiser Family Foundation study found that today's youth packed ten hours and forty-five minutes' worth of media content into the seven and a half hours they spent daily consuming media.[11] And even though much of this consumption involves social connections, are we really engaging with our friends when we communicate with them by texting or posting on Facebook or Twitter? Some critics and educators feel that media multitasking means that we are more distracted, that we engage less with each type of media we consume, and that we often pay much closer attention to the media device in our hand than to the person standing next to us.

However, media multitasking can have other effects. In the past, we would wait until the end of a TV program, or even the next day, to discuss it with our friends. Now, with the proliferation of social media, we can discuss that program with our friends—and with strangers—as we watch the show. Many TV shows now gauge their popularity with audiences by how many people are "live-tweeting" them and by how many related trending topics they have on Twitter. This type of participation could indicate that audiences are in fact engaging more with the media they consume, even though they are multitasking. Some media critics even posit that having more choice actually makes us more engaged media consumers, because we have to actively choose the media we want to consume from the growing list of options.

Stories: The Foundation of Media

The stories that circulate in the media can shape a society's perceptions and attitudes. During the first years of the wars in Afghanistan and Iraq, courageous professional journalists covered armed conflicts, telling stories that helped the public comprehend the magnitude and tragedy of such events. In the 1950s and 1960s, network television news stories on the Civil Rights movement led to crucial legislation that transformed the way many white people viewed the grievances and aspirations of African Americans. In the late 1990s, news and tabloid magazine stories about the President Clinton–Monica Lewinsky affair sparked heated debates over private codes of behavior and public abuses of authority. Today, impassioned discourse led by the eloquent survivors of the shooting at Marjory Stoneman Douglas High School has once again turned the topic of gun violence and control into a national dialogue. In each of these instances, the stories told through a variety of media outlets played a key role in changing individual awareness, cultural attitudes, and public perception.

Although we continue to look to the media for narratives today, the kinds of stories we seek out and tell are changing in the digital era. During Hollywood's Golden Age in the 1930s and 1940s, as many as ninety million people went to the movies each Saturday. In the 1980s, during TV's Network Era, most of us sat down each evening to watch professionally produced news or scripted sitcoms and dramas, written by paid writers and performed by seasoned actors. But in the digital age, many of the performances feature nonprofessionals. The stories we watch on YouTube and read on blog sites are mostly produced by amateurs. Audiences are fascinated by stories of couples finding love, relationships gone bad, and backstabbing friends on franchise shows like *The Bachelor* or *Real Housewives*. Some reality shows—like *Big Brother*, *Born This Way*, and *Shark Tank*—give us glimpses into the lives and careers of everyday people, while others entertain us by pitting amateurs against each other on talent, singing, and cooking competitions such as *America's Got Talent*, *The Voice*, and *Top Chef*. While these shows are all professionally produced, the performers are for the most part "ordinary" people (or celebrities and professionals performing alongside amateurs). This is part of the appeal of reality TV—relating to the characters or comparing our lives with theirs because they seem just like us. Part of the appeal, too, is feeling superior to characters who often make bad decisions that we can judge or laugh about.

Online, many of us are entertaining and informing one another with videos of our pets, Facebook posts about our achievements or relationship issues, photos of a good meal, or tweets about the latest school shooting and gun control. This cultural blending of old and new ways of telling stories and offering opinions—told by both professionals and amateurs—is just another form of convergence that has disrupted and altered the media landscape in the digital era. More than ever, ordinary citizens are able to participate in, and have an effect on, the stories told in the media. Our varied media institutions and outlets are, after all, in the **narrative**—or storytelling—business. Media stories put events in context, helping us better understand both our daily lives and the larger world. As psychologist Jerome Bruner argues, we are storytelling creatures, and as children, we acquire language to tell the stories we have inside us.[12] The common denominator, in fact, between our entertainment and information cultures is the narrative. It is the media's main cultural currency—whether it's a hilarious and heartwarming Super Bowl commercial, a post on a gossip blog, a Fox News "exclusive," a *New York Times*

On October 21, 1967, a crowd of 100,000 protesters marched on the Pentagon, demanding the end of the Vietnam War. Sadly, violence erupted when some protesters clashed with the U.S. Marshals protecting the Pentagon. However, this iconic image from the same protest appeared in the *Washington Post* the next day and went on to become a symbol for the peaceful ideals behind the protests. When has an image in the media made an event "real" to you?

Marc Riboud/Magnum Photos

article, or a tweet praising a local restaurant about a recent dining experience. The point is that the popular narratives of our culture are complex and varied. Narratives are, in the end, the dominant way we make sense and meaning of our experiences. As writer Joan Didion once put it, "We tell ourselves stories in order to live."[13]

Media Stories in Everyday Life

The earliest debates, at least in Western society, about the impact of cultural narratives on daily life date back to the ancient Greeks. Socrates, himself accused of corrupting young minds, worried that children exposed to popular art forms and stories "without distinction" would "take into their souls teachings that are wholly opposite to those we wish them to be possessed of when they are grown up."[14] He believed that art should uplift us from the ordinary routines of our lives. The playwright Euripides, however, believed that art should imitate life, that characters should be "real," and that artistic works should reflect the actual world—even when that reality is sordid.

In *The Republic*, Plato developed the classical view of art: It should aim to instruct and uplift. He worried that some staged performances glorified evil and that common folk watching might not be able to distinguish between art and reality. Aristotle, Plato's student, occupied a middle ground in these debates, arguing that art and stories should provide insight into the human condition but should entertain as well.

The cultural concerns of classical philosophers are still with us. In the early 1900s, for example, newly arrived immigrants to the United States, who spoke little English, gravitated toward cultural events whose enjoyment did not depend solely on understanding English. Consequently, these popular events—such as boxing, vaudeville, and the emerging medium of silent film—became a flash point for some groups, including the Daughters of the American Revolution, local politicians, religious leaders, and police vice squads, who not only resented the commercial success of immigrant culture but also feared that these "low" cultural forms would undermine what they saw as traditional American values and interests.

In the United States in the 1950s, the phenomenal popularity of Elvis Presley set the stage for many of today's debates over hip-hop lyrics and television's influence, especially on young people.

LaunchPad
macmillan learning
launchpadworks.com

Agenda Setting and Gatekeeping
Experts discuss how the media exert influence over public discourse.

Discussion: How might the rise of the Internet cancel out or reduce the agenda-setting effect in media?

Back in 2006, President George W. Bush criticized the news media for not showing enough "good news" about U.S. efforts to bring democracy to Iraq. Bush's remarks raised ethical questions about the complex relationship between the government and the news media during times of war: How much freedom should the news media have to cover a war? How much control, if any, should the military have over reporting a war? Are there topics that should not be covered?

These kinds of questions have also created ethical quagmires for local TV stations that cover war and its effects on communities where soldiers have been called to duty and then injured or killed. In one extreme case, the nation's largest TV station owner—Sinclair Broadcast Group—would not air the ABC News program *Nightline* in 2004 because it devoted an episode to reading the names of all U.S. soldiers killed in the Iraq War up to that time. Here is an excerpt from a *New York Times* account of that event:

> Sinclair Broadcast Group, one of the largest owners of local television stations, will preempt tonight's edition of the ABC News program "Nightline," saying the program's plan to have Ted Koppel [who then anchored the program] read aloud the names of every member of the armed forces killed in action in Iraq was motivated by an antiwar agenda and threatened to undermine American efforts there.
>
> The decision means viewers in eight cities, including St. Louis and Columbus, Ohio, will not see "Nightline." ABC News disputed that the program carried a political message, calling it "an expression of respect which simply seeks to honor those who have laid down their lives for their country."
>
> But Mark Hyman, the vice president of corporate relations for Sinclair, who is also a conservative commentator on the company's newscasts, said tonight's edition of "Nightline" is biased journalism. "Mr. Koppel's reading of the fallen will have no proportionality," he said in a telephone interview, pointing out that the program will ignore other aspects of the war effort.
>
> Mr. Koppel and the producers of "Nightline" said earlier this week that they had no political motivation behind the decision to devote an entire show, expanded to 40 minutes, to reading the names and displaying the photos of those killed. They said they only intended to honor the dead and document what Mr. Koppel called "the human cost" of the war.[1]

Given such a case, how might a local TV news director today—under pressure from the station's manager or owner—formulate guidelines to help negotiate such ethical territory? While most TV news divisions have ethical codes to guide journalists' behavior in certain situations, could ordinary citizens help shape ethical discussions and decisions? Following is a general plan for dealing with an array of ethical dilemmas that media practitioners face and for finding ways in which nonjournalists might participate in this decision-making process.

Arriving at ethical decisions about the appropriate use of photos and videos requires a particular kind of criticism involving several steps: (1) laying out the case; (2) pinpointing the key issues; (3) identifying the parties involved, their intents, and their potentially competing values; (4) studying ethical models and theories; (5) presenting strategies and options; and (6) formulating a decision or policy.[2]

As a test case, let's look at how local TV news directors might use the six steps to establish ethical guidelines for war-related events or domestic tragedies, such as mass shootings at schools, churches, movie theaters, and concerts. The goal of this exercise is to make ethical decisions and to lay the groundwork for policies that address videos or photographs that are disturbing, whether they are images of war or domestic terrorism. (See Chapter 14 for details on confronting ethical problems.)

Examining Ethics Activity

As a class or in smaller groups, design policies that address one or more of the issues raised here. Start by researching the topic, gathering as much information as possible. For example, you can research guidelines that local TV stations already use by contacting local news directors and TV journalists.

Do the local TV stations have guidelines in place? If so, are they adequate? Are there certain types of images they will not show? Based on your research and the six steps, design a set of policies that you believe local TV stations should follow when reporting on war or domestic tragedies. Regarding school shootings, for example, consider whether TV stations should air or post footage from the smartphones of victims. Finally, if time allows, send the policies you designed to various TV news directors or station managers. Request their evaluations, and ask whether they would consider implementing the policies.

FIGURE 1.2

CULTURE AS A SKYSCRAPER

Culture is diverse and difficult to categorize. Yet throughout the twentieth century, we tended to think of culture not as a social process but as a set of products sorted into high, low, or middle positions on a cultural skyscraper. Look at this highly arbitrary arrangement, and decide whether you agree or disagree. Write in some of your own examples.

Why do we categorize or classify culture in this way? Who controls this process? Is control of making cultural categories important? Why or why not?

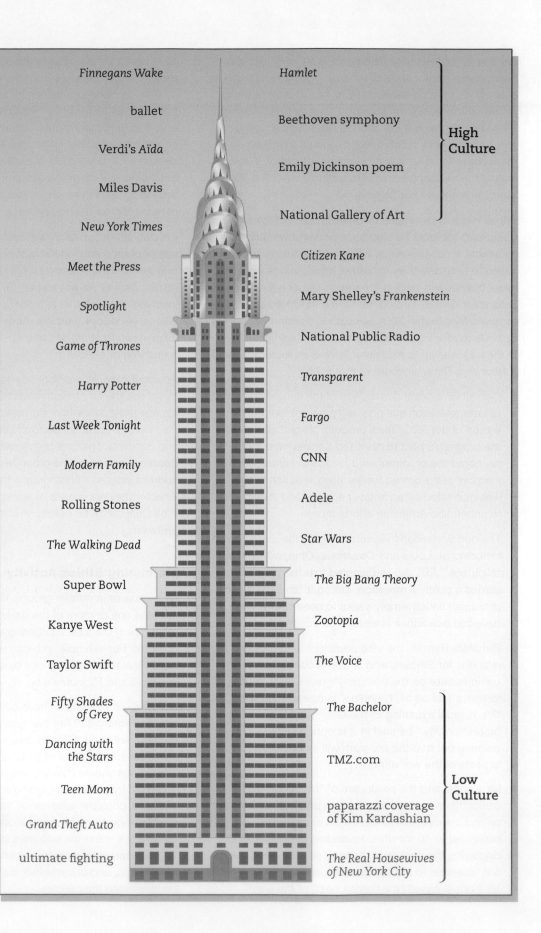

Finnegans Wake — Hamlet
ballet — Beethoven symphony
Verdi's Aïda — Emily Dickinson poem
Miles Davis
New York Times — National Gallery of Art

High Culture

Meet the Press — Citizen Kane
Spotlight — Mary Shelley's Frankenstein
Game of Thrones — National Public Radio
Harry Potter — Transparent
Last Week Tonight — Fargo
Modern Family — CNN
Rolling Stones — Adele
The Walking Dead — Star Wars
Super Bowl — The Big Bang Theory
Kanye West — Zootopia
Taylor Swift — The Voice
Fifty Shades of Grey — The Bachelor
Dancing with the Stars — TMZ.com
Teen Mom — paparazzi coverage of Kim Kardashian
Grand Theft Auto
ultimate fighting — The Real Housewives of New York City

Low Culture

"good taste" and higher education and supported by wealthy patrons and corporate donors, is associated with fine art, which is available primarily in libraries, theaters, and museums. In contrast, low or popular culture is aligned with the "questionable" tastes of the masses, who enjoy the commercial "junk" circulated by the mass media. Whether or not we agree with this cultural skyscraper model, the high–low hierarchy often determines or limits the way we view and discuss culture today.[16] Using this model, critics have developed at least five areas of concern about so-called low culture: the depreciation of fine art, the exploitation of high culture, the disposability of popular culture, the decline of high culture, and the deadening of our cultural taste buds.

An Inability to Appreciate Fine Art

Some critics claim that popular culture—in the form of contemporary movies, television, and music—distracts students from serious literature and philosophy, thus stunting their imagination and undermining their ability to recognize great art.[17] This critical view pits popular culture against high art, discounting a person's ability to value Bach and the Beatles or Shakespeare and *The Simpsons* concurrently. The assumption is that because popular forms of culture are made for profit, they cannot be experienced as valuable artistic experiences in the same way as more elite art forms, such as classical ballet, Italian opera, modern sculpture, or Renaissance painting, even though many of what we regard as elite art forms today were once supported and even commissioned by wealthy patrons.

A Tendency to Exploit High Culture

Another concern is that popular culture exploits classic works of literature and art. A good example is Mary Wollstonecraft Shelley's dark gothic novel *Frankenstein*, written in 1818 and ultimately transformed into multiple popular forms. Today, the tale is best remembered by virtue of two movies—a 1931 film version starring Boris Karloff as the towering and tragic monster, and the 1974 Mel Brooks comedy *Young Frankenstein*—alongside offshoots like the sitcom *The Munsters*, action movies like *I, Frankenstein*, and even a once popular cereal introduced in 1971. Shelley's powerful themes about abusing science and judging people on the basis of appearances are often lost or trivialized in favor of a simplistic horror story, a comedy spoof, or a form of junk food.

A Throwaway Ethic

Unlike an Italian opera or a Shakespearean tragedy, many elements of popular culture have a short life span; a hit song, for example, might top the charts for a few weeks at a time. Although endurance does not necessarily denote quality, many critics think that so-called better or higher forms of culture have more staying power. In this argument, lower or popular forms of culture are unstable and fleeting; they follow rather than lead public taste.

Photofest

20th Century Fox/Photofest

EXPLOITING HIGH CULTURE

Mary Shelley, the author of *Frankenstein*, might not recognize our popular culture mutations of her gothic classic. First published in 1818, the novel has inspired numerous interpretations, everything from the scary—Boris Karloff in the classic 1931 movie—to the silly—the Mel Brooks spoof *Young Frankenstein*. Can you think of another example of a story that has developed and changed over time and through various media transformations?

A Diminished Audience for High Culture

Some observers also warn that popular culture has inundated the cultural environment, driving out higher forms of culture and cheapening public life.[18] This concern is supported by data showing that TV sets are in use in the average American home for nearly eight hours a day, exposing adults and children each year to thousands of hours of trivial TV commercials, violent crime dramas, and superficial reality programs. According to one story critics tell, the prevalence of so many popular media products prevents the public from experiencing genuine art—though this view fails to note the number of choices and options now available to media consumers.

Dulling Our Cultural Taste Buds

Another cautionary story suggests that popular culture, especially its more visual forms (such as TV advertising and YouTube videos), undermines democratic ideals and reasoned argument. According to this view, popular media may inhibit not only rational thought but also social progress by transforming audiences into cultural dupes lured by the promise of products. Seductive advertising images showcasing the buffed and airbrushed bodies of professional models, for example, frequently contradict the actual lives of people who cannot hope to achieve a particular "look" or lifestyle and who may not have the means to obtain high-end cosmetics, clothing, or cars. In this environment, art and commerce have become blurred, restricting the audience's ability to make cultural and economic distinctions. Sometimes called the "Big Mac" theory, this view suggests that people are so addicted to mass-produced media menus that they lose their discriminating taste for finer fare and, much worse, their ability to see and challenge social inequities.

Culture as a Map

While the skyscraper model is one way to view culture, another way to view it is as a map. Here, culture is an ongoing and complicated process—rather than a high–low vertical hierarchy—that allows us to better account for our diverse and individual tastes. In the map model, we judge forms of culture as good or bad based on a combination of personal taste and the aesthetic judgments a society makes at particular historical times. Because such tastes and evaluations are "all over the map," a cultural map suggests that we can pursue many connections across various media choices and can appreciate a range of cultural experiences without simply ranking them from high to low.

Our attraction to and choice of cultural phenomena—such as the stories we read in books or watch at the movies—represent how we make our lives meaningful. Culture offers plenty of places to go that are conventional, familiar, and comforting. Yet at the same time, our culture's narrative storehouse contains other stories that tend toward the innovative, unfamiliar, and challenging. Most forms of culture, however, demonstrate multiple tendencies. We may use online social networks because they are both comforting (an easy way to keep up with friends) and innovative (new tools or apps that engage us). The map offered here (see Figure 1.3) is based on a subway grid. Each station represents tendencies or elements related to why a person would be attracted to particular cultural products. More popular cultural forms congregate in certain areas of the map, while less popular cultural forms are outliers. This multidirectional, antihierarchical model serves as a more flexible, multidimensional, and inclusive way of imagining how culture actually works.

The Comfort of Familiar Stories

The appeal of culture is often its familiar stories, pulling audiences toward the security of repetition and common landmarks on the cultural map. Consider, for instance, early television's *Lassie* series, about the adventures of a collie named Lassie and her owner, young Timmy. Of the more than five hundred episodes, many have a familiar and repetitive plotline: Timmy, who arguably possessed the poorest sense of direction and suffered more

THE POPULAR NETFLIX SERIES *STRANGER THINGS* represents many cultural forms with its elements of nostalgia, mystery, action, and sci-fi all rolled into one binge-able package. Where would you place *Stranger Things* on the map on the next page?

© Netflix/courtesy Everett Collection

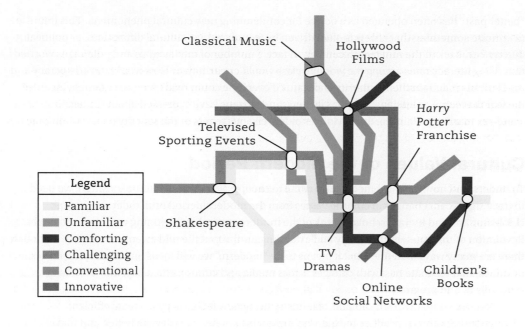

Classical Music

Hollywood
Films

Televised
Sporting Events

*Harry
Potter
Franchise*

Legend

| Familiar |
| Unfamiliar |
| Comforting |
| Challenging |
| Conventional |
| Innovative |

Shakespeare

TV
Dramas

Children's
Books

Online
Social Networks

FIGURE 1.3

CULTURE AS A MAP

In this map model, culture is not ranked as high or low. Instead, the model shows culture as spreading out in several directions across a variety of dimensions. For example, some cultural forms can be familiar, innovative, and challenging, like the *Harry Potter* books and movies. This model accounts for the complexity of individual tastes and experiences. The map model also suggests that culture is a process by which we produce meaning—that is, make our lives meaningful—as well as a complex collection of intersecting media products and texts. The map shown is just one interpretation of culture. What cultural products would you include in your own model? What dimensions and intersections would you identify with, and why?

concussions than any TV character in history, gets lost or knocked unconscious. After finding Timmy and licking his face, Lassie goes for help and saves the day. Adult critics might mock this melodramatic formula, but many children found comfort in the predictability of the story. This quality is also evident when children ask their parents to read *Goodnight Moon* or *Where the Wild Things Are* night after night.

Innovation and the Attraction of "What's New"

Like children, adults also seek comfort, often returning to an old Beatles or Guns N' Roses song, a William Butler Yeats or an Emily Dickinson poem, or a TV rerun of *Seinfeld* or *Andy Griffith*. But we also like cultural adventure. We may turn from a familiar film on cable's AMC to discover a new movie from Iran or India on the Sundance Channel. We seek new stories and new places to go—those aspects of culture that demonstrate originality and complexity. For instance, James Joyce's *Finnegans Wake* (1939) created language anew and challenged readers, as the novel's poetic first sentence illustrates: "riverrun, past Eve and Adam's, from swerve of shore to bend of bay, brings us by a commodius vicus of recirculation back to Howth Castle and Environs." A revolutionary work, crammed with historical names and topical references to events, myths, songs, jokes, and daily conversation, Joyce's novel remains a challenge to understand and decode. His work demonstrated that part of what culture provides is the impulse to explore new places, to strike out in new directions, searching for something different that may contribute to growth and change.

A Wide Range of Messages

We know that people have complex cultural tastes, needs, and interests based on different backgrounds and dispositions. It is not surprising, then, that our cultural treasures, from blues music and opera to comic books and classical literature, contain a variety of messages. Just as Shakespeare's plays—popular entertainments in his day—were packed with both obscure and popular references, TV episodes of *The Simpsons* have included allusions to the Beatles, Kafka, Tennessee Williams, Apple, *Star Trek*, *The X-Files*, Freud, *Psycho*, and *Citizen Kane*. In other words, as part of an ongoing process, cultural products and their meanings are "all over the map," spreading out in diverse directions.

Challenging the Nostalgia for a Better Past

Some critics of popular culture assert—often without presenting supportive evidence—that society was better off before the latest developments in mass media. These critics resist the idea of reimagining an established cultural hierarchy as a multidirectional map. The nostalgia for some imagined "better past" has often operated as a device for condemning new cultural phenomena. This impulse to criticize something that is new is often driven by fear of change, cultural differences, or political differences. Back in the nineteenth century, in fact, a number of intellectuals and politicians worried that rising literacy rates among the working class would create havoc: How would the aristocracy and intellectuals maintain their authority and status if everyone could read? A recent example includes the fear that some politicians, religious leaders, and citizens have expressed about the legalization of same-sex marriage, claiming that it violates older religious tenets or the sanctity of past traditions.

Cultural Values of the Modern Period

To understand how the mass media have come to occupy their current cultural position, we need to trace significant changes in cultural values from the modern period until today. In general, U.S. historians and literary scholars think of the **modern period** as beginning with the Industrial Revolution of the nineteenth century and extending until about the mid-twentieth century. Although there are many ways to define what it means to be "modern," we will focus on four major features, or values, that resonate best with changes across media and culture: efficiency, individualism, rationalism, and progress.

Modernization involved captains of industry using new technology to create efficient manufacturing centers, produce inexpensive products to make everyday life better, and make commerce more profitable. Printing presses and assembly lines made major contributions to this transformation, and then modern advertising spread the word to American consumers. In terms of culture, particularly in architecture, the modern mantra has been "form follows function." For example, the growing populations of big cities placed a premium on space, creating a new form of building that fulfilled that functional demand by building upward. Modern skyscrapers made of glass, steel, and concrete replaced the supposedly wasteful decorative and ornate styles of premodern Gothic cathedrals. This new value was echoed in journalism, where a front-page style rejected decorative and ornate adjectives and adverbs for "just the facts."

Cultural responses to and critiques of modern efficiency often manifested themselves in the mass media. For example, in *Brave New World* (1932), Aldous Huxley created a fictional world in which he cautioned readers that the efficiencies of modern science and technology posed a threat to individual dignity. Charlie Chaplin's film *Modern Times* (1936), set in a futuristic manufacturing plant, also told the story of the dehumanizing impact of modernization and machinery. Writers and artists, in their criticisms of the modern world, have often pointed to technology's ability to alienate people from one another, capitalism's tendency to foster greed, and government's inclination to create bureaucracies whose inefficiency oppresses rather than helps people.

While the values of the premodern period (before the Industrial Revolution) were guided by a strong belief in a natural or divine order, modernization elevated individual self-expression to a more central position. Modern print media allowed ordinary readers to engage with new ideas beyond what their religious leaders and local politicians communicated to them. Modern individualism and the Industrial Revolution also triggered new forms of hierarchy in which certain individuals and groups achieved higher standing in the social order.

To be modern also meant valuing the ability of logical and scientific minds to solve problems by working in organized groups and expert teams. Progressive thinkers maintained that the printing press, the telegraph, and the railroad, in combination with a scientific attitude, would foster a new type of informed society. At the core of this society, the printed mass media—particularly newspapers—would educate the citizenry, helping build and maintain an organized social framework.[19]

The idea of a well-informed rational society emerged out of the **Progressive Era**—a period of political and social reform that lasted roughly from the 1890s to the 1920s. On both local and national levels, Progressive Era reformers championed social movements that led to constitutional amendments for both Prohibition and women's suffrage, political reforms that led to the secret ballot during elections, and economic reforms that ushered in the federal income tax in order to foster a more equitable society. Muckrakers—journalists who exposed corruption, waste, and scandal in business and politics—represented media's significant contribution to this era (see Chapter 9).

Influenced by the Progressive movement, the notion of being modern in the twentieth century meant throwing off the chains of the past, breaking with tradition, and embracing progress. For example, twentieth-century journalists, in their quest for modern efficiency, focused on "the now" and the reporting of timely, new events. Newly standardized forms of front-page journalism that championed "just the facts" helped reporters efficiently meet tight deadlines. But modern newspapers often failed to take a historical perspective or to analyze sufficiently the ideas and interests underlying important events.

Shifting Values in Postmodern Culture

For many people, the changes occurring in the **postmodern period**—from roughly the mid-twentieth century to today—are identified by a confusing array of examples: music videos, remote controls, Nike ads, shopping malls, fax machines, e-mail, video games, blogs, *USA Today*, YouTube, iPads, hip-hop, and reality TV (see Table 1.1). Some critics argue that postmodern culture represents an entirely different way of seeing—a new condition, or even a malady, of the human spirit. Although there are many ways to define the postmodern, this textbook focuses on four major characteristics, or values, that resonate best with changes across media and culture: populism, diversity, nostalgia, and paradox.

As a political idea, *populism* tries to appeal to ordinary people by highlighting the differences or even creating an argument or conflict between "the people" and "the elite." In virtually every political campaign, politicians evoke populism by telling stories and running ads that pit one group of Americans against another. Meant to resonate with middle-class values and regional ties, campaign narratives generally pit southern or midwestern small-town "family values" against the supposedly coarser, even corrupt, urban lifestyles associated with big cities like New York or Los Angeles.

In postmodern culture, populism manifests itself in many ways. For example, some artists and performers—like Chuck Berry in "Roll Over Beethoven" (1956) or Queen in "Bohemian Rhapsody" (1975)—intentionally blur the border between high and low culture. In the visual arts, following Andy Warhol's 1960s pop art style, advertisers borrow from both fine art and street art, while artists appropriate styles from commerce and popular art.

Other forms of postmodern style blur modern distinctions not only between art and commerce but also between fact and fiction. For example, television programs—such as MTV's *Are You the One?* and *Teen Mom*—blur boundaries between the staged and the real, mixing serious themes and personal challenges with comedic interludes and romantic entanglements. Satiric news programs, like

TABLE 1.1

TRENDS ACROSS HISTORICAL PERIODS

Trend	Premodern (pre-1800s)	Modern Industrial Revolution (1800s–1950s)	Postmodern (1950s–present)
Work hierarchies	peasants/merchants/rulers	factory workers/managers/national CEOs	temp workers/global CEOs
Major work sites	field/farm	factory/office	office/home/"virtual" (or mobile) office
Communication reach	local	national	global
Communication transmission	oral/manuscript	print/electronic	electronic/digital
Communication channels	storytellers/elders/town criers	books/newspapers/magazines/radio	television/cable/Internet/multimedia
Communication at home	quill pen	typewriter/office computer	personal computer/laptop/smartphone/social networks
Key social values	belief in natural or divine order	individualism/rationalism/efficiency/antitradition	antihierarchy/skepticism (about science, business, government, etc.)/diversity/multiculturalism/irony and paradox
Journalism	oral and print based/partisan/controlled by political parties	print based/"objective"/efficient/timely/controlled by publishing families	TV and Internet based/opinionated/conversational/controlled by global entertainment conglomerates

HBO's *Last Week Tonight with John Oliver*, combine real, insightful news stories with biting (and often hilarious) critiques of traditional broadcast and cable news programs.

Closely associated with populism, another value (or vice) of the postmodern period is the emphasis on *diversity* and fragmentation, including the wild juxtaposition of old and new cultural styles. Part of this stylistic diversity involves borrowing and transforming earlier ideas from the modern period. In music, hip-hop deejays and performers sample R&B, soul, and rock classics, both reinventing old songs and creating something new. In postmodern architecture, such sampling is called "quoting," as new buildings (or sports stadiums) feature homages to old buildings. Critics of postmodern style contend that such borrowing devalues originality, emphasizing surface over depth and recycled ideas over new ones.

Another tendency of postmodern culture involves rejecting rational thought as "the answer" to every social problem, reveling instead in *nostalgia* for the premodern values of small communities, traditional religion, and even mystical experience. Rather than seeing science purely as enlightened thinking or rational deduction that relies on evidence, some artists, critics, and politicians criticize modern values for laying the groundwork for dehumanizing technological advances and bureaucratic problems. For example, in the renewed debates over evolution, one cultural narrative pits scientific evidence against religious belief and literal interpretations of the Bible. And in popular culture, many TV programs—such as *The X-Files*, *Fringe*, *The Walking Dead*, and *Stranger Things*—emerged to offer mystical and supernatural responses to the "evils" of our daily world and the limits of science and the purely rational.

Lastly, the fourth aspect of the postmodern period is the willingness to accept *paradox*. Whereas modern culture emphasized breaking with the past in the name of progress, postmodern culture stresses integrating—or converging—retro beliefs and contemporary culture. So at the same time that we seem nostalgic for the past, we embrace new technologies with a vengeance. For example, fundamentalist religious movements that promote outdated traditions (e.g., rejecting women's rights to own property or seek higher education) also embrace the Internet and modern technology as recruiting tools or as channels for spreading their messages. Culturally conservative politicians, who seem most comfortable championing the perceived values of the 1950s nuclear family, welcome talk shows, Twitter, Facebook, and Internet and social media ad campaigns as venues to advance their causes.

Although, as modernists predicted, new technologies can isolate people or encourage them to chase their personal agendas (e.g., a student following her individual interests online), new technologies can also draw people together to advance causes; to solve community problems; or to discuss politics on radio talk shows, blog sites, or smartphones. Our lives today are full of such incongruities.

FILMS OFTEN REFLECT THE KEY SOCIAL VALUES of an era, as represented by the modern and postmodern movies pictured here. Charlie Chaplin's *Modern Times* (1936, *left*) satirized modern industry and the dehumanizing impact of a futuristic factory on its overwhelmed workers. Similarly, the science-fiction TV series *Black Mirror* (2011–present, *right*) takes a dark and satirical look at technology's impact on today's society. In an interview with the *Guardian*, series creator Charlie Brooker explains how the series relates to our world: "Like an addict, I check my Twitter timeline the moment I wake up. . . . If technology is a drug—and it does feel like a drug—then what, precisely, are the side-effects? This area—between delight and discomfort—is where *Black Mirror* . . . is set."

CRITIQUING MEDIA AND CULTURE

In contemporary life, cultural boundaries are being tested; the arbitrary lines between information and entertainment have become blurred. Consumers now read newspapers on their smartphones and tablets. Media corporations do business globally. We are witnessing media convergence, in which everything from magazines to movies is channeled onto screens through the Internet, TV, tablets, and smartphones.

Considering the diversity of mass media, to paint them all with the same broad brush would be inaccurate and unfair. Yet that is often what we seem to do, which may in fact reflect the distrust many of us have of prominent social institutions, from local governments to daily newspapers. While revelations about phone hacking and government surveillance make this distrust understandable, it's ultimately more useful to replace cynicism with genuine criticism. To deal with these shifts in how we experience media and culture, as well as their impact, we need to develop a profound understanding of the media, focused on what they offer or produce and what they downplay or ignore.

Media Literacy and the Critical Process

Developing **media literacy**—that is, attaining an understanding of mass media and how they construct meaning—requires following a **critical process** that takes us through the steps of **description, analysis, interpretation, evaluation**, and **engagement** (see "Media Literacy and the Critical Process" on pages 26–27). We will be aided in our critical process by keeping an open mind, trying to understand the specific cultural forms we are critiquing, and acknowledging the complexity of contemporary culture.

Just as communication cannot always be reduced to the old linear sender-message-receiver model, many forms of media and culture are not easily represented by the high–low model. We should, perhaps, strip culture of such adjectives as *high*, *low*, *popular*, and *mass*, which can artificially force media into predetermined categories. We might instead look at a wide range of issues generated by culture, from the role of storytelling in the media to the global influence of media industries on the consumer marketplace. We should also be moving toward a critical perspective that takes into account the intricacies of the cultural landscape. A fair critique of any cultural form, regardless of its social or artistic reputation, requires a working knowledge of the particular book, program, or music under scrutiny. For example, to understand W. E. B. Du Bois's essays, critics immerse themselves in his work and in the historical context in which he wrote. Similarly, if we want to develop meaningful critiques of TV series such as *Stranger Things* or the media's obsession with celebrities like Katy Perry or Drake, it is essential to understand the contemporary context in which these cultural phenomena and icons are produced.

To begin this process of critical assessment, we must imagine culture as richer and more complicated than the high–low model allows. We must also assume a critical stance that enables us to get outside our own preferences. We may like or dislike hip-hop, R&B, pop, or country, but if we want to critique these musical genres intelligently, we should understand what the various types of music have to say and why their messages appeal to particular audiences that may be different from us. The same approach applies to other cultural forms. If we critique a newspaper article, we must account for the language that is chosen and what it means; if we analyze a film or TV program, we need to "rewind," or slow down the images, in order to understand how they make sense and create meaning.

Benefits of a Critical Perspective

Developing an informed critical perspective and becoming media literate allow us to participate in a debate about media culture as a force for both democracy and consumerism. On the one hand, the media can be a catalyst for democracy and social progress. Consider the role of television in spotlighting racism and injustice in the 1960s; the use of video technology to reveal oppressive conditions in

MEDIA LITERACY AND THE CRITICAL PROCESS

1 DESCRIPTION

If we decide to focus on how well the news media serve democracy, we might critique the fairness of several segments or individual stories from, say, *60 Minutes* or the *New York Times*. We would start by describing the segments or articles, accounting for their reporting strategies and noting those featured as interview subjects. We might further identify central characters, conflicts, topics, and themes. From the notes taken at this stage, we can begin comparing what we have found to other stories on similar topics. We can also document what we think is missing from these news narratives—the questions, viewpoints, and persons that were not included—and other ways to tell the story.

2 ANALYSIS

In the second stage of the critical process, we isolate patterns that call for closer attention. At this point, we decide how to focus the critique. Because *60 Minutes* has produced thousands of hours of programming in its nearly fifty-year history, our critique might spotlight just a few key patterns. For example, many of the program's reports are organized like detective stories, reporters are almost always visually represented at a medium distance, and interview subjects are generally shot in tight close-ups. In studying the *New York Times*, we might limit our analysis to social or political events in certain countries that get covered more often than events in other areas of the world. Or we could focus on recurring topics chosen for front-page treatment, or the number of quotes obtained from male and female experts.

It is easy to form a cynical view about the stream of TV advertising, reality programs, video games, celebrity gossip blogs, tweets, and news tabloids that floods the cultural landscape. But cynicism is no substitute for criticism. To become literate about media involves striking a balance between taking a critical position (developing knowledgeable interpretations and judgments) and becoming tolerant of diverse forms of expression (appreciating the distinctive variety of cultural products and processes).

A cynical view usually involves some form of intolerance and either too little or too much information. For example, after enduring the glut of news coverage and political advertising devoted to the 2016 presidential election, we might have easily become cynical about our political system. However, information in the form of "factual" news bits and knowledge about a complex social process such as a national election are not the same thing. The critical process stresses the subtle distinctions between amassing information and becoming media literate.

3 INTERPRETATION

In the interpretation stage, we try to determine the meanings of the patterns we have analyzed. The most difficult stage in criticism, interpretation demands an answer to the "So what?" question. For instance, the greater visual space granted to *60 Minutes* reporters—compared with the close-up shots used for interview subjects—might mean that the reporters appear to be in control. They are given more visual space in which to operate, whereas interview subjects have little room to maneuver within the visual frame. As a result, the subjects often look guilty and the reporters look heroic—or, at least, in charge. Likewise, if we look at the *New York Times*, its attention to particular countries could mean that the paper tends to cover nations in which the United States has more vital political or economic interests, even though the *Times* might claim to be neutral and evenhanded in its reporting of news from around the world.

Developing a media-literate critical perspective involves mastering five overlapping stages that build on one another:

- *Description:* paying close attention, taking notes, and researching the subject under study

- *Analysis:* discovering and focusing on significant patterns that emerge from the description stage

- *Interpretation:* asking and answering "What does that mean?" and "So what?" questions about one's findings

- *Evaluation:* arriving at a judgment about whether something is good, bad, or mediocre, which involves subordinating one's personal taste to the critical "bigger picture" resulting from the first three stages

- *Engagement:* taking some action that connects our critical perspective with our role as citizens and watchdogs to question our media institutions, adding our voice to the process of shaping the cultural environment

Let's look at each of these stages in greater detail.

4 EVALUATION

The fourth stage of the critical process focuses on making an informed judgment. Building on description, analysis, and interpretation, we are better able to evaluate the fairness of a group of *60 Minutes* or *New York Times* reports. At this stage, we can grasp the strengths and weaknesses of the news media under study and make critical judgments measured against our own frames of reference—what we like and dislike, as well as what seems good or bad or missing, in the stories and coverage we analyzed.

This fourth stage differentiates the reviewer (or previewer) from the critic. Most newspaper reviews, for example, are limited by daily time or space constraints. Although these reviews may give us key information about particular programs, they often begin and end with personal judgments— "This is a quality show" or "That was a waste of time"—which should be saved for this fourth stage in the critical process. Regrettably, many reviews do not reflect such a process; they do not move much beyond the writer's own frame of reference or personal taste.

5 ENGAGEMENT

To be fully media literate, we must actively work to create a media world that helps serve democracy. Thus, we have added a fifth stage in the critical process—engagement. In our *60 Minutes* and *New York Times* examples, engagement might involve something as simple as writing a formal letter or an e-mail to these media outlets to offer a critical take on the news narratives we are studying.

But engagement can also mean participating in online discussions; contacting various media producers or governmental bodies, such as the Federal Communications Commission, with critiques and ideas; organizing or participating in public media literacy forums; or learning to construct different types of media narratives ourselves— whether print, audio, video, or online— in order to participate directly in the creation of mainstream or alternative media. Producing actual work for media outlets might involve writing news stories for a local newspaper (and its website), producing a radio program or podcast on a controversial or significant community issue, or constructing a website that critiques various news media. The key to this stage is to challenge our civic imaginations, to refuse to sit back and cynically complain about the media without taking some action that lends our own voices and critiques to the process.

China and Eastern Europe or to document crimes by urban police departments; and the role of blogs and Twitter in debunking bogus claims or protesting fraudulent elections. The media have also helped renew interest in diverse cultures around the world and other emerging democracies.

On the other hand, competing against these democratic tendencies is a powerful commercial culture that reinforces a world economic order controlled by relatively few multinational corporations. For instance, when Poland threw off the shackles of the Soviet Union in the late 1980s, one of the first things its new leadership did was buy and dub the American soap operas *Santa Barbara* and *Dynasty*. For some, these shows were a relief from sober Soviet political propaganda, but others worried that Poles might inherit another kind of indoctrination—one starring American consumer culture and dominated by large international media companies.

This example illustrates that contemporary culture cannot easily be characterized as one thing or another. Binary terms such as *liberal* and *conservative* or *high* and *low* have less meaning in an environment where so many boundaries have been blurred, so many media forms have converged, and so many diverse styles and cultures coexist. Modern distinctions between print and electronic culture have begun to break down largely because of the increasing number of individuals who have come of age in what is a melting pot of print, electronic, and digital culture.[20] Either/or models of culture, such as the high–low approach, are giving way to more inclusive and varied ideas, like the map model for culture discussed earlier.

What are the social implications of the new, blended, and merging cultural phenomena? How do we deal with the fact that public debate and news about everyday life now seem to come more from Facebook, Twitter, John Oliver, *SNL*, and bloggers than from the *Wall Street Journal*, the *NBC Nightly News*, and *Time* magazine?[21] Clearly, such changes challenge us to reassess and rebuild the standards by which we judge our culture. The search for answers lies in recognizing the links between cultural expression and daily life. The search also involves monitoring how well the mass media serve democracy, not just by providing us with consumer culture but by encouraging us to help improve political, social, and economic practices. A healthy democracy requires the active involvement of everyone. Part of this involvement means watching over the role and impact of the mass media, a job that belongs to every one of us—not just paid media critics and watchdog organizations.

FIGURE 1.5

WHO USES THE INTERNET

The Internet and its availability are vitally important as so many people, both in the United States and around the world, rely on the information and resources that it provides. *Data from:* www.pewinternet.org/fact-sheet/internet-broadband/

By Age

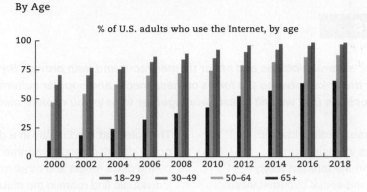

% of U.S. adults who use the Internet, by age

18–29 30–49 50–64 65+

By Race

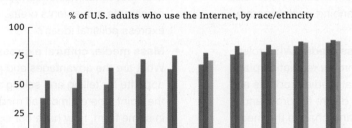

% of U.S. adults who use the Internet, by race/ethncity

White Black Hispanic

By Income

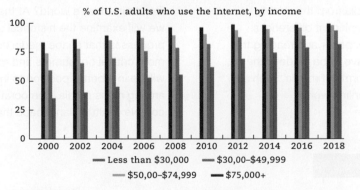

% of U.S. adults who use the Internet, by income

Less than $30,000 $30,00–$49,999
$50,00–$74,999 $75,000+

By Education

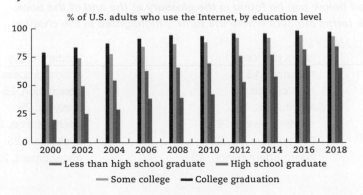

% of U.S. adults who use the Internet, by education level

Less than high school graduate High school graduate
Some college College graduation

Chapter Review

COMMON THREADS

In telling the story of mass media, several plotlines and major themes recur and help provide the big picture—the larger context for understanding the links between the forms of mass media and popular culture. Under each thread that follows, we pose a set of questions that we will investigate together to help you explore media and culture:

- **Developmental stages of mass media.** How did media evolve, from their origins in ancient oral traditions to their incarnation on the Internet today? What discoveries, inventions, and social circumstances drove the development of different media? What roles do new technologies play in changing contemporary media and culture?

- **The commercial nature of mass media.** What roles do media ownership and government regulation play in the presentation of commercial media products and serious journalism? How do the desire for profit and other business demands affect and change the media landscape? What role should government oversight play? What role do we play as ordinary viewers, readers, students, critics, and citizens?

- **The converged nature of media.** How has convergence changed the experience of media from the print to the digital era? What are the significant differences between reading a printed newspaper and reading the news online? What changes have to be made in the media business to help older forms of media, such as newspapers, transition to the online world?

- **The role that media play in a democracy.** How are policy decisions and government actions affected by the news media and other mass media? How do individuals find room in the media terrain to express alternative (nonmainstream) points of view? How do grassroots movements create media to influence and express political ideas?

- **Mass media, cultural expression, and storytelling.** What are the advantages and pitfalls of the media's appetite for telling and selling stories? As we reach the point where almost all media exist on the Internet in some form, how have our culture and our daily lives been affected?

- **Critical analysis of the mass media.** How can we use the critical process to understand, critique, and influence the media? How important is it to be media literate in today's world? At the end of each chapter, we will examine the historical contexts and current processes that shape media products. By becoming more critical consumers and more engaged citizens, we will be in a better position to influence the relationships among mass media, democratic participation, and the complex cultural landscape that we all inhabit.

KEY TERMS

The definitions for the terms listed below can be found in the glossary at the end of the book. The page numbers listed with the terms indicate where the term is highlighted in the chapter.

communication, 5
culture, 5
mass media, 6
mass communication, 6
digital communication, 8
selective exposure, 9
convergence, 10

cross platform, 11
narrative, 13
high culture, 15
low culture, 15
modern period, 22
Progressive Era, 22
postmodern period, 23

media literacy, 25
critical process, 25
description, 25
analysis, 25
interpretation, 25
evaluation, 25
engagement, 25

REVIEW QUESTIONS

Culture and the Evolution of Mass Communication

1. Define *culture*, *mass media*, and *mass communication*, and explain their interrelationships.

2. What key technological breakthroughs accompanied the transition to the print and electronic eras? Why were these changes significant?

3. Explain the limitations of the old linear model of mass communication.

The Development of Media and Their Role in Our Society

4. Describe the development of a mass medium from emergence to convergence.

5. In looking at the history of popular culture, explain why newer and emerging forms of media seem to threaten status quo values.

Surveying the Cultural Landscape

6. Describe the skyscraper model of culture. What are its strengths and limitations?

7. Describe the map model of culture. What are its strengths and limitations?

8. What are the chief differences between modern and postmodern values?

Critiquing Media and Culture

9. What are the five steps in the critical process? Which of these is the most difficult, and why?

10. What is the difference between cynicism and criticism?

11. Why is the critical process important?

QUESTIONING THE MEDIA

1. Drawing on your experience, list the kinds of media stories you like and dislike. You might think mostly of movies and TV shows, but remember that news, sports, political ads, and product ads are typically structured as stories. Conversations on Facebook can also be considered narratives. What kinds of stories do you like and dislike on Facebook, and why?

2. Cite some examples in which the media have been accused of unfairness. Draw on comments from parents, teachers, religious leaders, friends, news media, and so on. Discuss whether these criticisms were justified.

3. Pick an example of a popular media product that you think is harmful to children. How would you make your concerns known? Should the product be removed from circulation? Why or why not? If you think the product should be banned, how would you do so?

4. Make a critical case either defending or condemning Comedy Central's *South Park*, a TV or radio talk show, a hip-hop group, a soap opera, or TV news coverage of a recent mass shooting. Use the five-step critical process to develop your position.

5. Although in some ways postmodern forms of communication, such as e-mail, MTV, smartphones, and Twitter, have helped citizens participate in global life, in what ways might these forms have harmed more traditional or native cultures?

LAUNCHPAD FOR *MEDIA & CULTURE*

Visit LaunchPad for *Media & Culture* at launchpadworks.com for additional learning tools:

- REVIEW WITH LEARNINGCURVE
  LearningCurve, available on LaunchPad for *Media & Culture*, uses gamelike quizzing to help you master the concepts you need to learn from this chapter.

- VIDEO: *THE MEDIA AND DEMOCRACY*
  This video traces the history of the media's role in democracy, from newspapers and television to the Internet.

1 Digital Media and Convergence

Think about the media technologies in your life when you were growing up. How did you watch TV shows, listen to music, or communicate with friends? And how have those technologies changed since then?

Ever-increasing download speeds and more portable devices have fundamentally changed the ways in which we access and consume media. As you can see on the infographic on the opposite page, media didn't always develop this quickly; an early medium, like radio, could take decades to fully emerge, while today a website or an app can reach similar audience thresholds in a matter of years or even days. With these changes, the history of mass media has moved from *emergence* to *convergence*. While electronic media have been around for a long time, it was the emergence of the Internet as a mass medium that allowed an array of media to converge in one space and be easily shared, leading us to the **digital turn**. This shift will continue to shape our media consumption for years to come.

The digital turn has made us more fragmented—but also more connected. Facebook and Twitter have made it easier to tell friends—and strangers—what we're watching, reading, and listening to. And while digital media have led to positive social movements, they have also made it easier for bad actors to harass us or sow discord in our politics. For better and worse, mass media are more integrated into our lives than ever before.

LaunchPad
macmillan learning

launchpadworks.com

Visit **LaunchPad for *Media & Culture*** to explore an interactive time line of the history of mass communication; practice your media literacy skills; test your knowledge of the concepts in the textbook with LearningCurve; and explore and discuss current trends in mass communication with video activities, video assessment tools, and more.

FROM MEDIUM TO MASS MEDIA

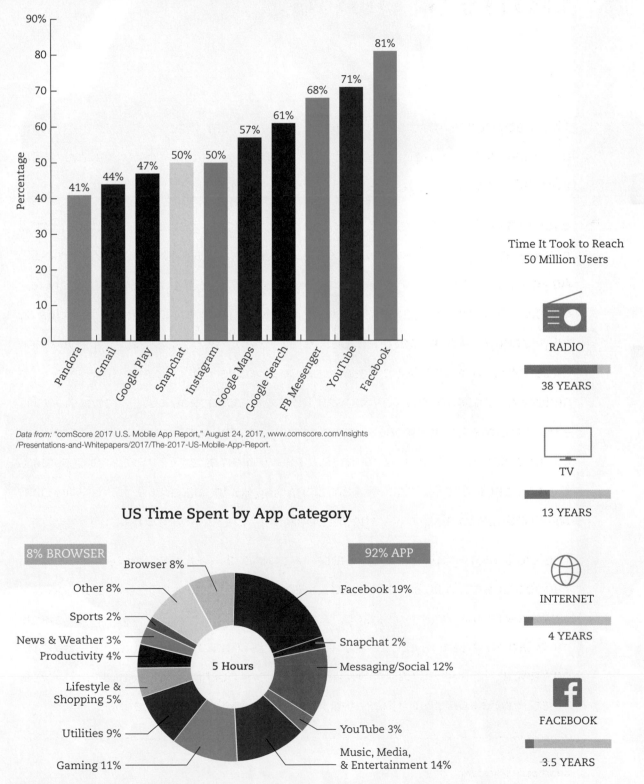

Top 10 Mobile Apps

The top mobile apps in the U.S., by users age 18+

Percentage

App	Percentage
Pandora	41%
Gmail	44%
Google Play	47%
Snapchat	50%
Instagram	50%
Google Maps	57%
Google Search	61%
FB Messenger	68%
YouTube	71%
Facebook	81%

Data from: "comScore 2017 U.S. Mobile App Report," August 24, 2017, www.comscore.com/Insights /Presentations-and-Whitepapers/2017/The-2017-US-Mobile-App-Report.

Time It Took to Reach 50 Million Users

RADIO — 38 YEARS

TV — 13 YEARS

INTERNET — 4 YEARS

FACEBOOK — 3.5 YEARS

US Time Spent by App Category

8% BROWSER   92% APP

5 Hours

- Browser 8%
- Other 8%
- Sports 2%
- News & Weather 3%
- Productivity 4%
- Lifestyle & Shopping 5%
- Utilities 9%
- Gaming 11%
- Facebook 19%
- Snapchat 2%
- Messaging/Social 12%
- YouTube 3%
- Music, Media, & Entertainment 14%

Data from: Simon Khalaf and Lali Kesiraju, "U.S. Consumers Time-Spent on Mobile Crosses 5 Hours a Day," Flurry, March 2, 2017, http://flurrymobile.tumblr.com/post/157921590345/us-consumers-time-spent-on-mobile-crosses-5.

The Internet, Digital Media, and Media Convergence

2

FOR AT LEAST some of us, the social mediated version of ourselves becomes the predominant way we experience the world. As *Time* magazine has noted, "Experiences don't feel fully real" until we have "tweeted them or tumbled them or YouTubed them—and the world has congratulated [us] for doing so."[1] Social media is all about us—we are simultaneously the creators and the subjects. But the flip side of promoting our own experiences on social media as the *most awesome happenings ever (and too bad you aren't here)* is the social anxiety associated with reading about other people's experiences and realizing that you are not actually there.

◄ FOMO, or Fear of Missing Out, is the anxiety that something exciting may be happening while you're off doing something else. The uninterrupted Internet connection we get from smartphones allows us to be in constant contact with friends through social media. But at what cost?

THE DEVELOPMENT OF THE INTERNET AND THE WEB
p. 37

SOCIAL MEDIA AND DEMOCRACY
p. 41

CONVERGENCE AND MOBILE MEDIA
p. 44

THE ECONOMICS AND ISSUES OF THE INTERNET
p. 47

THE INTERNET AND DEMOCRACY
p. 59

This problem is called Fear of Missing Out (FOMO), and it has been defined as "the uneasy and sometimes all-consuming feeling that you're missing out—that your peers are doing, in the know about or in possession of more or something better than you [are]."[2] There are plenty of platforms for posting about ourselves and anxiously creeping on others—Facebook, Twitter, Snapchat, LinkedIn, and Instagram are just a few of the sites that can feed our FOMO problem. The fear of missing out has been around since long before social media was invented. Party chatter, photos, postcards, and holiday letters usually put the most positive spin on people's lives. But social media and mobile technology make being exposed to the interactions you missed a 24/7 phenomenon. There is potentially *always* something better you could have/should have been doing, right?

With FOMO, there is a "desire to stay continually connected with what others are doing." Therefore, the person suffering from the anxiety continues to be tethered to social media, tracking "friends" and sacrificing time that might be spent having in-person, unmediated experiences.[3] And though spending all this time on social media is a personal choice, it may not make us happy. In fact, a study by University of Michigan researchers found that the use of Facebook makes college students feel worse about themselves. The two-week study found that the more the students used Facebook, the more two components of well-being declined: how people feel moment to moment, and how satisfied they are with their lives—regardless of how many Facebook "friends" they had in their network.[4]

Studies about happiness routinely conclude that the best path to subjective well-being (happiness) and life satisfaction is having a community of close personal relationships. Social psychologists Ed Diener and Robert Biswas-Diener acknowledge that the high use of mobile phones, text messaging, and social media is evidence that people want to connect. But they also explain that "we don't just need relationships: we need close ones." They conclude, "The close relationships that produce the most happiness are those characterized by mutual understanding, caring, and validation of the other person as worthwhile."[5] Thus, frequent contact isn't enough to produce the kinds of relationships that produce the most happiness.

Ironically, there has never been a medium better than the Internet and its social media platforms to bring people together. How many people do you know who met online and went on to have successful friendships or romantic relationships? How often have social media connections enhanced close relationships for you? Still, according to Diener and Biswas-Diener, maintaining close relationships may require a "vacation" from social media from time to time, experiencing something together with a friend or friends. Of course (and we hate to say it), you will still need to text, message, e-mail, or call to arrange that date (see also "Media Literacy and the Critical Process: *Note to Self* for Healthy Digital Consumption" on pages 54–55).

THE INTERNET—the vast network of telephone and cable lines, wireless connections, and satellite systems designed to link and carry digital information worldwide—was initially described as an *information superhighway*. This description implied that the goal of the Internet was to build a new media network—a new superhighway—to replace traditional media (e.g., books, newspapers, television, and radio)—the old highway system. In many ways, that description has turned out to be true. The Internet has expanded dramatically from its initial establishment in the 1960s to an enormous media powerhouse that encompasses—but has not replaced—all other media today.

In this chapter, we examine the many dimensions of the Internet, digital media, and convergence. We will:

- Review the birth of the Internet and the development of the web
- Provide an overview of the key features of the Internet, including e-mail, search engines, and social media
- Discuss the convergence of the Internet with mobile media, such as smartphones and tablets, and how the Internet has changed our relationship with media
- Examine the economics of the Internet, including the control of Internet content, ownership issues, and the five leading Internet companies
- Investigate the critical issues of the Internet, such as targeted advertising, free speech, security, net neutrality, and access

As you read through this chapter, think back to your first experiences with the Internet. What was your first encounter like? What were some of the things you remember using the Internet for back then? How did it compare with your first encounters with other mass media? How has the Internet changed since your first experiences with it? For more questions to help you think through the role of the Internet in our lives, see "Questioning the Media" in the Chapter Review.

THE DEVELOPMENT OF THE INTERNET AND THE WEB

From its humble origins as a military communications network in the 1960s, the **Internet** became increasingly interactive by the 1990s, allowing immediate two-way communication and one-to-many communication. By 2000, the Internet was a multimedia source for both information and entertainment, as it quickly became an integral part of our daily lives. For example, in 2000, about 50 percent of American adults were connected to the Internet; today, about nine out of ten American adults use the Internet.[6] Although the Internet is an American invention, the Internet is now global in scale and use. Asia has about half the world's Internet users, and in 2017, India surpassed the United States in the number of active Facebook accounts.[7]

The Birth of the Internet

The Internet originated as a military-government project, with computer time-sharing as one of its goals. In the 1960s, computers were relatively new, and there were only a few of the expensive, room-sized mainframe computers across the country for researchers to use. The Defense Department's Advanced Research Projects Agency (ARPA) developed a solution to enable researchers to share computer processing time beginning in the late 1960s. This original Internet—called **ARPAnet** and nicknamed the Net—enabled military and academic researchers to communicate on a distributed network system (see Figure 2.1). First, ARPA created a wired network system in which users from multiple locations could log into a computer whenever they needed it. Second, to prevent logjams in data communication, the network used a system called *packet switching*, which broke down messages into smaller pieces to more easily route them through the multiple paths on the network before reassembling them on the other end.

FIGURE 2.1

DISTRIBUTED NETWORKS

In a centralized network (*a*), all the paths lead to a single nerve center. Decentralized networks (*b*) contain several main nerve centers. In a distributed network (*c*), which resembles a net, there are no nerve centers; if any connection is severed, information can be immediately rerouted and delivered to its destination. But is there a downside to distributed networks when it comes to the circulation of network viruses?

Information from Katie Hafner and Matthew Lyon, *Where Wizards Stay Up Late* (New York: Simon & Schuster, 1996).

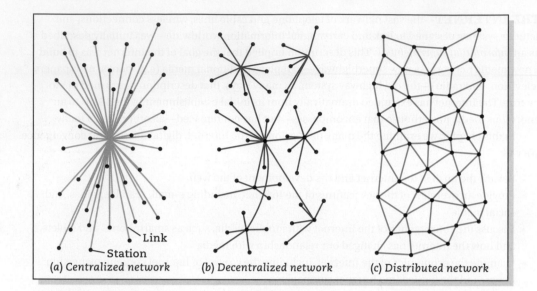

(a) Centralized network   (b) Decentralized network   (c) Distributed network

Ironically, one of the most hierarchically structured and centrally organized institutions in our culture—the national defense industry—created the Internet, possibly the least hierarchical and most decentralized social network ever conceived. Each computer hub in the Internet has similar status and power, so nobody can own the system outright, and nobody has the power to kick others off the network. There isn't even a master power switch, so authority figures cannot shut off the Internet—although as we will discuss later, some nations and corporations have attempted to restrict access for political or commercial benefit.

An essential innovation during the development stage of the Internet was e-mail. It was invented in 1971 by computer engineer Ray Tomlinson, who developed software to send electronic mail messages to any computer on ARPAnet. He decided to use the @ symbol to signify the location of the computer user, thus establishing the "login name@host computer" convention for e-mail addresses.

At this point in the development stage, the Internet was primarily a tool for universities, government research labs, and corporations involved in computer software and other high-tech products to exchange e-mail and post information. As the use of the Internet continued to proliferate, the entrepreneurial stage quickly came about.

The Net Widens

From the early 1970s until the late 1980s, a number of factors (both technological and historical) brought the Net to the entrepreneurial stage, in which it became a marketable medium. With the introduction in 1971 of **microprocessors**, or miniature circuits that process and store electronic signals, thousands of transistors and related circuitry could be integrated with thin strands of silicon, along which binary codes traveled. Microprocessors signaled the Net's marketability as manufacturers introduced the first *personal computers (PCs)*, which were smaller, cheaper, and more powerful than the bulky computer systems of the 1960s. With personal computers now readily available, a second opportunity for marketing the Net came in 1986, when the National Science Foundation developed a high-speed communications network (NSFNET) designed to link university research supercomputer centers around the country and also encourage private investment in the Net. This innovation led to a dramatic increase in Internet use and further opened the door to the widespread commercial possibilities of the Internet.

In the mid-1980s, **fiber-optic cable** had become the standard for transmitting communication data speedily. This development of thinner, faster cables made the commercial use of computers even

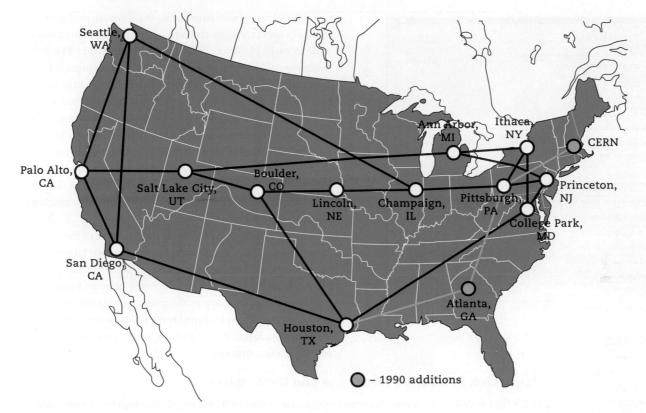

Seattle, WA

Palo Alto, CA

Salt Lake City, UT

Boulder, CO

San Diego, CA

Lincoln, NE

Houston, TX

Ann Arbor, MI

Champaign, IL

Ithaca, NY

Pittsburgh, PA

College Park, MD

Princeton, NJ

CERN

Atlanta, GA

○ – 1990 additions

more viable than before. With this increased speed, few limits existed with regard to the amount of information that digital technology could transport.

With the dissolution of the Soviet Union in the late 1980s, the ARPAnet military venture officially ended. By that time, a growing community of researchers, computer programmers, amateur hackers, and commercial interests had already tapped into the Net, creating tens of thousands of points on the network and the initial audience for its emergence as a mass medium.

The Commercialization of the Internet

The introduction of the World Wide Web and the first web browsers in the 1990s helped transform the Internet into a mass medium. Soon after these developments, the Internet quickly became commercialized, leading to battles between corporations vying to attract the most users and those who wished to preserve the original public, nonprofit nature of the Net.

The World Begins to Browse

Before the 1990s, most of the Internet's traffic was for e-mail, file transfers, and remote access of computer databases. The **World Wide Web** (or the web) changed all that. Developed in the late 1980s by software engineer Tim Berners-Lee at Switzerland's CERN particle physics lab to help scientists better collaborate, the web was initially a data-linking system that allowed computer-accessed information to associate with, or link to, other information no matter where it was on the Internet. Known as *hypertext*, this data-linking feature of the web was a breakthrough for those attempting to use the Internet. **HTML (hypertext markup language)**, the written code that creates web pages and links, is a language that all computers can read; thus, computers with different operating systems, such as Windows or Mac OS, can communicate easily. The development of the web and HTML allowed information to be organized in an easy-to-use, nonlinear manner, making way for the next step in using the Internet.

NSFNET NETWORK

The National Science Foundation developed NSFNET in 1986 to promote research and education. As part of this effort, the NSF funded several university supercomputing centers and linked them with a high-speed network, which became the basis for the commercial Internet of the 1990s.

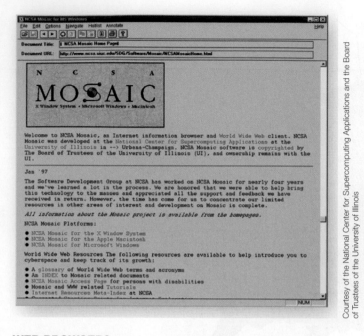

WEB BROWSERS

The GUI (graphical user interface) of the World Wide Web changed overnight with the release of Mosaic in 1993. As the first popular web browser, Mosaic unleashed the multimedia potential of the Internet. Mosaic was the inspiration for the commercial browser Netscape, which was released a year later.

The release of web **browsers**—the software packages that help users navigate the web—brought the web to mass audiences. In 1993, computer programmers led by Marc Andreessen at the National Center for Supercomputing Applications (NCSA) at the University of Illinois in Urbana-Champaign released Mosaic, the first window-based browser to load text and graphics together in a magazine-like layout, with attractive (for its time) fonts and easy-to-use back, forward, home, and bookmark buttons at the top. A year later, Andreessen joined investors in California's Silicon Valley to introduce a commercial browser, Netscape. These breakthroughs helped universities and businesses, and later home users, get connected.

As the web became the most popular part of the Internet, many thought that the key to commercial success on the Net would be through a web browser. In 1995, Microsoft released its own web browser, Internet Explorer, which overtook Netscape as the most popular web browser. Today, Microsoft has replaced Internet Explorer with its new browser, Edge, while Chrome, Safari, and Firefox remain leading browsers.

Users Link in through Telephone and Cable Wires

In the first decades of the Internet, most people connected to "cyberspace" through telephone wires. In 1985, AOL (formerly America Online) began connecting millions of home users to its proprietary web system via dial-up access, quickly becoming the United States' top **Internet service provider (ISP)**. AOL's success was so great that by 2001, the Internet start-up bought the world's largest media company, Time Warner—a deal that shocked the industry and signaled the Internet's economic significance as a vehicle for media content. As connections through **broadband**, which can quickly download multimedia content, became more available, users moved away from the slower telephone dial-up service and toward high-speed service from cable, telephone, or satellite companies.[8] Today, the major ISPs in the United States are AT&T, Comcast, Verizon, Spectrum (owned by Charter Communications), and Cox. There are also hundreds of local services, many offered by regional telephone and cable companies that compete to provide consumers with access to the Internet.

People Embrace Digital Communication

In **digital communication**, an image, a text, or a sound is converted into electronic signals (represented as a series of binary numbers—ones and zeros) that are then reassembled as a precise reproduction of the image, text, or sound. Digital signals operate as pieces, or bits (from *BI*nary digi*TS*), of information representing two values, such as yes/no, on/off, or 0/1. Used in various combinations, these digital codes can duplicate, store, and play back the most complex kinds of media content.

E-mail was one of the earliest services of the Internet, and people typically used the e-mail services connected to their ISPs before major web corporations—such as Google, Yahoo!, and Microsoft (Hotmail)—began to offer free web-based e-mail accounts to draw users to their sites. Today, all the top e-mail services—each of which now has millions of users—include advertisements in their users' e-mail messages, one of the costs of the "free" e-mail accounts. Google's Gmail goes one step further by scanning messages to dynamically match a relevant ad to the text each time an e-mail message is opened. Such targeted advertising has become a hallmark feature of the Internet.

Although e-mail remains a standard for business-related text communications in the digital era, it has been surpassed in popularity by social apps, which include Facebook, Instagram, Snapchat, and Twitter.

Search Engines Organize the Web

As the number of websites on the Internet quickly expanded, companies seized the opportunity to provide ways to navigate this vast amount of information by providing directories and search engines. One of the more popular search engines, Yahoo!, began as a directory. In 1994, Stanford University graduate students Jerry Yang and David Filo created a web page to organize their favorite websites, first into categories, then into more and more subcategories as the web grew. At that point, the entire World Wide Web was almost manageable, with only about twenty-two thousand websites.

Eventually, though, having employees catalog individual websites became impractical. **Search engines** offer a more automated route to finding content by allowing users to enter key words or queries to locate related web pages. Search engines are built on mathematical algorithms. Google, released in 1998, became a major success because it introduced a new algorithm that mathematically ranked a page's popularity based on how many other pages linked to it. In 2016, Google announced it was aware of more than 130 trillion web pages (although it had indexed only a portion of them), up from one billion in 2000.[9] By 2018, Google remained the dominant search engine, with a global market share across all platforms of approximately 91.8 percent of searches, with Microsoft's Bing at 2.8 percent, Baidu (based in China) at 1.7%, Yahoo! at 1.6 percent, and Russia's Yandex at 0.6 percent.[10]

Bettina Fabos

SOCIAL MEDIA AND DEMOCRACY

In just a decade, social media have changed the way we consume, relate to, and even produce media, as well as the way we communicate with others. We can share our thoughts and opinions, write or update an encyclopedic entry, start a petition or fund-raising campaign, post a video, create or explore virtual worlds, and instantly reach an audience of thousands of people. As such, social media has proven to be an effective tool for democratic action, bringing to light repressive regimes that thrive on serving up propaganda and hiding their atrocities from view.

One of the earliest instances of democratic action were the wave of protests in more than a dozen Arab nations in North Africa and the Middle East that began in late 2010 and resulted in four rulers' being forced from power by mid-2012. The period, dubbed "Arab Spring," began in Tunisia. Young activists, using mobile phones and social media, organized marches and protests across Tunisia. As satellite news networks spread the story and protesters' videos to the rest of the world, Tunisia's dictator of nearly twenty-four years fled the country. In the following spring, pro-democracy protests spread to other countries, including Egypt, Bahrain, Syria, Libya, Yemen, Algeria, Iraq, Jordan, Morocco, and Oman. In Libya and Yemen, it resulted in civil war, and in Syria, an ongoing civil war with multiple warring factions has thus far left at least 500,000 dead and more than five million displaced, causing the greatest global humanitarian crisis in decades.[11]

Soon, however, the effectiveness of social media for evil purposes also became clear. One of the warring parties in Syria and Iraq was the terrorist organization ISIS, which turned out to be successful in using the Internet and social media to recruit naïve young men and women from other countries to Syria and Iraq, and to inspire others to commit terrorism in their home countries.[12]

The events of the Arab Spring in 2011 inspired the Occupy Wall Street movement in the United States later that year, in which hundreds of people occupied a park in New York's financial district and made encampments in hundreds of other cities to protest economic inequality. The physical occupations didn't last, but the movement changed the language of economic inequality with the chant, "We are the 99 percent."[13] #OccupyWallStreet was the model for another social movement in 2013, Black Lives Matter. After the acquittal of George Zimmerman in the shooting of unarmed African American teenager Trayvon Martin in Florida, Alicia Garza wrote, "Black people, I love you. I love us. Our lives matter" in a Facebook post describing her anger and heartbreak. When Garza's friend Patrisse Cullors saw the post and shared it along with the hashtag #BlackLivesMatter, these same words inspired a new chapter in civil rights activism. Garza and Cullors brought in friend Opal Tometi, and the three women, all in their late twenties or early thirties, cofounded the Black Lives Matter movement. #BlackLivesMatter helped change the conversation about race in America, and was a leading group in protests following the 2014 shooting death of Michael Brown in Ferguson, Missouri. By 2018, the group had twenty-one chapters in North America. In 2017, another movement emerged in light of the sexual misconduct allegations against film producer Harvey Weinstein. The hashtag #metoo became a rallying point in social media for women to reveal stories of sexual harassment and assault in the workplace. The hashtag was first used by Tarana Burke in 2006 for women of color to share stories of sexual abuse.[14] In 2017, actor Alyssa Milano used the term to encourage women to acknowledge if they had been sexually harassed or assaulted. Millions of women responded, and the hashtag set off a national and international discussion, as powerful men in Hollywood and other communities were publicly accused of sexual abuse, which, in many cases, resulted in the accused abuser's downfall.

Hashtag activism—so called because of the use of the symbol # before a word or phrase that quickly communicates a larger idea, event, or cause—offers a compelling illustration of just how powerful social media can be when it is channeled toward a cause.

The flexible and decentralized nature of the Internet and social media is in large part what makes them such powerful tools for subverting control. In China, the Communist Party has tightly controlled mass communication for decades. As an increasing number of Chinese citizens take to the Internet, an estimated thirty thousand government censors monitor or even block web pages, blogs, chat rooms, and e-mails. The Chinese government frequently blocks social media sites. Repeated censoring of Google's Chinese search engine (Google.cn) caused Google to move it to Hong Kong. And for those who persist in practicing "subversive" free speech, there can be severe penalties: Paris-based Reporters without Borders reports that fifteen Chinese journalists and thirty-nine netizens were in prison in 2018 for writing articles and blogs that criticized the government.[15] Still, Chinese dissenters bravely play cat-and-mouse with Chinese censors, using free services like Hushmail, Freegate, and Ultrasurf (the latter two produced by Chinese immigrants in the United States) to break through the Chinese government's blockade. (For more on how the Internet can interact with politics, see "Examining Ethics: Social Media Fraud and Elections" on page 43.)

THE BLACK LIVES MATTER MOVEMENT, which began as a response to George Zimmerman's acquittal after he shot and killed Trayvon Martin, has grown to include dozens of chapters across the United States. Per the organization, "[o]ur intention from the very beginning was to connect Black people from all over the world who have a shared desire for justice to act together in their communities. The impetus for that commitment was, and still is, the rampant and deliberate violence inflicted on us by the state."

Scott Olson/Getty Images News/Getty Images

Social Media Fraud and Elections

In the early years of social media, it seemed as if democracy had a new friend. Ideally, social media sites like Facebook, Twitter, and YouTube would open up political conversation, enabling democratic discourse to flourish. In 2010, the London newspaper the *Guardian* optimistically called Facebook "the election's town square" and hoped "that people [were] prepared to let their politics show online."[1] The *Guardian* was right: People did let their politics show online, and many of them posted relevant news stories, offered thoughtful discussion, and organized friends to become more politically involved. It turned out, however, that there were a lot of jerks hanging out in the election's town square: people posting nasty political memes, heated arguments, and insults. It all came to a head with the 2016 presidential election. "What had been simmering all year suddenly boiled over as [the] presidential election cycle made online friends hostile and prompted many to mute or unfriend those whose political rantings were creating stress," the *Dayton Daily News* wrote.[2]

Unfortunately, that wasn't the worst of it. There were also criminals in the election's town square, as foreign countries infiltrated social media to spread political disinformation and disrupt America's 2016 presidential election. The assistant director of the FBI's Counterintelligence Division testified before a U.S. Senate committee in June 2017 regarding a report, "Assessing Russian Activities and Intentions in Recent Elections." He said, in part:

> Russia's 2016 presidential election influence effort was its boldest to date in the United States. Moscow employed a multi-faceted approach intended to undermine confidence in our democratic process. . . . This Russian effort included the weaponization of stolen cyber information, the use of Russia's English-language state media as a strategic messaging platform, and the mobilization of social media bots and trolls to spread disinformation and amplify Russian messaging.[3]

The extent of disinformation has been shocking. On Facebook, an estimated 126 million users might have been exposed to the fake ads and event posts produced by a Russian troll farm between 2015 and 2017. According to a Facebook official, "Many of the ads and posts we've seen so far are deeply disturbing—seemingly intended to amplify societal divisions and pit groups of people against each other."[4] By 2018, Twitter had identified more than 3,100 Russian-linked troll accounts spreading divisive information during the 2016 election, and said it had notified more than 677,000 people exposed to the fake messages.[5] Google also found at least two phony Russian accounts and eighteen fake YouTube channels with forty-three hours of content.[6]

That's what is known so far, as the U.S. Department of Justice continues its investigation. Russian trolls have also attempted to disrupt elections in the United Kingdom (where it tried to spread discord during the Brexit campaign), in France, and in several other European countries.

Because Europe has been dealing with Russian propaganda for decades, most of its nations have a head start on strategies to combat such disinformation. For example, in Sweden, there is a school literacy program to teach young people to identify Russian propaganda. Lithuania has citizen volunteers in the "Elves vs. Trolls" battle, with the good citizen investigators (elves) researching and revealing Russian trolls. Britain and France monitor Facebook closely and pressure the social media company to close down fake accounts. In Germany, political candidates all agreed not to use bots—fake accounts (mostly on Twitter) that make automated posts in an effort to boost a topic's profile—in their political social media campaigns. In Slovakia, fourteen hundred advertisers have pulled their business from websites identified by researchers as the work of trolls. In Brussels, a European Union task force has published thousands of phony stories to reveal their deception. In nearly all European countries affected, fact-checking and investigative journalism are additional countermeasures to the Russian troll offensive.[7]

What ideas do you think would work best in America to combat political social media fraud?

CONVERGENCE AND MOBILE MEDIA

The innovation of digital communication enables all media content to be created in the same basic way, which makes *media convergence*, the technological merging of content in different mass media, possible.

In recent years, the Internet has become the hub for convergence, a place where music, television shows, radio stations, newspapers, magazines, books, games, and movies are created, distributed, and presented. Although convergence initially happened on desktop computers, the popularity of notebook computers and then the introduction of smartphones and tablets have hastened the pace of media convergence and made the idea of accessing any media content anywhere a reality.

Media Converges on Our PCs and TVs

First there was the telephone, invented in the 1870s. Then came radio in the 1920s, TV in the 1950s, and eventually the personal computer in the 1970s. Each device had its own unique and distinct function. Aside from a few exceptions, such as the clock radio, that was how electronic devices worked.

The rise of the personal computer industry in the mid-1970s first opened the possibility for unprecedented technological convergence. However, PC-based convergence didn't truly materialize until a few decades later, when broadband Internet connections improved the multimedia capabilities of computers.

By the early 2000s, computers connected to the Internet allowed an array of digital media to converge in one space and be easily shared. Media are also converging on "smart" television sets that are manufactured to be Internet ready. Video game consoles like the Xbox One, Wii U, and PS4, and set-top devices like Apple TV, Google Chromecast, Roku, and Amazon Fire TV, offer additional entertainment-content access via their Internet connections. In the early years of the web, people would choose only one gateway to the Internet and media content, usually a computer or a television. Today, however, wireless networks and the recent technological developments in various media devices mean that consumers regularly use more than one avenue to access all types of media content.

Mobile Devices Propel Convergence

Mobile telephones have been around for decades (like the giant "brick" mobile phones of the 1970s and 1980s), but the smartphones of the twenty-first century are substantially different creatures. Introduced in 2002, the BlackBerry was the first popular Internet-capable smartphone in the United States. Mobile phones took another big leap in 2007 with Apple's introduction of the iPhone, which combined qualities of its iPod digital music player with telephone and Internet service, all accessed through a sleek touchscreen. The next year, Apple opened its App Store, featuring free and low-cost software applications for the iPhone (and the iPod Touch and, later, the iPad) created by third-party developers, vastly increasing the utility of the iPhone.

In 2008, the first smartphone to run on Google's competing Android platform was released. By 2017, Android phones (sold by companies such as Samsung, HTC, LG, and Motorola, and supported by the Google Play app market and the Amazon Appstore) held 53.3 percent of the smartphone market share in the United States, while Apple's iPhone had a 44.9 percent share; Microsoft and BlackBerry smartphones constituted the remainder of the market.[16] The precipitous drop of the BlackBerry's market standing (the company was late to add touchscreens and apps to its phones) illustrates the tumultuous competition among mobile devices.

In 2010, Apple introduced the iPad, a tablet computer suitable for reading magazines, newspapers, and books; watching video; and using visual applications. The tablets became Apple's fastest-growing product line, selling at a rate of twenty-five million a year. Apple added cameras, faster graphics, and a thinner design to subsequent generations of the iPad, as companies like Samsung (Galaxy), Amazon (Kindle Fire), Microsoft (Surface), and Google (Nexus) rolled out competing tablets.

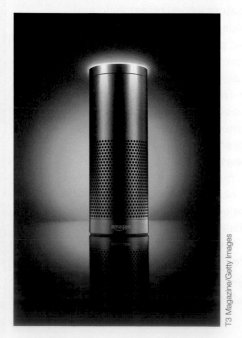

DEVICES LIKE AMAZON'S ECHO smart speaker allow users to control many aspects of their lives, such as playing music, ordering items, controlling their lights or thermostat, with just the sound of their voices.

T3 Magazine/Getty Images

The Impact of Media Convergence and Mobile Media

Convergence of media content and technology has forever changed our relationship with media. Today, media consumption is mobile and flexible; we don't have to miss out on media content just because we aren't home in time to catch a show, didn't find the book at the bookstore, or forgot to buy the newspaper. Increasingly, we demand and are able to get access to media when we want it, where we want it, and in multiple formats. In order to satisfy those demands and to stay relevant in such a converged world, traditional media companies have had to dramatically change their approach to media content and their business models.

Our Changing Relationship with the Media

The merging of all media onto one device, such as a tablet, smartphone, or smartwatch, blurs the distinctions of what used to be separate media. For example, *USA Today* newspaper and CBS network television news used to deliver the news in completely different formats; today, however, their web formats look quite similar, with listings of headlines, rankings of the most popular stories, local weather forecasts, photo galleries, and video. New forms of media are constantly challenging old categories. Is listening to an hour-long podcast of public radio's *This American Life* on a smartphone more like experiencing a radio program or more like experiencing an audio book?

Not only are the formats morphing, but we can now also experience the media in more than one manner simultaneously. Fans of television shows like *This Is Us*, *The Walking Dead*, and *Stranger Things*, or viewers of live events like NFL football, often multitask, reading live blogs during broadcasts or sharing their own commentary with friends on Facebook and Twitter. For those who miss the initial broadcasts, converged media offer a second life for media content through deep archive access and repurposed content on other platforms. For example, cable shows like *Game of Thrones* and *Ripper Street* have found audiences beyond their initial broadcasts through their DVD collections and online video services like Amazon Prime Video, Netflix, and Hulu. This has also led to the resurrection and continuation of many TV shows that would have stayed canceled in the past—for example, *Arrested Development*'s revival on Netflix.

Our Changing Relationship with the Internet

Mobile devices and social media have altered our relationship with the Internet. Two trends are noteworthy: (1) Apple now makes more than eight times as much money selling iPhones, iPads, services, and accessories as it does selling computers, and (2) the number of Facebook users (more than two billion in 2018) keeps increasing. The significance of these two trends is that through Apple devices and Facebook, we now inhabit a different kind of Internet—what some call a closed Internet, or a walled garden.[17]

In a world where the small screens of smartphones are becoming the preferred medium for linking to the Internet, we typically don't get the full, open Internet, one represented by the vast searches brought to us by Google. Instead, we get a more managed Internet, brought to us by apps or platforms that carry out specific functions via the Internet. Are you looking for a nearby restaurant? Don't search on the Internet—use this app especially designed for that purpose. And the distributors of these apps often act as gatekeepers. Apple has more than 2.2 million apps in its App Store, and Apple approves every one of them. The competing Android app store on Google Play has 2.7 million apps, but Google exercises less control over approval of apps than Apple does.

Facebook offers a similar walled garden experience. Facebook began as a highly managed environment, only allowing those with .edu e-mail addresses. Although anyone can now join Facebook, the interface and the user experience on the site are still highly managed by Facebook CEO Mark Zuckerberg and his staff. For example, Facebook has installed measures to stop search engines from indexing users' photos, Wall posts, videos, and other data. The effect of both Apple's devices and the Facebook interface is a clean, orderly, easy-to-use environment but one in which we are "tethered" to the Apple App Store or to Facebook.[18]

The open Internet—best represented by Google (but not its Google+ social networking service, which is more confining, like Facebook) and a web browser—promised to put the entire web at our fingertips. The appeal of the Internet is indeed its openness, its free-for-all nature. But the trade-off is that the open Internet can be chaotic and unruly. However, apps and other "walled garden" services have streamlined the cacophony of the Internet considerably, providing other options for users if they so choose.

The Changing Economics of Media and the Internet

The digital turn in the mass media has profoundly changed the economics of the Internet. Since the advent of Napster in 1999, which brought (illegal) file-sharing to the music industry, each media industry has struggled to rethink how to distribute its content for the digital age. The content itself remains important—people still want quality news, television, movies, music, and games—but they want it in digital formats and for mobile devices.

Apple's response to Napster established the new media economics. Late Apple CEO Steve Jobs struck a deal with the music industry: Apple would provide a new market for music on the iTunes store, selling digital music that customers could play on their iPods (and later on their iPhones and iPads). In return, Apple got a 30 percent cut of the revenue for all music sales on iTunes, simply for being the "pipes" that delivered the music. As music stores went out of business all across America, Apple sold billions of songs and hundreds of millions of iPods, all without requiring a large chain of retail stores.

Amazon started as a more traditional online retailer, taking orders online and delivering merchandise from its warehouses. As books took the turn into the digital era, Amazon created its own device, the Kindle, and followed Apple's model. Amazon started selling e-books, taking its cut for delivering the content. Along the way, Amazon and Apple (plus Google, Facebook, and Microsoft) have become leading media companies. They are among the top digital distributors of books, newspapers, magazines, music, television, movies, and games, and are now making their own content, too, including television, movies, digital games, and books.

The Next Era: The Semantic Web

Many Internet visionaries talk about the next generation of the Internet as the *Semantic Web*, a term that gained prominence after hypertext inventor Tim Berners-Lee and two coauthors published an influential article in a 2001 issue of *Scientific American*.[19] If semantics is the study of meanings, then the Semantic Web is about creating a more meaningful—or more organized and trustworthy—web. To do that, the future promises a layered, connected database of information that software agents will sift through and process automatically for us. Whereas the search engines of today generate relevant web pages for us to read, the software of the Semantic Web will make our lives even easier as it places the basic information of the web into meaningful categories—family, friends, calendars, mutual interests, location—and makes significant connections for us.

The best example of the Semantic Web is Apple's voice recognition assistant, Siri, first shipped with its iPhone 4S in 2011. Siri uses conversational voice recognition to answer questions, find locations, and interact with various iPhone functionalities, such as the calendar, reminders, the weather app, the music player, the web browser, and the maps function. Other Siri searches draw on the databases of external services, such as Yelp for restaurant locations and reviews, and StubHub for ticket information. Another example of the Semantic Web is the Samsung refrigerator that takes a photo of the interior every time the door closes. The owner may be away at the

THE SPIKE JONZE FILM *HER* (2013), set in the near future, explores the relationship between a human and an operating system. The voice-based operating system brings to mind Apple's Siri, which moves users toward a deeper, more personally relevant web. Google Now and Microsoft Cortana are similar voice-activated personal digital assistants for mobile devices.

© Warner Bros. Pictures/Everett Collection

supermarket but can call up a photo of the interior to be reminded of what should be on the shopping list. The refrigerator can also be used to order groceries, with its built-in touchscreen and Wi-Fi connection.[20] Voice recognition apps like Genie, Google Assistant, Cortana, and Bixby have brought voice recognition to Android devices as well. Voice recognition has also recently been pushed into a flourishing new market of home assistant and entertainment devices, like Amazon's Echo speakers (with Amazon's Alexa), Apple's HomePod (with Siri), and Google Home (with Google Assistant).

THE ECONOMICS AND ISSUES OF THE INTERNET

One of the unique things about the Internet is that no one owns it. But that hasn't stopped some corporations from trying to control it. Since the **Telecommunications Act of 1996**, which overhauled the nation's communications regulations, most regional and long-distance phone companies and cable operators have competed against one another to provide connections to the Internet. However, there is more to controlling the Internet than being the service provider for it. Companies have realized the potential of dominating the Internet through search engines, software, social networking, and access to content, all in order to sell the essential devices that display the content or to amass users who become an audience for advertising.

Ownership and control of the Internet are connected to three Internet issues that command much public attention: the security of personal and private information, the appropriateness of online materials, and the accessibility and openness of the Internet. Important questions have been raised: Should personal or sensitive government information be private, or should the Internet be an enormous public record? Should the Internet be a completely open forum, or should certain types of communication be limited or prohibited? Should all people have equal access to the Internet, or should it be available only to those who can afford it? For each of these issues, there have been heated debates but no easy resolutions.

Ownership: Controlling the Internet

By the end of the 1990s, four companies—AOL, Yahoo!, Microsoft, and Google—had emerged as the leading forces on the Internet. In today's converged world, in which mobile access to digital content prevails, Microsoft and Google still remain powerful. Those two, along with Apple, Amazon, and Facebook, constitute the leading companies of digital media's rapidly changing world. Of the five, all but Facebook also operate proprietary cloud services and encourage their customers to store all their files in their "walled garden" for easy access across all devices. This ultimately builds brand loyalty and generates customer fees for file storage.[21]

Microsoft, est. 1975

Microsoft, the oldest of the dominant digital firms (established by Bill Gates and Paul Allen in 1975), is an enormously wealthy software company that struggled for years to develop an Internet strategy. As its software business declined, its flourishing digital game business (Xbox) allowed it to continue to innovate and find a different path to a future in digital media. The company finally found moderate success on the Internet with its search engine Bing in 2009. With the 2012 release of the Windows Phone 8 mobile operating system and the Surface tablet and lightweight laptop, Microsoft made headway in the mobile media business. In 2014, Microsoft brought its venerable office software to mobile devices, with Office for iPad and Office Mobile for iPhones and Android phones, all of which work with OneDrive, Microsoft's cloud service. Microsoft is also developing the HoloLens, a holographic computer operated via a headset.

Nicole Rivelli / © Amazon / courtesy Everett Collection

AFTER YEARS IN THE RETAIL BUSINESS, Amazon has been experimenting with content creation, commissioning groups of series, making the pilots available on its Amazon Prime streaming service, and taking both viewer and critical feedback into account when deciding which pilot episodes to expand into series. *Transparent*, about a family adjusting to a parent's coming out as transgendered, established Amazon as a streaming video contender in 2014. Its first season received eleven Emmy nominations. Amazon has developed other successful shows, including the award-winning series *The Man in the High Castle* and *The Marvelous Mrs. Maisel* (pictured). In addition, Amazon Studios was the first streaming service to receive an Academy Awards Best Picture nomination, for *Manchester by the Sea* in 2017.

Apple, est. 1976

Apple, Inc., was founded by Steve Jobs and Steve Wozniak in 1976 as a home computer company. Apple was only moderately successful until 2001, when Jobs, having been forced out of the company for a decade, returned. Apple introduced the iPod and iTunes in 2003, two innovations that led the company to become the number one music retailer in the United States. Then in 2007, Jobs introduced the iPhone, transforming the mobile phone industry. The company further redefined wireless computing with the iPad in 2010, the Apple Watch in 2015, and the Siri-controlled Apple HomePod in 2018.

With the iPhone and iPad now at the core of Apple's business, the company expanded to include providing content—music, TV shows, movies, games, newspapers, magazines—to sell its media devices. The next wave of Apple's innovations was the iCloud, a new storage and syncing service that enables users to access media content anywhere (with a wireless connection) on its mobile devices. The iCloud also helps ensure that customers purchase their media content through Apple's iTunes store, further tethering users to its media systems. (For more on Apple devices and how they are made, see "Global Village: Designed in California, Assembled in China" on pages 52–53.)

Amazon, est. 1995

Amazon started its business in 1995 in Seattle, selling the world's oldest mass medium (books) online. Amazon has since developed into the world's largest e-commerce store, selling not only books but also electronics, garden tools, clothing, appliances, and toys. Still, with the introduction of its Kindle e-reader in 2007, Amazon was following Apple's model of using content to sell devices. The Kindle became the first widely successful e-reader, and by 2010, e-books were outselling hardcovers and paperbacks at Amazon. In 2011, in response to Apple's iPad, Amazon released its own color touchscreen tablet, the Kindle Fire, giving Amazon a device that can play all the media—including music, TV, movies, and games—it sells online and in its Appstore. Like Apple, Amazon has a Cloud Player for making media content portable. Amazon is now also competing with television, cable networks, and Netflix by producing Amazon Original television series for its streaming service and even breaking into feature films. In addition, Amazon's Alexa-controlled Echo speakers have become the best-selling voice-assisted home digital assistant.

Google, est. 1998

Google, established in 1998, had instant success with its algorithmic search engine and now controls over 90 percent of the global search market, generating billions of dollars of revenue yearly through the pay-per-click advertisements that accompany key-word searches. Google has also branched out into a number of other Internet offerings, including Google Shopping, Google Maps, Gmail, Blogger, the Chrome browser, YouTube, the Chromecast television device, and Google Home. Google has also challenged Microsoft's Office programs with Google Apps, a cloud-based bundle that includes word-processing, spreadsheet, calendar, messaging, and e-mail software. Google competes against Apple's iTunes with Google Play, an online media store; challenges Facebook with the social networking tool Google+; and vies with Amazon's voice-controlled Echo speakers with its own Google Home digital assistant.

ELSEWHERE IN
MEDIA & CULTURE

Netflix has more than twice as many subscribers as the largest cable company

p. 172

91%

The percentage of Facebook's advertising revenue that came from mobile ads in the first quarter of 2018

p. 341

SHOULD BLOGGERS DISCLOSE IF THEY ARE BEING PAID TO PROMOTE A PRODUCT?

p. 345

25,000

How many copies of an album an indie artist needs to sell to make a profit

p. 122

Does having more choices through the Internet make us more engaged media consumers?

p. 12

THE TRANSITION FROM WIRED TO WIRELESS HAPPENED FIRST IN RADIO

p. 130

Facebook, est. 2004

Established in 2004 by then-twenty-three-year-old Harvard psychology major and avid computer programmer Mark Zuckerberg, Facebook's immense, socially dynamic audience (about two-thirds of the U.S. population and more than 2.1 billion users around the globe)[22] is its biggest resource. Like Google, it has become a data processor as much as a social media service, collecting every tidbit of information about its users—what we "Like," where we live, what we read, and what we want—and selling this information to advertisers. Because Facebook users reveal so much about themselves in their profiles and the messages they share with others, Facebook can offer advertisers exceptionally tailored ads: A user who recently got engaged gets ads like "Impress Your Valentine," "Vacation in Hawaii," and "Are You Pregnant?" while a teenage girl sees ads for prom dresses, sweet-sixteen party venues, and "Chat with Other Teens" websites.

As a young company, Facebook has suffered growing pains while trying to balance its corporate interests (capitalizing on its millions of users) with its users' interest in controlling the privacy of their own information. Facebook has focused on becoming more mobile with its purchase of Instagram in 2012 for $1 billion and its 2014 purchase of WhatsApp, a global instant messaging service. Facebook made its first major investment in hardware with its purchase of Oculus VR, a virtual reality technology company, for $2 billion in 2014. The purchase set off a flurry of announcements and investments throughout the industry, as other digital companies aimed to compete with Facebook in the new virtual reality market.

Targeted Advertising and Data Mining

In the early years of the web, advertising took the form of traditional display ads placed on pages. The display ads were no more effective than newspaper or magazine advertisements, and because they reached small, general audiences, they weren't very profitable. But in the late 1990s, web advertising began to shift to search engines. Paid links appeared as "sponsored links" at the top, bottom, and side of a search engine result list and even, depending on the search engine, within the "objective" result list itself. Every time a user clicks on a sponsored link, the advertiser pays the search engine for the click-through. For online retailers, having paid placement in searches can be a good thing.

Advertising has since spread to other parts of the Internet, including social networking sites, e-mail, and mobile apps. For advertisers—who for years struggled with how to measure people's attention to ads—these activities make advertising easy to track, effective in reaching the desired niche audience, and relatively inexpensive, since ads get wasted less often on uninterested parties. For example, Google scans the contents of Gmail messages; Facebook uses profile information, status updates, and "Likes" to deliver individualized, real-time ads to users' screens; and Apple targets users through in-app ads. The rise in smartphone use has contributed to extraordinary growth in mobile advertising, which jumped from $3.4 billion in 2012 to $40 billion in 2017, and is predicted to reach $65 billion by 2020.[23]

Gathering users' location and purchasing habits has been a boon for advertising, but these data-collecting systems also function as consumer surveillance and **data mining** operations. The practice of data mining also raises issues of Internet security and privacy. Millions of people have embraced the ease of **e-commerce**: the buying and selling of products and services on the Internet. What many people don't know is that their personal information may be used without their knowledge. For example, in 2011, the Federal Trade Commission charged Facebook with a list of eight violations in which Facebook told consumers their information would be private but made it public to advertisers and third-party applications. Facebook settled with the FTC by fixing the problems and agreeing to submit to privacy audits through the year 2031.[24] But, Facebook came under fire in 2018 after it revealed that a political consulting firm, Cambridge Analytica, gained access to 87 million Facebook user accounts, and after reports that Facebook also gave phone and device makers access to data on users and their friends.

One common method that commercial interests use to track the browsing habits of computer users is **cookies**, or information profiles that are automatically collected and transferred between computer servers whenever users access websites.[25] The legitimate purpose of a cookie is to verify that a user has been cleared for access to a particular website, such as a library database that is open only to university faculty and students. However, cookies can also be used to create marketing profiles of web users to target them for advertising. Most commercial websites require the user to accept cookies in order to gain access to the site.

Even more unethical and intrusive is **spyware**, information-gathering software that is often secretly bundled with free downloaded software. Spyware can be used to send pop-up ads to users' computer screens, to enable unauthorized parties to collect personal or account information of users, or even to plant a malicious click-fraud program on a computer, which generates phony clicks on web ads that force an advertiser to pay for each click.

In 1998, the FTC developed fair information practice principles for online privacy to address the unauthorized collection of personal data, requiring disclosure, consumer control of data, and prohibiting unauthorized use. Unfortunately, the FTC has no power to enforce these principles, and most websites did not enforce them.[26] As a result, consumer and privacy advocates called for stronger regulations, such as requiring websites to adopt **opt-in** or **opt-out policies**. Opt-in policies, favored by consumer and privacy advocates, require websites to obtain explicit permission from consumers before the sites can collect browsing history data. Opt-out policies, favored by data-mining corporations, allow for the automatic collection of browsing history data unless the consumer requests to "opt out" of the practice. In 2012, the FTC approved a report recommending that Congress adopt "Do Not Track" legislation to limit tracking of user information on websites and mobile devices and to enable users to easily opt out of data collection. Several web browsers now offer "Do Not Track" options, while other web tools, like Ghostery, detect web tags, bugs, and other trackers, generating a list of all the sites following your moves. On May 25, 2018, the European Union's General Data Protection Regulation (GDPR) became effective, requiring informed consent before data is collected on any user. The GDPR also has new, stronger penalties for violations. Although the GDPR only applies to EU citizens, the rules became the default standard for global Internet companies, and many companies operating in the U.S. sent out notices to customers about their updated privacy policies.

Security: The Challenge to Keep Personal Information Private

When you watch television, listen to the radio, read a book, or go to the movies, you do not need to provide personal information to others. However, when you use the Internet, whether you are signing up for an e-mail account, shopping online, or even just surfing the web, you give away personal information—voluntarily or not. As a result, government surveillance, online fraud, and unethical data-gathering methods have become common, making the Internet a potentially treacherous place.

Government Surveillance

Since the inception of the Internet, government agencies worldwide have obtained communication logs, web browser histories, and the online records of individual users who thought their online activities were private. In the United States, for example, the USA PATRIOT Act (which became law about a month after the September 11 attacks in 2001, with most provisions renewed in 2006, 2011, and 2015) grants sweeping powers to law-enforcement agencies to intercept individuals' online communications, including e-mail and browsing records. The act was intended to allow the government to more easily uncover and track potential terrorists, but many now argue that it is too vaguely worded, allowing the government to unconstitutionally probe the personal records of citizens without probable cause and for reasons other than preventing terrorism. Moreover, searches of the Internet permit law-enforcement agencies to gather huge amounts of data, including the communications of people who are not the targets of an investigation. Documents leaked to the news media in 2013 by former CIA employee and former National Security Agency (NSA) contractor Edward Snowden revealed that the NSA has continued its domestic spying program, collecting bulk Internet and mobile phone data on millions of Americans for more than a decade.

Designed in California, Assembled in China

There is a now-famous story involving the release of the iPhone in 2007. The late Apple CEO Steve Jobs was carrying the prototype in his pocket about one month before its release and discovered that his keys, also in his pocket, were scratching the plastic screen. Known as a stickler for design perfection, Jobs reportedly gathered his fellow executives in a room and told them (angrily), "I want a glass screen, and I want it perfect in six weeks."[1] This demand would have implications for a factory complex in China, called Foxconn, where iPhones are assembled. When the order trickled down to a Foxconn supervisor, he woke up eight thousand workers in the middle of the night, gave them a biscuit and a cup of tea, then started them on twelve-hour shifts, fitting glass screens into the iPhone frames. Within four days, Foxconn workers were churning out ten thousand iPhones daily.

On its sleek packaging, Apple proudly proclaims that its products are "Designed by Apple in California"—a slogan that evokes beaches, sunshine, and Silicon Valley, where the best and brightest in American engineering ingenuity reside. The products also say, usually in a less visible location, "Assembled in China," which suggests little except that the components of the iPhone, iPad, iPod, or Apple computer were put together in a factory in the world's most populous country.

It wasn't until 2012 that most Apple customers learned that China's Foxconn was the company where their devices are assembled. Investigative reports by the *New York Times* revealed a company with ongoing problems in the areas of labor conditions and worker safety, including fatal explosions and a spate

of worker suicides.[2] (Foxconn responded in part by erecting nets around its buildings to prevent fatal jumps.)

Foxconn (also known as Hon Hai Precision Industry Co., Ltd., with headquarters in Taiwan) is China's largest and most prominent private employer, with 1.2 million employees—more than any American company except Walmart. Foxconn assembles an incredible 40 percent of the world's electronics and earns more revenue than ten of its competitors combined.[3] And Foxconn is not just Apple's favorite place to outsource production; nearly every global electronics company is connected to the manufacturing giant: Amazon (Kindle), Microsoft (Xbox), Sony (PlayStation), Dell, HP, IBM, Motorola, and Toshiba all feed their products to the vast Foxconn factory network.

Behind this manufacturing might is a network of factories now legendary for its enormity. Foxconn's largest factory compound is in Shenzhen. Dubbed "Factory City," the one-square-mile complex employs roughly 300,000 people, many of whom live in the dormitories (dorms sleep seven to a room) on the Foxconn campus.[4] The workers, many of whom come from rural areas in China, often begin their shift at 4:00 A.M. and work until late at night, performing monotonous, routinized tasks—for example, filing the aluminum shavings from iPad casings six thousand times a day. Thousands of these full-time workers are under the age of eighteen.

Conditions at Foxconn might, in some ways, be better than the conditions in the poverty-stricken small villages from which most of its workers come. But the low pay,

Guang Niu/Getty Images

long hours, dangerous work conditions, and suicide nets are likely *not* what the young workers had hoped for when they left their families behind.

In light of the news reports about the problems at Foxconn, Apple joined the Fair Labor Association (FLA), an international nonprofit that monitors labor conditions. The FLA inspected factories and surveyed more than thirty-five thousand Foxconn workers. Its 2012 study verified a range of serious issues. Workers regularly labored more than sixty hours per week, with some employees working more than seven days in a row. Other workers weren't compensated for overtime. More than 43 percent of the workers reported they had witnessed or experienced an accident, and 64 percent of the workers surveyed said that the compensation does not meet their basic needs. In addition, the FLA found the labor union at Foxconn to be an unsatisfactory channel for addressing worker concerns, as representatives from management dominated the union's membership.[5]

In 2014, Apple reported that its supplier responsibility program had resulted in improved labor conditions at supplier factories. But Apple might not have taken any steps had it not been for the *New York Times* investigative reports and the intense public scrutiny that followed.

Investigative journalism and other reports have revealed a few more interesting things about Apple and Foxconn. First, as Citizens for Tax Justice reported, at the end of 2015 (the most recent year data was available), more than three hundred top companies, including Apple, "collectively held $2.4 trillion offshore" to avoid paying taxes on it in the United States.[6] These stockpiled profits deprived the United States of up to $695 billion in taxes—money that could be spent on schools, infrastructure, paying down the national debt, and so on. Apple led the list of corporations in 2015 with $200.1 billion in income held offshore, skipping out on nearly $60.9 billion in U.S. tax collections. (Microsoft was also on the list, with $108.3 billion in income stashed offshore.)

Second, even though Apple is one of the wealthiest companies in the world, it regularly extracts concessions from states and municipalities for its building projects. For example, to get Apple to locate a $1.3 billion data center in Iowa in 2017, the state and the city of Waukee offered a package of $213 million in tax breaks and incentives. With the project creating only about fifty permanent jobs, it averaged out to a $4.26 million public subsidy for each job. At that same time, the state of Iowa was administering budget cuts for hundreds of millions of dollars in state revenue shortfalls. A *Los Angeles Times* headline summarized the situation: "Apple breaks new ground in squeezing locals for huge tax breaks while offering almost no jobs."[7]

Foxconn also made news in 2017 in the United States with a proposed flat-screen assembly plant near Kenosha, Wisconsin. To lure the manufacturer to Wisconsin, the state offered Foxconn $3 billion in cash incentives and tax breaks, and suspended environmental regulations for the project. The Village of Mount Pleasant and Racine County offered an additional $764 million in support for a plant expected to create up to thirteen thousand jobs. The state's public subsidy for each job is at least $230,700, assuming Foxconn creates the number of jobs anticipated. According to the state's nonpartisan legislative fiscal bureau, Wisconsin's $3 billion investment in the factory will not break even until the year 2042.[8]

The cases of Apple, Foxconn, and other companies raises the question: What is our role as citizens and consumers to ensure that digital companies are ethical and transparent in the treatment of the workers who make our electronic devices and in their financial dealings with our country and communities?

Note to Self with Manoush Zomorodi is a popular podcast about digital culture from WNYC public radio. Zomorodi questions common assumptions about tech culture, and offers a set of media literacy challenges to help us use technology more mindfully. How can we make information overload disappear and enjoy healthier digital consumption?

To answer these questions, get ready for the five-day "Infomagical" challenge.* Search "wnycinfomagical" for a project overview and links to instructions for each day of the challenge. Begin by clicking on "Why Infomagical" to access *Note to Self*'s "The Case for Infomagical" podcast to understand how to participate. Then pick a concrete goal for the week from the following list.

- I want to be more creative.

- I want to be more up to date on current events.

- I want to be more connected to friends and family.

- I want to be more focused on one topic or skill (pick one).

- I want to be more in tune with myself.

*NOTE: The project on the WNYC website is no longer interactive, so you don't have to sign up and "Join Infomagical."

You will want to stick with this goal the entire week.

Beginning on Monday, follow the basic instructions below. Every page on the Infomagical website contains helpful information and a worthwhile seven- to fourteen-minute podcast.

MONDAY, Day 1: "Magical Day"

The first challenge is about multitasking. Your instructions are to only do one thing at a time, because studies have shown us that our brain actually can't process more than one task simultaneously. We are, in fact, far more productive when we singletask. And yet most of us are so prone to multitasking we don't even think twice about it.

Here are the basic Monday instructions from *Note to Self*:

> All day long, do just one thing at a time. If you catch yourself doing two things, switch your focus back to one. Don't read an article and Tweet about it—read it, *then* Tweet. Write an e-mail until you've finished it and hit "send." Perhaps even take a moment to just drink your coffee. Use your Infomagical week goal to prioritize which thing to do when.

TUESDAY, Day 2: "Magical Phone"

The second challenge is about de-cluttering. Many of the apps on our phones are no longer useful to us, or maybe they no longer spark joy when we use them. Organizing our apps by concentrating on what to keep (rather than what to throw away) is a mindful exercise toward making our devices more task oriented. Think about this: Will uncluttering our apps, as Zomorodi suggests we do, also unclutter our brain?

Here are the basic Tuesday instructions from *Note to Self*:

> Today, you will rearrange the apps on your phone. You do not necessarily need to delete anything. You just need to

weigh the value of each one, delete the ones that (a) you do not use or (b) do not bring you joy. Pull all your remaining apps into folders—ideally, just one folder. When you've finished, set your phone's background wallpaper to an image that reminds you of your Infomagical week goal.

WEDNESDAY, Day 3: "Magical Brain"

The third challenge is about avoiding the emotional labor of keeping up with everything. Because information overload is both draining *and* stimulating, the goal here is to focus on only those things that actually matter to you. And in return for concentrating on your information choices, Zomorodi states, "You are going to reveal your brain's hidden capabilities."

Here are the basic Wednesday instructions from *Note to Self*:

Today, you will avoid clicking on something "everyone is talking about" unless it contributes to your information goal. This might be a trending topic or a "must read" or whichever article or video or .GIF everyone in your world is sharing. You've got a strict rule in place: "If this does not make me [insert your Infomagical week goal here], I won't click."

THURSDAY, Day 4: "Magical Connection"

The fourth challenge is about having meaningful conversations and trying out the seven-minute rule. According to social psychologist Sherry Turkle, we can only decide if a face-to-face conversation is "interesting" after we engage in it for seven minutes (or more). But today we are so impatient with—and afraid of—conversation lulls or any kind of awkwardness (inevitable with face-to-face talk, right?) that we avoid these discussions altogether. Students even avoid visiting their professors during office hours because it just seems easier to send an e-mail. But as a result, we are

missing out on the meaningful bits. Today, your goal is to skip the texting and e-mail and make at least one magical face-to-face connection.

Here are the basic Thursday instructions from *Note to Self*:

Do something with all that wonderful goal-oriented information you've been consuming. Discuss something you've heard/read/watched with someone by phone or in person for at least seven minutes.

FRIDAY, Day 5: "Magical Life"

The fifth challenge is about making technology serve you, instead of the other way around.

Here are the basic Friday instructions from *Note to Self*:

Apply whatever you learned or observed about yourself, and think about how to apply this magical feeling going forward. How can you use the idea of creating a priority, a goal, to create a magical life?

How was it? What did you learn? As *Note to Self*'s Zomorodi suggests, try to come up with a broader goal for tackling information overload (this can even be a sort of mantra). Put it on a sticky note, and affix it to your laptop. Here are two of her examples: Spend forty-five minutes of each hour online working or doing homework, and reserve the other fifteen minutes for fun; or think more about what you read. Perhaps you may want to give face-to-face conversations more of a try; or your mantra could be: "Read more [_____], text less," and talk, face-to-face, about your newfound ideas with your friends. Whatever you decide to do personally, bring your collective experiences to the entire class and have a class-wide discussion about digital technology and making information overload a thing of the past.

**THIS *NEW YORKER*
CARTOON**

illustrates an increasingly rare
phenomenon.

Online Fraud

In addition to being an avenue for surveillance, the Internet is
increasingly a conduit for online robbery and *identity theft*, the illegal
obtaining of personal credit and identity information in order to
fraudulently spend other people's money. Computer hackers have
the ability to infiltrate Internet databases (from banks to hospitals
to even the Pentagon) to obtain personal information and to steal
credit card numbers from online retailers. Identity theft victimizes
hundreds of thousands of people a year, and clearing one's name
can take a very long time and cost a lot of money. According to the
U.S. Department of Justice, about 6.15 percent of Americans were
victims of identity theft in 2017, totaling about $16 billion in losses.[27]
One particularly costly form of Internet identity theft is known as
phishing. This scam involves phony e-mail messages that appear
to be from official websites—such as eBay, PayPal, or the user's
university or bank—asking customers to update their credit card
numbers, account passwords, and other personal information.

Appropriateness: What Should Be Online?

The question of what constitutes appropriate content has been part of the story of most mass media,
from debates over the morality of lurid pulp-fiction books in the nineteenth century to arguments
over the appropriateness of racist, sexist, and homophobic content in films and music. Although it
is not the only material to come under intense scrutiny, most of the debate about appropriate media
content, despite the medium, has centered on sexually explicit imagery.

As has always been the case, eliminating some forms of sexual content from books, films,
television, and other media remains a top priority for many politicians and public interest groups. So
it should not be surprising that public objection to indecent and obscene Internet content has led to
various legislative efforts to tame the web. Although the Communications Decency Act of 1996 and
the Child Online Protection Act of 1998 were both judged unconstitutional, the Children's Internet
Protection Act of 2000 was passed and upheld in 2003. This act requires schools and libraries that
receive federal funding for Internet access to use software that filters out any visual content deemed
obscene, pornographic, or harmful to minors unless disabled at the request of adult users. Regardless
of new laws, pornography continues to flourish on commercial sites, individuals' blogs, and social
networking pages. As the American Library Association notes, there is "no filtering technology that
will block out all illegal content, but allow access to constitutionally protected materials."[28]

In addition to those sites featuring sexual content, Internet sites that carry potentially dangerous
information (bomb-building instructions, hate speech) have also incited calls for Internet censorship,
particularly after the terrorist attacks of September 11, 2001, several tragic school shootings, and the rise
in hate speech in recent years. Nevertheless, many people—fearing that government regulation of speech
would inhibit freedom of expression in a democratic society—want the web to be completely unregulated.

Access: The Fight to Prevent a Digital Divide

A key economic issue related to the Internet is whether the cost of purchasing a personal computer
and paying for Internet services will undermine equal access. Coined to echo the term *economic
divide* (the disparity of wealth between the rich and the poor), the term **digital divide** refers to the
growing contrast between the "information haves"—those who can afford to purchase computers and
pay for Internet services—and the "information have-nots"—those who may not be able to afford a
computer or pay for Internet services.

About 89 percent of U.S. households are connected to the Internet, but there are big gaps in access to advanced broadband service. For example, about 73 percent of Americans have home broadband service, but there is a large gap according to income: 93 percent of adults with household incomes of $75,000 or more have home broadband, whereas only 53 percent of adults with household incomes less than $30,000 have it. There is also a difference when it comes to the type of community, with broadband in 76 percent of suburban households, 73 percent of urban households, and 63 percent of rural households.[29] Although not a perfect substitute for a home broadband connection, smartphones are helping narrow the digital divide. The mobile phone industry forecasts that smartphone use in the United States will increase from 78 percent in 2016 to 81 percent by 2020, bringing more small-screen data connections to users.[30] The industry will begin to roll out the next generation of mobile phone data speeds—5G connections—in 2019.

Globally, though, the have-nots face an even greater obstacle to crossing the digital divide. Although the web claims to be worldwide, the most economically powerful countries—the United States, Sweden, Japan, South Korea, Australia, and the United Kingdom—account for most of its international flavor. In nations such as Jordan, Saudi Arabia, Syria, and Myanmar (Burma), the government permits limited or no access to the web. In other countries, an inadequate telecommunications infrastructure hampers access to the Internet. And in underdeveloped countries, phone lines and computers are almost nonexistent. For example, in Eritrea—an East African nation of about 6.5 million people, with poor public utilities and intermittent electrical service—about 71,000 people, or about 1.3 percent of the population, are Internet users.[31] However, as mobile phones become more popular in the developing world, they can provide one remedy for the global digital divide.

Even as the Internet matures and becomes more accessible, wealthy users are still able to buy higher levels of privacy and faster speeds of Internet access than are other users. Whereas traditional media made the same information available to everyone who owned a radio or a TV set, the Internet creates economic tiers and classes of service. Policy groups, media critics, and concerned citizens continue to debate the implications of the digital divide, valuing the equal opportunity to acquire knowledge.

CB2/ZOB/Supplied by WENN.com/Newscom

GOOGLE'S PROJECT LOON employs maneuverable high-altitude balloons that transmit wireless signals to Internet service providers across the globe. The project, which began in 2011, aims to provide Internet access to people in remote areas who would otherwise have no way of getting online. In its mission statement, Google cites the growing digital divide as its reason for launching the project: "Many of us think of the Internet as a global community. But two-thirds of the world's population does not yet have Internet access."

Net Neutrality: Maintaining an Open Internet

For more than a decade, the debate over net neutrality has framed the shape of the Internet's future. **Net neutrality** refers to the principle that every website and every user—whether a multinational corporation or you—has the right to the same Internet network speed and access. The idea of an open and neutral network has existed since the origins of the Internet, but there had never been a legal formal policy until 2015, when the Federal Communications Commission reclassified broadband Internet service and approved net neutrality rules.[32] Still, the debate forges on.

The dispute is dominated by some of the biggest communications corporations. These major telephone and cable companies—including Verizon, Comcast, AT&T, Spectrum, and Cox—control 98 percent of broadband access in the United States through DSL and cable modem service. They want to offer faster connections and priority to clients willing to pay higher rates, and provide preferential service for their own content or for content providers who make special deals with them, effectively eliminating net neutrality. For example, tiered Internet access might mean that these companies would charge customers more for data-heavy services like Netflix, YouTube, and Hulu. These companies argue that the profits they could make from tiered Internet access would allow them to build expensive new networks, benefiting everyone.

But supporters of net neutrality—such as bloggers, video gamers, educators, religious groups, unions, and small businesses—argue that the cable and telephone giants have incentive to rig their services and cause net congestion in order to force customers to pay a premium for higher-speed connections. They claim that an Internet without net neutrality would hurt small businesses, nonprofits, and Internet innovators, who might be stuck in the "slow lane," not being able to afford the same connection speeds that large corporations can afford. Large Internet corporations like Google, Yahoo!, Amazon, eBay, Microsoft, Skype, and Facebook also support net neutrality because their businesses depend on their millions of customers' having equal access to the web.

When Donald Trump became president in 2017, he appointed a new chairperson of the FCC, former Verizon lawyer Ajit Pai. On December 14, 2017, the FCC voted to repeal the 2015 FCC net neutrality policy on a three-to-two party-line vote. Yet after twelve years of debate about net neutrality, the battle continued. In January 2018, attorneys general from twenty-one states and the District of Columbia filed lawsuits to challenge the decision, stating that the FCC vote to repeal net neutrality was "arbitrary, capricious, and an abuse of discretion." The governor of Montana went one step further and ordered ISPs that have contracts with the state to follow net neutrality principles.[33]

Alternative Voices

Independent programmers continue to invent new ways to use the Internet and communicate over it. While some of their innovations have remained free of corporate control, others have been taken over by commercial interests. Despite commercial buyouts, however, the pioneering spirit of the Internet's independent early days endures; the Internet continues to be a participatory medium in which anyone can be involved. Two of the most prominent areas in which alternative voices continue to flourish relate to open-source software and digital archiving.

Open-Source Software

In the early days of computer code writing, amateur programmers were developing **open-source software** on the principle that it was a collective effort. They openly shared program source codes along with their ideas for upgrading and improving programs. Beginning in the 1970s, Microsoft put an end to much of this activity by transforming software development into a business in which programs were developed privately and users were required to pay for both the software and its periodic upgrades.

However, programmers are still developing noncommercial, open-source software, if on a more limited scale. One open-source operating system, Linux, was established in 1991 by Linus Torvalds, a twenty-one-year-old student at the University of Helsinki in Finland. Since the establishment of Linux, professional computer programmers and hobbyists around the world have participated in improving it, creating a sophisticated software system that even Microsoft has acknowledged is a credible alternative to expensive commercial programs. Linux can operate across disparate platforms, and companies such as IBM, Dell, and Oracle, as well as other corporations and governmental organizations, have developed applications and systems that run on it. Still, the greatest impact of Linux is evident not on the desktop screens of everyday computer users but in the operation of behind-the-scenes computer servers.

Digital Archiving

Librarians have worked tirelessly to build nonprofit digital archives that exist outside of any commercial system in order to preserve libraries' tradition of open access to information. One of the biggest and most impressive digital preservation initiatives is the Internet Archive, established in 1996. The Internet Archive aims to ensure that researchers, historians, scholars, and all citizens have universal access to human knowledge—that is, everything that's digital: text, moving images, audio, software, and more than 466 billion archived web pages reaching back to the earliest days of the Internet. The archive is growing at a staggering rate, as the general public and partners such as the Smithsonian Institution and the Library of Congress upload cultural artifacts. For example, the Internet Archive stores more than 186,000 live music concerts, including performances by Jack Johnson, the Grateful Dead, and the Smashing Pumpkins.

Media activist David Bollier has likened open-access initiatives to an information "commons," underscoring the idea that the public collectively owns (or should own) certain public resources, like the airwaves, the Internet, and public spaces (such as parks). Says Bollier, "Libraries are one of the few, if not the key, public institutions defending popular access and sharing of information as a right of all citizens, not just those who can afford access."[34]

THE INTERNET AND DEMOCRACY

Throughout the twentieth century, Americans closely examined emerging mass media for their potential contributions to democracy. Radio and television each developed with the promise of being able to reach everyone, even poor or illiterate citizens. Despite continuing concerns over the digital divide, many have praised the Internet for its democratic possibilities. Some advocates even tout the Internet as the most democratic social network ever conceived.

The biggest threat to the Internet's democratic potential may well be its increasing commercialization. As happened with radio and television, the growth of commercial "channels" on the Internet has far outpaced the emergence of viable nonprofit channels, as fewer and fewer corporations have gained more and more control. The passage of the 1996 Telecommunications Act cleared the way for cable TV systems, computer firms, and telephone companies to merge their interests and become even larger commercial powers. Although there was a great deal of buzz about lucrative Internet start-ups in the 1990s and 2000s, it has been large corporations—such as Microsoft, Apple, Amazon, Google, and Facebook—that have weathered the low points of the dot-com economy and maintained a controlling hand. If the histories of other media are any predictor, it seems realistic to expect that the Internet's potential for widespread use by all could be partially preempted by narrower commercial interests.

However, defenders of the digital age argue that inexpensive digital production and social media distribution allow greater participation than does any traditional medium. In response to these new media forms, older media are using Internet technology to increase their access to and feedback from varied audiences. Skeptics raise doubts about the participatory nature of discussions on the Internet. For instance, they warn that Internet users may be communicating with people whose beliefs and values are similar to their own. Although it is important to be able to communicate across vast distances with people who have similar viewpoints, these kinds of discussions may not serve to extend the diversity and tolerance that are central to democratic ideals. There are also those who may not be interacting with anyone at all. In the wide world of the web, we are in a shared environment of billions of people. In the emerging ecosystem of apps, we live in an efficient but gated community, walled off from the rest of the Internet. However, we are still in the early years of the Internet. The democratic possibilities of the Internet's future are endless.

2 Chapter Review

COMMON THREADS

One of the Common Threads discussed in Chapter 1 is the commercial nature of mass media. The Internet is no exception, as advertisers have capitalized on its ability to be customized. How might this affect other media industries?

People love the simplicity of Pinterest, the visual social media site where users "pin" images and videos to their "board," creating a customized site that reflects their own personal style on topics like home décor, apparel, food, crafts, or travel. To sign up for an account, users provide their name, e-mail address, and gender (male or female). The final choice is prechecked by Pinterest and says, "Let Pinterest personalize your experience based on other sites you visit."

Pinterest is just one example of the mass customization the Internet offers—something no other mass medium has been able to provide. (When is the last time a television set, radio, newspaper, or movie spoke directly to you or let you be the content producer?) This is one of the web's greatest strengths—it can connect us to the world in a personally meaningful way. But a casualty of the Internet may be our shared common culture. A generation ago, students and coworkers across the country gathered on Friday mornings to discuss what happened the previous night on NBC's "must-see" TV shows, like *Roseanne*, *Seinfeld*, *Friends*,

and *Will & Grace*. Today, it's more likely that they watched vastly different media the night before. And if they *did* view the same thing—say, a funny YouTube video—it's likely they all laughed alone because they watched it individually, although they may have later shared it with their friends on a social media site.

We have become a society divided by the media, often split into our basic entity: the individual. One would think that advertisers dislike this, since it is easier to reach a mass audience by showing commercials during *The Voice*. But mass customization gives advertisers the kind of personal information they once only dreamed about: your e-mail address, hometown, zip code, and birthday, and a record of your interests—what web pages you visit and what you buy online. If you have a Facebook profile or a Gmail account, they may know even more about you—what you did last night or what you are doing right now. What will advertisers have the best chance of selling to you with all this information? With the mass-customized Internet, you may have already told them.

KEY TERMS

The definitions for the terms listed below can be found in the glossary at the end of the book. The page numbers listed with the terms indicate where the term is highlighted in the chapter.

digital turn, 32
Internet, 37
ARPAnet, 37
microprocessors, 38
fiber-optic cable, 38
World Wide Web, 39
HTML (hypertext markup language), 39
browsers, 40

Internet service provider (ISP), 40
broadband, 40
digital communication, 40
search engines, 41
Telecommunications Act of 1996, 47
data mining, 50
e-commerce, 50
cookies, 50

spyware, 51
opt-in *or* opt-out policies, 51
phishing, 56
digital divide, 56
net neutrality, 58
open-source software, 58

REVIEW QUESTIONS

The Development of the Internet and the Web

1. When did the Internet reach the novelty (emergence), entrepreneurial, and mass medium stages?

2. How did the Internet originate? What role did the government play?

3. How does the World Wide Web work? What is its significance in the development of the Internet?

4. Why did Google become such a force in web searching?

Social Media and Democracy

5. What are the democratic possibilities of social media? How can social media aid political repression?

Convergence and Mobile Media

6. What conditions enabled media convergence?

7. What role do mobile devices play in media convergence, and what significant mobile milestones can you think of?

8. How has convergence changed our relationship with media and with the Internet?

9. What elements of today's digital world are part of the Semantic Web?

The Economics and Issues of the Internet

10. Which of the five major digital companies are most aligned with the "open Internet," and which are most aligned with the "closed Internet"?

11. What is the role of data mining in the digital economy? What are the ethical concerns?

12. What is the digital divide, and what is being done to close the gap?

13. Why is net neutrality such an important issue?

14. What are the major alternative voices on the Internet?

The Internet and Democracy

15. How can the Internet make democracy work better?

16. What are the key challenges to making the Internet itself more democratic?

QUESTIONING THE MEDIA

1. What possibilities for the Internet's future are you most excited about? Why? What possibilities are most troubling? Why?

2. What advantages of media convergence enable all types of media content to be accessed on a single device?

3. Google's corporate motto is "Don't be evil." Which of the five major digital corporations (Microsoft, Google, Apple, Amazon, and Facebook) seems to have the greatest tendency for evil? Which seems to do the most good? Why?

4. In the move from a print-oriented Industrial Age to a digitally based Information Age, how do you think individuals, communities, and nations have been affected positively? How have they been affected negatively?

LAUNCHPAD FOR *MEDIA & CULTURE*

Digital Gaming and the Media Playground

COLLEGE SCHOLARSHIPS, competitions to make the team, grueling practice sessions, matches in arenas drawing thirty thousand people or more, huge television audiences for championships, profiles in *Sports Illustrated*, and hopes to one day compete in the Olympics.

This is not swimming, track and field, soccer, hockey, or skiing. These "athletes" have no incentive to cheat with steroids, although they might fail a test for Mountain Dew and Doritos. These are eSports athletes: athletes who competitively play video games at the highest levels.

In the past two decades, eSports have followed the trajectory of traditional sports, with an increasing number of colleges and universities recruiting scholarship athletes, major sponsors underwriting teams and tournaments, big media corporations offering contracts, and, perhaps in the near future, the International Olympic Committee including them in the Olympic Games.

THE DEVELOPMENT
OF DIGITAL GAMING
p. 65

THE INTERNET
TRANSFORMS
GAMING
p. 70

THE MEDIA
PLAYGROUND
p. 72

TRENDS AND ISSUES
IN DIGITAL GAMING
p. 78

THE BUSINESS OF
DIGITAL GAMING
p. 84

DIGITAL GAMING,
FREE SPEECH, AND
DEMOCRACY
p. 89

◀ Video game players take part in a competitive video gaming event.

The Stanford University Artificial Intelligence Laboratory hosted the first video game tournament in October 1972. About two dozen people competed playing *Spacewar!*[1] (The Stanford AI Lab was funded by ARPA, the same Defense Department research agency that funded the original Internet, ARPANET.) Video games were still in their infancy, though; the breakthrough arcade game *Pong* wouldn't be released until the following month.

More organized eSports developed with leagues and tournaments in the late 1990s, as the Internet became a mass medium, connecting digital gamers globally. *Quake* and *Counter-Strike* were among the leading games for league play.[2] By the early 2000s, *StarCraft* and *Warcraft III* became the dominant eSports games, and South Korea fostered eSports with the first twenty-four-hour cable gaming channels, such as OGN.

Dozens of colleges and universities have had club eSports teams for years. In 2014, Robert Morris University, a small private school in Chicago, became the first university in the country to offer college scholarships to eSports athletes. In 2016, the University of California–Irvine became the first public research university to do so, and in 2017, the University of Utah established the first eSports program at a university belonging to one of the power five athletic conferences. The Utah team, consisting of thirty-three scholarship-supported students (who won positions against approximately two hundred players in tryouts), was launched to compete in four online digital games: *Overwatch*, *League of Legends*, *Rocket League*, and *Hearthstone*.[3]

With such a marked increase in college eSports,

professional eSports athletes sound increasingly plausible. Just like traditional sports, growing audience size has drawn media coverage, which has drawn big money into eSports. According to a report by technology consulting firm Activate, the eSports TV/streaming audience had already surpassed that of Major League Soccer (MLS) and the National Hockey League (NHL) by 2018. By 2021, eSports will have exceeded the National Basketball Association (NBA) and Major League Baseball (MLB) in viewership, trailing only the National Football League (NFL), and will have more than $5 billion in annual revenue.[4] Not surprisingly, a number of media corporations have invested in platforms to stream game competitions and content, including Amazon (with Twitch), Google (YouTube Gaming), and Disney (BAMtech). In early 2018, Facebook became the latest entry, signing a contract with ESL (the largest eSports company) to carry tournaments and gameplay for *Dota 2* and *Counter-Strike: Global Offensive* on its Facebook Watch platform.[5] Riot Games (maker of *League of Legends*) and Activision Blizzard (maker of *Overwatch*) are two of the biggest forces behind professional eSports leagues. The leagues have team franchise fees of between $10 million and $20 million, and interestingly, some of the leading investors in American eSports teams are owners of NFL, NBA, MLB, and NHL teams.[6]

And the Olympics? First, eSports will be a medal event in Hangzhou, China, at the 2022 Asian Games, the world's largest multisport event besides the Olympics. After that comes the 2024 Summer Olympic Games in Paris. The International Olympic Committee co-chair held open the possibility: "The youth, yes they are interested in eSport[s]. . . . Let's look at it. Let's meet them. Let's try if we can find some bridges."[7]

AFP Contributor/Getty Images

DIGITAL GAMES OFFER PLAY, ENTERTAINMENT, AND SOCIAL INTERACTION. Like the Internet, they combine text, audio, and moving images. But they go even further by enabling players to interact with aspects of the medium in the context of the game—from deciding when an onscreen character jumps or punches to controlling the direction of the "story." This interactive quality creates an experience so compelling that vibrant communities of fans have cropped up around the globe. And the games have shaped the everyday lives of millions of people. Indeed, for players around the world, digital gaming has become a social medium as compelling and distracting as other social media. The U.S. Supreme Court has even granted digital gaming First Amendment freedom of speech rights, ensuring its place as a mass medium.

In this chapter, we will take a look at the evolving mass medium of digital gaming and:

- Examine the early history of electronic gaming, including its roots in penny arcades
- Trace the evolution of electronic gaming, from arcades and bars to living rooms and our hands
- Discuss gaming as a social medium that forms communities of play
- Analyze the economics of gaming, including the industry's major players and various revenue streams
- Raise questions about the role of digital gaming in our democratic society

THE DEVELOPMENT OF DIGITAL GAMING

When the Industrial Revolution swept Western civilization two centuries ago, the technological advances involved weren't simply about mass production. They also promoted mass consumption and the emergence of *leisure time*—both of which created moneymaking opportunities for media makers. By the late nineteenth century, the availability of leisure time had sparked the creation of mechanical games like pinball. Technology continued to grow, and by the 1950s, computer science students in the United States had developed early versions of the video games we know today.

In their most basic form, digital games involve users in an interactive computerized environment where they strive to achieve a desired outcome. These days, most digital games go beyond a simple competition like the 1972 tennis-style arcade game of *Pong*: They often entail sweeping narratives and offer imaginative and exciting adventures, sophisticated problem-solving opportunities, a variety of gameplay, and multiple possible outcomes.

But the boundaries were not always so varied. Digital games evolved from their simplest forms in the arcade into four major formats: television, handheld devices, computers, and the Internet. As these formats evolved and graphics advanced, distinctive types of games emerged and became popular. Together, these varied formats constitute an industry that reached about $109 billion in annual revenues worldwide in 2017—and one that has become a socially driven mass medium.[8]

Mechanical Gaming

In the 1880s, the seeds of the modern entertainment industry were planted by a series of coin-operated contraptions devoted to cashing in on idleness. First appearing in train depots, hotel lobbies, bars, and restaurants, these leisure machines (also called "counter machines") would find a permanent home in the first thoroughly modern indoor playground: the **penny arcade**.[9]

Arcades were like nurseries for fledgling forms of amusement that would mature into mass entertainment industries during the twentieth century. For example, automated phonographs used in arcade machines evolved into the jukebox, while the kinetoscope (see Chapter 7) set the stage for

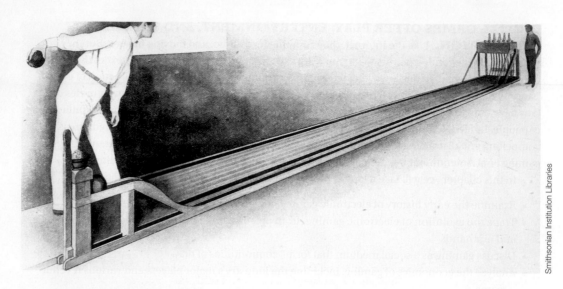

MODERN GAMING EVENTS

and obsessions can be traced back to the emergence of penny arcades in the late nineteenth century.

MAGNAVOX's ODYSSEY

This image of the first home game *Odyssey* was featured in its original German manual.

ODYSSEY

Elektronisches Fernsehspiel

Bedienungsanleitung

Bitte lesen Sie erst diese Bedienungsanleitung, dann die Spielregeln!

the coming wonders of the movies. But the machines most relevant to today's electronic gaming were more interactive and primitive than the phonograph and kinetoscope. Some were strength testers that dared young men to show off their muscles by punching a boxing bag or arm wrestling a robotlike Uncle Sam. Others required more refined skills and sustained play, such as those that simulated bowling, horse racing, and football.[10]

Another arcade game, the bagatelle, spawned the **pinball machine**, the most prominent of the mechanical games. In pinball, players score points by manipulating the path of a metal ball on a slanted table sealed within a glass-covered case. In the 1930s and 1940s, players could control only the launch of the ball. For this reason, pinball was considered a sinister game of chance that, like the slot machine, fed the coffers of the gambling underworld. As a result, pinball was banned in most American cities, including New York, Chicago, and Los Angeles.[11] However, pinball gained mainstream acceptance and popularity after World War II with the addition of the flipper bumper, which enables players to careen the ball back up the play table. This innovation transformed pinball into a challenging game of skill, touch, and timing—all of which would become vital abilities for video game players years later.

The First Video Games

Not long after the growth of pinball, the first video game patent was issued on December 14, 1948, to Thomas T. Goldsmith and Estle Ray Mann for what they described as a "Cathode Ray Tube Amusement Device."

The invention would not make much of a splash in the history of digital gaming, but it did feature the key component of the first video games: the cathode ray tube (CRT). CRT-powered screens provided the images for analog television and for early computer displays, where the first video games appeared a few years later. One such game was *Spacewar!*, a two-person game released by computer science students at MIT in 1962.[12] But because computers consisted of massive mainframes at the time, the games couldn't be easily distributed.

However, more and more people owned televisions, and this development provided a platform for video games. *Odyssey*, the first home video game, was developed by German immigrant and television engineer Ralph Baer. Released by Magnavox in 1972 and sold for a whopping $100, *Odyssey* used player controllers that moved dots of light around the screen in a twelve-game inventory of simple aiming and sports games.

In the next decade, a ripped-off version of one of the *Odyssey* games brought the delights of video gaming into modern **arcades**, establishments that gather together multiple coin-operated games. The same year that Magnavox released *Odyssey*, a young American computer engineer named Nolan Bushnell formed a video game development company, Atari, with a friend. The enterprise's first creation was *Pong*, a simple two-dimensional tennis-style game, with two vertical paddles that bounced a white dot back and forth. The game kept score on the screen and made blip noises when the ball hit the paddles or bounced off the sides of the court. *Pong* quickly became the first video game to become popular in arcades.

In 1975, Atari began successfully marketing a home version of *Pong* through an exclusive deal with Sears. This arrangement established the home video game market. Just two years later, Bushnell started the Chuck E. Cheese pizza–arcade restaurant chain and sold Atari to Warner Communications for an astounding $28 million. Although Atari folded in 1984, plenty of companies—including Nintendo, Sony, and Microsoft—followed its early lead, transforming the video game business into a full-fledged industry.

Arcades and Classic Games

By the late 1970s and early 1980s, games like *Asteroids*, *Pac-Man*, and *Donkey Kong* filled arcades and bars, competing directly with traditional pinball machines. Arcade games still attract fun-seekers to businesses like Dave and Buster's, a gaming–restaurant chain operating in more than ninety locations, as well as to amusement parks, malls, and casinos.

To play the classic arcade games, as well as many of today's popular console games, players use controllers to interact with graphical elements on a video screen. With a few notable exceptions (puzzle games like *Tetris*, for instance), these types of video games require players to identify with a position on the screen. After *Pac-Man*, the **avatar** (a graphic interactive "character" situated within the world of the game) became the most common figure of player control and position identification.

Consoles and Advancing Graphics

Home **consoles** have become increasingly more powerful since the appearance of the early Atari consoles in the 1970s. One way of charting the evolution of consoles is to track the number of bits (binary digits) that they can process at one time. The bit rating of a console is a measure of its power at rendering computer graphics. The higher the bit rating, the more detailed and sophisticated the graphics. The Atari 2600, released in 1977, used an 8-bit processor, as did the wildly popular Nintendo Entertainment System, first released in Japan in 1983. Sega Genesis, the first 16-bit console, appeared in 1989. In 1992, 32-bit computers appeared on the market; the following year, 64 bits became the new standard. The 128-bit era dawned with the marketing of Sega Dreamcast in 1999. With the current generation of consoles, 256-bit processors are the standard.

But more detailed graphics have not always replaced simpler games. Nintendo's NES Classic Edition, with thirty built-in classic games mostly from the 1980s, and the Atari Flashback series, with

Arcadelmages/Alamy Stock Photo

THE ATARI 2600 was followed by the Atari 400, Atari 800, and Atari 5200, but none matched the earlier success of the 2600 model.

built-in Atari games from the same era, have been hot commodities in recent years. Perhaps the best example of enduring games is the *Super Mario Bros.* series. Created by Nintendo mainstay Shigeru Miyamoto in 1983, the original *Mario Bros.* game began in arcades. The 1985 sequel *Super Mario Bros.*, developed for the 8-bit Nintendo Entertainment System, became the best-selling video game of all time (holding this title until 2009, when it was unseated by Nintendo's *Wii Sports*). Graphical elements from the *Mario Bros.* games, like the "1UP" mushroom that gives players an extra life, remain instantly recognizable to gamers of all ages.

Through decades of ups and downs in the electronic gaming industry (Atari folded in 1984, and Sega no longer makes video consoles), three major home console makers now compete for gamers: Nintendo, Sony, and Microsoft. Nintendo has been making consoles since the 1980s; Sony and Microsoft came later, but both companies were already major media conglomerates and thus well positioned to support and promote their interests in the video game market.

Nintendo

Nintendo got its start manufacturing Japanese playing cards in 1889. After seventy-seven years, the playing card business was becoming less profitable, and Nintendo began venturing into toy production in the 1960s—including eventually distributing Magnavox's *Odyssey* console. Nintendo would release its own video game console three years later. In the early 1980s, Nintendo had two major marketing successes. First, the company developed and released the very successful platform game *Donkey Kong* (1981), in which players help Jumpman rescue Lady from the giant ape, Donkey Kong. Developed for multiple consoles, the video game was the Japanese company's breakthrough into the U.S. console market. Second, Nintendo developed the Nintendo Entertainment System (NES) console, which reached U.S. markets in 1985 bundled with the *Super Mario Bros.* platform game. With this package, Nintendo set the standard for video game consoles, Mario and Luigi became household names, and *Super Mario Bros.* became the most successful video series for the next twenty-four years.

In 2006, Nintendo released a new kind of console, the Wii, which supported traditional video games like *New Super Mario Bros.* but was first to add a wireless motion-sensing controller that took the often-sedentary nature out of gameplay. Games like *Wii Sports* require the user to mimic the full-body motion of bowling or playing tennis, while *Wii Fit* uses a wireless balance board for interactive yoga, strength, aerobic, and balance games. Nintendo's Switch (2017) is a significant departure from previous Nintendo consoles, as it easily moves from a console to a portable system. When the tablet-size touchscreen is in a dock, it's a console for playing games on a TV monitor; when the touchscreen is removed, it "switches" into a portable system, with detachable joysticks/controllers.

Sony

Sony, also headquartered in Japan, emerged after World War II as a manufacturer of tape recorders and radios (the name Sony is rooted in the Latin word *sonus*, meaning "sound"). Since then, Sony has been a major player in the consumer electronics industry, producing televisions, VCRs, computers, cameras, and, beginning in the mid-1990s, video game consoles. Its venture into video games came about because of a deal gone bad with Nintendo. Sony had been partnering with Nintendo to create an add-on device to Nintendo's NES that would control music CDs (hence the name they proposed: "play station"). When the partnership fell through, Sony went into direct competition with Nintendo, launching in 1994 the impressive PlayStation console, which doubled the microprocessor size introduced by Sega (from 16 bits to 32 bits) and played both full-motion and three-dimensional (3-D) video.[13]

The PlayStation has a reputation as a high-performance gaming console. By 2018, its current version, the PlayStation 4 (PS4, launched in 2013), had sold more than 73.6 million units and 645 million copies of PS4 games globally.[14]

Sony's PlayStation Plus is a paid subscription service, with more than 31.5 million subscribers, that adds additional features—such as game downloads—to the PlayStation Network. Sony introduced PlayStation VR, its virtual reality headset, in 2016. Since 2014, Sony's PlayStation 4 has been the best-selling brand of the current generation of consoles.

Microsoft

In 2001, computer software goliath Microsoft entered into the world of serious gaming. The Xbox, which represented a $500 million commitment from Microsoft, had many firsts: the first console to feature a built-in hard disk drive; the first to be connected to an online service (Xbox Live); and the first to have Dolby Digital sound, for a cinematic sound experience. While Xbox could not offer the arsenal of games that PlayStation gamers had access to, the console did launch with one particular game, *Halo*. Game critics and players immediately recognized this sci-fi first-person shooter game—now a multibillion-dollar franchise—as Microsoft's "killer app."[15]

Microsoft linked to the Xbox Live online service in 2002 and released Xbox 360 in 2005. Xbox Live lets its 53 million subscribers play online and enables users to download new content directly to its console. In 2013, Microsoft released the Xbox One with an upgraded Kinect (a motion-sensing controller first introduced in 2010) as an advanced gaming device and voice-controlled entertainment system.

All three of the major consoles develop or license games for their own proprietary systems, and although some game content is released on all three platforms, game offerings become a major selling point for a particular system. For example, Xbox One has exclusive rights to *Forza Motorsport 7*; PS4 has *Uncharted: The Lost Legacy*; and Nintendo Switch has *Splatoon 2*. Once

Bettina Fabos

THE 3-D PLATFORM ACTION ADVENTURE GAME
Super Mario Odyssey was created by Nintendo for the Nintendo Switch. It features Mario in his never-ending quest to save Princess Peach from his evil archenemy, Bowser.

YOUNG MAN PLAYS
Ultimate Ninja Storm Revolution.

Joshua Mitchell

used exclusively for games, video game consoles also work as part computer, part cable box. They've become powerful entertainment centers, with multiple forms of media converging in a single device. For example, both Xbox One and PS4 offer access to Twitter, Facebook, and video chat, and can function as DVD and Blu-ray players and digital video recorders (with hard drives of up to 1 terabyte). PS4, Xbox, and Wii all offer connections to stream programming from sources like Netflix and Hulu. Microsoft's Xbox—which has Kinect's voice recognition system, allowing viewers to communicate with the box—has been the most successful in becoming a converged device for home entertainment.

Gaming on PCs

Like the early console games, very early home computer games often mimicked (and sometimes ripped off) popular arcade games like *Frogger*, *Centipede*, *Pac-Man*, and *Space Invaders*. Computer-based gaming also featured certain genres not often seen on consoles, like digitized card and board games. The early days of the personal computer saw the creation of electronic versions of games like Solitaire, Hearts, Spades, and Chess, all simple games still popular today. But for a time in the late 1980s and much of the 1990s, personal computers held some clear advantages over console gaming. The versatility of keyboards, compared with the relatively simple early console controllers, allowed for ambitious puzzle-solving games like *Myst*. Moreover, faster processing speeds gave some computer games richer, more detailed 3-D graphics. Many of the most popular early first-person shooter games, like *Doom* and *Quake*, were developed for home computers rather than consoles.

As consoles caught up with greater processing speeds and disc-based games in the late 1990s, elaborate personal computer games attracted less attention. But due to the advent of Internet-based free-to-play games (like *Spelunky* and *League of Legends*), subscription games (such as *World of Warcraft* and *Diablo 3*), social media games (such as *Candy Crush Saga* on Facebook), and the Steam PC game platform, PC gaming has experienced a resurgence. With powerful processors for handling rich graphics, and more stable Internet connectivity for downloading games or playing games via social media and other gaming sites, personal computers can adeptly handle a wide range of activities.

Portable Players

Nintendo popularized handheld digital games with the release of its Game Boy line of devices and sold nearly 120 million of them from 1989 to 2003, with games like *Tetris*, *Metroid*, and *Pokémon Red/Blue*.[16] The early handhelds gave way to later generations of devices offering more advanced graphics and wireless capabilities. These include the top-selling Nintendo 3DS, released in 2011, and PlayStation Portable (PSP), released in 2005 and succeeded by the PlayStation Vita in 2012, and the multipurpose Nintendo Switch, released in 2017.

While portable players remain immensely popular (the Nintendo 3DS sold more than 72 million units through 2017), they face competition from the widespread use of smartphones and touchscreen tablets like iPads. These devices are not designed principally for gaming, but their capabilities have provided another option for casual gamers who may not have been interested in owning a handheld console.

THE INTERNET TRANSFORMS GAMING

The connectivity of the Internet has opened the door to social gaming and enabled the spread of video games to converged devices—such as tablets and mobile phones—making games more portable and creating whole new segments in the gaming industry. This connectivity has also opened the door to virtual worlds, multiplayer online battle arenas, and massively multiplayer online games.

MMORPGs, MOBAs, Virtual Worlds, and Social Gaming

It is one of the longest acronyms in the world of gaming: **massively multiplayer online role-playing games (MMORPGs)**. These games are set in virtual worlds that require users to play through an avatar of their own design. The "massively multiplayer" aspect of MMORPGs indicates that electronic games—once designed for solo or small-group play—have expanded to reach large groups, like traditional mass media do.

The fantasy adventure game *World of Warcraft* remains a popular MMORPG, with about 5.5 million subscribers in 2016, down from a peak of 12 million in 2010. Users can select from twelve different "races" of avatars, including dwarves, gnomes, night elves, orcs, trolls, goblins, and humans, and form guilds or tribes with other players.

MMORPGs like *Overwatch* and MOBAs (multiplayer online battle arenas) like *League of Legends* are aimed at teenagers and adults. One of the most overlooked areas (at least by adults) in online gaming is the children's market. *Club Penguin*, a moderated virtual world purchased by Disney, enables kids to play games and chat as colorful penguins. Toy maker Ganz developed the online *Webkinz* game to revive its stuffed-animal sales. Each Webkinz stuffed animal comes with a code that lets players access the online game and care for the virtual version of their plush pets. All these virtual worlds offer younger players their own age-appropriate environment to experiment with virtual socializing, but they have also attracted criticism for their messages of consumerism. In many of these games, children can buy items with virtual currency or acquire "bling" more quickly through a premium membership.

Online fantasy sports games also reach a mass audience with a major social component. Players—real-life friends, virtual acquaintances, or a mix of both—assemble teams and use actual sports results to determine scores in their online games. But rather than experiencing the visceral thrills of, say, the most recent release of *Madden NFL*, fantasy football participants take a more detached, managerial perspective on the game—a departure from the classic video game experience. Fantasy sports' managerial angle makes it even more fun to watch almost any televised sporting event because players focus more on making strategic investments in individual performances scattered across the various professional teams than they do on rooting for local teams. In the process, players become statistically savvy aficionados of the game overall, rather than rabid fans of

OVERWATCH, a popular team based multi-player first person shooter game created by Blizzard Entertainment, won 102 separate "Game of the Year" awards when it came out in 2016.

a particular team. In 2017, over 59.3 million people played fantasy sports in the United States and Canada; the Fantasy Sports Trade Association estimates that fantasy sports players spend an average of $566 a year on single-player challenge games and league-related costs and materials.[17]

Gaming Apps

Google Play exceeds Apple's App Store in number of apps and provides a substantial platform for gaming on Android mobile phones and tablet devices like the Kindle, Galaxy, and Nexus. Microsoft got a later start with its Windows phones and Surface tablet, so its game offerings lag far behind those of the Android and Apple stores.

This portable and mobile gaming convergence is changing the way people look at digital games and their systems. While the games themselves are no longer confined to arcades or home television sets, the mobile media have gained power as entertainment tools, reaching a wider and more diverse audience. Thus, gaming has become an everyday form of entertainment rather than the niche pursuit of hard-core enthusiasts. Nintendo's Switch is an acknowledgment of this, in that it is a console system that can also be a handheld, portable player.

With its increased profile and flexibility across platforms, the gaming industry has achieved a mass medium status on a par with film or television. This rise in status has come with stiffer and more complex competition, not just within the gaming industry but across media. Rather than Sony competing with Nintendo, TV networks competing among themselves for viewers, or new movies facing off at the box office, media must now compete against other media for an audience's attention. Digital games have become a major player in these competitions.

THE MEDIA PLAYGROUND

To fully explore the larger media playground, we need to look beyond electronic gaming's technical aspects and consider the human faces of gaming. The attractions of this interactive playground validate electronic gaming's status as one of today's most powerful media industries. Electronic games occupy an enormous range of styles, from casual games like *Tetris*, *Angry Birds*, *Alto's Adventure*, and *Fruit Ninja* to full-blown, Hollywood-esque immersive adventure games like *Final Fantasy*.[18] No matter what the style, digital games are compelling entertainment and mass media because they pose challenges (mental and physical), allow us to engage in situations both realistic and fantastical, and allow us to socialize with others as we play with friends and form communities both inside and outside the games.

Video Game Genres

Electronic games inhabit so many playing platforms and devices, and cover so many genres, that they are not easy to categorize. The game industry, as represented by the Entertainment Software Association, organizes games by **gameplay**—the way in which the rules structure how players interact with the game—rather than by any sort of visual or narrative style. There are many hybrid forms, but the major gameplay genres are discussed in the following sections. (See Table 3.1 for a rundown of genres defined by gameplay and Figure 3.1 for a breakdown of top video game genres.)

Communities of Play: Inside the Game

Virtual communities often crop up around online video games and fantasy sports leagues. Indeed, players may get to know one another through games without ever meeting in person. They can interact in two basic types of groups. **PUGs** (short for "pick-up groups") are temporary teams usually assembled by matchmaking programs integrated into the game. The members of a PUG may range from **noobs** (clueless beginners) to elite players and may be geographically and generationally diverse. PUGs are notorious for harboring ninjas and trolls—two universally despised player types (not to be

Genre		Gameplay	Examples
Action		Player uses hand-eye coordination and motor skills to overcome physical challenges. Player controls most of the action to:	
	Platform games	- move character(s) between various platform levels in order to avoid or chase adversaries	*Super Mario Bros.*, *Never Alone*, *Canabalt*, *Super Mario Odyssey*, *Celeste*
	Shooter	- use a range of weapons to obliterate the enemy	*Overwatch*, *Call of Duty: Advanced Warfare*, *Halo*, *Half-Life*
	Fighting	- work in close-range combat against a small number of equally powerful opponents	*Street Fighter*, *Dragon Ball FighterZ*, *Soulcalibur*
	Stealth	- engage in subterfuge and precision strikes to beat the enemy	*Dishonored*, *Mark of the Ninja*
	Survival	- learn to survive in a hostile environment	*Paladins: Battlegrounds*, *Fortnite*, *PlayerUnknown's Battlegrounds (PUBG)*
	Rhythm	- challenge him- or herself in terms of rhythm, coordination, and musical precision	*Dance Dance Revolution*, *Guitar Hero*, *Rock Band*
Adventure		Player solves puzzles by interacting with people or the environment	*Myst*, *Tomb Raider*, *Lumino City*, *Monument Valley*, *Limbo*, *Hidden Folks*
Action-Adventure		Player navigates horror fiction elements or constant obstacles (e.g., doors) and acquires special tools or abilities to open them	*Zelda*, *Metroid*, *Castlevania*, *Resident Evil*, *Grand Theft Auto*
Role Playing		Player takes on specific characteristics and skill sets, goes on "adventures," and often amasses treasure; the most popular setting is a fantasy world	*Final Fantasy*, *Fallout*, *Grand Theft Auto*, *Minecraft*
MMPORG		Similar to role-playing games but distinguished by the high number of players interacting together	*World of Warcraft*, *Star Wars: The Old Republic*
Simulation		Player simulates a real or fictional reality to:	
	Construction/ Management	- expand or manage fictional communities or projects with limited resources	*SimCity*
	Life	- "realistically" live the life of a person or being (e.g., a wolf), possibly in a strange world	*SimLife*, *Spore*, *Creatures*
	Vehicle	- experience flight, race-car driving, train travel, combat vehicles, and so on	*FlightGear*, *Microsoft Flight Simulator*, *Nascar Racing*
Strategy		Player carefully plots out tactics to achieve a goal, usually military or world domination	*Master of Orion*, *Hogs of War*, *Starcraft*
	MOBA (Multiplayer Online Battle Arena)	Player on a team competes against another team to destroy the opposing team's main structure; similar to role-playing games but distinguished by the high number of players	*League of Legends*, *Data 2*, *Heroes of the Storm*, *Overwatch*
Sports		Player takes either a player's or management's perspective in simulating a sport, like soccer, Nascar racing, football, or fighting	*Pong*, *FIFA*, *Fight Night*, *Championship Manager*, *Madden NFL*
Casual Games		Player makes progress toward a simple reward, increasing the challenge if he or she feels like it; the rules are simple, and there is no long-term commitment	*Tetris*, *Candy Crush Saga*, *Run Sausage Run*

TABLE 3.1

VIDEO GAME GENRES

confused with ninja or troll avatars). **Ninjas** are players who snatch loot out of turn and then leave the group; **trolls** are players who delight in intentionally spoiling the gaming experience for others.

Because of the frustration of dealing with noobs, ninjas, and trolls, most experienced players join organized groups called **guilds** *or* **clans**. These groups can be small and easygoing or large and demanding. Players communicate in two forms of in-game chat—voice and text. Xbox Live, for example, uses three types of voice chat that allow players to socialize and strategize, in groups or one-on-one, even as they are playing the game. Other in-game chat systems are text-based, with chat channels for trading in-game goods or coordinating missions within a guild. These methods of communicating with fellow players who may or may not know one another outside the game create a sense of community around gameplay. Some players have formed lasting friendships or romantic relationships through their video game habit. Avid gamers have even held in-game

FIGURE 3.1

TOP VIDEO GAME GENRES BY UNITS SOLD, 2016

Data from: Entertainment Software Association, "Essential Facts about the Computer and Video Game Industry," 2017.

Note: Percentages were rounded.

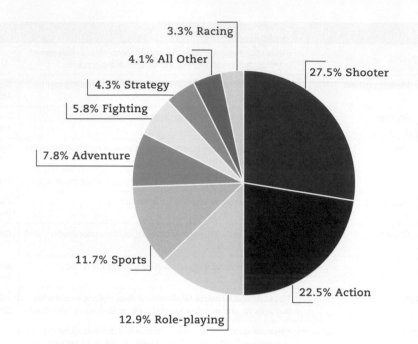

- 3.3% Racing
- 4.1% All Other
- 4.3% Strategy
- 5.8% Fighting
- 7.8% Adventure
- 27.5% Shooter
- 22.5% Action
- 11.7% Sports
- 12.9% Role-playing

ceremonies, such as weddings or funerals—sometimes for game-only characters, and sometimes for real-life events.

Communities of Play: Outside the Game

Communities also form outside games, through websites and even face-to-face gatherings (such as eSports events) dedicated to digital gaming in its many forms. This phenomenon is similar to the formation of online and in-person groups to discuss other mass media, like movies, TV shows, or books. These communities extend beyond gameplay, enhancing the social experience gained through the games.

Collective Intelligence

Mass media productions are almost always collaborative efforts, as is evident in the credits for movies, television shows, and music recordings. The same goes for digital games. But what is unusual about game developers and the game industry is their interest in listening to gamers and their communities in order to gather new ideas and constructive criticism and to gauge popularity. Gamers, too, collaborate with one another to share shortcuts and "cheats" to solving tasks and quests, and to create their own modifications to games. This sharing of knowledge and ideas is an excellent example of **collective intelligence**. French professor Pierre Lévy coined the term *collective intelligence* in 1997 to describe the Internet, "this new dimension of communication," and its ability to "enable us to share our knowledge and acknowledge it to others."[19] In the world of gaming, where users are active participants (more than in any other medium), the collective intelligence of players informs the entire game environment.

For example, collective intelligence (and action) is necessary to work through levels of many games. In *World of Warcraft*, collective intelligence is highly recommended. Gamers share ideas through chats and wikis, and those looking for tips and cheats provided by fellow players need only Google what they want. The largest of the sites devoted to sharing collective intelligence is the *World of*

THE *DANCE DANCE REVOLUTION* SERIES was a popular experiential game. The series—along with other rhythm-based games like *Just Dance* and *Rock Band*—provided a new revenue stream for the music industry, which could license songs to use with the games.

Bloomberg/Getty Images

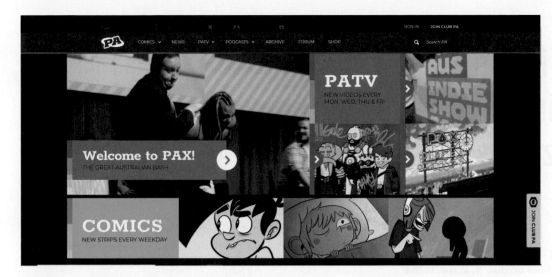

Warcraft wiki (www.wowwiki.com). Similar user-generated sites are dedicated to a range of digital games, including *Age of Conan*, *Assassin's Creed*, *Grand Theft Auto*, *Halo*, *Mario*, *Metal Gear*, *Pokémon*, *Sonic the Hedgehog*, *Spore*, and *Pokémon Go*. (See "Global Village: Phones in Hand, the World Finds Pokémon [and Wizards]" on pages 76–77 for more on *Pokémon Go*, collective intelligence, and global gaming.)

The most advanced form of collective intelligence in gaming is **modding**, slang for "modifying game software or hardware." In many mass communication industries, modifying hardware or content would land someone in a copyright lawsuit. In gaming, modding is often encouraged, as it is yet another way players become more deeply invested in a game, and it can improve the game for others. For example, *Counter-Strike*, a popular first-person shooter game, is a mod of Valve Corporation's first-person shooter game *Half-Life*. The developers of *Half-Life* encouraged mods by including software development tools with it. *Counter-Strike*, in which counterterrorists fight terrorists, emerged as the most popular among many mods, and Valve formed a partnership with the game's developers. *Counter-Strike* was released to retailers, eventually selling more copies than *Half-Life*. Today, many other games, such as *The Elder Scrolls*, have active modding communities.

Gaming Sites

Gaming sites and blogs are among the most popular external communities for gamers. IGN (owned by Ziff Davis), GameSpot (CBS Interactive), and Kotaku (Gizmodo Media Group) are three of the leading websites for gaming. Steam, the PC game software site, also has an active community, as well as the blog at Twitch, the gameplay streaming site.

Conventions

In addition to online gaming communities, there are conventions and expos where video game enthusiasts can come together in person to test out new games and other new products, play old games in competition, and meet video game developers. One of the most significant is the Electronic Entertainment Expo (E3), which draws more than 68,400 industry professionals, investors, developers, and retailers to its annual meeting. E3 is the place where the biggest new game titles and products are unveiled, and it is covered by hundreds of journalists and streamed to mobile devices and Xbox consoles.

The Penny Arcade Expo (PAX) is a convention created by gamers for gamers, held each year in Seattle and Boston. One of its main attractions is the Omegathon, a three-day elimination game tournament in which twenty randomly selected attendees compete in games across several genres, culminating in the championship match at the convention's closing. Other conventions include the Tokyo Game Show—the world's largest gaming convention, with more than 250,000 attendees annually.

Phones in Hand, the World Finds Pokémon (and Wizards)

The unique thing about the release of the digital game *Pokémon Go* on July 6, 2016, is that everyone played in open view. Millions of people were trying to catch wild Pokémon, not on consoles or computers in their living rooms or bedrooms but outdoors, in public, where individuals and groups of people scoured neighborhoods to locate PokéStops and Pokémon Gyms.

In a matter of hours, *Pokémon Go*—developed by Nintendo, the Pokémon Company, and Niantic Labs (a private company spun off from Google)—became the most popular mobile game app ever in America, and over the course of the month, it expanded into a global sensation, with over 100 million downloads.

Within a month, there were players in more than seventy countries, including Australia, New Zealand, Germany, the United Kingdom, Hungary, Canada, Greenland, Brazil, Peru, Costa Rica, Mexico, Malaysia, Laos, Philippines, Thailand, Vietnam, and the Solomon Islands. By early 2018, it had been downloaded over 800 million times and had earned almost $2 billion.[1] Although the game is free to play, in-game purchases and sponsorships helped it earn its revenue.

Pokémon Go is an augmented reality, geo-based game. Players (who are called Trainers and who adopt a unique nickname to play) create their own avatars and use their phone cameras as they walk through neighborhoods. The "augmented reality" technology overlays the game's map on a player's phone, and the map follows the real-world map of the place where the player is walking. Niantic Labs uses computer servers around the world to operate the game and locate Pokémon, PokéStops, and Pokémon Gyms, where teams can battle for control of the site. Niantic received complaints about some of its initial Gym sites, which sent people into graveyards, airports, a hospital delivery room, the 9/11 memorial in New York, the United States Holocaust Memorial Museum in Washington, D.C., the

Christopher Martin

Auschwitz Memorial in Poland, and the Demilitarized Zone in Korea, where "walking to the location would likely put them in imminent danger of being killed."[2] These days, *Pokémon Go* Gyms are mostly located in public parks and sponsored locations, like Starbucks cafés and Sprint stores.[3]

Although play of *Pokémon Go* peaked in summer 2016, it still remains popular, especially with worldwide *Pokémon Go* promotional events. For example, on Valentine's Day 2018, *Pokémon Go* tweeted, "Until February 15, schools of Luvdisc will be out swimming and awarding 3x Stardust for each one caught" (translation: a Luvdisc is a heart-shaped fish; Stardust is valuable because it increases Pokémon combat power). Other events—like the Pikachu Outbreak Japan 2017 and the *Pokémon Go* Fest Chicago Bonus Event 2017—offer geography-based play, where bonus encounters and catch rates occur for a limited period of time, drawing thousands of players.[4]

The success of *Pokémon Go* is its unique, inter-active augmented reality play, which, as few games

do, actually gets players out of the house and interacting in person. *Pokémon Go* also has the built-in bonus of nostalgia. Pokémon (short for Pocket Monsters) were invented in Japan and made their debut on the Nintendo Game Boy in 1996. Since that time, the franchise has expanded to trading card games, television shows, films, comic books, and toys.

Niantic continues to expand and refine *Pokémon Go*. Meanwhile, it is launching another augmented reality geo-hunt game. The game is also built on a well-known story with a massive supply of nostalgic fans. *Harry Potter: Wizards Unite* emerges from a partnership between Niantic and Warner Bros. Interactive Entertainment, a branch of the film studio that gave the world *Harry Potter* movies based on J. K. Rowling's series of seven books, the first of which was released in 1997, a year after Pikachu and the other Pokémon were born.[5] If the gameplay is immersive and authentic to the Harry Potter wizarding world, it is likely that millions more people will get on board with *Harry Potter: Wizards Unite.*

Christopher Martin

TRENDS AND ISSUES IN DIGITAL GAMING

The ever-growing relationship between video games and other media, such as books, movies, and television, leaves no doubt that digital gaming has a permanent place in our culture. Like other media, games are a venue for advertising. A virtual billboard in a video game is usually more than just a digital prop; as in some television shows and movies, it's a paid placement. And like other media, games are a subject of social concern. Violent and misogynistic content has from time to time spurred calls for more regulation of electronic games. But as games permeate more aspects of culture and become increasingly available in nonstandard formats and genres, they may also become harder to define and therefore regulate.

Electronic Gaming and Media Culture

Beyond the immediate industry, electronic games have had a pronounced effect on media culture. For example, fantasy league sports have spawned a number of draft specials on ESPN as well as a regular podcast, *Fantasy Focus*, on ESPN Radio. Fantasy football even inspired an adult comedy called *The League* on the cable channel FX (and later FXX). In the case of the website Twitch, streaming and archived video of digital games being played *is* the content. In just three years, the site became so popular that Amazon bought it for almost $1 billion to add to its collection of original video programming.

Like television shows, books, and comics before them, electronic games have inspired movies, such as the *Resident Evil* series (2001–2017), *Warcraft* (2016), and *Rampage* (2018). For many Hollywood blockbusters today, a video game spin-off is a must-have item. For example, the box-office hit *Guardians of the Galaxy* (2014) inspired the episodic digital game *Guardians of the Galaxy: The Telltale Series* (2017), which is available on console, PC, and mobile platforms.

Books and electronic games have also had a long history of influencing each other. Japanese manga and anime (comic books and animation) have also inspired video games, such as *Akira*, *Astro Boy*, and *Naruto*. *Batman: Arkham Asylum*, a top video game title introduced in 2009, is based closely on the *Batman* comic-book stories, while *The Witcher*, an action role-playing game for PCs, is based on Polish fantasy writer Andrzej Sapkowski's saga. Perhaps the most unusual link between books and electronic games is the *Marvel vs. Capcom* series. In this series, characters from Marvel comic books (Captain America, Hulk, Spider-Man, Wolverine) battle characters from Capcom games such as *Street Fighter* and *Resident Evil* (Akuma, Chun-Li, Ryu, Albert Wesker).

Electronic Gaming and Advertising

Commercialism is as prevalent in video games as it is in most entertainment media. **Advergames**— like television's infomercials or newspapers' and magazines' advertorials—are video games created for purely promotional purposes. The first notable advergame debuted in 1992, when Chester Cheetah, the official mascot for Cheetos snacks, starred in two video games for the Sega Genesis and Super Nintendo systems. **In-game advertisements** are more subtle; ads are integrated into the game as billboards, logos, or storefronts (e.g., a Farmers Insurance airship floating by in *FarmVille*, or Dove soap spas appearing in *The Sims Social*), or advertised products appear as components of the game (e.g., Mercedes-Benz automobiles in *Mario Kart 8 Deluxe*).[20]

Some in-game advertisements are static, which means the ads are permanently placed in the game. Other in-game ads are dynamic, which means the ads are digitally networked and can be altered remotely, so agencies can tailor them according to release time, geographical

FILM ADAPTATIONS OF VIDEO GAMES, such as *Resident Evil: The Final Chapter*, which is the sixth and final film of the series, give game makers another platform for promoting their games while giving gamers an opportunity to become even more immersed in the worlds of the games they love.

Entertainment Pictures/Alamy Stock Photo

location, or user preferences. A movie ad, for example, can have multiple configurations to reflect the movie's release date and screening markets. Advertisers can also record data on users who come in contact with a dynamic ad, such as how long they look at it, from what angle, and how often, and can thus determine how to alter their ad campaigns in the future. The Xbox Kinect has taken dynamic advertising one step further, enabling players to engage with the in-game ads using motion and voice control to learn more about a product.

Addiction and Other Concerns

Though many people view gaming as a simple leisure activity, the electronic gaming industry has sparked controversy. Parents, politicians, the medical establishment, and media scholars have expressed concern about the addictive quality of video games, especially MMORPGs and MOBAs, and have raised the alarm about violent and misogynistic game content—standard fare for many of the most heavily played games.

Addiction

No serious—and honest—gamer can deny the addictive qualities of electronic gaming. In a 2011 study of more than three thousand third through eighth graders from Singapore, one in ten were considered pathological gamers, meaning that their gaming addiction was jeopardizing multiple areas of their lives, including school, social and family relations, and psychological well-being. Indeed, the more the children were addicted, the more prone they were to depression, social phobias, and increased anxiety, which led to poorer grades in school. Singapore's high percentage of pathological youth gamers is in line with numbers reported in other countries, including the United States, where studies found 8.5 percent of gamers to be addicted. In China, the number is 10.3 percent, and in Germany, 11.9 percent.[21]

Gender is a factor in game addiction: A 2013 study found that males are much more susceptible to game addiction. This makes sense, given that the most popular games—action and shooter games— are heavily geared toward males.[22] These findings are also not entirely surprising, given that many electronic games are addictive not by accident but by design. Just as habit formation is a primary goal of virtually every commercial form of electronic media, from newspapers to television to radio, cultivating compulsiveness is the aim of most game designs. From recognizing high scores to incorporating various difficulty settings (encouraging players to try easy, medium, and hard versions) and levels that gradually increase in complexity, designers provide constant in-game incentives for obsessive play.

This is especially true of multiplayer online games—like *League of Legends*, *Call of Duty*, and *World of Warcraft*—which make money from long-term engagement by selling expansion packs; selling avatars, skins, or booster packs; or charging monthly subscription fees. These games have elaborate achievement systems with hard-to-resist rewards that include military ranks like "General" or fanciful titles like "King Slayer," as well as special armor, weapons, and mounts (creatures your avatar can ride, including bears, wolves, or even dragons), all aimed at turning casual players into habitual ones.

This strategy of promoting habit formation may not differ from the cultivation of other media obsessions, like watching televised sporting events. Even so, real-life stories—such as that of the South Korean couple whose three-month-old daughter died of malnutrition while the negligent parents spent ten-hour overnight sessions in an Internet café raising a virtual daughter—bring up serious questions about video games and addiction.[23] Meanwhile, industry executives and others cite the positive impact of digital games, such as the mental stimulation and educational benefits of games like *SimCity*, the health benefits of *Wii Fit* and *Pokémon Go*, and the socially rewarding benefits of playing games together as a family or with friends.

Violence and Misogyny

The Entertainment Software Association (ESA)—the main trade association of the gaming industry— likes to point out that nearly half of game players are women, that more than three-quarters of games sold are rated in the family- and teen-friendly categories, and that the average age of a game player is thirty-five. While these statements are true, they also mask a troubling aspect of some of game culture's most popular games: their violent and sexist imagery.

The Gender Problem in Digital Games

Anita Sarkeesian has a well-documented love of playing video games, from *Mario Kart* and *Rock Band* to *Plants vs. Zombies* and *Half-Life 2*. But that hasn't stopped her from becoming one of the most outspoken—and targeted—critics of how video games depict and treat women. In 2012, a successful Kickstarter campaign helped her launch her *Tropes vs. Women in Video Games* video series. As Sarkeesian explained, she was moved to examine video games because as a girl growing up and playing the games, she saw that so many of the troubling stereotypes about women were enmeshed in games and gaming culture.

"The games often reinforce a similar message, overwhelmingly casting men as heroes and relegating women to the roles of damsels, victims or hypersexualized playthings," Sarkeesian said. "The notion that gaming was not for women rippled out into society, until we heard it not just from the games industry, but from our families, teachers and friends. As a consequence, I, like many women, had a complicated, love–hate relationship with gaming culture."[1]

"Love–hate" is probably also a good way to describe the reaction to Sarkeesian's critique of games. On the one hand, she has gained critical acclaim and visibility for her videos and writing, appearing in the *New York Times*, *Businessweek*, and *Rolling Stone*, as well as on *The Colbert Report*. On the other hand, since she began releasing her videos on digital games, she has been the target of a global campaign of incredibly graphic and violent threats of rape, torture, and murder on social media. This ongoing online harassment reached a new low in the fall of 2014, when another of her Feminist Frequency video releases coincided with what has become known as the #GamerGate controversy.

The story surrounding the event that ostensibly touched off #GamerGate began when a computer programmer, Eron Gjoni, had a bad breakup with game designer Zoe Quinn. Gjoni then went online with their breakup in a 9,425-word blog post, claiming that Quinn had had an affair with a writer at Kotaku, an influential gamers' website that features information about a variety of games. The post went viral (as Gjoni intended). Male gamers who believed Gjoni assumed that the affair had led to a favorable review of Quinn's most recent game on Kotaku, pointing to this as indicative of a larger trend of shady journalistic ethics in the gaming press. They organized their criticisms under the hashtag #GamerGate. Very quickly, however, any supposed concerns over journalistic ethics were overshadowed by those focused on "slut-shaming" Quinn. As *Boston* magazine said, "Zoe Quinn's ex-boyfriend was obsessed with destroying her reputation—and thousands of online strangers were eager to help."[2] The misogynistic attacks by supporters of #GamerGate exploded into a global barrage of anonymous threats and attacks on a number of high-profile women in the gaming industry, including Sarkeesian, game developer Brianna Wu, and journalists Katherine Cross and Maddy Myers. A Reddit discussion board identified #GamerGate supporters in nearly every country around the world.[3]

It was at this point that Sarkeesian (and other critics) spoke up and pointed out that the deeply disturbing threats that female gamers and critics were experiencing proved her point about a deeper problem in the gaming culture, which in turn reflected broader cultural misogyny. In response to this criticism, many supporters of #GamerGate started behaving even worse.

Soon Sarkeesian and others weren't just receiving anonymous and graphic threats in places like Twitter; rather, they found themselves victims of doxing and swatting. To "dox" someone means to steal private or personal information (from addresses and personal phone numbers to social security and credit card information in some cases) and make it public. To "swat" someone means to call in an anonymous tip to a police department, giving the victim's address, in an attempt to provoke a raid—particularly by an armed SWAT team—on the person's home. In one such incident, approximately twenty Portland police officers were dispatched to the scene of a supposed armed hostage situation, when the target of the hoax saw someone bragging about it on a message board and called the police before the situation could escalate.[4] Quinn and Wu both had to flee their homes after being doxed and receiving threats that identified where they lived.

In another case, before a scheduled speech by Sarkeesian at Utah State University, an anonymous person threatened to carry out the biggest school shooting ever if the video game critic spoke. Sarkeesian canceled her speech after campus police said Utah's gun laws prohibited them from turning away any audience member who showed up with a gun. Sarkeesian went into hiding for a time, afraid to return to her home because of the various threats. Her Wikipedia page has been vandalized several times with pornographic pictures, and her Feminist Frequency website has been the target of denial-of-service attacks.

But Sarkeesian is far from giving up. In an ironic twist, the hatred leveled at the critic has brought many supporters her way as well. For example, donors have sent almost $400,000 to her crowdfunded Feminist Frequency website (which is now officially a nonprofit organization dedicated to providing commercial-free videos critiquing the portrayal of women in video games and mass media). Sarkeesian's Twitter feed (@femfreq) reaches over 740,000 followers, and her YouTube video commentary has drawn millions of views.[5]

Because the gaming news media was largely ignoring the misogyny of #GamerGate, Sarkeesian, Wu, and others began to speak out to mainstream news organizations, and coverage spread to Canada, the United Kingdom, Sweden, and elsewhere. With the #GamerGate controversy subject to greater international media scrutiny, the discussion began to change. "We finally shamed [the gaming news media] into finally addressing #GamerGate," Wu said in a university speech. After being subjected to more than fifty death threats and constant bullying, and still feeling "damaged from this experience," Wu perseveres. "We are making this better. We took #GamerGate and we turned it around in its tracks."[6] In 2018, Brianna Wu formed a campaign to run for Congress to represent a district in Massachusetts. Her campaign slogan: "She fought the Alt-Right and won—now she's fighting for you."[7]

David J. Green - Lifestyle/Alamy Stock Photo

**GAMES IN THE
GRAND THEFT AUTO**

series typically receive a rating of "Mature," indicating they should not be sold to players under seventeen. However, the ratings do not distinguish between overall game violence and misogynistic attitudes.

Most games involving combat, guns, and other weapons are intentionally violent, with representations of violence becoming all the more graphic as game visuals reach cinematic hyperrealism. The most violent video games, rated M for "Mature," often belong to the first-person shooter, dark fantasy, or survival horror genres (or a combination of all three) and cast players in a variety of sinister roles—serial killers, mortal combat soldiers, chain-gun-wielding assassins, mutated guys out for revenge, not-quite-executed death-row inmates, and underworld criminals (to name a few)—in which they earn points by killing and maiming their foes through the most horrendous means possible. In this genre of games, violence is a celebration, as is clear from one Top 10 list featuring the most "delightfully violent video games of all time."[24]

That some games can be violent and misogynistic is not a point of dispute. But the possible effects of such games have been debated for years, and video games have been accused of being a factor in violent episodes, such as the Columbine High School shootings in 1999. Earlier research linked playing violent video games to aggressive thoughts or hostility, but those effects don't necessarily transfer to real-world environments. Instead, more recent studies suggest that the personality traits of certain types of players should be of greater concern than the violence of video games. For example, a study in the *Review of General Psychology* noted that individuals with a combination of "high neuroticism (e.g., easily upset, angry, depressed, emotional, etc.), low agreeableness (e.g., little concern for others, indifferent to others' feelings, cold, etc.), and low conscientiousness (e.g., break rules, don't keep promises, act without thinking, etc.)" are more susceptible to the negative outcomes measured in studies of violent video games.[25] For the vast majority of players, the study concluded, violent video games have no adverse effects.

There is less research on misogyny (hatred of women) in video games. One of the most extreme game narratives is from the hugely successful *Grand Theft Auto* series, in which male characters earn points by picking up female prostitutes, paying money for sex, and then beating up or killing the hooker to get their money back. Women are close to half of the digital game audience in the United States, and it's likely that many aren't engaged by this story. The source of the problem may be the male insularity of the game development industry; for reasons that are unclear, few women are on the career path to be involved in game development. According to the National Center for Women & Information Technology, "Women hold 56% of all professional occupations in the U.S. workforce, but only 25% of IT occupations." And even as the digital game industry gets bigger, the impact of women gets smaller. "In 2009, just 18% of undergraduate Computing and Information Sciences degrees were awarded to women; in 1985, women earned 37% of these degrees."[26] (See "Examining Ethics: The Gender Problem in Digital Games" on pages 80–81 for more on violence and misogyny in video games.)

Regulating Gaming

For decades, concern about violence in video games has led to calls for regulation. Back in 1976, an arcade game called *Death Race* prompted the first public outcry over the violence of electronic gaming. The primitive graphics of the game depicted a blocky car running down stick-figure Gremlins that, if struck, turned into grave markers. Described as "sick and morbid" by the National Safety Council, *Death Race* inspired a *60 Minutes* report on the potential psychological damage of playing video games. Over the next forty years, violent video games would prompt citizen groups and politicians to call for government regulation of electronic game content.

Historical first-person shooter games are a significant subgenre of action games, the biggest-selling genre of the digital game industry. *Call of Duty: Modern Warfare 3* **(set in a fictional WWIII) made $775 million in its first five days. And with thirteen million units sold by 2012, Rockstar Games' critically acclaimed** *Red Dead Redemption* **(***RDR***, set in the Wild West) was applauded for its realism and called a "tour de force" by the** *New York Times*.[1] **But as these games proliferate through our culture, what are we learning as we are launched back and forth in time and into the worlds of these games?**

1 DESCRIPTION

Red Dead Redemption features John Madsen, a white outlaw turned federal agent, who journeys to the "uncivilized" West to capture or kill his old gang members. Within this game, gamers encounter breathtaking vistas and ghost towns with saloons, prostitutes, and gunslingers; large herds of cattle; and scenes of the Mexican Rebellion. Shootouts are common in towns and on the plains, and gamers earn points for killing animals and people. The *New York Times* review notes that *"Red Dead Redemption* is perhaps most distinguished by the brilliant voice acting and pungent, pitch-perfect writing we have come to expect from Rockstar."[2]

2 ANALYSIS

RDR may have "pitch-perfect writing," but a certain tune emerges. For example, African

Americans and Native Americans are absent from the story line (although they were clearly present in the West of 1911). The roles of women are limited: They are portrayed as untrustworthy and chronically nagging wives, prostitutes, or nuns—and they can be blithely killed in front of sheriffs and husbands without ramifications. One special mission is to hogtie a nun or prostitute and drop her onto tracks in front of an oncoming train. One gamer in his popular how-to demo on YouTube calls this mission "the coolest achievement I've ever seen in a game."[3]

3 INTERPRETATION

RDR may give us a technologically rich immersion into the Wild West of 1911, but it relies on clichés to do so (macho white gunslinger as leading man, weak or contemptible women, vigilante justice). If the macho/misogynistic narrative

possibilities and value system of *RDR* seem familiar, it's because the game is based on Rockstar's other video game hit, *Grand Theft Auto* (*GTA*), which lets players have sex with and then graphically kill hookers. *GTA* was heavily criticized for creating an "X-Rated wonderland" and was dubbed "Grand Theft Misogyny."[4] Indeed, Rockstar simply took the *GTA* engine and interface and overlaid new scenes, narratives, and characters, moving from the urban streets of Liberty City to American frontier towns.[5]

4 EVALUATION

The problem with *Red Dead Redemption* is its limited view of history, lack of imagination, and reliance on misogyny as entertainment. Since its gameplay is so similar to that of *GTA*, the specifics of time and place are beside the point—all that's left is killing and hating women. Video games are fun, but what effect do they have on men's attitudes toward women?

5 ENGAGEMENT

Talk to friends about games like *GTA*, *RDR*, and Rockstar's more recent *L.A. Noire*. (Set in 1940s Los Angeles, it also contains scenes of nudity and graphic violence against women.) Comment on blog sites about the ways some games can provide a mask for misogyny, and write to Rockstar itself (www.rockstargames.com), demanding less demeaning narratives regarding women and ethnic minorities.

In 1993, after the violence of *Mortal Kombat* and *Night Trap* attracted the attention of religious and educational organizations, Senator Joseph Lieberman conducted a hearing that proposed federal regulation of the gaming industry. Following a pattern established in the movie and music industries, the gaming industry implemented a self-regulation system enforced by an industry panel. The industry founded the **Entertainment Software Rating Board (ESRB)** in 1994 to institute a labeling system designed to inform parents of sexual and violent content that might not be suitable for younger players. Publishers aren't required to submit their games to the ESRB for a rating, but many retailers will only sell rated games, so gamemakers usually consent to the process. To get a rating, the game companies submit scripts that include any dialogue and music lyrics, and also fill out a questionnaire to describe the story and identify possibly offensive content.[27] Currently the ESRB sorts games into six categories: EC (Early Childhood), E (Everyone), E 10+ (Everyone 10+), T (Teens), M (Mature 17+), and AO (Adults Only 18+).

More restrictions on digital game sales seem unlikely for now. California passed a law in 2005 to fine stores $1,000 for selling video games rated M or AO to minors, but the U.S. Supreme Court struck down the law in a 7–2 decision in 2011, setting a difficult precedent for the establishment of other laws regulating electronic games.

The Future of Gaming and Interactive Environments

Gaming technology of the future promises a more immersive and portable experience that will touch even more aspects of our lives. The Wii introduced motion-controlled games in 2006. Microsoft's motion-sensing Xbox Kinect has been a hit since its introduction in late 2010, and with Avatar Kinect, users can control their avatar's motions, as the Kinect senses even small physical gestures. In 2012, Sony released its SOEmote facial-tracking and voice-font software with its popular *EverQuest II* game, enabling players to give their facial expressions and voices to their avatars. Virtual reality headsets such as the Oculus Rift, the HTC Vive VR, and PlayStation VR (all of which were introduced in 2016) now connect to PC and console games. Less expensive options like the ReTrak Utopia 360°, the Samsung Gear VR, and the ultra-low-tech Google Cardboard use mobile phones attached to the face of the headset to deliver a similar 360-degree virtual reality game experience.

Video games in the future will also continue to move beyond just entertainment. The term *gamification* describes how interactive game experiences are being embedded to bring competition and rewards to everyday activities.[28] Games are already used in workforce training, for social causes, in classrooms, and as part of multimedia journalism. All these developments continue to make games a larger part of our media experiences.

THE BUSINESS OF DIGITAL GAMING

Today, 65 percent of American households have someone at home who regularly plays video games, with 11 percent of households playing with a VR headset. The entire U.S. video game market, including portable and console hardware and accessories, adds up to about $25.1 billion annually, with global sales reaching an estimated $128.5 billion by 2020.[29] Thanks in part to the introduction of the Wii, mobile games, and a wide range of indie games, today's audience for digital games extends beyond the young-male gamer stereotype. According to the video and computer game industry's main trade group, the Entertainment Software Association, the average game player is thirty-five years old and has been playing games for eighteen years. Women constitute 41 percent of game players. Gamers are social, too: 41 percent of them play games with friends, either in person or online, and 18 percent play with parents.[30]

These numbers speak to the economic health of the electronic gaming industry. Digital gaming companies can make money selling not just consoles and games but also online subscriptions, companion books, and movie rights.

The Ownership and Organization of Digital Gaming

For years, the two major components of the gaming industry have been console makers and game publishers. The biggest blockbuster games are still produced and distributed by the leading game publishers, and many are designed to be played on the three leading game consoles connected to big television sets. At the same time, the emergence of game platforms on mobile devices and on social networks has expanded the game market and brought new game publishers into the field.

Game Publishers

As noted earlier, the three major console makers also publish games (sometimes making the games *proprietary*, meaning they will only play on that company's system). For example, Microsoft famously began publishing its *Halo* game series to drive sales of the Xbox. Similarly, Sony publishes the *Uncharted* game series just for PlayStation, and Nintendo publishes *The Legend of Zelda* series solely for its gaming platforms.

More often, game publishers are independent companies, distributing games that play across multiple platforms. Sometimes these publishers are also the developers—the people who write the actual code for the games. Other times these publishers serve as distributors for the game developers, in the same way that film studios may distribute the work of independent filmmakers. Activision Blizzard and Electronic Arts—two leading independent game publishing companies—have been particularly good at adaptation and innovation, producing the most imaginative and ambitious titles and selling the most games across multiple platforms.

Activision Blizzard was created through the merging of Activision and Vivendi's Blizzard division in 2008. One-half of the company—Activision—got its start in the 1970s as the first independent game developer and distributor, initially providing games for the Atari platform. Activision was unique in that it rewarded its developers with royalty payments and name credits on game box covers, something that hadn't yet been considered by other game publishing companies, which kept their developers anonymous. As a result, top game designers and programmers migrated to Activision, and Activision began to produce a number of top-selling games, including the *X-Men* series (2000–), the *Call of Duty* series (2003–), and *Guitar Hero* (2006–2011).

Meanwhile, Blizzard Entertainment, established in 1991 as an independent game publisher, has three famous franchises in game publishing: *Diablo* (1996–), *StarCraft* (1998–), and *World of Warcraft* (2004–). Its widely praised *Overwatch* (2016) reached thirty-five million players in a little over a year and has become Blizzard's fourth major franchise, particularly as a result of its becoming a widely used team-based first-person shooter game for eSports.[31] Known for its obsession with game quality, artistic achievement, and commitment to its fans, Blizzard has dominated in real-time strategy games and remains one of the most critically acclaimed game publishers in the world. As one company, Activision Blizzard has become a publishing giant in the industry, even expanding its offerings by purchasing mobile and social gamemaker King (*Candy Crush Saga*) in 2016.

Electronic Arts (EA) got its name by recognizing that the video game is an art form and that software developers are indeed artists; the name Electronic Arts is also a tribute to the United Artists film studio, established in 1919 by three actors and one director—Charlie Chaplin, Mary Pickford, Douglas Fairbanks, and D. W. Griffith—who broke away from the studio-dominated film industry (see pages 204–208). Operating under the same principle that Activision pioneered, EA was able to secure a stable of top talent and begin producing a promising lineup of titles: *Archon, Pinball Construction Set, M.U.L.E., Seven Cities of Gold, The Bard's Tale, Starflight, Wasteland,* and, perhaps most notably,

John Madden Football (now known as *Madden NFL*)—first released in 1988 and then updated annually beginning in 1990, a practice that has become the modus operandi for EA.

Like Activision Blizzard, EA has moved toward mobile and social gaming platforms. Electronic Arts acquired PopCap Games, the company that produces *Bejeweled* and *Plants vs. Zombies*. The company has also sought to compete directly with Activision Blizzard's *World of Warcraft* series by developing (through its Canadian subsidiary, BioWare) the lavish MMORPG game *Star Wars: The Old Republic* (2012)—the most expensive game made to date, with a price tag approaching $200 million.[32]

One of the newest major game publishers, Zynga, was established in 2007 and specializes in casual games. *FarmVille*, *Draw Something*, *Zynga Poker*, and *Looney Tunes Dash* are among its Facebook hits, though it is losing players to competing developers like Activision Blizzard subsidiary King (*Candy Crush Saga*, *Bubble Witch Saga*) and Wooga (*Diamond Dash*, *Bubble Island*). To decrease its reliance on Facebook, Zynga's plan going forward is to develop games for mobile devices.

The most well-known developer and publisher of games for mobile devices is Rovio, founded in Finland in 2003. In 2010, Rovio's *Angry Birds* became an international phenomenon, as millions of players downloaded the game on touchscreen devices for the chance to slingshot-launch birds at pigs hiding in increasingly complex structures. By 2012 (when Rovio released *Angry Birds Space*), downloads of all the company's *Angry Birds* titles reached one billion.[33] Like Zynga, Rovio has moved to diversify, and it brought *Angry Birds* to Facebook in 2012. In 2016, Sony Animation produced a feature film based on the game.

Other top game publishers around the world include Square Enix (*Deus Ex*, *Final Fantasy*), Ubisoft (*Assassin's Creed*, *Rayman*), Sega (*Sonic the Hedgehog*, *Super Monkey Ball*), and Bandai Namco (*Dark Souls: Remastered*, *Tekken 7*).

The Structure of Digital Game Publishing

AAA game titles (games that represent the current standard for technical excellence, pronounced "Triple-A") can cost as much as a blockbuster film to make and promote. For example, *The Witcher 3: Wild Hunt* (2015), *Destiny* (2014), and *Watch Dogs* (2014) all ranged between $80 million and $140 million in total costs to produce. Development, licensing, manufacturing, and marketing constitute the major expenditures in game publishing (see Figure 3.2).

Development

The largest part of the **development** budget—the money spent designing, coding, scoring, and testing a game—goes to paying talent, digital artists, and game testers. Each new generation of gaming platforms doubles the number of people involved in designing, programming, and mixing digitized images and sounds.

Licensing

Independent gamemakers must also deal with two types of licensing. First, they have to pay royalties to console manufacturers (Microsoft, Sony, or Nintendo) for the right to distribute a game using their system. These royalties vary from $3 to $10 per unit sold. (Of course, if a console

ANGRY BIRDS, Rovio's popular mobile video game, had over two billion downloads across all mobile platforms by 2014. With a mention on NBC's *30 Rock*, a tie-in with Twentieth Century Fox's animated film *Rio*, and a *New Yorker* cartoon, these fearsome birds permeated our media culture. A feature film followed in 2016.

"*Of course I'm angry—look at me.*"

© Kim Warp/The New Yorker Collection/www.CartoonBank.com

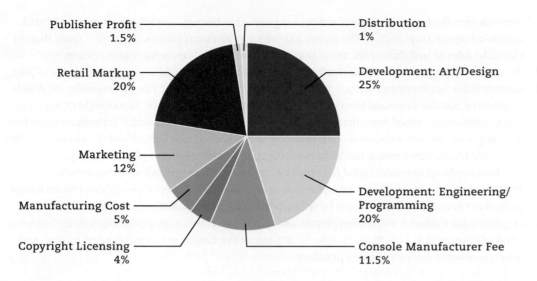

Publisher Profit
1.5%

Retail Markup
20%

Marketing
12%

Manufacturing Cost
5%

Copyright Licensing
4%

Distribution
1%

Development: Art/Design
25%

Development: Engineering/
Programming
20%

Console Manufacturer Fee
11.5%

FIGURE 3.2

WHERE THE MONEY GOES ON A $60 VIDEO GAME

Data from: Altered Gamer, March 30, 2012, www .alteredgamer.com/free-pc -gaming/21118-why-are-video -games-so-expensive.

manufacturer such as Nintendo makes its own games exclusively for the Wii, then it doesn't have to pay a console royalty to itself.) The other form of licensing involves **intellectual properties**—stories, characters, personalities, and music that require licensing agreements. In 2005, for instance, John Madden reportedly signed a $150 million deal with EA Sports that allowed the company to use his name and likeness for the next ten years.[34]

Marketing

The marketing costs of launching an electronic game often equal or exceed the development costs. The successful launch of a game involves online promotions, banner ads, magazine print ads, in-store displays, and the most expensive element of all: television advertising. In many ways, the marketing blitz associated with introducing a major new franchise title, including cinematic television trailers, resembles the promotional campaign surrounding the debut of a blockbuster movie. For example, Rockstar Games reportedly spent $150 million for the marketing of its 2013 blockbuster release *Grand Theft Auto V*, eclipsing its $115 million development budget. *GTAV* remains the most expensive digital game made to date.[35] Just as avid fans line up for the first showing of a new *Star Wars* or *Avengers* movie, devoted gamers mob participating retail outlets during the countdown to the midnight launch of a hotly anticipated new game.

Selling Digital Games

Just as digital distribution has altered the relationship between other mass media and their audiences, it has transformed the way electronic games are sold. Although the selling of $60 AAA console games at retail stores is an enduring model, many games are now free (with opportunities for hooked players to pay for additional play features), and digital stores are making access to games almost immediate.

Pay Models

There are three main pay models in the electronic game industry: the boxed game/retail model, the subscription model, and free-to-play.

The *boxed game/retail model* is the most traditional and dates back to the days of cartridges on Atari, Sega, and Nintendo console systems. By the 1990s, games were being released on CD-ROMs, and later DVDs, to better handle the richer game files. Many boxed games are now sold with offers of additional downloadable content. For blockbuster console games, retail sales of boxed games still reign as the venue for a game premiere. As of 2013, the biggest game launch ever—in fact, the biggest launch of *any* media product in history—was the September 17, 2013, release of *Grand Theft Auto V*. The game, published by Rockstar Games, generated more than $1 billion in sales in just three days, more than any other previous game or movie release.[36]

Some games are also sold via a *subscription model*, in which gamers pay a monthly fee to play. Notable subscription games include *World of Warcraft* and *Star Wars: The Old Republic*, for which players first buy the game and then pay a subscription of $14.99 a month. At its height of popularity, *World of Warcraft* earned more than $1 billion a year for Activision Blizzard.[37] Yet with so many free-to-play games, the subscription model hasn't expanded widely, and both *World of Warcraft* and *Star Wars: The Old Republic* now offer the free-to-play model, with premium play as an option.

Free-to-play (sometimes called *freemium*) is common with casual and online games like *100 Balls*. Free-to-play games are offered online or as downloads at no charge to gain or retain a large audience. These games make money by selling extras, like power boosters (to aid in gameplay), or in-game subscriptions for upgraded play. In addition to free casual games (like *Angry Birds Seasons*, *Clash of Clans*, and *Temple Run*), popular MOBA games like *League of Legends* are free-to-play, and generate revenue through in-game purchases.

Digital Distribution

With the advent and growing popularity of digital game distribution, game players don't need to go to a big-box store or retail game shop to buy video games. All three major consoles are Wi-Fi capable, and each has its own digital store—Xbox Games Store, Nintendo eShop, and PlayStation Store. Customers can purchase and download games, get extra downloadable content, and buy other media—including television shows and movies—as the consoles compete to be the sole entertainment center of people's living rooms.

Although the three major console companies control digital downloads to their devices, several companies compete for the download market in PC games. The largest is Steam, with more than 125 million subscribers and about 75 percent of the PC game distribution market.[39] Steam is owned by Valve Corporation, which used the digital store to help distribute its *Counter-Strike* game online beginning in 2003. Steam also carries more than 7,500 games from a wide range of game publishers. Other companies that sell digital game downloads for PCs include Amazon, GameStop, and Origin (owned by EA).

Of course, the most ubiquitous digital game distributors are Apple's App Store and Google Play, where users can purchase games on mobile devices. Although Google's Android system has surpassed the iPhone in market penetration, Apple customers are more likely to purchase apps, including games. This particularity has drawn more independent developers to work in the Apple operating system.[40]

Alternative Voices

The advent of mobile gaming has provided a new entry point for independent game developers. As *Canadian Business* magazine noted, the cost of entry has decreased substantially. "The average cost of making a major console game for Xbox 360 and PlayStation 3 is about $20 million, but almost anyone can churn out a new game app for the iPhone. And independent developers need only pay Apple's $99 fee for a developer's account to get their creations to the market—no Best Buy or Walmart shelf space required."[41]

VIDEO GAME STORES

Apart from buying boxed game titles at stores like Walmart, Best Buy, and Target, or online stores like Amazon, there is really only one major video game store chain devoted entirely to new and used video games: GameStop. The chain, which started in Dallas, Texas, in 1984 as Babbage's, today operates more than seventy-two hundred stores in fourteen countries.[38] GameStop is currently trying to negotiate the shifting ground of the digital turn by selling customers access codes to digital game downloads in the stores, selling Android tablets and refurbished iPads, and investing in other digital gaming companies.

Bettina Fabos

But even so, time and money are still required to develop quality games. Many independent game developers and smaller game companies are creating games that take a far different approach than blockbuster AAA games. For example, London-based State of Play Games developed *Lumino City*, an award-winning puzzle-adventure game that took three years to make. Hand painted and crafted entirely out of paper, cards, miniature lights, and motors, the game depicts an environment that is both tactile and gorgeous, which the animated character, Lumi, gently moves through. The story line puts Lumi on an epic journey as she hunts for her grandfather, who was kidnapped. As players solve puzzles to move the game forward, they explore unusual dwellings beyond the city gates and discover more about the grandfather's intriguing life along the way.

LUMINO CITY, a handcrafted puzzle game that took three years to make, has received many awards and recognition, including four awards for best indie game.

Two other award-winning independent games are *Limbo* and *Hidden Folks*. *Limbo*, developed by Playdead, is a 2-D side-scroller puzzle-platform game that guides an unnamed boy through harsh and sinister (film noir) environments as he searches for his sister. Reminiscent of the *Highlights for Children* magazine's "Hidden Pictures" feature, *Hidden Folks* asks players to search for hidden folks in multiple hand-drawn, interactive, miniature landscapes.

But for independent game developers, it can take incredible persistence against great odds to make a successful game. Rovio made fifty-one failed app games in six years, nearly folding before *Angry Birds* became a worldwide success in 2009.

DIGITAL GAMING, FREE SPEECH, AND DEMOCRACY

In a landmark decision handed down in 2011 over a California law enforcing fines for renting or selling M-rated games to minors, the Supreme Court granted electronic games speech protections afforded by the First Amendment. According to the opinion written by the late Justice Antonin Scalia, video games communicate ideas worthy of such protection:

Like the protected books, plays, and movies that preceded them, video games communicate ideas—and even social messages—through many familiar literary devices (such as characters, dialogue, plot, and music) and through features distinctive to the medium (such as the player's interaction with the virtual world).[42]

Scalia even mentioned *Mortal Kombat* in footnote 4 of the decision:

Reading Dante is unquestionably more cultured and intellectually edifying than playing Mortal Kombat. *But these cultural and intellectual differences are not constitutional ones. Crudely violent video games, tawdry TV shows, and cheap novels and magazines are no less forms of speech than* The Divine Comedy. . . . *Even if we can see in them "nothing of any possible value to society . . . they are as much entitled to the protection of free speech as the best of literature."*[43]

With the Supreme Court decision, electronic games achieved the same First Amendment protection afforded to other mass media. However, as in the music, television, and film industries, First Amendment protections will not make the rating system for the gaming industry go away. Parents continue to have legitimate concerns about the games their children play. Game publishers and retailers understand that it is still in their best interest to respect those concerns even though the ratings cannot be enforced by law.

3 Chapter Review

One of our favorite quotes that we like to use in our teaching is from writer Joan Didion, in her book The White Album. *She wrote: "We tell ourselves stories in order to live." Telling stories is one of the constants of cultural expression across the mass media. But with digital games, what is it that is being communicated if we are crafting our own individual narrative as we play through a game? Is it still a story?*

Books, television, movies, newspapers, magazines, and even musical recordings tell us stories about the human experience. Digital games, especially ones in which we play as a character or an avatar, offer perhaps the most immersive storytelling experience of any medium.

Gamers have already shifted away from traditional media stories to those of video games. The Entertainment Software Association reported that gamers who played more video games than they had three years earlier were spending less time going to the movies (40 percent of respondents), watching TV (39 percent), and watching movies at home (47 percent).[44] Clearly, video games are in competition with movies and television for consumers' attention. But as we move from the kind of storytelling we experience as viewers of TV shows and movies to the storytelling we experience as players of games, what happens to the story? Is it still a mass mediated story, or is it something else?

Jon Spaihts, screenwriter of the science-fiction film *Prometheus* (2012), identifies an essential difference between the stories and storytelling in games and in films. "The central character of a game is most often a cipher—an avatar into which the player projects himself or herself. The story has to have a looseness to accommodate the player's choices," Spaihts says. Conversely, "a filmmaker is trying to make you look at something a certain way—almost to force an experience on you," he adds.[45] Thus, the question of who is doing the storytelling—a producer/director or the game player—is a significant one.

Such was the case in the furor over *Mass Effect 3* in 2012. After players spent from 120 to 150 hours advancing through the trilogy, in which they could make hundreds of choices in the sequence of events, the final act took that power away from them with a tightly scripted finish. The players complained loudly, and the cofounder of BioWare, the game's developer, issued an apology. BioWare said that it would create a new ending with "a number of game content initiatives that will help answer the questions, providing more clarity for those seeking further closure to their journey."[46]

Certainly the audience at a movie will have a range of interpretations of the movie's story. But what of the stories we are telling ourselves as players of games like *Mass Effect*? Is such personally immersive storytelling better, worse, or just different? And who is doing the storytelling?

The definitions for the terms listed below can be found in the glossary at the end of the book. The page numbers listed with the terms indicate where the term is highlighted in the chapter.

penny arcade, 65
pinball machine, 66
arcades, 67
avatar, 67
consoles, 67
massively multiplayer online role-playing
   games (MMORPGs), 71
online fantasy sports, 71

gameplay, 72
PUGs, 72
noobs, 72
ninjas, 73
trolls, 73
guilds *or* clans, 73
collective intelligence, 74
modding, 75

advergames, 78
in-game advertisements, 78
Entertainment Software Rating Board
   (ESRB), 84
development, 86
intellectual properties, 87

REVIEW QUESTIONS

The Development of Digital Gaming

1. What sparked the creation of mechanical games in both the nineteenth and the twentieth centuries?
2. How are classic arcade games and the culture of the arcade similar to today's popular console games and gaming culture?
3. What advantages did personal computers have over video game consoles in the late 1980s and much of the 1990s?

The Internet Transforms Gaming

4. How are MMORPGs, MOBAs, virtual worlds, and online fantasy sports built around online social interaction?
5. How has digital convergence changed the function of gaming consoles?

The Media Playground

6. What are the main genres within digital gaming?
7. How do collective intelligence, gaming sites, and conventions enhance the social experience of gaming and make games different from other mass media?

Trends and Issues in Digital Gaming

8. How have digital games influenced media culture, and vice versa?
9. In what ways has advertising become incorporated into electronic games?
10. To what extent are video game addiction and violent and misogynistic representations problems for the gaming industry?

The Business of Digital Gaming

11. What are the roles of two major components of the gaming industry: console makers and game publishers?
12. How do game publishers develop, license, and market new titles?
13. What are the three major pay models for selling video games today?

Digital Gaming, Free Speech, and Democracy

14. Why did the U.S. Supreme Court rule that games count as speech?
15. Why does the game industry still rate digital games, even if it isn't required by law to do so?

QUESTIONING THE MEDIA

1. Do you have any strong memories from playing early video games? To what extent did these games define your childhood?
2. Have you ever been upset by the level of violence, misogyny, or racism in a video game you played (or watched being played)? Discuss the game narrative and what made it problematic.
3. Most electronic games have a white, male, heterosexual point of view. Why is that? If you were a game developer, what kinds of game narratives would you like to see developed?

LAUNCHPAD FOR *MEDIA & CULTURE*

Visit LaunchPad for *Media & Culture* at launchpadworks.com for additional learning tools:

- REVIEW WITH LEARNINGCURVE
  LearningCurve, available on LaunchPad for *Media & Culture*, uses gamelike quizzing to help you master the concepts you need to learn from this chapter.

Sounds and Images

The dominant media of the twentieth century were all about sounds and images: music, radio, television, and film. Each of these media industries was built around a handful of powerful groups that set the terms for creating and distributing this popular media content. The main story of these media industries was one of ever-improving technology.

Even today, music, radio, TV, and movies are still significant media in our lives. But convergence and the digital turn have changed the story of our sound and image media. We now live in a world where any and all media can be consumed via the Internet on laptops, tablets, smartphones, and video game consoles. As a result, we have seen the demise of record stores and video stores, local radio deejays, and the big network TV hit. Traditional media corporations are playing catch-up, devising new online services to bring their offerings to us while still making money.

The major media of the twentieth century are mostly still with us, but the twenty-first-century story of what form that content will take and how we will experience it is now being written.

HOW WE WATCH AND LISTEN TODAY

U.S. MUSIC GENRE, BY CONSUMPTION

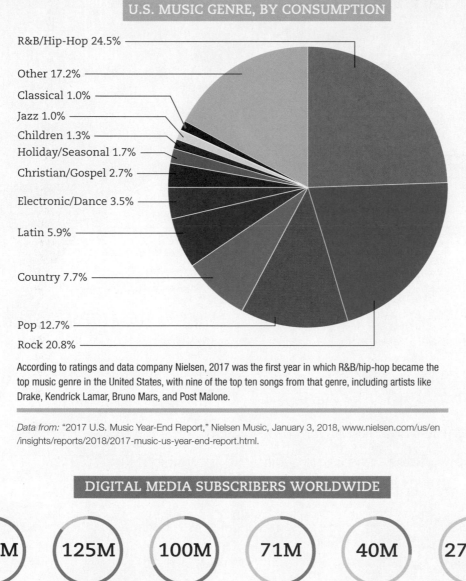

R&B/Hip-Hop 24.5%

Other 17.2%

Classical 1.0%

Jazz 1.0%

Children 1.3%

Holiday/Seasonal 1.7%

Christian/Gospel 2.7%

Electronic/Dance 3.5%

Latin 5.9%

Country 7.7%

Pop 12.7%

Rock 20.8%

According to ratings and data company Nielsen, 2017 was the first year in which R&B/hip-hop became the top music genre in the United States, with nine of the top ten songs from that genre, including artists like Drake, Kendrick Lamar, Bruno Mars, and Post Malone.

Data from: "2017 U.S. Music Year-End Report," Nielsen Music, January 3, 2018, www.nielsen.com/us/en /insights/reports/2018/2017-music-us-year-end-report.html.

DIGITAL MEDIA SUBSCRIBERS WORLDWIDE

142M	125M	100M	71M	40M	27.5M
HBO	NETFLIX	AMAZON PRIME	SPOTIFY	APPLE MUSIC	SIRIUS XM

17M	5.5M	3.6M	3M	2M	2M
HULU	PANDORA	NEW YORK TIMES	TINDER	CBS ALL ACCESS	MOVIEPASS

Data from: Rani Molla, "Amazon Prime Has 100 Million-Plus Prime Memberships—Here's How HBO, Netflix and Tinder Compare," Recode, April 19, 2018, www.recode.net/2018/4/19/17257942/amazon-prime-100-million-subscribers-hulu-hbo-tinder-members.

Sound Recording and Popular Music

4

IT WAS THE 2017 Grammy Awards in Los Angeles, and a twenty-three-year-old rapper from Chicago, Chancellor Johnathan Bennett, walked out with awards for best new artist, best rap performance, and best rap album. Bennett is better known as Chance the Rapper and is a major music artist who emerged from a very untraditional path. As *Billboard* magazine put it, "Chance the Rapper Is One of the Hottest Acts in Music, Has a Top 10 Album and His Own Festival—All Without a Label or Physical Release."

Other artists have paved the way for Chance's business approach. In 2007, British alternative rock group Radiohead decided to sell its album *In Rainbows* on its website for whatever price fans wished to pay, including nothing at all. Adele, Taylor Swift, and Rihanna all record for independent

◀ Artist Chance the Rapper shows off one of his signature "3" baseball caps at the 59th Grammy Awards.

THE DEVELOPMENT OF SOUND RECORDING
p. 97

U.S. POPULAR MUSIC AND THE FORMATION OF ROCK
p. 102

A CHANGING INDUSTRY: REFORMATIONS IN POPULAR MUSIC
p. 109

THE BUSINESS OF SOUND RECORDING
p. 116

SOUND RECORDING, FREE EXPRESSION, AND DEMOCRACY
p. 123

labels, and Macklemore sells music under his own label. Chance the Rapper has gone one step further by not selling any music at all.

His recording career began with the mixtapes *10 Day* (2012) and *Acid Rap* (2013), which he posted for free. Both mixtapes were critically praised, and he received offers from multiple music labels. Chance decided to make a business deal that would both earn him some money and help promote his next release, *Coloring Book* (2016). Rather than sign with a label, he agreed to a short-term contract with a streaming service. Apple Music got exclusive streaming rights to *Coloring Book* for two weeks, a deal that Chance later disclosed was worth $500,000.[1] The Apple Music connection gave his work an even greater audience. His album became the first to debut on the *Billboard* 200 chart (at No. 8) based on only the number of streams.[2] "I think artist[s] can gain a lot from the streaming wars as long as they remain in control of their own product," Chance said.[3] All of his recordings remain available for free streaming on SoundCloud (https://soundcloud.com /chancetherapper).

Why does Chance the Rapper remain independent and refuse to sell recordings? He sat down with journalist Katie Couric at Harold's Chicken Shack on the South Side of Chicago (one of his favorite restaurants) in 2017 to explain his approach to his career. When Couric asked him if he had ever considered signing with a record label, Chance replied, "I get to choose how much my music costs. I get to choose when my music gets released. I choose when I go

on tour, who I work with, what movies I work with."[4]

Instead, Chance makes his money selling merchandise and concert tickets on his website ChanceRaps.com. Among Chance's merchandise is his ubiquitous "3" baseball cap. Chance used to exclusively wear Chicago White Sox baseball caps, but when he and the team could not reach a deal for the publicity, he made his own trademark "3" cap to mark the release of his third album. In addition to merchandise and ticket sales, and revenue-generating streams on Apple Music, Spotify, and YouTube, Chance and his manager have put together other deals, such as sponsorship from Bud Light and Citibank for his sold-out 2016 Magnificent Coloring Day music festival at the White Sox's Cellular One Field.[5]

"My dad taught me to work hard, and my mom taught me to work for myself," Chance told Couric. "And so now I work for myself really hard."[6]

The rise of independent labels is one of the most significant developments in the music industry in the past two decades. The old route to success for musical artists was highly dependent on signing with a major label, which handled all the promotion to sell records. Now, with so many distribution forms for music—traditional CDs and vinyl; digital downloads and streaming; social media; music licensed for use in advertising, television, and film; and (of course) live, in-person concerts—there are multiple paths for talented artists to find an audience with an independent label or on their own.

THE MEDIUM OF SOUND RECORDING has had an immense impact on our culture. The music that helps shape our identities and comforts us during the transition from childhood to adulthood resonates throughout our lives. In the course of its history, popular music has also been banned by parents, school officials, and even governments under the guise of protecting young people from corrupting influences. As far back as the late eighteenth century, authorities in Europe, thinking that it was immoral for young people to dance close together, outlawed waltz music as "savagery." Popular music from the jazz age to today has also added its own chapters to the age-old musical battle between generations.

In this chapter, we will place the impact of popular music in context and:

- Investigate the origins of recording's technological "hardware," from Thomas Edison's early phonograph to Emile Berliner's invention of the flat disk record and the development of audiotape, compact discs, and MP3s
- Study radio's early threat to sound recording and the subsequent alliance between the two media when television arrived in the 1950s
- Explore the impact of the Internet on music, including the effects of online piracy and how the industry is adapting to the era of convergence with new models for distributing and promoting music, moving from downloads to streaming
- Examine the content and culture of the music industry, focusing on the predominant role of rock music and its extraordinary impact on mass media forms and a diverse array of cultures, both American and international
- Explore the economic and democratic issues facing the recording industry

As you consider these topics, think about your own relationship with popular music and sound recordings. Who was your first favorite group or singer? How old were you, and what was important to you about this music? How has the way you listen to music changed in the past five years? For more questions to help you think through the role of music in our lives, see "Questioning the Media" in the Chapter Review.

THE DEVELOPMENT OF SOUND RECORDING

aNew mass media have often been defined in terms of the communication technologies that preceded them. For example, movies were initially called *motion pictures*, a term that derived from photography; radio was known as *wireless telegraphy*, referring to telegraphs; and television was often called *picture radio*. Likewise, sound recording instruments were initially described as talking machines and later as phonographs, drawing on names of existing inventions, the tele*phone* and the tele*graph*. This early blending of technology foreshadowed our contemporary era, in which media as diverse as newspapers and movies converge on the Internet. Long before the Internet, however, the first major media convergence involved the relationship between two industries: sound recording and radio.

From Cylinders to Disks: Sound Recording Becomes a Mass Medium

In the 1850s, French printer Édouard-Léon Scott de Martinville conducted the first experiments with sound recording. Using a hog's hair bristle as a needle, he tied one end to a thin membrane stretched over the narrow part of a funnel. When the inventor spoke into the funnel, the membrane vibrated and the free end of the bristle made grooves on a revolving cylinder coated with a thick liquid called *lampblack*. De Martinville noticed that different sounds made different trails in the lampblack, but he could not figure out how to play back the sound. His experiments, however, ushered in the *development stage* of sound recording as a mass medium. In 2008, audio researchers using high-resolution scans of the recordings and a digital stylus were finally able to play back some of de Martinville's recordings for the first time.[7]

In 1877, Thomas Edison had success playing back sound. He recorded his voice by using a needle to press the sound waves onto tinfoil, which was wrapped around a metal cylinder about the size of a cardboard toilet-paper roll. After recording his voice, Edison played it back by repositioning the needle to retrace the grooves in the foil. The machine that played these cylinders became known as the *phonograph*, derived from the Greek terms for "sound" and "writing."

Thomas Edison was more than an inventor—he was also able to envision the practical uses of his inventions and ways to market them. Moving sound recording into its *entrepreneurial stage*, Edison patented his phonograph in 1878 as a kind of answering machine. He thought the phonograph would be used as a "telephone repeater" that would "provide invaluable records, instead of being the recipient of momentary and fleeting communication."[8] Edison's phonograph patent was specifically for a device that recorded and played back foil cylinders. Thanks to this narrow definition, in 1886 Chichester Bell (cousin of telephone inventor Alexander Graham Bell) and Charles Sumner Tainter were able to further sound recording by patenting an improvement on the phonograph. Their sound recording device, known as the *graphophone*, played back more durable wax cylinders.[9] Both Edison's phonograph and Bell and Tainter's graphophone had only marginal success as voice-recording office machines. Eventually, these inventors began to produce cylinders with prerecorded music, which proved to be more popular but difficult to mass-produce and not very durable for repeated plays.

Using ideas from Edison, Bell, and Tainter, Emile Berliner, a German engineer who had immigrated to America, developed a better machine that played round, flat disks, or records. Made of zinc and coated with beeswax, these records played on a turntable, which Berliner called a *gramophone* and patented in 1887. Berliner also developed a technique that enabled him to mass-produce his round records, bringing sound recording into its *mass medium stage*. Previously, using Edison's cylinder, performers had to play or sing into the speaker for each separate recording. Berliner's technique featured a master recording from which copies could be easily duplicated in mass quantities. In addition, Berliner's records could be stamped with labels, allowing the music to be differentiated by title, performer, and songwriter. This led to the development of a "star system," wherein fans could identify and choose their favorite artists across many records.

By the first decade of the twentieth century, record-playing phonographs were widely available for home use. In 1906, the Victor Talking Machine Company placed the hardware, or "guts," of the record player inside a piece of furniture. These early record players, known as Victrolas, were mechanical and had to be primed with a crank handle. As more homes were wired for electricity, electric record players, first available in 1925, gradually replaced Victrolas, and the gramophone soon became an essential appliance in most American homes.

The appeal of recorded music was limited at first due to sound quality. The original wax records were replaced by shellac discs, but these records were very fragile and did not improve the sound quality much. By the 1930s, in part because of the advent of radio and in part because of the Great Depression, record and phonograph sales declined dramatically. In the early 1940s, shellac was needed for World War II munitions production, so the record industry turned to manufacturing polyvinyl plastic records instead. Vinyl records turned out to be more durable than shellac records and less noisy, paving the way for a renewed consumer desire to buy recorded music.

In 1948, CBS Records introduced the 33⅓-rpm (revolutions per minute) *long-playing record* (LP), with about twenty minutes of music on each side, creating a market for multisong albums and classical music. This was an improvement over the three to four minutes of music contained on the existing 78-rpm records. The next year, RCA developed a competing 45-rpm record that featured a

Bettmann/Getty Images

THOMAS EDISON

In addition to inventing the phonograph, Edison (1847–1931) ran an industrial research lab that is credited with inventing the motion-picture camera, the first commercially successful lightbulb, and a system for distributing electricity.

quarter-size hole (best for jukeboxes), invigorating the sales of songs heard on jukeboxes throughout the country. Unfortunately, the two new record standards were not technically compatible, meaning the two types of records could not be played on each other's machines. A five-year marketing battle ensued, but in 1953, CBS and RCA compromised. The LP became the standard for long-playing albums, the 45 became the standard for singles, and record players were designed to accommodate 45s, LPs, and, for a while, 78s.

From Phonographs to CDs: Analog Goes Digital

The inventions of the phonograph and the record were the key sound recording advancements until the advent of magnetic **audiotape** and tape players in the 1940s. Magnetic-tape sound recording was first developed as early as 1929 and further refined in the 1930s, but it did not catch on right away because the first machines were bulky reel-to-reel devices, the amount of tape required to make a recording was unwieldy, and the tape itself broke or became damaged easily. However, owing largely to improvements made by German engineers, who developed plastic magnetic tape during World War II, audiotape eventually found its place.

Audiotape's lightweight magnetized strands finally made possible sound editing and multiple-track mixing, in which instrumentals and vocals can be recorded at one location and later mixed onto a master recording in another studio. By the mid-1960s, engineers had placed miniaturized reel-to-reel audiotape inside small plastic *cassettes* and developed portable cassette players, permitting listeners to bring recorded music anywhere and creating a market for prerecorded cassettes. Audiotape also permitted "home dubbing": Consumers could copy their favorite records onto tape or record songs from the radio.

FIGURE 4.1

THE EVOLUTION OF DIGITAL SOUND RECORDING SALES (REVENUE IN BILLIONS)

Data from: Recording Industry Association of America, Annual Year-End Statistics. Figures are rounded.

Note: The year 1999 is the year Napster arrived, and the peak year of industry revenue. In 2011, digital product revenue surpassed physical product revenue for the first time. Synchronization royalties are those from music being licensed for use in television, movies, and advertisements.

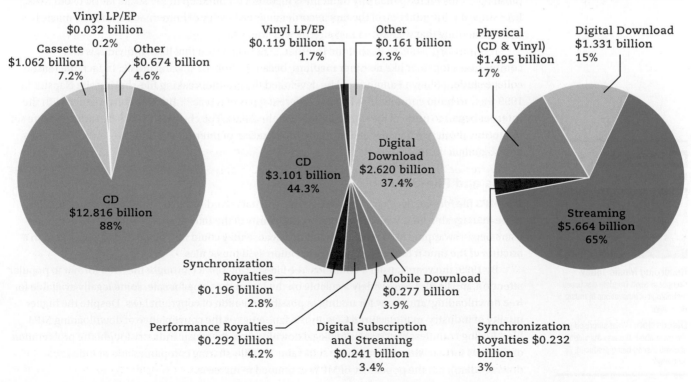

1999 Total Value: $14.584 billion

Vinyl LP/EP
$0.032 billion
0.2%

Cassette
$1.062 billion
7.2%

Other
$0.674 billion
4.6%

CD
$12.816 billion
88%

2011 Total Value: $7.007 billion

Vinyl LP/EP
$0.119 billion
1.7%

Other
$0.161 billion
2.3%

CD
$3.101 billion
44.3%

Digital Download
$2.620 billion
37.4%

Synchronization Royalties
$0.196 billion
2.8%

Performance Royalties
$0.292 billion
4.2%

Digital Subscription and Streaming
$0.241 billion
3.4%

Mobile Download
$0.277 billion
3.9%

2017 Total Value: $8.7 billion

Physical (CD & Vinyl)
$1.495 billion
17%

Digital Download
$1.331 billion
15%

Streaming
$5.664 billion
65%

Synchronization Royalties $0.232 billion
3%

The advances in audiotape technology opened the door to the development of other technologies. Although it had been invented by engineer Alan Blumlein in 1931, **stereo**—which permitted the recording of two separate channels, or tracks, of sound—was finally able to be put to commercial use in 1958, once audiotape became more accessible. Recording-studio engineers, using audiotape, could now record many instrumental or vocal tracks, which they "mixed down" to two stereo tracks. When played back through two loudspeakers, stereo creates a more natural sound distribution. By 1971, stereo sound had been advanced into *quadraphonic*, or four-track, sound, but that never caught on commercially.

The biggest recording advancement came in the 1970s, when electrical engineer Thomas Stockham made the first digital audio recordings on standard computer equipment. Although the digital recorder was invented in 1967, Stockham was the first to put it to practical use. In contrast to **analog recording**, which captures the fluctuations of sound waves and stores those signals in a record's grooves or a tape's continuous stream of magnetized particles, **digital recording** translates sound waves into binary on-off pulses and stores that information as numerical code. When a digital recording is played back, a microprocessor translates those numerical codes back into sounds and sends them to loudspeakers. By the late 1970s, Sony and Philips were jointly working on a way to design a digitally recorded disc and player to take advantage of this new technology, which could be produced at a lower cost than either vinyl records or audiocassettes. As a result of their efforts, digitally recorded **compact discs (CDs)** hit the market in 1983.

By 1987, CD sales were double the amount of LP sales. By 2000, CDs rendered records and audiocassettes nearly obsolete, except for deejays and record enthusiasts who continued to play and collect vinyl LPs. In an effort to create new product lines and maintain consumer sales, the music industry promoted two advanced digital disc formats in the late 1990s, which it hoped would eventually replace standard CDs. However, the introduction of these formats was ill-timed for the industry, because the biggest development in music formatting was already on the horizon—the MP3.

Convergence: Sound Recording in the Internet Age

Music, perhaps more so than any other mass medium, is bound up in the social fabric of our lives. Ever since the introduction of the tape recorder and the heyday of homemade mixtapes, music has been something that we have shared eagerly with friends.

It is not surprising, then, that the Internet, a mass medium that links individuals and communities together like no other medium, became a hub for sharing music. In fact, the reason college student Shawn Fanning said he developed the groundbreaking file-sharing site Napster in 1999 was "to build communities around different types of music."[10] But this convergence with the Internet began to unravel the music industry in the 2000s. The changes within the industry were set in motion about two decades ago, with the proliferation of Internet use and the development of a new digital file format.

MP3s and File-Sharing

The **MP3** file format, developed in 1992, enables digital recordings to be compressed into smaller, more manageable files. With the increasing popularity of the Internet in the mid-1990s, computer users began swapping MP3 music files online because they could be uploaded or downloaded in a fraction of the time it took to exchange noncompressed music files.

By 1999, the year Napster's infamous free file-sharing service brought the MP3 format to popular attention, music files were widely available on the Internet—some for sale, some legally available for free downloading, and many for trading in possible violation of copyright laws. Despite the higher quality of industry-manufactured CDs, music fans enjoyed the convenience of downloading MP3 files. Losing countless music sales to illegal downloading, the music industry fought the proliferation of the MP3 format with an array of lawsuits (aimed at file-sharing companies and at individual downloaders), but the popularity of MP3s continued to increase.

LaunchPad
macmillan learning
launchpadworks.com

Recording Music Today
Composer Scott Dugdale discusses technological innovations in music recording.

Discussion: What surprised you the most about the way the video showed a song being produced, and why?

In 2001, the U.S. Supreme Court ruled in favor of the music industry and against Napster, declaring free music file-swapping illegal and in violation of music copyrights held by recording labels and artists. It was relatively easy for the music industry to shut down Napster (which later relaunched as a legal service) because it required users to log into a centralized system. However, the music industry's elimination of file-sharing was not complete, as decentralized *peer-to-peer* (P2P) systems, such as Grokster, LimeWire, Morpheus, Kazaa, eDonkey, eMule, and BitTorrent, once again enabled free music file-sharing.

The recording industry fought back with thousands of lawsuits, many of them successful. By 2010, Grokster, eDonkey, Morpheus, and LimeWire had been shut down, while Kazaa settled a lawsuit with the music industry and became a legal service.[11] By 2011, several major Internet service providers, including AT&T, Comcast, and Verizon, had agreed to help the music industry identify customers who may have been illegally downloading music and try to prevent them from doing so by sending them "copyright alert" warning letters, redirecting them to web pages about digital piracy, and ultimately slowing download speeds or closing their broadband accounts.

As it cracked down on digital theft, the music industry—realizing that it would have to somehow adapt its business to the digital format—embraced services like iTunes (launched by Apple in 2003 to accompany the iPod), which had become the model for legal online distribution. In 2008, iTunes became the top music retailer in the United States. But by the time iTunes surpassed the twenty-five-billion-song milestone in 2013, global digital download sales had fallen for the first time.[12] What happened? The next big digital format had arrived.

The Next Big Thing: Streaming Music

If the history of recorded music tells us anything, it is that tastes change and formats change over time. Today, streaming music is quickly becoming the format of choice. In the language of the music industry, we are shifting from *ownership* of music to *access* to music.[13] The access model has been driven by the availability of streaming services such as the Sweden-based Spotify, which made its debut in the United States in 2011 and hit seventy-one million worldwide subscribers in 2018. Other services include Apple Music, Google Play Music, Amazon Music, Tidal, Deezer, and SoundCloud. With these services, listeners can pay a subscription fee (typically $5 to $10 per month) and instantly play millions of songs on demand via the Internet. YouTube and Vevo also supply ad-supported music streaming, and have wide international use.

Bettina Fabos

The key difference between streaming music (like Spotify) and streaming radio (like Pandora) is that streaming music enables the listener to select any song on demand. Streaming radio enables the listener to pick a style of music but lacks the option of songs on demand. Yet the line is often blurred, even by streaming services. For example, at $10 per month, premium Spotify is ad-free and allows subscribers to access any song on demand and stream offline. However, the free version of Spotify is more like radio in that listeners do not have complete control over song selection.

The Rocky Relationship between Records and Radio

The recording industry and radio have always been closely linked. Although they work almost in unison now, they had a tumultuous relationship at the beginning. Radio's very existence sparked the first battle. By 1915, the phonograph had become a popular form of entertainment. The recording industry sold thirty million records that year, and by the end of the decade, sales had more than tripled each year. In 1924, however, record sales dropped to only half of what they had been the previous year. Why? Because radio had arrived as a competing mass medium, providing free entertainment over the airwaves, independent of the recording industry.

The battle heated up when, to the alarm of the recording industry, radio stations began broadcasting recorded music without compensating the industry. The American Society of Composers, Authors, and Publishers (ASCAP), founded in 1914 to collect copyright fees for music publishers and writers, charged that radio was contributing to plummeting sales of records and sheet music. By 1925, ASCAP had established fees for radio, charging stations between $250 and $2,500 a week for the right to play recorded music—and causing many stations to leave the air.

But other stations countered by establishing their own live, in-house orchestras, disseminating "free" music to listeners. This time, the recording industry could do nothing, as original radio music did not infringe on any copyrights. Throughout the late 1920s and 1930s, record and phonograph sales continued to fall, although the recording industry got a small boost when Prohibition ended in 1933 and record-playing jukeboxes became the standard musical entertainment in neighborhood taverns.

The recording and radio industries only began to cooperate with each other after television became popular in the early 1950s. Television pilfered radio's variety shows, crime dramas, and comedy programs, along with much of its advertising revenue and audience. Seeking to reinvent itself, radio turned to the recording industry, and this time both industries greatly benefited from radio's new "hit-song" format. The alliance between the recording industry and radio was aided enormously by rock-and-roll music, which was just emerging in the 1950s. Rock created an enduring consumer youth market for sound recordings and provided much-needed content for radio precisely when television made it seem like an obsolete medium.

After the digital turn, the mutually beneficial arrangement between the recording and radio industries began to fray. While Internet streaming radio stations were being required to pay royalties to music companies when they played their songs, radio stations still got to play music royalty-free over the air. In 2012, Clear Channel—the largest radio station chain in the United States and one of the largest music streaming companies, with more than fifteen hundred live stations on iHeartRadio—was the first company to strike a new deal with the recording industry and pay royalties for music played over the air. Since that first deal, other radio groups have begun to forge agreements with music labels, paying royalties for on-air play while getting reduced rates for streaming music.

U.S. POPULAR MUSIC AND THE FORMATION OF ROCK

Popular music, or **pop music**, is music that appeals either to a wide cross section of the public or to sizable subdivisions within the larger public based on age, region, or ethnic background (e.g., teenagers, southerners, and Mexican Americans). Today, U.S. pop music encompasses styles as diverse as blues, country, Tejano, salsa, jazz, rock, reggae, punk, hip-hop, and dance. The word *pop* has also been used to distinguish popular music from classical music, which is written primarily for ballet, opera, ensemble, or symphony. As various subcultures have intersected, U.S. popular music has developed organically, constantly creating new forms and reinvigorating older musical styles.

The Rise of Pop Music

Although it is commonly assumed that pop music developed simultaneously with the phonograph and radio, it actually existed before these media. In the late nineteenth century, the sale of sheet music for piano and other instruments sprang from a section of Broadway in Manhattan known as Tin Pan Alley, a derisive term used to describe the sound of these quickly produced tunes, which supposedly resembled cheap pans clanging together. Tin Pan Alley's tradition of song publishing began in the late 1880s with such music as the marches of John Philip Sousa and the ragtime piano pieces of Scott Joplin. It continued through the first half of the twentieth century with the show tunes and vocal ballads of Irving Berlin, George Gershwin, and Cole Porter, and into the 1950s and 1960s with such rock-and-roll writing teams as Jerry Leiber–Mike Stoller and Carole King–Gerry Goffin.

At the turn of the twentieth century, with the newfound ability of song publishers to mass-produce sheet music for a growing middle class, popular songs moved from being a novelty to being a major business enterprise. With the emergence of the phonograph, song publishers also discovered that recorded tunes boosted interest in and sales of sheet music. Thus, songwriting and Tin Pan Alley played a key role in transforming popular music into a mass medium.

As sheet music grew in popularity, **jazz** developed in New Orleans. An improvisational and mostly instrumental musical form, jazz absorbed and integrated a diverse body of musical styles, including African rhythms, blues, and gospel. Jazz influenced many bandleaders throughout the 1930s and 1940s. Groups led by Louis Armstrong, Count Basie, Tommy Dorsey, Duke Ellington, Benny Goodman, and Glenn Miller were among the most popular of the "swing" jazz bands, whose rhythmic music also dominated radio, recordings, and dance halls in their day.

The first pop vocalists of the twentieth century were products of the vaudeville circuit, which radio, movies, and the Depression would bring to an end in the 1930s. In the 1920s, Eddie Cantor, Belle Baker, Sophie Tucker, and Al Jolson were extremely popular. By the 1930s, Rudy Vallée and Bing Crosby had established themselves as the first "crooners," or singers of pop standards. Bing Crosby also popularized Irving Berlin's "White Christmas," one of the most covered songs in recording history. (A song recorded or performed by another artist is known as **cover music**.) Meanwhile, the Andrews Sisters' boogie-woogie style helped them sell more than sixty million records in the late 1930s and 1940s. In one of the first mutually beneficial alliances between sound recording and radio, many early pop vocalists had their own network of regional radio programs, which vastly increased their exposure.

Frank Sinatra arrived in the 1940s, and his romantic ballads foreshadowed the teen love songs of rock and roll's early years. Nicknamed "the Voice" early in his career, Sinatra, like Crosby, parlayed his music and radio exposure into movie stardom. Helped by radio, pop vocalists like Sinatra were among the first vocalists to become popular with a large national teen audience.

Rock and Roll Is Here to Stay

The cultural storm called **rock and roll** hit in the mid-1950s. As with the term *jazz*, *rock and roll* was a blues slang term for "sex," lending it instant controversy. Early rock and roll was considered the first "integrationist music," merging the black sounds of rhythm and blues, gospel, and Robert Johnson's screeching blues guitar with the white influences of country, folk, and pop vocals.[14] From a cultural perspective, only a few musical forms have ever sprung from such a diverse set of influences, and no new style of music has ever had such a widespread impact on so many different cultures as rock and roll. From an economic perspective, rock and roll was the first musical form to simultaneously

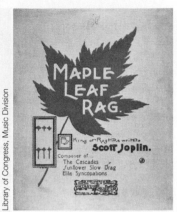

Library of Congress, Music Division

SCOTT JOPLIN

(1868–1917) published more than fifty compositions during his life, including "maple leaf rag"—arguably his most famous piece.

Photo by Robert Johnson Estate/Hulton Archive/Getty Images

ROBERT JOHNSON (LEFT) (1911–1938), who ranks among the most influential and innovative American guitarists, played Mississippi delta blues and was a major influence on early rock and rollers, especially the Rolling Stones and Eric Clapton. His intense slide-guitar and finger-style playing also inspired generations of blues artists, including Muddy Waters, Howlin' Wolf, Bonnie Raitt, and Stevie Ray Vaughan. To get a sense of his style, visit the Internet Archive's Robert Johnson collection: https://archive.org/details /RobertJohnson_666

Michael Ochs Archives/Getty Images

BESSIE SMITH (1895–1937) is considered the best female blues singer of the 1920s and 1930s. Mentored by the famous Ma Rainey, Smith had many hits, including "Down Hearted Blues" and "Gulf Coast Blues." She also appeared in the 1929 film *St. Louis Blues.*

transform the structure of sound recording and radio. Rock's development set the stage for how music is produced, distributed, and performed today. Many social, cultural, economic, and political factors leading up to the 1950s contributed to the growth of rock and roll, including black migration, the growth of youth culture, and the beginnings of racial integration.

The migration of southern blacks to northern cities in search of better jobs during the first half of the twentieth century helped spread different popular music styles. In particular, **blues** music—the foundation of rock and roll—came to the North. Influenced by African American spirituals, ballads, and work songs from the rural South, blues music was exemplified in the work of Robert Johnson, Ma Rainey, Son House, Bessie Smith, Charley Patton, and others. The introduction in the 1930s of the electric guitar—a major contribution to rock music— gave southern blues its urban style, popularized in the work of Muddy Waters, Howlin' Wolf, Sonny Boy Williamson, B. B. King, and Buddy Guy.[15]

During this time, blues-based urban black music began to be marketed under the name **rhythm and blues**, or **R&B**. Featuring "huge rhythm units smashing away behind screaming blues singers," R&B appealed to young listeners fascinated by the explicit (and forbidden) sexual lyrics in songs like "Annie Had a Baby," "Sexy Ways," and "Wild Wild Young Men."[16] Although it was banned on some stations, R&B was continuing to gain airtime by 1953. In those days, black and white musical forms were segregated: Trade magazines tracked R&B record sales on "race" charts, which were kept separate from white record sales, tracked on "pop" charts.

Perhaps the most significant factor in the growth of rock and roll was the beginning of the integration of white and black cultures. In addition to increased exposure to black literature, art, and music, several key historical events in the 1950s broke down the borders between black and white cultures. And with the Supreme Court's *Brown v. Board of Education* decision in 1954, "separate but equal" laws—which had kept white and black schools, hotels, restaurants, restrooms, and drinking fountains segregated for decades—were declared unconstitutional. A cultural reflection of the times, rock and roll would burst forth from the midst of the decade's social and political tensions.

Rock Muddies the Waters

In the 1950s, legal integration accompanied a cultural shift, and the music industry's race and pop charts blurred. White deejay Alan Freed had been playing black music for his young audiences in Cleveland and New York since the early 1950s, and such white performers as Johnnie Ray and Bill Haley had crossed over to the race charts to score R&B hits. Meanwhile, black artists like Chuck Berry were performing country songs, and for a time, Ray Charles even played in an otherwise all-white country band. Although continuing the work of breaking down racial borders was one of rock and roll's most important contributions, the genre also blurred other long-standing distinctions between high and low culture, masculinity and femininity, the country and the city, the North and the South, and the sacred and the secular.

High and Low Culture

In 1956, Chuck Berry's "Roll Over Beethoven" merged rock and roll, considered low culture by many, with high culture, forever blurring the traditional boundary between these cultural forms with lyrics like "You know my temperature's risin' / the jukebox is blowin' a fuse . . . / Roll over Beethoven / and tell Tchaikovsky the news." Although such early rock-and-roll lyrics seem tame by today's standards, at the time they sounded like sacrilege. Rock and rollers also challenged musical decorum and the rules governing how musicians should behave or misbehave: Berry's "duck walk" across the stage, Elvis Presley's pegged pants and gyrating hips, and Bo Diddley's use of the guitar as a phallic symbol were an affront to the norms of well-behaved, culturally elite audiences.

Masculinity and Femininity

Rock and roll was the first popular music genre to overtly confuse issues of sexual identity and orientation. Although early rock and roll largely attracted males as performers, the most fascinating feature of Elvis Presley, according to the Rolling Stones' Mick Jagger, was his androgynous appearance.[17] During this early period, though, the most sexually outrageous rock-and-roll performer was Little Richard (Penniman). Little Richard has said that given the reality of American racism, he blurred lines between masculinity and femininity because he feared the consequences of becoming a sex symbol for white girls: "I decided that my image should be crazy and way out so that adults would think I was harmless. I'd appear in one show dressed as the Queen of England and in the next as the pope."[18] Little Richard's playful blurring of gender identity and sexual orientation paved the way for performers like David Bowie, Elton John, Boy George, Annie Lennox, Prince, Grace Jones, Marilyn Manson, Lady Gaga, and Adam Lambert.

The Country and the City

Rock and roll also blurred geographic borders between country and city, between the white country & western music of Nashville and the black urban rhythms of Memphis. Early white rockers such as Buddy Holly and Carl Perkins combined country (or hillbilly) music, southern gospel, and Mississippi delta blues to create a sound called **rockabilly**. At the same time, an urban R&B influence on early rock came from Fats Domino ("Blueberry Hill"), Willie Mae "Big Mama" Thornton ("Hound Dog"), and Big Joe Turner ("Shake, Rattle, and Roll"). Soaring record sales and the crossover appeal of the music represented an enormous threat to long-standing racial and class boundaries. In 1956, the secretary of the North Alabama White Citizens Council bluntly spelled out the racism and white fear concerning the new blending of urban-black and rural-white culture: "Rock and roll is a means of pulling the white man down to the level of the Negro. It is part of a plot to undermine the morals of the youth of our nation."[19] Distinctions between traditionally rural and urban music have continued to blur, with older

Bettmann/Getty Images

ROCK-AND-ROLL PIONEER
A major influence on early rock and roll, Chuck Berry, born in 1926, scored major hits between 1955 and 1958, writing "Maybellene," "Roll Over Beethoven," "School Day," "Sweet Little Sixteen," and "Johnny B. Goode." At the time, he was criticized by some black artists for sounding white, and his popularity among white teenagers was bemoaned by conservative critics. Today, young guitar players routinely imitate his style.

ELVIS PRESLEY AND HIS LEGACY

Elvis Presley remains the most popular solo artist of all time. From 1956 to 1962, he recorded seventeen No. 1 hits, from "Heartbreak Hotel" to "Good Luck Charm." According to Little Richard, Presley's main legacy was that he opened doors for many young performers and made black music popular in mainstream America.

hybrids such as country rock (think of the Eagles) and newer forms like alternative country—performed by artists such as Ryan Adams, Steve Earle, the Avett Brothers, and Kings of Leon.

The North and the South

Not only did rock and roll muddy the urban and rural terrain, but it also combined northern and southern influences. In fact, with so much blues, R&B, and rock and roll rising from the South in the 1950s, this region regained some of its cultural flavor, which (along with a sizable portion of the population) had migrated to the North after the Civil War and during the early twentieth century. Meanwhile, musicians and audiences in the North had absorbed blues music as their own, eliminating the understanding of blues as a specifically southern style. Like the many white teens today who are fascinated by hip-hop, musicians such as Carl Perkins, Elvis Presley, and Buddy Holly—all from the rural South—were fascinated with and influenced by the black urban styles they had heard on the radio or seen in nightclubs. These artists in turn brought southern culture to northern listeners.

But the key to record sales and the spread of rock and roll, according to famed record producer Sam Phillips of Sun Records, was to find a white man who sounded black. Phillips found that man in Elvis Presley. Commenting on Presley's cultural importance, one critic wrote: "White rockabillies like Elvis took poor white southern mannerisms of speech and behavior deeper into mainstream culture than they had ever been taken."[20]

The Sacred and the Secular

Although many mainstream adults in the 1950s complained that rock and roll's sexuality and questioning of moral norms constituted an offense against God, many early rock figures actually had close ties to religion, often transforming gospel tunes into rock and roll. Still, many people did not appreciate the blurring of boundaries between the sacred and the secular. In the late 1950s, public outrage over rock and roll was so great that even Little Richard and Jerry Lee Lewis, both sons of

Michael Ochs Archives/Getty Images

Bettmann/Getty Images

southern preachers, became convinced that they were playing the "devil's music." By 1959, Little Richard had left rock and roll to become a minister. Lewis had to be coerced into recording "Great Balls of Fire," a song by Otis Blackwell that turned an apocalyptic biblical phrase into a sexually charged teen love song. The boundaries between sacred and secular music have continued to blur in the years since, with some churches using rock and roll to appeal to youth, and some Christian-themed rock groups recording music as seemingly incongruous as heavy metal.

Battles in Rock and Roll

The blurring of racial lines and the breakdown of other conventional boundaries meant that performers and producers were forced to play a tricky game to get rock and roll accepted by the masses. Two prominent white disc jockeys had different methods for achieving this end. Cleveland deejay Alan Freed, credited with popularizing the term *rock and roll*, played original R&B recordings from the race charts and black versions of early rock and roll on his program. In contrast, Philadelphia deejay Dick Clark believed that making black music acceptable to white audiences required cover versions by white artists. By the mid-1950s, rock and roll was gaining acceptance among the masses, but rock-and-roll artists and promoters faced further obstacles: Black artists found that their music was often undermined by white cover versions, the payola scandals portrayed rock and roll as a corrupt industry, and fears of rock and roll as a contributing factor in juvenile delinquency resulted in censorship.

White Cover Music Undermines Black Artists

By the mid-1960s, black and white artists routinely recorded and performed one another's original tunes. For example, established black R&B artist Otis Redding covered the Rolling Stones' "Satisfaction," Jimi Hendrix covered Bob Dylan's "All Along the Watchtower," and just about every white rock-and-roll band—including the Beatles and the Rolling Stones—established its career by covering R&B classics.

Although today we take such rerecordings for granted, in the 1950s the covering of black artists' songs by white musicians was almost always an attempt to capitalize on popular songs from the R&B "race" charts by transforming them into hits on the white pop charts. Often, not only would

IN 1955, LITTLE RICHARD (LEFT) wrote and recorded his first major hit record, "Tutti Frutti." The next year, Pat Boone (right) recorded a cover of "Tutti Frutti" that surpassed the original in popularity, reaching No. 12 on the *Billboard* Top 40 (Little Richard's original peaked at No. 17). In a 1984 interview with the *Washington Post*, Little Richard argued that this difference reflected the racial attitudes of the time: "The white kids would have Pat Boone up on the dresser and me in the drawer 'cause they liked my version better, but the families didn't want me because of the image that I was projecting."[21]

white producers give cowriting credit to white performers for the tunes they merely covered, but the producers would also buy the rights to potential hits from black songwriters, who seldom saw a penny in royalties or received songwriting credit.

During this period, black R&B artists, working for small record labels, saw many of their popular songs being covered by white artists working for major labels. These cover records, boosted by better marketing and ties to white deejays, usually outsold the original black versions. For instance, the 1954 R&B song "Sh-Boom," by the Chords on Atlantic's Cat label, was immediately covered by a white group, the Crew Cuts, for the major Mercury label. Record sales declined for the Chords, although jukebox and R&B radio play remained strong for the original version. By 1955, R&B hits regularly crossed over to the pop charts, but inevitably the white cover versions were more successful. Pat Boone's cover of Fats Domino's "Ain't That a Shame" went to No. 1 and stayed on the Top 40 pop chart for twenty weeks, whereas Domino's original made it only to No. 10. Slowly, however, the cover situation changed. After watching Boone outsell his song "Tutti Frutti" in 1956, Little Richard wrote "Long Tall Sally," which included lyrics written and delivered in such a way that he believed Boone would not be able to adequately replicate them. "Long Tall Sally" went to No. 6 for Little Richard and charted for twelve weeks; Boone's version got to No. 8 and stayed there for nine weeks.

Overt racism lingered in the music business well into the 1960s. A turning point, however, came in 1962, the last year that Pat Boone, then aged twenty-eight, ever had a Top 40 rock-and-roll hit. That year, Ray Charles covered "I Can't Stop Loving You," a 1958 country song by the Grand Ole Opry's Don Gibson. This marked the first time that a black artist, covering a white artist's song, had notched a No. 1 pop hit. With Charles's cover, the rock-and-roll merger between gospel and R&B, on the one hand, and white country and pop, on the other, was complete. In fact, the relative acceptance of black crossover music provided a more favorable cultural context for the political activism that spurred important Civil Rights legislation in the mid-1960s.

Payola Scandals Tarnish Rock and Roll

The payola scandals of the 1950s were another cloud over rock-and-roll music and its artists. In the music industry, *payola* is the practice of record promoters' paying deejays or radio programmers to play particular songs. As recorded rock and roll became central to commercial radio's success in the 1950s and the demand for airplay grew, independent promoters hired by record labels used payola to pressure deejays into playing songs by the artists they represented.

Although payola was considered a form of bribery, no laws prohibited its practice. However, following closely on the heels of television's quiz-show scandals (see Chapter 6), congressional hearings on radio payola began in December 1959. The hearings were partly a response to generally fraudulent business practices, but they were also an opportunity to blame deejays and radio for rock and roll's supposedly negative impact on teens by portraying rock and roll (and its radio advocates) as a corrupt industry.

The payola scandals threatened, ended, or damaged the careers of a number of rock-and-roll deejays and undermined rock and roll's credibility for a number of years. At the hearings in 1960, Alan Freed admitted to participating in payola, although he said he did not believe there was anything illegal about such deals, and his career soon ended. Dick Clark, then an influential deejay and the host of TV's *American Bandstand*, would not admit to participating in payola. The hearings committee nevertheless chastised Clark and alleged that some of his complicated business deals were ethically questionable, a censure that hung over him for years. Congress eventually added a law concerning payola to the Federal Communications Act, prescribing a $10,000 fine and/or a year in jail for each violation (see Chapter 5).

Fears of Rock and Roll as a Corrupting Influence Lead to Censorship

Since rock and roll's inception, one of the uphill battles the genre faced was the perception that it was a cause of juvenile delinquency, which was statistically on the rise in the 1950s. Looking for an easy culprit rather than considering contributing factors such as neglect, the rising consumer culture, or the growing youth population, many people assigned blame to rock and roll. The view that rock and roll corrupted youth was widely accepted by social authorities, and rock-and-roll music was often censored, eventually even by the industry itself.

By late 1959, many key figures in rock and roll had been tamed. Jerry Lee Lewis was exiled from the industry, labeled southern "white trash" for marrying his thirteen-year-old third cousin; Elvis Presley, having already been censored on television, was drafted into the army; Chuck Berry was run out of Mississippi and eventually jailed for gun possession and transporting a minor across state lines; and Little Richard felt forced to tone down his image and left rock and roll to sing gospel music. A tragic accident led to the final taming of rock and roll's first front line. In February 1959, Buddy Holly ("Peggy Sue"), Ritchie Valens ("La Bamba"), and the Big Bopper ("Chantilly Lace") all died in an Iowa plane crash—a tragedy mourned in Don McLean's 1971 hit "American Pie" as "the day the music died."

Although rock and roll did not die in the late 1950s, the U.S. recording industry decided that it needed a makeover. To protect the enormous profits the new music had been generating, record companies began to discipline some of rock and roll's rebellious impulses. In the early 1960s, the industry introduced a new generation of clean-cut white singers, like Frankie Avalon, Connie Francis, Ricky Nelson, Lesley Gore, and Fabian. Rock and roll's explosive violations of racial, class, and other boundaries were transformed into simpler generation-gap problems, and the music developed a milder reputation.

A CHANGING INDUSTRY: REFORMATIONS IN POPULAR MUSIC

As the 1960s began, rock and roll was tamer and "safer," as reflected in the surf and road music of the Beach Boys and Jan & Dean, but it was also beginning to branch out. For instance, the success of all-female groups, such as the Shangri-Las ("Leader of the Pack") and the Angels ("My Boyfriend's Back"), challenged the male-dominated world of early rock and roll. In the 1960s and the following decades, popular music went through cultural reformations that significantly changed the industry, including the international appeal of the "British invasion"; the development of soul and Motown; the political impact of folk-rock; the experimentalism of psychedelic music; the rejection of music's mainstream by punk, grunge, and indie rock movements; the reassertion of black urban style in hip-hop and R&B; and the transformation of music distribution, which resulted in an unprecedented market growth of music from independent labels.

The British Are Coming!

The global trade of pop music is evident in the exchanges and melding of rhythms, beats, vocal styles, and musical instruments across cultures. The origin of this global impact can be traced to England in the late 1950s, when the young Rolling Stones listened to the blues of Robert Johnson and Muddy Waters, and the young Beatles tried to imitate Chuck Berry and Little Richard.

Until 1964, rock-and-roll recordings had traveled on a one-way ticket to Europe. Even though American artists regularly reached the top of the charts overseas, no British performers had yet achieved the same in the States. This changed almost overnight. Following the Beatles' journey to America in 1964, British bands as diverse as the Kinks, the Rolling Stones, the Zombies, the Animals, Herman's Hermits, the Who, the Yardbirds, Them, and the Troggs hit the American Top 40 charts.

With the British invasion, "rock and roll" unofficially became "rock," sending popular music and the industry in two directions. On the one hand, the Rolling Stones would influence generations of musicians emphasizing gritty, chord-driven, high-volume rock, including those in the glam rock, hard rock, punk, heavy metal, and grunge genres. On the other hand, the Beatles would influence countless artists interested in a more accessible, melodic, and softer sound, in such genres as pop rock, power pop, new wave, and indie rock. The success of British groups helped change an industry arrangement in which most pop music was produced by songwriting teams hired by major labels and matched with

Paul Popper/Popperfoto/Getty Images

Dave Hogan/Getty Images

BRITISH ROCK GROUPS

Ed Sullivan, who booked the Beatles several times on his TV variety show in 1964, helped promote the band's early success. Sullivan, though, reacted differently to the Rolling Stones, who were perceived as the "bad boys" of rock and roll in contrast to the "good" Beatles. The Stones performed black-influenced music without "whitening" the sound and exuded a palpable aura of sexuality, particularly front-man Mick Jagger. Although the Stones appeared on the program as early as 1964 and returned on several occasions, Sullivan remained wary and forced the band to change the lyrics of "Let's Spend the Night Together" to "Let's Spend Some Time Together" for a 1967 broadcast.

selected performers. Even more important, the British invasion showed the recording industry how older American musical forms, especially blues and R&B, could be repackaged as rock and exported around the world.

Motor City Music: Detroit Gives America Soul

Ironically, the British invasion, which took much of its inspiration from black influences, drew many white listeners away from a new generation of black performers. Gradually, however, throughout the 1960s, black singers like James Brown, Aretha Franklin, Otis Redding, Ike and Tina Turner, and Wilson Pickett found large and diverse audiences. Transforming the rhythms and melodies of older R&B, pop, and early rock and roll into what became labeled as **soul**, these artists countered the British invaders with powerful vocal performances. Mixing gospel and blues with emotion and lyrics drawn from the American black experience, soul contrasted sharply with the emphasis on loud, fast instrumentals and lighter lyrical concerns that characterized much of rock music.[22]

The most prominent independent label that nourished soul and black popular music was Motown, established in 1959 by former Detroit autoworker and songwriter Berry Gordy with a $700 investment and named after Detroit's "Motor City" nickname. Beginning with Smokey Robinson and the Miracles' "Shop Around," Motown enjoyed a long string of hit records that rivaled the pop success of British bands throughout the decade. Motown's many successful artists included the Temptations ("My Girl"), Mary Wells ("My Guy"), the Four Tops ("I Can't Help Myself"), Martha and the Vandellas ("Heat Wave"), Marvin Gaye ("I Heard It through the Grapevine"), and, in the early 1970s, the Jackson 5 ("ABC"). But the label's most successful group was the Supremes, featuring Diana Ross, which scored twelve No. 1 singles between 1964 and 1969 ("Where Did Our Love Go," "Stop! In the Name of Love"). The Motown groups had a more stylized, softer sound than the grittier southern soul (later known as funk) of Brown and Pickett.

Folk and Psychedelic Music Reflect the Times

Popular music has always been a product of its time, so the social upheavals of the Civil Rights movement, the women's movement, the environmental movement, and the Vietnam War naturally brought social concerns into the music of the 1960s and early 1970s. By the late 1960s, the Beatles had transformed from a relatively lightweight pop band to one that spoke for the social and political concerns of its generation, and many other groups followed the same trajectory. (To explore how the times and

THE SUPREMES
One of the most successful groups in rock-and-roll history, the Supremes started out as the Primettes in Detroit in 1959. The group signed with Motown's Tamla label in 1960 and became the Supremes in 1961. Between 1964 and 1969, the group recorded twelve No. 1 hits, including "Where Did Our Love Go," "Baby Love," "Come See about Me," "Stop! In the Name of Love," "I Hear a Symphony," "You Can't Hurry Love," and "Someday We'll Be Together." Lead singer Diana Ross (*center*) left the group in 1969 for a solo career. The group was inducted into the Rock and Roll Hall of Fame in 1988.

personal taste influence music choices, see "Media Literacy and the Critical Process: Music Preferences across Generations" on page 112.)

Folk Inspires Protest

The musical genre that most clearly responded to the political happenings of the time was folk music, which had long been the sound of social activism. In its broadest sense, **folk music** in any culture refers to songs performed by untrained musicians and passed down mainly through oral traditions, from the banjo and fiddle tunes of Appalachia to the accordion-led zydeco of Louisiana and the folk-blues of the legendary Lead Belly (Huddie Ledbetter). During the 1930s, folk was defined by the music of Woody Guthrie ("This Land Is Your Land"), who not only brought folk to the city but also was extremely active in social reform. Groups such as the Weavers, featuring labor activist and songwriter Pete Seeger, carried on Guthrie's legacy and inspired a new generation of singer-songwriters, including Joan Baez; Arlo Guthrie; Peter, Paul, and Mary; Phil Ochs; and—perhaps the most influential—Bob Dylan. Significantly influenced by the blues, Dylan identified folk as "finger-pointing" music that addressed current social circumstances. At a key moment in popular music's history, Dylan walked onstage at the 1965 Newport Folk Festival fronting a full electric rock band. He was booed and cursed by traditional "folkies," who saw amplified music as a sellout to the commercial recording industry. However, Dylan's change inspired the formation of **folk-rock** artists like the Byrds, who had a No. 1 hit with a cover of Dylan's "Mr. Tambourine Man," and led millions to protest during the turbulent 1960s.

Rock Turns Psychedelic

Alcohol and drugs have long been associated with the private lives of blues, jazz, country, and rock musicians. These links, however, became much more public in the late 1960s and early 1970s, when authorities busted members of the Rolling Stones and the Beatles. With the increasing role of drugs in youth culture and the availability of LSD (not illegal until the mid-1960s), an increasing number

MEDIA LITERACY AND THE CRITICAL PROCESS

Music Preferences across Generations

We make judgments about music all the time. Older generations do not like some of the music younger people prefer, and young people often dismiss some of the music of previous generations. Even among our peers, we have different musical tastes and often reject certain kinds of music that have become too popular or that do not conform to our preferences. The following exercise aims to understand musical tastes beyond our individual choices. Be sure to include yourself in this project.

1 DESCRIPTION

Arrange to interview four to eight friends or relatives of different ages about their musical tastes and influences. Devise questions about what music they listen to and have listened to at different stages of their lives. What music do they buy or collect? What was the first album (or single) they acquired? What was the latest album? What stories or vivid memories do they relate to particular songs or artists? Collect demographic and consumer information: age, gender, occupation, educational background, place of birth, and current place of residence.

2 ANALYSIS

Chart and organize your results. Do you recognize any patterns emerging from the data or stories? What kinds of music did your interview subjects listen to when they were younger? What kinds of music do they listen to now? What formed/influenced their musical interests? If their musical interests changed, what happened? (If they stopped listening to music, note that and find out why.) Do they have any associations between music and their everyday lives? Are these music associations and lifetime interactions with songs and artists important to them?

3 INTERPRETATION

Based on what you have discovered and the patterns you have charted, determine what the patterns mean. Does age, gender, geographic location, or education matter when it comes to musical tastes? Are the changes in musical tastes and buying habits over time significant? Why or why not? What kind of music is most important to your subjects? Finally, and most important, why do you think your subjects' music preferences developed as they did?

4 EVALUATION

Determine how your interview subjects came to like particular kinds of music. What constitutes "good" and "bad" music for them? Did their ideas change over time? How? Are they open- or closed-minded about music? How do they form judgments about music? What criteria did your interview subjects offer for making judgments about music? Do you think their criteria are a valid way to judge music?

5 ENGAGEMENT

To expand on your findings, consider the connections of music across generations, geography, and genres. Take a musical artist you like and input the name at www.music-map.com. Use the output of related artists to discover new bands. Input favorite artists of the people you interviewed in Step 1, and share the results with them. Expand your musical tastes.

---

of rock musicians experimented with and sang about drugs in what were frequently labeled rock's psychedelic years. Many groups and performers of the *psychedelic* era (named for the mind-altering effects of LSD and other drugs), including Jefferson Airplane, Big Brother and the Holding Company (featuring Janis Joplin), the Jimi Hendrix Experience, the Doors, and the Grateful Dead, believed that artistic expression and responses to social problems could be enhanced through mind-altering drugs. But following the surge of optimism that culminated in the historic Woodstock concert in August 1969, the psychedelic movement was quickly overshadowed. In 1969, a similar concert at the Altamont racetrack in California started in chaos and ended in tragedy when one of the Hell's Angels hired as a bodyguard for the show murdered a concertgoer. Around the same time, the shocking multiple murders committed by the Charles Manson "family" cast a negative light on hippies, drug use, and psychedelic culture. Then, in quick succession, a number of the psychedelic movement's greatest stars died from drug overdoses, including Janis Joplin, Jimi Hendrix, and Jim Morrison of the Doors.

Punk and Indie Respond to Mainstream Rock

By the 1970s, rock music was increasingly viewed as just another part of mainstream consumer culture. With major music acts earning huge profits, rock soon became another product line for manufacturers and retailers to promote, package, and sell—primarily to middle-class white male teens. Rock musicians like Bruce Springsteen and Elton John; glam artists like David Bowie, Lou Reed, and Iggy Pop; and soul artists like Curtis Mayfield and Marvin Gaye continued to explore the social possibilities of rock or at least keep its legacy of outrageousness alive. But they had, for the most part, been replaced by "faceless" supergroups, like REO Speedwagon, Styx, Boston, and Kansas. By the late 1970s, rock could only seem to define itself by saying what it was not; "Disco Sucks" became a standard rock slogan against the popular dance music of the era.

Punk Revives Rock's Rebelliousness

Punk rock rose in the late 1970s to challenge the orthodoxy and commercialism of the record business. By this time, the glory days of rock's competitive independent labels had ended, and rock music was controlled by just a half-dozen major companies. By avoiding rock's consumer popularity, punk attempted to return to the basics of rock and roll: simple chord structures, catchy melodies, and politically or socially challenging lyrics.

The punk movement took root at CBGB, a small dive bar in New York City, around such bands as the Ramones, Blondie, and the Talking Heads. (The roots of punk essentially lay in four pre-punk groups from the late 1960s and early 1970s—the Velvet Underground, the Stooges, the New York Dolls, and the MC5—none of which experienced commercial success in their day.) Punk quickly spread to England, where a soaring unemployment rate and growing class inequality ensured the success of socially critical rock. Groups like the Sex Pistols, the Clash, the Buzzcocks, and Siouxsie and the Banshees sprang up and even scored Top 40 hits on the U.K. charts.

Punk was not a commercial success in the United States, where it was (not surprisingly) shunned by radio. However, punk's contributions continue to be felt. Punk broke down the "boys' club" mentality of rock, launching unapologetic and unadorned front women like Patti Smith, Joan Jett, Debbie Harry, and Chrissie Hynde, and it introduced all-women bands (writing and performing their own music) like the Go-Go's into the mainstream (see "Examining Ethics: The Music Industry's Day of Reckoning on Women" on page 120). It also reopened the door to rock experimentation at a time when the industry had turned music into a purely commercial enterprise. The influence of experimental, or post-punk, music is still felt today in alternative and indie bands such as the Yeah Yeah Yeahs, G.L.O.S.S., and State Champs.

Indie Groups Reinterpret Rock

Taking the spirit of punk and updating it, indie groups emerged from the do-it-yourself approach of independent labels and created music that found its audience in live shows and on alternative-format college radio stations beginning in the 1980s. Groups often associated with early indie rock include R.E.M., the Cure, Sonic Youth, the Pixies, the Minutemen, and Hüsker Dü. In the Pacific Northwest, a subgenre called **grunge** emerged in the 1980s. After years of limited commercial success, grunge broke into the American mainstream with Nirvana's "Smells Like Teen Spirit" on the 1991 album *Nevermind*. Nirvana opened the floodgates to other "alternative" bands, such as Green Day, Pearl Jam, Soundgarden, Stone Temple Pilots, Hole, and Sleater-Kinney.

Mainstream attention illustrates a key dilemma for successful indie acts: that their popularity results in commercial success, a situation that their music often criticizes. Still, independent acts like Arcade Fire, Vampire Weekend, and Belle and Sebastian are among many that have launched and

Andrew DeLory

BOB DYLAN
Born Robert Allen Zimmerman in Minnesota, Bob Dylan took his stage name from Welsh poet Dylan Thomas. He led a folk music movement in the early 1960s with engaging, socially provocative lyrics. He was also an astute media critic, as is evident in the seminal documentary *Don't Look Back* (1967).

sustained successful recording careers built on independent labels, playing concerts and using the
Internet and social media to promote their music and sell merchandise.

Hip-Hop Redraws Musical Lines

With the growing segregation of radio formats and the dominance of mainstream rock by white male
performers, the place of black artists in the rock world diminished from the late 1970s onward. These
trends, combined with the rise of "safe" dance disco by white bands (the Bee Gees), black artists
(Donna Summer), and integrated groups (the Village People), created a space for a new sound to
emerge: **hip-hop**, a term for the urban culture that includes *rapping, cutting* (or *sampling*) by deejays,
breakdancing, street clothing, poetry slams, and graffiti art.

In the same way that punk opposed commercial rock, hip-hop stood in direct opposition to
the polished, professional, and often less political world of soul. Its combination of social politics,
swagger, and confrontational lyrics carried forward long-standing traditions in blues, R&B,
soul, and rock and roll. Like punk and early rock and roll, hip-hop was driven by a democratic,
nonprofessional spirit and was cheap to produce, requiring only a few mikes, speakers, amps,
turntables, and vinyl records. Deejays, like the pioneering Jamaican émigré Clive Campbell (a.k.a.
DJ Kool Herc), emerged first in New York, scratching and re-cueing old reggae, disco, soul, and rock
albums. These deejays, or MCs (masters of ceremony), used humor, boasts, and trash talking to
entertain and keep the peace at parties.

The music industry initially saw hip-hop as a novelty, despite the enormous success of the
Sugarhill Gang's "Rapper's Delight" in 1979 (which sampled the bass beat of a disco hit from the
same year, Chic's "Good Times"). Then, in 1982, Grandmaster Flash and the Furious Five released
"The Message" and forever infused hip-hop with a political take on ghetto life, a tradition continued
by artists like Public Enemy and Ice-T. By 1985, hip-hop had exploded as a popular genre with the
commercial successes of groups like Run-DMC, the Fat Boys, and LL Cool J. That year, Run-DMC's
album *Raising Hell* became a major crossover hit, the first No. 1 hip-hop album on the popular charts
(thanks in part to a collaboration with Aerosmith on a rap version of the group's 1976 hit "Walk This
Way"). But because most major labels and many black radio stations rejected the rawness of hip-hop,

the music spawned hundreds of new independent labels. Although initially dominated by male performers, hip-hop was open to women, and some—Salt-N-Pepa and Queen Latifah among them— quickly became major players. Soon, white groups like the Beastie Boys, Limp Bizkit, and Kid Rock were combining hip-hop and punk rock in a commercially successful way, while Eminem found enormous success emulating black rap artists.

On the one hand, the conversational style of rap makes it a forum in which performers can debate issues of gender, class, sexuality, violence, and drugs. On the other hand, hip-hop, like punk, has often drawn criticism for lyrics that degrade women, espouse homophobia, and applaud violence. Although hip-hop encompasses many different styles, including various Latin and Asian offshoots, its most controversial subgenre is probably **gangster rap**, which, in seeking to tell the truth about gang violence in American culture, has been accused of creating violence. Gangster rap drew national attention in 1996 with the shooting death of Tupac Shakur, who lived the violent life he rapped about on albums like *Thug Life*. Then, in 1997, Notorious B.I.G. (Christopher Wallace, a.k.a. Biggie Smalls), whose followers were prominent suspects in Shakur's death, was shot to death in Hollywood. The result was a change in the hip-hop industry. Most prominently, Sean "Diddy" Combs led Bad Boy Entertainment (former home of Notorious B.I.G.) away from gangster rap to a more danceable hip-hop that combined singing and rapping with musical elements of rock and soul. Today, hip-hop's stars include artists such as Vince Staples, who revisits the gangster genre, and artists like Kendrick Lamar, Chance the Rapper, Future,

KENDRICK LAMAR
made history in 2018 when he became the first hip-hop musician—and, in fact, the first nonclassical or non-jazz musician—to win a Pulitzer Prize when his album *Damn* took home the award in April of that year.

ALESSIA CARA
got her start on YouTube, uploading homemade covers of songs by artists like Amy Winehouse and the Neighborhood. Her videos amassed a devoted online following and attracted the attention of major record label Def Jam Recordings, with whom Cara signed a deal in 2015. That year Cara released her first officially licensed single, "Here," which as of 2018 had over 145 million views on YouTube.

Drake, and Lizzo, who bring an old-school social consciousness to their performances. By 2017, R&B/hip-hop surpassed rock to become the top music genre in the United States, with the majority of the top recordings and songs from that genre.[23]

The Reemergence of Pop

After waves of punk, grunge, alternative, and hip-hop; the decline of Top 40 radio; and the demise of MTV's *Total Request Live* countdown show, it seemed as though pop music and the era of big pop stars were waning. But pop music has endured and even flourished in recent years, especially with the advent of iTunes. The era of digital downloads again made the single (as opposed to the album) the dominant unit of music, and this dominance has aided the reemergence of pop, since songs with catchy hooks generate the most digital sales. The reemergence of pop was allied with the rise of electronic dance music (EDM), as deejays/remixers/producers like David Guetta, Skrillex, Calvin Harris, and Avicii collaborated with a number of other pop stars. Similarly, streaming services such as Spotify, Apple Music, and Deezer have greatly expanded accessibility to music and new remixes. The digital formats in music have resulted in a leap in viability and market share for independent labels and have changed the cultural landscape of the music industry in the twenty-first century.

THE BUSINESS OF SOUND RECORDING

For many in the recording industry, the relationship between music's business and artistic elements is an uneasy one. The lyrics of hip-hop or punk rock, for example, often question the commercial value of popular music. But the line between commercial success and artistic expression is hazier than simply arguing that the business side is driven by commercialism and the artistic side is free of commercial concerns. The truth, in most cases, is that the business needs artists who are provocative, original, and appealing to the public, and the artists need the expertise of the industry's marketers, promoters, and producers to hone their sound and reach the public. And both sides stand to make a lot of money from this relationship. But such factors as the enormity of the major labels and the complexities of making, selling, and profiting from music in an industry still adapting to the digital turn affect the economies of sound recording.

Music Labels Influence the Industry

After several years of steady growth, revenues for the recording industry experienced significant losses beginning in 2000 as file-sharing began to undercut CD sales. In 2017, U.S. music sales were about $8.7 billion, down from a peak of $14.5 billion in 1999 but slowly growing again as subscription streaming music revenue continued to increase. The global music business was valued at about $15.7 billion in 2017.[24] The U.S. and global music business still constitutes an **oligopoly**: a business situation in which a few firms control most of an industry's production and distribution resources. This global reach gives these firms influence over what types of music gain worldwide distribution and popular acceptance, although the rise of independent-label market share has challenged the dominance of the big music corporations.

Fewer Major Labels and Falling Market Share

From the 1950s through the 1980s, the music industry, though powerful, consisted of a large number of competing major labels, along with numerous independent labels. Over time, the major labels began swallowing up the independents and then buying one another. By 1998, only six major labels remained—Universal, Warner, Sony, BMG, EMI, and Polygram. After a series of acquisitions and mergers, by 2012 only Universal Music Group, Sony Music Entertainment, and Warner Music

Group remained. Together, these companies control about 62 percent of the global recording industry market share (see Figure 4.2). Although their revenue has eroded over the past decade, the major music corporations still wield great power, with a number of music stars under contract and enormous back catalogs of recordings that continue to sell. Despite the oligopoly in the music industry, the biggest change has been the rise in market share for independent music labels.

The Indies Grow with Digital Music

The rise of rock and roll in the 1950s and early 1960s showcased a rich diversity of independent labels—including Sun, Stax, Chess, and Motown—all vying for a share of the new music. That tradition lives on today. In contrast to the three global players, some five thousand large and small independent production houses—or **indies**—record music that appears to be less commercial. Indies require only a handful of people to operate them. For years, indies accounted for 10 to 15 percent of all music releases. But with the advent of downloads and streaming, the enormous diversity of independent-label music became much more accessible, and the market share of indies grew to more than one-third of the U.S. recording industry. Indies often still have business relationships with major labels; about 52 percent of independent labels use major labels to distribute their music (not unlike how independent film companies rely on major studios for distribution).[25] Independent labels have produced some of the best-selling artists of recent years; these labels include Big Machine Records (Taylor Swift, Rascal Flatts), Broken Bow Records (Jason Aldean), Dualtone Records (the Lumineers), XL Recordings (Adele, Vampire Weekend), and Cash Money Records (Drake, Nicki Minaj). (See "Alternative Voices" at the end of this chapter.)

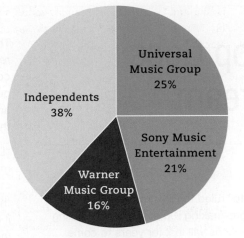

FIGURE 4.2

GLOBAL MARKET SHARE OF THE MAJOR LABELS IN THE RECORDING INDUSTRY, 2016
Data from: MusicBusinessWorldwide.com, 2017; *Wintel Worldwide Independent Market Report 2017.* Figures are rounded.

(Pie chart: Universal Music Group 25%; Sony Music Entertainment 21%; Warner Music Group 16%; Independents 38%)

Making, Selling, and Profiting from Music

Like most mass media, the music business is divided into several areas, each working in a different capacity. In the music industry, those areas are making the music (signing, developing, and recording the artist), selling the music (selling, distributing, advertising, and promoting the music), and dividing the profits. All these areas are essential to the industry but have always played a part in the conflict between business concerns and artistic concerns.

Making the Music

Labels are driven by **A&R (artist & repertoire) agents**, the talent scouts of the music business, who discover, develop, and sometimes manage artists. A&R agents seek out and listen to demonstration tapes, or *demos*, from new artists and decide whom to sign and which songs to record. (Today, demos are typically in digital form.) Naturally, these agents look for artists with commercial potential.

A typical recording session is a complex process that involves the artist, the producer, the session engineer, and audio technicians. In charge of the overall recording process, the producer handles most nontechnical elements of the session, including reserving studio space, hiring session musicians (if necessary), and making final decisions about the sound of the recording. The session engineer oversees the technical aspects of the recording session, everything from choosing recording equipment to managing the audio technicians. Most popular records are recorded part by part. Using separate microphones, the vocalists, guitarists, drummers, and so on, are digitally recorded onto separate audio tracks, which are edited and remixed during postproduction and ultimately mixed down to a two-track stereo master copy for digital reproduction.

Latin Pop Goes Mainstream

"**D**espacito" ruled the summer in 2017, but its record-making run and groundbreaking contributions will last for years to come.

For sixteen weeks, the Spanish-language song by artists Luis Fonsi and Daddy Yankee was the No. 1 song in the United States, and it spent thirty-five weeks at No. 1 on the Hot Latin Songs charts. A remix with Justin Bieber helped popularize the song even further with English-speaking audiences. "Despacito" is the first Spanish-language song to hit No. 1 on the music charts since the dance-craze song "Macarena" by Los Del Rio in 1996.

At 2.7 million downloads, it was the year's most purchased song; with 1.3 billion streams, it was also the year's most streamed song.[1] After the video topped more than 3 billion views by August 2017, it became YouTube's most popular video. By April 2018, it had accumulated more than 5 billion views, putting the video in its own stratosphere. (Most fans opted for the original; the Bieber remix had 620 million views by April 2018—a huge number, but not close to the all-Spanish-language original.)[2]

The impact of "Despacito" was felt around the world, where it hit No. 1 in more than forty countries, from Argentina to Ireland, Israel, Russia, and India. The song itself has an international background. It was cowritten by Fonsi (who went to high school in Orlando and studied music at Florida State) and Yankee, both Puerto Ricans, and Erika Ender, a Panamanian-born singer-songwriter. Bieber cowrote the remix, which came out three months after the original release. The music video was shot in the La Perla neighborhood of San Juan, between the rocky coast and the old city walls, and features Fonsi singing, Yankee rapping, and actor and former Miss Universe winner (and Puerto Rico native) Zuleyka Rivera as the object of the singer's love and desire (*despacito* means "slowly").

The sound of "Despacito" emerges from the *reggaeton* genre—a Latin-Caribbean music style that combines elements of dance hall with hip-hop. The genre is popular in Puerto Rico and the Caribbean and now—with the success of "Despacito"—around the world.

"Despacito" is part of a bigger story of how Latin music has gone mainstream. *Billboard* magazine, the music industry's top business publication, reported that in 2015, only three Spanish-language songs made it onto the Hot 100 chart. In 2016, just four made it. In 2017, with "Despacito" leading the way, nineteen Spanish-language songs made the Hot 100 chart, an unprecedented number.

Billboard argues that American Top-40 radio would never have promoted so many Spanish-language songs. But the now-dominant streaming music format means individual listeners are dramatically remaking what's popular. "Streaming numbers are a large part of what informs the Hot 100, and it's no secret that the global clout of platforms like Spotify and YouTube has allowed an increasing number of Latin tracks to seep into the upper echelons of streaming charts," *Billboard* says.[3]

Two other factors have also helped popularize Latin pop around the world. First, "thanks to the impact of reggaeton, we suddenly have an avalanche of danceable Latin tracks with a pop feel, and the combination is universally appealing," *Billboard* notes.[4]

Second, mainstream English-language artists have collaborated with Latin artists to make for more crossover success. Beyoncé did a remix of J Balvin and Willy William's "Mi Gente" to raise money for hurricane victims in Puerto Rico, Mexico, and other Caribbean islands, and the song moved high into the Hot 100. After "Despacito," Luis Fonsi teamed up with Demi Lovato on "Échame La Culpa." Similarly, Cardi B is featured on Ozuna's "La Modelo."

The trend of more Spanish-language songs in the Hot 100 continued into 2018. Americans and the rest of the world may have heard about Shakira and Enrique Iglesias, but based on streaming success, they may be soon be hearing more about other Latin music stars, including Ozuna, Nicky Jam, Romeo Santos, Maluma, and Wisin.

Selling the Music

Streaming services like Spotify, Apple Music, Google Play, and Amazon are the leading revenue generators in the music industry today and account for 65 percent of the U.S. music business.[26] As recently as 2011, physical recordings (CDs and some vinyl) accounted for about 50 percent of U.S. music sales, but CD sales continue to decline and now constitute about 12 percent of the U.S. market. In some countries, however—such as Japan and Germany—CDs retain a much larger market share. Vinyl album sales have carved out a successful niche as a classic format in the United States, accounting for about 4.5 percent of industry revenues. Digital downloads of singles and albums are about 15 percent of the market, down from the days in the early years of the century, when the iTunes store was the dominant seller of music.

Dividing the Profits

The digital upheaval in the music industry has shaken up the once-predictable sale of music through CDs or digital downloads. Now there are multiple digital venues for selling music and an equally large number of methods for dividing the profits.

With streaming as the leading music distribution format, figuring out what counts as a "sale" of a song or an album is important. The music industry developed an equivalency standard, with 1,500 song streams from an album equal to one album sale, and 150 song streams equal to the sale of a single.[27] The way in which songs are counted in music streaming is similar, but compensation can vary widely, depending on the streaming service. For example, the Recording Industry Association of America (RIAA) reports that Apple Music pays artists $12.50 per 1,000 streams, whereas Spotify pays $7.50 for the same number of streams. YouTube, which streams more music than any other service, pays only $1 per 1,000 streams.[28] This does not sit well with the music industry, which accuses YouTube of "exploiting legal loopholes and shortchanging artists of their fair share."[29]

For CDs, profits get divided more transparently. Let's take the example of a CD that retails at $17.98. The wholesale price for that CD is about $12.50, leaving the remainder as retail profit. Discount retailers like Walmart and Best Buy sell closer to the wholesale price to lure customers to buy other things (even if they make less profit on the CD itself). The wholesale price represents the actual cost of producing and promoting the recording, plus the music label's profits. The music label reaps the highest revenue (close to $9.74 on a typical CD) but, along with the artist, bears the bulk of the expenses: manufacturing costs, packaging and CD design, advertising and promotion, and artists' royalties (see Figure 4.3).

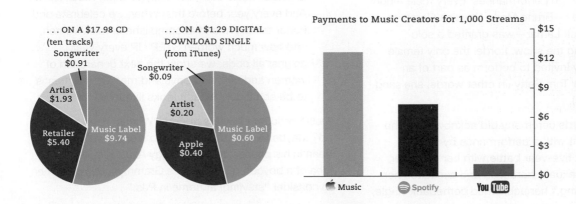

... ON A $17.98 CD
(ten tracks)
Songwriter $0.91
Artist $1.93
Retailer $5.40
Music Label $9.74

... ON A $1.29 DIGITAL DOWNLOAD SINGLE (from iTunes)
Songwriter $0.09
Artist $0.20
Apple $0.40
Music Label $0.60

Payments to Music Creators for 1,000 Streams
Music
Spotify
YouTube

FIGURE 4.3

WHERE THE MONEY GOES

Data from: Cary Sherman, "2016: A Year of Progress for Music," *Medium*, March 30, 2017, https://medium.com/@RIAA/2016-a-year-of-progress-for-music-4e9b77022635; and Steve Knopper, "The New Economics of the Music Industry," *Rolling Stone*, October 25, 2011, www.rollingstone.com/music/news/the-new-economics-of-the-music-industry-20111025.

The Music Industry's Day of Reckoning

What will the Grammys look like in the future? The 2018 Grammy Awards amounted to a day of reckoning for the music industry. In a year that had so many women writing, performing, and contributing to an astonishing number of standout songs and records, the spotlight should have been shining on these women. But it was not. In fact, this became the main narrative after the 2018 Grammys: the lack of women in the music industry.

First, there was the miniscule number of women awarded Grammys during the award ceremony itself: Alessia Cara won for best new artist, and Rihanna won as a featured artist (not in a solo capacity) on Kendrick Lamar's song "Loyalty." And that was it for the major awards—most women were shut out. In the best pop solo performance category, in which most of the nominees were women—Pink, Kesha, Lady Gaga, and Kelly Clarkson—the award went to Ed Sheeran (who wasn't even there to pick up his award). SZA was nominated in five categories but did not win a single Grammy. Cara was the only woman to accept a televised award.

Beyond the awards themselves, women were cut out of the program's onstage performances. Every male Album of the Year nominee—Bruno Mars, Childish Gambino, Jay-Z, and Kendrick Lamar—was granted a solo performance during the show. Lorde, the only female nominee, was only invited to perform as part of an ensemble to honor Tom Petty (in other words, she sang Tom Petty's music).

The Grammy Awards ceremony did acknowledge the #MeToo movement with a performance by Kesha. She had been in a five-year battle with her producer, who she alleged sexually harassed and assaulted her. Kesha sang "Praying," her acclaimed comeback single,

live with Camila Cabello, Cyndi Lauper, Julia Michaels, Bebe Rexha, and Andra Day. Despite that moment of personal triumph, another story emerged in the days following the Grammys, centered around the music industry's dominant male power structure, the need for change, and women in the industry who have had enough:

- The hashtag #GrammysSoMale appeared, inspired by the #OscarsSoWhite hashtag created in the wake of criticism following the 2016 Academy Awards.
- Former Sony Music employee Tristan Coopersmith revealed in an open letter that her former boss, music industry executive Charlie Walk, had sexually abused her and even cornered her in his bedroom, pushing her down on the bed. Other women wrote in with tales of Walk's sexual lewdness, prompting Walk to resign.[1]
- A coalition of female music executives demanded that the president of the Recording Academy, Neil Portnow, resign over comments he made immediately after the awards. When asked by reporters about the paucity of women nominations and awardees, Portnow told them that women needed to "step up," suggesting they weren't working hard or weren't talented enough. Pink was one of many women in the recording industry who was enraged by Portnow's comment. She tweeted an image she wrote on a whiteboard the next day:

    WOMEN IN MUSIC don't need to "step up"— Women have been stepping since the beginning of time. Stepping up, and also stepping aside. Women OWNED music this year. They've been KILLING IT. And every year before this. When we celebrate and honor the talent and accomplishments of women, and how much women STEP UP every year, against all odds, we show the next generation of women and girls and boys and men what it means to be equal, and what it looks like to be fair.

Music critic Ann Powers added, "Women need to step up? Maybe Neil Portnow needs to step down" (he has been in his post since 2002).[2] Iggy Azalea floated the idea of a boycott of next year's Grammys, telling women to consider "stay[ing] at home in PJs."

P!nk ✓
@Pink

Follow

WOMEN IN MUSIC dont need to "Step up". women have been stepping since the beginning of time. Stepping up, and also stepping aside women OWNED music this year. They've been KILLING IT. And every year before this. When we celebrate and honor the talent and accomplishments of women, and how much women STEP UP every year, against all odds, we show the next generation of women and girls and boy and men what it means to be equal, and what it looks like to be fair.

3:35 PM - 29 Jan 2018

32,391 Retweets **127,959** Likes

💬 1.9K   🔁 32K   ♡ 128K

PINK'S WHITEBOARD
message in response to the Recording Academy president Neil Portnow's suggestion for women in music to "step up." Four months later, Portnow announced he would step down from his position in July 2019.

In fact, the music industry does even worse than Hollywood in terms of gender equality. A study released by the Annenberg Inclusion Initiative at the University of Southern California found that of the 899 Grammy nominees in the last six years, only 9 percent were women. The report also analyzed top *Billboard* songs from 2012 to 2017 and found that women made up only 12 percent of songwriters and a mere 2 percent of producers.

The Grammys has previously dealt with criticisms related to issues of racial diversity. The institution did not recognize rap until 1989 (a decade too late), and even then did not televise the best rap category, leading to boycotts by the world's leading rap artists. Beyoncé lost Album of the Year three times: to Taylor Swift in 2010, to Beck in 2014, and to Adele in 2017. And black artists

were collectively enraged as hip-hop artists Macklemore and Ryan Lewis (who are white) swept the rap and new artist categories (overlooking Kendrick Lamar) in 2014. At the same time, the Annenberg Inclusion Initiative study found that of the 1,239 performing artists analyzed, 42 percent were from minority groups—a significantly better statistic than the gender breakdown.[3]

As Annenberg Inclusion Initiative@Inclusionists posted on Twitter the day after the 2018 Grammy Awards (and Neil Portnow's ill-conceived comment): "Instead of asking women to 'step` up,' what about asking about the systemic obstacles they face when trying to achieve sustainable careers in the music business? (And then, of course, ask the entire industry to take steps to demolish those barriers.)"[4]

New artists typically negotiate a royalty rate of between 8 and 12 percent on the retail price of a CD, while more established performers might negotiate for 15 percent or higher. An artist who has negotiated an 11 percent royalty rate would earn about $1.93 for each CD with a suggested retail price of $17.98. Therefore, a CD that "goes gold"—that is, sells 500,000 units—would net the artist around $965,000. But out of this amount, artists must repay the record company the money they have been advanced (from $100,000 to $500,000). The financial payout is more certain for the songwriter/publisher, who makes a standard mechanical royalty rate of about 9.1 cents per song, or 91 cents for a ten-song CD, without having to bear any production or promotional costs.

The profits are divided somewhat differently in digital download sales. A $1.29 iTunes download generates about $0.40 for Apple (it gets 30% of every song sale) and the standard $0.09 mechanical royalty for the song publisher and writer, leaving about $0.60 for the record company. Artists at a typical royalty rate of about 15 percent would get $0.20 from the song download. With no CD printing and packaging costs, record companies can retain more of the revenue on download sales.

Songs streamed on Internet radio, like Pandora, Slacker, or iHeartRadio, and satellite radio follow yet another formula for determining royalties. In 2003, the nonprofit group SoundExchange was established to collect royalties for Internet radio. SoundExchange charges fees of $0.0022 per stream for subscription (premium) services, and $0.0017 per stream for nonsubscription (free) services. Large Internet radio stations can pay up to 25 percent of their gross revenue (less for smaller Internet radio stations and a small flat fee for streaming nonprofit stations). About 50 percent of the fees go to the music label, 45 percent go to the featured artists, and 5 percent go to nonfeatured artists.

KISHI BASHI

is the stage name of singer, songwriter, and multi-instrumentalist Kaoru Ishibashi. A member of several indie bands—including Jupiter One and Of Montreal—Ishibashi has performed at major festivals, including SXSW and Austin City Limits. His original songs have been licensed in major commercials for Microsoft, Sony, and Smart USA.

Scott Dudelson/Getty Images

Alternative Voices

A vast network of independent (indie) labels, distributors, stores, publications, and Internet sites devoted to music outside the major label system has existed since the early days of rock and roll. The indie industry nonetheless continues to thrive, providing music fans access to all styles of music, including some of the world's most respected artists.

Independent labels have become even more viable by using the Internet as a low-cost distribution and promotional outlet for downloads, streaming, and merchandise sales, as well as for fan discussion groups, regular e-mail updates of tour schedules, and promotion of new releases. Consequently, bands that in previous years would have signed to a major label have found another path to success in the independent music industry, with labels like Merge Records (Arcade Fire, She & Him, the Mountain Goats), Matador (Yo La Tengo, Sonic Youth, Pavement), 4AD (the National, Bon Iver), and Epitaph (Bad Religion, Alkaline Trio, Frank Turner). Unlike artists on major labels who need to sell 500,000 copies or more to recoup expenses and make a profit, indie artists "can turn a profit after selling roughly 25,000 copies of an album."[30] One of the challenges of being an independent, unsigned artist is figuring out how to sell one's music on Spotify, Apple Music, iTunes, Google Play, Tidal, Amazon, YouTube, and other digital music services. TuneCore and CD Baby are two of the leading companies that have emerged to fulfill that need. For a fee, the companies will distribute recordings to online music services and then collect royalties for the artist (charging an additional percentage for recovered royalty fees).

Some established rock acts, like Radiohead, Macklemore, Nine Inch Nails, and Amanda Palmer, are taking another approach to their business model, shunning major labels and indies and using the Internet to directly reach their fans. By selling music on their own websites or selling CDs at live concerts, music acts generally do better, cutting out the retailer and keeping more of the revenue themselves. Artists and bands can also build online communities around their websites, listing shows, news, tours, photos, and downloadable songs. Social networking sites are another place for fans and music artists to connect. Myspace was one of the first dominant sites, but as a place to discover new music, it has been eclipsed by a number of music websites, such as Hype Machine and SoundCloud, as well as by video sites, including YouTube and Vevo.

SOUND RECORDING, FREE EXPRESSION, AND DEMOCRACY

From sound recording's earliest stages as a mass medium, when the music industry began stamping out flat records, to the breakthrough of MP3s and Internet-based music services, fans have been sharing music and pushing culture in unpredictable directions. The battle over pop music's controversial aspects speaks to the heart of democratic expression. Nevertheless, pop—like other art forms—also has a history of reproducing old stereotypes: limiting women's access as performers, fostering racist or homophobic attitudes, and celebrating violence and misogyny.

Popular musical forms that test cultural boundaries face a dilemma: how to uphold a legacy of free expression while resisting giant companies bent on consolidating independents and maximizing profits. Since the 1950s, forms of rock music have been in a recurring pattern of breaking boundaries, becoming commercial, then reemerging as rebellious. The congressional payola hearings of 1959 and the Senate hearings of the mid-1980s, triggered by Tipper Gore's Parents Music Resource Center (which led to music advisory labels), are just two of the many attempts to rein in popular music, whereas the infamous antics of performers from Elvis Presley onward, the blunt lyrics of rock and roll and rap artists, and the independent paths of the many garage and cult bands from the early rock-and-roll era through the present are among the things that pushed popular music's boundaries.

Still, this dynamic between popular music's clever innovations and capitalism's voracious appetite is crucial to sound recording's evolution and mass appeal. Ironically, successful commerce requires periodic infusions of the diverse sounds that come from ethnic communities, backyard garages, dance parties, and neighborhood clubs. No matter how it is produced and distributed, popular music endures because it speaks to both individual and universal themes, from a teenager's first romantic adventure to a nation's outrage over social injustice. Music often reflects the personal or political anxieties of a society. It also breaks down artificial or hurtful barriers better than many government programs do. Despite its tribulations, music at its best continues to champion a democratic spirit. Writer and free-speech advocate Nat Hentoff addressed this issue in the 1970s when he wrote, "Popular music always speaks, among other things, of dreams—which change with the times."[31] The recording industry continues to capitalize on and spread those dreams globally, but in each generation, musicians and their fans keep imagining new ones.

4 Chapter Review

COMMON THREADS

One of the Common Threads discussed in Chapter 1 is the developmental stages of mass media. But as new audio and sound recording technologies evolve, do they drive the kind of music we hear?

In the recent history of the music industry, it would seem as if technology has been the driving force behind the kind of music we hear. Case in point: The advent of the MP3 file as a new format in 1999 led to a new emphasis on single songs as the primary unit of music sales. In the past decade, we have come to live in a music business dominated by digital singles and streams.

What have we gained by this transition? Thankfully, there are fewer CD jewel boxes (which always shattered with the greatest of ease). And there is no requirement to buy the lackluster "filler" songs that often come with the price of an album, when all we really want are the two or three hit songs. But what have we lost culturally in the transition away from albums?

First, there is no physical album art for digital singles (although department stores now sell frames to turn vintage 12-inch album covers into art). And second, we have lost the concept of an album as a thematic collection of music and a medium that provides a much broader canvas to a talented musical artist. Consider this: How would the Beatles' *White Album* have been created in a business dominated by singles? A look at *Rolling Stone* magazine's 500 Greatest Albums and *Time* magazine's All-Time 100 Albums indicates the apex of album creativity in earlier decades, with such selections as Jimi Hendrix's *Are You Experienced* (1967), the Beatles' *Sgt. Pepper's Lonely Hearts Club Band* (1967), David Bowie's

The Rise and Fall of Ziggy Stardust (1972), Public Enemy's *It Takes a Nation of Millions to Hold Us Back* (1988), and Radiohead's *OK Computer* (1997). Has the movement away from albums changed possibilities for musical artists? That is, if an artist wants to be commercially successful, is there more pressure to generate hit singles rather than larger bodies of work that constitute an album? Have the styles of artists like Kesha, Nicki Minaj, OneRepublic, and Ed Sheeran been shaped by the predominance of the single?

Still, there is a clear case against technological determinism—the idea that technological innovations determine the direction of the culture. Back in the 1950s, the vinyl album caught on despite its newness—and despite the popularity of its competition: the 45-rpm single format. When the MP3 single format emerged in the late 1990s, the music industry had just rolled out two formats of album discs that were technological improvements on the CD. Neither caught on. Of course, music fans may have been lured both by the ease of acquiring music digitally via the Internet and by the price—usually free (but illegal).

Yet we may be seeing a revival of the idea of the concept album. Beyoncé's *Lemonade* (2016), Jay-Z's *4:44* (2017), and Kendrick Lamar's *DAMN* (2017) have all been critically acclaimed as cohesive works of art. Can you think of any other albums of the past few years that merit being listed among the greatest albums of all time?

KEY TERMS

The definitions for the terms listed below can be found in the glossary at the end of the book. The page numbers listed with the terms indicate where the term is highlighted in the chapter.

audiotape, 99
stereo, 100
analog recording, 100
digital recording, 100
compact discs (CDs), 100
MP3, 100
pop music, 102
jazz, 103

cover music, 103
rock and roll, 103
blues, 104
rhythm and blues (R&B), 104
rockabilly, 105
soul, 110
folk music, 111
folk-rock, 111

punk rock, 113
grunge, 113
hip-hop, 114
gangster rap, 115
oligopoly, 116
indies, 117
A&R (artist & repertoire) agents, 117

REVIEW QUESTIONS

The Development of Sound Recording

1. The technological configuration of a particular medium sometimes elevates it to mass market status. Why did Emile Berliner's flat disk replace the wax cylinder, and why did this reconfiguration of records matter in the history of mass media? Can you think of other mass media examples in which the size and shape of the technology have made a difference?

2. How did the music industry attempt to curb illegal downloading and file-sharing?

3. How did sound recording survive the advent of radio?

U.S. Popular Music and the Formation of Rock

4. How did rock and roll significantly influence two mass media industries?

5. Although many rock-and-roll lyrics from the 1950s are tame by today's standards, this new musical development represented a threat to many parents and adults at the time. Why?

6. What moral and cultural boundaries were blurred by rock and roll in the 1950s?

7. Why did cover music figure so prominently in the development of rock and roll and the record industry in the 1950s?

A Changing Industry: Reformations in Popular Music

8. Explain the British invasion. What was its impact on the recording industry?

9. What were the major influences of folk music on the recording industry?

10. Why did punk rock and hip-hop emerge as significant musical forms in the late 1970s and 1980s? What do their developments have in common, and how are they different?

11. Why does pop music continue to remain powerful today?

The Business of Sound Recording

12. What companies control the bulk of worldwide music production and distribution?

13. Why have independent labels grown to have a significantly larger market share in the 2010s?

14. Which major parties receive profits when a digital download, music stream, or physical CD is sold?

15. How is a mechanical royalty different from a performance royalty?

Sound Recording, Free Expression, and Democracy

16. Why is it ironic that so many forms of alternative music become commercially successful?

QUESTIONING THE MEDIA

1. If you ran a noncommercial campus radio station, what kind of music would you play, and why?

2. Think about the role of the 1960s drug culture in rock's history. How are drugs and alcohol treated in contemporary and alternative forms of rock and hip-hop today?

3. Is it healthy for or detrimental to the music business that so much of the recording industry is controlled by just a few large international companies? Explain.

4. Do you think the Internet as a technology helps or hurts musical artists? Why do so many contemporary musical performers differ in their opinions about the Internet?

5. Consider the platforms through which you most often listen to recorded music (and live music, too). Which of these modes delivers the most money to the artists you enjoy? Which of these modes results in little or no compensation for the artists? How should these modes be fixed to support musical artists?

LAUNCHPAD FOR *MEDIA & CULTURE*

Visit LaunchPad for *Media & Culture* at launchpadworks.com for additional learning tools:

- REVIEW WITH LEARNINGCURVE
  LearningCurve, available on LaunchPad for *Media &*

  Culture, uses gamelike quizzing to help you master the concepts you need to learn from this chapter.

Popular Radio and the Origins of Broadcasting

5

THE YEAR 2017 was a breakthrough year for podcasting: a third of Americans tuned into podcasts, and one out of six Americans listened to podcasts at least once a week.[1] Today, more than 400,000 podcast titles are available, and 1,000 more are added every week.[2] Just as listeners tuned in during the golden age of radio in the 1930s, when creative storytelling and sound effects transfixed American audiences, and welcomed inventive and entertaining talk radio, podcast listeners appreciate the intimate and authentic connection they have with their favorite hosts and the simple pleasure they get from listening to stories. These listeners have embraced the fresh perspectives that made sensations out of investigative journalism podcasts *Serial* (2014), *S-Town* (2017), and *Dirty John* (2017) and have made household names out of ongoing podcasts like *Pod Save America*, *Reply All*, *2 Dope Queens*, NPR's *Alt.Latino*, and the *New York Times' The Daily*.

EARLY TECHNOLOGY
AND THE
DEVELOPMENT
OF RADIO
p. 129

THE EVOLUTION OF
RADIO
p. 134

RADIO REINVENTS
ITSELF
p. 142

THE SOUNDS OF
COMMERCIAL RADIO
p. 145

THE ECONOMICS OF
BROADCAST RADIO
p. 154

RADIO AND THE
DEMOCRACY OF THE
AIRWAVES
p. 157

◀ Jasmine Garsd of NPR's podcast *Alt.Latino* interviews musician Ana Tijoux at the SXSW Music, Film + Interactive.

Forty-five percent of all podcasts currently address society and culture, with true-crime podcasts (*Criminal*, *My Favorite Murder*) tending to be the most popular. News and politics make up 34 percent of all podcast genres (*On the Media*, *Remainiacs*), followed by comedy (32 percent) and sports (23 percent).[3] Listeners have seamlessly integrated podcasts into their lives: while driving, washing dishes, exercising, working, or doing chores at home in the evenings or on weekends. And, not surprisingly, this new audio format has both challenged and invigorated radio broadcasting.

Since podcasts are so easy to make—anyone with a microphone can create a podcast and upload it to the Internet—they are flooding the listening market with inexpensive, accessible content. This new content tends to be less slick and polished than radio, taking a casual approach to conversation that many listeners find appealing. Also, since podcasts are not required to play along with broadcast rules that limit profane language, they are more akin to HBO and Netflix, offering flexible topics and content that broadcast radio isn't as easily able to explore, and presenting an exhilarating mix of diverse voices.

"Podcasts bring you to places you've never been, they give you the impression of sharing an animated kitchen-table banter (or a loud bar argument) with a couple of friends," Juliette De Maeyer noted in the *Atlantic Monthly*.[4] For the most part, broadcast radio stopped creating such listening experiences in the 1950s, as music formats ascended.

Perhaps most importantly, podcasts can be played at any time and on a variety of devices (especially mobile phones), are downloadable, and are not dependent on an on-air time slot. Because podcast listeners tend to be younger, college educated, digitally savvy, and well paid, the new format has been attracting advertising dollars away from radio.[5]

Radio has answered these challenges by creating podcasts out of its live programming. Perhaps National Public Radio (NPR) has been the most successful at making serious inroads in the podcasting space. NPR, and now the rest of the radio industry, has embraced podcasting as an extension of what it has been doing since the beginning of radio—creating intimate connections through sound—and making recorded broadcasts (now podcasts) available whenever people have time to listen. Tim Clarke of Cox Media thinks of podcasting as on-demand radio programming. "Consumers expect access to content they want, on their schedule, and on the device of their choice," he says. "We have to be able to deliver that."[6] Large radio conglomerates such as iHeartMedia now develop full podcasts with their biggest radio personalities (e.g., Elvis Duran, Bobby Bones, and Colin Cowherd).

The radio industry is also interested in exploring the expanding podcast environment to discover future broadcast radio personalities. It remains to be seen if podcast hosts will sacrifice their autonomy and abandon their niche audiences to join a broadcast network, or if radio content will change dramatically because of the podcasting challenge. Radio's biggest fear is that audiences will simply avoid radio altogether in search of new listening experiences that speak directly to their interests—a fear expressed succinctly by radio industry consultant Alan Burns: What if the increasing selection of podcasts create "infinite inventory, that is, too many audio avails chasing too few audio advertising dollars"?[7]

EVEN WITH THE ARRIVAL OF TELEVISION IN THE 1950s and the "corporatization" of broadcasting in the 1990s, the historical and contemporary roles played by radio have been immense. From the early days of network radio to the more customized, demographically segmented medium today, radio's influence continues to reverberate throughout our society. Though television displaced radio as our most common media experience, radio specialized and adapted. The daily music and persistent talk that resonate from radios all over the world continue to play a key role in contemporary culture.

In this chapter, we examine the scientific, cultural, political, and economic factors surrounding radio's development and perseverance. We will:

LaunchPad
macmillan learning
launchpadworks.com

Visit LaunchPad for *Media & Culture* and use LearningCurve to review concepts from this chapter.

- Explore the origins of broadcasting, from the early theories about radio waves to the critical formation of RCA as a national radio monopoly
- Probe the evolution of commercial radio, including the rise of NBC as the first network, the development of CBS, and the establishment of the first federal radio legislation
- Review the fascinating ways in which radio reinvented itself in the 1950s
- Examine television's impact on radio programming, the invention of FM radio, radio's convergence with sound recording, and the influence of various formats
- Investigate newer developments, like satellite and HD radio; radio's convergence with the Internet; and radio's hopes for greater convergence with the mobile phone industry
- Survey the economic health, increasing conglomeration, and cultural impact of commercial and noncommercial radio today, including the emergence of noncommercial low-power FM service and podcasting

As you read this chapter, think about your own relationship with radio. What are your earliest memories of radio listening? Do you remember a favorite song or station? How old were you when you started listening? Why did you listen? What types of radio stations are in your area today? How has the Internet made radio better? How has it made it worse? For more questions to help you think through the role of radio in our lives, see "Questioning the Media" in the Chapter Review.

EARLY TECHNOLOGY AND THE DEVELOPMENT OF RADIO

Radio did not emerge as a full-blown mass medium until the 1920s, though the technology that made radio possible had been evolving for years. The **telegraph**—the precursor of radio technology—was invented in the 1840s. American inventor Samuel Morse developed the first practical system, sending electrical impulses from a transmitter through a cable to a reception point. Using what became known as **Morse code**—a series of dots and dashes that stood for letters in the alphabet—telegraph operators transmitted news and messages simply by interrupting the electrical current along a wire cable. By 1844, Morse had set up the first telegraph line between Washington, D.C., and Baltimore. By 1861, telegraph lines ran coast to coast. By 1866, the first transatlantic cable, capable of transmitting about six words per minute, ran between Newfoundland and Ireland along the ocean floor.

Although it was a revolutionary technology, the telegraph had its limitations. For instance, while it dispatched complicated language codes, it was unable to transmit the human voice. Moreover, ships at sea still had no contact with the rest of the world. As a result, navies could not be alerted when wars had ceased on land, and they often continued fighting for months. Commercial shipping interests also lacked an efficient way to coordinate and relay information from land and between ships. What was needed was a telegraph without wires.

A TELEGRAPHY CLASS

at the Iowa State University, circa 1910. Sending messages using Morse code across telegraph wires was the precursor to radio, which did not fully become a mass medium until the 1920s. Like the Internet, radio was popularized through universities and high schools. Education-related clubs met to build radio transmitters and receivers, and teachers were among the first to develop radio content during the 1920s.

FIGURE 5.1

THE ELECTROMAGNETIC SPECTRUM

Data from: NASA, http://imagine .gsfc.nasa.gov/docs/science /know_l1/emspectrum.html.

Maxwell and Hertz Discover Radio Waves

The key development in wireless transmissions came from James Maxwell, a Scottish physicist who in the mid-1860s theorized the existence of **electromagnetic waves**: invisible electronic impulses similar to visible light. Maxwell's equations showed that electricity, magnetism, light, and heat are part of the same electromagnetic spectrum and that they radiate in space at the speed of light, about 186,000 miles per second (see Figure 5.1). Maxwell further theorized that a portion of these phenomena, later known as **radio waves**, could be harnessed so that signals could be sent from a transmission point to a reception point.

It was German physicist Heinrich Hertz, however, who in the 1880s proved Maxwell's theories. Hertz created a crude device that permitted an electrical spark to leap across a small gap between two steel balls. As the electricity jumped the gap, it emitted waves; this was the first recorded transmission and reception of an electromagnetic wave. Hertz's experiments significantly advanced the development of wireless communication.

Marconi and the Inventors of Wireless Telegraphy

In 1894, Guglielmo Marconi—a twenty-year-old, self-educated Italian engineer—read Hertz's work and understood that developing a way to send high-speed messages over great distances would transform communication, the military, and commercial shipping. Although revolutionary, the telephone and the telegraph were limited by their wires, so Marconi set about trying to make wireless technology practical. First, he attached Hertz's spark-gap transmitter to a Morse telegraph key, which could send out dot-dash signals. The electrical impulses traveled into a Morse inker, the machine that telegraph operators used to record the dots and dashes onto narrow strips of paper. Second, Marconi discovered that grounding—connecting the transmitter and receiver to the earth—greatly increased the distance over which he could send signals.

In 1896, Marconi traveled to England, where he received a patent for **wireless telegraphy**, a form of voiceless point-to-point communication. In London in 1897, he formed the Wireless Telegraph and Signal Company, later known as British Marconi, and began installing wireless technology on British naval and private commercial ships. In 1899, he opened a branch of the company in the United States, nicknamed American Marconi. That same year, he sent the first wireless Morse-code signal across the English Channel to France; and in 1901, he relayed the first wireless signal across the Atlantic Ocean. Although Marconi was a successful innovator and entrepreneur, he saw wireless telegraphy only as a

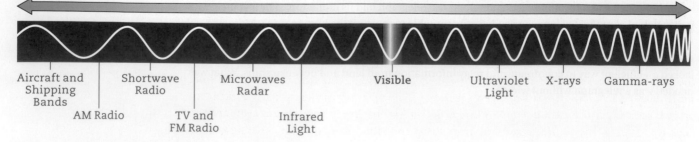

Long Wavelength
Low Frequency
Low Energy

Short Wavelength
High Frequency
High Energy

Aircraft and Shipping Bands | Shortwave Radio | Microwaves Radar | Visible | Ultraviolet Light | X-rays | Gamma-rays

AM Radio | TV and FM Radio | Infrared Light

method of point-to-point communication, much like the telegraph and the telephone, not as a one-to-many mass medium. He also confined his applications to Morse-code messages for military and commercial ships, leaving others to explore the wireless transmission of voice and music.

History often cites Marconi as the "father of radio," but another inventor unknown to him was making parallel discoveries about wireless telegraphy in Russia. Alexander Popov, a professor of physics in St. Petersburg, was also experimenting with sending wireless messages over distances. Popov announced to the Russian Physicist Society of St. Petersburg on May 7, 1895, that he had transmitted and received signals over a distance of six hundred yards.[8] Yet Popov was an academic, not an entrepreneur, and after Marconi accomplished a similar feat that same summer, Marconi was the first to apply for and receive a patent.

It is important to note that the work of Popov and Marconi was preceded by that of Nikola Tesla, a Serbian-Croatian inventor who immigrated to New York in 1884. Tesla, who also conceived the high-capacity alternating current systems that made worldwide electrification possible, invented a wireless system in 1892 and successfully demonstrated his device a year later.[9] However, Tesla's work was overshadowed by Marconi's. In fact, Marconi used much of Tesla's work in his own developments, and for years Tesla was not associated with the invention of radio. Tesla never received great financial benefit from his breakthroughs, but in 1943 (a few months after he died penniless in New York), the U.S. Supreme Court overturned Marconi's wireless patent and deemed Tesla the inventor of radio.[10]

Wireless Telephony: De Forest and Fessenden

In 1899, inventor Lee De Forest (who, in defiance of other inventors, liked to call himself the "father of radio") wrote the first Ph.D. dissertation on wireless technology, building on others' innovations. In 1901, De Forest challenged Marconi, who was covering New York's International Yacht Races for the Associated Press, by signing up to report the races for a rival news service. The competing transmitters jammed each other's signals so badly, however, that officials ended up relaying information on the races in the traditional way—with flags and hand signals. The event exemplified a problem that would persist throughout radio's early development: noise and interference from competition for the finite supply of radio frequencies.

In 1902, De Forest set up the Wireless Telephone Company to compete head-on with American Marconi, by then the leader in wireless communication. A major difference between Marconi and De Forest was the latter's interest in wireless voice and music transmissions, later known as **wireless telephony** and, eventually, radio. Although sometimes an unscrupulous competitor (inventor Reginald Fessenden won a lawsuit against De Forest for using one of his patents without permission), De Forest went on to patent more than three hundred inventions.

De Forest's biggest breakthrough was the development of the Audion, or triode, vacuum tube, which detected radio signals and then amplified them. De Forest's improvements greatly increased listeners' ability to hear dots and dashes and, later, speech and music on a receiver set. His modifications were essential to the development of voice transmission, long-distance radio, and television. In fact, the Audion vacuum tube, which powered radios until the arrival of transistors and solid-state circuits in the 1950s, is considered by many historians to be the beginning of modern electronics. But again, bitter competition taints De Forest's legacy; although De Forest won a twenty-year court battle for the rights to the Audion patent, most engineers at the time agreed that Edwin Armstrong (who later developed FM radio) was the true inventor and disagreed with the U.S. Supreme Court's 1934 decision on the case that favored De Forest.[11]

The credit for the first voice broadcast belongs to Canadian engineer Reginald Fessenden, formerly a chief chemist for Thomas Edison. Fessenden went to work for the U.S. Navy and eventually for General Electric (GE), where he played a central role in improving wireless signals. Both the navy and GE were interested in the potential for voice transmissions. On Christmas Eve in 1906, after GE built Fessenden a powerful transmitter, he gave his first public demonstration, sending a voice

NIKOLA TESLA
A double-exposed photograph combines the image of inventor Nikola Tesla reading a book in his Colorado Springs, Colorado, laboratory in 1899 with the image of his Tesla coil discharging several million volts.

through the airwaves from his station at Brant Rock, Massachusetts. A radio historian describes what happened:

> *That night, ship operators and amateurs around Brant Rock heard the results: "someone speaking! . . . a woman's voice rose in song. . . . Next someone was heard reading a poem." Fessenden himself played "O Holy Night" on his violin. Though the fidelity was not all that it might be, listeners were captivated by the voices and notes they heard. No more would sounds be restricted to mere dots and dashes of the Morse code.*[12]

Ship operators were astonished to hear voices rather than the familiar Morse code. (Some operators actually thought they were having a supernatural encounter.) This event showed that the wireless medium was moving from a point-to-point communication tool (wireless operator to wireless operator) toward a one-to-many communication tool. **Broadcasting**, once an agricultural term that referred to the process of casting seeds over a large area, would come to mean the transmission of radio waves (and, later, TV signals) to a broad public audience. Before radio broadcasting, wireless was considered a form of **narrowcasting**, or person-to-person communication, like the telegraph and the telephone.

In 1910, De Forest transmitted a performance of *Tosca* by the Metropolitan Opera to friends in the New York area with wireless receivers. At this moment, radio passed from the novelty stage to the entrepreneurial stage, during which various practical uses would be tested before radio would launch as a mass medium.

Regulating a New Medium

The two most important international issues affecting radio in the first decade of the twentieth century were ship radio requirements and signal interference. Congress passed the Wireless Ship Act in 1910, which required that all major U.S. seagoing ships carrying more than fifty passengers and traveling more than two hundred miles off the coast be equipped with wireless equipment with a one-hundred-mile range. The importance of this act would be underscored two years later, when Britain's brand-new luxury steamship, the *Titanic*, sank in 1912. Although more than fifteen hundred people died in the tragedy, wireless reports played a critical role in pinpointing the *Titanic*'s location, enabling rescue ships to save over seven hundred lives.

Radio Waves as a Natural Resource

In the wake of the *Titanic* tragedy, Congress passed the **Radio Act of 1912**, which addressed the problem of amateur radio operators increasingly cramming the airwaves. Because radio waves crossed state and national borders, legislators determined that broadcasting constituted a "natural resource"—a kind of interstate commerce. This meant that radio waves could not be owned; they were the collective property of all Americans, just like national parks. Therefore, transmitting on radio waves would require licensing from the Commerce Department. This act, which governed radio until 1927, also formally adopted the SOS Morse-code distress signal, which other countries had been using for several years. Further, the "natural resource" mandate led to the idea that radio, and eventually television, should provide a benefit to society—in the form of education and public service. The eventual establishment of public radio stations was one consequence of this idea; the Fairness Doctrine was another.

The Impact of World War I

By 1915, more than twenty American companies sold wireless point-to-point communication systems, primarily for use in ship-to-shore communication. Having established a reputation for efficiency and honesty, American Marconi was the biggest and best of these companies. But in 1914, with the outbreak of World War I in Europe, and America warily watching the conflict, the U.S. Navy questioned the wisdom of allowing a foreign-controlled company to wield so much power. American corporations, especially GE and AT&T, capitalized on the navy's xenophobia and succeeded in undercutting Marconi's influence.

As wireless telegraphy played an increasingly large role in military operations, the navy sought tight controls on information. When the United States entered the war in 1917, the navy closed down all amateur radio operations and took control of key radio transmitters to ensure military security. In 1919, after the end of the war, British Marconi placed an order with GE for twenty-four potent new alternators, which were strong enough to power a transoceanic system of radio stations that could connect the world. But the U.S. Navy grew concerned and moved to ensure that such powerful new radio technology would not fall under foreign control.

At this time, President Woodrow Wilson and the navy saw an opportunity to slow Britain's influence over communication and to promote a U.S. plan for the control of emerging wireless operations as part of the larger goal of developing the United States as an international power. Thus, corporate heads and government leaders conspired to make sure radio communication would serve American interests.

The Formation of RCA

Some members of Congress and the corporate community opposed federal legislation that would grant the government or the navy a radio monopoly. Consequently, GE developed a compromise plan that would create a *private sector monopoly*—that is, a private company that would have the

NEWS OF THE *TITANIC*

Despite the headline in the *St. Louis Post-Dispatch*, 1,523 people died and 705 were rescued when the *Titanic* hit an iceberg on April 14, 1912 (the ship technically sank at 2:20 A.M. on April 15). The crew of the *Titanic* used the Marconi wireless equipment on board to send distress signals to other ships. Of the eight ships nearby, the *Carpathia* was the first to respond with lifeboats.

government's approval to dominate the radio industry. First, GE broke off negotiations to sell key radio technologies to European-owned companies like British Marconi, thereby limiting those companies' global reach. Second, GE took the lead in founding a new company, **Radio Corporation of America (RCA)**, which soon acquired American Marconi and radio patents of other U.S. companies. Upon its founding in 1919, RCA had pooled the necessary technology and patents to monopolize the wireless industry and expand American communication technology throughout the world.[13]

Under RCA's patent pool arrangement, wireless patents from the navy, AT&T, GE, the former American Marconi, and other companies were combined to ensure U.S. control over the manufacture of radio transmitters and receivers. Initially AT&T, then the government-sanctioned monopoly provider of telephone services, manufactured most transmitters, while GE (and later Westinghouse) made radio receivers. RCA administered the pool, collecting patent royalties and distributing them to pool members. To protect these profits, the government did not permit RCA to manufacture equipment or to operate radio stations under its own name for several years. Instead, RCA's initial function was to ensure that radio parts were standardized by manufacturers and to control frequency interference by amateur radio operators, which increasingly became a problem after the war.

A government restriction at the time mandated that no more than 20 percent of RCA could be owned by foreigners. This restriction, later raised to 25 percent, became law in 1927 and applied to all U.S. broadcasting stocks and facilities. Because of this rule, Rupert Murdoch—the head of Australia's News Corp.—became a U.S. citizen in 1985, so he could buy a number of TV stations and form the Fox television network. In 2013, the Federal Communications Commission ruled that it would allow exemptions to the 25 percent foreign ownership limit on a case-by-case basis.

RCA's most significant impact was that it gave the United States almost total control over the emerging mass medium of broadcasting. At the time, the United States was the only country that placed broadcasting under the care of commercial, rather than military or government, interests. By pooling more than two thousand patents and sharing research developments, RCA ensured the global dominance of the United States in mass communication, a position it maintained in electronic hardware into the 1960s and maintains in program content today.

THE EVOLUTION OF RADIO

When Westinghouse engineer Frank Conrad set up a crude radio studio above his Pittsburgh garage in 1916, placing a microphone in front of a phonograph to broadcast music and news to his friends (whom Conrad supplied with receivers) two evenings a week on experimental station 8XK, he unofficially became one of the medium's first disc jockeys. In 1920, a Westinghouse executive, intrigued by Conrad's curious hobby, realized the potential of radio as a mass medium. Westinghouse then established station KDKA, which is generally regarded as the first commercial broadcast station. KDKA is most noted for airing national returns from the Cox–Harding presidential election on November 2, 1920, an event most historians consider the first professional broadcast.

Other amateur broadcasters could also lay claim to being first. One of the earliest stations, operated by Charles "Doc" Herrold in San Jose, California, began in 1909 and later became KCBS. Additional experimental stations—in places like New York; Detroit; Medford, Massachusetts; and Pierre, South Dakota—broadcast voices and music prior to the establishment of KDKA. But KDKA's success, with the financial backing of Westinghouse, signaled the start of broadcast radio.

In 1921, the U.S. Commerce Department officially licensed five radio stations for operation; by early 1923, more than six hundred commercial and noncommercial stations were operating. Some of these stations were owned by AT&T, GE, and Westinghouse, but many were run by amateurs or were independently owned by universities or businesses. By the end of 1923, as many as 550,000 radio receivers, most manufactured by GE and Westinghouse, had been sold for about $55 each (about $701 in today's dollars). Just as the "guts" of the phonograph had been put inside a piece of furniture to create a consumer product, the vacuum tubes, electrical posts, and bulky batteries that made up the radio receiver were placed inside stylish furniture and marketed to households. By 1925, 5.5 million radio sets were in use across America, and radio was officially a mass medium.

Building the First Networks

In a major power grab in 1922, AT&T, which already had a government-sanctioned monopoly in the telephone business, decided to break its RCA agreements in an attempt to monopolize radio as well. Identifying the new medium as the "wireless telephone," AT&T argued that broadcasting was merely an extension of its control over the telephone. Ultimately, the corporate giant complained that RCA had gained too much monopoly power. In violation of its early agreements with RCA, AT&T began making and selling its own radio receivers.

In the same year, AT&T started WEAF (now WNBC) in New York, the first radio station to regularly sell commercial time to advertisers. AT&T claimed that under the RCA agreements it had the exclusive right to sell ads, which AT&T called *toll broadcasting*. Most people in radio at the time recoiled at the idea of using the medium for crass advertising, viewing it instead as a public information service. In fact, stations that had earlier tried to sell ads received "cease and desist" letters from the Department of Commerce. Yet by August 1922, AT&T had sold its first ad to a New York real estate developer for $50. The idea of promoting the new medium as a public service, along the lines of today's noncommercial NPR, ended when executives realized that radio ads offered another opportunity for profits long after radio-set sales had saturated the consumer market.

The initial strategy behind AT&T's toll broadcasting idea was an effort to conquer radio. Through its agreements with RCA, AT&T retained the rights to interconnect the signals between two or more radio stations via telephone wires. In 1923, when AT&T aired a program simultaneously on its flagship WEAF station and on WNAC in Boston, the phone company created the first **network**: a cost-saving operation that links (at that time, through special phone lines; today, through satellite relays) a group of broadcast stations that share programming produced at a central location. By the end of 1924, AT&T had interconnected twenty-two stations to air a talk by President Calvin Coolidge. Some of these stations were owned by AT&T, but most simply consented to become AT&T "affiliates," agreeing to air the phone company's programs. These network stations informally became known as the *telephone group* and later as the Broadcasting Corporation of America (BCA).

In response, GE, Westinghouse, and RCA interconnected a smaller set of competing stations, known as the *radio group*. Initially, their network linked WGY in Schenectady, New York (then GE's national headquarters), and WJZ in Manhattan. The radio group had to use inferior Western Union telegraph lines when AT&T denied the group access to its telephone wires. By this time, AT&T had sold its stock in RCA and refused to lease its lines to competing radio networks. The telephone monopoly was now enmeshed in a battle to defeat RCA for control of radio.

This clash, among other problems, eventually led to a government investigation and an arbitration settlement in 1925. In the agreement, the Justice Department, irritated by AT&T's power grab, redefined patent agreements. AT&T received a monopoly on providing the wires, known as *long lines*, to interconnect stations nationwide. In exchange, AT&T sold its BCA network to RCA for $1 million and agreed not to reenter broadcasting for eight years (a banishment that actually extended into the 1990s).

Bettmann/Getty Images

WESTINGHOUSE ENGINEER FRANK CONRAD

Broadcasting from his garage, Conrad transformed his hobby into Pittsburgh's KDKA, one of the first radio stations. Although this early station is widely celebrated in history books as the first broadcasting outlet, one cannot underestimate the influence Westinghouse had in promoting this "historical first." Westinghouse clearly saw the celebration of Conrad's garage studio as a way to market the company and its radio equipment. The resulting legacy of Conrad's garage studio has thus overshadowed other individuals who also experimented with radio broadcasting.

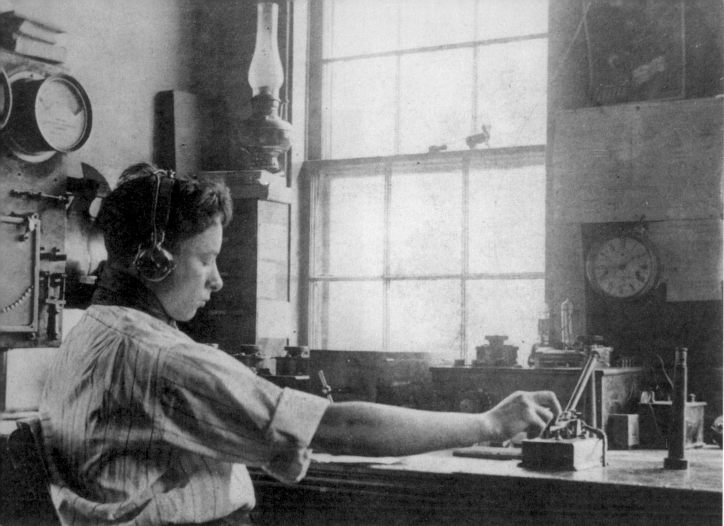

Bettmann/Getty Images

DAVID SARNOFF

As a young man, Sarnoff taught himself Morse code and learned as much as possible in Marconi's experimental shop in New York, after which he earned the job of wireless telegraph operator at Marconi's station on Nantucket Island. Sarnoff steadily rose through the ranks, ultimately creating NBC and network radio. Sarnoff's calculated ambition in the radio industry can easily be compared to Bill Gates's drive to control the computer software and Internet industries.

Sarnoff and NBC: Building the "Blue" and "Red" Networks

After Lee De Forest, David Sarnoff was among the first to envision wireless telegraphy as a modern mass medium. From the time he served as Marconi's personal messenger (at age fifteen), Sarnoff rose rapidly at American Marconi. He became a wireless operator, helping relay information about the *Titanic* survivors in 1912. Promoted to a series of management positions, Sarnoff was closely involved in RCA's creation in 1919, when most radio executives saw wireless merely as point-to-point communication. But with Sarnoff as RCA's first commercial manager, radio's potential as a mass medium was quickly realized. In 1921, at age thirty, Sarnoff became RCA's general manager.

In September 1926, soon after RCA bought AT&T's telephone group network (BCA), Sarnoff created a subsidiary called the National Broadcasting Company (NBC). Its ownership was shared by RCA (50 percent), General Electric (30 percent), and Westinghouse (20 percent). The loose network of stations that made up the new subsidiary would be connected by AT&T long lines. Shortly thereafter, the original telephone group became known as the NBC-Red network, and the radio group (the network established by RCA, GE, and Westinghouse) became the NBC-Blue network.

Although NBC owned a number of stations by the late 1920s, many independent stations began affiliating with the NBC networks to receive programming. NBC affiliates, though independently owned, signed contracts to be part of the network and paid NBC to carry their programs. In exchange, NBC reserved time slots, which it sold to national advertisers. NBC centralized costs and programming by bringing the best musical, dramatic, and comedic talent to one place, from which programs could be produced and then distributed all over the country. By 1933, NBC-Red had twenty-eight affiliates, and NBC-Blue had twenty-four. One result of this is that network radio may have actually helped modernize

America by de-emphasizing the local and the regional in favor of national programs broadcast to nearly everyone.

David Sarnoff's leadership at RCA was capped in 1929 by two negotiations that would solidify his stature as the driving force behind radio's development as a modern medium: cutting a deal with General Motors for the manufacture of car radios (under the brand name Motorola) and merging RCA with the Victor Talking Machine Company. From 1930 through the mid-1960s, the record and phonograph company would be known as RCA Victor, adopting as its corporate symbol the famous terrier sitting alertly next to a Victrola radio-phonograph. The merger gave RCA control over Victor's records and recording equipment, making the radio company a major player in the sound recording industry. In 1930, David Sarnoff became president of RCA, and he ran it for the next forty years.

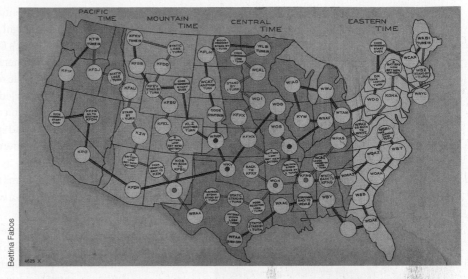

Bettina Fabos

THE RADIO GAME was released by Milton Bradley soon after David Sarnoff launched the National Broadcasting Company (NBC). This family-friendly board game is played on a stylized map of the United States, illustrated in four colors that represent the four U.S. time zones. Some circles on the map are linked by red lines, while others are linked by blue lines—representing the NBC-Red and NBC-Blue networks.

Government Scrutiny Ends RCA-NBC Monopoly

As early as 1923, the Federal Trade Commission (FTC) had charged RCA with violations of antitrust laws, but the FTC allowed the monopoly to continue. By the late 1920s, the government, concerned about NBC's growing control over radio content, intensified its scrutiny. Then, in 1930, federal marshals charged RCA-NBC with a number of violations, including exercising too much control over manufacturing and programming. The government had originally sanctioned a closely supervised monopoly for wireless communication, but after the collapse of the stock market in 1929, the public became increasingly distrustful of big business.

RCA acted quickly. To eliminate its monopolizing partnerships, Sarnoff's company proposed buying out GE's and Westinghouse's remaining shares in RCA's manufacturing business. Now RCA would compete directly against GE, Westinghouse, and other radio manufacturers, encouraging more competition in the radio manufacturing industry. In 1932, days before the antitrust case against RCA was to go to trial, the government accepted RCA's proposal for breaking up its monopoly. Ironically, in the mid-1980s GE bought RCA, a shell of its former self and no longer competitive with foreign electronics firms.[14] GE was chiefly interested in RCA's brand-name status and its still-lucrative subsidiary, NBC.

CBS and Paley: Challenging NBC

Even with RCA's head start and its favored status, the two NBC networks faced competitors in the late 1920s. These competitors, however, found it tough going. One group, United Independent Broadcasters (UIB), even lined up twelve prospective affiliates and offered them $500 a week for access to ten hours of station time in exchange for quality programs. UIB was cash poor, however, and AT&T would not rent the new company its lines to link the affiliates.

Enter the Columbia Phonograph Company, which was looking for a way to preempt RCA's merger with the Victor Talking Machine Company, then the record company's major competitor. With backing from Columbia, UIB launched the new Columbia Phonograph Broadcasting System (CPBS), a wobbly sixteen-affiliate network, in 1927. But after losing $100,000 in the first month, the record company pulled out. Later, CPBS dropped "Phonograph" from its title, creating the Columbia Broadcasting System (CBS).

CBS HELPED ESTABLISH ITSELF as a premier radio network by attracting top talent from NBC, like Eddie Cantor. *The Eddie Cantor Show* featured lighthearted comedy (Cantor would often tell stories about his wife and four daughters) and singers such as Ethel Merman (shown here), Deanna Durbin, and Dinah Shore. In 1934, Cantor introduced the song "Santa Claus Is Comin' to Town" (other singers had rejected it as being too silly), and by the next day, the song was a hit, having sold 100,000 copies of sheet music.

In 1928, William Paley, the twenty-seven-year-old son of Sam Paley, owner of a Philadelphia cigar company, bought a controlling interest in CBS to sponsor the cigar brand, La Palina. One of Paley's first moves was to hire public relations pioneer Edward Bernays to polish the new network's image. (Bernays played a significant role in the development of the public relations industry; see Chapter 12.) Paley and Bernays modified a concept called **option time**, in which CBS paid affiliate stations $50 per hour for an option on a portion of their time. The network provided programs to the affiliates and sold ad space or sponsorships to various product companies. In theory, CBS could now control up to twenty-four hours a day of its affiliates' radio time. Some affiliates received thousands of dollars per week merely to serve as conduits for CBS programs and ads. Because NBC was still charging some of its affiliates as much as $96 a week to carry its network programs, the CBS offer was extremely appealing.

By 1933, Paley's efforts had netted CBS more than ninety affiliates, many of them defecting from NBC. Paley also concentrated on developing news programs and entertainment shows, particularly soap operas and comedy-variety series. In the process, CBS successfully raided NBC, not just for affiliates but for top talent as well. Throughout the 1930s and 1940s, Paley lured a number of radio stars from NBC, including Jack Benny, Frank Sinatra, George Burns and Gracie Allen, and Groucho Marx. During World War II, Edward R. Murrow's powerful firsthand news reports from bomb-riddled London established CBS as the premier radio news network, a reputation it carried forward to television. In 1949, near the end of big-time network radio, CBS finally surpassed NBC as the highest-rated network. Although William Paley had intended to run CBS for only six months to help get it off the ground, he ultimately ran it for more than fifty years.

Bringing Order to Chaos with the Radio Act of 1927

In the 1920s, as radio moved from narrowcasting to broadcasting, the battle for more frequency space and less channel interference intensified. Manufacturers, engineers, station operators, network executives, and the listening public demanded action. Many wanted more sweeping regulation than the simple licensing function granted under the Radio Act of 1912, which gave the Commerce Department little power to deny a license or to unclog the airwaves.

Beginning in 1924, Commerce Secretary Herbert Hoover ordered radio stations to share time by setting aside certain frequencies for entertainment and news, and others for farm and weather reports. To challenge Hoover, a station in Chicago jammed the airwaves, intentionally moving its signal onto an unauthorized frequency. In 1926, the courts decided that based on the existing Radio Act, Hoover had the power only to grant licenses, not to restrict stations from operating. Within the year, two hundred new stations clogged the airwaves, creating a chaotic period in which nearly all radios had poor reception. By early 1927, sales of radio sets had declined sharply.

To restore order to the airwaves, Congress passed the **Radio Act of 1927**, which stated an extremely important principle—licensees did not *own* their channels but could only license them as long as they operated to serve the "public interest, convenience, or necessity." To oversee licenses and negotiate channel problems, the 1927 act created the **Federal Radio Commission (FRC)**, whose members were appointed by the president. Although the FRC was intended as a temporary committee, it grew into a powerful regulatory agency. With passage of the **Communications Act of 1934**, the FRC became the **Federal Communications Commission (FCC)**. Its jurisdiction covered not only radio but also the telephone and the telegraph (and later television, cable, and the Internet). More significantly, by this time Congress and the president had sided with the already-powerful radio networks and acceded to a system of advertising-supported commercial broadcasting as best serving the "public interest, convenience, or necessity," overriding the concerns of educational, labor, and citizen broadcasting advocates.[15] (See Table 5.1.)

Act	Provisions	Effects
Wireless Ship Act of 1910	Required U.S. seagoing ships carrying more than fifty passengers and traveling more than two hundred miles off the coast to be equipped with wireless equipment with a one-hundred-mile range.	Saved lives at sea, including more than seven hundred rescued by ships responding to the *Titanic*'s distress signals two years later.
Radio Act of 1912	Required radio operators to obtain a license, gave the Commerce Department the power to deny a license, and began a uniform system of assigning call letters to identify stations.	The federal government began to assert control over radio. Penalties were established for stations that interfere with other stations' signals.
Radio Act of 1927	Established the Federal Radio Commission (FRC) as a temporary agency to oversee licenses and negotiate channel assignments.	First expressed the now-fundamental principle that licensees did not *own* their channels but could only license them as long as they operated to serve the "public interest, convenience, or necessity."
Communications Act of 1934	Established the Federal Communications Commission (FCC) to replace the FRC. The FCC regulated radio; the telephone; the telegraph; and later television, cable, and the Internet.	Congress tacitly agreed to a system of advertising-supported commercial broadcasting despite concerns of the public.
Telecommunications Act of 1996	Eliminated most radio and television station ownership rules, some dating back more than fifty years.	Enormous national and regional station groups formed, dramatically changing the sound and localism of radio in the United States.

TABLE 5.1

MAJOR ACTS IN THE HISTORY OF U.S. RADIO

In 1941, an activist FCC went after the networks. Declaring that NBC and CBS could no longer force affiliates to carry programs they did not want, the government outlawed the practice of option time, which Paley had used to build CBS into a major network. The FCC also demanded that RCA sell one of its two NBC networks. RCA and NBC claimed that the rulings would bankrupt them. The Supreme Court sided with the FCC, however, and RCA eventually sold NBC-Blue for $8 million. Soon after, in mid-1944, the network became the American Broadcasting Company (ABC). These government crackdowns brought long-overdue reform to the radio industry, but they had not come soon enough to prevent considerable damage to noncommercial radio.

The Golden Age of Radio

Many programs on television today were initially formulated for radio. The first weather forecasts and farm reports on radio began in the 1920s. Regularly scheduled radio news analysis began in 1927, with H. V. Kaltenborn, a reporter for the *Brooklyn Eagle*, providing commentary on AT&T's WEAF. The first regular network news analysis began on CBS in 1930 and featured Lowell Thomas, who would remain on radio for forty-four years.

Early Radio Programming

Early on, only a handful of stations operated in most large radio markets, and popular stations were affiliated with CBS, NBC-Red, or NBC-Blue. Many large stations employed their own in-house orchestras and aired live music daily. Listeners had favorite evening programs, usually fifteen minutes long, to which they would tune in each night. Families gathered around the radio to hear such shows as *Amos 'n' Andy*, *The Shadow*, *The Lone Ranger*, *The Green Hornet*, and *Fibber McGee and Molly*, or one of President Franklin Roosevelt's fireside chats.

Among the most popular early programs on radio, the variety show was the forerunner to popular TV shows like the *Ed Sullivan Show*. The variety show, developed from stage acts and vaudeville, began with the *Eveready Hour* in 1923 on WEAF. Considered experimental, the program presented classical music, minstrel shows, comedy sketches, and dramatic readings. Stars from vaudeville, musical comedy, and New York theater and opera would occasionally make guest appearances.

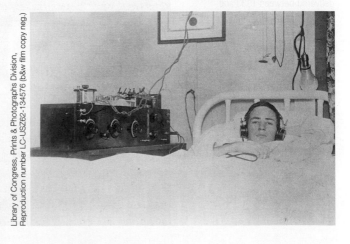

Library of Congress, Prints & Photographs Division, Reproduction number LC-USZ62-134576 (b&w film copy neg.)

A YOUNG MAN, who had broken his back while building a radio tower, sits in a hospital bed convalescing and listening to the radio.

By the 1930s, studio-audience quiz shows—*Professor Quiz* and the *Old Time Spelling Bee*—had emerged. The quiz format was later copied by television, particularly in the 1950s. *Truth or Consequences*, based on a nineteenth-century parlor game, first aired on radio in 1940 and featured guests performing goofy stunts. It ran for seventeen years on radio and another twenty-seven years on television, influencing TV stunt shows like CBS's *Beat the Clock* in the 1950s and NBC's *Fear Factor* in the early 2000s.

Dramatic programs, mostly radio plays that were broadcast live from theaters, developed as early as 1922. Historians mark the appearance of *Clara, Lu, and Em* on WGN in 1931 as the first soap opera. One year later, Colgate-Palmolive bought the program, put it on NBC, and began selling the soap products that gave this dramatic genre its distinctive nickname. Early "soaps" were fifteen minutes in length and ran five or six days a week. By 1940, sixty different soap operas occupied nearly eighty hours of network radio time each week.

Most radio programs had a single sponsor that created and produced each show. The networks distributed these programs live around the country, charging each sponsor advertising fees. Many shows—the *Palmolive Hour*, *General Motors Family Party*, *Lucky Strike Orchestra*, and the *Eveready Hour* among them—were named after the sole sponsor's product.

Radio Programming as a Cultural Mirror

The situation comedy, a major staple of TV programming today, began on radio in the mid-1920s. By the early 1930s, the most popular comedy was *Amos 'n' Andy*, which started on Chicago radio in 1925 before moving to NBC-Blue in 1929. *Amos 'n' Andy* was based on the conventions of the nineteenth-century minstrel show and featured black characters stereotyped as shiftless and stupid. Created as a blackface stage act by two white comedians, Charles Correll and Freeman Gosden, the program was criticized as racist. But NBC and the program's producers claimed that *Amos 'n' Andy* was as popular among black audiences as it was among white audiences.[16]

FIRESIDE CHATS

This giant bank of radio network microphones makes us wonder today how President Franklin D. Roosevelt managed to project such an intimate and reassuring tone in his famous fireside chats. Conceived originally to promote FDR's New Deal policies amid the Great Depression, these chats were delivered between 1933 and 1944 and touched on topics of national interest. Roosevelt was the first president to effectively use broadcasting to communicate with citizens; he also gave nearly a thousand press conferences during his twelve-plus years as president, revealing a strong commitment to using media and news to speak early and often with the American people.

Amos 'n' Andy also launched the idea of the serial show: a program that featured continuing story lines from one day to the next. The serial format would soon be copied by soap operas and other radio dramas. *Amos 'n' Andy* aired six nights a week from 7:00 to 7:15 P.M. During the show's first year on the network, radio-set sales rose nearly 25 percent nationally. To keep people coming to restaurants and movie theaters, owners broadcast *Amos 'n' Andy* in lobbies, restrooms, and entryways. Early radio research estimated that the program aired in more than half of all radio homes in the nation during the 1930–31 season, making it the most popular radio series in history. In 1951, it made a brief transition to television (Correll and Gosden sold the rights to CBS for $1 million), becoming the first TV series to have an entirely black cast. But amid a strengthening Civil Rights movement and a formal protest by the NAACP (which argued that "every character is either a clown or a crook"), CBS canceled the program in 1953.[17]

The Authority of Radio

The most famous single radio broadcast of all time was an adaptation of H. G. Wells's *War of the Worlds* on the radio series *Mercury Theatre on the Air*. Orson Welles produced, hosted, and acted in this popular series, which adapted science fiction, mystery, and historical adventure dramas for radio. On Halloween eve in 1938, the twenty-three-year-old Welles aired the 1898 Martian invasion novel in the style of a radio news program. For people who missed the opening disclaimer, the program sounded like a real news report, with eyewitness accounts of battles between Martian invaders and the U.S. Army.

The program created a panic that lasted several hours. In New Jersey, some people walked through the streets with wet towels around their heads for protection from deadly Martian heat rays. In New York, young men reported to their National Guard headquarters to prepare for battle. Across the nation, calls jammed police switchboards. Afterward, Orson Welles, once the radio voice of *The Shadow*, used the notoriety of this broadcast to launch his film career. Meanwhile, the FCC called for stricter warnings both before and during programs that imitated the style of radio news.

Bettmann/Getty Images

Bettmann/Getty Images

EARLY RADIO'S EFFECT AS A MASS MEDIUM

On Halloween eve in 1938, Orson Welles *(left)* broadcast a radio dramatization of *War of the Worlds* that created a panic up and down the East Coast, especially in Grover's Mill, New Jersey—the setting for the fictional Martian invasion that many listeners assumed was real. A seventy-six-year-old Grover's Mill resident *(right)* guards a warehouse against alien invaders.

RADIO REINVENTS ITSELF

Older media forms do not generally disappear when confronted by newer forms. Instead, they adapt. Although radio threatened sound recording in the 1920s, the recording industry adjusted to the economic and social challenges posed by radio's arrival. Remarkably, the arrival of television in the 1950s marked the only time in media history when a new medium stole virtually every national programming and advertising strategy from an older medium. Television snatched radio's advertisers, program genres, major celebrities, and large evening audiences. The TV set even physically displaced the radio as the living room centerpiece of choice across America.

Nevertheless, radio adapted and survived, a story that is especially important today, as newspapers, magazines, books, and other media appear in new digital formats. In contemporary culture, we have grown accustomed to such media convergence, but to better understand this blurring of the boundaries between media forms, it is useful to look at the 1950s and the ways in which radio responded to the advent of television with adaptive innovations in technology and program content.

Transistors Make Radio Portable

ADVERTISEMENTS for pocket transistor radios, which became popular in the 1950s, emphasized their portability.

A key development in radio's adaptation to television occurred with the invention of the transistor by Bell Laboratories in 1947. **Transistors** were small electrical devices that, like vacuum tubes, could receive and amplify radio signals. However, they used less power and produced less heat than vacuum tubes, and they were more durable and less expensive. Best of all, they were tiny. Transistors, which also revolutionized hearing aids, constituted the first step in replacing bulky and delicate tubes, eventually leading to today's integrated circuits.

Texas Instruments marketed the first transistor radio in 1953 for about $40. Using even smaller transistors, Sony introduced the pocket radio in 1957. But it wasn't until the 1960s that transistor radios became cheaper than conventional tube and battery radios. For a while, the term *transistor* became a synonym for a small portable radio.

The development of transistors let radio go where television could not—to the beach, to the office, into bedrooms and bathrooms, and into nearly all new cars. (Before the transistor, car radios were a luxury item.) By the 1960s, most radio listening took place outside the home.

New from Motorola
ALL-TRANSISTOR
Shirt-pocket radio
with powerful built-in speaker

Slips into your pocket...plays with the sound of a set twice its size.
New miniaturized transistor radio lets you enjoy favorite programs wherever you go. Powerful chassis pulls in stations loud and clean . . . plays them clear and mellow through a newly designed built-in speaker. A *single* low-cost battery gives many hours of listening pleasure. Motorola extras include magnifying lens for easy-to-read dial . . . durable case in black, blue, red, or green. 90-day warranty on all parts and labor at no additional cost.

Perfect gift for you or someone extra special

ONLY $**29**$^{**95**}* MODEL X11

ACTUAL SIZE . . . 4¼ inches high . . . weighs only 9 oz. with battery

Built-In Easel Stand in back for stable "stand-up" position.
Power-Packed Chassis with 6 transistors provides plenty of volume.
Built-In Antenna pulls in stations like a magnet for finest reception.
Perfect Companion for sports events. Earphone jack for private listening.

More to enjoy **MOTOROLA**

The FM Revolution and Edwin Armstrong

By the time the broadcast industry launched commercial television in the 1950s, many people, including David Sarnoff of RCA, were predicting radio's demise. To fund television's development and to protect his radio holdings, Sarnoff had even delayed a dramatic breakthrough in broadcast sound, what even he called a "revolution"—FM radio.

Edwin Armstrong, who first discovered and developed FM radio in the 1920s and early 1930s, is often considered the most prolific and influential inventor in radio history. He used De Forest's vacuum tube to invent an amplifying system that enabled radio receivers to pick up distant signals, rendering the enormous alternators used for generating power in early radio transmitters obsolete. In 1922, he sold a "super" version of his circuit to RCA for $200,000 and sixty thousand shares of RCA stock, which made him a millionaire as well as RCA's largest private stockholder.

Armstrong also worked on the major problem of radio reception: electrical interference. Between 1930 and 1933, the inventor filed five patents on **FM**, or frequency modulation. Offering static-free radio reception, FM supplied greater fidelity and clarity than AM did, making FM ideal for music. **AM**, or amplitude modulation (modulation refers to the variation in waveforms), stressed the volume, or height, of radio waves; FM accentuated the pitch, or distance, between radio waves (see Figure 5.2).

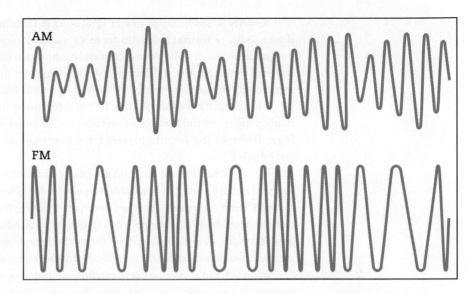

FIGURE 5.2

AM AND FM WAVES

Although David Sarnoff, RCA's president, thought that television would replace radio, he helped Armstrong set up the first experimental FM station atop the Empire State Building in New York City. Eventually, though, Sarnoff thwarted FM's development (which he was able to do because RCA had an option on Armstrong's new patents). Instead, in 1935, Sarnoff threw RCA's considerable weight behind the development of television. With the FCC allocating and reassigning scarce frequency spaces, RCA wanted to ensure that channels went to television before they went to FM. Most of all, however, Sarnoff wanted to protect RCA's existing AM empire. Thus, Sarnoff decided to close down Armstrong's station.

Armstrong forged ahead without RCA. He founded a new FM station and instructed other engineers, who established more than twenty experimental stations between 1935 and the early 1940s. In 1941, the FCC approved limited space allocations for commercial FM licenses. During the next few years, FM grew in fits and starts. Between 1946 and early 1949, the number of commercial FM stations expanded from forty-eight to seven hundred. But then the FCC (with RCA's urging) moved FM's frequency space to a new band on the electromagnetic spectrum, rendering some 400,000 prewar FM receiver sets useless. FM's future became uncertain, and by 1954, the number of FM stations had fallen to 560. On January 31, 1954, Edwin Armstrong—weary from years of legal skirmishes over patents with RCA, Lee De Forest, and others—wrote a note apologizing to his wife, removed the air conditioner from his thirteenth-story New York apartment window, and jumped to his death.

Although AM stations had greater reach, they could not match the crisp fidelity of FM, which made FM preferable for music. In the early 1960s, the FCC opened up more spectrum space for the superior sound of FM, infusing new life into radio. In the early 1970s, about 70 percent of listeners tuned almost exclusively to AM radio, but by the 1980s, FM had surpassed AM in profitability. By the 2010s, more than 75 percent of all listeners preferred FM. This expansion of FM represented one of the chief ways radio survived the advent of television.

The Rise of Format and Top 40 Radio

Live and recorded music had long been radio's single biggest staple, accounting for 48 percent of all programming in 1938. Although live music on radio was generally considered superior to recorded music, early disc jockeys made a significant contribution to the latter, demonstrating that music alone could drive radio. In fact, when television snatched radio's program ideas and national sponsors, radio's dependence on recorded music became a necessity and helped the medium survive the 1950s.

As early as 1949, station owner Todd Storz in Omaha, Nebraska, experimented with formula-driven radio, or **format radio**. Under this system, management rather than deejays controlled programming each hour. When Storz and his program manager noticed that bar patrons and waitstaff repeatedly played certain favorite songs from the records available in a jukebox, they began researching record sales to identify the most popular tunes. From observing jukebox culture, Storz hit on the idea of **rotation**: playing the top songs many times during the day. By the mid-1950s, the management-control idea combined with the rock-and-roll explosion, and the **Top 40 format** was born. The term *Top 40* came to refer to the forty most popular hits in a given week as measured by record sales.

As format radio grew, program directors combined rapid deejay chatter with the best-selling songs of the day and occasional oldies—popular songs from a few months earlier. By the early 1960s, to avoid "dead air," managers asked deejays to talk over the beginning and the end of a song so that listeners would feel less compelled to switch stations. Ads, news, weather forecasts, and station identifications were all designed to fit a consistent station environment. Listeners, tuning in at any moment, would recognize the station by its distinctive sound.

In format radio, management carefully coordinates, or programs, each hour, dictating what the deejay will do at various intervals throughout each hour of the day. Management creates a program log—once called a *hot clock* in radio jargon—that deejays must follow. By the mid-1960s, one study had determined that in a typical hour on Top 40 radio, listeners could expect to hear about twenty ads; numerous weather, time, and contest announcements; multiple recitations of the station's call letters; about three minutes of news; and approximately twelve songs.

Radio managers further sectioned off programming into day parts, which typically consisted of time blocks covering 6 to 10 A.M., 10 A.M. to 3 P.M., 3 to 7 P.M., and 7 P.M. to midnight. Each day part, or block, was programmed through ratings research according to who was listening. For instance, a Top 40 station would feature its top deejays in the morning and afternoon blocks, when audiences—many riding in cars—were largest. From 10 A.M. to 3 P.M., research determined that women at home and secretaries at work usually controlled the dial, so program managers, capitalizing on the gender stereotypes of the day, played more romantic ballads and less hard rock. Teenagers tended to be heavy evening listeners, so program managers often discarded news breaks at this time, since research showed that teens turned the dial when news came on.

Critics of format radio argued that only the top songs received play and that lesser-known songs deserving airtime received meager attention. Although a few popular star deejays continued to play a role in programming, many others quit when managers introduced formats. Program directors approached programming as a science, whereas deejays considered it an art form. The program directors' position, which generated more revenue, triumphed.

Resisting the Top 40

The expansion of FM in the mid-1960s created room for experimenting, particularly with classical music, jazz, blues, and non–Top 40 rock songs. **Progressive rock** emerged as an alternative to conventional formats. Many noncommercial stations broadcast from college campuses, where student deejays and managers rejected the commercialism associated with Top 40 tunes and began playing lesser-known alternative music and longer album cuts (such as Bob Dylan's "Desolation Row" and the Doors' "The End"). Until that time, most rock on the radio had been consigned almost exclusively to Top 40 formats, with song length averaging about three minutes.

Experimental FM stations, both commercial and noncommercial, offered a cultural space for hard-edged political folk music and for rock music that commented on the Civil Rights movement and protested America's

JUKEBOXES often played the same favorite songs over and over as requested by their listeners, who chose the songs. This inspired the idea of rotation in the radio industry.

WIN-Initiative/Getty Images

involvement in the Vietnam War. By the 1970s, however, progressive rock had been copied, tamed, and absorbed by mainstream radio under the format labeled **album-oriented rock (AOR)**. By 1972, AOR-driven album sales accounted for more than 85 percent of the retail record business. By the 1980s, as first-generation rock and rollers aged and became more affluent, AOR stations became less political and played mostly white, post-Beatles music, featuring such groups as Pink Floyd, Genesis, AC/DC, and Queen.

THE SOUNDS OF COMMERCIAL RADIO

Contemporary radio sounds very different from its predecessor. In contrast to the few stations per market in the 1930s, most large markets today include more than forty stations that vie for listener loyalty. Although a few radio personalities—such as Glenn Beck, Ryan Seacrest, Rush Limbaugh, Tom Joyner, Tavis Smiley, and Jim Rome—are nationally prominent, and some shows are syndicated nationally, local deejays and their music are the stars at most radio stations.

However, listeners today are unlike radio's first audiences in several ways. First, listeners in the 1930s tuned in to their favorite shows at set times. Today, less driven by particular shows, radio has become a secondary, or background, medium that follows the rhythms of daily life. In addition, people can listen to radio programs as podcasts any time of the day or night. Second, in the 1930s, peak listening time occurred during the evening hours—dubbed *prime time* in the TV era—while today's heaviest radio listening occurs during **drive time**, between 6 and 9 A.M. and between 4 and 7 P.M. Third, stations today are more specialized. Listeners are loyal to favorite stations, music formats, and even radio personalities, rather than to specific shows. Although more than fifteen thousand radio stations now operate in the United States, people generally listen to only four or five stations that target them.

Format Specialization

Stations today use a variety of formats based on managed program logs and day parts. All told, more than forty different radio formats, plus variations, serve diverse groups of listeners (see Figure 5.3). To please advertisers, who want to know exactly who is listening, formats usually target audiences

FIGURE 5.3

THE MOST POPULAR RADIO FORMATS IN THE UNITED STATES AMONG PERSONS AGE TWELVE AND OLDER

Data from: Nielsen report: "State of the Media: Audio Today 2018, How America Listens," April 2018, www.nielsen.com /content/dam/corporate/us/en /reports-downloads/2018 -reports/audio-today-report -apr-2018.pdf.

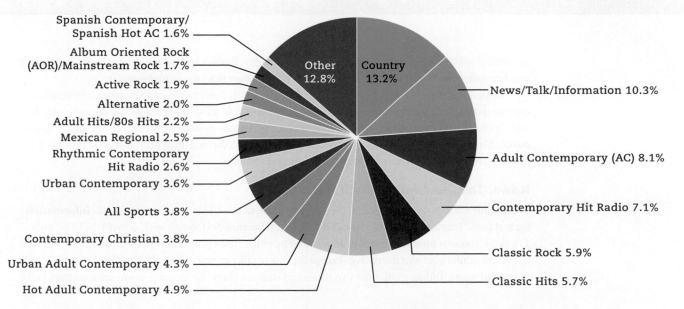

How Did Talk Radio Become So One-Sided?

For young adults, news/talk/information radio is in another universe. Radio listeners ages eighteen to thirty-four are all about music, with country, pop contemporary hit radio, and urban contemporary as their top radio formats.

It turns out that radio listeners ages fifty-five to sixty-four live in that other universe. Their top radio format is news/talk/information.[1] According to Nielsen research, the news/talk/information universe is also mostly white and male. The masters of that universe—the leading radio personalities—are Rush Limbaugh, Sean Hannity, Dave Ramsey, Michael Savage, Glenn Beck, Mark Levin, George Noory, Laura Ingraham, Mike Gallagher, and Hugh Hewitt (see Table 5.2). Although there are some moderates (e.g., Jim Bohannon) and progressives/liberals (e.g., Thom Hartmann and Stephanie Miller)

among the top fifteen, their rarity suggests one other thing about the news/talk/information universe: it's predominantly politically conservative.[2]

How did one point of view come to dominate news/talk/information in the United States? Its roots were in the repeal of a little-known regulation that had been on the books of the Federal Communications Commission for decades. Since 1949, the FCC enforced what was called the Fairness Doctrine. This allowed "a station to editorialize, provided it made air time available for 'balanced presentation of all responsible viewpoints on particular issues.'"[3]

The rationale behind the doctrine was that there were a limited number of stations on the public airwaves, and that broadcast stations should serve the public interest of the communities where they were located. Consumer advocate Ralph Nader argued that "such issues as women's rights, the health effects of smoking, and the safety of nuclear power plants would have come to far less public prominence had the fairness doctrine not been in effect."[4]

But by 1987, President Reagan was pushing business-friendly deregulation. A chief target for the broadcasting industry was the Fairness Doctrine, since broadcasters did not like the additional demands of reporting contrasting positions on controversial public issues. The National Association of Broadcasters (NAB) stated

according to their age, income, gender, or race/ethnicity. Radio's specialization enables advertisers to reach smaller target audiences at costs that are much lower than those for television.

Targeting listeners has become extremely competitive, however, because forty or fifty stations may be available in a large radio market. About 10 percent of all stations across the country switch formats each year in an effort to find a formula that generates more advertising money. Some stations, particularly those in large cities, even rent blocks of time to various local ethnic or civic groups; this enables the groups to dictate their own formats and sell ads.

News, Talk, and Information Radio

The nation's fastest-growing format throughout much of the 1990s was the **news/talk/information** format (see "Examining Ethics: How Did Talk Radio Become So One-Sided?" above). In 1987, only 170 radio stations operated formats dominated by either news programs or talk shows, which tend to appeal to adults over age thirty-five (except for sports talk programs, which draw mostly male sports fans of all ages). Today, more than two thousand stations carry the format—more stations than carry that broadcasters could report evenhandedly without regulation. "Broadcasters believe in fairness and generally report both sides of controversial issues, but want to do so without Uncle Sam looking over our shoulders," the NAB's executive director said.

After its 1987 repeal, radio broadcasters did not continue to "report both sides of controversial issues," as the NAB had promised, but instead rolled out new programs that *created controversy* with very one-sided political opinions. As media historians Robert Hilliard and Michael Keith explain, the demise of the Fairness Doctrine changed the tenor of talk radio. "Ostensibly this put no limits on any ideas, philosophies, or other political matter a station might wish to advocate. In reality, it swung the tide of radio and television political advocacy to the right."[5]

Limbaugh, still talk radio's biggest star, was the first conservative talk show host to go national in 1988. He moved from Sacramento to New York City and was a huge hit for ABC Radio, after which a host of conservative personalities flooded the airwaves. "My success has spawned dozens of imitators. It has touched off a frantic scramble to cash in," Limbaugh wrote.[6] Limbaugh's support of conservative causes in his national radio program led to the Republicans gaining control of the House of Representatives in 1994. Republicans acknowledged their debt to Limbaugh and named him an "honorary member of their class."[7]

There was an attempt at a liberal talk radio network with Air America from 2004 to 2010. It featured personalities like Thom Hartmann, Al Franken, Montel Williams, Janeane Garofalo, and Marc Maron and helped introduce America to current MSNBC host Rachel Maddow. Yet Air America could never build the critical mass that conservative talk had. Rush Limbaugh has about 590 affiliate stations for his three-hour weekday show. Air America could never get more than 70 affiliate stations to run its programs.

But another alternative to commercial news/talk/information has thrived: noncommercial news/talk/information. While Limbaugh's rise was meteoric, since the 1970s NPR has slowly built a broad base of listeners for its nonprofit, nonpartisan public radio network.

Rush Limbaugh's audience is commercial talk radio's largest, at 14 million weekly listeners. NPR's two-hour flagship *Morning Edition* program has a weekly audience of 14.9 million listeners at more than 800 affiliate stations.[8] As a noncommercial alternative, NPR does not focus on personalities (*Morning Edition*'s four hosts are largely unrecognizable compared to Limbaugh or Hannity) and is heavily based in reporting, not commentary, with reporters in seventeen U.S. locations as well as seventeen countries.

Still, commercial news/talk/information holds a significant edge on the airwaves, in politics, and in overall radio ratings, with 8.3 percent of the U.S. listening audience compared to 4 percent of the national listening audience for noncommercial news/talk.[9]

any other format. It is the most dominant format on AM radio and the second most popular format (by number of listeners) in the nation (see Figure 5.3 and Table 5.2). A news/talk/information format, though more expensive to produce than a music format, appeals to advertisers looking to target working- and middle-class adult consumers. Nevertheless, most radio stations continue to be driven by a variety of less expensive music formats.

TABLE 5.2

TOP TALK RADIO WEEKLY AUDIENCE (IN MILLIONS)

Data from: Talkers magazine, "The Top Talk Radio Audiences," March 2018.

Note: * = Information unavailable; N/A = Talk-show host not nationally broadcast.

Talk-Show Host	2003	2008	2016	2018
Rush Limbaugh (Conservative)	14.50	14.25	13.25	14
Sean Hannity (Conservative)	11.75	13.25	12.50	13.50
Dave Ramsey (Financial Advice)	*	4.50	8.25	13
Michael Savage (Conservative)	7.00	8.25	5.25	11
Glenn Beck (Conservative)	*	6.75	7.00	10
Mark Levin (Conservative)	N/A	5.50	7.00	10

Music Formats

The **adult contemporary (AC)** format, also known as middle-of-the-road, or MOR, is among radio's oldest and most popular formats, reaching about 8.1 percent of all listeners, most of them over age forty, with an eclectic mix of news, talk, oldies, and soft rock music—what *Broadcasting* magazine describes as "not too soft, not too loud, not too fast, not too slow, not too hard, not too lush, not too old, not too new." Now encompassing everything from rap to pop-punk songs, Top 40 radio—also called **contemporary hit radio (CHR)**—still appeals to many teens and young adults. A renewed focus on producing pop singles in the sound recording industry has recently boosted listenership of this format.

Country is the most popular format in the nation (except during morning drive time, when news/talk/information is number one). Many stations are in tiny markets, where country is traditionally the default format for communities with only one radio station. Country music has old roots in radio, beginning in 1925 with the influential *Grand Ole Opry* program on WSM in Nashville. Although Top 40 drove country music out of many radio markets in the 1950s, the growth of FM in the 1960s brought it back, as station managers looked for market niches not served by rock music.

Many formats appeal to particular ethnic or racial groups. In 1947, WDIA in Memphis was the first station to program exclusively for black listeners. Now called **urban contemporary**, this format targets a wide variety of African American listeners, primarily in large cities. Urban contemporary, which typically plays popular dance, rap, R&B, and hip-hop music (featuring performers like Drake and Cardi B), also subdivides by age, featuring an urban AC category with performers like Maxwell, Alicia Keys, and Bruno Mars.

Spanish-language radio, one of radio's fastest-growing formats, is concentrated mostly in large Hispanic markets, such as Miami, New York, Chicago, Las Vegas, California, Arizona, New Mexico, and Texas (where KCOR, the first all-Spanish-language station, originated in San Antonio in 1947). Besides talk shows and news segments in Spanish, this format features a variety of Spanish, Caribbean, and Latin American musical styles, including calypso, flamenco, mariachi, merengue, reggae, samba, salsa, and Tejano.

In addition, today there are formats that are spin-offs from album-oriented rock. Classic rock serves up rock favorites from the mid-1960s through the 1980s to the baby-boom generation and other listeners who have outgrown Top 40. The oldies format originally served adults who grew up on 1950s and early-1960s rock and roll. As that audience has aged, oldies formats now target younger audiences with the classic hits format, featuring songs from the 1970s, 1980s, and 1990s. The alternative format recaptures some of the experimental approach of the FM stations of the 1960s, although with much more controlled playlists, and has helped introduce such artists as Awolnation and Cage the Elephant.

Research indicates that most people identify closely with the music they listened to as adolescents and young adults. This tendency partially explains why classic hits and classic rock stations combined have surpassed CHR stations today. It also helps explain the recent nostalgia for music from the 1980s and 1990s.

Nonprofit Radio and NPR

Nonprofit radio maintains a voice in a landscape dominated by commercial radio conglomerates. But the road to viability for nonprofit radio in the United States has not been easy. In the 1930s, the Wagner-Hatfield Amendment to the 1934 Communications Act intended to set aside 25 percent of radio for

WENDY WILLIAMS
refers to herself as the "queen of all media," but before her daytime TV talk show, she got her start with a nearly two-decade career in radio. She began as a substitute deejay on an urban contemporary station in New York before gaining notoriety with her celebrity interviews and gossip.

Julie Jacobson/AP Images

a wide variety of nonprofit stations. When the amendment was defeated in 1935, the future of educational and noncommercial radio looked bleak. Many nonprofits had sold out to for-profit owners during the Great Depression of the 1930s. The stations that remained were often banished from the air during the evening hours or assigned weak signals by federal regulators who favored commercial owners and their lobbying agents. Still, nonprofit public radio survived. Today, more than six thousand full-power and low-power nonprofit stations operate, most of them on the FM band.

The Early Years of Nonprofit Radio

Two government rulings, both in 1948, aided nonprofit radio. First, the government began authorizing noncommercial licenses to stations not affiliated with labor, religious, education, or civic groups. The first license went to Lewis Kimball Hill, a radio reporter and pacifist during World War II who started the **Pacifica Foundation** to run experimental public stations. Pacifica stations, like Hill, have often challenged the status quo in radio as well as in government. Most notably, in the 1950s, they aired the poetry, prose, and music of performers who were considered radical, left-wing, or communist and who were blacklisted by television and seldom acknowledged by AM stations. Over the years, Pacifica has been fined and reprimanded by the FCC and Congress for airing programs that critics considered inappropriate for public airwaves. Today, Pacifica has more than one hundred affiliate stations.

Second, the FCC approved 10-watt FM stations. A 10-watt station with a broadcast range of only about seven miles took very little capital to operate, allowing more people to participate (before this, radio stations had to have at least 250 watts to get licensed). Such stations became training sites for students interested in broadcasting. Although the FCC stopped licensing new 10-watt stations in 1978, about one hundred longtime 10-watters are still in operation.

Creation of the First Noncommercial Networks

During the 1960s, nonprofit broadcasting found a Congress sympathetic to an old idea: using radio and television as educational tools. As a result, **National Public Radio (NPR)** and the **Public Broadcasting Service (PBS)** were created as the first noncommercial networks. Under the provisions of the **Public Broadcasting Act of 1967** and the **Corporation for Public Broadcasting (CPB)**, NPR and PBS were mandated to provide alternatives to commercial broadcasting. Today, NPR's popular news and interview programs, such as *Morning Edition* and *All Things Considered*, are thriving, contributing to the network's weekly audience of thirty-two million listeners.

Over the years, however, public radio has faced waning government support and the threat of losing its federal funding. In 1994, a conservative majority in Congress cut financial support and threatened to scrap the CPB, the funding authority for public broadcasting. In 2011, the House voted to end financing for the CPB, but the Senate voted against the measure. Consequently, stations have become more reliant on private donations and corporate sponsorship, which could cause some public broadcasters to steer clear of controversial subjects, especially those that critically examine corporations (see "Media Literacy and the Critical Process: Comparing Commercial and Noncommercial Radio" on page 150).

Like commercial stations, nonprofit radio has adopted the format style. However, the dominant style in public radio is a loose variety format whereby a station may actually switch from jazz, classical music, and alternative rock to news and talk during different parts of the day. Noncommercial radio remains the place for both tradition and experimentation, as well as for programs that do not draw enough listeners for commercial success.

New Radio Technologies Offer More Stations

Over the past decade or so, two alternative radio technologies have helped expand radio beyond its traditional AM and FM bands and bring more diverse sounds to listeners: satellite and HD (digital) radio.

LaunchPad
macmillan learning
launchpadworks.com

Going Visual: Video, Radio, and the Web
This video looks at how radio stations adapted to the Internet by providing multimedia on their websites to attract online listeners.

Discussion: If video is now important to radio, what might that mean for journalism and broadcasting students who are considering a job in radio?

MEDIA LITERACY AND THE CRITICAL PROCESS

Comparing Commercial and Noncommercial Radio

1 DESCRIPTION Listen to a typical morning or late-afternoon hour of a popular local commercial news/talk radio station and a typical hour of your local NPR station from the same time period for two to three days. Keep a log of what topics are covered and what news stories are reported. For the commercial station, log what commercials are carried and how much time in an hour is devoted to ads. For the noncommercial station, note both how much time is devoted to recognizing the station's sources of funding and who the supporters are.

2 ANALYSIS Look for patterns. What kinds of stories are covered? What kinds of topics are discussed? Create a chart to categorize the stories. To cover events and issues, do the stations use actual reporters at the scene? How much time is given to reporting compared to time devoted to opinion? How many sources are cited in each story? What kinds of interview sources are used? Are they expert sources or person-on-the-street interviews? How many sources are men, and how many are women?

3 INTERPRETATION What do these patterns mean? Is there a balance between reporting and opinion? Do you detect any bias, and if so, what is it? Are

the stations serving as watchdogs to ensure that democracy's best interests are being served? What effect, if any, do you think the advertisers/supporters have on the programming? What arguments might you make about commercial and noncommercial radio based on your findings?

4 EVALUATION Which station seems to be doing a better job serving its local audience? Why? Do you buy the 1930s argument that noncommercial stations serve narrow, special interests while commercial stations serve capitalism

After the arrival and growth of commercial TV, the Corporation for Public Broadcasting (CPB) was created in 1967 as the funding agent for public broadcasting— an alternative to commercial TV and radio featuring educational and cultural programming that could not be easily sustained by commercial broadcasters in search of large general audiences. As a result, National Public Radio (NPR) developed to provide national programming to public stations to supplement local programming efforts. Today, NPR affiliates get just 2 percent of their funding from the federal government. Most money for public radio comes from corporate sponsorships, individual grants, and private donations.

and the public interest? Why or why not? From which station did you learn the most? Explain. Which station did you find most entertaining? Why? What did you like and dislike about each station?

5 ENGAGEMENT Join your college radio station. Talk to the station manager about the goals for a typical hour of programming and what audience the station is trying to reach. Finally, pitch program or topic ideas that would improve your college station's programming.

Satellite Radio

A series of satellites launched to cover the continental United States created a subscription-based national **satellite radio** service. Two companies, XM and Sirius, completed their national introduction by 2002 and merged into a single provider in 2008. The merger was precipitated by the companies' struggles to make a profit after building competing satellite systems and battling for listeners. SiriusXM offers about 174 digital music, news, and talk channels to the continental United States, with monthly prices starting at $14.99 and satellite radio receivers costing from $50 to $200. SiriusXM access is also available on mobile devices via an app.

Programming includes a range of music channels, from rock and reggae to Spanish Top 40 and opera, as well as channels dedicated to NASCAR, NPR, cooking, and comedy. Another feature of satellite radio's programming is popular personalities who host their own shows or have their own channels, including Howard Stern, Martha Stewart, Oprah Winfrey, and Bruce Springsteen. U.S. automakers (investors in the satellite radio companies) now equip most new cars with a satellite band, in addition to AM and FM, in order to promote further adoption of satellite radio. SiriusXM had about 32.7 million subscribers by 2018 (for comparison, Spotify had more than twice that number).

HD Radio

Available to the public since 2004, **HD radio** is a digital technology that enables AM and FM radio broadcasters to multicast up to three additional compressed digital signals within their traditional analog frequency. For example, KNOW, a public radio station at 91.1 FM in Minneapolis–St. Paul, runs its National Public Radio news/talk/information format on 91.1 HD1, runs Radio Heartland (acoustic and Americana music) on 91.1 HD2, and runs the BBC News service on 91.1 HD3. About twenty-two hundred radio stations now broadcast in HD. To tune in, listeners need a radio with the HD band, which brings in high-quality digital signals. Digital HD radio also provides program data, such as artist name and song title, and enables listeners to tag songs for playlists that can later be downloaded to an iPod and purchased on iTunes. The rollout of HD has been slow, but by 2016, every major auto manufacturer was selling automobile models with built-in HD radio receivers.

Radio and Convergence

Like every other mass medium, radio is moving into the future by converging with the Internet. Interestingly, this convergence is taking radio back to its roots in some respects. Internet radio allows for much more variety in radio, which is reminiscent of radio's earliest years, when nearly any individual or group with some technical skill could start a radio station. Moreover, *podcasts* bring back such content as storytelling, instructional programs, and local topics of interest, which have largely been missing in corporate radio. And portable listening devices like smartphones, tablets, and iPods hark back to the compact portability that first came with the popularization of transistor radios in the 1950s.

Internet Radio

Internet radio emerged in the 1990s with the popularity of the web. Internet radio stations come in two types. The first involves an existing AM, FM, satellite, or HD station "streaming" a simulcast version of its on-air signal over the web. Many radio stations currently stream programming over the web and often facilitate the listening with an app. iHeartRadio is one of the major streaming sites for broadcast and custom digital stations. The second kind of online radio station is one that has been created exclusively for the Internet. Pandora, 8tracks, Slacker, and Last.fm are some of the leading Internet radio services. In fact, services like Pandora allow users to have more control over their listening experience and the selections that are played. Listeners can create individualized stations based on a specific artist or song that they request.

Beginning in 2002, a Copyright Royalty Board established by the Library of Congress began to assess royalty fees for streaming copyrighted songs over the Internet based on a percentage of each station's revenue. Webcasters complained that royalty rates set by the board were too high and threatened their financial viability—particularly compared to satellite radio, which pays a lower royalty rate, and broadcasters, who pay no royalty rates at all. For decades, radio broadcasters have paid mechanical royalties to songwriters and music publishers but no royalties to the performing artists or record companies. Broadcasters have argued that the promotional value of getting songs played is sufficient compensation.

In 2009, Congress passed the Webcaster Settlement Act, which was considered a lifeline for Internet radio. The act enabled Internet stations to negotiate royalty fees directly with the music industry, at rates presumably more reasonable than what the Copyright Royalty Board had proposed.

RADIO STORIES FROM AROUND THE WORLD

Radio can make us laugh, save our lives, confound us with technical advances, and weaken our democratic self-governance with its absence. Here are four stories of radio from four countries.

England

What could the radio station, Mansfield 103.2, do? In July 2017, a radio hacker (also called a pirate) with a high-quality transmitter was hijacking its signal and playing a deliberately offensive song about masturbation over the airwaves. It was happening over and over, and children were heard humming the ditty, called "The Winker's Song," in their parents' cars. Written and performed by Doc Cox (a.k.a. Ivor Biggun) in the 1970s, "The Winker's Song"—also called "The Wanker's Song" or "I'm a Wanker"—refers to a "wanker" thirty-six times; the song was never broadcast during the 1970s because of its obscene content.[1]

While the masturbation song was causing some listeners to laugh, others were aghast and incredulous that Britain's communications regulator could not catch the pirate(s). Hacking a radio signal is surprisingly easy; as long as a person has a portable transmitter and the know-how to lock into the same frequency and modulation as a radio station's receiving equipment, he or she can override the signal at the receiver. The tactic saw significant use during World War II and the Cold War. Today, signal jamming happens throughout China, Russia, the Middle East, Africa, and Pakistan. However, it is still uncommon in Britain and the United States. According to Mansfield 103.2's managing director, "There [was] absolutely nothing we could do about it."

Norway

In December 2017, Norway did something drastic: the country switched off its entire national FM network in favor of digital technology. (The national radio channels switched, but the local radio stations stayed on FM for the time being.) As the first country to do this, Norway cited numerous benefits: better sound quality, the possibility of many more channels, and significant cost savings (digital is one-eighth the cost of FM radio). However, the move has been controversial. At the time of the transition, digital audio broadcasting had not yet reached the entire country and was available in only 49 percent of Norwegians' cars. In addition, many radio users opposed having to buy expensive new radio receivers ($150–$300) if they wanted to keep on listening. To help Norwegians get used to digital radio, the country transitioned one section at a time over the course of an entire year, and although national radio listening took a temporary nosedive, it is on its way up

In 2012, Clear Channel (now iHeartMedia) became the first company to strike a deal directly with the recording industry. The company pledged to pay royalties to Big Machine Label Group for broadcasting the songs of Taylor Swift and its other artists in exchange for a limit on the royalties it had to pay for streaming those artists' music on its iHeartRadio.com site.

Clear Channel's deal with the music industry opened up a new dialogue about equalizing the royalty rates paid by broadcast radio, satellite radio, and Internet radio. Tim Westergren, founder of Pandora, argued before Congress in 2012 that the rates were most unfair to companies like his. In the previous year, Westergren said, Pandora had paid 50 percent of its revenue for performance royalties, whereas satellite radio service SiriusXM had paid 7.5 percent, and broadcast radio had paid nothing.

again. Countries planning to go all digital in the coming years are Switzerland, Britain, and Denmark.[2]

India

Radio saves lives in India. The fishermen of Kerala, a state in southern India, have begun to venture farther and farther away from the coast to catch their fish. The reason is overfishing (fish stocks has been depleted) and climate change (fish are migrating to different waters). Because their boats are small and flimsy, Kerala fishermen are at risk: one bad monsoon storm and they might not come home. Fortunately, a radio station called Radio Monsoon has begun providing daily weather forecasts in a number of local languages along the coast. Radio weather broadcasts have made fishing much safer for about thirty thousand families in the area, who depend on fishing for their livelihood.[3]

Hungary

As a post-communist country entering the twenty-first century, Hungary looked as if it would become a leading democracy in eastern Europe. Instead, the country has more recently slid backward, with an authoritarian leader, Viktor Orbán, taking control of nearly every institution (political, legal, cultural) in Hungary. After gaining a political majority in 2010, Orbán's next step was to take over the news media. Radio was an immediate target.

Orbán and his Fidesz Party appointed several new managers to head up Hungarian public radio, who then pushed out about one thousand employees (one-third of the entire radio staff) and enforced a propaganda mentality. The leader also created a National Media and Communications Authority, which set out to impose heavy fines for any news (both print and broadcast) that was critical of the government. Because the government of Hungary is a major advertiser in the national media, Orbán's government regularly withheld advertising from media organizations that it disfavored, which often brought financial ruin to the organization. The surviving privately owned media are held by Orbán's allies.[4]

In April 2018, the latest casualty in Hungarian independent media was the popular commercial radio station Lánchíd Rádió. It was "the last independent commercial radio station to broadcast countrywide," and closed at the same time as *Magyar Nemzet*, the last major independent opposition newspaper in Hungary.[5] Both were owned by a political opponent of Orbán and closed within days of Orbán's party retaining power after the election. A Hungarian analyst explained that with the win by Orbán, the newspaper and radio station owner decided that "it was no longer worth his while" to maintain these businesses: "He [saw] the results [of the election], anticipate[d] government revenge, and is shutting down unprofitable media organisations."[6]

As Reuters reported, "Orban's Fidesz party, in power since 2010, has turned public broadcasters into obedient mouthpieces, his closest allies have bought big stakes in privately owned media and advertising has been channelled to heavily benefit government-friendly outlets. Businessmen close to the premier purchased then shuttered *Nepszabadsag*, the country's top opposition newspaper, in 2016. They also bought up nearly all regional dailies and acquired dozens of radio licenses covering the entire country."[7]

He noted that a car equipped with an AM/FM radio, satellite radio, and streaming Internet radio could deliver the same song to a listener through all three technologies, but the various radio services would pay markedly different levels of performance royalties to the artist and record company.[18]

Podcasting and Portable Listening

Developed in 2004, **podcasting** (the term marries *iPod* and *broadcasting*) refers to the practice of making audio files available on the Internet so that listeners can download and listen to them on their phones, iPods, or computers. This distribution method quickly became mainstream, as mass media companies created commercial podcasts to promote and extend existing content, such as news and

LaunchPad
macmillan learning
launchpadworks.com

Radio: Yesterday, Today, and Tomorrow

Scholars and radio producers explain how radio adapts to and influences other media.

Discussion: Do you expect that the Internet will be the end of radio, or will radio stations still be around decades from now?

reality TV, while independent producers developed new programs, such as public radio's *Serial*, a popular weekly audio nonfiction narrative. As noted earlier, by 2017 a third of Americans were tuning in to podcasts, and one out of six Americans listened to podcasts at least once a week.[19]

For the broadcast radio industry, portability used to mean listening on a transistor or a car radio. But with the digital turn to iPods and mobile phones, broadcasters have not been as easily available on today's primary portable audio devices. Hoping to change that, the National Association of Broadcasters has been lobbying the FCC and the mobile phone industry to include FM radio capability in all mobile phones. New mobile phones in the United States now have FM radio chips, but by 2018, Sprint, Samsung, and LG were the only major cell phone companies or manufacturers to enable the chips with the NextRadio app.[20] Although the NAB argues that the enabled radio chip would be most important for enabling listeners to access local broadcast radio in times of emergencies and disasters, the chip would also be commercially beneficial for radio broadcasters, putting them on the same digital devices as their nonbroadcast radio competitors, like Pandora. At the same time, radio streaming apps like iHeartRadio and TuneIn offer an alternative means for listening to thousands of radio stations on mobile phones.

THE ECONOMICS OF BROADCAST RADIO

Radio continues to be one of the most used mass media, reaching about 90 percent of American teenagers and adults every week.[21] Because of radio's broad reach, the airwaves are very desirable real estate for advertisers, who want to reach people in and out of their homes; for record labels, who want their songs played; and for radio station owners, who want to create large radio groups to dominate multiple markets.

Local and National Advertising

About 10 percent of all U.S. spending on media advertising goes to radio stations. Like newspapers, radio generates its largest profits by selling local and regional ads. Thirty-second radio spot ads range from $1,500 in large markets to just a few dollars in the smallest markets. Today, gross advertising receipts for radio are between $13.9 and $17 billion.[22] (The radio industry stopped reporting annual revenue in 2016, a signal that radio's revenue growth trend is declining.)[23] About 75 percent of radio revenues are from local ad sales, with the remainder in national spot, network, and digital radio sales. Digital sales—advertisements on web pages and apps, for example—are an area of advertising growth for radio.[24] Although industry revenue has dropped from a peak of $21.7 billion in 2006, the number of stations keeps growing, now totaling 15,499 stations (4,633 AM stations, 6,741 FM commercial stations, and 4,125 FM educational stations).[25] Unlike television, in which nearly 40 percent of a station's expenses goes toward buying syndicated programs, local radio stations get much of their content free from the recording industry. Therefore, only about 20 percent of a typical radio station's budget goes toward covering programming costs. But, as noted earlier, that free music content is in doubt, as the music industry—which already charges performance royalties for Internet radio stations—moves toward charging radio broadcasters performance royalties for playing music on the air.

When radio stations want to purchase programming, they often turn to national network radio, which generates more than $1 billion in ad sales annually by offering dozens of specialized services. For example, Westwood One—the nation's largest radio network service, managed by Cumulus Media—reaches more than 245 million consumers a week with a range of programming, including regular network radio news (CBS, CNBC, CNN), entertainment programs (*The Bob & Tom Show*), talk shows (*The Mark Levin Show*), and complete twenty-four-hour formats (*Hot Country, Hits Now!, Jack FM*). Dozens of companies offer national program and format services, typically providing local stations with programming in exchange for time slots for national ads. The most successful radio network programs are the shows broadcast by affiliates in the Top 20 markets, which offer advertisers half of the country's radio audience.

Manipulating Playlists with Payola

Radio's impact on music industry profits has required ongoing government oversight to expose illegal playlist manipulation. **Payola**, the practice by which record promoters pay deejays to play particular records, was rampant during the 1950s as record companies sought to guarantee record sales (radio airplay serves to popularize recordings; see Chapter 4). In response, management took control of programming, arguing that if individual deejays had less impact on which records would be played, the deejays would be less susceptible to bribery.

Despite congressional hearings and new regulations, payola persisted. Record promoters showered their favors on a few influential high-profile deejays, whose backing could make or break a record nationally, or on key program managers in charge of Top 40 formats in large urban markets. In 2010, Univision Radio paid $1 million to settle allegations of payola and end an FCC investigation.

More recently, as streaming music and streaming radio services have grown, the practice of payola has resurfaced. But because streaming services are not broadcasting, they fall outside the FCC's oversight. *Billboard* magazine reports that music promoters have been paying to influence playlists at services like Spotify, Deezer, and Apple Music. These playlists, used by hundreds of thousands of subscribers as a way to discover music, are created by the streaming services, influential individuals, or the music labels themselves. Spotify announced in 2015 that it would prohibit any playlists that had been influenced by money or other compensation. Yet the three major music corporations are themselves invested in influencing streaming music. Universal Music Group features its music playlists on Digster, Sony showcases its music on Filtr, and Warner Music Group promotes its playlists on Topsify.[26]

Radio Ownership: From Diversity to Consolidation

The **Telecommunications Act of 1996** substantially changed the rules concerning ownership of the public airwaves because the FCC eliminated most ownership restrictions on radio. As a result, twenty-one hundred stations and $15 billion changed hands that year alone. From 1995 to 2005, the number of radio station owners declined by one-third, from sixty-six hundred to about forty-four hundred.[27]

Once upon a time, the FCC tried to encourage diversity in broadcast ownership. From the 1950s through the 1980s, a media company could not own more than seven AM, seven FM, and seven TV stations nationally and could own only one radio station per market. Just prior to the 1996 act, the ownership rules were relaxed to allow any single person or company to own up to twenty AM, twenty FM, and twelve TV stations nationwide, but only two in the same market.

The 1996 act allows individuals and companies to acquire as many radio stations as they want, with relaxed restrictions on the number of stations a single broadcaster may own in the same city: The larger the market or area, the more stations a company may own within that market. For example, in areas where forty-five or more stations are available to listeners, a broadcaster may own up to eight stations, but not more than five of one type (AM or FM). In areas with fourteen or fewer stations, a broadcaster may own up to five stations (three of any one type). In very small markets with a handful of stations, a broadcast company may not own more than half the stations. As a result of the consolidations permitted by the 1996 deregulation, in most American cities, just a few corporations dominate the radio market.

After passage of the 1996 Telecommunications Act, several enormous radio corporations came to dominate American radio. Consider the cases of Clear Channel Communications and Cumulus, two of the largest radio chain owners in terms of number of stations owned (see Table 5.3). Clear Channel Communications was formed in 1972 with one San Antonio station. Eventually, it gobbled up enough conglomerates to become the largest radio chain owner in the country, peaking in a pre-recession 2005 with 1,205 stations. Today, as iHeartMedia, it owns 849 radio stations and almost 600,000 billboard and outdoor displays in twenty countries, including about 99,000 displays in forty-three of the fifty largest U.S. markets. iHeartMedia also distributes many of the leading syndicated programs—including *The Rush Limbaugh Show, The Glenn Beck Program, On Air with Ryan Seacrest*, and *Delilah*—through its Premiere Networks business. iHeartMedia is also an Internet

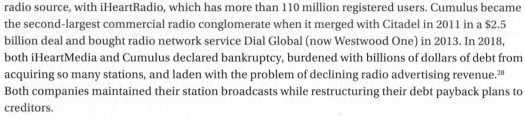

Rank	Company	Number of Stations
1	iHeartMedia (Top property: WLTW-FM, New York)	849
2	Educational Media Foundation (KLVB, Citrus Heights, CA)	664
3	Cumulus Media (KNBR-AM, San Francisco)	445
4	Townsquare Media (KSAS-FM, Boise)	317
5	Entercom (WEEI-AM, Boston)	235
6	Alpha Media (KINK-FM, Portland, OR)	229
7	American Family Radio (WAFR, Tupelo, MS)	188
8	Salem Media Group (KLTY, Dallas–Ft. Worth)	115
9	Saga Communications (WSNY, Columbus, OH)	108
10	Midwest Communications (WTAQ-FM, Green Bay)	75

TABLE 5.3

TOP TEN RADIO COMPANIES (BY NUMBER OF STATIONS), 2018

Data from: The 10-K annual reports and business profiles for each radio company.

ALTERNATIVE RADIO VOICES

can also be found on college stations, typically started by students and community members. There are around 520 such stations currently active in the United States, broadcasting in an eclectic variety of formats. Throughout the years, college radio has become a major outlet for new indie bands.

radio source, with iHeartRadio, which has more than 110 million registered users. Cumulus became the second-largest commercial radio conglomerate when it merged with Citadel in 2011 in a $2.5 billion deal and bought radio network service Dial Global (now Westwood One) in 2013. In 2018, both iHeartMedia and Cumulus declared bankruptcy, burdened with billions of dollars of debt from acquiring so many stations, and laden with the problem of declining radio advertising revenue.[28] Both companies maintained their station broadcasts while restructuring their debt payback plans to creditors.

Townsquare Media, the fourth largest radio company, launched in 2010 with the buyout of a 62-station group and grew to 317 stations by 2018 by focusing on acquiring stations in midsize markets. Entercom, the Pennsylvania-based radio chain, nearly doubled its number of stations after its 2017 acquisition of CBS Radio. Two other major radio groups, the Educational Media Foundation and American Family Radio, are nonprofit religious broadcasters. The Educational Media Foundation also syndicates the K-Love and Air1 contemporary Christian music formats to hundreds of stations. American Family Radio is a conservative Christian activist organization that was originally established by Rev. Donald Wildmon in 1977 as the National Federation for Decency. Salem Media Group is a commercial Christian-format radio chain.

A smaller radio conglomerate, but one that is perhaps the most dominant in a single-format area, is Univision. Univision is the top Spanish-language radio broadcaster in the United States (with about 70 broadcast and digital stations); the largest Spanish-language television broadcaster in the United States (see Chapter 6); and the owner of the top Spanish-language cable networks (Galavisión, UniMás, and Univision Deportes Network) and Univision Online, the most popular Spanish-language website in the United States.

Alternative Voices

As large corporations gained control of America's radio airwaves, activists in hundreds of communities across the United States protested in the 1990s by starting up their own noncommercial "pirate" radio stations, capable of broadcasting over a few miles with low-power FM signals of 1 to 10 watts. The NAB and other industry groups pressed to have the pirate broadcasters shut down, citing their illegality and their potential to create interference with existing stations. Between 1995 and 2000, more than five hundred illegal micropower radio stations were shut down. Still, an estimated one hundred to one thousand pirate stations are in operation in the United States, in both large urban areas and small rural towns.

The major complaint of pirate radio station operators was that the FCC had long ago ceased licensing low-power community radio stations. In 2000, the FCC, responding to tens of thousands of inquiries about the development of a new local radio broadcasting service, approved a new noncommercial **low-power FM (LPFM)** class of 100-watt stations (with a broadcast reach of about five miles) to give voice to local groups lacking access to the public airwaves. LPFM station licensees included mostly religious groups but also high schools, colleges and universities, Native American tribes, labor groups, and museums.

LPFM stations are located in unused frequencies on the FM dial. Still, the NAB and NPR fought to delay and limit the number of LPFM stations, arguing that such stations would cause interference with existing full-power FM stations. The passage of the Local Community Radio Act in 2011 created opportunities for more LPFM station applications in 2013. By 2018, more than 2,170 LPFM stations were licensed to broadcast. A major advocate of LPFM stations is the Prometheus Radio Project, a nonprofit formed by radio activists in 1998. Prometheus has helped educate community organizations about low-power radio and has sponsored at least a dozen "barn raisings" to build community stations in places like Hudson, New York; Opelousas, Louisiana; and Woodburn, Oregon.

LOW-POWER FM RADIO
To help communities or organizations set up LPFM stations, nonprofit groups like the Prometheus Radio Project provide support in obtaining government licenses and also construct the stations. For construction endeavors known as "barn raisings," Prometheus will send volunteers "to raise the antenna mast, build the studio, and flip on the station switch." Shown here is the barn raising for station WRFU 104.5 FM in Urbana, Illinois.

RADIO AND THE DEMOCRACY OF THE AIRWAVES

As radio was the first national electronic mass medium, its influence in the formation of American culture cannot be overestimated. Radio has given us soap operas, situation comedies, and broadcast news; it helped popularize rock and roll, car culture, and the politics of talk radio. Yet for all its national influence, broadcast radio in the United States is still a supremely local medium (see "Global Village: Radio Stories from around the World" on page 152). For decades, listeners have tuned in to hear the familiar voices of their community's deejays and talk-show hosts and hear the regional flavor of popular music over publicly owned airwaves.

The early debates over radio gave us one of the most important and enduring ideas in communication policy: a requirement to operate in the "public interest, convenience, or necessity." But the broadcasting industry has long been at odds with this policy, arguing that radio corporations invest heavily in technology and should be able not only to have more control over the radio frequencies on which they operate but also to own as many stations as they want. Deregulation in the past few decades has moved the industry closer to that corporate vision, as nearly every radio market in the nation is dominated by a few owners, who are required to renew their broadcasting licenses only every eight years.

This trend in ownership has moved radio away from its localism, as radio groups often manage hundreds of stations from afar. Given broadcasters' reluctance to publicly raise questions about their own economic arrangements, public debate regarding radio as a natural resource has remained minuscule. As citizens look to the future, a big question remains to be answered: With a few large broadcast companies now permitted to dominate radio ownership nationwide, how much is consolidation of power restricting the number and kinds of voices permitted to speak over the public airwaves? To ensure that mass media industries continue to serve democracy and local communities, the public needs to play a role in developing the answer to this question.

5 Chapter Review

COMMON THREADS

One of the Common Threads discussed in Chapter 1 is the developmental stages of mass media. Like other mass media, radio evolved in three stages, but it also influenced an important dichotomy in mass media technology: wired versus wireless.

In radio's novelty stage, several inventors transcended the wires of the telegraph and telephone to solve the problem of wireless communication. In the entrepreneurial stage, inventors tested ship-to-shore radio, while others developed person-to-person toll radio transmissions and other schemes to make money from wireless communication. Finally, when radio stations began broadcasting to the general public (who bought radio receivers for their homes), radio became a mass medium.

As the first electronic mass medium, radio set the pattern for an ongoing battle between wired and wireless technologies. For example, television brought images to wireless broadcasting. Then, cable television's wires brought television signals to places where receiving antennas did not work. Satellite television (wireless from outer space) followed as an innovation to bring TV where cable did not exist. Now, broadcast, cable, and satellite all compete against one another.

Similarly, think about how cell phones have eliminated millions of traditional phone, or land, lines. The Internet, like the telephone, also began with wires, but Wi-Fi and home wireless systems are eliminating those wires, too. And radio? Most listeners get traditional local (wireless) radio broadcast signals, but now listeners may use a wired Internet connection to stream Internet radio or download webcasts and podcasts. The radio industry's push for the future is to ensure that all mobile phones have enabled FM radio chips so that listeners can access local broadcast radio wirelessly, anytime and anyplace.

Both wired and wireless technologies have advantages and disadvantages. Do we want the stability and the tethers of a wired connection? Or do we want the freedom and occasional instability ("Can you hear me now?") of wireless media? Can radio's development help us understand wired-versus-wireless battles in other media?

KEY TERMS

The definitions for the terms listed below can be found in the glossary at the end of the book. The page numbers listed with the terms indicate where the term is highlighted in the chapter.

telegraph, 129
Morse code, 129
electromagnetic waves, 130
radio waves, 130
wireless telegraphy, 130
wireless telephony, 131
broadcasting, 132
narrowcasting, 132
Radio Act of 1912, 133
Radio Corporation of America (RCA), 134
network, 135
option time, 138
Radio Act of 1927, 138
Federal Radio Commission (FRC), 138

Communications Act of 1934, 138
Federal Communications Commission (FCC), 138
transistors, 142
FM, 143
AM, 143
format radio, 144
rotation, 144
Top 40 format, 144
progressive rock, 144
album-oriented rock (AOR), 145
drive time, 145
news/talk/information, 146
adult contemporary (AC), 148
contemporary hit radio (CHR), 148

country, 148
urban contemporary, 148
Pacifica Foundation, 149
National Public Radio (NPR), 149
Public Broadcasting Service (PBS), 149
Public Broadcasting Act of 1967, 149
Corporation for Public Broadcasting (CPB), 149
satellite radio, 150
HD radio, 151
Internet radio, 151
podcasting, 153
payola, 155
Telecommunications Act of 1996, 155
low-power FM (LPFM), 157

REVIEW QUESTIONS

Early Technology and the Development of Radio

1. Why was the development of the telegraph important in media history? What were some of the disadvantages of telegraph technology?

2. How is the concept of wireless different from that of radio?

3. What was Guglielmo Marconi's role in the development of wireless telegraphy?

4. What were Lee De Forest's contributions to radio?

5. Why was the RCA monopoly formed?

6. How did broadcasting, unlike print media, come to be federally regulated?

The Evolution of Radio

7. What was AT&T's role in the early days of radio?

8. Why did the government-sanctioned RCA monopoly end?

9. What is the significance of the Radio Act of 1927 and the Communications Act of 1934?

Radio Reinvents Itself

10. How did radio adapt to the arrival of television?

11. What was Edwin Armstrong's role in the advancement of radio technology? Why did RCA hamper Armstrong's work?

12. What is format radio, and why was it important to the survival of radio?

The Sounds of Commercial Radio

13. Why are there so many radio formats today?

14. Why did Top 40 radio diminish as a format in the 1980s and 1990s?

15. What is the state of nonprofit radio today?

16. Why are performance royalties a topic of debate between broadcast radio, satellite radio, Internet radio, and the recording industry?

The Economics of Broadcast Radio

17. What are the current ownership rules governing American radio?

18. What has been the main effect of the Telecommunications Act of 1996 on radio station ownership?

19. Why did the FCC create a new class of low-power FM stations?

Radio and the Democracy of the Airwaves

20. Throughout the history of radio, why did the government encourage monopoly or oligopoly ownership of radio broadcasting?

21. What is the relevance of localism to debates about ownership in radio?

QUESTIONING THE MEDIA

1. Count the number and types of radio stations in your area today. What formats do they use? Do a little research, and find out who owns the stations in your market. How much diversity is there among the highest-rated stations?

2. If you could own and manage a commercial radio station, what format would you choose, and why?

3. How might radio be used to improve social and political discussions in the United States?

4. If you were a broadcast radio executive, what arguments would you make in favor of broadcast radio over Internet radio?

LAUNCHPAD FOR *MEDIA & CULTURE*

Visit LaunchPad for *Media & Culture* at launchpadworks.com for additional learning tools:

- REVIEW WITH LEARNINGCURVE
  LearningCurve, available on LaunchPad for *Media &*

Culture, uses gamelike quizzing to help you master the concepts you need to learn from this chapter.

Television and Cable

The Power of Visual Culture

ON A FRIDAY NIGHT (and into Saturday morning) in early November 2017, 361,000 viewers binge-watched all nine episodes of the just-released second season of *Stranger Things*, one of Netflix's biggest hits. The audience ratings service Nielsen called this a "significant viewing experience." On that night, the second season's first episode alone—an homage to Steven Spielberg's *E.T.* and *Close Encounters of Third Kind*—drew an estimated 15.8 million viewers.[1] By contrast, the second season premiere of *Big Bang Theory*, a perennial Top 5 network show, drew a measly 10 million viewers back in 2008.

With more than 120 million subscribers around the world by mid-2018, the streaming juggernaut has stepped up its game and struck fear into network executives. It acquired the rights to Jerry Seinfeld's *Comedians in Cars Getting Coffee*, a web series the comedian started in 2012, signed

◄ Original content from streaming providers, like Netflix's *Stranger Things*, has shifted the way we consume our TV.

THE ORIGINS AND DEVELOPMENT OF TELEVISION
p. 163

THE DEVELOPMENT OF CABLE
p. 168

TECHNOLOGY AND CONVERGENCE CHANGE VIEWING HABITS
p. 172

MAJOR PROGRAMMING TRENDS
p. 173

REGULATORY CHALLENGES TO TELEVISION AND CABLE
p. 182

THE ECONOMICS AND OWNERSHIP OF TELEVISION AND CABLE
p. 187

TELEVISION, CABLE, AND DEMOCRACY
p. 194

up late night talk-show host David Letterman to do a six-episode interview program titled *My Next Guest Needs No Introduction*, and enlisted producer and screenwriting mastermind Shonda Rhimes to create new projects."[2]

For 2018, Netflix planned to spend "$8 billion on original TV shows and movies . . . and expects to have about 700 programs available for customers."[3] What is surprising, even to Netflix executives, is the appetite viewers have for programming from other nations and their willingness to watch movies and TV shows that are subtitled, a taboo in the old network era of television. In 2018, the streaming behemoth aired its first series in Arabic (a supernatural thriller titled *Jinn*) and in Danish (a postapocalyptic series titled *The Rain*). Overall, Netflix planned to stream about eighty new foreign-language TV shows and movies in 2018 alone.

Historically, United States film studios, networks, and cable services have adapted programs from other countries, like *The Office*, *Big Brother*, and *The Voice*. It is, of course, a lot cheaper to stream a subtitled original program than produce a whole new U.S. version, as media analyst Rich Greenfield notes when commenting on the cost-effectiveness of Netflix's global strategy: "We had this assumption in our brains, this kind of believed fact, that people only wanted content in their own native language in this country. I think what Netflix has proven over the last year is that subtitles, in many ways, have been a way of life overseas for a lot of content."[4]

Many media analysts and traditional network executives view Netflix as a disruptive force, turning the TV and cable programming business on its head. First, streaming services like Amazon and Netflix are financed mostly by inexpensive monthly subscription packages. Therefore, they are not subject to the TV ratings game or advertiser pressure that has dictated what is available on network television for half a century. Second, Netflix has a stable of executives authorized to find good stories from all over the world. Netflix's chief content officer, Ted Sarandos, has noted, "Every one of our creative executives has buying power. . . . They can greenlight a big-budget show in the room without me."[5] Third, in doing original programming, Netflix is not locked into the old network dictate of making twenty-two to twenty-four shows per season, often shooting a single episode in less than two weeks. Instead, Netflix has adopted the cable model of HBO and Showtime, producing series with as few as six and usually no more than ten or twelve episodes per season. A postproduction sound editor in Los Angeles notes that for an episode of a hit show like CBS's *NCIS*, his team might get three days to finish the sound, whereas for an HBO program or a Netflix production, he usually gets eight days to complete the work.[6] This kind of production schedule promotes quality, with fewer shows and more time to do each show. Finally, Netflix is not beholden to a traditional fall launch schedule, when the most promising network shows debut. Netflix promotes and releases new programs—some original productions and some licensed from other countries— pretty much every week.

Netflix's enormous subscriber base demonstrates its appeal to viewers who ultimately appreciate the wide international choice of stories. Netflix, probably more so than any other entertainment company, understands the cross-cultural power of storytelling and is thus gambling on a model for story distribution that seems to be a safe bet. What is yet unclear is the future of network television. How are the traditional networks adapting to the Netflix model, and what will happen to the networks over the next decade or so?

THE LEGACY BROADCAST NETWORKS TODAY may resent the development of original programming by streaming services like Netflix, but in the beginning, network television actually stole most of its programming and business ideas from radio. Old radio scripts began reappearing in TV form, snatching radio's sponsors, its program ideas, and even its prime-time evening audience. For example, in 1949, *The Lone Ranger* rode over to television from radio, where it had originated in 1933. Since replacing radio in the 1950s as our most popular mass medium, television has sparked repeated arguments about its social and cultural impact. Television has not only been accused of having a negative impact on children but also faced criticism for enabling and sustaining a sharply partisan political system. But there are other sides to this story. In times of crisis, our fragmented and pluralistic society has embraced television as common ground. It was TV that exposed many to Civil Rights violations in the South and to the shared loss after the Kennedy and King assassinations in the 1960s. On September 11, 2001—in shock and horror—we turned on our TV sets to learn that nearly three thousand people had been killed in that day's terrorist attacks. In 2013, we viewed the Boston Marathon bombing attacks on TV and online, and in 2018, we watched yet another school shooting when a gunman killed seventeen students and teachers in Parkland, Florida. For better or worse, television remains a central touchstone in our daily lives.

LaunchPad
macmillan learning

launchpadworks.com

Visit LaunchPad for *Media & Culture* and use LearningCurve to review concepts from this chapter.

In this chapter, we examine television and cable's cultural, social, and economic impact. We will:

- Review television's early technological development
- Discuss the TV boom in the 1950s and the impact of the quiz-show scandals
- Examine cable's technological development and basic services
- Explore new viewing technologies, such as computers, smartphones, and tablets
- Learn about major programming genres: comedy, drama, news, and reality TV
- Trace the key rules and regulations of television and cable
- Inspect the costs related to the production, distribution, and syndication of programs
- Investigate the impact of television and cable on democracy and culture

As you read this chapter, think about your own experiences with television programs and the impact they have on you. What was your favorite show growing up? Were there shows you weren't allowed to watch when you were young? If so, why? Were there shows your whole family watched together? Which ones? What attracts you to your favorite programs today? For more questions to help you think through the role of television and cable in our lives, see "Questioning the Media" in the Chapter Review.

THE ORIGINS AND DEVELOPMENT OF TELEVISION

In 1948, only 1 percent of America's households had a TV set; by 1953, more than 50 percent had one; and since the early 1960s, more than 90 percent of all homes have at least one. Television's rise throughout the 1950s created fears that radio—as well as books, magazines, and movies—would become irrelevant and unnecessary, but both radio and print media adapted. In fact, today more radio stations are operating and more books and magazines are published than ever before; only ticket sales for movies have declined slightly since the 1960s.

Three major historical developments in television's early years helped shape its growth: (1) technological innovations and patent wars, (2) the wresting of content control from advertisers, and (3) the sociocultural impact of the infamous quiz-show scandals.

Early Innovations in TV Technology

In its novelty stage, television's earliest pioneers were trying to isolate TV waves from the electromagnetic spectrum (as radio's pioneers had done with radio waves). The big question was, if a person could transmit audio signals from one place to another, why not visual images as well? Inventors from a number of nations toyed with the idea of sending "tele-visual" images for nearly a hundred years before what we know as TV developed.

Bettmann/Getty Images

From roughly 1897 to 1907, the development by several inventors of the *cathode ray tube*, the forerunner of the TV picture tube, combined principles of the camera and electricity. Because television images could not physically float through the air, technicians and inventors developed a method of encoding them at a transmission point (TV station) and decoding them at a reception point (TV set). In the 1880s, German inventor Paul Nipkow developed the *scanning disk*, a large flat metal disk with a series of small perforations organized in a spiral pattern. As the disk rotated, it separated pictures into pinpoints of light that could be transmitted as a series of electronic lines. As the disk spun, each small hole scanned one line of a scene to be televised. For years, Nipkow's mechanical disk served as the foundation for experiments on the transmission of visual images.

Electronic Technology: Zworykin and Farnsworth

The story of television's invention included a complex patents battle between two independent inventors: Vladimir Zworykin and Philo Farnsworth. It began in Russia in 1907, when physicist Boris Rosing improved Nipkow's mechanical scanning device. Rosing's lab assistant, Vladimir Zworykin, left Russia for America in 1919 and went to work for Westinghouse and then RCA. In 1923, Zworykin invented the *iconoscope*, the first TV camera tube to convert light rays into electrical signals, and he received a patent for it in 1928.

Around the same time, Idaho teenager Philo Farnsworth also figured out that a mechanical scanning system would not send pictures through the air over long distances. On September 7, 1927, the twenty-one-year-old Farnsworth transmitted the first electronic TV picture: He rotated a straight line scratched on a square of painted glass by 90 degrees. RCA, then the world leader in broadcasting technology, challenged Farnsworth in a major patents battle, in part over Zworykin's innovations for Westinghouse and RCA. Farnsworth had to rely on his high school science teacher to retrieve his original drawings from 1922. Finally, in 1930, Farnsworth received a patent for the first electronic television.

After the company's court defeat, RCA's president, David Sarnoff, had to negotiate to use Farnsworth's patents. Farnsworth later licensed these patents to RCA and AT&T for use in the commercial development of television. At the end of television's development stage, Farnsworth conducted the first public demonstration of television at the Franklin Institute in Philadelphia in 1934—five years *before* RCA's famous public demonstration at the 1939 World's Fair.

Setting Technical Standards

Figuring out how to push TV as a business and elevate it to a mass medium meant creating a coherent set of technical standards for product manufacturers. In the late 1930s, the National Television Systems Committee (NTSC), a group representing major electronics firms, began outlining industry-wide manufacturing practices and compromising on technical standards. As a result, the Federal Communications Commission (FCC) adopted an **analog** standard (based on radio waves) for all U.S. TV sets in 1941. About thirty countries, including Japan, Canada, Mexico, Saudi Arabia, and most Latin American nations, also adopted this system. (Most of Europe and Asia, however, adopted a slightly superior technical system shortly thereafter.)

The United States continued to use analog signals until 2009, when they were replaced by **digital** signals. These signals translate TV images and sounds into binary codes (ones and zeros like computers use) and allow for increased channel capacity and improved image quality and sound. HDTV, or *high-definition television*, digital signals offer the highest resolution and sharpest image.

Assigning Frequencies and Freezing TV Licenses

In the early days of television, the number of TV stations a city or market could support was limited because airwave spectrum frequencies interfered with one another. Thus, a market could have a channel 2 and a channel 4 but not a channel 3. Cable systems "fixed" this problem by sending channels through cable wires that don't interfere with one another. Today, a frequency that once carried one analog TV signal can carry eight or nine compressed digital channels.

PHILO FARNSWORTH, one of the inventors of television, experiments with an early version of an electronic TV set.

In the 1940s, the FCC began assigning channels in specific geographic areas to make sure there was no interference. In fact, there were many years when New Jersey had no TV stations because the signals would have interfered with the New York stations. By 1948, however, the FCC had issued nearly one hundred TV licenses, and there was growing concern about the finite number of channels and the frequency-interference problems. As a result, the FCC declared a freeze on new licenses from 1948 to 1952.

During this time, cities such as New York, Chicago, and Los Angeles had several TV stations, while other areas—including Little Rock, Arkansas, and Portland, Oregon—had none. In non-TV cities, movie audiences increased. Cities with TV stations, however, saw a 20 to 40 percent drop in movie attendance during this period. Taxi receipts and nightclub attendance also fell in TV cities, as did library book circulation. Radio listening also declined.

After a second NTSC conference in 1952 sorted out the technical problems, the FCC ended the licensing freeze, and almost thirteen hundred communities received TV channel allocations. By the mid-1950s, there were more than four hundred television stations in operation—a 400 percent surge since the prefreeze era—and television became a mass medium. Today, about seventeen hundred TV stations are in operation.

The Introduction of Color Television

In 1952, the FCC tentatively approved an experimental CBS color system. However, because black-and-white TV sets could not receive its signal, the system was incompatible with the sets most Americans owned. In 1954, RCA's color system, which sent TV images in color but allowed older sets to receive the color images as black-and-white, usurped CBS's system to become the color standard. Although NBC began broadcasting a few shows in color in the mid-1950s, it wasn't until 1966, when the consumer market for color sets had taken off, that the Big Three networks (CBS, NBC, and ABC) broadcast their entire evening lineups in color.

Controlling Content—TV Grows Up

By the early 1960s, television had become a dominant mass medium and cultural force, with more than 90 percent of U.S. households owning at least one set. Television's new standing came as its programs moved away from the influence of radio and established a separate identity. Two important contributors to this identity were a major change in the sponsorship structure of television programming and, more significant, a major scandal.

Program Format Changes Inhibit Sponsorship

Like radio in the 1930s and 1940s, early TV programs were often developed, produced, and supported by a single sponsor. Many of the top-rated programs in the 1950s included the sponsor's name in the title: *Buick Circus Hour*, *Camel News Caravan*, and *Colgate Comedy Hour*. Having a single sponsor for a show meant that the advertiser could easily influence the program's content. In the early 1950s, the broadcast networks became increasingly unhappy with the lack of creative control in this arrangement. Luckily, the growing popularity—and growing cost—of television offered opportunities to alter this financial setup. In 1952, for example, a single one-hour TV show cost a sponsor about $35,000, a figure that would rise to $90,000 by the end of the decade.

David Sarnoff, then head of RCA-NBC, and William Paley, head of CBS, saw an opportunity to diminish the sponsors' role. In 1953, Sarnoff appointed Sylvester "Pat" Weaver (father of actor Sigourney Weaver) as the president of NBC. Previously an advertising executive, Weaver undermined his former profession by increasing program length from fifteen minutes (then the standard for radio programs) to thirty minutes or longer, substantially raising program costs for advertisers and discouraging some of them from sponsoring programs.

In addition, the introduction of two new types of programs—the magazine format and the TV spectacular—greatly helped the networks gain control over content. The *magazine program* featured multiple segments—news, talk, comedy, and music—similar to the varied content found in a general-interest publication or a newsmagazine of the day, such as *Life* or *Time*. In January 1952, NBC introduced the *Today* show as a three-hour morning talk-news program. Then, in September 1954, NBC premiered the ninety-minute *Tonight Show*. Because both shows ran daily rather than weekly, studio production costs were prohibitive for a single sponsor. Consequently, NBC offered spot ads within the shows: Advertisers paid the network for thirty- or sixty-second time slots. The network, not the sponsor, now either produced and owned the programs or bought them from independent producers.

The television spectacular is today recognized by a more modest term, the *television special*. At NBC, Weaver bought the rights to special programs, like the Broadway production of *Peter Pan*, and sold spot ads to multiple sponsors. The 1955 TV version of *Peter Pan* was a particular success, with sixty-five million viewers. More typical specials featured music-variety shows hosted by famous singers, such as Judy Garland, Frank Sinatra, and Nat King Cole.

The Rise and Fall of Quiz Shows

In 1955, CBS aired the *$64,000 Question*, reviving radio's quiz-show genre (radio's version was the more modest *$64 Question*). Sponsored by Revlon, the program ran in **prime time** (the hours between 8 and 11 P.M., when networks traditionally draw their largest audiences and charge their highest advertising rates) and became the most popular TV show in America during its first year. Revlon followed the show's success with the *$64,000 Challenge* in 1956; by the end of 1958, twenty-two quiz shows aired on network television. Revlon's cosmetics sales skyrocketed from $1.2 million before its sponsorship of the quiz shows to nearly $10 million by 1959.

Compared with dramas and sitcoms, quiz shows were (and are) cheap to produce, with inexpensive sets and mostly nonactors as guests. The problem was that most of these shows were rigged. To heighten the drama, key contestants were rehearsed and given the answers.

The most notorious rigging occurred on *Twenty-One*, a quiz show owned by Geritol (whose profits climbed by $4 million one year after it began to sponsor the program in 1956). A young Columbia University English professor from a famous literary family, Charles Van Doren, won $129,000 in 1957 during his fifteen-week run on the program; his fame even landed him a job on NBC's *Today* show. But in 1958, after a series of contestants accused the quiz show *Dotto* of being fixed, the networks quickly dropped twenty quiz shows. Following further rumors, a *TV Guide* story, a New York grand jury probe, and a 1959 congressional investigation during which Van Doren admitted to cheating, big-money prime-time quiz shows ended.

Quiz-Show Scandal Hurts the Promise of TV

The impact of the quiz-show scandal was enormous. First, the sponsors' pressure on TV executives to rig the programs and the subsequent fraud put an end to any role that major sponsors had in creating TV content. Second, and more important, the fraud undermined Americans' expectation of the democratic promise of television—to bring inexpensive information and entertainment into every household. Many people had trusted their own eyes—what they saw on TV—more than the *words* they heard on radio or read in print. But the scandal provided the first dramatic indication that TV images could be manipulated. In fact, our contemporary love-hate relationship with electronic culture and new gadgets got its start during this time.

The third, and most important, impact of the quiz-show scandal was that it magnified the division between "high" and "low" culture attitudes toward television. The fact that Charles Van Doren had come from a family of Ivy League intellectuals and cheated for fame and money drove a wedge between skeptical intellectuals and the popular new medium. This was best expressed in 1961 by FCC commissioner Newton Minow, who labeled game shows, westerns, cartoons, and other popular genres as part of television's "vast wasteland." Critics have used the "wasteland" metaphor ever since to admonish the TV industry for failing to live up to its potential. Prime-time quiz shows did have a brief comeback in 1999, when ABC's *Who Wants to Be a Millionaire* emerged as that season's No. 1 program.

TWENTY-ONE

In 1957, the most popular contestant on the quiz show *Twenty-One* was college professor Charles Van Doren *(left)*. Congressional hearings on rigged quiz shows revealed that Van Doren had been given some answers. Host Jack Barry, pictured here above the sponsor's logo, nearly had his career ruined but made a comeback in the late 1960s with the syndicated game show *The Joker's Wild*.

Everett Collection

THE DEVELOPMENT OF CABLE

Most historians mark the period from the late 1950s, when the networks gained control over TV's content, to the end of the 1970s as the **network era**. Except for British and American anthology dramas on PBS, this was a time when the Big Three broadcast networks—CBS, NBC, and ABC—dictated virtually every trend in programming and collectively accounted for more than 95 percent of all prime-time TV viewing. By 2014, however, this figure was less than 35 percent. Why the drastic drop? Because cable television systems—along with home video and early streaming technology—had cut into the broadcast networks' audience. With the rise of Netflix and Amazon streaming services and the loss of younger viewers to digital devices, some TV industry watchers predicted that by 2020, traditional networks would capture only about 20 percent of viewers on a typical evening in prime time.

CATV—Community Antenna Television

The first small cable systems—called **CATV**, or community antenna television—originated in the late 1940s in Oregon, Pennsylvania, and New York City, where mountains or tall buildings blocked TV signals. These systems served roughly 10 percent of the country and, because of early technical and regulatory limits, contained only twelve channels. Even at this early stage, though, TV sales personnel, broadcasters, and electronics firms recognized two big advantages of cable. First, by routing and reamplifying each channel in a separate wire, cable eliminated over-the-air interference. Second, running signals through coaxial cable increased channel capacity.

In the beginning, small communities with CATV often received twice as many channels as were available over the air in much larger cities. That technological advantage, combined with cable's ability to deliver clear reception, would soon propel the new industry into competition with conventional broadcast television. But unlike radio, which freed mass communication from unwieldy wires, early cable technology relied on wires.

The Wires and Satellites behind Cable Television

The idea of using space satellites to receive and transmit communication signals is right out of science fiction. In 1945, Arthur C. Clarke (who studied physics and mathematics and would later write dozens of sci-fi books, including *2001: A Space Odyssey*) published the original theories for a global communications system based on three satellites spaced equally apart from one another, rotating with the earth's orbit. In the mid-1950s, these theories became reality, as the Soviet Union and then the United States successfully sent satellites into orbit around the earth.

In 1960, AT&T launched Telstar, the first communication satellite capable of receiving, amplifying, and returning signals. Telstar was able to process and relay telephone and occasional television signals between the United States and Europe. By the mid-1960s, scientists had figured out how to lock communication satellites into *geosynchronous orbit*, in which they circled the earth at the same speed as the earth revolves on its axis. For cable television, the breakthrough was the launch of domestic communication satellites: Canada's *Anik* in 1972 and the United States' *Westar* in 1974.

Advances in satellite technology in the 1970s dramatically changed the fortunes of cable by creating a reliable system for the distribution of programming to cable companies across the nation. The first cable network to use satellites for regular transmission of TV programming was Home Box Office (HBO), which began delivering such programming as uncut, commercial-free movies and exclusive live coverage of major boxing matches for a monthly fee in 1975. The second cable network began in 1976, when media owner Ted Turner distributed his small Atlanta broadcast TV station, WTBS, to cable systems across the country.

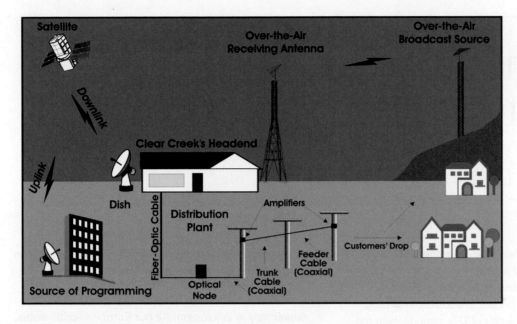

FIGURE 6.1

A BASIC CABLE TELEVISION SYSTEM

Information from Clear Creek Communications, www.ccmtc.com.

Cable Threatens Broadcasting

While only 14 percent of all U.S. homes received cable in 1977, by 1985 that percentage had climbed to 46. By the summer of 1997, basic cable channels had captured a larger prime-time audience than the broadcast networks had. The cable industry's rapid rise to prominence was partly due to the shortcomings of broadcast television. Beyond improving signal reception in most communities, the cable era introduced **narrowcasting**—the providing of specialized programming for diverse and fragmented groups. Attracting both advertisers and audiences, cable programs provide access to certain target audiences (like young male viewers for ESPN's numerous channels) that cannot be guaranteed in broadcasting. For example, a golf-equipment manufacturer can buy ads on the Golf Channel and reach only golf enthusiasts.

As cable channels have become more and more like specialized magazines or radio formats, they have siphoned off network viewers, and the networks' role as the chief programmer of our shared culture has eroded. For example, back in 1980, the Big Three evening news programs had a combined audience of more than fifty million on a typical weekday evening. By 2017, that audience was less than half that size—about twenty-three million.[7]

Cable Services

Cable consumers usually choose programming from a two-tiered structure: basic cable services like CNN and premium cable services like HBO. These services are the production arm of the cable industry, supplying programming to the nation's six-thousand-plus cable operations, which function as program distributors to cable households.

Basic Cable Services

A typical **basic cable** system today includes a hundred-plus channel lineup composed of local broadcast signals; access channels (for local government, education, and general public use); regional PBS stations; and a variety of cable channels, such as ESPN, CNN, MTV, USA, Bravo, Disney, Comedy Central, BET, Telemundo, the Weather Channel, and **superstations** (independent TV stations uplinked to a satellite, such as WGN in Chicago). Typically, local cable companies pay each of these satellite-delivered services between a few cents per month per subscriber ($.06 per month per subscriber for low-cost, low-demand channels like C-SPAN) and over $6 per month per subscriber (for high-cost, high-demand channels like ESPN). That fee is passed along to consumers

Telling and Selling Stories around the World

The United States has long been the world's leading supplier of aircraft—both commercial and military. In 2017, aircraft was the top revenue-generating product we exported. In addition, in what is referred to as the service sector of U.S. exports, near the top of the list is our popular culture. This includes global license fees for the rights to U.S. movies and TV programs. These fees generated over $124 billion in 2017.[1]

As one European analysis puts it: "Turn on the radio, check the TV listings, look what's playing at the local cinema, pull out a computer game or just go online and search for a nice chat room—do any of these things and within a short time you will run into American cultural influence."[2]

So what's the deal? Why is our popular culture so popular?

There are at least three reasons. One is our large affluent domestic market of over 325 million people. So "Americans can profitably produce a great many TV programs, films, songs, computer games and other products for use at home and then export the same programs abroad at very low prices. No other country has this advantage in both numbers and language."[3] For example, the U.S. television industry earns significant profits from telling and selling its stories in the United States. Then the industry makes these programs available throughout the world. Since these products are already "Made in the USA," TV producers and film studios collect billions in license fees from hundreds of countries. This is pure gravy. Contributing to much of these additional profits are the more than two billion people in the world who speak English.

A second reason often cited for U.S. pop culture supremacy is innovation. As our European critic notes, "It is often in the United States that new forms of communication have either been invented or perfected. TV broadcasting is a good example of this. In the 1950s American TV networks created a zoo of new program types including game shows, soap operas, mystery shows, westerns and, of course, situation comedies (sit-coms) that were later exported internationally. Later, cable TV expanded the variety and quality of American shows creating such international best sellers as *The Sopranos*, *Sex and the City* and *Heroes*."[4] Most recently, of course, the U.S. development of the World Wide Web in the early 1990s enabled the rise of Netflix and Amazon, the world's top pop cultural powerhouses in creating and streaming movies and TV programs that dominate the world market.

Finally, Americans are good at telling stories. As our European critic observes, "The fact is that American programming *is* popular. It successfully appeals to the emotions and interests of a global audience." U.S.-made sitcoms and dramas "have made fans around the world because they stick to the basics—they portray regular people everyone can recognize and identify with, however dramatic or fanciful the situation they may find themselves in. American culture celebrates the commonplace, the average, the universal and as a result it has gained a universal audience."[5]

as part of their basic monthly cable rate, which averaged—depending on the study and the location—between $76 and $100 per month in 2017. By 2018, the purchase of faster bandwidth speeds, additional premium channels, and video-on-demand drove many monthly cable bills to the $200 level.

Premium Cable Services

Besides basic programming, cable offers a wide range of special channels, known as **premium channels**, which lure customers with the promise of no advertising; recent and classic Hollywood movies; and original movies or series, like HBO's *Game of Thrones* and Showtime's *Homeland*. These channels are a major source of revenue for cable companies: The cost to them is around $6 per month per subscriber to carry a premium channel, but the cable company can charge customers $12–$16 or more per month and reap a nice profit. Premium services also include pay-per-view (PPV) programs; video-on-demand (VOD); and interactive services that enable consumers to use their televisions to bank, shop, play games, and access the Internet.

Beginning in 1985, cable companies began introducing new viewing options for their customers. **Pay-per-view (PPV)** channels came first, offering recently released movies or special one-time sporting events to subscribers who paid a designated charge to their cable company, allowing them to view the program. In the early 2000s, cable companies introduced **video-on-demand (VOD)**. This service enables customers to choose among hundreds of titles and watch their selection whenever they want in the same way as a video, pausing and fast-forwarding when desired. Along with online downloading and streaming services and digital video recorders (DVRs), VOD services today are ending the era of the local video store.

Pictorial Press Ltd/Alamy Stock Photo

HBO'S *WESTWORLD,* based on Michael Crichton's 1973 film of the same name, features many gruesome and graphic scenes of violence not usually found on basic cable channels.

DBS: Cable without Wires

By 1999, cable penetration had hit 70 percent. But **direct broadcast satellite (DBS)** services presented a big challenge to cable—especially in regions with rugged terrain and isolated homes, where the installation of cable wiring hadn't always been possible or profitable. Instead of using wires, DBS transmits its signal directly to small satellite dishes near or on customers' homes. Consumers now had a viable alternative to cable. As a result, cable and broadcast-only penetration had dropped to 50 percent by 2018. In addition, new over-the-air digital signals and better online options meant that many customers began moving away from either cable or DBS subscriptions.

Satellite service began in the mid-1970s, when satellite dishes were set up to receive cable programming. Small-town and rural residents bypassed FCC restrictions by buying receiving dishes and downlinking, for free, the same channels that cable companies were supplying to wired communities. Not surprisingly, satellite programmers filed a flurry of legal challenges against those who were receiving their signals for free. Because the law was unclear, a number of cable channels began scrambling their signals, and most satellite users had to buy or rent descramblers and subscribe to services, just as cable customers did. By 1994, full-scale DBS service was available. Today, DBS companies like DirecTV (now owned by AT&T) and Dish (formerly the Dish Network) offer consumers most of the channels and tiers of service that cable companies carry (including Internet, television, and phone services) at a comparable and often cheaper monthly cost. But with over-the-air digital signals and online streaming options like Netflix and Amazon Prime now offering services for under $10 per month, many customers are **cord cutting**, moving away from both cable and DBS subscriptions.

TECHNOLOGY AND CONVERGENCE CHANGE VIEWING HABITS

launchpadworks.com

David Gale
VP of New Media, MTV

Television Networks Evolve
Insiders discuss how cable and satellite have changed the television market.

Discussion: How might definitions of a TV network change in the realm of new digital media?

Among the biggest technical innovations in TV viewing are non-television delivery systems. We can skip a network broadcast and still watch our favorite shows on laptops or mobile devices for free or for a nominal cost. Not only is television being reinvented, but its audiences—although fragmented—are also growing. A few years ago, televisions glimmered in the average U.S. household just over seven hours a day; but by 2014, when you add in downloading, streaming, DVR playback, and smartphone/tablet viewing, that figure has expanded to and remained at more than eight hours a day. All these options mean that we are still watching television—just at different times, in different places, and on different kinds of screens.

Home Video

In 1975–76, the consumer introduction of videocassettes and *videocassette recorders (VCRs)* enabled viewers to tape-record TV programs and play them back later. VCRs got a boost from a failed suit brought against Sony by Disney and MCA (now NBC Universal) in 1976: The two film studios alleged that home taping violated their movie copyrights. In 1979, a federal court ruled in favor of Sony and permitted home taping for personal use. In response, the movie studios quickly set up videotaping facilities so that they could rent and sell movies in video stores, which became popular in the early 1980s.

Over time, the VHS format gave way to DVDs, but today the standard DVD is also disappearing. Although many public libraries stock extensive movie and TV show DVD collections, there is only one significant home video chain left—Family Video, based in Illinois—which in 2018 operated more the seven hundred stores in the United States and Canada, mostly in small towns and rural communities. Blockbuster, once the king of video stores with more than nine thousand outlets, went bankrupt in 2012.[8]

Most homes today have *DVRs (digital video recorders)*, which enable users to download specific programs onto the DVR's computer memory and watch at a later time. While offering greater flexibility for viewers, DVRs also provide a means to "watch" the watchers. DVRs give advertisers information about what each household views, allowing them to target viewers with specific ads when they play back their programs. This kind of technology has raised concerns among some lawmakers and consumer groups over the tracking of personal viewing and buying habits by marketers.

The DVD and now DVRs contributed to two major developments in TV viewing: video rentals and time shifting. Video rentals, formerly the province of walk-in video stores like Blockbuster, have given way to streaming services like Netflix and Amazon or online services like iTunes. **Time shifting**, which began during the VCR era, occurs when viewers record shows and watch them at a later, more convenient time. Video rentals and time shifting, however, have threatened the TV industry's advertising-driven business model; when viewers watch programs on DVDs and DVRs, they often fast-forward through the ads.

The Third Screen: TV Converges with the Internet

The Internet has transformed the way many of us, especially younger generations, watch movies, TV, and cable programming. These new online viewing experiences are often labeled **third screens**, usually meaning that computer screens are the third major way we view content (movie screens and traditional TV sets are the first and second screens, respectively). By far the most popular site for viewing video online is YouTube, owned by Google. Containing some original shows, classic TV episodes, full-length films, and the homemade user-uploaded clips that first made the site famous, YouTube remains at the center of video consumption online.

But YouTube has competition from sites that offer full-length episodes of current and recent programming. While viewers might be able to watch blurry snippets of a show on YouTube, it's hard to find a full episode of popular TV shows like *The Walking Dead* or *Stranger Things*. Services like iTunes or Amazon Instant Video offer downloads of full seasons of popular TV shows for under $20 or a single episode for under $3.

In late 2010, Hulu started Hulu Plus, a paid subscription service. For as little as $8 a month, viewers can stream full seasons of current and older programs and some movies and documentaries on their computer, TV, or mobile device. Hulu Plus had more than seventeen million subscribers by 2018. Netflix, which started streaming videos back in 2008, has moved further away from a DVD-through-the-mail model to become the world's biggest online streaming service. With over fifty-six million U.S. subscribers in 2018, Netflix is much bigger than Comcast, the nation's largest cable company, with its twenty-two million U.S. subscribers (down from twenty-seven million in 2016).[9] Netflix's biggest rival is Amazon Prime, which had over ninety million U.S. subscribers in early 2018, up from sixty-three million just a year earlier.[10] Like cable companies, Netflix and Amazon (in addition to creating their own programs) routinely negotiate with major film and TV studios for the rights to stream current episodes of prime-time television shows—which typically cost between $70,000 and $100,000 per episode.[11]

Fourth Screens: Smartphones and Mobile Video

Back in 2014, according to Nielsen's "Digital Consumer" report, 84 percent of smartphone and tablet owners said they used those devices as an additional screen while watching television "at the same time."[12] Such multitasking has further accelerated with new **fourth screen** technologies, like smartphones, iPads, and mobile TV devices. For the past few years, these devices have forced major changes in consumer viewing habits and media content creation.

The multifunctionality and portability of third- and fourth-screen devices mean that consumers may no longer need television sets—just as landline telephones have fallen out of favor as more people rely solely on their mobile phones. If *where* we watch TV programming changes, does TV programming also need to change to keep up? Reality shows like *The Voice* and sci-fi dramas like *Stranger Things*—with many contestants or characters and multiple plotlines—are considered best suited for the digital age, enabling viewers to talk to one another on various social networks about favorite singers, characters, and plot twists at the same time as they watch these programs on traditional—or nontraditional—TV.

Still, it is hard to imagine the giant flat-screen TV experience going away anytime soon. Late in 2017, *Consumer Reports* accurately predicted that TV screens would get even bigger in 2018. This seems counter to the small-screen digital turn to smartphone and tablet devices that grab much of our daily attention. But the trend to 65- and 75-inch models with 4K technology is due in part to the resolution on the new large screens—about four times better than previous digital images from the "old days," when 42-inch screens seemed enormous. TV industry analyst Stephen Baker offers an explanation: "Consumers want bigger screens because the biggest, best screen in the house—the TV— is where communal watching happens, where you watch sports, or movies or Netflix with your wife or your kids. . . . People are willing to spend the money on [the] biggest TV they can for the main room in the house, and then use the [other devices] for content away from the main TV room."[13]

MAJOR PROGRAMMING TRENDS

Television programming began by borrowing genres from radio, such as variety shows, sitcoms, soap operas, and newscasts. Beginning in 1955, the Big Three networks gradually moved their entertainment divisions to Los Angeles because of its proximity to Hollywood production studios. Network news operations, however, remained in New York. Ever since, Los Angeles and New York came to represent the two major branches of TV programming: *entertainment* and *information*.

#MeToo and TV Station Policy

In the wake of the #MeToo movement in 2017 and 2018, famous men across the television landscape lost their jobs (and, in some cases, their TV shows)—from Charlie Rose (CBS's *60 Minutes* and PBS's *Charlie Rose*) to Matt Lauer (NBC's *Today* show) to Louis C.K. (FX's *Louie*) to Kevin Spacey (Netflix's *House of Cards*). In a 2018 *New Yorker* article, reporter Dana Goodyear quotes a very worried (and anonymous) Hollywood TV executive: "All people want to know is, who's next and what happens? How long do these people stay off the playing field? Are they done for good, does this provide opportunities for women, is this permanent, temporary, what? Is this an overreaction? Should all doors literally be glass? Nobody knows how to act now. The rules have been so changed."[1]

Clearly, here is a TV exec unnerved by #MeToo.

The #MeToo phenomenon raised a host of ethical concerns on top of a wide range of behaviors—everything from sexist comments in an office to criminal assaults in a hotel room. What is most telling about the TV executive's reaction to #MeToo is that he seems to be clueless about how to react and what to do next.

Let's see if local TV executives have a clue. Contact a local TV station (either in your hometown or near where you attend college) and ask about the station's policy on sexual harassment. Ask for a copy or where the policy can be found online. What does the policy say? Does it list levels of inappropriate behavior? Are there specific behaviors mentioned? How does the station deal with these issues? What are the procedures and steps followed? Who handles each case? Is there a range of disciplinary actions, such as forcing the employee to seek professional help or reporting transgressions to local law enforcement? What are the grounds for dismissal, and can a person return to his or her job? If there is no policy, ask why not. If one is in the process of being developed, who is in charge of developing it?

Share your findings in class. Did you find a good model for dealing with these issues? What constitutes a good policy? Share your findings with the TV station you contacted.

Richard Drew/AP Images

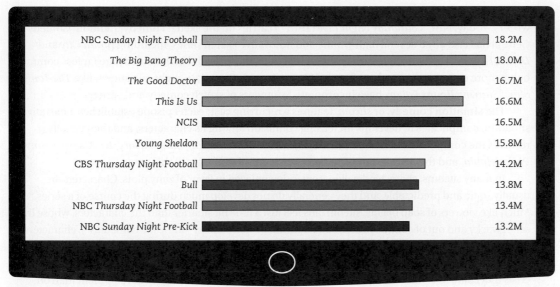

FIGURE 6.2

THE TOP 10 MOST WATCHED TV SHOWS OF THE 2017–18 SEASON

Data from: Lynette Rice, "The Top 75 Most-Watched Shows of the 2017–18 Season," *Entertainment Weekly*, December 19, 2017, http://ew.com/tv/2017/12/19/75-most-watched-tv-shows-2017-18-season.

NBC *Sunday Night Football*	18.2M
The Big Bang Theory	18.0M
The Good Doctor	16.7M
This Is Us	16.6M
NCIS	16.5M
Young Sheldon	15.8M
CBS *Thursday Night Football*	14.2M
Bull	13.8M
NBC *Thursday Night Football*	13.4M
NBC *Sunday Night Pre-Kick*	13.2M

Although there is considerable blurring between these categories today, the two were once more distinct. In the sections that follow, we focus on these long-standing program developments and explore newer trends (see Figure 6.2).

TV Entertainment: Our Comic Culture

The networks began to move their entertainment divisions to Los Angeles partly because of the success of the pioneering comedy series *I Love Lucy* (1951–1957). *Lucy*'s owners and costars, Lucille Ball and Desi Arnaz, began filming the top-rated sitcom in California near their home. In 1951, *Lucy* became the first TV program to be filmed before a live Hollywood audience. Before the days of videotape (invented in 1956), the only way to preserve a live broadcast, other than filming it like a movie, was through a technique called **kinescope**. In this process, a film camera recorded a live TV show off a studio monitor. The quality of the kinescope was poor, and most series that were saved in this way have not survived. *I Love Lucy*, *Alfred Hitchcock Presents*, and *Dragnet* are among a handful of series from the 1950s that have endured because they were originally shot and preserved on film, like movies. In capturing *I Love Lucy* on film for future generations, the program's producers understood the enduring appeal of comedy, which is a central programming strategy both for broadcast networks and for cable. TV comedy is usually delivered in two formats: sketch comedy and situation comedy (usually referred to as sitcoms).

Sketch comedy, or short comedy skits, was a key element in early TV variety shows, which also included singers, dancers, acrobats, animal acts, stand-up comics, and ventriloquists. According to one TV historian, variety shows "resurrected the essentials of stage variety entertainment" and played to noisy studio audiences.[14] Vaudeville and stage performers were TV's first stars of sketch comedy. They included Milton Berle, TV's first major celebrity, in *Texaco Star Theater* (1948–1967), and Sid Caesar, Imogene Coca, and Carl Reiner in *Your Show of Shows* (1950–1954), on which playwright Neil Simon,

COMEDIES are often among the most popular shows on television. *I Love Lucy* was the top-ranked show from 1952 to 1955 and was a model for other shows, such as *Dick Van Dyke*, *Laverne & Shirley*, and the rebooted *Will & Grace* and *Roseanne*.

CBS Photo Archive/Getty Images

filmmakers Mel Brooks and Woody Allen, and writer Larry Gelbart (*M*A*S*H*) all served for a time as writers. Today, NBC's *Saturday Night Live* (1975–) carries on the sketch comedy tradition. Comedy Central has also aired several high-profile and innovative sketch series, including *Broad City* and *Drunk History*. The hour-long variety shows that once showcased sketch comedy are far less common, being more expensive to produce than half-hour sitcoms. Some late-night talk shows, like *The Tonight Show Starring Jimmy Fallon*, have incorporated elements of sketch comedy and variety.

The **situation comedy**, or *sitcom*, features a recurring cast; each episode establishes a narrative situation, complicates it, develops increasing confusion among its characters, and then usually resolves the complications.[15] *I Love Lucy*, *Seinfeld*, *New Girl*, *The Big Bang Theory*, *It's Always Sunny in Philadelphia*, and the British show *The Detectorists* are all examples of this genre.

In many sitcoms, character development is downplayed in favor of zany plots. Characters are usually static and predictable, and they generally do not develop much during the course of a series. Much like viewers of soap operas, sitcom fans feel just a little bit smarter than the characters, whose lives seem wacky and out of control. In some sitcoms (once referred to as "domestic comedies"), characters and settings are typically more important than complicated predicaments. Although an episode might offer a goofy situation as a subplot, the main narrative usually features a personal problem or family crisis that characters have to resolve. Greater emphasis is placed on character development than on reestablishing the order that has been disrupted by confusion. Such comedies take place primarily at home (*Modern Family*), at the workplace (*Parks and Recreation*), or at both (*Curb Your Enthusiasm*).

In TV history, some sitcoms have mixed dramatic and comedic elements. This blurring of serious and comic themes marks a contemporary hybrid, sometimes labeled *dramedy*, which has included such series as ABC's *The Wonder Years* (1988–1993), Fox's *Ally McBeal* (1997–2002), HBO's *Sex and the City* (1999–2004), Fox's musical-dramedy *Glee* (2009–2015), and Netflix's *Orange Is the New Black* (2013–).

TV Entertainment: Our Dramatic Culture

Because the production of TV entertainment was centered in New York City in its early days, many of its ideas, sets, technicians, actors, and directors came from New York theater. Young stage actors—including Anne Bancroft, Ossie Davis, James Dean, Grace Kelly, Paul Newman, Sidney Poitier, Robert Redford, and Joanne Woodward—often worked in television if they could not find stage work. The TV dramas that grew from these early influences fit roughly into two categories: the anthology drama and the episodic series.

AMERICAN HORROR STORY

Each season of this anthology horror series takes place in a different time and place and features fresh characters who are not directly connected to the previous season's story, though many of the actors return, playing different roles in each season. The series, which has aired on FX since 2011, is part of a recent resurgence of season-based anthology programs. Other examples include HBO's *True Detective* and FX's *Fargo*, both of which have introduced all-new casts and a new story line with each new season.

Everett Collection

The Anthology Drama and the Miniseries

In the early 1950s, television—like cable in the early 1980s—served a more elite and wealthier audience. **Anthology dramas** brought live dramatic theater to that audience. Influenced by stage plays, anthologies offered new, artistically significant *teleplays* (scripts written for television), casts, directors, writers, and sets from one week to the next. In the 1952–53 season alone, there were eighteen anthology dramas, including *Alfred Hitchcock Presents* (1955–1965), the *Twilight Zone* (1959–1964), and *Kraft Television Theater* (1947–1958), which was created to introduce Kraft's Cheez Whiz.

The anthology's brief run as a dramatic staple on television ended for both economic and political reasons. First, advertisers disliked anthologies, as they often presented stories containing complex human problems that were not easily resolved—this in sharp contrast to the commercials that interrupted the drama, which told upbeat stories in which problems were easily solved by purchasing a product. Thus, anthologies made the simplicity of the commercial pitch ring false. A second reason for the demise of anthology dramas was a change in audience. The people who could afford TV sets in the early 1950s could also afford tickets to a play. For these viewers, the anthology drama was a welcome addition given their cultural tastes. By 1956, however, working- and middle-class families were increasingly able to afford television sets, and the prices of sets dropped. Anthology dramas were not as popular in this newly expanded market. Third, anthology dramas were expensive to produce—double the cost of most other TV genres in the 1950s—because each week meant a new story line, along with new writers, casts, and sets. Sponsors and networks came to realize that it would be easier and less expensive to build audience allegiance with an ongoing program featuring the same cast and set.

Finally, anthologies that dealt seriously with the changing social landscape often attracted controversy. This was especially true during the attempts by Senator Joseph McCarthy and his followers to rid media industries and government agencies of left-leaning political influences. (See Chapter 16 for more on blacklisting.) By the early 1960s, this dramatic form had virtually disappeared from network television, although its legacy continues on public television with the imported British program *Masterpiece Theatre* (1971–)—now known as either *Masterpiece Classic* or *Masterpiece Mystery!*—the longest-running prime-time drama series on U.S. television.

In fact, these British shows resemble U.S. TV *miniseries*—serialized TV shows that run over a two-day to two-week period, usually on consecutive evenings. A cross between an extended anthology drama and a network serial, the most famous U.S. miniseries was probably *Roots* (1977), based on Alex Haley's novelized version of his family's slave history. The final episode of *Roots*, which ran on eight consecutive nights, drew an audience of more than 100 million viewers. Contemporary British series like *Doc Martin* (2005–), *Downton Abbey* (2010–2016), and *Sherlock* (2011–) last three to eight episodes over a few weeks, making them more like miniseries than traditional network dramas, even though they have multiple seasons. The miniseries has also experienced a recent resurgence in the United States, with high-quality and popular miniseries on cable, like *True Detective* (HBO), *American Horror Story* (FX), and *Hatfields and McCoys* (History Channel).

Episodic Series

Abandoning anthologies, producers and writers increasingly developed **episodic series**, first used on radio in 1929. In this format, main characters continue from week to week, sets and locales remain the same, and technical crews stay with the program. The episodic series comes in two general types: chapter shows and serial programs.

Chapter shows are self-contained stories with a recurring set of main characters who confront a problem, face a series of conflicts, and find a resolution. This structure can be used in a wide range of sitcoms—like *The Big Bang Theory* (2007–)—and dramatic genres, including adult westerns like *Gunsmoke* (1955–1975); police/detective shows like *CSI: Crime Scene Investigation* (2000–2015); and science fiction like *Star Trek* (1966–1969). Culturally, television dramas often function as a window into the hopes and fears of the American psyche. For example, in the 1970s, police/detective dramas became a staple, mirroring anxieties about the urban unrest of the time, precipitated by the decline of manufacturing and the loss of factory jobs. Americans' popular entertainment reflected the idea of heroic police and tenacious detectives protecting a nation from menacing forces that were undermining the economy and the cities. Such shows as *Hawaii Five-O* (1968–1980), *The Mod Squad* (1968–1973), and *The Rockford Files* (1974–1980) all ranked among the nation's top-rated programs during that time.

In contrast to chapter shows, **serial programs** are open-ended episodic shows; that is, most story lines continue from episode to episode. Cheaper to produce than chapter shows, employing just a few indoor sets, and running five days a week, daytime *soap operas* are among the longest-running serial

LaunchPad
macmillan learning
launchpadworks.com

Television Drama: Then and Now
Head to LaunchPad to watch clips from two different drama series: one several decades old, and one recent.

Discussion: What evidence of storytelling changes can you see by comparing and contrasting the two clips?

programs in the history of television. Acquiring their name from soap manufacturers that sponsored these programs in the days of fifteen-minute radio dramas, soaps feature cliff-hanging story lines and intimate close-up shots that tend to create strong audience allegiance. Soaps also probably do the best job of any genre at imitating the actual open-ended rhythms of daily life. However, popular daytime network soaps have mostly disappeared in the digital age, with so many choices and small screens drawing away viewers, especially younger ones. In 2017–18, just four remained on the networks, including *General Hospital* (1963–) and *The Young and the Restless* (1973–), which remains the most popular of the four with about 4.4 million viewers each weekday.

Another type of drama is the *hybrid*, which developed in the early 1980s with the appearance of *Hill Street Blues* (1981–1987). Often mixing comic situations and grim plots, this multiple-cast show looked like an open-ended soap opera. On occasion, as in real life, crimes were not solved and recurring characters died. As a hybrid form, *Hill Street Blues* combined elements of both chapter and serial television by featuring some self-contained plots that were resolved in a single episode as well as other plotlines that continued from week to week. This blend has been used by many successful dramatic hybrids, including *The X-Files* (1993–2002), *Buffy the Vampire Slayer* (1997–2003), *Lost* (2004–2010), *The Closer* (2005–2012), *Breaking Bad* (2008–2013), and *The Walking Dead* (2010–).

TV Information: Our Daily News Culture

For about forty years (from the 1960s to the 2000s), broadcast news, especially on local TV stations, consistently topped print journalism in national research polls that asked which news medium was most trustworthy. Most studies at the time suggested that this had to do with TV's intimacy as a medium—its ability to create loyalty with viewers who connect personally with the news anchors we "invite" into our living rooms each evening. Print reporters and editors, by comparison, seemed anonymous and detached. But this distinction began breaking down as print reporters started discussing their work on cable TV news programs and became more accessible to their readers through e-mail, blogs, and newspaper websites. In this section, we focus on the traditional network evening news, its history, and the changes in TV news ushered in by twenty-four-hour cable news channels.

Network News

Originally featuring a panel of reporters interrogating political figures, NBC's weekly *Meet the Press* (1947–) is the oldest show on television. Daily evening newscasts began on NBC in February 1948 with the *Camel Newsreel Theater*, sponsored by the cigarette company. Originally a ten-minute Fox Movietone newsreel that was also shown in theaters, it became a live fifteen-minute broadcast in 1949. In 1956, the *Huntley Brinkley Report* debuted with Chet Huntley in New York and David Brinkley in Washington, D.C. This coanchored NBC program became the most popular evening news show at the time and served as the dual-anchor model for hundreds of local news broadcasts. After Huntley retired in 1970, the program was renamed *NBC Nightly News*. Tom Brokaw eventually settled in as sole anchor in September 1983 and passed the chair to Brian Williams in 2004. In 2015, amid a scandal over inaccurate statements, Williams was replaced by Lester Holt, the first African American solo anchor on network news.

RACHEL MADDOW

hosts one of the most widely viewed daily opinion shows, the Emmy Award–winning *Rachel Maddow Show*, on MSNBC. Maddow has been honored with the Walter Cronkite Faith and Freedom Award, the John Steinbeck Award, and two Gracie Awards for excellence. Recently, Maddow's reporting on the water crisis in Flint, Michigan, helped raise the crisis to national attention.

D. Dipasupil/Getty Images

Over at CBS, the network's flagship evening news program, *The CBS-TV News* with Douglas Edwards, premiered in May 1948. In 1956, the program became the first news show to be videotaped for rebroadcast on **affiliate stations** (stations that contract with a network to carry its programs) in Central and Western time zones. Walter Cronkite succeeded Edwards in 1962, starting a nineteen-year run as the influential anchor of the renamed *CBS Evening News*. Some critics believe Cronkite's eventual on-air opposition to the Vietnam War helped convince mainstream Americans to oppose it. Cronkite retired and gave way to Dan Rather in 1981. In 2006, CBS hired Katie Couric to serve as the first woman solo anchor on a network evening news program. But with stagnant ratings, she was replaced in 2011 by Scott Pelley. Jeff Glor took over the anchor chair in 2017.

After premiering an unsuccessful daily program in 1948, ABC launched a daily news show in 1953, anchored by John Daly—the head of ABC News and the host of CBS's evening game show *What's My Line?* After Daly left in 1960, John Cameron Swayze, Peter Jennings, Harry Reasoner, and Howard K. Smith all took a turn in the anchor's chair. In 1978, *ABC World News Tonight* premiered, featuring four anchors: Frank Reynolds in Washington, D.C.; Jennings in London; Barbara Walters in New York; and Max Robinson in Chicago. Robinson was the first black reporter to coanchor a network news program, and Walters was the first woman. In 1983, Jennings became the sole anchor of the broadcast until his death in 2005. The desk was then shared by coanchors Elizabeth Vargas and Bob Woodruff (who was severely injured covering the Iraq War in 2006) until Charles Gibson—from ABC's *Good Morning America*—took over in 2006. Gibson retired in 2009 and was replaced by Diane Sawyer, formerly of CBS's *60 Minutes* and ABC's *Good Morning America*. David Muir took over in 2014.

Cable News Changes the Game

The first 24/7 cable TV news channel, Cable News Network (CNN), premiered in 1980 and was the brainchild of Ted Turner, who had already revolutionized cable with his Atlanta-based superstation WTBS (Turner Broadcast Service). When Turner turned a profit with CNN in 1985 (along with its sister Headline News channel), he revealed a need and a lucrative market for twenty-four-hour news. Spawning a host of competitors in the United States and worldwide, CNN now battles for viewers with other twenty-four-hour news providers, including the Fox News Channel; MSNBC; CNBC; Euronews; British Sky Broadcasting; and thousands of web and blog sites, such as *Politico*, the *Huffington Post*, the *Drudge Report*, and *Salon*.

Cable news has significantly changed the TV news game by offering viewers information and stories in a 24/7 loop. Rather than waiting until 5:30 or 6:30 P.M. to watch the national network news, viewers can access news updates and breaking stories at any time. Cable news also challenges the network program formulas. Daily opinion programs, such as MSNBC's *Rachel Maddow Show* and Fox News' *Sean Hannity Show*, often celebrate argument, opinion, and speculation over traditional reporting based on verified facts. These programs emerged primarily because of their low cost compared with that of traditional network news. At the same time, satirical (originally called "fake news") programs like *The Daily Show with Trevor Noah* have challenged traditional news outlets by discussing the news in larger contexts, something the conventional thirty-minute daily broadcasts rarely do. (See Chapter 14 for more on fake news programs.)

CBS Photo Archive/Getty Images

WALTER CRONKITE

In 1968, after popular CBS news anchor Walter Cronkite visited Vietnam, CBS produced the documentary *Report from Vietnam by Walter Cronkite*. At the end of the program, Cronkite offered this terse observation: "It is increasingly clear to this reporter that the only rational way out then will be to negotiate, not as victors but as an honorable people who lived up to their pledge to defend democracy, and did the best they could." Most political observers said that Cronkite's opposition to the war influenced President Johnson's decision not to seek reelection.

Reality TV and Other Enduring Genres

Dramas, comedies, and news are some of the longest-standing TV genres, but others have played major roles in the medium's history, including talk shows, game shows, variety shows, and newsmagazines. Reality-based programs are the newest significant trend; they include everything from *The Voice* and *Deadliest Catch* to *Top Chef* and *Teen Mom*. One reason for their popularity is that these shows introduce us to characters and people who seem more "like us" and less like celebrities. Additionally, these programs have helped the networks and cable providers deal with the high cost of programming. Featuring non-actors, cheap sets, and no extensive scripts, reality shows are much less expensive to produce than sitcoms and dramas. While reality-based programs have played a major role in network prime time since the late 1990s, the genre was actually inspired by cable's *The Real World* (1992–), the longest-running program on MTV. Changing locations and casts from season to season, *The Real World* follows a group of strangers who live and work together for a few months and records their interpersonal entanglements and up-and-down relationships. *The Real World* has significantly influenced the structure of today's reality TV programs, including *The Bachelor, Survivor, Project Runway, Teen Mom,* and *Dancing with the Stars.* (See "Media Literacy and the Critical Process: TV and the State of Storytelling" on page 181.)

Another key trend is Spanish-language television, like the Univision and Telemundo networks. Back in the 2013–14 TV season, the popular network Univision reached about three million viewers in prime time each day (more than the CW but only about a third of the prime-time viewership for CBS and NBC, the top-rated networks). Then, in June 2014, Univision's ratings soared during soccer's World Cup. Sometimes beating ESPN throughout the tournament, Univision had nearly seven million viewers for the Brazil–Mexico match.

Univision, the first foreign-language U.S. network, had its start in 1961, when the owners of the nation's first Spanish-language TV station in San Antonio acquired a TV station in Los Angeles, setting up what was then called the Spanish International Network. It officially became Univision in 1986 and has built audiences in major urban areas with large Hispanic populations through its popular talk-variety programs and *telenovelas* (Spanish-language soap operas, mostly produced in Mexico), which air each weekday evening. Today, Univision Communications owns and operates more than sixty TV stations in the United States.

In 2018, the *Wall Street Journal* reported that Univision's prime-time audience has been in steady decline since the 2012–13 television season, in large part because of the slowdown and reversal of Mexican and Latino immigration to the United States over the last decade.[16] For the 2017–18 television season, Telemundo (owned by cable giant Comcast) averaged 751,000 viewers during prime time, compared with Univision's 789,000 viewers.

Public Television Struggles to Find Its Place

Another key programmer in TV history has been public television. Under President Lyndon Johnson, and in response to a report from the Carnegie Commission on Educational Television, Congress passed the Public Broadcasting Act of 1967, establishing the Corporation for Public Broadcasting (CPB) and later, in 1969, the Public Broadcasting Service (PBS). In part, Congress intended public television to target viewers who were "less attractive" to commercial networks and advertisers. Besides providing programs for viewers over age fifty, public television has figured prominently in programming for audiences under age twelve, with children's series like *Mister Rogers' Neighborhood* (1968–2001), *Sesame Street* (1969–), and *Barney & Friends* (1991–2009). The major networks have largely abdicated the responsibility of developing educational series aimed at children under age twelve. When Congress passed a law in 1996 ordering the networks to offer three hours of children's educational programming per week, the networks sidestepped the mandate by taking advantage of the law's vagueness on what constituted "educational" to claim that many of their routine sitcoms, cartoons, and dramatic shows satisfied the legislation's requirements.

The original Carnegie Commission report also recommended that Congress create a financial plan to provide long-term support for public television, in part to protect it from political

The rise of the reality program over the past decade has more to do with the cheaper cost of this genre than with the wild popularity of these programs. In fact, in the history of television and viewer numbers, traditional sitcoms and dramas—and even prime-time news programs like *60 Minutes* and *20/20*—have been far more popular than successful reality programs like *American Idol*. But when national broadcast TV executives cut costs by reducing writing and production staffs and hiring "regular people" instead of trained actors, does the craft of storytelling suffer at the expense of commercial savings? Can good stories be told in a reality program? In this exercise, let's compare the storytelling competence of a reality program with that of a more traditional comedy sitcom or drama.

1 DESCRIPTION
Pick a current reality program and a current sitcom or drama. Choose programs that either started in the last year or two or have been on television for roughly the same period of time. Now develop a "viewing sheet" that allows you to take notes as you watch the two programs over a three- to four-week period. Keep track of main characters, plotlines, settings, conflicts, and resolutions. Also track the main problems that are posed in the programs and how they are portrayed or worked out in each episode. Find out and compare the basic production costs of each program.

2 ANALYSIS
Look for patterns and differences in the ways stories are told in the two programs. At a general level, what are the conflicts about? (For example, are they about men versus women, managers versus employees, tradition versus change, individuals versus institutions, honesty versus dishonesty, authenticity versus artificiality?) How complicated or simple are the tensions in the two programs, and how are problems resolved? Are there some conflicts that you feel should not be permitted—like pitting older contestants against younger contestants or white against black? Are there noticeable differences between "the look" of one program and that of the other?

3 INTERPRETATION
What do some of the patterns mean? What seems to be the point of each program? What do the programs say about relationships, values, masculinity or femininity, power, social class, and so on? What is the value of each program for its viewers?

4 EVALUATION
What are the strengths and weaknesses of each program? Which program would you judge as being better at telling a compelling story that you want to watch each week? How could each program improve its storytelling?

5 ENGAGEMENT
Through either online forums or personal contacts, find other viewers of these programs. Ask them follow-up questions about what they like or do not like about such shows, what they might change, and what the programs' creators might do differently. Then report your findings to the programs' producers through a letter, a phone call, or an e-mail. Try to elicit responses from the producers about the status of their programs. How did they respond to your findings?

---

interference. However, Congress did not do this, nor did it require wealthy commercial broadcasters to subsidize public television (as many other countries do). As federal funding levels dropped in the 1980s, PBS increasingly depended on corporate underwriting. By the early 2000s, corporate sponsors funded more than 25 percent of all public television, although corporate sponsorship declined in 2009 as the economy suffered. In 2010, Congress gave an extra $25 million to PBS to help sustain it during the economic downturn.[17] However, only about 15 percent of funding for public broadcasting (which includes both television and radio) has come from the federal government, with the bulk of support being provided by viewers, listeners, and corporations.

PUBLIC TELEVISION

The most influential children's show in TV history, *Sesame Street* (1969–) has been teaching children their letters and numbers for more than forty-five years. The program has also helped break down ethnic, racial, and class barriers by introducing TV audiences to a rich and diverse cast of puppets and people. However, in 2015, a controversy erupted over the production company's decision to move the program from PBS to the subscription network HBO.

Photofest

Despite support from the Obama administration, there have been attempts to reduce or eliminate CPB funds in recent years. Because public television is a visible target, some politicians have used it as an example of government waste. However, a 2012 ProPublica study showed that CPB's $440 million subsidy amounted to "0.12 percent of the $3.8 trillion federal budget—or about $1.35 per person per year."[18] This percentage remains about the same in 2018. To counter proposed cutbacks, in the fall of 2011 PBS began inserting promotional messages from sponsors into some of their programs, every fifteen minutes.[19] Some critics and public TV executives worry that such messaging could compromise public television's mission to air programs that might be considered controversial or commercially less viable.

Also troubling to public television (in contrast to public radio, which increased its audience from two million listeners per week in 1980 to more than thirty million per week in 2010) is that its audience has declined. PBS content chief John Boland attributed the loss to the same market fragmentation and third-screen technology that has plagued the broadcast networks: "We are spread thin in trying to maintain our TV service and meet the needs of consumers on other platforms."[20] One viewer segment that PBS is watching closely is the children's audience—which declined 22 percent between 2010 and 2014, as it did on several cable channels aimed at children. One report suggests that parents are increasingly using on-demand services like Netflix to control what their children watch, while other reports indicate that educational video games and tablets are commanding more attention from younger viewers.[21]

REGULATORY CHALLENGES TO TELEVISION AND CABLE

Though cable cut into broadcast TV's viewership, both types of programming came under scrutiny from the U.S. government. Initially, thanks to extensive lobbying efforts, cable's growth was suppressed to ensure that no harm came to local broadcasters and traditional TV networks' ad revenue streams. Later, as cable developed, FCC officials worried that power and profits were growing increasingly concentrated in fewer and fewer industry players' hands. Thus, the FCC set out to mitigate the situation through a variety of rules and regulations.

Government Regulations Temporarily Restrict Network Control

By the late 1960s, a progressive and active FCC, increasingly concerned about the monopoly-like impact of the Big Three networks, passed a series of regulations that began undercutting their power. The first, the **Prime Time Access Rule (PTAR)**, introduced in April 1970, reduced the networks' control of prime-time programming from four to three hours. This move was an effort to encourage more local news and public affairs programs, usually slated for the 6–7 P.M. time block. However, most stations simply ran thirty minutes of local news at 6 P.M. and then acquired syndicated quiz shows (*Wheel of Fortune*) or *infotainment* programs (*Entertainment Tonight*) to fill the remaining half hour, during which they could sell lucrative regional ads.

In a second move, in 1970 the FCC created the Financial Interest and Syndication Rules—called **fin-syn**—which "constituted the most damaging attack against the network TV monopoly in FCC history," according to one historian.[22] Throughout the 1960s, the networks had run their own syndication companies. The networks sometimes demanded as much as 50 percent of the profits that TV producers earned from airing older shows as reruns in local TV markets. This was the case even though those shows were no longer on the networks and most of them had been developed not by the networks but by independent companies. The networks claimed that because popular TV series had gained a national audience due to the networks' reach, production companies owed them compensation even after shows completed their prime-time runs. The FCC banned the networks from reaping such profits from program syndication.

The Justice Department instituted a third policy action in 1975. Reacting to a number of legal claims against monopolistic practices, the department limited the networks' production of non-news shows, requiring them to seek most of their programming from independent production companies and film studios. Initially, the limit was three hours of network-created prime-time entertainment programs per week (raised to five hours by the late 1980s). In addition, the networks were limited to producing eight hours per week of in-house entertainment or non-news programs outside prime time, most of which were devoted to soap operas (which were inexpensive to produce and popular with advertisers). However, given that the networks could produce their own TV newsmagazines and select which programs to license, they retained a great deal of power over the content of prime-time television.

With the growth of cable and home video in the 1990s, which made the TV market much more competitive, the FCC gradually phased out the rule limiting network production. Beginning in 1995, the networks were again allowed to syndicate and profit from rerun programs, but only from those they produced. The elimination of fin-syn and other rules opened the door for megadeals (such as Disney's acquisition of ABC in 1995), which constrained independent producers from creating new shows and competing in prime time. Many independent companies and TV critics complained that the corporations that owned the networks (Disney, CBS, 21st Century Fox, and Comcast) exerted too much power and control over broadcast television content. The digital turn, however, has largely changed that picture, with the explosion of available entertainment—from YouTube videos to streaming services to smartphone podcasts. Then there's Netflix, a company that planned to spend $8 billion on new programming in 2018. In 2002, 182 new scripted shows debuted on network television and cable; in 2017, that number was 487.[23]

Balancing Cable's Growth against Broadcasters' Interests

By the early 1970s, cable's rapid growth, capacity for more channels, and better reception led the FCC to seriously examine industry issues. In 1972, the commission updated or enacted two regulations with long-term effects on cable's expansion: must-carry rules and access-channel mandates.

Must-Carry Rules

First established by the FCC in 1965 and reaffirmed in 1972, the **must-carry rules** required all cable operators to assign channels to and carry all local TV broadcasts on their systems. This rule ensured that local network affiliates, independent stations (those not carrying network programs), and public television channels would benefit from cable's clearer reception. However, to protect regional TV stations and their local advertising, the guidelines limited the number of distant commercial TV signals that a cable system could import to two or three independent stations per market. The guidelines

© Castle Rock Entertainment/ Everett Collection

SEINFELD

(1989–1998) was not an immediate hit, but it was in the ratings top three for the final five of its nine seasons. Now, thirty years after its first episode, the show can still be seen in heavy syndication on broadcast and cable TV. Produced by Sony Pictures Television and NBC, *Seinfeld* is the type of successful show the fin-syn rules targeted to keep out of the networks' hands. The show also made news in 2015 when Hulu acquired exclusive streaming rights to all 180 episodes—for a reported $180 million.

also prohibited cable companies from bringing in network-affiliated stations from another city when a local station already carried that network's programming.

Access-Channel Mandates

In 1972, the FCC also mandated **access channels** in the nation's top one hundred TV markets, requiring cable systems to provide and fund a tier of nonbroadcast channels dedicated to local education, government, and the public. The FCC required large-market cable operators to assign separate channels for each access service, while cable operators in smaller markets (and with fewer channels) could require education, government, and the public to share one channel. In addition to free public-access channels, the FCC called for **leased channels**. Citizens could buy time on these channels and produce their own programs or present controversial views.

Cable's Role: Electronic Publisher or Common Carrier?

Because the Communications Act of 1934 had not anticipated cable, the industry's regulatory status was unclear at first. In the 1970s, cable operators argued that they should be considered **electronic publishers** and be able to choose which channels and content to carry. Cable companies wanted the same "publishing" freedoms and legal protections that broadcast and print media enjoyed in selecting content. Just as local broadcasters could choose to carry local news or *Jeopardy!* at 6 P.M., cable companies wanted to choose what channels to carry.

At the time, the FCC argued the opposite: Cable systems were **common carriers**, providing services that do not get involved in content. Like telephone operators, who do not question the topics of personal conversations ("Hi, I'm the phone company, and what are you going to be talking about today?"), cable companies, the FCC argued, should offer at least part of their services on a first-come, first-served basis to whoever can pay the rate.

In 1979, the debate over this issue ended in the landmark *Midwest Video* case, when the U.S. Supreme Court upheld the rights of cable companies to determine channel content and defined the industry as a form of "electronic publishing."[24] Although the FCC could no longer mandate channels' content, the court said that communities could "request" access channels as part of contract negotiations in the franchising process. Access channels are no longer a requirement, but most cable companies continue to offer them in some form to remain on good terms with their communities.

Intriguingly, must-carry rules seem to contradict the *Midwest Video* ruling, since they require cable operators to carry certain local content. But this is a quirky exception to the *Midwest Video* ruling—mostly due to politics and economics. Must-carry rules have endured because of the lobbying power of the National Association of Broadcasters and the major TV networks. Over the years, these groups have successfully argued that cable companies should carry most local over-the-air broadcast stations on their systems so that local broadcasters can stay financially viable as cable systems expand their menu of channels and services.

Franchising Frenzy

After the *Midwest Video* decision, the future of cable programming was secure, and competition to obtain franchises to supply local cable service became intense. Essentially, a cable franchise is a mini-monopoly awarded by a local community to the most attractive bidder, usually for a fifteen-year period.

ELSEWHERE IN
MEDIA & CULTURE

MEDIA STORIES HAVE SHIFTED OVER TIME TO FOCUS ON "ORDINARY" PEOPLE
p. 180

8
number of hours we watch TV per week, on average
p. 172

Our first TV networks—NBC, CBS, and ABC—started out as radio networks
p. 163

WAS HAPPY TALK INVENTED TO COUNTER MUCH OF THE "BAD NEWS" IN THE 1970s?
p. 441

300
THE NUMBER OF BRANDS PROCTER & GAMBLE, THE WORLD'S LEADING ADVERTISER, DISPLAYS ON TV SHOWS VIEWED PRIMARILY BY WOMEN
p. 338

Although a few large cities permitted two companies to build different parts of their cable systems, most communities granted franchises to only one company so that there wouldn't be more than one operator trampling over private property to string wire from utility poles or to bury cables underground. Most of the nation's cable systems were built between the late 1970s and the early 1990s.

During the franchising process, a city (or state) would outline its cable system needs and request bids from various cable companies. (Potential cable companies were prohibited from also owning broadcast stations or newspapers in the community.) In its bid, a company would make a list of promises to the city about construction schedules, system design, subscription rates, channel capacity, types of programming, financial backing, deadlines, and a *franchise fee*: the money the cable company would pay the city annually for the right to operate the local cable system. Lots of wheeling and dealing transpired in these negotiations, along with occasional corruption (e.g., paying off local city officials who voted on which company got the franchise), as few laws existed to regulate franchise negotiations. Often, battles over broken promises, unreasonable contracts, or escalating rates ended up in court.

Today, a federal cable policy act from 1984 dictates the franchise fees for most U.S. municipalities. This act helps cities and towns use such fees to establish and fund access channels for local government, educational, and community programming as part of their license agreement. For example, Groton, Massachusetts (population around ten thousand), has a cable contract with Charter Communications. According to the terms of the contract, Charter returns 4.25 percent of its revenue to the town (5% is the maximum a city can charge a cable operator). This money, which has amounted to about $100,000 a year, helps underwrite Groton's cable-access programs and other community services.

The Telecommunications Act of 1996

Between 1984 and 1996, lawmakers went back and forth on cable rates and rules, creating a number of cable acts. One Congress would try to end must-carry rules or abandon rate regulation, and then a later one would restore the rules. Congress finally rewrote the nation's communications laws in the **Telecommunications Act of 1996**, bringing cable fully under the federal rules that had long governed the telephone, radio, and TV industries. In its most significant move, Congress used the Telecommunications Act to knock down regulatory barriers, allowing regional phone companies, long-distance carriers, and cable companies to enter one another's markets. The act allows cable companies to offer telephone services, and it permits phone companies to offer Internet services and buy or construct cable systems in communities with fewer than fifty thousand residents. For the first time, owners could operate TV or radio stations in the same market where they owned a cable system. Congress had hoped that the new rules would spur competition and lower both phone and cable rates, but this has not typically happened. Instead, phone and cable companies have merged operations in many markets, keeping prices at a premium and competition to a minimum.

The 1996 act has had a mixed impact on cable customers. Although cable companies argued that it would lead to more competition and innovations in programming, services, and technology, there is in fact little competition in cable. About 90 percent of communities in the United States still have only one local cable company, and in these areas, cable rates have risen faster. In communities with multiple cable providers, the competition does make a difference—monthly rates are an average of 10 percent lower, according to one FCC study.[25] The rise of DBS companies like Dish in the last few years has also made cable prices more competitive. As more customers eventually "cut the cord" and move to cheaper streaming services, cable rates are predicted to drop.

Still, the cable industry has delivered on some of its technology promises, investing $275 billion in technological infrastructure between 1998 and 2017, with most of the funds used for installing high-speed fiber-optic wires to carry TV and phone services. This has enabled cable companies to offer what they call the "triple play"—or the *bundling* of digital cable television, broadband Internet, and telephone service. By 2015, U.S. cable companies had signed more than forty-six million households to digital programming packages, while 67 percent of households had high-speed cable Internet service, and more than thirty million households received their telephone service from cable companies.[26]

THE ECONOMICS AND OWNERSHIP OF TELEVISION AND CABLE

It is not much of a stretch to define TV programming as a system that mostly delivers viewers to merchandise displayed in blocks of ads. And with more than $60 billion at stake in advertising revenues each year, networks and cable services work hard to attract the audiences and subscribers that bring in the advertising dollars. But although broadcast and cable advertising have declined in prominence, one recent study reported that more than 80 percent of consumers say that TV advertising—of all ad formats—has the most impact or influence on their buying decisions. A distant second, third, and fourth in the study were magazines (50%), online (47%), and newspapers (44%).[27] (See Figure 6.3 for costs for a thirty-second commercial during prime-time programs.) To understand the TV economy today, we need to examine the production, distribution, and syndication of programming; the rating system that sets advertising rates; and the ownership structure that controls programming and delivers content to our homes.

Monday

	8:00 P.M.	8:30 P.M.	9:00 P.M.	9:30 P.M.	10:00 P.M.
ABC	Dancing with the Stars ($115,962)				Castle ($113,149)
CBS	The Big Bang Theory ($348,300)	Life in Pieces ($192,379)	Scorpion ($142,108)		NCIS Los Angeles ($109,940)
NBC	The Voice ($240,502)				Blindspot ($209,700)
FOX	Gotham ($151,080)		Minority Report ($120,388)		no network programming

Thursday

	8:00 P.M.	8:30 P.M.	9:00 P.M.	9:30 P.M.	10:00 P.M.
ABC	Grey's Anatomy ($157,609)		Scandal ($224,505)		How to Get Away with Murder ($252,934)
CBS	NFL Thursday Night Football ($464,625)				Elementary ($106,695)
NBC	Heroes Reborn ($126,830)		The Blacklist ($193,793)		The Player* ($108,082)
FOX	Bones ($94,681)		Sleepy Hollow ($98,253)		no network programming

FIGURE 6.3

PRIME-TIME NETWORK TV PRICING, 2018

The average costs are shown for a thirty-second commercial during prime-time programs on Monday and Thursday nights in 2018.

Data from: "TV's most expensive ads: Brands pay for football and tears" (AdAge.com, Oct. 2, 2017)

Note: * = Canceled show

Production

The key to the TV industry's success is offering programs that viewers will habitually watch each week—whether at scheduled times or via catch-up viewing. The networks, producers, and film studios spend fortunes creating programs that they hope will keep us coming back.

Production costs generally fall into two categories: below-the-line and above-the-line. *Below-the-line* costs, which account for roughly 40 percent of a new program's production budget, include the technical, or "hardware," side of production: equipment, special effects, cameras and crews, sets and designers, carpenters, electricians, art directors, wardrobe, lighting, and transportation. *Above-the-line*, or "software," costs include the creative talent: actors, writers, producers, editors, and directors. These costs account for about 60 percent of a program's budget, except in the case of successful long-running series (like *Friends* or *The Big Bang Theory*), in which salary demands by actors can drive up above-the-line costs to more than 90 percent.

Most prime-time programs today are developed by independent production companies that are owned or backed by a major film studio, such as Sony or Disney. In addition to providing and renting production facilities, these film studios serve as a bank, offering enough capital to carry producers through one or more seasons. In television, programs are funded through **deficit financing**. This means that the production company leases the show to a network or cable channel for a license fee that is actually lower than the cost of production. (The company hopes to recoup this loss later in lucrative rerun syndication.) Typically, a network leases an episode of a one-hour drama for about $1.5 million for two airings. Each episode, however, might cost the program's producers about $2.5 million to make, meaning they lose about $1 million per episode. After two years of production (usually forty-four to forty-six episodes), an average network show builds up a large deficit.

Because of smaller audiences and fewer episodes per season, costs for original programs on cable channels are lower than those for network broadcasts.[28] In 2014–15, cable channels paid over $1 million per episode in licensing fees to production companies. Some cable shows, like AMC's *Breaking Bad*, cost about $3 million per episode, but since cable seasons are shorter (usually ten to thirteen episodes per season, compared to twenty-two or twenty-three for broadcast networks), cable channels build up smaller deficits. And unlike networks, cable channels air far fewer programs each year and have two revenue streams to pay for original programs—monthly subscription fees and advertising. (However, because network audiences are usually larger, ad revenue is higher for the traditional networks.) Cable channels also keep costs down by introducing three or four new programs a year, compared to the ten to twenty new shows that a broadcast network might air.

By 2017, competition from HBO and Netflix had driven production costs up, especially for cable programs. *Variety* reported that a new hour-long cable TV drama costs between $3 million and $4 million, whereas a new half-hour sitcom price tag came in between $1 million and $1.5 million. However, as *Variety* noted, "Netflix often exceeds the new, higher averages. The first season of its supernatural sensation *Stranger Things* was shot to look like a 1980s Steven Spielberg movie and came with a price tag of $6 million an episode for season one, rising to $8 million in season two. Netflix's sumptuous period drama *The Crown* cost an estimated $10 million an episode." Probably the most expensive series on television in 2018 was *Game of Thrones*, which *Variety* estimated cost $15 million per episode in its final season.[29]

OFF-NETWORK SYNDICATION

programs often include reruns of popular network sitcoms like *The Big Bang Theory*, which airs on local stations as well as cable channel TBS—where it sometimes beats network programming in the ratings.

© CBS/Photofest

Still, both networks and cable channels build up deficits. This is where film studios like Disney, Sony, and Twentieth (now 21st) Century Fox have been playing a crucial role: They finance the deficit and hope to profit on lucrative deals when the show—such as *NCIS*, *Friends*, or *The Office*—goes into domestic and international syndication.

To save money and control content, many networks and cable stations create programs that are less expensive than sitcoms and dramas. These include TV newsmagazines and reality programs. For example, NBC's *Dateline* requires only about half the outlay (between $700,000 and $900,000 per episode) demanded by a new hour-long drama. In addition, by producing projects in-house, networks and cable channels avoid paying license fees to independent producers and movie production companies.

Distribution

Programs are paid for in a variety of ways. Cable service providers (e.g., Comcast or Cablevision) rely mostly on customer subscriptions to pay for distributing their channels, but they also have to pay the broadcast networks **retransmission fees** to carry network channels and programming. While broadcast networks do earn carriage fees from cable and DBS providers, they pay *affiliate stations* license fees to carry their programs. In return, the networks sell the bulk of advertising time to recoup their fees and their investments in these programs. In this arrangement, local stations receive national programs that attract large local audiences and are allotted some local ad time to sell during the programs to generate their own revenue.

A common misconception is that TV networks own their affiliated stations. This is not usually true. Although traditional networks like NBC own stations in major markets like New York, Los Angeles, and Chicago, throughout most of the country networks sign short-term contracts to rent time on local stations. Years ago, the FCC placed restrictions on network owned-and-operated stations (called **O & Os**). But the sweeping Telecommunications Act of 1996 abolished most ownership restrictions. Today, owners can buy many stations as long as they reach no more than 39 percent of the nation's 120 million–plus TV households.

Although a local affiliate typically carries a network's entire lineup, a station may substitute another program. According to *clearance rules* established in the 1940s by the Justice Department and the FCC, all local affiliates are ultimately responsible for the content of their channels and must clear, or approve, all network programming. Over the years, some of the circumstances in which local affiliates have rejected a network's programming have been controversial. For example, in 1956 singer Nat King Cole was one of the first African American performers to host a network variety program. However, as a result of pressure applied by several white southern organizations, the program had trouble attracting a national sponsor. When some affiliates, both southern and northern, refused to carry the program, NBC canceled it in 1957. Affiliates may occasionally substitute other programming for network programs they think may offend their local audiences, especially if the programs contain explicit sexual content.

Syndication Keeps Shows Going and Going . . .

Syndication—leasing TV stations or cable networks the exclusive right to air TV shows—is a critical component of the distribution process. Each year, executives from thousands of local TV stations and cable firms gather at the National Association of Television Program Executives (NATPE) convention to buy or barter for programs that are up for syndication. In so doing, they acquire the exclusive local market rights, usually for two- or three-year periods, to game shows, talk shows, and **evergreens**— popular old network reruns, such as *I Love Lucy*.

Syndication plays a large role in programming for both broadcast and cable networks. For local network-affiliated stations, syndicated programs are often used during **fringe time**—programming immediately before the evening's prime-time schedule (*early fringe*) and following the local evening news or a network late-night talk show (*late fringe*). Cable channels also syndicate network shows but are more flexible with time slots; for example, TNT may run older network syndicated episodes of

MANDEL NGAN/Getty Images

FIRST-RUN SYNDICATION

programs often include talk shows like *The Ellen DeGeneres Show*, which debuted in 2003 and is now one of the highest-rated daytime series.

Law & Order or *Bones* during its prime-time schedule, along with original cable programs like *Rizzoli & Isles*.

Types of Syndication

In **off-network syndication** (commonly called "reruns"), older programs that no longer run during network prime time are made available for reruns to local stations, cable operators, online services, and foreign markets. This type of syndication occurs when a program builds up a supply of episodes (usually three or four seasons' worth) that are then leased to hundreds of TV stations and cable or DBS providers in the United States and overseas. A show can be put into rerun syndication even if new episodes are airing on network television. Rerun, or off-network, syndication is the key to erasing the losses generated by deficit financing. With a successful program, the profits can be enormous. For instance, the early rerun cycle of *Friends* earned, on average, $4 million an episode from syndication in 250-plus markets, plus cable, totaling over $1 billion. Because the show's success meant the original production costs were already covered, the syndication market became almost pure profit for the producers and their backers. This is why deficit financing endures: Although investors rarely hit the jackpot, when they do, the revenues more than cover a lot of losses and failed programs.

First-run syndication relates to any program specifically produced for sale into syndication markets. Quiz programs such as *Wheel of Fortune* and daytime talk or advice shows like *The Ellen DeGeneres Show* or *Dr. Phil* are made for first-run syndication. The producers of these programs usually sell them directly to local markets around the country and the world.

Barter versus Cash Deals

Most financing of television syndication is either a cash deal or a barter deal. In a *cash deal*, the distributor offers a series for syndication to the highest bidder. Because of exclusive contractual arrangements, programs air on only one broadcast outlet per city in a major TV market or, in the case of cable, on one cable channel's service across the country. Whoever bids the most gets to syndicate the program (which can range from a few thousand dollars for a week's worth of episodes in a small market to $250,000 per week in a large market). In a variation of a cash deal called *cash-plus*, distributors retain some time to sell national commercial spots in successful syndicated shows (when the show is distributed, it already contains the national ads). While this means the local station has less ad time to sell, the station usually pays less for the syndicated show.

Although syndicators prefer cash deals, *barter deals* are usually arranged for new, untested, or older but less popular programs. In a straight barter deal, no money changes hands. Instead, a syndicator offers a program to a local TV station in exchange for a split of the advertising revenue. For example, in a 7/5 barter deal, during each airing the show's producers and syndicator retain seven minutes of ad time for national spots and leave stations with five minutes of ad time for local spots. As programs become more profitable, syndicators repackage and lease the shows as cash-plus deals.

Measuring Television Viewing

Primarily, TV shows live or die based on how satisfied advertisers are with the quantity and quality of the viewing audience. Since 1950, the major organization that tracks and rates prime-time viewing has been the

Nielsen Corporation, which estimates what viewers are watching in the nation's major markets. Ratings services like Nielsen provide advertisers, broadcast networks, local stations, and cable channels with considerable details about viewers—from race and gender to age, occupation, and educational background.

The Impact of Ratings and Shares on Programming

In TV measurement, a **rating** is a statistical estimate expressed as the percentage of households that are tuned to a program in the market being sampled. Another audience measure is the **share**, a statistical estimate of the percentage of homes that are tuned to a specific program but expressed as a percentage of households that are actually using their sets at the time of the sample. For instance, let's say on a typical night that Nielsen samples five thousand metered homes in 210 large U.S. cities, and four thousand of those households have their TV sets turned on. Of those four thousand, about one thousand are tuned to *The Voice* on NBC. The rating for that show is 20 percent—that is, one thousand households watching *The Voice* out of five thousand TV sets monitored. The share is 25 percent—one thousand homes watching *The Voice* out of a total of four thousand sets turned on.

The importance of ratings and shares to the survival of TV programs cannot be overestimated. In practice, television is an industry in which networks, producers, and distributors target, guarantee, and "sell" viewers in blocks to advertisers. Audience measurement tells advertisers not only how many people are watching but, more important, what kinds of people are watching. Prime-time advertisers on the broadcast networks have mainly been interested in reaching relatively affluent eighteen- to forty-nine-year-old viewers, who account for most consumer spending. If a show is attracting those viewers, advertisers will compete to buy time during that program. Typically, as many as nine out of ten new shows introduced each fall on the networks either do not attain the required ratings or fail to reach the "right" viewers. The result is cancellation. Cable, in contrast, targets smaller audiences, so programs that do not attract a large audience might survive on cable because most of cable's revenues come from subscription fees rather than advertising. For example, on cable, AMC's award-winning *Breaking Bad* was considered successful. However, that show rarely attracted an audience of over two million in its first two seasons. By the fifth and final season, its audience had grown to six million viewers, and the show's finale drew over ten million viewers in 2013. (The show's creator, Vince Gilligan, has credited Netflix with *Breaking Bad*'s rating surge, because its streaming service allowed viewers to catch up with the series.) By comparison, CBS's *NCIS* drew an average audience of 16.5 million for each show in 2017–18.

Assessing Today's Converged and Multiscreen Markets

During the height of the network era, a prime-time series with a rating of 17 or 18 and a share of between 28 and 30 was generally a success. By the late 2000s, though, with increasing competition from cable, DVDs, and the Internet, the threshold for success had dropped to a rating of 3 or 4 and a share of under 10. In fact, with all the screen options and targeted audiences, it is almost impossible for a TV program today to crack the highest-rated series list (see Table 6.1). Unfortunately, many popular programs have been canceled over the years because advertisers considered their audiences too young, too old, or too poor. To account for the rise of DVRs, Nielsen now offers three versions of its ratings: live; live plus twenty-four hours, counting how many DVR users played shows within a day of recording; and live plus seven days, adding in how many viewers played the shows within a week. TV series that benefit from large boosts in live plus seven numbers include huge hits like *The*

Scott Green/© IFC/Courtesy: Everett Collection

NICHE MARKETS

As TV's audience gets fragmented among broadcast, cable, DVRs, and the Internet, some shows have focused on targeting smaller niche audiences instead of the broad public. IFC's *Portlandia*, for example, had a relatively small but devoted fan base that supported the show's culturally specific satire.

TABLE 6.1

THE TOP 10 HIGHEST-RATED TV SERIES; INDIVIDUAL PROGRAMS (SINCE 1960)

Note: The *Seinfeld* finale, which aired in May 1998, drew a rating of 41-plus and a total viewership of 76 million; in contrast, the final episode of *Friends* in May 2004 had a 25 rating and drew about 52 million viewers. (The *M*A*S*H* finale in 1983 had more than 100 million viewers.)

Data from: The World Almanac and Book of Facts, 1997 (Mahwah, N.J.: World Almanac Books, 1996), 296; Corbett Steinberg, *TV Facts* (New York: Facts on File Publications, 1985); A.C. Nielsen Media Research.

Program	Network	Date	Rating
1 *M*A*S*H* (final episode)	CBS	2/28/83	60.2
2 *Dallas* ("Who Shot J.R.?" episode)	CBS	11/21/80	53.3
3 *The Fugitive* (final episode)	ABC	8/29/67	45.9
4 *Cheers* (final episode)	NBC	5/20/93	45.5
5 *Ed Sullivan Show* (Beatles' first U.S. TV appearance)	CBS	2/9/64	45.3
6 *Beverly Hillbillies*	CBS	1/8/64	44.0
7 *Ed Sullivan Show* (Beatles' second U.S. TV appearance)	CBS	2/16/64	43.8
8 *Beverly Hillbillies*	CBS	1/15/64	42.8
9 *Beverly Hillbillies*	CBS	2/26/64	42.4
10 *Beverly Hillbillies*	CBS	3/25/64	42.2

Big Bang Theory, moderate performers like *Agents of S.H.I.E.L.D.*, and more niche-specific shows like *New Girl*.[30]

In its efforts to keep up with TV's move to smaller screens, Nielsen is also using special software to track TV viewing on computers and mobile devices. Today, with the fragmentation of media audiences, the increase in third- and fourth-screen technologies, and the decline in traditional TV set viewing, targeting smaller niche markets and consumers has become advertisers' main game.

The biggest revenue game changer in the small-screen world will probably be Google's YouTube, which in 2011 and 2012 entered into a joint venture with nearly a hundred content producers to create niche online channels. YouTube advances up to $5 million to each content producer, and it keeps the ad money it collects until the advance is paid off; revenue after that is split between YouTube and the content producer. Some familiar names have signed on, including Madonna, Shaquille O'Neal, and Amy Poehler. Among the popular channels already launched are the music video site Noisey, which had twenty-seven million visits in its first two months, and Drive, a channel for auto fans, which had seven million views in its first four months.

The way advertising works online differs substantially from the way it works on network TV, where advertisers pay as much as $400,000 to buy one thirty-second ad during Fox's *Empire*. Online advertisers pay a rate called a CPM ("cost per mille"; *mille* is Latin for "one thousand"), meaning the rate per one thousand *impressions*—which is a single ad shown to a person visiting an online site. If a product company or ad agency purchases one thousand online impressions at a $1 CPM rate, that means the company or agency would spend $10 to have its advertisement displayed ten thousand times. Popular online sites where advertisers are reaching targeted audiences could set a CPM rate between $10 and $100, while less popular sites might command only a $.10 to $.20 CPM rate from ad agencies and product companies. For some of its new YouTube channels, analysts are predicting that Google might be able to charge as much as a $20 CPM for a relatively popular site.

The Major Programming Corporations

After deregulation began in the 1980s, many players in TV and cable consolidated to broaden their offerings, expand their market share, and lower expenses. For example, Disney now owns both ABC and ESPN and can spread the costs of sports programming over its networks and its various ESPN cable channels. This business strategy has produced an *oligopoly* in which just a handful of media corporations now controls programming.

The Major Broadcast Networks

Despite their declining reach and the rise of cable, the traditional networks have remained attractive business investments. In 1985, General Electric, which once helped start RCA-NBC, bought back NBC. In 1995, Disney bought ABC for $19 billion; in 1999, Viacom acquired CBS for $37 billion (Viacom and

CBS split in 2005, but Viacom's CEO, Sumner Redstone, has remained CBS's main stockholder and executive chair; in 2014, his holdings in both CBS and Viacom totaled $6 billion). And in January 2011, the FCC and the Department of Justice approved Comcast's purchase of NBC Universal from GE—a deal valued at $30 billion.

To combat audience erosion in the 1990s, the major networks began acquiring or developing cable channels to recapture viewers. Thus, what appears to be competition between TV and cable is sometimes an illusion. NBC, for example, operates MSNBC, CNBC, and Bravo, while ABC owns ESPN along with portions of Lifetime, A&E, and History.

Major Cable and DBS Companies

In the late 1990s, cable became a coveted investment, not so much for its ability to carry TV programming as for its access to households connected with high-bandwidth wires. Today, there are about 5,000 U.S. cable systems, down from 11,200 in 1994. Since the 1990s, thousands of cable systems have been bought by large **multiple-system operators (MSOs)**, corporations like Comcast and Charter Communications that own many cable systems. For years the industry called its major players **multichannel video programming distributors (MVPDs)**, a term that included DBS providers like DirecTV and Dish. By 2014, cable's main trade organization, the National Cable & Telecommunications Association (NCTA), had moved away from the MVPD classification and started using the term **video subscription services**, which now also includes Netflix and Hulu (see Table 6.2). Some critics say that the new classification term has provided new hope for mergers, like the recent purchase of TWC by Charter Communications. Cable attorneys argue that the streaming service Netflix now dwarfs Comcast and Charter Communications—with forty-three million U. S. subscribers in 2016, more than those of Comcast and Charter combined. In addition, with AT&T's acquisition of DirecTV in 2015, the subscriber numbers of the merged phone and DBS providers also surpassed those of Comcast.

In the cable industry, Comcast became the top player after its takeover of NBC and move into network broadcasting. Back in 2001, AT&T had merged its cable and broadband industry in a $72 billion deal with Comcast, then the third-largest MSO. The new Comcast instantly became the cable industry leader. In 2015, Comcast also owned E!, NBCSN, the Golf Channel, Universal Studios, Fandango (the online movie ticket site), and a 32 percent stake in Hulu (with Fox and Disney). In 2017, there were about 650 companies still operating the nation's 5,000 cable systems. Along with Comcast, the other large MSOs included TWC, Cox Communications, Charter Communications, and Cablevision Systems.

In the DBS market, DirecTV and Dish control virtually all the DBS service in the continental United States. In 2008, News Corp. sold DirecTV to cable service provider Liberty Media, which also owned the Encore and Starz movie channels. The independently owned Dish was founded as EchoStar Communications in 1980. In 2015, to counter the merger talks between Comcast and TWC, DirecTV merged with AT&T. Over the last few years, TV services (combined with existing voice and

Rank	Video Subscription Service	Subscribers
1	Netflix	56.7 million
2	Amazon	26.0 million
3	DIRECTV	25.4 million
4	Comcast	22.3 million
5	Hulu	20.0 million
6	Charter Communications	16.4 million
7	Dish	10.9 million
8	Verizon FiOS	4.6 million
9	Cox Communications	3.8 million
10	Altice	3.6 million

TABLE 6.2

TOP 10 VIDEO SUBSCRIPTION SERVICES IN 2018

Data from: National Cable & Telecommunications Association, "Industry Data," www.ncta.com /industry-data?industry=true www.ncta.com/chart/top-10-video -subscription-services.

Internet services) offered by telephone giants AT&T (U-verse) and Verizon (FiOS) have developed into viable competitors for cable and DBS.

The Effects of Consolidation

There are some concerns that the trend toward mergers of cable, DBS, broadcasting, and telephone companies will limit expression of political viewpoints, programming options, and technical innovation, and lead to price-fixing. These concerns raise an important question: *In an economic climate in which fewer owners control the circulation of communication, what happens to new ideas or controversial views that may not always be profitable to circulate?*

The response from the industries is that, given the tremendous capital investment it takes to run television, cable, and other media enterprises, it is necessary to form business conglomerates in order to buy up struggling companies and keep them afloat. This argument suggests that without today's video subscription services, many smaller ventures in programming would not be possible. However, there is evidence that large MSOs and other big media companies can wield their monopoly power unfairly. Business disputes have caused disruptions as networks and cable providers have dropped one another from their services, leaving customers in the dark. For example, in August 2013, Time Warner Cable took CBS off its systems for a month in a bitter dispute over retransmission fee hikes the network sought. In addition to blacking out WCBS in New York, Los Angeles, Dallas, and five other markets, the cable company yanked Showtime from its systems. This is one of many examples that illustrate what can happen when a few large corporations engage in arguments over prices and programs: In markets with minimal or no competition and programming from just a handful of large media companies, consumers are often left with little recourse.

Alternative Voices

After suffering through years of rising rates and limited expansion of services, some small U.S. cities have decided to challenge the private monopolies of cable giants by building competing, publicly owned cable systems. So far, the municipally owned cable systems number in the hundreds and can be found in places like Glasgow, Kentucky; Kutztown, Pennsylvania; Cedar Falls, Iowa; and Provo, Utah. In most cases, they're operated by the community-owned, nonprofit electric utilities. There are more than two thousand such municipal utilities across the United States, serving about 14 percent of the population and creating the potential for more municipal utilities to expand into communications services. As nonprofit entities, the municipal operations are less expensive for cable subscribers, too.

More than a quarter of the country's two-thousand-plus municipal utilities offer broadband services, including cable, high-speed Internet, and telephone. How will commercial cable operators fend off this unprecedented competition? In 2016 in Glasgow, Kentucky, the local Electric Plant Board offered bundled services that were about $20 a month cheaper than Comcast's $100-per-month cost. According to William Ray, superintendent of the board, "If cable operators are afraid of cities competing with them, there is a defense that is impregnable—they can charge reasonable rates, offer consummate customer service, improve their product, and conduct their business as if they were a guest that owes their existence to the benevolence of the city that has invited them in."[31]

TELEVISION, CABLE, AND DEMOCRACY

In the 1950s, television's arrival significantly changed the media landscape—particularly the radio and magazine industries, both of which had to cultivate specialized audiences and markets to survive. In its heyday, television carried the egalitarian promise that it could bypass traditional print literacy and reach all segments of society. This promise was reenergized in the 1970s when cable-access channels gave local communities the chance to create their own TV programming. In such a heterogeneous and diverse nation, the concept of a visual, affordable mass medium, giving citizens entertainment and information that they could talk about the next day, held great appeal. However, since its creation, commercial television has tended to serve the interests of profit more often than those of democracy. Despite this, television remains the main storytelling medium of our time.

The development of cable, VCRs and DVD players, DVRs, the Internet, and smartphone services has fragmented television's audience by appealing to viewers' individual and special needs. These changes and services, by providing more specialized and individual choices, also alter television's role as a national unifying cultural force, potentially de-emphasizing the idea that we are all citizens of a larger nation and world. Moreover, many cable channels have survived mostly by offering live sports or recycling old television shows and movies. Although cable and on-demand streaming services like Netflix are creating an increasing number of original high-quality programs, they rarely reach even the diminished audience numbers commanded by the traditional broadcast networks. In fact, given that the television networks and many leading cable channels are now owned by the same media conglomerates, cable has evolved into something of an extension of the networks.

Even though cable audiences are growing and network viewership is contracting, the division between the two is blurring. New generations who have grown up on cable and the Internet rarely make a distinction between a broadcast network, a cable service, DBS, and an on-demand program. In addition, tablets, smartphones, and Internet services that now offer or create our favorite "TV" programs are breaking down the distinctions between mobile devices and TV screens. Cable, which once offered promise as a place for alternative programming and noncommercial voices, is now being usurped by the Internet, where all kinds of TV experiments are under way.

The bottom line is that despite the audience fragmentation, television still provides a gathering place for friends and family, while providing anytime, anywhere access to a favorite show. Like all media forms before it, television is adapting to changing technology and shifting economics. As the technology becomes more portable and personal, TV-related industries continue to search for less expensive ways to produce stories and more channels on which to deliver them. But what will remain common ground on this shifting terrain is that television continues as our nation's chief storyteller, whether those stories come in the form of news bulletins, sporting events, cable dramas, network sitcoms, or YouTube vignettes.

TV's future will be about serving smaller rather than larger audiences. As sites like YouTube develop original programming and as niche cable services like the Weather Channel produce reality TV series about storms, no audience seems too small and no subject matter too narrow for today's TV world. For example, by 2013, *Duck Dynasty*—a program about an eccentric Louisiana family that got rich making products for duck hunters—had become a hit series on A&E. The program averaged 12.4 million viewers in 2012–13, a cable record, but then lost 75 percent of those viewers by 2015, as many viewers grew weary of the series. The show ended in 2017, with the finale drawing only 1.5 million viewers. An overwhelming number of programming choices now exist for big and small TV screens alike. How might this converged TV landscape—with its volatile ups and downs in viewer numbers—change how audiences watch, and pay for, TV? With hundreds of shows available, will we adopt à la carte viewing habits, in which we download or stream only the shows that interest us, rather than pay for cable (or DBS) packages with hundreds of channels we don't watch?

Series: Photographic Materials, ca. 1926 - ca. 1994 Collection: Richard Nixon Foundation Collection of Audiovisual Materials, ca. 1926 - ca. 1994/National Archives and Records Administration

TV AND DEMOCRACY
The first televised presidential debates took place in 1960, pitting Massachusetts senator John F. Kennedy against Vice President Richard Nixon. Don Hewitt, who later created the long-running TV newsmagazine *60 Minutes*, directed the first debate and has argued that the TV makeup that Nixon turned down would have helped create a better appearance alongside that of his tanned opponent. In fact, one study at the time reported that a majority of radio listeners thought Nixon won the debate, while a majority of TV viewers thought Kennedy won.

6 Chapter Review

COMMON THREADS

One of the Common Threads discussed in Chapter 1 is mass media, cultural expression, and storytelling. As television and cable change their shape and size, do they remain the dominant way our culture tells stories?

By the end of the 1950s, television had become an "electronic hearth," where families gathered in living rooms to share cultural experiences. By 2012, though, the television experience had splintered. Now we are watching programming on our laptops, smartphones, and tablets, making the experience increasingly individual rather than communal. Still, television remains the mass medium that can reach most of us at a single moment in time, whether it's during a popular sitcom or during a presidential debate.

In this shift, what has been lost, and what has been gained? As an electronic hearth, television has offered coverage of special or historic moments—inaugurations, assassinations, moonwalks, space disasters, Super Bowls, *Roots*, the Olympics, 9/11, hurricanes, presidential campaigns, Arab uprisings, World Cups—that brought large heterogeneous groups together for the common experience of sharing information, celebrating triumphs, mourning loss, and electing presidents. Accessible now in multiple

digitized versions, the TV image has become portable—just as radio became portable in the 1950s. Today, we can watch television in cars, in the park, and in class on our smartphones (even when we're not supposed to).

The bottom line is that television in all its configurations is now both electronic hearth and digital encounter. It still provides a gathering place for friends and family, but now we can also watch a favorite show almost whenever or wherever we want. Like all media forms before it, television is adapting to changing technology and shifting economics. As technology becomes more portable and personal, the network TV, cable, and video subscription industries search for less expensive ways to produce and deliver television. Still, television remains the main place—whether it's the big LED screen or the handheld smartphone—where we go for stories. In what ways do you think this will change or remain the case in the future? Where do you prefer to get your stories?

KEY TERMS

The definitions for the terms listed below can be found in the glossary at the end of the book. The page numbers listed with the terms indicate where the term is highlighted in the chapter.

analog, 164
digital, 164
prime time, 166
network era, 168
CATV, 168
narrowcasting, 169
basic cable, 169
superstations, 169
premium channels, 171
pay-per-view (PPV), 171
video-on-demand (VOD), 171
direct broadcast satellite (DBS), 171
cord cutting, 171
time shifting, 172
third screens, 172
fourth screens, 173

kinescope, 175
sketch comedy, 175
situation comedy, 176
anthology dramas, 176
episodic series, 177
chapter shows, 177
serial programs, 177
affiliate stations, 179
Prime Time Access Rule (PTAR), 182
fin-syn, 183
must-carry rules, 183
access channels, 184
leased channels, 184
electronic publishers, 184
common carriers, 184
Telecommunications Act of 1996, 186

deficit financing, 188
retransmission fees, 189
O & Os, 189
syndication, 189
evergreens, 189
fringe time, 189
off-network syndication, 190
first-run syndication, 190
rating, 191
share, 191
multiple-system operators (MSOs), 193
multichannel video programming distributors (MVPDs), 193
video subscription services, 193

REVIEW QUESTIONS

The Origins and Development of Television

1. What were the major technical standards established for television in the 1940s? What happened to analog television?

2. Why did the FCC freeze the allocation of TV licenses between 1948 and 1952?

3. How did the sponsorship of network programs change during the 1950s?

The Development of Cable

4. What is CATV, and what were its advantages over broadcast television?

5. How did satellite distribution change the cable industry?

6. What is DBS? How well does it compete with the cable industry?

Technology and Convergence Change Viewing Habits

7. How have computers and mobile devices challenged the TV and cable industries?

8. What has happened to the audience in the digital era of third and fourth screens?

Major Programming Trends

9. What are the differences between sketch comedy and sitcoms on television?

10. How did news develop at the networks in the late 1940s and 1950s?

11. What are the challenges faced by public broadcasting today?

Regulatory Challenges to Television and Cable

12. What rules and regulations did the government impose to restrict the networks' power?

13. How did cable pose a challenge to broadcasting, and how did the FCC respond to cable's early development?

14. How did the Telecommunications Act of 1996 change the economic shape and future of the television and cable industries?

The Economics and Ownership of Television and Cable

15. Why has it become more difficult for independent producers to create programs for television?

16. What are the differences between off-network syndication and first-run syndication?

17. What are ratings and shares in TV audience measurement?

Television, Cable, and Democracy

18. Why has television's role as a national cultural center changed over the years? What are programmers doing to retain some of their influence?

QUESTIONING THE MEDIA

1. How much television do you watch today? How has technology influenced your current viewing habits?

2. If you were a television or cable executive, what changes would you make in today's programs? How would you try to adapt to third- and fourth-screen technologies?

3. Do you think the must-carry rules violate a cable company's First Amendment rights? Why or why not?

4. How do you think new technologies will further change TV viewing habits?

5. How could television be used to improve our social and political life?

LAUNCHPAD FOR *MEDIA & CULTURE*

Visit LaunchPad for *Media & Culture* at launchpadworks.com for additional learning tools:

- **REVIEW WITH LEARNINGCURVE**
  LearningCurve, available on LaunchPad for *Media & Culture*, uses gamelike quizzing to help you master the concepts you need to learn from this chapter.

- **VIDEO: WIRED OR WIRELESS: TELEVISION DELIVERY TODAY**
  This video explores the switch to digital TV signals in 2009 and how it is changing television delivery.

Movies and the Impact of Images

7

"A LONG TIME AGO in a galaxy far, far away . . ." So begins the now-famous opening credit crawl of *Star Wars*. The first appearance of those words was in movie theaters on earth, but the time now is rather long ago: May 25, 1977.

The space epic changed the culture of the movie industry. *Star Wars*—produced, written, and directed by George Lucas—departed from the personal filmmaking of the early 1970s and spawned a blockbuster mentality that formed a new primary audience for Hollywood: teenagers. It had all of the now-typical blockbuster characteristics, including massive promotion and lucrative merchandising tie-ins. Repeat attendance and positive buzz among young people made the first *Star Wars* the most successful movie of its generation.

◄ Fans of the classic 1970s *Star Wars* films were skeptical when George Lucas sold Lucasfilm to the Walt Disney Company in 2012 for $4.06 billion, but a new trilogy of films starting with *The Force Awakens* has brought new life to the *Star Wars* franchise.

EARLY TECHNOLOGY AND THE EVOLUTION OF MOVIES
p. 201

THE RISE OF THE HOLLYWOOD STUDIO SYSTEM
p. 204

THE STUDIO SYSTEM'S GOLDEN AGE
p. 208

THE TRANSFORMATION OF THE STUDIO SYSTEM
p. 218

THE ECONOMICS OF THE MOVIE BUSINESS
p. 221

POPULAR MOVIES AND DEMOCRACY
p. 228

Star Wars has influenced not only the cultural side of moviemaking but also the technical form. In the first *Star Wars* trilogy, produced in the 1970s and 1980s, Lucas developed technologies that are now commonplace in moviemaking: digital animation, special effects, and computer-based film editing. With the second trilogy (which was a prequel to the narrative of the original *Star Wars*), Lucas again broke new ground in the film industry, using digital video for several scenes, which eased integration with digital special effects. By the time the last installment of the second trilogy—*Star Wars: Episode III—Revenge of the Sith* (2005)—was released, *Star Wars* was firmly in place as one of the most successful film series of all time, with more than $4.5 billion in worldwide box office revenue.[1]

The third *Star Wars* trilogy opened in late 2015 with *Star Wars: Episode VII—The Force Awakens*. The story picks up thirty years after *Star Wars: Episode VI—Return of the Jedi* (1983) and includes characters Luke Skywalker, Han Solo, and Princess Leia played by original actors Mark Hamill, Harrison Ford, and Carrie Fisher. However, perhaps the biggest news regarding *The Force Awakens* was on the business side: For the first time, *Star Wars* was a Disney property. In 2012, Disney paid $4 billion for Lucasfilm—George Lucas's independent production company, which had controlled the *Star Wars* legacy from its inception.

At the time of the announcement, Disney CEO Robert Iger spoke about the business possibilities: "This transaction combines a world-class portfolio of content including *Star Wars*, one of the greatest family entertainment franchises of all time, with Disney's unique and unparalleled creativity across multiple platforms, businesses, and markets to generate sustained growth and drive

significant long-term value."[2] In plain language, this means more *Star Wars* on television, in digital games, in theme parks, and in consumer products.

Some purists may groan at the volume of these ancillaries, but Disney's track record at turning its acquisitions into even greater media and merchandise franchises is enviable. Two other important movie brand acquisitions were its purchase of Pixar for $7.6 billion in 2006, and Marvel for $3.96 billion in 2009.[3] Pixar has created some of the most successful animated movies of the past two decades, such as *Toy Story 3* (2010), *Coco* (2017), and *The Incredibles 2* (2018). Marvel, in retrospect, appears to be even more of a bargain. Disney-produced films from the Marvel cinematic universe include *Guardians of the Galaxy* (2014), *Black Panther* (2018), and *Avengers: Infinity War* (2018).

In fact, Disney's business for the first film in the third *Star Wars* trilogy (*Episode VII*) exceeded all expectations. Four months after its December 2015 premiere in the United States, *The Force Awakens* had grossed $936.7 million in domestic box-office receipts and totaled more than $2 billion worldwide, becoming the highest-earning film in U.S. box-office history. *Star Wars Episode VIII—The Last Jedi*, had more than $620 million in domestic box office for its 2017 release, putting it at No. 7 on the blockbuster list. The story continues in *Episode IX*, expected in December 2019.

Disney's purchase of the *Star Wars* franchise is yielding more than just another trilogy. In between each new episode premiere, Disney is releasing individual anthology films that fill in parts of the entire *Star Wars* saga, the schedule of which ensures a new *Star Wars* film for every year through 2020. The plan is likely to please fans and generate an enormous return on investment for Disney's *Star Wars* franchise.

DATING BACK TO THE LATE 1800s, films have had a substantial social and cultural impact on society. Blockbuster movies such as *Star Wars, E.T., Titanic, Lord of the Rings, Avatar,* and *The Avengers* represent what Hollywood has become—America's storyteller. Movies tell communal stories that evoke and symbolize our most enduring values and our secret desires (from *The Wizard of Oz* to *The Godfather* to the *Batman* series).

Films have also helped moviegoers sort through experiences that either affirmed or deviated from their own values. Some movies—for instance, *Last Tango in Paris* (1972), *Scarface* (1983), *Fahrenheit 9/11* (2004), *Brokeback Mountain* (2005), and *Three Billboards Outside Ebbing, Missouri* (2017)—have allowed audiences to survey "the boundary between the permitted and the forbidden" and to experience, in a controlled way, "the possibility of stepping across this boundary."[4] Such films— criticized by some for appearing to glorify crime and violence, verge on pornography, trample on sacred beliefs, or promote unpatriotic viewpoints—have even, on occasion, been banned from public viewing.

Finally, movies have acted to bring people together. Movies distract us from our daily struggles: They evoke and symbolize universal themes of human experience (that of childhood, coming of age, family relations, growing older, and coping with death); they can help us understand and respond to major historical events and tragedies (for instance, the Holocaust and 9/11); and they encourage us to reexamine contemporary ideas as the world evolves, particularly in terms of how we think about race, class, spirituality, gender, and sexuality.

In this chapter, we examine the rich legacy and current standing of movies. We will:

- Consider film's early technology and the evolution of film as a mass medium
- Look at the arrival of silent feature films; the emergence of Hollywood; and the development of the studio system with regard to production, distribution, and exhibition
- Explore the coming of sound and the power of movie storytelling
- Analyze major film genres, directors, and alternatives to Hollywood's style, including independent films, foreign films, and documentaries
- Survey the movie business today—its major players, economic clout, technological advances, and implications for democracy
- Examine how convergence has changed the way the industry distributes movies and the way we experience them

As you consider these topics, think about your own relationship with movies. What is the first movie you remember watching? What are your movie-watching experiences like today? How have certain movies made you think differently about an issue, yourself, or others? For more questions to help you think through the role of movies in our lives, see "Questioning the Media" in the Chapter Review.

LaunchPad
macmillan learning

launchpadworks.com

Visit LaunchPad for *Media & Culture* and use LearningCurve to review concepts from this chapter.

EARLY TECHNOLOGY AND THE EVOLUTION OF MOVIES

History often credits a handful of enterprising individuals with developing the new technologies that lead to new categories of mass media. Such innovations, however, are usually the result of simultaneous investigations by numerous people. In addition, the innovations of both known and unknown inventors are propelled by economic and social forces as well as by individual abilities.[5]

The Development of Film

The concept of film goes back as early as Leonardo da Vinci, who theorized in the late fifteenth century about creating a device that would reproduce reality. Other early precursors to film included the Magic Lantern, developed in the seventeenth century, which projected images painted on glass plates using an oil lamp as a light source; the *thaumatrope*, invented in 1824, a two-sided card with different images on each side that appeared to combine the images when twirled; and the *zoetrope*,

EADWEARD MUYBRIDGE'S

study of horses in motion proved that a racehorse gets all four feet off the ground during a gallop. In his various studies of motion, Muybridge would use up to twelve cameras at a time.

'A galloping horse and rider.' by Eadweard Muybridge and University of Pennsylvania/Wellcome Collection.

introduced in 1834, a cylindrical device that rapidly twirled images inside a cylinder, which appeared to make the images move.

Muybridge and Goodwin Make Pictures Move

The development stage of movies began when inventors started manipulating photographs to make them appear to move while simultaneously projecting them onto a screen. Eadweard Muybridge, an English photographer living in America, is credited with being the first to do both. He studied motion by using multiple cameras to take successive photographs of humans and animals in motion. One of Muybridge's first projects involved using photography to determine if a racehorse actually lifts all four feet from the ground at full gallop (it does). By 1880, Muybridge had developed a method for projecting the photographic images onto a wall for public viewing. These early image sequences were extremely brief, showing a horse jumping over a fence or a man running a few feet, because only so many photographs could be mounted inside the spinning cylinder that projected the images.

Meanwhile, other inventors were also working on capturing moving images and projecting them. In 1884, George Eastman (founder of Eastman Kodak) developed the first roll film—a huge improvement over the heavy metal and glass plates used to make individual photos. The first roll film had a paper backing that had to be stripped off during the film developing stage. Louis Aimé Augustin Le Prince, a Frenchman living in England, invented the first motion picture camera using roll film. Le Prince, who disappeared mysteriously on a train ride to Paris in 1890, is credited with filming the first motion picture, *Roundhay Garden Scene*, in 1888. About two seconds' worth of the film survives today.

In 1889, a New Jersey minister, Hannibal Goodwin, improved Eastman's roll film by using thin strips of transparent, pliable material called **celluloid**, which could hold a coating of chemicals sensitive to light. Goodwin's breakthrough solved a major problem: It enabled a strip of film to move through a camera and be photographed in rapid succession, producing a series of pictures. Because celluloid was transparent (except for the images made on it during filming), it was ideal for projection, as light could easily shine through it. George Eastman, who also announced the development of celluloid film, legally battled Goodwin for years over the patent rights. The courts eventually awarded Goodwin the invention, but Eastman's company became the major manufacturer of film stock for motion pictures after buying Goodwin's patents.

Edison and the Lumières Create Motion Pictures

As with the development of sound recording, Thomas Edison takes center stage in most accounts of the invention of motion pictures. In the late 1800s, Edison planned to merge phonograph technology and moving images to create talking pictures (which would not happen in feature films until 1927). With no breakthrough, however, Edison lost interest. He directed an assistant, William Kennedy Dickson, to combine his incandescent lightbulb, Goodwin's celluloid, and Le Prince's camera to create another early movie camera, the **kinetograph**, and a single-person viewing system, the **kinetoscope**. This small projection system housed fifty feet of film that revolved on spools (the device was similar to those in a library microfilm reader). Viewers looked through a hole and saw images moving on a tiny plate. In 1894, the first kinetoscope parlor, featuring two rows of coin-operated machines, opened on Broadway in New York. ·

Meanwhile, in France, brothers Louis and Auguste Lumière developed the *cinematograph*, a combined camera, film developer, and projection system. The projection system was particularly important, as it allowed more than one person at a time to see the moving images on a large screen. In a Paris café on December 28, 1895, the Lumières projected ten short movies for viewers who paid one franc each, on such subjects as a man falling off a horse and a child trying to grab a fish from a bowl. Within three weeks, twenty-five hundred people were coming each night to see how, according to one Paris paper, film "perpetuates the image of movement."

With innovators around the world now dabbling in moving pictures, Edison's lab renewed its interest in film. Edison patented several inventions and manufactured a new large-screen system called the **vitascope**, which enabled filmstrips of longer lengths to be projected without interruption and hinted at the potential of movies as a future mass medium. Staged at a music hall in New York in April 1896, Edison's first public showing of the vitascope featured shots from a boxing match and waves rolling onto a beach. Some members of the audience were so taken with the realism of the film images that they stepped back from the screen's crashing waves to avoid getting their feet wet. Early movie demonstrations such as these marked the beginning of the film industry's entrepreneurial stage. By 1900, short movies had become part of the entertainment industry and were showing up in amusement arcades, traveling carnivals, wax museums, and vaudeville theater.

Everett Collection

KINETOSCOPES
allowed individuals to view motion pictures through a window in a cabinet that held the film. The first kinetoscope parlor opened in 1894 and was such a hit that many others quickly followed.

The Introduction of Narrative

The shift to the mass medium stage for movies occurred with the introduction of **narrative films**: movies that tell stories. Audiences quickly tired of static films of waves breaking on beaches or vaudeville acts recorded by immobile cameras. To become a mass medium, the early silent films had to offer what books achieved: the suspension of disbelief. They had to create narrative worlds that engaged an audience's imagination.

Some of the earliest narrative films were produced and directed by French magician and inventor Georges Méliès, who opened the first public movie theater in France in 1896. Méliès may have been the first director to realize that a movie was not simply a means of recording reality, that it could be artificially planned and controlled like a staged play. Méliès began producing short fantasy and fairy-tale films—including *The Vanishing Lady* (1896), *Cinderella* (1899), and *A Trip to the Moon* (1902)—employing editing and existing camera tricks and techniques, such as slow motion and cartoon animation, which became key ingredients in future narrative filmmaking.

The first American filmmaker to adapt Méliès's innovations to narrative film was Edwin S. Porter. A camera operator who had studied Méliès's work in an Edison lab, Porter mastered the technique of editing diverse shots together to tell a coherent story. Porter shot narrative scenes out of order (for instance, some in a studio and some outdoors) and reassembled, or edited, them to make a story. In 1902, he made what is regarded as America's first narrative film, *The Life of an American Fireman*. The film also contained the first close-up shot in U.S. narrative film history—a ringing fire alarm. Until then, moviemakers thought close-ups cheated the audience of the opportunity to see an entire scene. Porter's most important film, *The Great Train Robbery* (1903), introduced the western genre as well as chase scenes. In this popular eleven-minute movie, which inspired many copycats, Porter demonstrated the art of film suspense by alternating shots of the robbers with those of a posse in hot pursuit.

The Arrival of Nickelodeons

Another major development in the evolution of film as a mass medium was the arrival of **nickelodeons**—a form of movie theater whose name combines the admission price with the Greek word for "theater." According to media historian Douglas Gomery, these small and uncomfortable makeshift theaters were often converted storefronts redecorated to mimic vaudeville theaters: "In front, large, hand-painted posters announced the movies for the day. Inside, the screening of news, documentary, comedy, fantasy, and dramatic shorts lasted about one hour."[6] Usually a piano player added live music, and sometimes theater operators used sound effects to simulate gunshots or loud crashes. Because they showed silent films that transcended language barriers, nickelodeons flourished during the great European immigration at the turn of the twentieth century. These theaters filled a need for many newly arrived people struggling to learn English and seeking an inexpensive escape from the hard life of the city. Often managed by immigrants, nickelodeons required a minimal investment: just a secondhand projector and a large white sheet. Between 1907 and 1909, the number of nickelodeons grew from five thousand to ten thousand. The craze peaked by 1910, when entrepreneurs began to seek more affluent spectators, attracting them with larger and more lavish movie theaters.

THE RISE OF THE HOLLYWOOD STUDIO SYSTEM

By the 1910s, movies had become a major industry. Among the first to try his hand at dominating the movie business and reaping its profits, Thomas Edison formed the Motion Picture Patents Company, known as the *Trust*, in 1908. A cartel of major U.S. and French film producers, the company pooled patents in an effort to control film's major technology, acquired most major film distributorships, and signed an exclusive deal with George Eastman, who agreed to supply movie film only to Trust-approved companies.

However, some independent producers refused to bow to the Trust's terms. They saw too much demand for films, too much money to be made, and too many ways to avoid the Trust's scrutiny. Some producers began to relocate from the centers of film production in New York and New Jersey to Cuba and Florida. Ultimately, though, Hollywood became the film capital of the world. Southern California offered cheap labor, diverse scenery for outdoor shooting, and a mild climate suitable for year-round production. Geographically far from the Trust's headquarters in New Jersey, independent producers in Hollywood could easily slip over the border into Mexico to escape legal prosecution brought by the Trust for patent violations.

Wanting to free their movie operations from the Trust's tyrannical grasp, two Hungarian immigrants—Adolph Zukor, who would eventually run Paramount Pictures, and William Fox, who would found the Fox Film Corporation (which later became Twentieth Century Fox)—played a role in the collapse of Edison's Trust. Zukor's early companies figured out ways to bypass the Trust, and a suit by Fox, a nickelodeon operator turned film distributor, resulted in the Trust's breakup due to restraint-of-trade violations in 1917.

Ironically, entrepreneurs like Zukor developed other tactics for controlling the industry. The strategies, many of which are still used today, were more ambitious than just monopolizing patents and technology. They aimed at dominating the movie business at all three essential levels—*production*, everything involved in making a movie, from securing a script and actors to raising money and filming; *distribution*, getting the films into theaters; and *exhibition*, playing films in theaters. This control—or **vertical integration**—of all levels of the movie business gave certain studios great power and eventually spawned a film industry that turned into an **oligopoly**, a situation in which a few firms control the bulk of the business.

Production

In the early days of film, producers and distributors had not yet recognized that fans would seek not only particular film stories—like dramas, westerns, and romances—but also particular film actors. Responding to discerning audiences and competing against Edison's Trust, Adolph Zukor hired a number of popular actors and formed the Famous Players Company in 1912. His idea was to control movie production not through patents but through exclusive contracts with actors. One Famous Players performer was Mary Pickford. Known as "America's Sweetheart" for her portrayal of spunky and innocent heroines, Pickford was "unspoiled" by a theater background and better suited to the more subtle and intimate new medium. She became so popular that audiences waited in line to see her movies, and producers were forced to pay her increasingly higher salaries.

An astute business owner, Mary Pickford was the key figure in elevating the financial status and professional role of film actors. In 1910, Pickford made about $100 a week, but by 1914 she was earning

MARY PICKFORD
With legions of fans, Mary Pickford became the first woman ever to make a salary of $1 million in a year, gaining the freedom to take artistic risks with her roles. (She would famously tell Adolph Zukor in 1915, "No, I really cannot afford to work for only $10,000 a week.") In 1919 she launched United Artists, a film distributing company, with Douglas Fairbanks, Charlie Chaplin, and D. W. Griffith. No woman since has been as powerful a player in the movie industry.

$1,000 a week, and by 1917, $15,000 a week. Having appeared in nearly two hundred films, Pickford was so influential that in 1919 she broke from Zukor to form her own company, United Artists. Joining her were actor Douglas Fairbanks (her future husband), comedian-director Charlie Chaplin, and director D. W. Griffith.

Although United Artists represented a brief triumph of autonomy for a few powerful actors, by the 1920s the **studio system** firmly controlled creative talent in the industry. Pioneered by director Thomas Ince and his company, Triangle, the studio system constituted a sort of assembly-line process for moviemaking: actors, directors, editors, writers, and others all worked under exclusive contracts for the major studios. Ince also developed the notion of the studio head; he appointed producers to handle hiring, logistics, and finances so that he could more easily supervise many pictures at one time. The system was so efficient that each major studio was producing a feature film every week. Pooling talent, rather than patents, was a more ingenious approach for movie studios aiming to dominate film production.

Distribution

An early effort to control movie distribution occurred around 1904, when movie companies provided vaudeville theaters with films and projectors on a *film exchange* system. In exchange for their short films, shown between live acts, movie producers received a small percentage of the vaudeville ticket-gate receipts. Gradually, as the number of production companies and the popularity of narrative films grew, demand for a distribution system serving national and international markets increased as well. One of the ways Edison's Trust sought to control distribution was by withholding equipment from companies not willing to pay the Trust's patent-use fees.

However, as with the production of film, independent film companies looked for distribution strategies outside the Trust. Again, Adolph Zukor led the fight, developing **block booking**. Under this system, which was eventually outlawed as monopolistic, exhibitors had to agree to rent new or marginal films with no stars in order to gain access to popular films with big stars like Mary Pickford. Such contracts enabled the new studios to test-market new stars without taking much financial risk.

Another distribution strategy involved the marketing of American films in Europe. When World War I disrupted the once-powerful European film production industry, only U.S. studios were able to meet the demand for films in Europe. The war marked a turning point and made the United States the leader in the commercial movie business worldwide. After the war, no other nation's film industry could compete economically with Hollywood. By the mid-1920s, foreign revenue from U.S. films totaled $100 million. Today, Hollywood continues to dominate the world market.

Exhibition

Edison's Trust attempted to monopolize exhibition by controlling the flow of films to theater owners. If theaters wanted to ensure they had films to show their patrons, they had to purchase a license from the Trust and pay whatever price it asked. Otherwise, they would be locked out of the Trust and have to try to find enough films from independent producers to show. Eventually, the flow of films from independents in Hollywood and foreign films enabled theater owners to resist the Trust's scheme.

After the collapse of the Trust, emerging studios in Hollywood had their own ideas on how to control exhibition. When industrious theater owners began forming film cooperatives to compete with block-booking tactics, producers like Zukor conspired to dominate exhibition by buying up theaters. By 1921, Zukor's Paramount owned three hundred theaters, solidifying its ability to show the movies it produced. In 1925, a business merger between Paramount and Publix (then the country's largest theater chain, with more than five hundred screens) gave Zukor enormous influence over movie exhibition.

MOVIE PALACES

Part of the ornate auditorium of the Ohio Theatre in Columbus, Ohio, which, after its deterioration and closing in 1969, came as close as the width of the gap between a wrecking ball and three determined preservationists, standing in the way, to demolition.

BUSTER KEATON (1895–1966)

Born into a vaudeville family, Keaton honed his comic skills early on. He got his start acting in a few shorts in 1917 and went on to star in some of the most memorable silent films of the 1920s, including classics such as *Sherlock Jr.* (1924), *The General* (1927), and *Steamboat Bill Jr.* (1928). Because of Keaton's ability to match physical comedy with an unfailingly deadpan and stoic face, he gained the nickname the Great Stone Face.

Zukor and the heads of several major studios understood that they did not have to own all the theaters to ensure that their movies would be shown. Instead, the major studios (which would eventually include MGM, RKO, Warner Brothers, Twentieth Century Fox, and Paramount) only needed to own the first-run theaters (about 15% of the nation's theaters), which premiered new films in major downtown areas and generated 85 to 95 percent of all film revenue.

The studios quickly realized that to earn revenue from these first-run theaters, they would have to draw the middle and upper-middle classes to the movies. To do so, they built **movie palaces**—full-time single-screen movie theaters that offered a more hospitable moviegoing environment, providing elegant décor usually reserved for high-society opera, ballet, symphony, and live theater. Another major innovation in exhibition was the development of *mid-city movie theaters*, built in convenient locations near urban mass-transit stations to attract the business of the urban and suburban middle class. This idea continues today, as **multiplexes** featuring multiple screens lure middle-class crowds to interstate highway crossroads.

By the late 1920s, the major studios had clearly established vertical integration in the industry. What had been many small competitive firms in the early 1900s was now a few powerful studios, including the **Big Five**—Paramount, MGM, Warner Brothers, Twentieth Century Fox, and RKO—and the **Little Three** (which did not

own theaters)—Columbia, Universal, and United Artists. Together, these eight companies formed a powerful oligopoly, which made it increasingly difficult for independent companies to make, distribute, and exhibit commercial films.

THE STUDIO SYSTEM'S GOLDEN AGE

Many consider Hollywood's Golden Age as beginning in 1915 with innovations in feature-length narrative film in the silent era, peaking with the introduction of sound and the development of the classic Hollywood style, and ending with the transformation of the Hollywood studio system after World War II.

Hollywood Narrative and the Silent Era

D. W. Griffith, among the first "star" directors, was the single most important director in Hollywood's early days. Griffith paved the way for all future narrative filmmakers by refining many of the narrative techniques introduced by Méliès and Porter and using nearly all of them in one film for the first time, including varied camera distances, close-up shots, multiple story lines, fast-paced editing, and symbolic imagery. Despite the cringe-inducing racism of this pioneering and controversial film, *The Birth of a Nation* (1915) was the first *feature-length film* (more than an hour long) produced in America. The three-hour epic was also the first **blockbuster** and cost moviegoers a record $2 admission. Although considered a technical masterpiece, the film glorified the Ku Klux Klan and stereotyped southern blacks, leading to a campaign against the film by the NAACP and protests and riots at many screenings. Nevertheless, the movie triggered Hollywood's fascination with narrative films.

Feature films became the standard throughout the 1920s and introduced many of the film genres we continue to see today. The most popular films during the silent era were historical and religious epics, including *Napoleon* (1927), *Ben-Hur* (1925), and *The Ten Commandments* (1923), but the silent era also produced pioneering social dramas, mysteries, comedies, horror films, science-fiction films, war films, crime dramas, westerns, and spy films. The silent era also introduced numerous technical innovations, established the Hollywood star system, and cemented the reputation of movies as a viable art form, when they had previously been seen as nothing more than novelty entertainment.

The Introduction of Sound

With the studio system and Hollywood's worldwide dominance firmly in place, the next big challenge was to bring sound to moving pictures. Various attempts at **talkies** had failed since Edison first tried to link phonograph and moving picture technologies in the 1890s. During the 1910s, however, technical breakthroughs at AT&T's research arm, Bell Labs, produced prototypes of loudspeakers and sound amplifiers. Experiments with sound continued during the 1920s, particularly at Warner Brothers studios, which released numerous short sound films of vaudeville acts featuring singers and comedians. The studio packaged them as a novelty along with silent feature films.

THE JAZZ SINGER (1927),

one of the first commercially successful talkies, helped bring about Hollywood's transition from silent movies to movies with sound. The film stars Al Jolson as Jack Rabinowitz, a Jewish American who defies his family's wishes by putting on blackface makeup and pursuing a career as a jazz musician.

Everett Collection

In 1927, Warner Brothers produced *The Jazz Singer*, a feature-length film starring Al Jolson, a charismatic and popular vaudeville singer who wore blackface makeup as part of his act. This further demonstrated, as did *The Birth of a Nation*, that racism in America carried into the film industry. An experiment, *The Jazz Singer* was basically a silent film interspersed with musical numbers and brief dialogue ("Wait a minute, wait a minute, you ain't heard nothin' yet"). At first there was only modest interest in the movie, which featured just 354 spoken words. But the film grew in popularity as it toured the Midwest, where audiences stood and cheered the short bursts of dialogue. The breakthrough film, however, was Warner Brothers' 1928 release *The Singing Fool*, which also starred Jolson. Costing $200,000 to make, the film took in $5 million and "proved to all doubters that talkies were here to stay."[7]

Warner Brothers, however, was not the only studio exploring sound technology. Five months before *The Jazz Singer* opened, Fox studio premiered sound-film **newsreels**. Fox's newsreel company, Movietone, captured the first film footage with sound of the takeoff and return of Charles Lindbergh, who piloted the first solo, nonstop flight across the Atlantic Ocean in May 1927. Fox's Movietone system recorded sound directly onto the film, running it on a narrow filmstrip that ran alongside the larger image portion of the film. Superior to the sound-on-record system, the Movietone method eventually became film's standard sound system.

Boosted by the innovation of sound, annual movie attendance in the United States rose from sixty million a week in 1927 to ninety million a week in 1929. By 1935, the world had adopted talking films as the commercial standard.

The Development of the Hollywood Style

By the time sound came to movies, Hollywood dictated not only the business but also the style of most moviemaking worldwide. That style, or model, for storytelling developed with the rise of the studio system in the 1920s, solidified during the first two decades of the sound era, and continues to dominate American filmmaking today. The model serves up three ingredients that give Hollywood movies their distinctive flavor: the narrative, the genre, and the author (or director). The right blend of these ingredients—combined with timing, marketing, and luck—has led to many movie hits, from 1930s and 1940s classics like *It Happened One Night*, *Gone with the Wind*, *The Philadelphia Story*, and *Casablanca* to recent successes like *Get Out* (2017) and *The Shape of Water* (2017).

Hollywood Narratives

American filmmakers from D. W. Griffith to Steven Spielberg have understood the allure of *narrative*, which always includes two basic components: the story (what happens to whom) and the discourse (how the story is told). Further, Hollywood codified a familiar narrative structure across all genres. Most movies, like most TV shows and novels, feature recognizable character types (protagonist, antagonist, romantic interest, sidekick); a clear beginning, middle, and end (even with flashbacks and flash-forwards, the sequence of events is usually clear to the viewer); and a plot propelled by the main character's experiencing and resolving a conflict by the end of the movie.

Within Hollywood's classic narratives, filmgoers find an amazing array of intriguing cultural variations. For example, familiar narrative conventions of heroes, villains, conflicts, and resolutions may be made more unique with inventions like computer-generated imagery (CGI) or digital remastering for an IMAX 3D Experience release. This combination of convention and invention—standardized Hollywood stories and differentiated special effects—provides a powerful economic package that satisfies most audiences' appetites for both the familiar and the distinctive.

Hollywood Genres

In general, Hollywood narratives fit a **genre**, or category, in which conventions regarding similar characters, scenes, structures, and themes recur in combination. Grouping films by category is another way for the industry to achieve the two related economic goals of *product standardization* and *product differentiation*. By making films that fall into popular genres, the movie industry provides familiar models that can be imitated. It is much easier for a studio to promote a film that already fits into a preexisting category with which viewers are familiar. Among the most familiar genres are comedy, adventure, drama, action, thriller/suspense, horror, romantic comedy, musical, documentary/performance, western, gangster, fantasy–science fiction, and film noir.

Because most Hollywood narratives try to create believable worlds, the artificial style of musicals is sometimes a disruption of what many viewers expect. Musicals' popularity peaked in the 1940s and 1950s, but they showed a small resurgence in the 2000s with *Moulin Rouge!* (2001), *Chicago* (2002), and *The Greatest Showman* (2017). Still, no live-action musicals rank among the top fifty highest-grossing films of all time.

One fascinating genre is the horror film, which also claims none of the top fifty highest-grossing films of all time. In fact, from *Psycho* (1960) to *A Quiet Place* (2018), this lightly regarded genre has earned only one Oscar for best picture—*Silence of the Lambs* (1991)—and one for original screenplay: *Get Out* (2017). Yet these movies are extremely popular with teenagers, among the largest theatergoing audience, who are in search of cultural choices distinct from those of their parents. Critics suggest that the teen appeal of horror movies is similar to the allure of gangster rap or heavy-metal music; they believe teens enjoy the horror genre because it is a cultural form that often carries anti-adult messages and does not appeal to most adults.

The *film noir* genre (French for "black film") developed in the United States in the late 1920s and hit its peak after World War II. Still, the genre continues to influence movies today. Using low-lighting techniques, few daytime scenes, and bleak urban settings, films in this genre (such as *The Big Sleep*, 1946, and *Sunset Boulevard*, 1950) explore unstable characters and the sinister side of human nature. Although the French critics who first identified noir as a genre place these films in the 1940s, their influence resonates in contemporary films—sometimes called *neo-noir*—including *Se7en* (1995), *L.A. Confidential* (1997), and *Under the Silver Lake* (2018).

Hollywood "Authors"

In commercial filmmaking, the director serves as the main author of a film. Sometimes called "auteurs," successful directors develop a particular cinematic style or an interest in particular topics that differentiates their narratives from those of other directors. Alfred Hitchcock, for instance, redefined the suspense drama through editing techniques that heightened tension (*Rear Window*, 1954; *Vertigo*, 1958; *North by Northwest*, 1959; *Psycho*, 1960).

The contemporary status of directors stems from two breakthrough films: Dennis Hopper's *Easy Rider* (1969) and George Lucas's *American Graffiti* (1973), which became surprise box-office hits. Their inexpensive budgets, rock-and-roll soundtracks, and big payoffs created opportunities for a new generation of directors. The success of these films exposed cracks in the Hollywood system, which was losing money in the late 1960s and early 1970s. Studio executives seemed at a loss to explain and predict the tastes of a new generation of movie-goers. Yet Hopper and Lucas had tapped into the anxieties of the postwar baby-boom generation in its search for self-realization, its longing for an innocent past, and its efforts to cope with the turbulence of the 1960s.

This opened the door for a new wave of directors who were trained in California or New York film schools and were also products of the 1960s, such as Francis Ford Coppola (*The Godfather*, 1972), William Friedkin (*The Exorcist*, 1973), Steven Spielberg (*Jaws*, 1975), Martin Scorsese (*Taxi Driver*, 1976), Brian De Palma (*Carrie*, 1976), and George Lucas

FILM GENRES
Psycho (1960), a classic horror film, tells the story of Marion Crane (played by Janet Leigh), who flees to a motel after embezzling $40,000 from her employer. There, she meets the motel owner, Norman Bates (played by Anthony Perkins), and her untimely death. The infamous shower scene, pictured here, is widely considered one of the most iconic horror film sequences.

Everett Collection

(*Star Wars*, 1977). Combining news or documentary techniques and Hollywood narratives, these films demonstrated how mass media borders had become blurred and how movies had become dependent on audiences who were used to television and rock and roll. These films signaled the start of a period that Scorsese has called "the deification of the director." A handful of successful directors gained the kind of economic clout and celebrity standing that had previously belonged almost exclusively to top movie stars.

Although the status of directors grew in the 1960s and 1970s, recognition for women directors of Hollywood features remained rare.[8] A breakthrough came with Kathryn Bigelow's best director Academy Award for *The Hurt Locker* (2009), which also won the award for best picture. Prior to Bigelow's win, only three women had received an Academy Award nomination for directing a feature film: Lina Wertmüller in 1976 for *Seven Beauties*, Jane Campion in 1994 for *The Piano*, and Sofia Coppola in 2004 for *Lost in Translation*. Both Wertmüller and Campion are from countries outside the United States, where women directors frequently receive more opportunities for film development. Some women in the United States get an opportunity to direct because of their prominent standing as popular actors; Barbra Streisand, Jodie Foster, Penny Marshall, and Sally Field all fall into this category. Other women have come to direct films via their scriptwriting achievements. For example, Jennifer Lee, who wrote *Wreck-It Ralph* (2012), followed up by writing and directing *Frozen* (2013). Other women directors—like Bigelow, Catherine Hardwicke (*Twilight*, 2008), Debra Granik (*Winter's Bone*, 2010), Kimberly Peirce (*Carrie*, 2013), and Sarah Gavron (*Suffragette*, 2015)—have moved past debut films and proven themselves as experienced studio auteurs.

Nevertheless, a recent study finds that women were hired to direct only 3.4 percent of major Hollywood releases, calling attention to the film industry's gender problem.[9] In light of women's persistently low status in Hollywood, and the dozens of charges of sexual harassment, assault, and rape against producer Harvey Weinstein (spurring the #MeToo movement of women sharing similar stories), a number of powerful women in the entertainment industry formed Time's Up in 2018. The advocacy group, which established a legal defense fund for those who have experienced sexual harassment or retaliation in the workplace, had more than three hundred signers to its founding letter, including Oprah Winfrey, Shonda Rhimes, Reese Witherspoon, Constance Wu, and Ava DuVernay.[10]

Members of minority groups, including African Americans, Asian Americans, and Native Americans, have also struggled for recognition in Hollywood. Still, some have succeeded as directors, crossing over from careers as actors or gaining notoriety through independent filmmaking. Among the most successful contemporary African American directors are Ryan Coogler (*Black Panther*, 2018), Ava DuVernay (*A Wrinkle in Time*, 2018; *Selma*, 2014), Tyler Perry (*A Madea Family Funeral*, 2018), Jordan Peele (*Get Out*, 2017), Barry Jenkins (*Moonlight*, 2017), Spike Lee (the TV series *She's Gotta Have It*, 2017; *Chi-Raq*, 2015), Lee Daniels (*The Butler*, 2013; *Precious*, 2009; and the TV series *Empire*), and John Singleton (*Abduction*, 2011, and the TV series *Snowfall*). (See "Examining Ethics: Breaking through Hollywood's Race Barrier" on page 212.) Asian Americans such as M. Night Shyamalan (*Split*, 2016; *After Earth*, 2013), Ang Lee (*Billy Lynn's Long Halftime Walk*, 2016; *Life of Pi*, 2012), Wayne Wang (*Snow Flower and the Secret Fan*, 2011), and documentarian Arthur Dong (*The Killing Fields of Dr. Haing S. Ngor*, 2015) have built accomplished directing careers. Chris Eyre (*Hide Away*, 2011) remains the most noted Native American director, working mainly as an independent filmmaker, but the Sundance Institute's Native American and Indigenous Program works to support Native American artists, and the 2018 Sundance Film Festival featured eight films made by indigenous filmmakers.[11]

Outside the Hollywood System

Since the rise of the studio system, Hollywood has focused on feature-length movies that command popular attention and earn the most money. However, the movie industry has a long tradition of films made outside the Hollywood studio system. In the following sections, we look at three alternatives to Hollywood: international films, documentaries, and independent films.

Breaking through Hollywood's Race Barrier

The problem of the term *black cinema* is that such a term needs to exist. (Do we, for example, talk about a *white cinema* in the United States?) But there is a long history of blacks' exclusion from the industry as writers, directors, and actors—not to mention even as audience members at theaters—so when a film like *Dope* (2015) by director Rick Famuyiwa gets praised as "revolutionary" and "subversive," it's because this teen coming-of-age story dares to feature a cast that for the most part isn't white.

Despite African Americans' long support of the film industry, their moviegoing experience has not been the same as that of whites. From the late 1800s until the passage of Civil Rights legislation in the mid-1960s, many theater owners discriminated against black patrons. In large cities, blacks often had to attend separate theaters, where new movies might not appear until a year or two after white theaters had shown them. In smaller towns and in the South, blacks were often allowed to patronize local theaters only after midnight. In addition, some theater managers required black patrons to sit in less desirable areas of the theater.[1]

Changes began taking place during and after World War II. In response to the "white flight" from central cities during the suburbanization of the 1950s, many downtown and neighborhood theaters began catering to black customers in order to keep from going out of business. By the late 1960s and early 1970s, these theaters had become major venues for popular commercial films, even featuring a few movies about African Americans, including *Guess Who's Coming to Dinner* (1967), *In the Heat of the Night* (1967), *The Learning Tree* (1969), and *Sounder* (1972).

Based on the popularity of these films, Gordon Parks, the black photographer turned filmmaker who directed *The Learning Tree* (adapted from his own novel), went on to make commercial action/adventure films, including *Shaft* (1971, remade by John Singleton in 2000) and, with his son, Gordon Parks Jr., *Super Fly* (1972).

Opportunities for black film directors have expanded since the 1980s and 1990s, but only recently have black filmmakers achieved a measure of mainstream success. Lee Daniels received only the second Academy Award nomination for a black director for *Precious: Based on the Novel "Push" by Sapphire* in 2009 (the first was John Singleton, for *Boyz N the Hood* in 1991). In 2013, *12 Years a Slave*, a film adaptation of Solomon Northup's 1853 memoir by black British director Steve McQueen, won three Academy Awards, including best picture, and a best director nomination for McQueen. McQueen became the first black director to win a best picture award. But the lack of regular recognition of nonwhite actors, writers, and directors for the Academy Awards in 2016 led to much discussion and a trending #OscarsSoWhite hashtag. In 2017, *Moonlight*, a coming-of-age drama with an all-black cast by black director Barry Jenkins, won the best picture award.

But in Hollywood, nothing speaks more loudly than a blockbuster. Thus, *Black Panther* might be a turning point in the history of blacks in American cinema. In less than a month after its February 2018 release, *Black Panther* (directed by Ryan Coogler, Marvel/Disney) generated more than $1.1 billion in global box-office revenue, and over $570 million in domestic box-office receipts.[2] Shortly after its release, it became the third highest-grossing movie in the United States. The film, which is the eighteenth film in the Marvel Cinematic Universe, is particularly notable for its director, cast, and story. Jamil Smith of *Time* magazine noted, "It may be the first mega-budget movie—not just about superheroes, but about anyone—to have an African-American director and a predominantly black cast. Hollywood has never produced a blockbuster this splendidly black." Smith related the movie's cultural significance to his own experience. "Those of us who are not white have considerably more trouble not only finding representation of ourselves in mass media and other arenas of public life, but also finding representation that indicates that our humanity is multifaceted. Relating to characters onscreen is necessary not merely for us to feel seen and understood, but also for others who need to see and understand us."[3] As Vox's Sean Rameswaram observes, "Representation matters, and it's good for business."[4]

Atsushi Nishijima/© Paramount Pictures/Everett Collection

Global Cinema

For generations, Hollywood has dominated the global movie scene. In many countries, American films capture up to 90 percent of the market. In striking contrast, foreign films constitute only a tiny fraction—less than 2 percent—of motion pictures seen in the United States today. Despite Hollywood's domination of global film distribution, other countries have a rich history of producing both successful and provocative short-subject and feature films. For example, cinematic movements of the twentieth century—such as German expressionism (capturing psychological moods), Soviet social realism (presenting a positive view of Soviet life), Italian neorealism (focusing on the everyday lives of Italians), and European new-wave cinema (experimenting with the language of film)—and post–World War II Japanese, Hong Kong, Korean, Australian, Indian, Canadian, and British cinema have all been extremely influential, demonstrating alternatives to the Hollywood approach.

Early on, Americans showed interest in British and French short films and in experimental films, such as Germany's *The Cabinet of Dr. Caligari* (1919). Foreign-language movies did reasonably well throughout the 1920s, especially in ethnic neighborhood theaters in large American cities. For a time, Hollywood studios even dubbed some popular American movies into Spanish, Italian, French, and German for these theaters. But the Depression brought cutbacks, and by the 1930s, the daughters and sons of turn-of-the-century immigrants—many of whom were trying to assimilate into mainstream American culture—preferred their Hollywood movies in English.[12]

Postwar prosperity, rising globalism, and the gradual decline of the studios' hold over theater exhibition in the 1950s and 1960s stimulated the rise of art-house theaters, and these decades saw a rebirth of interest in foreign-language films by such prominent directors as Sweden's Ingmar Bergman (*Wild Strawberries*, 1957), Italy's Federico Fellini (*La Dolce Vita*, 1960), France's François Truffaut (*Jules and Jim*, 1961), Japan's Akira Kurosawa (*Seven Samurai*, 1954), and India's Satyajit Ray (*Apu Trilogy*, 1955–1959). Catering to academic audiences, art houses made a statement against Hollywood commercialism as they sought to show alternative movies.

By the late 1970s, however, the home video market had emerged, and audiences began staying home to watch both foreign and domestic films. New multiplex theater owners rejected the smaller profit margins of most foreign titles, which lacked the promotional hype of U.S. films. As a result,

GLOBALIZATION OF FILM

Today, U.S. production companies often partner with foreign crews to make big-budget movies like *The Great Wall* (2016, released in the United States in 2017), starring Matt Damon and directed by Zhang Yimou. Featuring a predominantly Chinese cast but with English dialogue, this film was produced jointly by the China Film Group and the U.S.-based Legendary Entertainment. The movie received a wide theatrical release in both countries and is the biggest Hollywood-China coproduction to date.

Entertainment Pictures/Alamy Stock Photo

between 1966 and 1990 the number of foreign films released annually in the United States dropped by two-thirds, from nearly three hundred to about one hundred titles per year.

With the growth of superstore video chains like Blockbuster in the 1990s, which would be supplanted by streaming services like Netflix in the 2000s, viewers gained access to a larger selection of foreign-language titles. The success of *Amélie* (France, 2001), *The Girl with the Dragon Tattoo* (Sweden, 2009), and *Instructions Not Included* (Mexico, 2013) illustrate that U.S. audiences are willing to watch subtitled films with non-Hollywood perspectives. Yet foreign films are losing ground as they compete with the expanding independent American film market for screen space.

Today, the largest film industry is in India, out of Bollywood (a play on words combining city names Bombay—now Mumbai—and Hollywood), where close to two thousand films a year are produced—mostly romance or adventure musicals in a distinct style.[13] In comparison, U.S. moviemakers release more than seven hundred films a year, and the growing film industry in China produces more than six hundred movies annually. (The United States and China are first and second in terms of film revenue.) Japan, France, and Nigeria are also major film producing nations. (For a broader perspective, see "Global Village: Beyond Hollywood: Asian Cinema" on pages 216–217.)

The Documentary Tradition

Both TV news and nonfiction films trace their roots to the movie industry's *interest films* and *newsreels* of the late 1890s. In Britain, interest films compiled footage of regional wars, political leaders, industrial workers, and agricultural scenes, and were screened with fiction shorts. Pioneered in France and England, newsreels consisted of weekly ten-minute magazine-style compilations of filmed news events from around the world. International news services began supplying theaters and movie studios with newsreels, and by 1911, they had become a regular part of the moviegoing menu.

DOCUMENTARY FILMS

Faces Places, a documentary released in 2017, features director Agnès Varda following photographer and muralist J.R. through France, and the friendship the two strike up along the journey. The film was nominated for the Academy Award for best documentary feature in 2018.

Everett Collection

Over time, the **documentary** film genre developed as a style that interprets reality by recording actual people and settings. As an educational, noncommercial form, the documentary typically required the backing of industry, government, or philanthropy to cover costs. In support of a clear alternative to Hollywood cinema, some nations began creating special units, such as Canada's National Film Board, to sponsor documentaries. In the United States, art and film received considerable support from the Roosevelt administration during the Depression.

By the late 1950s and early 1960s, the development of portable cameras had led to **cinema verité** (a French term for "truth film"). This documentary style allowed filmmakers to go where cameras could not go before and record fragments of everyday life more unobtrusively. Directly opposed to packaged, high-gloss Hollywood features, verité aimed to track reality, employing a rough, grainy look and shaky, handheld camera work. Among the key innovators in cinema verité was Drew Associates, led by Robert Drew, a former *Life* magazine photographer. Through his connection to Time Inc. (which owned *Life*) and its chain of TV stations, Drew shot the groundbreaking documentary *Primary*, which followed the 1960 Democratic presidential primary race between Hubert Humphrey and John F. Kennedy.

Perhaps the major contribution of documentaries has been their willingness to tackle controversial or unpopular subject matter. For example, American documentary filmmakers Kirby Dick and Amy Ziering address complex topics about sex and power. Their films include *The Invisible War*, about sexual assault in the military; *The Hunting Ground*, about campus assault at Harvard University; and their yet-to-be-named documentary about Harvey Weinstein and the reality of sexual assault and harassment in Hollywood. "What our film will capture," Dick explains, "especially at this pivotal turning point in Hollywood history, is the underlying current of abuse and manipulation at the hands of power."[14] Dick and Ziering's films are part of a resurgence in high-profile documentary filmmaking in the United States, which includes *The Cove* (2009), *Hell and Back Again* (2011), *The Queen of Versailles* (2012), *Icarus* (2017), *Step* (2017), and *Won't You Be My Neighbor* (2018).

The Rise of Independent Films

The success of documentary films dovetails with the rise of **indies,** or independently produced films. As opposed to directors working in the Hollywood system, independent filmmakers typically operate on a shoestring budget and show their movies in thousands of campus auditoriums and at hundreds of small film festivals. The decreasing costs of portable technology, including smaller digital cameras and computer editing, have kept many documentary and independent filmmakers in business. Successful independents like Sofia Coppola (*Lost in Translation*, 2003; *The Bling Ring*, 2013) and Jim Jarmusch (*Dead Man*, 1995; *Only Lovers Left Alive*, 2014) continue to find substantial audiences in college and art-house theaters and through streaming services like Netflix, which promote work produced outside the studio system. Meanwhile, independent-minded filmmakers like Wes Anderson (*Isle of Dogs*, 2018; *The Grand Budapest Hotel*, 2014), Darren Aronofsky (*Mother!*, 2017; *Noah*, 2014; *Black Swan*, 2010), and David O. Russell (*Joy*, 2015; *American Hustle*, 2013) have established careers somewhere between fully independent and studio backed, often with smaller companies financing their films before they're picked up by bigger studios.

Distributing smaller films can be big business for the studios. The rise of independent film festivals in the 1990s—especially the Sundance Film

INDEPENDENT FILM FESTIVALS, like the Sundance Film Festival, are widely recognized in the film industry as a place to discover new talent and acquire independently made films on topics that might otherwise be too controversial, too niche-specific, or too original for a major studio-backed picture. One of the breakout hits of Sundance 2018 was *Eighth Grade*, a look at the awkward middle-school years through the eyes of a shy and insecure eighth grade girl. After the festival, A24 picked up the film for a wider release.

Everett Collection

Beyond Hollywood: Asian Cinema

Asian nations easily outstrip Hollywood in the quantity of films produced. India alone produces about a thousand movies a year. But from India to South Korea, Asian films are increasingly challenging Hollywood in terms of quality, and they have become more influential as Asian directors, actors, and film styles are exported to Hollywood and the world.

India

Part musical, part action, part romance, and part suspense, the epic films of Bollywood typically have fantastic sets, hordes of extras, plenty of wet saris, and symbolic fountain bursts (as a substitute for kissing and sex, which are prohibited from being shown). Indian movie fans pay from $.75 to $5 to see these films, and they feel shortchanged if the movies are shorter than three hours. With many films produced in less than a week, however, most of the Bollywood fare is cheaply produced and badly acted. Yet these production aesthetics are changing, as bigger-budget releases target the middle and upper classes in India, the twenty-five million Indians living abroad, and Western audiences. *Baahubali 2: The Conclusion* (2017), a fantasy-action film set in medieval India, stars Prabhas—one of India's most famous leading men. Appearing on seven hundred standard screens and another fifty-eight IMAX screens across the United States and Canada, and playing in three different languages (Telugu, Tamil, and Hindi), the film is the most successful U.S. box-office opening of any Bollywood film, grossing $155 million in just ten days.[1]

2017 CHINESE ACTION FILM *WOLF WARRIOR II* broke many box office records, including the biggest single day gross for a Chinese film and the first to cross the $800 million (U.S.) box office mark.

Everett Collection

China

Since the late 1980s, Chinese cinema has developed an international reputation. Leading this generation of directors are Yimou Zhang (*House of Flying Daggers*, 2004; *Coming Home*, 2014) and Kaige Chen (*Farewell My Concubine*, 1993; *Monk Comes Down the Mountain*, 2015), whose work has spanned such genres as historical epics, love stories, contemporary tales of city life, and action fantasy. These directors have also helped make international stars out of Li Gong (*Memoirs of a Geisha*, 2005; *Coming Home*, 2014) and Ziyi Zhang (*Memoirs of a Geisha*, 2005; *Dangerous Liaisons*, 2012). *Wolf Warrior 2* (2017), pictured here, about realizing the "Chinese Dream" of cultural power and international dominance, is the current highest-grossing Chinese film of all time, having made over $870 million (US) at the box office.

Hong Kong

Hong Kong films were the most talked about—and the most influential—film genre in cinema throughout the late 1980s and 1990s. The style of highly choreographed action with often breathtaking, ballet-like violence became hugely popular around the world, reaching American audiences and in some cases even outselling Hollywood blockbusters. Hong Kong directors like John Woo, Ringo Lam, and Jackie Chan (who also acts in his movies) have directed Hollywood action films; and stars like Jet Li (*Lethal Weapon 4*, 1998; *The Expendables 3*, 2014), Yun-Fat Chow (*Pirates of the Caribbean: At World's End*, 2007; *The Monkey King: The Legend Begins*, 2016), and Malaysia's Michelle Yeoh (*Guardians of the Galaxy Vol. 2*, 2017) are landing leading roles in American movies.

Japan

Americans may be most familiar with low-budget monster movies like *Godzilla*, but the widely heralded films of the late director Akira Kurosawa have had an even greater impact: His *Seven Samurai* (1954) was remade by Hollywood as the film masterpiece *The Magnificent Seven* (1960), and *The Hidden Fortress* (1958) was George Lucas's inspiration for *Star Wars*. Hayao Miyazaki (*Ponyo*, 2009; *The Wind Rises*, 2013) was the country's top director of anime movies, and with his retirement a new anime successor has emerged, Makoto Shinkai, with his cultural sensation *Your Name* (2016). Japanese thrillers like *Ringu* (1998), *Ringu 2* (1999), and *Ju-on: The Grudge* (2003) were remade into successful American horror films. Hirokazu Kore-eda's drama *Like Father, Like Son* (2013) won the Jury Prize at the Cannes Film Festival and caught the attention of Steven Spielberg, who acquired the remake rights for his company DreamWorks.

South Korea

The end of military regimes in the late 1980s and corporate investment in the film business in the 1990s created a new era in Korean moviemaking. Leading directors include Kim Jee-woon; Lee Chang-dong (nominated for the Palme d'Or award at Cannes for *Poetry*, 2010); and Chan-wook Park, whose Vengeance Trilogy films (*Sympathy for Mr. Vengeance*, 2002; *Oldboy*, 2003; and *Lady Vengeance*, 2005) have won international acclaim, including the Grand Prix at Cannes for *Oldboy*, which was remade in the United States in 2013 by director Spike Lee. Joon-ho Bong's science-fiction film *Snowpiercer* (2013)—based on a French graphic novel, filmed in the Czech Republic, and starring a mostly English-speaking cast (including Chris Evans and Tilda Swinton)—epitomizes the international outlook of Korean cinema.

Festival held every January in Park City, Utah—helped Hollywood rediscover low-cost independent films as an alternative to traditional movies with *Titanic*-size budgets. Films such as *Get Out* (2017), *Call Me by Your Name* (2017), and *Eighth Grade* (2018) were able to generate industry buzz and garner major studio distribution deals through Sundance screenings, becoming star vehicles for several directors and actors. As with the recording industry, the major studios see these festivals—which also include New York's Tribeca Film Festival, the South by Southwest festival in Austin, and international film festivals in Toronto and Cannes—as important venues for discovering new talent. Some major studios developed in-house indie divisions (Sony's Sony Pictures Classics) to specifically handle the development and distribution of indies. Netflix and Amazon have also established themselves as buyers of festival-screened films for their streaming services.

THE TRANSFORMATION OF THE STUDIO SYSTEM

After years of thriving, the Hollywood movie industry began to falter after 1946. Weekly movie attendance in the United States peaked at ninety million in 1946, then fell to under twenty-five million by 1963. Critics and observers began talking about the death of Hollywood, claiming that the Golden Age was over. However, the movie industry adapted and survived, just as it continues to do today. Among the changing conditions facing the film industry were the communist witch-hunts in Hollywood, the end of the industry's vertical integration, suburbanization, the arrival of television, and the appearance of home entertainment.

The Hollywood Ten

In 1947, in the wake of the unfolding Cold War with the Soviet Union, conservative members of Congress began investigating Hollywood for alleged subversive and communist ties. That year, aggressive witch-hunts for political radicals in the film industry by the House Un-American Activities

THE HOLLYWOOD TEN

While many studio heads, producers, and actors "named names" to HUAC, others, such as the group shown here, held protests to demand the release of the Hollywood Ten.

Committee (HUAC) led to the famous **Hollywood Ten** hearings and subsequent trial. (HUAC included future president Richard M. Nixon, then a congressman from California.)

During the investigations, HUAC coerced prominent people from the film industry to declare their patriotism and to give up the names of colleagues suspected of having politically unfriendly tendencies. Upset over labor union strikes and outspoken writers, many film executives were eager to testify and provide names. For instance, Jack L. Warner of Warner Brothers suggested that whenever film writers made fun of the wealthy or America's political system in their work, or if their movies were sympathetic to "Indians and the colored folks,"[15] they were engaging in communist propaganda. Other "friendly" HUAC witnesses included actors Gary Cooper and Ronald Reagan, director Elia Kazan, and producer Walt Disney. Whether they believed it was their patriotic duty or they feared losing their jobs, many prominent actors, directors, and other film executives also "named names."

Eventually, HUAC subpoenaed ten unwilling witnesses who were questioned about their memberships in various organizations. The so-called Hollywood Ten—nine screenwriters and one director—refused to discuss their memberships or to identify communist sympathizers. Charged with contempt of Congress in November 1947, they were eventually sent to prison. Although jailing the Hollywood Ten clearly violated their free-speech rights, in the atmosphere of the Cold War many people worried that "the American way" could be sabotaged via unpatriotic messages planted in films. Upon release from jail, the Hollywood Ten found themselves blacklisted, or boycotted, by the major studios, and their careers in the film industry were all but ruined. The national fervor over communism continued to plague Hollywood well into the 1950s.

The Paramount Decision

Coinciding with the HUAC investigations, the government also increased its scrutiny of the movie industry's aggressive business practices. By the mid-1940s, the Justice Department had demanded that the five major film companies—Paramount, Warner Brothers, Twentieth Century Fox, MGM, and RKO—end vertical integration, which involved the simultaneous control over production, distribution, and exhibition. In 1948, after a series of court appeals, the Supreme Court ruled against the film industry in what is commonly known as the **Paramount decision**, forcing the studios to gradually divest themselves of their theaters.

Although the government had hoped to increase competition, the Paramount case never really changed the oligopoly structure of the Hollywood film industry because it failed to challenge the industry's control over distribution. However, the 1948 decision did create opportunities in the exhibition part of the industry for those outside Hollywood. In addition to art houses showing documentaries or foreign films, thousands of drive-in theaters sprang up in farmers' fields, welcoming new suburbanites who embraced the automobile. Although drive-ins had been around since the 1930s, by the end of the 1950s, more than four thousand existed. The Paramount decision encouraged new indoor theater openings as well, but the major studios continued to dominate distribution.

Moving to the Suburbs

Common sense might suggest that television alone precipitated the decline in post–World War II movie attendance, but the most dramatic drop actually occurred in the late 1940s—before most Americans even owned TV sets.[16]

The transformation from a wartime economy and a surge in consumer production had a significant impact on moviegoing. With industries turning from armaments to appliances, Americans started cashing in their wartime savings bonds for household goods and new cars. Discretionary income that formerly went to buying movie tickets now went to acquiring consumer products, and the biggest product of all was a new house far from the downtown movie theaters—in the suburbs, where tax bases were lower. Home ownership in the United States doubled between 1945 and 1950, while the moviegoing public decreased just as quickly. Additionally, after the war, the average age for couples

MOVIES TAKE ON SOCIAL ISSUES
Rebel without a Cause (1955), starring James Dean and Natalie Wood, was marketed in movie posters as "Warner Bros.' Challenging Drama of Today's Teenage Violence!" James Dean's memorable portrayal of a troubled youth forever fixed his place in movie history. He was killed in a car crash a month before the movie opened.

entering marriage dropped from twenty-four to nineteen. Unlike their parents, many postwar couples had their first child before they turned twenty-one. The combination of social and economic changes meant there were significantly fewer couples dating at the movies. Then, when television exploded in the late 1950s, there was even less discretionary income—and less reason to go to the movies.

Television Changes Hollywood

In the late 1940s, radio's popularity had a strong impact on film. Not only were 1948 and 1949 high points in radio listenership, but with the mass migration to the suburbs, radio offered Americans an inexpensive entertainment alternative to the movies (as it had during the Great Depression). As a result, many people stayed home and listened to radio programs—that is, until the mid-1950s, when both radio and movies were displaced by television as the medium of national entertainment. The movie industry responded to this change in a variety of ways.

First, with growing legions of people gathering around their living room TV sets, movie content slowly shifted toward more serious subjects. At first, this shift was a response to the war and an acknowledgment of life's complexity, but later movies focused on subject matter that television did not encourage. This shift had begun with film noir in the 1940s but it continued into the 1950s, as commercial movies, for the first time, explored larger social problems, such as alcoholism (*The Lost Weekend*, 1945), anti-Semitism (*Gentleman's Agreement*, 1947), mental illness (*The Snake Pit*, 1948), racism (*Pinky*, 1949), adult–teen relationships (*Rebel without a Cause*, 1955), drug abuse (*The Man with the Golden Arm*, 1955), and—perhaps most controversial—sexuality (*Peyton Place*, 1957; *Butterfield 8*, 1960; *Lolita*, 1962).

These and other films challenged the authority of the industry's own prohibitive Motion Picture Production Code. Hollywood adopted the Code in the early 1930s to restrict film depictions of violence, crime, drug use, and sexual behavior and to quiet public and political concerns that the movie business was lowering the moral standards of America. (For more on the Code, see Chapter 16.) In 1967, after the Code had been ignored by producers for several years, the Motion Picture Association of America initiated the current ratings system, which rated films for age appropriateness rather than censoring all adult content.

Second, just as radio worked to improve sound to maintain an advantage over television in the 1950s, the film industry introduced a host of technological improvements to lure Americans away from their TV sets. Technicolor, invented by an MIT scientist in 1917, had improved and was being used in more movies to draw people away from their black-and-white TV sets. In addition, Cinerama, CinemaScope, and VistaVision all arrived in movie theaters, featuring striking wide-screen images, multiple synchronized projectors, and stereophonic sound. Then 3-D (three-dimensional) movies appeared, although they wore off quickly as a novelty. Finally, Panavision, which used special Eastman color film and camera lenses that decreased the fuzziness of images, became the wide-screen standard throughout the industry. These developments, however, generally failed to address the movies' primary problem: the middle-class flight to the suburbs, away from downtown theaters.

Hollywood Adapts to Home Entertainment

Just as nickelodeons, movie palaces, and drive-ins transformed movie exhibition in earlier times, the introduction of cable television and the videocassette in the 1970s transformed contemporary movie exhibition. Although the video market became a financial bonanza for the movie industry, Hollywood ironically tried to stall the arrival of the VCR in the 1970s—even filing lawsuits to prohibit customers from copying movies from television. The 1997 introduction of the DVD helped reinvigorate the flat sales of the home video market as people began to acquire new movie collections on DVD. Today, home movie exhibition is again in transition, this time from DVD to Internet streaming. As DVD purchases began to decline, Hollywood endorsed the high-definition format Blu-ray in 2008 to revive sales, but the format didn't grow quickly enough to help the video store business. The Movie Gallery–Hollywood Video chain shuttered its stores in 2010, and the biggest chain, Blockbuster, closed most of its stores by 2013. The only bright spot in DVD rentals has been at the low end of the market—automated kiosks like Redbox that rent movies for $1.50 to $2.00 a day—but even the kiosk rental business began to flatline by 2013.

The future of the video business is in Internet distribution. Movie fans can rent or purchase from services like Netflix, Amazon, Hulu, Google Play, and the iTunes store and view on smart TVs or with devices like Roku, Apple TV, Amazon Fire TV Stick, Google Chromecast, TiVo Premiere, or video game consoles. As people invest in wide-screen TVs and sophisticated sound systems, home entertainment is getting bigger and keeping pace with the movie theater experience. Interestingly, home entertainment is also getting smaller—movies are becoming increasingly available to stream and download on portable devices like tablets, laptop computers, and smartphones.

THE ECONOMICS OF THE MOVIE BUSINESS

Despite the development of network and cable television, video-on-demand, DVDs, and Internet downloads and streaming, the movie business has continued to thrive. In fact, since 1963, Americans have purchased roughly 1 billion movie tickets each year; in 2017, 1.24 billion tickets were sold in the United States and Canada.[17] With first-run movie tickets in some areas rising to $15 (and 3-D movies costing even more), gross revenues from North American box-office sales have climbed above the $11 billion mark, up from $9.2 billion annually in 2006 (see Figure 7.1). The bigger news for Hollywood studios is that global box-office revenues have grown at a much faster rate, especially in China (though it returns less money to studios), Russia, and Mexico.[18]

The growing global market for Hollywood films has helped cushion the industry as the home video market undergoes a significant transformation, with the demise of the video rental business and the rise of video streaming. In order to flourish, the movie industry has had to continually revamp its production, distribution, and exhibition system and consolidate its ownership.

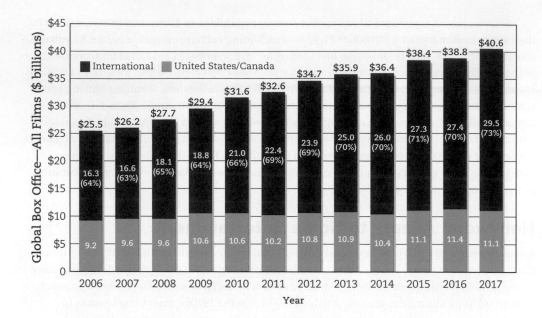

FIGURE 7.1

NORTH AMERICAN AND GLOBAL BOX-OFFICE REVENUE, 2017 (IN $ BILLIONS)

Data from: Motion Picture Association of America, "Theme Report 2017," 2018, www.mpaa.org/wp-content /uploads/2018/04/MPAA -THEME-Report-2017_Final.pdf, pp. 10–15.

Production, Distribution, and Exhibition Today

The 1970s marked the rise of blockbuster movies in suburban multiplex theaters, beginning with *The Godfather* (1972), *The Exorcist* (1973), *Jaws* (1975), *Rocky* (1976), and *Star Wars* (1977). Two films, *Jaws* and *Star Wars*, were the first movies to gross more than $100 million in a single year. Studios have been trying to copy this success in every subsequent decade (see "Media Literacy and the Critical Process: The Blockbuster Mentality" on page 226).

Making Money on Movies Today

With 80 to 90 percent of newly released movies failing to make money at the domestic box office, studios need a couple of major hits each year to offset losses on other films (see Table 7.1 for a list of the highest-grossing films of all time). The potential losses are great: Over the past decade, a major studio film, on average, cost about $66 million to produce and about $37 million for domestic marketing, advertising, and print costs.[19]

With climbing film costs, creating revenue from a movie is a formidable task. Studios make money on movies from six major sources:

- First, the studios get a portion of the theater box-office revenue—about 40 percent of the box-office take (the theaters get the rest). More recently, studios have found that they can often reel in bigger box-office receipts for 3-D films and their higher ticket prices. For example, admission to the 2-D

TABLE 7.1

THE TOP 10 ALL-TIME BOX-OFFICE CHAMPIONS*

Data from: "All-Time Domestic Blockbusters," Box Office Guru, accessed April 24, 2018, www.box officeguru.com/blockbusters.htm.

*Most rankings of the Top 10 most popular films are based on American box-office receipts. If these were adjusted for inflation, *Gone with the Wind* (1939) would become No. 2 in U.S. theater revenue.

**Gross is shown in absolute dollars based on box-office sales in the United States and Canada.

Rank	Title/Date	Domestic Gross** ($ millions)
1	*Star Wars: Episode VII—The Force Awakens* (incl. 3D & Imax, 2015)	$936.7
2	*Avatar* (2009)	760.5
3	*Black Panther* (incl. 3D & Imax, 2018)	699.9
4	*Avengers: Infinity War* (incl. 3D & Imax, 2018)	674.8
5	*Titanic* (1997, 2012 3D)	658.6
6	*Jurassic World* (incl. 3D & Imax, 2015)	652.3
7	*The Avengers* (2012)	623.4
8	*Star Wars: The Last Jedi* (incl. 3D & Imax, 2017)	620.2
9	*The Dark Knight* (incl. Imax, 2008)	533.3
10	*Rogue One* (incl. 3D & Imax, 2016)	532.2

version of a film costs $16 at a New York City multiplex, while the 3-D version costs more than $20 at the same theater. As Hollywood makes more 3-D films (the latest form of product differentiation), the challenge for major studios has been to increase the number of digital 3-D screens across the country. By 2017, about 39 percent of U.S. theater screens were capable of showing digital 3-D.

- Second, about three to four months after the theatrical release comes the home video market, which includes subscription streaming, video-on-demand (VOD), and the remaining Blu-ray and DVD sales and rental business. This second release "window" generates more revenue than the domestic box-office income for major studios, but it has been in transition as VOD has replaced the Blu-ray and DVD formats. Video-on-demand includes services like iTunes, Amazon, Google Play, Vudu, Hulu Plus, and Netflix, and the VOD services of cable companies like Comcast, Cox, AT&T, and Verizon, and satellite providers DirecTV and Dish. Depending on the agreement with the film distributer, movies may be purchased for instant viewing, rented for a limited time at a lower price, or instantly streamed as part of a monthly fee for access to a company's entire library of licensed offerings. (Netflix, the largest streaming service, has over fifty-six million subscribers in the United States.)

  Generally, discount rental kiosk companies like Redbox must wait twenty-eight days after films go on sale before they can rent them. Netflix has entered into a similar agreement with movie studios in exchange for more video-streaming content—a concession to Hollywood's preference to try to reap the greater profits from selling movies as digital downloads or as DVDs before renting them or licensing them to a streaming service. Independent films and documentaries often bypass the theatrical box-office release window entirely because of the necessary steep marketing expenses and instead go straight to home video for release. There is pressure from services like Netflix for Hollywood to release films simultaneously to the home video market and to theaters, but the theater industry and its major studio allies have fiercely protected the three- to four-month exclusive window that theaters have for movie releases, arguing that to lose exclusivity would destroy the movie theater business.[20] Netflix and Amazon have begun to make their own films, which enables them to control the release dates at least on those films.

- Third are the next "windows" of release for a film: premium cable (such as HBO and Showtime), then network and basic cable showings, and finally the syndicated TV market. The price these cable and television outlets pay to the studios is negotiated on a film-by-film basis.

- Fourth, studios earn revenue from distributing films in foreign markets. In fact, at a record-breaking $39.9 billion in 2017, international box-office gross revenues are more than triple the U.S. and Canadian box-office receipts, and they continue to climb annually, even as other countries produce more of their own films.

- Fifth, studios make money by distributing the work of independent producers and filmmakers, who hire the studios to gain wider circulation. Independents pay the studios between 30 and 50 percent of the box-office and home video dollars they make from movies.

- Sixth, revenue is earned from merchandise licensing and *product placements* in movies. In the early days of television and film, characters generally used generic products, or product labels weren't highlighted in shots. But with soaring film production costs, product placements are adding extra revenue

David James/© Walt Disney Studios Motion Pictures/Lucasfilm Ltd./Everett Collection while lending an element of authenticity to the staging. Famous product placements in movies include Reese's Pieces in *E.T.* (1982), Pepsi-Cola in *Back to the Future II* (1989), and an entire line of toy products in *The Lego Movie* (2014).

Theater Chains Consolidate Exhibition

Film exhibition is controlled by a handful of theater chains; the leading five companies operate more than 50 percent of U.S. screens. The major chains—AMC Entertainment, Regal Entertainment Group, Cinemark USA, Cineplex Entertainment, and Marcus Theatres—own thousands of screens in suburban malls and at highway crossroads, and most have expanded into international markets as well. Because distributors require access to movie screens, they do business with the chains that control the most screens. In a multiplex, an exhibitor can project a potential hit on two or three screens at the same time; films that do not debut well are relegated to the smallest theaters or bumped quickly for a new release.

The strategy of the leading theater chains during the mid-1990s was to build more **megaplexes** (facilities with fourteen or more screens), featuring upscale concession services and luxurious screening rooms equipped with stadium-style seating and digital sound to make moviegoing a special event. By 2017, the movie exhibition business growth had leveled off at 39,651 indoor screens, most of them at megaplex locations. To further combat the home theater market, movie theater chains were experimenting with bigger screens (the ultrawide 270-degree views of ScreenX, for example), responsive 4-D seating (with "sway" and "twist" motions to further immerse viewers of action movies), and virtual reality (VR) experiences in which viewers wear VR headsets and sit in special full-motion chairs. IMAX is also testing "VR Centres," with small 12-by-12-foot "pods" where individuals or small groups have 5- to 15-minute VR experiences that cost from $7 to $25.[21]

The Major Studio Players

The current Hollywood commercial film business is ruled primarily by six companies: Warner Brothers, Paramount, 21st Century Fox, Universal, Columbia Pictures, and Disney—the **Big Six**. Except for Disney and Fox, all these companies are owned by large parent conglomerates (see Figure 7.2).

FIGURE 7.2

MARKET SHARE OF U.S. FILM STUDIOS AND DISTRIBUTORS, 2017 (IN $ MILLIONS)

Note: Based on gross box-office revenue, January 1, 2017–December 31, 2017. Overall gross for the period: $11.1 billion.

Data from: Box Office Mojo, "Studio Market Share, 2017," www.boxofficemojo.com/studio.

Note: The Weinstein Company and Open Road were both out of business by 2018. Disney's plan to acquire 21st Century Fox was pending in 2018.

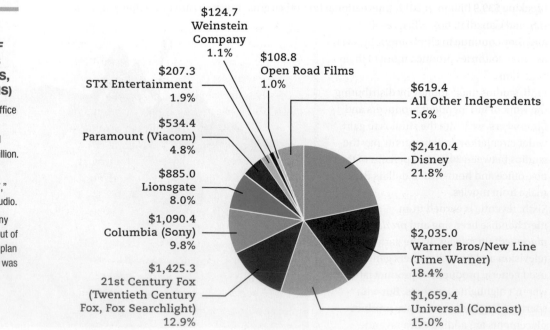

The six major studios account for about 86 percent of the revenue generated by commercial films. They also control more than half the movie market in Europe and Asia. (The Big Six may become the Big Five if Disney's plan to acquire 21st Century Fox is approved; Disney announced the plan in late 2017.) Independent studios that have maintained modest market share are sometimes called mini-majors. Lionsgate (*The Hunger Games*, the *Twilight* series, the *Divergent* series), which purchased indie Summit Entertainment in 2012, was the only established mini-major by 2018. The Weinstein Company (*Django Unchained*, *The Imitation Game*) had been a successful mini-major, but it folded quickly in 2018 after more than fifty women publicly charged co-owner Harvey Weinstein of instances of sexual harassment, assault, and rape over several decades. The charges were brought to light in 2017 in Pulitzer Prize–winning investigative reports by the *New York Times* and the *New Yorker* magazine.

In the 1980s, to offset losses resulting from box-office failures, the movie industry began to diversify, expanding into other product lines and other mass media. This expansion included television programming, print media, sound recordings, and home videos/DVDs, as well as cable and computers, electronic hardware and software, retail stores, and theme parks such as Universal Studios. To maintain the industry's economic stability, management strategies today rely on both heavy advance promotion (which can double the cost of a commercial film) and **synergy**—the promotion and sale of a product throughout the various subsidiaries of the media conglomerate. Companies promote not only the new movie itself but also its book form, soundtrack, calendars, T-shirts, website, and toy action figures, as well as "the-making-of" story on television and the Internet. The Disney studio, in particular, has been successful with its multiple repackaging of youth-targeted movies, including comic books, toys, television specials, fast-food tie-ins, and theme-park attractions. Since the 1950s, this synergy has been a key characteristic of the film industry and an important element in the flood of corporate mergers that have made today's Big Six even bigger.

The biggest corporate mergers have involved the internationalization of the American film business. Investment in American popular culture by the international electronics industry is particularly significant. This business strategy represents a new, high-tech kind of vertical integration—an attempt to control both the production of electronic equipment that consumers buy for their homes and the production and distribution of the content that runs on that equipment. This began in 1985, when Australia's News Corp. bought Twentieth Century Fox

SYNERGIES

in feature films can be easy for Disney, which is a $55.1 billion multinational corporation. *Frozen* (2013) is one of Disney's biggest animated hits ever, and *Frozen* merchandise was in short supply in North America for fans wanting to celebrate the story of Anna and Elsa, two princess sisters who also became attractions at Disney resort parks. The movie's soundtrack hit No. 1 in sales, and Disney Cruise Line and the Adventures by Disney tour company experienced a huge increase in holiday business to Geirangerfjord, Norway, the fjord that inspired the film's fantasy kingdom of Arendelle.

The Blockbuster Mentality

In the beginning of this chapter, we noted Hollywood's shift toward a blockbuster mentality after the success of films like *Star Wars*. How pervasive is this blockbuster mentality, which targets an audience of young adults, releases action-packed big-budget films featuring heavy merchandising tie-ins, and produces sequels?

1 DESCRIPTION
Consider a list of the all-time highest-grossing movies in the United States, such as the one on Box Office Mojo, www.boxofficemojo.com /alltime/domestic.htm.

2 ANALYSIS
Note patterns in the list. For example, of the thirty top-grossing films, nearly all of them target young audiences. Nearly all of the top-grossing films feature animated or digitally composited characters (*Frozen*, *Shrek 2*, *Jurassic Park*) or extensive special effects (*Transformers: Revenge of the Fallen*, *Avengers: Age of Ultron*). Nearly all of the films either spawned or are part of a series, like *Transformers*, *The Dark Knight*, and *Harry Potter*. More than half of the films fit into the action movie genre. Nearly all of the Top 30 had intense merchandising campaigns that featured action figures, fast-food tie-ins, and an incredible variety of products for sale; that is, hardly any were "surprise" hits.

3 INTERPRETATION
What do the patterns mean? It's clear, economically, why Hollywood likes to have successful blockbuster movie franchises. But what kinds of films get left out of the mix? Hits like *Forrest Gump* (now bumped way out of the Top 30), which may have had big-budget releases but lack some of the other attributes of blockbusters, are clearly anomalies of the blockbuster mentality, although they illustrate that strong characters and compelling stories can carry a film to great commercial success.

4 EVALUATION
It is likely that we will continue to see an increase in youth-oriented, animated/action movie franchises that are heavily merchandised and intended for wide international distribution. Indeed, Hollywood does not have a lot of motivation to put out the kinds of movies that don't fit these categories. Is this a good thing? Can you think of a film that you thought was excellent and that would have probably been a bigger hit with better promotion and wider distribution?

5 ENGAGEMENT
Watch independent and foreign films to see what you're missing. Visit the Sundance Film Festival site and browse through the many films listed. Find these films on Netflix, Amazon, Google Play, or iTunes (and if the films are unavailable, let these services know). Write your cable company and request to have the Sundance Channel on your cable lineup. Organize an independent film night on your college campus and bring these films to a crowd.

(News Corp. has since split into two separate companies; the film division is under the umbrella of 21st Century Fox). Sony bought Columbia in 1989 for $4 billion. Vivendi, a French utility, acquired Universal in 2000 but sold it to General Electric, the parent of NBC, in 2003. Comcast bought a controlling stake in NBC Universal in 2009, and government agencies approved the merger in 2011. In 2006, Disney bought its animation partner, Pixar. It also bought Marvel in 2009, which gave Disney the rights to a host of characters, including Spider-Man, Iron Man, the Hulk, the X-Men, and the Fantastic Four. In 2012, Disney bought Lucasfilm, gaining control of the *Indiana Jones* and *Star Wars* franchises, plus the innovative technologies of George Lucas's famed Industrial Light & Magic special-effects company.

Convergence: Movies Adjust to the Digital Turn

The biggest challenge the movie industry faces today is the Internet. As broadband Internet service connects more households, movie fans are increasingly getting movies from the web. After witnessing the difficulties that illegal file-sharing brought on the music labels (some of which share the same corporate parent as the Big Six), the movie industry has more quickly embraced the Internet for movie distribution. Apple's iTunes store began selling digital downloads of a limited selection of movies in 2006, and in 2008, iTunes began renting new movies from all the major studios for just $3.99. In the same year, online DVD rental service Netflix began streaming some movies and television shows to customers' computer screens and televisions.

The popularity of Netflix's streaming service opened the door to other similar services. Hulu, a joint venture by NBC Universal (Universal Studios), 21st Century Fox, and Disney, was created as the studios' attempt to divert attention from YouTube and get viewers to either watch free, ad-supported streaming movies and television shows online or subscribe to Hulu Plus, Hulu's premium service. Comcast operates a similar website, called Xfinity. Google's YouTube, the most popular online video service, began offering commercial films in 2010 by redesigning its interface to be more film-friendly and offering online rentals. Amazon and Vudu (owned by Walmart) also operate digital movie stores.

The year 2012 marked a turning point: For the first time, movie fans accessed more movies through digital online media than through physical copies, like DVDs and Blu-ray discs.[22] For the movie industry, this shift to Internet distribution has mixed consequences. On the one hand, the industry needs to offer movies where people want to access them, and digital distribution is a growing market. "We're agnostic about where the money comes from," says Eamonn Bowles, president of the independent distributor Magnolia Pictures. "We don't care. Basically, our philosophy is we want to make the film available for however the customer wants to purchase it."[23] On the other hand, although providing streaming is less expensive than producing physical DVDs, the revenue is still much lower compared to DVD sales; this shift has had a larger impact on the major studios, which had grown reliant on healthy DVD revenue.

The digital turn creates two long-term paths for Hollywood. One path is that studios and theaters will lean even more heavily toward making and showing big-budget blockbuster film franchises with a lot of special effects, since people will want to watch those on the big screen (especially IMAX and 3-D) for the full effect—and they are easy to export for international audiences. The other path involves inexpensive digital distribution of lower-budget documentaries and independent films, which probably wouldn't get wide theatrical distribution anyway but could find an audience in those who watch at home.

The Internet has also become an essential tool for movie marketing, and one that studios are finding less expensive than traditional methods, like television ads or billboards. Films regularly have web pages, but many studios now also use a full menu of social media to promote films in advance of their release. For example, the marketing plan for Lionsgate's 2012 movie *The Hunger Games*, which launched an enormously successful movie franchise, employed "near-constant use of Facebook and Twitter, a YouTube channel, a Tumblr blog, iPhone games and live Yahoo streaming from the premiere" to build interest that would make it into a hit film.[24]

Alternative Voices

With the major studios exerting such a profound influence on the worldwide production, distribution, and exhibition of movies, new alternatives have helped open and redefine the movie industry. The digital revolution in movie production is the most recent opportunity to wrest some power away from the Hollywood studios. Substantially cheaper and more accessible than standard film equipment, **digital video** is a shift from celluloid film; it allows filmmakers to replace expensive and bulky 16-mm and 35-mm film cameras with less expensive, lightweight digital video cameras. For moviemakers, digital video also means seeing camera work instantly, instead of waiting for film to be developed, and being able to capture additional footage without concern for the high cost of film stock and processing.

Everett Collection

HARDCORE HENRY (2015),

an action film by Russian director Ilya Naishuller, was shot with an inexpensive GoPro Hero 3 helmet camera, worn by various actors playing the title character to achieve the first-person shooter point of view. The producers raised about $255,000 from more than two thousand backers on the Indiegogo crowdfunding platform to make the film's first version. American-based STX Entertainment then acquired the film for $10 million, made improvements, and released it worldwide in 2016.

Though digital video has become commonplace on big studio productions, the greatest impact of digital technology has been on independent filmmakers. Low-cost digital video opened up the creative process to countless new artists. With digital video camera equipment and computer-based desktop editors, movies can be made for a fraction of what the cost would be on film. Some feature films—*Unsane* (2018) and *Tangerine* (2015), for example—were actually shot on iPhones. Digital cameras are now the norm for independent filmmakers. Ironically, both independent and Hollywood filmmakers have to contend with issues of preserving digital content: Celluloid film stock can last a hundred years, whereas digital formats can be lost as storage formats fail and devices become obsolete.[25]

Because digital production puts movies in the same format as the Internet, independent filmmakers have new distribution venues beyond film festivals or the major studios. For example, Vimeo, YouTube, Netflix, and Amazon have grown into leading Internet sites for the screening and distribution of short films and film festival entries, providing filmmakers with their most valuable asset—an audience.

POPULAR MOVIES AND DEMOCRACY

At the cultural level, movies function as **consensus narratives**, a term that describes cultural products that become popular and provide shared cultural experiences. These consensus narratives operate across different times and cultures. In this sense, movies are part of a long narrative tradition, encompassing "the oral formulaic of Homer's day, the theater of Sophocles, the Elizabethan theater, the English novel from Defoe to Dickens, . . . the silent film, the sound film, and television during the Network Era."[26] Consensus narratives—whether they are dramas, romances, westerns, or mysteries—speak to central myths and values in an accessible language that often bridges global boundaries.

At the international level, countries continue to struggle with questions about the influence of American films on local customs and culture. As with other American mass media industries, the long reach of Hollywood movies is one of the key contradictions of contemporary life: Do such films contribute to a global village in which people throughout the world share a universal culture that breaks down barriers? Or does an American-based common culture stifle the development of local cultures worldwide and diversity in moviemaking? Clearly, the steady production of profitable action/adventure movies—whether they originate in the United States, Africa, France, or China—continues, not only because these movies appeal to mass audiences but also because they translate easily into other languages.

With the rise of international media conglomerates, it has become more difficult to awaken public debate over issues of movie diversity and America's domination of the film business. Consequently, issues concerning increased competition and a greater variety of movies sometimes fall by the wayside. As critical consumers, those of us who enjoy movies and recognize their cultural significance must raise these broader issues in public forums as well as in our personal conversations.

LaunchPad
macmillan learning
launchpadworks.com

More Than a Movie: Social Issues and Film
Independent filmmakers are using social media to get moviegoers involved.

Discussion: Do you think the convergence of digital media with social-issue movies helps such films make a larger impact? Why or why not?

7 Chapter Review

COMMON THREADS

One of the Common Threads discussed in Chapter 1 is mass media, cultural expression, and storytelling. The movie industry is a particularly potent example of this, as Hollywood movies dominate international screens. But Hollywood dominates our domestic screens as well. Does this limit our exposure to other kinds of stories?

In the 1920s, when the burgeoning film industries in Europe lay in ruins after World War I, Hollywood gained an international dominance it has never relinquished. Critics have long cited America's *cultural imperialism*, claiming America floods the world with its movies, music, television shows, fashion, and products. The strength of American cultural and economic power is evident when you witness a Thai man in a Tommy Hilfiger shirt watching *Transformers* at a Bangkok bar while eating a hamburger and drinking a Coke. Critics feel that American-produced culture overwhelms indigenous cultural industries, which will never be able to compete at the same level.

But other cultures are good at bending and blending our content. Hip-hop has been remade into regional music in places like Senegal, Portugal, Taiwan, and the Philippines. McDonald's is global, but in India you can get a McAloo Tikki sandwich—a spicy fried potato and pea vegetarian patty. In Turkey you can get a McTurco, a kebab with lamb or chicken. And in France you can order a beer with your meal.

While some may be proud of the success of America's cultural exports, we might also ask ourselves this: What is the impact of our cultural dominance on our own media environment? Foreign films, for example, account for less than 2 percent of all releases in the United States. Is this because we find subtitles or other languages too challenging? At points in the twentieth century, American moviegoers were much more likely to see foreign films. Did our taste in movies change of our own accord, or did we simply forget how to appreciate different narratives and styles?

Of course, international content does make it to our shores. We exported rock and roll, and the British sent it back to us, with long hair. They also gave us *The Office* and *House of Cards*. Japan gave us anime, Pokémon, *Iron Chef*, and Hello Kitty.

But in a world where globalization is a key phenomenon, Hollywood rarely shows us the world through another's eyes. The burden falls to us to search out and watch those movies until Hollywood finally gets the message.

KEY TERMS

The definitions for the terms listed below can be found in the glossary at the end of the book. The page numbers listed with the terms indicate where the term is highlighted in the chapter.

celluloid, 202
kinetograph, 203
kinetoscope, 203
vitascope, 203
narrative films, 204
nickelodeons, 204
vertical integration, 205
oligopoly, 205
studio system, 206
block booking, 206

movie palaces, 207
multiplexes, 207
Big Five, 207
Little Three, 207
blockbuster, 208
talkies, 208
newsreels, 209
genre, 209
documentary, 215
cinema verité, 215

indies, 215
Hollywood Ten, 219
Paramount decision, 219
megaplexes, 224
Big Six, 224
synergy, 225
digital video, 227
consensus narratives, 228

REVIEW QUESTIONS

Early Technology and the Evolution of Movies

1. How did film go from the novelty stage to the mass medium stage?

2. Why were early silent films popular?

3. What contribution did nickelodeons make to film history?

The Rise of the Hollywood Studio System

4. Why did Hollywood end up as the center of film production?

5. Why did Thomas Edison and the Trust fail to shape and control the film industry, and why did Adolph Zukor of Paramount succeed?

6. How does vertical integration work in the film business?

The Studio System's Golden Age

7. Why did a certain structure of film—called classic Hollywood narrative—become so dominant in moviemaking?

8. Why are genres and directors important to the film industry?

9. Why are documentaries an important alternative to traditional Hollywood filmmaking? What contributions have they made to the film industry?

The Transformation of the Studio System

10. What political and cultural forces changed the Hollywood system in the late 1940s and 1950s?

11. How did the movie industry respond to the advent of television?

12. How has the home entertainment industry developed and changed since the 1970s?

The Economics of the Movie Business

13. What are the various ways in which major movie studios make money from the film business?

14. How do a few large film studios manage to control most of the commercial industry?

15. How is the movie industry adapting to the Internet?

16. What is the impact of inexpensive digital technology on filmmaking?

Popular Movies and Democracy

17. Do films contribute to a global village in which people throughout the world share a universal culture? Or do U.S.-based films overwhelm the development of other cultures worldwide? Discuss.

QUESTIONING THE MEDIA

1. Do some research among family members, then compare your earliest memory of going to a movie with a parent's or grandparent's earliest memory.

2. Do you remember seeing a movie you were not allowed to see? Discuss the experience.

3. Do you prefer viewing films at a movie theater or at home? How might your viewing preferences connect to the way in which the film industry is evolving?

4. If you were a Hollywood film producer or executive, what kinds of films would you like to see made? What changes would you make in what we see at the movies?

LAUNCHPAD FOR *MEDIA & CULTURE*

Visit LaunchPad for *Media & Culture* at launchpadworks.com for additional learning tools:

- REVIEW WITH LEARNINGCURVE
  LearningCurve, available on LaunchPad for *Media & Culture*, uses gamelike quizzing to help you master the concepts you need to learn from this chapter.

- VIDEO: *GRAVITY*
  Watch a brief clip from *Gravity*, then discuss how the movie uses the most advanced technical tools in service of classical storytelling.

PART 3

Words and Pictures

The dominant media of the nineteenth century featured printed material, with pictures supplementing the written text of newspapers, magazines, and books—our oldest mass media. When music, radio, and TV came along in the twentieth century, the newspaper, magazine, and book industries did not disappear; instead, they adapted. And in the twenty-first century, the story of our oldest media is still about adapting, but this time in the age of Apple, Amazon, Google, and Twitter. We are still reading newspapers, subscribing to magazines, and buying books, but they now come in multiple forms from multiple places, most of them online.

As we wrestle with the changes of the digital age, does it make any difference whether we get our news from a printed newspaper or an online website? Does it matter if we hold a physical magazine or even this textbook in our hands, or is an online version just as good? What *is* clear is that newspapers, magazines, and books will continue in some form. Perhaps these forms will represent something entirely new, but the earlier, physical versions of these texts will continue to shape their digital content even as the ways they are read and interpreted change.

LaunchPad
macmillan learning

launchpadworks.com

Visit **LaunchPad for *Media & Culture*** to explore an interactive time line of the history of mass communication, practice your media literacy skills, test your knowledge of the concepts in the textbook with LearningCurve, explore and discuss current trends in mass communication with video activities and video assessment tools, and more.

HOW WE READ NOW

FORMAT TRENDS FOR BOOKS

From 2012 to 2016, the market for print books held steady, e-books became less popular, and sales of audio books increased.

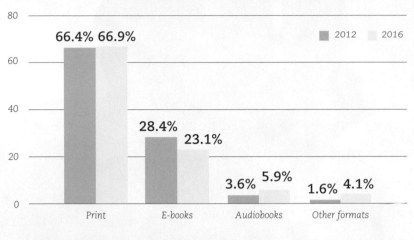

66.4% 66.9%   Print
28.4% 23.1%   E-books
3.6% 5.9%   Audiobooks
1.6% 4.1%   Other formats

■ 2012 ■ 2016

MEDIA USAGE BY GENERATION

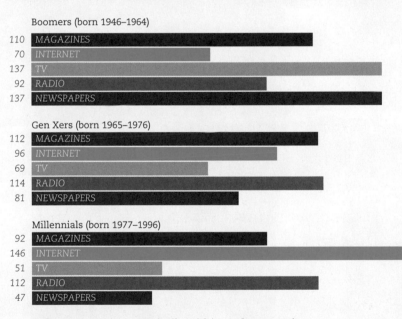

Boomers (born 1946–1964)
- 110 MAGAZINES
- 70 INTERNET
- 137 TV
- 92 RADIO
- 137 NEWSPAPERS

Gen Xers (born 1965–1976)
- 112 MAGAZINES
- 96 INTERNET
- 69 TV
- 114 RADIO
- 81 NEWSPAPERS

Millennials (born 1977–1996)
- 92 MAGAZINES
- 146 INTERNET
- 51 TV
- 112 RADIO
- 47 NEWSPAPERS

Index: Percent in top quintile within each generation vs. percent in top quintile among adults 18+.
Data from: GfK MRI, Fall 2016

THE TOP 20 MOST WELL-READ CITIES IN THE UNITED STATES

1. Seattle, Wash.
2. Portland, Ore.
3. Washington, D.C.
4. San Francisco, Calif.
5. Austin, Texas
6. Las Vegas, Nev.
7. Tucson, Ariz.
8. Denver, Colo.
9. Albuquerque, N.M.
10. San Diego, Calif.
11. Baltimore, Md.
12. Charlotte, N.C.
13. Louisville, Ky.
14. San Jose, Calif.
15. Houston, Texas
16. Nashville, Tenn.
17. Chicago, Ill.
18. Indianapolis, Ind.
19. Dallas, Texas
20. San Antonio, Texas

Data from: "Amazon.com Announces the Most Well-Read Cities in America," BusinessWire, May 24, 2016, https://www.businesswire.com/news/home/20160524005123/en/Amazon.com-Announces-Well-Read-Cities-America.

NOTE: based on sales data from cities with more than 500,000 residents on a per capita basis, including purchases of all books, magazines and newspapers in both Kindle and print format

MEDIASHIFT'S BEST NEWS APPS

1. Buzzfeed News
2. Reddit
3. AP Mobile
4. Apple News
5. Inkl
6. CNN
7. Flipboard
8. BBC News
9. Al Jazeera English

HONORABLE MENTIONS

1. Pocket
2. NPR News
3. Pulse
4. New York Times
5. Washington Post
6. Reuters

Data from: Phil Corso, "The Best News Apps of 2017," MediaShift, December 2017, http://mediashift.org/2017/12/best-news-apps-for-each-of-your-news-needs/.

Newspapers

The Rise and Decline of Modern Journalism

8

WHILE TODAY IT SEEMS AS IF printed newspapers are in perpetual decline, the fact is that more people read news from newspapers than at any other time in U.S. history—it's just that they mostly read the news online, delivered "free" from Google or Facebook, who rake in all the digital ad money. Back in 2001, reporters working at daily newspapers numbered over fifty-six thousand. In 2018, that number was less than twenty-five thousand—more than half the daily print news workforce wiped out. In 2017, the number of reporters working in TV news outnumbered those at daily papers for the first time, totaling about 27,100 to 25,000.[1]

Back in 2016, the movie *Spotlight*, which won the Academy Award for best picture, showcased the kind of journalism that is in jeopardy today with the loss of so many reporters.

THE EVOLUTION OF
AMERICAN
NEWSPAPERS
p. 237

COMPETING MODELS
OF MODERN PRINT
JOURNALISM
p. 242

THE BUSINESS AND
OWNERSHIP OF
NEWSPAPERS
p. 247

CHALLENGES
FACING
NEWSPAPERS
TODAY
p. 259

NEWSPAPERS AND
DEMOCRACY
p. 265

The movie depicted the work of the *Boston Globe*'s investigative reporting team, Spotlight, which won the Pulitzer Prize for public service in 2003 for its coverage of sexual abuse by Catholic priests in Boston and across Massachusetts. The movie celebrated the kind of journalism that not only holds people in power accountable but also changes lives. Recognizing, let alone acknowledging, this kind of work is difficult in a time when we are awash in the noise and drama of social media and "fake news."

Spotlight also distinguished itself for portraying good journalism as a team effort rather than just the work of a single heroic reporter. More broadly, journalism often dramatizes the exploits of individuals rather than the ways in which institutions and organizations work—or don't work. For example, CBS's *60 Minutes*—the gold standard for investigative TV journalism since 1968—often portrays socioeconomic problems like homelessness by dramatizing the plight of an individual person or family.[2] In doing so, the larger social problem of homelessness, which requires collective social action to actually solve, often plays out in the news as isolated personal problems demanding individual remedies.

In *Spotlight*, however, the reporters moved in a different direction. They pointed to institutional failure and dysfunction, rather than just presenting a series of isolated reports about the church covering up for various rogue priests. In other words, the Spotlight team portrayed the abuse as a major social and institutional problem that demanded collective engagement by both the church and the press. The movie's script was inspired by a 2009 case study from Columbia Journalism School, which argued that in the past, priest abuse stories from across the country were being treated as isolated instances: "The church, and to some degree the press, seemed content to portray the growing list of cases as stories of individual priests who had sinned, been exposed, and brought to justice."[3]

Sadly, with the loss of thirty-thousand reporters over the past two decades, the kind of daily newspaper journalism portrayed in *Spotlight* is the exception rather than the rule. Investigative journalism that holds the powerful accountable is time consuming and expensive and on the decline. In today's newspaper world, the bottom line is often about managing costs and explaining the value of newspapers to stockholders.

Despite the decline of newspapers, some big investors have been buying them. Amazon's Jeff Bezos paid $250 million in 2013 for the *Washington Post*. Investment guru Warren Buffett bought more than sixty newspapers in 2012 and 2013—at a time when many traditional print companies, looking at the decline in newspaper readership, were trying to unload their papers. In 2018, a Los Angeles investment firm, owned by biotech billionaire Dr. Patrick Soon-Shiong, purchased the *Los Angeles Times*, the *San Diego Union-Tribune*, and Spanish-language *Hoy Los Angeles* for a reported $500 million.

If the journalism portrayed in *Spotlight* is to thrive, it will take more than the underwriting of a handful of billionaires who understand the value of good journalism to their communities. Operating like the *Spotlight* team, individual communities need to think about the falloff in investigative journalism as a systemic problem that requires collective action in order to foster the kind of reporting that not only better informs us but strengthens our democracy. One hopeful sign is the emergence of the nonprofit Report for America (RFA). Borrowing ideas from Teach for America and the Peace Corps, RFA hopes to add more than a thousand reporters to daily journalism by the early 2020s. RFA is partly funded by Google News Lab.[4]

DESPITE THEIR CURRENT PREDICAMENTS, newspapers and their online offspring play many roles in contemporary culture. As chroniclers of daily life, newspapers both inform and entertain. By reporting on scientific, technological, and medical issues, newspapers disseminate specialized knowledge to the public. In reviews of films, concerts, and plays, they shape cultural trends. Investigative teams like the *Boston Globe*'s Spotlight unit expose corruption. Opinion pages trigger public debates and offer differing points of view. Columnists provide everything from advice on raising children to opinions on the United States' role as an economic and military superpower. Newspapers help readers make choices about everything from what kind of food to eat to what kinds of leaders to elect.

Although newspapers have played a central role in daily life, in today's digital age the industry is losing both papers and readers. Newspapers have lost their near monopoly on classified advertising, much of which has shifted to free websites, like craigslist and eBay. According to a 2017 report from the Pew Research Center, total print and digital newspaper ad revenues totaled $16.5 billion in 2017, with $11.2 billion coming from print ads, and $5.3 billion coming from online ads.[5] By comparison, print ads brought in $47 billion back in 2005, with online ads accounting for an additional $2 billion in revenue.[6] The slow growth of digital revenue for newspapers has not come close to offsetting the major declines in print ads between 2005 and 2015.

In terms of circulation, Pew reports that after two years of slight gains in 2012 and 2013, both weekday and Sunday circulation declined in 2014. Pew's analysis of readership data shows that weekday circulation fell 3.3 percent from 2013, and Sunday circulation dropped 3.4 percent. Still, about 56 percent of newspaper readers report that they get their news from print editions exclusively.[7]

In this chapter, we examine the cultural, social, and economic impact of newspapers. We will:

- Trace the history of newspapers through a number of influential periods and styles
- Explore the early political-commercial press, the penny press, and yellow journalism
- Examine the modern era through the influence of the *New York Times* and journalism's embrace of objectivity
- Look at interpretive journalism in the 1920s and 1930s and the revival of literary journalism in the 1960s
- Review issues of newspaper ownership, new technologies, citizen journalism, declining revenue, and the crucial role of newspapers in our democracy

As you read this chapter, think about your own early experiences with newspapers and the impact they have had on you and your family. Did you read certain sections of the paper, like sports or comics? What do you remember from your childhood about your parents' reading habits? What are your own newspaper reading habits today? How often do you actually hold a newspaper in your hands? How often do you get your news online? For more questions to help you think through the role of newspapers in our lives, see "Questioning the Media" in the Chapter Review.

LaunchPad
macmillan learning
launchpadworks.com

Visit LaunchPad for *Media & Culture* and use LearningCurve to review concepts from this chapter.

THE EVOLUTION OF AMERICAN NEWSPAPERS

The idea of news is as old as language itself. The earliest news was passed along orally from family to family, from tribe to tribe, by community leaders and oral historians. The earliest known written news sheet, *Acta Diurna* (Latin for "daily events"), was developed by Julius Caesar and posted in public spaces and on buildings in Rome in 59 BCE. Even in its oral and early written stages, news informed people on the state of their relations with neighboring tribes and towns. With the development of the printing press in the fifteenth century, a society's ability to send and receive information was greatly accelerated. Throughout history, news has satisfied our need to know things we cannot experience

Bettmann/Getty Images

COLONIAL NEWSPAPERS

During the colonial period, New York printer John Peter Zenger was arrested for seditious libel. He eventually won his case, which established the precedent that today allows U.S. journalists and citizens to criticize public officials.

personally. Newspapers today continue to document daily life and bear witness to both ordinary and extraordinary events.

Colonial Newspapers and the Partisan Press

The novelty and entrepreneurial stages of print-media development first happened in Europe with the rise of the printing press. In North America, the first newspaper, *Publick Occurrences, Both Foreign and Domestick*, was published on September 25, 1690, by Boston printer Benjamin Harris. The colonial government objected to Harris's negative tone regarding British rule, and local ministers were offended by his published report that the king of France had once had an affair with his son's wife. The newspaper was banned after one issue.

Because European news took weeks to travel by ship, early colonial papers were not very timely. In their more spirited sections, however, the papers did report local illnesses, public floggings, and even suicides. In 1704, the first regularly published newspaper appeared in the American colonies—the *Boston News-Letter*, published by John Campbell. In 1721, also in Boston, James Franklin, the older brother of Benjamin Franklin, started the *New England Courant*. The *Courant* established a tradition of running stories that interested ordinary readers rather than printing articles that appealed primarily to business and colonial leaders. In 1729, Benjamin Franklin, at age twenty-four, took over the *Pennsylvania Gazette* and created, according to historians, the best of the colonial papers. Although a number of colonial papers operated solely on subsidies from political parties, the *Gazette* also made money by advertising products.

Another important colonial paper, the *New-York Weekly Journal*, appeared in 1733. John Peter Zenger had been installed as the printer of the *Journal* by the Popular Party, a political group that opposed British rule and ran articles that criticized the royal governor of New York. After a Popular Party judge was dismissed from office, the *Journal* escalated its attack on the governor. When Zenger shielded the writers of the critical articles, he was arrested in 1734 for *seditious libel*—defaming a public official's character in print. Championed by famed Philadelphia lawyer Andrew Hamilton, Zenger ultimately won his case in 1735. A sympathetic jury, in revolt against the colonial government, decided that newspapers had the right to criticize government leaders as long as the reports were true. After the Zenger case, the British never prosecuted another colonial printer. The Zenger decision would later provide a key foundation—the right of a democratic press to criticize public officials—for the First Amendment to the Constitution, adopted as part of the Bill of Rights in 1791. (See Chapter 16 for more on the First Amendment.)

By 1765, about thirty newspapers operated in the American colonies, with the first daily paper beginning in 1784. Newspapers were of two general types: political or commercial. Their development was shaped in large part by social, cultural, and political responses to British rule and by its eventual overthrow. Although the political and commercial papers carried both party news and business news, they had different agendas. Political papers, known as the **partisan press**, generally pushed the plan of the particular political group that subsidized the paper. The *commercial press*, by contrast, served business leaders, who were interested in economic issues. Both types of journalism left a legacy. The partisan press gave us the editorial pages, while the early commercial press was the forerunner of the business section.

In the eighteenth and early nineteenth centuries, even the largest of these papers rarely reached a circulation of fifteen hundred. Readership was primarily confined to educated or wealthy men who controlled local politics and commerce. During this time, however, a few pioneering women operated newspapers, including Elizabeth Timothy, the first American woman newspaper publisher (and mother of eight children). After her husband died of smallpox in 1738, Timothy took over the

South Carolina Gazette, established in 1734 by Benjamin Franklin and the Timothy family. In addition, Anna Maul Zenger ran the *New-York Weekly Journal* throughout her husband's 1734–35 incarceration and trial and after his death in 1746.[8]

The Penny Press Era: Newspapers Become Mass Media

By the late 1820s, the average newspaper cost six cents a copy and was sold through yearly subscriptions priced at ten to twelve dollars. Because that price was more than a week's salary for most skilled workers, newspaper readers were mostly affluent. By the 1830s, however, the Industrial Revolution made possible the replacement of expensive handmade paper with cheaper machine-made paper. During this time, the rise of the middle class spurred the growth of literacy, setting the stage for a more popular and inclusive press. In addition, breakthroughs in technology, particularly the replacement of mechanical presses with steam-powered presses, permitted publishers to produce as many as four thousand newspapers an hour, which lowered the cost of newspapers. **Penny papers** soon began competing with six-cent papers. Though subscriptions remained the preferred sales tool of many penny papers, they began relying increasingly on daily street sales of individual copies.

Day and the *New York Sun*

In 1833, printer Benjamin Day founded the *New York Sun* with no subscriptions and the price set at one penny. The *Sun*—whose slogan was "It shines for all"—highlighted local events, scandals, police reports, and serialized stories. Like today's supermarket tabloids, the *Sun* fabricated stories, including the infamous moon hoax, which reported "scientific" evidence of life on the moon. Within six months, the *Sun*'s lower price had generated a circulation of eight thousand, twice that of its nearest New York competitor.

The *Sun*'s success initiated a wave of penny papers that favored **human-interest stories**: news accounts that focus on the daily trials and triumphs of the human condition, often featuring ordinary individuals facing extraordinary challenges. These kinds of stories reveal journalism's ties to literary traditions, such as the archetypal conflicts between good and evil, normal and deviant, or individuals and institutions.

Bennett and the *New York Morning Herald*

The penny press era also featured James Gordon Bennett's *New York Morning Herald*, founded in 1835. Bennett, considered the first U.S. press baron, freed his newspaper from political influence. He established an independent paper serving middle- and working-class readers as well as his own business ambitions. The *Herald* carried political essays, news about scandals, business stories, a letters section, fashion notes, moral reflections, religious news, society gossip, colloquial tales and jokes, sports stories, and eventually reports from the Civil War. In addition, Bennett's paper sponsored balloon races, financed safaris, and overplayed crime stories. By 1860, the *Herald* reached nearly eighty thousand readers, making it the world's largest daily paper at the time.

Changing Economics and the Founding of the Associated Press

The penny papers were innovative. For example, they were the first to assign reporters to cover crime, which readers enthusiastically embraced, along with the reporting of local news. By gradually separating daily front-page reporting from overt political viewpoints on an editorial page, penny papers shifted their economic base from political parties to the market—that is, to advertising revenue, classified ads, and street sales. Although many partisan papers had taken a moral stand against advertising certain controversial products and "services"—such as medical "miracle" cures, abortionists, and especially the slave trade—the penny press became more neutral toward advertisers and printed virtually any ad. In fact, many penny papers regarded advertising as consumer news. The rise in ad revenues and circulation accelerated the growth of the newspaper industry. In 1830, 650

NEWSIES

sold Hearst and Pulitzer papers on the streets of New York in the 1890s. With more than a dozen dailies competing, street tactics were ferocious, and publishers often made young "newsies"—newsboys and newsgirls—buy the papers they could not sell.

weekly and 65 daily papers operated in the United States, reaching a circulation of 80,000. By 1840, a total of 1,140 weeklies and 140 dailies attracted more than 300,000 readers.

In 1848, six New York newspapers formed a cooperative arrangement and founded the Associated Press (AP), the first major news wire service. **Wire services** began as commercial organizations that relayed news stories and information around the country and the world using telegraph lines and, later, radio waves and digital transmissions. In the case of the AP, the New York papers provided access to both their own stories and those from other newspapers. In the 1850s, papers started sending reporters to cover Washington, D.C., and in the early 1860s, more than a hundred reporters from northern papers went south to cover the Civil War, relaying their reports back to their home papers via telegraph and wire services. The news wire companies enabled news to travel rapidly from coast to coast, setting the stage for modern journalism.

The marketing of news as a product and the use of modern technology to dramatically cut costs gradually elevated newspapers from the entrepreneurial stage to the status of a mass medium. By adapting news content, penny papers captured the middle- and working-class readers who could now afford the paper and also had more leisure time to read it. As newspapers sought to sustain their mass appeal, news and "factual" reports about crimes and other items of human interest eventually became more important than partisan articles about politics and commerce.

The Age of Yellow Journalism: Sensationalism and Investigation

The rise of competitive dailies and the penny press triggered the next significant period in American journalism. In the late 1800s, **yellow journalism** emphasized profitable papers that carried exciting human-interest stories, crime news, large headlines, and more readable copy. Generally regarded as sensationalistic and the direct forerunner of today's tabloid papers, reality TV, and celebrity-centered shows like *Access Hollywood*, yellow journalism featured two major developments: the emphasis on sensational or overly dramatic stories and early in-depth "detective" stories—the legacy for twentieth-century **investigative journalism** (news reports that hunt out and expose corruption, particularly in business and government). Reporting during this yellow journalism period increasingly became a crusading force for common people, with the press assuming a watchdog role on their behalf.

During this period, a newspaper circulation war pitted Joseph Pulitzer's *New York World* against William Randolph Hearst's *New York Journal*. A key player in the war was the Yellow Kid, the main character in the first popular cartoon strip, *Hogan's Alley*, created in 1895 by artist R. F. Outcault, who once worked for Thomas Edison. The phrase *yellow journalism* has since become associated with the strip, which shuttled back and forth between the Hearst and Pulitzer papers during their furious battle for readers in the mid- to late 1890s.

Pulitzer and the *New York World*

Joseph Pulitzer, a Jewish-Hungarian immigrant, began his career in newspaper publishing in the early 1870s as part owner of the *St. Louis Post*. He then bought the bankrupt *St. Louis Dispatch* for $2,500 at an auction in 1878 and merged it with the *Post*. The *Post-Dispatch* became known for stories that highlighted "sex and sin" ("A Denver Maiden Taken from Disreputable House") and satires of the upper class ("St. Louis Swells"). Pulitzer also viewed the *Post-Dispatch* as a "national conscience" that promoted the public good. He carried on the legacies of James Gordon Bennett: making money and developing a "free and impartial" paper that would "serve no party but the people." Within five years, the *Post-Dispatch* had become one of the most influential newspapers in the Midwest.

In 1883, Pulitzer bought the *New York World* for $346,000. He encouraged plain writing and the inclusion of maps and illustrations to help immigrant and working-class readers understand the written text. In addition to running sensational stories on crime and sex, Pulitzer instituted advice columns and women's pages. Like Bennett, Pulitzer treated advertising as a kind of news that displayed consumer products for readers. In fact, department stores became major advertisers during this period. This development contributed directly to the expansion of consumer culture and indirectly to the acknowledgment of women as newspaper readers. Eventually (because of pioneers like Nellie Bly—see Chapter 14), newspapers began employing women as reporters.

The *World* reflected the contradictory spirit of the yellow press. It crusaded for improved urban housing, better conditions for women, and equal labor laws. It campaigned against monopoly practices by AT&T, Standard Oil, and Equitable Insurance. Such popular crusades helped lay the groundwork for tightening federal antitrust laws in the early 1910s. At the same time, Pulitzer's paper manufactured news events and staged stunts, such as sending star reporter Nellie Bly around the world in seventy-two days to beat the fictional "record" in the popular 1873 Jules Verne novel *Around the World in Eighty Days*. By 1887, the *World*'s Sunday circulation had soared to more than 250,000, the largest anywhere.

Pulitzer created a lasting legacy by leaving $2 million to start the graduate school of journalism at Columbia University in 1912. In 1917, part of Pulitzer's Columbia endowment established the Pulitzer Prizes, the prestigious awards given each year for achievements in journalism, literature, drama, and music.

Hearst and the *New York Journal*

The *World* faced its fiercest competition when William Randolph Hearst bought the *New York Journal* (a penny paper founded by Pulitzer's brother Albert). Before moving to New York, the twenty-four-year-old Hearst took control of the *San Francisco Examiner* when his father, George Hearst, was elected to the U.S. Senate in 1887 (the younger Hearst had recently been expelled from Harvard for playing a practical joke on his professors). In 1895, with an inheritance from his father, Hearst bought the ailing *Journal* and then raided Joseph Pulitzer's paper for editors, writers, and cartoonists.

YELLOW JOURNALISM

Generally considered America's first comic-strip character, the Yellow Kid was created in the mid-1890s by cartoonist Richard (R. F.) Outcault. The cartoon was so popular that newspaper barons Joseph Pulitzer and William Randolph Hearst fought over Outcault's services, giving yellow journalism its name.

THE PENNY PRESS

The *World* (*near right*) and the *New York Journal* (*far right*) cover the same story in May 1898.

Taking his cue from Bennett and Pulitzer, Hearst focused on lurid, sensational stories and appealed to immigrant readers by using large headlines and bold layout designs. To boost circulation, the *Journal* invented interviews, faked pictures, and encouraged conflicts that might result in a story. In promoting journalism as mere dramatic storytelling, Hearst reportedly said, "The modern editor of the popular journal does not care for facts. The editor wants novelty. The editor has no objection to facts if they are also novel. But he would prefer a novelty that is not a fact to a fact that is not a novelty."[9]

Hearst is remembered as an unscrupulous publisher who once hired gangsters to distribute his newspapers. He was also, however, considered a champion of the underdog, and his paper's readership soared among the working and middle classes. In 1896, the *Journal*'s daily circulation reached 450,000, and by 1897, the Sunday edition of the paper rivaled the 600,000 circulation of the *World*. By the 1930s, Hearst's holdings included more than forty daily and Sunday papers, thirteen magazines (including *Good Housekeeping* and *Cosmopolitan*), eight radio stations, and two film companies. In addition, he controlled King Features Syndicate, which sold and distributed articles, comics, and features to many of the nation's dailies. Hearst—the model for Charles Foster Kane, the ruthless publisher in Orson Welles's classic 1940 film *Citizen Kane*—operated the largest media business in the world, comparable to today's Disney or Google.

COMPETING MODELS OF MODERN PRINT JOURNALISM

To some extent, the early commercial and partisan presses were covering important events impartially. These papers often carried verbatim reports of presidential addresses and murder trials, or the annual statements of the U.S. Treasury. In the late nineteenth century, as newspapers pushed for greater circulation, newspaper reporting changed. Two distinct types of journalism emerged: the *story-driven model*, which dramatized important events and was favored by the penny papers and the yellow press; and the *"just the facts" model*, which appeared to package information more impartially.[10] Implicit in these efforts was a question that is still debated today, especially in this era of "fake news" posts on social media and political attacks on legitimate news media. Is there some ideal, attainable objective model out there, or does the quest for objectivity actually conflict with journalists' traditional roles of telling news stories, revealing corruption, and questioning abuses of power, especially in government and business?

"Objectivity" in Modern Journalism

As the consumer marketplace expanded during the Industrial Revolution, facts and news became marketable products. Throughout the mid-nineteenth century, the more a newspaper appeared not to take sides on its front pages, the more its readership base grew (although, as they are today, editorial pages were still often partisan). In addition, wire service organizations were serving a variety of newspaper clients in different regions of the country. To satisfy all clients, readers, and the wide range of political views, newspapers tried to appear more impartial.

Ochs and the *New York Times*

The ideal of an impartial, or purely informational, news model was championed by Adolph Ochs, who bought the *New York Times* in 1896. The son of immigrant German Jews, Ochs grew up in Ohio and Tennessee, where at age twenty-one he took over the *Chattanooga Times* in 1878. Known more for his business and organizational ability than for his writing and editing skills, he transformed the Tennessee paper. Seeking a national stage and business expansion, Ochs moved to New York and invested $75,000 in the struggling *Times*. Through strategic hiring, Ochs and his editors rebuilt the paper around substantial news coverage and provocative editorial pages. To distance his New York paper from the yellow press, the editors also downplayed sensational stories, favoring the documentation of major events or issues.

Pool/Getty Images

CINCINNATI ENQUIRER staff won the 2018 Pulitzer Prize for local reporting, "for a riveting and insightful narrative and video documenting seven days of greater Cincinnati's heroin epidemic, revealing how the deadly addiction has ravaged families and communities." The series, "Seven Days of Heroin," devoted more than sixty journalists to telling a number of stories through the eyes of addicts, family members, first responders, and courtroom officials.

Partly as a marketing strategy, Ochs offered a distinct contrast to the more sensational Hearst and Pulitzer newspapers: an informational paper that provided stock and real estate reports to businesses, court reports to legal professionals, treaty summaries to political leaders, and theater and book reviews to educated general readers and intellectuals. Ochs's promotional gimmicks took direct aim at yellow journalism, advertising the *Times* under the motto "It does not soil the breakfast cloth." Ochs's strategy is similar to today's advertising tactic of targeting upscale viewers and readers, who control a disproportionate share of consumer dollars.

With the Hearst and Pulitzer papers capturing the bulk of working- and middle-class readers, managers at the *Times* first tried to use their straightforward, "no frills" reporting to appeal to more affluent and educated readers. In 1898, however, Ochs lowered the paper's price to a penny. He believed that people bought the *World* and the *Journal* primarily because they were cheap, not because of their stories. The *Times* began attracting middle-class readers who gravitated to the now-affordable paper as a status marker for the educated and well informed. Between 1898 and 1899, its circulation rose from 25,000 to 75,000. By 1921, the *Times* had a daily circulation of 330,000, and 500,000 on Sunday.

"Just the Facts, Please"

Early in the twentieth century, with reporters adopting a more "scientific" attitude to news- and fact-gathering, the ideal of objectivity began to anchor journalism. In **objective journalism**, which distinguishes factual reports from opinion columns, modern reporters strive to maintain a neutral attitude toward the issue or event they cover; they also search out competing points of view among the sources for a story.

The story form for packaging and presenting this kind of reporting has been traditionally labeled the **inverted-pyramid style**. According to some historians, Civil War correspondents developed this style by imitating the terse, compact press releases (summarizing or imitating telegrams to generals) that came from President Abraham Lincoln and his secretary of war, Edwin M. Stanton.[11] Often stripped of adverbs and adjectives, inverted-pyramid reports began—as they do today—with the most dramatic or newsworthy information. They answered who, what, where, when (and, less frequently, why or how) questions at the top of the story and then narrowed down the information to presumably less significant details. If wars or natural disasters disrupted the telegraph transmission of these dispatches, the information the reporter led with had the best chance of getting through.

For much of the twentieth century, the inverted-pyramid style served as an efficient way to arrange a timely story. It also had the advantage of appearing to present news as straightforward factual information, thereby not offending readers of differing political affiliations. Among other things, the importance of seeming objective and the reliance on the inverted pyramid signaled journalism's break from the partisan tradition. Although impossible to achieve (journalism is, after all, a literary practice, not a science), objectivity nonetheless became a guiding ideal of the modern press.

Interpretive Journalism

By the 1920s, there was a sense, especially after the trauma of World War I, that the impartial approach to reporting was insufficient for explaining complex national and global conditions. It was partly as a result of "drab, factual, objective reporting," one news scholar contended, that "the American people were utterly amazed when war broke out in August 1914, as they had no understanding of the foreign scene to prepare them for it."[12]

The Promise of Interpretive Journalism

Under the sway of objectivity, modern journalism had downplayed an early role of the partisan press: to offer analysis and opinion. But with the world becoming more complex, some papers began to revisit the analytical function of news. The result was the rise of **interpretive journalism**, which aims to explain key issues or events and place them in a broader historical or social context. This shift allowed journalism to take an analytic turn in a world grown more interconnected and complicated.

By the 1920s, editor and columnist Walter Lippmann insisted that the press should do more. Noting that objectivity and factuality should serve as the foundation for journalism, Lippmann ranked three press responsibilities: (1) "to make a current record"; (2) "to make a running analysis of it"; and (3) "on the basis of both, to suggest plans."[13] Indeed, reporters and readers alike have historically distinguished between informational reports and editorial (interpretive) pieces, which offer particular viewpoints or deeper analyses of the issues. Since the boundary between information and interpretation can be somewhat ambiguous, American papers have traditionally placed news analysis in separate labeled columns and placed opinion articles on certain pages so that readers do not confuse them with "straight news." It was during this time that political columns developed to evaluate and provide context for news. Moving beyond the informational and storytelling functions of news, journalists and newspapers began to extend their role as analysts.

Of course, in today's social media world, analysis and opinion are everywhere. In the nineteenth century, the problem was too little information; today, the problem is too much information. Thus, in this digital age, how do we find reliable sources and the best resources? As always, the best opinions and interpretations are those based on evidence and documentation. What is true of good scholarship is also true of the best journalism: It relies on investigating what happened, verifying information, and documenting multiple sides of the story—as there are usually more than two.

Broadcast News Embraces Interpretive Journalism

In a surprising twist, the rise of broadcast radio in the 1930s also forced newspapers to become more analytical in their approach to news. At the time, the newspaper industry was upset that broadcasters took their news directly from papers and wire services. As a result, a battle developed between radio journalism and print news. Although mainstream newspapers tried to copyright the facts they reported and sued radio stations for routinely using newspapers as their main news sources, the papers lost many of these court battles. Editors and newspaper lobbyists argued that radio personalities should be permitted to broadcast only commentary. By conceding this interpretive role to radio, the print press tried to protect its dominion over "the facts." It was in this environment that radio analysis began to flourish as a form of interpretive news. Lowell Thomas delivered the first daily network analysis for CBS on September 29, 1930, attacking Hitler's rise to power in Germany. By 1941, twenty regular commentators—the forerunners of today's radio talk-show hosts, "talking heads" on cable, and political bloggers—were explaining their version of the world to millions of listeners.

In this environment, some print journalists and editors came to believe that interpretive stories, rather than objective reports, could better compete with radio. They realized that interpretation was a way to counter radio's (and later television's) superior ability to report breaking news quickly—or even live. In 1933, the American Society of News Editors (ASNE) supported the idea of interpretive journalism. Most newspapers, however, did not embrace probing analysis during the 1930s. In most U.S. dailies, then, interpretation remained relegated to a few editorial and opinion pages. It wasn't until the 1950s—with the Korean War, the development of atomic power, tensions with the Soviet Union, and the anticommunist movement—that news analysis resurfaced on the newest medium: television. Interpretive journalism in newspapers grew at the same time, especially in such areas as the environment, science, agriculture, sports, health, politics, and business. Following the lead of the *New York Times*, many papers by the 1980s had developed an *op-ed page*—an opinion page opposite the traditional editorial page, which allowed a greater variety of columnists, news analyses, and letters to the editor.

Literary Forms of Journalism

By the late 1960s, many people were criticizing America's major social institutions. Political assassinations, Civil Rights protests, the Vietnam War, the drug culture, and the women's movement were not easily explained. Faced with so much change and turmoil, many individuals began to lose faith in the ability of institutions to oversee and ensure the social order. Members of protest movements as well as many middle- and working-class Americans began to suspect the privileges and power of traditional authority. As a result, key institutions—including journalism—lost some of their credibility.

Journalism as an Art Form

Throughout the first part of the twentieth century—journalism's modern era—journalistic storytelling was downplayed in favor of the inverted-pyramid style and the separation of fact from opinion. Dissatisfied with these limitations, some reporters began exploring a new model of reporting. **Literary journalism**, sometimes dubbed "new journalism," adapted fictional techniques—such as descriptive details and settings and extensive character dialogue—to nonfiction material and in-depth reporting. In the United States, literary journalism's roots are evident in the work of nineteenth-century novelists like Mark Twain, Stephen Crane, and Theodore Dreiser, all of whom started out as reporters. In the late 1930s and 1940s, literary journalism surfaced: Journalists, such as James Agee and John Hersey, began to demonstrate how writing about real events could achieve an artistry often associated only with fiction.

In the 1960s, Tom Wolfe, a leading practitioner of new journalism, argued for mixing the *content* of reporting with the *form* of fiction to create "both the kind of objective reality of journalism" and "the subjective reality" of the novel.[14] Writers such as Wolfe (*The Electric Kool-Aid Acid Test*), Truman Capote (*In Cold Blood*), Joan Didion (*The White Album*), Norman Mailer (*Armies of the Night*), and Hunter S. Thompson (*Hell's Angels*) turned to new journalism to overcome the flaws they perceived in routine reporting. Their often self-conscious treatment of social problems gave their writing a perspective that conventional journalism did not offer. After the 1960s' tide of intense social upheaval ebbed, new journalism subsided as well. However, literary journalism not only influenced magazines like *Mother Jones* and *Rolling Stone* but also affected daily newspapers by emphasizing longer feature stories on cultural trends and social issues, with detailed description or dialogue. Today, writers such as Adrian Nicole LeBlanc (*Random Family*), Dexter Filkins (*The Forever War*), and Åsne Seierstad (*The Bookseller of Kabul*) keep this tradition alive.

The Attack on Journalistic Objectivity

Former *New York Times* columnist Tom Wicker argued that in the early 1960s, an objective approach to news remained the dominant model. According to Wicker, the "press had so wrapped itself in the paper chains of 'objective journalism' that it had little ability to report anything beyond the bare and undeniable facts."[15] Eventually, the ideal of objectivity became suspect, along with the authority of experts and professionals in various fields.

A number of reporters responded to the criticism by rethinking the framework of conventional journalism and adopting a variety of alternative techniques. One of these was *advocacy journalism*, in which the reporter actively promotes a particular cause or viewpoint. *Precision journalism*, another technique, attempts to make the news more scientifically accurate by using poll surveys and questionnaires. Today we call this "data journalism," and it has increased in importance as newspapers and other news organizations take advantage of the availability of Internet data and the lack of space and time constraints in online journalism.

Contemporary Journalism in the TV and Internet Age

In the early 1980s, a postmodern brand of journalism arose from two important developments. In 1980, the *Columbus Dispatch* became the first paper to go online (today, nearly all U.S. papers offer some web services). And in 1982, the colorful *USA Today*, started by Gannett, radically changed the look of most major U.S. dailies.

USA Today Colors the Print Landscape

USA Today made its mark by incorporating features closely associated with postmodern forms, including an emphasis on visual style over substantive news or analysis and the use of brief news items to appeal to readers' busy schedules and shortened attention spans.

Now the second most widely circulated paper in the nation, *USA Today* represents the only successful launch of a new major U.S. daily newspaper in the last several decades. Showing its marketing savvy, *USA Today* was the first newspaper to acknowledge television's central role in mass culture: The paper used TV-inspired color and designed its first vending boxes to look like color TVs. Even the writing style of *USA Today* mimics TV news by casting many reports in the present tense rather than the past tense (which was the print-news norm throughout the twentieth century).

Writing for *Rolling Stone* in March 1992, media critic Jon Katz argued that the authority of modern newspapers suffered in the wake of a variety of "new news" forms that combined immediacy, information, entertainment, persuasion, and analysis. Katz claimed that the news supremacy of most prominent daily papers, such as the *New York Times* and the *Washington Post*, was being challenged by "news" coming from talk shows, television sitcoms, popular films, and even rap music. In other words, society was changing from one in which the transmission of knowledge depended mainly on books, newspapers, and magazines to one dominated by a mix of print, visual, and digital information.

Online Journalism Redefines News

What started out in the 1980s as simple, text-only experiments for newspapers developed into more robust websites in the 1990s, allowing newspapers to develop an online presence. Today, online journalism has completely changed the news industry. First, rather than subscribing to a traditional paper, most readers now begin their day on their iPads, smartphones, or computers, scanning a wide variety of news websites—including those of print papers, cable news channels, newsmagazines, bloggers, and online-only news organizations. Increasingly, news consumers use their Facebook friends and Twitter posts to direct them to key news stories on any particular day. Such resources and digital sites are taking over the role of more traditional forms of news, helping set the nation's cultural, social, and political agendas. One of the biggest changes is that digital news has sped up the news cycle to a constant stream of information and has challenged traditional news services to keep up. In an early example, Matt Drudge, the conservative Internet gossip and news source behind the *Drudge*

Report, hijacked the traditional news agenda in January 1998 and launched a scandal when he posted a report that *Newsweek* had delayed the story about President Clinton's affair with White House intern Monica Lewinsky.

With the election of Donald Trump as president in 2016, several critics noted the savvy way he hijacked the national news agenda through Twitter. For the first two years of his presidency, he tweeted almost every morning. Thus, the national news media—particularly cable TV outlets like CNN, Fox News, and MSNBC—would spend the rest of their day dissecting his tweets, verifying whether they were true and sometimes even what they meant. The president tweeted so often that it even became a story when he did not tweet. As a number of media critics have noted, one result of President Trump's tweeting habits was that many important national news stories were neglected, overlooked, or underreported. At the local level, a number of small-town newspaper editors started to notice that letters-to-the-editor were just as likely to be about national cable news "talking points" as about local community issues.

Another change is the way nontraditional sources and even newer digital technology help drive news stories. For example, the Occupy Wall Street (OWS) movement, inspired by the Arab Spring uprisings, began in September 2011 when a group of protesters gathered in Zuccotti Park in New York's financial district to express discontentment with overpaid CEOs, big banks, and Wall Street, all of which helped cause the 2008–09 financial collapse but still enjoyed a government bailout.

Mainstream media were slow to cover OWS, with early coverage simply pitting angry protesters against dismissive Wall Street executives and politicians, many of whom questioned the movement's longevity as well as its vague agenda. But as retirees, teachers, labor unions, off-duty police officers, firefighters, and other government workers joined the college students, the jobless, and the homeless in OWS protests across the country, the coverage and narratives in the media became more complicated and nuanced. As in the Arab uprisings, sites like Tumblr, Facebook, and Twitter became key organizational tools. But more than that, they became alternative media sources, documenting incidents of police brutality and arrests, and covering the issues protesters championed. In both the Arab Spring and the OWS stories, the Internet and social media gave ordinary people more agency than ever before. Still, it's important to remember that while successful movements need good communication and media coverage, they also require enough people willing to challenge power, just as they did in the days of the American Revolution and the Civil Rights movement.

In the digital age, newsrooms are integrating their digital and print operations and asking their journalists to tweet breaking news that links back to newspapers' websites. At first, there was resistance to the digital turn, with executive editors trying to get older reporters and editors to embrace what news executives regard as a reporter's online responsibilities. Back in 2011, for example, then executive editor of the *New York Times* Jill Abramson noted that although the *Times* had fully integrated its online and print operations, some sub-editors still tried to hold back on publishing a timely story online, hoping that it would make the front page of the print paper instead. "That's a culture I'd like to break down, without diminishing the [reporters'] thrill of having their story on the front page of the paper," said Abramson.[16] As a younger generation of journalists—raised on social media and digital technology—move into newsrooms, this resistance to online innovations has largely fallen away. (For more about how online news ventures are changing the newspaper industry, see "Convergence: Newspapers Struggle in the Move to Digital.")

Newspapers and the Internet: Convergence
This video discusses the ways that newspapers are adapting to online delivery of news.

Discussion: What different kinds of skills are needed to be effective in the new online world? What skills might remain the same?

THE BUSINESS AND OWNERSHIP OF NEWSPAPERS

In the news industry today, there are several kinds of papers. *National newspapers* (such as the *Wall Street Journal*, the *New York Times*, the *Washington Post*, and *USA Today*) serve a broad readership across the country. Other papers primarily serve specific geographic regions. Roughly

Mark Edward Atkinson/Tracey Lee/Getty Images

sixty *metropolitan dailies* have a weekday paid circulation of approximately 100,000 (much more if we count digital hits on their websites). About thirty of these papers have a circulation of more than 200,000 during the workweek. In addition, about ninety daily newspapers are classified as medium dailies, with circulations between 50,000 and 100,000. By far the largest number of U.S. dailies—about one thousand papers—fall into the small-daily category, with circulations under 50,000. While dailies serve urban and suburban centers, over 7,000 nondaily and *weekly newspapers* (down from fourteen thousand back in 1910) serve smaller communities and average over 8,000 copies per issue. No matter the size of the paper, each must determine its approach, target readers, establish social media strategies, and deal with ownership issues in a time of technological transition and declining revenue.

Consensus versus Conflict: Newspapers Play Different Roles

Smaller nondaily papers tend to promote social and economic harmony in their communities. Besides providing community calendars and meeting notices, nondaily papers focus on **consensus-oriented journalism**, carrying articles on local schools, social events, town government, property crimes, and zoning issues. Recalling the partisan spirit of an earlier era, small newspapers are often owned by business leaders who may also serve in local politics. Because consensus-oriented papers have a small advertising base, they are generally careful not to offend local advertisers, who provide the financial underpinnings for many of these papers. At their best, these small-town papers foster a sense of community; at their worst, they overlook or downplay discord and problems.

In contrast, national and metro dailies practice **conflict-oriented journalism**, in which front-page news is often defined primarily as events, issues, or experiences that deviate from social norms. Under this news orientation, journalists see their role not merely as neutral fact-gatherers but as observers who monitor their city's institutions and problems. They often maintain an adversarial relationship with local politicians and public officials. Newspapers practicing this form of journalism offer competing perspectives on such issues as education, government, poverty, crime, and the economy; and their publishers, editors, and reporters avoid playing overt roles in community politics. In theory, modern newspapers believe their role in large cities is to point out problems. However, some newsrooms are asking how they can be more solution oriented in their news coverage. For example, an organization called My Voice Ohio, staffed by former journalists and activists, is training journalists and citizens to confront problems and consider solutions. In 2018, one of its primary initiatives focused on "evaluating data, collecting solutions, and supplying resources to help Ohio confront [its] opioid epidemic."[17]

In telling stories about complex and controversial topics, conflict-oriented journalists often turn such topics into two-dimensional accounts, pitting one idea or person against another. This convention, or "telling both sides of a story," allows a reporter to take the position of a detached observer. Although this practice offers the appearance of balance, its function is mainly to generate conflict and sustain a lively news story. Sometimes, though, good reporters ignore the notion that there are two sides to *every* story in order to tell the fullest and best story possible. And yet these reporters, often faced with deadline pressures, do not always have the time or space to develop a multifaceted and complex report or series of reports. However, with the digital revolution releasing journalism from time and space constraints, news observers see the potential for more complex and longer stories developing online (see "Media Literacy and the Critical Process: Covering the News Media Business" on page 249).

MEDIA LITERACY AND THE CRITICAL PROCESS

Covering the News Media Business

With the economic challenges in journalism over the last decade, the loss of jobs has affected what gets covered as news. We already know that many local newspapers have closed or consolidated their statehouse and federal news bureaus. But what about coverage of the changing news media business itself? Over the years, critics have claimed that business news pages tend to favor issues related to management and downplay the role of everyday employees, focusing on positive business stories—such as managers' promotions—and minimizing negative news. So do local newspapers today cover business in general and their own business owners well? Are there any stories in the news about editors and reporters and the challenges they face? Using the LexisNexis database or the **Pew Research Center**, check the business coverage in a regional daily newspaper to see how the paper covers itself and the news media business in general. You can also call business editors and reporters at your local paper and ask them about how they cover economic issues related to their own business.

1 DESCRIPTION

Track three to four weeks' worth of business and economic news in your local paper or a regional paper you have access to through LexisNexis or the Pew Research Center. You could pick a story about a paper that has recently been sold, such as the sale of the *Los Angeles Times* and *San Diego Union-Tribune* to Nant Capital in 2018. Examine both the business pages and the front and local sections for business/economic stories in general and media business stories in particular. Devise a chart and create categories for sorting stories (e.g., business scandal stories, earnings reports, home foreclosures, job promotion reports, and news-media-related stories), and gauge whether these stories are positive or negative. If possible, compare your local or regional paper's coverage of the news media business to coverage in one of the nation's dailies, like the *New York Times* or the *Wall Street Journal*, over the same period.

2 ANALYSIS

Look for patterns in the coverage. How many economic or business stories were produced over the period? How many were positive? How many were negative? How many stories did you find in which individual reporters or columnists discuss the impact of the economy and the Internet on the newspaper business? Compared to the local or regional paper, are there differences in the frequency and kinds of coverage offered in the national newspaper? Does your paper cover the business of the parent company that owns the local paper? Does it cover national or international business stories? What are the differences between local/regional coverage and national coverage of business in general and the news media in particular?

3 INTERPRETATION

What do some of the patterns mean? Did you find examples in which the coverage of business seems comprehensive and fair? If business news gets more positive coverage than does political news, what might this mean? What does it mean if certain businesses are not being covered adequately by local/regional and national news operations? If men are quoted as sources more often than women are quoted in these stories, what might this mean? What does it mean if there are very few stories about the news business in general and about the paper you are studying specifically? What does it mean if there are differences between local/regional coverage and national coverage of business and news media?

4 EVALUATION

Determine which papers and stories you would judge as stronger models for how business and news media get covered, and which ones you would judge as weaker models. What do you think makes a good business or media story, and what makes a weak one? Are some elements that should be included missing from the coverage? If so, make suggestions.

5 ENGAGEMENT

Either write to or e-mail the editor or a business reporter to offer your findings, or make an appointment with the editor or business reporter to discuss what you discovered or to ask questions about the kind of coverage you have found. Note what the newspaper is doing well, and make a recommendation on how to improve business and news media coverage. Possibly recommend issues and trends of concern to college students—college loans, credit card debt, the rise of college tuition costs—that aren't being covered well, and suggest ways to better report on these. Recommend stories about the news media (and your newspaper's owner) that you would like to see covered.

ELSEWHERE IN
MEDIA & CULTURE

5.9%
THE PERCENTAGE OF BOOKS THAT WERE CONSUMED AS AUDIOBOOKS IN 2016
p. 233

HOW HAS THE DIGITAL TURN CHANGED A JOURNALIST'S EVERYDAY ACTIVITIES?
pp. 261–264

1887
the year that Nellie Bly caused a sensation in the *New York World*
p. 423

$10.6B
the revenue of Facebook's mobile ads in the first quarter of 2018
p. 341

1980s
WHEN THE TERM *SOUND BITE* WAS INVENTED
p. 441

Newspapers Target Specific Readers

Historically, small-town weeklies and daily newspapers have served predominantly white, mainstream readers. However, ever since Benjamin Franklin launched the short-lived German-language *Philadelphische Zeitung* in 1732, newspapers aimed at ethnic groups have played a major role in initiating immigrants into American society. During the nineteenth century, Swedish- and Norwegian-language papers informed various immigrant communities in the Midwest. The early twentieth century gave rise to papers written in German, Yiddish, Russian, and Polish, assisting the massive influx of European immigrants.

Throughout the 1990s and into the twenty-first century, several hundred foreign-language daily and nondaily presses published papers in at least forty different languages in the United States. Many are financially healthy today, supported by classified ads, local businesses, and increased ad revenue from long-distance phone companies and Internet services. These companies have long seen the value of the ethnic press to reach customers most likely to need international communication services.[18] Although the financial crisis took its toll and some ethnic newspapers failed, loyal readers allowed such papers to fare better overall than the mainstream press.[19]

Most of these weekly and monthly newspapers serve some of the same functions for their constituencies—minorities and immigrants, as well as disabled veterans, retired workers, gay and lesbian communities, and the homeless—that the "majority" papers do. These papers, however, are often published outside the social mainstream. Consequently, they provide viewpoints that are different from the mostly middle- and upper-class establishment attitudes that have shaped the media throughout much of America's history. As noted by the Pew Research Center's Excellence in Journalism project, ethnic newspapers and media "cover stories about the activities of those ethnic groups in the United States that are largely ignored by the mainstream press, they provide ethnic angles to news that actually is covered more widely, and they report on events and issues taking place back in the home countries from which those populations or their family members emigrated. These outlets have also traditionally been leaders in their communities."[20]

African American Newspapers

Between 1827 and the end of the Civil War in 1865, forty newspapers directed at black readers and opposed to slavery struggled for survival. These papers faced not only higher rates of illiteracy among potential readers but also hostility from white society and the majority press of the day. The first black newspaper, *Freedom's Journal*, operated from 1827 to 1829 and opposed the racism of many New York newspapers. In addition, it offered a public voice for antislavery societies. Other notable papers included the *Alienated American* (1852–1856) and the *New Orleans Daily Creole*, which began its short life in 1856 as the first black-owned daily in the South. The most influential oppositional newspaper was Frederick Douglass's *North Star*, a weekly antislavery newspaper in Rochester, New York, which was published from 1847 to 1860 and reached a circulation of three thousand. Douglass, a former slave, wrote essays on slavery and on a variety of national and international topics.

Since 1827, fifty-five hundred newspapers have been edited or started by African Americans.[21] These papers, with an average life span of nine years, have taken stands against race baiting, lynching, and the Ku Klux Klan. They also promoted racial pride long before the Civil Rights movement. The most widely circulated black-owned paper was Robert C. Vann's weekly *Pittsburgh Courier*, founded in 1910. Its circulation peaked at 350,000 in 1947—the year professional baseball was integrated by Jackie Robinson, thanks in part to relentless editorials in the *Courier* that denounced the color barrier in pro sports. As they have throughout their history, these papers offer oppositional viewpoints to the mainstream press and record the daily activities of black communities by listing weddings, births, deaths, graduations, meetings, and church functions. Today, the National Association of Black

Library of Congress/Getty Images

FREDERICK DOUGLASS

helped found the *North Star* in 1847. It was printed in the basement of the Memorial African Methodist Episcopal Zion Church, a gathering spot for abolitionists and "underground" activities in Rochester, New York. At the time, the white-owned *New York Herald* urged Rochester's citizens to throw the *North Star*'s printing press into Lake Ontario. Under Douglass's leadership, the paper came out weekly until 1860, addressing problems facing blacks around the country and offering a forum for Douglass to debate his fellow black activists.

Hansel Mieth/Getty Images

AFRICAN AMERICAN NEWSPAPERS

This 1936 scene reveals the newsroom of Harlem's *Amsterdam News*, one of the nation's leading African American newspapers. Ironically, the Civil Rights movement and affirmative action policies since the 1960s served to drain talented reporters from the black press by encouraging them to work for larger, mainstream newspapers.

Journalists (NABJ) reports that there are roughly two hundred African American newspapers, including Baltimore's *Afro-American*, New York's *Amsterdam News*, and the *Chicago Defender*, which celebrated its one hundredth anniversary in 2005.[22] None of these publish daily editions any longer, and most are weeklies.

The circulation rates of most black papers dropped sharply after the 1960s. The combined circulation of the local and national editions of the *Pittsburgh Courier*, for instance, dropped from 202,080 in 1944 to 20,000 in 1966, when it was reorganized as the *New Pittsburgh Courier*. Several factors contributed to these declines. First, television and black radio stations tapped into the limited pool of money that businesses allocated for advertising. Second, some advertisers, to avoid controversy, withdrew their support when the black press started giving favorable coverage to the Civil Rights movement in the 1960s. Third, the loss of industrial urban jobs in the 1970s and 1980s not only diminished readership but also hurt small neighborhood businesses, which could no longer afford to advertise in both the mainstream and the black press. Finally, after the enactment of Civil Rights and affirmative action laws, mainstream papers raided black papers, seeking to integrate their newsrooms with African American journalists. Black papers could seldom match the offers from large white-owned dailies.

While a more integrated mainstream press initially hurt black papers—an ironic effect of the Civil Rights laws—by 2011 that trend had reversed a bit, as some black reporters and editors returned to black press newsrooms.[23] Overall, however, the number of African Americans in newsrooms is declining. The ASNE reports that in each year between 1998 and 2007, nearly three thousand African Americans worked in various journalistic jobs at daily newspapers, but by 2015, that number had fallen to fewer than sixteen hundred.[24] Most of this decline is due to newsroom cutbacks in response to declining print ad revenue and the 2008–09 economic crisis.

According to ASNE data, the total workforce at daily newspapers hovered between 54,000 and 56,000 from 1986 to 2007. But during that time, the number of minorities working in newsrooms grew from 3,400 to 7,400, or about 12 to 13 percent of the workforce. However, by 2015, the total newspaper workforce had shrunk to under 33,000, with the number of minorities falling to 4,200.[25] By 2017, ASNE no longer trusted its ability to accurately count the total number of reporters. Nevertheless, according to a survey of 598 newspapers and 63 online-only news sites, ASNE, in partnership with Google News Lab, reported that in 2017, minorities made up 16.6 percent of all working journalists and 24.3 percent of the workforce in online-only newsrooms.[26] (A 2017 Radio Television Digital News Association survey reported that the total number of working journalists at daily papers had fallen to 25,000—down by about 8,000 since ASNE's 2015 report.)[27]

Spanish-Language Newspapers

Bilingual and Spanish-language newspapers have served a variety of Mexican, Puerto Rican, Cuban, and other Hispanic readerships since 1808, when *El Misisipi* was founded in New Orleans. Throughout the 1800s, Texas had more than 150 Spanish-language papers.[28] Los Angeles' *La Opinión*, founded in 1926, is now the nation's largest Spanish-language daily. Other prominent publications are in Miami (*La Voz* and *Diario Las Américas*), Houston (*La Información*), Chicago (*El Mañana Daily News* and *La Raza*), and New York (*El Diario–La Prensa*). By 2011, about eight hundred

Spanish-language papers operated in the United States, most of them weekly and nondaily papers, although since 2004, no new Hispanic papers have been founded.[29] Until the late 1960s, mainstream newspapers virtually ignored Hispanic issues and culture. But with the influx of Mexican, Puerto Rican, and Cuban immigrants throughout the 1980s and 1990s, many mainstream papers began to feature weekly Spanish-language supplements. The first was the *Miami Herald*'s "El Nuevo Herald," introduced in 1976. Other mainstream papers also joined in, but many had folded their Spanish-language supplements by the mid-1990s. In 1995, the *Los Angeles Times* discontinued its supplement, "Nuestro Tiempo," and the *Miami Herald* trimmed budgets and staff for "El Nuevo Herald." Spanish-language radio and television had beaten newspapers to these potential customers and advertisers. As the U.S. Hispanic population reached 17 percent in 2013, Hispanic journalists accounted for about 4 percent of the newsroom workforce at U.S. daily newspapers.[30] According to ASNE, Hispanic journalists in daily newsrooms peaked at just over twenty-four hundred in 2006 but had declined to fewer than fourteen hundred by 2015.[31] The ASNE/Google News Lab 2017 survey did not break out Hispanic reporters as a separate category.

Asian American Newspapers

In the 1980s, hundreds of small papers emerged to serve immigrants from Pakistan, Laos, Cambodia, and China. Although people of Asian descent made up only about 5.3 percent of the U.S. population in 2013, this percentage is expected to rise to 9 percent by 2050.[32] Today, fifty small U.S. papers are printed in Vietnamese. Ethnic papers like these help readers both adjust to foreign surroundings and retain ties to their traditional heritage. In addition, these papers often cover major stories downplayed in the mainstream press. For example, in the aftermath of 9/11, airport security teams detained thousands of Middle Eastern–looking men. The *Weekly Bangla Patrika*—a Long Island, New York, paper—reported on the one hundred people the Bangladeshi community lost in the 9/11 attacks and on how it feels to be innocent yet targeted by ethnic profiling.[33]

A growth area in newspapers is Chinese publications. Even amid a poor economy, a new Chinese newspaper, *News for Chinese*, started in 2008. The Chinese-language paper began as a free monthly distributed in the San Francisco area. In early 2009, it began publishing twice a week. By 2014, the *World Journal*, the largest U.S.-based Chinese-language paper, was publishing editions in seven U.S. and Canadian cities: New York, Los Angeles, San Francisco, Chicago, Dallas, Vancouver, and Toronto.[34] According to ASNE, Asian American journalists working in newsrooms peaked at almost eighteen hundred in 2007 but had declined to fewer than one thousand by 2015.[35] The ASNE/Google News Lab 2017 survey did not break out Asian American reporters as a separate category.

Native American Newspapers

An activist Native American press has provided oppositional voices to mainstream American media since 1828, when the *Cherokee Phoenix* appeared in Georgia. Another prominent early paper was the *Cherokee Rose Bud*, founded in 1848 by tribal women in the Oklahoma territory. The Native American Press Association has documented more than 350 Native American papers, most of them printed in English but a few printed in tribal languages. Currently, two national papers are the *Native American Times*, which offers perspectives on "sovereign rights, civil rights, and government-to-government relationships with the federal government," and *Indian Country Today*, owned by the Oneida Nation in New York. According to ASNE data, Native American journalists in daily

ASIAN NEWSPAPERS, such as the Hindi newspaper seen here, can help readers stay up to date with important events that are sometimes downplayed by traditional media.

Emmanuel Dunand/Getty Images

newsrooms peaked at 324 in 2007 but had declined to 118 by 2015.[36] The ASNE/Google News Lab 2017 minority survey did not break out Native American reporters as a separate category.

To counter the neglect of Native American culture's viewpoints by the mainstream press, Native American newspapers have both helped educate various tribes about their heritage and helped build community solidarity. These papers have also reported on the problems as well as the progress among tribes that have opened casinos and gambling resorts. Overall, these smaller papers provide a forum for debates on tribal conflicts and concerns, and they often signal the mainstream press on issues—such as gambling or hunting and fishing rights—that have particular significance for the larger culture.

The Underground Press

The mid- to late 1960s saw an explosion of alternative newspapers. Labeled the **underground press** at the time, these papers questioned mainstream political policies and conventional values, often voicing radical opinions. Generally running on shoestring budgets, they were also erratic in meeting publication schedules. Springing up on college campuses and in major cities, underground papers were inspired by the writings of socialists and intellectuals from the 1930s and 1940s and by a new wave of thinkers and artists. Particularly inspirational were poets and writers (such as Allen Ginsberg, Jack Kerouac, LeRoi Jones, and Eldridge Cleaver) and "protest" musicians (including Bob Dylan, Pete Seeger, and Joan Baez). In criticizing social institutions, alternative papers questioned the official reports distributed by public relations agents, government spokespeople, and the conventional press (see "Examining Ethics: Alternative Journalism: The Activism of Dorothy Day and I. F. Stone" on page 256).

During the 1960s, underground papers played a unique role in documenting social tension by including the voices of students, women, African Americans, Native Americans, gay men and lesbians, and others whose opinions were often excluded from the mainstream press. The first and largest underground paper, the *Village Voice*, was founded in Greenwich Village in 1955. Until the publication of its final print edition on September 21, 2017, the *Village Voice* had been distributed free, surviving through advertising. The paper then continued through its significant online presence, the website winning two national awards, including the *Editor and Publisher* EPPY Award for best overall U.S. weekly newspaper online.[37] Sadly, the site ceased online publication as well on August 31, 2018.

Among campus underground papers, the *Berkeley Barb* was the most influential, developing amid the free-speech movement in the mid-1960s. Despite their irreverent tone, many underground papers turned a spotlight on racial and gender inequities and occasionally goaded mainstream journalism to examine social issues. Like the black press, though, many early underground papers folded after the 1960s. Given their radical outlook, it was difficult for them to appeal to advertisers. In addition, as with the black press, mainstream papers raided alternatives and expanded their own coverage of culture by hiring the underground's best writers. Still, today more than 130 papers, reaching twenty-five million readers, are members of the Association of Alternative Newsmedia.

Newspaper Operations

Today, a weekly paper might employ only two or three people, while a major metro daily might have a staff of more than one thousand, including those in the newsroom and online operations, and those in circulation (distributing the newspaper), advertising (selling ad space), and mechanical operations (assembling and printing the paper). In either situation, however, most newspapers distinguish business operations from editorial or news functions. Journalists' and readers' praise or criticism usually rests on the quality of a paper's news and editorial components, but today, business and advertising concerns dictate whether papers will survive.

Most major daily papers would like to devote one-half to two-thirds of their pages to advertisements. Newspapers carry everything from full-page spreads for department stores to shrinking classified ads, which consumers can purchase for a few dollars to advertise used cars or old furniture (although many websites now do this for free). In most cases, ads are positioned in the paper first. The **newshole**—space not taken up by ads—accounts for the remaining 35 to 50 percent of the content of daily newspapers, including front-page news. The newshole and the overall size of many newspapers had shrunk substantially by 2010.

News and Editorial Responsibilities

The chain of command at most larger papers begins with the publisher and owner at the top and then moves, on the news and editorial side, to the editor in chief and managing editor, who are in charge of the daily news-gathering and writing processes. Under the main editors, assistant editors have traditionally run different news divisions, including features, sports, photos, local news, state news, and wire service reports that contain major national and international news. Increasingly, many editorial positions are being eliminated or condensed to the job of a single editor, whose chief responsibility is often ensuring that stories are posted first online (to give them the immediacy that radio and TV news have always had), then updated, and then prepared for the print edition.

R.J. Matson, courtesy of Cagle Cartoons

POLITICAL CARTOONS
are often syndicated features in newspapers that reflect the issues of the day.

Reporters work for editors. *General assignment reporters* handle all sorts of stories that might emerge—or "break"—in a given day. *Specialty reporters* are assigned to particular beats (police, courts, schools, local and national government) or topics (education, religion, health, environment, technology). On large dailies, *bureau reporters* also file reports from other major cities. Large daily papers feature columnists and critics who cover various aspects of culture, such as politics, books, television, movies, and food. While papers used to employ a separate staff for their online operations, the current trend is to have traditional reporters file both online and print versions of their stories, accompanied by images or video they are responsible for gathering.

Recent consolidation and cutbacks have led to layoffs and the closing of bureaus outside a paper's city limits. For example, in 1985, more than six hundred newspapers had reporters stationed in Washington, D.C.[38] By 2016, Pew reported that 21 states had no local newspapers sending reporters to cover Washington.[39] By 2018, the situation had not improved. The downside of these money-saving measures in our nation's capital and in various U.S. state capitals is that far fewer versions of stories are being produced, and readers must often rely on a single version of a news report. According to the ASNE, the workforce in daily U.S. newsrooms declined by 11,100 jobs during the height of the recession in 2008 and 2009.[40] A small turnaround occurred in 2010, with 100 new jobs created overall, driven by the increase in digital news organizations.[41] But ASNE reported that from 2011 to 2015, the total number of daily newsroom jobs fell by almost 8,000, from 40,600 to 32,900.[42] By 2017, that number had fallen to 25,000.[43]

Wire Services and Feature Syndication

Major daily papers might have one hundred or so local reporters and writers, but they still cannot cover the world or produce enough material to fill up the newshole each day. Newspapers rely on wire services and syndicated feature services to supplement local coverage. A few major dailies, such as the *New York Times*, run their own wire services, selling their stories to other papers to reprint. Other agencies, such as the Associated Press (AP) and United Press International (UPI), have hundreds of staffers stationed in major U.S. cities and world capitals, submitting stories and photos daily for

Alternative Journalism: The Activism of Dorothy Day and I. F. Stone

Over the years, a number of unconventional reporters have struggled against the status quo to find a place for unheard voices and alternative ways to practice their craft. While social activism by reporters goes against the ethical standards of conventional journalism, it has a long and rich history as part of American journalism. For example, reporter Ida B. Wells fearlessly investigated violence against blacks for the *Memphis Free Speech* in the late nineteenth century. As an activist, Wells led the anti-lynching crusade throughout the 1890s. Twentieth-century newspaper history offers a pair of influential alternative journalists and their publications: Dorothy Day's *Catholic Worker* and *I. F. Stone's Weekly*.

In 1933, Dorothy Day (1897–1980) cofounded a radical religious organization with a monthly newspaper, the *Catholic Worker*, that opposed war and supported social reforms. Like many young intellectual writers during World War I, Day was a pacifist; she also joined the Socialist Party. Quitting college at age eighteen to work as an activist reporter for socialist newspapers, Day participated in the ongoing suffrage movement to give women the right to vote. Throughout the 1930s, her Catholic Worker organization invested in thirty hospices for the poor and homeless, providing food and shelter for five thousand people a day. This legacy endures today, with the organization continuing to fund soup kitchens and homeless shelters throughout the country.

For more than eighty years, the *Worker* has consistently advocated personal activism to further social justice,

opposing anti-Semitism, Japanese American internment camps during World War II, nuclear weapons, the Korean War, military drafts, and the communist witch-hunts of the 1950s. The *Worker*'s circulation peaked in 1938 at 190,000, then fell dramatically during World War II, when Day's pacifism was at odds with much of America. Today, the *Catholic Worker* has a circulation of about thirty thousand.

I. F. Stone (1907–1989) shared Dorothy Day's passion for social activism. He also started early, publishing his own monthly paper at the age of fourteen and becoming a full-time reporter by age twenty. He worked as a Washington political writer for the *Nation* in the early 1940s and later for the *New York Daily Compass*. Throughout his career, Stone challenged the conventions and privileges of both politics and journalism. In 1941, for example, he resigned from the National Press Club when it refused to serve his guest, the nation's first African American federal judge. In the early 1950s, he actively opposed Joseph McCarthy's rabid campaign to rid government and the media of alleged communists.

When the *Daily Compass* failed in 1952, the radical Stone was unable to find a newspaper job and decided to create his own newsletter, *I. F. Stone's Weekly*, which he published for nineteen years. Practicing interpretive and investigative reporting, Stone became as adept as any major journalist at tracking down government records to discover contradictions, inaccuracies, and lies. Over the years, Stone questioned decisions by the Supreme Court, investigated the substandard living conditions of many African Americans, and criticized political corruption. He guided the *Weekly* to a circulation that reached seventy thousand during the 1960s, when he probed American investments of money and military might in Vietnam.

I. F. Stone and Dorothy Day embodied a spirit of independent reporting that has been threatened by first the rise of chain ownership, then the decline in readership. Stone, who believed that alternative ideas were crucial to maintaining a healthy democracy, once wrote that "there must be free play for so-called 'subversive' ideas—every idea 'subverts' the old to make way for the new. To shut off 'subversion' is to shut off peaceful progress and to invite revolution and war."[1]

AP Images

Bettmann/Getty Images

distribution to newspapers across the country. Some U.S. papers also subscribe to foreign wire services, such as Agence France-Presse in Paris or Reuters in London.

Daily papers generally pay monthly fees for access to all wire stories. Although they use only a fraction of what is available over the wires, editors monitor wire services each day for important stories and ideas for local angles. Wire services have greatly expanded the reach and scope of news, as local editors depend on them when selecting statewide, national, or international reports for reprinting.

In addition, traditional **feature syndicates**, such as United Features (now known as Andrews McMeel Syndication) and Tribune Media Services (now known as Tribune Content Agency), operated historically as commercial outlets that contracted with newspapers to provide work from the nation's best political writers, editorial cartoonists, comic-strip artists, and self-help columnists. These companies served as brokers, distributing horoscopes and crossword puzzles as well as the political columns and comic strips that appealed to a wide audience. When a paper bid on and acquired the rights to a cartoonist or columnist, it signed exclusivity agreements with a syndicate to ensure that it was the only paper in the region to carry, say, Clarence Page, Maureen Dowd, Leonard Pitts, Connie Schultz, George Will, or cartoonist Mike Peters. Feature syndicates, like wire services, wielded great influence in determining which writers and cartoonists gained national prominence.

Newspaper Ownership: Chains Lose Their Grip

Edward Wyllis Scripps founded the first **newspaper chain**—a company that owns several papers throughout the country—in the 1890s. By the 1920s, there were about thirty chains in the United States, each owning an average of five papers. The emergence of chains paralleled the major business trend during the twentieth century: the movement toward oligopolies, in which a handful of corporations control each industry.

By the 1980s, more than 130 chains owned an average of nine papers each, with the 12 largest chains accounting for 40 percent of total circulation in the United States. By 2001, the top 10 chains controlled more than one-half of the nation's total daily newspaper circulation. Gannett, for example, the nation's largest chain, owns over eighty daily papers (and hundreds of nondailies worldwide), ranging from small suburban papers to the *Cincinnati Enquirer*, the Nashville *Tennessean*, and *USA Today*.

Consolidation in newspaper ownership leveled off around 2005, when a decline in newspaper circulation and ad sales panicked investors, leading to drops in the stock value of newspapers. Many newspaper chains responded by significantly reducing their newsroom staffs and selling off individual papers.

About the same time, large chains started to break up, selling individual newspapers to private equity firms and big banks (like Bank of America and JPMorgan Chase) that deal in distressed and overleveraged companies with too much debt. For example, in 2006, Knight Ridder—then the nation's second-leading chain—was sold for $4.5 billion to the McClatchy Company. McClatchy then broke up the chain by selling off twelve of its thirty-two papers, including the *San Jose Mercury News* and Philadelphia Newspapers (which included the *Philadelphia Inquirer*). McClatchy also sold its leading newspaper, the *Minneapolis Star Tribune*, to a private equity company for $530 million, less than half of what it had paid to buy it eight years earlier.

On a more promising note, in 2012, billionaire philanthropist Warren Buffett, CEO of the investment firm Berkshire Hathaway, spent $344 million and bought more than sixty newspapers (the company planned to retain about thirty). A newspaper junkie and former paperboy, Buffett has owned the *Buffalo News* in New York since 1977 and has run it profitably. In 2011, he also bought his hometown paper, the *Omaha World-Herald*, for $200 million. Buffett has argued that many smaller and regional newspapers will thrive if they have a strong sense of their local communities and do a good job of mixing their print and digital products. The *New York Times* reported that Buffett planned to buy more papers—"three years after telling shareholders that he would not buy a newspaper at any price."[44] In 2013, Buffett's BH Media Group bought the *Tulsa World* in Oklahoma and the *Roanoke Times* in Virginia. In 2015, Buffett bought two more small dailies in Virginia and retained ownership of nearly thirty small and midsize daily newspapers. By 2017, he was pessimistic once again: "If you look, there are 1,300 daily newspapers left," Buffett said. "There were 1,700 or 1,800 not too long ago. Now, you've got the internet. . . . [Most papers] haven't figured out a way to make the digital model complement the print model."[45]

While Warren Buffett concentrated on purchasing smaller regional papers, ownership of one of the nation's three national newspapers also changed hands. Back in 2007, the *Wall Street Journal*, held by the Bancroft family for more than a hundred years, accepted a bid of nearly $5.8 billion from News Corp. head Rupert Murdoch (News Corp. also owns the *New York Post* and many papers in the United Kingdom and Australia). At the time, critics raised serious concerns about takeovers of newspapers by large entertainment conglomerates (Murdoch's company also owned TV stations, a network, cable channels, and a movie studio). As small subsidiaries in large media empires, newspapers are increasingly treated as just another product line that is expected to perform in the same way that a movie or TV program does. But in 2012, News Corp. decided to split its news and entertainment divisions, leading some critics to hope that Murdoch's news operations would no longer be subject to the same high-profit expectations of Hollywood movies and sitcoms.

As chains lose their grip, there are concerns about who will own papers in the future and the effect the papers' owners will have on content and press freedoms. Recent purchases by private equity groups are alarming, since these companies are usually more interested in turning a profit than supporting journalism. However, ideas exist for how to avoid this fate. For example, more support could be rallied for small independent owners, who could then make decisions based on what's best for the paper—not just what's best for the quarterly report. (For more on how newspapers and owners are trying new business models, see "New Models for Journalism.")

Joint Operating Agreements Combat Declining Competition

Although the amount of regulation preventing newspaper monopolies has decreased, the government continues to monitor the declining number of newspapers in various American cities as well as mergers in cities where competition among papers might be endangered. In the mid-1920s, about five hundred American cities had two or more newspapers with separate owners. However, by 2010, fewer than fifteen cities had independent, competing papers.

In 1970, Congress passed the Newspaper Preservation Act, which enabled failing papers to continue operating through a **joint operating agreement (JOA)**. Under a JOA, two competing papers keep separate news divisions while merging business and production operations for a period of years. Following the act's passage, twenty-eight cities adopted JOAs. By 2003, sixteen of those JOAs had been terminated. In 2018, just five JOAs remained in place—in Detroit; Fort Wayne, Indiana; Las Vegas; Salt Lake City; and York, Pennsylvania. Although JOAs and mergers have monopolistic tendencies, they have typically been the only way to maintain competition between newspapers.

For example, before 1989, Detroit was one of the most competitive newspaper cities in the nation. The *Detroit News* and the *Detroit Free Press*—then owned by Gannett and Knight Ridder, respectively—both ranked among the ten most widely circulated papers in the country and sold their weekday editions for just fifteen cents a copy. Faced with declining revenue and increased costs, the papers' managers asked for and received a JOA in 1989. Problems, however, continued. Then, in 1995, a prolonged and bitter strike by several unions sharply reduced circulation, as strikers formed a union-backed paper to compete against the existing newspapers. Many readers dropped their subscriptions to the *News* and the *Free Press* to support the strikers. Before the strike (and the rise of the Internet), Gannett and Knight Ridder had both reported profit margins of well over 15 percent on all their newspaper holdings.[46] By 2010, Knight Ridder was out of the newspaper chain business, and neither Detroit paper ranked in the Top 20. In addition, the *News* and the *Free Press* became the first major papers to stop daily home delivery for part of the week, instead directing readers to the web or to brief newsstand editions.

CHALLENGES FACING NEWSPAPERS TODAY

Publishers and journalists today face worrisome issues, such as the decline in newspaper readership and the failure of many papers to attract younger readers. However, other problems persist as newspapers continue to converge with the Internet and grapple with the future of digital news. Still, most newspaper editors report that more people are reading their papers in combined print and digital form than at any time in history; however, those readers are often doing so for free on the various websites that the newspapers support.

Readership Declines in the United States

The decline in daily newspaper readership actually began during the Great Depression with the rise of radio. Between 1931 and 1939, six hundred newspapers ceased operation. Another circulation crisis occurred from the late 1960s through the 1970s with the rise in network television viewing and greater competition from suburban weeklies. In addition, with an increasing number of women working full-time outside the home, newspapers could no longer consistently count on one of their core readership groups. Throughout the first decade of the twenty-first century, U.S. newspaper circulation dropped again, this time by more than 25 percent.[47] Yet despite such steep circulation and print readership declines, overall audiences in 2018 are growing again thanks to online readers.

Going Local: How Small and Campus Papers Retain Readers

Despite the doomsday headlines and predictions about the future of newspapers, it is important to note, as Pew's *State of the News Media* report has indicated, that the problems of the newspaper business "are not uniform across the industry." In fact, according to the report, "Small dailies and community weeklies, with the exception of some that are badly positioned or badly managed," still do better than many "big-city papers."[48] That report back in 2010 also suggested that smaller papers in smaller communities remain "the dominant source for local information and the place for local merchants to advertise."[49] While the importance of small papers remains true in 2018, there are still many areas of the country increasingly referred to as **media deserts**: "places where it is difficult to access daily, local news and information."[50] This problem stems partly from larger regional city papers, like those in Dayton or Cincinnati, Ohio, whose staffs used to cover outlying counties in their regions but have increasingly lost rural area reporters to cutbacks, leaving these remote counties partially or even completely uncovered.

Smaller newspapers continue to do better today for several reasons. First, small towns and cities often don't have local TV stations, big-city magazines, or numerous radio stations competing against newspapers for ad space. This means that smaller papers are more likely to retain their revenue from local advertisers. Second, whether they are tiny weekly papers serving small towns or campus newspapers serving university towns, such papers have a loyal and steady base of readers who cannot get information on their small communities from any other source. In fact, many college newspaper editors report that the most popular feature in their papers is the police report: It serves as a kind of local gossip column, listing the names of students arrested over the weekend for underage drinking or public intoxication.

Finally, because smaller newspapers tend to be more consensus-oriented than conflict-driven in their approach to news, these papers do not usually see the big dips in ad revenue that may occur when editors tackle complex or controversial topics that are divisive. For example, when a major regional newspaper does an investigative series on local auto dealers for poor service or shady business practices, those dealers can suspend or cancel advertising that the paper sorely needs. Still, as local papers fill in the gaps left by large mainstream papers and other news media sources, they will

LaunchPad
macmillan learning
launchpadworks.com

Community Voices: Weekly Newspapers
Journalists discuss the role of local newspapers in their communities.

Discussion: In a democratic society, why might having many community voices in the news media be a good thing?

Newspaper Readership across the Globe

While the United States continues to experience declines in newspaper readership and print advertising dollars, many other nations—where Internet news is still emerging—are experiencing increases. For example, the World Association of Newspapers (WAN) reported that between 2003 and 2009, there was an 8.8 percent growth in newspaper readership worldwide, mostly concentrated in Asia, Africa, and South America.[1] In 2013, WAN reported that between 2008 and 2013, "newspaper circulation dropped by 13 per cent in North America but rose 9.8 per cent in Asia," while ad revenue "declined by 42.1 per cent in North America but rose 6.2 per cent in Asia."[2] In 2014, circulation rose 9.8 percent in Asia, 1.2 percent in the Middle East and Africa, and 0.6 percent in Latin America, while it fell 1.3 percent in North America, 4.5 percent in Europe, and 5.3 percent in Australia and Oceania.[3] In 2014, WAN reported that around 2.7 billion people worldwide read newspapers in print and about 770 million read them in digital forms. While digital ad sales continue to grow for newspapers worldwide, this still represents a small percentage of print news revenue. According to WAN, "Globally, 93 per cent of all newspaper revenues continue to come from print."[4]

By 2017, WAN estimated that about 2.7 billion people around the world read print newspapers: "Print circulations continue to decline in the west, but globally circulation levels grew by almost 5 percent in 2016 and 21 per cent over five years. The increase is largely the result of strong print markets in India and elsewhere in Asia."[5] In the three years since its 2014 report, WAN showed that print advertising still made up about 93 percent of ad revenue: "Digital advertising revenue continues to grow worldwide (5.4 percent in 2016 and 32 percent over five years), even though it still represents a relatively small part—6 percent—of overall newspaper revenue. Meanwhile revenue from digital circulation continues to grow at a double-digit rate, having increased 20 percent between 2016 and 2015."[6]

Following are WAN's estimates of the world's most widely circulated newspapers.

TOP 10 PAID-FOR DAILIES (2016)

	TITLE	COUNTRY	LANGUAGE	CIRCULATION (IN THOUSANDS)
1	Yomiuri Shimbun	Japan	Japanese	9101
2	Asahi Shimbun	Japan	Japanese	6622
3	USA Today	USA	English	4139
4	Dainik Bhaskar	India	Hindi	3818
5	Dainik Jagran	India	Hindi	3308
6	The Mainichi Newspapers	Japan	Japanese	3166
7	Cankao Xiaoxi	China	Chinese	3073
8	Amar Ujala	India	Hindi	2935
9	Times of India	India	English	2836
10	Nikkei	Japan	Japanese	2729

Data from: "World Press Trends 2017: Facts and Figures," www.wptdatabase.org/world-press-trends-2017-facts-and-figures.

face some of the same challenges as large papers and must continue to adapt to retain readers and advertisers.

Convergence: Newspapers Struggle in the Move to Digital

Because of their local monopoly status, many newspapers were slower than other media to confront the challenges of the Internet. But when faced with competition from the 24/7 news cycle on cable, newspapers responded by developing online versions of their papers. While some observers think that newspapers are on the verge of extinction as the digital age eclipses the print era, the industry is no dinosaur. In fact, the history of communication demonstrates that older mass media have always adapted; so far, books, newspapers, and magazines have adjusted to the radio, television, and movie industries. And with nearly all fourteen hundred U.S. daily papers now online, newspapers are slowly solving one of the industry's major economic headaches: the cost of newsprint. After salaries, paper is the industry's largest expense, typically accounting for more than 25 percent of a newspaper's total cost.

Online newspapers are truly taking advantage of the flexibility the Internet offers. Because space is not an issue online, newspapers can post stories and readers' letters that they aren't able to print in the paper edition. They can also run longer stories with more in-depth coverage, as well as offer immediate updates to breaking news. Also, most stories appear online before they appear in print, and they can be posted at any time and updated several times a day.

Among the valuable resources that online newspaper stories offer are hyperlinks, which give readers access to related websites or to an archive of similar articles. Free of charge or for a modest fee, a reader can search the newspaper's database from home and investigate the entire sequence and history of an ongoing story, such as a trial, over the course of several months. Taking advantage of the Internet's multimedia capabilities, online newspapers offer readers the ability to stream audio and video files—everything from presidential news conferences to local sports highlights to original video footage from a storm disaster. Today's online newspapers offer readers a dynamic, rather than a static, resource.

However, these advances have yet to pay off. Online ads in the United States accounted for about 18 percent of the newspaper industry's advertising in 2014—up from 13 percent back in 2010.[51]

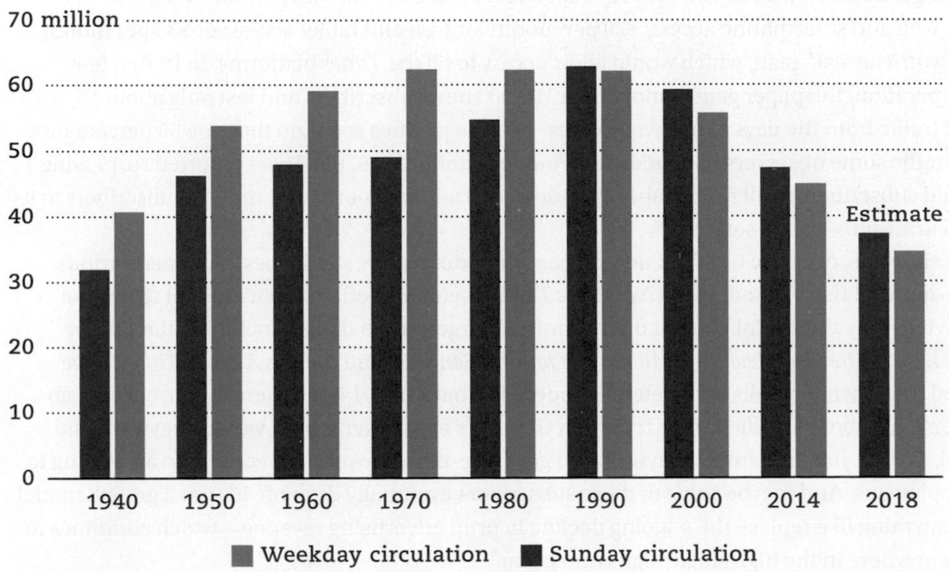

FIGURE 8.1

NEWSPAPER CIRCULATION CONTINUES TO FALL

Data from: Pew Research Center, "Despite Subscription Surges for Largest U.S. Newspapers, Circulation and Revenue Fall for Industry Overall," www.pewresearch.org/fact-tank/2017/06/01/circulation-and-revenue-fall-for-newspaper-industry.

So newspapers, even in decline, are still heavily dependent on print ads. But this trend does not seem likely to sustain papers for long. Ad revenue for newspaper print ads in 2009 declined 25 to 35 percent at many newspapers.[52] To jump-start online revenue streams, more than four hundred daily newspapers collaborated with Yahoo! (the number-one portal to newspapers online) in 2006 to begin an advertising venture that aimed to increase papers' online revenue by 10 to 20 percent. By summer 2010, with the addition of the large Gannett chain, Yahoo! had nearly nine hundred papers in the ad partnership. During an eighteen-month period in 2009–10, the Yahoo! consortium sold over thirty thousand online ad campaigns in local markets, with most revenue shared 50/50 between Yahoo! and its partner papers.[53]

By 2014, online ad sales for newspapers accounted for about 17 percent of U.S. newspapers' advertising revenue, suggesting that online sales on average had risen just 1 percent a year since 2010. The Newspaper Association of America reported that print ad sales in 2013 had declined another 8.6 percent, which represented a loss of $1.6 billion. In terms of digital advertising—the revenue stream that could provide the foundation for a new business model for newspapers—sales were up just 1.5 percent in 2013. As the Nieman Journalism Lab noted: "In 2014, American newspapers still [got] 83 percent of their advertising revenue from print."[54]

One of the business mistakes that most newspaper executives made near the beginning of the Internet age was giving away online content for free. Whereas their print versions always had two revenue streams—ads and subscriptions—newspaper executives weren't convinced that online revenue would amount to much, so they used their online version as an advertisement for the printed paper. Since those early years, most newspapers are now trying to establish a **paywall**—charging a fee for online access to news content—but customers used to getting online content for free have shunned most online subscriptions. One paper that did charge early for online content was the *Wall Street Journal*, which pioneered one of the few successful paywalls in the digital era. In fact, the *Journal*, helped by the public's interest in the economic crisis and 400,000 paid subscriptions to its online service, replaced *USA Today* as the nation's most widely circulated newspaper in 2009. In early 2011, a University of Missouri study found that 46 percent of papers with circulations under 25,000 charged for some online content, while only 24 percent of papers with more than 25,000 in circulation charged for content.[55]

An interesting case in the paywall experiments is the *New York Times*. In 2005, the paper began charging online readers for access to its editorials and columns, but the rest of the site was free. This system lasted only until 2007. But starting in March 2011, the paper added a paywall—a metered system that was mostly aimed at getting the *New York Times*' most loyal online readers, rather than the casual online reader, to pay for online access. Under this paywall system, print subscribers would continue to get free web access. Online-only subscribers could opt for one of three plans: $15 per month for web and smartphone access; $20 per month for web and tablet access; or $35 per month for an "all-you-can-eat" plan, which would allow access to all the *Times* platforms. In its first few weeks of operation, the paper gained more than 100,000 new subscribers and lost only about 15 percent of traffic from the days of free web access—a more positive scenario than the 50 percent loss in online traffic some observers had predicted. And in October 2015, the *Times* reported surpassing 1 million paid subscribers to all its digital-only options and adding another 1.1 million subscribers to its combined print-plus-online services.[56]

In recent years, over two hundred newspapers, including many small ones, launched various paywalls—many of them based on the *New York Times*' metered model—in an attempt to reverse years of giving away their print content online for free. Larger metro dailies, including the *Boston Globe*, the *Dallas Morning News*, the *Milwaukee Journal Sentinel*, and the *Los Angeles Times*, have also started their own paywalls and metered models. But back in 2014, the Nieman Journalism Lab reported on a number of studies and a report on Gannett's experiments with various paywalls and concluded, "When you announce a paywall, you get a one-time boost from people who are willing to pay. But it plateaus. And maybe some of those subscribers eventually drop off. It's not a growth model that does anything like replace the ongoing decline in print advertising revenue—which continues to decline somewhere in the high single digits every year."[57]

New Models for Journalism

In response to the challenges newspapers face, a number of journalists, economists, and citizens are calling for new business models—with more potential than paywalls—for combating newspapers' decline. One avenue is developing new business ventures, such as the online-only papers begun by former print reporters, such as *Politico*. Another idea is for wealthy universities like Harvard and Yale to buy and support papers, thereby better insulating their public service and watchdog operations from the high profit expectations of the marketplace. Another possibility might be to get Internet companies involved. Amazon founder Jeff Bezos's purchase of the *Washington Post* in 2013 is one example. Earlier, Google—worried that a decline in the quality of journalism would mean fewer sites on which to post ads and earn online revenue—pledged $5 million to news foundations and companies to encourage innovation in digital journalism. As mentioned earlier, Google in 2017 began supporting Report for America, which hopes to employ a thousand early career reporters over the next few years. Back in 2010, Yahoo! began hiring reporters to increase the presence of its online news site. The company has since been hiring reporters from *Politico*, *Businessweek*, the *New York Observer*, the *Washington Post*, and *Talking Points Memo*, among others.

Additional ideas are coming from universities (where journalism school enrollments are actually increasing). For example, the dean of Columbia University's Journalism School (started once upon a time with money bequeathed by nineteenth-century newspaper mogul Joseph Pulitzer) commissioned a study from Leonard Downie, former executive editor of the *Washington Post*, and Michael Schudson, Columbia journalism professor and media scholar. Their report, "The Reconstruction of American Journalism," focuses on lost circulation, advertising revenue, and news jobs, and aims to create a strategy for reporting that would hold public and government officials accountable.[58] After all, citizens in democracies require basic access to reports, data, and documentation in order to be well informed. Here is an overview of their recommendations, some of which have already been implemented:

- News organizations "substantially devoted to reporting on public affairs" should be allowed to operate as nonprofit entities in order to take in tax-deductible contributions while still collecting ad and subscription revenues. For example, the Poynter Institute owns and operates the *Tampa Bay Times* (formerly the *St. Petersburg Times*), Florida's largest newspaper. As a nonprofit, the *Times* is protected from the unrealistic 16 to 20 percent profit margins that publicly held newspapers had been expected to earn in the 1980s and 1990s.
- Public radio and TV, through federal reforms in the Corporation for Public Broadcasting, should reorient their focus to "significant local news reporting in every community served by public stations and their Web sites."
- Operating their own news services or supporting regional news organizations, public and private universities "should become ongoing sources of local, state, specialized subject and accountability news reporting as part of their educational mission."
- News services, nonprofit organizations, and government agencies should use the Internet to "increase the accessibility and usefulness of public information collected by federal, state, and local governments."

As the newspaper industry continues to reinvent itself and tries new avenues to ensure its future, not every "great" idea will work out. Some of the immediate backlash to Downie and Schudson's report raised questions about the government's becoming involved with traditionally independent news media. The RFA model, launched after the 2016 election, seeks to avoid government funding by supporting partnerships between existing newsrooms and philanthropy. Whether government-funded models like NPR or private enterprises like RFA, the important thing is that newspapers continue to experiment with new ideas and business models so that they can adapt and even thrive in the Internet age. (For more on the challenges facing journalism, see Chapter 14.)

Alternative Voices

The combination of the online news surge and traditional newsroom cutbacks has led to a phenomenon known as **citizen journalism**, or *citizen media* (or *community journalism* for those projects in which the participants might not be citizens). As a grassroots movement, citizen journalism refers to people—activist amateurs and concerned citizens, not professional journalists—who use the Internet and blogs to disseminate news and information. In fact, with steep declines in newsroom staffs, many professional news media organizations—like CNN's iReport and many regional newspapers—are increasingly trying to corral citizen journalists as an inexpensive way to make up for the journalists lost to newsroom downsizing.

Back in 2008, one study reported that more than one thousand community-based websites were in operation, posting citizen stories about local government, police, and city development.[59] By 2015, more than fifteen hundred such sites were running. Some sites simply aggregate video footage from YouTube, mostly from natural disasters and crises, such as the Boston Marathon terrorist bombing in 2013. These disaster and crisis videos represent the biggest contribution to news by amateurs. According to the Pew Research Center, more than 40 percent of the "most watched news videos" over a fifteen-month period in 2011 and 2012 "came directly from citizens."[60]

Beyond the citizen model, another 2013 Pew study identified 170 specific nonprofit news organizations "with minimal staffs and modest budgets," ranging "from the nationally known [like the investigative site ProPublica] to the hyperlocal," that are trying to compensate for the loss of close to 20,000 commercial newsroom jobs over the last decade.[61] In 2014, Pew studied 438 of these newer digital sites: "Of the 402 outlets that identified a business model, slightly more than half (204) are nonprofits compared with 196 that are commercial entities. In recent years, the nonprofit model has attracted a significant amount of foundation funding for news gathering." In its *State of the News Media 2014* report, Pew "estimated that roughly $150 million in philanthropy now goes to journalism annually. Some of that is used as seed money for digital nonprofit news organizations: 61% of the nonprofit news organizations

A vision for a Public-Spirited Free Press

IowaWatch.org
The Iowa Center for Public Affairs Journalism

Business Education Environment Government & Politics Health About Contact

Don't Miss The IowaWatch Connection Databases News Quizzes Center News

CAMPUS SPEECH   12 hours ago

Free Speech Battles Come To Boil at Cornell College This Spring

By Christina Rueth and Clare McCarthy

f RECOMMEND   TWEET   PRINT   MORE

Christina Rueth/IowaWatch

"Free speech matters" reads the writing on three posts at Cornell College in mid-April 2016. This was a response to an initial painting on April 11 that read, "Build a Wall. Build it Tall." That initial painting was replaced with "Wall or No Wall We Stand Tall. Land of Immigrants."

On April 11, Cornell College students found the words "Build a Wall. Build it Tall." painted on three tall cement blocks that have been used traditionally to write messages on campus.

THE IOWA CENTER for Public Affairs Journalism is an "independent, nonprofit and nonpartisan news service" founded in 2009 by Pulitzer Prize–winning journalist Stephen J. Berry. The center's goal is to publish rigorously researched investigative stories about events at the state level—an unusual approach in a landscape dominated by clickbait headlines and the national news media.

surveyed by Pew Research began with a large start-up grant." Pew also noted that the "goal for these organizations is ultimately finding a sustainable business model less reliant on big giving."[62]

Most journalists and many citizens want to see more professional models of journalism develop in the digital age so that people can decrease their reliance on unedited video footage and untrained amateurs as key sources for news. While many community-based sites and ordinary citizen reporters do not have the resources to provide the kind of regional news coverage that local newspapers once provided, there is still a lot of hope for community journalism moving forward. Some new digital sites have adopted what could be called a "pro-am" model for journalism, in which amateurs are trained by professionals. This practice is already followed at many universities, where students first train with former and current journalists, then collaborate on print, broadcast, and online news projects with local news media.

NEWSPAPERS AND DEMOCRACY

Of all mass media, newspapers have played the leading role in sustaining democracy and championing freedom. Over the years, newspapers have fought heroic battles in places that had little tolerance for differing points of view. According to the Committee to Protect Journalists (CPJ), from

1992 through mid-2018, 1,305 reporters from around the world were killed while doing their jobs. Back in 2016, CPJ reported that since 1992, the five deadliest countries for journalists have been Iraq (174 killed), Syria (94 killed), the Philippines (77 killed), Algeria (60 killed), and Somalia (59 killed). Of those killed, 13 percent died while "on dangerous assignment," 21 percent were killed in cross fire or combat, and 66 percent were murdered.[63]

In 2017, forty journalists were killed around the world—the lowest number since 2002.

Many journalist deaths in the twenty-first century reported by CPJ came from the war in Iraq. From 2003 to 2011, 225 reporters, media workers, and support staff died in Iraq. For comparison, 63 reporters were killed while covering the Vietnam War, 17 died covering the Korean War, and 69 were killed during World War II.[64] Our nation and many others remain dependent on journalists who are willing to do this very dangerous reporting in order to keep us informed about what is going on around the world.

In addition to the physical danger, newsroom cutbacks, and the closing of foreign bureaus, a number of smaller concerns remain as we consider the future of newspapers. For instance, some charge that newspapers have become so formulaic in their design and reporting styles that they may actually discourage new approaches to telling stories and reporting news. Another criticism is that in many one-newspaper cities, only issues and events of interest to middle- and upper-middle-class readers are covered, resulting in the underreporting of the experiences and events that affect poorer and working-class citizens. In addition, given the rise of newspaper chains, the likelihood of including new opinions, ideas, and information in mainstream daily papers may be diminishing. Moreover, chain ownership tends to discourage watchdog journalism and the crusading traditions of newspapers. Like other business managers, many news executives have preferred not to offend investors or outrage potential advertisers by running too many investigative reports—especially business probes. This may be most evident in the fact that reporters have generally not reported adequately on the business and ownership arrangements in their own industry.

Finally, as print journalism shifts to digital platforms, the greatest challenge is the upheaval of print journalism's business model. Most economists say that newspapers need new business models, but some observers think that many local small-town papers—those that are not part of big, overleveraged chains—will survive on the basis of local ads and coupons or "big sale" inserts. Increasingly, independent online firms will help bolster national reporting through special projects. In 2009, the Associated Press initiated an experiment to distribute investigative reports from several nonprofit groups—including the Center for Public Integrity, the Center for Investigative Reporting, and ProPublica—to its fifteen hundred members as a news source for struggling papers that have cut back on staff. Also in 2009, the news aggregator *Huffington Post* hired a team of reporters to cover the economic crisis. Back in 2011, AOL (which had just purchased the *Huffington Post* for $315 million) had more than thirteen hundred reporters—most of them for Patch, a hyperlocal news initiative with over eight hundred separate editorial units serving small to midsize towns and cities across the United States. The Patch experiment aimed to restore local news coverage to areas that had been neglected due to newsroom cutbacks.[65] But by 2014, AOL had not made money, so it cut the number of local sites to six hundred and entered into a new joint venture controlled by Hale Global.[66] In mid-2015, Verizon agreed to buy AOL and the *Huffington Post* for $4.4 billion. With the departure of its founder and publisher, Ariana Huffington, in 2017, the *Post* rebranded itself as *HuffPost*.

Among the success stories in digital journalism, ProPublica has published more than a hundred investigative stories a year, often teaming up with traditional newspapers or public radio stations from around the country. It then offers these reports to traditional news outlets for free. ProPublica won its first Pulitzer Prize in 2010, and in 2017, it teamed up with the *New York Daily News* to win a Pulitzer for public service reporting: "For uncovering . . . widespread abuse of eviction rules by the police to oust hundreds of people, most of them poor minorities."[67]

Regional examples of this kind of public service news include the *Voice of San Diego* and *MinnPost*, both nonprofit online news ventures that feature news about the San Diego and Twin Cities areas, respectively. Many of these news services have tried to provide reports for news outlets that have downsized and no longer have the reporting resources to do extensive and extended investigations.

As print journalism loses readers and advertisers to digital culture, what will become of newspapers, which do most of the nation's primary journalistic work? What role will they play in national elections? Will more and more people rely on TV ads, Twitter, Facebook, and ever newer social media for the political and policy information that an informed citizenry needs? In many instances, these newer websites deliver readers to newspaper sites where actual reporting and documentation is still being done. But will these readers be able to distinguish opinionated, partisan blogging from actual evidence-based reporting?

John Carroll presided over thirteen Pulitzer Prize–winning reports at the *Los Angeles Times* as editor from 2000 to 2005, but he left the paper to protest deep corporate cuts to the newsroom. He has lamented the future of newspapers and their unique role: "Newspapers are doing the reporting in this country. Google and Yahoo! and those people aren't putting reporters on the street in any numbers at all. Blogs can't afford it. Network television is taking reporters off the street. Commercial radio is almost nonexistent. And newspapers are the last ones standing, and newspapers are threatened. And reporting is absolutely an essential thing for democratic self-government. Who's going to do it? Who's going to pay for the news? If newspapers fall by the wayside, what will we know?"[68] In the end, there will be no return to any "golden age" of newspapers. The Internet is transforming journalism and relocating where we get our news; the print era is passing the news baton to the digital age.

8 Chapter Review

One of the Common Threads discussed in Chapter 1 is the role that media play in a democracy. The newspaper industry has always played a strong role in our democracy by reporting news and investigating stories. Even in the Internet age, newspapers remain our primary source for content. How will the industry's current financial struggles affect our ability to demand and access reliable news?

With the coming of radio and television, newspapers in the twentieth century surrendered their title as the mass medium shared by the largest audience. However, to this day, newspapers remain the single most important source of news for the nation, even in the age of the Internet. Although today's readers may cite search engines like Google or social media sites like Facebook as the primary places they search for news, such sites are really directories and aggregators that guide readers to news stories—most often to online newspaper sites. This means that newspaper organizations are still the primary institutions doing the work of gathering and reporting the news. Even with all the newsroom cutbacks across the United States, newspapers remain the only journalistic organization in most towns and cities that still employs a significant staff to report news and tell the community's stories.

Newspapers link people to what matters in their communities, their nation, and their world. Few other journalistic institutions serve society as well. But with smaller news resources and the industry no longer able to sustain high profit margins, what will become of newspapers? Are digital news sites serving readers in their communities as well as newspapers once did? Who will gather the information needed to sustain a democracy, to serve as the watchdog over our key institutions, to document the comings and goings of everyday life? And perhaps more important, who will act on behalf of the people who don't have the news media's access to authorities or the ability to influence them?

KEY TERMS

The definitions for the terms listed below can be found in the glossary at the end of the book.
The page numbers listed with the terms indicate where the term is highlighted in the chapter.

partisan press, 238
penny papers, 239
human-interest stories, 239
wire services, 240
yellow journalism, 240
investigative journalism, 241
objective journalism, 243

inverted-pyramid style, 243
interpretive journalism, 244
literary journalism, 245
consensus-oriented journalism, 248
conflict-oriented journalism, 248
underground press, 254
newshole, 254

feature syndicates, 257
newspaper chain, 257
joint operating agreement (JOA), 258
media deserts, 259
paywall, 262
citizen journalism, 264

REVIEW QUESTIONS

The Evolution of American Newspapers

1. What are the limitations of a press that serves only partisan interests? Why did the earliest papers appeal mainly to more privileged readers?

2. How did newspapers emerge as a mass medium during the penny press era? How did content changes make this happen?

3. What are the two main features of yellow journalism? How have Joseph Pulitzer and William Randolph Hearst contributed to newspaper history?

Competing Models of Modern Print Journalism

4. Why did "objective" journalism develop? What are its characteristics? What are its strengths and limitations?

5. Why did interpretive forms of journalism develop in the modern era? What are the limits of objectivity?

6. How would you define *literary journalism*? Why did it emerge in such an intense way in the 1960s? How did literary journalism provide a critique of so-called objective news?

The Business and Ownership of Newspapers

7. What is the difference between consensus- and conflict-oriented newspapers?

8. What role have ethnic, minority, and oppositional newspapers played in the United States?

9. Define *wire service* and *syndication*.

10. Why did newspaper chains become an economic trend in the twentieth century?

Challenges Facing Newspapers Today

11. What are the major reasons for the decline in U.S. newspaper circulation figures? How do these figures compare with circulations in other nations?

12. What major challenges does new technology pose to the newspaper industry?

13. With traditional ownership in jeopardy today, what are some other possible business models for running a newspaper?

14. What is citizen journalism? What are its pros and cons?

15. What challenges do new online news sites face?

Newspapers and Democracy

16. What is a newspaper's role in a democracy?

17. What makes newspaper journalism different from the journalism of other mass media?

QUESTIONING THE MEDIA

1. What kinds of stories, topics, or issues are not being covered well by mainstream papers?

2. Why do you think people aren't reading U.S. daily newspapers as frequently as they once did? Why is newspaper readership going up in other countries?

3. Discuss whether newspaper chains are ultimately good or bad for the future of journalism.

4. What are "media deserts," and why should we care about this?

5. Do newspapers today play a vigorous role as watchdogs of our powerful institutions? Why or why not? What impact will the downsizing and closing of newspapers have on this watchdog role?

6. Will tablets, or some other format, eventually replace the printed newspaper? Explain your response.

LAUNCHPAD FOR *MEDIA & CULTURE*

Visit LaunchPad for *Media & Culture* at **launchpadworks.com** for additional learning tools:

- REVIEW WITH LEARNINGCURVE
  LearningCurve, available on LaunchPad for *Media & Culture*, uses gamelike quizzing to help you master the concepts you need to learn from this chapter.

- VIDEO: THE MEDIA AND DEMOCRACY
  This video traces the history of media's role in democracy from newspapers and television to the Internet.

Magazines in the Age of Specialization

9

THE MAGAZINE INDUSTRY WEBSITE *Folio* got to the point quickly: "America can't get enough of Chip and Joanna."[1] Married couple Chip and Joanna Gaines became a household name with their show *Fixer Upper*, a popular home renovation program that aired on HGTV from 2013 to 2018 (a follow-up show, *Fixer Upper: Behind the Design*, began airing in 2018). On each episode of *Fixer Upper*, Chip and Joanna take clients to visit three potential houses to buy and renovate. Once the client selects one of them, Chip leads the messy work of the renovation while Joanna handles the design and decorating details. The final reveal comes when a billboard-size image of the old house is pulled away to show the homeowners the dramatic transformation of the house.

THE EARLY HISTORY
OF MAGAZINES
p. 273

THE DEVELOPMENT
OF MODERN
AMERICAN
MAGAZINES
p. 276

THE DOMINATION OF
SPECIALIZATION
p. 284

THE ORGANIZATION
AND ECONOMICS OF
MAGAZINES
p. 291

MAGAZINES IN
A DEMOCRATIC
SOCIETY
p. 295

◀ HGTV's Joanna Gaines and her husband Chip are expanding their media reach even further as they venture into the world of magazine publishing with their latest venture, *Magnolia Journal*.

Chip and Joanna's Magnolia Homes and Magnolia Realty businesses have since expanded to the Magnolia Market—a renovated market, bakery, and garden that has turned the old industrial silo district of Waco, Texas, into a tourist attraction. The key to the couple's TV success is their often-funny on-screen chemistry. Chip is a jokester who likes to take sledgehammers to walls, and Joanna is the more organized taskmaster, with an eye for getting everything just right for the reveal. Viewers also sense their genuine dedication to their family (the couple has five children).

The Gaineses' television sensation has translated into one of the most successful magazine launches in years. *Magnolia Journal* publishes four times a year and gives America even more Chip and Joanna. The magazine was launched by Meredith Corporation, which publishes titles based on other lifestyle television celebrities, including *Martha Stewart Living* and *Rachael Ray Every Day.* The company describes the magazine this way:

> The *Magnolia Journal* is a quarterly lifestyle magazine that marks the first print extension of Joanna and Chip Gaines' powerhouse Magnolia brand. Inspiring readers to create their best homes, families and lives while making every moment count, the magazine covers entertaining, seasonally-driven celebrations, outdoor living, family, food, healthy lifestyle and more—all showcased through the Gaineses' signature

rustic, back-to-our-roots aesthetic and focus on idea-rich content that encourages readers to dive in and try something new.[2]

With its base of millions of TV fans, the first issue of *Magnolia Journal* was so popular in October 2016 that Meredith had to go back to press after two weeks to increase the number of copies from 400,000 to 600,000. The company printed 750,000 copies to meet demand for the second issue, and in May 2017, Meredith announced that it would print over one million copies of the third issue: 700,000 just for the magazine's subscribers, and the rest for single-issue newsstand sales. Meredith reports that "the magazine has been a hit particularly with millennials."[3]

One significant way in which the Gaineses' built their television and magazine audience is through their social media activity. Joanna, Chip, and @magnolia post frequently to Facebook, Twitter, Instagram, and Pinterest. Fans who want even more Chip and Joanna can buy something from their ever-expanding retail empire: Joanna's paint, textile, and furniture lines; an online Magnolia Market shop; and overnight stays at the Magnolia House or Hillcrest Estate, large historic homes in the Waco area that Chip and Joanna renovated and rent to guests for between $695 and $1,295 a night. Alternatively, fans can follow the couple on social media, watch the spinoff show, or read the latest *Magnolia Journal*.

SINCE THE 1740s, magazines have played a key role in our social and cultural lives, becoming America's earliest national mass medium. They created some of the first spaces for discussing the broad issues of the age, including public education, the abolition of slavery, women's suffrage, literacy, and the Civil War.

In the nineteenth century, magazines became an educational forum for women, who were barred from higher education and from the nation's political life. At the turn of the twentieth century, magazines' probing reports paved the way for investigative journalism, while their use of engraving and photography provided a hint of the visual culture to come. Economically, magazines brought advertised products into households, hastening the rise of a consumer society.

Today, more than twenty thousand commercial, alternative, and noncommercial magazines are published in the United States annually. Like newspapers, radio, movies, and television, magazines reflect and construct portraits of American life. They are catalogues of daily events and experiences, but they also show us the latest products, fostering our consumer culture. We read magazines to learn something about our community, our nation, our world, and ourselves.

In this chapter, we will:

- Investigate the history of the magazine industry, highlighting the colonial and early American eras, the arrival of national magazines, and the development of photojournalism
- Focus on the age of muckraking and the rise of general-interest and consumer magazines in the modern American era
- Look at the decline of mass market magazines, the impact of TV and the Internet, and how magazines have specialized in order to survive in a fragmented and converged market
- Investigate the organization and economics of magazines and their function in a democracy

As you think about the evolution of magazine culture, consider your own experiences. When did you first start reading magazines, and what magazines were they? What sort of magazines do you read today—popular mainstream magazines, like *Cosmopolitan* or *Sports Illustrated*, or niche publications that target specific subcultures? How do you think printed magazines can best adapt to the age of the Internet? For more questions to help you think through the role of magazines in our lives, see "Questioning the Media" in the Chapter Review.

THE EARLY HISTORY OF MAGAZINES

The first magazines appeared in seventeenth-century France in the form of bookseller catalogues and notices that book publishers inserted in newspapers. In fact, the word *magazine* derives from the French term *magasin*, meaning "storehouse." The earliest magazines were storehouses of writing and reports taken mostly from newspapers. Today, the word **magazine** broadly refers to collections of articles, stories, and advertisements appearing in nondaily (such as weekly or monthly) periodicals that are published in the smaller tabloid style rather than the larger broadsheet newspaper style.

The First Magazines

The first political magazine, called the *Review*, appeared in London in 1704. Edited by political activist and novelist Daniel Defoe (author of *Robinson Crusoe*), the *Review* was printed sporadically until 1713. Like the *Nation*, the *National Review*, and the *Progressive* in the United States today, early European magazines were channels for political commentary and argument. These periodicals looked like newspapers of the time, but they appeared less frequently and were oriented toward broad domestic and political commentary rather than recent news.

Regularly published magazines or pamphlets, such as the *Tatler* and the *Spectator*, also appeared in England around this time. They offered poetry, politics, and philosophy for London's elite, and they served readerships of a few thousand. The first publication to use the term *magazine* was *Gentleman's Magazine*, which appeared in London in 1731 and consisted of reprinted articles from newspapers, books, and political pamphlets. Later, the magazine began publishing original work by such writers as Defoe, Samuel Johnson, and Alexander Pope.

Magazines in Colonial America

Without a substantial middle class, widespread literacy, or advanced printing technology, magazines developed slowly in colonial America. Like the partisan newspapers of the time, these magazines served politicians, the educated, and the merchant classes. Paid circulations were low—between one hundred and fifteen hundred copies. However, early magazines did serve the more widespread purpose of documenting a new nation coming to terms with issues of taxation, state versus federal power, Indian treaties, public education, and the end of colonialism. George Washington, Alexander Hamilton, and John Hancock all wrote for early magazines, and Paul Revere worked as a magazine illustrator for a time.

The first colonial magazines appeared in Philadelphia in 1741, about fifty years after the first newspapers. Andrew Bradford started it all with *American Magazine, or A Monthly View of the Political State of the British Colonies*. Three days later, Benjamin Franklin's *General Magazine and Historical Chronicle* appeared. Bradford's magazine lasted for only three issues, due to circulation and postal obstacles that Franklin, who had replaced Bradford as Philadelphia's postmaster, put in its way. For example, Franklin mailed his magazine without paying the high postal rates that he subsequently charged others. However, as Franklin's magazine primarily duplicated what was already available in the local papers, it stopped publication after six months.

Nonetheless, following the Philadelphia experiments, magazines began to emerge in the other colonies, beginning in Boston in the 1740s. The most successful magazines simply reprinted articles from leading London periodicals, keeping readers abreast of European events. These magazines included New York's *Independent Reflector* and the *Pennsylvania Magazine*, edited by activist Thomas Paine, which helped rally the colonies against British rule. By 1776, about a hundred colonial magazines had appeared and disappeared. Although historians consider them dull and uninspired for the most part, these magazines helped launch a new medium that caught on after the American Revolution.

U.S. Magazines in the Nineteenth Century

After the revolution, the growth of the magazine industry in the newly independent United States remained slow. Delivery costs remained high, and some postal carriers refused to carry magazines because of their weight. Only twelve magazines operated in 1800. By 1825, approximately one hundred magazines existed, although another five hundred or so had failed between 1800 and 1825. Nevertheless, during the first quarter of the nineteenth century, most communities had their own weekly magazines. Although these magazines did sell some advertising, they were usually in precarious financial straits due to their small circulations.

As the nineteenth century progressed, the idea of specialized magazines devoted to certain categories of readers developed. Many early magazines were overtly religious and boasted the largest readerships of the day. Literary magazines also emerged at this time. The *North American Review*, for instance, established the work of important writers, such as Ralph Waldo Emerson, Henry David Thoreau, and Mark Twain. In addition to religious and literary magazines, specialty magazines that addressed various professions, lifestyles, and topics also appeared, including the *American Farmer*, the *American Journal of Education*, the *American Law Journal*, *Medical Repository*, and the *American Journal of Science*. Such specialization spawned the modern trend of reaching readers who share a profession, a set of beliefs, cultural tastes, or a social identity.

Library of Congress

COLONIAL MAGAZINES

The first issue of Benjamin Franklin's *General Magazine and Historical Chronicle* appeared in January 1741. Although it lasted only six months, Franklin found success in other publications, like his annual *Poor Richard's Almanack*, which first appeared in 1732 and lasted twenty-five years.

The nineteenth century also saw the birth of the first general-interest magazine aimed at a national audience. In 1821, two young Philadelphia printers, Charles Alexander and Samuel Coate Atkinson, launched the *Saturday Evening Post*, which became the longest-running magazine in U.S. history. Like most magazines of the day, the early *Post* included a few original essays but "borrowed" many pieces from other sources. Eventually, however, the *Post* grew to incorporate news, poetry, essays, play reviews, and more. The *Post* published the writings of such prominent popular authors as Nathaniel Hawthorne and Harriet Beecher Stowe. Although the *Post* was a general-interest magazine, it was also the first major magazine to appeal directly to women, via its "Lady's Friend" column, which addressed women's issues.

Northwind Picture Archives

National, Women's, and Illustrated Magazines

With increases in literacy and public education, the development of faster printing technologies, and improvements in mail delivery (due to rail transportation), a market was created for more national magazines, like the *Saturday Evening Post*. Whereas in 1825 one hundred magazines struggled for survival, by 1850 nearly six hundred magazines were being published regularly. (Thousands of others lasted less than a year.)

Besides the move to national circulation, other important developments in the magazine industry were under way. In 1828, Sarah Josepha Hale started the first magazine directed exclusively

COLOR ILLUSTRATIONS
first became popular in the fashion sections of women's magazines in the mid-nineteenth century. The color for this fashion image from *Godey's Lady's Book* was added to the illustration by hand.

Bettmann/Getty Images

CIVIL WAR PHOTOGRAPHY
Famed portrait photographer Mathew Brady commissioned many photographers to help him document the Civil War. (Although all the resulting photos were credited "Photograph by Brady," he did not actually take them all.) This effort allowed people at home to see and understand the true carnage of the war. Photo critics now acknowledge that some of Brady's photos were posed or reenactments.

to a female audience: the *Ladies' Magazine*. In addition to carrying general-interest articles, the magazine advocated for women's education, work, and property rights. After nine years and marginal success, Hale merged her magazine with its main rival, *Godey's Lady's Book* (1830–1898), which she edited for the next forty years. By 1850, *Godey's*, known for its colorful fashion illustrations as well as its advocacy, achieved a circulation of forty thousand—at the time, the biggest distribution ever for a U.S. magazine. By 1860, circulation had swelled to 150,000. Hale's magazine played a central role in educating working- and middle-class women, who were denied access to higher education throughout the nineteenth century.

The other major development in magazine publishing during the mid-nineteenth century was the arrival of illustration. Like the first newspapers, early magazines were totally dependent on the printed word. By the mid-1850s, drawings, engravings, woodcuts, and other forms of illustration had become a major feature of magazines. During the Civil War, many readers relied on *Harper's New Monthly Magazine* for its elaborate battlefield sketches. Publications like *Harper's* married visual language to the printed word, helping transform magazines into a mass medium. Bringing photographs into magazines took a bit longer. Mathew Brady and his colleagues, whose thirty-five hundred photos documented the Civil War, helped popularize photography by the 1860s. But it was not until the 1890s that magazines and newspapers possessed the technology to reproduce photos in print media.

THE DEVELOPMENT OF MODERN AMERICAN MAGAZINES

In 1870, about twelve hundred magazines were produced in the United States. By 1890, that number had reached forty-five hundred, and by 1905, more than six thousand magazines existed (see Figure 9.1). Part of this surge in titles and readership was facilitated by the Postal Act of 1879, which assigned magazines lower postage rates and put them on an equal footing with newspapers delivered by mail, reducing distribution costs. Meanwhile, faster presses and advances in mass-production printing, conveyor systems, and assembly lines reduced production costs and made large-circulation national magazines possible.[4]

The combination of reduced distribution and production costs enabled publishers to slash magazine prices. As prices dropped from thirty-five cents to fifteen cents and then to ten cents, the working class was gradually able to purchase national publications. By 1905, there were about twenty-five national magazines, available from coast to coast and serving millions of readers.[5] As jobs and the population began shifting from farms and small towns to urban areas, magazines helped readers imagine themselves as part of a nation rather than as individuals with only local or regional identities. In addition, the dramatic growth of drugstores and dime stores, supermarkets, and department stores offered new venues and shelf space for selling consumer goods, including magazines.

As magazine circulation began to skyrocket, advertising revenue soared. The economics behind the rise of advertising was simple: A magazine publisher could dramatically expand circulation by dropping the price of an issue below the actual production cost for a single copy. The publisher recouped the loss through ad revenue, guaranteeing large readerships to advertisers who were willing to pay to reach more readers. The number of ad pages in national magazines proliferated. *Harper's*, for instance, devoted only seven pages to ads in the mid-1880s, nearly fifty pages in 1890, and more than ninety pages in 1900.[6]

Social Reform and the Muckrakers

Better distribution and lower costs had attracted readers, but to maintain sales, magazines had to change content as well. Whereas printing the fiction and essays of the best writers of the day was one way to maintain circulation, many magazines also engaged in one aspect of *yellow journalism*—crusading for social reform on behalf of the public good. In the 1890s, for example, *Ladies' Home Journal* (*LHJ*) and its editor, Edward Bok, led the fight against unregulated patent medicines (which often contained nearly 50 percent alcohol), while other magazines took on poor living and working conditions, exposed unsanitary practices in various food industries, and joined the fight against phony medicines.

The rise in magazine circulation coincided with rapid social change in America. While hundreds of thousands of Americans moved from the country to the city in search of industrial jobs, millions of new immigrants poured in. Thus, the nation that journalists had long written about had grown increasingly complex by the turn of the century. Many newspaper reporters became dissatisfied with the simplistic and conventional style of newspaper journalism and turned to magazines, where they were able to write at greater length and in greater depth about broader issues. With this new freedom, reporters wrote about corruption in big business and government, urban problems faced by immigrants, labor conflicts, race relations, and so on.

In 1902, *McClure's Magazine* (1893–1933) touched off an investigative era in magazine reporting with a series of probing stories, including Ida Tarbell's "History of the Standard Oil Company," which took on John D. Rockefeller's oil monopoly, and Lincoln Steffens's "Shame of the Cities," which tackled urban problems. In 1906, *Cosmopolitan* joined the fray with a series called "The Treason of the Senate," and *Collier's* magazine (1888–1957) developed "The Great American Fraud" series, focusing on patent medicines (whose ads accounted for 30 percent of the profits made by the American press by the 1890s). Much of this new reporting style was critical of American institutions. Angry with so much negative reporting, in 1906 President Theodore Roosevelt dubbed these investigative reporters **muckrakers** because they were willing to crawl through society's muck to uncover a story. "Muckraking" was a label that Roosevelt used with disdain, but it was worn with pride by reporters such as Ray Stannard Baker, Frank Norris, and Lincoln Steffens.

Influenced by Upton Sinclair's novel *The Jungle*—a fictional account of Chicago's meatpacking industry—and by the muckraking reports of *Collier's* and *LHJ*, in 1906 Congress passed the Pure Food and Drug Act and the Meat Inspection Act. Other reforms stemming from muckraking journalism and the politics of the era include antitrust laws for increased government oversight of business, a fair and progressive income tax, and the direct election of U.S. senators.

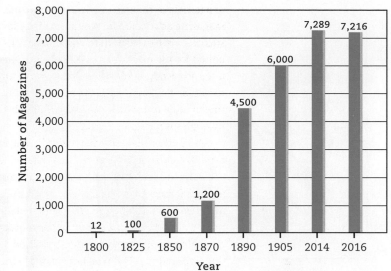

FIGURE 9.1

THE GROWTH OF CONSUMER MAGAZINES PUBLISHED IN THE UNITED STATES

Data from: Association of Magazine Media, *2017/18 Magazine Media Factbook*, www.magazine.org/sites /default/files/FACTBOOK-17 -18-f2.pdf. Historical data from John Tebbel and Mary Ellen Zuckerman, *The Magazine in America, 1741–1990* (New York: Oxford University Press, 1991) and Theodore Peterson, *Magazines in the Twentieth Century* (Urbana: University of Illinois Press, 1964).

The Rise of General-Interest Magazines

The heyday of the muckraking era lasted into the mid-1910s, when America was drawn into World War I. After the war and through the 1950s, **general-interest magazines** were the most prominent publications, offering occasional investigative articles but also covering a wide variety of topics aimed at a broad national audience. A key aspect of these magazines was **photojournalism**—the use of photos to document the rhythms of daily life. High-quality photos gave general-interest magazines a visual advantage over radio, which was the most popular medium of the day. In 1920, about fifty-five magazines fit the general-interest category; by 1946, more than one hundred such magazines competed with radio networks for the national audience.

Saturday Evening Post

Although it had been around since 1821, the *Saturday Evening Post* concluded the nineteenth century as only a modest success, with a circulation of about ten thousand. In 1897, Cyrus Curtis, who had already made *Ladies' Home Journal* the nation's top magazine, bought the *Post* and remade it into

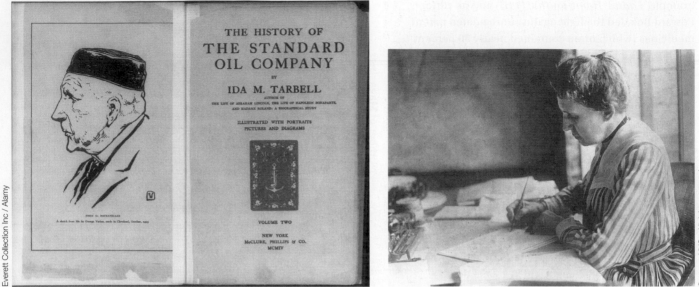

MUCKRAKERS SUCH AS IDA TARBELL (1857–1944),
who is best known for her "History of the Standard Oil Company," once remarked on why she dedicated years of her life to investigating the company: "They had never played fair, and that ruined their greatness for me." For Tarbell and other investigative journalists—or "muckrakers," a term coined by Teddy Roosevelt—exposing such corruption was a driving force behind their work.

the first widely popular general-interest magazine. Curtis's strategy for reinvigorating the magazine included printing popular fiction and romanticizing American virtues through words and pictures (a *Post* tradition best depicted in the three-hundred-plus cover illustrations by Norman Rockwell). Curtis also featured articles that celebrated the business boom of the 1920s. This reversed the journalistic direction of the muckraking era, in which business corruption was often the focus. By the 1920s, the *Post* had reached two million in circulation, the first magazine to hit that mark.

Reader's Digest

The most widely circulated general-interest magazine during this period was *Reader's Digest*. Started in a Greenwich Village basement in 1922 by Dewitt Wallace and Lila Acheson Wallace, *Reader's Digest* championed one of the earliest functions of magazines: printing condensed versions of selected articles from other magazines. With its inexpensive production costs, low price, and popular pocket-size format, the magazine's circulation climbed to over one million during the Great Depression, and by 1946, it was the nation's most popular magazine. By the mid-1980s, it was the most popular magazine in the world, with a circulation of 20 million in America and 10 to 12 million abroad. However, by 2014 it was recovering from bankruptcy, and its circulation base had dropped to about 4.2 million, less than a quarter of its circulation thirty years earlier.

Time

During the general-interest era, national newsmagazines such as *Time* were also major commercial successes. Begun in 1923 by Henry Luce and Briton Hadden, *Time* developed a magazine brand of interpretive journalism, assigning reporter-researcher teams to cover stories, after which a rewrite editor would put the article in narrative form with an interpretive point of view. *Time* had a circulation of 200,000 by 1930, increasing to more than 3 million by the mid-1960s. *Time*'s success encouraged prominent imitators, including *Newsweek* (established in 1933); *U.S. News & World Report* (1948); and, more recently, *The Week* (2001). By 2014, economic decline, competition from the web, and a shrinking

MARGARET BOURKE-WHITE (1904–1971) was a photojournalist of many "firsts": first female photographer for *Life* magazine, first Western photographer allowed into the Soviet Union, first photographer to shoot the cover photo for *Life*, and first female war correspondent. Bourke-White (*near left*) was well known for her photos of World War II—including concentration camps—but also for her documentation of the India-Pakistan partition, including a photo of Gandhi at his spinning wheel (*far left*).

number of readers and advertisers took their toll on the three top newsweeklies. *Time*'s circulation stagnated at 3.2 million, while *U.S. News* became a monthly magazine in 2008 and switched to an all-digital format in 2010 (and is now most famous for its "America's Best Colleges" reports).

Life

Despite the commercial success of *Reader's Digest* and *Time* in the twentieth century, the magazines that truly symbolized the general-interest genre during this era were the oversized pictorial weeklies *Look* and *Life*. More than any other magazine of its day, *Life* developed an effective strategy for competing with popular radio by advancing photojournalism. Launched as a weekly by Henry Luce in 1936, *Life* appealed to the public's fascination with images (invigorated by the movie industry), radio journalism, and advertising and fashion photography. By the end of the 1930s, *Life* had a **pass-along readership**—the total number of people who come into contact with a single copy of a magazine—of more than seventeen million, rivaling the ratings of popular national radio programs.

Life's first editor, Wilson Hicks—formerly a picture editor for the Associated Press—built a staff of renowned photographer-reporters who chronicled the world's ordinary and extraordinary events from the late 1930s through the 1960s. Among *Life*'s most famous photojournalists were Margaret Bourke-White, the first female war correspondent to fly combat missions during World War II, and Gordon Parks, who later became Hollywood's first African American director of major feature films. Today, *Life*'s photographic archive is hosted online by Google (images.google.com/hosted/life).

The Fall of General-Interest Magazines

The decline of weekly general-interest magazines, which had dominated the industry for thirty years, began in the 1950s. By 1957, both *Collier's* (founded in 1888) and *Woman's Home Companion* (founded in 1873) had folded. Each magazine had a national circulation of more than four million the year it died. No magazine with this kind of circulation had ever shut down before. Together, the two publications brought in advertising revenues of more than $26 million in 1956. Although some critics blamed poor management, both magazines were victims of changing consumer tastes, rising postal costs, falling ad revenues, and, perhaps most important, television, which began usurping the role of magazines as the preferred family medium.

TV Guide Is Born

While other magazines were just beginning to make sense of the impact of television on their readers, *TV Guide* appeared in 1953. Taking its cue from the pocket-size format of *Reader's Digest* and the supermarket sales strategy used by women's magazines, *TV Guide*—started by Walter Annenberg's

The Evolution of Photojournalism

BY CHRISTOPHER R. HARRIS

What we now recognize as photojournalism began with the assignment of photographer Roger Fenton, of the *Sunday Times of London*, to document the Crimean War in 1856. However, technical limitations did not allow direct reproduction of photodocumentary images in the publications of the day. Woodcut artists had to interpret the photographic images as black-and-white-toned woodblocks that could be reproduced by the presses of the period. Images interpreted by artists therefore lost the inherent qualities of photographic visual documentation: an on-site visual representation of facts for those who weren't present.

Woodcuts remained the basic method of press reproduction until 1880, when *New York Daily Graphic* photographer Stephen Horgan invented halftone reproduction using a dot-pattern screen. This screen enabled metallic plates to directly represent photographic images in the printing process; now periodicals could bring exciting visual reportage to their pages.

In the mid-1890s, Jimmy Hare became the first photographer recognized as a photojournalist in the United States. Taken for *Collier's Weekly*, Hare's photoreportage on the sinking of the battleship *Maine* in 1898 near Havana, Cuba, established his reputation as a newsman traveling the world to bring back images of news events. Hare's images fed into growing popular support for Cuban independence from Spain and eventual U.S. involvement in the Spanish-American War.

In 1888, George Eastman brought photography to the working and middle classes when he introduced the first flexible-film camera from Kodak, his company in Rochester, New York. Gone were the bulky equipment and fragile photographic plates of the past. Now families and journalists could more easily and affordably document gatherings and events.

As photography became easier and more widespread, photojournalism began to take on an increasingly important social role. At the turn of the century, the documentary photography of Jacob Riis and Lewis Hine captured the harsh living and working conditions of the nation's many child laborers, including crowded ghettos and unsafe mills and factories. Reaction to these shockingly honest photographs resulted in public outcry and new laws against the exploitation of children. Photographs also brought the horrors of World War I to people far from the battlefields.

In 1923, visionaries Henry Luce and Briton Hadden published *Time*, the first modern photographic newsweekly; *Life* and *Fortune* soon followed. From coverage of the Roaring Twenties to the Great Depression, these magazines used images that changed the way people viewed the world.

Life, with its spacious 10-by-13-inch format and large photographs, became one of the most influential magazines in America, printing what are now classic images from World War II and the Korean War. Often, *Life* offered images that were unavailable anywhere else: Margaret Bourke-White's photographic proof of the unspeakably horrific concentration camps; W. Eugene

Triangle Publications—soon rivaled the success of *Reader's Digest* by addressing the nation's growing fascination with television by publishing TV listings. The first issue sold a record 1.5 million copies in ten urban markets. Because many newspapers were not yet listing TV programs, by 1962 the magazine had become the first weekly to reach a circulation of 8 million, with its seventy regional editions tailoring its listings to TV channels in specific areas of the country. (See Table 9.1 for circulation figures of the Top 10 U.S. magazine print editions.)

Smith's gentle portraits of the humanitarian Albert Schweitzer in Africa; David Duncan's gritty images of the faces of U.S. troops fighting in Korea.

Television photojournalism made its quantum leap into the public mind as it documented the assassination of President Kennedy in 1963. In televised images that were broadcast and rebroadcast, the public witnessed the actual assassination and the confusing aftermath, including live coverage of both the murder of alleged assassin Lee Harvey Oswald and President Kennedy's funeral procession. Photojournalism also provided visual documentation of the turbulent 1960s, including aggressive photographic coverage of the Vietnam War—its protesters and supporters. Pulitzer Prize–winning photographer Eddie Adams shook the emotions of the American public with his photographs of a South Vietnamese general's summary execution of a suspected Vietcong terrorist. Closer to home, shocking images of the Civil Rights movement culminated in pictures of Birmingham police and police dogs attacking Civil Rights protesters.

In the 1970s, new computer technologies emerged and were embraced by print and television media worldwide. By the late 1980s, computers could transform images into digital form and easily manipulate them with sophisticated software programs. Today, a reporter can take a picture and within minutes send it to news offices in Tokyo, Berlin, and New York; moments later, the image can be used in a late-breaking TV story or sent directly to that organization's Twitter followers. Such digital technology has revolutionized photojournalism, perhaps even more than the advent of roll film did in the late nineteenth century. Today's photojournalists post entire interactive photo slide shows alongside stories, sometimes adding audio explaining their artistic and journalistic process. Their photographs live on through online news archives and through photojournalism blogs, such as the *Lens* of the *New York Times*, where photojournalists are able to gain recognition for their work and find new audiences.

However, there is a dark side to all this digital technology. Because of the absence of physical film, there is a loss of proof, or veracity, of the authenticity of images. Original film has qualities that make it easy to determine whether it has been tampered with. Digital images, by contrast, can be easily altered, and such alteration can be very difficult to detect.

An egregious example of image-tampering involved the Ralph Lauren fashion model Filippa Hamilton. She appeared in a drastically Photoshopped advertisement that showed her hips as being thinner than her head—like a Bratz doll. The ad, published only in Japan, received intense criticism when the picture went viral. The five-foot-ten, 120-pound model was subsequently dropped by the fashion label because, as Hamilton explained, "they said I was overweight and I couldn't fit in their clothes anymore."[1] In today's age of Photoshop, it is common practice to make thin female models look even thinner and make male models look unnaturally muscled. "Every picture has been worked on, some twenty, thirty rounds," Ken Harris, a fashion magazine photo-retoucher said; "going between the retoucher, the client, and the agency . . . [photos] are retouched to death."[2] And since there is no disclaimer saying these images have been retouched, it can be hard for viewers to know the truth.

Photojournalists and news sources are confronted today with unprecedented concerns over truth-telling. In the past, trust in documentary photojournalism rested solely on the verifiability of images ("what you see is what you get"). This is no longer the case. Just as we must evaluate the words we read, now we must also take a more critical eye to the images we view.

Christopher R. Harris is a professor emeritus of the Department of Media Arts at Middle Tennessee State University.

In 1988, media baron Rupert Murdoch acquired Triangle Publications for $3 billion. Murdoch's News Corp. owned the new Fox network, and buying the then influential *TV Guide* ensured that the fledgling network would have its programs listed. In 2005, after years of declining circulation (TV schedules in local newspapers had increasingly undermined its regional editions), *TV Guide* became a full-size entertainment magazine, dropping its smaller digest format and its 140 regional editions. In 2008, *TV Guide*, once the most widely distributed magazine, was sold to a private venture capital firm

TABLE 9.1

THE TOP 10 MAGAZINES (RANKED BY PAID AND NONPAID U.S. CIRCULATION AND SINGLE-COPY SALES, 1972 VERSUS 2017

Data from: "Total Paid, Verified and Analyzed Non-Paid Circulation," Alliance for Audited Media, December 31, 2017, http://abcas3.auditedmedia.com/ecirc/magtitlesearch.asp.

1972		2017	
Rank/Publication	Circulation	Rank/Publication	Circulation
1 *Reader's Digest*	17,825,661	1 *AARP The Magazine*	23,802,452
2 *TV Guide*	16,410,858	2 *AARP Bulletin*	23,337,835
3 *Woman's Day*	8,191,731	3 *Costco Connection*	12,851,336
4 *Better Homes and Gardens*	7,996,050	4 *Better Homes and Gardens*	7,636,682
5 *Family Circle*	7,889,587	5 *Game Informer*	7,585,296
6 *McCall's*	7,516,960	6 *AAA Living*	4,854,409
7 *National Geographic*	7,260,179	7 *Good Housekeeping*	4,315,905
8 *Ladies' Home Journal*	7,014,251	8 *Family Circle*	4,046,353
9 *Playboy*	6,400,573	9 *People*	3,411,860
10 *Good Housekeeping*	5,801,446	10 *Woman's Day*	3,254,234

for $1—less than the cost of a single issue. However, the TV Guide Network and TVGuide.com—both deemed the more valuable assets—were sold to the film company Lionsgate Entertainment for $255 million in 2009. As *TV Guide* fell out of favor, *Game Informer*—a magazine about digital games—became a top title, as it chronicled the rise of another mass media industry.

Saturday Evening Post, Look, and Life Expire

Although *Reader's Digest* and women's supermarket magazines were not greatly affected by television, other general-interest magazines were. The *Saturday Evening Post* folded in 1969, *Look* in 1971, and *Life* in 1972. At the time, all three magazines were rated in the Top 10 in terms of paid circulation, and each had a readership that exceeded six million per issue. (A look at today's top-selling magazines—see Table 9.1—indicates just how large a readership this was.) Why did these magazines fold? First, to maintain these high circulation figures, their publishers were selling the magazines for far less than the cost of production.

Second, the national advertising revenue pie that helped make up the cost differences for *Life* and *Look* now had to be shared with network television—and magazines' slices were getting smaller. *Life*'s high pass-along readership meant that it had a larger audience than many prime-time TV shows. But it cost more to have a single full-page ad in *Life* than it did to buy a minute of ad time during evening television. National advertisers were often forced to choose between the two, and in the late 1960s and early 1970s, television seemed a better buy to advertisers looking for the biggest audience.

Third, dramatic increases in postal rates had a particularly negative effect on oversized publications (those larger than the 8-by-10.5-inch standard). In the 1970s, postal rates increased by more than 400 percent for these magazines. *Post* and *Life* cut their circulations drastically to save money. The economic rationale here was that limiting the number of copies would reduce production and postal costs, enabling the magazines to lower their ad rates to compete with network television. Yet with their decreased circulation, these magazines became less attractive to advertisers trying to reach the largest general audience.

The general-interest magazines that survived the competition for national ad dollars tended to be women's magazines, such as *Good Housekeeping, Better Homes and Gardens, Family Circle, Ladies' Home Journal,* and *Woman's Day.* These publications had smaller formats and depended primarily on supermarket sales rather than on expensive mail-delivered subscriptions (like *Life* and *Look*). However, the most popular magazines—*TV Guide* and *Reader's Digest*—benefited not only from supermarket sales but also from their larger circulations (twice that of *Life*), their pocket size, and their small photo budgets. The failure of the *Saturday Evening Post, Look,* and *Life* as oversized general-audience weeklies ushered in a new era of specialization.

People Puts Life Back into Magazines

In March 1974, Time Inc. launched *People*, the first successful mass market magazine to appear in decades. With an abundance of celebrity profiles and human-interest stories, *People* showed a profit in two years and reached a circulation of more than two million within five years. *People* now ranks first in revenue from advertising and circulation sales—more than $1.5 billion a year—and ranks ninth in the United States in terms of circulation (see Table 9.1).

The success of *People* is instructive, particularly because only two years earlier television had helped kill *Life* by draining away national ad dollars. Instead of using a bulky oversized format and relying on subscriptions, *People* downsized and generated most of its circulation revenue from newsstand and supermarket sales. For content, it took its cue from our culture's fascination with celebrities. Supported by plenty of photos, its short articles are about one-third the length of the articles in a typical newsmagazine.

If *People* is viewed, as one argument suggests, as a specialty magazine rather than as a mass market magazine, its financial success makes much more sense. It also helps explain the host of magazines that try to emulate it, including *Us Weekly*, *Entertainment Weekly*, *In Touch Weekly*, *Star*, and *OK! People* has even spawned its own spin-offs, including *People en Español* and *People StyleWatch*—the latter a low-cost fashion magazine that began in 2007 and features celebrity styles at discount prices.

COMMUNIST INFILTRATION IN THE PROTESTANT CLERGY: TWO VIEWS

THE RISE AND FALL OF *LOOK*

With large pages, beautiful photographs, and compelling stories on celebrities like Marilyn Monroe, *Look* entertained millions of readers from 1937 to 1971, emphasizing photojournalism to compete with radio. By the late 1960s, however, television had lured away national advertisers, postal rates increased, and production costs rose, forcing *Look* to fold despite a readership of more than eight million.

Convergence: Magazines Confront the Digital Age

Although the Internet was initially viewed as the death knell of print magazines, the industry now embraces it. The Internet has become the place where print magazines like *Time* and *Entertainment Weekly* can extend their reach; where magazines like *FHM* and *PCWorld* can survive when their print version ends; and where online magazines like *Salon*, *Slate*, and *Wonderwall* can exist exclusively.

Magazines Move Online

Given the costs of paper, printing, and postage, and the flexibility of the web, mobile devices, and social media, magazines are increasingly being distributed across multiple digital formats.

For example, *Wired* has a print circulation of about 869,000. It estimates its print edition reaches 2.8 million readers, but with its digital versions, social media pages, and video, it reaches nearly 62 million people monthly.

The magazine industry has adapted to the changing environment by thinking about magazines as not just paper publications but brands that find audiences across print and digital editions, desktop/laptop computers, the mobile web, and video. Even the shares of these platform categories are shifting quickly, as Figure 9.2 illustrates. Mobile web and video magazine content continued to expand their share, while print and digital editions and web (desktop/laptop) platforms remain large but declining formats. The good news for the magazine industry is that although its platforms for reaching its audience are changing rapidly, its total monthly brand audience increased from 1.55 billion to 1.74 billion from 2014 to 2018.

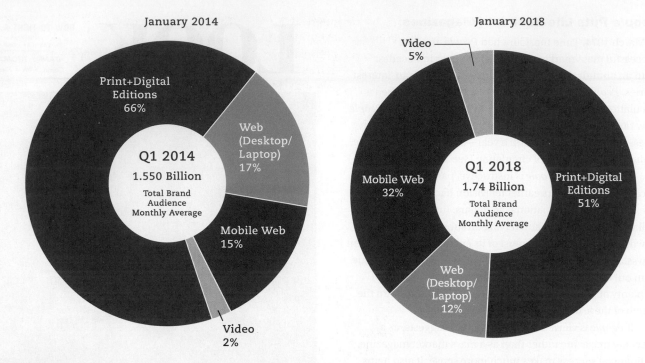

January 2014

Print+Digital Editions
66%

Web (Desktop/Laptop)
17%

Q1 2014
1.550 Billion
Total Brand Audience Monthly Average

Mobile Web
15%

Video
2%

January 2018

Video
5%

Mobile Web
32%

Q1 2018
1.74 Billion
Total Brand Audience Monthly Average

Print+Digital Editions
51%

Web (Desktop/Laptop)
12%

FIGURE 9.2

MAGAZINE BRAND AUDIENCE SHARE BY FORMAT, 2014–2018

Data from: Magazine Media Factbook 2015 (New York: Association of Magazine Media, 2015) and the Association of Magazine Media, "Magazine Media 360° Brand Audience Report Shows That Media Mix Has Shifted, Total Audience Remains Strong," March 7, 2018, www.magazine.org /industry-news/press-releases /mpa/magazine-media -360%C2%B0-brand-audience -report-shows-media-mix-has.

Paperless: Magazines Embrace Digital Content

Salon and *Slate*, which began as magazines exclusively online, were pioneers in making the web a legitimate site for reporting breaking news and discussing culture and politics. *Salon* was founded in 1995 by five former reporters from the *San Francisco Examiner* who wanted to break from the traditions of newspaper publishing and build "a different kind of newsroom" in order to create well-developed stories and commentary.[7] *Salon* is a leading online magazine, claiming twenty million unique monthly visitors in 2018. Its main online competitor, *Slate*—founded in 1996 and now owned by the Graham Holdings Company—has a similar online news and commentary presence but differentiates itself by producing more than fifteen profitable podcasts.

Other digital-only magazines include *Rookie*, created by fashion blogger Tavi Gevinson for teenage girls, and *Primer*, founded by Andrew Snavely as a fashion and lifestyle DIY for young men. Some have tried to reinvent the idea of a magazine, rather than just adapting the print product to the web. For example, *Lonny*—an interior design magazine—enables readers to flip through digital pages and then click on items (such as pillows, chairs, or fabrics) for purchase.

Allrecipes, established in 1997 and owned by Meredith, and *Epicurious*, founded in 1995 by Condé Nast (and affiliated with Conde Nast brand *Bon Appétit* since 2015), are the leading online food and recipe magazine sites. Both have flourished, as people increasingly search online for recipes and cooking videos.

THE DOMINATION OF SPECIALIZATION

The general trend away from mass market publications and toward specialty magazines coincided with radio's move to specialized formats in the 1950s. With the rise of television, magazines ultimately reacted the same way that radio and movies did: They adapted. Radio developed formats for older and younger audiences, for rock fans and classical music fans. At the movies, filmmakers focused on more adult subject matter, which was off-limits to television's image as a family medium. And magazines traded their mass audience for smaller, discrete audiences that could be guaranteed to advertisers. This specialization continues today as the magazine industry adapts to the Internet. At least seven of the nation's top twenty-five magazines in circulation are now linked to membership in a specialized organization: *AARP The Magazine* and *AARP Bulletin* (for members of AARP), *Costco Connection* (for Costco warehouse club members), *Game Informer* (for a Pro membership card at GameStop stores), *AAA Living* (for members of the automobile organization AAA), *American Rifleman* (one of four magazines for members of the National Rifle Association), and *American Legion* (for members of the American Legion veterans organization). Linking a magazine subscription to organizational membership helps ensure audience loyalty to the magazine in the face of many competing media options.

Magazines are now divided by advertiser type: *consumer magazines* (*O: The Oprah Magazine, Cosmopolitan*), which carry a host of general consumer product ads; *business* or *trade magazines* (*Advertising Age, Progressive Grocer*), which include ads for products and services for various occupational groups; and *farm magazines* (*Dairy Herd Management, Dakota Farmer*), which contain ads for agricultural products and farming lifestyles. Grouping by advertiser type further distinguishes commercial magazines from noncommercial magazine-like periodicals. The noncommercial category includes everything from activist newsletters and scholarly journals to business newsletters created by companies for distribution to employees. Magazines such as *Ms., Consumer Reports,* and *Cook's Illustrated,* which rely solely on subscription and newsstand sales, accept no advertising and thus fit into the noncommercial periodical category.

In addition to grouping magazines by advertising style, we can categorize popular consumer magazine styles by the demographic characteristics of their target audience—such as gender, age, or ethnic group—or by an audience interest area, such as entertainment, sports, literature, or tabloids.

Men's and Women's Magazines

One way the magazine industry competed with television was to reach niche audiences that were not being served by the new medium, creating magazines focused on more adult subject matter. *Playboy*, launched in 1953 by Hugh Hefner, was the first magazine to do this by undermining the conventional values of pre–World War II America and emphasizing previously taboo subject matter. Scraping together $7,000, Hefner published his first issue, which contained a nude calendar reprint of the actress Marilyn Monroe, along with male-focused articles that criticized alimony payments and gold-digging women. With the financial success of that first issue, which sold more than fifty thousand copies, Hefner was in business.

Playboy's circulation peaked in the 1960s at more than seven million, but it fell gradually throughout the 1970s as the magazine faced competition from imitators and video, as well as criticism for "packaging" and objectifying women for the enjoyment of men. *Playboy* and similar publications continue to publish, but newer men's magazines have shifted their focus to include health (*Men's Health*) and lifestyle (*Details* and *Maxim*). In an attempt to create new interest in the magazine, *Playboy* announced it would stop publishing nude pictures of women beginning in early 2016, but it reversed its decision a year later.

Women's magazines had long demonstrated that gender-based publications were highly marketable, but during the era of specialization, the magazine industry sought the enormous market of magazine-reading women even more aggressively. *Better Homes and Gardens, Good Housekeeping, Ladies' Home Journal,* and *Woman's Day* focused on cultivating the image of women as homemakers and consumers. In the conservative 1950s and early 1960s, this formula proved to be enormously successful, but as the women's movement advanced in the late 1960s and into the 1970s, women's magazines grew more contemporary and sophisticated, incorporating content related to feminism (such as in Gloria Steinem's *Ms.* magazine, which first appeared in 1972), women's sexuality (such as in *Cosmopolitan*, which became a young women's magazine in the 1960s [see "Global Village: Cosmopolitan Style Travels the World" on page 286]), and career and politics—topics previously geared primarily toward men. Even so, *Better Homes and Gardens, Good Housekeeping,* and *Woman's Day* are still in the Top 10 list of the highest-circulation magazines in the United States (see Table 9.1).

LaunchPad
macmillan learning
launchpadworks.com

Magazine Specialization Today
Editors discuss motivations for magazine specialization and how the Internet is changing the industry.

Discussion: How have the types of magazines you read changed over the past ten years? Have their formats changed, too?

Cosmopolitan Style Travels the World

In 1962, Helen Gurley Brown, one of the country's top advertising copywriters, wrote the best-selling book *Sex and the Single Girl*. After proposing a magazine modeled on the book's vision of strong, sexually liberated women, the Hearst Corporation hired her as editor in chief in 1965 to reinvent *Cosmopolitan*, at that time a women's illustrated literary monthly. The new *Cosmopolitan* helped spark a sexual revolution and was marketed to the "Cosmo Girl": a woman aged eighteen to thirty-four with an interest in love, sex, fashion, and her career.

Brown's vision of *Cosmo* continues today. It's the top women's fashion magazine in America, surpassing competitors like *Glamour*, *Marie Claire*, and *Vogue*. Beyond U.S. borders, *Cosmopolitan* is a global publication that publishes in more than eighty countries around the world, including Chile, Argentina, the UK,

Italy, Spain, France, Germany, the Netherlands, Russia, Malaysia, Singapore, Taiwan, Japan, Australia, South Africa, and the Middle East.

Although it looks much the same in every country, with a fashionable young woman on the cover and racy headlines ("Sofort Super Sex!" in Germany and "¡Ohhhh! Verdades Y Mentiras sobre el Orgasmo" in Spain), some countries have to make adjustments for regional standards. For example, the editor of *Cosmopolitan Middle East*, which is mostly read in Dubai and Beirut, says, "We can't even publish the word 'sex,' . . . but [readers] are still thinking about sex and they're still wanting to meet a guy and they are still dating. We've just got to wrap it up and present it in a slightly more conservative fashion."[1] In Chile, the editor of *Cosmopolitan* says she covers contraception and women's reproductive health issues "a lot" because Chile has some of the most restrictive abortion laws in the world.[2] Oddly, news about one topic seems to transcend all cultural boundaries and be universally acceptable for *Cosmopolitan* international editions: the Kardashians.

Cosmopolitan didn't always have cover photos of women with plunging necklines or cover lines like "67 New Sex Tricks" and "The Sexiest Things to Do after Sex." In fact, *Cosmopolitan* had at least four format changes before

Sports, Entertainment, and Leisure Magazines

In the age of specialization, magazine executives have developed multiple magazines for fans of soap operas, running, tennis, golf, hunting, quilting, antiquing, surfing, and video games, to name only a few. Within categories, magazines specialize further, targeting older or younger runners, men or women golfers, duck hunters or bird-watchers, and midwestern or southern antique collectors.

The most popular sports and leisure magazine is *Sports Illustrated*, which took its name from a failed 1935 publication. Launched in 1954 by Henry Luce's Time Inc., *Sports Illustrated* was initially aimed at well-educated middle-class men. In the years since, it has become the most successful general sports magazine in history, covering everything from major-league sports and mountain climbing to foxhunting and snorkeling. Although frequently criticized for its immensely profitable but exploitative yearly swimsuit edition, *Sports Illustrated* has also done major investigative pieces—for example, on racketeering in boxing and on land conservation. Its circulation held at 2.7 million in 2018 through its print and digital platforms. *Sports Illustrated* competes directly with *ESPN The Magazine* and indirectly with dozens of leisure and niche sports magazines, like *Golf Digest*, *Outside*, and the website *Bleacher Report*.

Helen Gurley Brown came along. The magazine was launched in 1886 as an illustrated monthly for the modern family (meaning it was targeted at married women), with articles on cooking, child care, household decoration, and occasionally fashion, featuring illustrated images of women in the hats and high collars of late-Victorian fashion.[3]

But the magazine was thin on content and almost folded. *Cosmopolitan* was saved in 1889, when journalist and entrepreneur John Brisben Walker gave it a second chance as an illustrated magazine of literature and insightful reporting. The magazine featured writers like Edith Wharton, Rudyard Kipling, and Theodore Dreiser, and it serialized entire books, including H. G. Wells's *The War of the Worlds*. And Walker, seeing the success of contemporary newspapers in New York, was not above stunt reporting. When Joseph Pulitzer's *New York World* sent reporter Nellie Bly to travel the world in less than eighty days in 1889 (challenging the premise of Jules Verne's 1873 novel, *Around the World in Eighty Days*), Walker sent reporter Elizabeth Bisland around the world in the opposite direction for a more literary travel account.[4] Walker's leadership turned *Cosmopolitan* into a respected magazine with increased circulation and a strong advertising base.

Walker sold *Cosmopolitan* at a profit to William Randolph Hearst (Pulitzer's main competitor) in 1905.

Under Hearst, *Cosmopolitan* had its third rebirth—this time as a muckraking magazine. As magazine historians explain, Hearst was a U.S. representative who "had his eye on the presidency and planned to use his newspapers and the recently bought *Cosmopolitan* to stir up further discontent over the trusts and big business."[5] *Cosmopolitan*'s first big muckraking series, David Graham Phillips's "The Treason of the Senate" in 1906, didn't help Hearst's political career, but it did boost the circulation of the magazine by 50 percent and was reprinted in Hearst newspapers for even more exposure.

By 1912, the progressive political movement that had given impetus to muckraking journalism was waning. *Cosmopolitan*, in its fourth incarnation, became a version of its former self—an illustrated literary monthly targeted to women, featuring short stories and serialized novels by such popular writers as Damon Runyon, Sinclair Lewis, and Faith Baldwin.

Cosmopolitan had great success as an upscale literary magazine, but by the early 1960s, the format had become outdated, and readership and advertising was on the decline. At this point, the magazine had its most radical makeover and became, under Brown's reign, the *Cosmo* we and young women around much of the world know today.

Founded in 1888 by Boston lawyer Gardiner Greene Hubbard and his famous son-in-law, Alexander Graham Bell, *National Geographic* promoted "humanized geography" and helped pioneer color photography in 1910. It was also the first publication to publish both undersea and aerial color photographs. In addition, many of *National Geographic*'s nature and culture specials on television, which began in 1965, rank among the most popular programs in the history of public television. *National Geographic*'s popularity grew slowly and steadily throughout the twentieth century, reaching one million in circulation in 1935 and ten million in the 1970s. In the late 1990s, its circulation of paid subscriptions slipped to under nine million. Other media ventures (for example, a cable channel and atlases) provided new revenue as circulation for the magazine continued to slide, falling to three million in 2018. Despite its falling circulation, *National Geographic* is often recognized as one of the country's best magazines for its reporting and photojournalism. Today, *National Geographic* competes with other travel and geography magazines, such as *Discover, Smithsonian, Travel + Leisure, Condé Nast Traveler,* and its own *National Geographic Traveler*. The brand has also been extended to the National Geographic channel (launched in 2001 in the United States), National Geographic Films, and a museum in Washington, D.C.

Joshua Mitchell

SPECIALIZED MAGAZINES

target a wide range of interests, from mainstream sports to hobbies, such as model airplanes. Some of the more successful specialized magazines include *National Geographic* and *Sports Illustrated*.

Magazines for the Ages

In the age of specialization, magazines have further delineated readers along ever-narrowing age lines, catering increasingly to very young readers and older readers, groups often ignored by mainstream television.

The first children's magazines appeared in New England in the late eighteenth century. Ever since, magazines such as *Youth's Companion*, *Boy's Life* (the Boy Scouts' national publication since 1912), *Highlights for Children*, and *Ranger Rick* have successfully targeted preschool and elementary-school children. The ad-free and subscription-only *Highlights for Children* topped the children's magazine category in 2018 with a circulation of about two million. In the popular arena, the leading female teen magazines have shown substantial growth; the top magazine for thirteen- to nineteen-year-olds is *Seventeen*, with a circulation of two million in 2018. (For a critical take on women's fashion magazines, see "Media Literacy and the Critical Process: Uncovering American Beauty" on page 289.)

In targeting audiences by age, the most dramatic success has come from magazines aimed at readers over fifty, America's fastest-growing age segment. These publications have tried to meet the cultural interests of older Americans, who historically have not been prominently featured in mainstream consumer culture. AARP and its magazine, *AARP The Magazine*, were founded in 1958 by retired California teacher Ethel Percy Andrus. Subscriptions to the bimonthly *AARP The Magazine* and the monthly *AARP Bulletin* come free when someone joins AARP and pays the modest membership fee ($16 in 2018). By the early 1980s, *AARP The Magazine*'s circulation was approaching seven million. However, with AARP signing up thirty thousand new members each week by the late 1980s, both *AARP The Magazine* and the bulletin overtook *TV Guide* and *Reader's Digest* as the top circulated magazines. By 2017, both of these publications were reaching more than twenty-three million people a month, far surpassing the circulations of all other magazines (see Table 9.1). Article topics in the magazine cover a range of lifestyle, travel, money, health, and entertainment issues, such as sex at age fifty-plus, secrets for spectacular vacations, and how poker can create a sharper mind.

Elite Magazines

Although long in existence, *elite magazines* grew in popularity during the age of specialization. Elite magazines are characterized by their combination of literature, criticism, humor, and journalism and by their appeal to highly educated audiences, often living in urban areas. Among the numerous elite publications that grew in stature during the twentieth century were the *Atlantic Monthly* (now the *Atlantic*), *Vanity Fair*, and *Harper's*.

However, the most widely circulated elite magazine is the *New Yorker*. Launched in 1925 by Harold Ross, the *New Yorker* became the first city magazine aimed at a national upscale audience. Over the years, the *New Yorker* has featured many of the twentieth century's most prominent biographers, writers, reporters, and humorists, including A. J. Liebling, Dorothy Parker, Lillian Ross, John Updike, E. B. White, and Garrison Keillor, as well as James Thurber's cartoons and Ogden Nash's poetry. By the mid-1960s, the *New Yorker*'s circulation hovered around 500,000; by 2018, its print circulation had expanded to 1.2 million. Along with the *New York Times*, the *New Yorker* in 2017 broke the story of dozens of women's charges of sexual harassment, assault, and rape against film producer Harvey Weinstein. The reports won Pulitzer Prizes for each publication and spurred a nationwide and global #MeToo movement of women sharing their stories of workplace harassment, assault, and rape.

How does the United States' leading fashion magazine define *beauty*? One way to explore this question is by critically analyzing the covers of *Cosmopolitan*.

1 DESCRIPTION

If you review a number of *Cosmopolitan* covers, you'll notice that they typically feature a body shot of a female model surrounded by blaring headlines often featuring the words *Hot* and *Sex* to usher a reader inside the magazine. The cover model is dressed provocatively and is positioned against a solid-color background. She looks confident. Everything about the cover is loud and brassy.

2 ANALYSIS

Looking at covers from the last decade and then the decade before it, what are some significant patterns? One thing you'll notice is that all the models look incredibly similar, particularly when it comes to race: There is a disproportionate number of white cover models. However, you'll probably notice that things are improving somewhat in this regard; *Cosmo* has used several Hispanic and African American cover models in recent years, but they are still few and far between. Besides race, there is an even more consistent pattern regarding body type. Of cover model Kylie Jenner, *Cosmo* fashion editor Rachel Torgeson wrote, "Kylie Jenner Is RAWRRRRR in This Low-Cut, Leopard-Print Dress. I'm, like, literally realizing stuff, and that stuff is that Kylie Jenner looks hawt." In *Cosmo*-speak, "rawrrrrr" and "hawt" means ultrathin and curvy.[1]

3 INTERPRETATION

What does this mean? Although *Cosmo* doesn't provide height and weight figures for its models, the magazine is probably selling an unhealthy body weight (in fact, photos can be digitally altered to make the models look even thinner). In its guidelines for the fashion industry, the Academy for Eating Disorders suggests "for women and men over the age of 18, adoption of a minimum body mass index threshold of 18.5 kg/m^2 (e.g., a female model who is 5'9" [1.75 m] must weigh more than 126 pounds [57.3 kg]), which recognizes that weight below this is considered underweight by the World Health Organization."[2]

4 EVALUATION

Cosmopolitan uses thin cover models as aspirational objects for its readers—that is, as women its readers would like to look like. Thus, these cover models become the image of what a "terrific" body is for its readers, who—by *Cosmopolitan*'s own account—are women ages eighteen to twenty-four. *Cosmo* also notes that it's been the best-selling women's magazine in college bookstores for twenty-five years. But that target audience also happens to be the one most susceptible to body issues. As the Academy for Eating Disorders notes, "About one in 20 young women in the community has an eating disorder," which can include anorexia, bulimia, and binge eating.[3]

5 ENGAGEMENT

Contact *Cosmo*'s editor in chief, Michele Promaulayko, and request representation of healthy body types on the magazine's covers. You can contact her and the editorial department via e-mail (inbox@cosmopolitan.com), telephone (212-649-3570), or U.S. mail: Michele Promaulayko, Editor, *Cosmopolitan*, 300 West 57th Street, New York, NY 10019. Your voice can be effective: In 2012, a thirteen-year-old girl started a petition on change.org and successfully got *Seventeen* to respond to the way it Photoshops images of models.

Minority-Targeted Magazines

Minority-targeted magazines, like newspapers, have existed since before the Civil War, including the African American antislavery magazines *Emancipator*, *Liberator*, and *Reformer*. One of the most influential early African American magazines, the *Crisis*, was founded by W. E. B. Du Bois in 1910 and is the official magazine of the NAACP (National Association for the Advancement of Colored People).

In the modern age, the major magazine publisher for African Americans was John H. Johnson. While working on a newsletter at a Chicago life insurance company, Johnson got the idea of starting a publication for blacks. In 1942, Johnson started *Negro Digest* on $500 borrowed against his mother's furniture. By 1945, the *Digest* had a circulation of more than 100,000, and its profits enabled Johnson and a small group of editors to start *Ebony*, a picture-text magazine modeled on *Life* but serving black readers.

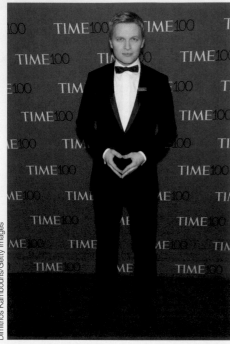

RONAN FARROW,
son of actress and activist Mia Farrow and director and writer Woody Allen, is the Pulitzer Prize–winning journalist whose exposé in the *New Yorker* prompted the beginning of the #MeToo movement.

Dimitrios Kambouris/Getty Images

The Johnson Publishing Company also successfully introduced *Jet*, a pocket-size supermarket magazine, in 1951. By 2017, *Ebony* had a monthly circulation of 1,050,000 and a readership of 8.5 million.

Essence, the first major magazine geared toward African American women, debuted in 1969; by 2017, the magazine had a readership of 10.6 million people a month. *Jet*, trailing the other two African American market magazines, announced in 2014 that it would begin publishing in a digital-only format.

Other minority groups have magazines aimed at their own interests as well. The *Advocate*, founded in 1967 as a twelve-page newsletter, was the first major magazine to address issues of interest to gay men and lesbians. In the ensuing years, the *Advocate* has published some of the best journalism about antigay violence, policy issues affecting the LGBT community, and AIDS—topics often not well covered by the mainstream press. *Out* is the top gay style magazine. Both are owned by Here Media, which also owns Here TV and several LGBT websites.

With increases in the Hispanic population and immigration, magazines appealing to Spanish-speaking readers have developed rapidly since the 1980s. In 1983, the De Armas Spanish Magazine Network began distributing Spanish-language versions of mainstream American magazines, including *Cosmopolitan en Español*; *Harper's Bazaar en Español*; and *Ring*, the prominent boxing magazine. *Latina* magazine was founded in 1996 and is the most successful English-language publication for Hispanic women. The new magazines target the most upwardly mobile segments of the growing American Hispanic population, which numbered more than fifty-three million—about 18 percent of the U.S. population—by 2018. Today, *People en Español*, *Latina*, and *Vanidades* rank as the top three Hispanic magazines by ad revenue.

Although national magazines aimed at other minority groups were slow to arrive, there are magazines now that target virtually every race, culture, and ethnicity, including *Asian Week*, *Native Peoples*, and *Tikkun*.

Supermarket Tabloids

With headlines like "Obama Birth Certificate Is Fake!," "Hillary: 6 Months to Live" (published in 2015), and "Miracle After 67 Years of Blindness . . . Stevie Wonder Can See Again!," **supermarket tabloids** push the limits of both decency and credibility. Tabloid history can be traced to newspapers' use of graphics and pictorial layouts in the 1860s and 1870s, but the modern U.S. tabloid began with the founding of the *National Enquirer* by William Randolph Hearst in 1926. The *Enquirer* struggled until it was purchased in 1952 by Generoso Pope, who originally intended to use it to "fight for the rights of man" and "human decency and dignity."[8] In the interest of profit, however, Pope settled on the "gore formula" to transform the paper's anemic weekly circulation of seven thousand: "I noticed how auto accidents drew crowds and I decided that if it was blood that interested people, I'd give it to them."[9]

By the mid-1960s, the *Enquirer*'s circulation had jumped to over one million through the publication of bizarre human-interest stories, gruesome murder tales, violent accident accounts, unexplained-phenomena stories, and malicious celebrity gossip. By 1974, the magazine's weekly circulation had topped four million. Its popularity inspired the creation of other tabloids—like *Globe* (founded in 1954) and *Star* (founded by News Corp. in 1974)—and the adoption of a tabloid style by general-interest magazines such as *People* and *Us Weekly*. Today, tabloid magazine sales are down from their peak in the 1980s, but they continue to be popular. New York–based American Media, Inc., publishes the leading tabloids the *National Enquirer*, *Globe*, and *Star*, as well as gossip brands *Us Weekly*, *OK!*, and Radaronline.com.

SELECTA

is an upscale fashion magazine targeted at Hispanic women. The magazine is published in Spanish, although it maintains Twitter and Instagram feeds in English. Other popular magazines aimed at this audience include *Latina* and *People en Español*.

GALA *GLAM*
Vestidos para ocasiones *black tie*, al estilo del verano

EDICIÓN DE
MODA

La arquitectura Latinoamericana se presenta en el MOMA

JOYAS LUJOSAS
Los tonos más vibrantes de la temporada

HAUTE HORLOGERIE
Tesoros desde las ferias de alta relojería más prestigiosas del mundo

DAISY FUENTES
FELIZ Y SOÑANDO EN GRANDE

JUNIO 2015 $3.95

THE ORGANIZATION AND ECONOMICS OF MAGAZINES

Given the great diversity in magazine content and ownership, it is hard to offer a common profile of a successful magazine. However, large or small, online or in print, most magazines deal with the same basic functions: production, content, ads, and sales. In this section, we discuss how magazines operate, the ownership structure behind major magazines, and how smaller publications fulfill niche areas that even specialized magazines do not reach.

Magazine Departments and Duties

Unlike a broadcast station or a daily newspaper, a small newsletter or magazine can be created inexpensively on a computer, which enables an aspiring publisher-editor to write, design, lay out, and print or post online a modest publication. For larger operations, however, the work is divided into departments.

Editorial and Production

The lifeblood of a magazine is its *editorial department*, which produces the magazine's content, excluding advertisements. Like newspapers, most magazines have a chain of command that begins with a publisher and extends to the editor in chief, the managing editor, and a variety of subeditors. These subeditors oversee such editorial functions as photography, illustrations, reporting and

launchpadworks.com

Narrowcasting in Magazines
Magazine editors explain the benefits and consequences of narrowcasting.

Discussion: Think of magazines that might be considered good examples of narrowcasting. What makes them good examples, and would you consider them successful? Why or why not?

writing, copyediting, layout, and print and multimedia design. Magazine writers generally include contributing staff writers, who are specialists in certain fields, and freelance writers: non-staff professionals who are assigned to cover particular stories or a region of the country. Many magazines, especially those with small budgets, also rely on well-written unsolicited manuscripts to fill their pages. Most commercial magazines, however, reject more than 95 percent of unsolicited pieces.

A magazine's *production and technology department* maintains the computer and printing hardware necessary for mass market production. Because magazines are printed weekly, monthly, or bimonthly, it is not economically practical for most magazine publishers to maintain expensive print facilities. Most national magazines send digital magazine copy to various regional printing sites for the insertion of local ads and for faster distribution.

Advertising and Sales

The *advertising and sales department* of a magazine secures clients, arranges promotions, and places ads. Like radio stations, network television stations, and basic cable television stations, consumer magazines are heavily reliant on advertising revenue. Magazines provide their advertisers with rate cards, which indicate how much they charge for a certain amount of advertising space on a page. A top-rated consumer magazine like *People* might charge more than $371,500 for a full-page color ad and about $119,800 for a third of a page black-and-white ad. However, in today's competitive world, most rate cards are not very meaningful: Almost all magazines offer 25 to 50 percent rate discounts to advertisers, particularly when they buy ads in multiple issues. Although fashion and general-interest magazines carry a higher percentage of ads than do political or literary magazines, the average magazine contains about 40 percent ad copy and 60 percent editorial material, a figure that has remained fairly constant for the past decade.

The traditional display ad has been the staple of magazine advertising for more than a century. As magazines have become digital brands, the advertising opportunities have become more creative. For example, Condé Nast offers multiple opportunities for advertisers to connect with audiences. The company states, "We connect consumers to their passions, to the culture and ultimately to you, our marketing partners."[10] If that sounds somewhat vague, it's because the new world of magazine brand advertising is still being invented. In addition to traditional display ads in its print and digital magazine versions, Condé Nast offers data information about its digital readers to its customers, opportunities for **branded content** (specialized print, online, or video content produced and funded by individual advertisers), paid social media placements on platforms like Facebook and Instagram, and custom video stories and features. By offering these varied advertising opportunities, magazine publishers hope to generate new revenue to replace declining print display ad earnings.

A few contemporary magazines, such as *Highlights for Children*, have decided not to carry ads and rely solely on subscriptions and newsstand sales. To protect the integrity of their various tests and product comparisons, *Consumer Reports* and *Cook's Illustrated* carry no advertising. To strengthen its editorial independence, *Ms.* magazine abandoned ads in 1990 after years of pressure from the food, cosmetics, and fashion industries to feature recipes and more complimentary copy.

Some advertisers and companies have canceled ads when a magazine featured an unflattering or critical article about a company or an industry.[11] In some instances, this practice has put enormous pressure on editors not to offend advertisers. The cozy relationships between some advertisers and magazines have led to a dramatic decline in investigative reporting, once central to popular magazines during the muckraking era.

As television advertising siphoned off national ad revenues in the 1950s, publishers began introducing different editions of their magazines to attract advertisers. **Regional editions** are national magazines whose content is tailored to the interests of different geographic areas. For example, *Sports Illustrated* often prints several different regional versions of its College Football Preview and March Madness Preview editions, picturing regional stars on each of the covers. In **split-run editions**, the editorial content remains the same, but the magazine includes a few pages of ads purchased by local or regional companies. Most editions of *Time* and *Sports Illustrated*, for example, contain a number of pages reserved for regional ads. **Demographic editions**, meanwhile,

TEXTURE, launched in 2012, is a Netflix-like app for magazines. It allows users to access an array of digital magazines, from *People* to *National Geographic* to *Sports Illustrated*. Users can choose between a Basic plan and the more expensive Premium access, which includes a wider selection of magazines. Apple bought Texture in 2018, and reports have surfaced that it plans to integrate the subscription service into its Apple News app.

are editions of magazines targeted to particular groups of consumers. In this case, market researchers identify subscribers primarily by occupation, class, and zip code. *Time* magazine, for example, developed special editions of its magazine to target high-income professional/managerial households. Demographic editions guarantee advertisers a particular magazine audience, one that enables them to pay lower rates for their ads because the ads will be run in only a limited number of copies of the magazine. The magazine can then compete with advertising in regional television or cable markets and in newspaper supplements.

Circulation and Distribution

In the era in which magazines came only in the paper format, the focus of *circulation and distribution departments* were single-copy and subscription sales. These days, paper is still a leading format, but subscriptions account for more than 90 percent of print magazine distribution, as sales of more expensive single copies at retailers have declined.

One tactic used by magazine circulation departments to increase subscription revenue is to encourage consumers to renew well in advance of their actual renewal dates. Magazines can thus invest and earn interest on early renewal money as a hedge against consumers who drop their subscriptions. Other strategies include **evergreen subscriptions**—those that automatically renew on a credit card account unless subscribers request that the automatic renewal be stopped—and *controlled circulations*, which provide readers with a magazine at no charge by targeting captive audiences, such as airline passengers or association members. These magazines' financial support comes solely from advertising or corporate sponsorship.

The biggest trend in magazine sales is the migration to digital distribution (see Figure 9.2). By 2018, combined print and digital editions accounted for about 51 percent of the magazine audience. Mobile editions (usually via apps) attract about 32 percent of the industry's audience, while web versions of magazines (via desktops and laptops) account for 12 percent, and video content comprises 5 percent.[12] As Figure 9.3 demonstrates, certain magazines that might not have the highest annual

FIGURE 9.3

TOP TEN MAGAZINE BRANDS—AVERAGE MONTHLY AUDIENCE ACROSS PLATFORMS

Data from: Association of Magazine Media, "Magazine Media 360° Brand Audience Report," March 2018, www .magazine.org/march-2018-1.

Print+Digital

MAGAZINE BRAND	AUDIENCE
1 People	39,141
2 AARP	38,557
3 Better Homes and Gardens	36,324
4 National Geographic	32,225
5 Good Housekeeping	19,451
6 Time	18,337
7 Reader's Digest	18,133
8 Sports Illustrated	17,643
9 ESPN The Magazine	17,459
10 Cosmopolitan	16,158

Web

MAGAZINE BRAND	UNIQUE VISITORS
1 ESPN The Magazine	24,805
2 WebMD Magazine	12,787
3 Time	10,434
4 Allrecipes	9,214
5 New York Magazine	6,707
6 People	6,244
7 The Atlantic	6,065
8 Taste of Home	4,005
9 AARP	3,912
10 National Geographic	3,606

Mobile

MAGAZINE BRAND	UNIQUE VISITORS
1 ESPN The Magazine	42,168
2 WebMD Magazine	35,938
3 People	28,690
4 Allrecipes	28,047
5 Time	25,150
6 New York Magazine	20,766
7 Cosmopolitan	17,076
8 Us Weekly	15,542
9 Entertainment Weekly	13,147
10 The Atlantic	12,500

Video

MAGAZINE BRAND	UNIQUE VISITORS
1 ESPN The Magazine	12,081
2 Entrepreneur	9,628
3 Vanity Fair	6,548
4 GQ	4,767
5 Vogue	4,460
6 Time	4,203
7 Bon Appétit/Epicurious	4,168
8 Wired	4,072
9 People	3,924
10 Allure	2,987

Total Brand

MAGAZINE BRAND	TOTAL BRAND AUDIENCE
1 ESPN The Magazine	96,513
2 People	77,999
3 WebMD Magazine	60,849
4 Time	58,124
5 AARP	49,359
6 Allrecipes	46,210
7 Better Homes and Gardens	45,152
8 National Geographic	41,507
9 Cosmopolitan	36,217
10 Sports Illustrated	32,934

print circulation figures are nevertheless thriving in newer distribution platforms. Other models for magazine distribution, such as the Texture app, offer a subscription plan, with more than two hundred weekly and monthly titles accessible for $9.99 to $14.99 a month.

Major Magazine Chains

In terms of ownership, the commercial magazine industry most closely resembles the cable television business, which patterned its specialized channels on the consumer magazine market. Even though more than two hundred new commercial magazine titles appear each year—many of them independently owned—it is a struggle to survive in the competitive magazine marketplace.

The Meredith Corporation, based in Des Moines, Iowa, specializes in women's and home lifestyle magazines, and it became the world's largest magazine publisher with its 2018 purchase of Time Inc. The $1.8 billion deal puts the eponymously named *Time* magazine and other popular titles—like *People, Sports Illustrated, Fortune, Golf Magazine, Travel + Leisure, Real Simple,* and *Entertainment Weekly*—under the same corporate umbrella with Meredith's magazine titles, including *Better Homes and Gardens, Family Circle, Midwest Living,* and *Rachael Ray Every Day*. Meredith's focus on women's and lifestyle magazines did not mesh with all of its new Time Inc. magazines, and within weeks of the purchase, Meredith announced it had already sold Time Inc. UK and *Golf Magazine,* and it would be putting *Time, Sports Illustrated, Fortune,* and *Money* up for sale. Meredith's properties also include seventeen local television stations in the United States.

The Hearst Corporation, the leading magazine (and newspaper) chain in the early twentieth century, still remains a formidable publisher, with titles like *Cosmopolitan, Esquire, Elle, Car and Driver,* and *O: The Oprah Magazine*. In 2018, Hearst bought Rodale, a family-owned magazine company that published health and wellness titles such as *Prevention, Runner's World,* and *Men's Health*. Hearst also owns interests in cable channels A&E, History, Lifetime, and ESPN; thirty local television stations, and a number of major newspapers. Long a force in upscale consumer magazines, Condé Nast is a division of Advance Publications, which operates the Newhouse newspaper chain. The Condé Nast group controls several key magazines, including *Vanity Fair, GQ,* and *Vogue*. In addition, a number of American magazines have carved out market niches worldwide. *Reader's Digest, Cosmopolitan, National Geographic,* and *Time,* for example, all produce international editions in several languages. In general, though, most American magazines are local, regional, or specialized and therefore less exportable than movies and television. Of the more than seven thousand consumer titles, only about two hundred magazines from the United States circulate routinely in the world market. Such magazines, however—like exported American TV shows and films—play a key role in determining the look of global culture (see "Global Village: Cosmopolitan Style Travels the World" on page 286).

Many magazine publishers generate additional revenue through custom publishing divisions, producing limited-distribution publications, sometimes called **magalogs**, which combine glossy magazine style with the sales pitch of retail catalogues. Magalogs are often used to market goods or services to customers or employees. For example, international clothing retailer H&M has *H&M Magazine,* Bloomingdale's department store in New York publishes its *Bloomingdale's* magalog, Ford Motor Co. produces *My Ford* (also available via Apple's App Store), and Midwest grocer Hy-Vee offers its *Seasons* magazine, featuring food and recipes.

Alternative Voices

Only eighty-five of the twenty thousand American magazines have circulations that top one million, so most alternative magazines struggle to satisfy small but loyal groups of readers. At any given time, there are over two thousand alternative magazines in circulation, with many failing and others starting up every month.

Alternative magazines have historically defined themselves in terms of politics—published by either the Left (the *Progressive, In These Times,* the *Nation*) or the Right (the *National Review,*

American Spectator, the *Weekly Standard*). However, what constitutes an alternative magazine has broadened over time to include just about any publication considered outside the mainstream, ranging from environmental magazines to alternative lifestyle magazines to punk-zines—the magazine world's answer to punk rock. (**Zines**, pronounced "zeens," is a term used to describe self-published magazines.) *Utne Reader*, widely regarded as "the *Reader's Digest* of alternative magazines," has defined *alternative* as any sort of "thinking that doesn't reinvent the status quo, that broadens issues you might see on TV or in the daily paper."

Occasionally, alternative magazines have become marginally mainstream. For example, during the conservative Reagan era in the 1980s, William F. Buckley's *National Review* saw its circulation swell to more than 100,000—enormous by alternative standards—only to grow to 170,390 in 2011 as a conservative counterpoint to President Barack Obama. However, the magazine didn't support Donald Trump as a Republican candidate, and it was ridiculed by him after he won the presidency. By 2017, the magazine's circulation had shrunk to about 90,000.[13] On the Left, *Mother Jones* (named after labor organizer Mary Harris Jones), which champions muckraking and investigative journalism, had a circulation of about 200,000 in 2018, and about 11 million monthly online readers.

Most alternative magazines, however, are content to swim outside the mainstream. These are the small magazines that typically include diverse political, cultural, religious, international, and environmental subject matter, such as *Against the Current, Y'all, Buddhadharma, Hot VWs, Jewish Currents, Small Farmer's Journal*, and *Humor Times*.

MAGAZINES IN A DEMOCRATIC SOCIETY

Like other mass media, magazines are a major part of the cluttered media landscape. To keep pace, the magazine industry has become fast-paced and high-risk. Of the seven hundred to one thousand new magazines that start up each year, fewer than two hundred will survive longer than a year.

As an industry, magazine publishing—like advertising and public relations—has played a central role in transforming the United States from a producer society to a consumer society. Since the 1950s, though, individual magazines have not had the powerful national voice they once possessed, uniting separate communities around important issues such as abolition and suffrage. Today, with so many specialized magazines appealing to distinct groups of consumers, magazines play a much-diminished role in creating a sense of national identity.

Contemporary commercial magazines provide essential information about politics, society, and culture, thus helping us think about ourselves as participants in a democracy. Unfortunately, however, these magazines have often identified their readers as consumers first and citizens second. With magazines growing increasingly dependent on advertising, and some of them being primarily *about* the advertising, controversial content sometimes has difficulty finding its way into print. Increasingly, magazines are defining their readers merely as viewers of displayed products and purchasers of material goods.

At the same time, magazines have arguably had more freedom than other media to encourage and participate in democratic debates. More magazine voices circulate in the marketplace than do broadcast or cable television channels. Moreover, many new magazines play an important role in uniting dispersed groups of readers, often giving cultural minorities, newly arrived immigrants, or alternative groups a sense of membership in a broader community. In addition, because magazines are distributed weekly, monthly, or bimonthly, they are less restricted by the deadline pressures experienced by newspaper publishers or radio and television broadcasters. Good magazines can usually offer more analysis of and insight into society than other media outlets can. In the midst of today's swirl of images, magazines and their advertisements certainly contribute to the commotion. But good magazines also maintain our connection to words, sustaining their vital role in an increasingly electronic and digital culture.

9 Chapter Review

One of the Common Threads discussed in Chapter 1 is the commercial nature of mass media. The magazine industry is an unusual example of this. Big media corporations control some of the most popular magazines, and commercialism runs deep in many consumer magazines. At the same time, magazines are one of the most democratic mass media. How can that be?

There are more than twenty thousand magazine titles in the United States. But the largest and most profitable magazines are typically owned by some of the biggest media corporations. Advance Publications, for example, counts *GQ*, the *New Yorker*, *Vanity Fair*, and *Vogue* among its holdings. Even niche magazines that seem small are often controlled by chains. Supermarket tabloids like *Star* and the *National Enquirer* are owned by Florida-based American Media, which also publishes *Muscle & Fitness*, *Men's Fitness*, and *Hers*.

High-revenue magazines, especially those focusing on fashion, fitness, and lifestyle, can also shamelessly break down the firewall between the editorial and business departments. "Fluff" story copy serves as a promotional background for cosmetic, clothing, and gadget advertisements. Many titles in the new generation of online and tablet magazines further break down that firewall; with a single click on a story or an image, readers are linked to an e-commerce site where they can purchase the item they clicked on. Digital retouching makes every model and celebrity thinner or more muscular and always blemish-free. This altered view of their "perfection" becomes our ever-hopeful aspiration, spurring us to purchase the advertised products.

Yet the huge number of magazine titles—more than the number of radio stations, TV stations, cable networks, or yearly Hollywood releases—means that magazines span a huge range of activities and thought. Although some magazines may think of readers as consumers, others view them as citizens—and several hundred new launches each year bring new voices to the marketplace, searching for their own community to serve and sustain.

So there is the glitzy, commercial world of the big magazine industry, with *Time*'s Person of the Year, the latest *Cosmo* girl, and the band on the cover of *Rolling Stone*. But many smaller magazines (like the *Georgia Review*, *Bitch*, and *E—The Environmental Magazine*) account for the majority of magazine titles and the broad democratic spectrum of communities that are their readers.

KEY TERMS

The definitions for the terms listed below can be found in the glossary at the end of the book. The page numbers listed with the terms indicate where the term is highlighted in the chapter.

magazine, 273
muckrakers, 277
general-interest magazines, 277
photojournalism, 277
pass-along readership, 279

supermarket tabloids, 290
branded content, 292
regional editions, 292
split-run editions, 292
demographic editions, 292

evergreen subscriptions, 293
magalogs, 294
zines, 295

REVIEW QUESTIONS

The Early History of Magazines

1. Why did magazines develop later than newspapers in the American colonies?

2. Why did most of the earliest magazines have so much trouble staying financially solvent?

3. How did magazines become national in scope?

4. What was the social impact of the most popular women's magazines in the nineteenth century?

The Development of Modern American Magazines

5. What role did magazines play in social reform at the turn of the twentieth century?

6. When and why did general-interest magazines become so popular?

7. Why did some of the major general-interest magazines fail in the twentieth century?

8. What are the advantages of magazines' movement to digital formats?

The Domination of Specialization

9. What triggered the move toward magazine specialization?

10. What are the most useful ways to categorize the magazine industry? Why?

The Organization and Economics of Magazines

11. What are the four main departments at a typical consumer magazine?

12. How do digital editions of magazines change the format of magazine advertising?

13. What are the differences between regional and demographic editions?

14. What are some of the models for digital distribution of magazines?

15. What are the major magazine chains, and what is their impact on the mass media industry in general?

Magazines in a Democratic Society

16. How do magazines serve a democratic society?

17. How does advertising affect what gets published in the editorial side of magazines?

QUESTIONING THE MEDIA

1. What role did magazines play in America's political and social shift from being colonies of Great Britain to becoming an independent nation?

2. Why is the muckraking spirit—so important in popular magazines at the turn of the twentieth century—generally missing from magazines today?

3. If you were the marketing director at your favorite magazine, how would you increase circulation through the use of digital editions?

4. Think of stories, ideas, and images (illustrations and photos) that do not appear in mainstream magazines.

Why do you think this is so? (Use the Internet, LexisNexis, or the library to compare your list with Project Censored, an annual list of the year's most underreported stories.)

5. Discuss whether your favorite magazines define you primarily as a consumer or as a citizen. Do you think magazines have a responsibility to educate their readers as both? What can they do to promote responsible citizenship?

6. Do you think mobile phone editions will become the dominant format for magazines? Why or why not?

LAUNCHPAD FOR *MEDIA & CULTURE*

Visit LaunchPad for *Media & Culture* at launchpadworks.com for additional learning tools:

- REVIEW WITH LEARNINGCURVE
  LearningCurve, available on LaunchPad for *Media & Culture*, uses gamelike quizzing to help you master the concepts you need to learn from this chapter.

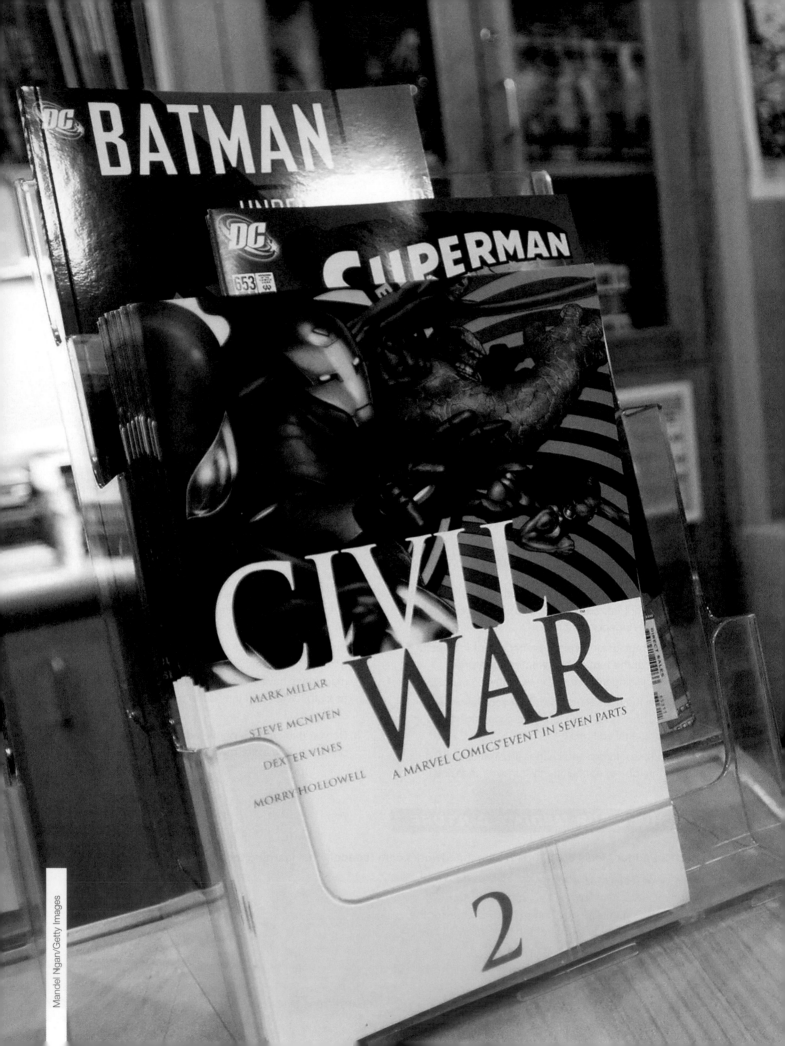

Books and the Power of Print

10

TRADE BOOKS ARE the largest segment of the book industry, and one of the fastest-growing segments within trade books are graphic novels and comics.[1] According to the business consultant NPD Group, "the comics and graphic novels category in the U.S. trade book market has experienced compound annual unit sales growth of 15 percent over the last three years" and has had generally "robust" growth for more than five years.[2] Graphic novels now comprise 6 percent of the U.S. book market.[3]

Although adults sometimes lament that younger people don't read books, "buyers in the 13–29 age group account for 57 percent of purchasing of comics and graphic novels overall," NPD Group reports.[4]

Manga, a graphic style originating in Japan, has the youngest and most racially diverse audience of the graphic novel and comics categories, "with 76 percent of the purchasing being done by those ages 13–29."[5]

THE HISTORY OF BOOKS, FROM PAPYRUS TO PAPERBACKS
p. 301

MODERN PUBLISHING AND THE BOOK INDUSTRY
p. 304

TRENDS AND ISSUES IN BOOK PUBLISHING
p. 309

THE ORGANIZATION AND OWNERSHIP OF THE BOOK INDUSTRY
p. 314

BOOKS AND THE FUTURE OF DEMOCRACY
p. 320

◀ Despite their popularity, graphic novels got snubbed by the *New York Times*, which dropped the graphic novel best-seller list in 2017.

Overall, comics and graphic novels have made a big impact in the book industry and in popular culture, especially as the stories have been transformed into television and movie narratives. Moreover, graphic novelists have received some of the highest honors and cultural acclaim. Graphic novelists Alison Bechdel and Gene Luen Yang have won MacArthur Fellowships, and for the first time, a graphic novel won a National Book Award (*March: Book 3*, the third part of the memoir by Civil Rights leader and U.S. representative John Lewis, awarded in 2016).[6]

Yet people in the graphic novel business have felt dismayed by the *New York Times*' decision in 2017 to drop its graphic novel best-seller lists, which had been in existence for eight years. The *Times*' lists of best-sellers are the most influential in the industry and can increase sales by communicating the most important books of the week. Starting with a single list of best-selling books in 1931, the *Times* now includes weekly lists for Combined Print & E-Book Fiction; Hardcover Fiction; Paperback Trade Fiction; similar categories for nonfiction; a category for Advice, How-To & Miscellaneous; children's and young adult categories; and monthly lists for audio, business, science, and sports and fitness.

In the wake of the *Times* dropping its Hardcover Graphic Novel, Paperback Graphic Novel, and Manga best-seller charts, more than nine hundred people signed a letter in February 2018 asking the *Times*' publisher to "increase coverage of the comics medium and bring back the graphic novel bestseller list."[7]

The *New York Times* best-seller lists are important to the graphic novel industry, argues Susana Polo at *Polygon*. "Historically, comics in newspapers belonged to the gutter of journalistic practices," she explains, dating all the way back to the time of the Yellow Kid, the popular late nineteenth-century comic character over which Joseph Pulitzer and William Randolph Hearst battled to publish in their New York newspapers.[8] The *New York Times* shunned comic strips, treating them as the stuff of the sensationalistic "yellow journalism" newspapers, so named after their fight over the Yellow Kid.

"The mere existence of The New York Times Graphic Novel bestseller lists was evidence of a sea change in the way its audience and its editors viewed sequential art (a fancy umbrella term for comics, comic strips, cartoons and the like)," Polo says.[9] Yet graphic novels and comics, one of the brightest segments of the book industry, are once again getting second-rate treatment from the *Times*.

According to Charlie Olsen, a literary agent for graphic novelists and the organizer of the letter to the *New York Times*, "Comics are a vibrant medium and shouldn't be on the sidelines of the book world."[10]

IN THE 1950s AND 1960s, cultural forecasters thought that the popularity of television might spell the demise of a healthy book industry, just as they thought television would replace the movie, sound recording, radio, newspaper, and magazine industries. Obviously, this did not happen. In 1950, more than 11,000 new book titles were introduced, and by 2014, publishers were producing over eighteen times that number—more than 200,000 titles per year.[11] Despite the absorption of small publishing houses by big media corporations, thousands of publishers—mostly small independents—issue at least one title a year in the United States alone.

Our oldest mass medium is also still our most influential and diverse one. The portability and compactness of books make them the preferred medium in many situations (relaxing at the beach, resting in bed, traveling on buses or commuter trains), and books are still the main repository of history and everyday experience, passing along stories, knowledge, and wisdom from generation to generation.

In this chapter, we consider the long and significant relationship between books and culture.

We will:

- Trace the history of books, from Egyptian papyrus to downloadable e-books
- Examine the development of the printing press and investigate the rise of the book industry, from early publishers in Europe and colonial America to the development of publishing houses in the nineteenth and twentieth centuries
- Review the various types of books, and explore recent trends in the industry—including audio books, the convergence of books onto online platforms, and book digitization
- Consider the economic forces facing the book industry as a whole, from the decline of bookstore chains to the rise of Amazon in the digital age
- Explore how books play a pivotal role in our culture by influencing everything from educational curricula to popular movies

As you read this chapter, think about the pivotal role books have played in your life. What are your earliest recollections of reading? Is there a specific book that considerably influenced the way you think? How do you discover new books? Do you envision yourself reading more books on a phone or tablet in the future, or do you prefer holding a paper copy and leafing through the pages? For more questions to help you understand the role of books in our lives, see "Questioning the Media" in the Chapter Review.

Historical/Getty Images

IN THE EARLY 1950s,
the popularity of crime and horror comics led to a moral panic about their effects on society. Fredric Wertham, a prominent psychiatrist, campaigned against them, claiming they led to juvenile delinquency. Wertham was joined by many religious and parent groups, and Senate hearings were held on the issue. In October 1954, the Comics Magazine Association of America adopted a code of acceptable conduct for publishers of comic books. One of the most restrictive examples of industry self-censorship in mass media history, the code kept the government from legislating its own code or restricting the sale of comic books to minors.

macmillan learning
launchpadworks.com

Visit LaunchPad for *Media & Culture* and use LearningCurve to review concepts from this chapter.

THE HISTORY OF BOOKS, FROM PAPYRUS TO PAPERBACKS

Before books, or writing in general, oral cultures passed on information and values through the wisdom and memories of a community's elders or tribal storytellers. Sometimes these rich traditions were lost. Print culture and the book, however, gave future generations different and often more enduring records of authors' words.

Ever since the ancient Babylonians and Egyptians began experimenting with alphabets some five thousand years ago, people have found ways to preserve their written symbols. These first alphabets mark the development stage for books. Initially, pictorial symbols and letters were drawn on wood strips or pressed with a stylus into clay tablets, then tied or stacked together to form the first "books." As early as 2400 BCE, the Egyptians wrote on **papyrus** (from which the word *paper* is derived), made from plant reeds found along the Nile River. They rolled these writings into scrolls, much as builders do today with blueprints. This method was adopted by the Greeks in 650 BCE and by the Romans (who imported papyrus from Egypt) in 300 BCE. Gradually, **parchment**—treated animal skin—replaced papyrus in Europe. Parchment was stronger, smoother, more durable, and less expensive because it did not have to be imported from Egypt.

At about the same time the Egyptians began using papyrus, the Babylonians recorded business transactions, government records, favorite stories, and local history on small tablets of clay. Around 1000 BCE, the Chinese began creating book-like objects, using strips of wood and bamboo tied together in bundles. Although the Chinese began making paper from cotton and linen around 105 CE, paper did not replace parchment in Europe until the thirteenth century because of questionable durability.

The first protomodern book was probably produced in the fourth century by the Romans, who created the **codex**, a type of book made of sheets of parchment and sewn together along the edge, then bound with thin pieces of wood and covered with leather. Whereas scrolls had to be wound, unwound, and rewound, a codex could be opened to any page, and its configuration allowed writing on both sides of a page.

The Development of Manuscript Culture

During the Middle Ages (400–1500 CE), the Christian clergy strongly influenced what is known as **manuscript culture**, a period in which books were painstakingly lettered, decorated, and bound by hand. This period also marks the entrepreneurial stage in the evolution of books. During this time, priests and monks advanced the art of bookmaking; in many ways, they may be considered the earliest professional editors. Known as *scribes*, they transcribed most of the existing philosophical tracts and religious texts of the period, especially versions of the Bible. Through tedious and painstaking work, scribes became the chief caretakers of recorded history and culture, promoting ideas they favored and censoring ideas that were out of line with contemporary Christian thought.

Many books from the Middle Ages were **illuminated manuscripts**. Often made for churches or wealthy clients, these books featured decorative, colorful designs and illustrations on each page. Their covers were made from leather, and some were embedded with precious gems or trimmed with gold and silver. During this period, scribes developed rules of punctuation, making distinctions between small and capital letters and placing space between words to make reading easier. (Older Roman writing used all capital letters, and the words ran together on a page, making reading a torturous experience.) Hundreds of illuminated manuscripts still survive today in the rare-book collections of museums and libraries.

The Innovations of Block Printing and Movable Type

Whereas the work of the scribes in the Middle Ages led to advances in written language and the design of books, it did not lead to the mass proliferation of books, simply because each manuscript had to be painstakingly created one copy at a time. To make mechanically produced copies of pages, Chinese printers developed **block printing**—a technique in which sheets of paper were applied to blocks of inked wood with raised surfaces depicting hand-carved letters and illustrations—as early as the third century. This constituted the basic technique used in printing newspapers, magazines, and books throughout much of modern history. Although hand-carving each block, or "page," was time consuming, this printing breakthrough enabled multiple copies to be printed and then bound together. The oldest dated printed book still in existence is China's *Diamond Sutra* by Wang Chieh, from 868 CE. It consists of seven sheets pasted together and rolled up in a scroll. In 1295, explorer Marco Polo introduced the block-printing technique to Europe after his excursion to China. The first block-printed books appeared in Europe during the fifteenth century, and demand for them began to grow among the literate middle-class populace emerging in large European cities.

The next step in printing was the radical development of movable type, first invented in China around the year 1000. Movable type featured individual characters made from reusable pieces of wood or metal, rather than entire hand-carved pages. Printers arranged the characters into various word combinations, greatly speeding up the time it took to create block pages. This process, also used in Korea as early as the thirteenth century, developed independently in Europe in the fifteenth century.

The Gutenberg Revolution: The Invention of the Printing Press

Germany inventor Johannes Gutenberg was responsible for the next great leap forward in printing. Between 1453 and 1456, Gutenberg used the principles of movable type to develop a mechanical **printing press**, which he adapted from the design of wine presses. Gutenberg's staff of printers produced the first so-called modern books, including two hundred copies of a Latin Bible, twenty-one copies of which still exist. The Gutenberg Bible (as it's now known) required six presses, many printers, and several months to produce. It was printed on a fine calfskin-based parchment called **vellum**. The pages were hand-decorated, and the use of woodcuts made illustrations possible. Gutenberg and his printing assistants had not only found a way to make books a mass medium but also formed the prototype for all mass production.

Printing presses spread rapidly across Europe in the late fifteenth and early sixteenth centuries. Chaucer's *Canterbury Tales* became the first English work to be printed in book form. Many early books were large, elaborate, and expensive, taking months to illustrate and publish; as such, they were typically purchased by aristocrats, royal families, religious leaders, and ruling politicians. Printers, however, gradually reduced the size of books and developed less expensive grades of paper, making books cheaper so that more people could afford them.

The social and cultural transformations ushered in by the spread of printing presses and books cannot be overestimated. As historian Elizabeth Eisenstein has noted, when people had the means and opportunity to learn for themselves by using maps, dictionaries, Bibles, and the writings of others, they could differentiate themselves as individuals; their social identities were no longer solely dependent on what their leaders told them or on the habits of their families, communities, or social class. The technology of printing presses permitted information and knowledge to spread outside local jurisdictions. Gradually, individuals had access to ideas far beyond their isolated experiences, and this permitted them to challenge the traditional wisdom and customs of their tribes and leaders.[12]

ILLUMINATED MANUSCRIPTS were handwritten by scribes and illustrated with colorful and decorative images and designs.

Fine Art Images/Heritage/The Image Works

The Birth of Publishing in the United States

In colonial America, English locksmith Stephen Daye set up a print shop in the late 1630s in Cambridge, Massachusetts. In 1640, Daye and his son Matthew printed the first colonial book, *The Whole Booke of Psalms* (known today as *The Bay Psalm Book*), marking the beginning of book publishing in the colonies. This collection of biblical psalms quickly sold out its first printing of 1,750 copies, even though fewer than 3,500 families lived in the colonies at the time. By the mid-1760s, all thirteen colonies had printing shops.

The New York Public Library/Art Resource, NY

PULP FICTION

The weekly paperback series *Tip Top Weekly*, published between 1896 and 1912, featured stories of the most popular dime novel hero of the day, the fictional Yale football star and heroic adventurer Frank Merriwell. This issue, from 1905, follows Frank as he battles the "railroad wolves."

In 1744, Benjamin Franklin, who had worked in printing shops, imported Samuel Richardson's *Pamela; or, Virtue Rewarded* (1740) from Britain, the first novel reprinted and sold in colonial America. Both *Pamela* and Richardson's second novel, *Clarissa; or, The History of a Young Lady* (1747), connected with the newly emerging and literate middle classes—especially women, who were just beginning to gain a social identity as individuals apart from their fathers, husbands, and employers. Richardson's novels portrayed women in subordinate roles; however, they also depicted women triumphing over tragedy, so he is credited as one of the first popular writers to take the domestic life of women seriously.

By the early nineteenth century, the demand for books was growing. To meet this demand, the cost of producing books needed to be reduced. By the 1830s, machine-made paper replaced more expensive handmade varieties, cloth covers supplanted more expensive leather ones, and **paperback books** with cheaper paper covers (introduced from Europe) helped make books more accessible to the masses. Further reducing the cost of books, Erastus and Irwin Beadle introduced paperback **dime novels** (so called because they sold for five or ten cents) in 1860. Ann Stephens authored the first dime novel, *Malaeska: The Indian Wife of the White Hunter*, a reprint of a serialized story Stephens wrote in 1839 for the *Ladies' Companion* magazine.[13] By 1870, dime novels had sold seven million copies. By 1885, one-third of all books published in the United States were popular paperbacks and dime novels, sometimes identified as **pulp fiction**—a reference to the cheap, machine-made pulp paper they were printed on.

In addition, the printing process became quicker and more mechanized. In the 1880s, the introduction of **linotype** machines enabled printers to save time by setting type mechanically using a typewriter-style keyboard, while the introduction of steam-powered and high-speed rotary presses permitted the production of more books at a lower cost. In the early 1900s, the development of **offset lithography** allowed books to be printed from photographic plates rather than from metal casts, greatly reducing the cost of color and illustrations and accelerating book production. With these developments, books disseminated further, preserving culture and knowledge and supporting a vibrant publishing industry.

MODERN PUBLISHING AND THE BOOK INDUSTRY

Throughout the nineteenth century, the rapid spread of knowledge and literacy as well as the Industrial Revolution spurred the emergence of the middle class. Its demand for books promoted the development of the publishing industry, which capitalized on increased literacy and widespread compulsory education. Many early publishers were mostly interested in finding quality authors and publishing books of importance. But with the growth of advertising and the rise of a market economy in the latter half of the nineteenth century, publishing gradually became more competitive and more concerned with sales.

The Formation of Publishing Houses

The modern book industry developed gradually in the nineteenth century with the formation of the early "prestigious" publishing houses: companies that tried to identify and produce the works of good writers.[14] Among the oldest American houses established at the time (all are now part of major media conglomerates) were J. B. Lippincott (1792); Harper & Bros. (1817), which became Harper & Row in 1962 and HarperCollins in 1990; Houghton Mifflin (1832); Little, Brown (1837); G. P. Putnam (1838); Scribner's (1842); E. P. Dutton (1852); Rand McNally (1856); and Macmillan (1869).

Between 1880 and 1920, as the center of social and economic life shifted from rural farm production to an industrialized urban culture, the demand for books grew. The book industry also helped assimilate European immigrants to the English language and American culture. In fact, 1910 marked a peak year in the number of new titles produced: 13,470, a record that would not be challenged until the 1950s. These changes marked the emergence of the next wave of publishing houses, as entrepreneurs began to better understand the marketing potential of books. These houses included Doubleday & McClure Company (1897), the McGraw-Hill Book Company (1909), Prentice-Hall (1913), Alfred A. Knopf (1915), Simon & Schuster (1924), and Random House (1925).

Despite the growth of the industry in the early twentieth century, book publishing sputtered from 1910 into the 1950s, as profits were adversely affected by the two world wars and the Great Depression. Radio and magazines fared better because they were generally less expensive and could more immediately cover topical issues during times of crisis. After World War II, the book publishing industry bounced back.

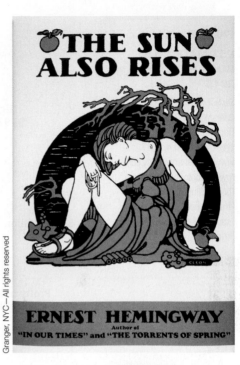

SCRIBNER'S— known more for its magazines in the late nineteenth century than for its books—became the most prestigious literary house of the 1920s and 1930s, publishing F. Scott Fitzgerald (*The Great Gatsby*, 1925) and Ernest Hemingway (*The Sun Also Rises*, 1926).

Types of Books

The divisions of the modern book industry come from economic and structural categories developed by both publishers and trade organizations, such as the Association of American Publishers (AAP), the Book Industry Study Group (BISG), and the American Booksellers Association (ABA). The categories of book publishing that exist today include trade books (both adult and juvenile), professional books, textbooks (both elementary through high school, often called "el-hi," and college), religious books, and university press books. (For sales figures for the book types, see Figure 10.1.)

Trade Books

One of the most lucrative parts of the industry, **trade books** include hardbound and paperback books aimed at general readers and sold at commercial retail outlets. The industry distinguishes among adult trade books (including hardbound and paperback fiction; current nonfiction and biographies; literary classics; books on hobbies, art, and travel; popular science, technology, and computer publications; self-help books; and cookbooks), juvenile books (ranging from preschool picture books to young-adult or young-reader books), and, beginning in 2003, comics and graphic novels. In the changing world of modern trade publishing, young-adult books and graphic novels have boosted the industry. The *Harry Potter* series alone created record-breaking first-press runs: 10.8 million for *Harry Potter and the Half-Blood Prince* (2005), and 12 million for the final book in the series, *Harry Potter and the Deathly Hallows* (2007).

Since the 1978 release of Will Eisner's *A Contract with God*, generally credited as the first graphic novel, interest in graphic novels has grown; in 2006, sales of graphic novels surpassed those of comic books. Given their strong stories and visual nature, many comics and graphic novels—including *X-Men*, *The Dark Knight*, *Watchmen*, and *Captain America*—have inspired movies. But graphic novels aren't only about warriors and superheroes; Maira Kalman's *Principles of Uncertainty* and Alison Bechdel's *Are You My Mother?* are both acclaimed graphic novels, but their characters are regular mortals in real settings.

FIGURE 10.1

ESTIMATED U.S. BOOK REVENUE, 2016

Data from: Jim Milliot, "Trade Sales Were a Bright Spot in a Dark Year for Sales," *Publishers Weekly*, August 4, 2017, www.publishersweekly.com /pw/by-topic/industry-news /bookselling/article/74418 -trade-sales-were-a-bright -spot-in-a-dark-year-for-sales .html.

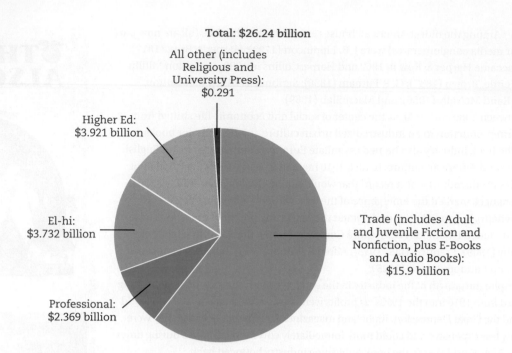

Total: $26.24 billion

All other (includes Religious and University Press): $0.291

Higher Ed: $3.921 billion

El-hi: $3.732 billion

Professional: $2.369 billion

Trade (includes Adult and Juvenile Fiction and Nonfiction, plus E-Books and Audio Books): $15.9 billion

Professional Books

The counterpart to professional trade magazines, **professional books** target various occupational groups and are not intended for the general consumer market. This area of publishing capitalizes on the growth of professional specialization that has characterized the job market. Traditionally, the industry has subdivided professional books into the areas of law, business, medicine, and technical-scientific works, with books in other professional areas accounting for a very small segment. These books are often bought by professional schools and university libraries; however, as a result of stagnating and declining library budgets, professional book sales have declined in recent years.

Textbooks

The most widely read secular book in U.S. history was *The Eclectic Reader*, an elementary-level reading textbook first written by William Holmes McGuffey, a Presbyterian minister and college professor. From 1836 to 1920, more than 100 million copies of this text were sold. Through stories, poems, and illustrations, *The Eclectic Reader* taught nineteenth-century schoolchildren to spell and read simultaneously—and to respect the nation's political and economic systems. Ever since the publication of the McGuffey reader (as it is often nicknamed), **textbooks** have served a nation intent on improving literacy rates and public education. Elementary school textbooks found a solid market niche in the nineteenth century, while college textbooks boomed in the 1950s, when the GI Bill enabled hundreds of thousands of working- and middle-class men returning from World War II to attend college. The demand for textbooks further accelerated in the 1960s, as opportunities for women and minorities expanded. Textbooks are divided into elementary through high school (el-hi) texts, college texts, and vocational texts.

In about half of the states, local school districts determine which el-hi textbooks are appropriate for their students. In the other half of the states, including Texas and California—the two largest states—statewide adoption policies determine which texts can be used. If individual schools choose to use books other than those mandated, they are not reimbursed by the state for their purchases.

Ariel Skelley/Getty Images

TEXTBOOKS
Even though they may not be as much fun to read for some students as, say, graphic novels, textbooks and learning materials are an important part of education today.

Unlike el-hi texts, which are subsidized by various states and school districts, college texts are paid for by individual students (and parents). The cost of textbooks, the markup on used books, and the profit margins of local college bookstores (which in many cases face no on-campus competition) have caused disputes on most college campuses. Yet even as tuition at most colleges and universities has been rising, the price of an academic year's worth of textbooks has been dropping due to the lower cost of digital textbooks and greater access to online retailers and used books. Surveys indicate that each college student spent an average of $579 annually on required course materials in 2016–17, down from $701 during the 2007–08 academic year.[15] As an alternative, some enterprising students have developed social media sites to trade, resell, and rent textbooks. Other students have turned to online purchasing, through e-commerce sites like Amazon, Barnes & Noble, eBay, eCampus.com, and textbooks.com, or renting digital or physical books through companies like Chegg or Campus Book Rentals.

Religious Books

The best-selling book of all time is the Bible, in all its diverse versions. Over the years, the success of Bible sales has created a large industry for religious books. After World War II, sales of religious books soared. Historians attribute the sales boom to economic growth and a nation seeking peace and security while facing the threat of "godless communism" and the Soviet Union.[16] By the 1960s, though, the scene had changed dramatically. The impact of the Civil Rights struggle, the Vietnam War, the sexual revolution, and the youth rebellion against authority led to declines in formal church membership. Not surprisingly, sales of some types of religious books dropped as well. To compete, many religious-book publishers extended their offerings to include serious secular titles on such topics as war and peace, race, poverty, gender, and civic responsibility.

Throughout this period of change, the publication of fundamentalist and evangelical literature remained steady. It then expanded rapidly during the 1980s, when the Republican Party began making political overtures to conservative groups and prominent TV evangelists. Inspirational books in this segment, including Chip and Joanna Gaineses' *The Magnolia Story* (2016), have been top sellers in recent years.

Contemporary Politics Revives Interest in Classic Novels

Just over one week into Donald Trump's presidency, a book nearly seventy years old shot to the top of the best-seller list. The book? George Orwell's *1984*, the dystopian novel that gave us the cultural terms *Big Brother*, *doublethink*, *newspeak*, *thoughtcrime*, and *Orwellian*—the adjective for an authoritative, deceptive surveillance state. The main character, Winston Smith, works in the Ministry of Truth, rewriting old newspaper articles so that they revise history and conform to the party line. Winston starts to have thoughts about rebelling against the political regime, thus committing a thoughtcrime in a world in which every space is monitored electronically with two-way telescreens (which carry images of the leader, Big Brother, and also keep a watchful eye on everyone).

The surge in sales for *1984* came in the days just after White House adviser and former Trump campaign manager Kellyanne Conway used the term "alternative facts" to defend the inaccurate information White House press secretary Sean Spicer gave to the news media. Several media analysts called Conway's use of language "Orwellian."[1] A lot of readers were apparently interested in delving into the notion of "Orwellian," and the book vaulted to the top of Amazon and other best-seller lists. The book's publisher, Signet Classics, reprinted a half million copies of *1984* in one week. "That's more than we sell in a typical year," Signet vice president and executive publicity director Craig Burke noted.[2]

Another book that jumped in sales with the new presidency was Margaret Atwood's classic from 1985, *The Handmaid's Tale*. Atwood's novel, also dystopian, tells the story of the Republic of Gilead, a fundamentalist authoritarian regime that has taken over the United States and imposes strict rule along class, gender, racial, and sexual orientation lines. White men are in control, and women are their property and have no rights. The main character, Offred (meaning "of Fred"—she belongs to the Commander named Fred) is a Handmaid, one of the rare fertile women (in a time when pollution and disease have rendered most infertile) whose function is to produce children for Commanders and their Wives. The Handmaids wear red cloaks with white winged bonnets to shield their faces. Handmaids are "re-educated" by other women, called Aunts, who control and monitor them. "Non-persons" (e.g., racial minorities, people of other religions, and "Unwomen") are sent away to the "Colonies," toxic labor camps where they die a slow death. Like Winston in *1984*, Offred learns of a resistance movement, but it's unclear who to trust.

An estimated 2.6 million people in the United States and around the world participated in the Women's March on January 21, 2017, the day after Trump's inauguration.[3] In Washington, D.C., where the largest of all the marches occurred, people held signs that made the political connection to Atwood's novel, including "Make Margaret Atwood Fiction Again!" and "The Handmaid's Tale is NOT an Instruction Manual!"[4] The book's publisher printed 100,000 additional copies to keep up with demand after Trump's election. The new acclaimed Hulu TV version of *The Handmaid's Tale* in 2017 further boosted sales of the book, although plans to make the book into a series started five years earlier, long before anyone might have predicted a Trump presidency.[5]

Usually it is movies, a television show, or a mention on a talk show that spurs renewed interest in classic books. The fact that a political movement can provide the inspiration to read speaks to the power that books have in addressing ethical debates in our society.

University Press Books

The smallest division in the book industry is the nonprofit **university press**, which publishes scholarly works for small groups of readers interested in intellectually specialized areas, such as literary theory and criticism, history of art movements, and contemporary philosophy. Professors often try to secure book contracts from reputable university presses to increase their chances for *tenure*, a lifetime teaching contract. University presses range in size from very small, often producing fewer than a dozen titles a year, to the largest, Oxford University Press, which publishes more than six thousand titles a year.

University presses have not traditionally faced pressure to produce commercially viable books, preferring to encourage books about highly specialized topics by innovative thinkers. In fact, most university presses routinely lose money and are subsidized by their university. Even when they publish more commercially accessible titles, the lack of large marketing budgets prevents such books from reaching mass audiences. While large commercial trade houses are often criticized for publishing only blockbuster books, university presses often suffer the opposite criticism—that they produce mostly obscure books that only a handful of scholars read. To offset costs and increase revenue, some presses are trying to form alliances with commercial houses to help promote and produce academic books that have wider appeal.

TRENDS AND ISSUES IN BOOK PUBLISHING

Ever since Harriet Beecher Stowe's abolitionist novel *Uncle Tom's Cabin* sold fifteen thousand copies in fifteen days back in 1852 (and three million total copies prior to the Civil War), many American publishers have stalked the *best-seller*, or blockbuster (just like in the movie business). While most authors are professional writers, the book industry also reaches out to famous media figures, who may pen a best-selling book (Anna Kendrick's *Scrappy Little Nobody*, Misty Copeland's *Life in Motion*, Trevor Noah's *Born a Crime*) or a commercial failure (Amy Schumer's *The Girl with the Lower Back Tattoo*). Other ways publishers attempt to ensure popular success include acquiring the rights to license popular film and television programs or experimenting with formats like audio books and e-books. In addition to selling new books, other industry issues include the preservation of older books and the history of banned books and censorship.

Based On: Making Books into Movies
Writers and producers discuss the process that brings a book to the big screen.

Discussion: How is the creative process of writing a novel different from making a movie? Which would you rather do, and why?

Influences of Television and Film

There are two major facets in the relationship among books, television, and film: how TV can help sell books, and how books can serve as ideas for TV shows and movies. Through TV exposure, books by or about talk-show hosts, actors, and politicians, such as Stephen Colbert, John Oliver, Barack and Michelle Obama, and Hillary Clinton, sell millions of copies—enormous numbers in a business in which selling 100,000 copies constitutes remarkable success. In national polls conducted from the 1980s through today, nearly 30 percent of respondents said they had read a book after seeing a story about it or a promotion on television.

One of the most influential forces in promoting books on TV has been Oprah Winfrey. Even before the development of Oprah's Book Club in 1996, Oprah's afternoon talk show had become a major power broker in terms of selling books. In 1993, for example, Holocaust survivor and Nobel Prize recipient Elie Wiesel appeared on *Oprah*. Afterward, his 1960 memoir, *Night*, which had been issued as a Bantam paperback in 1982, returned to the best-seller lists. In 1996, novelist Toni Morrison's nineteen-year-old book *Song of Solomon* became a paperback best-seller after Morrison appeared on *Oprah*. In 1998, after Winfrey brought Morrison's *Beloved* to movie screens, the book version was back on the best-seller lists. Each Oprah's Book Club selection became an immediate

Pictorial Press Ltd/Alamy Stock Photo

**THE 2018 FILM
*A WRINKLE IN TIME,***
based on the 1960s book of
the same name by Madeline
L'Engle, featured a star-studded
cast that included breakout
star Storm Reid, Oprah Winfrey,
Chris Pine, Reese Witherspoon,
and Mindy Kaling. Director
Ava DuVernay became the
first woman of color to direct a
live-action film with a nine-digit
budget.

best-seller, generating tremendous excitement within the book industry. *The Oprah Winfrey Show* ended in 2011, but the book club was revived online in 2012.

The film industry gets many of its story ideas from books (more than 1,450 feature-length movie adaptations in the United States since 1980), which results in enormous movie-rights revenues for the book industry and its authors.[17] Madeleine L'Engle's *A Wrinkle in Time* (1962), W. Bruce Cameron's *A Dog's Purpose* (2010), Ernest Cline's *Ready Player One* (2011), and R. J. Palacio's *Wonder* (2012) are just a few classic and recent books made into movies. The most profitable movie successes for the book industry in recent years emerged from fantasy works. J. K. Rowling's best-selling *Harry Potter* books have become hugely popular movies, as has Peter Jackson's film trilogy of J. R. R. Tolkien's enduringly popular *The Lord of the Rings* (first published in the 1950s). The *Twilight* movie series has created a huge surge in sales of Stephenie Meyer's four-book saga, a success repeated by Suzanne Collins's *Hunger Games* trilogy. Books have also inspired popular television programs, including *Game of Thrones* on HBO and *A Handmaid's Tale* on Hulu. In each case, the television shows boosted the sales of the original books, too (see Examining Ethics: Contemporary Politics Revives Interest in Classic Novels on page 308). Newer adaptations of books to television include Lemony Snicket's (real name Daniel Handler) *A Series of Unfortunate Events* books, featuring Neil Patrick Harris, for Netflix; and Caleb Carr's *The Alienist*, starring Daniel Brühl and Dakota Fanning, for Amazon.

Audio Books

Another major development in publishing has been the merger of sound recording with publishing. *Audio books* generally feature actors or authors reading entire works or abridged versions of popular fiction and nonfiction trade books. Indispensable to many sightless readers and older readers whose vision is diminished, audio books are also popular among readers who do a lot of commuter driving or who want to listen to a book at home while doing something else, like exercising. Audio books are readily available on the Internet for downloading to smartphones and other portable devices; in fact, between 2012 and 2016, book downloads more than doubled in sales.[18] Amazon owns Audible, the largest provider of audio books.

Convergence: Books in the Digital Age

In 1971, Michael Hart, a student computer operator at the University of Illinois, typed up the text of the U.S. Declaration of Independence, and thus the idea of the **e-book**—a digital book read on a computer or a digital reading device—was born. Hart soon founded Project Gutenberg, which now offers more than forty thousand public domain books (older texts with expired copyrights) for free at www.gutenberg.org. However, the idea of *commercial e-books*—putting copyrighted books like current best-sellers in digital form—took a lot longer to gain traction.

Print Books Move Online

In the 1990s, early portable reading devices were criticized for being too heavy, too expensive, or too difficult to read, while their e-book titles were scarce and had little cost advantage over full-price hardcover books. But in 2007, Amazon—the largest online bookseller—developed an e-reader (the Kindle) and an e-book store that seemed inspired by Apple's iPod and iTunes, which changed the music industry. The first Kindle had an easy-on-the-eyes electronic paper display, held more than two hundred books, and did something no other device before could do: wirelessly download e-books from Amazon's online bookstore. Moreover, most Kindle e-books sold for $9.99, less than half the price of most new hardcovers. This time, e-books caught on quickly.

Amazon has continued to refine its e-reader, and in 2011 it introduced the Kindle Fire, a color touchscreen tablet with web browsing, access to all the media on Amazon, and access to Amazon's Appstore. Apps also have transformed the iPod Touch, the iPhone, and other smartphones into e-readers. In 2010, Apple introduced the iPad, a color touchscreen tablet that quickly outsold the Kindle. The immediate initial success of the iPad (introduced at a starting price of $499 and up) spurred other e-readers to drop their prices below $200.

By 2016, e-books accounted for 14 percent of the U.S. trade book market, and 33 percent of the adult fiction category. Yet revenue and unit sales of e-books declined for the third year in 2016, suggesting a limit to reader demand for e-books and a resurgence in sales of printed books.[19]

The Future of E-Books

E-books are demonstrating how digital technology can help the oldest mass medium adapt and survive. Distributors, publishers, and bookstores also use digital technology to print books on demand, reviving books that would otherwise go out of print and avoiding the inconveniences of carrying unsold books. But perhaps the most exciting part of e-books is their potential for reimagining what a book can be. Computers or tablet touchscreens such as an iPad can host e-books with embedded video, hyperlinks, and dynamic content, enabling, for example, a professor to reorganize, add to, or delete the content of an e-textbook to tailor it to the needs of a specific class. Children's books may also never be the same. An *Alice in Wonderland* e-book developed for the iPad uses the device's motion and touchscreen technologies to make "the pop-up book of the 21st-century." Such developments are changing the reading experience: "Users don't just flip the 'pages' of the e-book— they're meant to shake it, turn it, twist it, jiggle it, and watch the characters and settings in the book react."[20] E-books have also made the distribution of long-form journalism and novellas easier with products like the inexpensive Kindle Singles.

Preserving and Digitizing Books

Another recent trend in the book industry involves the preservation of older books, especially those from the nineteenth century printed on acid-based paper, which gradually deteriorates. At the turn of the twentieth century, research initiated by libraries concerned with losing valuable older collections provided evidence that acid-based paper would eventually turn brittle and self-destruct. The paper industry, however, did not respond, so in the 1970s, leading libraries began developing techniques to halt any further deterioration (these processes could not restore books to their original state). Finally, by the early 1990s, motivated almost entirely by economics rather than by the cultural value of books, the paper industry began producing acid-free paper. Libraries and book conservationists, however, still focused their attention on older, at-risk books. Some institutions began photocopying original books onto acid-free paper and making the copies available to the public. Libraries then stored the originals, which were treated to halt further wear.

Sam Abell/Getty Images

E-BOOKS

have opened up many new possibilities for children's books and are even going so far as to redefine how a book looks and acts. The classic *Alice in Wonderland* has been reimagined into a fully interactive experience. You can tilt your iPad to make Alice grow bigger or smaller, and shake your iPad to make the Mad Hatter even madder.

Another way to preserve books is through digital imaging. The most extensive digitization project is Google Books, which began in 2004 and features partnerships with the New York Public Library and about twenty major university research libraries—including Harvard, Michigan, Oxford, and Stanford—to scan millions of books and make them available online. The Authors Guild and the Association of American Publishers initially sued Google for digitizing copyrighted books without permission. Google argued that displaying only a limited portion of the books was legal under fair-use rules. After years of legal battles, a U.S. Court of Appeals sided with Google's fair-use argument in 2013 and dismissed the lawsuit. The Authors Guild vowed to appeal the decision. An alternative group, dissatisfied by Google Books' restriction of its scanned book content from use by other commercial search services, started a nonprofit service in 2007. The Internet Archive's Open Library works with the Boston Public Library, several university libraries, Amazon, Microsoft, and Yahoo! to digitize millions of books with expired copyrights and make them freely available at openlibrary.org. In 2008, another group of universities formed the HathiTrust Digital Library to further archive and share digital collections. In 2010, these nonprofit archives joined other libraries to create the Digital Public Library of America.

Censorship and Banned Books

Over time, the wide circulation of books gave many ordinary people the same opportunities to learn that were once available to only the privileged few. However, as societies discovered the power associated with knowledge and the printed word, books were subjected to a variety of censors. Imposed by various rulers and groups intent on maintaining their authority, the censorship of books often prevented people from learning about the rituals and moral standards of other cultures. Political censors sought to banish "dangerous" books that promoted radical ideas or challenged conventional authority. In various parts of the world, some versions of the Bible, Karl Marx's *Das Kapital* (1867), *The Autobiography of Malcolm X* (1965), and Salman Rushdie's *The Satanic Verses* (1989) have all been banned at one time or another. In fact, one of the triumphs of the Internet is that it allows the digital passage of banned books into nations where printed versions have been outlawed. (For more on banned books, see "Media Literacy and the Critical Process: Banned Books and 'Family Values'" on page 314.)

Each year, the American Library Association (ALA) compiles a list of the most challenged books in the United States. Unlike an enforced ban, a **book challenge** is a formal request to have a book removed from a public or school library's collection. Common reasons for challenges include sexually explicit passages, offensive language, occult themes, violence, homosexual themes, promotion of a religious viewpoint, nudity, and racism. (The ALA defends the right of libraries to offer material with a wide range of views and does not support removing material on the basis of partisan or doctrinal disapproval.) Some of the most challenged books of the past decade include *I Know Why the Caged Bird Sings* by Maya Angelou, *Forever* by Judy Blume, the *Harry Potter* series by J. K. Rowling, and the *Captain Underpants* series by Dav Pilkey.

Buenos Aires, the World's Bookstore Capital

Buenos Aires, Argentina, has more bookstores per capita than any other city in the world, about 700, or about 25 per 100,000 people.[1] By comparison, Madrid has 16 bookstores per 100,000 people, Tokyo has 13, London has 10, Paris and New York each have 9, Amsterdam and Berlin each have 7, Los Angeles and Rio de Janeiro each have 5, Mumbai has 4, and Singapore has 3.

Buenos Aires also has some of the best bookstores in the world, including El Ateneo Gran Splendid. A former theater palace built in 1919, the ornate building was repurposed as a bookstore in 2007. The main floor and balconies are filled with bookshelves; the former theater boxes are now reading nooks; and the stage, framed by a crimson curtain, is a café. Juan Pablo Marciani, manager of El Ateneo, says books are a significant part of Argentinian culture: "Books represent us like the tango. We have a culture very rooted in print."[2] So how did Buenos Aires come to have such a bookish culture?

Partly it's due to chance; the country's literary community grew and flourished with the influx of Spanish writers and publishers who fled to Argentina during the Spanish Civil War in the 1930s. It is also because of choice: Argentina doesn't charge sales tax on books. Heavy taxes on e-readers and tablets have kept e-book use low, too.[3] The local bookstore industry is also helped by the fact that Amazon.com doesn't have a retail website in Argentina. Even if Argentina did have Amazon, it's likely that the company wouldn't gain the dominant foothold it now has in the United States and the United Kingdom in digital and print book sales.

The main reason behind the country's thriving bookstore culture, though, is that Argentina has fixed book pricing (FBP). Thirteen other countries have FBP as well: Austria, France, Germany, Greece, Italy, Japan, Lebanon, the Netherlands, Norway, Portugal, Slovenia, South Korea, and Spain. FBP rules among countries vary, but they generally require bookstores to limit price discounts during the first six months to two years following the release of a book. The rules usually apply to digital books as well. The effect is that all bookstores in a country sell the latest titles for roughly the same price, even digital books. Countries without FBP tend to have large book chains and Internet retailers, which can offer deep discounts on new releases and easily dominate the market.[4] In the United States, Amazon used the Internet to change the distribution rules and undercut the brick-and-mortar bookstores.

The effect of FBP can be seen when comparing the number of independent bookstores in various countries. The United Kingdom, which gave up FBP in the late 1990s, has lost one-third of its bookstores since 2005, and independents represent only about 4 percent of the bookseller market. In France, however (which has FBP), independent booksellers represent 22 percent of the market. France has about twenty-five hundred booksellers, more than the nineteen hundred booksellers in the United States, even though France is five times smaller in population.[5]

Catherine Blache of the French Publishers Association explains that in France, "booksellers compete not on price, therefore, but in terms of the variety of books they offer, their location and the quality of their customer service."[6] This is what the Buenos Aires bookselling market looks like, too. *Travel + Leisure* magazine recommends this special feature of life in Argentina's capital. "Buenos Aires is bursting with bookstores. . . . Enjoy the land that Amazon forgot."[7]

MEDIA LITERACY AND THE CRITICAL PROCESS

Banned Books and "Family Values"

In *Free Speech for Me—but Not for Thee: How the American Left and Right Relentlessly Censor Each Other*, Nat Hentoff writes that "the lust to suppress can come from any direction." Indeed, *Ulysses* by James Joyce, *The Scarlet Letter* by Nathaniel Hawthorne, *Leaves of Grass* by Walt Whitman, *The Diary of a Young Girl* by Anne Frank, *Lolita* by Vladimir Nabokov, and *To Kill a Mockingbird* by Harper Lee have all been banned by some U.S. community, school, or library at one time or another. In fact, the most censored book in U.S. history is Mark Twain's *The Adventures of Huckleberry Finn*, the 1884 classic that still sells tens of thousands of copies each year. Often, the impulse behind calling for a book's banishment is to protect children in the name of a community's "family values."

1 DESCRIPTION

Identify two contemporary books that have been challenged in two separate communities. (Check the American Library Association's Banned and Challenged Books website [www.ala.org/advocacy/bbooks] for information on the most frequently challenged books.) Describe the communities involved and what sparked the challenges. Describe the issues at stake and the positions students, teachers, parents, administrators, citizens, religious leaders, and politicians took with regard to the books. Discuss what happened and the final outcomes.

2 ANALYSIS

What patterns emerge? What are the main arguments given for censoring the books? What are the main arguments of those defending

these particular books? Are there any middle-ground positions or unusual viewpoints raised in your book controversies? Did these communities take similar or different approaches when dealing with these books?

3 INTERPRETATION

Why did these issues arise? What do you think are the actual reasons why people would challenge or ban a book? (For example, can you tell whether people seem genuinely concerned about protecting young readers or are just personally offended by particular books?) How do people handle book banning and issues raised by First Amendment protections of printed materials?

4 EVALUATION

Who do you think is right and wrong in these controversies? Why?

5 ENGAGEMENT

Read the two challenged books. Then write a book review and publish it in a student or local paper, on a blog, or on Facebook. Using social media, post a link to the ALA's list of challenged books, and encourage people to read and review them.

THE ORGANIZATION AND OWNERSHIP OF THE BOOK INDUSTRY

Compared with other mass media industries, book publishing has adapted to the digital turn and has been able to avoid huge declines in revenues. From the mid-1980s to 2016, total revenue rose from $9 billion to about $26.24 billion.[21] Within the industry, the concept of who or what constitutes a publisher varies widely. A publisher may be a large company that is a subsidiary of a global media conglomerate and occupies an entire office building, or a one-person home office operation that uses a laptop computer.

FIGURE 10.3

CHALLENGED AND
BANNED BOOKS

Ownership Patterns

Like most mass media, commercial publishing is dominated by a handful of major corporations with ties to international media conglomerates. Mergers and consolidations have driven the book industry. For example, the world's largest publisher is Pearson, based in the U.K. Pearson established its book business in the 1920s and at one point owned the *Financial Times*, a 50 percent share in the *Economist* magazine, and nearly half of Penguin Random House (PRH)—the largest trade book publisher in the world. But in 2015, Pearson committed its focus to the el-hi, college, and professional publishing business, and is deeply involved in publishing textbooks, digital materials, and assessment exams for the education market.

Germany's Bertelsmann shook up the book industry by adding Random House, the largest U.S. book publisher, to its fold for $1.4 billion. Bertelsmann's book company subsidiaries include Ballantine Bantam Dell, Doubleday Broadway, Alfred A. Knopf, and the Random House Publishing Group. In 2013, Random House merged with Penguin Books (then owned by Pearson), creating Penguin Random House, the largest trade book publisher (see Table 10.1). Bertelsmann also owns large European magazine and television divisions.

TABLE 10.1

WORLD'S FIFTEEN LARGEST BOOK PUBLISHERS (REVENUE IN MILLIONS OF DOLLARS), 2017

Data from: Jim Milliot, "The World's 54 Largest Publishers, 2017," *Publishers Weekly,* August 25, 2017, www.publishersweekly.com/pw/by-topic/international/international-book-news/article/74505-the-world-s-50-largest-publishers-2017.html.

Rank 2017	Rank 2016	Publishing Group or Division	Parent Company	Parent Country	2016 Revenue (in $M)	2015 Revenue (in $M)
1	1	Pearson	Pearson PLC	UK	$5,617	$6,625
2	3	RELX Group	Reed Elsevier PLC & Reed Elsevier NV	UK/NL/US	$4,864	$5,209
3	2	ThomsonReuters	The Woodbridge Company	Canada	$4,819	$5,776
4	not listed	Bertelsmann	Bertelsmann AG	Germany	$3,697	$5,259
5	4	Wolters Kluwer	Wolters Kluwer	NL	$3,384	$4,592
6	8	Hachette Livre	Lagardère	France	$2,390	$2,407
7	10	Grupo Planeta	Grupo Planeta	Spain	$1,889	$1,809
8	9	McGraw-Hill Education	Apollo Global Management	US	$1,757	$1,835
9	11	Wiley	Wiley	US	$1,727	$1,822
10	15	Springer Nature	Springer Nature	Germany	$1,715	$1,605
11	14	Scholastic	Scholastic	US	$1,673	$1,636
12	12	HarperCollins	News Corp.	US	$1,646	$1,667
13	13	Cengage Learning Holdings II	Apax and Omers Capital Partners	US/Canada	$1,631	$1,633
14	16	Houghton Mifflin Harcourt	Houghton Mifflin Harcourt Company	US/Cayman Islands	$1,373	$1,416
15	19	Holtzbrinck	Verlagsgruppe Georg	Germany	$1,226	$1,231

Penguin Random House, Simon & Schuster (owned by CBS), Hachette (owned by French-based Lagardère), HarperCollins (owned by News Corp.), and Macmillan (owned by German-based Holtzbrinck) are the five largest trade book publishers in the United States. From a corporate viewpoint, executives have argued that large companies can financially support a number of smaller firms or imprints while allowing their editorial ideas to remain independent from the parent corporation. With thousands of independent presses competing with bigger corporations, book publishing continues to produce volumes on an enormous range of topics. Still, the largest trade book publishers and independents alike find themselves struggling in the face of the industry's digital upheaval and the dominance of Amazon in the distribution of books.

The Structure of Book Publishing

A small publishing house may be staffed with a few to twenty people. Medium-size and large publishing houses employ hundreds of people. In the larger houses, divisions usually include acquisitions and development; copyediting, design, and production; marketing and sales; and administration and business. Unlike daily newspapers but similar to magazines, most publishing houses contract independent printers to produce their books.

Most publishers employ **acquisitions editors** to seek out and sign authors to contracts. For fiction, this might mean discovering talented writers through book agents or reading unsolicited manuscripts. For nonfiction, editors might examine manuscripts and letters of inquiry or match a known writer to a project (such as a celebrity biography). Acquisitions editors also handle **subsidiary rights** for an author—that is, selling the rights to a book for use in other media, such as the basis for a screenplay.

As part of their contracts, writers sometimes receive *advance money*, an early payment that is subtracted from royalties earned from book sales. Typically, an author's royalty is between 5 and 15 percent of the net price of the book. Amazon and book publishers have been experimenting with different price points for e-books—low enough to ensure good online sales but high enough to make publishing still profitable. Thus, while an author's royalty percentage may be much higher for e-books, it's a percentage of a lower book price. New authors may receive little or no advance from a publisher, but commercially successful authors can receive millions. For example, author J. K. Rowling hauled

TWO FEUDING BUNNY BOOKS,

Marlon Bundo's Day in the Life of the Vice President (left) written by Mike Pence's daughter Charlotte and illustrated by his wife Karen, and *A Day in the Life of Marlon Bundo* (right) written by comedian John Oliver, tell two very different stories of a familiar White House bunny. John Oliver's parody book, which was released the day before the Pences' book and outstripped it in sales, tells the story of a gay Marlon Bundo who falls in love with a boy bunny named Wesley. Proceeds of Oliver's book, which is dedicated "to every bunny who has ever felt different," are being donated to AIDS United and the LGBTQ charity the Trevor Project.

in an estimated $7 million advance from Little, Brown & Company/Hachette for *The Casual Vacancy* (2012), her first novel after the *Harry Potter* series. Nationally recognized authors—including political leaders, sports figures, comedians, or movie stars—can also command large advances from publishers who are banking on the well-known person's commercial potential. For example, fresh off their television series *The Office*, Mindy Kaling and B.J. Novak received a reported $7.5 million advance from Penguin Random House in 2015 to collaborate on a book.

After a contract is signed, the acquisitions editor may turn the book over to a **developmental editor**, who provides the author with feedback, makes suggestions for improvements, and, in educational publishing, obtains advice from knowledgeable members of the academic community. If a book contains images, editors work with photo researchers to select photographs and pieces of art. Then the production staff enters the picture. While **copy editors** attend to specific problems in writing or length, production and **design managers** work on the look of the book, making decisions about type style, paper, cover design, and layout.

Simultaneously, plans are under way to market and sell the book. Decisions need to be made concerning the number of copies to print, ways to reach potential readers, and costs for promotion and advertising. For trade books and some scholarly books, publishing houses may send advance copies of a book to appropriate magazines and newspapers with the hope of receiving favorable reviews that can be used in promotional material. Prominent trade writers typically have book signings and travel the radio and TV talk-show circuit to promote their books. Unlike trade publishers, college textbook firms rarely sell directly to bookstores. Instead, they contact instructors through direct-mail brochures or sales representatives assigned to geographic regions.

To help create a best-seller, trade houses often distribute large illustrated cardboard bins, called *dumps*, to thousands of stores to display a book in bulk quantity. Like food merchants who buy eye-level shelf placement for their products in supermarkets, large trade houses buy shelf space from major chains to ensure prominent locations in bookstores. Similarly, publishers are required to pay (co-op payments) for featured treatment on Amazon. Publishers also buy ad space in newspapers and magazines and on buses, billboards, television, radio, and the web—all in an effort to generate interest in a new book.

INDEPENDENT BOOKSTORES

City Lights Books in San Francisco is both an independent bookstore and an independent publisher, publishing nearly two hundred titles since launching in 1955, including poet Allen Ginsberg's revolutionary work *Howl*. Customers from around the world now come to browse through the landmark store's three floors and to see the place where beatniks like Ginsberg got their start.

Selling Books: Book Superstores and Independent Booksellers

Traditionally, the final part of the publishing process involves the business and order fulfillment stages—shipping books to thousands of commercial outlets and college bookstores. Warehouse inventories are monitored to ensure that enough copies of a book will be available to meet demand. Anticipating such demand, though, is tricky. No publisher wants to be caught short if a book becomes more popular than originally predicted or get stuck with books it cannot sell, as publishers must absorb the cost of returned books. Independent bookstores, which tend to order more carefully, return about 20 percent of books ordered; in contrast, mass merchandisers such as Walmart, Sam's Club, Target, and Costco, which routinely overstock popular titles, often return up to 40 percent. Returns this high can have a serious impact on a publisher's bottom line. For years, publishers have talked about doing away with the practice of allowing bookstores to return unsold books to the publisher for credit.

Today, about fifteen thousand outlets sell books in the United States, including traditional bookstores, department stores, drugstores, used-book stores, and toy stores. Shopping-mall bookstores strengthened book sales beginning in the late 1960s. But it was the development of book superstores in the 1980s that truly reinvigorated the business. Following the success of a single Borders store established in Ann Arbor, Michigan, in 1971, a number of book chains began developing book superstores to cater to suburban areas as well as avid readers. A typical Barnes & Noble superstore stocks up to 200,000 titles. As superstores expanded, they began to sell music and coffee. Superstores like Border and Barnes & Noble began to push out small, independent bookstores. (In the 1998 movie *You've Got Mail*, Tom Hanks's giant corporate bookstore threatens Meg Ryan's independent bookshop.) In fact, between 1995 and 2000, 43 percent of independent bookstores in the United States closed.[22] Yet the next wave of bookselling had already arrived. As Amazon (established 1995) grew as an online bookseller, Borders lost business and closed its last brick-and-mortar store in 2011. Barnes & Noble became the last national bookstore retail chain in the United States, operating 630 bookstores. By 2018, book sales continued to fall at Barnes & Noble stores, leading a *New York Times* columnist to conclude, "It's depressing to imagine that more than 600 Barnes & Noble stores might simply disappear. . . . But the death of Barnes & Noble is now plausible."[23]

As the superstores fell on hard times, an amazing thing happened: independent bookstores came back. From 2009 to 2018, there has been an almost 40 percent increase in the number of independent bookstores. A professor at the Harvard Business School says the success of independent bookstores are in the three Cs: community (responding to the distinct local needs of the place), curation (providing a thoughtfully selected inventory for customers), and convening (making the store a place for meetings, reading groups, events, and even parties).[24]

Selling Books Online

Since the late 1990s, online booksellers have created an entirely new book distribution system on the Internet. The strength of online sellers lies in their convenience and low prices, and especially their ability to offer backlist titles and the works of less famous authors that retail stores aren't able to carry on their shelves. Online customers are also drawn to the interactive nature of these sites, which allow readers to post their own book reviews, read those of fellow customers, and receive book recommendations based on book searches and past purchases.

The trailblazer is Amazon, established in 1995 by then thirty-year-old Jeff Bezos, who left Wall Street to start a web-based business. Bezos realized that books were an untapped and ideal market for the Internet, with more than three million publications in print and plenty of distributors to fulfill orders. He moved to Seattle and started Amazon, so named because search engines like Yahoo! listed categories in alphabetical order, putting Amazon near the top of the list. In 1997, Barnes & Noble, the leading retail store bookseller, launched its own online book site, BN.com. The site's success, however, remains dwarfed by Amazon.

Beyond selling books, Amazon's bigger objective was to transform the entire book industry itself, from one based on bound paper volumes to one based on digital files. The introduction of the Kindle in 2007 made Amazon the fastest book delivery system in the world. Instead of going to a bookstore or ordering from Amazon and waiting for the book to be delivered in a box, one could buy a digital version in a few seconds from the Amazon store. Amazon quickly grew to control 90 percent of the e-book market, which it used as leverage to force book publishers to comply with its low prices or risk getting dropped from Amazon's bookstore (something that has happened to several independent book publishers who complained).[25] Amazon has done the same in print book sales, where it is also a major player.

Amazon's price slashing caused most of the major trade book publishing corporations to endorse Apple's agency-model pricing, in which the publishers set the book prices and the digital bookseller gets a 30 percent commission. When the U.S. Department of Justice ruled in 2013 that Apple and the major publishers had colluded to set book prices (thus denying consumers the lower prices that Amazon's deep discounts might offer), the booksellers responded that government investigators should be more concerned about Amazon. Of particular concern to publishers is that Amazon has been expanding into the domain of traditional publishers with the establishment of Amazon Publishing, which has grown rapidly since 2009. With a publishing arm that can sign authors to book contracts, distribution provided by the Amazon store, and millions of Kindle devices in the hands of readers, Amazon is becoming a vertically integrated company and a too-powerful entity, traditional publishers fear. Amazon ultimately agreed with the five major book publishers in 2014 and let them set e-book prices. At the same time, Amazon began undercutting the major publishers' e-books (often costing $12.99 to $14.99) with e-books from independent publishers or from its own in-house publishing business, which typically cost from $2.99 to $5.99.

Amazon's biggest rivals in the digital book business are those with their own tablet devices. Apple has its iBook Store, which is available for iPads and iPhones through an app in the iTunes store.

Google Play, Google's digital media store, combines newly released and backlist books, along with the out-of-print titles that Google has been digitizing since 2004. Google also introduced its Nexus 7 tablet in 2012 to promote its store. Barnes & Noble has been less successful in shoring up its flagging brick-and-mortar bookstores with its Nook device and online store. The Kobo e-book device, introduced in 2010 by a Toronto-based company, has become the most popular e-book device in Canada and is making some inroads with independent booksellers in the United States.

By 2017, Amazon still dominated the U.S. e-book market, with a 79.6 percent share of sales, while Apple iBooks accounted for 12 percent; B&N Nook, 4.2 percent; Google 1.9 percent; Kobo, 0.3 percent; and others, 2.1 percent.[26] Moreover, Amazon dominates in print books, selling 45.5 percent of U.S. print books in 2017.[27]

Alternative Voices

Even though the book industry is dominated by large book publishers and one big online retailer (Amazon), there are still alternatives for both publishing and selling books. One idea is to make books freely available to everyone. This idea is not a new one; in the late nineteenth and early twentieth centuries, industrialist Andrew Carnegie used millions of dollars from his vast steel fortune to build more than twenty-five hundred public libraries in the United States, Britain, Australia, and New Zealand. Carnegie believed that libraries created great learning opportunities for citizens, especially for immigrants like himself.

One Internet source, NewPages, is offering another alternative to conglomerate publishing and chain bookselling by bringing together a vast array of alternative and university presses, independent bookstores, and guides to literary and alternative magazines. The site's listing of independent publishers, for example, includes hundreds, mostly based in the United States and Canada, ranging from Academy Chicago Publishers (which publishes a range of fiction and nonfiction books) to Zubaan (an imprint of South Asia's first feminist publishing house).

Finally, because e-books make publishing and distribution costs low, **e-publishing** has enabled authors to sidestep traditional publishers. A new breed of large Internet-based publishing houses, such as Xlibris, iUniverse, Hillcrest Media, Amazon's CreateSpace, and Author Solutions, design and distribute books for a comparatively small price for aspiring authors who want to self-publish a title, which can even be formatted for the Kindle or iPad. Although sales are typically low for such books, the low overhead costs allow higher royalty rates for the authors and lower retail prices for readers.

Sometimes self-published books make it to the best-seller lists. British writer E. L. James's blockbuster erotic novel *Fifty Shades of Grey* was written as fan fiction and posted to a busy *Twilight* fan forum beginning in 2009, where thousands read and commented on it. In 2012, Vintage bought the rights to the *Fifty Shades* trilogy for more than $1 million. Some traditional publishers are considering the straight-to-e-book route themselves. Little, Brown & Company released Pete Hamill's *They Are Us* in digital format only.

AMAZON'S WAREHOUSES go far beyond the stockrooms of a typical brick-and-mortar store, housing more than one hundred employees at each location, of which there are dozens across the United States and around the world. Though Amazon still uses these warehouses to support its massive fulfillment needs, it owns a lot of virtual businesses, too, including cloud storage, e-publishing, e-commerce sites like Zappos, and social media like Goodreads, which Amazon bought in 2013.

Sean Gallup/Getty Images

BOOKS AND THE FUTURE OF DEMOCRACY

As we enter the digital age, the book-reading habits of children and adults have become a social concern. After all, books have played an important role not only in spreading the idea of democracy but also in connecting us to new ideas beyond our local experience. The impact of our oldest mass medium—the book—remains immense. Without the development of printing presses and books, the idea of

Randy Duchaine / Alamy Stock Photo

democracy would be hard to imagine. From Harriet Beecher Stowe's *Uncle Tom's Cabin*, which helped bring an end to slavery in the 1860s, to Rachel Carson's *Silent Spring*, which led to reforms in the pesticide industry in the 1960s, books have made a difference. They have told us things that we wanted—and needed—to know, and they have inspired us to action. And, despite what some people might believe, Americans are still reading books. A Pew Research Center study found that 76 percent of Americans age eighteen and older had read at least one book in the past year. Moreover, they experience books across several formats: 69 percent read a book in print, 28 percent read an e-book, and 14 percent listened to an audio book. Among all Americans, the average number of books read per year is twelve, and the median is five (that is, half of adults read more than five books, half read fewer). Although some might conclude that the proliferation of digital devices has drawn readers away from books, Pew reported that the rate of book reading in the United States has not changed significantly from previous years. Although reading e-books is on the rise, only 4 percent read only e-books. Print books have a more dedicated audience: 52 percent of readers read only print books. Finally, despite the concerns of some that young adults are rejecting reading, the Pew study found "no significant differences by age group for rates of reading overall." The only difference in age was the tendency toward reading format: Young adults are more likely to read e-books than are those over age sixty-five.[28]

Although there is a sustained interest in books, many people are concerned about their quality. Often, editors and executives prefer to invest in commercially successful authors or those who have a built-in television, sports, or movie audience. In his book *The Death of Literature*, Alvin Kernan argues that serious literary work has been increasingly overwhelmed by the triumph of consumerism. People jump at craftily marketed celebrity biographies and popular fiction, he argues, but seldom read serious works. He contends that cultural standards have been undermined by marketing ploys that divert attention away from serious books and toward mass-produced works that are more easily consumed.[29]

Yet books and reading have survived the challenge of visual and digital culture. Developments such as digital publishing, audio books, graphic novels, and online services have integrated aspects of print and electronic culture into our daily lives. Most of these new forms carry on the legacy of books, transcending borders to provide personal stories, world history, and general knowledge to all who can read.

Since the early days of the printing press, books have helped us understand ideas and customs outside our own experiences. For democracy to work well, we must read. When we examine other cultures through books, we discover not only who we are and what we value but also who others are and what our common ties might be.

10 Chapter Review

One of the Common Threads discussed in Chapter 1 is the commercial nature of mass media. Books have been products of a publishing industry in the United States since at least the early nineteenth century, but with the advent of digital technologies, the structure of the publishing industry is either evolving or dying. Is this a good or bad thing for the future of books?

Since the popularization of Gutenberg's printing press, there has always been some kind of gatekeeper in the publishing industry. Initially, it was religious institutions (which, for example, determined what would constitute the books of the Bible), then intellectuals, educators, and—with the development of publishing houses in the early nineteenth century—a fully formed commercial publishing industry.

Now, with the digital turn in publishing, anyone can be an author. Clay Shirky, a digital theorist at New York University, argues that this completely undercuts the work of publishers. "Publishing is going away," Shirky says. "Because the word 'publishing' means a cadre of professionals who are taking on the incredible difficulty and complexity and expense of making something public.

That's not a *job* anymore. That's a *button*. There's a button that says 'publish,' and when you press it, it's done."[30] Indeed, self-publishing is already a huge part of what the industry has become. As the *New York Times* noted in 2012, "Nearly 350,000 new print titles were published in 2011, and 150,000 to 200,000 of them were produced by self-publishing companies."[31]

An increase in the number of books in circulation is great for democracy in that it includes a multitude of voices. But is there still value to the acquisition, editing, and marketing of books that publishers do? Are these traditional gate-keepers worth keeping around? Is it a legitimate concern that the quality of book content will suffer without publishers to find, develop, and promote the work of the best authors?

KEY TERMS

The definitions for the terms listed below can be found in the glossary at the end of the book. The page numbers listed with the terms indicate where the term is highlighted in the chapter.

papyrus, 302
parchment, 302
codex, 302
manuscript culture, 302
illuminated manuscripts, 302
block printing, 302
printing press, 303
vellum, 303
paperback books, 304

dime novels, 304
pulp fiction, 304
linotype, 304
offset lithography, 304
trade books, 305
professional books, 306
textbooks, 306
university press, 309
e-book, 310

book challenge, 312
acquisitions editors, 316
subsidiary rights, 316
developmental editor, 317
copy editors, 317
design managers, 317
e-publishing, 320

REVIEW QUESTIONS

The History of Books, from Papyrus to Paperbacks

1. What distinguishes the manuscript culture of the Middle Ages from the oral and print eras in communication?

2. Why was the printing press such an important and revolutionary invention?

3. Why were books particularly important to women readers during the early periods of American history?

Modern Publishing and the Book Industry

4. Why did publishing houses develop?

5. Why is the trade book segment one of the most lucrative parts of the book industry?

6. What factors have been causing a decline in the cost of an academic year's worth of college textbooks?

Trends and Issues in Book Publishing

7. What is the relationship between the book and movie industries?

8. Why did the Kindle succeed in the e-book market where other devices had failed?

9. In what ways have e-books reimagined what a book can be?

10. What are the major issues in the debate over digitizing millions of books for web search engines?

The Organization and Ownership of the Book Industry

11. What are the general divisions within a typical publishing house?

12. How have online booksellers affected bookstores and the publishing industry?

13. What are the concerns over Amazon's powerful role in determining book pricing and having its own publishing division?

14. What is Andrew Carnegie's legacy in regard to libraries in the United States and elsewhere?

Books and the Future of Democracy

15. Why is an increasing interest in reading a signal for improved democratic life?

QUESTIONING THE MEDIA

1. As books shift to digital formats, what advantages of the bound-book format are we sacrificing?

2. Given the digital turn in the book industry, if you were to self-publish a book, what strategies would you use in marketing and distribution to help an audience find it?

3. Imagine that you are on a committee that oversees book choices for a high school library in your town.

What policies do you think should guide the committee's selection of controversial books?

4. What is the cultural significance of a bound volume, particularly a religious holy book, such as the Bible or the Qur'an? If holy books are in digital form, does the format change their meaning?

LAUNCHPAD FOR *MEDIA & CULTURE*

Visit LaunchPad for *Media & Culture* at launchpadworks.com for additional learning tools:

- REVIEW WITH LEARNINGCURVE
  LearningCurve, available on LaunchPad for *Media & Culture*, uses gamelike quizzing to help you master the concepts you need to learn from this chapter.

PART 4

The Business of Mass Media

The digital turn has brought about a shift in the locus of power in the mass media. For decades, the mass media have been dominated by giant corporations. Now a new digital market has grown up around them, displacing the way traditional mass media work and breaking down the barriers of entry to start-up media companies:

- **Changes in the structure of media economics.** In just a few short years, legacy media companies have lost some of their power due to the rise of major digital companies, which are the new media conglomerates. Traditional media companies now find themselves in a position in which they have to work with these companies or risk losing their audience.

- **The new digital ecosystem for advertising and public relations.** Professional media communicators are negotiating new terrain in the digital age, too, figuring out what kinds of advertising or PR campaigns work best in the age of social media and mobile devices. This new environment can be both good and bad. Everyone on the Internet is a potential customer but also a potential public critic.

- **Democracy and the redistribution of power.** The digital turn has allowed more voices to participate in various media industries. Content creators can now enter the marketplace more easily: It's simple to get songs listed in the iTunes store, books placed in the Amazon catalog, and videos posted to YouTube.

LaunchPad
macmillan learning

Visit **LaunchPad** for *Media & Culture* to explore an interactive time line of the history of mass communication, practice your media literacy skills, test your knowledge of the concepts in the textbook with LearningCurve, explore and discuss current trends in mass communication with video activities and video assessment tools, and more.

THE BIG FIVE DIGITAL COMPANIES

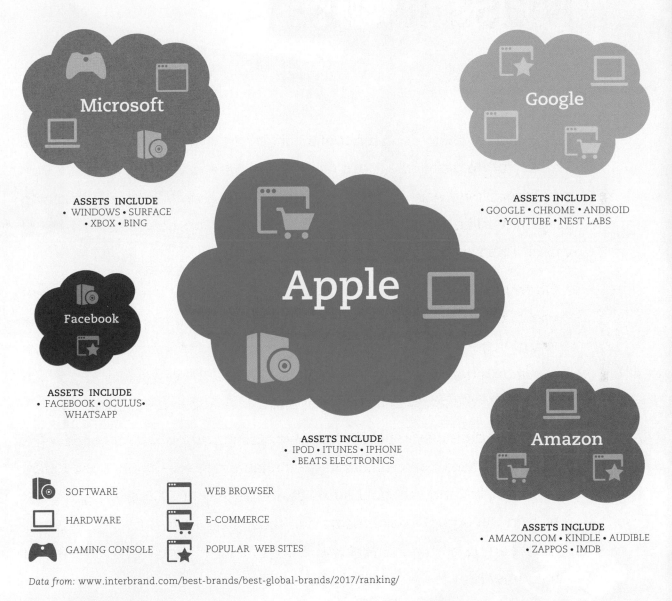

Microsoft

ASSETS INCLUDE
- WINDOWS • SURFACE
- XBOX • BING

Google

ASSETS INCLUDE
- GOOGLE • CHROME • ANDROID
- YOUTUBE • NEST LABS

Facebook

ASSETS INCLUDE
- FACEBOOK • OCULUS• WHATSAPP

Apple

ASSETS INCLUDE
- IPOD • ITUNES • IPHONE
- BEATS ELECTRONICS

Amazon

ASSETS INCLUDE
- AMAZON.COM • KINDLE • AUDIBLE
- ZAPPOS • IMDB

SOFTWARE

WEB BROWSER

HARDWARE

E-COMMERCE

GAMING CONSOLE

POPULAR WEB SITES

Data from: www.interbrand.com/best-brands/best-global-brands/2017/ranking/

2017 REVENUE

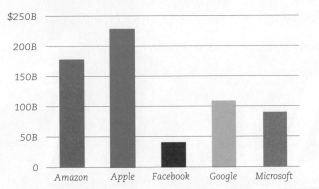

BRAND VALUE

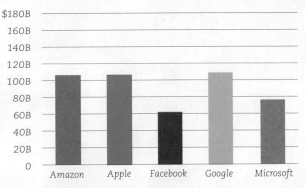

Data from: http://investor.shareholder.com/alphabet/investorkit.cfm; http://investor.apple.com/sec.cfm; investor.fb.com;
https://www.microsoft.com/en-us/Investor/sec-filings.aspx; http://phx.corporate-ir.net/phoenix.zhtml?c=97664&p=irol-reportsannual

Advertising and Commercial Culture

THE DIGITAL TURN over the last several years has dramatically changed the way that products and advertising are bought, sold, and consumed. By 2016, the only older, or "legacy," mass medium whose global advertising revenue was not totally disrupted by the Internet was television—both cable and broadcast, which includes ABC, CBS, Fox, and NBC. In fact, television's nearly 38 percent share of worldwide ad revenue in 2015 represented a 2 percent rise between 2007 and 2015. However, in 2017, Internet advertising surpassed TV advertising for the first time, rising to 35.1 percent while TV's share fell to 34.7 percent. Print newspapers (8.4%) and magazines (7.8%) continued on the decline (down from 30% and 14%, respectively, in 2005).[1]

◄ Digital streaming services—like Hulu, Netflix, and Amazon Prime—have provided an opportunity to give new life to shows that have been canceled by TV networks. Mindy Kaling's *The Mindy Project* was canceled by Fox after three seasons in 2015 but was picked up by Hulu and renewed for several more seasons.

EARLY
DEVELOPMENTS
IN AMERICAN
ADVERTISING
p. 330

THE SHAPE OF U.S.
ADVERTISING TODAY
p. 334

PERSUASIVE
TECHNIQUES IN
CONTEMPORARY
ADVERTISING
p. 343

COMMERCIAL
SPEECH AND
REGULATING
ADVERTISING
p. 348

ADVERTISING,
POLITICS, AND
DEMOCRACY
p. 356

Analyzing data from *Ad Age*'s yearly *Marketing Fact Pack* reveals what's happening. In 2013, "time spent using digital media overtook time spent watching television" for the first time. In 2015, the average time U.S. adults spent watching TV came in at four hours a day, whereas the average time spent with digital devices and services—from computers to YouTube to smartphones to tablets—amounted to almost six hours a day. Back in the first half of 2015, traditional U.S. TV viewing declined almost 10 percent, with Netflix's digital streaming services accounting for almost half that decline.[2] And, of course, we are often watching ads on TV and texting on our smartphones at the same time.[3]

ABC, CBS, Fox, and NBC are worried about these trends. While these once-dominant TV networks have started their own digital streaming services—including Hulu—they trail Netflix and Amazon Prime, which remain ad-free, subscription-only services. In 2015 and 2016, spending declined during the TV "upfronts"—that time each spring when advertisers spend about 75 percent of their TV budgets buying ads on popular programs like CBS's long-running *Big Bang Theory*, which earned the network about $348,000 per thirty-second ad in 2015 but slipped to $286,000 in 2017, or NBC's *The Blacklist*, which drew $115,000 per thirty seconds in 2017, down from $194,000 in 2015. However, CBS's *Thursday Night Football* was a bright spot, averaging $464,000 for a thirty-second spot in 2015 and $551,000 in 2017.[4]

Traditional TV has managed to hold on to nearly a third of the advertising pie because in a fragmented marketplace, the "mass" prime-time TV audience—only a quarter of what it was in the 1980s—still remains significantly larger than the audience a YouTube video or a Netflix series can generate. Once in a while, a brief hit the size of Fox's *Empire* will come along and instill faith in the networks' ability to capture a mass audience. However, the great-grandchildren of those baby boomers who grew up on TV in the 1950s and 1960s will be raised on smartphones and tablets, with no loyalty to (or patience for) ad-based broadcast networks and no memory of gathering with the family around the electronic hearth to watch a favorite "must-see" network sitcom—and the ads that accompany it.

But people will always want stories. So the challenge for the advertising industry is to figure out how its ads can be tied into the consumption of those stories. What will cable and broadcast networks do to get younger viewers to watch those stories on their smartphones? Will Netflix, with 130 million subscribers in 190 countries in mid-2018, look to advertising for another revenue stream? Will some of the ad budgets for Procter & Gamble, AT&T, GM, Ford, and Verizon—five of the biggest U.S. advertisers—shift from TV to digital platforms? In short: What will advertisers do to keep people watching ads, especially in a world of digital devices that either let us skip ads or offer ad-free story services, like HBO, Amazon Prime, and Netflix?

TODAY, ADVERTISEMENTS ARE EVERYWHERE AND IN EVERY MEDIA FORM. Ads take up more than half the space in most daily newspapers and consumer magazines. They are inserted into trade books and textbooks. They clutter websites on the Internet. They fill our mailboxes and wallpaper the buses we ride. Dotting the nation's highways, billboards promote fast-food and hotel chains, while neon signs announce the names of stores along major streets and strip malls. Ads are even found in the restrooms of malls, restaurants, and bars.

At local theaters and on DVDs, ads now precede the latest Hollywood movie trailers. Corporate sponsors spend millions for **product placement**: the purchase of spaces for particular goods to appear in a TV show, movie, or music video. Ads are part of a deejay's morning patter, and ads routinely interrupt our favorite TV and cable programs. By 2015, nearly sixteen minutes of each hour of prime-time network television carried commercials, program promos, and public service announcements—an increase from thirteen minutes an hour in 1992. In addition, each hour of prime-time network TV carried about eleven minutes of product placements.[5] This means that about twenty-six minutes of each hour (or 43 percent) include some sort of paid sponsorship. In addition, according to the Food Marketing Institute, the typical supermarket's shelves are filled with thirty thousand to fifty thousand different brand-name packages, all functioning like miniature billboards. By some research estimates, the average American comes into contact with five thousand forms of advertising each day.[6]

Advertising comes in many forms, from classified ads to business-to-business ads, which provide detailed information on specific products. However, in this chapter, we will concentrate on the more conspicuous advertisements that shape product images and brand-name identities. Because so much consumer advertising intrudes into daily life, ads are often viewed in a negative light. Although business managers agree that advertising is the foundation of a healthy media economy—far preferable to government-controlled media—audiences routinely complain about how many ads they are forced to endure, and they increasingly find ways to avoid them, like zipping through television ads with TiVo and blocking pop-up ads with web browsers. In response, market researchers routinely weigh consumers' tolerance—how long an ad or how many ads they are willing to tolerate to get "free" media content. Without consumer advertisements, however, mass communication industries would cease to function in their present forms. Advertising is the economic glue that holds most media industries together.

In this chapter, we will:

- Examine the historical development of advertising—an industry that helped transform numerous nations into consumer societies
- Look at the first U.S. ad agencies; early advertisements; and the emergence of packaging, trademarks, and brand-name recognition
- Consider the growth of advertising in the last century, such as the increasing influence of ad agencies and the shift to a more visually oriented culture
- Outline the key persuasive techniques used in consumer advertising
- Investigate ads as a form of commercial speech, and discuss the measures aimed at regulating advertising
- Look at political advertising and its impact on democracy

It's increasingly rare to find spaces in our society that don't contain advertising. As you read this chapter, think about your own exposure to advertising. What are some things you like or admire about advertising? For example, are there particular ad campaigns that give

THE "GOT MILK?" advertising campaign was originally designed by Goodby, Silverstein & Partners for the California Milk Processor Board in 1993. From 1998 to 2014, the National Milk Processor Board licensed the "got milk?" slogan for its celebrity milk-mustache ads, like this one.

you enormous pleasure? How and when do ads annoy you? Can you think of any ways you intentionally avoid advertising? For more questions to help you understand the role of advertising in our lives, see "Questioning the Media" in the Chapter Review.

EARLY DEVELOPMENTS IN AMERICAN ADVERTISING

Advertising has existed since 3000 BCE, when shop owners in ancient Babylon hung outdoor signs carved in stone and wood so that customers could spot their stores. Merchants in early Egyptian society hired town criers to walk through the streets, announcing the arrival of ships and listing the goods on board. Archaeologists searching Pompeii, the ancient Italian city destroyed when Mount Vesuvius erupted in 79 CE, found advertising messages painted on walls. By 900 CE, many European cities featured town criers who not only called out the news of the day but also directed customers to various stores.

Other early media ads were on handbills, posters, and broadsides (long, newsprint-quality posters). English booksellers printed brochures and bills announcing new publications as early as the 1470s, when posters advertising religious books were tacked onto church doors. In 1622, print ads imitating the oral style of criers appeared in the first English newspapers. Announcing land deals and ship cargoes, the first newspaper ads in colonial America ran in the *Boston News-Letter* in 1704.

To distinguish their approach from the commercialism of newspapers, early magazines refused to carry advertisements. By the mid-nineteenth century, though, most magazines contained ads, and most publishers started magazines hoping to earn advertising dollars. About 80 percent of these early advertisements covered three subjects: land sales, transportation announcements (stagecoach and ship schedules), and "runaways" (ads placed by farm and plantation owners whose slaves had fled).

The First Advertising Agencies

Until the 1830s, little need existed for elaborate advertising, as few goods and services were available for sale. Before the Industrial Revolution, 90 percent of Americans lived in isolated areas and produced most of their own tools, clothes, and food. The minimal advertising that did exist usually featured local merchants selling goods and services in their own communities. In the United States, national advertising, which initially focused on patent medicines, didn't begin in earnest until the 1850s, when railroads linking the East Coast to the Mississippi River valley began carrying newspapers, handbills, and broadsides—as well as national consumer goods—across the country.

The first American advertising agencies were newspaper **space brokers**, individuals who purchased space in newspapers and sold it to various merchants. Newspapers, accustomed to a 25 percent nonpayment rate from advertisers, welcomed the space brokers, who paid up front. Brokers usually received discounts of 15 to 30 percent but sold the space to advertisers at the going rate. In 1841, Volney Palmer opened a prototype of the first ad agency in Boston; for a 25 percent commission from newspaper publishers, he sold space to advertisers.

Advertising in the 1800s

The first full-service modern ad agency, N. W. Ayer & Son, worked primarily for advertisers and product companies rather than for newspapers. Opening in 1869 in Philadelphia, the agency helped create, write, produce, and place ads in selected newspapers and magazines. The traditional payment structure at this time had the agency collecting a fee from its advertising client for each ad placed; the fee covered the price that each media outlet charged for placement of the ad, plus a 15 percent commission for the agency. The more ads an agency placed, the larger the agency's revenue. Thus, agencies had little incentive to buy fewer ads on behalf of their clients. Nowadays, however, many advertising agencies work for a flat fee, and others are paid on a performance basis.

Trademarks and Packaging

During the mid-1800s, most manufacturers served retail store owners, who usually set their own prices by purchasing goods in large quantities. Manufacturers, however, came to realize that if their products were distinctive and associated with quality, customers would ask for them by name. This would allow manufacturers to dictate prices without worrying about being undersold by stores' generic products or bulk items. Advertising let manufacturers establish a special identity for their products, separate from those of their competitors.

Like many ads today, nineteenth-century advertisements often created the impression of significant differences among products when in fact very few differences actually existed. But when consumers began demanding certain products—either because of quality or because of advertising— manufacturers were able to raise the prices of their goods. With ads creating and maintaining brand-name recognition, retail stores had to stock the desired brands.

One of the first brand names, Smith Brothers, has been advertising cough drops since the early 1850s. Quaker Oats, the first cereal company to register a trademark, has used the image of William Penn, the Quaker who founded Pennsylvania in 1681, to project a company image of honesty, decency, and hard work since 1877. Other early and enduring brands include Campbell Soup, which came along in 1869; Levi Strauss overalls in 1873; Ivory Soap in 1879; and Eastman Kodak film in 1888. Many of these companies packaged their products in small quantities, thereby distinguishing them from the generic products sold in large barrels and bins.

Product differentiation associated with brand-name packaged goods represents the single biggest triumph of advertising. Studies suggest that although most ads are not very effective in the short run, over time they create demand by leading consumers to associate particular brands with quality. Not surprisingly, building or sustaining brand-name recognition is the focus of many product-marketing campaigns. But the costs that packaging and advertising add to products generate many consumer complaints. The high price of many contemporary products results from advertising costs. For example, high-end jeans that cost $150 (or more) today are made from roughly the same inexpensive denim that has outfitted farmworkers since the 1800s. The difference now is that more than 90 percent of the jeans' cost goes toward advertising and profit.

Patent Medicines and Department Stores

By the end of the 1800s, patent medicines and department stores accounted for half of the revenue taken in by ad agencies. Meanwhile, one-sixth of all print ads came from patent medicine and drug companies. Such ads ensured the financial survival of numerous magazines as "the role of the publisher changed from being a seller of a product to consumers to being a gatherer of consumers for the advertisers," according to Goodrum and Dalrymple in *Advertising in America*.[7] Bearing names like Lydia Pinkham's Vegetable Compound, Dr. Lin's Chinese Blood Pills, and William Radam's Microbe Killer, patent medicines were often made with water and 15 to 40 percent concentrations of ethyl alcohol. One patent medicine—Mrs. Winslow's Soothing Syrup—actually contained morphine. Powerful drugs in these medicines explain why people felt "better" after taking them; at the same time, they triggered lifelong addiction problems for many customers.

Many contemporary products, in fact, originated as medicines. Coca-Cola, for instance, was initially sold as a medicinal tonic and even contained traces of cocaine until 1903, when it was replaced with caffeine. Early Post and Kellogg's cereal ads promised to cure stomach and digestive problems. Many patent medicines made outrageous claims about what they could cure, leading to increased public cynicism. As a result, advertisers began to police their ranks and developed industry codes to restore consumer confidence. Partly to monitor patent medicine claims, the Federal Food and Drug Act was passed in 1906.

PATENT MEDICINES
Unregulated patent medicines, such as the ones represented in these ads, created a bonanza for nineteenth-century print media in search of advertising revenue. After several muckraking magazine reports about deceptive patent medicine claims, Congress created the Food and Drug Administration in 1906.

Along with patent medicine ads, department store ads were also becoming prominent in newspapers and magazines. By the early 1890s, more than 20 percent of ad space was devoted to department stores. At the time, these stores were frequently criticized for undermining small shops and businesses, where shopkeepers personally served customers. The more impersonal department stores allowed shoppers to browse and find brand-name goods themselves. Because these stores purchased merchandise in large quantities, they could generally sell the same products for less.

Advertising's Impact on Newspapers

With the advent of the Industrial Revolution, "continuous-process machinery" kept company factories operating at peak efficiency, helping produce an abundance of inexpensive packaged consumer goods.[8] The companies that produced those goods—Procter & Gamble, Colgate-Palmolive, Heinz, Borden, Pillsbury, Eastman Kodak, Carnation, and American Tobacco—were some of the first to advertise, and they remain major advertisers today (although many of these brand names have been absorbed by larger conglomerates).

The demand for newspaper advertising by product companies and retail stores significantly changed the ratio of copy at most newspapers. Whereas newspapers in the mid-1880s featured 70 to 75 percent news and editorial material and only 25 to 30 percent advertisements, by the early 1900s, more than half the space in daily papers was devoted to advertising. However, newspapers have recently been hit hard: Their advertising revenue fell by nearly two-thirds—from a peak of $49 billion in 2005 to $16.8 billion in 2017—as the number of car, real estate, and help-wanted ads dropped significantly following the 2008–09 financial crisis and as Internet ads continued their ascendance.[9] For many newspapers, fewer ads mean smaller papers—not room for more articles.

Promoting Social Change and Dictating Values

As U.S. advertising became more pervasive, it contributed to major social changes in the twentieth century. First, it significantly influenced the transition from a producer-directed to a consumer-driven society. By stimulating demand for new products, advertising helped manufacturers create new markets and recover product start-up costs quickly. From farms to cities, advertising spread the word—first in newspapers and magazines and later on radio and television. Second, advertising promoted technological advances by showing how new machines—such as vacuum cleaners, washing machines, and cars—could improve daily life. Third, advertising encouraged economic growth by increasing sales. To meet the demand generated by ads, manufacturers produced greater quantities, which reduced their costs per unit; however, they did not always pass these savings on to consumers.

Appealing to Female Consumers

By the early 1900s, advertisers and ad agencies came to believe that women, who constituted 70 to 80 percent of newspaper and magazine readers, controlled most household purchasing decisions. (This is still a fundamental principle of advertising today.) Ironically, more than 99 percent of the copywriters and ad executives at that time were men, based primarily in Chicago and New York. Copywriters emphasized stereotyped appeals to women, believing that simple ads with emotional and even irrational content worked best. Thus, early ad copy featured personal tales of "heroic" cleaning products and household appliances. The intention was to help female consumers feel good about defeating life's problems—an advertising strategy that endured throughout much of the twentieth century.

Dealing with Criticism

Although ad revenues fell during the Great Depression in the 1930s, World War II rejuvenated advertising. For the first time, the federal government bought large quantities of advertising space to promote U.S. involvement in a war. These purchases helped offset a decline in traditional advertising, as many industries had turned their attention and production facilities to the war effort.

Also during the 1940s, the industry began to actively deflect criticism that advertising created needs that ordinary citizens never knew they had. Criticism of advertising grew as the industry appeared to be dictating values as well as driving the economy. To promote a more positive image, the industry developed the War Advertising Council—a voluntary group of agencies and advertisers that organized war bond sales, blood donor drives, and the rationing of scarce goods.

The postwar extension of advertising's voluntary efforts became known as the Ad Council. This organization has earned praise over the years for its Smokey the Bear campaign

Bettmann/Getty Images

WAR ADVERTISING COUNCIL
During World War II, the federal government engaged the advertising industry to create messages to support the U.S. war effort. Advertisers promoted the sale of war bonds; conservation of natural resources, such as tin and gasoline; and even saving kitchen waste, so that it could be fed to farm animals.

National Safety Council

**PUBLIC SERVICE
ANNOUNCEMENTS**

The Ad Council has been creating public service announcements (PSAs) since 1942. Supported by contributions from individuals, corporations, and foundations, the council's PSAs are produced pro bono by ad agencies. This PSA is the result of the Ad Council's long-standing relationship with the National Safety Council.

("Only you can prevent forest fires"); its fund-raising campaign for the United Negro College Fund ("A mind is a terrible thing to waste"); and its crash test dummy spots for the Department of Transportation, which substantially increased seat belt use. Choosing a dozen worthy causes annually, the Ad Council continues to produce pro bono *public service announcements* (PSAs) on a wide range of topics, including suicide prevention, cancer screening, sexual harassment, opioids, and teen bullying.

Early Ad Regulation

The early 1900s saw the formation of several watchdog organizations. Partly to keep tabs on deceptive advertising, advocates in the business community in 1913 created the nonprofit Better Business Bureau, which now has more than one hundred branch offices in the United States. At the same time, advertisers wanted a formal service that would track newspaper readership, guarantee accurate audience measures, and ensure that papers would not overcharge ad agencies and their clients. As a result, publishers formed the Audit Bureau of Circulations (ABC) in 1914 (now known as the Alliance for Audited Media).

That same year, the government created the Federal Trade Commission (FTC), in part to help monitor advertising abuses. Thereafter, the industry urged self-regulatory measures to keep government interference at bay. For example, the American Association of Advertising Agencies (AAAA)—established in 1917—tried to minimize government oversight by urging ad agencies to refrain from making misleading product claims.

Finally, the advent of television dramatically altered advertising. With this new visual medium, ads increasingly intruded on daily life. Critics also discovered that some agencies were using **subliminal advertising**. This term, coined in the 1950s, refers to hidden or disguised print and visual messages that allegedly register in the subconscious and fool people into buying products. Noted examples of subliminal ads from that time include a "Drink Coca-Cola" ad embedded in a few frames of a movie and alleged hidden sexual activity drawn into liquor ads. Although research suggests that such ads are no more effective than regular ads, the National Association of Broadcasters banned the use of subliminal ads in 1958.

THE SHAPE OF U.S. ADVERTISING TODAY

Until the 1960s, the shape and pitch of most U.S. ads were determined by a **slogan**, the phrase that attempts to sell a product by capturing its essence in words. With slogans such as "A Diamond Is Forever" (which De Beers first used in 1948), the visual dimension of ads was merely a complement. Eventually, however, through the increasing influence of European design, television, and multimedia devices such as the iPad, images asserted themselves, and visual style became dominant in U.S. advertising and ad agencies.

The Influence of Visual Design

Just as a postmodern design phase developed in art and architecture during the 1960s and 1970s, a new design era began to affect advertising at the same time. Part of this visual revolution was imported from non-U.S. schools of design; indeed, ad-rich magazines such as *Vogue* and *Vanity Fair* increasingly hired

European designers as art directors. These directors tended to be less tied to U.S. word-driven radio advertising because most European countries had government-sponsored radio systems with no ads.

By the early 1970s, agencies had developed teams of writers and artists, thus granting equal status to images and words in the creative process. By the mid-1980s, the visual techniques of MTV, which initially modeled its style on advertising, influenced many ads and most agencies. MTV promoted a particular visual aesthetic—rapid edits, creative camera angles, compressed narratives, and staged performances. Video-style ads soon saturated television and featured such prominent performers as Paula Abdul, Ray Charles, Michael Jackson, Elton John, and Madonna. The popularity of MTV's visual style also started a trend in the 1980s to license hit songs for commercial tie-ins. By the twenty-first century, a wide range of short, polished musical performances and familiar songs—including the work of Train (Samsung), the Shins (McDonald's), LMFAO (Kia Motors), and classic Louis Armstrong (Apple iPhone)—were routinely used in TV ads to encourage consumers not to click the remote control.

Most recently, the Internet and multimedia devices, such as smartphones, laptops, and tablets, have had a significant impact on visual design in advertising. As the web became a mass medium in the 1990s, TV and print designs often mimicked the drop-down menu of computer interfaces. In the twenty-first century, visual design has evolved in other ways, becoming more realistic and interactive as full-motion 3-D animation becomes a high-bandwidth multimedia standard. Design is also simpler, as ads and logos need to appear clearly on the small screens of smartphones and portable media players, and more international, as agencies need to appeal to the global audiences of many companies by reflecting styles from around the world.

Types of Advertising Agencies

About fourteen thousand ad agencies currently operate in the United States. In general, these agencies are classified as either **mega-agencies**—large ad firms that form when several agencies merge and that maintain regional offices worldwide—or small **boutique agencies**, which devote their talents to only a handful of select clients. As a result of the economic crisis, both types of ad agencies suffered revenue declines in 2008 and 2009, but profits slowly improved within about five years.

Mega-Agencies

Mega-agencies provide a full range of services, from advertising and public relations to operating their own in-house radio and TV production studios. In 2017, the four global mega-agencies were WPP, Omnicom, Publicis, and Interpublic (see Figure 11.1). London-based WPP grew quickly in the 1980s with the purchases of J. Walter Thompson, the largest U.S. ad firm at the time; Hill+Knowlton, one of the largest U.S. public relations agencies; and Ogilvy & Mather Worldwide. (The original company, founded in 1971, was named Wire and Plastic Products.) WPP's revenue in 2017 was more than $19 billion. The company today has more than 200,000 employees worldwide and controls a number of leading U.S. advertising and PR agencies, including Young & Rubicam and Burson-Marsteller.

Back in 2013, the number two and three agencies, Omnicom and Publicis, challenged WPP's dominance by proposing a merger that would have created the world's largest mega-agency. But that plan fell apart in 2014, according to the *New York Times*, over a "mix of clashing personalities, disagreements about how the companies would be integrated and complications over legal and tax issues."[10] In 2017, New York–based Omnicom Group had more than 78,000 employees operating in over one hundred countries; today, the company owns the global advertising firms BBDO Worldwide, DDB Worldwide, and TBWA Worldwide. Omnicom also owns three leading public relations agencies: Fleishman-Hillard,

MAD MEN

AMC's hit series *Mad Men* depicts the male-dominated world of Madison Avenue in the 1960s, as the U.S. consumer economy kicked into high gear and agencies developed ad campaigns for cigarettes, exercise belts, and presidential candidates. The show ended its run in 2015 after seven seasons and many awards.

FIGURE 11.1

GLOBAL REVENUE FOR THE WORLD'S LARGEST AGENCIES (IN BILLIONS OF DOLLARS)

Data from: Ad Age, Marketing Fact Pack, 2018 edition. Numbers rounded.

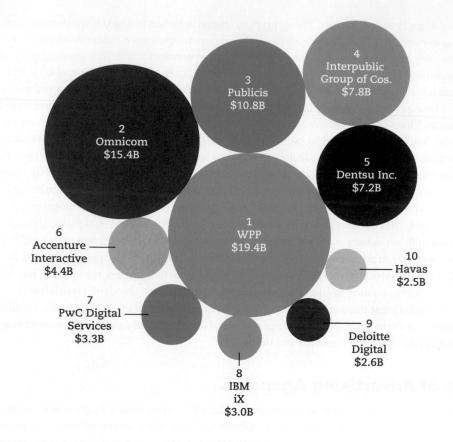

Ketchum, and Porter Novelli. Paris-based Publicis Groupe has a global reach through agencies like Leo Burnett Worldwide, the British agency Saatchi & Saatchi, and the public relations firm MSL Group. Publicis employees numbered more than 79,000 worldwide in 2017.

The Interpublic Group, based in New York with about 50,000 employees worldwide, holds global agencies like McCann Erickson (the top U.S. ad agency) and public relations firms Golin and Weber Shandwick.

This mega-agency trend has stirred debate among consumer and media watchdog groups. Some consider large agencies a threat to the independence of smaller firms, which are slowly being bought out. An additional concern is that these four firms now control more than half the distribution of advertising dollars globally. As a result, the cultural values represented by U.S. and European ads may undermine or overwhelm the values and products of developing countries. (See Figure 11.2 for a look at how advertising dollars are spent by medium.)

Boutique Agencies

The visual revolutions in advertising during the 1960s elevated the standing of designers and graphic artists, who became closely identified with the look of particular ads. Breaking away from bigger agencies, many of these creative individuals formed small boutique agencies. Offering more personal services, the boutiques prospered, bolstered by innovative ad campaigns and increasing profits from TV accounts. By the 1980s, large agencies had bought up many of the boutiques. Nevertheless, these boutiques continue to operate as fairly autonomous subsidiaries within multinational corporate structures.

One independent boutique agency in Minneapolis, Peterson Milla Hooks (PMH), made its name in 1999 with a boldly graphic national branding ad campaign for Target department stores. Target moved its business to another agency in 2011, but PMH—which employs only about sixty people—rebounded. By 2015, the agency's client list included Gap, Kohl's, Nine West, Mattel, Kmart, Sephora, Rooms To Go, Sleep Number, JCPenney, and Chico's.[11]

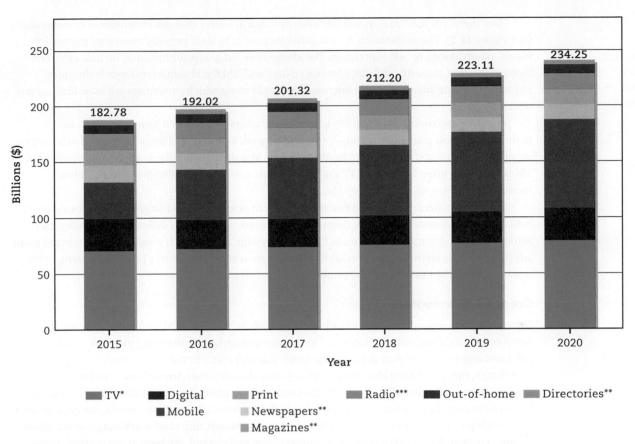

FIGURE 11.2

**WHERE WILL THE
ADVERTISING
DOLLARS GO?**

Data from: eMarketer, "US
Spending on Paid Media
Expected to Climb 5.1% in
2016," March 25, 2016.

Note: *excludes digital; **print only, excludes digital; ***excludes off-air
radio and digital; years 2016–2020 are projections.

The Structure of Ad Agencies

Traditional ad agencies, regardless of their size, generally divide the labor of creating and maintaining advertising campaigns among four departments: account planning, creative development, media coordination, and account management. Expenses incurred for producing the ads are part of a separate negotiation between the agency and the advertiser. As a result of this commission arrangement, it generally costs most large-volume advertisers no more to use an agency than it does to use their own staff.

Account Planning, Market Research, and VALS

The account planner's role is to develop an effective advertising strategy by combining the views of the client, the creative team, and consumers. Consumers' views are the most difficult to understand, so account planners coordinate **market research** to assess the behaviors and attitudes of consumers toward particular products long before any ads are created. Researchers may study everything from possible names for a new product to the size of the copy for a print ad. Researchers also test new ideas and products with consumers to get feedback before developing final ad strategies. In addition, some researchers contract with outside polling firms to conduct regional and national studies of consumer preferences.

In 1978, the Stanford Research Institute (SRI), now called Strategic Business Insights (SBI), instituted its **Values and Lifestyles (VALS)** strategy. Using questionnaires, VALS researchers measure psychological factors and divide consumers into types. VALS research assumes that not every product suits every consumer and encourages advertisers to vary their sales slants to find market niches.

Over the years, the VALS system has been updated to reflect changes in consumer orientations (see Figure 11.3). The most recent system classifies people by their primary consumer motivations: ideals, achievement, or self-expression. The ideals-oriented group, for instance, includes *thinkers*—those who "plan, research, and consider before they act." VALS and similar research techniques ultimately provide advertisers with microscopic details about which consumers are most likely to buy which products.

Agencies and clients—particularly auto manufacturers—have relied heavily on VALS to determine the best placement for ads. VALS data suggest, for example, that *achievers* and *experiencers* watch more sports and news programs; these groups also prefer luxury cars or sport-utility vehicles. *Thinkers*, on the other hand, favor TV dramas and documentaries and like the functionality of minivans or the gas efficiency of hybrids.

VALS researchers do not claim that most people fit neatly into one category. But many agencies believe that VALS research can give them an edge in markets where few differences in quality may actually exist among top-selling brands. Consumer groups, wary of such research, argue that too many ads promote only an image and provide little information about a product's price, its content, or the work conditions under which it was produced.

Creative Development

Teams of writers and artists—many of whom regard ads as a commercial art form—make up the nerve center of the advertising business. The creative department outlines the rough sketches for print and online ads and then develops the words and graphics. For radio, the creative side prepares a working script, generating ideas for everything from choosing the narrator's voice to determining background sound effects. For television, the creative department develops a **storyboard**, a sort of blueprint or roughly drawn comic-strip version of the potential ad. For digital media, the creative team may develop websites, interactive tools, flash games, downloads, and **viral marketing**—short videos or other content that (marketers hope) will quickly gain widespread attention as users share it with friends online or by word of mouth.

Often the creative side of the business finds itself in conflict with the research side. In the 1960s, for example, both Doyle Dane Bernbach (DDB) and Ogilvy & Mather downplayed research, instead championing the art of persuasion and what "felt right." Still, both the creative and the strategic sides of the business acknowledge that they cannot predict with any certainty which ads and which campaigns will succeed. Agencies say ads work best by slowly creating brand-name identities—by associating certain products over time with quality and reliability in the minds of consumers. Some economists, however, believe that much of the money spent on advertising is ultimately wasted because it simply encourages consumers to change from one brand name to another. Such switching may lead to increased profits for a particular manufacturer, but it has little positive impact on the overall economy.

Media Coordination: Planning and Placing Advertising

Ad agency media departments are staffed by media planners and **media buyers**: people who choose and purchase the types of media that are best suited to carry a client's ads, reach the targeted audience, and measure the effectiveness of those ad placements. For instance, a company like Procter & Gamble, currently the world's leading advertiser, displays its more than three hundred major brands—most of them household products like Crest toothpaste and Pampers diapers—on TV shows viewed primarily by women. To reach male viewers, however, media buyers encourage beer advertisers to spend their ad budgets on cable and network sports programming, evening talk radio, or sports magazines.

Along with commissions or fees, advertisers often add incentive clauses to their contracts with agencies, raising the fee if sales goals are met and lowering it if goals are missed. Incentive clauses can sometimes encourage agencies to conduct repetitive **saturation advertising**, in which a variety of media are inundated with ads aimed at target audiences. The initial Miller Lite beer campaign

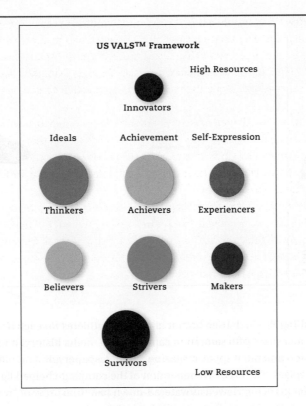

US VALS™ Framework

High Resources

Innovators

Ideals · Achievement · Self-Expression

Thinkers · Achievers · Experiencers

Believers · Strivers · Makers

Survivors

Low Resources

VALS™ Types and Characteristics

Innovators Typically, Innovators are always taking in information, are confident enough to experiment, make the highest number of financial transactions, are skeptical about advertising, have international exposure, are future oriented, are self-directed consumers, believe science and R&D are credible, are most receptive to new ideas and technologies, enjoy the challenge of problem solving, and have the widest variety of interests and activities.

Thinkers Typically, Thinkers have "ought" and "should" benchmarks for social conduct; have a tendency toward analysis paralysis; plan, research, and consider before they act; enjoy a historical perspective; are financially established; are not influenced by what's hot; use technology in functional ways; prefer traditional intellectual pursuits; and buy proven products.

Achievers Typically, Achievers have a "me first, my family first" attitude; believe money is the source of authority; are committed to family and job; are fully scheduled; are goal oriented; are hardworking; are moderate; act as anchors of the status quo; are peer conscious; are private; are professional; and value technology that provides a productivity boost.

Experiencers Typically, Experiencers want everything, are first in and first out of trend adoption, go against the current mainstream, are up on the latest fashions, love physical activity, are sensation seeking, see themselves as very sociable, believe that friends are extremely important, are spontaneous, and have a heightened sense of visual stimulation.

Believers Typically, Believers believe in basic rights and wrongs to lead a good life, rely on spirituality and faith to provide inspiration, want friendly communities, watch TV and read romance novels to find an escape, want to know where things stand and have no tolerance for ambiguity, are not looking to change society, find advertising a legitimate source of information, value constancy and stability and can appear to be loyal, and have strong me-too fashion attitudes.

Strivers Typically, Strivers have revolving employment and high temporary unemployment, use video and video games as a form of fantasy, are fun loving, are imitative, rely heavily on public transportation, are at the center of low-status street culture, desire to better their lives but have difficulty realizing their desire, and wear their wealth.

Makers Typically, Makers are distrustful of government; have a strong interest in all things automotive; have strong outdoor interests, like hunting and fishing; believe in sharp gender roles; want to protect what they perceive to be theirs; see themselves as straightforward and appear to others as anti-intellectual; and want to own land.

Survivors Typically, Survivors are cautious and risk averse; are the oldest consumers; are thrifty; are not concerned about appearing traditional or trendy; take comfort in routine, familiar people, and familiar places; are heavy TV viewers; are loyal to brands and products; spend most of their time alone; are the least likely to use the Internet; and are the most likely to have a landline-only household.

FIGURE 11.3

VALS TYPES AND CHARACTERISTICS

Data from: Strategic Business Insights, 2016, http://strategicbusinessinsights.com/vals/ustypes.shtml.

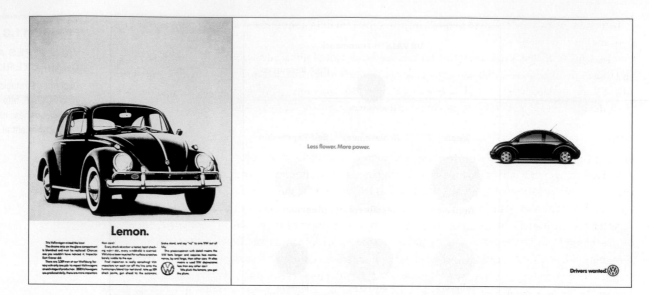

Less flower. More power.

Drivers wanted. VW

Lemon.

("Tastes great, less filling"), which used humor and retired athletes to reach its male audience, became one of the most successful saturation campaigns in media history. It ran from 1973 to 1991 and included television and radio spots, magazine and newspaper ads, and billboards and point-of-purchase store displays. The excessive repetition of the campaign helped light beer overcome a potential image problem: being viewed as watered-down beer unworthy of "real" men.

The cost of advertising, especially on network television, increases each year. The Super Bowl remains the most expensive program for purchasing TV advertising, with thirty seconds of time costing an average of $5 million in 2016 on CBS—up from $4 million in 2014 on Fox. Running a thirty-second ad during a national prime-time TV show can cost anywhere from $50,000 to more than $500,000, depending on the popularity and ratings of the program. The prime-time average for a thirty-second TV spot was $107,000 in 2015, down from an all-time high of $129,600 in the prerecession year 2005.[12]

Trends in Online Advertising

The earliest form of web advertising appeared in the mid-1990s and featured *banner ads*, the print-like display ads that load across the top or side of a web page. Since that time, other formats have emerged, including video ads, sponsorships, and "rich media"—like pop-up ads, pop-under ads, flash multimedia ads, and **interstitials**, which pop up in new screen windows as a user clicks to a new web page. Other forms of Internet advertising include classified ads and e-mail ads. Unsolicited commercial e-mail—known as **spam**—accounted for more than 85 percent of e-mail messages by 2010. Spam today is still a big business. By 2016, unsolicited junk mail made up 86 percent of all e-mails in the world's Internet traffic, with over 400 billion spam messages sent each day.[13]

Paid search advertising has become the dominant format of web advertising. Even though their original mission was to provide impartial search results, search sites such as Google, Yahoo!, and Bing morphed over time into advertising companies, selling sponsored links associated with search terms and distributing online ads to affiliated web pages.[14] In 2016, Google revealed Analytics 360, its latest multiscreen strategy for helping advertisers better target consumers. According to the *New York Times*, "Analytics 360 involves figuring out someone's habits over numerous screens, including desktop web surfing, television, and the web and app parts of smartphones. There are ways to tailor page designs for many of these screens, and place ads using both Google properties and third-party services."[15] In May 2018, Google introduced Advanced Analysis, which allows organizations that use Analytics 360 to break down the purchase process into ten smaller steps so that website owners can have access to more information and data about how consumers engage with their media and progress.[16]

Back in 2004, digital ads accounted for just over 4 percent of global ad spending. By 2007, that share had more than doubled—to 9.3 percent. And by 2015, the Internet held a 29 percent share of worldwide ad spending, making it the second-largest global advertising medium, behind only television/cable. By 2017, the Internet accounted for 35 percent of all ad spending in the United States.[17]

Online Advertising Challenges Traditional Media

Because Internet advertising is the leading growth area, advertising mega-agencies have added digital media agencies and departments to develop and sell ads online. For example, WPP has Xaxis, Omnicom owns Proximity Worldwide, Publicis has Digitas and SapientRazorfish, and Interpublic operates R/GA. Realizing the potential of their online ad businesses, major web services have also aggressively expanded into the advertising market by acquiring smaller Internet advertising agencies. Google bought DoubleClick, the biggest online ad server; Yahoo! purchased Right Media, which auctions online ad space; and Microsoft acquired aQuantive, an online ad server and network that enables advertisers to place ads on multiple websites with a single buy. Google, as the top search engine, has surpassed the traditional mega-agencies in revenue, earning nearly $110 billion in 2017, with almost all of that coming from advertising. Facebook, the top social networking site, is not yet in Google's league but remains a strong challenger, with over 2.1 billion users worldwide in early 2018. Facebook earned just over $40 billion in 2017, most of that profit also coming from ads.[18]

By far the biggest jumps in advertising revenue through social media are in the area of mobile ad sales. While Google accounted for the largest share of mobile ad revenue back in 2014, earning $10 billion, Facebook finished second that year, with nearly $6 billion in mobile ad sales. Twitter placed a distant third, earning just $700 million.[19] By 2018, however, media analysts estimated that Google would earn more than $61 billion through worldwide net mobile advertising, and 91 percent of all ad revenue received by Facebook in the first quarter of 2018 alone was through mobile ad sales of $10.6 billion. Twitter still lagged behind both social media giants, with nearly $3.6 billion in mobile ad revenue in 2018.[20]

It is not just social media advertising on Google and Facebook that explains why the Internet has surpassed TV ad sales as the number-one place to advertise. Amazon, for example, reported over $2 billion in digital ad sales for the first quarter of 2018. In addition, Microsoft was expected to earn over $4 billion in digital advertising revenue in 2018—more than a quarter of all U.S. newspaper ad revenue for an entire year. Microsoft's upsurge in ad growth "is fueled largely by the acquisition of professional networking site LinkedIn and its search site, Bing."[21]

As the Internet draws people's attention away from traditional mass media, leading advertisers are moving more of their ad campaigns and budget dollars to digital media. For example, back in 2010, the CEO of consumer product giant Unilever—a company with more than four hundred brands (including Dove, Hellmann's, and Lipton) and a multibillion-dollar advertising budget—doubled its spending on digital media, since customers were spending much more time on the Internet and mobile phones. "I think you need to fish where the fish are," the Unilever CEO said. "So I've made it fairly clear that I'm driving Unilever to be at the leading edge of digital marketing."[22] The average time spent on mobile phones per day was one hour and thirty minutes back in 2012, but by 2017, daily use had more than doubled—to over three hours per day. Thus, we should expect an increase in ad dollars to chase our mobile devices.[23]

Online Marketers Target Individuals

Compared to ads in traditional media outlets, such as newspapers, magazines, radio, and television, Internet ads offer many advantages to advertisers. Perhaps the biggest advantage—and potentially the

SOCIAL MEDIA ADVERTISING is growing rapidly. Sites like Facebook, Twitter, and Instagram gather a huge amount of information from their users every day, allowing advertisers to reach specific users by displaying ads for products related to those users' unique preferences and behaviors.

SNAPCHAT'S 3V
(vertical video views) advertising strategy seeks to harness the app's key strengths: its dominance on mobile devices and its ability to reach the highly sought-after thirteen- to twenty-four-year-old demographic. The smartphone-friendly ad strategy has proven effective. According to a 2016 study by research firm Millward Brown Digital, Snapchat users who saw 3V ads for the film *Furious 7* were three times more likely to see the film than users who did not see the ads.

most disturbing part for citizens—is that marketers can develop consumer profiles that direct targeted ads to specific website visitors. They do this by collecting information about each Internet user through cookies (see Chapter 2 for more on cookies) and online surveys. For example, when an ESPN.com contest requires you to fill out a survey to be eligible to win sports tickets, or when washingtonpost.com requires that you create an account for free access to the site, marketers use that information to build a profile about you. The cookies they attach to your profile allow them to track your activities on a certain site. They can also add to your profile by tracking what you search for and even by mining your profiles and data on social networking sites. Agencies can also add online and retail sales data (what you bought and where) to user profiles to create an unprecedented database, largely without your knowledge. Such data mining is a boon to marketers, but it is very troubling to consumer privacy advocates.

Internet advertising agencies can also track ad *impressions* (how often ads are seen) and *click-throughs* (how often ads are clicked on). This provides advertisers with specific data on the number of people who not only viewed the ad but also showed real interest by clicking on it. For advertisers, online ads are more beneficial because they can be precisely targeted and easily measured. For example, an advertiser can use Google AdWords to create small ads that are linked to selected key words and geographic targeting (from global coverage to a small radius around a given location). AdWords tracks and graphs the performance of the ad's key words (through click-through and sales rates) and lets the advertiser update the campaign at any time. This kind of targeted advertising enables smaller companies with a $500 ad budget, for example, to place their ads in the same location as larger companies with multimillion-dollar ad budgets.

Beyond computers, smartphones—the "third screen" for advertisers—are of increasing importance. Smartphones offer effective targeting to individuals, as does Internet advertising, but they also offer advertisers the bonus of tailoring ads according to either a specific geographic location (e.g., a restaurant ad goes to someone in close proximity) or the user's demographic, since wireless providers already have that information. Google has also developed unique applications for mobile advertising and searching. For example, the Google Goggles smartphone app enables the user to take a photo of an object—such as a book cover, a landmark, a logo, or text—and then have Google return related search results. Google's Voice Search app lets users speak their search terms. Such apps are designed to maintain Google's dominant search engine position on mobile platforms as ad dollars move there and away from computer websites.

Advertising Invades Social Media

Social media, such as Facebook, Twitter, and Instagram, provide a wealth of data for advertisers to mine. These sites and apps create an unprecedented public display of likes, dislikes, locations, and other personal information. And advertisers are using such information to further refine their ability to send targeted ads that might interest users. Facebook and other sites (like Hulu) go even further by asking users if they like a particular ad. For example, clicking off a display ad in Facebook results in the question "Why didn't you like it?" followed by the choices "uninteresting," "misleading," "offensive," "repetitive," and "other." All that information goes straight back to advertisers, so that they can revise their advertising and try to engage you the next time. Beyond allowing advertisers to target and monitor their ad campaigns, most social media encourage advertisers to create their own online identity. For example, by 2016, the Ben & Jerry's Facebook page had more than eight million "Likes." Despite appearances, such profiles and identities still constitute a form of advertising and serve to promote products to a growing online audience for virtually no cost.

Vertical ads for vertical screens.

Companies and organizations also buy traditional paid advertisements on social media sites. A major objective of their *paid media* is to get *earned media*, or to convince online consumers to promote products on their own. Imagine that the National Resources Defense Council buys an ad on Facebook that attracts your interest. That's a successful paid media ad for the council, but it's even more effective if it becomes earned media—that is, when you mark that you "Like" it, you essentially give the organization a personal endorsement. Knowing that you like the ad, your friends view it; as they pass it along, it gets more earned media and eventually becomes viral—an even greater advertising achievement. As the Nielsen rating service says about online earned media, "Study after study has shown that consumers trust their friends and peers more than anyone else when it comes to making a purchase decision."[24] Social media are helping advertisers use such personal endorsements to further their own products and marketing messages—basically, letting consumers do the work for them.

One controversy in online advertising is whether people have to disclose if they are being paid to promote a product. For example, bloggers often review products or restaurants as part of their content. Some bloggers with large followings have been paid (either directly or with gifts of free products or trips) to give positive reviews or promote products on their site. When such instances, dubbed "blog-ola" by the press, came to light in 2008 and 2009, the bloggers argued that they did not have to reveal that they were being compensated for posting their opinions. At the time, they were right. However, in 2009, the FTC released new guidelines that require bloggers to disclose when an advertiser is compensating them to discuss a product. In 2010, a similar controversy erupted when the FTC revealed that celebrities were being paid to tweet about their "favorite" products. In 2016, the FTC found Lord & Taylor in violation of the disclosure rules when the clothing company hired fifty bloggers (or "influencers") to wear the same designer dress within days of one another: "The dress not only sold out, but these sponsored posts reached 11.4 million Instagram users."[25] The bloggers did not disclose that their posts were sponsored, that the expensive dresses had been "gifted" to them, and that in addition they earned between $1,000 and $4,000 each. The FTC fined Lord & Taylor an undisclosed amount.

A much bigger controversy and problem, especially for Facebook, involved a major data breach that undermined the trust of consumers using any social media platform. In late spring of 2018, news outlets reported that a firm known as Cambridge Analytica had collected private data from over fifty million Facebook users. The British company had then used the information in 2016 to try to influence voter behavior during the U.S. presidential election. In explaining the breach, TechAdvisory.org noted, "Cambridge Analytica analyzed the collected data to create psychological profiles and invent better political drives to influence whom people would vote for. Although there is still a huge debate about how effective the plans were, there's no doubt that tens of thousands of users were manipulated into signing away their data without knowing it."[26] TechAdvisory.org recommends that consumers "remove third-party apps that use your Facebook account." While this is a good first step, issues of privacy and data breaches will continue to haunt digital companies and jeopardize their users as we move out of the infancy stage of the digital age.

PERSUASIVE TECHNIQUES IN CONTEMPORARY ADVERTISING

Ad agencies and product companies often argue that the main purpose of advertising is to inform consumers about available products in a straightforward way. Most consumer ads, however, merely create a mood or tell stories about products without revealing much else. A one-page magazine ad, a giant billboard, or a thirty-second TV spot gives consumers little information about how a product was made, how much it costs, or how it compares with similar brands. In managing space and time constraints, advertising agencies engage in a variety of persuasive techniques.

"IS NOT A KISS THE VERY AUTOGRAPH OF LOVE?"
HENRY FINCK, AUTHOR

ROMANCE IS ON

NEW REVLON
ULTRA HD™ LIPSTICK

Revolutionary **wax-free gel technology** for a weightless feel and **true colour clarity** in one smooth swipe.
14 high-definition shades to love.

EMMA STONE WEARS HD GLADIOLUS
#LoveIsOn

REVLON
LOVE IS ON

Image Courtesy of The Advertising Archives

FAMOUS-PERSON TESTIMONIALS

Major stars used to be somewhat wary of appearing in ads (at least in the United States), but many brands now use celebrity endorsements. This recent Revlon campaign, for example, features actress Emma Stone.

Conventional Persuasive Strategies

One of the most frequently used advertising approaches is the **famous-person testimonial**, in which a product is endorsed by a well-known person. Famous endorsers include Justin Timberlake for Bud Light, Taylor Swift for Diet Coke, and Beyoncé for Pepsi. Athletes earn some of the biggest endorsement contracts. For example, in 2015, Golden State Warrior guard Steph Curry made $12 million in endorsements for Under Armour, Degree, Kaiser Permanente, and Brita, among other companies. In 2016, JPMorgan Chase also added Curry (after buying the naming rights for Golden State's new arena). In 2017, Curry—the NBA's top scorer—earned $35 million in endorsements, as did soccer superstar Cristiano Ronaldo. That same year, the two top endorsement earners were Roger Federer and LeBron James—at $58 million and $55 million, respectively.[27]

Another technique, the **plain-folks pitch**, associates a product with simplicity. Over the years, Volkswagen ("Drivers wanted"), General Electric ("We bring good things to life"), and Microsoft ("I'm a PC and Windows 7 was my idea") have each used slogans that stress how new technologies fit into the lives of ordinary people. In a way, the Facebook technique of sponsored stories fits this model, since it depends on friends' endorsements of products rather than the words or images of stars or athletes.

By contrast, the **snob-appeal approach** attempts to persuade consumers that using a product will maintain or elevate their social status. Advertisers selling jewelry, perfume, clothing, and luxury automobiles often use snob appeal. For example, the pricey bottled water brand Fiji ran ads in *Esquire* and other national magazines that said, "The label says Fiji because it's not bottled in Cleveland"—a jab intended to favorably compare the water bottled in the South Pacific to the drinking water of an industrial city in Ohio. (Fiji ended up withdrawing the ad after the Cleveland Water Department released test data showing that its water was purer than Fiji water.)

Another approach, the **bandwagon effect**, points out in exaggerated claims that *everyone* is using a particular product. Brands that refer to themselves as "America's favorite" or "the best" imply that consumers will be left behind if they ignore these products. A different technique, the **hidden-fear appeal**, plays on consumers' sense of insecurity. Deodorant, mouthwash, and shampoo ads frequently invoke anxiety, pointing out that only a specific product could relieve embarrassing personal hygiene problems and restore a person to social acceptability.

A final ad strategy, used more in local TV and radio campaigns than in national ones, has been labeled **irritation advertising**: creating product-name recognition by being annoying or obnoxious. Although both research and common sense suggest that irritating ads do not work very well, there have been exceptions. In the 1950s and 1960s, for instance, an aspirin company ran a TV ad illustrating a hammer pounding inside a person's brain. Critics and the product's own agency suggested that people bought the product, which sold well, to get relief from the ad as well as from their headaches. On the regional level, irritation ads are often used by appliance discount stores or local car dealers, who dress in outrageous costumes and yell at the camera.

The Association Principle

Historically, American car advertisements have shown automobiles in natural settings—on winding roads that cut through rugged mountain passes or across shimmering wheat fields—but rarely on congested city streets or in other urban settings where most driving actually occurs. Instead, the car—an example of advanced technology—merges seamlessly into the natural world.

This type of advertising exemplifies the **association principle**, a widely used persuasive technique that associates a product with a positive cultural value or image even if it has little connection to the product. For example, many ads displayed visual symbols of American patriotism in the wake of the 9/11 terrorist attacks in an attempt to associate products and companies with national pride. Media critic Leslie Savan noted that in trying "to convince us that there's an innate relationship between a brand name and an attitude," advertising may associate products with nationalism, happy families, success at school or work, natural scenery, freedom, or humor.[28]

One of the more controversial uses of the association principle has been the linkage of products to stereotyped caricatures of women. In numerous instances, women have been portrayed either as sex objects or as clueless housewives who, during many a daytime TV commercial, need the powerful off-screen voice of a male narrator to instruct them in their own homes.

Another popular use of the association principle is to claim that products are "real" and "natural"—possibly the most familiar adjectives associated with advertising. For example, Coke sells itself as "the real thing," and the cosmetics industry offers synthetic products that promise to make women look "natural." The adjectives *real* and *natural* saturate American ads yet almost always describe processed or synthetic goods. Green marketing has a similar problem, as it is associated with goods and services that aren't always environmentally friendly.

Philip Morris's Marlboro brand has used the association principle to completely transform its product image. In the 1920s, Marlboro began as a fashionable women's cigarette. Back then, the company's ads equated smoking with a sense of freedom, attempting to appeal to women who had just won the right to vote. Marlboro, though, did poorly as a women's product, and new campaigns in the 1950s and 1960s transformed the brand into a man's cigarette. Powerful images of active, rugged men dominated the ads. Often, Marlboro associated its product with nature, displaying an image of a lone cowboy roping a calf, building a fence, or riding over a snow-covered landscape. The branding consultancy BrandZ (a division of WPP) dropped Marlboro from the world's tenth "most valuable global brand" in 2015 to the thirteenth in 2018, citing the rise in technology/digital-based brands as one of the main reasons for the dip. (Google, Apple, Amazon, Microsoft, and the Chinese multinational investment conglomerate Tencent were the top five brand names in 2018.)[29]

Disassociation as an Advertising Strategy

As a response to corporate mergers and public skepticism toward impersonal and large companies, a *disassociation corollary* emerged in advertising. The nation's largest winery, Gallo, pioneered the idea in the 1980s by establishing a dummy corporation, Bartles & Jaymes, to sell jug wine and wine coolers, thereby avoiding the use of the Gallo corporate image in ads and on its bottles. The ads featured Frank and Ed, two low-key grandfatherly types, as "co-owners" and ad spokespersons. On the one hand, as a *BusinessWeek* article observed, the ad was "a way to connect with younger consumers who yearn for products that are handmade, quirky, and authentic."[30] On the other hand, this technique, by concealing the Gallo tie-in, allowed the wine giant to disassociate from the negative publicity of the 1970s—a period when labor leader Cesar Chavez organized migrant workers in a long boycott of Gallo.

Advertising as Myth and Story

Another way to understand ads is to use **myth analysis**, which provides insight into how ads work at a general cultural level. Here, the term *myth* does not refer simply to an untrue story or an outright falsehood. Rather, myths help us define people, organizations, and social norms. According to myth analysis, most ads are narratives with stories to tell and social conflicts to resolve. Three common mythical elements are found in many types of ads:

- Ads incorporate myths in mini-story form, featuring characters, settings, and plots.
- Most stories in ads involve conflicts, pitting one set of characters or social values against another.
- Such conflicts are negotiated or resolved by the end of the ad, usually by applying or purchasing a product. In advertising, the product and those who use it often emerge as the heroes of the story.

Even though the stories that ads tell are usually compressed into thirty seconds or onto a single page, they still include the traditional elements of narrative. For instance, many SUV ads ask us to imagine ourselves driving out into the raw, untamed wilderness, to a quiet, natural place that only, say, a Jeep can reach. The audience implicitly understands that the SUV can somehow, almost magically, take us out of our fast-paced, freeway-wrapped urban world, plagued with long commutes, traffic jams, and automobile exhaust. This implied conflict between the natural world and the manufactured world is apparently resolved by the image of the SUV in a natural setting. Although SUVs typically clog our urban and suburban highways, get low gas mileage, and create tons of air pollution particulates, the ads ignore these facts. Instead, they offer an alternative story about the wonders of nature, and the SUV amazingly becomes the vehicle that negotiates the conflict between city/suburban blight and the unspoiled wilderness.

Most advertisers do not expect consumers to accept without question the stories or associations they make in ads. As media scholar Michael Schudson observed in his book *Advertising: The Uneasy Persuasion*, ads do not "make the mistake of *asking* for belief."[31] Instead, they are most effective when they operate like popular fiction, creating attitudes and reinforcing values while encouraging us to suspend our disbelief. Although most of us realize that ads create a fictional world, we often get caught up in their stories and myths. Indeed, ads often work because the stories offer comfort about our deepest desires and conflicts—between men and women, nature and technology, tradition and change, the real and the artificial. Most contemporary consumer advertising does not provide much useful information about products. Rather, it tries to reassure us that through the use of familiar brand names, everyday tensions and problems can be managed (see "Media Literacy and the Critical Process: The Branded You" on page 348).

PRODUCT PLACEMENT in movies and television is more prevalent than ever. On television, placement is often most visible in reality shows, while scripted series and films tend to be more subtle—but not all the time. In this scene from the Netflix series *Orange Is the New Black*, a bag of Funyuns (a brand owned by Frito-Lay) is prominently featured.

Jessica Miglio/© Netflix/Everett Collection

Product Placement

Product companies and ad agencies have become adept in recent years at *product placement*: strategically placing ads or buying space in movies, TV shows, comic books, video games, blogs, and music videos so that products appear as part of a story's set environment. For example, a 2015 episode of *Modern Family* was told entirely through a character's MacBook Pro and apps filmed on Apple devices, though the idea came from the show rather than from Apple. In 2013, the Superman movie *Man of Steel* had the most product placements ever for a film up to that time, with two-hundred-plus marketing partners in deals worth $160 million, including those with Hardee's, Gillette, Sears, Nikon, Nokia, 7-Eleven, IHOP, and the National Guard.

EXAMINING ETHICS

Do Alcohol Ads Encourage Binge Drinking?

With clear evidence that cigarettes caused lung cancer, the tobacco industry in the early 1970s chose to pull all TV ads for cigarettes, in part to ward off the planned increase in public service ads that the government and nonprofit agencies were airing about the dangers of smoking. Similarly, for decades ads for hard liquor (called "distilled spirits" by the industry) were not shown in TV markets across the United States for fear of igniting anti-alcohol public service spots warning about alcoholism and heavy drinking, and countering TV commercials. Some ads for hard liquor have reappeared in recent years, but not all channels or shows will air them; often they appear on late-night or specialized programming.

Beer ads, however, have never been interrupted and remain ubiquitous, usually associating beer drinking with young people, sex appeal, and general good times. As such, the debates over alcohol ads continue, especially in light of the ritual of binge drinking that has bedeviled universities

BUD LIGHT
attracted negative attention with a campaign about "turning no into yes," evoking the language of sexual assault.

throughout the United States. According to the Centers for Disease Control and Prevention, "More than half of the 88,000 alcohol-attributable deaths" result from binge drinking, which is generally defined as five or more drinks for men, four or more drinks for women, in one sitting.[1]

A Dartmouth University study, first released in 2015 and published in *JAMA Pediatrics*, demonstrated that "familiarity with and response to images of television alcohol marketing was associated with the subsequent onset of drinking across a range of outcomes."[2] The study, "Cued Recall of Alcohol Advertising on Television and Underage Drinking Behavior," surveyed more than twenty-five hundred people between the ages of fifteen and twenty-three in 2011, then reinterviewed fifteen hundred of them in 2013.

In 2013, 66 percent of high school students said they had tried alcohol, whereas only 21 percent said they had engaged in binge drinking. However, 29 percent of the fifteen- to seventeen-year-olds reinterviewed after exposure to alcohol ads reported binge drinking. One coauthor of the study said, "It's very strong evidence that underage drinkers are not only exposed to the television advertising, but they also assimilate the messages. That process moves them forward in their drinking behavior."[3] Although the study argues that the efforts by hard liquor advertisers to protect young people from the messages in their ads are ineffective, the Distilled Spirits Council disagrees, saying that the Dartmouth study was "driven by advocacy, not science."[4]

One ethical question raised by the 2015 study has to do with those who work in the ad business and the work they are asked to do. Many reputable ad agencies will ask new or potential employees if there are clients and products that they would not represent. Some agencies might specifically ask newly hired account executives if they would be willing to work for a tobacco or a liquor company—or, given what they know about childhood obesity and the low nutrition content in many fast foods, sugared cereals, and popular sodas, if they could represent these types of products.

It might be a useful exercise, then, to ask yourself, Are there products or companies you would not work for or represent in some capacity? Why or why not? Would you be willing to represent tobacco companies that wanted to place ads in magazines or a hard liquor company that wanted to advertise on TV? Why or why not?

MEDIA LITERACY AND THE CRITICAL PROCESS

The Branded You

To what extent are you influenced by brands?

1 DESCRIPTION

Take a look around your home or dormitory room and list all the branded products you've purchased, including food, electronics, clothes, shoes, toiletries, and cleaning products.

2 ANALYSIS

Now organize your branded items into categories. For example, how many items of clothing are branded with athletic, university, or designer logos? What patterns emerge, and what kind of psychographic profile do these brands suggest about you? (As a reference, use the VALS chart on page 339.)

3 INTERPRETATION

Why did you buy each particular product? Was it because you thought it was of superior quality?

Because it was cheaper? Because your parents used this product (making it tried, trusted, and familiar)? Because it made you feel a certain way about yourself and you wanted to project that image to others? Have you ever purchased items without brands or removed logos once you bought the product? Why?

4 EVALUATION

As you become more conscious of our branded environment (and your participation in it), what is your assessment of U.S. consumer culture? Is there too much conspicuous branding? What is good and bad about the ubiquity of brand names in our culture? How does branding relate to the common American ethic of individualism?

5 ENGAGEMENT

Visit Adbusters (www.adbusters .org) and read about action projects that confront commercialism, including Buy Nothing Day, Media Carta, TV Turnoff, the Culture Jammers Network, the Blackspot nonbrand sneaker, and Unbrand America. Also visit the home page for the advocacy organization Commercial Alert (www.commercialalert .org) to learn about the most recent commercial incursions into everyday life and what can be done about them. Or write a letter to a company about a product or ad that you think is a problem. How does the company respond?

For many critics, product placement has gotten out of hand. What started out as subtle appearances in realistic settings—like Reese's Pieces in the 1982 movie *E.T.*—has turned into Coca-Cola being almost an honorary cast member on Fox's *American Idol* set. The practice is now so pronounced that it was a subject of Hollywood parody in the 2006 film *Talladega Nights: The Ballad of Ricky Bobby*, starring Will Ferrell.

In 2005, watchdog organization Commercial Alert asked both the FTC and the FCC to mandate that consumers be warned about product placement on television. Although the FTC rejected the petition, the FCC proposed product placement rules, but it had still not approved them by the summer of 2018. In contrast, the European Union approved product placement for television in 2007 but required programs to alert viewers of such paid placements. In Britain, for example, the letter *P* must appear in the corner of the screen at commercial breaks and at the beginning and end of a show to signal product placements.[32]

COMMERCIAL SPEECH AND REGULATING ADVERTISING

In 1791, Congress passed and the states ratified the First Amendment to the U.S. Constitution, promising, among other guarantees, to "make no law . . . abridging the freedom of speech, or of the press." Over time, we have developed a shorthand label for the First Amendment, misnaming it the free-speech clause. The amendment ensures that citizens and journalists can generally say and write what they want, but it says nothing directly about **commercial speech**—any print or broadcast expression for which a fee is charged to organizations and individuals buying time or space in the mass media.

Whereas freedom of speech refers to the right to express thoughts, beliefs, and opinions in the abstract marketplace of ideas, commercial speech is about the right to circulate goods, services, and images in the concrete marketplace of products. For most of the history of mass media, only very wealthy citizens established political parties, and only multinational companies could routinely afford to purchase speech that reached millions. The Internet, however, has helped level that playing field. A cleverly edited mash-up or an entertaining speech—or apparently any video featuring cats captured on a smartphone—has the potential to go viral. For example, in April 2018, eleven-year-old Mason Ramsey sang a version of Hank Williams's classic "Lovesick Blues" in a Walmart in Harrisburg, Illinois, that was shot on a smartphone and then tweeted. The tweet reached millions, rivaling the most expensive commercial speech.

Although the mass media have not hesitated to carry product and service-selling advertisements and have embraced the concepts of infomercials and cable home-shopping channels, they have also refused certain issue-based advertising that might upset their traditional advertisers. For example, whereas corporations experience little resistance when placing paid ads, many labor unions have had their print and broadcast ads rejected as "controversial." The nonprofit Adbusters Media Foundation, based in Vancouver, British Columbia, has had difficulty getting networks to air its "uncommercials." One of its spots promotes the Friday after Thanksgiving (traditionally, the beginning of the holiday shopping season) as Buy Nothing Day.

Critical Issues in Advertising

In his 1957 book *The Hidden Persuaders*, Vance Packard expresses concern that advertising manipulates helpless consumers, attacks our dignity, and invades "the privacy of our minds."[33] According to this view, the advertising industry is all-powerful. Although consumers have historically been regarded as dupes by many critics, research reveals that the consumer mind is not as easy to predict as some advertisers once thought. One of the most disastrous campaigns of all time featured the now-famous "This is not your father's Oldsmobile" spots, which began running in 1989 and starred celebrities like former Beatles drummer Ringo Starr and his daughter. Oldsmobile (which became part of General Motors in 1908) and its ad agency, Leo Burnett, decided to market to a younger generation after sales declined from a high of 1.1 million vehicles in 1985 to just 715,000 in 1988. But the campaign backfired, apparently alienating its older loyal customers (who may have felt abandoned by Olds and its catchy new slogan) and failing to lure younger buyers (who probably still had trouble getting past the name Olds). In 2000, Oldsmobile sold only 260,000 cars; and by 2005, GM had phased out its Olds division.[34]

As this example illustrates, most people are not easily persuaded by advertising. Over the years, studies have suggested that between 75 and 90 percent of new consumer products typically fail because they are not embraced by the buying public.[35] But despite public resistance to many new products, the ad industry has made contributions, including raising the American standard of living and financing

WARNING
TO STOP THE OBESITY CRISIS, GOVERNMENTS MUST APPLY THE LESSONS LEARNED FROM SUCCESSFUL ANTI-TOBACCO CAMPAIGNS

www.oma.org
Ontario Medical Association   @Ontariosdoctors

$OMA

most media industries. Yet serious concerns over the impact of advertising remain. Watchdog groups worry about the expansion of advertising's reach, and critics continue to condemn ads that stereotype or associate products with sex appeal, youth, and narrow definitions of beauty. Some of the most serious concerns involve children, teens, and health.

Children and Advertising

Children and teenagers, living in a culture dominated by TV ads, are often viewed as "consumer trainees." For years, groups such as Action for Children's Television (ACT) worked to limit advertising aimed at children. In the 1980s, ACT fought particularly hard to curb program-length commercials: thirty-minute cartoon programs (such as *G.I. Joe*, *My Little Pony and Friends*, *The Care Bear Family*, and *He-Man and the Masters of the Universe*) developed for television syndication primarily to promote a line of toys. This commercial tradition continued with programs such as *Pokémon* and *SpongeBob SquarePants*.

In addition, parent groups have worried about the heavy promotion of sugar-coated cereals and similar products during children's programs. Pointing to European countries, where children's advertising is banned, these groups have pushed to minimize advertising directed at children. Congress, hesitant to limit the protection that the First Amendment offers to commercial speech and faced with lobbying by the advertising industry, has responded weakly. The Children's Television Act of 1990 mandated that networks provide some educational and informational children's programming, but the act has been difficult to enforce and has done little to restrict advertising aimed at kids.

Because children and teenagers influence nearly $500 billion a year in family spending— on everything from snacks to cars—they are increasingly targeted by advertisers.[36] A Stanford University study found that a single thirty-second TV ad can influence the brand choices of children as young as age two. Still, the pull to use these methods for marketing to children is becoming increasingly seductive as product placement and merchandising tie-ins become more prevalent. Most recently, companies have used seemingly innocuous online games to sell products like breakfast cereal to children.

Advertising in Schools

A controversial development in advertising was the introduction of Channel One into thousands of schools during the 1989–90 school year. The brainchild of Whittle Communications, Channel One offered "free" video and satellite equipment (tuned exclusively to Channel One) in exchange for a twelve-minute package of current events programming that included two minutes of commercials. Public pressure managed to get most junk-food ads removed from Channel One schools by 2006.

Over the years, the National Dairy Council and other organizations have also used schools to promote products, providing free filmstrips, posters, magazines, folders, and study guides adorned with corporate logos. Teachers, especially in underfunded districts, have usually been grateful for the support. Early on, however, Channel One was viewed as a more intrusive threat, violating the implicit cultural border between an entertainment situation (watching commercial television) and a learning situation (going to school). One study showed that schools with a high concentration of low-income students were more than twice as likely as affluent schools to receive Channel One.[37]

Texas and Ohio contain the highest concentrations of Channel One contracts, but many individual school districts and some state systems, including New York and California, have banned Channel One News. These school systems have argued that Channel One provides students with only slight additional knowledge about current affairs, and fear that students deem the products advertised—sneakers, clothing, cereal, and controversial sugar-flavored juices like SunnyD—more worthy of purchase because they are advertised in educational environments.[38] A 2006 study found that students remember "more of the advertising than they do the news stories shown on Channel One."[39] Channel One's owner, publisher Houghton Mifflin Harcourt, shut the service down in 2018 after it had been losing subscribers.

LaunchPad
macmillan learning
launchpadworks.com

Advertising and Effects on Children
Scholars and advertisers analyze the effects of advertising on children.

Discussion: In the video, some argue that using cute, kid-friendly imagery in ads can lead children to begin drinking; others dispute this claim. What do you think, and why?

Health and Advertising

Eating Disorders. Advertising has a powerful impact on the standards of beauty in our culture. A long-standing trend in advertising is the association of certain products with ultrathin female models, promoting a style of "attractiveness" that girls and women are invited to emulate. Even today, despite the popularity of fitness programs, most fashion models are much thinner than the average woman. Some forms of fashion and cosmetics advertising actually pander to individuals' insecurities and low self-esteem by promising the ideal body. Such advertising suggests standards of style and behavior that may not only be unattainable but also be harmful, leading to eating disorders such as anorexia and bulimia and an increase in cosmetic surgeries.

If advertising has been criticized for promoting skeleton-like beauty, it has also been blamed for the tripling of obesity rates in the United States since the 1980s, with more than two-thirds of adult Americans identified in 2015 as being overweight or obese. Corn syrup–laden soft drinks, fast food, and processed food are the staples of media ads and are major contributors to the nationwide weight problem. More troubling is that because an obese nation is good for business (creating a multibillion-dollar market for diet products, exercise equipment, and self-help books), media outlets see little reason to change current ad practices. The food and restaurant industry at first denied any connection between ads and the rise of U.S. obesity rates, instead blaming individuals who make bad choices. Increasingly, however, fast-food chains are offering healthier meals and calorie counts on various food items.

Tobacco. One of the most sustained criticisms of advertising is its promotion of tobacco consumption. Opponents of tobacco advertising have become more vocal in the face of grim statistics: Each year, an estimated 400,000 Americans die from diseases related to nicotine addiction and poisoning. Tobacco ads disappeared from television in 1971 under pressure from Congress and the FCC. However, over the years, numerous ad campaigns have targeted teenage consumers of cigarettes. In 1988, for example, R. J. Reynolds—a subdivision of RJR Nabisco—updated its Joe Camel cartoon character, outfitting him with hipper clothes and sunglasses. Spending $75 million annually, the company put Joe on billboards and store posters and in sports stadiums and magazines. One study revealed that before 1988, fewer than 1 percent of teens under the age of eighteen smoked Camels. After the ad blitz, however, 33 percent of this age group preferred Camels.

In addition to young smokers, the tobacco industry has targeted other groups. In the 1960s, for instance, the advertising campaigns for Eve and Virginia Slims cigarettes (reminiscent of ads during the suffrage movement in the early 1900s) associated their products with women's liberation, equality, and slim fashion models. And in 1989, R. J. Reynolds introduced a cigarette called Uptown, targeting African American consumers. The ad campaign fizzled due to public protests by black leaders and government officials. When these leaders pointed to the high concentration of cigarette billboards in poor urban areas and the high mortality rates among black male smokers, the tobacco company withdrew the brand.

The government's position regarding the tobacco industry began to change in the mid-1990s, when new reports revealed that tobacco companies had known that nicotine was addictive as early as the 1950s and had withheld that information from the public. In 1998, after four states won settlements against the tobacco industry and the remaining states threatened to bring more expensive lawsuits against the companies, the

LIFESTYLE AD APPEALS

TBWA (now a unit of Omnicom) introduced Absolut Vodka's distinctive advertising campaign in 1980. The campaign marketed a little-known Swedish vodka as an exclusive lifestyle brand, an untraditional approach that parlayed it into one of the world's best-selling spirits. The long-running ad campaign ended in 2006, with more than 1,450 ads serving to maintain the brand's premium status by referencing fashion, artists, and contemporary music.

The Advertising Archives

ABSOLUT OBSESSION.

Smoking Up the Global Market

John van Hasselt–Corbis/Getty Images

By 2000, the status of tobacco companies and their advertising in the United States had hit a low point. A $206 billion settlement in 1998 between tobacco companies and state attorneys general ended tobacco advertising on billboards and severely limited the ways in which cigarette companies can promote their products in the United States. Advertising bans and antismoking public service announcements contributed to tobacco's growing disfavor in America, with smoking rates dropping from a high of 42.5 percent of the population in 1965 to just 18 percent fifty years later.

As Western cultural attitudes have turned against tobacco, the large tobacco multinationals have shifted their global marketing focus, targeting Asia in particular. In 2015, China had approximately 254 million male smokers, India had about 91 million, and Indonesia had about 50 million. Additionally, countries with the highest percentage of female smokers in 2015 were the United States (17 million), China (14 million), and India (13.5 million). However, according to a surgeon general's report from April 2017, the highest rate of female smoking in 2015 was in Greenland, where 44 percent of women smoked daily. According to the study, 11.5 percent of worldwide deaths in 2015 were due to smoking, and just over half of these deaths occurred in four countries: China, India, the United States, and Russia.[1]

Underfunded government health programs and populations that generally admire American and European cultural products make Asian nations ill-equipped to resist cigarette marketing efforts. For example, in spite of China's efforts to control smoking (several Chinese cities have banned smoking in public

tobacco industry agreed to an unprecedented $206 billion settlement, which carried significant limits on the advertising and marketing of tobacco products.

The agreement's provisions banned cartoon characters in advertising, thus ending the use of the Joe Camel character; prohibited the industry from targeting young people in ads and marketing and from giving away free samples, tobacco-brand clothing, and other merchandise; and ended outdoor billboard and transit advertising. The agreement also banned tobacco company sponsorship of concerts and athletic events, and strictly limited its other corporate sponsorships. These provisions, however, do not apply to tobacco advertising abroad (see "Global Village: Smoking Up the Global Market" above).

Alcohol.   In 2016, about ninety thousand people in the United States died from alcohol-related or alcohol-induced diseases, and another ten-thousand-plus died in car crashes involving drunk drivers. As you might guess, many of the same complaints regarding tobacco advertising are being directed at alcohol ads. (The hard liquor industry had voluntarily banned TV and radio ads for decades.) For example, one of the most popular beer ad campaigns of the late 1990s, featuring the Budweiser frogs (which croak "Budweis-errrr"), has been accused of using cartoonlike animal places), recent studies have shown that nearly two-thirds of Chinese men and 10 percent of Chinese women are addicted to tobacco. Chinese women, who are now starting to smoke at increasing rates, are associating smoking with slimness, feminism, and independence.[2]

Advertising bans have actually forced tobacco companies to find alternative and, as it turns out, better ways to promote smoking. Philip Morris, the largest private tobacco company, and its global rival, British American Tobacco (BAT), practice "brand stretching"—linking their logos to race-car events, soccer leagues, youth festivals, concerts, TV shows, and popular cafés. The higher price for Western cigarettes in Asia has increased their prestige and has made packs of Marlboros symbols of middle-class aspiration.

The unmistakable silhouette of the Marlboro Man is ubiquitous throughout developing countries, particularly in Asia. In Hanoi, Vietnam, almost every corner boasts a street vendor with a trolley cart, the bottom half of which carries the Marlboro logo or one of the other premium foreign brands. Vietnam's Ho Chi Minh City has two thousand such trolleys. Children in Malaysia are especially keen on Marlboro clothing, which—along with watches, binoculars, radios, knives, and backpacks—they can win by collecting a certain number of empty Marlboro packages. (It is now illegal to sell tobacco-brand clothing and merchandise in the United States.)

Sporting events have proved to be an especially successful brand-stretching technique with men. In addition to Philip Morris's sponsorship of the Marlboro soccer league in China in the mid to late 1990s, cigarette ads flourished on Chinese television (in the United States, such ads have been banned by FCC rules since 1971). For the last twenty years, however, cigarette ads have been banned in China on TV and radio and in newspapers and magazines. But in 2014, the powerful government-controlled Chinese tobacco industry blocked a complete ban, according to Reuters, still permitting "cigarette product launches, and tobacco sponsorship for sporting events and schools."[3]

Critics suggest that the same marketing strategies will make their way into the United States and other Western countries, but that's unlikely. Tobacco companies are mainly interested in developing regions like Asia for two reasons. First, the potential market is staggering: Only one in twenty cigarettes now sold in China is a foreign brand, and women are just beginning to develop the habit. Second, many smokers in countries like China are unaware that smoking causes lung cancer. In fact, a million Chinese people die each year from tobacco-related health problems—around 50 percent of Chinese men will die before they are sixty-five years old, and lung cancer among Chinese women has increased by 30 percent in the past few years.[4] Smoking is projected to cause about eight million deaths a year by 2030.[5]

characters to appeal to young viewers. In fact, the Budweiser ads would be banned under the tough standards of the tobacco industry settlement, which prohibits the attribution of human characteristics to animals, plants, or other objects.

Alcohol ads have also targeted minority populations. Malt liquors, which contain higher concentrations of alcohol than beers do, have been touted in high-profile television ads for such labels as Colt 45 and Magnum. There is also a trend toward marketing high-end liquors to African American and Hispanic male populations. In a recent marketing campaign, Hennessy targeted young African American men with ads featuring hip-hop star Nas and sponsored events in Times Square and at the Governors Ball and Coachella music festivals. Hennessy also sponsored VIP parties with Latino deejays and hip-hop acts in Miami and Houston.

College students, too, have been heavily targeted by alcohol ads, particularly by the beer industry. Although colleges and universities have outlawed "beer bashes" hosted and supplied directly by major brewers, both Coors and Miller still employ student representatives to help "create brand awareness." These students notify brewers of special events that might be sponsored by and linked to a specific beer label. The images and slogans in alcohol ads often associate the products with power, romance, sexual prowess, or athletic skill. In reality, though, alcohol is a chemical depressant; it diminishes athletic ability and sexual performance, triggers addiction in roughly 10 percent of the U.S. population, and factors into many domestic abuse cases. One national study demonstrated "that young people who see more ads for alcoholic beverages tend to drink more."[40]

Prescription Drugs.   Another area of concern is the surge in prescription drug advertising. Spending on direct-to-consumer advertising for prescription drugs increased from $266 million in 1994 to $4.5 billion in 2014—largely due to the growth in television advertising, which today accounts for about two-thirds of such ads. These ads have made household names of prescription drugs such as Nexium, Claritin, Paxil, and Viagra. The ads are also very effective: One survey found that nearly one in three adults has talked to a doctor, and one in eight has received a prescription in response to seeing an ad for a prescription drug.[41] Between 2007 and 2011, direct-to-consumer TV advertising for prescription drugs dropped 23 percent—from $3.1 billion in 2007 to $2.3 billion in 2011—due both to doctors' concerns about being pressured by patients who see the TV ads for new drugs and to notable recalls of heavily advertised drugs like Vioxx, a pain reliever that was later found to have harsh side effects. Still, in 2011, Pfizer spent $156 million on TV ads for Lipitor (a cholesterol-lowering drug that reduces the risk of heart attack and stroke), the highest amount spent for any prescription drug that year. In 2012, prescription-drug ad spending rose again to over $3 billion.[42]

The tremendous growth of prescription drug ads brings the potential for false and misleading claims, particularly because a brief TV advertisement cannot possibly communicate all the relevant cautionary information. More recently, direct-to-consumer prescription drug advertising has appeared in text messages and on Facebook. Pharmaceutical companies have also engaged in "disease awareness" campaigns to build markets for their products. As of 2014, the United States and New Zealand were the only two nations to allow prescription drugs to be advertised directly to consumers.

Watching Over Advertising

A few nonprofit watchdog and advocacy organizations—Commercial Alert, as well as the Better Business Bureau and the National Consumers League—compensate in many ways for some of the shortcomings of the Federal Trade Commission and other government agencies in monitoring the excesses of commercialism and false and deceptive ads.

Excessive Commercialism

Since 1998, Commercial Alert—a nonprofit organization founded in part by longtime consumer advocate Ralph Nader and based in Portland, Oregon—has been working to "limit excessive commercialism in society" by informing the public about the ways that advertising has crept out of its "proper sphere." For example, Commercial Alert highlights the numerous deals for cross-promotion made between Hollywood studios and fast-food companies. These include DreamWorks' partnership with Hardee's for *TrollHunters: Tales of Arcadia* and Disney's partnership with McDonald's for family-friendly flicks like *The Incredibles 2* and *Wreck It Ralph 2*.

These deals have not only helped movie studios make money in an era of reduced DVD

CELEBRITY SPOKESPEOPLE

In 2017, actress Jennifer Lawrence appeared as the face of Dior's advertising campaign. Such celebrity endorsements bring attention to a brand or a line while promoting a desired image.

Robert Alexander/Getty Images

sales but also helped movies reach audiences that traditional advertising can't. As Jeffrey Godsick, president of consumer products at 21st Century Fox, has said, "We want to hit all the lifestyle points for consumers. Partners get us into places that are nonpurchasable (as media buys). McDonald's has access to tens of millions of people on a daily basis—that helps us penetrate the culture."[43]

Commercial Alert is a lonely voice in checking the commercialization of U.S. culture. Its other activities have included challenges to specific marketing tactics, such as the potentially deceptive advertising practices to which the new Instagram video app IGTV may expose users. In constantly questioning the role of advertising in democracy, the organization has aimed to strengthen noncommercial culture and limit the amount of corporate influence on publicly elected government bodies.

The FTC Takes On Puffery and Deception

Since the days when Lydia Pinkham's Vegetable Compound promised "a sure cure for all female weakness," false and misleading claims have haunted advertising. Over the years, the FTC, through its truth-in-advertising rules, has played an investigative role in substantiating the claims of various advertisers. A certain amount of *puffery*—ads featuring hyperbole and exaggeration—has usually been permitted, particularly when a product says it is "new and improved." However, ads become deceptive when they are likely to mislead reasonable consumers based on statements in the ad or because they omit information. Moreover, when a product claims to be "the best," "the greatest," or "preferred by four out of five doctors," FTC rules require scientific evidence to back up those claims.

Some famous examples of deceptive advertising have included the Campbell Soup TV ad in which marbles in the bottom of a soup bowl forced more bulky ingredients—and less water—to the surface. In another instance, a 1990 Volvo commercial featured a monster truck driving over a line of cars and crushing all but the Volvo; the company later admitted that the Volvo had been specially reinforced and the other cars' support columns had been weakened. Finally, a more subtle form of deception featured the Klondike Lite ice cream bar—"the 93 percent fat-free dessert with chocolate-flavored coating." The bars were indeed 93 percent fat-free—but only after the chocolate coating was removed.[44]

In 2003, the FTC brought enforcement actions against companies marketing the herbal weight-loss supplement ephedra. Ephedra has a long-standing connection to elevated blood pressure, strokes, and heart attacks and has contributed to numerous deaths. Nevertheless, companies advertised ephedra as a safe and miraculous weight-loss supplement and, incredibly, as "a beneficial treatment for hypertension and coronary disease." According to the FTC, one misleading ad said, "Teacher loses 70 pounds in only eight weeks. . . . This is how over one million people have safely lost millions of pounds! No calorie counting! No hunger! Guaranteed to work for you too!" As the director of the FTC's Bureau of Consumer Protection summed up, "There is no such thing as weight loss in a bottle. Claims that you'll lose substantial amounts of weight and still eat everything you want are simply false."[45] In 2004, the United States banned ephedra.

When the FTC discovers deceptive ads, it usually requires advertisers to change them or remove them from circulation. The FTC can also impose monetary civil penalties for companies, and it occasionally requires an advertiser to run spots to correct the deceptive ads.

kourtneykardash ✓   Follow

kourtneykardash Popeyes on the PJ. #cheatday

Load more comments

whynotblya @brigs1984 🌍visit ▶titsgram .me◀

sadam.diab @ashleighoke 💧visit ↳titsgram .me↵

kira_alexandrova13 @m8ttty| ♥ visit 🔲titsgram .me🔲

katerina_vels_ @golfpro23 🔲visit

♡ ○

427,293 likes

MAY 16, 2016

Log in to like or comment.   ···

STEALTH ADS, like Kourtney Kardashian's Popeyes endorsement posted to her Instagram page, have been criticized for being deceptive and unethical as consumers may not be aware that they are being subjected to an advertisement.

BE THE GENERATION TO END SMOKING

Truth Initiative

ALTERNATIVE ADS
In 2005, truth, the national youth smoking prevention campaign, won an Emmy Award in the national public service announcement category. Ads from truth were created by Arnold Worldwide, Crispin Porter & Bogusky, and 72andSunny.

Alternative Voices

In 1998, the largest civil litigation settlement in U.S. history took place between forty-six U.S. states, five U.S. territories, the District of Columbia, and the major heads of the tobacco industry. This Master Settlement Agreement was focused on reducing smoking—especially smoking among America's youth.

In 2000, that goal was realized through the Truth Initiative®, which launched the truth® campaign—an antismoking/anti–tobacco industry ad campaign. Truth Initiative takes the ad campaign far beyond traditional methods and has been doing so for nearly twenty years. By reaching out to teens both online (specifically offering them an opportunity to engage with the website, volunteer, and become informed) and through a grassroots approach that includes summer tours and events, the Truth Initiative has seen real results. Since summer 2000, the organization has reached nearly five million people and given away almost four million T-shirts, hats, bandannas, and other branded gear.

Additionally, truth has won multiple Emmy, Cannes Lions, Effie, Clio, and Webby awards, among many others for creative ads like "Body Bags" and "Singing Cowboy." In 2014, Ad Age—a global media brand that analyzes marketing and media—named truth one of the top fifteen campaigns of the twenty-first century. The truth campaign at least partly explains the reported decline in teen smoking. Back in 2000, according to University of Michigan studies, 23 percent of all teens smoked. In 2017, that figure was down to 6 percent.[46]

ADVERTISING, POLITICS, AND DEMOCRACY

Advertising as a profession came of age in the twentieth century, facilitating the shift of U.S. society from production-oriented small-town values to consumer-oriented urban lifestyles. With its ability to create consumers, advertising became the central economic support system for our mass media industries. Through its seemingly endless supply of pervasive and persuasive strategies, advertising today saturates the cultural landscape. Products now blend in as props or even as "characters" in TV shows and movies. In addition, almost every national consumer product now has its own website to market itself to a global audience 365 days a year. With today's digital technology, ad images can be made to appear in places where they don't really exist. For example, advertisements can be superimposed on the backstop wall behind the batter during a nationally televised baseball broadcast. Viewers at home see the ads, but fans at the game do not.

Advertising's ubiquity, especially in the age of social media, raises serious questions about our privacy and the ease with which companies can gather data on our consumer habits. But an even more serious issue is the influence of ads on our lives as democratic citizens. With fewer and fewer large media conglomerates controlling advertising and commercial speech, what is the effect on free speech and political debate? In the future, how easy will it be to get heard in a marketplace where only a few large companies control access to that space?

Advertising's Role in Politics

Since the 1950s, political consultants have been imitating market-research and advertising techniques to sell their candidates, giving rise to **political advertising**, the use of ad techniques to promote a candidate's image and persuade the public to adopt a particular viewpoint. In the early days of television, politicians running for major offices either bought or were offered half-hour blocks of time to discuss their views and the issues of the day. As advertising time became more valuable, however, local stations and the networks became reluctant to give away time in large chunks. Gradually, TV managers began selling thirty-second spots to political campaigns, just as they sold time to product advertisers.

During the 1992 and 1996 presidential campaigns, third-party candidate Ross Perot restored the use of the half-hour time block when he ran political infomercials on cable and the networks. In 2008, Barack Obama also ran a half-hour infomercial; and in the 2012 presidential race, both major candidates and various political organizations supporting them ran many online infomercials that were much longer than the standard thirty- to sixty-second TV spot. However, only very wealthy or well-funded candidates can afford such promotional strategies, and television does not usually provide free airtime to politicians. Questions about political ads continue to be asked: Can serious information on political issues be conveyed in thirty-second spots? Do repeated attack ads, which assault another candidate's character, so undermine citizens' confidence in the electoral process that they stop voting?[47] And how does a democratic society ensure that alternative political voices, which are not well financed or commercially viable, still receive a hearing?

Although broadcasters use the public's airwaves, they have long opposed providing free time for political campaigns and issues, since political advertising is big business for television stations. In the historic 2008 election, more than $5.28 billion was spent on advertising by all presidential and congressional candidates and interest groups. In 2012 (with a total of $6.28 billion spent on all elections), more than $1.1 billion alone went to local broadcast TV stations in the twelve most highly contested states, with local cable raking in another $200 million in those states.[48] According to Borrell Associates, political campaign ad spending in 2016 totaled $9.8 billion during the election cycle— short of predictions. Borrell cited a decline in traditional media spending (outlets such as broadcast television, magazine/newspaper ads, and even radio).[49] The lower revenue total is partly connected to President Trump's use of his celebrity status and his Twitter account to garner free media coverage.

The Future of Advertising

Although commercialism—through packaging both products and politicians—has generated cultural feedback that is often critical of advertising's pervasiveness, the growth of the industry has not diminished. Ads continue to fascinate. Many consumers buy magazines or watch the Super Bowl just for the advertisements. Adolescents decorate their rooms with their favorite ads and identify with the images certain products convey. In 2014, the fifth straight year of increases, advertising spending in the United States totaled more than $141 billion.[50]

A number of factors have made advertising's largely unchecked growth possible. Many Americans tolerate advertising as a necessary evil for maintaining the economy, and many others dismiss advertising as not believable and trivial. Thus, unwilling to admit its centrality to global culture, many citizens do not think advertising is significant enough to monitor or reform. Such attitudes have ensured advertising's pervasiveness and suggest the need to escalate our critical vigilance.

As individuals and as a society, we have developed an uneasy relationship with advertising. Favorite ads and commercial jingles remain part of our cultural world for a lifetime, yet we detest irritating and repetitive commercials. We realize that without ads, many mass media would need to reinvent themselves. At the same time, we need to remain critical of what advertising has come to represent: the overemphasis on commercial acquisitions and images of material success, and the disparity between those who can afford to live comfortably in a commercialized society and those who cannot.

11 Chapter Review

COMMON THREADS

One of the Common Threads discussed in Chapter 1 is the commercial nature of mass media. The U.S. media system, due to policy choices made in the early and mid-twentieth century, was built largely on a system of commercial sponsorship. Consumers' acceptance of this arrangement was based on a sense that media content and sponsors should remain independent of each other. In other words, sponsors and product companies should not control and create media content. Today, is that line between media content and advertising shifting—or even completely disappearing?

Although media consumers have not always been comfortable with advertising, they developed a resigned acceptance of it because it "pays the bills" of the media system. Yet media consumers have their limits. Moments in which sponsors stepped over the usual borders of advertising into the realm of media content—including the TV quiz-show and radio payola scandals, complimentary newspaper reports about advertisers' businesses, product placement in TV shows and movies, and now "sponsored stories" on Facebook—have generated the greatest legal and ethical debates about advertising.

Still, as advertising has become more pervasive and consumers have become more discriminating, ad practitioners have searched for ways to weave their work more seamlessly into the cultural fabric. Products now blend in as props or even as "characters" in TV shows and movies. Search engines deliver paid placements along with regular search results. Product placements are woven into video games. Advertising messages can also be the subject of viral videos—and consumers do the work of distributing the message.

Among the more intriguing efforts to become enmeshed in the culture are the ads that exploit, distort, or transform the political and cultural meanings of popular music. When Nike used the Beatles' song "Revolution" (1968) to promote Nike shoes in 1987 ("Nike Air is not a shoe . . . it's a revolution," the ad said), many music fans were outraged to hear the Beatles' music being used for the first time to sell products.

That was more than thirty years ago. These days, having a popular song used in a TV commercial is considered a good career move for musicians—even better than radio airplay. Similarly, while product placement in TV shows and movies was hotly debated in the 1980s and 1990s, the explosive growth of paid placements in video games hardly raises an eyebrow today. Even the lessons of the quiz-show scandals, which forced advertisers out of TV program production in the late 1950s, are forgotten or ignored today as advertisers have been warmly invited to help develop TV programs.

Are we as a society giving up on trying to set limits on the never-ending onslaught of advertising? Are we weary of trying to keep advertising out of media production? How do we feel about the growing encroachment of ads into social networks like Facebook and Twitter? Why do we now seem less concerned about the integration of advertising into the core of media culture?

KEY TERMS

The definitions for the terms listed below can be found in the glossary at the end of the book. The page numbers listed with the terms indicate where the term is highlighted in the chapter.

product placement, 329
space brokers, 330
subliminal advertising, 334
slogan, 334
mega-agencies, 335
boutique agencies, 335
market research, 337
Values and Lifestyles (VALS), 337

storyboard, 338
viral marketing, 338
media buyers, 338
saturation advertising, 338
interstitials, 340
spam, 340
famous-person testimonial, 344
plain-folks pitch, 344

snob-appeal approach, 344
bandwagon effect, 344
hidden-fear appeal, 344
irritation advertising, 344
association principle, 345
myth analysis, 345
commercial speech, 349
political advertising, 357

REVIEW QUESTIONS

Early Developments in American Advertising

1. Whom did the first ad agencies serve?

2. How did trademarks and packaging influence advertising?

3. Explain why patent medicines and department stores figured so prominently in advertising in the late nineteenth century.

4. What role did advertising play in transforming America into a consumer society?

The Shape of U.S. Advertising Today

5. What influences did visual culture exert on advertising?

6. What are the differences between boutique agencies and mega-agencies?

7. What are the major divisions at most ad agencies? What is the function of each department?

8. What are the advantages of Internet and mobile advertising over traditional media, like newspapers and television?

Persuasive Techniques in Contemporary Advertising

9. How do the common persuasive techniques used in advertising work?

10. How does the association principle work, and why is it an effective way to analyze advertising?

11. What is the disassociation corollary?

12. What is product placement? Cite examples.

Commercial Speech and Regulating Advertising

13. What is commercial speech?

14. What are four serious contemporary issues regarding health and advertising? Why is each issue controversial?

15. What is the difference between puffery and deception in advertising? How can the FTC regulate deceptive ads?

Advertising, Politics, and Democracy

16. What are some of the major issues involving political advertising?

17. What role does advertising play in a democratic society?

QUESTIONING THE MEDIA

1. What is your earliest recollection of watching a television commercial? Do you think the ad had a significant influence on you?

2. Why are so many people critical of advertising?

3. If you were (or are) a parent, what strategies would you use to explain an objectionable ad to your child or teenager? Provide an example.

4. Should advertising aimed at children be regulated? Support your response.

5. Should tobacco or alcohol advertising be prohibited? Why or why not? How would you deal with First Amendment issues regarding controversial ads?

6. Would you be in favor of regular advertising on public television and radio as a means of financial support for these media? Explain your answer.

7. Is advertising at odds with the ideals of democracy? Why or why not?

LAUNCHPAD FOR *MEDIA & CULTURE*

Public Relations and Framing the Message

12

AMERICA'S BIGGEST SPORT is having major public relations problems. While the NFL continues to deal with the fallout from incidents and research findings related to concussion and chronic traumatic encephalopathy (CTE), the league has also had to react to public scrutiny from the #MeToo and Black Lives Matter movements. The NFL has often responded to bad press by downplaying the incidents or covering them up, which has led critics to call the NFL's public relations (PR) strategy a fiasco. In addition, the NFL's ratings are in decline.[1]

The first PR problem is CTE, a serious head-trauma disease afflicting a number of players and former players. After San Diego Chargers linebacker Junior Seau committed suicide in 2012 at age forty-three (he shot himself in the chest), it seemed as though the NFL was committed to

EARLY
DEVELOPMENTS IN
PUBLIC RELATIONS
p. 363

THE PRACTICE OF
PUBLIC RELATIONS
p. 368

TENSIONS BETWEEN
PUBLIC RELATIONS
AND THE PRESS
p. 378

PUBLIC RELATIONS
AND DEMOCRACY
p. 381

◄ San Francisco 49ers players Eli Harold and Colin Kaepernick take a knee during the national anthem to protest the oppression of black people and people of color in the United States.

taking head trauma seriously. A few months after the suicide, the NFL pledged $30 million to the National Institutes of Health (NIH) toward independent CTE research led by top neuropathologists. But when one of these researchers designed a study to find CTE in living patients, the NFL moved to veto the research and withdrew the $16 million the NIH had earmarked for it.[2]

In August 2017, the NFL funded another NIH study which found that 99 percent of NFL players' brains and 91 percent of college players' brains had CTE.[3] The NFL's public relations response to this study was to downplay its damning results as insignificant or misleading.[4] Part of the tepid response, critics suggested, was influenced by the $1 billion concussion settlement between thousands of players and the NFL, which was being finalized around the time the new CTE study came out. The lawsuit in question alleged that the NFL had concealed the link between football and brain damage, clearing the way for payouts to more than twenty thousand retired players. The NFL's response to the study, critics supposed, was aimed at avoiding any challenges to the settlement or any new lawsuits.[5]

The NFL's most recent public relations strategy was to pledge $100 million toward its Play Smart, Play Safe initiative, which funds newly engineered headgear and "medical and neuroscience research."[6] Significantly, this new research will be done in-house, not among NIH's top independent, peer-reviewed neuropathologists. "The NFL is going to insulting lengths to prove that CTE isn't a problem," wrote NFL critic Louis Bien for Vox Media's fan site SB Nation: "The NFL is funding its own concussion studies now. The first thing it did was study horse jockeys, not football players." Indeed, the NFL issued only one study with its $100 million in pledged funding—on horse jockeys and CTE. Disturbingly, the study

was headed up by an Australian researcher who was critical of U.S. CTE media coverage (he called it "hoo-hah") and a British doctor who minimized CTE and gave slapstick presentations that were peppered with inappropriate jokes.[7]

Meanwhile, the NFL had to field a continuous stream of stories throughout the 2017 season about numerous NFL players who chose to publicly support the Black Lives Matter movement by kneeling, sitting, or raising their fists during the national anthem played before every game, a moment when players and audience members are expected to stand and visibly honor the American flag. In the early stages of the controversy, the NFL issued a public statement: "Players are encouraged but not required to stand during the playing of the national anthem." The next year, the NFL pledged $89 million over the next seven years toward social justice causes. But before the 2018 season, the NFL reversed itself, with the owners voting to require players on the field to stand for the national anthem. The NFL owners made an even larger symbolic statement by continuing their refusal to offer a contract to the talented quarterback Colin Kaepernick, who had initiated the protests in August 2016.

The NFL Network was also plagued by sexual harassment and assault lawsuits from women in the first few months of 2018, as the #MeToo movement came to sports television. Five former NFL football players and a former NFL Network executive were suspended by three media organizations after a former wardrobe stylist for the network, Jami Cantor, brought a lawsuit against them, alleging sexual harassment;[8] an NFL Network executive was forced to resign because of a stream of sexually explicit tweets;[9] and a former NFL cheerleader filed an antidiscrimination suit against the New Orleans Saints.[10] The NFL, and football itself, swings from bad PR to bad PR.

THE STORY OF THE NFL ILLUSTRATES A MAJOR DIFFERENCE between advertising and public relations: Advertising is controlled publicity that a company or an individual buys; public relations attempts to secure favorable media publicity (which is more difficult to control) to promote a company or a client.

Public relations covers a wide array of practices, such as shaping the public image of a politician or a celebrity, establishing or repairing communication between consumers and companies, and promoting government agencies and actions, especially during wartime. Broadly defined, **public relations** refers to the total communication strategy conducted by a person, a government, or an organization attempting to reach and persuade an audience to adopt a point of view.[11] While public relations may sound very similar to advertising, which also seeks to persuade audiences, it is a different skill in a variety of ways. Advertising uses simple and fixed messages (e.g., "our appliance is the most efficient and affordable") that are transmitted directly to the public through the purchase of ads. Public relations involves more complex messages that may evolve over time (e.g., a political campaign or a long-term strategy to dispel unfavorable reports about "fatty processed foods") and that may be transmitted to the public indirectly, often through the news media.

The social and cultural impact of public relations has been immense. In its infancy, PR helped convince many American businesses of the value of nurturing the public, whose members became purchasers rather than producers of their own goods after the Industrial Revolution. PR set the tone for the corporate image-building that characterized the economic environment of the twentieth century and for the battles of organizations taking sides on today's environmental, energy, and labor issues. Perhaps PR's most significant effect, however, has been on the political process, in which individuals and organizations—on both the Right and the Left—hire spin doctors to shape their media images.

In this chapter, we will:

- Study the impact of public relations and the historical conditions that affected its development as a modern profession
- Look at nineteenth-century press agents and the role that railroad and utility companies played in developing corporate PR
- Consider the rise of modern PR, particularly the influences of former reporters Ivy Lee and Edward Bernays
- Explore the major practices and specialties of public relations
- Examine the reasons for the long-standing antagonism between journalists and members of the PR profession, and the social responsibilities of public relations in a democracy

As you read this chapter, think about what knowledge you might already have about what public relations practitioners do, given that PR is an immensely powerful media industry and yet remains largely invisible. Can you think of a company or an organization, either national (like BP) or local (like your university or college), that might have engaged the help of a public relations team to handle a crisis? What did the team do to make the public trust the organization more? When you see political campaign coverage, are you sometimes aware of the spin doctors who are responsible for making sure their candidate says or does the "right" thing at the "right" time to foster the most favorable public image that will gain the candidate the most votes? For more questions to help you understand the role of public relations in our lives, see "Questioning the Media" in the Chapter Review.

LaunchPad
macmillan learning
launchpadworks.com

Visit LaunchPad for *Media & Culture* and use LearningCurve to review concepts from this chapter.

EARLY DEVELOPMENTS IN PUBLIC RELATIONS

At the beginning of the twentieth century, the United States shifted to a consumer-oriented, industrial society, which fostered the development of new products and services as people moved to cities to find work. During this transformation from farm to factory, advertising and PR emerged as professions. While advertising drew attention and customers to new products, PR began in part to help businesses fend off increased scrutiny from the muckraking journalists and emerging labor unions of the time.[12]

The first PR practitioners were simply theatrical **press agents**: those who sought to advance a client's image through media exposure, primarily via stunts staged for newspapers. The advantages of these early PR techniques soon became obvious. For instance, press agents were used by people like Daniel Boone, who engineered various land-grab and real estate ventures, and Davy Crockett, who in addition to performing heroic exploits was involved in the massacre of Native Americans. Such individuals often wanted press agents to repair and reshape their reputations as cherished frontier legends or as respectable candidates for public office.

P. T. Barnum and Buffalo Bill

The most notorious press agent of the nineteenth century was Phineas Taylor (P. T.) Barnum, who used gross exaggeration, fraudulent stories, and staged events to secure newspaper coverage for his clients, his American Museum, and later his circus. Barnum's circus, dubbed "The Greatest Show on Earth," included the "midget" General Tom Thumb, Swedish soprano Jenny Lind, Jumbo the Elephant, and Joice Heth (who Barnum claimed was the 161-year-old nurse of George Washington but who was actually 80 when she died). These performers became some of the earliest nationally known celebrities because of Barnum's skill in using the media for promotion. Decrying outright fraud and cheating, Barnum understood that his audiences liked to be tricked. In newspapers and on handbills, he later often revealed the strategies behind his more elaborate hoaxes.

From 1883 to 1916, William F. Cody, who once killed buffalo for the railroads, promoted himself and his traveling show: "Buffalo Bill's Wild West and Congress of Rough Riders of the World." Cody's troupe—which featured Bedouins, Cossacks, and gauchos, as well as "cowboys and Indians"— re-created dramatic gunfights, the Civil War, and battles of the Old West. The show employed sharpshooter Annie Oakley and Lakota chief and healer Sitting Bull, whose legends were partially shaped by Cody's nine press agents. These agents were led by John Burke, who successfully promoted the show for its entire thirty-four-year run. Burke was one of the first press agents to use a wide variety of media channels to generate publicity: promotional newspaper stories, magazine articles and ads, dime novels, theater marquees, poster art, and early films. Burke and Buffalo Bill shaped many of the lasting myths about rugged American individualism and frontier expansion that were later adopted by books, radio programs, and Hollywood films depicting the American West. Along with Barnum, they were among the first to use **publicity**—a type of PR communication that uses various media messages to spread information about a person, a corporation, an issue, or a policy—to elevate entertainment culture to an international level.

Big Business and Press Agents

As P. T. Barnum, Buffalo Bill, and John Burke demonstrated, the use of press agents brought with it enormous power to sway the public and to generate business. So it is not surprising that during the nineteenth century, America's largest industrial companies—particularly the railroads—also employed press agents to win favor in the court of public opinion.

EARLY PUBLIC RELATIONS
Originally called "P. T. Barnum's Great Traveling Museum, Menagerie, Caravan, and Hippodrome," Barnum's circus merged with Bailey's circus in 1881 and again with the Ringling Bros. in 1919. Even with the ups and downs of the Ringling Bros. and Barnum & Bailey Circus over the decades, Barnum's original catchphrase, "The Greatest Show on Earth," endured through the circus's final performance on May 21, 2017.

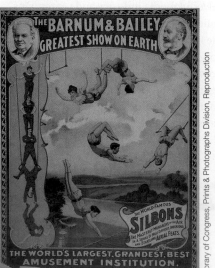

Library of Congress, Prints & Photographs Division, Reproduction number LC-DIG-ppmsca-54807 (digital file from original) LC-USZC4-9668 (color film copy transparency) LC-USZ62-24475 (b&w film copy neg.)

The railroads began to use press agents to help them obtain federal funds. Initially, local businesses raised funds to finance the spread of rail service. Around 1850, however, the railroads began pushing for federal subsidies, complaining that local fund-raising efforts took too long. For example, Illinois Central was one of the first companies to use government *lobbyists* (people who try to influence the voting of lawmakers) to argue that railroad service between the North and the South was in the public interest and would ease tensions, unite the two regions, and prevent a war.

The railroad press agents successfully gained government support by developing some of the earliest publicity tactics. Their first strategy was simply to buy favorable news stories about rail travel from newspapers through direct bribes. Another practice was to engage in *deadheading*—giving reporters free rail passes with the tacit understanding that they would write glowing reports about rail travel. Eventually, wealthy railroads received the federal subsidies they wanted and increased their profits, while the American public shouldered much of the financial burden of rail expansion.

Having obtained construction subsidies, the larger rail companies turned their attention to bigger game—persuading the government to control rates and reduce competition, especially from smaller, aggressive regional lines. Railroad lobbyists argued that federal support would lead to improved service and guaranteed quality because the government would be keeping a close watch. These lobbying efforts, accompanied by favorable publicity, led to passage of the Interstate Commerce Act in 1887, the first federal law to regulate private industry, which required railroads to publicize their shipping rates, banned special lower rates for certain freights or passengers, and established a commission to oversee enforcement of the law.[13] Historians have argued that, ironically, the PR campaign's success actually led to the decline of the railroads: Artificially maintained higher rates and burdensome government regulations forced smaller firms out of business and eventually drove many customers to other modes of transportation.

The Birth of Modern Public Relations

By the first decade of the twentieth century, reporters and muckraking journalists were investigating the promotional practices behind many companies. As an informed citizenry paid more attention, it became increasingly difficult for large firms to fool the press and mislead the public. With the rise of the middle class, increasing literacy among the working classes, and the spread of information through print media, democratic ideals began to threaten the established order of business and politics—and the elite groups who managed them. Two pioneers of public relations—Ivy Lee and Edward Bernays—emerged in this atmosphere to popularize an approach that emphasized shaping the interpretation of facts and "engineering consent."

Ivy Ledbetter Lee

Most nineteenth-century corporations and manufacturers cared little about public sentiment. By the early 1900s, though, executives had realized that their companies could sell more products if they were associated with positive public images and values. Into this public space stepped Ivy Ledbetter Lee, considered one of the founders of modern public relations. Lee understood that the public's attitude toward big corporations had changed. He counseled his corporate clients that honesty and directness were better PR devices than the deceptive practices of the nineteenth century, which had fostered suspicion and an anti-big-business sentiment.

A minister's son, an economics student at Princeton University, and a former reporter, Lee opened one of the first PR firms in the early 1900s with George Park. Lee quit the firm in 1906 to work for the Pennsylvania Railroad, which, following a rail accident, had hired him to help downplay unfavorable publicity. Lee's advice, however, was that Penn Railroad admit its mistake, vow to do better, and let newspapers in on the story. These suggestions ran counter to the then standard practice of hiring press agents to manipulate the media, yet Lee argued that an open relationship between

IT'S GREAT TO BE A NEW YORKER

Our Men KNOW Their Jobs

Elevated Express

Published now and then by the Interborough Rapid Transit Company

Always Dependable

VOLUME VI · OCTOBER · NUMBER 27

Your Children and you will enjoy seeing the thousand and one wonders in the Museum of Natural History

Take the West Side Elevated to 81st Street

Interborough Rapid Transit Co.

The Subway Station at 79th Street is only 2½ Blocks away

Bettmann/Getty Images

Photo courtesy of Princeton University. Reprinted by permission.

IVY LEE,
a founding father of public relations (*above*), did more than just crisis work with large companies and business magnates. His PR clients also included transportation companies in New York City (*above right*) and aviator Charles Lindbergh.

business and the press would lead to a more favorable public image. In the end, Penn and subsequent clients, notably John D. Rockefeller, adopted Lee's successful strategies.

By the 1880s, Rockefeller controlled 90 percent of the nation's oil industry and suffered from periodic image problems, particularly after Ida Tarbell's powerful muckraking series about the ruthless business tactics practiced by Rockefeller and his Standard Oil Company appeared in *McClure's Magazine* in 1904. The Rockefeller and Standard Oil reputations reached a low point in April 1914, when tactics to stop union organizing erupted in tragedy at a coal company in Ludlow, Colorado. During a violent strike, fifty-three workers and their family members died, including thirteen women and children.

Lee was hired to contain the damaging publicity fallout. He immediately distributed a series of "fact" sheets to the press, telling the corporate side of the story and discrediting the tactics of the United Mine Workers, who had organized the strike. As he had done for Penn Railroad, Lee also brought in the press and staged photo opportunities. John D. Rockefeller Jr., who now ran the company, donned overalls and a miner's helmet and posed with the families of workers and union leaders. This was probably the first use of a PR campaign in a labor-versus-management dispute. Over the years, Lee completely transformed the wealthy family's image, urging the discreet Rockefellers to publicize their charitable work. To improve his image, the senior Rockefeller took to handing out dimes to children wherever he went—a strategic ritual that historians attribute to Lee.

Called "Poison Ivy" by corporate foes and critics within the press, Lee had a complex understanding of facts. For Lee, facts were elusive and malleable, begging to be forged and shaped. "Since crowds do not reason," he noted in 1917, "they can only be organized and stimulated through symbols and phrases."[14] In the Ludlow case, for instance, Lee noted that the women and children who died while retreating from the charging company-backed militia had overturned a stove, which caught fire and caused their deaths. One of his PR fact sheets implied that they had, in part, been victims of their own carelessness.

Edward Bernays

The nephew of Sigmund Freud, former reporter Edward Bernays inherited the public relations mantle from Ivy Lee. Beginning in 1919, when he opened his own office, Bernays was the first person to apply the findings of psychology and sociology to public relations, referring to himself as

EDWARD BERNAYS
with his business partner and wife, Doris Fleischman (*left*). Bernays worked on behalf of the American Tobacco Company to make smoking socially acceptable for women. For one of American Tobacco's brands, Lucky Strike, Bernays was also asked to change public attitudes toward the color green. (Women weren't buying the brand because surveys indicated that the forest green package clashed with their wardrobes.) Bernays and Fleischman organized events such as green fashion shows and sold the idea of a new trend in green to the press. By 1934, green had become the fashion color of the season, making Lucky Strike cigarettes the perfect accessory for the female smoker. Interestingly, Bernays forbade his own wife to smoke, flushing her cigarettes down the toilet and calling smoking a nasty habit.

a "public relations counselor" rather than a "publicity agent." Over the years, Bernays's client list included General Electric, the American Tobacco Company, General Motors, *Good Housekeeping* and *Time* magazines, Procter & Gamble, RCA, the government of India, the city of Vienna, and President Coolidge.

Bernays also worked for the Committee on Public Information (CPI) during World War I, developing propaganda that supported America's entry into that conflict and promoting the image of President Woodrow Wilson as a peacemaker. Both efforts were among the first full-scale governmental attempts to mobilize public opinion. In addition, Bernays made key contributions to public relations education, teaching the first class called "public relations"—at New York University in 1923—and writing the field's first textbook, *Crystallizing Public Opinion*. For many years, his definition of PR was the standard: "Public relations is the attempt, by information, persuasion, and adjustment, to engineer public support for an activity, cause, movement, or institution."[15]

In the 1920s, Bernays was hired by the American Tobacco Company to develop a campaign to make smoking more publicly acceptable for women. Among other strategies, Bernays staged an event: placing women smokers in New York's 1929 Easter parade. He labeled cigarettes "torches of freedom" and encouraged women to smoke as a symbol of their newly acquired suffrage and independence from men. He also asked the women he placed in the parade to contact newspaper and newsreel companies in advance—to announce their symbolic protest. The campaign received plenty of free publicity from newspapers and magazines. Within weeks of the parade, men-only smoking rooms in New York theaters began opening up to women.

Through much of his writing, Bernays suggested that emerging freedoms threatened the established hierarchical order. He thought it was important for experts and leaders to control the direction of American society: "The duty of the higher strata of society—the cultivated, the learned, the expert, the intellectual—is therefore clear. They must inject moral and spiritual motives into public opinion."[16] For the cultural elite to maintain order and control, they would have to win the consent of the larger public. As a result, Bernays described the shaping of public opinion through PR as the "engineering of consent." Like Ivy Lee, Bernays believed that public opinion was malleable and not always rational: In the hands of the right experts, leaders, and PR counselors, public opinion could be shaped into forms people could rally behind.[17] However, journalists like Walter Lippmann, who wrote the famous book *Public Opinion* in 1922, worried that PR professionals with hidden agendas, as opposed to journalists with professional detachment, held too much power over American public opinion.

Throughout Bernays's most active years, his business partner and later wife, Doris Fleischman, worked on many of his campaigns as a researcher and coauthor. Beginning in the 1920s, she was one of the first women to work in public relations, and she introduced PR to America's most powerful leaders through a pamphlet she edited called *Contact*. Because she opened up the profession to women from its inception, PR emerged as one of the few professions—apart from teaching and nursing—accessible to women who chose to work outside the home at that time. Today, more than 60 percent of PR professionals are women.

THE PRACTICE OF PUBLIC RELATIONS

Today, there are more than twelve thousand PR firms in the United States, plus thousands of additional PR departments within corporate, government, and nonprofit organizations.[18] Since the 1980s, the formal study of public relations has grown significantly at colleges and universities. By 2018, the Public Relations Student Society of America (PRSSA) had more than ten thousand members and over three hundred chapters in colleges and universities. As certified PR programs have expanded (often requiring courses in journalism), the profession has relied less and less on its traditional practice of recruiting journalists for its workforce. At the same time, new courses in professional ethics, issues management, and integrated marketing have expanded the responsibility of future practitioners. In this section, we discuss the differences between public relations agencies and in-house PR services and the various practices involved in performing PR.

Approaches to Organized Public Relations

The Public Relations Society of America (PRSA) offers this simple and useful definition of PR: "Public relations is a strategic communication process that builds mutually beneficial relationships between organizations and their publics." To carry out this mutual communication process, the PR industry uses two approaches. First, there are independent PR agencies whose sole job is to provide clients with PR services. Second, most companies, which may or may not also hire independent PR firms, maintain their own in-house PR staffs to handle routine tasks, such as writing press releases, managing various media requests, staging special events, updating web and social media sites, and dealing with internal and external publics.

Many large PR firms are owned by, or are affiliated with, multinational communications holding companies, such as Omnicom, WPP, and Interpublic (see Table 12.1). The largest PR agency is Edelman, started by Daniel J. Edelman in Chicago in 1952. Edelman was an innovator; his was the first public relations firm to bring clients and their products on television media tours, and one of the first American PR companies to do business in Asia. His son, Richard Edelman, now leads the company, which has represented corporate clients like Heinz, Butterball, Starbucks, Microsoft, and Samsung for decades, and has sixty-five global offices.

In contrast to external agencies, most PR work is done in-house at companies and organizations. Although America's largest companies typically retain external PR firms, almost every company involved in the manufacturing and service industries has an in-house PR department. Such departments are also a vital part of many professional organizations, such as the American Medical

Rank	Agency	Parent Firm	Headquarters	Revenue
1	Edelman	Independent	Chicago	$893.6
2	Weber Shandwick	Interpublic	New York	$719.1
3	Burson Cohn & Wolfe	WPP	New York	$669.7
4	FleishmanHillard	Omnicom	St. Louis	$598.1
5	Ketchum	Omnicom	New York	$510.4

TABLE 12.1

THE TOP 5 PUBLIC RELATIONS FIRMS, 2017 (BY WORLDWIDE REVENUE, IN MILLIONS OF U.S. DOLLARS)

Data from: "Public Relations Worldwide," *Advertising Age,* April 30, 2018, p. 19.

Association, the AFL-CIO, and the National Association of Broadcasters, as well as large nonprofit organizations, such as the American Cancer Society, the Arthritis Foundation, and most universities and colleges.

Performing Public Relations

Public relations, like advertising, pays careful attention to the needs of its clients—politicians, small businesses, industries, and nonprofit organizations—and to the perspectives of its targeted audiences: consumers and the general public, company employees, shareholders, media organizations, government agencies, and community and industry leaders. To do so, PR involves providing a multitude of services, including publicity, communication, public affairs, issues management, government relations, financial PR, community relations, industry relations, minority relations, advertising, press agentry, promotion, media relations, social networking, and propaganda. This last service, **propaganda**, is communication strategically placed, either as advertising or as publicity, to gain public support for a special issue, program, or policy, such as a nation's war effort.

In addition, PR personnel (both PR technicians, who handle daily short-term activities, and PR managers, who counsel clients and manage activities over the long term) produce employee newsletters, manage client trade shows and conferences, conduct historical tours, appear on news programs, organize damage control after negative publicity, analyze complex issues and trends that may affect a client's future, manage Twitter and other social media accounts, and much more. Basic among these activities, however, are formulating a message through research, conveying the message through various channels, sustaining public support through community and consumer relations, and maintaining client interests through government relations.

Research: Formulating the Message

One of the most essential practices in the PR profession is doing research. Just as advertising is driven today by demographic and psychographic research, PR uses similar strategies to project messages to appropriate audiences. Because it has historically been difficult to determine why particular PR campaigns succeed or fail, research has become the key ingredient in PR forecasting. Like advertising, PR makes use of mail, telephone, and Internet

WORLD WAR II
was a time when the U.S. government used propaganda and other PR strategies to drum up support for the war. One of the more iconic posters at the time asked women to join the workforce.

MPI/Getty Images

MESSAGE FORMULATION

One of the social media commercials developed in the FDA's "The Real Cost" anti-tobacco campaign confronted smokeless tobacco. In this ad, the narrator says, "Dip doesn't just leave a mark on your jeans. Dip can cause mouth cancer. Smokeless doesn't mean harmless."

surveys; focus group interviews; and social media analytics tools—such as Google Analytics, Klear, Keyhole, Sprout Social, and Twitter Analytics—to get a fix on an audience's perceptions of an issue, a policy, a program, or a client's image.

Research also helps PR professionals focus a campaign message. For example, after years of declining smoking rates, the Food and Drug Administration (FDA) was alarmed to discover an increase in youth smoking, particularly in hookah pipes and e-cigarettes. The FDA conducted research with at-risk youths to determine what messages would be most effective among youths who were open to smoking or already experimenting with cigarettes. As a result, "The Real Cost" campaign launched nationwide in 2014 across a number of media platforms. The FDA even hired independent researchers to assess the effectiveness of the campaign among its target group. Over time, the campaign has evolved to keep up with tobacco use trends. In 2016, the campaign expanded to prevent smokeless tobacco use, targeting rural male teens in thirty-five markets. In 2017, it set its sights on youth e-cigarette use, communicating the dangers of nicotine on developing brains. The FDA planned an even larger e-cigarette campaign beginning in 2018.[19]

Conveying the Message

One of the chief day-to-day functions in public relations is creating and distributing PR messages for the news media or the public. There are several possible message forms, including press releases, VNRs, and various online options.

Press releases, or news releases, are announcements written in the style of news reports that present new information about an individual, a company, or an organization and pitch a story idea to the news media. In issuing press releases, PR agents hope that their client information will be picked up by the news media and transformed into news reports. Through press releases, PR firms manage the flow of information, controlling which media get what material in which order. (A PR agent may even reward a cooperative reporter by strategically releasing information.) News editors and broadcasters sort through hundreds of releases daily to determine which ones contain the most original ideas or are the most current. Most large media institutions rewrite and double-check the releases, but small media companies often use them verbatim because of limited editorial resources. Usually, the more closely a press release resembles actual news copy, the more likely it is to be used. Twitter has also become a popular format for releasing information to the news media. More than half of journalists follow Twitter to get news tips. Today, a tweet can be just as successful as a complete press release in gaining news media coverage.

PUBLIC RELATIONS CRISIS ON TWITTER

Public relations crises can result from a poorly considered tweet and then play out in real time on the social media platform. For example, when actor Roseanne Barr posted a tweet in May 2018 that likened Valerie Jarrett, an African American woman and former Obama aide, to an ape, an enormous public relations crisis opened up on Twitter. Shortly after reviewing the tweet, ABC posted its own tweet, firing Barr and canceling her show. Later, Barr posted an apology to Jarrett, characterizing it as a bad joke. Then Barr made another post, blaming the sleeping drug Ambien for her racist tweet. Sanofi, the maker of Ambien, responded with its own pointed tweet, saying that "racism is not a known side effect of any Sanofi medication." Other members of the *Roseanne* show posted on Twitter to distance themselves from Barr. President Trump, a fan of Barr's TV show, joined the viral tweetstorm, not criticizing Barr but posting his own grievances about ABC.

Since the introduction of portable video equipment in the 1970s, PR agencies and departments have also been issuing **video news releases (VNRs)**—thirty- to ninety-second visual press releases designed to mimic the style of a broadcast news report. Although networks and large TV news stations do not usually broadcast VNRs, news stations in small TV markets regularly use material from VNRs. On occasion, news stations have been criticized for using video footage from a VNR without acknowledging the source. In 2005, the FCC mandated that broadcast stations and cable operators must disclose the source of the VNRs they air.

The equivalent of VNRs for nonprofits are **public service announcements (PSAs)**: fifteen- to sixty-second audio or video reports that promote government programs, educational projects, volunteer agencies, or social reform. As part of their requirement to serve the public interest, broadcasters have been encouraged to carry free PSAs. Since the deregulation of broadcasting began in the 1980s, however, there has been less pressure and no minimum obligation for TV and radio stations to air PSAs. When PSAs *do* run, they are frequently scheduled between midnight and 6:00 A.M., a less commercially valuable time slot.

The Internet is an essential avenue for distributing PR messages. Companies upload or e-mail press releases, press kits, and VNRs for targeted groups. Social media have also transformed traditional PR communications. For example, a social media press release pulls together "remixable" multimedia elements, such as text, graphics, video, podcasts, and hyperlinks, giving journalists ample material to develop their own stories.

Media Relations

PR managers specializing in media relations promote a client or an organization by securing publicity or favorable coverage in the news media. This often requires an in-house PR person to speak on behalf of an organization or to direct reporters to experts who can provide information. Media-relations specialists also perform damage control or crisis management when negative publicity occurs. Occasionally, in times of crisis—such as a scandal at a university or a safety recall by a car manufacturer—a PR spokesperson might be designated as the only source of information available to news media. Although journalists often resent being cut off from higher administrative levels and leaders, the institution or company in question wants to ensure that rumors and inaccurate stories do not circulate in the media. In these situations, a game often develops between PR specialists and the media in which reporters attempt to circumvent the spokesperson and induce a knowledgeable insider to talk off the record, providing background details without being named directly as a source.

PR agents who specialize in media relations also recommend advertising to their clients when it seems appropriate. Unlike publicity, which is sometimes outside a PR agency's control, paid advertising may help focus a complex issue or a client's image. Publicity, however, carries the aura of legitimate news and thus has more credibility than advertising does. In addition, media specialists cultivate associations with editors, reporters, freelance writers, and broadcast news directors to ensure that their work on behalf of their client is favorably received (see "Examining Ethics: Public Relations and 'Alternative Facts'" on page 372).

Special Events and Pseudo-Events

Another public relations practice involves coordinating *special events* to raise the profile of corporate, organizational, or government clients. Typical special-events publicity often includes a corporate sponsor aligning itself with a cause or an organization that has positive stature among the general public. For example, John Hancock Financial has been the primary sponsor of the Boston Marathon since 1986 and funds the race's prize money. The company's corporate communications department also serves as the PR office for the race, operating the pressroom and creating the marathon's media guide and other press materials. Eighteen other sponsors—including Adidas, Gatorade, Clif Bar, and JetBlue Airways—also pay to affiliate themselves with the Boston Marathon. At the local level, companies often sponsor a community parade or a charitable fund-raising activity.

EXAMINING ETHICS

Public Relations and "Alternative Facts"

On Sunday, January 22, 2017, White House adviser Kellyanne Conway appeared on NBC's *Meet the Press* with host Chuck Todd. The Trump administration was brand new, with Trump's inauguration just two days earlier. According to *Guardian* columnist Jill Abramson, Conway "made the absurd claim that the new White House press secretary, Sean Spicer, hadn't lied to reporters about the size of the inaugural crowd, he had merely presented them with 'alternative facts.'"[1]

For context, here is the excerpt of the Todd and Conway exchange:

Chuck Todd: . . . *Answer the question of why the president asked the White House press secretary to come out in front of the podium for the first time and utter a falsehood. Why did he do that? It undermines the credibility of the entire White House press office . . .*

Kellyanne Conway: *No it doesn't.*

Chuck Todd: . . . *on day one.*

Kellyanne Conway: *Don't be so overly dramatic about it, Chuck. What . . . You're saying it's a falsehood. And they're giving Sean Spicer, our press secretary, gave alternative facts to that. But the point remains . . .*

Chuck Todd: *Wait a minute . . . alternative facts? Alternative facts? Four of the five facts he uttered, the one thing he got right was Zeke Miller. Four of the five facts he uttered were just not true. Look, alternative facts are not facts. They're falsehoods.*[2]

Conway's suggestion that "alternative facts" are a legitimate form of truth caught the ire of the Public Relations Society of America (PRSA) as well. Jane Dvorak, chair of the PRSA, released a statement making it clear that the organization has no regard for dishonesty in public communications:

January 24, 2017

PRSA Statement on "Alternative Facts"

Truth is the foundation of all effective communications. By being truthful, we build and maintain trust with the media and our customers, clients and employees. As professional communicators, we take very seriously our responsibility to communicate with honesty and accuracy.

The Public Relations Society of America, the nation's largest communications association, sets the standard of ethical behavior for our 22,000 members through our Code of Ethics. Encouraging and perpetuating the use of alternative facts by a high-profile spokesperson reflects poorly on all communications professionals.

PRSA strongly objects to any effort to deliberately misrepresent information. Honest, ethical professionals never spin, mislead or alter facts. We applaud our colleagues and professional journalists who work hard to find and report the truth.[3]

Conway's "alternative facts" statement found little backing across the United States (and the world); many compared it to "newspeak," the government-approved language to eliminate free thought in the totalitarian state featured in George Orwell's classic dystopian novel *1984*. For more on the relationship between current political events and the surge in popularity of classic novels, see Examining Ethics: Contemporary Politics Revives Interest in Classic Novels in Chapter 10.[4]

For the PRSA's Dvorak, rejecting "alternative facts" and defending truth is a matter of defending public relations itself. In a March 22 tweet, Dvorak (@JKDJane) stated, "We can't stand by & allow others to imply these unethical behaviors apply to #PR pros. It diminishes ALL of us. #ethicsmatter."[5]

The Advertising Archives/Alamy Stock Photo

In contrast to a special event, a **pseudo-event** is any circumstance created for the sole purpose of gaining coverage in the media. Historian Daniel Boorstin coined the term in his influential book *The Image* when pointing out the key contributions of PR and advertising in the twentieth century. Typical pseudo-events are press conferences, TV and radio talk-show appearances, or any other staged activity aimed at drawing public attention and media coverage. Although the success of such events depends on the participation of clients and often on paid performers, the biggest factor is the media's attention to the event. In business, pseudo-events extend at least as far back as P. T. Barnum's publicity stunts, such as parading Jumbo the Elephant across the Brooklyn Bridge in the 1880s. In politics, Theodore Roosevelt's administration set up the first White House pressroom and held the first presidential press conferences in the early 1900s. By the twenty-first century, presidential pseudo-events involved a multimillion-dollar White House Communications Office. One of the most successful pseudo-events in recent years was a record-breaking space-diving project. On October 14, 2012, a helium balloon took Austrian skydiver Felix Baumgartner twenty-four miles into the stratosphere. He jumped from the capsule and went into a free dive for about four minutes, reaching a speed of 833.9 mph before deploying his parachute. Red Bull sponsored the project, which took more than five years of preparation.

Community and Consumer Relations

Another responsibility of PR is to sustain goodwill between an agency's clients and the public. The public is often seen as two distinct audiences: communities and consumers. Companies have learned that sustaining close ties with their communities and neighbors not only enhances their image and attracts potential customers but also promotes the idea that the companies are good citizens. As a result, PR firms encourage companies to participate in community activities, such as hosting plant tours and open houses, making donations to national and local charities, and participating in town events like parades and festivals. In addition, more progressive companies may also get involved in unemployment and job-retraining programs, or donate equipment and workers to urban revitalization projects, such as Habitat for Humanity.

Public Relations and Bananas

Doing public relations on behalf of bananas doesn't sound particularly necessary. After all, bananas are the number-one fresh fruit eaten in the United States, having long ago displaced apples in the top position. Yet the seemingly uncomplicated banana figures into the history of public relations, and not always in a good way.

In the early twentieth century, huge banana plantations were established in Colombia, Ecuador, Peru, Costa Rica, Guatemala, and Honduras. United Fruit (the predecessor of today's Chiquita Brands) was the dominant grower and importer of bananas and was particularly powerful in the small nations of Central America—in fact, too powerful. In 1951, Jacobo Árbenz, the new democratically elected president of Guatemala, proposed a number of reforms to raise the status of poor agrarian Guatemalans. One of the reforms included redistributing idle, cultivatable lands to peasants to lift them from poverty. United Fruit owned some of those lands (which it had been given years earlier and on which it didn't pay property taxes). Unwilling to tolerate any limits on its control, United Fruit hired public relations pioneer Edward Bernays to work behind the scenes to build U.S. public opinion against the liberal Árbenz government, branding it as "communist." In one of the worst moments for public relations and U.S. foreign policy, the CIA led a covert operation that deposed Guatemala's democratically elected administration in 1954 and installed a right-wing military dictator who was more to United Fruit's liking. Guatemala then endured decades of war, while the CIA repeated similar covert interventions on behalf of U.S. business interests in several Latin American countries, giving rise to the term *banana republic*—a country in which a single dominant industry controls business and politics.

In another black eye for the banana industry, Dole and Del Monte, two of today's largest banana producers,

were sued in 2012 by more than one thousand banana plantation workers for using a pesticide that had been banned in the United States in 1979. Bloomberg reported that the pesticide, dibromochloropropane (DBCP), "has been linked to sterility, miscarriages, birth defects, cancer, eye problems, skin disorders and kidney damage," and that workers argued they had not been informed of the dangers or issued protective equipment.[1]

Now the good news for bananas and public relations: In 2001, Dole Food Company responded to increasing consumer interest by producing organic bananas for the first time. Although it still produces bananas that are not certified as organic, it is now the leading producer of organic bananas in the world. In 2007, Dole improved communication of its organic program by launching Doleorganic.com and labeling each bunch of organic bananas with a sticker that identifies the farm that produced them. The sticker reads "Visit the Farm at doleorganic.com" and includes the country of origin and a three-digit farm code. The website includes information about the banana farm in question; a Google map (viewers can zoom in on the satellite view to see the expanse of the farm); and photo albums containing shots of workers, plants, and facilities. The company says its Dole Organic site is evidence of the company's "corporate philosophy of adhering to the highest ethical conduct in all its business dealings, treatment of its employees, and social and environmental policies."[2] Considering the lack of transparency in the history of public relations for bananas, this is a good thing—for the countries where Dole does business, the company's workers, and its consumers.

Romeo Gacad/AFP/Getty Images

Government Relations and Lobbying

While sustaining good relations with the public is a priority, so is maintaining connections with government agencies that have some say in how companies operate in a particular community, state, or nation. Both PR firms and the PR divisions within major corporations are especially interested in making sure that government regulation neither becomes burdensome nor reduces their control over their businesses.

Government PR specialists monitor new and existing legislation, create opportunities to ensure favorable publicity, and write press releases and direct-mail letters to persuade the public about the pros and cons of new regulations. In many industries, government relations has evolved into **lobbying**: the process of attempting to influence lawmakers to support and vote in favor of an organization's or industry's best interests. In seeking favorable legislation, some lobbyists contact government officials on a daily basis. In Washington, D.C., alone, there are about twelve thousand registered lobbyists—and thousands more government-relations workers who aren't required to register under federal disclosure rules. Lobbying expenditures targeting the federal government were at $3.37 billion in 2017, down from a peak in 2010 but climbing once again after six years of incremental decline (see Figure 12.1).[20]

Lobbying can often lead to ethical problems, as in the case of earmarks and astroturf lobbying. *Earmarks* are specific spending directives that are slipped into bills to accommodate the interests of lobbyists and are often the result of political favors or outright bribes. In 2006, lobbyist Jack Abramoff (dubbed "the Man Who Bought Washington" in *Time*) and several of his associates were convicted of corruption related to earmarks, leading to the resignation of leading House members and a decline in the use of earmarks.

Astroturf lobbying is phony grassroots public affairs campaigns engineered by public relations firms. PR firms deploy massive phone banks and computerized mailing lists to drum up support and create the impression that millions of citizens back their client's side of an issue. For instance, the Center for Consumer Freedom (CCF), an organization that appears to serve the interests of consumers, is actually a creation of the Washington, D.C.–based PR firm Berman & Co. and is funded by the restaurant, food, alcohol, and tobacco industries. According to SourceWatch, which tracks astroturf lobbying, anyone who criticizes tobacco, alcohol, processed food, fatty food, soda pop, pharmaceuticals, animal testing, overfishing, or pesticides "is likely to come under attack from CCF."[21]

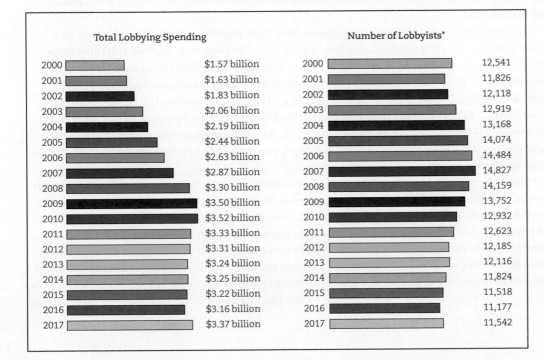

Total Lobbying Spending		Number of Lobbyists*	
2000	$1.57 billion	2000	12,541
2001	$1.63 billion	2001	11,826
2002	$1.83 billion	2002	12,118
2003	$2.06 billion	2003	12,919
2004	$2.19 billion	2004	13,168
2005	$2.44 billion	2005	14,074
2006	$2.63 billion	2006	14,484
2007	$2.87 billion	2007	14,827
2008	$3.30 billion	2008	14,159
2009	$3.50 billion	2009	13,752
2010	$3.52 billion	2010	12,932
2011	$3.33 billion	2011	12,623
2012	$3.31 billion	2012	12,185
2013	$3.24 billion	2013	12,116
2014	$3.25 billion	2014	11,824
2015	$3.22 billion	2015	11,518
2016	$3.16 billion	2016	11,177
2017	$3.37 billion	2017	11,542

FIGURE 12.1

TOTAL LOBBYING SPENDING AND NUMBER OF LOBBYISTS (2000–2017)

Data from: Figures are calculations by the Center for Responsive Politics based on data from the Senate Office of Public Records, accessed May 31, 2018, www.opensecrets.org/lobby.

*The number of unique, registered lobbyists who have actively lobbied.

Public relations firms do not always work for the interests of corporations, however. They also work for other clients, including consumer groups, labor unions, professional groups, religious organizations, and even foreign governments. For example, after the horrific 2016 mass shooting at Pulse, a gay nightclub in Orlando, Florida, the Edelman Orlando office helped organize and assist the One Orlando Alliance, which connected community leaders and more than thirty nonprofit organizations to unify the LGBTQ+ community in Orlando. The alliance sponsored events to honor the families of the forty-nine killed and the sixty-eight injured, and initiated a movement called "acts of love and kindness" to make Orlando a more inclusive community. Edelman's public relations work on behalf of One Orlando Alliance was a finalist for one of PRSA's 2018 Silver Anvil Awards.[22]

Presidential administrations also use public relations—with varying degrees of success—to support their policies. From 2002 to 2008, the Bush administration's Defense Department operated a "Pentagon Pundit" program, secretly cultivating more than seventy retired military officers to appear on radio and television talk shows in order to shape public opinion about the Bush agenda. In 2008, the *New York Times* exposed the unethical program, and its story earned a Pulitzer Prize.[23] Barack Obama pledged to be more transparent on day one of his administration, but an Associated Press analysis during Obama's second term concluded that "the administration has made few meaningful improvements in the way it releases records."[24]

Public Relations Adapts to the Internet Age

Historically, public relations practitioners have tried to earn news media coverage (as opposed to buying advertising) to communicate their clients' messages to the public. While this is still true, the Internet, with its instant accessibility, offers public relations professionals a number of new routes for communicating with the public.

A company or an organization's website has become the home base of public relations efforts. Companies and organizations can upload and maintain their media kits (including press releases, VNRs, images, executive bios, and organizational profiles), giving the traditional news media access to the information at any time. And because everyone can access these corporate websites, the barriers between the organization and the groups that PR professionals ultimately want to reach are broken down.

The web also enables PR professionals to have their clients interact with audiences on a more personal, direct basis through social media tools like Facebook, Twitter, YouTube, Instagram, Wikipedia, and blogs. Now people can be "friends" and "followers" of companies and organizations. Corporate executives can share their professional and personal observations and seem downright chummy through a blog (e.g., *The Counterintuitive CEO* blog by George Colony, the CEO of Forrester Research). Executives, celebrities, and politicians can seem more accessible and personable through a Twitter feed. But social media's immediacy can also be a problem, especially for those who send messages into the public sphere without considering the ramifications.

Another concern about social media is that sometimes such communications appear without complete disclosure, which is an unethical practice. Some PR firms have edited Wikipedia entries for their clients' benefit, a practice Wikipedia founder Jimmy Wales has repudiated as a conflict of interest. A growing number of companies also compensate bloggers to subtly promote their products, unbeknownst to most readers. Public relations firms and marketers are particularly keen on working with "mom bloggers," who appear to be independent voices in discussions about consumer products but may receive gifts in exchange for their opinions. In 2009, the Federal Trade Commission instituted new rules requiring online product endorsers to disclose their connections to companies.

Public Relations during a Crisis

Since the Ludlow strike, one important duty of PR has been helping a corporation handle a public crisis or tragedy, especially if the public assumes the company is at fault. Disaster management may reveal the best and the worst attributes of the company and its PR firm. Let's look at two examples of crisis management and the different ways they were handled.

One of the largest environmental disasters so far in the twenty-first century occurred in 2010. BP's Deepwater Horizon oil rig exploded on April 10 of that year, killing eleven workers. The oil gushed from the ocean floor for months, spreading into a vast area of the Gulf of Mexico, killing wildlife, and washing tar balls onto beaches. Although the company, formerly British Petroleum, officially changed its name to BP in 2001, adopting the motto Beyond Petroleum and a sunny new yellow and green logo in an effort to appear more "green-friendly," the disaster linked the company back to the hazards of its main business in oil. BP's many public relations missteps included its multiple underestimations of the amount of oil leaking, the company chair's reference to the "small people" of the Gulf region, the CEO's wish that he could "get his life back," and the CEO's attendance at an elite yacht race in England even as the oil leak persisted. In short, many people felt that BP failed to show enough remorse or compassion for the affected people and wildlife. BP tried to salvage its reputation by vowing to clean up the damaged areas, establishing a $20 billion fund to reimburse those economically affected by the spill, and creating a campaign of TV commercials to communicate its efforts. Nevertheless, harsh criticism persisted, and BP's ads were overwhelmed by online parodies and satires of its efforts. Years later, entire communities of anglers and rig workers continue to be affected, and BP made its first $1 billion payment for Gulf restoration projects.

A decidedly different approach was taken in the 1982 tragedy involving Tylenol pain-relief capsules. Seven people died in the Chicago area after someone tampered with several bottles and laced them with poison. Discussions between the parent company, Johnson & Johnson, and its PR representatives focused on whether or not withdrawing all Tylenol capsules from store shelves might

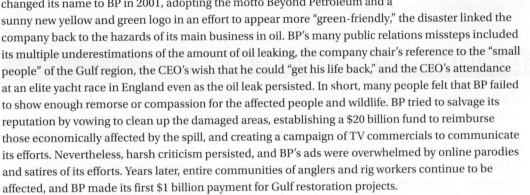

Doug Mills/The New York Times/Redux Pictures

Christopher Martin

A PR CRISIS HITS STARBUCKS

In April 2018, Starbucks suffered a devastating crisis in public goodwill after a manager at a Philadelphia store called the police on two African American men because they were sitting in the store but had not ordered anything. By the time the person they were waiting for arrived for their business meeting, the two men were being handcuffed and arrested, which was caught on video by another customer. Starbucks' management apologized, calling the incident "reprehensible"; met with the two men and city leaders in Philadelphia; and in the following month closed more than eight thousand company-owned locations across the United States for an afternoon of mandatory anti-bias training. "This is just one step in the journey," Starbucks CEO Kevin Johnson said.[25]

RALPH LAUREN

attracted media scrutiny when it was discovered that the uniforms the company designed for the 2012 U.S. Olympic Team had been manufactured in China. After lawmakers publicly chastised the decision to outsource the uniforms, Lauren released a statement promising to produce the 2014 U.S. Olympic Team's uniforms in the United States.

send a signal that corporations could be intimidated by a single deranged person. Nevertheless, Johnson & Johnson's chair, James E. Burke, and the company's PR agency, Burson-Marsteller (now Burson Cohn & Wolfe), opted for full disclosure to the media and the immediate recall of the capsules nationally, costing the company an estimated $100 million and cutting its market share in half. As part of its PR strategy to overcome the negative publicity and to restore Tylenol's market share, Burson-Marsteller tracked public opinion nightly through telephone surveys and organized satellite press conferences to debrief the news media. In addition, emergency phone lines were set up to take calls from consumers and health-care providers. When the company reintroduced Tylenol three months later, it did so with tamper-resistant bottles that were soon copied by almost every major drug manufacturer. Burson-Marsteller, which received PRSA awards for its handling of the crisis, found that the public thought Johnson & Johnson had responded admirably to the crisis and did not hold Tylenol responsible for the deaths. In less than three years, Tylenol had recaptured its former (and dominant) share of the market.

TENSIONS BETWEEN PUBLIC RELATIONS AND THE PRESS

In 1932, Stanley Walker, an editor at the *New York Herald Tribune*, identified public relations agents as "mass-mind molders, fronts, mouthpieces, chiselers, moochers, and special assistants to the president."[26] Walker added that newspapers and PR firms would always remain enemies, even if PR professionals adopted a code of ethics (which they did in the 1950s) to "take them out of the red-light district of human relations."[27] Walker's tone captures the spirit of one of the most mutually dependent—and antagonistic—relationships in all of mass media.

Much of this antagonism, directed at public relations from the journalism profession, is historical. Journalists have long considered themselves part of a public service profession, and some regard PR as having emerged as a pseudo-profession created to distort the facts that reporters work hard to gather. Over time, reporters and editors developed the derogatory term **flack** to refer to a PR agent. The term—derived from the military word *flak*, meaning an antiaircraft artillery shell or a protective military jacket—symbolizes for journalists the protective barrier PR agents insert between their clients and the press. Today, the Associated Press manual for editors defines *flack* simply as "slang for *press agent*." Yet this antagonism belies journalism's dependence on public relations. Many editors, for instance, admit that more than half of their story ideas each day originate with PR people. In this section, we take a closer look at the relationship between journalism and public relations, which can be both adversarial and symbiotic.

Elements of Professional Friction

The relationship between journalism and PR is important and complex. Although journalism lays claim to independent traditions, the news media have become ever more reliant on public relations because of the increasing amount of information now available. Newspaper staff cutbacks, combined with television's need for local news events, have expanded the news media's need for PR story ideas.

Another cause of tension is that PR firms often raid the ranks of reporting for new talent. Because most press releases are written to imitate news reports, the PR profession has always sought good writers who are well connected to sources and savvy about the news business. For instance, the fashion industry likes to hire former style or fashion news writers for its PR staff, and university information offices seek reporters who once covered higher education. But although reporters frequently move into PR, public relations practitioners seldom move into journalism; the news profession rarely accepts prodigal sons or daughters back into the fold once they have left reporting for public relations. Nevertheless, the professions remain codependent: PR needs journalists for publicity, and journalism needs PR for story ideas and access.

LaunchPad
macmillan learning
launchpadworks.com

Give and Take: Public Relations and Journalism
This video debates the relationship between public relations and journalism.

Discussion: Are the similarities between public relations and journalism practices a good thing for the public? Why or why not?

Undermining Facts and Blocking Access

Journalism's most prevalent criticism of public relations is that it works to counter the truths reporters seek to bring to the public. Modern public relations redefined and complicated the notion of what "facts" are. PR professionals demonstrated that the facts can be spun in a variety of ways, depending on what information is emphasized and what is downplayed. As Ivy Lee noted in 1925: "The effort to state an absolute fact is simply an attempt to achieve what is humanly impossible; all I can do is to give you my interpretation of the facts."[28] With practitioners like Lee showing the emerging PR profession how the truth could be interpreted, the journalist's role as a custodian of accurate information became much more difficult.

Journalists have also objected that PR professionals block press access to key business leaders, political figures, and other newsworthy people. Before the prevalence of PR, reporters could talk to such leaders directly and obtain quotable information for their news stories. Now, however, journalists complain that PR agents insert themselves between the press and the newsworthy, thus disrupting the journalistic tradition in which reporters would vie for interviews with top government and business leaders. Journalists further argue that PR agents are now able to manipulate reporters by giving exclusives only to journalists who are likely to cast a story in a favorable light or by cutting off a reporter's access to one of their newsworthy clients if that reporter has written unfavorably about the client in the past.

Promoting Publicity and Business as News

Another explanation for the professional friction between the press and PR involves simple economics. As Michael Schudson noted in his book *Discovering the News: A Social History of American Newspapers*, PR agents help companies "promote as news what otherwise would have been purchased in advertising."[29] Accordingly, Ivy Lee wrote to John D. Rockefeller after he gave money to Johns Hopkins University: "In view of the fact that this was not really news, and that the newspapers gave so much attention to it, it would seem that this was wholly due to the manner in which the material was 'dressed up' for newspaper consumption. It seems to suggest very considerable possibilities along this line."[30] News critics worry that this type of PR is taking media space and time away from those who do not have the financial resources or sophistication to become visible in the public eye. And there is another issue: If public relations can secure news publicity for clients, the added credibility of a journalistic context gives clients a status that the purchase of advertising cannot offer.

Another criticism is that PR firms with abundant resources clearly get more client coverage from the news media than do their lesser-known counterparts. For example, a business reporter at a large metro daily sometimes receives as many as a hundred press releases a day—far outnumbering the fraction of handouts generated by organized labor or grassroots organizations. Workers and union leaders have long argued that the money that corporations allocate to PR leads to more favorable coverage for management positions in labor disputes. For example, standard news reports may feature subtle language choices, with "rational, coolheaded management making offers" and "hotheaded workers making demands." Walter Lippmann saw such differences in 1922 when he wrote, "If you study the way many a strike is reported in the press, you will find very often that [labor] issues are rarely in the headlines, barely in the leading paragraph, and sometimes not even mentioned anywhere."[31] This imbalance is particularly significant in that the great majority of workers are neither managers nor CEOs, and yet these workers receive little if any media coverage on a regular basis. Most newspapers now have business sections that focus on the work of various managers, but few have a labor, worker, or employee section.[32]

THE INVISIBILITY OF PUBLIC RELATIONS is addressed in a series of books by John Stauber and Sheldon Rampton.

TOXIC SLUDGE IS GOOD FOR YOU!

LIES, DAMN LIES AND THE PUBLIC RELATIONS INDUSTRY

JOHN STAUBER AND SHELDON RAMPTON

INTRODUCTION BY MARK DOWIE

"Terrific! Don't miss it." —Molly Ivins

Shaping the Image of Public Relations

Dealing with a tainted past and journalism's hostility has led to the development of several image-enhancing strategies. In 1947, the PR industry formed its own professional organization, the PRSA (Public Relations Society of America). The PRSA is the largest organization devoted to the professional development of communications professionals. It is the recognized voice on ethics and professional standards, and it provides learning and networking opportunities for its members. It also offers operational support to the Universal Accreditation Board (UAB), a diverse group of educators and professionals who oversee the accreditation program for public relations. In addition to the PRSA, independent agencies devoted to uncovering shady or unethical public relations activities publish their findings in publications like *Public Relations Tactics*, *PRWeek*, and *PRWatch*. Ethical issues have become a major focus of the profession, with self-examination of these issues routinely appearing in public relations textbooks and professional newsletters (see Table 12.2).

Over the years, as PR has subdivided itself into specialized areas, it has used more positive phrases—such as *institutional relations*, *corporate communications*, and *news and information services*—to describe what it does. Public relations' best press strategy, however, may be the limitations of the journalism profession itself. For most of the twentieth century, many reporters and editors clung to the ideal that journalism is, at its best, an objective institution that gathers information on behalf of the public. Reporters have only occasionally turned their pens, computers, and cameras on themselves to examine their own practices or their vulnerability to manipulation. Thus, by not challenging PR's more subtle strategies, many journalists have allowed PR professionals to interpret "facts" to their clients' advantage.

Alternative Voices

Because public relations professionals work so closely with the press, their practices are not often the subject of media reports or investigations. Indeed, the multibillion-dollar industry remains virtually

TABLE 12.2

PUBLIC RELATIONS SOCIETY OF AMERICA ETHICS CODE

In 2000, the PRSA approved a completely revised Code of Ethics, which included core principles, guidelines, and examples of improper conduct. Here is one section of the code.

The full text of the PRSA Code of Ethics is available at www.prsa.org.

PRSA Member Statement of Professional Values
The PRSA Member Statement of Professional Values below represents the values of both the PRSA members and of the public relations profession in general. These values, which provide the foundation for the Member Code of Ethics, are the fundamental beliefs that guide members' behaviors and decision-making processes. They are as follows.
ADVOCACY PRSA members serve the public interest by acting as responsible advocates for those they represent and by providing a voice in the marketplace of ideas, facts, and viewpoints to aid informed public debate.
HONESTY PRSA members adhere to the highest standards of accuracy and truth in advancing the interests of those they represent and in communicating with the public.
EXPERTISE PRSA members acquire and responsibly use specialized knowledge and experience; advance the profession through continued professional development, research, and education; and build mutual understanding, credibility, and relationships among a wide array of institutions and audiences.
INDEPENDENCE PRSA members provide objective counsel to those they represent and are accountable for their actions.
LOYALTY PRSA members are faithful to those they represent, while honoring their obligation to serve the public interest.
FAIRNESS PRSA members deal fairly with clients, employers, competitors, peers, vendors, the media, and the general public while respecting all opinions and supporting the right of free expression.

invisible to the public, most of whom have never heard of Burson Cohn & Wolfe, Weber Shandwick, or Edelman. The Center for Media and Democracy (CMD) in Madison, Wisconsin, is concerned about the invisibility of PR practices and has sought to expose the hidden activities of large PR firms since 1993. Its *PRWatch* publication reports on the PR industry, with the goal of "investigating and countering PR campaigns and spin by corporations, industries and government agencies."[33] (See "Media Literacy and the Critical Process: The Invisible Hand of PR" on page 382.)

CMD staff members have also written books targeting public relations practices having to do with the Republican Party's lobbying establishment (*Banana Republicans*), U.S. propaganda on the Iraq War (*The Best War Ever*), industrial waste (*Toxic Sludge Is Good for You!*), mad cow disease (*Mad Cow USA*), and PR uses of scientific research (*Trust Us, We're Experts!*). Their work helps bring an alternative angle to the well-moneyed battles over public opinion. "You know, we feel that in a democracy, it's very, very critical that everyone knows who the players are, and what they're up to," said CMD founder and book author John Stauber.[34]

PUBLIC RELATIONS AND DEMOCRACY

From the days of PR's origins in the early twentieth century, many people—especially journalists—have been skeptical of communications originating from public relations professionals. The bulk of the criticism leveled at public relations argues that the crush of information produced by PR professionals overwhelms traditional journalism. However, PR's most significant impact may be on the political process, especially when organizations hire spin doctors to favorably shape or reshape a candidate's media image. In one example, former president Richard Nixon, who resigned from office in 1974 to avoid impeachment hearings regarding his role in the Watergate scandal, hired Hill+Knowlton to restore his postpresidency image. Through the firm's guidance, Nixon's writings—mostly on international politics—began appearing in Sunday op-ed pages. Nixon himself started showing up on television news programs like *Nightline* and spoke frequently before such groups as the American Newspaper Publishers Association and the Economic Club of New York. In 1984, after a media blitz by Nixon's PR handlers, the *New York Times* announced, "After a decade, Nixon is gaining favor," and *USA Today* trumpeted, "Richard Nixon is back." Before his death in 1994, Nixon, who never publicly apologized for his role in Watergate, saw a large portion of his public image shift from that of an arrogant, disgraced politician to that of a revered elder statesman.[35] Many media critics have charged that the press did not counterbalance this PR campaign and treated Nixon too reverently. In 2014, on the fortieth anniversary of the Watergate scandal, former CBS news anchor Dan Rather remembered Nixon's administration as a "criminal presidency" but added, "There has been an effort to change history, and in some ways it has been successful the last 40 years, saying well, it wasn't all that bad."[36]

Another critical area for public relations and democracy is how organizations integrate environmental claims into their public communications. In 1992, the Federal Trade Commission first issued its "Green Guides"—guidelines to ensure that environmental marketing practices don't run afoul of its prohibition against unfair or deceptive acts or practices, sometimes called **greenwashing**. As concern about global warming has grown in recent years, green marketing and public relations now extend into nearly every part of business and industry: product packaging (buzzwords include *recyclable, biodegradable, compostable, refillable, sustainable,* and *renewable*), buildings and textiles, renewable energy certificates, carbon offsets (funding projects to reduce greenhouse gas emissions in one place to offset carbon emissions produced elsewhere), labor conditions, and fair trade. Although there have been plenty of companies that make claims about providing green products and services, only some have infused environmentally sustainable practices throughout their corporate culture, and being able to tell the difference is essential to the public's understanding of environmental issues.

John Stauber, founder of the Center for Media and Democracy and its publication *PRWatch*, has described the PR industry as "a huge, invisible industry . . . that's really only available to wealthy individuals, large multinational corporations, politicians and government agencies."[1] How true is this? Is the PR industry so invisible?

to influencing the public image of corporations, government bodies, and public policy initiatives in the United States and abroad. PR firms also have enormous influence over news content, yet the U.S. media are silent on this influence. Public relations firms aren't likely to reveal their power, but should journalism be more forthcoming about its role as a publicity vehicle for PR?

1 DESCRIPTION

Test the so-called invisibility of the PR industry by seeing how often, and in what way, PR firms are discussed in the print media. Using LexisNexis, search U.S. newspapers—over the last six months—for any mention of three prominent PR firms: Edelman, Weber Shandwick, and FleishmanHillard.

2 ANALYSIS

What patterns emerge from the search? Possible patterns may have to do with personnel: Someone was hired or fired. (These articles may be extremely brief, with only a quick mention of the firms.) Or these personnel-related articles may reveal connections between politicians or corporations and the PR industry. What about specific PR campaigns or articles that quote "experts" who work for Edelman, Weber Shandwick, or FleishmanHillard?

3 INTERPRETATION

What do these patterns tell you about how the news media covers the PR industry? Was the coverage favorable? Was it critical or analytical? Did you learn anything about how the industry operates? Was the industry itself, its influencing strategies, and its wide reach across the globe visible in your search?

4 EVALUATION

PR firms—such as the three major firms in this search—have enormous power when it comes

5 ENGAGEMENT

Visit the Center for Media and Democracy's website (prwatch .org) and begin to learn about the unseen operations of the public relations industry. (You can also visit SpinWatch. org for similar critical analyses of PR in the United Kingdom.) Follow the CMD's Twitter feed. Read some of the organization's books, join forum discussions, or attend a *PRWatch* event. Visit the organization's wiki site, SourceWatch (sourcewatch.org), and if you can, do some research of your own on PR and contribute an entry.

Though public relations often provides political information and story ideas, the PR profession bears only part of the responsibility for "spun" news; after all, it is the job of a PR agency to get favorable news coverage for the individual or group it represents. PR professionals police their own ranks for unethical or irresponsible practices, but the news media should also monitor the public relations industry, as they do other government and business activities. Journalism itself also needs to institute changes that will make it less dependent on PR and more conscious of how its own practices play into the hands of spin strategies. A positive example of change on this front is that many major newspapers and news networks now offer regular critiques of the facts and falsehoods contained in political advertising and messaging. This media vigilance should be on behalf of citizens, who are entitled to robust, well-rounded debates on important social and political issues.

Like advertising and other forms of commercial speech, PR campaigns that result in free media exposure raise a number of questions regarding democracy and the expression of ideas. And like well-financed politicians, large companies and PR agencies can afford to invest in figuring out how to obtain favorable publicity. The question is not how to prevent that but how to ensure that other voices—less well financed and less commercial—also receive an adequate hearing. To that end, journalists need to become less willing conduits in the distribution of publicity. PR agencies, for their part, need to show clients that participating in the democratic process as responsible citizens can serve them well and enhance their image.

12 Chapter Review

COMMON THREADS

One of the Common Threads in Chapter 1 is the role that media play in a democracy. One key ethical contradiction that can emerge in PR is that (according to the PRSA Code of Ethics) PR should be honest and accurate in disclosing information while being loyal and faithful to clients and their requests for confidentiality and privacy. In this case, how does the general public know when public communications are the work of paid advocacy, particularly when public relations plays such a strong role in U.S. politics?

Public relations practitioners who are members of the Public Relations Society of America are obligated to follow the PRSA Code of Ethics. Members are asked to sign a pledge to conduct themselves "professionally, with truth, accuracy, fairness, and responsibility to the public."

Yet the code is not enforceable, and many public relations professionals simply ignore the PRSA. For example, most employees of PR firms are not PRSA members.[37] Most lobbyists in Washington have to register with the House and Senate, so that there is some public record of their activities to influence politics. Conversely, public relations professionals working to influence the political process don't have to register, so unless they act with the highest ethical standards and disclose what they are doing and who their clients are, they operate in relative secrecy.

According to National Public Radio (NPR), public relations professionals in Washington, D.C., work to engineer public opinion in advance of lobbying efforts to influence legislation. As NPR reported, "For PR folks, conditioning the legislative landscape means trying to shape public perception. So their primary target is journalists like Lyndsey Layton, who writes for the *Washington Post*. She says she gets about a dozen emails or phone calls in a day."[38]

Less ethical work includes assembling phony "astroturf" front groups to engage in communication campaigns to influence legislators, spreading unfounded rumors about an opposing side, and entertaining government officials in violation of government reporting requirements—all things the PRSA code prohibits. Yet these are all-too-frequent practices in the realm of political public relations.

PRSA CEO Rosanna Fiske decries this kind of unethical behavior in her profession. "It's not that ethical public relations equals good public relations," Fiske says. "It is, however, that those who do not practice ethical public relations affect all of us, regardless of the environment in which we work, and the causes we represent."[39]

KEY TERMS

The definitions for the terms listed below can be found in the glossary at the end of the book. The page numbers listed with the terms indicate where the term is highlighted in the chapter.

public relations, 363
press agents, 364
publicity, 364
propaganda, 369
press releases, 370

video news releases (VNRs), 371
public service announcements (PSAs), 371
pseudo-event, 373
lobbying, 375

astroturf lobbying, 375
flack, 378
greenwashing, 381

REVIEW QUESTIONS

Early Developments in Public Relations

1. What did people like P. T. Barnum and Buffalo Bill Cody contribute to the development of modern public relations in the twentieth century?

2. How did railroads give the early forms of corporate public relations a bad name?

3. What contributions did Ivy Lee make toward the development of modern PR?

4. How did Edward Bernays affect public relations?

The Practice of Public Relations

5. What are two approaches to organizing a PR firm?

6. What are press releases, and why are they important to reporters?

7. Why have research and lobbying become increasingly important to the practice of PR?

8. What are some socially responsible strategies that a PR specialist can use during a crisis to help a client manage unfavorable publicity?

Tensions between Public Relations and the Press

9. Explain the historical background of the antagonism between journalism and public relations.

10. How did PR change old relationships between journalists and their sources?

11. In what ways is conventional news like public relations?

Public Relations and Democracy

12. In what ways does the profession of public relations serve the rebranding of public officials and other famous people to obtain favorable publicity?

13. How do organizations integrate environmental claims into their public communications (greenwashing), and why?

14. How do we prevent unethical or irresponsible PR?

QUESTIONING THE MEDIA

1. What do you think of when you hear the term *public relations*? What images come to mind? Where did these impressions come from?

2. What steps can reporters and editors take to monitor PR agents who manipulate the news media?

3. Considering the BP, Tylenol, Starbucks, and NFL concussion cases cited in this chapter, what are some key things an organization can do to respond effectively once a crisis hits?

LAUNCHPAD FOR *MEDIA & CULTURE*

Media Economics and the Global Marketplace

13

IN MAY 2018, NETFLIX MOVED CLOSER TO JOINING THE SELECT GROUP OF THE WORLD'S TOP DIGITAL COMPANIES. Netflix's stock-market value surged to $153 billion, surpassing traditional media companies Disney and Comcast, which owns NBC Universal. Although just over twenty years old and a streaming company for only about ten years, Netflix has revolutionized television in the United States and around the world.

Netflix began as a modest idea in 1997. Two software engineers in California founded the company to rent movie DVDs online and ship them through the mail. In this model, customers would pay a flat monthly fee, rent and return as many videos as they liked each month, and incur no late fees (unlike at its biggest competitor, Blockbuster video

ANALYZING THE
MEDIA ECONOMY
p. 389

THE TRANSITION TO
AN INFORMATION
ECONOMY
p. 391

SPECIALIZATION,
GLOBAL MARKETS,
AND CONVERGENCE
p. 400

SOCIAL ISSUES IN
MEDIA ECONOMICS
p. 408

THE MEDIA
MARKETPLACE
AND DEMOCRACY
p. 415

◄ At the Netflix headquarters—based in Los Gatos, California, about an hour south of San Francisco—employees enjoy many perks, including free breakfast, lunch, and popcorn daily; a car borrowing service; and a flexible vacation schedule. Jim Bennett, left, Vice President of Recommendation Systems, and Reed Hastings, Netflix CEO, are seen here in a screening room at headquarters.

stores). By its own admission, the company struggled for the first five years, even unsuccessfully offering to sell itself to Blockbuster and Amazon during that time.[1]

Eventually, though, DVD-rental-by-mail caught on, and Netflix continued to grow its customer base. Then, in 2007, Netflix developed Internet streaming—a better movie distribution system that proved to be immensely popular, as there was no need to wait for a new DVD by mail or to drive over to the local video store. In 2010, Netflix began expanding to a number of global markets, which now include Canada, Latin America, Europe, Japan, and Australia.

In 2013, Netflix came up with another significant innovation when it began creating its own original series. Some of the company's biggest and most critically acclaimed hits include *House of Cards*, *Orange Is the New Black*, *BoJack Horseman*, *Master of None*, *Unbreakable Kimmy Schmidt*, and *Bloodline*.

By 2018, Netflix was generating about $6.8 billion in annual revenue, making it "the world's leading Internet television network with over 130 million streaming members in over 190 countries enjoying more than 140 million hours of TV shows and movies per day, including original series, documentaries and feature films."[2]

Netflix has changed TV culture. By releasing entire seasons of its own original programming and licensing series such as *Breaking Bad*, *The Walking Dead*, *Nurse Jackie*, *Mad Men*, and *The Office*, Netflix gave rise to the practice of binge-watching.[3]

The key to Netflix's success has been providing excellent content and a superior user experience (easy access, reasonable price) that is being continuously improved. In doing so, not only did Netflix kill the video store, but it's in the process of killing regular broadcast and cable television.

Netflix itself argues that it is leading this transformation:

> People love TV content, but they don't love the linear TV experience, where channels present programs only at particular times on non-portable screens with complicated remote controls. Now Internet TV—which is on-demand, personalized, and available on any screen—is replacing the linear TV experience. Changes of this magnitude are rare. . . . The new era of Internet TV is likely to be very big and enduring also, given the flexibility and ubiquity of the Internet around the world.[4]

As media citizens, we have witnessed these kinds of transformations before. For example, in 1999, Napster offered a better way to access music: on the Internet, with a quick (and illegal) download. The new format marked the beginning of the death of the CD album. Apple improved the user experience a few years later, with a large (and legal) music catalog on the iTunes store and new iPod devices on which to play the music. Now, music streaming and Internet radio businesses like Spotify and Apple Music have offered better user experiences for accessing music.

Netflix's leading position in the transition from linear to Internet TV puts the company in position to join the top five digital conglomerates: Amazon, Apple, Facebook, Google, and Microsoft. With annual revenues of $11.7 billion (2017), Netflix is still much smaller than the largest, Apple, with $229.23 billion in annual revenue (2017). Yet Netflix has enormous potential for growth over the next decade, as new generations of global binge-watchers emerge, demanding TV and movies on small digital screens—and on their own time.

THE MEDIA TAKEOVERS, MULTIPLE MERGERS, AND CORPORATE CONSOLIDATION over the last two decades have made our modern world very distinct from that of earlier generations—at least in economic terms. What's at the heart of this "brave new media world" is a media landscape that has been forever altered by the emergence of the Internet and a changing of the guard, from traditional media giants like Comcast and Disney to new digital giants like Amazon, Apple, Facebook, Google (Alphabet), and Microsoft. (See "Examining Ethics: Are the Big Digital Companies Too Big?" on page 392.) As the Netflix venture demonstrates, the media industry is marked by shifting and unpredictable terrain. In usurping the classified ads of newspapers and altering distribution for music, movies, and TV programs, the Internet has forced almost all media businesses to rethink not only the content they provide but also the entire economic structure within which our capitalist media system operates.

LaunchPad
macmillan learning

launchpadworks.com

Visit LaunchPad for *Media & Culture* and use LearningCurve to review concepts from this chapter.

In this chapter, as we examine the economic impact of business strategies on various media, we will:

- Explore the issues and tensions that are part of the current media economy
- Examine the rise of the Information Age, distinguished by flexible, specialized, and global markets
- Investigate the breakdown of economic borders, focusing on media consolidation, corporate mergers, synergy, deregulation, and the emergence of an economic global village
- Address ethical and social issues in media economics, investigating the limits of antitrust laws, the concept of consumer control, and the threat of cultural imperialism
- Examine the rise of new digital media conglomerates
- Consider the impact of media consolidation on democracy and on the diversity of the marketplace

As you read this chapter, think about the different media you use on a daily basis. What media products or content did you consume over the past week? Do you know who owns them? How important is it to know this? Do you consume popular culture or read news from other countries? Why or why not? For more questions to help you understand the role of media economics in our lives, see "Questioning the Media" in the Chapter Review.

ANALYZING THE MEDIA ECONOMY

Given the sprawling scope of the mass media, the study of their economic conditions poses a number of complicated questions:

- What role does the government need to play in determining who owns the mass media and what kinds of media products are manufactured? Should it be a strong role, or should the government step back and let competition and market forces dictate what happens to mass media industries?

- Should citizen groups play a larger role in demanding that media organizations help maintain the quality of social and cultural life?

- Does the influence of American popular culture worldwide smother or encourage the growth of democracy and local cultures?

- Does the increasing concentration of economic power in the hands of several international corporations too severely restrict the number of players and voices in the media?

Answers to such questions span the economic and social spectrums. On the one hand, critics express concerns about the increasing power and reach of large media conglomerates. On the other hand, many free-market advocates maintain that as long as these structures ensure efficient operation and generous profits, they measure up as quality media organizations.

In order to probe these issues fully, we need to understand key economic concepts across two broad areas: media structure and media performance.[5]

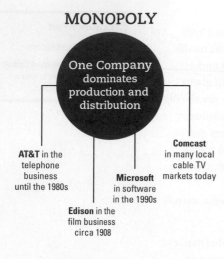

MONOPOLY

One Company dominates production and distribution

AT&T in the telephone business until the 1980s

Microsoft in software in the 1990s

Edison in the film business circa 1908

Comcast in many local cable TV markets today

On the local level, monopoly situations have been more plentiful, occurring in any city that has only one newspaper or cable company. Although the federal government has encouraged owner diversity since the 1970s by prohibiting a newspaper from operating a broadcast or cable company in the same city, many individual local media monopolies have been purchased by national and international firms.

OLIGOPOLY

A Few Firms dominate an industry

Advertising/PR
WPP
Omnicom
Publicis
Interpublic

Internet
Google
Amazon
Apple
Facebook

Book Retail
Amazon
Apple
Google Play

Internet Streaming
Pandora
Spotify
Deezer

Music
Sony
Universal
Warner

Video Games
Nintendo
Microsoft
Sony
Activision
Blizzard

Film/TV
Sony
Viacom
Time Warner
Disney
21st Century Fox
NBC Universal
Netflix
Google/YouTube

Theaters
Regal
AMC Entertainment
Cinemark
Cineplex
Marcus

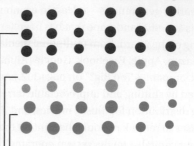

LIMITED COMPETITION
(sometimes called "monopolistic competition")

In limited competition, there are many producers and sellers but only a few products, as in the example of radio.

Contemporary Hits stations
News/Talk stations
Country stations

Because commercial broadcast radio is a difficult market to enter—requiring an FCC license and major capital investment—most stations play one of the few formats that attract sizable audiences. Under these circumstances, fans of blues, jazz, or classical music may not be able to find a radio station. That is changing, though, with the Internet.

FIGURE 13.1

MEDIA INDUSTRY STRUCTURES

The Structure of the Media Industry

Media industries are typically structured in one of three ways: as a **monopoly**, an **oligopoly** (the most common structure), or a **limited competition** (typical of the radio and newspaper industries).[6] For a detailed explanation of these structures, refer to Figure 13.1.

The Business of Media Organizations

Media organizations develop or distribute content, set prices, and generate profit. They are often asked to live up to society's expectations as well—that is, to operate with a sense of social responsibility in their role as mass communicators. These two main activities—maximizing profits while being socially responsible—are sometimes contradictory functions.

Maximizing Profits

Media companies make money in two main ways. First, they generate revenue when consumers buy a book, song, game, movie, newspaper, magazine, or subscription—whether directly through them or through a retailer. This monetary transaction used to rely on brick-and-mortar stores or the mail, and we used to be able to hold a media product—like a magazine or a music CD—in our hands. Now we buy much of our media online, often through the devices of media companies themselves (such as a Google Pixel phone), and most of our media purchases are digital.

The other way media companies generate revenue is through advertisements that support the product, such as TV and radio shows, newspapers, most magazines, and many websites. These media products seem free to us, but actually advertisers are paying for our attention as we engage with the content. As consumers of advertising-based media, we have to work for the "free" content by giving our time and attention to commercial sponsors. Advertisers pay more depending on how many of us are getting exposed to the ads and our potential buying power as an audience, often determined by demographics and psychographics and other data collected about us (see Chapter 11). This is the main revenue structure for "free" over-the-air radio and TV broadcasting and most websites. Media companies similarly make money through product placement advertising in movies, television, and video games.

Media corporations generate the most money when they can get us to buy a media product or pay for a subscription (like a cable TV package or a newspaper or magazine subscription) and subsequently to be the target audience for advertising that comes with that media product.

Balancing Profits and the Public Good

The harshest critics of capitalism suggest that running a business is all about maximizing profits, which often means keeping wages low and production high. How this plays out in terms of social responsibility for media corporations is twofold. First, in their own operations, should they compensate their workers with a fair and sustaining wage? Second, should they produce media content that is more than just profitable and contributes to society in some positive way?

In regard to fair wages, a national "Fight for $15" movement toward a $15 minimum wage has been active since 2012.[7] Opponents say a higher wage results in having to cut jobs, whereas advocates argue that a higher wage means that workers can buy more products, leading to more hiring and an improved economy. In 2016, the U.S. Department of Labor tried to settle the matter, citing a letter signed by "more than 600 economists, including 7 Nobel Prize winners," that made the following argument: "In recent years there have been important developments in the academic literature on the effect of increases in the minimum wage on employment, with the weight of evidence now showing that increases in the minimum wage have had little or no negative effect on the employment of minimum-wage workers, even during times of weakness in the labor market. Research suggests that a minimum-wage increase could have a small stimulative effect on the economy as low-wage workers spend their additional earnings, raising demand and job growth, and providing some help on the jobs front."[8]

In addition, many business executives have argued that there is an obligation in flourishing democracies to balance earning profits with serving the larger public. Recent decisions of billionaires like Warren Buffett of Berkshire Hathaway and Jeff Bezos of Amazon to buy struggling newspapers resonate with the founders' belief that a robust free press has a central role in helping democracy work well. Media corporations can also serve the public good in not only providing information necessary for democracy but also creating content that reflects the full diversity of their audience. For example, television producers in recent years have increased the diversity of their stories and representations both to make more money by attracting younger audiences and "because it's the right thing to do," as one television critic put it.[9] In examining business strategies, what are other ways media businesses can balance profit motives and public-good obligations?

Don Arnold/Getty Images

OPRAH WINFREY
has built a remarkable media empire over the course of her long career. From book publishing to filmmaking and television, where she got her start, Winfrey has established an expansive sphere of influence. After ending her talk show, she launched the cable TV network OWN in 2011, which, after a slow start, moved toward stability on the strength of scripted television programs. Discovery Communications is now the majority owner of OWN, but Winfrey remains its CEO.

THE TRANSITION TO AN INFORMATION ECONOMY

The twentieth century can be divided in two. The first half of the century emphasized mass production, assembly lines, the rise of manufacturing plants, and the intense rivalry between U.S.-based businesses and businesses from other nations that produced competing products. By the 1950s, however, the U.S. economy was beginning a transition to a new cooperative global economy, as the

EXAMINING ETHICS

Are the Big Digital Companies Too Big?

In the past few years, Americans have come to the realization that Apple, Google, Amazon, Microsoft, and Facebook structure much of our everyday lives. Can one imagine living without these five companies? But perhaps that is the problem. As CNN reporter Dylan Byers says of the biggest tech companies, "It's their century. We're just living in it."[1]

With that realization comes reminders that all is not good with our big digital companies. Over the course of their relatively brief histories, all these companies have been under fire for a number of problems: deploying anticompetitive practices (Microsoft and Amazon), recording users' private conversations on home digital assistants (Amazon), gobbling up too much of the advertising industry (Google and Facebook), being manipulated by trolls during the 2016 presidential election (Google and Facebook), violating user privacy (Facebook), and slowing down mobile phone performance to spur sales (Apple).

But Amanda Lotz, a professor of media studies at the University of Michigan, warns us not to lump these companies together like we do for Big Oil, Big Pharma, and Big Tobacco: "Because all of these companies provide services relating to computers, there is a tendency to lump them together, calling them 'Big Tech' or the 'Frightful Five' or even 'GAFA'—the acronym for the first four of them, leaving Microsoft out. Conceiving of 'big tech' as a single industry makes the threat and influence overwhelming."[2] She continues, "The so-called big tech companies certainly are big: In 2017, they were the top five most valuable public companies in the U.S. But, as a scholar of the media marketplace that many of these firms are beginning to explore, I know that lumping them together hides the fact they're very separate and distinct—not just as companies, but in terms of their business models and practices."[3]

In fact, some analysts are differentiating between the Big Five in terms of which ones might actually be too big. There is evidence that three of these companies have far too much dominance in their industries. The *Wall Street Journal* notes that "Facebook Inc., Google parent Alphabet Inc. and Amazon.com Inc. are enjoying profit margins, market dominance and clout that, according to economists and historians, suggest they're developing into a new category of monopolists."[4] Consider that Google and Facebook control 73 percent of digital advertising in the United States, or that Amazon controls 44 percent of U.S. online sales. Google and Facebook's ability to corner the market on digital advertising has decimated the newspaper industry as it has moved online. Local advertisers that once supported local newspapers with their ads now often just place ads with one or both of these companies.

Yet there can be an impermanence to seemingly powerful companies. For example, Amazon's powerful control over book sales online first devastated the big bookstore chains (which themselves had earlier hurt small independent bookstores). Amazon now sells everything and threatens brick-and-mortar grocery stores and department stores, including Walmart (whose superstores earlier shattered many small-town business districts). It is also important to remember that in the 1990s, it seemed that Microsoft had completely beaten its main rival, Apple, yet Apple came back. However, the U.S. Department of Justice's scrutiny of Microsoft during the 1990s resulted in the company avoiding any engagement in anticompetitive practices, which cleared a path for Apple and other competitors.[5]

machines that drove the Industrial Age changed gears for the new Information Age. Offices slowly displaced factories as major work sites; centralized mass production declined and often gave way to internationalized, decentralized, and lower-paid service work; and the information-based economy became driven by computers and data.

As part of the shift to an information-based economy, various mass media industries began marketing music, movies, television programs, and computer software on a global level. The emphasis on mass production (e.g., television programs targeted to mass audiences, or magazines designed to appeal to a broad cross section of the U.S. population) slowly shifted to the cultivation of specialized niche media markets. The political and economic forces swung from regulating media industries (and industries in general) in the first half of the twentieth century to deregulating them in the second half. Decades of deregulation have led to media mergers and acquisitions, resulting in media powerhouses and more concentrated ownership in nearly every media sector.

From Regulation to Deregulation

During the rise of industry in the nineteenth century, entrepreneurs such as John D. Rockefeller in oil, Cornelius Vanderbilt in shipping and railroads, and Andrew Carnegie in steel created monopolies in their respective industries. There was so little regulation of these newly powerful industries that the companies became notorious for their exploitative labor practices (including child labor), corrupt corporate conduct, and manipulation of the competitive landscape. Corporations and their business partners were often organized as "trusts," but soon the word *trust* became equated with any large corporation—particularly large unethical corporations that tried to drive out fair competition. Congress responded by passing three significant antitrust laws between 1890 and 1950 to increase competition between companies and prevent any one company from having too much control over the market:

- **1890—Sherman Antitrust Act**
  Outlawed monopoly practices and corporate trusts that often fix prices to force competitors out of business.

- **1914—Clayton Antitrust Act**
  Prohibited manufacturers from selling only to dealers and contractors who agree to reject the products of business rivals.

- **1950—The Celler-Kefauver Act**
  Limited any corporate mergers and joint ventures that reduced competition.

Today, the Federal Trade Commission (established in 1914) and the Antitrust Division of the Department of Justice are responsible for enforcing these laws.

Deregulation Spurs Formation of Media Conglomerates

Corporations chafed under antitrust rules and other regulations, and with the rise of public relations tactics and aggressive lobbying campaigns from the 1920s onward, they worked to turn the anticorporate rhetoric so prominent throughout the first half of the twentieth century (particularly in light of the Great Depression) into a commonsense narrative that government regulation was bad for business and bad for America.[10] Although the administration of President Jimmy Carter (1977–1981) actually initiated deregulation, most controls on business were drastically weakened under the presidency of Ronald Reagan (1981–1989). Deregulation led to easier mergers, corporate diversifications, and increased tendencies in some sectors toward oligopolies (especially in air travel, energy, finance, and communications).[11]

One of the media sectors most visibly deregulated was broadcasting. In 1953, as television was expanding across the country, the FCC adopted the 7-7-7 Rule, limiting companies to owning no more than seven AM radio stations, seven FM radio stations, and seven television stations.[12] For more than

ANTITRUST REGULATION

During the late nineteenth century, John D. Rockefeller Sr., considered the richest man in the world, controlled more than 90 percent of the U.S. oil refining business. But in 1911, antitrust regulations were used to bust up Rockefeller's powerful Standard Oil into more than thirty separate companies. He later hired PR guru Ivy Lee to refashion his negative image as a greedy corporate mogul.

thirty years, these ownership limitations helped ensure diversity among broadcast media ownership—and, with it, diverse and alternative viewpoints. However, by the 1980s, the ownership limits had been slowly whittled away. In 1984, the FCC expanded the ownership rule to 12-12-12; it was increased to 18-18-12 in 1992, and then to 20-20-12 in 1994.

The Telecommunications Act of 1996 (signed by President Bill Clinton) brought unprecedented deregulation to a broadcast industry that had been closely regulated for more than sixty years. From 1996 onward, the following held true:

- A single company could now own an almost unlimited number of radio and TV stations.
- Telephone companies could now own TV and radio stations.
- Cable companies could now compete in the local telephone business.
- Cable companies could now freely raise rates.

For more on deregulation's effect on broadcast ownership consolidation, see Figure 13.2 on page 395.

Proponents of the Telecommunications Act of 1996 argued that the new competition would lower consumer prices. Instead, ever-larger corporations now control cable, telephone, and broadband service to households, and they have charged ever-increasing prices. For example, the average monthly price of expanded basic cable service grew to $69.03 by 2015, a price increase almost triple the rate of inflation since 1995.[13] Of course, cable, telephone, and satellite companies are delivering even more channels to consumers. But because the industry "bundles" channels, most consumers pay for far more channels than they watch. The steep cost of cable has spurred consumer groups to push for "à la carte" cable, which would allow customers to pay for only the channels they use. An even bigger problem for cable, however, has been the much cheaper costs of streaming services offered by Netflix, Amazon, and Hulu. An increasing number of young people have "cut the cable cord," willing to wait and binge-watch their favorite shows on one or more streaming services, whose subscription costs are often paid by their parents, who share their streaming passwords. In fact, in 2018 the average monthly subscription costs for Netflix, Amazon Prime, and Hulu Plus (no ads) combined was $32.90.

Media Powerhouses: Consolidation, Partnerships, and Mergers

Despite their strength, the antitrust laws of the twentieth century have been unevenly applied, especially in terms of the media. When International Telephone & Telegraph (ITT) tried to acquire ABC in the 1960s, loud protests and government investigations sank the deal. But in the mid-1980s, just as the Justice Department was breaking up AT&T's century-old monopoly—creating telephone competition—the government was authorizing a number of mass media mergers that consolidated power in the hands of a few large companies. For example, when General Electric set out to purchase RCA-NBC in the 1980s, the FTC, the FCC, and the Justice Department had few objections. When NBC Universal changed hands again—in its 2011 purchase by cable giant Comcast, which created the nation's largest traditional media conglomerate—the *New York Times* reported that "Comcast said it faced few onerous restrictions" from federal regulatory agencies and no requirements to sell any assets.[14]

In 1995, Disney acquired ABC for $19 billion. To ensure its rank as the world's largest media conglomerate, Time Warner countered and bought Turner Broadcasting in 1995 for $7.5 billion. In 2001, AOL acquired Time Warner for $164 billion—the largest media merger in history at the time. The company was originally called AOL–Time Warner. However, when the online giant saw its subscription service decline in the face of new high-speed broadband services from cable firms, the company went back to the Time Warner name and spun off AOL in 2009. Time Warner's failed venture in the volatile world of the Internet proved disastrous. The companies together were valued at $350 billion in 2000 but only at $50 billion in 2010. After suffering losses of over $700 million in 2010, AOL in 2011

FIGURE 13.2

U.S. BROADCAST OWNERSHIP DEREGULATION

From 1953 to 1984, the FCC enacted rules that prohibited a single company from owning more than seven AM radio stations, seven FM radio stations, and seven TV stations (called the 7-7-7 Rule):

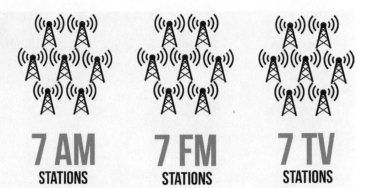

7 AM STATIONS   **7 FM** STATIONS   **7 TV** STATIONS

Also, a single person or company could own only one radio station per market. But ownership rules relaxed during the 1980s, and by 1994, the following was allowed:

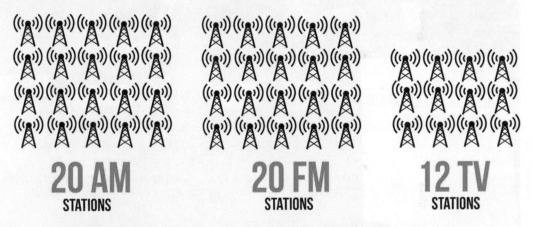

20 AM STATIONS   **20 FM** STATIONS   **12 TV** STATIONS

After the Telecommunications Act of 1996, several radio corporations quickly ballooned to include hundreds of stations. As a result, radio and television ownership became increasingly consolidated. Since 1996, the largest radio company is iHeartMedia (formerly Clear Channel Communications).

CLEAR CHANNEL COMMUNICATIONS GREW ASTRONOMICALLY AFTER THE TELECOMMUNICATIONS ACT OF 1996 WAS PASSED

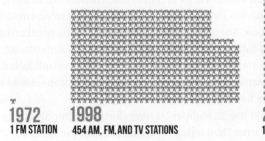

1972
1 FM STATION

1998
454 AM, FM, AND TV STATIONS

2005
1,200 AM, FM, AND TV STATIONS

Bloomberg/Getty Images

IN JUNE OF 2018, AT&T INC.,

led by chairman and chief executive officer Randall Stephenson (left), successfully acquired Time Warner Inc., led by chairman and chief executive officer Jeffrey "Jeff" Bewkes (right). The approval of the merger worried many, and by July of that same year, the federal government sought to overturn the deal.

bought the *Huffington Post* for $315 million in an attempt to reverse its decline. AOL itself was bought by Verizon in 2015 for $4.4 billion. Meanwhile, AT&T proposed to buy Time Warner in 2016 so that it could compete, the company said, with digital giants like Google and Facebook. The U.S. government sued to stop the merger, but in June 2018, a federal judge allowed AT&T to proceed with one of the biggest media deals in history. Shortly after, Disney's purchase of 21st Century Fox was approved, making Disney an even more enormous entertainment conglomerate.

Also in 2001, the federal government approved a $72 billion deal uniting AT&T's cable division with Comcast, creating a cable company twice the size of its nearest competitor. (AT&T quickly left the merger, selling its cable holdings to Comcast for $47 billion in late 2001.) In 2009, Comcast struck a deal with GE to purchase a majority stake in NBC Universal, stirring up antitrust complaints from some consumer groups. In 2010, Congress began hearings on whether uniting a major cable company and a major broadcasting network under a single owner would decrease healthy competition between cable and broadcast TV and thus hurt consumers. In 2011, the FCC approved the deal.

Until the 1980s, antitrust rules attempted to ensure diversity of ownership among competing businesses. Sometimes this happened, as in the breakup of AT&T, and sometimes it did not, as in the cases of cable monopolies and the mergers just discussed. What has occurred consistently, however, is media competition being usurped by media consolidation. Today, the same anticompetitive mind-set exists that allowed a few utility and railroad companies to control their industries in the days before antitrust laws.

Most media companies have skirted monopoly charges by purchasing diverse types of mass media rather than trying to control just one medium. For example, Disney provides programming to

TV, cable, and movie theaters. In 1995, then CEO Michael Eisner defended the company's practices, arguing that as long as large companies remain dedicated to quality—and as long as Disney did not try to buy the phone lines and TV cables running into homes—such mergers benefit America.

But Eisner's position raises questions: How is the quality of cultural products determined? If companies cannot make money on quality products, what happens? If ABC News cannot make a substantial profit, should Disney's managers cut back its national or international news staff? What are the potential effects of such layoffs on the public mission of the news media and, consequently, on our political system? How should the government and citizens respond?

Business Tendencies in Media Industries

In addition to the consolidation trend, a number of other factors characterize the economics of mass media businesses. These are general trends or tendencies that cut across most business sectors and demonstrate how contemporary global economies operate.

Flexible Markets and the Decline of Labor Unions

Geographer David Harvey has observed that today's information culture is characterized by what business executives call flexibility—a tendency to emphasize "the new, the fleeting . . . and the contingent in modern life, rather than the more solid values implanted" during Henry Ford's day, when relatively stable mass production drove mass consumption.[15] The new elastic economy features the expansion of the service sector (most notably in health care, banking, real estate, fast food, Internet ventures, and computer software) and the need to serve individual consumer preferences. This type of economy has relied on cheap labor—sometimes exploiting poor workers in sweatshops—and quick, high-volume sales to offset the costs of making so many niche products for specialized markets.

Given that 80 to 90 percent of new consumer and media products typically fail, a flexible economy has demanded rapid product development and efficient market research. Companies need to score a few hits to offset investments in failed products. For instance, during the peak summer movie season, studios premiere dozens of new feature films, such as 2018's *Solo: A Star Wars Story*, *The Incredibles 2*, and *Jurassic World: Fallen Kingdom*. A few are big hits, but many more miss, and studios hope to recoup their losses via merchandising tie-ins and movie rentals and sales. Similarly, TV networks introduce scores of new programs each year but quickly replace those that fail to attract a large audience or an audience that fits a network's preferred demographics. Of course, this flexible media system heavily favors large companies with greater access to capital over small businesses that cannot easily absorb the losses incurred from failed products.

The era of flexible markets also coincided with the decline in the number of workers who belonged to labor unions. Having made strong gains on behalf of workers after World War II, labor unions, at their peak in 1954, represented 34.8 percent of U.S. workers. Manufacturers and other large industries soon began to look for ways to cut labor costs, which had increased as powerful labor unions successfully bargained for middle-class wages. With the shift to an information economy, many jobs—such as the manufacture of computers, stereo systems, TV sets, and DVD players—were exported to avoid the high price of U.S. unionized labor. (See "Global Village: Designed in California, Assembled in China" in Chapter 2, which describes the conditions in which the Chinese company Foxconn currently makes electronic devices for Apple, Amazon, Microsoft, Sony, and a number of other electronics brands.) As large companies bought up small companies across national boundaries, commerce developed rapidly at the global level. According to the U.S. Department of Labor, union membership fell to 20.1 percent in 1983 and 10.7 percent in 2017, flattening out at the lowest rate in more than seventy years.[16]

Downsizing and the Wage Gap

With the apparent advantage to large companies in this flexible age, who is disadvantaged? From the beginning of the recession in December 2007 through 2009, the United States lost more than 8.4 million jobs (affecting 6.1 percent of all employers), creating the highest unemployment

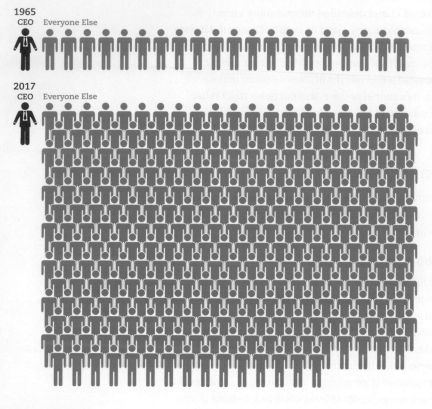

FIGURE 13.3

CEO-TO-WORKER WAGE GAP, 1965 AND 2017

Data from: David Gelles, "Want to Make Money Like a C.E.O.? Work for 275 Years," *New York Times,* May 25, 2018, www .nytimes.com/2018/05/25 /business/highest-paid -ceos-2017.html.

contraction since the Great Depression.[17] The unemployment rate began to recede in 2009, but from 2009 to 2012, as the economy slowly recovered, 95 percent of postrecession income growth was captured by the top 1 percent—those Americans with the greatest income.[18]

Inequality in the United States between the richest and everyone else has been growing since the 1970s. This is apparent in the skyrocketing rate of executive compensation and the growing ratio between executive pay and the typical pay of workers in corresponding industries. In 1965, the CEO-to-worker compensation ratio was 20:1, meaning the typical CEO earned twenty times the salary of the typical worker in that industry. By 2017, the ratio was 275:1 (see Figure 13.3).[19] Media corporations are among those with the highest wage gaps. In 2017, Leslie Moonves of CBS ($68.4 million), Jeffrey Bewkes of Time Warner ($49 million), David Zaslov of Discovery Communications ($42.2 million), and Robert Iger of Disney ($36.3 million) were among the highest-paid CEOs of all publicly traded companies in the United States. At CBS, for example, Moonves was awarded 595 times the median employee salary.[20]

Corporate downsizing—often employed to make companies more flexible and more profitable—has served CEOs well but has had a negative effect on workers. This trend, spurred by government deregulation and a decline in worker protections, means that many employees today scramble for jobs, often working two or three part-time positions. Increasingly, the available positions have substandard pay. In 2012, the National Employment Law Project reported that "more than one in four private sector jobs (26%) were low-wage positions paying less than $10 per hour."[21] This translates to a salary of about $20,000 a year or less. And the flexible economy keeps moving in that direction. The U.S. Bureau of Labor Statistics estimated in 2012 that 70 percent of the leading growth occupations for the next decade are low-wage ones.[22] Even as most big businesses had recovered from the recession and experienced record profits by 2011, their low-wage workers' wages still suffered. For example, at the top fifty low-wage employers—including Target, McDonald's, Panera, Macy's, and Abercrombie & Fitch—the highest paid executives earned an average of $9.4 million a year. At that rate, they earned about $4,520 an hour, an amount it would take more than six hundred minimum-wage employees to earn in the same period.[23]

Economics, Hegemony, and Storytelling

To understand why our society hasn't (until recently) participated in much public discussion about wealth disparity and salary gaps, it is helpful to understand the concept of hegemony. The word *hegemony* has roots in ancient Greek, but in the 1920s and 1930s, Italian philosopher and activist Antonio Gramsci worked out a modern understanding of hegemony: how a ruling class in a society maintains its power—not simply by military or police force but more commonly by citizens' consent and deference to power. He explained that people who are without power—the disenfranchised, the poor, the disaffected, the unemployed, the exploited workers—do not routinely rise up against those in power because "the rule of one class over another does not depend on economic or physical power alone but rather on persuading the ruled to accept the system of beliefs of the ruling class and to share their social, cultural, and moral values."[24] **Hegemony**, then, is the acceptance of the dominant values in a culture by those who are subordinate to those who hold economic and political power.

How, then, does this process actually work in our society? How do lobbyists, the rich, and our powerful two-party political system convince regular citizens that they should go along with the status quo? Edward Bernays, one of the founders of modern public relations (see Chapter 12), wrote in his 1947 article "The Engineering of Consent" that companies and rulers couldn't lead people—or get them to do what they wanted—until the people consented to what those companies or rulers were trying to do, whether it was convincing the public to support women smoking cigarettes or convincing them to support going to war. To pull this off, Bernays would convert his clients' goals into "common sense," then convince the public that these commonsense ideas were the "natural" way things worked.

By convincing consumers and voters that the interests of the powerful were normal and natural, companies and politicians created an atmosphere and context in which there was less chance for challenge and criticism. Common sense, after all, repels self-scrutiny ("that's just plain common sense—end of discussion"). In this case, status quo values and conventional wisdom (e.g., hard work and religious belief are rewarded with economic success) and political arrangements (e.g., the traditional two-party system serves democracy best) become accepted as normal and natural ways to organize and see the world.

To argue that a particular view or value is common sense is often an effective strategy for stopping conversation and debate. Yet common sense is socially and symbolically constructed and shifts over time. For example, it was once common sense that the world was flat and that people who were not property-owning white males shouldn't be allowed to vote. Common sense is particularly powerful because it contains no analytical strategies for criticizing elite or dominant points of view and therefore certifies class, race, or sexual orientation divisions or mainstream political views as natural and given.

To buy uncritically into concepts presented as common sense inadvertently serves to maintain such concepts as natural, shutting down discussions about the ways in which economic divisions or political hierarchies are *not* natural and given. So when Democratic and Republican candidates run for office, the stories they tell about themselves espouse their connection to Middle American common sense and down-home virtues—for example, a photo of Donald Trump eating pork on a stick or images of New York gubernatorial candidate Cynthia Nixon riding the subway in New York City. These ties to ordinary commonsense values and experience connect the powerful to the everyday, making their interests and ours appear to be seamless.

To understand how hegemony works as a process, let's examine how common sense is practically and symbolically transmitted. Here it is crucial to understand the central importance of storytelling to culture. The narrative—as the dominant symbolic way we make sense of experience and articulate our values—is often a vehicle for delivering common sense. Therefore, ideas, values, and beliefs can be carried in our mainstream stories—the stories we tell and find in daily conversations; in the local paper; in political ads; on the evening news; in books, magazines, movies, and favorite TV shows; and online. The narrative, then, is the normal and familiar structure that aids in converting ideas, values, and beliefs to common sense—normalizing them into "just the way things are."

The reason that common narratives work is that they identify with a culture's dominant values. Middle American values include allegiances to family, honesty, hard work, religion, capitalism, health, democracy, moderation, loyalty, fairness, authenticity, and modesty. These values are the ones that our politicians most frequently align themselves with in the political

Everett Collection

AMERICAN DREAM STORIES

are distributed through the media. This was especially true of television shows in the 1950s and 1960s like *The Donna Reed Show*, which idealized the American nuclear family as central to the American Dream.

ads that tell their stories. They lie at the heart of powerful American Dream stories that for centuries have told us that if we work hard and practice such values, we will triumph and be successful. Hollywood, too, distributes these shared narratives, celebrating characters and heroes who are loyal, honest, and hardworking. Through this process, the media (and the powerful companies that control them) provide the commonsense narratives that keep the economic status quo relatively unchallenged and leave little room for alternatives.

In the end, hegemony helps explain why we occasionally support economic plans and structures that may not be in our best interest. We may do this out of altruism, as when wealthy people or companies favor higher taxes because of a sense of obligation to support those who are less fortunate. But more often, the American Dream story is so powerful in our media and popular culture that many of us believe we have an equal chance of becoming rich and therefore successful and happy. So why would we do anything to disturb the economic structures that the dream is built on? In fact, in many versions of our American Dream story—from Hollywood films to political ads—the government often plays the role of villain, seeking to raise our taxes or undermine rugged individualism and hard work. Pitted against the government in these stories, the protagonist is the little guy, at odds with burdensome regulations and bureaucratic oversight. However, many of these stories are produced and distributed by large media corporations and political leaders who rely on the rest of us to consent to the American Dream narrative in order to keep their privileged place in the status quo and reinforce this "commonsense" story as the way the world works.

SPECIALIZATION, GLOBAL MARKETS, AND CONVERGENCE

In today's complex and often turbulent economic environment, global firms have sought greater profits by moving labor to less economically developed countries that need jobs but have poor health and safety regulations for workers. The continuous outsourcing of many U.S. jobs and the breakdown of global economic borders accompanied this transformation. Bolstered by the passage of GATT (General Agreement on Tariffs and Trade) in 1947, the signing of NAFTA (North American Free Trade Agreement) in 1994, and the formation of the WTO (World Trade Organization, which succeeded GATT in 1995), global cooperation fostered transnational media corporations and business deals across international terrain.

But in many cases, this global expansion by U.S. companies ran counter to America's early-twentieth-century vision of itself. Henry Ford, for example, followed his wife's suggestion to lower prices so workers could afford Ford cars. In many countries today, however, most workers cannot even afford the computers and TV sets they are making primarily for U.S. and European markets.

The Rise of Specialization and Synergy

The new globalism coincided with the rise of specialization. The magazine, radio, and cable industries sought specialized markets both in the United States and overseas, in part to counter television's mass appeal. By the 1980s, however, even television—confronted with the growing popularity of home video and cable—began niche marketing, targeting affluent eighteen- to thirty-four-year-old viewers, whose buying habits are generally not as stable or predictable as those of older consumers. Younger and older audiences, abandoned by the networks, were sought by other media outlets and advertisers. Magazines such as *J-14* and *AARP The Magazine* now flourish. Cable channels such as Nickelodeon and the Cartoon Network serve the under-eighteen market, while the Hallmark Channel and Lifetime address female viewers over age fifty; in addition, cable channel BET targets young African Americans, helping define them as a consumer group.

Beyond specialization, though, what really distinguishes current media economics is the extension of **synergy** to international levels. *Synergy* typically refers to the promotion and sale of different versions of a media product across the various subsidiaries of a media conglomerate (e.g., a Weather Channel segment on NBC's *Today Show*, or an NBC News reporter appearing on MSNBC for election coverage—all part of Comcast and its NBC Universal subsidiary). However, it also refers to global companies like Sony buying up popular culture—in this case, movie studios and record labels—to play on its various electronic products. Today, synergy is an important goal for large media corporations and is often the reason given for expensive mergers and acquisitions. But historically, half of all mergers and acquisitions are failures, and synergies are never realized.[25] (Consider, for example, the disastrous AOL–Time Warner merger of 2001 or News Corp.'s expensive bad bet on the success of Myspace in 2005.)

Disney: A Postmodern Media Conglomerate

The Walt Disney Company is one of the most successful companies in leveraging its many properties to create synergies. For example, in 2014, ABC broadcast the prime-time special *The Story of "Frozen": Making a Disney Animated Classic* to promote the Disney movie studio's enormous hit movie and soundtrack—and to hype ABC's *Once Upon a Time* series (which would soon feature a character from *Frozen*) along with Disney's next animated film, *Big Hero 6*. *Frozen* also tapped into a huge array of licensed merchandise and even *Frozen*-themed vacation trips by Disney's tour company and cruise line (see Chapter 7). Such promotional events and merchandise helped maintain interest in the story and characters while *Frozen 2* awaited its 2019 release. To fully understand the contemporary story of media economics and synergy, we need only examine the transformation of Disney from a struggling cartoon creator to one of the world's largest media conglomerates.

The Early Years

After Walt Disney's first cartoon company, Laugh-O-gram, went bankrupt in 1922, Disney moved to Hollywood and found his niche. He created Mickey Mouse (originally named Mortimer) for the first sound cartoons in the late 1920s, then developed the first feature-length cartoon, *Snow White and the Seven Dwarfs*, completed in 1937.

For much of the twentieth century, the Disney company set the standard for popular cartoons and children's culture. The *Silly Symphonies* series (1929–1939) established the studio's reputation for high-quality hand-drawn cartoons. Although Disney remained a minor studio, *Fantasia* and *Pinocchio* each made more than $40 million. Nonetheless, the studio barely broke even because cartoon projects took time—four years for *Snow White*—and commanded the company's entire attention.

Around the time of the demise of the cartoon film short in movie theaters, Disney expanded into other areas with its first nature documentary short, *Seal Island* (1949); its first live-action feature, *Treasure Island* (1950); and its first feature documentary, *The Living Desert* (1953).

Disney was also among the first film studios to embrace television, launching a long-running prime-time show in 1954. Then, in 1955, Disneyland opened in Southern California. Eventually, Disney's theme parks would produce the bulk of the studio's revenues. (Walt Disney World in Orlando, Florida, began operation in 1971.)

In 1953, Disney started Buena Vista, a distribution company. This was the first step in making the studio into a major player. The company also began exploiting the power of its early cartoon features. *Snow White*, for example, was successfully rereleased in theaters to new generations of children before eventually going to videocassette and much later to DVD.

Global Expansion

The death of Walt Disney in 1966 triggered a period of decline for the studio. But in 1984, a new management team, led by Michael Eisner, initiated a turnaround. The newly created Touchstone movie division reinvented the live-action cartoon for adults as well as for children in *Who Framed Roger Rabbit* (1988). A string of hand-drawn animated hits followed, including *The Little Mermaid* (1989), *Beauty and the Beast* (1991), *The Lion King* (1994), *Mulan* (1998), and *Lilo & Stitch* (2002). Disney also distributed a string of computer-animated blockbusters from Pixar Animation Studios, including *Toy Story* (1995), *Monsters, Inc.* (2001), *Finding Nemo* (2003), and *The Incredibles* (2004); it later acquired Pixar outright and released additional movies, including *Up* (2009), *Toy Story 3* (2010), *Brave* (2012), *Inside Out* (2015), *Coco* (2017), and *Incredibles 2* (2018). Disney's in-house animation studio eventually got into the computer-animation business and had several major successes with *Wreck-It Ralph* (2012), *Frozen* (2013), *Big Hero 6* (2014), *Moana* (2016), and *Zootopia* (2016).

In the mid-1990s, Disney changed from a media company to a media conglomerate. Through its purchase of ABC in 1995, Disney became the owner of the cable sports channels ESPN and ESPN2, and later expanded the brand with ESPNEWS, ESPN Classic, and ESPNU channels; *ESPN The Magazine*; ESPN Radio; and ESPN.go.com, beginning an era of sports monopolization. In addition, it came to epitomize the synergistic possibilities of media consolidation; for example, Disney can

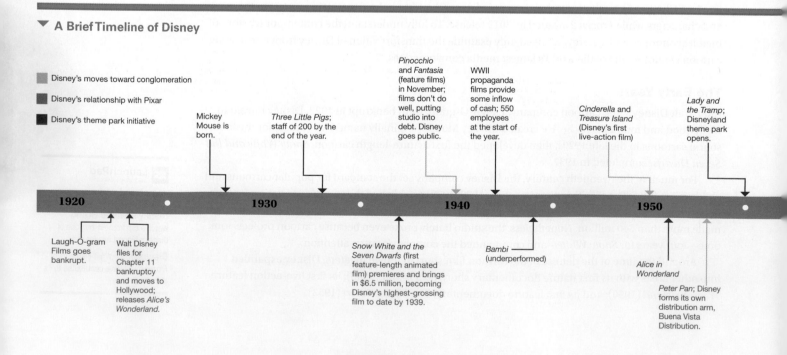

▼ A Brief Timeline of Disney

■ Disney's moves toward conglomeration
■ Disney's relationship with Pixar
■ Disney's theme park initiative

Mickey Mouse is born.

Three Little Pigs; staff of 200 by the end of the year.

Pinocchio and *Fantasia* (feature films) in November; films don't do well, putting studio into debt. Disney goes public.

WWII propaganda films provide some inflow of cash; 550 employees at the start of the year.

Cinderella and *Treasure Island* (Disney's first live-action film)

Lady and the Tramp; Disneyland theme park opens.

1920   **1930**   **1940**   **1950**

Laugh-O-gram Films goes bankrupt.

Walt Disney files for Chapter 11 bankruptcy and moves to Hollywood; releases *Alice's Wonderland*.

Snow White and the Seven Dwarfs (first feature-length animated film) premieres and brings in $6.5 million, becoming Disney's highest-grossing film to date by 1939.

Bambi (underperformed)

Alice in Wonderland

Peter Pan; Disney forms its own distribution arm, Buena Vista Distribution.

produce an animated feature for both theatrical release and DVD distribution. With its ABC network, it can promote Disney movies and television shows on programs like *Good Morning America*. A book version can be released through Disney's publishing arm, Disney Publishing Worldwide, and "the-making-of" versions can appear on cable's Disney Channel or ABC Family (now called Freeform). Characters can become attractions at Disney's theme parks, which themselves have spawned Hollywood movies, such as the lucrative *Pirates of the Caribbean* franchise. In New York City, Disney renovated several theaters and launched versions of *Beauty and the Beast*, *The Lion King*, *Spider-Man*, *Tarzan*, *Mary Poppins*, *The Little Mermaid*, *Aladdin*, and *Frozen* as successful Broadway musicals.

Building on the international appeal of its cartoon features, Disney extended its global reach by opening Tokyo Disney Resort in 1983 and Disneyland Paris in 1991. Disney opened more venues in Asia, with Hong Kong Disneyland Resort in 2005 and Shanghai Disney Resort in 2016.

FOR ABOUT A DECADE, DISNEY ANIMATION WAS DEFINED more by Pixar, the computer-animation studio it purchased in 2006, than by its original in-house animation studio. But Disney's original studio has seen a resurgence in recent years with movies like *Tangled* (2010), *Wreck-It Ralph* (2012), *Frozen* (2013), *Moana* (2016), and *Zootopia* (2016). In 2013, *Frozen* became an international phenomenon, grossing over $1 billion worldwide, and won the Academy Award for best animated feature. Dolls of the *Frozen* characters sold out at stores around the world. In 2016, Disney launched a *Frozen*-themed ride, Frozen Ever After, at its Epcot Center theme park in Florida; and in 2017, the *Frozen* musical opened on Broadway.

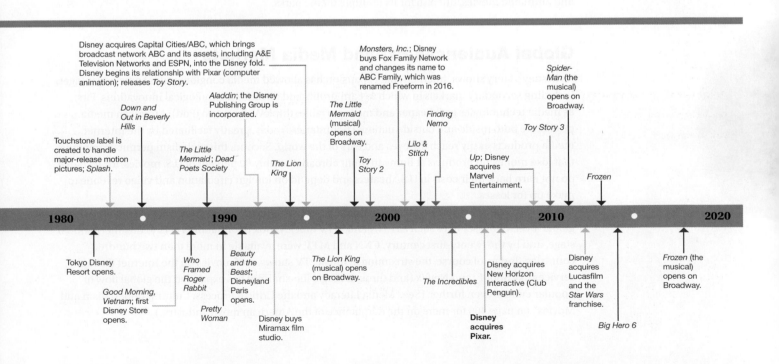

Disney acquires Capital Cities/ABC, which brings broadcast network ABC and its assets, including A&E Television Networks and ESPN, into the Disney fold. Disney begins its relationship with Pixar (computer animation); releases *Toy Story*.

Monsters, Inc.; Disney buys Fox Family Network and changes its name to ABC Family, which was renamed Freeform in 2016.

Aladdin; the Disney Publishing Group is incorporated.

Down and Out in Beverly Hills

The Little Mermaid; *Dead Poets Society*

The Lion King

The Little Mermaid (musical) opens on Broadway.

Finding Nemo

Lilo & Stitch

Toy Story 2

Up; Disney acquires Marvel Entertainment.

Spider-Man (the musical) opens on Broadway.

Toy Story 3

Frozen

Touchstone label is created to handle major-release motion pictures; *Splash*.

1980 ● **1990** ● **2000** ● **2010** ● **2020**

Tokyo Disney Resort opens.

Good Morning, Vietnam; first Disney Store opens.

Who Framed Roger Rabbit

Pretty Woman

Beauty and the Beast; Disneyland Paris opens.

Disney buys Miramax film studio.

The Lion King (musical) opens on Broadway.

The Incredibles

Disney acquires Pixar.

Disney acquires New Horizon Interactive (Club Penguin).

Disney acquires Lucasfilm and the *Star Wars* franchise.

Big Hero 6

Frozen (the musical) opens on Broadway.

FIGURE 13.5

SYNERGY

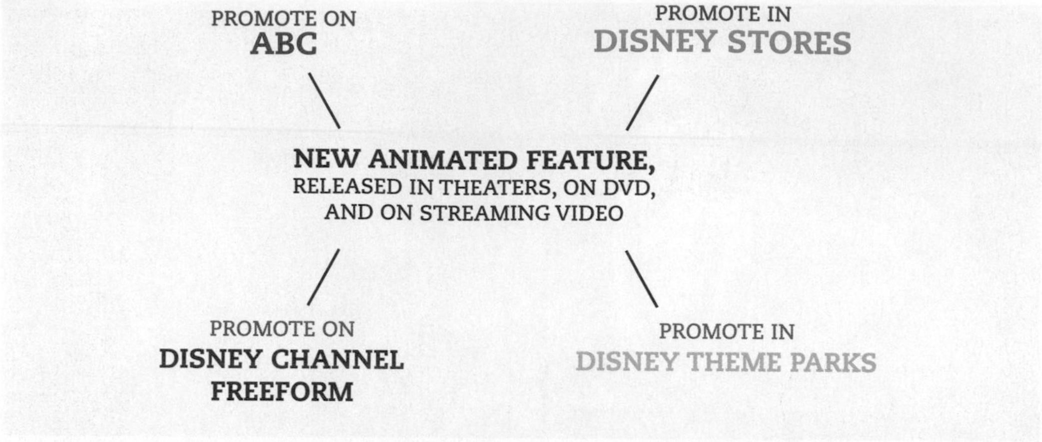

PROMOTE ON
ABC

PROMOTE IN
DISNEY STORES

NEW ANIMATED FEATURE,
RELEASED IN THEATERS, ON DVD,
AND ON STREAMING VIDEO

PROMOTE ON
**DISNEY CHANNEL
FREEFORM**

PROMOTE IN
DISNEY THEME PARKS

Disney exemplifies the formula for becoming a "great media conglomerate" as defined in the book *Global Dreams*: "Companies able to use visuals to sell sound, movies to sell books, or software to sell hardware [will] become the winners in the new global commercial order."[26]

Disney Today

Even as Disney grew into the world's No. 2 media conglomerate by the beginning of the twenty-first century, the cartoon pioneer experienced the multiple shocks of a recession, failed films and Internet ventures, and declining theme park attendance. By 2005, Disney had fallen to No. 5 among movie studios in U.S. box-office sales—down from No. 1 in 2003. The new course for Disney was to develop (through acquisitions) new stories for movies and its other corporate offerings. In 2006, new CEO Robert Iger merged Disney and Pixar. In 2009, Disney purchased Marvel Entertainment for $4 billion, bringing Iron Man, Spider-Man, and X-Men into the Disney family; in 2012, it purchased Lucasfilm and, with it, the rights to the *Star Wars* and *Indiana Jones* movies and characters. This means that Disney now has access to whole casts of "new" characters—not just for TV programs, feature films, and animated movies, but also for its multiple theme parks.

Global Audiences Expand Media Markets

As Disney's story shows, international expansion has allowed media conglomerates some advantages, including secondary markets in which to earn profits and advance technological innovations. First, as media technologies get cheaper and more portable (think Walkman to iPod), American media proliferate both inside and outside national boundaries. Today, greatly facilitated by the Internet, media products easily reach the eyes and ears of the world. Second, this globalism permits companies that lose money on products at home to profit abroad. Roughly 80 percent of U.S. movies, for instance, do not earn back their costs in U.S. theaters and depend on foreign circulation and video revenue to make up for losses.

In addition, satellite transmission has made North American and European TV available at the global level. Cable services such as CNN and MTV quickly took their national acts to the international stage, and by the twenty-first century, CNN and MTV were available in more than two hundred countries. Today, of course, the streaming of music, TV shows, and movies on the Internet through services like Spotify and Netflix (and through illegal file-sharing) has expanded the global flow of popular culture even further. (See "Media Literacy and the Critical Process: Cultural Imperialism and Movies" on page 406 for more on the dominance of the American movie industry.)

HBO GO AND HBO NOW
Acclaimed HBO original programming, including *Game of Thrones* and a variety of other TV series and movies, is available online through the company's HBO Go online service. Initially, it was available only to those who already subscribed to the premium channel through their cable company, but in 2015, HBO introduced the stand-alone subscription service HBO Now, which offers HBO content through non-cable providers like Apple.

The Internet and Convergence Change the Game

For much of their history, media companies have usually been part of discrete industries—that is, the newspaper business stood apart from book publishing, which was different from radio, which was different from the film industry. But the Internet and convergence have changed that—not only by offering a portal to view or read older media forms but also by requiring virtually all older media companies to establish an online presence. Today, newspapers, magazines, book publishers, music companies, radio and TV stations, and film studios all have websites that offer online versions of their product or web services that enhance their original media form.

The Rise of the New Digital Media Conglomerates

The digital turn marks a shift in the media environment, from the legacy media powerhouses like Time Warner and Disney to the new digital media conglomerates (see "Global Village: China's Dominant Media Corporations Rival America's" on page 411). Five companies—Microsoft, Apple, Amazon, Google, and Facebook—reign in digital media, and Netflix is poised to join them, as detailed in Figure 13.6 and the chapter opener.

Even though these digital corporations have proven to be technologically adept, they still need to provide compelling narratives to attract people (to repeat a point from earlier in the chapter). The five largest companies are weak in this regard, as they rely on other companies' media narratives (e.g., the sounds, images, words, and pictures) or the stories that their own users provide (as in Facebook posts or YouTube videos). Netflix, the smallest of the companies, is the leader in content development, although Amazon now has its own publishing divisions (to compete with publishing companies) and its own original television series and online channels, like Twitch (to compete with Netflix, Hulu, and

In the 1920s, the U.S. film industry became the leader in the worldwide film business. The images and stories of American films are well known in nearly every corner of the world. But with major film production centers in places like India, China, Hong Kong, Japan, South Korea, Mexico, the United Kingdom, Germany, France, Russia, and Nigeria, to what extent do U.S. films dominate international markets today? Conversely, how often do international films get much attention in the United States?

1 DESCRIPTION

Using international box-office revenue listings (www.boxofficemojo.com/intl/ is a good place to start), compare the recent weekly box-office rankings of the United States to those of five other countries. (Your sample could extend across several continents or focus on a specific region, like Southeast Asia.) Limit yourself to the top ten or fifteen films in box-office rank. Note where each film is produced (some films are joint productions of studios from two or more countries), and put your results in a table for comparison.

2 ANALYSIS

What patterns emerged in each country's box-office rankings?

What percentage of films came from the United States? What percentage of films were domestic productions in each country? What percentage of films came from countries other than the United States? In the United States, what percentage of films originated with studios from other countries?

3 INTERPRETATION

So what do your discoveries mean? Can you make an argument for or against the existence of cultural imperialism by the United States? Are there film industries in other countries that dominate movie theaters in their region of the world? How would you critique the reverse of cultural imperialism, wherein films from other countries rarely break into the Top 10 box-office list? Does this happen in any countries you sampled?

4 EVALUATION

Given your interpretation, is cultural dominance by one country a good thing or a bad thing? Consider the potential advantages of creating a global village of shared popular culture versus the potential disadvantages of cultural imperialism. Also, is there any potential harm in a country's Top 10 box-office list being filled with domestic productions and rarely featuring international films?

5 ENGAGEMENT

Contact managers of your local movie theater (or executives at the headquarters of the chain that owns it). Ask them how they decide which films to screen. If they don't show many international films, ask them why. Be ready to provide a list of three to five international films released in the United States (see the full list of current U.S. releases at www.boxofficemojo.com) that haven't yet been screened in the theater.

YouTube). It's likely that the other digital companies will eventually do the same. The history of mass communication suggests that it is the content—the narratives—that endures, while the devices and distribution systems do not.

The Digital Age Favors Small, Flexible Start-Up Companies

All the leading digital companies of today were once small start-ups that emerged at important junctures of the digital age. The earliest, Microsoft and Apple, were established in the mid-1970s with the rise of the personal computer. Amazon began in 1995 with the popularization of the web and the beginnings of e-commerce. Google was established in 1998, as search engines became the best way of navigating the web. Facebook, beginning in 2004, proved to be the best social media site to emerge in the 2000s, and Netflix began in 1997 as just another way to deliver DVDs. For each success story, though, hundreds of other firms failed or flamed out quickly (e.g., Myspace).

MICROSOFT

est. 1975

Strengths:
search
game console

APPLE

est. 1976

Strengths:
technology
infrastructure

AMAZON

est. 1995

Strength:
e-commerce

GOOGLE

est. 1998

Strengths:
search
advertising

FACEBOOK

est. 2004

Strengths:
communication
social media

NETFLIX

est. 1997

Strengths:
Internet video
original
programming

Microsoft, one of the wealthiest digital companies in the world, is making the transition from being the top software company (a business that is slowly in decline) to competing in the digital media world with its Bing search engine and devices like its successful Xbox game console, Surface tablet, and Windows phone. Microsoft holds a small ownership share in Facebook and purchased the social media businesses LinkedIn ($26.2 billion) and GitHub ($7.5 billion) in 2016 and 2018, respectively.

Apple's strength has been creating the technology and the infrastructure to bring any media content to users' fingertips. When many traditional media companies didn't have the means to distribute online content easily, Apple developed the shiny devices (the iPod, iPhone, and iPad) and easy-to-use systems (the iTunes store) to do it, immediately transforming the media. Today, Apple has a hand in every media industry. However, iPhone sales have slowed somewhat, putting Apple's always-rising profits at risk.

Amazon's entrée is that it has grown into the largest e-commerce site in the world. In recent years, Amazon has begun shifting from delivering physical products (e.g., bound books) to distributing digital products (e-books and downloadable music, movies, television shows, and more) on its digital devices (Kindle, Fire TV, and Fire Phone). Amazon, the top digital retailer, is also moving into physical locations, with Amazon bookstores and the purchase of the Whole Foods grocery chain.

Google's search advertising business is about 86 percent of its $119.9 billion annual revenue (2017). Google moved into the same digital media distribution business that Apple and Amazon offer via its Android phone operating system, Nexus 7 tablet, Chromebook, and Chromecast. The company used YouTube to be part of the streaming video revolution; now it's also a platform for music videos and original shows. Google's parent company is Alphabet.

Facebook had more than 2.2 billion users worldwide in 2018, and the company leverages those users (and the massive amounts of data they share about themselves) into advertising sales. Like the four larger digital companies, Facebook now has a hardware device to access the Internet and digital media following its purchase of the Oculus Rift virtual reality gaming headset for $2 billion in 2014. Facebook introduced live streaming on its site in 2016.

Netflix started out as a DVD-by-mail service in 1997 and began streaming in 2007. With over 130 million streaming members in over 190 countries, Netflix is the leading Internet television channel. Netflix does not market any hardware devices, but that may be an advantage in the fast-changing media business, where devices can quickly become obsolete. Netflix's popular original programming also gives it insurance against the high costs of buying programming from other media corporations and against competing streaming channels.

FIGURE 13.6
RISE OF THE NEW
DIGITAL MEDIA
CONGLOMERATES

Today, the juncture in the digital era is the growing importance of social media and mobile devices. As in the earlier periods, the strategy for start-up companies is to find a niche market, connect with consumers, and get big fast, swallowing up or overwhelming competitors. Instagram, YouTube, Snapchat, and Zynga are recent examples of this. The successful start-ups then take one of two paths—either be acquired by a larger company (e.g., Google buying YouTube, Facebook buying Instagram) or go it alone and try to get even bigger (e.g., Snapchat). Either way, success might not last long, especially in an age when people's interests can change very quickly. Witness Zynga, which had the top social media game when *FarmVille* debuted in 2009 but began to fizzle out a few years later without another hit game.

SOCIAL ISSUES IN MEDIA ECONOMICS

As the Disney-ABC merger demonstrates, recent years have brought a surplus of billion-dollar takeovers and mergers, including those between Time Inc. and Warner Communications, Time Warner and Turner, AOL and Time Warner, UPN and WB, Comcast and NBC Universal, Sirius and XM, Universal Music Group and EMI, Yahoo! and Tumblr, and AT&T and DirecTV (see Figure 13.7). By 2018, a number of other mergers and acquisitions had been proposed or approved, including Disney's purchase of 21st Century Fox, a Sprint and T-Mobile merger, and a re-merger of CBS and Viacom. The 2018 court approval of AT&T's purchase of Time Warner signaled a new era of lax enforcement of antitrust law.

This mergermania has accompanied stripped-down regulation, which has virtually suspended most ownership limits on media industries. As a result, a number of consumer advocates and citizen groups have raised questions about deregulation and ownership consolidation. Still, the 2008 financial crisis saw many of these megamedia firms overleveraged—that is, not making enough from stock investments to offset the debt they took on to add more companies to their empires. Thus, in recent years we have seen Time Warner send AOL and Time Inc. adrift, the New York Times Company sell the *Boston Globe*, the Washington Post Company sell *Newsweek*, News Corp. spin off its newspaper and publishing divisions, and the Tribune Company and Gannett split off their newspaper divisions.

One longtime critic of media mergers is Ben Bagdikian, author of *The Media Monopoly*. Bagdikian has argued that although there are abundant products in the market—thousands of daily and weekly newspapers, radio and television stations, magazines, and book publishers— only a limited number of companies are in charge of those products.[27] Bagdikian and others fear that this represents a dangerous antidemocratic tendency, in which a handful of media moguls wield a disproportionate amount of economic control. Moreover, there is little diversity in media ownership. For example, the distribution of U.S. airwaves in the 1930s went only to white male owners. According to media journalist Kristal Brent Zook, "African American ownership remains particularly low, hovering at less than 1 percent of all television properties, and less than 2 percent of radio."[28]

The Limits of Antitrust Laws

Although meant to ensure multiple voices and owners, American antitrust laws have been easily subverted since the 1980s, as companies expanded by diversifying holdings and merging product lines with other big media firms. Large media firms have also become among the most active and powerful lobbyists in Washington, D.C., and other political capitals. The resulting consolidation of media owners has limited the number of independent voices in the market and reduced the number of owners who might be able to innovate and challenge established economic powers. All of this has led to renewed interest in enforcing antitrust laws.

MERGER AND ACQUISITION	PRICE	OUTCOME
New York Times + *Boston Globe* (1993)	$1.1 billion	The *Times* sells the *Globe* to the owner of the Boston Red Sox for $70 million in 2013.
Disney + ABC (1995)	$19 billion	The television network and ESPN become huge profit centers for Disney.
Time Warner + Turner Broadcasting (1995)	$7.5 billion	Time Warner grows even bigger than the combined Disney and ABC and adds CNN, TBS, and other cable channels.
Tribune Media Company + Times Mirror Company (2000)	$8.3 billion	Biggest newspaper merger ever combines the *Chicago Tribune*, the *Los Angeles Times*, and several others. The company files for bankruptcy in 2008 and spins off its newspaper division in 2014 (like several other newspaper conglomerates).
AOL + Time Warner (2001)	$164 billion	Biggest media merger failure ever. Time Warner spins off AOL in 2009.
Google + YouTube (2006)	$1.65 billion	One of Google's best acquisitions—YouTube makes several billion dollars each year.
Sirius + XM (2008)	$13 billion	A merger of equals makes a bigger company but reduces the number of satellite radio companies to one.
Google + Motorola (2011)	$12.5 billion	Google sells the Motorola mobile phone business to Lenovo in 2014 for $2.91 billion.
Comcast + NBC Universal (2011)	$28 billion	The biggest cable company becomes even bigger with a TV network, a movie studio, and more—though some of the media holdings are not at peak performance.
AT&T + T-Mobile (2011)	$39 billion	The Department of Justice opposes this merger, which would have reduced the number of cell phone carriers from four to three. AT&T loses, but consumers win with more choices and competitive pricing.
Universal Music Group + EMI (2012)	$1.3 billion	Universal becomes the biggest music company in the world, leaving only three major sound recording corporations.
Comcast + Time Warner Cable (2014)	$45.2 billion	A merger creating the most dominant wired broadband network in the United States is abandoned by Comcast in the face of regulatory opposition.
AT&T + DirecTV (2014)	$48.5 billion	The merger of the largest mobile phone service and the largest satellite television provider comes with a number of conditions imposed by the FCC to ensure that the company doesn't discriminate against other content providers.
Charter Cable + Time Warner Cable + Bright House Networks (2016)	$67.1 billion	The merger of three cable companies creates the second-largest cable and broadband firm, serving markets in forty states.

FIGURE 13.7

MAJOR MEDIA MERGERS AND ACQUISITIONS

Diversification

Most media companies diversify among media products (such as television stations and film studios), never fully dominating a particular media industry. Disney, for example, spreads its holdings among its television programming, film, and theme parks and resorts. However, the media giant actually competes with a handful of other big companies, including Comcast, CBS, and even digital media companies like Amazon and Netflix.

Such diversification promotes oligopolies in which a few behemoth companies control most media production and distribution. This kind of economic arrangement makes it difficult for products offered outside an oligopoly to compete in the marketplace. For instance, music streaming companies like Apple and Google have a distinct advantage because they have their own mobile devices and

ELSEWHERE IN
MEDIA & CULTURE

SIX MEDIA COMPANIES THAT WILL DOMINATE OUR FUTURE MEDIA LANDSCAPE
pp. 47–50

For the first time in 2017, Internet advertising surpassed TV advertising

p. 337

$39.9 billion
the total international box-office gross revenues in 2017

p. 223

$348,300
THE COST OF A THIRTY-SECOND ADVERTISEMENT DURING *THE BIG BANG THEORY*

p. 187

WHERE CAN YOU FIND MORE THAN 466 BILLION ARCHIVED WEB PAGES FOR FREE?
p. 59

China's Dominant Media Corporations Rival America's

The 2018 rankings of the most valuable global brands show the dominance of digital media in our world. In 2006, just four of the Top 10 global brands were digital technology companies. In 2018, eight of the Top 10 global brands were digital media related. And although Google, Apple, Amazon, Microsoft, Facebook, and AT&T are recognizable brands in the United States, two Chinese companies—Tencent and Alibaba—are the fastest-growing brands in the global Top 10.[1]

Both companies are leading forces in China's 770-million-plus Internet-user market and are stretching beyond. Both are conglomerates like Amazon, spreading into a wide range of businesses. Founded in 1998, Tencent is currently one of China's largest web portals (at QQ.com); has the popular WeChat messaging, social media, and mobile payment app, and Tenpay payment services; owns China's (and the world's) largest music streaming service; and runs hundreds of other businesses in the areas of financial services, insurance, mobile games, smartphones, and artificial intelligence.

Alibaba was started in 1999 as an e-commerce site, and today it (not Amazon) is the world's largest online retailer. It also runs Taobao Marketplace (bigger than eBay), the Fliggy travel platform, Alibaba Cloud, Alipay (an online payment business run by subsidiary Ant Financial), and music streaming and film production businesses.

In a 2018 article, the *New York Times* highlighted the high level of competition between Tencent and Alibaba. "They have both funded ventures that offer online education, make electric cars and rent out bicycles. For the giants, such initiatives represent new opportunities for people to use their digital wallets—Ant Financial's Alipay and Tencent's WeChat Pay—and new ways to collect data on consumer behavior," the *Times* reported. "Once the companies have locked people into their payment systems, they can become the enablers of commerce and financial services of even more kinds."[2]

Whereas the U.S. government and the European Union are increasingly interested in checking the power and size of American digital giants like Google, Facebook, and Amazon, Tencent and Alibaba seem to have no such governmental limits on them: "China's internet titans have a powerful ally found nowhere else, though: the Chinese government. Tencent and Alibaba have avoided antimonopoly clampdowns by staying in Beijing's good graces, said Hu Wenyou, a partner at the Beijing law firm Yingke. Their sheer size also makes them easier for the authorities to control. They simply have too much to lose."[3]

TOP 10 U.S MEDIA COMPANIES

Revenue in $billions
(Numbers have been rounded)

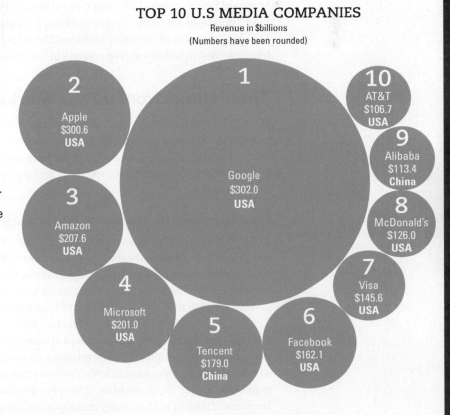

- 1. Google $302.0 USA
- 2. Apple $300.6 USA
- 3. Amazon $207.6 USA
- 4. Microsoft $201.0 USA
- 5. Tencent $179.0 China
- 6. Facebook $162.1 USA
- 7. Visa $145.6 USA
- 8. McDonald's $126.0 USA
- 9. Alibaba $113.4 China
- 10. AT&T $106.7 USA

ecosystems as well as enormous cash reserves to patiently build their music businesses. Meanwhile, Pandora and Spotify helped launch the streaming business, but as independent companies, they may struggle in the long term because they don't have the same level of resources and don't have exclusive control over the music content.

Applying Antitrust Laws Today

Occasionally, independent voices raise issues that aid the Justice Department and the FTC in their antitrust cases. For example, when EchoStar (now the Dish Network) proposed to purchase DirecTV in 2001, a number of rural, consumer, and Latino organizations spoke out against the merger for several reasons. Latino organizations opposed the merger because in many U.S. markets, direct broadcast satellite (DBS) service offers the only available Spanish-language television programming. The merger would have left the United States with just one major DBS company and created a virtual monopoly for EchoStar, which had fewer Spanish-language offerings than DirecTV. In 2002, the FCC declined to approve the merger, saying it would not serve the public interest, convenience, and necessity.

In 2011, AT&T moved to acquire T-Mobile, another wireless telecom giant, for $39 billion. The Justice Department opposed the merger on antitrust grounds (media watchdog groups said it would have left the country with just three major mobile phone companies, giving consumers far fewer options), leading AT&T to eventually scrap the deal. AT&T, still looking to grow, bought DirecTV in 2014 for $48.5 billion. This bigger merger was approved because the two companies are generally involved in different businesses, although government regulators imposed certain conditions to ensure that the new company wouldn't discriminate against carrying other content providers.

But U.S. antitrust laws have no teeth globally. Although international copyright laws offer some protection to musicians and writers, no international antitrust rules exist to prohibit transnational companies from buying up as many media companies as they can afford. Still, as legal scholar Harry First points out, antitrust concerns are "alive and well and living in Europe."[29] For example, when Sony and Bertelsmann's BMG unit merged their music businesses, only the European Union (EU) raised questions about the merger on behalf of independent labels and musicians worried about the oligopoly structure of the music business. The EU repeatedly reviewed the merger beginning in 2004, but it decided to withdraw its opposition in late 2008.

The Fallout from a Free Market

Since the wave of media mergers began with gusto in the 1980s, a number of consumer critics have pointed to the lack of public debate surrounding the tightening oligopoly structure of international media. Economists and media critics have traced the causes and history of this void to two major issues: a reluctance to criticize capitalism, and the debate over how much control consumers have in the marketplace.

Equating Free Markets with Democracy

In the 1920s and 1930s, commercial radio executives, many of whom had befriended FCC members, succeeded in portraying themselves as operating in the public interest while labeling their noncommercial radio counterparts in education, labor, or religion as mere voices of propaganda. In these early debates, corporate interests succeeded in misleadingly aligning the political ideas of democracy with the economic structures of capitalism.

Throughout the Cold War period in the 1950s and 1960s, it became increasingly difficult to criticize capitalism, which had become a synonym for democracy in many circles. In this context, any criticism of capitalism became an attack on the free marketplace. This, in turn, appeared to be a criticism of free speech because the business community often sees its right to operate in a free marketplace as an extension of its right to buy commercial speech in the form of advertising. As longtime CBS chief William Paley told a group of educators in 1937, "He who attacks the fundamentals of the American system" of commercial broadcasting "attacks democracy itself."[30]

Broadcast historian Robert McChesney, discussing the rise of commercial radio during the 1930s, has noted that leaders like Paley "equated capitalism with the free and equal marketplace, the free and equal marketplace with democracy, and democracy with 'Americanism.'"[31] The collapse of the former Soviet Union's communist economy in the 1990s is often portrayed as a triumph for democracy. As we now realize, however, it was primarily a victory for capitalism and free-market economies.

Consumer Choice versus Consumer Control

As many economists point out, capitalism is not structured democratically but arranged vertically, with powerful corporate leaders at the top and hourly-wage workers at the bottom. But democracy, in principle, is built on a more horizontal model, in which each individual has an equal opportunity to have his or her voice heard and vote counted. In discussing free markets, economists distinguish between similar types of consumer power: *consumer control* over marketplace goods and freedom of *consumer choice*.[32] Most Americans and the citizens of other economically developed nations clearly have *consumer choice*: options among a range of media products. Yet consumers and even media employees have limited *consumer control*: power in deciding what kinds of media get created and circulated.

One recurring place for democratic production is the work of independent and alternative producers, artists, writers, and publishers. Despite the movement toward economic consolidation, the fringes of media industries still offer a diversity of opinions, ideas, and alternative products. In fact, when independent companies become even marginally popular, they are often pursued by large companies that seek to make them subsidiaries. For example, alternative music often taps into social concerns that are not normally discussed in the recording industry's corporate boardrooms. Moreover, business leaders "at the top" depend on independent ideas "from below" to generate new product lines. A number of transnational corporations encourage the development of local artists—talented individuals who might have the capacity to transcend the regional or national level and become the next global phenomenon.

Cultural Imperialism

The influence of American popular culture has created considerable debate in international circles. On the one hand, the notion of freedom that is associated with innovation and rebellion in American culture has been embraced internationally. The global spread of media—and increased access to it—have made it harder for political leaders to secretly repress dissident groups, as police and state activity (such as the torture of illegally detained citizens) can now be documented digitally and easily dispatched by satellite, the Internet, and cell phones around the world.

On the other hand, American media are shaping the cultures and identities of other nations. American styles in fashion and food, as well as media fare, dominate the global market—a process known as **cultural imperialism**. Today, many international observers contend that the idea of consumer control or input is even more remote in countries inundated by American movies, music, television, and images of beauty. For example, consumer product giant Unilever sells Dove soap with its "Campaign for Real Beauty" in the United States but markets Fair & Lovely products—a skin-lightening line—to poor women in India.

Although many indigenous forms of media culture—such as Brazil's telenovela, Jamaica's reggae, and Japan's anime—are extremely popular, U.S. dominance in producing and distributing mass media puts a severe burden on countries attempting to produce their own cultural products. For example, American TV producers have generally recouped their production costs by the time their TV shows are exported. This enables American distributors to offer these programs to other countries at bargain rates, undercutting local production companies that are trying to create original programs.

CULTURAL IMPERIALISM

Ever since Hollywood gained an edge in film production and distribution during World War I, U.S. movies have dominated the box office in Europe, in some years accounting for more than 80 percent of the revenues taken in by European theaters. Hollywood's reach has since extended throughout the world, including previously difficult markets such as China.

Defenders of American popular culture argue that because some aspects of our culture challenge authority, national boundaries, and outmoded traditions, they create an arena in which citizens can raise questions. Supporters also argue that a universal popular culture creates a global village and fosters communication across national boundaries.

Critics, however, such as the authors of the book *Global Dreams*, believe that although American popular culture often contains protests against social wrongs, such protests "can be turned into consumer products and lose their bite. Protest itself becomes something to sell."[33] The harshest critics have also argued that American cultural imperialism both hampers the development of native cultures and negatively influences teenagers, who abandon their own rituals to adopt American tastes. The exportation of U.S. entertainment media is sometimes viewed as "cultural dumping," because it discourages the development of original local products and value systems.

Perhaps the greatest concern regarding a global village is the cultural disconnection for people whose standards of living are not routinely portrayed in contemporary media. About two-thirds of the world's population cannot afford most of the products advertised on American, Japanese, and European television. Yet more and more of the world's populations are able to glimpse consumer abundance and middle-class values through television, magazines, and the Internet.

As early as the 1950s, media managers feared political fallout, or a backlash of rising expectations, in that ads and products would raise the hopes of poor people but not keep pace with their actual living conditions.[34] Furthermore, the conspicuousness of consumer culture makes it difficult for many of us to imagine—and thus appreciate—ways of living that are not heavily dependent on the mass media and brand-name products.

THE MEDIA MARKETPLACE AND DEMOCRACY

In the midst of today's major global transformations of economies, cultures, and societies, the best way to monitor the impact of transnational economies is through vigorous news attention and lively public discussion. Clearly, however, this process is being hampered. Beginning in the 1990s, for example, news organizations, concerned about the bottom line, severely cut back the number of reporters assigned to cover international developments. This occurred—especially after 9/11—just as global news became more critical than ever to an informed citizenry.

We live in a society in which often-superficial consumer concerns, stock market quotes, and profit aspirations—rather than broader social issues—increasingly dominate the media agenda. In response, critics have posed some key questions: As consumers, do we care who owns the media as long as most of us have a broad selection of products? Do we care who owns the media as long as multiple voices *seem* to exist in the market?

The Effects of Media Consolidation on Democracy

Merged and multinational media corporations will continue to control more aspects of production and distribution. Of pressing concern is the impact of mergers on news operations, particularly the influence of large corporations on their news subsidiaries. These organizations have the capacity to use major news resources to promote their products and determine national coverage.

THE PRESIDENT AND COFOUNDER

of Free Press, a national nonpartisan organization dedicated to media reform, Robert McChesney is one of the foremost scholars of media economics in the United States. For ten years he hosted *Media Matters*, a radio call-in show in Central Illinois that discussed the relationship between politics and media. McChesney (*left*) most recently published *People Get Ready: The Fight Against a Jobless Economy and a Citizenless Democracy* (2016) with journalist and Free Press cofounder John Nichols (*right*).

Because of the growing consolidation of mass media, it has become increasingly difficult to sustain a public debate on economic issues. From a democratic perspective, the relationship of our mass media system to politics has been highly dysfunctional. Politicians in Washington, D.C., have regularly accepted millions of dollars in contributions from large media conglomerates and their lobbying groups to finance their campaigns. This changed in 2008 when the Obama campaign raised much of its financing from small donors. Still, corporations got a big boost from the Supreme Court in early 2010 in the *Citizens United* case. In a five-to-four vote, the court "ruled that the government may not ban political spending by corporations in candidate elections."[35] Writing for the majority, Justice Anthony Kennedy stated, "If the First Amendment has any force, it prohibits Congress from fining or jailing citizens, or associations of citizens, for simply engaging in political speech." The ruling overturned two decades of precedents that had limited direct corporate spending on campaigns, including the Bipartisan Campaign Reform Act of 2002 (often called the McCain-Feingold Act, after the senators who sponsored the bill), which placed restrictions on buying TV and radio campaign ads.

As unfettered corporate political contributions count as "political speech," some corporations are experiencing backlash (or praise) once their customers discover their political positions. For example, in 2012, fast-food outlet Chick-fil-A's charitable foundation "was revealed to be funneling millions to groups that oppose gay marriage and, until recently, promoted gay 'cure' therapies," resulting in a firestorm of criticism but also a wave of support from others, the *Daily Beast* reported. In the same year, Amazon founder and CEO Jeff Bezos and his wife donated $2.5 million of their own money to support a same-sex marriage referendum in Washington State, gaining both praise and criticism from some Amazon customers.[36]

Politicians have often turned to local television stations, spending record amounts during each election period to get their political ads on the air. In 2004, spending on the federal elections in the United States totaled $5.3 billion, with a large portion of that going to local broadcasters for commercials for congressional candidates and—in swing states like Ohio, Iowa, and Florida—for presidential candidates. In 2008, spending on federal elections topped $5.92 billion, and in 2016, it surpassed $6.44 billion.[37] But although local television stations have been happy to get part of the ever-increasing bounty of political ad money, the actual content of their news broadcasts has become less and less substantial, particularly when it comes to covering politics.

The Pew Research Center's Project for Excellence in Journalism reported that from 2005 to 2013, the amount of airtime given to weather, traffic, and sports on local news broadcasts expanded from 32 percent to 40 percent. Meanwhile, over that same period, the amount of time spent on politics and government-related stories slipped from 7 percent to 3 percent. The study's authors noted, "For some time, television consultants have been advising local television stations that viewers aren't interested in politics and government, and it appears that advice is being taken."[38]

Although television consultants might have concluded that local viewers aren't interested in politics and government, political consultants are only increasing the onslaught of political television ads every campaign season. Thus, there is little news content to provide a counterpoint to all the allegations that might be hurled in the barrage of political ads.

The Media Reform Movement

Robert McChesney and John Nichols described the state of concern about the gathering consolidation of mainstream media power: "'Media Reform' has become a catch-all phrase to describe the broad goals of a movement that says consolidated ownership of broadcast and cable media, chain ownership of newspapers, and telephone and cable-company colonization of the Internet pose a threat not just to the culture of the Republic but to democracy itself."[39] While our current era has spawned numerous grassroots organizations that challenge media to do a better job for the sake of democracy, there has not been much of an outcry from the general public for the kinds of concerns described by McChesney and Nichols. There is a reason for that. One key paradox of the Information Age is that for such economic discussions to be meaningful and democratic, they must be carried out in the popular media as well as in educational settings. Yet public debates and disclosures about the structure and ownership of the media are often not in the best economic interests of media owners.

Still, in some places, local groups and consumer movements are trying to address media issues that affect individual and community life. Such movements—like the National Conference for Media Reform—are generally united by geographic ties, common political backgrounds, or shared concerns about the state of the media. The Internet has also made it possible for media reform groups to form globally, uniting around such issues as contesting censorship or monitoring the activities of multinational corporations. The movement was also largely responsible for the success of preserving "net neutrality," which prevents Internet service providers from censoring or penalizing particular websites and online services (see Chapter 2), and then battling to bring it back when it was rejected by the Trump administration in 2018.

Given the exploitation of Facebook and Google by trolls during the 2016 election, and the revelation that millions of Facebook users had their data shared without their knowledge, perhaps we are more ready than ever to question some of the hierarchical and undemocratic arrangements of what McChesney, Nichols, and other reform critics call "Big Media." Even in the face of so many media mergers, the general public today seems open to such examinations, which might improve the global economy, improve worker conditions, and serve the public good. By better understanding media economics, we can play a more knowledgeable role in critiquing media organizations and evaluating their impact on democracy.

13 Chapter Review

One of the Common Threads discussed in Chapter 1 is the commercial nature of mass media. In thinking about media ownership regulations, it is important to consider how the media wield their influence.

During the 2000 presidential election, two marginal candidates—Pat Buchanan on the Right and Ralph Nader on the Left—shared a common view that both major-party candidates largely ignored. Buchanan and Nader warned of the increasing power of corporations to influence the economy and our democracy. In fact, between 2000 and 2017, total spending on lobbying in the nation's capital grew from $1.57 billion to more than $3.37 billion.[40] (See Chapter 12 for more on lobbyists.)

These warnings have generally gone unnoticed and unreported by the mainstream media, whose reporters, editors, and pundits often work for the giant media corporations that not only are well represented by Washington lobbyists but also contribute generously to the campaigns of the major parties to influence legislation that governs media ownership and commercial speech.

Fast-forward to 2012. While politicians spoke of transparency and truth-telling, their campaign-funding process had few of those characteristics. In the aftermath of the U.S. Supreme Court's *Citizens United* (2010) decision, new Super PACs (political action committees) were formed to channel unlimited funds into political races—legal as long as the Super PACs didn't officially "coordinate" with the political campaigns. With his own Super PAC (named Americans for a Better Tomorrow, Tomorrow), comedian Stephen Colbert satirized the lax standards of Super PAC rules that enable hundreds of millions of dollars to be channeled into politics while obscuring disclosure of the contributors' identities. By December 2012, Super PACs had spent more than $644 million on the 2012 election cycle (mostly in negative attack ads), with the majority of contributions coming from a few dozen elite ultrawealthy donors. For example, Las Vegas casino magnate Sheldon Adelson and his wife donated in excess of $54 million to candidates and Super PACs during the 2012 election cycle.[41] In the 2014 midterm elections, billionaire Tom Steyer surpassed the Adelsons by donating at least $58 million, mostly through the NextGen Climate Action Super PAC. During the 2016 election cycle, the "dark money" of Super PACs exceeded $1.4 billion, including $20 million for pro-Trump and anti-Clinton ads from an organization linked to Chicago Cubs owner Todd Ricketts.[42] The huge influx of money was a boon for media advertising profits.

What both Buchanan and Nader argued in 2000 was that corporate influence is a bipartisan concern that we have in common, and that all of us in a democracy need to be vigilant about how powerful and influential corporations become. This is especially true for the media companies that report the news and distribute many of our cultural stories. As media-literate consumers, we need to demand that the media serve as watchdogs over the economy and our democratic values. And when they fall down on the job, we need to demand accountability (through alternative media channels or the Internet), especially from those mainstream media—radio, television, and cable—that are licensed to operate in the public interest.

The definitions for the terms listed below can be found in the glossary at the end of the book. The page numbers listed with the terms indicate where the term is highlighted in the chapter.

monopoly, 390
oligopoly, 390

limited competition, 390
hegemony, 399

synergy, 401
cultural imperialism, 413

REVIEW QUESTIONS

Analyzing the Media Economy

1. How are the three basic structures of mass media organizations—monopoly, oligopoly, and limited competition—different from one another?

2. How do media companies distribute content, set prices, and generate profit while living up to society's expectations?

The Transition to an Information Economy

3. Why has the federal government emphasized deregulation at a time when so many media companies are growing so large?

4. How have media mergers changed the economics of mass media?

Specialization, Global Markets, and Convergence

5. How do global and specialized markets factor into the new media economy? How are regular workers affected?

6. Using Disney as an example, what is the role of synergy in the current climate of media mergers?

7. Why have Amazon, Apple, Facebook, Google, Microsoft, and Netflix emerged as the leading corporations of the digital era?

Social Issues in Media Economics

8. What are the differences between consumer choice and consumer control?

9. What is cultural imperialism, and what does it have to do with the United States?

The Media Marketplace and Democracy

10. What do critics and activists fear most about the concentration of media ownership? How do media managers and executives respond to these fears?

11. What are some promising signs regarding the relationship between media economics and democracy?

QUESTIONING THE MEDIA

1. Why are consumers more likely to pay to download some digital content, like music and books, and less likely to pay for other content, like sports and news?

2. Why are narratives—media content—crucial to the success of a media corporation?

3. How does the concentration of media ownership limit the number of voices in the marketplace? Do we need rules limiting media ownership?

4. Is there such a thing as a global village? What does this concept mean to you?

LAUNCHPAD FOR *MEDIA & CULTURE*

Visit LaunchPad for *Media & Culture* at launchpadworks.com for additional learning tools:

- REVIEW WITH LEARNINGCURVE

  LearningCurve, available on LaunchPad for *Media & Culture*, uses gamelike quizzing to help you master the concepts you need to learn from this chapter.

- VIDEO: THE MONEY BEHIND THE MEDIA

  Producers, advertisers, and advocates discuss how ownership systems and profits shape media production.

PART 5

Democratic Expression and the Mass Media

The freedom and openness of the Internet is a double-edged sword. In a digital world overloaded with data and news, it has become much easier to obtain information. With so many people paying attention to the details of everyday life, it is also easier to uncover wrongdoing and hold institutions to higher levels of transparency. The news media are helping to do this, but the digital turn and online outlets have provided new methods that allow ordinary citizens and nonprofit groups to do some of the work once performed by investigative journalists.

The rise in the accessibility of and participation in social media platforms has both opened up more opportunities to hold authorities, like the police, accountable, and also contributed to the capacity for user manipulation of these sites. This user manipulation was demonstrated throughout the 2016 U.S. presidential election when *bots*—computer-generated accounts and pages on Twitter and Facebook—were used to advocate certain ideas, support campaigns, and promote propaganda and may have had a direct hand in influencing the election.[1]

The fragmented and accessible nature of the Internet has led to concerns about how best to police the online world. We may be seeing similar conflicts, changes, and compromises in the years ahead as we continue to explore how powerful mass media fit into a democracy.

LaunchPad
macmillan learning

launchpadworks.com

Visit **LaunchPad for *Media & Culture*** to explore an interactive timeline of the history of mass communication, practice your media literacy skills, test your knowledge of the concepts in the textbook with LearningCurve, explore and discuss current trends in mass communication with video activities and video tools, and more.

EXPRESSION AND THE MASS MEDIA

Note: Numbers may not add up to total shown due to rounding.

PRESS FREEDOM RANKINGS

Sample Rankings from 1 to 200

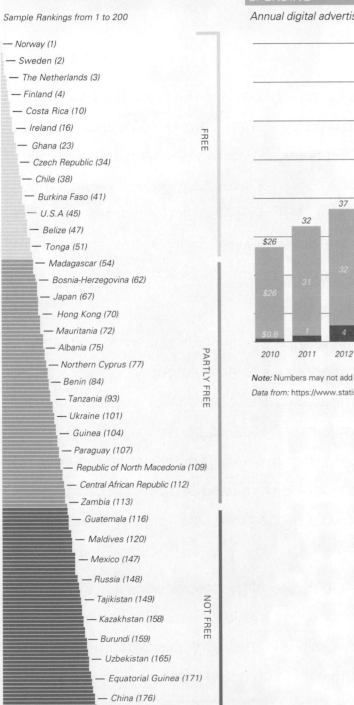

FREE

— Norway (1)
— Sweden (2)
— The Netherlands (3)
— Finland (4)
— Costa Rica (10)
— Ireland (16)
— Ghana (23)
— Czech Republic (34)
— Chile (38)
— Burkina Faso (41)
— U.S.A (45)
— Belize (47)
— Tonga (51)

PARTLY FREE

— Madagascar (54)
— Bosnia-Herzegovina (62)
— Japan (67)
— Hong Kong (70)
— Mauritania (72)
— Albania (75)
— Northern Cyprus (77)
— Benin (84)
— Tanzania (93)
— Ukraine (101)
— Guinea (104)
— Paraguay (107)
— Republic of North Macedonia (109)
— Central African Republic (112)
— Zambia (113)
— Guatemala (116)
— Maldives (120)

NOT FREE

— Mexico (147)
— Russia (148)
— Tajikistan (149)
— Kazakhstan (158)
— Burundi (159)
— Uzbekistan (165)
— Equatorial Guinea (171)
— China (176)
— North Korea (180)

Data from: https://rsf.org/en/ranking

MOBILE NOW MORE THAN HALF OF ALL DIGITAL ADVERTISING SPENDING

Annual digital advertising spending (in billions of U.S. dollars)

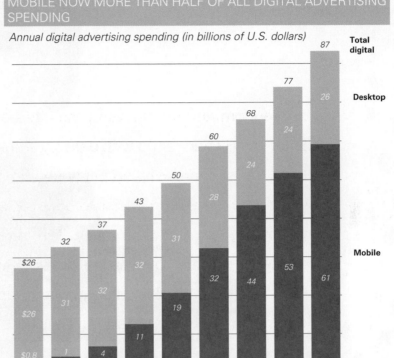

Total digital

Desktop

Mobile

Year	Total	Desktop	Mobile
2010	$26	$26	$0.8
2011	32	31	1
2012	37	32	4
2013	43	32	11
2014	50	31	19
2015	60	28	32
2016	68	24	44
2017	77	24	53
2018 (projected)	87	26	61

Note: Numbers may not add up to total shown due to rounding.

Data from: https://www.statista.com/statistics/237974/online-advertising-spending-worldwide/

The Culture of Journalism

14

Values, Ethics, and Democracy

IN 1887, a young reporter left her job at the *Pittsburgh Dispatch* to seek her fortune in New York City. Only twenty-three years old, Elizabeth "Pink" Cochrane had grown tired of writing for the society pages and answering letters to the editor. She wanted to be on the front page. But at that time, it was considered "unladylike" for women journalists to use their real names, so the *Dispatch* editors, borrowing from a Stephen Foster song, had dubbed her "Nellie Bly."

After four months of persistent job-hunting and freelance writing, Nellie Bly earned a tryout at Joseph Pulitzer's *New York World*, the nation's largest paper. Her assignment: to investigate the deplorable conditions at the Women's Lunatic Asylum on Blackwell's Island. Her method: to get herself declared mad and committed to the asylum.

◀ Journalist Nellie Bly dedicated her life to helping women and the poor as she laid the groundwork for what we know today as investigative journalism. Her undercover work—including time spent posing as a mental patient at the Women's Lunatic Asylum, an unwed mother looking to rid herself of an unwanted child, and a sinner at a home for unfortunate women—exposed a need for reforms in the care of the mentally ill and of underprivileged members of society.

MODERN JOURNALISM IN THE INFORMATION AGE
p. 425

ETHICS AND THE NEWS MEDIA
p. 429

REPORTING RITUALS AND THE LEGACY OF PRINT JOURNALISM
p. 435

JOURNALISM IN THE AGE OF TV AND THE INTERNET
p. 440

ALTERNATIVE MODELS: PUBLIC JOURNALISM AND "FAKE NEWS"
p. 444

DEMOCRACY AND REIMAGINING JOURNALISM'S ROLE
p. 448

After practicing the look of a disheveled lunatic in front of mirrors, wandering city streets unwashed and seemingly dazed, and terrifying her fellow boarders in a New York rooming house by acting crazy, she succeeded in convincing doctors and officials to commit her. Other New York newspapers reported her incarceration, speculating on the identity of this "mysterious waif," this "pretty crazy girl" with the "wild, hunted look in her eyes."[1]

Her two-part story appeared in October 1887 and caused a sensation. Bly was the first reporter to pull off such a stunt. In the days before so-called objective journalism, Nellie Bly's dramatic first-person accounts documented harsh cold baths ("three buckets of water over my head—ice cold water—into my eyes, my ears, my nose and my mouth"); attendants who abused and taunted patients; and newly arrived immigrant women, completely sane, who were committed to this "rat trap" simply because no one could understand them. After the exposé, Bly was famous. Pulitzer gave her a permanent job, and New York City committed $1 million toward improving its asylums.

Within a year, Nellie Bly had exposed a variety of shady scam artists, corrupt politicians and lobbyists, and unscrupulous business practices. Posing as an "unwed mother" with an unwanted child, she uncovered an outfit trafficking in newborn babies. And disguised as a sinner in need of reform, she revealed the appalling conditions at a home for "unfortunate women." A lifetime champion of women and the poor, Bly pioneered what was then called *detective* or *stunt* journalism. Her work inspired the twentieth-century practice of investigative journalism—from Ida Tarbell's exposés of oil corporations in 1902–1904 to the Pulitzer Prizes for investigative reporting, awarded in

2016 to Leonora LaPeter Anton and Anthony Cormier of the *Tampa Bay Times* and Michael Braga of the *Sarasota Herald-Tribune* "for a stellar example of collaborative reporting by two news organizations that revealed escalating violence and neglect in Florida mental hospitals and laid the blame at the door of state officials."[2]

One problem facing journalism today is that in the last few years, traditional print and broadcast newsrooms have dramatically cut back on news investigations, which are expensive and time consuming, even though readers and viewers want more of them, not fewer. Mary Walton, writing about the state of investigative reporting for *American Journalism Review*, made this point in 2010: "Kicked out, bought out or barely hanging on, investigative reporters are a vanishing species in the forests of dead tree media and missing in action on Action News. I-Teams are shrinking or, more often, disappearing altogether. Assigned to cover multiple beats, multitasking backpacking reporters no longer have time to sniff out hidden stories, much less write them." She reported that Investigative Reporters and Editors (IRE) membership "fell more than 30 percent, from 5,391 in 2003, to a 10-year low of 3,695 in 2009."[3] But encouragingly, the slack has been picked up, at least partially, by nontraditional and online media. Jason Stverak, writing for Watchdog.org, has noted, "Today, nonprofit news groups across the country are providing the 'unsexy and repetitive' coverage that the old-guard press began abandoning at the turn of the century. . . . Nonprofit news groups will lead the way in conducting investigative reports and keeping elected officials open and honest."[4] And in 2017, IRE reported that its membership had climbed to more than 5,000.

JOURNALISM IS THE ONLY MEDIA ENTERPRISE that democracy absolutely requires—and it is the only media practice and business that is specifically mentioned and protected by the U.S. Constitution. However, with the major decline in investigative reporting and traditional news audiences, the collapse of many newspapers, and the rise of twenty-four-hour cable news channels and Internet news blogs, mainstream journalism is searching for new business models and better ways to connect with the public.

In this chapter, we examine the changing news landscape and definitions of journalism. We will:

- Explore the values underlying news and ethical problems confronting journalists
- Investigate the shift from more neutral news models to partisan cable and online news
- Study the legacy of print-news conventions and rituals
- Investigate the impact of television and the Internet on news
- Consider contemporary controversial developments in journalism and democracy—specifically, the public journalism movement and satirical forms of news

As you read this chapter, think about how often you look at the news in a typical day. What are some of the recent events or issues you remember reading about in the news? Where is the first place you go to find information about a news event or current issue? If you start with a search engine, what newspapers or news organizations do you usually end up looking at? Do you prefer opinion blogs over news organizations for your information? Why or why not? Do you pay for news—either by buying a newspaper or newsmagazine or by going online? For more questions to help you understand the role of journalism in our lives, see "Questioning the Media" in the Chapter Review.

LaunchPad
macmillan learning

launchpadworks.com

Visit LaunchPad for *Media & Culture* and use LearningCurve to review concepts from this chapter.

MODERN JOURNALISM IN THE INFORMATION AGE

In modern America, serious journalism has sought to provide information that enables citizens to make intelligent decisions. Today, this guiding principle faces serious threats. Why? First, we may just be producing too much information. According to social critic Neil Postman, as a result of developments in media technology, society has developed an "information glut" that transforms news and information into "a form of garbage."[5] Postman believes that scientists, technicians, managers, and journalists merely pile up mountains of new data, which add to the problems and anxieties of everyday life. As a result, too much unchecked data—especially on the Internet—and too little thoughtful discussion emanate from too many channels of communication.

A second, related problem suggests that all the data (and distractions) the media now provide have questionable impact on improving public and political life. Many people feel cut off from our major institutions, including journalism. As a result, some citizens are looking to take part in public conversations and civic debates—to renew a democracy in which many voices participate. For example, while the election of Donald Trump in 2016 invigorated and infuriated Americans across the political spectrum, his controversial presidency has engaged the American public on a much deeper level than have the more predictable presidencies of the past.

What Is News?

In a 1963 staff memo, NBC news president Reuven Frank outlined the narrative strategies integral to all news: "Every news story should . . . display the attributes of fiction, of drama. It should have structure and conflict, problem and denouement, rising and falling action, a beginning, a middle, and an end."[6] Despite Frank's candid insights, many journalists today are uncomfortable thinking of themselves as storytellers. Instead, they tend to describe themselves mainly as information-gatherers.

News is defined here as the process of gathering information and making narrative reports—edited by individuals for news organizations—that offer selected frames of reference; within those

Ben Margot/AP Images

AP Images

"DEEP THROAT"
The major symbol of twentieth-century investigative journalism, Carl Bernstein and Bob Woodward's (*above right*) coverage of the Watergate scandal for the *Washington Post* helped topple the Nixon White House. In *All the President's Men*—the newsmen's book about their investigation—a major character is Deep Throat, the key unidentified source for much of Woodward's reporting. Deep Throat's identity was protected by the two reporters for more than thirty years. Then, in the summer of 2005, he revealed himself as Mark Felt (*above*), the former No. 2 official in the FBI during the Nixon administration. (Felt died in 2008.)

frames, news helps the public make sense of important events, political issues, cultural trends, prominent people, and unusual happenings in everyday life.

Characteristics of News

Over time, a set of conventional criteria for determining **newsworthiness**—information most worthy of transformation into news stories—has evolved. Journalists are taught to select and develop news stories relying on one or more of these criteria: timeliness, proximity, conflict, prominence, human interest, consequence, usefulness, novelty, and deviance.

Most issues and events that journalists select as news are *timely*, or *new*. Reporters, for example, cover speeches, meetings, crimes, and court cases that have just happened. In addition, most of these events have to occur close by, or in *proximity* to, readers and viewers. Although local TV news and papers offer some national and international news, readers and viewers expect to find the bulk of news devoted to their own towns and communities.

Most news stories are narratives and thus contain a healthy dose of *conflict*—a key ingredient in narrative writing. In developing news narratives, reporters are encouraged to seek contentious quotes from those with opposing views. For example, stories on presidential elections almost always feature the most dramatic opposing Republican and Democratic positions. And many stories in the aftermath of the terrorist attacks of September 11, 2001, pitted the values of other cultures against those of Western culture—for example, Islam versus Christianity or premodern traditional values versus contemporary consumerism.

Reader and viewer surveys indicate that most people identify more closely with an individual than with an abstract issue. Therefore, the news media tend to report stories that feature *prominent*, powerful, or influential people. Because these individuals often play a role in shaping the rules and values of a community, journalists have traditionally been responsible for keeping a watchful eye on them and relying on them for quotes.

But reporters also look for *human-interest* stories: extraordinary incidents that happen to "ordinary" people. In fact, reporters often relate a story about a complicated issue (such as unemployment, war, tax rates, health care, or homelessness) by illustrating its impact on one "average" person, family, or town.

Two other criteria for newsworthiness are *consequence* and *usefulness*. Stories about isolated or bizarre crimes, even though they might be new, near, or notorious, often have little impact on our daily lives. To balance these kinds of stories, many editors and reporters believe that some news must also be of consequence to a majority of readers or viewers. For example, stories about issues or events that affect a family's income or change a community's laws have consequence. Likewise, many people look for stories with a practical use: hints on buying a used car or choosing a college, strategies for training a pet or removing a stain.

Finally, news is often about the *novel* and the *deviant*. When events happen that are outside the routine of daily life, such as a seven-year-old girl trying to pilot a plane across the country or an ex-celebrity involved in a drug deal, the news media are there. Reporters also cover events that appear to deviate from social norms, including murders, rapes, fatal car crashes, fires, political scandals, and gang activities. For example, as the war in Iraq escalated, any suicide bombing in the Middle East represented the kind of novel and deviant behavior that qualified as major news.

Values in American Journalism

Although newsworthiness criteria are a useful way to define news, they do not reveal much about the cultural aspects of news. News is both a product and a process. It is both the morning paper or evening newscast and a set of subtle values and shifting rituals that have been adapted to historical and social circumstances, such as the partisan press values of the eighteenth century or the informational standards of the twentieth century.

For example, in 1841, Horace Greeley described the newly founded *New York Tribune* as "a journal removed alike from servile partisanship on the one hand and from gagged, mincing neutrality on the other."[7] Greeley feared that too much neutrality would make reporters into wimps who stood for nothing. Yet the neutrality Greeley warned against is today a major value of conventional journalism, with mainstream reporters assuming they are acting as detached and all-seeing observers of social experience.

Neutrality Boosts Credibility—and Sales

As former journalism professor and reporter David Eason notes, "Reporters . . . have no special method for determining the truth of a situation nor a special language for reporting their findings. They make sense of events by telling stories about them."[8]

Even though journalists transform events into stories, they generally believe that they are—or should be—neutral observers who present facts without passing judgment on them. Conventions such as the inverted-pyramid news lead, the careful attribution of sources, the minimal use of adverbs and adjectives, and a detached third-person point of view all help reporters perform their work in an apparently neutral way.

Like lawyers, therapists, and other professionals, many modern journalists believe that their credibility derives from personal detachment. Yet the roots of this view reside in less noble territory. Jon Katz, media critic and former CBS News producer, discusses the history of the neutral pose:

The idea of respectable detachment wasn't conceived as a moral principle so much as a marketing device. Once newspapers began to mass market themselves in the mid-1880s, . . . publishers ceased being working, opinionated journalists. They mutated instead into businessmen eager to reach the broadest number of readers and antagonize the fewest. . . . Objectivity works well for publishers, protecting the status quo and keeping journalism's voice militantly moderate.[9]

To reach as many people as possible across a wide spectrum, publishers and editors realized as early as the 1840s that softening their partisanship might boost sales.

Partisanship Trumps Neutrality, Especially Online and on Cable

Since the rise of cable and the Internet, today's media marketplace has offered a fragmented world where appealing to the widest audience no longer makes the best economic sense. More options than ever exist, with newspaper readers and TV viewers embracing cable news, social networks,

Roger Kisby/Redux

ON MARCH 24, 2018, more than 1.2 million people supported March for Our Lives, a student-led demonstration organized to support gun control legislation following the mass shooting at Marjory Stoneman Douglas High School, which left fourteen students and three staff members dead just one month prior. Since the march, the organization continues to grow and fight against the endemic gun violence in the United States by demanding that government leaders pass gun control legislation.

blogs, and Twitter. The old "mass" audience has morphed into smaller niche audiences that embrace particular hobbies, story genres, politics, and social networks. News media outlets that hope to survive appeal no longer to mass audiences but to interest groups—be they sports fans or history buffs, conservatives or liberals. So, mimicking the news business of the eighteenth century, partisanship has become good business. For the news media today, muting political leanings to reach a mass audience makes no sense because such an audience no longer exists in the way it once did—especially in the days when only three major TV networks offered evening news for a half hour, once a day. Instead, news media now make money by targeting and catering to niche groups on a 24/7 news cycle.

In such a marketplace, we see the decline of a more neutral journalistic model that promoted fact-gathering, documents, and expertise and held up "objectivity" as the ideal for news practice. Rising in its place is a new era of partisan news—what Bill Kovach and Tom Rosenstiel call a "journalism of assertion"—marked partly by a return to journalism's colonial roots and partly by the downsizing of the "journalism of verification" that kept watch over our central institutions.[10] This transition is symbolized by the rise of the cable news pundit on Fox News or MSNBC as a kind of "expert," with more standing than verified facts, authentic documents, and actual experts.

Today, the new partisan fervor found in news, both online and on cable, has been a major catalyst for escalating the nation's intense political and ideological divide. In the Trump era, ratings and revenue have gone up across cable news but especially on those networks that are the most partisan. On the conservative spectrum, Fox News' evening hosts have generally operated as loyal supporters of the Trump administration. On the left in cable news, MSNBC hosts have emerged as President Trump's harshest daily critics. CNN has tried to position itself as more neutral—but it also has the lowest evening ratings. Whereas in 2018 Sean Hannity on Fox News and Rachel Maddow on MSNBC occasionally draw an audience of three million or more, CNN's most popular evening host/reporter, Anderson Cooper, had an average viewership of just under one million. Of the three, Cooper (by far) did the most actual reporting in the field.

Other Cultural Values in Journalism

Even the neutral journalism model, which most reporters and editors still aspire to, remains a selective and uneven process. Reporters and editors turn some events into reports and discard many others. This process is governed by a deeper set of subjective beliefs that are not neutral. Sociologist Herbert Gans, who studied the newsroom cultures of CBS, NBC, *Newsweek*, and *Time* in the 1970s, generalized that several basic "enduring values" have been shared by most American reporters and editors. The most prominent of these values, which persist to this day, are ethnocentrism, responsible capitalism, small-town pastoralism, and individualism.[11]

By **ethnocentrism**, Gans meant that in most news reporting, especially foreign coverage, reporters judge other countries and cultures on the basis of how "they live up to or imitate American practices and values." In identifying **responsible capitalism** as an underlying value, Gans contended that journalists sometimes naïvely assume that businesspeople compete with one another not primarily to maximize profits but "to create increased prosperity for all." Gans pointed out that although most reporters and editors condemn monopolies, "there is little implicit or explicit criticism of the oligopolistic nature of much of today's economy."[12]

Another value that Gans found was the romanticization of **small-town pastoralism**: favoring the small over the large and the rural over the urban. Many journalists equate small-town life with innocence and harbor suspicions of cities, their governments, and urban experiences. Consequently, stories about rustic communities with crime or drug problems have often been framed as if the purity of country life had been contaminated by "mean" big-city values.

Finally, **individualism**, according to Gans, remains the most prominent value underpinning daily journalism. Many idealistic reporters are attracted to this profession because it rewards the rugged tenacity needed to confront and expose corruption. Beyond this, individuals who overcome personal adversity are the subjects of many enterprising news stories.

Often, however, journalism that focuses on personal triumphs neglects to explain how large organizations and institutions work or fail. Many conventional reporters and editors are unwilling or unsure of how to tackle the problems raised by institutional decay. In addition, because they value their own individualism and are accustomed to working alone, many journalists dislike cooperating on team projects or participating in forums in which community members discuss their own interests and alternative definitions of news.[13]

Facts, Values, and Bias

Traditionally, reporters have aligned facts with an objective position and values with subjective feelings.[14] Within this context, news reports offer readers and viewers details, data, and description. It then becomes the citizen's responsibility to judge and take a stand about the social problems represented by the news. Given these assumptions, reporters are responsible only for adhering to the tradition of the trade—"getting the facts." As a result, many reporters view themselves as neutral "channels" of information rather than selective storytellers or citizens actively involved in public life.

Still, most public surveys have shown that while journalists may work hard to stay neutral, the addition of partisan cable channels such as Fox News and MSNBC has undermined reporters who try to report fairly. So while conservatives tend to see the media as liberally biased, liberals tend to see the media as favoring conservative positions. But political bias is complicated. During the early years of Barack Obama's presidency, many pundits on the political Right argued that Obama got much more favorable media coverage than did former president George W. Bush. But left-wing politicians and critics maintained that the right-wing media—especially news analysts associated with conservative talk radio and Fox's cable channel—rarely reported evenhandedly on Obama, painting him as a "socialist" or as "anti-American."

ETHICS AND THE NEWS MEDIA

National journalists occasionally face a profound ethical dilemma, especially in the aftermath of 9/11: When is it right to protect government secrets, and when should those secrets be revealed to the public? How must editors weigh such decisions when national security bumps up against citizens' need for information?

In 2006, Dean Baquet, then editor of the *Los Angeles Times* (in 2014, he became the executive editor of the *New York Times*), and Bill Keller, then executive editor of the *New York Times*, wrestled with these questions in a coauthored editorial:

Finally, we weigh the merits of publishing against the risks of publishing. There is no magic formula. . . . We make our best judgment.

News Bias around the Globe

News consumers throughout the world generally agree that news coverage should be politically unbiased, but many do not believe that their country's news media achieves this goal particularly well. A recent survey conducted by the Pew Research Center questioned media consumers from thirty-eight countries to gauge how unbiased they believed their news media to be. Perhaps not surprisingly, in light of recent political events, consumers in the United States expressed a marked distrust in the news media in terms of bias; although 78 percent of American respondents felt the news media *should* be free of political bias, only 47 percent of respondents believed that political issues were covered fairly across the news.

The following table highlights consumer perceptions of media bias around the globe. Take a look to see where media consumers are most (or least) trusting about the lack of bias in their news, as well as how they feel about the media's ability to present news about government leaders and officials, portray news accurately, and cover the most important news events.

	Political issues fairly	News about govt. leaders and officials	News accurately	Most important news events
Tanzania	83%	89%	93%	92%
Vietnam	78%	78%	80%	85%
Canada	73%	79%	78%	82%
Germany	72%	77%	75%	85%
Nigeria	67%	68%	71%	74%
Sweden	66%	78%	78%	86%
South Africa	65%	69%	73%	76%
India	65%	72%	80%	72%
Mexico	58%	55%	62%	68%
Russia	55%	68%	60%	79%
Japan	55%	55%	65%	74%
UK	52%	64%	63%	74%
Venezuela	52%	50%	58%	62%
U.S.	47%	58%	56%	61%
Brazil	45%	54%	57%	66%
Israel	42%	50%	63%	78%
Argentina	37%	38%	45%	56%
Spain	33%	48%	48%	63%
South Korea	27%	26%	36%	44%
Greece	18%	25%	22%	42%

Data from: Pew Research Center, accessed July 31, 2018, www.pewglobal.org/2018/01/11/publics-globally-want-unbiased-news-coverage-but-are-divided-on-whether-their-news-media-deliver.

When we come down on the side of publishing, of course, everyone hears about it. Few people are aware when we decide to hold an article. But each of us, in the past few years, has had the experience of withholding or delaying articles when the administration convinces us that the risk of publication outweighed the benefits. . . .

We understand that honorable people may disagree . . . to publish or not to publish. But making those decisions is a responsibility that falls to editors, a corollary to the great gift of our independence. It is not a responsibility we take lightly. And it is not one we can surrender to the government.[15]

What makes the predicament of these national editors so tricky is that in the war against terrorism, some politicians maintain that one value terrorists truly hate is "our freedom." At the same time, some of these same politicians criticized the *Times* for carefully editing and then publishing the WikiLeaks documents. There is irony here: What is more integral to liberty than the freedom of an independent press—so independent that for more than two hundred years U.S. courts have protected the news media's right to criticize our political leaders and, within boundaries, reveal government secrets?

Ethical Predicaments

What is the moral and social responsibility of journalists, not only for the stories they report but also for the actual events or issues they are shaping for millions of people? Wrestling with such media ethics involves determining the moral response to a situation through critical reasoning. Although national security issues raise problems for a few of our largest news organizations, the most frequent ethical dilemmas encountered in most newsrooms across the United States involve intentional deception, privacy invasions, and conflicts of interest.

Deploying Deception

Ever since Nellie Bly faked insanity to get inside an asylum in the 1880s, investigative journalists have used deception to get stories. Today, journalists continue to use disguises and assume false identities to gather information on social transgressions. Beyond legal considerations, though, a key ethical question comes into play: Does the end justify the means? For example, can a newspaper or TV newsmagazine use deceptive ploys to go undercover and expose a suspected fraudulent clinic that promises miracle cures at a high cost? Are news professionals justified in posing as clients desperate for a cure?

In terms of ethics, there are at least two major positions and multiple variations. At one end of the spectrum, *absolutist ethics* suggests that a moral society has laws and codes, including honesty, that everyone must live by. This means citizens, including members of the news media, should tell the truth at all times and in all cases. In other words, the ends (exposing a phony clinic) never justify the means (using deception to get the story). An editor who is an absolutist would cover this story by asking a reporter to find victims who have been ripped off by the clinic and then telling the story through their eyes. At the other end of the spectrum is *situational ethics*, which promotes ethical decisions on a case-by-case basis. If a greater public good could be served by using deceit, journalists and editors who believe in situational ethics would sanction deception as a practice.

Should a journalist withhold information about his or her professional identity to get a quote or a story from an interview subject? Many sources and witnesses are reluctant to talk with journalists, especially about a sensitive subject that might jeopardize a job or hurt another person's reputation. Journalists know they can sometimes obtain information by posing as someone other than a journalist, such as a curious student or a concerned citizen.

Most newsrooms frown on such deception. In particular situations, though, such a practice might be condoned if reporters and their editors believed that the public needed the information. The ethics code adopted by the Society of Professional Journalists (SPJ) is mostly silent on issues of deception. The code does say that "journalists should be honest, fair and courageous in gathering, reporting and interpreting information," and it also calls on journalists to "seek truth and report it" (see Figure 14.1). So is it being "honest" for reporters to use deceptive tactics in the pursuit of truth?

Society of Professional Journalists

CODE of ETHICS

PREAMBLE

Members of the Society of Professional Journalists believe that public enlightenment is the forerunner of justice and the foundation of democracy. Ethical journalism strives to ensure the free exchange of information that is accurate, fair and thorough. An ethical journalist acts with integrity.

The Society declares these four principles as the foundation of ethical journalism and encourages their use in its practice by all people in all media.

SEEK TRUTH AND REPORT IT

Ethical journalism should be accurate and fair. Journalists should be honest and courageous in gathering, reporting and interpreting information.

Journalists should:

▶ Take responsibility for the accuracy of their work. Verify information before releasing it. Use original sources whenever possible.

▶ Remember that neither speed nor format excuses inaccuracy.

▶ Provide context. Take special care not to misrepresent or oversimplify in promoting, previewing or summarizing a story.

▶ Gather, update and correct information throughout the life of a news story.

▶ Be cautious when making promises, but keep the promises they make.

▶ Identify sources clearly. The public is entitled to as much information as possible to judge the reliability and motivations of sources.

▶ Consider sources' motives before promising anonymity. Reserve anonymity for sources who may face danger, retribution or other harm, and have information that cannot be obtained elsewhere. Explain why anonymity was granted.

▶ Diligently seek subjects of news coverage to allow them to respond to criticism or allegations of wrongdoing.

▶ Avoid undercover or other surreptitious methods of gathering information unless traditional, open methods will not yield information vital to the public.

▶ Be vigilant and courageous about holding those with power accountable. Give voice to the voiceless.

▶ Support the open and civil exchange of views, even views they find repugnant.

▶ Recognize a special obligation to serve as watchdogs over public affairs and government. Seek to ensure that the public's business is conducted in the open, and that public records are open to all.

▶ Provide access to source material when it is relevant and appropriate.

▶ Boldly tell the story of the diversity and magnitude of the human experience. Seek sources whose voices we seldom hear.

▶ Avoid stereotyping. Journalists should examine the ways their values and experiences may shape their reporting.

▶ Label advocacy and commentary.

▶ Never deliberately distort facts or context, including visual information. Clearly label illustrations and re-enactments.

▶ Never plagiarize. Always attribute.

MINIMIZE HARM

Ethical journalism treats sources, subjects, colleagues and members of the public as human beings deserving of respect.

Journalists should:

▶ Balance the public's need for information against potential harm or discomfort. Pursuit of the news is not a license for arrogance or undue intrusiveness.

▶ Show compassion for those who may be affected by news coverage. Use heightened sensitivity when dealing with juveniles, victims of sex crimes, and sources or subjects who are inexperienced or unable to give consent. Consider cultural differences in approach and treatment.

▶ Recognize that legal access to information differs from an ethical justification to publish or broadcast.

▶ Realize that private people have a greater right to control information about themselves than public figures and others who seek power, influence or attention. Weigh the consequences of publishing or broadcasting personal information.

▶ Avoid pandering to lurid curiosity, even if others do.

▶ Balance a suspect's right to a fair trial with the public's right to know. Consider the implications of identifying criminal suspects before they face legal charges.

▶ Consider the long-term implications of the extended reach and permanence of publication. Provide updated and more complete information as appropriate.

ACT INDEPENDENTLY

The highest and primary obligation of ethical journalism is to serve the public.

Journalists should:

▶ Avoid conflicts of interest, real or perceived. Disclose unavoidable conflicts.

▶ Refuse gifts, favors, fees, free travel and special treatment, and avoid political and other outside activities that may compromise integrity or impartiality, or may damage credibility.

▶ Be wary of sources offering information for favors or money; do not pay for access to news. Identify content provided by outside sources, whether paid or not.

▶ Deny favored treatment to advertisers, donors or any other special interests, and resist internal and external pressure to influence coverage.

▶ Distinguish news from advertising and shun hybrids that blur the lines between the two. Prominently label sponsored content.

BE ACCOUNTABLE AND TRANSPARENT

Ethical journalism means taking responsibility for one's work and explaining one's decisions to the public.

Journalists should:

▶ Explain ethical choices and processes to audiences. Encourage a civil dialogue with the public about journalistic practices, coverage and news content.

▶ Respond quickly to questions about accuracy, clarity and fairness.

▶ Acknowledge mistakes and correct them promptly and prominently. Explain corrections and clarifications carefully and clearly.

▶ Expose unethical conduct in journalism, including within their organizations.

▶ Abide by the same high standards they expect of others.

The SPJ Code of Ethics is a statement of abiding principles supported by additional explanations and position papers (at spj.org) that address changing journalistic practices. It is not a set of rules, rather a guide that encourages all who engage in journalism to take responsibility for the information they provide, regardless of medium. The code should be read as a whole; individual principles should not be taken out of context. It is not, nor can it be under the First Amendment, legally enforceable.

FIGURE 14.1

SOCIETY OF PROFESSIONAL JOURNALISTS' CODE OF ETHICS

Courtesy Society of Professional Journalists (SPJ).

Invading Privacy

To achieve "the truth" or to "get the facts," journalists routinely straddle a line between "the public's right to know" and a person's right to privacy. One infamous example is the phone hacking scandal involving News Corp.'s now-shuttered U.K. newspaper, *News of the World*. In 2011, the *Guardian* reported that *News of the World* reporters had hired a private investigator to hack into the voice mail of thirteen-year-old murder victim Milly Dowler and had deleted some messages. Although there had been past allegations that reporters from *News of the World* had hacked into the private voice mails of the British royal family, government officials, and celebrities, this revelation on the extent of *News of the World*'s phone hacking activities caused a huge scandal and led to the arrests and resignations of several senior executives. Today, in the digital age, when reporters can gain access to private e-mail messages, Twitter accounts, and Facebook pages, as well as voice mail, such practices raise serious questions about how far a reporter should go to get information.

In the case of privacy issues, media companies and journalists should always ask these ethical questions: What public good is being served here? What significant public knowledge will be gained through the exploitation of a tragic private moment? Although journalism's code of ethics says, "The news media must guard against invading a person's right to privacy," this clashes with another part of the code: "The public's right to know of events of public importance and interest is the overriding mission of the mass media."[16] When these two ethical standards collide, should journalists err on the side of the public's right to know?

Conflict of Interest

Journalism's code of ethics also warns reporters and editors not to place themselves in positions that produce a **conflict of interest**—that is, any situation in which journalists may stand to benefit personally from stories they produce. "Gifts, favors, free travel, special treatment or privileges," the code states, "can compromise the integrity of journalists and their employers. Nothing of value should be accepted."[17] Although small newspapers with limited resources and poorly paid reporters might accept such "freebies" as game tickets for their sportswriters and free meals for their restaurant critics, this practice does increase the likelihood of a conflict of interest that produces favorable or uncritical coverage.

On a broader level, ethical guidelines at many news outlets attempt to protect journalists from compromising positions. For instance, in most cities, U.S. journalists do not actively participate in politics or support social causes. Some journalists will not reveal their political affiliations, and some even decline to vote.

For these journalists, the rationale behind their decision is straightforward: Journalists should not place themselves in a situation in which they might have to report on the misdeeds of an organization or a political party to which they belong. If a journalist has a tie to any group, and that group is later suspected of involvement in shady or criminal activity, the reporter's ability to report on that group would be compromised— along with the credibility of the news outlet for which he or she works. Conversely, other journalists believe that not actively

MICHAEL FINKEL was let go from the *New York Times* in 2001, after it was revealed that he had created composite characters for a story. His subsequent experiences with an accused murderer who had used Finkel's name while on the lam were documented in his memoir *True Story*, which was made into a 2015 movie (*below*) starring Jonah Hill as Finkel alongside James Franco as Christian Longo, eventually convicted of murder.

participating in politics or social causes means abandoning their civic obligations. They believe that fairness in their reporting, not total detachment from civic life, is their primary obligation.

Resolving Ethical Problems

When a journalist is criticized for ethical lapses or questionable reporting tactics, a typical response might be "I'm just doing my job" or "I was just getting the facts." Such explanations are troubling, though, because in responding this way, reporters are transferring personal responsibility for the story to a set of institutional rituals.

There are, of course, ethical alternatives to self-justifications such as "I'm just doing my job" that force journalists to think through complex issues. With the crush of deadlines and daily duties, most media professionals deal with ethical situations only on a case-by-case basis as issues arise. However, examining major ethical models and theories is a common strategy for addressing ethics on a general rather than a situational basis. The most well-known ethical standard, the Judeo-Christian command to "love your neighbor as yourself," provides one foundation for constructing ethical guidelines. Although we cannot address all major moral codes here, a few key precepts can guide us.

Aristotle, Kant, and Bentham and Mill

The Greek philosopher Aristotle offered an early ethical concept, the "golden mean"—a guideline for seeking balance between competing positions. For Aristotle, this was a desirable middle ground between extreme positions, usually with one regarded as deficient and the other as excessive. For example, Aristotle saw ambition as the balance between sloth and greed.

Another ethical principle entails the "categorical imperative" developed by German philosopher Immanuel Kant (1724–1804). This idea maintains that a society must adhere to moral codes that are universal and unconditional, applicable in all situations at all times. For example, the Golden Rule ("Do unto others as you would have them do unto you") is articulated in one form or another in most of the world's major religious and philosophical traditions and operates as an absolute moral principle. The First Amendment, which prevents Congress from abridging free speech and other rights, could be considered an example of an unconditional national law.

British philosophers Jeremy Bentham (1748–1832) and John Stuart Mill (1806–1873) promoted an ethical principle derived from "the greatest good for the greatest number," directing us "to distribute a good consequence to more people rather than to fewer, whenever we have a choice."[18]

Developing Ethical Policy

Arriving at ethical decisions involves several steps. These include laying out the case; pinpointing the key issues; identifying involved parties, their intents, and their competing values; studying ethical models; presenting strategies and options; and formulating a decision.

One area that requires ethics is covering the private lives of people who have unintentionally become prominent in the news. Consider Richard Jewell, the Atlanta security guard who, for eighty-eight days, was the FBI's prime suspect in the city park bombing at the 1996 Olympics. During this time, at least two key ethical questions emerged: (1) Should the news media have named Jewell as a suspect even though he was never charged with a crime? (2) Should the media have camped out daily in front of his mother's house in an attempt to interview him and his mother? The Jewell case pitted the media's right to tell stories and earn profits against a person's right to be left alone.

Working through the various ethical stages, journalists formulate policies grounded in overarching moral principles.[19] Should reporters, for instance, follow the Golden Rule and be willing to treat themselves, their families, or their friends the way they treated the Jewells? Or should they invoke Aristotle's "golden mean" and seek moral virtue between extreme positions? In Richard Jewell's situation, how might journalists have developed guidelines to balance Jewell's interests and those of the news media?

Unfamiliar with being questioned themselves, many reporters are uncomfortable discussing their personal values or their strategies for getting stories. Nevertheless, a stock of rituals, derived from basic American values, underlie the practice of reporting. These include focusing on the present, relying on experts, balancing story conflict, and acting as adversaries toward leaders and institutions.

Focusing on the Present

In the 1840s, when the telegraph first enabled news to crisscross America instantly, modern journalism was born. To complement the new technical advances, editors called for a focus on the immediacy of the present. Modern front-page print journalism began to de-emphasize political analysis and historical context, accenting instead the new and the now.

As a result, the profession began drawing criticism for failing to offer historical, political, and social analyses. Modern journalism tends to reject "old news" for whatever new event or idea disrupts today's routines. During the 1996 elections, when statistics revealed that drug use among middle-class high school students was rising, reporters latched on to new versions of the drug narrative, which had surfaced about crack cocaine during the 1986 and 1988 national elections.[20] But these 1990s reports made only limited references to the 1980s. And although drug problems and addiction rates did not diminish in subsequent years, these topics were virtually ignored by journalists during national elections from 2000 to 2016. Indeed, given the space and time constraints of current news practices, reporters seldom link stories to the past or to the ebb and flow of history. (To analyze current news stories, see "Media Literacy and the Critical Process: Telling Stories and Covering Disaster" on page 436.)

Getting a Good Story

Early in the 1980s, the Janet Cooke hoax demonstrated the difference between the mere telling of a good story and the social responsibility to tell the truth.[21] Cooke, a former *Washington Post* reporter, was fired for fabricating an investigative report for which she initially won a Pulitzer Prize. (It was later revoked.) She had created a cast of characters, featuring a mother who contributed to the heroin addiction of her eight-year-old son.

At the time the hoax was exposed, Chicago columnist Mike Royko criticized conventional journalism for allowing narrative conventions—getting a good story—to trump journalism's responsibility to the daily lives it documents: "There's something more important than a story here. This eight-year-old kid is being murdered. The editors should have said forget the story, find the kid. . . . People in any other profession would have gone right to the police."[22] Had editors at the *Post* done so, Cooke's hoax would not have gone as far as it did.

According to Don Hewitt, the creator and longtime executive producer of *60 Minutes*, "There's a very simple formula if you're in Hollywood, Broadway, opera, publishing, broadcasting, newspapering. It's four very simple words—tell me a story."[23] For most journalists, the bottom line is "Get the story"— an edict that overrides most other concerns. It is the standard against which many reporters measure themselves and their profession.

Getting the Story First

In a discussion on public television about the press coverage of a fatal airline crash in Milwaukee in the 1980s, a news photographer was asked to talk about his role in covering the tragedy. Rather than discussing the poignant, heartbreaking aspects of witnessing the aftermath of such an event, the excited photographer launched into a dramatic recounting of how he had slipped behind police barricades to snap the first grim photos, which later appeared in the *Milwaukee Journal*.

MEDIA LITERACY AND THE CRITICAL PROCESS

Telling Stories and Covering Disaster

Covering difficult stories—such as natural disasters like hurricanes or floods—may present challenges to journalists about how to frame their coverage. The opening sections, or leads, of news stories can vary depending on the source— whether it is print, broadcast, or online news—or even the editorial style of the news organization (e.g., some story leads are straightforward; some are very dramatic). And, although modern journalists claim objectivity as a goal, it is unlikely that a professional in the storytelling business can approximate any sort of scientific objectivity. The best journalists can do is be fair, reporting and telling stories to their communities and nation by explaining the complicated and tragic experiences in words or pictures. To explore this type of coverage, try this exercise with examples from recent disaster coverage of a regional or national event.

1 DESCRIPTION
Find print and broadcast news versions of the same disaster story (use LexisNexis if available). Make copies of each story, and note the pictures chosen to tell the story.

2 ANALYSIS
Find patterns in the coverage. How are the stories treated differently in print and on television? Are there similarities in the words chosen or images used? What kinds of experiences are depicted? Who are the sources the reporters use to verify their information?

3 INTERPRETATION
What do these patterns suggest? Can you make any interpretations or arguments based on the kinds of disasters covered, sources used, areas covered, or words/images chosen? How are the stories told in relation to their importance to the entire community or nation? How complex are the stories?

4 EVALUATION
Which stories are the strongest? Why? Which are the weakest? Why? Make a judgment on how well these disaster stories serve your interests as a citizen and the interests of the larger community or nation.

5 ENGAGEMENT
In an e-mail or letter to the editor, share your findings with relevant editors and TV news directors. Make suggestions for improved coverage, and cite strong stories that you admired. Share with the class how the editors and news directors responded.

As part of their socialization into the profession, reporters often learn not only to emotionally detach from a tragic event but also to evade authority figures in order to secure a story ahead of the competition.

The photographer's recollection points to the important role journalism plays in calling public attention to serious events and issues. Yet he also talked about the news-gathering process as a game that journalists play. It's now routine for local television stations, 24/7 cable news, and newspapers to run self-promotions about how they beat competitors to a story. In addition, during political elections, local television stations and networks project winners in particular races and often hype their projections when they are able to forecast results before the competition does.

Journalistic *scoops* and exclusive stories attempt to portray reporters in a heroic light: They have won a race for facts, which they have gathered and presented ahead of their rivals. It is not always clear, though, how the public is better served by a journalist's claim to have gotten a story first. In some ways, the 24/7 cable news, the Internet, and bloggers have intensified the race for getting a story first. With a fragmented audience and more media competing for news, the mainstream news often feels more pressure to lure an audience with exclusive, and sometimes sensational, stories. Although readers and viewers might value the aggressiveness of reporters, the earliest reports are not necessarily better, more accurate, or as complete as stories written later, with more context and perspective.

This kind of scoop behavior, which has become rampant in the digital age, demonstrates pack or **herd journalism**, which occurs when reporters stake out a house; chase celebrities in packs; or follow a story in such herds that the entire profession comes under attack for invading people's privacy, exploiting their personal problems, or just plain getting the story wrong.

Relying on Experts . . . Usually Men

Another ritual of modern print journalism—relying on outside sources—has made reporters heavily dependent on experts. Reporters, though often experts themselves in certain areas by virtue of having covered them over time, are not typically allowed to display their expertise overtly. Instead, they must seek outside authorities to give credibility to seemingly neutral reports. *What* daily reporters know is generally subordinate to *whom* they know.

During the early twentieth century, progressive politicians and leaders of opinion such as President Woodrow Wilson and columnist Walter Lippmann believed in the cultivation of strong ties among national reporters, government officials, scientists, business managers, and researchers. They wanted journalists supplied with expertise across a variety of areas. Today, the widening gap between those with expertise and those without it has created a need for public mediators. Reporters have assumed this role as surrogates who represent both leaders' and readers' interests. With their access to experts, reporters transform specialized and insider knowledge into the everyday commonsense language of news stories.

Reporters also frequently use experts to create narrative conflict by pitting a series of quotes against one another or, on occasion, use experts to support a particular position. In addition, the use of experts enables journalists to distance themselves from daily experience; they are able to attribute the responsibility for the events or issues reported in a story to those who are quoted.

To use experts, journalists must make direct contact with a source—by phone or e-mail or in person. Journalists do not, however, heavily cite the work of other writers; that would violate reporters' desire not only to get a story first but to get it on their own. Telephone calls and face-to-face interviews, rather than extensively researched interpretations, are the stuff of daily journalism.

In addition, expert sources have historically been predominantly white and male. Fairness and Accuracy in Reporting (FAIR) conducted a major study of the 14,632 sources used during 2001 on evening news programs on ABC, CBS, and NBC. FAIR found that only 15 percent of sources were women—and 52 percent of these women represented "average citizens" or "non-experts." By contrast, of the male sources, 86 percent were cast in "authoritative" or "expert" roles. Among U.S. sources for whom race could be determined, the study found that white sources "made up 92 percent of the total, blacks 7 percent, Latinos and Arab Americans 0.6 percent each, and Asian Americans 0.2 percent."[24] (At that time, the 2000 census reported that the U.S. population stood at 69 percent white, 13 percent Hispanic, 12 percent black, and 4 percent Asian.) So as mainstream journalists increased their reliance on a small pool of experts, they probably alienated many viewers, who may have felt excluded even from vicarious participation in day-to-day social and political life.

By 2012, the evidence suggested little improvement. In fact, a study from the 4th Estate showed that over a six-month period during the 2012 election, men were "much more likely to be quoted on their subjective insight in newspapers and on television." This held true even on stories specifically dealing with women's issues. The 4th Estate study showed that "in front page articles about the 2012

WALTER LIPPMANN, often hailed as the father of modern journalism, believed that journalists should act as mediators between the general public and the political elite. In addition to treating journalism as a research-based science, Lippmann believed that the role of a journalist was essential to democracy, as citizens were otherwise uninformed about sociopolitical issues.

election that mention[ed] abortion or birth control, men [were] 4 to 7 times more likely to be cited than women." The study concluded by noting that such a "gender gap undermines the media's credibility."[25]

These gender and source representation numbers have not changed much, even recently. Adrienne LaFrance, a staff writer for the *Atlantic*, found similar numbers borne out in her own work in both 2013 and 2015: "Male dominance in global media is well documented, and has been for many decades. Both in newsrooms and in news articles, men are leaders—they make more money, get more bylines, spend more time on-camera, and are quoted far more often than women—by a ratio of about 3:1." LaFrance cites an *American Sociological Review* study summarizing these data over the last forty years: "'The findings of these studies are consistent: They all report substantial underrepresentation of female names, and they typically find that female names constitute approximately one fourth of all mentions.'"[26]

These numbers should not be surprising when we look at recent data on the number of women who actually lead print and broadcast newsrooms as top editors and managers. A key 2018 Women's Media Center study found that in the United States, 86.47 percent of newsroom leaders were white, "down slightly from 86.97 percent" in the center's 2016 survey. Of all leaders, about 33 percent were white women, while just over 2 percent were black women, and less than 2 percent were Hispanic or Asian women. As Nikole Hannah-Jones, racial injustice reporter for the *New York Times Magazine* noted in the study, "It's rare to see a woman of color in a mainstream newsroom in a very high management position, and, for those who are there, it's [often] been a struggle."[27] It is reasonable to conclude that if more women were in charge of newsrooms, more news sources would be women.

By the late 1990s, many journalists were criticized for blurring the line between remaining neutral and being an expert. The boom in twenty-four-hour cable news programs at this time led to a news vacuum that was eventually filled with talk shows and interviews with journalists willing to give their views. During events with intense media coverage—such as the 2000 through 2016 presidential elections, 9/11, and the Iraq and Afghanistan wars—many print journalists appeared several times a day on cable programs acting as experts on the story, often providing factual information but sometimes offering only opinion and speculation.

Some editors even encourage their reporters to go on these shows for marketing reasons. Today, many big-city newspapers have office space set aside for reporters to use for cable, TV, and Internet interviews. Critics contend that these practices erode the credibility of the profession by blending journalism with celebrity culture and commercialism. Daniel Schorr, who worked as a journalist for seven decades (he died in 2010), resigned from CNN when the cable network asked him to be a commentator during the 1984 Republican National Convention along with former Texas governor John Connally. Schorr believed that it was improper to blend a journalist and a politician in this way, but the idea seems innocent by today's blurry standards. As the late media writer David Carr pointed out in the *New York Times* in 2010, "Where there was once a pretty bright line between journalist and political operative, there is now a kind of continuum, with politicians becoming media providers in their own right, and pundits, entertainers and journalists often driving political discussions."[28]

Balancing Story Conflict

For most journalists, *balance* means presenting all sides of an issue without appearing to favor any one position. The quest for balance presents problems for journalists. On the one hand, time and space constraints do not always permit the presentation of *all* sides; in practice, this value has often been reduced to "telling *both* sides of a story." In recounting news stories as two-sided dramas, reporters often misrepresent the complexity of social issues. The abortion controversy, for example, is often treated as a story that pits two extreme positions (staunchly pro-life versus resolutely pro-choice) against each other. Yet people whose views fall somewhere between these positions are seldom represented (studies show that this group actually represents the majority of Americans). In this manner, "balance" becomes a narrative device to generate story conflict.

On the other hand, although many journalists claim to be detached, they often stake out a moderate or middle-of-the-road position between the two sides represented in a story. In claiming neutrality and inviting readers to share their "detached" point of view, journalists offer a distant, third-person, all-knowing point of view (a narrative device that many novelists use as well), enhancing the impression of neutrality by making the reporter appear value-free (or valueless).

The claim for balanced stories, like the claim for neutrality, disguises journalism's narrative functions. After all, when reporters choose quotes for a story, these are usually the most dramatic or conflict-oriented words that emerge from an interview, press conference, or public meeting. Choosing quotes sometimes has more to do with enhancing drama than with being fair, documenting an event, or establishing neutrality.

Until the recent shift to appealing to smaller niche audiences in the Internet age, the balance claim long served the financial interests of twentieth-century news organizations that staked out the middle ground. William Greider, a former *Washington Post* editor, saw the tie between good business and balanced news: "If you [were] going to be a mass circulation journal, that mean[t] you [were] going to be talking simultaneously to lots of groups that [had] opposing views. So you [had] to modulate your voice and pretend to be talking to all of them."[29]

Acting as Adversaries

The value that many journalists take the most pride in is their adversarial relationship with the prominent leaders and major institutions they cover. The prime narrative frame for portraying this relationship is sometimes called a *gotcha story*, which refers to the moment when, through questioning, the reporter nabs "the bad guy," or wrongdoer.

This narrative strategy—part of the *tough questioning style* of some reporters—is frequently used in political reporting. Many journalists assume that leaders are hiding something and that the reporter's main job is to ferret out the truth through tenacious fact-gathering and gotcha questions. An extension of the search for balance, this stance locates the reporter in the middle, between "them" and "us," between political leaders and the people they represent.

Critics of the tough questioning style of reporting argue that while it can reveal significant information, when overused it fosters a cynicism among journalists that actually harms the democratic process. Although journalists need to guard against becoming too cozy with their political sources, they sometimes go to the other extreme. By constantly searching for what politicians may be hiding, some reporters may miss other issues or other key stories.

When journalists employ the gotcha model to cover news, being tough often becomes an end in itself. Thus, reporters believe they have done their job just by roughing up an interview subject or by answering the limited "What is going on here?" question. Yet the Pulitzer Prize, the highest award honoring journalism, often goes to the reporter who asks ethically charged and open-ended questions, such as "Why is this going on?" and "What ought to be done about it?"

JOURNALISM IN THE AGE OF TV AND THE INTERNET

The rules and rituals governing American journalism began shifting in the 1950s. At the time, former radio reporter John Daly hosted the CBS network game show *What's My Line?* When he began moonlighting as the evening news anchor on ABC, the network blurred the entertainment and information border, foreshadowing what was to come.

In the early days, the most influential and respected television news program was CBS's *See It Now*. Coproduced by Fred Friendly and Edward R. Murrow, *See It Now* practiced a kind of TV journalism lodged somewhere between the neutral and narrative traditions. Generally regarded as "the first and definitive" news documentary on American television, *See It Now* sought "to report in depth—to tell and show the American audience what was happening in the world using film as a narrative tool," according to A. William Bluem, author of *Documentary in American Television*.[30] Murrow worked as both the program's anchor and its main reporter, introducing the investigative model of journalism to television—a model that programs like *60 Minutes* and *Dateline* would imitate. Later, of course, Internet news-gathering and reporting would further alter journalism.

Differences between Print, TV, and Internet News

Although TV news reporters share many values, beliefs, and conventions with their print counterparts, television transformed journalism in a number of ways.

First, while print editors traditionally cut stories to fit the physical space around ads, TV news directors had to time their stories to fit between commercials. Despite the fact that a much higher percentage of space is devoted to print ads (about 60 percent at most dailies), TV ads (which take up less than 25 percent of a typical thirty-minute news program) generally seem more intrusive to viewers, perhaps because TV ads take up time rather than space. The Internet has "solved" these old space and time problems by freeing stories from those constraints.

Second, while modern print journalists are expected to be detached, TV news derives its credibility from live, on-the-spot reporting; believable imagery; and viewers' trust in the reporters and anchors. In fact, from the early 1970s through the early 2000s, most annual polls indicated that the majority of viewers found TV news a more credible resource than print news. Indeed, viewers have tended to feel a personal regard for the local and national anchors who appear each evening on TV sets in their living rooms. Today, however, the credibility gap has disappeared, partly because of the growing distrust people have of all news media and partly because of print reporters' growing star status as guests on (or even hosts of) local or cable TV news programs.

By the mid-1970s, the public's fascination with the Watergate scandal, combined with the improved quality of TV journalism, helped local news departments realize profits. In an effort to retain high ratings, stations began hiring consultants, who advised news directors to invest in national prepackaged formats—such as Action News or Eyewitness News—which employ the same theme music and opening graphic visuals from market to market. Consultants also suggested that stations lead their newscasts with *crime blocks*: a group of TV stories that recount the worst local criminal transgressions of the day. A cynical slogan soon developed in the industry: "If it bleeds, it leads." Depending on the local

MORNING NEWS SHOWS are closely tended patches of the network news landscape. Competition between shows like *Today* and *Good Morning America* remains intense, and network executives sometimes intervene to make "fixes," like the controversial 2012 reassignment of former *Today* anchor Ann Curry, who had come forward and accused Matt Lauer of sexual assault. Five years later in the midst of the #MeToo movement, similar accusations were made against Lauer by multiple women, and he was eventually fired from NBC, leaving Willie Geist, Samantha Guthrie, Carson Daly, and Al Roker (pictured here) to run the show, with Hoda Kotb (not pictured) replacing Lauer as Guthrie's main coanchor.

Chance Yeh/Getty Images

station, multiple studies continue to show that crime stories still dominate as the lead story on any typical evening newscast—far more than any other category of news.

Pretty-Face and Happy-Talk Culture

In the early 1970s at a Milwaukee TV station, consultants advised the station's news director that the evening anchor looked too old. The anchor, who showed a bit of gray, was replaced and went on to serve as the station's editorial director. He was thirty-two years old at the time. In the late 1970s, a reporter at the same station was fired because of a "weight problem," although that was not given as the official reason. Earlier that year, she had given birth to her first child. In 1983, Christine Craft, a former Kansas City television news anchor, was awarded $500,000 in damages in a sex discrimination suit against station KMBC (she eventually lost the monetary award when the station appealed). She had been fired because consultants believed she was too old, too unattractive, and not deferential enough to men.

Such stories are rampant in the annals of TV news, and they have helped create the stereotype of the half-witted but physically attractive news anchor, reinforced by images from popular culture—from Ted Baxter on TV's *Mary Tyler Moore Show* to Ron Burgundy in the *Anchorman* films. Although the situation has improved slightly, national news consultants set the agenda for what local reporters should cover (lots of crime) as well as how they should look and sound (young, attractive, pleasant, and with no regional accent). Essentially, news consultants—also known as *news doctors*—have advised stations to replicate the predominant male and female advertising images of the 1960s and 1970s in modern local TV news.

Another strategy favored by news consultants is *happy talk*: the ad-libbed or scripted banter that goes on among local news anchors, reporters, meteorologists, and sports reporters before and after news reports. During the 1970s, consultants often recommended such chatter to create a more relaxed feeling on the news set and to foster the illusion of conversational intimacy with viewers. Some also believed that happy talk would counter much of that era's "bad news," which included coverage of urban riots and the Vietnam War. A strategy still used today, happy talk often appears forced and may create awkward transitions, especially when anchors transition to reports on events that are sad or tragic.

Sound Bitten

Beginning in the 1980s, the term **sound bite** became part of the public lexicon. The TV equivalent of a quote in print news, a sound bite is the part of a broadcast news report in which an expert, a celebrity, a victim, or a person-in-the-street responds to some aspect of an event or issue. With increasing demands for more commercial time, there is less time for interview subjects to explain their views. As a result, sound bites have become the focus of intense criticism. With shorter comments from interview subjects, TV news sometimes seems like dueling sound bites, with reporters creating dramatic tension by editing competing viewpoints together, as if interviewees had actually been in the same location speaking to one another. Of course, print news also pits one quote against another in a story, even though the actual interview subjects may never have met. Once again, these reporting techniques, also at work in online journalism, are evidence of the profession's reliance on storytelling devices to replicate or create conflict.

Ted Soqui/Getty Images

ANDERSON COOPER has been the primary anchor of *Anderson Cooper 360°* since 2003. Although the program is mainly taped and broadcast from its New York City studio and typically features reports of the day's main news stories, with added analyses from experts, Cooper is one of the few "talking heads" who reports live fairly often from the field for major news stories. Notably, he has done extensive coverage of the 2010 BP oil spill in the Gulf of Mexico; the February 2011 uprisings in Egypt; the 2016 massacre at Pulse—a gay nightclub in Orlando—which claimed forty-nine lives, making it the worst mass shooting in U.S. history at that time; and the aftermath of Hurricane Maria in Puerto Rico in September 2017.

Pundits, "Talking Heads," and Politics

The transformation of TV news by cable—with the arrival of CNN in 1980—led to dramatic changes in TV news delivery at the national level. Prior to cable news (and the Internet), most people tuned to their local and national news late in the afternoon or evening on a typical weekday, with each program lasting just thirty minutes. But today, the 24/7 news cycle means that we can get TV news anytime, day or night, and constant new content has led to major changes in what is considered news. Because it is expensive to dispatch reporters to document stories or maintain foreign news bureaus to cover international issues, the much less expensive "talking head" pundit has become a standard for cable news channels. Such a programming strategy requires few resources beyond the studio and a few guests.

Today's main cable channels have built their evening programs along partisan lines and follow the model of journalism as opinion and assertion: Fox News goes right with pundit stars like Tucker Carlson, Sean Hannity, and Laura Ingraham; MSNBC leans left with Rachel Maddow, Chris Hayes, and Lawrence O'Donnell; and CNN stakes out the middle with hosts who try to strike a more neutral pose, like Jake Tapper, Anderson Cooper, and Don Lemon.

Today's cable and Internet audiences seem to prefer partisan talking heads over traditional reporting. This suggests that in today's fragmented media marketplace, going after niche audiences along political lines is smart business—although not necessarily good journalism. What should concern us today is the jettisoning of journalism—anchored in reporting and verification—that uses reporters to document stories and interview key sources. In its place, on cable and online, are highly partisan pundits who may have strong opinions and charisma but who probably do no reporting themselves and therefore may not have all their facts straight.

Convergence Enhances and Changes Journalism

For mainstream print and TV reporters and editors, online news has added new dimensions to journalism. Both print and TV news can continually update breaking stories online, and many reporters now post their online stories first and then work on the traditional versions. This means that readers and viewers no longer have to wait until the next day for the morning paper or for the local evening newscast for important stories. To enhance the online reports, which do not have the time or space constraints of television or print, newspaper reporters are increasingly required to provide video or audio for their stories. This might allow readers and viewers to see full interviews rather than just selected print quotes in the paper or short sound bites on the TV report.

However, use of technology in the newsroom comes with a special set of problems. Print reporters, for example, can conduct e-mail interviews rather than leave the office to question a subject in person. Many editors discourage this practice because they think relying on e-mail gives interviewees the chance to control and shape their answers. While some might argue that this provides more thoughtful answers, journalists say it takes the elements of surprise and spontaneity out of the traditional news interview, during which a subject might accidentally reveal information—something less likely to occur in an online setting.

Another problem for journalists, ironically, is the wide-ranging resources of the Internet. This includes access to versions of stories from other papers or broadcast stations. The mountain of information available on the Internet has made it all too easy for journalists to—unwittingly or intentionally—copy other journalists' work. In addition, access to databases and other informational sites can keep reporters at their computers rather than out cultivating sources, tracking down new kinds of information, and staying in touch with their communities.

Most notable for journalists in the digital age, however, are the demands that convergence has made on their reporting and writing. Print journalists at newspapers (and magazines) are expected to carry digital cameras so that they can post video along with the print versions of their stories. TV reporters are expected to write print-style news reports for their station's website to

LaunchPad
macmillan learning
launchpadworks.com

The Contemporary Journalist: Pundit or Reporter?
Journalists discuss whether the 24/7 news cycle encourages reporters to offer opinions more than facts.

Discussion: What might be the reasons why reporters should give opinions, and what might be the reasons why they shouldn't?

supplement the streaming video of their original TV stories. And both print and TV reporters are often expected to post the Internet versions of their stories first, before the versions they do for the morning paper or the six o'clock news. And journalists today are increasingly expected to tweet and blog.

The Power of Visual Language

The shift from a print-dominated culture to an electronic-digital culture requires that we look carefully at differences among various approaches to journalism. For example, the visual language of TV news and the Internet often captures events more powerfully than do words. Over the past fifty years, television news has dramatized America's key events. Civil Rights activists, for instance, acknowledge that the movement benefited enormously from televised news that documented the plight of southern blacks in the 1960s. The news footage of southern police officers turning powerful water hoses on peaceful Civil Rights demonstrators, as well as the news images of "white only" and "colored only" signs in hotels and restaurants, created a context for understanding the disparity between black and white in the 1950s and 1960s.

Other TV images are also embedded in the collective memory of many Americans: the Kennedy and King assassinations in the 1960s; the turmoil of Watergate in the 1970s; the first space shuttle disaster and the Chinese student uprisings in the 1980s; the Oklahoma City federal building bombing in the 1990s; the terrorist attacks on the Pentagon and World Trade Center in 2001; Hurricane Katrina in 2005; the historic election of President Obama in 2008; and the Arab Spring uprisings in 2011. More recently, the visual images etched in our collective consciousness have been of mass shootings: the murders of twenty schoolchildren and six adults at the Sandy Hook Elementary School in Newtown, Connecticut, in 2012; the murders of forty-nine people in an Orlando nightclub in 2016; the Las Vegas gunman who opened fire on a concert crowd in 2017, killing 58 and injuring more than 850; and the 2018 school shooting at Marjory Stoneman Douglas High School in Parkland, Florida, where seventeen people—fourteen students and three staff members—were killed. During these critical events, TV news has been a cultural reference point, often sparking national debates, most recently over gun control and the meaning of the Second Amendment.

Today, the Internet, for good or bad, functions as a repository for news images and video, alerting us to stories that the mainstream media missed or to videos captured by amateurs. In 2013, CIA employee Edward Snowden chose a civil liberties advocate and columnist for the London-based *Guardian* to receive leaked material on systematic surveillance of ordinary Americans by the National Security Agency. The video interview with the *Guardian* scored 1.5 million YouTube hits shortly after its release. As *New York Times* columnist David Carr noted at the time, "News no longer needs the permission of traditional gatekeepers to break through. Scoops can now come from all corners of the media map and find an audience just by virtue of what they reveal."[31] More recently, during the 2016 presidential campaign, a video from 2005 surfaced in which candidate Donald Trump could be heard bragging "in vulgar terms about kissing, groping and trying to have sex with women . . . saying that

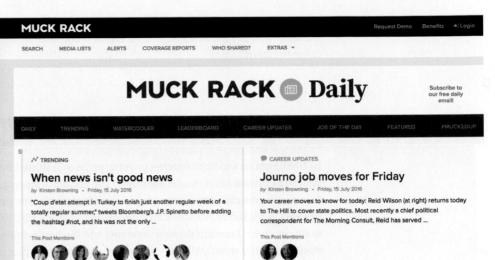

Courtesy of Muckrack.com

NEWS IN THE DIGITAL AGE

Today, more and more journalists use Twitter in addition to performing their regular reporting duties. Muck Rack collects journalists' tweets in one place, making it easier than ever to access breaking news and real-time, online reporting.

'when you're a star, they let you do it.'"[32] The incident and video got a second life during the #MeToo movement in 2018, when a number of critics pointed to the infamous Trump tape as the beginning of the movement.

ALTERNATIVE MODELS: PUBLIC JOURNALISM AND "FAKE NEWS"

In 1990, Poland was experiencing growing pains as it shifted from a state-controlled economic system to a more open market economy. The country's leading newspaper, *Gazeta Wyborcza*—the first noncommunist newspaper to appear in Eastern Europe since the 1940s—was also undergoing challenges. Based in Warsaw with a circulation of about 350,000 at the time, *Gazeta Wyborcza* had to report on and explain the new economy and the new crime wave that accompanied it. Especially troubling to the news staff and Polish citizens were gangs that robbed American and Western European tourists at railway stations, sometimes assaulting them in the process. The stolen goods would then pass to an outer circle, whose members transferred the goods to still another exterior ring of thieves. Even if the police caught the inner circle members, the loot usually disappeared.

These developments triggered heated discussions in the newsroom. A small group of young reporters, some of whom had recently worked in the United States, argued that the best way to cover the story was to describe the new crime wave and relay the facts to readers in a neutral manner. Another group, many of whom were older and more experienced, felt that the paper should take an advocacy stance and condemn the criminals through interpretive columns on the front page. The older guard won this particular debate, and more interpretive pieces appeared.[33]

This story illustrates the two competing models that have influenced American and European journalism since the early twentieth century. The first—the *informational* or *modern model*—emphasizes describing events and issues from a seemingly neutral point of view. The second—a more *partisan* or *European model*—stresses analyzing occurrences and advocating remedies from an acknowledged point of view. For a fictionalized representation of these differences, contrast the depiction of journalists on HBO's U.S. program *The Newsroom* (2012–2014) with that on the Danish TV series *Borgen* (2010–2013). In *The Newsroom*, discussions of remedies and viewpoints take place off camera; in *Borgen*, journalists talk about these issues on and off camera.

In most American newspapers today, the informational model dominates the front page, while the partisan model remains confined to the editorial pages and an occasional front-page piece. However, alternative models of news—from the serious to the satirical—have emerged to challenge modern journalistic ideals.

The Rise and Decline of the Public Journalism Movement

From the late 1980s through the 1990s, a number of papers experimented with ways to involve readers more actively in the news process. These experiments surfaced primarily at midsize daily papers, including the *Charlotte Observer*, the *Wichita Eagle*, the *Virginian-Pilot*, and the *Minneapolis Star Tribune*. Davis "Buzz" Merritt, editor of the *Wichita Eagle* at the time, defined key aspects of **public journalism**, including moving "beyond the limited mission of 'telling the news' to a broader mission of helping public life go well," and moving "from seeing people as consumers—as readers or nonreaders, as bystanders to be informed—to seeing them as a public, as potential actors in arriving at democratic solutions to public problems."[34]

In 1990, historian Christopher Lasch argued that "the job of the press is to encourage debate, not to supply the public with information."[35] Although he overstated his case—journalism does both and more—Lasch made a cogent point about how conventional journalism had lost its bearings. In the so-called objective era of modern journalism, mainstream news media had lost touch with its partisan roots. The early mission of journalism—to advocate opinions and encourage public debate—had been relegated to alternative magazines, the editorial pages, news blogs, and cable news channels starring allegedly elite reporters. Tellingly, Lasch connected the gradual decline in voter participation, which began in the 1920s, to more professionalized conduct on the part of journalists. With a modern "objective" press, he contended, the public increasingly began to defer to the "more professional" news media to watch over civic life on its behalf.

CITIZEN JOURNALISM
One way technology has allowed citizens to become involved in the reporting of news is through cell phone photos and videos uploaded online. Witnesses can now pass on what they have captured to major mainstream news sources, like CNN's iReports, or post to their own blogs and websites.

Public journalism is best imagined as a conversational model for news practice. Modern journalism had drawn a distinct line between reporter detachment and community involvement; public journalism—driven by citizen forums, community conversations, and even talk shows—obscured this line.

Throughout the 1990s—before people felt the full impact of the Internet—public journalism served as a response to the many citizens who felt alienated from participating in public life. This alienation arose, in part, from viewers who watched passively as the political process seemed to play out in the news and on TV between party operatives and media pundits. Public journalism seemed to involve both the public and journalists more centrally in civic and political life. Editors and reporters interested in addressing citizen alienation—and reporter cynicism—began devising ways to engage people as conversational partners in determining the news. In an effort to draw the public into discussions about community priorities, these journalists began sponsoring citizen forums, where readers would have a voice in shaping aspects of the news that directly affected them.

The public journalism movement was in decline by 2000, partly because it failed to gain the support of many mainstream editors and reporters, many beholden to a detachment model of journalism and wary of becoming too involved in the communities they covered. However, the leaders of the movement had also not foreseen or addressed the changing economic structure of the news business. In the wake of lost classified ad revenue amid the rise of free advertising online, newspaper executives furiously cut reporting staffs and expensive investigative projects, reduced the print space for news, or converted to online-only operations. While such trends temporarily helped profits and satisfied stockholders, they limited both the range of stories told and the views represented in a community.

As the advocates of public journalism acknowledged, people had grown used to letting their representatives think and act for them. Today, more community-oriented journalism and other civic projects offer citizens an opportunity to deliberate and to influence their leaders. This may include broadening the story models and frames they use to recount experiences, paying more attention to the historical and economic contexts of these stories, doing more investigative reports that analyze both news conventions and social issues, taking more responsibility for their news narratives, participating more fully in the public life of their communities, admitting to their cultural biases and occasional mistakes, and ensuring that the verification model of reporting is not overwhelmed by cable's journalism of assertion.

Arguing that for too long journalism had defined its role only in negative terms, news scholar Jay Rosen noted: "To be adversarial, critical, to ask tough questions, to expose scandal and wrongdoing . . . these are necessary tasks, even noble tasks, but they are negative tasks." In addition, he suggested that journalism should assert itself as a positive force, not merely as a watchdog or as a neutral information conduit to readers but as "a support system for public life."[36]

The Shifting Meanings of "Fake News" and the Rise of Satiric Journalism

For many young people, it is especially frustrating that two wealthy, established political parties— beholden to special interests and their lobbyists—control the nation's government. In part, this frustration explained the popularity of both Donald Trump and Bernie Sanders during the 2016 presidential campaign season, as they were considered outside the political establishment. After all, 98 percent of congressional incumbents get reelected each year—not always because they've done a good job but often because they've made promises and done favors for the lobbyists and interests that helped get them elected in the first place.

Why shouldn't people, then, be cynical about politics? It is this cynicism that has drawn increasingly young audiences to so-called fake news shows like Comedy Central's *The Daily Show with Trevor Noah*; TBS's *Full Frontal with Samantha Bee*; HBO's *Last Week Tonight with John Oliver*, and Seth Meyers's "A Closer Look" segments on NBC's *Late Night* program. Following in the tradition of *Saturday Night Live* (*SNL*), which began in 1975, news satires tell their audiences something that seems truthful about politicians and how they try to manipulate media and public opinion. But most important, these shows use humor and detailed research to critique the news media and our political system. *SNL*'s sketches on GOP vice presidential candidate Sarah Palin in 2008, when Seth Meyers served as the show's head writer, drew large audiences and shaped the way younger viewers thought about the election. By the 2016 campaign, all the current news satires were aiming their sharp acerbic lenses at Hillary Clinton and Donald Trump, as well as at CNN, Fox News, and MSNBC. In reality, at their best, these programs, which employ numerous researchers and writers, do some of the best reporting on the state of our politics and provide some of the best criticism of the so-called non-fake-news media.

In critiquing the limits of news stories and politics, *The Daily Show* has historically parodied the narrative conventions of evening and cable news programs: the clipped eight-second sound bite that limits meaning; the formulaic shot of the TV news "stand up," depicting reporters "on location" to establish credibility by revealing that they were really there; and the talking heads and opinionated pundits of CNN, Fox News, and MSNBC. In a now famous 2004 exchange with actor-comedian Rob Corddry, former host Jon Stewart asked his "political correspondent" for his opinion about presidential campaign tactics. "My opinion? I don't have opinions," Corddry answered. "I'm a reporter, Jon. My job is to spend half the time repeating what one side says, and half the time repeating the other. Little thing called objectivity; might want to look it up."

During his reign as news court jester, Stewart, who stepped down from *The Daily Show* in 2015, exposed the melodrama of TV news that nightly depicts the world in various stages of disorder while offering the stalwart, comforting presence of celebrity-anchors overseeing it all from their high-tech command centers. Even before CBS's usually neutral and aloof Walter Cronkite signed off the evening news with "And that's the way it is," network news anchors tried to offer a sense of order through the reassurance of their individual personalities.

Before the Trump era, "fake news" had generally referred to the kind of satirical news found on *SNL*'s "Weekend Update" or Comedy Central. But during the 2016 presidential campaign, "fake news" took on a new meaning, increasingly referring to inaccurate and false news stories that emerged on Facebook during the election and originated in Eastern Europe. Following the election of Donald Trump, the phrase began to take on newer meanings. As the BBC reported

Eric Liebowitz/© HBO/Everett Collection

Richard Shotwell/AP Images

NEWS AS SATIRE

Satirical news has become something of a cottage industry in recent years, stemming from *SNL*'s "Weekend Update" segment and dominated by *The Daily Show*. Several *Daily Show* correspondents have gone on to their own news-related shows and have interviewed a variety of political leaders and prominent figures in the process. For example, John Oliver (*left*) of *Last Week Tonight* scored a major interview with Edward Snowden in 2015. In addition, the *Daily Show*'s hiring of South African comedian Trevor Noah (*right*) as Jon Stewart's replacement and Samantha Bee's *Full Frontal* have brought much more diversity to the fake news business.

during President Trump's first year, "all sorts of things—misinformation, spin, conspiracy theories, mistakes, and reporting that people just don't like—have been rolled into it."[37] In fact, as the BBC report suggests, President Trump managed to expand the definition to encompass any news report or news analysis—evidence based or not—that he did not like, especially those that portrayed his administration in a negative light.

While fake news programs often mock the formulas that real TV news programs have long used, they also present an informative and insightful look at current events and the way "traditional" media cover them. For example, they expose hypocrisy by juxtaposing what a politician said recently in the news with the opposite position articulated by the same politician months or years earlier. Indeed, many Americans have admitted that they watch news satires not only to be entertained but also to stay current with what's going on in the world. In fact, a prominent Pew Research Center study back in 2007 found that people who watched these satiric shows were more often "better informed" than most other news consumers, usually because these viewers tended to get their news from multiple sources and a cross section of news media.[38]

Although the world has changed, local TV news formulas (except for splashy opening graphics and Doppler weather radar) have gone virtually unaltered since the 1970s, when *SNL* first started making fun of TV news. Local newscasts still limit most reporters' stories to two minutes or less and promote stylish anchors, a "sports guy," and a certified meteorologist as familiar personalities whom we invite into our homes each evening. Now that a generation of viewers has been raised on the TV satire and political cynicism of "Weekend Update," David Letterman, Jimmy Fallon, Conan O'Brien, Stephen Colbert, Seth Meyers, Samantha Bee, Jimmy Kimmel, and *The Daily Show*, the slick, formulaic packaging of political ads and the canned, cautious sound bites offered in news packages are simply not as effective. Maybe younger audiences would value news more if it matched the complicated storytelling that surrounds them—in everything from TV dramas to interactive video games to their own conversations.

DEMOCRACY AND REIMAGINING JOURNALISM'S ROLE

Journalism is central to democracy: Both citizens and the media must have access to the information that we need to make important decisions. As this chapter illustrates, however, this is a complicated idea. For example, in the aftermath of 9/11, some government officials claimed that reporters or columnists who raised questions about fighting terrorism, invading Iraq, or developing secret government programs were being unpatriotic. Yet the basic principles of democracy require citizens and the media to question our leaders and government. Isn't this, after all, what the American Revolution was all about? (See "Examining Ethics: WikiLeaks, Secret Documents, and Good Journalism" on page 449.)

Conventional journalists will fight ferociously for the principles that underpin journalism's basic tenets—freedom of the press, the obligation to question government, the public's right to know, and the belief that there are two sides to every story. These are mostly worthy ideals, but they do have limitations. These tenets, for example, generally do not acknowledge any moral or ethical duty for journalists to improve the quality of daily life. Rather, conventional journalism values its news-gathering capabilities and the well-constructed news narrative, leaving the improvement of civic life to political groups, nonprofit organizations, business philanthropists, individual citizens, and TV comedians.

Social Responsibility

Although reporters have traditionally thought of themselves first and foremost as observers and recorders, some journalists have acknowledged a social responsibility. Among them was James Agee in the 1930s. In his book *Let Us Now Praise Famous Men*, which was accompanied by the Depression-era photography of Walker Evans, Agee said that he regarded conventional journalism as dishonest, partly because the act of observing intruded on people and turned them into story characters that newspapers and magazines then exploited for profit.

Agee also worried that readers would retreat into the comfort of his writing—his narrative—instead of confronting what for many families was the horror of the Great Depression. For Agee, the question of responsibility extended not only to journalism and to himself but to the readers of his stories as well: "The reader is no less centrally involved than the authors and those of whom they tell."[39] Agee's self-conscious analysis provides insights into journalism's hidden agendas and the responsibility of all citizens to make public life better.

Deliberative Democracy

According to advocates of public journalism, when reporters are chiefly concerned with maintaining their antagonistic relationship to politics and are less willing to improve political discourse, news and democracy suffer. The late *Washington Post* columnist David Broder thought that national journalists like him—through rising salaries, prestige, and formal education—have distanced themselves "from the people that [they] are writing for and have become much, much closer to people [they] are writing about."[40] Broder believed that journalists need to become activists, not for a particular party but for the political process and in the interest of reenergizing public life. For those who advocate for public journalism, this might also involve mainstream media spearheading voter registration drives or setting up pressrooms or news bureaus in public libraries or shopping malls, where people converge in large numbers.

Public journalism offers people models for how to deliberate in forums, and then it covers those deliberations. This kind of community journalism aims to reinvigorate a *deliberative democracy* in which citizen groups, local government, and the news media work together more actively to shape

EXAMINING ETHICS

WikiLeaks, Secret Documents, and Good Journalism

Since its inception in 2006, the controversial website WikiLeaks has released millions of documents—from revelations of toxic dumps in Africa to the 2013 release of 1.5 million U.S. diplomatic records, many involving President Nixon's secretary of state, Henry Kissinger. In 2016, WikiLeaks offered reports on the NSA's "bugging" operation of multiple foreign leaders and a searchable database of thirty thousand of former secretary of state Hillary Clinton's e-mails. WikiLeaks' controversial spokesperson and self-identified "editor in chief," Julian Assange—an Australian online activist—has been called everything from a staunch free-speech advocate to a "hi-tech terrorist" (by former U.S. vice president Joe Biden). Certainly, government leaders around the world have faced embarrassment from the site's many document dumps and secrecy breaches.

In its most controversial move, in 2010 WikiLeaks offered 500,000-plus documents, called the "War Logs," to three mainstream print outlets—the *Guardian* in the United Kingdom, the German magazine *Der Spiegel*, and the *New York Times*. These documents were mainly U.S. military and state department dispatches and internal memos related to the Afghan and Iraq wars—what Bill Keller, then executive editor of the *New York Times*, called a "huge breach of secrecy" for those running the wars. Keller described working with WikiLeaks as an adventure that "combined the cloak-and-dagger intrigue of handling a vast secret archive with the more mundane feat of sorting, searching and understanding a mountain

of data."[1] Indeed, one of the first major stories the *Times* wrote, based on the "War Logs" project, reported on "Pakistan's ambiguous role as an American ally."[2] Then, just a few months later, Osama bin Laden was found hiding in the middle of a Pakistani suburb.

WikiLeaks presents a number of ethical dilemmas and concerns for both journalists and citizens. News critic and journalism professor Jay Rosen has called WikiLeaks "the world's first stateless news organization."[3] But is WikiLeaks actually engaging in journalism—and therefore entitled to First Amendment protections? Or is it merely an important "news source, news provider, content host, [or] whistle-blower," exposing things that governments would rather keep secret, as one critic from the Nieman Journalism Lab suggests?[4] And should *any* document or material obtained by WikiLeaks be released for public scrutiny, or should some kinds of documents and materials be withheld?

Examining Ethics Activity

As a class or in smaller groups, consider the ethical concerns laid out above. Following the ethical template outlined on page 17 in Chapter 1, begin by researching the topic, finding as much information and analysis as possible. Read Bill Keller's *New York Times Magazine* piece "Dealing with Assange and the WikiLeaks Secrets" (January 26, 2011). See also Nikki Usher's work for Harvard's Nieman Journalism Lab and Jay Rosen's blog, *PressThink*. Consider also journalism criticism and news study sites, such as the *Columbia Journalism Review*, the Pew Research Center, and the First Amendment Center. Watch Julian Assange's interview on CBS's *60 Minutes* from January 2011.

Next, based on your research and informed analysis, decide whether WikiLeaks is a legitimate form of journalism and whether there should be newsroom policies that restrict the release of some kinds of documents when in partnership with a resource like WikiLeaks (such as the "War Logs" project described here). Create an outline for such policies.

social, economic, and political agendas. In a more deliberative democracy, a large segment of the community discusses public life and social policy before advising or electing officials who represent the community's interests.

A Lost Generation of Journalists

In the aftermath of the November 2016 election that installed reality-television star Donald Trump as the forty-fifth U.S. president, we might think that the biggest challenge facing journalism would be the Trump administration's almost daily attacks—without supporting evidence—on the "fake media." But the real crisis in journalism started years before Trump, with the catastrophic loss of ad revenue to the Internet and the loss of reporters in print and broadcast newsrooms.

Following the election, most U.S. news professionals conceded that they had missed a story of monumental proportions. The factors behind this historic journalistic failing are numerous and complex, but the most important one is perfectly simple: In the last decade, the number of journalists working at daily newspapers in the United States has been cut in half, and this radical reduction has brought a remorseless cutback in coverage of the working-class and rural communities where Trump built his electoral-college majority. The press simply did not have the reporters on the ground to document this historic shift and the appeal of Trump. For years, the anxieties of a vast swath of the public had been overlooked, leaving them isolated and voiceless—forgotten communities that found a voice in the Trump campaign. Much of the news that these communities did get came from the pundit class, mostly from cable (especially Fox News) and regional talk radio.

This news-media failure is the most striking evidence yet that the United States needs to replenish its ranks of working journalists, who must rededicate to the press's fundamental mission—in the words of Bill Kovach and Tom Rosenstiel in their now-classic *The Elements of Journalism*—"to provide citizens with the information they need to be free and self-governing."[41]

A few numbers reveal the problem:

- In the fifteen-year transition from the newsprint era to the digital age, the United States lost nearly 24,000 daily newspaper reporters—from a high of 56,400 in 2001 to fewer than 30,000 in 2017—according to the American Society of Newspaper Editors and the U.S. Bureau of Labor Statistics.
- In that same period, America's trust in the mass media ("to report the news fully, accurately and fairly") has fallen from 53 percent to 32 percent, according to annual Gallup polls.
- In the 1970s, the ratio of public relations specialists to working reporters was roughly 1:1. By 2001, that ratio had become 2:1. And by 2015, according to the U.S. Bureau of Statistics, the ratio had reached an astonishing imbalance of nearly 5:1.

The decline in the number of reporters and the rise of PR and political spin doctors raise significant concerns. During and following the digital turn, journalists have increasingly relied on press releases both for story ideas and for news copy. However, according to Robert McChesney and John Nichols in *The Death and Life of American Journalism*, "as editorial staffs shrink, there is less ability for news media to interrogate and counter the claims in press releases."[42] As an example, a 2012 Pew study reported that during the national election that year, journalists "often functioned as megaphones for political partisans, relaying assertions rather than contextualizing them."[43]

With the decrease in reporters and the increase in PR practitioners, far fewer journalists are available to vet information and fact-check the press releases that PR specialists pitch daily to multiple news organizations. For example, on the subject of health news, Pew researchers in 2014 reported on a *JAMA Internal Medicine* finding "that half of the stories examined relied on a single source or failed to disclose conflicts of interest from sources."[44]

Finally, more students coming from journalism schools are taking jobs as business writers and PR workers. The journalism profession, then, needs to not only figure out a new business model for the twenty-first century but also figure out how to recruit the best and brightest journalism students. Back in 1791, our founders offered special protection to journalists under the First Amendment—not to public relations specialists. Good journalism, after all, helps democracy work: It makes sense of key issues, documents events, keeps watch over our central institutions, and tells a community's significant stories. In the partisan era in which we now live, overloaded with decontextualized information and undocumented punditry, these skills are more important than ever. Good journalism and compelling stories will eventually save and sustain the profession, no matter how the marketplace continues to fracture.

14 Chapter Review

COMMON THREADS

One of the Common Threads discussed in Chapter 1 is the role that media plays in a democracy. Today, one of the major concerns is the proliferation of news sources. How well is our society being served by this trend—especially on cable and the Internet—compared with the time when just a few major news media sources dominated journalism?

Historians, media critics, citizens, and even many politicians argue that a strong democracy is only possible with a strong, healthy, skeptical press. In the old days, a few legacy or traditional media—key national newspapers, three major networks, and three newsmagazines—provided most of the journalistic common ground for discussing major issues confronting U.S. society.

In today's online and 24/7 cable world, though, the legacy media have ceded some of their power and many of their fact-checking duties to new media forms, especially in the blogosphere. As discussed in this chapter and in Chapter 8, this power shortage is partly because substantial losses in advertising (which has gone to the Internet) have led to severe cutbacks in newsroom staffs, and partly because bloggers, 24/7 cable news media, and news satire shows like *The Daily Show*, *Full Frontal*, and *Last Week Tonight* are fact-checking the media as well as reporting

stories that used to be the domain of professional news organizations.

The case before us, then, goes something like this: In the old days, the major news media provided us with reports and narratives to share, discuss, and argue about. But in today's explosion of news and information, that common ground has eroded or is shifting. Instead, today we often rely only on those media sources that match our comfort level, cultural values, or political affiliations; increasingly, these are blog sites, radio talk shows, or cable channels. Sometimes these opinion sites and channels are not supported with the careful fact-gathering and verification that has long been a pillar of the best kinds of journalism.

So in today's media environment, how severely have technological and cultural transformations undermined the common-ground function of mainstream media? And are these changes ultimately good or bad for democracy?

KEY TERMS

The definitions for the terms listed below can be found in the glossary at the end of the book. The page numbers listed with the terms indicate where the term is highlighted in the chapter.

news, 425
newsworthiness, 426
ethnocentrism, 428
responsible capitalism, 429

small-town pastoralism, 429
individualism, 429
conflict of interest, 433
herd journalism, 437

sound bite, 441
public journalism, 444

LaunchPad
macmillan learning

For review quizzes, chapter summaries, links to media-related websites, and more, go to launchpadworks.com.

REVIEW QUESTIONS

Modern Journalism in the Information Age

1. What are the criteria used for determining newsworthiness?
2. Explain the values shift in journalism today from a more detached or neutral model to a more partisan or assertion model.

Ethics and the News Media

3. How do issues such as deception and privacy present ethical problems for journalists?
4. What are the connections between so-called neutral journalism and the business side of a news organization?

Reporting Rituals and the Legacy of Print Journalism

5. Why is getting a story first important to reporters?
6. Why have reporters become so dependent on experts?

Journalism in the Age of TV and the Internet

7. How is credibility established in TV news as compared with print journalism?

8. In what ways has the Internet influenced traditional forms of journalism?

Alternative Models: Public Journalism and "Fake News"

9. What is public journalism? In what ways is it believed to make journalism better?
10. Explain how the definition of "fake news" has shifted over time.
11. What role do satirical news programs like *SNL*'s "Weekend Update," *The Daily Show*, and *Last Week Tonight* play in the world of journalism?

Democracy and Reimagining Journalism's Role

12. What is deliberative democracy, and what does it have to do with journalism?
13. What are some of the factors affecting the decline in the number of journalists?

QUESTIONING THE MEDIA

1. What are your main criticisms of the state of news today? In your opinion, what are the news media doing well?
2. Is the trend toward opinion-based partisan news programs on cable and the Internet a good thing or a bad thing for democracy?
3. Is there political bias in front-page news stories? If so, cite some current examples.
4. How would you go about formulating an ethical policy with regard to using deceptive means to get a story?

5. For a reporter, what are the dangers of both detachment from and involvement in public life?
6. Do satirical news programs make us more cynical about politics and less inclined to vote? Why or why not?
7. How do you feel about attacking the news media being used as a political strategy? How can good journalists best defend themselves from this strategy?

LAUNCHPAD FOR *MEDIA & CULTURE*

Visit LaunchPad for *Media & Culture* at launchpadworks.com for additional learning tools:

- REVIEW WITH LEARNINGCURVE
  LearningCurve, available on LaunchPad for *Media & Culture*, uses gamelike quizzing to help you master the concepts you need to learn from this chapter.

- VIDEO: THE OBJECTIVITY MYTH
  Pulitzer Prize–winning journalist Clarence Page and *Onion* editor Joe Randazzo explore how objectivity began in journalism and how reporter biases may nonetheless influence news stories.

BASED ON THE BEST SELLING MYSTERY

13 REASONS WHY ▶

IF YOU'RE LISTENING,
YOU'RE TOO LATE.

MARCH 31 | NETFLIX

Media Effects and Cultural Approaches to Research

15

IS IT EVER POSSIBLE to depict suicide in a television show without also glamorizing it?

That was the predicament for the creators of *13 Reasons Why*, a 2017 series on Netflix adapted by Brian Yorkey from the 2007 debut young-adult novel of the same name by Jay Asher.

The story, which spins out in thirteen episodes in its first Netflix season, "follows teenager Clay Jensen (Dylan Minnette) as he returns home from school to find a mysterious box with his name on it lying on his porch. Inside he discovers cassette tapes recorded by Hannah Baker (Katherine Langford)—his classmate and

EARLY MEDIA
RESEARCH
METHODS
p. 457

RESEARCH ON
MEDIA EFFECTS
p. 460

CULTURAL
APPROACHES TO
MEDIA RESEARCH
p. 469

MEDIA RESEARCH
AND DEMOCRACY
p. 478

◀ Hit Netflix original series *13 Reasons Why* raises important questions about teenage suicide. But does it go too far?

crush—who tragically died from suicide two weeks earlier. On tape, Hannah explains that there are thirteen reasons why she decided to end her life. The reasons catalog betrayals, bullying, slut-shaming, binge drinking, drunk driving, drug use, and rape. Hannah's suicide is depicted in the final episode. A reviewer for the *Guardian* concluded that the series was "too bleak to binge," but plenty of people did binge on it, leading to a second season in 2018 and a third in 2019.[1]

Like the book, the series prompted a debate about bullying, depression, sexual consent, drug and alcohol abuse, and self-harm. From a media effects perspective, there was concern that portrayals of suicide might glamorize suicide and induce copycats.

Mark Henick, a mental health advocate, argued that TV programs like *13 Reasons Why* can have several problematic features in their portrayal of suicide, including simplifying or romanticizing suicide, and portraying suicide as a viable option instead of seeking proper care for mental health issues. Graphic representations of suicide can also harm viewers, especially young and impressionable ones.[2]

In 2017, the *Atlantic* reported on a study in which public health researchers found that "Google queries about suicide rose by almost 20 percent in 19 days after the show came out, representing between 900,000 and 1.5 million more searches than usual regarding the subject."[3] The concern among many experts—referred to as the contagion effect—is that although the television series can increase awareness of the tragedy of suicide, it can also idealize it.

The show's creators defended the program and its story.[4] Nevertheless,

about two months after the 2017 release of *13 Reasons Why* (which was already rated TV-MA), Netflix added stronger advisory warnings at the beginning of certain episodes and supplementary content to its companion 13ReasonsWhy .info website. The site contains videos addressing a number of the show's disturbing topics, such as sexual assault; a discussion guide; and links to mental health resources for help, including the Crisis Text Line and the National Suicide Prevention Lifeline. In a statement, Netflix said, "While many of our members find the show to be a valuable driver for starting important conversation with their families, we have also heard concern from those who feel the series should carry additional advisories."[5] The Netflix page for the series states, "This series contains scenes that viewers may find disturbing, including graphic depictions of sexual assault, substance abuse, and suicide. If you or anyone you know needs help finding support or crisis resources, please go to 13ReasonsWhy.info for more information."[6]

Dan Reidenberg, psychologist and executive director of the national organization Suicide Awareness Voices of Education (SAVE), weighed in: "Although it's created a conversation about suicide, it's not the right conversation." When Reidenberg was contacted by Netflix for guidance before the release of *13 Reasons Why*, he recommended that the company not release the show. That, of course, did not happen. In response, SAVE issued talking points for *13 Reasons Why* for people to share, to try to create the right conversation. The first point was this: "*13 Reasons Why* is a fictional story based on a widely known novel and is meant to be a cautionary tale."[7]

MANY BELIEVE THAT MEDIA HAVE A POWERFUL EFFECT on individuals and society. This belief has led media researchers to focus most of their efforts on two types of research: media effects research and cultural studies research.

Media effects research attempts to understand, explain, and predict the effects of mass media on individuals and society. The main goal of this type of research is to uncover whether there is a connection between aggressive behavior and violence in the media, particularly in children and teens. In the late 1960s, government leaders—reacting to the social upheavals of that decade—set aside $1 million to examine this potential connection. Since that time, thousands of studies have told us what most teachers and parents believe instinctively: Violent scenes on television and in movies stimulate aggressive behavior in children and teens—especially young boys.

The other major area of mass media research is **cultural studies**. This research approach focuses on how people make meaning, apprehend reality, articulate values, and order experience through their use of cultural symbols. Cultural studies scholars also examine the way status quo groups in society, particularly corporate and political elites, use media to circulate their messages and sustain their interests. This research has attempted to make daily cultural experience the focus of media studies, centering on the subtle intersections among mass communication, history, politics, and economics.

In this chapter, we will:

- Examine the evolution of media research over time
- Focus on the two major strains of media research, investigating the strengths and limitations of each
- Conclude with a discussion of how media research interacts with democratic ideals

As you get a sense of media effects and cultural studies research, think of some research questions of your own. Consider your own Internet habits. How do the number of hours you spend online every day, the types of online content you view, and your motivations for where you spend your time online shape your everyday behavior? Also, think about the ways your gender, race, sexuality, or class play into other media you consume—like the movies and television you watch and the music you like. For more questions to help you understand the effects of media in our lives, see "Questioning the Media" in the Chapter Review.

EARLY MEDIA RESEARCH METHODS

In the early days of the United States, philosophical and historical writings tried to explain the nature of news and print media. For instance, the French political philosopher Alexis de Tocqueville, author of *Democracy in America*, noted differences between French and American newspapers in the early 1830s:

In France the space allotted to commercial advertisements is very limited, and . . . the essential part of the journal is the discussion of the politics of the day. In America three quarters of the enormous sheet are filled with advertisements and the remainder is frequently occupied by political intelligence or trivial anecdotes; it is only from time to time that one finds a corner devoted to the passionate discussions like those which the journalists of France every day give to their readers.[8]

During most of the nineteenth century, media analysis was based on moral and political arguments, as demonstrated by the Tocqueville quote.[9]

More scientific approaches to mass media research did not begin to develop until the late 1920s and 1930s. In 1920, Walter Lippmann's *Liberty and the News* called on journalists to operate more like scientific researchers in gathering and analyzing factual material. Lippmann's next book, *Public Opinion* (1922), was the first to apply the principles of psychology to journalism. Described by media historian James Carey as "the founding book in American media studies,"[10] it led to an expanded understanding of the effects of the media, emphasizing data collection and numerical measurement. According to media historian Daniel Czitrom, by the 1930s "an aggressively empirical spirit, stressing new and increasingly sophisticated research techniques, characterized the study of modern communication in America."[11] Czitrom traces four trends between 1930 and 1960 that contributed to the rise of modern media research: propaganda analysis, public opinion research, social psychology studies, and marketing research.

Propaganda Analysis

After World War I, some media researchers began studying how governments used propaganda to advance the war effort. They found that during the war, governments routinely relied on propaganda divisions to spread "information" to the public. According to Czitrom, though propaganda was considered a positive force for mobilizing public opinion during the war, researchers after the war labeled propaganda negatively, calling it "partisan appeal based on half-truths and devious manipulation of communication channels."[12] Harold Lasswell's important 1927 study *Propaganda Technique in the World War* focused on propaganda in the media, defining it as "the control of opinion by significant symbols, . . . by stories, rumors, reports, pictures and other forms of social communication."[13] **Propaganda analysis** thus became a major early focus of mass media research.

Public Opinion Research

Researchers soon went beyond the study of war propaganda and began to focus on more general concerns about how the mass media filtered information and shaped public attitudes. In the face of growing media influence, Walter Lippmann distrusted the public's ability to function as knowledgeable citizens as well as journalism's ability to help the public separate truth from lies. In promoting the place of the expert in modern life, Lippmann celebrated the social scientist as part of a new expert class that could best make "unseen facts intelligible to those who have to make decisions."[14]

Today, social scientists conduct *public opinion research*, or citizen surveys; these have become especially influential during political elections. On the upside, public opinion research on diverse populations has provided insights into citizen behavior and social differences, especially during election periods or following major national events. For example, a 2018 Pew Research poll confirmed what many other polls reported: Young adults tend to be less religious than their elders by several measures; the opposite is rarely true. This pattern is consistent across many countries with different religious, economic, and social profiles.[15]

On the downside, journalism has become increasingly dependent on polls, particularly for political insight. Some critics argue that this heavy reliance on measured public opinion has begun to adversely affect the active political involvement of American citizens. Many people do not vote because they have seen or read poll projections and have decided that their votes will not make a difference. Furthermore, some critics of incessant polling argue that the public is just passively responding to surveys that mainly measure opinions on topics of interest to business, government, academics, and the mainstream news media. A final problem is the pervasive use of

PUBLIC OPINION RESEARCH

Public opinion polls suggest that the American public's attitude toward same-sex marriage has evolved. Just weeks before the Supreme Court ruled same-sex marriage legal nationwide, a 2015 Pew Research poll reported that 57 percent of Americans were in favor of it—the same percentage of people who opposed it in a poll back in 2001.

Ethan Miller/Getty Images

unreliable **pseudo-polls**, typically call-in, online, or person-in-the-street polls that the news media use to address a "question of the day." The National Council on Public Polls notes that "unscientific pseudo-polls are widespread and sometimes entertaining, but they never provide the kind of information that belongs in a serious report," and discourages news media from conducting them.[16]

Social Psychology Studies

While opinion polls measure public attitudes, *social psychology studies* measure the behavior and cognition of individuals. The most influential early social psychology study, the Payne Fund Studies, encompassed a series of thirteen research projects conducted by social psychologists between 1929 and 1932. Named after the private philanthropic organization that funded the research, the Payne Fund Studies were a response to a growing national concern about the effects of motion pictures, which had become a popular pastime for young people in the 1920s. These studies, which were later used by some politicians to attack the movie industry, linked frequent movie attendance to juvenile delinquency, promiscuity, and other antisocial behaviors, arguing that movies took "emotional possession" of young filmgoers.[17]

In one of the Payne studies, for example, children and teenagers were wired with electrodes and galvanometers, mechanisms that detected any heightened response via the subject's skin. The researchers interpreted changes in the skin as evidence of emotional arousal. In retrospect, the findings hardly seem surprising: The youngest subjects in the group had the strongest reaction to violent or tragic movie scenes, whereas the teenage subjects reacted most strongly to scenes with romantic and sexual content. The researchers concluded that films could be dangerous for young children and might foster sexual promiscuity among teenagers. The conclusions of this and other Payne Fund Studies contributed to the establishment of the Motion Picture Production Code, which tamed movie content from the 1930s through the 1950s (see Chapter 16). As forerunners of today's TV violence and aggression research, the Payne Fund Studies became the model for media research. (See Figure 15.1 for one example of a contemporary policy that developed out of media research.)

SOCIAL AND PSYCHOLOGICAL EFFECTS OF MEDIA Concerns about film violence are not new. The 1930 movie *Little Caesar* follows the career of gangster Rico Bandello (played by Edward G. Robinson, shown), who kills his way to the top of the crime establishment and gets the girl as well. The Motion Picture Production Code, which was established a few years after this movie's release, reined in sexual themes and profane language, set restrictions on film violence, and attempted to prevent audiences from sympathizing with bad guys like Rico.

FIGURE 15.1

TV PARENTAL GUIDELINES

The TV industry continues to study its self-imposed rating categories, promising to fine-tune them to ensure that the government keeps its distance. These standards are one example of a policy that was shaped in part by media research. Since the 1960s, research has attempted to demonstrate links between violent TV images and increased levels of aggression among children and adolescents.

Data from: TV Parental Guidelines Monitoring Board, accessed June 19, 2018, www.tvguidelines.org.

The following categories apply to programs designed solely for children:

 All Children
This program is designed to be appropriate for all children. Whether animated or live-action, the themes and elements in this program are specifically designed for a very young audience, including children from ages 2–6. This program is not expected to frighten young children.

Directed to Older Children
This program is designed for children age 7 and above. It may be more appropriate for children who have acquired the developmental skills needed to distinguish between make-believe and reality. Themes and elements in this program may include mild fantasy violence or comedic violence, or may frighten children under the age of 7. Therefore, parents may wish to consider the suitability of this program for their very young children.

Directed to Older Children— Fantasy Violence
For those programs where fantasy violence may be more intense or more combative than other programs in this category, such programs will be designated **TV-Y7-FV**.

The following categories apply to programs designed for the entire audience:

General Audience
Most parents would find this program suitable for all ages. Although this rating does not signify a program designed specifically for children, most parents may let younger children watch this program unattended. It contains little or no violence, no strong language, and little or no sexual dialogue or situations.

Parental Guidance Suggested
This program contains material that parents may find unsuitable for younger children. Many parents may want to watch it with their younger children. The theme itself may call for parental guidance and/or the program may contain one or more of the following: some suggestive dialogue (D), infrequent coarse language (L), some sexual situations (S), or moderate violence (V).

Parents Strongly Cautioned
This program contains some material that many parents would find unsuitable for children under 14 years of age. Parents are strongly urged to exercise greater care in monitoring this program and are cautioned against letting children under the age of 14 watch unattended. This program may contain one or more of the following: intensely suggestive dialogue (D), strong coarse language (L), intense sexual situations (S), or intense violence (V).

Mature Audiences Only
This program is specifically designed to be viewed by adults and therefore may be unsuitable for children under 17. This program may contain one or more of the following: crude indecent language (L), explicit sexual activity (S), or graphic violence (V).

Marketing Research

A fourth influential area of early media research, *marketing research*, developed when advertisers and product companies began conducting surveys on consumer buying habits in the 1920s. The emergence of commercial radio led to the first ratings system, which measured how many people were listening on a given night. By the 1930s, radio networks, advertisers, large stations, and advertising agencies all subscribed to ratings services. However, compared with print media, whose circulation departments kept careful track of customers' names and addresses, radio listeners were more difficult to trace. This problem precipitated the development of increasingly sophisticated marketing research methods to determine consumer preferences and media use, such as direct-mail diaries, television meters, phone surveys, telemarketing, and Internet tracking. In many instances, product companies paid consumers nominal amounts of money to take part in these studies.

RESEARCH ON MEDIA EFFECTS

As concern about public opinion, propaganda, and the impact of the media merged with the growth of journalism and mass communication departments in colleges and universities, media researchers looked more and more to behavioral science as the basis of their research. Between 1930 and 1970, as media historian Daniel Czitrom has noted, "Who says what to whom with what effect?" became the key question "defining the scope and problems of American communications research."[18] In addressing this question specifically, media effects researchers asked follow-up questions such as this: If children watch a lot of TV cartoons (stimulus or cause), will this repeated act influence their behavior toward their peers (response or effect)? For most of the twentieth century, media researchers and news reporters used different methods to answer similar sets of questions—who, what, when, and where—about our daily experiences (see "Media Literacy and the Critical Process: Wedding Media and the Meaning of the Perfect Wedding Day" on page 465).

Early Theories of Media Effects

A major goal of scientific research is to develop theories or laws that can consistently explain or predict human behavior. The varied impacts of the mass media and the diverse ways in which people create popular culture, however, tend to defy predictable rules. Historical, economic, and political factors influence media industries, making it difficult to develop systematic theories that explain communication. Researchers developed a number of small theories, or models, that help explain individual behavior rather than the impact of the media on large populations. But before these small theories began to emerge in the 1970s, mass media research followed several other models. Developing between the 1930s and the 1970s, these major approaches included the hypodermic-needle model, the minimal-effects model, and the uses and gratifications model.

The Hypodermic-Needle Model

One of the earliest media theories attributed powerful effects to the mass media. A number of intellectuals and academics were fearful of the influence and popularity of film and radio in the 1920s and 1930s. Some social psychologists and sociologists who arrived in the United States after fleeing Germany and Nazism in the 1930s had watched Hitler use radio, film, and print media as propaganda tools. They worried that the popular media in America also had a strong hold over vulnerable audiences. The concept that powerful media affect weak audiences has been labeled the **hypodermic-needle model**, sometimes also called the *magic bullet theory* or the *direct-effects model*. It suggests that the media shoot their potent effects directly into unsuspecting victims.

One of the earliest challenges to this theory involved a study of Orson Welles's legendary October 30, 1938, radio broadcast of *War of the Worlds*, which presented H. G. Wells's Martian invasion novel in the form of a news report and frightened millions of listeners who didn't realize it was fictional (see Chapter 5). In a 1940 book-length study of the broadcast, *The Invasion from Mars: A Study in the Psychology of Panic*, radio researcher Hadley Cantril argued that contrary to expectations based on the hypodermic-needle model, not all listeners thought the radio program was a real news report. Instead, Cantril—after conducting personal interviews and a nationwide survey of listeners, and analyzing newspaper reports and listener mail to CBS Radio and the FCC—noted that although some did believe the radio report to be real (mostly those who missed the disclaimer at the beginning of the broadcast), the majority reacted out of collective panic, not out of a gullible belief in anything transmitted through the media. Although the hypodermic-needle model has been disproved over the years by social scientists, many people still attribute direct effects to the mass media, particularly in the case of children.

The Minimal-Effects Model

Cantril's research helped lay the groundwork for the **minimal-effects model**, or *limited model*. With the rise of empirical research techniques, social scientists began discovering and demonstrating that media alone cannot cause people to change their attitudes and behaviors. Based on tightly controlled experiments and surveys, researchers argued that people generally engage in **selective exposure** and **selective retention** with regard to the media. That is, people expose themselves to the media messages that are most familiar to them, and they retain the messages that confirm the values and attitudes they already hold. Minimal-effects researchers have argued that in most cases, mass media

LaunchPad
macmillan learning
launchpadworks.com

Media Effects Research
Experts discuss how media effects research informs media development.

Discussion: Why do you think the question of media's effects on children has continued to be such a big concern among researchers?

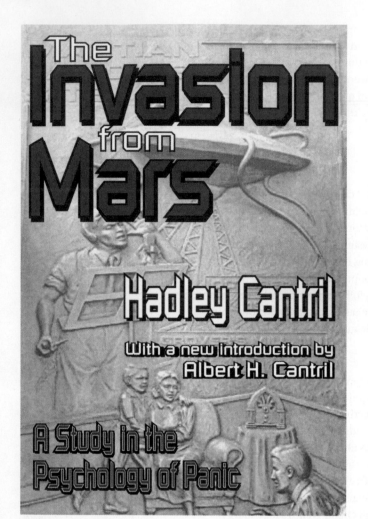

MEDIA EFFECTS?

In *The Invasion from Mars: A Study in the Psychology of Panic*, Hadley Cantril (1906–1969) argued against the hypodermic-needle model as an explanation for the panic that broke out after the *War of the Worlds* radio broadcast (see photo under "The Authority of Radio" in Chapter 5). A lifelong social researcher, Cantril also did a lot of work in public opinion research, even working with the government during World War II.

reinforce existing behaviors and attitudes rather than change them. The findings from the first comprehensive study of children and television—by Wilbur Schramm, Jack Lyle, and Edwin Parker in the late 1950s—best capture the minimal-effects theory:

For some children, under some conditions, some television is harmful. For other children under the same conditions, or for the same children under other conditions, it may be beneficial. For most children, under most conditions, most television is probably neither particularly harmful nor particularly beneficial.[19]

In addition, Joseph Klapper's important 1960 research study, *The Effects of Mass Communication*, found that the mass media only influenced individuals who did not already hold strong views on an issue and that the media had a greater impact on poor and uneducated audiences. Solidifying the minimal-effects argument, Klapper concluded that strong media effects occur largely at an individual level and do not appear to have large-scale, measurable, and direct effects on society as a whole.[20]

The Uses and Gratifications Model

A response to the minimal-effects theory, the **uses and gratifications model** was proposed to contest the notion of a passive media audience. Under this model, researchers—usually using in-depth interviews to supplement survey questionnaires—studied the ways in which people used the media to satisfy various emotional or intellectual needs. Instead of asking, "What effects do the media have on us?" researchers asked, "Why do we use the media?" Asking the *why* question enabled media researchers to develop inventories cataloguing how people employed the media to fulfill their needs. For example, researchers noted that some individuals used the media to see authority figures elevated or toppled, to seek a sense of community and connectedness, to fulfill a need for drama and stories, and to confirm moral or spiritual values.[21]

Although the uses and gratifications model addressed the *functions* of the mass media for individuals, it did not address important questions related to the impact of the media on society. Once researchers had accumulated substantial inventories of the uses and functions of media, they often did not move in new directions. Consequently, uses and gratifications never became a dominant or an enduring theory in media research.

Conducting Media Effects Research

Media research generally comes from the private or public sector, and each type has distinguishing features. *Private research*, sometimes called *proprietary research*, is generally conducted for a business, a corporation, or even a political campaign. It is usually applied research in the sense that the information it uncovers typically addresses some real-life problem or need. *Public research*, in contrast, usually takes place in academic and government settings. It involves information that is often more *theoretical* than applied; it tries to clarify, explain, or predict the effects of mass media rather than to address a consumer problem.

Most media research today focuses on the effects of the media in such areas as learning, attitudes, aggression, and voting habits. This research employs the **scientific method**, a blueprint long used by scientists and scholars to study phenomena in systematic stages. The steps in the scientific method include the following:

1. Identifying the research problem
2. Reviewing existing research and theories related to the problem
3. Developing working hypotheses or predictions about what the study might find
4. Determining an appropriate method or research design
5. Collecting information or relevant data
6. Analyzing results to see if the hypotheses have been verified
7. Interpreting the implications of the study to determine whether they explain or predict the problem

The scientific method relies on *objectivity* (eliminating bias and judgments on the part of researchers); *reliability* (getting the same answers or outcomes from a study or measure during repeated testing); and *validity* (demonstrating that a study actually measures what it claims to measure).

In scientific studies, researchers pose one or more **hypotheses**: tentative general statements that predict the influence of an *independent variable* on a *dependent variable*. For example, a researcher might hypothesize that frequent TV viewing among adolescents (independent variable) causes poor academic performance (dependent variable). Or another researcher might hypothesize that playing first-person shooter video games (independent variable) is associated with aggression in children (dependent variable).

Broadly speaking, the methods for studying media effects on audiences have taken two forms—experiments and survey research. To supplement these approaches, researchers also use content analysis to count and document specific messages that circulate throughout mass media.

Experiments

Like all studies that use the scientific method, **experiments** in media research isolate some aspect of content; suggest a hypothesis; and manipulate variables to discover a particular medium's effect on attitude, emotion, or behavior. To test whether a hypothesis is true, researchers expose an *experimental group*—the group under study—to a selected media program or text. To ensure valid results, researchers also use a *control group*, which serves as a basis for comparison; this group is not exposed to the selected media content. Subjects are picked for each group through **random assignment**, which simply means that each subject has an equal chance of being placed in either group. Random assignment ensures that the independent variables researchers want to control are distributed to both groups in the same way.

For instance, to test the effects of violent films on preadolescent boys, a research study might take a group of ten-year-olds and randomly assign them to two groups. Researchers expose the experimental group to a violent action movie that the control group does not see. Later, both groups are exposed to a staged fight between two other boys so that the researchers can observe how each group responds to an actual physical confrontation. Researchers then determine whether or not there is a statistically measurable difference between the two groups' responses to the fight. For example, perhaps the control subjects try to break up the fight but the experimental subjects do not. Because the groups were randomly selected and the only measurable difference between them was the viewing of the movie, researchers may conclude that under these conditions, the violent film

J. R. Eyerman/Getty Images

USES AND GRATIFICATIONS

In 1952, audience members at the Paramount Theater in Hollywood donned 3-D glasses for the opening-night screening of *Bwana Devil*, the first full-length color 3-D film. The uses and gratifications model of research investigates the appeal of mass media, such as going out to the movies.

caused a different behavior (see the "Bobo doll" experiment photos under "Contemporary Media Effects Theories").

When experiments carefully account for independent variables through random assignment, they generally work well to substantiate direct cause-effect hypotheses. Such research takes place both in laboratory settings and in field settings, where people can be observed using the media in their everyday environments. In field experiments, however, it is more difficult for researchers to control variables. In lab settings, researchers have more control, but other problems may occur. For example, when subjects are removed from the environments in which they regularly use the media, they may act differently—often with fewer inhibitions—than they would in their everyday surroundings.

Experiments have other limitations as well. First, they are not generalizable to a larger population; they cannot tell us whether cause-effect results can be duplicated outside the laboratory. Second, most academic experiments today are performed on college students, who are convenient subjects for research but are not representative of the general public. Third, while most experiments are fairly good at predicting short-term media effects under controlled conditions, they do not predict how subjects will behave months or years later in the real world.

Survey Research

In the simplest terms, **survey research** is the collecting and measuring of data taken from a group of respondents. Using random sampling techniques that give each potential subject an equal chance to be included in the survey, this research method draws on much larger populations than those used in experimental studies. Surveys may be conducted through direct mail, personal interviews, telephone calls, e-mail, and websites, enabling survey researchers to accumulate large amounts of information by surveying diverse cross sections of people. These data help researchers examine demographic factors such as educational background, income level, race, ethnicity, gender, age, sexual orientation, and political affiliation, along with questions directly related to the survey topic.

Two other benefits of surveys are that they are usually generalizable to the larger society and that they enable researchers to investigate populations in long-term studies. For example, survey research can measure subjects when they are ten, twenty, and thirty years old to track changes in how frequently they watch television and what kinds of programs they prefer at different ages. In addition, large government and academic survey databases are now widely available and contribute to the development of more long-range or **longitudinal studies**, which make it possible for social scientists to compare new studies with those conducted years earlier.

Like experiments, surveys have several drawbacks. First, survey investigators cannot account for all the variables that might affect media use; therefore, they cannot show cause-effect relationships. Survey research can, however, reveal **correlations**—or associations—between two variables. Second, the validity of survey questions is a chronic problem for survey practitioners. Surveys are only as good as the wording of their questions and the answer choices they present.

Content Analysis

Over the years, researchers recognized that experiments and surveys focused on general topics (violence) while ignoring the effects of specific media messages (gun violence, fistfights). As a corrective, researchers developed a method known as **content analysis** to study these messages. Such analysis is a systematic method of coding and measuring media content.

Although content analysis was first used during World War II for radio, more recent studies have focused on television, film, and the Internet. Probably the most influential content analysis studies were conducted by George Gerbner and his colleagues at the University of Pennsylvania. Beginning in the late 1960s, they coded and counted acts of violence on network television. Combined with surveys, their annual "violence profiles" showed that heavy watchers of television, ranging from children to retired Americans, tend to overestimate the amount of violence that exists in the actual world.[22]

MEDIA LITERACY AND THE CRITICAL PROCESS

Wedding Media and the Meaning of the Perfect Wedding Day

According to media researcher Erika Engstrom, the bridal industry in the United States generates $50 to $70 billion annually, with more than two million marriages a year.[1] Supporting that massive industry are books, magazines, websites, reality TV shows, and digital games (in addition to fictional accounts in movies and music) that promote the idea of what a "perfect" wedding should be. What values are wrapped up in these wedding narratives?

1 DESCRIPTION
Select three or four types of wedding media, and compare them. Possible choices include magazines such as *Brides*, *Bridal Guide*, and *Martha Stewart Weddings*; reality TV shows like *David Tutera's Celebrations*, *Say Yes to the Dress*, *My Big Fat American Gypsy Wedding*, *Something Borrowed, Something New*, and *Four Weddings*; websites like The Knot, Southern Bride, and Project Wedding; and games like *My Fantasy Wedding*, *Wedding Dash*, and *Imagine Wedding Designer*.

2 ANALYSIS
What patterns do you find in the wedding media? (Consider what isn't depicted as well.) Are there limited ways in which femininity is defined? Do men have an equal role in the planning of wedding events? Are weddings depicted as something just for heterosexuals? Do the wedding media presume that weddings are first-time experiences for the couple getting married? What seem to be the standards in terms of consumption—the expense, size, and number of things to buy and rent to make a "perfect" day?

3 INTERPRETATION
What do the wedding media seem to say about what it is to be a woman or a man on her or his wedding day? What do these gender roles for the wedding suggest about appropriate gender roles for married life after the wedding? What do the wedding media infer about the appropriate level of consumption? In other words, consider the role of wedding media in constructing *hegemony*: In their depiction of what makes a perfect wedding, do the stories attempt to get us to accept the dominant cultural values related to things like gender relations and consumerism?

4 EVALUATION
Come to a judgment about the wedding media analyzed. Are they good or bad regarding certain elements? Do they promote gender equality? Do they promote marriage equality (that is, gay marriage)? Do they offer alternatives to having a "perfect" day without buying into all the trappings of traditional weddings?

5 ENGAGEMENT
Talk to friends about what weddings are supposed to celebrate and whether an alternative conception of a wedding would be a better way to celebrate a union of two people. (In real life, if there is discomfort in talking about alternative ways to celebrate a wedding, that's probably the pressure of hegemony. Why is that pressure so strong?) Share your criticisms and ideas on wedding websites as well.

The limits of content analysis, however, have been well documented. First, this technique does not measure the effects of the messages on audiences, nor does it explain how those messages are presented. For example, a content analysis sponsored by the Kaiser Family Foundation examined more than eleven hundred television shows and found that 70 percent featured sexual content.[23] However, the study didn't explain how viewers interpreted the content or the context of the messages.

Second, problems of definition occur in content analysis. For instance, in the case of coding and counting acts of violence, how do researchers distinguish slapstick cartoon aggression from the violent murders or rapes in an evening police drama? Critics point out that such varied depictions may have diverse and subtle effects that are not differentiated by content analysis. Third, as content analysis grew to be a primary tool in media research, it sometimes pushed to the sidelines other

Courtesy of Albert Bandura

SOCIAL LEARNING THEORY

These photos document the "Bobo doll" experiments conducted by Albert Bandura and his colleagues at Stanford University in the early 1960s. Seventy-two children from the Stanford University Nursery School were divided into experimental and control groups. The "aggressive condition" experimental group subjects watched an adult in the room sit on, kick, and hit the Bobo doll with hands and a wooden mallet while saying such things as "Sock him in the nose," "Throw him in the air," and "Pow." (In later versions of the experiment, children watched filmed versions of the adult with the Bobo doll.) Afterward, in a separate room filled with toys, the children in the "aggressive condition" group were more likely than the other children to imitate the adult model's behavior toward the Bobo doll.

ways of thinking about television and media content. Broad questions concerning the media as a popular art form, as a measure of culture, as a democratic influence, or as a force for social control are difficult to address through strict measurement techniques. Critics of content analysis, in fact, have objected to the kind of social science that reduces culture to acts of counting. Such criticism has addressed the tendency by some researchers to favor measurement accuracy over intellectual discipline and inquiry.[24]

Contemporary Media Effects Theories

By the 1960s, the first departments of mass communication began graduating Ph.D.-level researchers schooled in experiment and survey research techniques as well as content analysis. These researchers began documenting consistent patterns in mass communication and developing new theories. Five of the most influential contemporary theories that help explain media effects are social learning theory, agenda-setting, the cultivation effect, the spiral of silence, and the third-person effect.

Social Learning Theory

Some of the most well-known studies that suggest a link between the mass media and behavior are the "Bobo doll" experiments, conducted on children by psychologist Albert Bandura and his colleagues at Stanford University in the 1960s. Bandura concluded that the experiments demonstrated a link between violent media programs, such as those on television, and aggressive behavior. Bandura developed **social learning theory** as a four-step process: *attention* (the subject must attend to the media and witness the aggressive behavior), *retention* (the subject must retain the memory for later retrieval), *motor reproduction* (the subject must be able to physically imitate the behavior), and *motivation* (there must be a social reward or reinforcement to encourage modeling of the behavior).

Supporters of social learning theory often cite real-life imitations of media aggression as evidence of social learning theory at work. Yet critics note that many studies conclude just the opposite— that there is no link between media content and aggression. For example, millions of people have watched episodes of *How to Get Away with Murder* and *Breaking Bad* without subsequently exhibiting aggressive behavior. As these critics point out, social learning theory simply makes television, film, and other media scapegoats for larger social problems relating to violence. Others suggest that experiencing media depictions of aggression can actually help viewers let off steam peacefully through a catharsis effect.

Agenda-Setting

A key phenomenon posited by contemporary media effects researchers is **agenda-setting**: the idea that when the mass media focus their attention on particular events or issues, they determine—that is, set the agenda for—the major topics of discussion for individuals and society. Essentially, agenda-setting researchers have argued that the mass media do not so much tell us what to think as *what to think about*. Traceable to Walter Lippmann's notion in the early 1920s that the media "create pictures in our heads," the first investigations into agenda-setting began in the 1970s.[25]

Over the years, agenda-setting research has demonstrated that the more stories the news media do on a particular subject, the more importance audiences attach to that subject. For instance, when the media seriously began to cover ecology issues after the first Earth Day in 1970, a much higher percentage of the population began listing the environment as a primary social concern in surveys. When *Jaws* became a blockbuster in 1975, the news media started featuring more shark attack stories; even landlocked people in the Midwest began ranking sharks as a major problem, despite the rarity of such incidents worldwide. More recently, extensive news coverage about the documentary *An Inconvenient Truth* and its companion best-selling book in 2006 sparked the highest-ever public concern about global warming, according to national surveys. But in the following years, the public's sense of urgency faltered somewhat as stories about the economy and other topics dominated the news agenda.

Carolyn Cole/Getty Images

POST-HURRICANE MEDIA COVERAGE
Despite causing catastrophic damage to the island of Puerto Rico back in 2017, the landfall of Hurricane Maria on the U.S. territory drew a negligible amount of U.S. media coverage, especially compared to the coverage devoted to the large hurricanes that made landfall in the continental United States just weeks before.

The Cultivation Effect

Another mass media phenomenon—the **cultivation effect**—suggests that heavy viewing of television leads individuals to perceive the world in ways that are consistent with television portrayals. This area of media effects research has pushed researchers beyond a focus on how the media affects individual behavior toward larger ideas about the impact of the media on perception.

The major research in this area grew from the attempts of George Gerbner and his colleagues to make generalizations about the influence of televised violence. The cultivation effect suggests that the more time individuals spend viewing television and absorbing its viewpoints, the more likely their views of social reality will be "cultivated" by the images and portrayals they have seen.[26] For example, Gerbner's studies concluded that although fewer than 1 percent of Americans are victims of violent crime in any single year, people who watch a lot of television tend to overestimate this percentage. Such exaggerated perceptions, Gerbner and his colleagues argued, are part of a "mean world" syndrome, in which viewers with heavy, long-term exposure to television violence are more likely to believe that the external world is a mean and dangerous place.

According to the cultivation effect, media messages interact in complicated ways with personal, social, political, and cultural factors; they are one of a number of important factors in determining individual behavior and defining social values. Some critics have charged that cultivation research has provided limited evidence to support its findings. In addition, some have argued that the cultivation effects recorded by Gerbner's studies have been so minimal as to be benign and that when compared side by side, the perceptions of heavy television viewers and nonviewers in terms of the "mean world" syndrome are virtually identical.

The Spiral of Silence

Developed by German communication theorist Elisabeth Noelle-Neumann in the 1970s and 1980s, the **spiral of silence** theory links the mass media, social psychology, and the formation of public opinion. The theory proposes that those who believe that their views on controversial issues are in the minority will keep their views to themselves—that is, become silent—out of fear of social isolation, which diminishes or even silences alternative perspectives. The theory is based on social psychology studies, such as the classic conformity research studies of Solomon Asch in 1951. In Asch's study on the effects of group pressure, he demonstrated that a test subject is more likely to give clearly wrong answers to questions about line lengths if all other people in the room unanimously state the same incorrect answers. Noelle-Neumann argued that mass media, particularly television, can exacerbate this effect by communicating real or presumed majority opinions widely and quickly.

According to the theory, the mass media can help create a false, overrated majority; that is, a true majority of people holding a certain position can grow silent when they sense an opposing majority in the media. One criticism of the theory is that some people may fail to fall into a spiral of silence either because they don't monitor the media or because they mistakenly perceive that more people hold their position than really do. Noelle-Neumann acknowledges that in many cases, "hard-core" non-conformists exist and remain vocal even in the face of social isolation and can ultimately prevail in changing public opinion.[27]

The Third-Person Effect

Identified in a 1983 study by W. Phillips Davison, the **third-person effect** theory suggests that people believe others are more affected by media messages than they are themselves.[28] In other words, it proposes the idea that "we" can escape the worst effects of media while still worrying about people who are younger, less educated, more impressionable, or otherwise less capable of guarding against media influence.

Under this theory, we might fear that other people will, for example, take tabloid newspapers seriously, imitate violent movies, or get addicted to the Internet, while dismissing the idea that any of those things could happen to us. It has been argued that the third-person effect is instrumental in censorship, as it would allow censors to assume immunity to the negative effects of any supposedly dangerous media they must examine.

Evaluating Research on Media Effects

The mainstream models of media research have made valuable contributions to our understanding of mass media, submitting content and audiences to rigorous testing. This wealth of research exists partly because funding for studies on the effects of media on young people remains popular among politicians and has drawn ready government support since the 1960s. Media critic Richard Rhodes argues that media effects research is inconsistent and often flawed but continues to resonate with politicians and parents because it offers an easy-to-blame social cause for real-world violence.[29] (For more on real-world gun violence in the United States, see "Examining Ethics: Our Masculinity Problem" on page 474.)

Funding restricts the scope of some media effects and survey research, particularly if government, business, or other administrative agendas do not align with researchers' interests. Other limits also exist, including the inability to address how media affect communities and social institutions. Because most media research operates best when examining media and individual behavior, fewer research studies explore media's impact on community and social life. Some research has begun to address these deficits and also to turn more attention to the increasing influence of media technology on international communication.

CULTURAL APPROACHES TO MEDIA RESEARCH

During the rise of modern media research, approaches with a stronger historical and interpretive edge developed as well, often in direct opposition to the scientific models. In the late 1930s, some social scientists began to warn about the limits of "gathering data" and "charting trends," particularly when these kinds of research projects served only advertisers and media organizations and tended to be narrowly focused on individual behavior, ignoring questions like "Where are institutions taking us?" and "Where do we want them to take us?"[30]

In the United States in the 1960s, an important body of research—loosely labeled *cultural studies*—arose to challenge mainstream media effects theories. Since that time, cultural studies research has focused on how people make meaning, understand reality, and order experience by using cultural symbols that appear in the media. This research has attempted to make everyday culture the centerpiece of media studies, focusing on how subtly mass communication shapes and is shaped by history, politics, and economics. Other cultural studies work examines the relationships between elite individuals and groups in government and politics, and how media play a role in sustaining the authority of elites and—occasionally—in challenging their power (see "Global Village: International Media Research" on page 470).

Early Developments in Cultural Studies Research

In Europe, media studies have always favored interpretive rather than scientific approaches; in other words, researchers there have approached the media as if they were literary or cultural critics rather than experimental or survey researchers. These approaches were built on the writings of political philosophers such as Karl Marx and Antonio Gramsci, who investigated how mass media support

International Media Research

Charlie Fong

LUWEI ROSE LUQIU, a renowned Chinese journalist who is pursuing her doctorate in media studies at Penn State University, uses a microblog and social media to encourage conversation surrounding her journalistic work.

Outside the borders of the United States, the mass media can create markedly different types of content, generate diverse meanings among its audience, and be part of a distinctive media economy. Mass media researchers inside and outside the United States often engage in international and comparative studies to illustrate the various effects and meanings of media in a variety of contexts. Here are four examples of recent international media research:

China

How does political satire work in China, a country that is notorious for media censorship? For her article "The Cost of Humour: Political Satire on Social Media and Censorship in China" (2017), media researcher Luwei Rose Luqiu of Pennsylvania State University interviewed many notable political satirists in China and conducted a content analysis of several satirical texts. Luqiu, a former journalist and blogger from Hong Kong, explains, "This study demonstrates how censorship has been strengthened since the creation of the State Internet Information Office in 2011." The government's threat of censorship on social media "causes political satirists to self-censor, abandon their creations and reduce their output. The influence of those who continue to work is diminished because the government controls all Chinese social media platforms. However, political satire still has strong vitality thanks to collective action, such as the anonymous production, distribution and sharing of work on Chinese social media."[1]

Nigeria

Is Nigeria's film industry integrated into the larger global film entertainment industry? In "Global Nollywood: The

existing hierarchies in society. They examined how popular culture and sports distract people from redressing social injustices, and they addressed the subordinate status of particular social groups, something emerging media effects researchers were seldom doing.

In the United States, early criticism of media effects research came from the Frankfurt School, a group of European researchers who emigrated from Germany to America to escape Nazi persecution

Nigerian Movie Industry and Alternative Global Networks in Production and Distribution" (2012), Jade Miller—now an assistant professor at Wilfrid Laurier University in Canada—looks at "Nollywood," Nigeria's film industry. Miller investigated the global linkages of the Nigerian film industry by interviewing "those populating these networks, from key Nollywood producers to shop owners thousands of miles from Lagos." She found that Nollywood is international in scope but operates outside the dominant Hollywood-based film industry by working "via alternative global networks." This distinctive political economy "renders Nollywood as situated in an alternative media capital, central to alternative networks, while too informal to integrate into dominant networks, and it is from this position that we can best understand Nollywood's position in global media flows."[2]

Switzerland/France

How does news travel when it moves in multilingual newsrooms and across regions with different languages? Is anything lost in translation? Researcher Lucile Davier investigated these questions in "The Paradoxical Invisibility of Translation in the Highly Multilingual Context of News Agencies" (2014). Davier, of the University of Geneva and the University of Paris III, studied two European-based news agencies: Agence France-Presse (AFP) and Agence télégraphique suisse (ATS). Davier, who has worked as a professional translator herself, did fieldwork observations and interviews at the regional office of AFP in Geneva (in the French-speaking region of Switzerland) and at the head office of ATS in Bern (in Switzerland's German-speaking region). According to Davier, the goal of the study was "to evaluate the potential consequences of a highly plurilingual production process on the one hand, and of the ostensible invisibility of multilingualism/translation on

the other hand." Working on a deadline already presents challenges for journalists to remain accurate; adding in the presence of multiple languages in a workplace and the need to translate news into other languages increases the chance of inaccuracies. Davier found that "some of the interviewed journalists acknowledge the risks that may be posed by interlingual and intercultural transfer (translation), given the working norms of news agencies (rapidity, accuracy of information, and adaptation to the audience). However, the institutional denial of these possible biases may prevent news agencies from reducing them."[3]

Bahrain

What were the news media narrative frames in Bahrain during the Arab Spring protests there in 2011? Ahmed K. Al-Rawi, now an assistant professor at Concordia University in Montreal, Canada, analyzed this in the article "Sectarianism and the Arab Spring: Framing the Popular Protests in Bahrain" (2015). Al-Rawi noted that the anti-government protests in this Persian Gulf nation started in February 2011 and "resulted in the death of one protestor. Hundreds of other protests followed, and popular anger against the Sunni monarchy is still a vital issue in the Kingdom." Al-Rawi explained that the monarchy in Bahrain framed the protests not as pleas for democracy but as the work of outside agitators. "From the earliest stages, the Bahraini government, which is closely aided by other Gulf Cooperation Council (GCC) countries, framed the protests as an Iran-backed conspiracy against the Gulf in an attempt to spread Shiism and infiltrate into the region. This sectarian dimension became the dominant frame in order to discredit the cause of the mostly Shiite protestors who were asking for equal rights and job opportunities."[4]

in the 1930s. Under the leadership of Max Horkheimer, T. W. Adorno, and Leo Lowenthal, this group pointed to at least three inadequacies of traditional scientific approaches to media research, arguing that they (1) reduced large "cultural questions" to measurable and "verifiable categories"; (2) depended on "an atmosphere of rigidly enforced neutrality"; and (3) refused to place "the phenomena of modern life" in a "historical and moral context."[31] The researchers of the Frankfurt

School did not completely reject the usefulness of measuring and counting data. They contended, however, that historical and cultural approaches were also necessary to focus critical attention on the long-range effects of the mass media on audiences.

Since the time of the Frankfurt School, criticisms of the media effects tradition and its methods have continued, with calls for more interpretive studies of the rituals of mass communication. Academics who have embraced a cultural approach to media research try to understand how media and culture are tied to the actual patterns of communication in daily life.

Conducting Cultural Studies Research

Cultural studies research focuses on the investigation of daily experience, especially concerning issues of race, gender, class, and sexuality and the unequal arrangements of power and status in contemporary society. Such research emphasizes how some social and cultural groups have been marginalized and ignored throughout history. Consequently, cultural studies have attempted to recover lost or silenced voices, particularly among African American, Native American, Asian and Asian American, Arab, Latino, Appalachian, LGBT (lesbian, gay, bisexual, and transgender), immigrant, and women's cultures. The major analytical approaches in cultural studies research today are textual analysis, audience studies, and political economy studies.

Textual Analysis

In cultural studies research, **textual analysis** highlights the close reading and interpretation of cultural messages, including those found in books, movies, and TV programs. It is the equivalent of measurement methods like experiments, surveys, and content analysis. While media effects research approaches media messages with the tools of modern science—replicability, objectivity, and data—textual analysis looks at rituals, narratives, and meaning. One type of textual analysis is *framing research*, which looks at recurring media story structures, particularly in news stories. Media sociologist Todd Gitlin defines media frames as "persistent patterns of cognition, interpretation, and presentation, of selection, emphasis, and exclusion, by which symbol-handlers routinely organize discourse, whether verbal or visual."[32]

Although textual analysis has a long and rich history in film and literary studies, it became significant to media in 1974, when Horace Newcomb's *TV: The Most Popular Art* became the first serious academic book to analyze television shows. Newcomb studied why certain TV programs and formats became popular, especially comedies, westerns, mysteries, soap operas, news reports, and sports programs. Newcomb took television programs seriously, examining patterns in the most popular programs at the time, such as the *Beverly Hillbillies*, *Bewitched*, and *Dragnet*, which traditional researchers had usually snubbed or ignored. Trained as a literary scholar, Newcomb argued that content analysis and other social science approaches to popular media often ignored artistic traditions and social context. For Newcomb, "the task for the student of the popular arts is to find a technique through which many different qualities of the work—aesthetic, social, psychological—may be explored" and to discover "why certain formulas . . . are popular in American television."[33]

Before Newcomb's work, textual analysis generally focused only on "important" or highly regarded works of art—debates, films, poems, and books. But by the end of the 1970s, a new generation of media studies scholars, who had grown up on television and rock and roll, began to study less elite forms of culture. These scholars extended the concept of what a "text" is to include architecture, fashion, tabloid magazines, pop icons like Madonna, rock music, hip-hop, soap operas and telenovelas, movies, cockfights, shopping malls, reality TV, Martha Stewart, and professional wrestling in an attempt to make sense of the most taken-for-granted aspects of everyday media culture. Often the study of these seemingly minor elements of popular culture provides insight into

Lisa Wiltse/Getty Images

broader meanings within our society. By shifting the focus to daily popular culture artifacts, cultural studies succeeded in focusing scholarly attention not just on significant presidents, important religious leaders, prominent political speeches, or military battles but on the more ordinary ways that "normal" people organize experience and understand their daily lives.

Audience Studies

Cultural studies research that focuses on how people use and interpret cultural content is called **audience studies**, or *reader-response research*. Audience studies differ from textual analysis because the subject being researched is the audience for the text, not the text itself. For example, in *Reading the Romance: Women, Patriarchy, and Popular Literature*, Janice Radway studied a group of midwestern women who were fans of romance novels. Using her training in literary criticism and employing interviews and questionnaires, Radway investigated the meaning of romance novels to the women. She argued that reading romance novels functions as personal time for some women, whose complex family and work lives leave them very little time for themselves. The study also suggested that these particular romance-novel fans identified with the active, independent qualities of the romantic heroines they most admired. As a cultural study, Radway's work did not claim to be scientific, and her findings are not generalizable to all women. Rather, Radway was interested in investigating and interpreting the relationship between reading romantic fiction and living a conventional life.[34]

Radway's influential cultural research used a variety of interpretive methods, including literary analysis, interviews, and questionnaires. Most important, these studies helped define culture in broad terms—as being made up of both the *products* a society fashions and the *processes* that forge those products.

Political Economy Studies

A focus on the production of popular culture and the forces behind it is the topic of **political economy studies**, which specifically examine interconnections among economic interests, political power, and

Our Masculinity Problem

There have been at least 154 mass shootings (defined as four or more killed) in the United States from 1966 through July 2018 (1,102 people killed, 185 of which were children and teenagers). Half of these shootings have taken place since 2004, and the deadliest have occurred within the past few years.[1] Just some of those that made headlines include the Marjory Stoneman Douglas High School shooting in Parkland, Florida, in 2018 (17 dead, 15 injured); the First Baptist Church shooting in Sutherland Springs, Texas, in 2017 (27 dead, 20 injured); the Route 91 Harvest festival shooting in Las Vegas in 2017 (59 dead, 851 injured); the Pulse nightclub shooting in Orlando in 2016 (49 dead, 53 injured); the Sandy Hook Elementary School shooting in Newtown, Connecticut, in 2012 (28 dead, 2 injured); the Century 16 movie theater shooting in Aurora, Colorado, in 2012 (12 dead, 58 injured); and the Virginia Tech shooting in 2007 (33 dead, 23 injured).

What are the reasons? Our news media respond with a number of usual suspects: the easy availability of guns in the United States; influential movies, television shows, and video games; mental illness; bad parenting. But Jackson Katz—educator, author, and filmmaker (of *Tough Guise* and *Tough Guise 2*)—sees another major factor. The least-talked-about commonality in these shootings is the one so obvious most of us miss it: Nearly all the mass murderers are male (and usually white).

What would psychologists, pundits, and other talking heads be saying if women were responsible for nearly every mass shooting for more than three decades? "If a woman were the shooter," Katz says, "you can bet there would be all sorts of commentary about shifting cultural notions of femininity and how they might have contributed to her act, such as discussions in recent years about girl gang violence."[2]

But women were involved in only three of the 152 mass shootings; all the others had a man (or men) behind the trigger. "Because men represent the dominant gender, their gender is rendered invisible in the discourse about violence," Katz says.[3] In fact, the dominance of masculinity is the norm in our mainstream mass media. Dramatic content is often about the performance of heroic, powerful masculinity (e.g., many action films, digital games, and sports). Similarly, humorous content often derives from calling into question the standards of masculinity (e.g., a man trying to cook, clean, or take care of a child). The same principles apply for the advertising that supports the content. How many

how that power is used. Among the major concerns of political economy studies is the increasing conglomeration of media ownership. This growing concentration of ownership means that the production of media content is being controlled by fewer and fewer organizations, investing those companies with more and more power. In addition, the domination of public discourse by for-profit corporations may mean that the bottom line for all public communication and popular culture is money, not democratic expression.

Political economy studies work best when combined with textual analysis and audience studies, which provide context for understanding the cultural content of a media product, its production process, and how the audience responds. For example, a major media corporation might, for commercial reasons, create a film and market it through a number of venues (political economy),

Archive Photos/Getty Images

automobile, beer, shaving cream, and food commercials peddle products that offer men a chance to maintain or regain their rightful masculinity?

Rachel Kalish and Michael Kimmel, sociologists at SUNY Stonybrook, analyzed the problem of mass shootings that usually end in suicide. They found that males and females have similar rates of suicide attempts. "Feeling aggrieved, wronged by the world— these are typical adolescent feelings, common to many boys and girls," they report.

The results of these attempts, though, differ by gender. Female suicide behaviors are more likely to be a cry for help. Male suicide behaviors, informed by social norms of masculinity, often result in a different outcome:

"aggrieved entitlement." Kalish and Kimmel define this as "a gendered emotion, a fusion of that humiliating loss of manhood and the moral obligation and entitlement to get it back. And its gender is masculine."[4] Retaliation, which is considered acceptable in lesser forms (think of all the cultural narratives in which the weak or aggrieved character finally gets his revenge), becomes horrifying when combined with the immediacy and lethal force of assault firearms. "Aggrieved entitlement" exactly fit the profile of Omar Mateen, the Orlando shooter with a record of misogyny and homophobia.[5]

There is some evidence that the gun industry understands the sense of masculine entitlement but uses that knowledge to sell guns, not to consider how they might be misused. A marketing campaign begun in 2010 for the Bushmaster .223-caliber semiautomatic rifle showed an image of the rifle with the large tagline "Consider Your Man Card Reissued." The Bushmaster was the same civilian assault rifle used by the shooter who massacred twenty-eight people at the Newtown elementary school in 2012.

How do we find a way out of this cultural cycle? "Make gender—specifically the idea that men are gendered beings—a central part of the national conversation about rampage killings," Katz says. "It means looking carefully at how our culture defines manhood, how boys are socialized, and how pressure to stay in the 'man box' not only constrains boys' and men's emotional and relational development, but also their range of choices when faced with life crises."[6]

but the film's meaning or popularity will make sense only within the historical and narrative contexts of the culture (textual analysis), and it may be interpreted by various audiences in ways both anticipated and unexpected (audience studies).

Cultural Studies' Theoretical Perspectives

Developed as an alternative to the predictive theories of social science research (e.g., if X happens, the result will be Y), cultural studies research on media is informed by more general perspectives about how the mass media interact with the world. Two foundational concepts in cultural studies research are (1) the public sphere and (2) the idea of communication as culture.

The Public Sphere

The idea of the **public sphere**, defined as a space for critical public debate, was first advanced by German philosopher Jürgen Habermas in 1962.[35] Habermas, a professor of philosophy, studied late seventeenth-century and eighteenth-century England and France, and he found those societies to be increasingly influenced by free trade and the rise of the printing press. At that historical moment, an emerging middle class began to gather to discuss public life in coffeehouses, meeting halls, and pubs, and to debate the ideas of novels and other publications in literary salons and clubs. In doing so, this group (which did not yet include women, peasants, the working classes, and other minority groups) began to build a society beyond the control of aristocrats, royalty, and religious elites. The outcome of such critical public debate led to support for the right to assembly, free speech, and a free press.

Habermas's research is useful to cultural studies researchers when they consider how democratic societies and the mass media operate today. For Habermas, a democratic society should always work to create the most favorable communication situation possible—a public sphere. Basically, without an open communication system, there can be no democratically functioning society. This fundamental notion is the basis for some arguments on why an open, accessible mass media system is essential. However, Habermas warned that the mass media could also be an enemy of democracy; he cautioned modern societies to be aware of "the manipulative deployment of media power to procure mass loyalty, consumer demand, and 'compliance' with systematic imperatives" by those in power.[36]

Communication as Culture

As Habermas considered the relationship between communication and democracy, media historian James Carey considered the relationship between communication and culture. Carey rejected the "transmission" view of communication—that is, that a message goes simply from sender to receiver. Carey argued that communication is more of a cultural ritual; he famously defined communication as "a symbolic process whereby reality is produced, maintained, repaired, and transformed."[37] Thus, communication creates our reality and maintains that reality in the stories we tell ourselves. For example, think about the novels; movies; and other stories, representations, and symbols that explicitly or tacitly supported discrimination against African Americans in the United States before the Civil Rights movement. When events occur that question reality (like protests and sit-ins in the 1950s and 1960s), communication may repair the culture with adjusted narratives or symbols, or it may completely transform the culture with new dominant symbols. Indeed, analysis of media culture in the 1960s and afterward (including books, movies, TV, and music) suggests a U.S. culture undergoing repair and transformation.

Carey's ritual view of communication leads cultural studies researchers to consider communication's symbolic process as culture itself. Everything that defines our culture—our language, food, clothing, architecture, mass media content, and the like—is a form of symbolic communication that signifies shared (but often still-contested) beliefs about culture at a point in historical time. From this viewpoint, then, cultural studies is tightly linked with communication studies.

PUBLIC SPHERE

Conversations in eighteenth-century English coffeehouses (like the one shown) inspired Jürgen Habermas's public-sphere theory. However, Habermas expressed concerns that the mass media could weaken the public sphere by allowing people to become passive consumers of the information distributed by the media instead of entering into debates with one another about what is best for society. What do you think of such concerns? Has the proliferation of political cable shows, Internet bloggers, and other mediated forums decreased serious public debate, or has it just shifted the conversation to places besides coffeehouses?

CULTURAL STUDIES
researchers are interested in the production and meaning of a wide range of elements within communication culture, as well as audiences' responses to these. ABC's *Blackish* seeks to challenge ideas about black identity by satirically questioning stereotypes, biases, and myths.[38]

Evaluating Cultural Studies Research

In opposition to media effects research, cultural studies research involves interpreting written and visual "texts" or artifacts as symbolic representations that contain cultural, historical, and political meaning. For example, the wave of police and crime TV shows that appeared in the mid-1960s can be interpreted as a cultural response to concerns and fears people had about urban unrest and income disparity. Audiences were drawn to the heroes of these dramas, who often exerted control over forces that, among society in general, seemed out of control. As James Carey put it, the cultural approach—unlike media effects research, which is grounded in the social sciences—"does not seek to explain human behavior, but to understand it. . . . It does not attempt to predict human behavior, but to diagnose human meanings."[39] In other words, a cultural approach does not provide explanations for laws that govern how mass media behave. Rather, it offers interpretations of the stories, messages, and meanings that circulate throughout our culture.

One of the main strengths of cultural studies is the freedom it affords researchers to broadly interpret the impact of the mass media. Because cultural work is not bound by the precise control of variables, researchers can more easily examine the ties between media messages and the broader social, economic, and political world. For example, media effects research on politics has generally concentrated on election polls and voting patterns, while cultural research has broadened the discussion to examine class, gender, and cultural differences among voters and the various uses of power by individuals and institutions in authority. Following Horace Newcomb's work, cultural investigators have expanded the study of media content beyond "serious" works. These researchers have studied many popular forms, including music, movies, and prime-time television.

Just as media effects research has its limits, so does cultural studies research. Sometimes cultural studies have focused exclusively on the meanings of media programs or texts, ignoring their effect on audiences. Some cultural studies, however, have tried to address this deficiency by incorporating audience studies. Today, both media effects and cultural studies researchers have begun to look at the limitations of their work more closely, borrowing ideas from one another to better assess the complexity of the media's meaning and influence.

MEDIA RESEARCH AND DEMOCRACY

One charge frequently leveled at academic studies is that they fail to address the everyday problems of life, often seeming to have little practical application. The growth of mass media departments in colleges and universities has led to an increase in specialized jargon, which tends to alienate and exclude nonacademics. Although media research has built a growing knowledge base and dramatically advanced what we know about the effect of mass media on individuals and societies, the academic world has also built a barrier to that knowledge. That is, the larger public has often been excluded from access to the research process even though cultural research tends to identify with marginalized groups. The scholarship is self-defeating if its complexity removes it from the daily experience of the groups it addresses. Researchers themselves have even found it difficult to speak to one another across domains because of discipline-specific language used to analyze and report findings. For example, understanding the elaborate statistical analyses used to document media effects requires special training.

In some cultural research, the language used is often incomprehensible to students and to other audiences who use mass media. A famous hoax in 1996 pointed out just how inaccessible some academic jargon can be. Alan Sokal, a New York University physics professor, submitted an impenetrable article, "Transgressing the Boundaries: Toward a Transformative Hermeneutics of Quantum Gravity," to a special issue of the academic journal *Social Text* devoted to science and postmodernism. As he had expected, the article—a hoax designed to point out how dense academic jargon can sometimes mask sloppy thinking—was published. According to the journal's editor, about six reviewers had read the article but didn't suspect that it was phony. A public debate ensued after Sokal revealed his hoax. Sokal said he worries that jargon and intellectual fads cause academics to lose contact with the real world and "undermine the prospect for progressive social critique."[40]

In addition, increasing specialization in the 1970s began isolating many researchers from life outside the university. Academics were locked away in their ivory towers, concerned with seemingly obscure matters to which the general public could not relate. Academics across many fields, however, began responding to this isolation and became increasingly active in political and cultural life in the 1980s and 1990s.

PUBLIC INTELLECTUALS

Melissa Harris-Perry is an author, a professor at Wake Forest University, and editor-at-large at ELLE.com. From 2012 to 2016, she hosted an opinion show for MSNBC. Her most recent book is *Sister Citizen: Shame, Stereotypes, and Black Women in America.*

Fred R. Conrad/The New York Times/Redux

In recent years, public intellectuals have encouraged discussion about media production in a digital world. Harvard law professor Lawrence Lessig has been a leading advocate of efforts to rewrite the nation's copyright laws to enable noncommercial "amateur culture" to flourish on the Internet. (Lessig also ran a long-shot campaign for the Democratic presidential nomination in 2016 to advocate for campaign finance reform.) American University's Pat Aufderheide, longtime media critic for the alternative magazine *In These Times*, worked with independent filmmakers to develop the Documentary Filmmakers' Statement of Best Practices in Fair Use, which calls for documentary filmmakers to have reasonable access to copyrighted material for their work.

Like public journalists, public intellectuals based on campuses help carry on the conversations of society and culture, actively circulating the most important new ideas of the day and serving as models for how to participate in public life.

15 Chapter Review

COMMON THREADS

One of the Common Threads discussed in Chapter 1 is the commercial nature of mass media. In controversies about media content, how much of what society finds troubling in the mass media is due more to the commercial nature of the media than to any intrinsic quality of the media themselves?

For some media critics, such as Jaron Lanier in his popular book *Ten Arguments for Deleting Your Social Media Accounts Right Now* (2018), the problems of the mass media are inherent in the technology of the medium (e.g., the immersive nature of social media) and cannot be fixed or reformed. Other researchers focus primarily on the effects of media on individual behavior.

But how much of what critics dislike about social media, television, and other mass media—including violence, indecency, immorality, inadequate journalism, and unfair representations of people and issues—derives from the way in which the mass media are organized in our culture rather than from anything about the technologies themselves or their effects on behavior? In other words, are many of the criticisms of television and other mass media merely masking what should be broader criticisms of capitalism?

One of the keys to accurately analyzing social media and other mass media is to tease apart the effects of a capitalist economy (which organizes media industries and relies on advertising, corporate underwriting, and other forms of sponsorship to profit from them) from the effects of the actual medium (television, movies, the Internet, radio, newspapers). If our media system wasn't commercial in nature—if it wasn't controlled by large corporations—would the same "effects" exist? Would the content change? Would different kinds of movies fill theaters? Would radio play the same music? What would the news be about? Would search engines generate other results?

Basically, would society be learning other things if the mass media were organized in a noncommercial way? Would noncommercial mass media set the same kind of political agenda, or would they cultivate a different kind of reality? What would the spiral of silence theory look like in a noncommercial media system?

Perhaps noncommercial mass media would have their own problems. Indeed, there may be effects that can't be unhitched from the technology of a mass medium no matter what the economy is. But it's worth considering whether any effects are due to the economic system that brings the content to us. If we determine that the commercial nature of the media is a source of negative effects, then we should also reconsider our policy solutions for trying to deal with those effects.

KEY TERMS

The definitions for the terms listed below can be found in the glossary at the end of the book. The page numbers listed with the terms indicate where the term is highlighted in the chapter.

media effects research, 457
cultural studies, 457
propaganda analysis, 458
pseudo-polls, 458
hypodermic-needle model, 461
minimal-effects model, 461
selective exposure, 461
selective retention, 461
uses and gratifications model, 462

scientific method, 462
hypotheses, 463
experiments, 463
random assignment, 463
survey research, 464
longitudinal studies, 464
correlations, 464
content analysis, 464
social learning theory, 466

agenda-setting, 467
cultivation effect, 468
spiral of silence, 468
third-person effect, 468
textual analysis, 472
audience studies, 473
political economy studies, 473
public sphere, 476

REVIEW QUESTIONS

Early Media Research Methods

1. What were the earliest types of media studies, and what were their shortcomings as social scientific approaches?

2. What were the major influences that led to scientific media research?

Research on Media Effects

3. What are the differences between the hypodermic-needle model and the minimal-effects model in the history of media research?

4. What are the differences between experiments and surveys as media research strategies?

5. What is content analysis, and why is it significant?

6. What are the main ideas behind social learning theory, agenda-setting, the cultivation effect, the spiral of silence, and the third-person effect?

7. What are some strengths and limitations of modern media research?

Cultural Approaches to Media Research

8. Why did cultural studies develop in opposition to media effects research?

9. What are the features of cultural studies?

10. How is textual analysis different from content analysis?

11. What are some of the strengths and limitations of cultural studies research?

Media Research and Democracy

12. What is a major criticism about specialization in academic research at universities?

13. How have public intellectuals contributed to society's debates about the mass media?

QUESTIONING THE MEDIA

1. Think about instances in which the mass media have been blamed for a social problem. Could there be another, more accurate cause (an underlying variable) of that problem?

2. One charge leveled against a lot of media research—both the effects and the cultural models—is that it has very little impact on our media institutions. Do you agree or disagree, and why?

3. Do you have a major concern about media in society that hasn't been, but should be, addressed by research? Explain your answer.

4. Can you think of a media issue on which researchers from different fields at a university could team up to study together? Explain.

LAUNCHPAD FOR *MEDIA & CULTURE*

Visit LaunchPad for *Media & Culture* at **launchpadworks.com** for additional learning tools:

- REVIEW WITH LEARNINGCURVE
  LearningCurve, available on LaunchPad for *Media & Culture*, uses gamelike quizzing to help you master the concepts you need to learn from this chapter.

Legal Controls and Freedom of Expression

16

POLITICIANS AND THEIR CONSTITUENTS can talk, but money as speech speaks much louder. Aspects of our present political system amount to a legal pay-to-play system in which the wealthiest can leverage indirect influence over elections (manipulating issues by buying lots of advertising) and more direct influence over legislation (manipulating politicians who desperately want money to pay for campaign advertising).[1] There is plenty of evidence that a majority of Americans dislike this system. For example, a national survey in 2016 found that 76 percent of likely U.S. voters "believe the wealthiest individuals and companies have too much influence over elections."[2] Yet at the same time, the oversized influence of wealthy contributors and businesses is protected by the First Amendment as a form of speech, even though it says nothing explicitly about money. So how did we end up here?

◀ Protesters here are speaking out against the 2010 Supreme Court decision in the *Citizens United v. Federal Election Commission* case. This ruling protects corporations and labor unions, allowing them to spend unlimited amounts of money on TV and radio advertising during elections.

THE ORIGINS OF
FREE EXPRESSION
AND A FREE PRESS
p. 485

FILM AND THE FIRST
AMENDMENT
p. 497

EXPRESSION IN
THE MEDIA: PRINT,
BROADCAST, AND
ONLINE
p. 501

THE FIRST
AMENDMENT AND
DEMOCRACY
p. 507

Ironically, it began with Congress's intention to control the amount of money in elections. In 1974, emerging from the Watergate scandal (President Nixon's illegal tactics in the 1972 election), Congress amended federal election law to further limit campaign contributions. Two years later, in *Buckley v. Valeo* (1976), the U.S. Supreme Court suggested for the first time that political contributions count as speech. The court argued that restrictions on campaign money "necessarily reduce[d] the quantity of expression by restricting the number of issues discussed, the depth of the exploration, and the size of the audience reached. This is because virtually every means of communicating ideas in today's mass society requires the expenditure of money."

Over the ensuing years, Congress has tried to again rein in campaign finance with new laws, but federal courts, beholden to the idea that money equals speech, have always struck them down. This brings us to the current state of our national elections. The two main political parties and their supporters spent $6.2 billion on campaign advertising for the 2012 presidential and congressional election and $6.4 billion for the 2016 election. (Social media and candidate Trump's extensive news coverage gave him an estimated $5.6 billion in free media coverage, an unprecedented amount, which kept the cost of the presidential election slightly lower than in 2012.)[3] The main explanation for why corporations and rich individuals can now spend extraordinary amounts lies in another decision by the Supreme Court, *Citizens United v. Federal Election Commission* (2010). The five-to-four decision said that it was a violation of First Amendment free-speech rights for the federal government to limit spending for TV and radio advertising, usually done through organized Super PACs (political action committees), which are most often sponsored by corporate interests or super-rich donors.

While the Supreme Court decision ran counter to public opinion, many advocates on the political Right and some on the Left offered that the First Amendment means what it says: "Congress shall make no law." Traditional First Amendment supporters like Gene Policinski of the First Amendment Center argue that the "good intentions" behind the idea of limiting campaign spending "don't justify ignoring a basic concept that the Supreme Court majority pointed out in its ruling: Nothing in the First Amendment provides for 'more or less' free-speech protection depending on who is speaking."[4]

An advantage in advertising spending is only one of many variables. Nevertheless, those with limited means are at a clear disadvantage compared to those who have money when it comes to buying expensive commercial speech and shaping the direction of a presidential campaign. Harvard Law School professor Lawrence Lessig argues that money corrupted American politics long before the *Citizens United* ruling. "Politicians are dependent upon 'the funders'—spending anywhere from 30 percent to 70 percent of their time raising money from these funders," he wrote. "But 'the funders' are not 'the People': .26 percent of Americans give more than $200 in a congressional campaign; .05 percent give the max to any congressional candidate; .01 percent—the 1 percent of the 1 percent—give more than $10,000 in an election cycle; and .0000063 percent have given close to 80 percent of the super PAC money spent in this election so far. That's 196 Americans."[5] Given the *Citizens United* ruling, what can be done to give all citizens a voice in the campaign finance system and make them "patrons" of the political process?

THE CULTURAL AND POLITICAL STRUGGLES OVER WHAT CONSTITUTES FREE SPEECH or free expression have defined American democracy. In 1989, when Supreme Court justice William Brennan Jr. was asked to comment on his favorite part of the Constitution, he replied, "The First Amendment, I expect. Its enforcement gives us this society. The other provisions of the Constitution really only embellish it." Of all the issues that involve the mass media and popular culture, none is more central—or explosive—than freedom of expression and the First Amendment. Our nation's historical development can often be traced to how much or how little we tolerated speech during particular periods.

The current era is as volatile a time as ever for free-speech issues. Contemporary free-speech debates include copyright issues, hate-speech codes on college and university campuses, explicit lyrics in music, violent images in film and television, the swapping of media files on the Internet, and the right of the press to publish government secrets.

In this chapter, we will:

- Examine free-expression issues, focusing on the implications of the First Amendment for a variety of mass media
- Investigate the models of expression, the origins of free expression, and the First Amendment
- Examine the prohibition of censorship and how the First Amendment has been challenged and limited throughout U.S. history
- Focus on the impact of gag orders, shield laws, the use of cameras in the courtroom, and some of the clashes between the First Amendment and the Sixth Amendment
- Review the social and political pressures that gave rise to early censorship boards and the current film ratings system
- Discuss First Amendment issues in broadcasting, considering why broadcasting has been treated differently from print media
- Explore the newest frontier in free expression—the Internet

One of the most important laws relating to the media is the First Amendment. While you've surely heard about its protections, do you know how or why it was put in place? Have you ever known someone who had to fight to express an idea—for example, was anyone in your high school ever sent home for wearing a certain T-shirt or hat that school officials deemed "offensive"? Have you ever felt that your access to some media content was restricted or censored? What were the circumstances, and how did you respond? For more questions to help you understand the role of freedom of expression in our lives, see "Questioning the Media" in the Chapter Review.

THE ORIGINS OF FREE EXPRESSION AND A FREE PRESS

When students from other cultures attend school in the United States, many are astounded by the number of books, news articles, editorials, cartoons, films, TV shows, and websites that make fun of U.S. presidents, the military, and the police. Many countries' governments throughout history have jailed, or even killed, their citizens for such speech "violations." For instance, between 1992 and July 2018, more than thirteen hundred international journalists were killed in the line of duty, often because someone disagreed with what they wrote or reported.[6] In the United States, however, we have generally taken for granted our right to criticize and poke fun at the government and other authority figures. Moreover, many of us are unaware of the ideas that underpin our freedoms and don't realize the extent to which those freedoms surpass those in most other countries.

In fact, a 2017 survey related that 45 percent of the world's population live in countries with virtually no freedom of the press, with those governments exercising tight control over the news media and even intimidating, jailing, and executing journalists. Only 13 percent of people on the planet live in a country with a free media system.[7]

John Moore/AP Images

JOURNALISTS IN IRAQ

During the Iraq War, journalists were embedded with troops to provide "frontline" coverage. The freedom the U.S. press had to report on the war came at a cost. According to the Committee to Protect Journalists, 277 journalists and media workers were killed or went missing in Iraq between 2003 and 2018 as a result of hostile actions.

Today, given the diversity among nations, the experimentation of journalists, and the collapse of many communist press systems, these categories are no longer as relevant. Nevertheless, they offer a good point of departure for discussing the press and democracy.

The First Amendment of the U.S. Constitution

To understand the development of free expression in the United States, we must first understand how the idea for a free press came about. In various European countries throughout the seventeenth century, in order to monitor—and punish, if necessary—the speech of editors and writers, governments controlled the circulation of ideas through the press by requiring printers to obtain licenses from them. However, in 1644, English poet John Milton, author of *Paradise Lost*, published his essay *Areopagitica*, which opposed government licenses for printers and defended a free press. Milton argued that all sorts of ideas, even false ones, should be allowed to circulate freely in a democratic society because eventually the truth would emerge. In 1695, England stopped licensing newspapers, and

TABLE 16.1

MODELS OF EXPRESSION

MODELS OF EXPRESSION	
Since the mid-1950s, four conventional models for speech and journalism have been used to categorize the widely differing ideas underlying free expression.[8] These models are distinguished by the levels of freedom permitted and by the attitudes of the ruling and political classes toward the freedoms granted to the average citizen.	
AUTHORITARIAN	Developed in sixteenth-century England (at about the time the printing press first arrived), advocates of this model believe the general public needs guidance from an elite, educated ruling class. An authoritarian government censors the media that critiques its actions, and supports the media that is sympathetic to its agenda and the agenda of the ruling class. Today, authoritarian systems operate in many developing countries throughout Asia, Latin America, and Africa, where journalism often joins with government and business to foster economic growth, minimize political dissent, and promote social stability. Authoritarianism has also reemerged in European countries such as Hungary and Poland. In these societies, both reporters and citizens may be punished if they question leaders and the status quo too fiercely.
COMMUNIST OR **STATE**	The government controls the press because state leaders believe the press should serve government goals. Ideas that challenge the basic premises of state authority are not tolerated. A few countries still using this model include China, Cuba, North Korea, and Turkmenistan.
SOCIAL RESPONSIBILITY	Social responsibility characterizes the ideals of mainstream journalism in the United States. The press is usually privately owned (although the government technically operates the broadcast media in most European democracies). The press is also free to function as a *Fourth Estate*— that is, an unofficial branch of government that monitors the legislative, judicial, and executive branches for abuses of power and provides information necessary for self-governance.
LIBERTARIAN	A more radical extension of the social responsibility model is libertarianism, which encourages vigorous government criticism and supports the highest degree of individual and press freedoms. Under this model, no restrictions are placed on the mass media or on individual speech. Libertarians tolerate the expression of everything, from publishing pornography to advocating anarchy. In North America and Europe, many alternative newspapers and magazines operate on such a model.

Data from: Fred Siebert, Theodore Peterson, and Wilbur Schramm, *Four Theories of the Press* (Urbana: University of Illinois Press, 1956).

most of Europe followed. In many democracies today, publishing a newspaper, magazine, or newsletter remains one of the few public or service enterprises that requires no license.

Less than a hundred years later, the writers of the U.S. Constitution were ambivalent about the freedom of the press. In fact, the Constitution as originally ratified in 1788 didn't include a guarantee of freedom of the press. Constitutional framer Alexander Hamilton thought it impractical to attempt to define "liberty of the press" and believed that whatever declarations might be added to the Constitution, its security would ultimately depend on public opinion. At that time, though, nine of the original thirteen states had charters defending the freedom of the press, and the states pushed to have federal guarantees of free speech and a free press approved at the first session of the new Congress. The Bill of Rights, which contained the first ten amendments to the Constitution, was adopted in 1791.

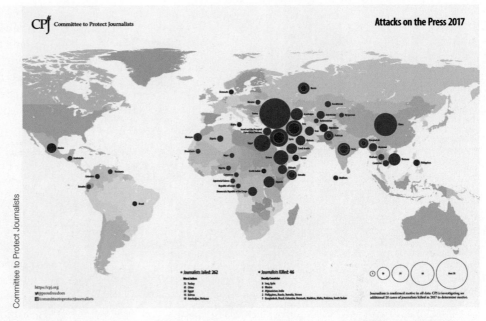

Committee to Protect Journalists

PRESS FREEDOM
This map shows the number and location of journalists killed between 1992 and 2018.

The commitment to freedom of the press, however, was not resolute. In 1798, the Federalist Party, which controlled the presidency and Congress, passed the Sedition Act to silence opposition to an anticipated war against France. Led by President John Adams, the Federalists believed that defamatory articles by the opposition Democratic-Republican Party might stir up discontent against the government and undermine its authority. Over the next three years, twenty-five individuals were arrested and ten were convicted under the act, which was also used to prosecute anti-Federalist newspapers. After failing to curb opposition, the Sedition Act expired in 1801 during Thomas Jefferson's presidency. Jefferson, a Democratic-Republican who had challenged the act's constitutionality, pardoned all defendants convicted under it.[9] Ironically, the Sedition Act, the first major attempt to constrain the First Amendment, became the defining act in solidifying American support behind the notion of a free press. As journalism historian Michael Schudson explained, "Only in the wake of the Sedition Act did Americans boldly embrace a free press as a necessary bulwark of a liberal civil order."[10]

Censorship as Prior Restraint

In the United States, the First Amendment has theoretically prohibited censorship. Over time, Supreme Court decisions have defined censorship as **prior restraint**. This means that courts and governments cannot block any publication or speech before it actually occurs, on the principle that a law has not been broken until an illegal act has been committed. In 1931, for example, the Supreme Court determined in *Near v. Minnesota* that a Minneapolis newspaper could not be stopped from publishing "scandalous and defamatory" material about police and law officials whom they felt were negligent in arresting and punishing local gangsters.[11] However, the Court left open the idea that the news media could be ordered to halt publication in exceptional cases. During a declared war, for instance, if a U.S. court judged that the publication of an article would threaten national security, such expression could be restrained prior to its printing. In fact, during World War I, the U.S. Navy seized all wireless radio transmitters. This was done to ensure control over critical information about weather conditions and troop movements that might inadvertently aid the enemy. In the 1970s, though, the Pentagon Papers decision and the *Progressive* magazine case tested important concepts underlying prior restraint.

Bettmann/Getty Images

PRIOR RESTRAINT

In 1971, Daniel Ellsberg surrendered to government prosecutors in Boston. Ellsberg was a former Pentagon researcher who turned against America's military policy in Vietnam and leaked information to the press. He was charged with unauthorized possession of top-secret federal documents. Later called the Pentagon Papers, the documents contained evidence on the military's bungled handling of the Vietnam War. In 1973, an exasperated federal judge dismissed the case when illegal government-sponsored wiretaps of Ellsberg's psychoanalyst came to light during the Watergate scandal.

The Pentagon Papers Case

In 1971, with the Vietnam War still in progress, Daniel Ellsberg, a former Defense Department employee, stole a copy of the forty-seven-volume report *History of U.S. Decision-Making Process on Vietnam Policy*. A thorough study of U.S. involvement in Vietnam since World War II, the report was classified by the government as top secret. Ellsberg and a friend leaked the study—nicknamed the Pentagon Papers—to the *New York Times* and the *Washington Post*. In June 1971, the *Times* began publishing articles based on the study. To block any further publication, the Nixon administration applied for and received a federal court injunction against the *Times*, arguing that the publication of these documents posed "a clear and present danger" to national security.

A lower U.S. district court supported the newspaper's right to publish, but the government's appeal put the case before the Supreme Court less than three weeks after the first article was published. In a six-to-three vote, the Court sided with the newspaper. Justice Hugo Black, in his majority opinion, attacked the government's attempt to suppress publication: "Both the history and language of the First Amendment support the view that the press must be left free to publish news, whatever the source, without censorship, injunctions, or prior restraints."[12] (See "Media Literacy and the Critical Process: Who Knows the First Amendment?" on page 490.)

The *Progressive* Magazine Case

The issue of prior restraint for national security surfaced again in 1979 with an injunction being issued to the editors of the *Progressive*—a national left-wing magazine—to stop publication of an article titled "The H-Bomb Secret: How We Got It, Why We're Telling It." The dispute began when the editor of the magazine sent a draft to the Department of Energy to verify technical portions of the article. Believing that the article contained sensitive data that might damage U.S. efforts to halt the proliferation of nuclear weapons, the Energy Department asked the magazine not to publish it. When the magazine said it would proceed anyway, the government sued the *Progressive* and asked a federal district court to block publication.

Judge Robert Warren sought to balance the *Progressive*'s First Amendment rights against the government's claim that the article would spread dangerous information and undermine national security. In an unprecedented action, Warren sided with the government, deciding that "a mistake in ruling against the United States could pave the way for thermonuclear annihilation for us all. In that event, our right to life is extinguished and the right to publish becomes moot."[13] During appeals and further litigation, several other publications, including the *Milwaukee Sentinel* and *Scientific American*, published their own articles related to the H-bomb, getting much of their information from publications already in circulation. None of these articles—including the one eventually published in the *Progressive* after the government dropped the case during an appeal—contained the precise technical details needed to actually design a nuclear weapon, nor did they provide information on where to obtain the sensitive ingredients.

Even though the article was eventually published, Warren's decision stands as the first time in American history that a prior-restraint order imposed in the name of national security actually stopped the initial publication of a controversial news report.

Unprotected Forms of Expression

Despite the First Amendment's provision that "Congress shall make no law" restricting speech, the federal government has made a number of laws that do just that, especially concerning false or misleading advertising, expressions that intentionally threaten public safety, and certain speech that compromises war strategy and other issues of national security.

Beyond the federal government, state laws and local ordinances have on occasion curbed expression, and over the years the court system has determined that some kinds of expression do not merit protection under the Constitution, including seditious expression, copyright infringement, libel, obscenity, the right to privacy, and expression that interferes with the Sixth Amendment.

Seditious Expression

For more than a century after the Sedition Act of 1798, Congress passed no laws prohibiting dissenting opinion. But by the twentieth century, the sentiments of the Sedition Act reappeared in times of war. For instance, the Espionage Acts of 1917 and 1918, which were enforced during World Wars I and II, made it a federal crime to disrupt the nation's war effort, authorizing severe punishment for seditious statements.

In the landmark *Schenck v. United States* (1919) appeal case during World War I, the Supreme Court upheld the conviction of a Socialist Party leader, Charles T. Schenck, for distributing leaflets urging American men to protest the draft, in violation of the recently passed Espionage Act. In upholding the conviction, Justice Oliver Wendell Holmes wrote two of the more famous interpretations and phrases in the First Amendment's legal history:

But the character of every act depends upon the circumstances in which it is done. The most stringent protection of free speech would not protect a man in falsely shouting fire in a theater and causing a panic.

The question in every case is whether the words used are used in such circumstances and are of such a nature as to create a clear and present danger that they will bring about the substantive evils that Congress has a right to prevent.

In supporting Schenck's sentence—a ten-year prison term—Holmes noted that the Socialist leaflets were entitled to First Amendment protection, but only during times of peace. In establishing the "clear and present danger" criterion for expression, the Supreme Court demonstrated the limits of the First Amendment.

Copyright Infringement

Appropriating a writer's or an artist's words or music without consent or payment is also a form of expression that is not protected as speech. A **copyright** legally protects the rights of authors and producers to their published or unpublished writing, music, lyrics, TV programs, movies, or graphic art designs. When Congress passed the first Copyright Act in 1790, it gave authors the right to control their published works for fourteen years, with the opportunity for a renewal for another fourteen

Enacted in 1791, the First Amendment supports not just press and speech freedoms but also religious freedom and the right of people to protest and to "petition the government for a redress of grievances." It also says that "Congress shall make no law" abridging or prohibiting these five freedoms. To investigate some critics' charge that many citizens don't exactly know the protections offered in the First Amendment, conduct your own survey. Discuss with friends, family, or colleagues what they know or think about the First Amendment.

1 DESCRIPTION

Working alone or in small groups, find eight to ten people you know from two different age groups: (1) from your peers and friends or younger siblings, and (2) from your parents' or grandparents' generations. (Do not choose students from your class.) Interview your subjects individually, in person, by phone, or by e-mail, and ask them this question: "Would you approve of the following law if Congress were considering it?" Then offer the First Amendment, but don't tell them what it is. Then ask them to respond to the following series of questions, adding any other questions that you think would be appropriate:

1. Do you agree or disagree with the freedoms? Explain.
2. Which do you support, and which do you think are excessive or provide too much freedom?
3. Do you recognize the law? (Note how many of your subjects identify it as the First Amendment to the U.S. Constitution and how many do not. Note the percentage from each age group.)
4. Optional: If you are willing to do so, please share your political leanings—Republican, Democrat, Independent, not sure, disaffected, apathetic, or other.

Record their answers.

2 ANALYSIS

What patterns emerge in the answers from the two groups? Are the answers similar or different? How? Note any differences in the answers based on gender, level of education, or occupation.

3 INTERPRETATION

What do these patterns mean? Are your interview subjects supportive or unsupportive of the First Amendment? What are their reasons?

4 EVALUATION

How do your interviewees judge the freedoms? In general, what did your interview subjects know about the First Amendment? What impresses you about your subjects' answers? Do you find anything alarming or troubling in their answers?

5 ENGAGEMENT

Research free expression, and locate any national studies that are similar to this assignment. Then, check the recent national surveys on attitudes toward the First Amendment at www.freedomforuminstitute.org /first-amendment-center/state-of -the-first-amendment. Based on your research, educate others. Do a presentation in class or at your college or university about the First Amendment.

---

years. At the end of the copyright period, the work would enter the **public domain**, which would give the public free access to the work. The idea was that a period of copyright control would give authors financial incentive to create original works, and that the public domain would give others incentive to create derivative works.

Over the years, as artists lived longer and, more important, as corporate copyright owners became more common, copyright periods were extended by Congress. In 1976, Congress extended the copyright period to the life of the author plus fifty years, or seventy-five years for a corporate copyright owner. In 1998, as copyrights on such works as Disney's Mickey Mouse were approaching expiration, Congress again extended the copyright period for twenty additional years—the eleventh time in forty years that the terms for copyright had been extended.[14] Barring any last-minute extensions of the copyright period, a number of works from 1923—including *The Great American Novel* by William Carlos Williams, *The Prophet* by Kahlil Gibran, *The World Crisis* by Winston Churchill, Charlie

Chaplin's film *The Pilgrim*, Cecil B. DeMille's *The 10 Commandments*, and a number of music compositions and artwork—will finally fall into the public domain on January 1, 2019, with more to come on the first day of subsequent years.[15]

Corporate owners have millions of dollars to gain by keeping their properties out of the public domain. Disney, a major lobbyist for the 1998 extension, would have lost its copyright to Mickey Mouse in 2004 but now continues to earn millions on its movies, T-shirts, and Mickey Mouse watches through 2024. Warner/Chappell Music, which made up to $2 million a year in royalties from the popular "Happy Birthday to You" song, lost its copyright in a 2015 lawsuit in which a U.S. district court judge ruled that it didn't have a valid claim to the 120-year-old song.

Today, nearly every innovation in digital culture creates new questions about copyright law. For example, is a video mash-up that samples copyrighted sounds and images a copyright violation or a creative accomplishment protected under the concept of *fair use* (the same standard that enables students to legally quote attributed text from other works in their research papers)? Is it fair use for a blog to quote an entire newspaper article as long as it has a link and an attribution? Should news aggregators like Google News and Facebook pay something to financially strapped newspapers when they link to their articles? One of the laws that tips the debates toward stricter enforcement of copyright is the Digital Millennium Copyright Act of 1998, which outlaws any action or technology that circumvents copyright protection systems. In other words, it may be illegal to merely create or distribute technology that enables someone to make illegal copies of digital content, such as a music file or a movie.

Libel

The biggest legal worry that haunts editors and publishers is the issue of libel, a form of expression that, unlike political expression, is not protected as free speech under the First Amendment. **Libel** refers to defamation of character in written or broadcast form; libel is different from **slander**, which is spoken language that defames a person's character. Inherited from British common law, libel is generally defined as a false statement that holds a person up to public ridicule, contempt, or hatred or injures a person's business or occupation. Examples of libelous statements include falsely accusing someone of professional dishonesty or incompetence (such as medical malpractice), falsely accusing a person of a crime (such as drug dealing), falsely stating that someone is mentally ill or engages in unacceptable behavior (such as public drunkenness), or falsely accusing a person of associating with a disreputable organization or cause (such as the Mafia or a neo-Nazi military group).

Since 1964, the *New York Times v. Sullivan* case has served as the standard for libel law. The case stems from a 1960 full-page advertisement placed in the *New York Times* by the Committee to Defend Martin Luther King and the Struggle for Freedom in the South. Without naming names, the ad criticized the law-enforcement tactics used in southern cities—including Montgomery, Alabama—to break up Civil Rights demonstrations. The ad condemned "southern violators of the Constitution" bent on destroying King and the movement. Taking exception, the city commissioner of Montgomery, L. B. Sullivan, sued the *Times* for libel, claiming the ad defamed him indirectly. Although Alabama civil courts awarded Sullivan $500,000, the newspaper's lawyers appealed to the Supreme Court, which unanimously reversed the ruling, holding that Alabama libel law violated the *Times'* First Amendment rights.[16]

Richard Stonehouse/Camera Press/Redux

Andy Warhol

THE LIMITS OF COPYRIGHT

The iconic album art for the Velvet Underground's 1967 debut—a banana print designed by artist Andy Warhol—has been a subject of controversy in recent years, as a copyright dispute between the Andy Warhol Foundation for the Visual Arts and the rock band has continued to flourish. The most recent disagreement occurred when the Warhol Foundation, which had previously accused the Velvet Underground of violating its claim to the print, announced plans to license the banana design for iPhone cases. Accusing the foundation of copyright violation, the band filed a copyright claim to the design, which a federal judge later dismissed.

LIBEL AND THE MEDIA

A 1960 *New York Times* advertisement triggered one of the most influential and important libel cases in U.S. history by criticizing law-enforcement tactics used against Martin Luther King (pictured above) and the Civil Rights movement. The behind-the-scenes machinations of King's later Alabama demonstrations are the subject of the film *Selma*.

As part of the *Sullivan* decision, the Supreme Court asked future civil courts to distinguish whether plaintiffs in libel cases are public officials or private individuals. Citizens with more "ordinary" jobs, such as city sanitation employees, undercover police informants, nurses, or unknown actors, are normally classified as private individuals. Private individuals have to prove (1) that the public statement about them was false, (2) that damages or actual injury occurred (such as the loss of a job, harm to reputation, public humiliation, or mental anguish), and (3) that the publisher or broadcaster was negligent in failing to determine the truthfulness of the statement.

There are two categories of public figures: (1) public celebrities (movie or sports stars) or people who "occupy positions of such pervasive power and influence that they are deemed public figures for all purposes" (presidents, senators, mayors), and (2) individuals who have thrown themselves—usually voluntarily but sometimes involuntarily—into the middle of "a significant public controversy," such as a lawyer defending a prominent client, an advocate for an antismoking ordinance, or a labor union activist.

Public officials also have to prove falsehood, damages, negligence, and actual malice on the part of the news medium; **actual malice** means that the reporter or editor knew that the statement was false and either printed (or broadcast) it anyway or acted with a reckless disregard for the truth. Because actual malice against a public official is hard to prove, it is difficult for public figures to win libel suits. The *Sullivan* decision allowed news operations to aggressively pursue legitimate news stories without fear of continuous litigation. However, the mere threat of a libel suit still scares off many in the news media. Plaintiffs may also belong to one of many vague classification categories, such as public high school teachers, police officers, and court-appointed attorneys. Individuals from these professions end up as public or private citizens depending on a particular court's ruling.

Defenses against Libel Charges

Since the 1730s, the best defense against libel in American courts has been the truth. In most cases, if libel defendants can demonstrate that they printed or broadcast statements that were essentially true, such evidence usually bars plaintiffs from recovering any damages—even if their reputations were harmed.

In addition, there are other defenses against libel. Prosecutors, for example, who would otherwise be vulnerable to being accused of libel, are granted *absolute privilege* in a court of law so that they are not prevented from making accusatory statements toward defendants. The reporters who print or broadcast statements made in court are also protected against libel; they are granted conditional or **qualified privilege**, allowing them to report judicial or legislative proceedings even though the public statements being reported may be libelous.

Another defense against libel is the rule of **opinion and fair comment**. Generally, libel applies only to intentional misstatements of factual information rather than opinion, and therefore opinions are protected from libel. However, because the line between fact and opinion is often hazy, lawyers advise journalists to first set forth the facts on which a viewpoint is based and then state their opinion based on those facts. In other words, journalists should make it clear that a statement of opinion is a criticism and not an allegation of fact.

Libel laws also protect satire, comedy, and opinions expressed in reviews of books, plays, movies, and restaurants. Such laws may not, however, protect malicious statements in which plaintiffs can prove that defendants used their free-speech rights to mount a damaging personal attack.

Obscenity

For most of this nation's history, legislators have argued that **obscenity** does not constitute a legitimate form of expression protected by the First Amendment. The problem, however, is that little agreement has existed on how to define an obscene work. In the 1860s, a court could judge an entire

Howard Sochurek/Getty Images

book obscene if it contained a single passage believed capable of "corrupting" a person. In fact, throughout the nineteenth century, certain government authorities outside the courts—especially U.S. post office and customs officials—held the power to censor or destroy material they deemed obscene.

This began to change in the 1930s, during the trial involving the celebrated novel *Ulysses* by Irish writer James Joyce. Portions of *Ulysses* had been serialized in the early 1920s in an American magazine, *Little Review*, copies of which were later seized and burned by postal officials. The publishers of the magazine were fined $50 and nearly sent to prison. Because of the four-letter words contained in the novel and the book-burning and fining incidents, British and American publishing houses backed away from the book, and in 1928, the U.S. Customs Office officially banned *Ulysses* as an

John Phillips/Getty Images

obscene work. Ultimately, however, Random House agreed to publish the work in the United States if it was declared "legal." Finally, in 1933, a U.S. judge ruled that an important literary work such as *Ulysses* was a legitimate, protected form of expression, even if portions of the book were deemed objectionable by segments of the population.

The current legal definition of obscenity derives from the 1973 *Miller v. California* case, which stated that to qualify as obscenity, the material must meet three criteria: (1) the average person, applying contemporary community standards, would find that the material as a whole appeals to prurient interest; (2) the material depicts or describes sexual conduct in a patently offensive way; and (3) the material, as a whole, lacks serious literary, artistic, political, or scientific value. The *Miller* decision contained two important ideas. First, it acknowledged that different communities and regions of the country have different values and standards with which to judge obscenity. Second, it required that a work be judged *as a whole*, so that publishers could not use the loophole of inserting a political essay or literary poem into pornographic materials to demonstrate in court that their publications contained redeeming features.

Since the *Miller* decision, courts have granted great latitude to printed and visual obscenity. By the 1990s, major prosecutions had become rare—aimed mostly at child pornography—as the legal system accepted the concept that a free and democratic society must tolerate even repulsive kinds of speech. Most battles over obscenity are now online, where the global reach of the Internet has eclipsed the concept of community standards. A new complication in defining pornography has emerged with cases of "sexting," in which minors produce and send sexually graphic images of themselves via cell phones or the Internet.

The Right to Privacy

Whereas libel laws safeguard a person's character and reputation, the right to privacy protects an individual's peace of mind and personal feelings. In the simplest terms, the **right to privacy** addresses a person's right to be left alone, without his or her name, image, or daily activities becoming public property. Invasions of privacy occur in different situations, the most common of which are intrusion into someone's personal space via unauthorized tape recording, photographing, wiretapping, and the like; making available to the public personal records, such as health and

ACTOR JOHNNY DEPP brought a £200,000 libel lawsuit against the tabloid newspaper the *Sun* in 2018. In late 2017, during production of the latest installment of the *Fantastic Beasts* movie series, Depp was accused of assault by his ex-wife Amber Heard, right. When *Harry Potter* and *Fantastic Beasts* author J. K. Rowling publicly supported Depp, who was starring in this latest movie of her franchise, the *Sun* criticized her for her support of a "wife-beater," as it referred to Depp.

HULK HOGAN'S

successful lawsuit against the entertainment website *Gawker* set an important precedent for celebrities and other public figures, who are normally not protected against invasions of privacy.

phone records; disclosure of personal information, such as religion, sexual activities, or personal activities; and unauthorized appropriation of someone's image or name for advertising or other commercial purposes. In general, the news media have been granted wide protections under the First Amendment to do their work.

Public figures, however, have received some legal relief, as many local municipalities and states have passed "anti-paparazzi" laws that protect individuals from unwarranted scrutiny and surveillance of personal activities on private property or outside public forums.

In a recent test of the boundaries of privacy for public figures, a Florida jury in 2016 ordered gossip entertainment website *Gawker* to pay more than $140 million to Terry G. Bollea, better known as the former professional wrestler Hulk Hogan. In 2012, *Gawker* posted a brief excerpt of a grainy sex tape that showed Bollea having sex with his best friend's wife. *Gawker* argued that its actions were protected by the First Amendment and that Bollea was a public figure who had often talked about his sex life in media interviews. But the jury determined that Bollea's privacy had been violated, and it awarded him the huge sum for emotional distress, economic distress, and punitive damages. Gawker and Bollea reached a settlement of $31 million, but the litigation shattered Gawker, which declared bankruptcy and then sold itself to Univision for $135 million.

A number of laws also protect the privacy of regular citizens. For example, the Privacy Act of 1974 protects individuals' records from public disclosure unless individuals give written consent. The Electronic Communications Privacy Act of 1986 extended the law to computer-stored data and the Internet, although subsequent court decisions ruled that employees have no privacy rights in electronic communications conducted on their employer's equipment. The USA PATRIOT Act of 2001, however, weakened the earlier laws and gave the federal government more latitude in searching private citizens' records and intercepting electronic communications without a court order.

In early 2016, there was a brief but significant standoff between the FBI and Apple over the FBI's getting access to an iPhone. The phone in question was recovered from one of the terrorists in the December 2015 attack in San Bernardino, California. A court ordered Apple to create a software key for the FBI to unlock the iPhone. Apple responded that writing such software would potentially make all iPhones subject to FBI scrutiny and could make them more susceptible to other hackers. A day before a court hearing on the matter, the FBI withdrew its case, saying that it had cracked the code to access the iPhone itself. Yet the question remains whether technology companies like Apple should provide customers (most of whom have the best intentions) with the most robust privacy possible or assist law-enforcement agencies (which could include those from authoritarian nations) in gaining access to their products. In 2018, Apple announced it would close the software loophole that enabled the FBI to gain access to the iPhone.

First Amendment versus Sixth Amendment

Over the years, First Amendment protections of speech and the press have often clashed with the Sixth Amendment, which guarantees an accused individual in "all criminal prosecutions . . . the right to a speedy and public trial, by an impartial jury." In 1954, for example, the Sam Sheppard case garnered enormous nationwide publicity and became the inspiration for the TV show and film *The Fugitive*. Featuring lurid details about the murder of Sheppard's wife, the press editorialized in favor of Sheppard's quick arrest; some papers even pronounced him guilty. A prominent and wealthy osteopath, Sheppard was convicted of the murder, but twelve years later Sheppard's new lawyer, F. Lee Bailey, argued before the Supreme Court that his client had not received a fair trial because of prejudicial publicity in the press. The Court overturned the conviction and freed Sheppard.

Gag Orders and Shield Laws

A major criticism of recent criminal cases concerns the ways in which lawyers use the news media to comment publicly on cases that are pending or are in trial. After the Sheppard reversal in the 1960s, the Supreme Court introduced safeguards that judges could employ to ensure fair trials in heavily publicized cases. These included sequestering juries (Sheppard's jury was not sequestered); moving cases to other jurisdictions; limiting the number of reporters; and placing restrictions, or **gag orders**, on lawyers and witnesses. In some countries, courts have issued gag orders to prohibit the press from releasing information or giving commentary that might prejudice jury selection or cause an unfair trial. In the United States, however, especially since a Supreme Court review in 1976, gag orders have been struck down as a prior-restraint violation of the First Amendment.

In opposition to gag orders, **shield laws** have favored the First Amendment rights of reporters, protecting them from having to reveal their sources for controversial information used in news stories. The news media have argued that protecting the confidentiality of key sources maintains a reporter's credibility, protects a source from possible retaliation, and serves the public interest by providing information that citizens might not otherwise receive. In the 1960s, when the First Amendment rights of reporters clashed with Sixth Amendment fair-trial concerns, judges usually favored the Sixth Amendment arguments. In 1972, a New Jersey journalist became the first reporter jailed for contempt of court for refusing to identify sources in a probe of the Newark housing authority. Since that case, forty states and the District of Columbia have adopted some type of shield law, and other states (except Wyoming) have established some shield law protection through legal precedent. There is no federal shield law in the United States, leaving journalists exposed to subpoenas from federal prosecutors and courts. Revelations that the U.S. Department of Justice had obtained phone records of the Associated Press renewed calls for a federal shield law in 2013.

Cameras in the Courtroom

The debates over limiting intrusive electronic broadcast equipment and photographers in the courtroom actually date to the sensationalized coverage of the Bruno Hauptmann trial in the mid-1930s. Hauptmann was convicted and executed for the kidnap-murder of the nineteen-month-old son of Anne and Charles Lindbergh (the aviation hero who made the first solo flight across the Atlantic Ocean in 1927). During the trial, Hauptmann and his attorney complained that the circus atmosphere fueled by the presence of radio and flash cameras prejudiced the jury and turned the public against him.

After the trial, the American Bar Association amended its professional ethics code, Canon 35, stating that electronic equipment in the courtroom detracted "from the essential dignity of the proceedings." Calling for a ban on photographers and radio equipment, the association believed that if such elements were not banned, lawyers would begin playing to audiences and negatively alter the

MEDIA IN THE COURTROOM

Photographers surround aviator Charles A. Lindbergh (without hat) as he leaves the courthouse in Flemington, New Jersey, during the trial in 1935 of Bruno Hauptmann on charges of kidnapping and murdering Lindbergh's infant son.

judicial process. For years after the Hauptmann trial, almost every state banned photographic, radio, and TV equipment from courtrooms.

As broadcast equipment became more portable and less obtrusive, however, and as television became the major news source for most Americans, courts gradually reevaluated their bans on broadcast equipment. In fact, in the early 1980s, the Supreme Court ruled that the presence of TV equipment did not make it impossible for a fair trial to occur, leaving it up to each state to implement its own system. The ruling opened the door for the debut of Court TV (now truTV) in 1991 and the televised O.J. Simpson trial of 1994 (the most publicized case in history). All states today allow television coverage of cases, although most states place certain restrictions on coverage of courtrooms, often leaving it up to the discretion of the presiding judge. While U.S. federal courts now allow limited TV coverage of their trials, the Supreme Court continues to ban TV from its proceedings; in 2000, however, the Court broke its anti-radio rule by permitting delayed radio broadcasts of the hearings on the Florida vote recount case that determined the winner of the 2000 presidential election.

As libel law and the growing acceptance of courtroom cameras indicate, the legal process has generally, though not always, tried to ensure that print and other news media are able to cover public issues broadly, without fear of reprisals.

FILM AND THE FIRST AMENDMENT

When the First Amendment was ratified in 1791, even the most enlightened leaders of our nation could not have predicted the coming of visual media such as film and television. Consequently, new communication technologies have not always received the same kinds of protection under the First Amendment as those granted to speech or print media, including newspapers, magazines, and books. Movies, in existence since the late 1890s, earned legal speech protection only after a 1952 Supreme Court decision. Prior to that, social and political pressures led to both censorship and self-censorship in the movie industry (see "Global Village: The Challenges of Film Censorship in China" on page 498).

Social and Political Pressures on the Movies

During the early part of the twentieth century, movies rose in popularity among European immigrants and others from modest socioeconomic groups. This, in turn, spurred the formation of censorship groups, which believed that the movies would undermine morality. During this time, according to media historian Douglas Gomery, criticism of movies converged on four areas: "the effects on children, the potential health problems, the negative influences on morals and manners, and the lack of a proper role for educational and religious institutions in the development of movies."[17]

Public pressure on movies came both from conservatives, who saw them as a potential threat to the authority of traditional institutions, and from progressives, who worried that children and adults were more attracted to movie houses than to social organizations and urban education centers. As a result, civic leaders publicly escalated their pressure, organizing local *review boards* that screened movies for their communities. In 1907, the Chicago City Council created an ordinance that gave the police authority to issue permits for the exhibition of movies. By 1920, more than ninety cities in the United States had some type of movie censorship board made up of vice squad officers, politicians, and citizens. By 1923, twenty-two states had established such boards.

Meanwhile, social pressure began to translate into law as politicians, wanting to please their constituencies, began to legislate against films. Support mounted for a federal censorship bill. When Jack Johnson won the heavyweight championship in 1908, boxing films became the target of the first federal censorship law aimed at the motion-picture industry. In 1912, the government outlawed the transportation of boxing movies across state lines. The laws against boxing films, however, had more to do with Johnson's race than with concern over violence in movies. The first black heavyweight

The Challenges of Film Censorship in China

With Netflix and Amazon Prime Video each available in about 200 countries around the globe, and YouTube Go in more than 130 countries, the flow of international movie and television content is becoming stronger. Yet these digital streaming services aren't available in China, the world's No. 2 box-office market. Getting international films onto movie screens in China remains a challenge.

As it works to expand its domestic film audience by building more movie theaters in smaller-tier cities throughout the country, China maintains a strong government censorship office. There are no movie ratings in China, so if a film gains the approval of the censors, it can be shown to any age group without restriction.

The lack of age guidelines in China can result in a unique audience mix in theaters. As a writer for the *South China Morning Post* reported, "It's common, therefore, to see parents take young children to adult-oriented movies. Over the years, I've seen things you would never see in other countries: from impatient kids crying and then running around the aisles during a screening of Greek rape-revenge thriller *The Enemy Within* (2013) in a suburban cinema at the Beijing International Film Festival, to small boys egging on Jackie Chan and his co-stars as they dispose of caricatured Japanese villains—sometimes very violently—in recent second world war caper *Railroad Tigers*."[1]

Before 2013, filmmakers had to submit screenplays for review. Now they are relieved of that requirement, but all films still need to be reviewed before screening. Hong Kong filmmaker Jevons Au listed some of the content limitations for filmmakers: "The censors have the last word. Crime stories cannot have too many details. Stories of corruption must end with the bad guy behind bars. No ghosts. No gay love stories. No religion. No nudity. No politics."[2]

In fact, the U.S.-produced *Ghostbusters* (2016) remake was banned in China because its guidelines reject movies that "promote cults or superstition." Sony's attempt to rename the movie "Super Power Dare Die Team" for the Chinese market did not move the censors to change their position.[3] Chinese censors also reject films that portray time travel. *Back to the Future* (1985) was banned because Chinese censors said it was a "disrespectful portrayal of history." Since 2011, all films and television shows with time-travel stories are banned, eliminating screenings of such movies as *Bill and Ted's Excellent Adventure*, *12 Monkeys*, *Austin Powers*, and the *Star Trek* and *Terminator* films.[4]

Making films in China is a challenge as well, and the rules are reminiscent of the United States' Motion Picture Production Code, which lasted from the 1930s to the 1950s. "Can you make a movie with a bad cop in it in China? Of course. But then he has to end up in jail. Can you have much blood? No. A kid is going to see it. Foreigners who want to make movies in China need to understand the country first," said Barbara Wong Chun-Chun, a Hong Kong filmmaker, actor, and screenwriter. "The regulations are blurry, you can tackle things in a different way: shoot a film where the corruption is in America, not in China. Then it's OK. As an artist, you must find ways of getting around it."[5]

Hong Kong filmmaker Johnnie To agreed. "Does it mean compromises? Yes, very many. But the alternative is no movie in China. There are many political issues that China is still stuck with, because it has an old-fashioned system of government, and even if there is more freedom than there used to be, the Communist party is unable to relax. Yet you see it very clearly—everybody is ready to shut up to make money."[6]

champion, he was perceived as a threat to some in the white community.

The first Supreme Court decision regarding film's protection under the First Amendment was handed down in 1915 and went against the movie industry. In *Mutual v. Ohio*, the Mutual Film Company of Detroit sued the state of Ohio, whose review board had censored a number of the distributor's films. On appeal, the case arrived at the Supreme Court, which unanimously ruled that motion pictures were not a form of speech but "a business pure and simple" and, like a circus, merely a "spectacle" for entertainment with "a special capacity for evil." This ruling would stand as a precedent for thirty-seven years, although a movement to create a national censorship board failed.

Bettmann/Getty Images

Self-Regulation in the Movie Industry

As the film industry expanded after World War I, the influence of public pressure and review boards began to affect movie studios and executives who wanted to ensure control over their economic well-being. In the early 1920s, a series of scandals rocked Hollywood: actress Mary Pickford's divorce and quick marriage to actor Douglas Fairbanks, director William Desmond Taylor's unsolved murder, and actor Wallace Reid's death from a drug overdose. But the most sensational scandal involved aspiring actress Virginia Rappe, who died a few days after a wild party in a San Francisco hotel hosted by popular silent-film comedian Fatty Arbuckle. After Rappe's death, the comedian was indicted for rape and manslaughter in a case that was sensationalized in the press. Although two hung juries could not reach a verdict, Arbuckle's career was ruined. Censorship boards across the country banned his films. And even though Arbuckle was acquitted at his third trial in 1922, the movie industry chose to send a signal about the kinds of values and lifestyles it would tolerate: Arbuckle was banned from acting in Hollywood. He later resurfaced to direct several films under the name Will B. Goode.

In response to the scandals, particularly the first Arbuckle trial, the movie industry formed the Motion Picture Producers and Distributors of America (MPPDA) and hired as its president Will Hays, a former Republican National Committee chair. Also known as the Hays Office, the MPPDA attempted to smooth out problems between the public and the industry. Hays blacklisted promising actors or movie extras with even minor police records. He also developed an MPPDA public relations division, which stopped a national movement for a federal law censoring movies.

The Motion Picture Production Code

During the 1930s, the movie business faced a new round of challenges. First, various conservative and religious groups—including the influential Catholic Legion of Decency—increased their scrutiny of the industry. Second, deteriorating economic conditions during the Great Depression forced the industry to tighten self-regulation in order to maintain profits and keep harmful public pressure at bay. In 1927, the Hays Office had developed a list of "Don'ts and Be Carefuls" to steer producers and directors away from questionable sexual, moral, and social themes. Nevertheless, pressure for a more formal and sweeping code mounted. As a result, in the early 1930s the Hays Office established the Motion Picture Production Code, whose overseers were charged with officially stamping Hollywood films with a moral seal of approval.

CENSORSHIP

A native of Galveston, Texas, Jack Johnson (1878–1946) was the first black heavyweight boxing champion, from 1908 to 1914. His stunning victory over white champion Jim Jeffries (who had earlier refused to fight black boxers) in 1910 resulted in race riots across the country and led to a ban on the interstate transportation of boxing films. A 2005 Ken Burns documentary, *Unforgivable Blackness*, chronicles Johnson's life.

The Code laid out its mission in its first general principle: "No picture shall be produced which will lower the moral standards of those who see it. Hence the sympathy of the audience shall never be thrown to the side of crime, wrong-doing, evil or sin." The Code dictated how producers and directors should handle "methods of crime," "repellent subjects," and "sex hygiene." A section on profanity outlawed a long list of phrases and topics, including "toilet gags" and "traveling salesmen and farmer's daughter jokes." Under "scenes of passion," the Code dictated that "excessive and lustful kissing, lustful embraces, suggestive postures and gestures are not to be shown," and it required that "passion should be treated in such a manner as not to stimulate the lower and baser emotions." The section on religion revealed the influences of a Jesuit priest and a Catholic publisher, who helped write the Code: "No film or episode may throw ridicule on any religious faith," and "ministers of religion . . . should not be used as comic characters or as villains."

Adopted by 95 percent of the industry, the Code influenced nearly every commercial movie made between the mid-1930s and the early 1950s. It also gave the industry a relative degree of freedom, enabling the major studios to remain independent of outside regulation. When television arrived, however, competition from the new family medium forced movie producers to explore more adult subjects.

The *Miracle* Case

In 1952, the Supreme Court heard the *Miracle* case—officially *Burstyn v. Wilson*—named after Roberto Rossellini's film *Il Miracolo* (*The Miracle*). The movie's distributor sued the head of the New York Film Licensing Board for banning the film. A few New York City religious and political leaders considered the 1948 Italian film sacrilegious and pressured the film board for the ban. In the film, an unmarried peasant girl is impregnated by a scheming vagrant who tells her that he is St. Joseph and she has conceived the baby Jesus. The importers of the film argued that censoring it constituted illegal prior restraint under the First Amendment. Because such an action could not be imposed on a print version of the same story, the film's distributor argued that the same freedom should apply to the film. The Supreme Court agreed, declaring movies "a significant medium for the communication of ideas." The decision granted films the same constitutional protections as those enjoyed by the print media and other forms of speech. Even more important, the decision rendered most activities of film review boards unconstitutional because these boards had been engaged in prior restraint. Although a few local boards survived into the 1990s to handle complaints about obscenity, most of them had disbanded by the early 1970s.

The MPAA Ratings System

The current voluntary movie rating system—the model for the advisory labels for music, television, and video games—developed in the late 1960s after discontent again mounted over movie content, spurred on by such films as 1965's *The Pawnbroker*, which contained brief female nudity, and 1966's *Who's Afraid of Virginia Woolf?*, which featured a level of profanity and sexual frankness that had not been seen before in a major studio film. In 1966, the movie industry hired Jack Valenti to run the MPAA (the Motion Picture Association of America, formerly the MPPDA), and in 1968 he established an industry board to rate movies. Eventually, G, PG, R, and X ratings emerged as guideposts for the suitability of films for various age groups. In 1984, prompted by the releases of *Gremlins* and *Indiana Jones and the Temple of Doom*, the MPAA added the PG-13 rating and sandwiched it between PG and R to distinguish slightly higher levels of violence or adult themes in movies that might otherwise qualify as PG-rated films.

The MPAA copyrighted all ratings designations as trademarks except for the X rating, which was gradually appropriated as a promotional tool by the pornographic film industry. In fact, between 1972 and 1989, the MPAA stopped issuing the X rating. In 1990, however, based on protests from filmmakers over movies with adult sexual themes that they did not consider pornographic, the industry copyrighted the NC-17 rating—no children age seventeen or under. In 1995, *Showgirls* became the first movie to intentionally seek an NC-17 to demonstrate that the rating was commercially viable. However, many theater chains refused to carry NC-17 movies, fearing economic sanctions and boycotts by their customers or religious groups. Many newspapers also refused to carry ads for NC-17 films. Panned by the critics, *Showgirls* flopped at the box office. Since then, the NC–17 rating has not proved commercially viable, and distributors avoid releasing films with the rating, preferring either to label such films "unrated" or to cut the films to earn an R rating, as happened with *Clerks* (1994), *Eyes Wide Shut* (1999), *Brüno* (2009), and *The Wolf of Wall Street* (2013). Today, there is mounting protest against the MPAA, which many argue is essentially a censorship board that limits the First Amendment rights of filmmakers.

EXPRESSION IN THE MEDIA: PRINT, BROADCAST, AND ONLINE

During the Cold War, a vigorous campaign led by Joseph McCarthy, an ultraconservative senator from Wisconsin, tried to rid both government and the media of so-called communist subversives who were allegedly challenging the American way of life. In 1950, a publication called *Red Channels: The Report of Communist Influence in Radio and Television* aimed "to show how the Communists have been able to carry out their plan of infiltration of the radio and television industry." *Red Channels*, inspired by McCarthy and produced by a group of former FBI agents, named 151 performers, writers, and musicians who were "sympathetic" to communist or left-wing causes. Among those named were Leonard Bernstein, Will Geer, Dashiell Hammett, Lillian Hellman, Lena Horne, Burgess Meredith, Arthur Miller, Dorothy Parker, Pete Seeger, Irwin Shaw, and Orson Welles. For a time, all were banned from working in television and radio even though no one on the list was ever charged with a crime.[18]

Although the First Amendment protects an individual's right to hold controversial political views, network executives either sympathized with the anticommunist movement or feared losing ad revenue. At any rate, the networks did not stand up to the communist witch-hunters. In order to work, a blacklisted or "suspected" performer required the support of the program's sponsor. Though *I Love Lucy*'s Lucille Ball, who in sympathy with her father once registered to vote as a communist in the 1930s, retained Philip Morris's sponsorship of her popular program, other performers were not as fortunate. Although no evidence was ever introduced to show how entertainment programs circulated communist propaganda, by the early 1950s the TV networks were asking actors and other workers to sign loyalty oaths denouncing communism—a low point for the First Amendment.

The communist witch-hunts demonstrated key differences between print and broadcast protections under the First Amendment. Whereas licenses for printers and publishers had been outlawed since the eighteenth century, commercial broadcasters themselves had asked the federal government to step in and regulate the airwaves in the late 1920s. At that time, the broadcasters had wanted the government to clear up technical problems, channel noise, noncommercial competition, and amateur interference. Ever since, most broadcasters have been trying to free themselves from the government intrusion they once demanded.

The FCC Regulates Broadcasting

Drawing on the argument that limited broadcast signals constitute a scarce national resource, the Communications Act of 1934 mandated that radio

THE HOUSE UN-AMERICAN ACTIVITIES COMMITTEE attempted to expose performers, writers, and musicians as "communist subversives," blacklisting them from working in Hollywood without any evidence of criminal wrongdoing. In 1947, movie stars like Humphrey Bogart, Evelyn Keyes, and Lauren Bacall, pictured here, visited Washington to protest the committee's methods.

Bettmann/Getty Images

Everett Collection

FAMILY GUY

has been the target of hundreds of thousands of indecency complaints, a majority of which have been filed by the Parents Television Council. The Federal Communications Commission evaluates shows based on occurrences of explicit language, violent content, or sexually obscene depictions. *Family Guy* has been at the center of moral controversy and criticism since its debut in 1999.

broadcasters operate in "the public interest, convenience, and necessity." Since the 1980s, however, with cable and, later, DBS increasing channel capacity, station managers have lobbied to own their airwave assignments. Although the 1996 Telecommunications Act did not grant such ownership, stations continue to challenge the "public interest" statute. They argue that because the government is not allowed to dictate content in newspapers, it should not be allowed to control broadcasting via licenses or mandate any broadcast programming.

Two cases—*Red Lion Broadcasting Co. v. FCC* (1969) and *Miami Herald Publishing Co. v. Tornillo* (1974)—demonstrate the historic legal differences between broadcast and print. The *Red Lion* case began when WGCB, a small-town radio station in Red Lion, Pennsylvania, refused to give airtime to Fred Cook, author of a book that criticized Barry Goldwater, the Republican Party's presidential candidate in 1964. The Reverend Billy James Hargis, a conservative radio preacher and Goldwater fan, verbally attacked Cook on the air. Cook asked for response time from the two hundred stations that carried the Hargis attack. Most stations complied, granting Cook free reply time. But WGCB offered only to sell Cook time. He appealed to the FCC, which ordered the station to give Cook free time. The station refused, claiming that its First Amendment rights granted it control over its program content. On appeal, the Supreme Court sided with the FCC, deciding that whenever a broadcaster's rights conflict with the public interest, the public interest must prevail. In interpreting broadcasting as different from print, the Supreme Court upheld the 1934 Communications Act by reaffirming that broadcasters' responsibilities to program in the public interest may outweigh their right to program whatever they want.

In contrast, five years later, in *Miami Herald Publishing Co. v. Tornillo*, the Supreme Court sided with the newspaper. A political candidate, Pat Tornillo Jr., requested space to reply to an editorial opposing his candidacy. Previously, Florida had a right-to-reply law, which permitted a candidate to respond, in print, to editorial criticisms from newspapers. Counter to the *Red Lion* decision, the Court in this case struck down the Florida state law as unconstitutional. The Court argued that mandating that a newspaper give a candidate space to reply violated the paper's First Amendment right to control what it chose to publish. The two decisions demonstrate that the unlicensed print media receive protections under the First Amendment that have not always been available to licensed broadcast media.

Dirty Words, Indecent Speech, and Hefty Fines

In theory, communication law prevents the government from censoring broadcast content. Accordingly, the government may not interfere with programs or engage in prior restraint, although it may punish broadcasters for **indecency** or profanity after the fact.

The current precedent for regulating broadcast indecency stems from a complaint to the FCC in 1973. In the middle of the afternoon, WBAI, a nonprofit Pacifica network station in New York, aired George Carlin's famous comedy sketch about the seven dirty words that could not be uttered by broadcasters. A father, riding in a car with his fifteen-year-old son, heard the program and complained to the FCC, which sent WBAI a letter of reprimand. Although no fine was issued, the station appealed on principle and won its case in court. The FCC, however, appealed to the Supreme Court. Although

ELSEWHERE IN
MEDIA & CULTURE

ARE VIDEO GAMES MISOGYNISTIC?
pp. 79–82

THE ADVENTURES OF HUCKLEBERRY FINN IS STILL THE MOST BANNED BOOK IN U.S. HISTORY
p. 314

HOW IS ADVERTISING SPENDING CHANGING?

35%

Share of U.S. advertising dollars
spent on Internet advertising, up from 9.3% in 2007

p. 341

HOW PIRACY CHANGED THE MUSIC INDUSTRY
p. 101

no court had legally defined indecency (and still hasn't), the Supreme Court's unexpected ruling in the 1978 *FCC v. Pacifica Foundation* case sided with the FCC and upheld the agency's authority to require broadcasters to air adult programming at times when children are not likely to be listening. The Court ruled that so-called indecent programming, though not in violation of federal obscenity laws, was a nuisance and could be restricted to late-evening hours. As a result, the FCC banned indecent programs from most stations between 6:00 A.M. and 10:00 P.M. In 1990, the FCC tried to ban such programs entirely. Although a federal court ruled this move unconstitutional, it still upheld the time restrictions intended to protect children.

This ruling provides the rationale for the indecency fines that the FCC has frequently leveled against programs and stations that have carried indecent programming during daytime and evening hours. While Howard Stern and his various bosses held the early record for racking up millions in FCC indecency fines in the 1990s—before Stern moved to unregulated satellite radio—the largest-ever fine was for $3.6 million, leveled in 2006 against 111 TV stations that broadcast a 2004 episode of the popular CBS program *Without a Trace* that depicted teenage characters taking part in a sexual orgy.

After the FCC later fined broadcasters for several instances of "fleeting expletives" during live TV shows, the four major networks sued the FCC on the grounds that their First Amendment rights had been violated. In its fining flurry, the FCC was partly responding to organized campaigns aimed at Howard Stern's vulgarity and at the Janet Jackson exposed-breast incident during the 2004 Super Bowl halftime show. In 2006, Congress substantially increased the FCC's maximum allowable fine to $325,000 per incident of indecency—meaning that one fleeting expletive in a live entertainment, news, or sports program could cost millions of dollars in fines, as it is repeated on affiliate stations across the country. But in 2010, a federal appeals court rejected the FCC's policy against fleeting expletives, arguing that it was constitutionally vague and had a chilling effect on free speech "because broadcasters have no way of knowing what the FCC will find offensive."[19]

Political Broadcasts and Equal Opportunity

In addition to indecency rules, another law that the print media do not encounter is **Section 315** of the 1934 Communications Act, which mandates that during elections, broadcast stations must provide equal opportunity and response time for qualified political candidates. In other words, if broadcasters give or sell time to one candidate, they must give or sell the same opportunity to others. Local broadcasters and networks have fought this law for years, complaining that it has required them to give marginal third-party candidates with little hope of success equal airtime in political discussions. Broadcasters claim that because no similar rule applies to newspapers or magazines, the law violates their First Amendment right to control content. In fact, because of this rule, many stations avoid all political programming, ironically reversing the rule's original intention. The TV networks managed to get the law amended in 1959 to exempt newscasts, press conferences, and other events— such as political debates—that qualify as news. For instance, if a senator running for office appears in a news story, opposing candidates cannot invoke Section 315 and demand free time. The FCC has subsequently ruled that interview portions of programs like the *700 Club* and *TMZ* also count as news.

Due to Section 315, many stations from the late 1960s through the 1980s refused to air movies starring Ronald Reagan. Because his film appearances did not count as bona fide news stories, politicians opposing Reagan as a presidential candidate could demand free time in markets that ran old Reagan movies. For the same reason, TV stations in California banned the broadcast of Arnold Schwarzenegger movies in 2003, when he became a candidate for governor. And in November 2015, Donald Trump's twelve minutes of screen time as the host of *SNL* opened the door for his competitors to demand equal screen time from NBC.

However, supporters of the equal opportunity law argue that it has provided forums for lesser-known candidates representing views counter to those of the Democratic and Republican parties, further noting that the other main way for alternative candidates to circulate their messages widely is to buy political ads, thus limiting serious outside contenders to wealthy candidates.

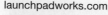

LaunchPad
macmillan learning
launchpadworks.com

Bloggers and Legal Rights
Legal and journalism scholars discuss the legal rights and responsibilities of bloggers.

Discussion: What are some of the advantages and disadvantages of the audience's turning to blogs— rather than traditional sources—for news?

The Demise of the Fairness Doctrine

Considered an important corollary to Section 315, the **Fairness Doctrine** was to controversial issues what Section 315 is to political speech. Initiated in 1949, this FCC rule required stations (1) to air and engage in controversial-issue programs that affected their communities and (2) to provide competing points of view when offering such programming. Over the years, broadcasters argued that mandating opposing views every time a program covered a controversial issue was a burden not required of the print media, and that it forced many of them to refrain from airing controversial issues. As a result, the Fairness Doctrine ended with little public debate in 1987 after a federal court ruled that it was merely a regulation rather than an extension of Section 315 law.

Since 1987, however, periodic support for reviving the Fairness Doctrine has surfaced. Its supporters argue that broadcasting is fundamentally different from—and more pervasive than— print media, requiring greater accountability to the public. Although many broadcasters disagree, supporters of fairness rules insist that as long as broadcasters are licensed as public trustees of the airwaves—unlike newspaper or magazine publishers—legal precedent permits the courts and the FCC to demand responsible content and behavior from radio and TV stations.

Communication Policy and the Internet

Many have looked to the Internet as the one true venue for unlimited free speech under the First Amendment because it is not regulated by the government, it is not subject to the Communications Act of 1934, and little has been done in regard to self-regulation. Its current global expansion is comparable to that of the early days of broadcasting, when economic and technological growth outstripped law and regulation. At that time, noncommercial experiments by amateurs and engineering students provided a testing ground that commercial interests later exploited for profit. In much the same way, amateurs, students, and various interest groups have explored and extended the communication possibilities of the Internet. In fact, they have experimented so successfully that commercial vendors have raced to buy up pieces of the Internet since the 1990s.

Public conversations about the Internet have not typically revolved around ownership. Instead, the debates have focused on First Amendment issues, such as civility and pornography. However, as we watch the rapid expansion of the Internet, an important question confronts us: Will the Internet continue to develop as a democratic medium? In late 2010, the FCC created net neutrality rules for wired (cable and DSL) broadband providers, requiring that they provide the same access to all Internet services and content. But the FCC's net neutrality rules were rejected by federal courts twice. The courts argued that because the FCC had not defined the Internet as a utility, it couldn't regulate it in this manner. Telecommunication companies were pleased with the decision, as they don't want any rules governing how they distribute access to the Internet. However, citizens and entrepreneurs opposed an unregulated system that would allow telecommunication companies to create fast lanes (for those who pay more) and slow lanes on the Internet. The debate generated a record number of comments to the FCC, the vast majority in favor of net neutrality.[20] In February 2015, the FCC reclassified broadband Internet as a Title II utility and voted to approve net neutrality rules, which were

Senate Democrats

NET NEUTRALITY HEARINGS
The long-debated issue of net neutrality—which was successfully reclassified as a Title II utility as advocated by Senator Edward Markey, Senator Bernie Sanders, and Senator Al Franken, seen here speaking at a news conference—became mainstream news again not long after President Trump came into office. Ajit Pai, whom the president appointed to chair the FCC—is an outspoken opponent of net neutrality and swiftly worked to overturn the Obama-era change. By June 2018, the FCC's repeal of net neutrality rules officially came into effect.

Is "Sexting" Pornography?

© Mother Image/ulltura/Aurora Photos

According to U.S. federal and state laws, when someone produces, transmits, or possesses images with graphic sexual depictions of minors, it is considered child pornography. Digital media have made the circulation of child pornography even more pervasive, according to a 2006 study on child pornography on the Internet. About one thousand people are arrested each year in the United States for child pornography, and according to a U.S. Department of Justice guide for police, they have few distinguishing characteristics other than being "likely to be white, male, and between the ages of 26 and 40."[1]

Now, a social practice has challenged the common wisdom of what is obscenity and who are child pornographers: What happens when the people who produce, transmit, and possess images with graphic sexual depictions of minors are minors themselves?

The practice in question is "sexting," the sending or receiving of sexual images via mobile phone text messages or via the Internet. Sexting occupies a gray area of obscenity law—yes, these are images of minors; but no, they don't fit the intent of child pornography laws, which are designed to stop the exploitation of children by adults.

While such messages are usually meant to be completely personal, technology makes it otherwise. "All control over the image is lost—it can be forwarded repeatedly all over the school, town, state, country and world," says Steven M. Dettelbach, U.S. attorney for the Northern District of Ohio.[2] And given the endless archives of the Internet, such images never really go away but can be accessed by anyone with enough skills to find them.

Research published in the journal *JAMA Pediatrics* in 2018 found that 14.8 percent of teenagers sent sexts, while 27.4 percent received them. Other sexting behaviors raise issues of privacy and bullying: 12 percent of teens forwarded a sext without consent, and 8.4 percent had a sext of them forwarded without

consent.[3] Some cases illustrate how young people engaging in sexting have gotten caught up in a legal system designed to punish pedophiles. In 2008, Florida resident Phillip Alpert, then eighteen, sent nude images of his sixteen-year-old girlfriend to friends after they got in an argument. He was convicted of child pornography and is required to be registered as a sex offender for the next twenty-five years. In 2009, three Pennsylvania girls took seminude pictures of themselves and sent the photos to three boys. All six minors were charged with child pornography. A judge later halted the charges in the interest of freedom of speech and parental rights. In Cañon City, Colorado, a 2015 texting scandal involving middle and high school students exchanging hundreds of nude photos resulted in student suspensions, a canceled high school football game, and a criminal investigation. Ultimately, the state district attorney didn't bring charges against the students involved, but felony charges were a possibility. Twenty states (Arizona, Arkansas, Connecticut, Florida, Georgia, Hawaii, Illinois, Louisiana, Nebraska, Nevada, New Jersey, New York, North Dakota, Pennsylvania, Rhode Island, South Dakota, Texas, Utah, Vermont, and West Virginia) have responded with new sexting laws, so that teens involved in sexting generally face misdemeanor charges rather than being subject to the harsher felony laws against child pornography.[4] In the states without such laws, the charges are often at the discretion of prosecutors and courts and could be as harsh as a felony crime, with the accompanying fine, jail time, and permanent criminal record. How do you think sexting should be handled by the law?

upheld by the U.S. Court of Appeals in 2016, enabling the FCC to enforce open Internet standards on wired and mobile networks. Yet the battle over net neutrality continued. Donald Trump's appointee to chair the FCC moved to reconsider net neutrality, and in December 2017, the FCC voted to repeal the 2015 FCC net neutrality policy on a 3–2 party-line vote, effective June 2018. Attorneys general from twenty-one states and the District of Columbia filed lawsuits to challenge the decision.

Critics and observers hope that a vigorous debate about ownership will develop—a debate that will go beyond First Amendment issues. The promise of the Internet as a democratic forum encourages the formation of all sorts of regional, national, and global interest groups. In fact, many global movements use the Internet to fight political forms of censorship. Human Rights Watch, for example, encourages free-expression advocates to use blogs "for disseminating information about, and ending, human rights abuses around the world."[21] Where oppressive regimes have tried to monitor and control Internet communication, Human Rights Watch suggests bloggers post anonymously to safeguard their identity. Just as fax machines, satellites, and home videos helped expedite and document the fall of totalitarian regimes in Eastern Europe in the late 1980s, the Internet helps spread the word and activate social change today.

THE FIRST AMENDMENT AND DEMOCRACY

For most of our nation's history, citizens have counted on journalism to monitor abuses in government and business. During the muckraking period, writers like Upton Sinclair, Ida Tarbell, and Sinclair Lewis made strong contributions by reporting on corporate expansion and the corruption that accompanied it. Unfortunately, however, news stories about business issues today are usually reduced to consumer affairs reporting. In other words, when covering a labor strike, factory recall, or business shutdown, the reporter mainly tries to answer the question, How do these events affect consumers? Although this is an important news angle, discussions about media ownership or labor management ethics are no longer part of the news that journalists typically report. Similarly, when companies announce mergers, reporters do not routinely question the economic wisdom or social impact of such changes but focus on how consumers will be affected.

At one level, journalists have been compromised by the ongoing upheavals of their own media businesses. As newspapers, magazines, and broadcast stations consolidate, downsize, outsource, or close down completely, and digital outlets spring up without a history or mission of news reporting, there are fewer journalists available to adequately cover and lead discussions on issues of politics, the economy, and media ownership. In fact, the very companies they work for are the prime buyers and sellers of major news-media outlets and are often participants in a political system rife with advertising money during campaign season.

As a result, it is becoming increasingly important that the civic role of watchdog be shared by citizens and journalists. Citizen action groups like Free Press, the Media Access Project, and the Center for Digital Democracy have worked to bring media ownership issues into the mainstream. However, it is important to remember that the First Amendment protects not only the news media's free-speech rights but also the rights of all of us to speak out. Mounting concerns over who can afford access to the media go to the heart of free expression. As we struggle to determine the future of converging print, electronic, and digital media and to strengthen the democratic spirit underlying media technology, we need to stay engaged in spirited public debates about media ownership and control and about the differences between commercial speech and free expression. As citizens, we need to pay attention to who is included and excluded from opportunities not only to buy products but also to speak out and shape the cultural landscape. To accomplish this, we need to challenge our journalists and our leaders. More important, we need to challenge ourselves to become watchdogs—critical consumers and engaged citizens—who learn from the past, care about the present, and map mass media's future.

16 Chapter Review

One of the Common Threads discussed in Chapter 1 is the role that media play in a democracy. Is a free media system necessary for democracy to exist, or must democracy be established before a media system can operate freely? What do the mass media do to enhance or secure democracy?

In 1787, as the Constitution was being formed, Thomas Jefferson famously said, "Were it left to me to decide whether we should have a government without newspapers, or newspapers without a government, I should not hesitate a moment to prefer the latter." Jefferson supported the notion of a free press and free speech. He stood against the Sedition Act, which penalized free speech, and did not support its renewal when he became president in 1801.

Nevertheless, as president, Jefferson had to withstand the vitriol and allegations of a partisan press. In 1807, near the end of his second term, Jefferson's idealism about the press had cooled, as he remarked, "The man who never looks into a newspaper is better informed than he who reads them, inasmuch as he who knows nothing is nearer the truth than he whose mind is filled with falsehoods and errors."

Today, we contend with mass media that extend far beyond newspapers—a media system that is among the biggest and most powerful institutions in the country. Unfortunately, it is also a media system that too often envisions us as consumers of capitalism, not citizens of a democracy. Media sociologist Herbert Gans argues that the media alone can't guarantee a democracy.[22] "Despite much disingenuous talk about citizen empowerment by politicians and merchandisers, citizens have never had much clout. Countries as big as America operate largely through organizations," Gans explains.

But in a country as big as America, the media constitute one of those critical organizations that can either help or hurt us in creating a more economically and politically democratic society. At their worst, the media can distract or misinform us with falsehoods and errors. But at their Jeffersonian best, the media can shed light on the issues, tell meaningful stories, and foster the discussions that can help a citizens' democracy flourish.

KEY TERMS

The definitions for the terms listed below can be found in the glossary at the end of the book. The page numbers listed with the terms indicate where the term is highlighted in the chapter.

authoritarian model, 486
communist or state model, 486
social responsibility model, 486
Fourth Estate, 486
libertarian model, 486
prior restraint, 487
copyright, 489

public domain, 490
libel, 491
slander, 491
actual malice, 492
qualified privilege, 492
opinion and fair comment, 492
obscenity, 492

right to privacy, 493
gag orders, 495
shield laws, 495
indecency, 502
Section 315, 504
Fairness Doctrine, 505

LaunchPad
macmillan learning

For review quizzes, chapter summaries, links to media-related websites, and more, go to launchpadworks.com.

REVIEW QUESTIONS

The Origins of Free Expression and a Free Press

1. Explain the various models of the news media that exist under different political systems.

2. What is the basic philosophical concept that underlies America's notion of free expression?

3. How has censorship been defined historically?

4. What is the public domain, and why is it an important element in American culture?

5. Why is the case of *New York Times v. Sullivan* so significant in First Amendment history?

6. How has the Internet changed battles over what constitutes obscenity?

7. What issues are at stake when First Amendment and Sixth Amendment concerns clash?

Film and the First Amendment

8. Why were films not constitutionally protected as a form of speech until 1952?

9. Why did film review boards develop, and why did they eventually disband?

10. How did both the Motion Picture Production Code and the current movie rating system come into being?

Expression in the Media: Print, Broadcast, and Online

11. What's the difference between obscenity and indecency?

12. What is the significance of Section 315 of the Communications Act of 1934?

13. Why didn't broadcasters like the Fairness Doctrine?

The First Amendment and Democracy

14. Why is the future of watchdog journalism in jeopardy?

QUESTIONING THE MEDIA

1. Have you ever had an experience in which you thought personal or public expression went too far and should be curbed? Explain. How might you remedy this situation?

2. If you owned a community newspaper and had to formulate a policy about which letters to the editor could appear in the limited space available on your editorial page, what kinds of letters would you eliminate, and why? Would you be acting as a censor in this situation? Why or why not?

3. Should the United States have a federal shield law to protect reporters?

4. What do you think of the current movie rating system? Should it be changed? Why or why not?

5. Should corporations, unions, and rich individuals be able to contribute any amount of money they want to support particular candidates and pay for TV ads? Why or why not?

LAUNCHPAD FOR *MEDIA & CULTURE*

Visit LaunchPad for *Media & Culture* at launchpadworks.com for additional learning tools:

- REVIEW WITH LEARNINGCURVE
  LearningCurve, available on LaunchPad for *Media & Culture*, uses gamelike quizzing to help you master the concepts you need to learn from this chapter.

- VIDEO: THE FIRST AMENDMENT AND STUDENT SPEECH
  Legal and newspaper professionals explain how student newspapers are protected by the First Amendment.

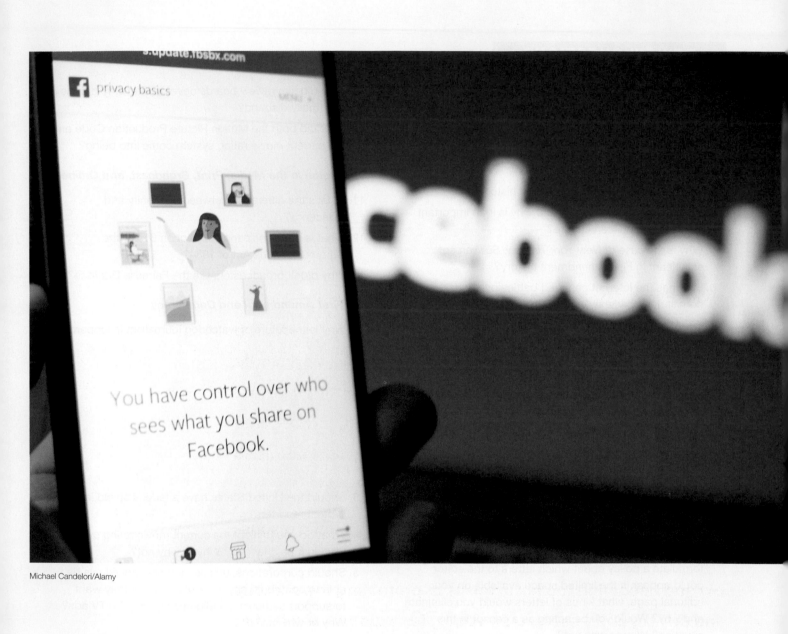

Michael Candelori/Alamy

Extended Case Study

Can We Trust Facebook with Our Personal Data?

THE FIRST HALF OF 2018 was a rough one for Facebook. On the surface, things appeared to be going well. The company had more than 2.2 billion monthly users.[1] Its revenue was $40.65 billion, more than twice as much as just two years prior. Along with Google, Facebook had become a digital advertising powerhouse, with nearly all—about 98 percent—of its revenue coming from advertising.

Yet in recent years, there has been increasing public discussion in America about digital media companies growing too big and becoming too lax in terms of protecting the security and privacy of its users. *USA Today*, for example, wrote that the big digital companies "have grown too big, too influential, too unmonitored—too much the Big Brother that dystopian stories warn about."[2]

◄ Social media behemoth Facebook confronted some serious questions after a data breach placed the personal information of about eighty-seven million users at risk.

Of all the major digital companies, Facebook was the one with the most obvious missteps, and those missteps became serious stumbles by 2018.

First was the problem of the 2016 presidential campaign in the United States. In February 2018, the U.S. Justice Department's special counsel indicted thirteen individuals connected to a Russian internet troll farm that placed at least three thousand Facebook ads to influence American voters and increase polarization on certain social issues. The Russian trolls were responsible for eighty thousand posts reaching 126 million people on Facebook.[3]

Then, in March 2018, the *New York Times* and the *Observer* revealed a huge unauthorized use of Facebook user data by Cambridge Analytica, a British firm that consulted with candidate Donald Trump's campaign in 2016. According to the account of a whistleblower who worked with Cambridge Analytica, the company "used personal information taken without authorization in early 2014 to build a system that could profile individual US voters, in order to target them with personalized political advertisements."[4] It all started in 2014, when 270,000 Facebook users participated in a survey and downloaded an app, consenting to have their data accessed for academic use. It then veered off into a violation of privacy for millions of Facebook users. Cambridge Analytica and its partners, without authorization, bought the data set and scraped information from the survey participants' friends, ultimately gaining access to information on about 87 million Facebook users.[5]

In April 2018, Facebook revealed that *most of its two billion users* could have had their user information accessed without authorization, but that it would disable the feature that had allowed it to happen. Bloomberg reported that this was yet more "evidence of the ways the social-media giant failed to protect people's privacy while generating billions of dollars in revenue from the information."[6]

Facebook founder and CEO Mark Zuckerberg (and the fifth richest person in the world, with a $71 billion net worth) was called to testify before the U.S. Congress and the European Parliament. By most accounts, Zuckerberg got off easy, fielding largely clueless questions from older elected officials. As the *Guardian* put it, "At times Zuckerberg resembled the polite teenager who visits his grandparents, only to spend the afternoon showing them how to turn on the wifi."[7] (Zuckerberg's testimony did generate an avalanche of critical memes, though.)[8] But one candid comment from a European official in May 2018 had a sharp point:

> "In total you apologized 15 or 16 times in the last decade," Guy Verhofstadt, leader of the Alliance of Liberals and Democrats for Europe, said after Zuckerberg apologized, again. "Every year you have one or another wrongdoing with your company. . . . Are you able to fix it? And if you've already confronted so many dysfunctions, there clearly has to be a problem."[9]

Dylan Byers, a technology reporter for CNN, argued that "Facebook's problem is Facebook." In other words, the very nature of how Facebook operates leads to problems: "Facebook's data privacy problem isn't a glitch, it's the central feature. Facebook succeeds by collecting, harvesting and profiting off your data. In fact, many of Facebook's proposed solutions to its myriad problems are structured to give them more access to your data."[10] By July 2018, even investors were alarmed by Facebook's ongoing privacy problems and long-term future for growth. In one day, the value of Facebook's shares plunged about 20 percent, the largest drop in its Wall Street history.

Is Facebook's business model of profiting from our personal data also an ever-present problem for our data privacy and security? Are Facebook's constant apologies for violating the privacy of our data evidence of a serious problem? For this extended case study, we will look at news stories about instances of unauthorized data use and data breaches at Facebook and what Facebook promised to do in its apologies.

As developed in Chapter 1, a media-literate perspective involves mastering five overlapping critical stages that build on one another: (1) description: paying close attention, taking notes, and researching the subject under study; (2) analysis: discovering and focusing on significant patterns that emerge from the description stage; (3) interpretation: asking and answering the "What does that mean?" and "So what?" questions about your findings; (4) evaluation: arriving at a judgment about whether something is good, bad, poor, or mediocre, which involves subordinating one's personal views to the critical assessment resulting from the first three stages; and (5) engagement: taking some action that connects our critical interpretations and evaluations with our responsibility as citizens.

STEP 1: DESCRIPTION

Given our research question, in the description phase you would look at news stories that reveal data-security problems at Facebook.

A good starting point is 2011, when the Federal Trade Commission charged Facebook with a list of eight violations in which Facebook told consumers their information would be private but made it public to advertisers and third-party applications. At the time, the chair of the FTC said, "Facebook's innovation does not have to come at the expense of consumer privacy."[11] Facebook settled with the FTC by fixing the problem and agreeing to submit to privacy audits through the year 2031. "Today's announcement formalizes our commitment to providing you with control over your privacy and sharing—and it also provides protection to ensure that your information is only shared in the way you intend," said Zuckerberg in his statement in regard to the settlement.[12]

Since that time, what are some other unauthorized uses of data or data breaches at Facebook, and how has the company responded to them?

- In 2013, Facebook reported that it "inadvertently exposed six million users' phone numbers and e-mail addresses to unauthorized viewers over the last year." The company also noted, "It's still something we're upset and embarrassed by, and we'll work doubly hard to make sure nothing like this happens again."[13]

IN APRIL 2018,

Mark Zuckerberg testified on Capitol Hill, answering difficult and important questions about privacy, foreign interference, and abuse of social media tools.

- In 2014, Facebook faced criticism from European regulators after it disclosed "that it deliberately manipulated the emotional content of the news feeds by changing the posts displayed to nearly 700,000 users to see if emotions were contagious. The company did not seek explicit permission from the affected people—roughly one out of every 2,500 users of the social network at the time of the experiment—and some critics have suggested that the research violated its terms of service with its customers. Facebook has said that customers gave blanket permission for research as a condition of using the service." In a news report, "Richard Allan, Facebook's director of policy in Europe, said that it was clear that people had been upset by the study. 'We want to do better in the future and are improving our process based on this feedback,' he said in a statement."[14]

- In 2016, WhatsApp—the world's largest messaging service, purchased by Facebook in 2014—said it would begin to share users' information with Facebook. Regulators in Hamburg, Germany, objected and ordered Facebook to stop and to delete any information from WhatsApp's thirty-five million German users that had been shared with Facebook. "'It has to be their decision, whether they want to connect their account with Facebook,' Johannes Caspar, the Hamburg data protection commissioner, said."[15] According to the report, "Facebook said . . . after the order had been issued, that it had complied with Europe's privacy rules and that it was willing to work with the regulator to address its concerns."[16]

- In June 2018 (after the European Union officially chastised Zuckerberg), the *New York Times* revealed that Facebook had agreements with at least sixty digital device makers, including Apple, Amazon, Microsoft, and Samsung, allowing them "access to vast amounts of its users' personal information," including users' friends. According to the article, "The partnerships, whose scope has not previously been reported, raise concerns about the company's privacy protections and compliance with a 2011 consent decree with the Federal Trade Commission."[17] In a statement on Facebook titled "Why We Disagree with the *New York Times*," Facebook's vice president of product partnerships responded that "friends' information, like photos, was only accessible on devices when people made a decision to share their information with those friends. We are not aware of any abuse by these companies." He further noted that Facebook had earlier announced that it would be "winding down" the software-sharing agreements with the digital device makers.[18]

- Just a few days later in June 2018, another *New York Times* investigative report revealed that "Facebook has data-sharing partnerships with at least four Chinese electronics companies, including a manufacturing giant that has a close relationship with China's government." The agreements dated back to at least 2010, the paper reported.[19] According to the *Times*, "Facebook officials said in an interview that the company would wind down the Huawei deal by the end of the week." Huawei was the Chinese telecommunications company that "has been flagged by American intelligence officials as a national security threat" to the United States.[20] Facebook did not post a statement on its website responding to this article.

STEP 2: ANALYSIS

In the second stage of the critical process, you isolate patterns that call for closer attention. What patterns emerged from the news stories just discussed? For example, was there a consistent pattern of unauthorized data use by Facebook, or a pushing of the boundaries of data collection? Are Facebook's policies on personal data clear to its users and the public? Did Facebook have a consistent pattern in dealing with concerns and complaints about its ability to secure users' data and privacy?

The New York Times

Facebook Says Cambridge Analytica Harvested Data of Up to 87 Million Users

The Facebook chief executive, Mark Zuckerberg, is expected to appear before multiple congressional committees. Steven Senne/Associated Press

CNBC HOME U.S. ▾ NEWS MARKETS INVESTING TECH MAKE IT VIDEO SHOWS MORE   SUBSCRIBE ›

Facebook-Cambridge Analytica: A timeline of the data hijacking scandal

Sam Meredith | @smeredith19 | Published 7:22 AM ET Tue, 10 April 2018
| Updated 9:51 AM ET Tue, 10 April 2018

CNBC

NEWS COVERAGE
of the Cambridge Analytica Facebook data breach reached far and wide. Were you following the news stories surrounding this event? How was the story covered differently by various types of news outlets?

STEP 3: INTERPRETATION

In the interpretation stage, you determine the larger meanings of the patterns you have analyzed. The most difficult stage in criticism, interpretation demands an answer to the questions "So what?" and "What does all this mean?"

One interpretation might be (to quote Dylan Byers) that "Facebook's problem is Facebook." Facebook has regularly fallen short in transparency in data use and its commitment to users' privacy and data security, particularly given the provisions of its 2011 agreement with the FTC. It seems that Facebook's main method of making money—appealing to advertisers by providing substantial information on its users—motivates it to constantly develop new ways to harvest data. Thus, it's always pushing the boundaries of privacy rules, and by sharing user information with its clients, users' data security is at risk. (This can be seen in the Cambridge Analytica case—yes, it violated Facebook policies, but sharing user data with so many third-party developers increases the opportunities for violations to happen.)

STEP 4: EVALUATION

The evaluation stage of the critical process is about making informed judgments. Building on description, analysis, and interpretation, you can better evaluate Facebook's performance.

Based on your critical research, what would you conclude about Facebook's record in terms of privacy and security? Remember that for any problems you identify in your evaluation, you will need to weigh them against the value of Facebook: What good does this particular social medium offer you, your community, the country, and the world?

STEP 5: ENGAGEMENT

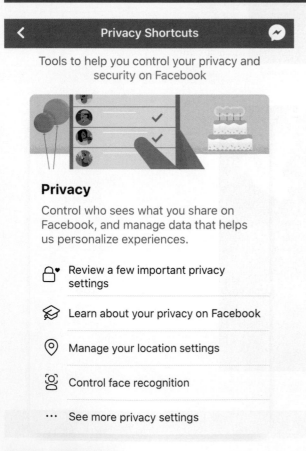

< **Privacy Shortcuts** 📧

Tools to help you control your privacy and security on Facebook

Privacy

Control who sees what you share on Facebook, and manage data that helps us personalize experiences.

🔒• Review a few important privacy settings

🎓 Learn about your privacy on Facebook

◎ Manage your location settings

😃 Control face recognition

⋯ See more privacy settings

IN THE AFTERMATH of the massive data breach, Facebook attempted to make things right with its users by updating its privacy policy and features. How effective do you think these efforts were?

The fifth stage of the critical process—engagement—encourages you to take action, adding your own voice to the process of shaping our culture and environment.

Given more than a decade of Facebook's existence, a number of ideas for engagement already exist. At the global level, the General Data Protection Regulation (or GDPR) became effective in May 2018. The new European law establishes common rules for digital companies in handling user data and is supported by heavy fines for violations. European Parliament member Viviane Reding explained that with the GDPR, "you cannot hand over the personal data of citizens without having asked if the citizens agree that you hand it over. And you cannot steal it and just tell them after. That is not possible anymore, according to the new law. If you do, then the penalties will be very, very severe."[21]

Because all of the major digital companies—including Amazon, Apple, Facebook, Google, Microsoft—do business in Europe, they have effectively adopted the higher standards of the GDPR for their operations in the United States and other countries, so as not to have multiple rules to follow. (Users in the United States might remember receiving notices from their digital services on changes in user agreements at the time the GDPR went into effect.) The GDPR exists because of the concerns of European citizens about data privacy. You might be further engaged to ensure that the new standards are followed in the United States. Also, if you have a complaint about your personal data being misused on a social media platform, you can make an online report at the FTC Complaint Assistant (www .ftccomplaintassistant.gov).

You can also make a switch to other social media platforms. Ironically, a *New York Times* writer suggests that users upset with the shortcomings of Facebook might find a solution with one of Facebook's own subsidiaries: Instagram. He argued that the two social media platforms are almost a side-by-side test. Facebook is "designed as a giant megaphone, with an emphasis on public sharing and an algorithmic feed capable of sending posts rocketing around the world in seconds." Conversely, Instagram is "more minimalist, designed for intimate sharing rather than viral broadcasting. Users of this app, many of whom have private accounts with modest followings, can post photos or videos, but

external links do not work and there is no re-share button, making it harder for users to amplify one another's posts."[22]

Finally, you can tell people what you think: you can respond directly to Facebook on its help pages (www.facebook.com/help), you can monitor and set your Facebook and other social media sharing settings to the most restrictive, you can weigh in regarding social media privacy with your elected officials (you can find them at www.govtrack.us/congress/members), and you can share your ideas with friends on social media—including Facebook.

Notes

① Mass Communication: A Critical Approach

1. Phillip Bum, "Eighteen Years of Gun Violence in U.S. Schools, Mapped," *Washington Post*, February 14, 2018, www.washingtonpost.com/news/politics/wp/2018/02/14/eighteen-years-of-gun-violence-in-u-s-schools-mapped.

2. Ali Breland, "Teen Shooting Survivors Leverage Huge Social Media Followings for Gun Control," March 3, 2018, http://thehill.com/policy/technology/376530-teen-shooting-survivors-leverage-huge-social-media-followings-for-gun.

3. Julia Carrie Wong, "Florida Students Have Turned Social Media into a Weapon for Good," *Guardian*, February 21, 2018, www.theguardian.com/us-news/2018/feb/21/florida-students-have-turned-social-media-into-a-weapon-for-good.

4. Jessica Taylor, "Most Still Favor Stricter Gun Laws, but It's Fading as a 2018 Voting Issue," April 19, 2918, www.npr.org/2018/04/19/603909072/most-still-favor-stricter-gun-laws-but-its-fading-as-a-2018-voting-issue.

5. Darrell M. West, "How Millennials and Gun Control Can Change the 2018 Midterm Landscape," April 5, 2018, www.brookings.edu/blog/fixgov/2018/04/05/how-millennials-and-gun-control-can-change-the-2018-midterm-landscape.

6. Neil Postman, *Amusing Ourselves to Death: Public Discourse in the Age of Show Business* (New York: Penguin Books, 1985), 19.

7. James W. Carey, *Communication as Culture: Essays on Media and Society* (Boston: Unwin Hyman, 1989), 203.

8. Postman, *Amusing Ourselves to Death*, 65. See also Elizabeth Eisenstein, *The Printing Press as an Agent of Change*, 2 vols. (Cambridge: Cambridge University Press, 1979).

9. James Fallows, "How to Save the News," *Atlantic*, June 2010, www.theatlantic.com/magazine/archive/2010/06/how-to-save-the-news/8095.

10. Raymond Wong, "Google's Taking Another Big Step to Stop the Spread of Fake News," December 17, 2017, https://mashable.com/2017/12/17/google-news-no-hiding-country-origin-stop-fake-news/#5TGkc0fhimqu.

11. "Generation M2: Media in the Lives of 8- to 18-Year-Olds," January 1, 2010, http://www.kff.org/entmedia/upload/8010.pdf, p. 2.

12. Jerome Bruner, *Making Stories: Law, Literature, Life* (New York: Farrar, Straus & Giroux, 2002), 8.

13. Joan Didion, *The White Album* (New York: Pocket Books, 1979), 14.

14. See Plato, *The Republic*, Book II, 377B.

15. Romeo Vitelli, "Television, Commercials, and Your Child," *Psychology Today*, July 22, 2013, www.psychologytoday.com/blog/media-spotlight/201307/television-commercials-and-your-child.

16. For a historical discussion of culture, see Lawrence Levine, *Highbrow/Lowbrow: The Emergence of Cultural Hierarchy in America* (Cambridge, Mass.: Harvard University Press, 1988).

17. For an example of this critical position, see Allan Bloom, *The Closing of the American Mind: How Higher Education Has Failed Democracy and Impoverished the Souls of Today's Students* (New York: Simon & Schuster, 1987).

18. For overviews of this position, see Postman, *Amusing Ourselves to Death*; and Stuart Ewen, *Captains of Consciousness: Advertising and the Social Roots of the Consumer Culture* (New York: McGraw-Hill, 1976).

19. See Carey, *Communication as Culture* (see 7).

20. For more on this idea, see Cecelia Tichi, *Electronic Hearth: Creating an American Television Culture* (New York: Oxford University Press, 1991), 187–188.

21. See Jon Katz, "Rock, Rap and Movies Bring You the News," *Rolling Stone*, March 5, 1992, p. 33.

▣ EXAMINING ETHICS Covering War, p. 16

1. Bill Carter, "Some Stations to Block 'Nightline' War Tribute," *New York Times*, April 30, 2004, p. A13.

2. For reference and guidance on media ethics, see Clifford Christians, Mark Fackler, and Kim Rotzoll, *Media Ethics: Cases and Moral Reasoning*, 4th ed. (White Plains, N.Y.: Longman, 1995); Thomas H. Bivins, "A Worksheet for Ethics Instruction and Exercises in Reason," *Journalism Educator* (Summer 1993): 4–16.

PART 1: DIGITAL MEDIA AND CONVERGENCE

Infographic sources:

www.digitalbuzzblog.com/infographic-2013-mobile-growth-statistics/comment-page-3/

www.cnet.com/news/vine-grows-to-40-million-users-despite-instagram-challenge/

http://techcrunch.com/2015/06/22/consumers-spend-85-of-time-on-smartphones-in-apps-but-only-5-apps-see-heavy-use/#.wzzhvrr:5bJy

www.nielsen.com/us/en/insights/reports/2015/the-comparable-metrics-report-q2-2015.html

② The Internet, Digital Media, and Media Convergence

1. Lev Grossman and Matt Vella, "iNeed?" *Time*, September 22, 2014, p. 44.

2. "Fear of Missing Out," J. Walter Thompson Intelligence, May 2011, quoted in Eric Barker, "This Is the Best Way to Overcome Fear of Missing Out," *Time*, accessed April 27, 2018, http://time.com/collection/guide-to-happiness/4358140/overcome-fomo.

3. Andrew K. Przybylski et al., "Motivational, Emotional, and Behavioral Correlates of Fear of Missing Out," *Computers in Human Behavior* 29 (2013): 1841–1848.

4. Ethan Kross et al., "Facebook Use Predicts Declines in Subjective Well-Being in Young Adults," *PLOS ONE* 8, no. 8 (2013), doi:10.1371/journal.pone.0069841.

5. Ed Diener and Robert Biswas-Diener, *Happiness: Unlocking the Mysteries of Psychological Wealth* (Malden, Mass.: Wiley-Blackwell, 2008), 51.

6. "Internet/Broadband Fact Sheet," Pew Research Center, January 12, 2017, www.pewinternet.org/fact-sheet/internet-broadband.

7. "Internet Usage Statistics," Internet World Stats, June 30, 2017, http://www.internetworldstats.com/stats.htm; Donna Fuscaldo, "Facebook Now Has More Users in India Than in Any Other Country," Investopedia, June 13, 2017, www.investopedia.com/news/facebook-now-has-more-users-india-any-other-country.

8. "Broadband vs. Dial-Up Adoption over Time," Pew Research Internet Project, September 2013, www.pewinternet.org/data-trend/internet-use/connection-type.

9. Barry Schwartz, "Google's Search Knows about over 130 Trillion Pages," November 14, 2016, https://searchengineland.com/googles-search-indexes-hits-130-trillion-pages-documents-263378.

10. "Search Engine Market Share Worldwide, Dec 2016–Dec 2017," StatCounter Global Stats, http://gs.statcounter.com/search-engine-market-share.

11. "Operation Portal Refugee Situations," United Nations High Commissioner for Refugees, https://data2.unhcr.org/en/situations/syria; "Death Tolls," I Am Syria, www.iamsyria.org/death-tolls.html.

12. Brendan I. Koerner, "Why ISIS Is Winning the Social Media War," *Wired*, March 2016, www.wired.com/2016/03/isis-winning-social-media-war-heres-beat.

13. Renee Guarriello Heath, Courtney Vail Fletcher, and Ricardo Munoz, eds., *Understanding Occupy from Wall Street to Portland: Applied Studies in Communication Theory* (Lanham, Md.: Lexington Books, 2013).

14. Sandra E. Garcia, "The Woman Who Created #MeToo Long Before Hashtags," *New York Times*, October 20, 2017, www.nytimes.com/2017/10/20/us/me-too-movement-tarana-burke.html.

15. "Chinese Regime's True Face—One of the Worst Free Speech Predators," Reporters without Borders, January 9, 2018, https://rsf.org/en/news/chinese-regimes-true-face-one-worst-free-speech-predators.

16. "ComScore Reports June 2017 U.S. Smartphone Subscriber Market Share," ComScore, August 3, 2017, www.prnewswire.com/news-releases/comscore-reports-june-2017-us-smartphone-subscriber-market-share-300498296.html.

17. Chris Anderson and Michael Wolff, "The Web Is Dead. Long Live the Internet," *Wired*, August 17, 2010, www.wired.com/magazine/2010/08/ff_webrip. See also Charles Arthur, "Walled Gardens Look Rosy for Facebook, Apple—and Would-Be Censors," *Guardian*, April 17, 2012, www.guardian.co.uk/technology/2012/apr/17/walled-gardens-facebook-apple-censors.

18. Arthur, "Walled Gardens."

19. Tim Berners-Lee, James Hendler, and Ora Lassila, "The Semantic Web," *Scientific American*, May 17, 2001.

20. Alex Colon, "Samsung's Family Hub Fridge Could Be the First Truly Smart Appliance," *PC Magazine*, January 7, 2016, www.pcmag.com/article2/0,2817,2497578,00.asp.

21. Farhad Manjoo, "The Great Tech War of 2012: Apple, Facebook, Google, and Amazon Battle for the Future of the Innovation Economy," *Fast Company*, October 19, 2011, www.fastcompany.com/magazine/160/tech-wars-2012-amazon-apple-google-facebook.

22. "Company Info," Facebook Newsroom, accessed April 2018, https://newsroom.fb.com/company-info.

23. Julie Bernard, "Five Bleeding-Edge Mobile Marketing Trends in 2017," *Ad Age*, January 5, 2017, http://adage.com/article/digitalnext/mobile-marketing-trends-2017/307343.

24. Mark Zuckerberg, "Our Commitment to the Facebook Community," *The Facebook Blog*, November 29, 2011, www.facebook.com/notes/facebook/our-commitment-to-the-facebook-community/10150378701937131.

25. "Online Tracking: Understanding Cookies," Federal Trade Commission, June 2016, www.consumer.ftc.gov/articles/0042-cookies-leaving-trail-web.

26. See Federal Trade Commission, *Privacy Online: Fair Information Practices in the Electronic Marketplace*, May 2000, www.ftc.gov/sites/default/files/documents/reports/privacy-online-fair-information-practices-electronic-marketplace-federal-trade-commission-report/privacy2000.pdf.

27. Erika Harrell, "Victims of Identity Theft, 2014," U.S. Department of Justice, September 2015, www.bjs.gov/content/pub/pdf/vit14.pdf.

28. American Library Association, "CIPA Questions and Answers," July 16, 2003, www.ala.org/advocacy/sites/ala.org.advocacy/files/content/advleg/federallegislation/cipa/cipaqa-1.pdf.

29. "Internet/Broadband Fact Sheet," Pew Research Center, February 5, 2018, www.pewinternet.org/fact-sheet/internet-broadband.

30. GSMA, "The Mobile Economy North America 2017," September 12, 2017, www.gsma.com/mobileeconomy/northamerica.

31. Internet World Stats, "Internet Users Statistics for Africa," June 30, 2017, www.internetworldstats.com/stats1.htm#africa.

32. Rebecca R. Ruiz, "F.C.C. Sets Net Neutrality Rules," March 12, 2015, *New York Times*, www.nytimes.com/2015/03/13/technology/fcc-releases-net-neutrality-rules.html.

33. Ted Johnson, "State Attorneys General File Suit over FCC's Net Neutrality Repeal," *Variety*, January 16, 2018, http://variety.com/2018/biz/news/net-neutrality-fcc-state-attorneys-general-sue-1202665803/. See also "Montana Pushes Back on FCC Ruling to Enforce Net Neutrality," NPR, January 27, 2018, www.npr.org/2018/01/27/581343532/montana-pushes-back-on-fcc-ruling-to-enforce-net-neutrality.

34. David Bollier, "Saving the Information Commons," Remarks to American Library Association Convention, Atlanta, June 15, 2002, www.ala.org/acrl/aboutacrl/directoryofleadership/committees/copyright/piratesbollier.

◘ **EXAMINING ETHICS** Social Media Fraud and Elections, p. 43

1. Alan Finlayson, "Facebook: The Election's Town Square," *Guardian*, February 14, 2010, www.theguardian.com/commentisfree/2010/feb/14/social-networking-facebook-general-election.

2. Omar L. Gallaga, "We've Reached a Turning Point for Facebook—and Its Users," *Dayton Daily News*, December 3, 2016, D6.

3. Bill Priestap, "Statement Before the Senate Select Committee on Intelligence," Washington, D.C., June 21, 2017, www.fbi.gov/news/testimony/assessing-russian-activities-and-intentions-in-recent-elections.

4. Elizabeth Weise, "Russian Fake Accounts Showed Posts to 126 Million Facebook Users," *USA Today*, October 30, 2017, www.usatoday.com/story/tech/2017/10/30/russian-fake-accounts-showed-posts-126-million-facebook-users/815342001.

5. Jessica Guynn, "Twitter: There Were More Russian Trolls Than We Thought," *USA Today*, January 19, 2018, www.usatoday.com/story/tech/news/2018/01/19/twitter-there-were-more-russian-trolls-than-we-thought/1050091001.

6. Wiese, "Russian Fake Accounts."

7. Dana Priest and Michael Birnbaum, "Europe Has Been Working to Expose Russian Meddling for Years," *Washington Post*, June 25, 2017, www.washingtonpost.com/world/europe/europe-has-been-working-to-expose-russian-meddling-for-years/2017/06/25/e42dcece-4a09-11e7-9669-250d0b15f83b_story.html.

◘ **GLOBAL VILLAGE** Designed in California, Assembled in China, p. 52

1. Charles Duhigg and Keith Bradsher, "How the U.S. Lost Out on iPhone Work," *New York Times*, January 21, 2012, www.nytimes.com/2012/01/22/business/apple-america-and-a-squeezed-middle-class.html.

2. Ibid. See also Charles Duhigg and David Barboza, "In China, Human Costs Are Built into an iPad," *New York Times*, January 25, 2012, www.nytimes.com/2012/01/26/business/ieconomy-apples-ipad-and-the-human-costs-for-workers-in-china.html.

3. Bill Weir, "A Trip to the iFactory: 'Nightline' Gets an Unprecedented Glimpse inside Apple's Chinese Core," *ABC News*, February 20, 2012, http://abcnews.go.com/International/trip-ifactory-nightline-unprecedented-glimpse-inside-apples-chinese/story?id=15748745#.T9AQTu2PfpA.

4. Barbara Demick and David Sarno, "Firm Shaken by Suicides," *Los Angeles Times*, May 26, 2010, http://articles.latimes.com/2010/may/26/world/la-fg-china-suicides-20100526.

5. Fair Labor Association, "Fair Labor Association Secures Commitment to Limit Workers' Hours, Protect Pay at Apple's Largest Supplier," March 29, 2012, www.fairlabor.org/blog/entry/fair-labor-association-secures-commitment-limit-workers-hours-protect-pay-apples-largest.

6. Citizens for Tax Justice, "Fortune 500 Companies Hold a Record $2.4 Trillion Offshore," March 3, 2016, http://ctj.org/pdf/pre0316.pdf.

7. Kevin Hardy, Kim Norvell, and Pat Johnson, "Apple's Billion-Dollar Data Center 'Puts Iowa on World Stage,'" *Des Moines Register*, August 24, 2017, www.desmoinesregister.com/story/money/business/2017/08/24/iowa-incentives-waukee-apple-data-center/596822001/. See also Michael Hiltzik, "Apple Breaks New Ground in Squeezing Locals for Huge Tax Breaks While Offering Almost No Jobs," *Los Angeles Times*, August 25, 2017, www.latimes.com/business/hiltzik/la-fi-hiltzik-apple-iowa-20170825-story.html.

8. Rick Romell and Lee Bergquist, "State, Local Tab for Foxconn: $4.5 Billion, Democratic Leader Says," *Milwaukee Journal Sentinel*, January 17, 2018, www.jsonline.com/story/news/2018/01/16/state-local-tab-foxconn-4-5-billion-democratic-leader-says/1037038001. See also Legislative Fiscal Bureau, "August 2017 Special Session Assembly Bill 1: Foxconn/Fiserv Legislation," August 8, 2017, www.documentcloud.org/documents/3935827-Wisconsin-Legislative-Fiscal-Bureau-Memo-on.html.

③ Digital Gaming and the Media Playground

1. See Megan Farokhmanesh, "First Game Tournament, 'Intergalactic Spacewar Olympics,' Held 40 Years Ago," Polygon, October 20, 2012, www.polygon.com/2012/10/20/3529662/first-game-tournament-intergalactic-spacewar-olympics-held-40-years. See also Chris Baker, "Stewart Brand Recalls First 'Spacewar' Video Game Tournament," *Rolling Stone*, May 25, 2016, www.rollingstone.com/culture/news/stewart-brand-recalls-first-spacewar-video-game-tournament-20160525.

2. Andrew Paradise, "The History Behind a $5 Billion eSports Industry," TechCrunch, November 3, 2016, https://techcrunch.com/gallery/the-history-behind-a-5-billion-esports-industry.

3. "U Unveils Roster for First Varsity eSports Team," University of Utah, October 4, 2017, https://unews.utah.edu/university-of-utah-unveils-roster-for-first-varsity-esports-team. See also Aaron Reiss, "What It's Like to Be a Varsity Esports Player," *Sports Illustrated*, January 4, 2017, www.si.com/tech-media/2017/01/04/varsity-esports-team-columbia-college-league-legends.

4. Activate, *Activate Tech & Media Outlook 2018*, October 17, 2017, www.slideshare.net/ActivateInc/activate-tech-media-outlook-2018. See also Paradise, "The History Behind."

5. Phuc Pham, "Facebook's Giant Step into eSports May Be a Look at Its Future," *Wired*, January 18, 2018, www.wired.com/story/facebook-esl-esports-streaming-partnership.

6. Irwin A. Kishner, "Esports Leagues Set to Level Up with Permanent Franchises," *Forbes*, October 3, 2017, www.forbes.com/sites/kurtbadenhausen/2017/10/03/esports-leagues-grow-up-with-permanent-franchises/#3f3f9be121d6.

7. Phuc Pham, "Esports Zerg-Rush the Olympics—but Can They Become Official Events?" *Wired*, February 9, 2018, www.wired.com/story/esports-pyeongchang-olympics.

8. Emma McDonald, "The Global Games Market Will Reach $108.9 Billion in 2017 with Mobile Taking 42%," Newzoo, April 20, 2017, https://newzoo.com/insights/articles/the-global-games-market-will-reach-108-9-billion-in-2017-with-mobile-taking-42.

9. Erkki Huhtamo, "Slots of Fun, Slots of Trouble: An Archaeology of Arcade Gaming," in Joost Raessens and Jeffrey Goldstein, eds., *Handbook of Computer Game Studies* (Cambridge, Mass.: MIT, 2005), 10.

10. Ibid., 9–10.

11. Seth Porges, "11 Things You Didn't Know about Pinball History," *Popular Mechanics*, September 1, 2009, www.popularmechanics.com/technology/g284/4328211-new.

12. Matthew Lasar, "*Spacewar!*, the First 2D Top-Down Shooter Turns 50," *Ars Technica*, October 25, 2011, http://arstechnica.com/gaming/2011/10/spacewar-the-first-2d-top-down-shooter-turns-50.

13. John Markoff, "Company News; Sony Starts a Division to Sell Game Machines," *New York Times*, May 19, 1994, www.nytimes.com/1994/05/19/business/company-news-sony-starts-a-division-to-sell-game-machines.html.

14. "PlayStation 4 Sells 5.9 Million Units Worldwide during the 2017 Holiday Season," Sony Interactive Entertainment, January 8, 2018, www.playstation.com/en-us/corporate/press-releases/2018/playstation-4-sells-59-million-units-worldwide-during-the-2017-holiday-season.

15. Craig Glenday, ed., "Hardware History II," in *Guinness World Records Gamer's Edition 2008* (London: Guinness World Records, 2008), 27.

16. Keith Stuart, "Nintendo Game Boy—25 Facts for Its 25th Anniversary," *Guardian*, April 21, 2014, www.theguardian.com/technology/2014/apr/21/nintendo-game-boy-25-facts-for-its-25th-anniversary.

17. "Industry Demographics," Fantasy Sports Trade Association, accessed February 7, 2018, https://fsta.org/research/industry-demographics.

18. Sam Anderson, "Just One More Game . . . Angry Birds, Farmville and Other Hyperaddictive 'Stupid Games,'" *New York Times*, April 4, 2012, www.nytimes.com/2012/04/08/magazine/angry-birds-farmville-and-other-hyperaddictive-stupid-games.html.

19. Pierre Lévy, *Collective Intelligence: Mankind's Emerging World in Cyberspace* (New York: Basic Books, 1997), xxviii.

20. Entertainment Software Association, *In-Game Advertising*, 2012, http://www.theesa.com/games-improving-what-matters/advertising.asp.

21. D. A. Gentile et al., "Pathological Video Game Use among Youths: A Two-Year Longitudinal Study," *Pediatrics* 127, no. 2 (2011), doi:10.1542/peds.2010-1353.

22. Florian Rehbein and Dirk Baier, "Family-, Media-, and School-Related Factors of Video Game Addiction: A 5-Year Longitudinal Study," *Journal of Media Psychology: Theories, Methods, and Application* 25, no. 3 (2013): 118–128.

23. Andrew Salmon, "Couple: Internet Gaming Addiction Led to Baby's Death," CNN, April 1, 2010, www.cnn.com/2010/WORLD/asiapcf/04/01/korea.parents.starved.baby/index.html.

24. Jason Epstein, "10 of the Most Delightfully Violent Video Games of All Time," Guyism, February 13, 2012, https://brobible.com/guyism/article/10-of-the-most-violent-video-games-of-all-time.

25. Patrick Markey and Charlotte N. Markey, "Vulnerability to Violent Video Games: A Review and Integration of Personality Research," *Review of General Psychology* 14, no. 2 (2010): 82–91.

26. National Center for Women & Information Technology, "NCWIT Factsheet," accessed June 26, 2012, www.ncwit.org/sites/default/files /resources/ncwitfactsheet.pdf. See also Claire Cain Miller, "Technology's Man Problem," *New York Times*, April 5, 2014, www.nytimes .com/2014/04/06/technology/technologys-man-problem.html.

27. Daniel Engber, "How Do Video Games Get Rated?" *Slate*, July 15, 2005, www.slate.com/articles/news_and_politics/explainer/2005/07 /how_do_video_games_get_rated.html.

28. Janna Anderson and Lee Rainie, "The Future of Gamification," Pew Internet & American Life Project, May 18, 2012, http://pewinternet.org /Reports/2012/Future-of-Gamification/Overview.aspx.

29. McDonald, "Global Games Market."

30. Entertainment Software Association, *2017: Essential Facts about the Computer and Video Game Industry*, April 2017, www.theesa.com /wp-content/uploads/2017/09/EF2017_Design_FinalDigital.pdf.

31. Ben Barrett, "Overwatch Just Reached 35 Million Players," PCGamesN, October 16, 2017, www.pcgamesn.com/overwatch/overwatch-sales -numbers.

32. Alex Pham, "Star Wars: The Old Republic—the Costliest Game of All Time?" *Los Angeles Times*, January 20, 2012, http://latimesblogs.latimes .com/entertainmentnewsbuzz/2012/01/star-wars-old-republic-cost .html.

33. Matt Brian, "Rovio's Angry Birds Titles Hit 1 Billion Cumulative Downloads," *TNW Blog*, May 9, 2012, http://thenextweb.com /mobile/2012/05/09/rovios-angry-birds-titles-hit-1-billion-cumulative --downloads.

34. "John Madden Net Worth," Celebrity Networth, accessed July 5, 2012, www.celebritynetworth.com/richest-athletes/nfl/john-madden-net -worth.

35. Joshua Brustein, "Grand Theft Auto V Is the Most Expensive Game Ever—and It's Almost Obsolete," *Bloomberg Businessweek*, September 18, 2013, www.businessweek.com/articles/2013-09-18/grand-theft-auto-v -is-the-most-expensive-game-ever-and-it-s-almost-obsolete. See also Superannuation, "How Much Does It Cost to Make a Big Video Game?" *Kotaku*, January 15, 2014, http://kotaku.com/how-much-does-it-cost-to -make-a-big-video-game-1501413649.

36. Erik Kain, "'Grand Theft Auto V' Crosses $1B in Sales, Biggest Entertainment Launch in History," *Forbes*, September 20, 2013, www .forbes.com/sites/erikkain/2013/09/20/grand-theft-auto-v-crosses-1b -in-sales-biggest-entertainment-launch-in-history.

37. Ian Hamilton, "Blizzard's World of Warcraft Revenue Down," *Orange County Register*, November 8, 2010, www.ocregister.com/2010/11/08 /blizzards-world-of-warcraft-revenue-down.

38. GameStop Corp., "Fact Sheet," accessed February 17, 2018, http:// news.gamestop.com/phoenix.zhtml?c=130125&p=factsheet.

39. "Steam: Valve's Ingenious Digital Store," Daily Infographic, February 24, 2012, http://dailyinfographic.com/steam-valves-ingenious-digital -store-infographic.

40. Don Reisinger, "Here's How Many iPhones Are Currently Being Used Worldwide," *Fortune*, March 6, 2017, http://fortune.com/2017/03/06 /apple-iphone-use-worldwide. See also Shara Tibken, "Six Takeaways from Apple CEO Cook's Earnings Call," CNET, April 24, 2014, www.cnet .com/news/six-takeaways-from-apple-ceo-cooks-earnings-call.

41. Jeff Beer, "Rise of Mobile Gaming Surprises Big Video-Game Developers," *Canadian Business*, April 2, 2012, p. 30.

42. Scalia, quoted in Evan Narcisse, "Supreme Court: 'Video Games Qualify for First Amendment Protection,'" *Time*, June 27, 2011, http:// techland.time.com/2011/06/27/supreme-court-video-games-qualify-for -first-amendment-protection.

43. Ibid.

44. Entertainment Software Association, *2015: Essential Facts about the Computer and Video Game Industry*, April 2015, www.theesa.com /wp-content/uploads/2015/04/ESA-Essential-Facts-2015.pdf.

45. Charlie Jane Anders, "*Prometheus* Writer Jon Spaihts on How to Create a Great Space Movie," *io9*, May 10, 2012, http://io9.com/5909279 /prometheus-writer-jon-spaihts-on-how-to-create-a-great-space-movie.

46. Ray Muzyka, "To Mass Effect 3 Players, from Dr. Ray Muzyka, Co-founder of BioWare," *BioWare*, March 21, 2012, http://blog.bioware .com/2012/03/21/4108.

◉ **GLOBAL VILLAGE** Phones in Hand, the World Finds Pokémon (and Wizards), p. 76

1. J. V. Chamary, "Why 'Pokémon GO' Is the World's Most Important Game," *Forbes*, February 10, 2018, www.forbes.com/sites /jvchamary/2018/02/10/pokemon-go-science-health -benefits/#2d728a153ab0.

2. See "'Pokemon Go': 10 Strangest Pokestop Locations," *Rolling Stone*, July 13, 2016, www.rollingstone.com/culture/pictures/pokemon-go -10-worst-pokestop-locations-20160713; and Charles Pulliam-Moore, "Is There a Pokémon Go Gym in the Korean Demilitarized Zone?" Splinter, July 11, 2016, https://splinternews.com/is-there-a-pokemon-go-gym-in -the-korean-demilitarized-z-1793860155.

3. Paul Tassi, "Niantic and 'Pokémon GO' Have Turned an Important Corner This Past Week," *Forbes*, November 24, 2017, www.forbes.com /sites/insertcoin/2017/11/24/niantic-and-pokemon-go-have-turned-an -important-corner-this-past-week/#646df3d472d1.

4. Rene Ritchie, "Pokémon Go Fest Chicago," "Pokémon Go Events: What's Coming in 2018," iMore, February 16, 2018, www.imore.com /pokemon-go-events.

5. "New Augmented Reality Mobile Game Harry Potter: Wizards Unite Announced," Pottermore, November 8, 2017, www.pottermore.com /news/new-augmented-reality-mobile-game-harry-potter-wizards-unite -announced.

◉ **EXAMINING ETHICS** The Gender Problem in Digital Games, p. 80

1. Anita Sarkeesian, "It's Game Over for 'Gamers,'" *New York Times*, October 28, 2014, www.nytimes.com/2014/10/29/opinion/anita -sarkeesian-on-video-games-great-future.html.

2. Zachary Jason, "Game of Fear," *Boston Magazine*, April 2015, www .bostonmagazine.com/news/article/2015/04/28/gamergate.

3. KotakuInAction, "The Global Reach of Gamer-Gate?" May 12, 2015, www.reddit.com/r/KotakuInAction/comments/35ptw7/the_global_ reach_of_gamergate.

4. Cory Marshall, "Dozens of Police, SWAT Respond to 'Swatting' Hoax in Southwest Portland," Katu.com, January 4, 2015, www.katu.com/news /local/Dozens-of-police-SWAT-respond-to-Swatting-hoax-in-Southwest -Portland--287467591.html.

5. Ross Miller, "Anita Sarkeesian to Create New Series Looking at Masculinity in Video Games," *Verge*, January 26, 2015, www.theverge .com/2015/1/26/7915385/new-feminist-frequency-series-on -masculinity-in-video-games. See also https://twitter.com/femfreq and www.youtube.com/user/feministfrequency.

6. Brianna Wu, "Can I Play, Too? Gender Equity in the Age of #Gamer-gate," University of Northern Iowa, March 31, 2015, 7, www.youtube.com /watch?v=N-6fHFM_DdM.

7. Brianna Wu for Congress, www.briannawu2018.com.

◻ **MEDIA LITERACY AND THE CRITICAL PROCESS** First-Person Shooter Games: Misogyny as Entertainment? p. 83

1. Seth Schiesel, "Way Down Deep in the Wild, Wild West," *New York Times*, May 16, 2010, www.nytimes.com/2010/05/17/arts/television/17dead.html.

2. Ibid.

3. The Red Dragon, "Red Dead Redemption Coolest Achievement Ever—Dastardly Tutorial," YouTube video, posted May 19, 2010, www.youtube.com/watch?v=Vmtdvpp9dMc&feature=related.

4. Tracy Clark-Flory, "Grand Theft Misogyny," *Salon*, May 3, 2008, www.salon.com/2008/05/03/gta_2.

5. Matt Cabral, "A History of GTA and How It Helped Shape Red Dead Redemption," *PCWorld Australia*, July 13, 2010, www.pcworld.idg.com.au/article/352981/history_gta_how_it_helped_shape_red_dead_redemption.

PART 2: SOUNDS AND IMAGES

Infographic sources:

"2017 U.S. Music Year-End Report," Nielsen Music, January 3, 2018, www.nielsen.com/us/en/insights/reports/2018/2017-music-us-year-end-report.html.

Rani Molla, "Amazon Prime Has 100 Million-Plus Prime Memberships—Here's How HBO, Netflix and Tinder Compare," Recode, April 19, 2018, www.recode.net/2018/4/19/17257942/amazon-prime-100-million-subscribers-hulu-hbo-tinder-members.

④ Sound Recording and Popular Music

1. Joe Coscarelli, "Chance the Rapper Says His Apple Music Deal Was Worth $500,000," *New York Times*, March 17, 2017, www.nytimes.com/2017/03/17/arts/music/chance-the-rapper-apple-deal.html.

2. Dan Rys and Ben Austen, "How Chance the Rapper Turned Down Leading Labels, Then Teamed with Apple Music," *Billboard*, August 11, 2016, www.billboard.com/articles/columns/hip-hop/7469373/chance-the-rapper-manager-interview.

3. Coscarelli, "Chance the Rapper."

4. Katie Couric, "The Magnificent Rise of Chance the Rapper," Yahoo! News, February 27, 2017, www.yahoo.com/katiecouric/chance-the-rapper-talks-grammys-chicago-and-why-he-doesnt-need-a-label-211356146.html.

5. David Drake, "Chance the Rapper Puts on Magnificent Show for 'Coloring Day' Festival in Chicago," *Billboard*, September 26, 2016, www.billboard.com/articles/columns/hip-hop/7518992/chance-the-rapper-magnificent-coloring-day-festival.

6. Couric, "Magnificent Rise of Chance the Rapper."

7. "The Phonautograms of Édouard-Léon Scott de Martinville," First Sounds, accessed August 21, 2014, www.firstsounds.org/sounds/scott.php.

8. Thomas Edison, quoted in Marshall McLuhan, *Understanding Media* (New York: McGraw-Hill, 1964), 276.

9. Mark Coleman, *Playback: From the Victrola to MP3* (Cambridge, Mass.: Da Capo Press, 2003).

10. Shawn Fanning, quoted in Steven Levy, "The Noisy War over Napster," *Newsweek*, June 5, 2000, p. 46.

11. Ethan Smith, "LimeWire Found to Infringe Copyrights," *Wall Street Journal*, May 12, 2010, www.wsj.com/articles/SB10001424052748704247904575240572654422514.

12. Ben Sisario, "Spotify Hits 10 Million Subscribers, a Milestone," *New York Times*, May 21, 2014, www.nytimes.com/2014/05/22/business/media/spotify-hits-milestone-with-10-million-paid-subscribers.html.

13. IFPI, "IFPI Global Music Report 2016," 2016, www.ifpi.org/downloads/GMR2016.pdf.

14. See Bruce Tucker, "'Tell Tchaikovsky the News': Postmodernism, Popular Culture and the Emergence of Rock 'n' Roll," *Black Music Research Journal* 9, no. 2 (Fall 1989): 280.

15. Robert Palmer, *Deep Blues: A Musical and Cultural History of the Mississippi Delta* (New York: Penguin, 1982), 15.

16. LeRoi Jones, *Blues People* (New York: Morrow Quill, 1963), 168.

17. Mick Jagger, quoted in Jann S. Wenner, "Jagger Remembers," *Rolling Stone,* December 14, 1995, p. 66.

18. Little Richard, quoted in Charles White, *The Life and Times of Little Richard: The Quasar of Rock* (New York: Harmony Books, 1984), 65–66.

19. Quoted in Dave Marsh and James Bernard, *The New Book of Rock Lists* (New York: Fireside, 1994), 15.

20. Tucker, "'Tell Tchaikovsky the News,'" 287.

21. Richard Harrington, "'A Wopbopaloobop'; and 'Alopbamboom,' as Little Richard Himself Would Be (and Was) First to Admit," *Washington Post*, November 12, 1984, final edition, sec. C1.

22. See Gerri Hershey, *Nowhere to Run: The Story of Soul Music* (New York: Penguin Books, 1984).

23. "2017 U.S. Music Year-End Report," Nielsen Music, January 3, 2018, www.nielsen.com/us/en/insights/reports/2018/2017-music-us-year-end-report.html.

24. See Tim Ingham, "The Major Labels' Revenues Grew by $1BN in 2017. But Who Had the Biggest Year?" Music Business Worldwide, February 28, 2018, www.musicbusinessworldwide.com/major-labels-revenues-grew-1bn-2017-biggest-year; "Wintel Worldwide Independent Market Report 2017," October 23, 2017, http://winformusic.org/files/WINTEL%202017/WINTEL%202017.pdf.

25. "Independent Labels Have a 37.6% Market Share, Says New Report," Music Business Worldwide, June 6, 2016, www.musicbusinessworldwide.com/independent-labels-37-6-global-market-share-says-new-report.

26. Joshua Friedlander, "News and Notes on 2017 RIAA Revenue Statistics," March 22, 2018, www.riaa.com/wp-content/uploads/2018/03/RIAA-Year-End-2017-News-and-Notes.pdf.

27. Billboard Staff, "Billboard's Genre Album Charts Will Now Incorporate Streams and Track Sales," *Billboard*, January 26, 2017, www.billboard.com/articles/columns/chart-beat/7669133/billboard-genre-album-charts-consumption-streams-track-sales; Paul Resnikoff, "Billboard's New Math: 1,500 Streams = One Album Sale; Digital Music News," November 20, 2014, www.digitalmusicnews.com/2014/11/20/billboards-new-math-1500-streams-one-album-sale.

28. Cary Sherman, "2016: A Year of Progress for Music," Medium, March 30, 2017, https://medium.com/@RIAA/2016-a-year-of-progress-for-music-4e9b77022635.

29. Value the Music, https://valuethemusic.com.

30. Jeff Leeds, "The Net Is a Boon for Indie Labels," *New York Times*, December 27, 2005, p. E1.

31. Nat Hentoff, "Many Dreams Fueled Long Development of U.S. Music," Milwaukee Journal/United Press International, February 26, 1978, p. 2.

◻ **GLOBAL VILLAGE** Latin Pop Goes Mainstream, p. 118

1. "2017 U.S. Music Year-End Report," Nielsen Music, January 3, 2018, www.nielsen.com/us/en/insights/reports/2018/2017-music-us-year-end-report.html.

2. Todd Spangler, "'Despacito' Sets YouTube Record as First Video to Top 5 Billion Views," *Variety*, April 5, 2018, http://variety.com/2018/digital/news/despacito-youtube-record-5-billion-views-1202744690.

3. Leila Cobo, "How Latin Went Mainstream, and Why It Will Continue to Happen in 2018," *Billboard*, January 26, 2018, www.billboard.com/articles/columns/latin/8096420/latin-mainstream-crossover-how-it-happened-2018.

4. Ibid. See also Cydney Adams, "Why You're Dancing to So Many Irresistible Reggaeton Beats," CBS News, January 26, 2018, www.cbsnews.com/news/reggaeton-movement-grooves-to-the-top-of-the-charts.

◉ **EXAMINING ETHICS** The Music Industry's Day of Reckoning, p. 120

1. Ben Sisario, "In Days After Grammys, a #MeToo Spark Comes to Music," *New York Times*, February 1, 2018, www.nytimes.com/2018/02/01/arts/music/music-metoo-charlie-walk-neil-portnow.html.

2. Joe Coscarelli, "Grammys President Faces Backlash After Saying Women Need to 'Step Up,'" *New York Times*, January 30, 2018, www.nytimes.com/2018/01/30/arts/music/grammys-step-up-neil-portnow-backlash.html.

3. Ben Sisario, "Gender Diversity in the Music Industry? The Numbers Are Grim," *New York Times*, January 25, 2018, www.nytimes.com/2018/01/25/arts/music/music-industry-gender-study-women-artists-producers.html.

4. Coscarelli, "Grammys President Faces Backlash."

5 **Popular Radio and the Origins of Broadcasting**

1. Brendan Regan, "Podcasts Took Off This Year; What Will the New Year Bring?" *Newsweek*, December 26, 2017, www.newsweek.com/podcasts-took-year-what-will-new-year-bring-758304.

2. "Best of the Blogs: What Kind of Shows Dominate Podcasting?" Inside Radio, December 6, 2017, www.insideradio.com/free/best-of-the-blogs-what-kind-of-shows-dominate-podcasting/article_57b18af4-da5e-11e7-9d35-9bf13c627d23.html; and "2018's Top Programming Trend Isn't a Format: It's Podcasting," Inside Radio, January 3, 2018, www.insideradio.com/s-top-programming-trend-isn-t-a-format-it-s/article_eee906ae-f057-11e7-a4e2-bb5440d19573.html.

3. Ibid.

4. Juliette De Maeyer, "Podcasting Is the New Talk-Radio," *Atlantic*, May 24, 2017, www.theatlantic.com/technology/archive/2017/05/how-podcasting-is-shaping-democracy/524028.

5. "Study: How to Use Podcasts to Bring Ears to Radio," Inside Radio, February 7, 2017, www.insideradio.com/free/study-how-to-use-podcasts-to-bring-ears-to-radio/article_42865dd4-ed07-11e6-b430-6fda005c6b66.html.

6. "Must Haves in 2018: Podcasting, Voice-Activated Listening," Inside Radio, January 9, 2018, www.insideradio.com/must-haves-in-podcasting-voice-activated-listening/article_9628c4b4-f51b-11e7-9910-d7cfa7bdfc7c.html.

7. "2018's Top Programming Trend Isn't a Format."

8. Captain Linwood S. Howeth, USN (Retired), *History of Communications-Electronics in the United States Navy* (Washington, D.C.: Government Printing Office, 1963), http://earlyradiohistory.us/1963hw.htm.

9. Margaret Cheney, *Tesla: Man out of Time* (New York: Touchstone, 2001).

10. William J. Broad, "Tesla, a Bizarre Genius, Regains Aura of Greatness," *New York Times*, August 28, 1984, http://query.nytimes.com/gst/fullpage.html?res=9400E4DD1038F93BA1575BC0A962948260&sec=health&spon=&partner=permalink&exprod=permalink.

11. Michael Pupin, "Objections Entered to Court's Decision," *New York Times*, June 10, 1934, p. E5.

12. Tom Lewis, *Empire of the Air: The Men Who Made Radio* (New York: HarperCollins, 1991), 73.

13. For a full discussion of early broadcast history and the formation of RCA, see Eric Barnouw, *Tube of Plenty* (New York: Oxford University Press, 1982); Susan Douglas, *Inventing American Broadcasting, 1899–1922* (Baltimore: Johns Hopkins University Press, 1987); and Christopher Sterling and John Kitross, *Stay Tuned: A Concise History of American Broadcasting* (Belmont, Calif.: Wadsworth, 1990).

14. See Jefferson Cowie, *Capital Moves: RCA's Seventy-Year Quest for Cheap Labor* (New York: New Press, 2001).

15. Robert W. McChesney, *Telecommunications, Mass Media, and Democracy: The Battle for Control of U.S. Broadcasting, 1928–1935* (New York: Oxford University Press, 1994).

16. Michele Hilmes, *Radio Voices: American Broadcasting, 1922–1952* (Minneapolis: University of Minnesota Press, 1997).

17. "Amos 'n' Andy Show," Museum of Broadcast Communications, www.museum.tv/eotv/amosnandy.htm.

18. Ed Christman, "RIAA, Pandora, NARAS, NAB Square Off on Capitol Hill," Billboard.biz, June 7, 2012, www.billboard.com/biz/articles/news/1094327/riaa-pandora-naras-nab-square-off-on-capitol-hill.

19. Regan, "Podcasts Took Off This Year."

20. Swapna Krishna, "Samsung Phones Will Have Functioning FM Chips from Now On," Engadget, January 11, 2018, www.engadget.com/2018/01/11/samsung-activate-fm-chips-smartphones-nextradio.

21. Radio Advertising Bureau, "Why Radio: FAQs," March 2018, www.rab.com/whyradio/WRnew/faq/faq.cfm.

22. Emily M. Reigart, "U.S. Commercial Radio Revenue Down in 2017," Radio World, April 5, 2018, www.radioworld.com/news-and-business/radio-revenue-down-in-2017.

23. Susan Ashworth, "RAB Will No Longer Release Revenue Estimates," Radio World, August 10, 2016, www.radioworld.com/news-and-business/rab-will-no-longer-release-revenue-estimates.

24. "Digital Revenue for Radio Hits $700 Million in 2017," Radio Ink, February 8, 2018, https://radioink.com/2018/02/08/digital-revenue-radio-hits-700-million-2017.

25. Federal Communications Commission, "Broadcast Station Totals as of March 31, 2018," April 9, 2018, https://apps.fcc.gov/edocs_public/attachmatch/DOC-350110A1.pdf.

26. Glenn Peoples, "How 'Playola' Is Infiltrating Streaming Services: Pay for Play Is 'Definitely Happening,'" *Billboard*, August 19, 2015, www.billboard.com/articles/business/6670475/playola-promotion-streaming-services; see also Robert Cookson, "Spotify Bans 'Payola' on Playlists," *Financial Times*, August 20, 2015, www.ft.com/content/af1728ca-4740-11e5-af2f-4d6e0e5eda22.

27. Peter DiCola, "False Premises, False Promises: A Quantitative History of Ownership Consolidation in the Radio Industry," Future of Music Coalition, December 13, 2006, http://futureofmusic.org/article/research/false-premises-false-promises.

28. Ben Sisario, "IHeartMedia, U.S.'s Largest Radio Broadcaster, Files for Bankruptcy," *New York Times*, March 15, 2018, www.nytimes.com/2018/03/15/business/media/iheartmedia-bankruptcy.html.

◉ **EXAMINING ETHICS** How Did Talk Radio Become So One-Sided?, p. 146

1. "State of the Media: Audio Today 2018, How America Listens," April 2018, www.nielsen.com/content/dam/corporate/us/en/reports-downloads/2018-reports/audio-today-report-apr-2018.pdf.

2. "The Top Talk Radio Audiences," *Talkers*, March 2018, www.talkers.com/top-talk-audiences.

3. Robert L. Hilliard and Michael C. Keith, *Waves of Rancor: Tuning in the Radical Right* (Armonk, N.Y.: M.E. Sharpe, 1999), 15.

4. Robert D. Hershey Jr., "F.C.C. Votes Down Fairness Doctrine in a 4–0 Decision," *New York Times*, August 5, 1987, www.nytimes.com/1987/08/05/arts/fcc-votes-down-fairness-doctrine-in-a-4-0-decision.html.

5. Hilliard and Keith, *Waves of Rancor*, 17.

6. Rush Limbaugh, *See I Told You So* (New York: Pocket Star Books, 1993), 372.

7. Kathleen Hall Jamieson and Joseph N. Cappella, *Echo Chamber: Rush Limbaugh and the Conservative Media Establishment* (New York: Oxford University Press, 2008), 46.

8. See "The Top Talk Radio Audiences" and *Morning Edition*, www.nationalpublicmedia.com/npr/programs/morning-edition.

9. "State of the Media."

▣ **GLOBAL VILLAGE** Radio Stories from Around the World, p. 152

1. Matthew Weaver, "Local Radio Station Keeps Getting Hijacked by Song about Masturbation," *Guardian*, July 11, 2017, www.theguardian.com/tv-and-radio/2017/jul/11/local-radio-station-mansfield-hijacked-masturbation-winkers-song.

2. "Norway Becomes First Country to End National Radio Broadcasts on FM," *Guardian*, December 13, 2017, www.theguardian.com/world/2017/dec/13/norway-becomes-first-country-to-end-national-radio-broadcasts-on-fm; "Norway First to Start Switching Off FM Radio," *Guardian*, January 5, 2017, www.theguardian.com/world/2017/jan/05/norway-first-to-start-switching-off-fm-radio.

3. Nicola Slawson, "Radio Monsoon Aims to Ensure Safety Reigns among Fishermen in South India," *Guardian*, April 24, 2017, www.theguardian.com/global-development/2017/apr/24/radio-monsoon-safety-fishermen-south-india-kerala.

4. "Explore the Government-Friendly Media Empire in Hungary," Center for Media, Data and Society, January 16, 2018, https://cmds.ceu.edu/article/2018-01-16/explore-government-friendly-media-empire-hungary.

5. "*Magyar Nemzet*, Lánchíd Rádió to Cease Operations Effective April 11th," *Budapest Beacon*, April 10, 2018, https://budapestbeacon.com/magyar-nemzet-lanchid-radio-to-cease-operations-effective-april-11th.

6. Marton Dunai, "Major Hungarian Opposition Newspaper to Close after Orban Victory," Reuters, April 10, 2018, www.reuters.com/article/us-hungary-election-media/major-hungarian-opposition-newspaper-to-close-after-orban-victory-idUSKBN1HH10S.

7. Ibid.

⑥ Television and Cable: The Power of Visual Culture

1. Quinn Keaney, "When You Find Out How Many People Watched *Stranger Things* Season 2, Your Jaw Will Drop," Pop Sugar, November 8, 2017, www.popsugar.com/entertainment/How-Many-People-Watch-Stranger-Things-44215482.

2. Lesley Goldberg, "Shonda Rhimes' Netflix Deal Ups the Stakes in Hollywood's Battle for Ownership," *Hollywood Reporter*, August 16, 2017, www.hollywoodreporter.com/live-feed/shonda-rhimes-netflix-deal-ups-stakes-hollywoods-battle-ownership-1029850.

3. David Sims, "Why Netflix Is Releasing So Many New Shows in 2018," *Atlantic*, August 29, 2017, www.theatlantic.com/entertainment/archive/2017/08/now-dawns-the-age-of-peak-netflix/538263.

4. Jill Disis, "Netflix Looks All over the World to Feed a Growing Audience," CNN, February 27, 2018, http://money.cnn.com/2018/02/27/media/netflix-worldwide-content/index.html.

5. Sims, "Why Netflix Is Releasing So Many New Shows in 2018."

6. Author interview with *NCIS* postproduction sound editor in Los Angeles, January, 8, 2018.

7. Amanda Kondolojy, "*ABC World News with Diane Sawyer* Closes Total Viewing Gap with *NBC Nightly News* by 3%," TV by the Numbers, June 5, 2012, http://tvbythenumbers.zap2it.com/2012/06/05/abc-world-news-with-diane-sawyer-closes-total-viewing-gap-with-nbc-nightly-news-by-3/136864. See also Stephen Battaglio, "*ABC World News Tonight* Takes Ratings Crown, but Broadcast News Audiences Continue to Shrink," *Los Angeles Times*, September 26, 2017, www.latimes.com/business/hollywood/la-fi-ct-network-news-ratings-20170927-story.html.

8. Noah Kirsch, "The Last Video Chain: The Inside Story of Family Video and Its $400 Million Owner," *Forbes*, February 21, 2017, www.forbes.com/sites/noahkirsch/2017/02/21/the-last-video-chain-the-inside-story-of-family-video-and-its-400-million-owner/#1aef5dcda607.

9. Rani Molla, "Netflix Now Has Nearly 118 Million Streaming Subscribers Globally," Recode, January 22, 2018, www.recode.net/2018/1/22/16920150/netflix-q4-2017-earnings-subscribers.

10. "Number of Amazon Prime Members in the United States as of September 2017 (in Millions)," Statista, October 2017, www.statista.com/statistics/546894/number-of-amazon-prime-paying-members.

11. Edmund Lee, "Netflix CEO Reed Hastings: We Won't Compete with Cable TV," *Advertising Age*, May 4, 2011, http://adage.com/article/media/netflix-ceo-reed-hastings-compete-cable-tv/227364.

12. Nielsen, "The Digital Consumer," February 2014, www.nielsen.com/content/dam/corporate/us/en/reports-downloads/2014%20Reports/the-digital-consumer-report-feb-2014.pdf.

13. James K. Willcox, "TV Trends to Watch for in 2018," *Consumer Reports*, December 22, 2017, www.consumerreports.org/lcd-led-oled-tvs/tv-trends-to-watch-for.

14. J. Fred MacDonald, *One Nation under Television: The Rise and Decline of Network TV* (Chicago: Nelson-Hall, 1994), 70.

15. See Horace Newcomb, *TV: The Most Popular Art* (Garden City, N.Y.: Anchor Books, 1974), 31, 39.

16. Keach Hagey, "Inside Telemundo's Battle with Univision for American Hispanics," March 16, 2018, www.wsj.com/articles/inside-telemundos-battle-with-univision-for-american-hispanics-1521198000.

17. Association of Public Television Stations, "Congress Provides Critical Funding Increases to Public Broadcasting for FY2010," December 15, 2009, http://archive.today/Ue9iE.

18. Suevon Lee, "Big Bird Debate: How Much Does Federal Funding Matter to Public Broadcasting?" ProPublica, October 11, 2012, www.propublica.org/article/big-bird-debate-how-much-does-federal-funding-matter-to-public-broadcasting.

19. See Elizabeth Jensen, "PBS Plans Promotional Breaks within Programs," *New York Times*, May 31, 2011, www.nytimes.com/2011/05/31/business/media/31adco.html.

20. John Boland, quoted in Katy June-Friesen, "Surge of Channels . . . Depress PBS Ratings," *Current*, December 8, 2008, www.current.org/2008/12/surge-of-channels-people-meter-chaos-depress-pbs-ratings.

21. See Dru Sefton, "PBS Mulls Strategy to Boost Kids' Ratings," *Current*, March 11, 2014, www.current.org/2014/03/pbs-mulls-strategy-to-boost-kids-ratings.

22. MacDonald, *One Nation under Television*, 181.

23. "487 Original Programs Aired in 2017; Bet You Didn't Watch Them All," January 7, 2018, https://www.nytimes.com/2018/01/05/business/media/487-original-programs-aired-in-2017.html.

24. *United States v. Midwest Video Corp.*, 440 U.S. 689 (1979).

25. Federal Communications Commission, "Report on Cable Industry Prices," January 16, 2009, http://hraunfoss.fcc.gov/edocs_public /attachmatch/DA-09-53A1.pdf.

26. "Broadband by the Numbers," NCTA, March 27, 2016, www.ncta.com /broadband-by-the-numbers; "Operating Metrics," NCTA, accessed July 12, 2012, www.ncta.com/broadband-by-the-numbers.

27. See Jack Loechner, "TV Advertising Most Influential," MediaPost, March 23, 2011, www.mediapost.com/publications/article/147033.

28. Bill Carter, "Cable TV, the Home of High Drama," *New York Times*, April 5, 2010, pp. B1, B3.

29. Maureen Ryan and Cynthia Littleton, "TV Series Budgets Hit the Breaking Point as Costs Skyrocket in Peak TV Era," *Variety*, September 26, 2017, http://variety.com/2017/tv/news/tv-series-budgets-costs-rising -peak-tv-1202570158.

30. See Sara Bibel, "Live+7 DVR Ratings: Complete 2013–2014 Season," TV by the Numbers, June 9, 2014, http://tvbythenumbers.zap2it .com/2014/06/09/live7-dvr-ratings-complete-2013-14-season-the-big -bang-theory-leads-adults-18-49-ratings-increase-raising-hope-earns -biggest-percentage-increase-the-blacklist-tope-viewership -gains/271900.

31. William J. Ray, "Private Enterprise, Privileged Enterprise, or Free Enterprise," accessed February 21, 2012, www.glasgow-ky.com /papers/#Private Enterprise.

◨ **GLOBAL VILLAGE** Telling and Selling Stories around the World,   p. 170

1. Kimberly Amadeo, "U.S. Exports, Including Top Categories, Challeng-es, and Opportunities: Why Isn't America the World's Largest Exporter?" The Balance, February 22, 2018, www.thebalance .com/u-s-exports-top-categories-challenges-opportunities-3306282.

2. "America's Cultural Role in the World Today," Access to International English, accessed May 31, 2018, access-internationalvg2.cappelendamm .no/c951212/artikkel/vis.html?tid=385685.

3. Ibid.

4. Ibid.

5. Ibid.

◨ **EXAMINING ETHICS** #MeToo and TV Station Policy,   p. 174

1. Dana Goodyear, "Can Hollywood Change Its Ways?" January 8, 2018, www.newyorker.com/magazine/2018/01/08/can-hollywood-change -its-ways.

⑦ Movies and the Impact of Images

1. "*Star Wars*," Box Office Mojo, accessed June 14, 2015, www .boxofficemojo.com/franchises/chart/?id=starwars.htm.

2. Walt Disney Company, "Disney to Acquire Lucasfilm Ltd.," October 30, 2012, www.thewaltdisneycompany.com/disney-to-acquire-lucasfilm-ltd.

3. Matt Krantz, Mike Snider, Marco Della Cava, and Bryan Alexander, "Disney Buys Lucasfilm for $4 Billion," *USA Today*, October 30, 2012, www.usatoday.com/story/money/business/2012/10/30/disney-star -wars-lucasfilm/1669739.

4. John Cawelti, *Adventure, Mystery, and Romance: Formula Stories as Art and Popular Culture* (Chicago: University of Chicago Press, 1976), 35.

5. See Charles Musser, *The Emergence of Cinema: The American Screen to 1907* (New York: Scribner's, 1991).

6. Douglas Gomery, *Shared Pleasures: A History of Movie Presentation in the United States* (Madison: University of Wisconsin Press, 1992), 18.

7. Douglas Gomery, *Movie History: A Survey* (Belmont, Calif.: Wadsworth, 1991), 167.

8. See Barbara Koenig Quart, *Women Directors: The Emergence of a New Cinema* (New York: Praeger, 1988).

9. Mike McPhate, "Hollywood's Inclusion Problem Extends beyond the Oscars, Study Says," *New York Times*, February 22, 2016, www.nytimes .com/2016/02/23/movies/hollywoods-inclusion-problem-extends -beyond-the-oscars-study-says.html.

10. Time's Up, January 1, 2018, www.timesupnow.com.

11. "8 Indigenous-Made Films Premiering at the Sundance Film Festival—and a 20th Anniversary Screening of 'Smoke Signals,'" Sundance Institute, January 10, 2018, www.sundance.org/blogs /program-spotlight/8-indigenous-made-films-premiering-at-the -2018-sundance-film-festival#/10.

12. See Gomery, *Shared Pleasures*, 171–180.

13. "Record Number of Films Produced," UNESCO, March 31, 2016, http://uis.unesco.org/en/news/record-number-films-produced; "Indian Feature Films Certified during the Year 2017," Film Federation of India, 2017, www.filmfed.org/IFF2017.html; Zheping Huang, "China's Top 10 Box Office Hits of All Time Include Four Domestic Films Released in 2017," Quartz, January 2, 2018, https://qz.com/1169192/chinas-all-time -top-10-box-office-list-has-four-domestic-films-released-in-2017 -including-wolf-warrior-2.

14. Daniel Kreps, "Hunting Ground Team Plan Hollywood Sexual Assault Documentary," *Rolling Stone*, October 23, 2017, www.rollingstone.com /movies/news/hunting-ground-team-plan-hollywood-sexual -assault-film-w509976.

15. Eric Barnouw, *Tube of Plenty: The Evolution of American Television*, rev. ed. (New York: Oxford University Press, 1982), 108–109.

16. See Douglas Gomery, "Who Killed Hollywood?" *Wilson Quarterly* (Summer 1991): 106–112.

17. Motion Picture Association of America, "Theme Report 2017," 2018, www.mpaa.org/wp-content/uploads/2018/04/MPAA-THEME -Report-2017_Final.pdf, p. 19

18. Chris Dodd, "CinemaCon 2014—Remarks as Prepared for Delivery," March 25, 2014, www.mpaa.org/wp-content/uploads/2014/03 /MPAA-DODD-CinemaCon-2014-As-Prepared-For-Delivery-MG.pdf.

19. Dave McNary, "U.S. Movie Ticket Sales Plunged 6% in 2017, Thanks to Lousy Summer," *Variety*, January 17, 2018, https://variety.com/2018/film /box-office/u-s-movie-tickets-sold-2017-1202667483.

20. Andrew Wallenstein and Ramin Setoodeh, "The Movie Deal Netflix Wants to Make—and It's Not Day-and-Date," *Variety*, November 5, 2013, http://variety.com/2013/biz/news/netflix-to-preem-movies-the-same -day-they-bow-in-theaters-1200796130.

21. IMAX, "IMAX and Warner Bros. Home Entertainment Announce Groundbreaking Virtual Reality Blockbuster Content Deal," March 28, 2017, www.imax.com/content/imax-and-warner-bros-home -entertainment-announce-groundbreaking-virtual-reality-blockbuster.

22. Julianne Pepitone, "Americans Now Watch More Online Movies Than DVDs," CNN/Money, March 22, 2012, http://money.cnn .com/2012/03/22/technology/streaming-movie-sales/index.htm.

23. Jake Coyle, "Clicking through the Wild West of Video-on-Demand," *Bloomberg Businessweek*, March 29, 2012, www.deseretnews.com /article/765564153/Clicking-through-the-wild-west-of-video-on -demand.amp?pg=all.

24. Brooks Barnes, "How 'Hunger Games' Built Up Must-See Fever," *New York Times*, March 18, 2012, www.nytimes.com/2012/03/19/business /media/how-hunger-games-built-up-must-see-fever.html.

25. David S. Cohen, "Academy to Preserve Digital Content," *Variety*, August 3, 2007, www.variety.com/article/VR1117969687.html.

26. David Thorburn, "Television as an Aesthetic Medium," *Critical Studies in Mass Communication* 4 (June 1987): 168.

▣ **EXAMINING ETHICS** Breaking through Hollywood's Race Barrier, p. 212

1. Gomery, *Shared Pleasures*, 155–170.

2. Scott Mendelson, "Box Office: Marvel's 'Black Panther' Tops $1.1 Billion Worldwide," *Forbes*, March 14, 2018, www.forbes.com/sites /scottmendelson/2018/03/14/box-office-marvels-black-panther-tops -1-1-billion-worldwide/#6d47c4935ecb.

3. Jamil Smith, "The Revolutionary Power of *Black Panther*," *Time*, February 19, 2018, http://time.com/black-panther.

4. Sean Rameswaram, "Black Panther Is the Most Important Movie of 2018," *Today, Explained*, February 20, 2018, www.stitcher.com/podcast /stitcher/today-explained/e/53403504.

▣ **GLOBAL VILLAGE** Beyond Hollywood: Asian Cinema, p. 216

1. Rob Cain, "Indian Movies Are Booming in America," *Forbes*, May 5, 2017, www.forbes.com/sites/robcain/2017/05/05/these-are-the-best-of -times-for-indian-movies-in-america/#17411a842b97; Box Office India, "Bahubali 2 Hits 1000 Crore Worldwide in Ten Days," May 8, 2017, www .boxofficeindia.com/report-details.php?articleid=2914.

PART 3: WORDS AND PICTURES

Infographic sources:

http://newsroom.publishers.org/book-publishing-annual-statshot -survey-reveals-religious-crossover-and-inspirational-books-supported -trade-book-growth-in-2016

www.magazine.org/sites/default/files/FACTBOOK-17-18-f2.pdf

www.businesswire.com/news/home/20160524005123/en/Amazon .com-Announces-Well-Read-Cities-America

http://mediashift.org/2017/12/best-news-apps-for-each-of-your-news -needs

8 Newspapers: The Rise and Decline of Modern Journalism

1. Bob Papper, "Research: TV News Employment Surpasses Newspapers," Radio Television Digital News Association, April 16, 2018, https://rtdna .org/article/research_tv_news_employment_surpasses_newspapers.

2. Richard Campbell and Jimmie L. Reeves, "Covering the Homeless: The Joyce Brown Story," *Critical Studies in Mass Communication* 6, no. 1 (March 1989): 21–42.

3. David Mizner, "Reporting an Explosive Truth: The *Boston Globe* and Sexual Abuse in the Catholic Church," Knight Case Studies Initiative, Graduate School of Journalism, Columbia University, 2009, p. 7.

4. See "Google News Lab," newsinitiative.withgoogle.com/google-news -lab.

5. Michael Barthel, "Newspapers Fact Sheet," Pew Research Journalism Project, June 13, 2018, www.journalism.org/fact-sheet/newspapers.

6. Michael Barthel, "*State of the News Media 2015*: Newspapers: Fact Sheet," Pew Research Journalism Project, April 29, 2015, www.journalism .org/2015/04/29/newspapers-fact-sheet.

7. Ibid.

8. See Kay Mills, *A Place in the News: From the Women's Pages to the Front Page* (New York: Dodd, Mead, 1988).

9. William Randolph Hearst, quoted in Piers Brendon, *The Life and Death of the Press Barons* (New York: Atheneum, 1983), 134.

10. Michael Schudson, *Discovering the News: A Social History of American Newspapers* (New York: Basic Books, 1978), 23.

11. See David T. Z. Mindich, "Edwin M. Stanton, the Inverted Pyramid, and Information Control," *Journalism Monographs* 140 (August 1993).

12. Curtis D. MacDougall, *The Press and Its Problems* (Dubuque: William C. Brown, 1964), 143, 189.

13. Walter Lippmann, *Liberty and the News* (New York: Harcourt, Brace and Howe, 1920), 92.

14. Tom Wolfe, quoted in Leonard W. Robinson, "The New Journalism: A Panel Discussion," in Ronald Weber, ed., *The Reporter as Artist: A Look at the New Journalism Controversy* (New York: Hastings House, 1974), 67. See also Tom Wolfe and E. E. Johnson, eds., *The New Journalism* (New York: Harper & Row, 1973).

15. Tom Wicker, *On Press* (New York: Viking, 1978), 3–5.

16. Jill Abramson, quoted in Nat Ives, "Abramson and Keller, NYT's Incoming and Outgoing Top Editors, Talk Challenges and Changes," *Advertising Age*, June 2, 2011, http://adage.com/article /mediaworks/q-a-york-times-jill-abramson-bill-keller/227928.

17. Your Voice Ohio, accessed June 3, 2018, https://yourvoiceohio.org.

18. See Sreenath Sreenivasan, "As Mainstream Papers Struggle, the Ethnic Press Is Thriving," *New York Times*, July 22, 1996, p. C7.

19. Pew Research Center's Project for Excellence in Journalism, "Ethnic: Summary Essay," *State of the News Media 2010*, http://stateofthemedia .org/2010/ethnic-summary-essay.

20. Ibid.

21. See Barbara K. Henritze, *Bibliographic Checklist of American Newspapers* (Baltimore: Clearfield, 2009).

22. Aprill Turner, "Black Journalists' Ranks Cut by Nearly 1,000 in Past Decade," National Association of Black Journalists newsletter, April 4, 2012, www.nabj.org/news/88558.

23. Pamela Newkirk, "The Not-So-Great Migration," *Columbia Journalism Review*, May 25, 2011, www.cjr.org/feature/the_not_so_great_migration .php.

24. ASNE, "Table B: Minority Employment by Race and Job Category," http://asne.org/content.asp?pl=140&sl=416&contentid=416.

25. ASNE, "Table A: Minority Employment in Daily Newspapers," http:// asne.org/content.asp?contentid=129.

26. ASNE, "ASNE, Google News Lab Release 2017 Diversity Survey Results with Interactive Website," October 10, 2017, http://asne.org/diversity -survey-2017.

27. Papper, "Research: TV News Employment Surpasses Newspapers."

28. Special thanks to Mary Lamonica and her students at New Mexico State University.

29. Pew Research Center's Project for Excellence in Journalism, *State of the News Media 2010*, www.stateofthenewsmedia.org/2010. See also Emily Guskin and Monica Anderson, "Developments in the Hispanic Media Market," Pew Research Journalism Project, March 26, 2014, www .journalism.org/2014/03/26/developments-in-the-hispanic-media -market.

30. ASNE, "Table A: Minority Employment in Daily Newspapers" and "Table B: Minority Employment by Race and Job Category."

31. ASNE, "Table B: Minority Employment by Race and Job Category."

32. United States Census Bureau, "State & County Quick Facts," July 8, 2014, http://quickfacts.census.gov/qfd/states/00000.html. See also Pew Research Center's Project for Excellence in Journalism, *State of the News Media 2010*.

33. Wil Cruz, "The New *New Yorker*: Ethnic Media Fill the Void," *Newsday*, June 26, 2002, p. A25.

34. Chinese Advertising Agencies, "About *Chinese Daily News*," accessed September 3, 2014, www.chineseadvertisingagencies.com/mediaguide /Chinese-Daily-News.html.

35. ASNE, "Table B: Minority Employment by Race and Job Category."

36. Ibid.

37. "About the *Village Voice*," accessed June 4, 2018, www.villagevoice .com/about.

38. Pew Research Center Publications, "The New Washington Press Corps," July 16, 2009, www.journalism.org/2009/07/16/new-washington -press-corps.

39. Kristine Lu and Jesse Holcomb, "In 21 States, Local Newspapers Lack a Dedicated D.C. Reporter Covering Congress," January 7, 2016, www .pewresearch.org/fact-tank/2016/01/07/in-21-states-local-newspapers -lack-a-dedicated-reporter-keeping-tabs-on-congress.

40. American Society of News Editors, "Decline in Newsroom Jobs Slows," April 11, 2010, http://asne.org/content.asp?pl=121&sl=150&contentid=150.

41. Rick Edmonds, "ASNE Newsroom Census Total Reflects Decline in Traditional Journalism Jobs, Growth in Online," Poynter, May 5, 2011, www.poynter.org/news/asne-newsroom-census-total-reflects-decline -traditional-journalism-jobs-growth-online.

42. ASNE, "2013 Census," June 25, 2013, http://asne.org/diversity -survey-2013; ASNE, "2015 Census," July 28, 2015, http://asne.org /content.asp?pl=121&sl=415&contentid=415.

43. Papper, "Research: TV News Employment Surpasses Newspapers."

44. See Mac Ryan, "Amid Industry Cuts, Warren Buffett Says He Is Looking to Buy More Newspapers," *Forbes*, May 24, 2012, www.forbes .com/sites/ryanmac/2012/05/24/warren-buffett-says-he-is-looking-to -buy-more-newspapers; Christine Haughney, "Newspaper Work, with Warren Buffett as Boss," *New York Times*, June 17, 2012, www.nytimes .com/2012/06/18/business/media/newspaper-work-with-warren -buffett-as-the-boss.html?_r=0.

45. Warren Buffett, quoted in Mathew Ingram, "Warren Buffett Says Most Newspapers, Including His Own, Are Doomed," *Forbes*, February 28, 2017, http://fortune.com/2017/02/28/buffett-newspapers-doomed.

46. See Philip Meyer, "Learning to Love Lower Profits," *American Journalism Review*, December 1995, 40–44.

47. Pew Research Center's Project for Excellence in Journalism, "Newspapers: Summary Essay," *State of the News Media 2010*, http:// stateofthemedia.org/2010/newspapers-summary-essay.

48. Pew Research Center's Project for Excellence in Journalism, "Newspapers: Summary Essay," *State of the News Media 2010*.

49. Ibid.

50. "Media Deserts Project Creates Searchable Media Access Research Atlas," April 9, 2018, www.ohio.edu/compass/stories/17-18/04 /media-deserts-research-ferrier.cfm.

51. Joshua Benton, "American Newspaper Revenue Is Still Dropping, Just Not Quite as Much as Before," April 21, 2014, www.niemanlab .org/2014/04/american-newspaper-revenue-is-still-dropping-just-not -quite-as-much-as-before.

52. Richard Pérez-Peña, "Newspaper Ad Revenue Could Fall as Much as 30%," *New York Times*, April 15, 2009, p. B3.

53. See "Gannett Newspapers and Yahoo Create Local Advertising Partnership," Chicago Press Release Services, July 19, 2010, http:// chicagopressrelease.com/technology/gannett-newspapers-and-yahoo; Evan Hessel, "Yahoo!'s Dangerous Newspaper Deal?" *Forbes*, June 22, 2009, www.forbes.com/2009/06/22/advertising-newspapers-internet -business-media-yahoo.html; Kate Kaye, "Media General Expands Yahoo Partnership to TV-Only Markets," Clickz Marketing News, June 11, 2010, www.clickz.com/clickz/news/1721928/media-general-xpands-yahoo -partnership.

54. Benton, "American Newspaper Revenue Is Still Dropping."

55. D. M. Levine, "Small Papers Lead the Way on Paywalls," *Adweek*, June 3, 2011, www.adweek.com/news/press/small-papers-lead-way -paywalls-132203.

56. Dean Baquet, "The New York Times Reaches a Milestone, Thanks to Our Readers," October 5, 2015, www.nytimes.com/2015/10/05/business /the-new-york-times-reaches-a-milestone-thanks-to-our-readers .html?_r=0.

57. Joshua Benton, "Paywalls Are Not a Cure-All: Evidence from Gannett," February 4, 2014, www.niemanlab.org/2014/02/paywalls-are-not-a -cure-all-evidence-from-gannett.

58. Leonard Downie and Michael Schudson, "The Reconstruction of American Journalism," *Columbia Journalism Review*, October 19, 2009, pp. 77–91, https://archives.cjr.org/reconstruction/the_reconstruction_ of_american.php. (All quoted material is from this report.) See also Leonard Downie Jr. and Michael Schudson, "New-Model Journalism Needs Community Support," *Washington Post*, October 19, 2009, www .washingtonpost.com/wp-dyn/content/article/2009/10/18 /AR2009101801461.html?noredirect=on.

59. Brian Deagon, "You, Reporting Live: Citizen Journalism Relies on Audience; Now, Everyone's a Stringer," *Investor's Business Daily*, March 31, 2008, p. A4.

60. Mark Jurkowitz and Paul Hitlin, "Citizen Eyewitnesses Provide Majority of Top Online News Videos in Oklahoma Tornado Disaster," Pew Research Center, May 20, 2013, www.pewresearch.org/fact -tank/2013/05/22/citizen-eyewitnesses-provide-majority-of-top-online -news-videos.

61. Amy Mitchell, Mark Jurkowitz, Jesse Holcomb, Jodi Enda, and Monica Anderson, "Nonprofit Journalism—a Growing but Fragile Part of the U.S. News System," Pew Research Journalism Project, June 10, 2013, www .journalism.org/2013/06/10/nonprofit-journalism.

62. Jesse Holcomb and Amy Mitchell, "Personal Wealth, Capital Investments, and Philanthropy," Pew Research Journalism Project, March 26, 2014, www.journalism.org/2014/03/26/personal-wealth-capital -investments-and-philanthropy.

63. Committee to Protect Journalists, accessed June 2016, www.cpj.org /killed.

64. Marc Santora and Bill Carter, "War in Iraq Becomes the Deadliest Assignment for Journalists in Modern Times," *New York Times*, May 30, 2006, p. A10.

65. See Matthew Ingram, "Which Will Save AOL: *Huffington Post* or Patch?" *Gigaom*, June 9, 2011, www.gigaom.com/2011/06/09/which-will -save-aol-huffington-post-or-patch.

66. Jondi Gumz, "Patch.com Shuts News Websites, Lays Off Hundreds," *Santa Cruz Sentinel*, January 29, 2014, Business and Financial section.

67. See "2017 Pulitzer Prizes: Journalism," www.pulitzer.org/prize -winners-by-year/2017.

68. John Carroll, "News War, Part 3," *Frontline*, PBS, February 27, 2007, www.pbs.org/wgbh/pages/frontline/newswar/etc/script3.html.

■ **EXAMINING ETHICS** Alternative Journalism: The Activism of Dorothy Day and I. F. Stone, p. 256

1. I. F. Stone, quoted in Jack Lule, "I. F. Stone: Professional Excellence in Raising Hell," *QS News* (Summer 1989): 3.

◼ **GLOBAL VILLAGE** Newspaper Readership across the Globe, p. 260

1. World Association of Newspapers (WAN), "Newspaper Circulation Grows Despite Economic Downturn," May 27, 2009, www.wan-press.org /article18148.html.

2. Achara Deboonme, "Floppy Discs, Walkmans and Now Newspapers?" *Nation* (Thailand), June 4, 2013, www.nationmultimedia.com/opinion /Floppy-discs-Walkmans-and-now-newspapers-30207480.html.

3. World Association of Newspapers (WAN), "World Press Trends: Newspaper Revenues Shift to New Sources," June 1, 2015, www.wan-ifra .org/press-releases/2015/06/01/world-press-trends-newspaper -revenues-shift-to-new-sources.

4. World Association of Newspapers (WAN), "World Press Trends: Print and Digital Together Increasing Newspaper Audiences," June 9, 2014, www.wan-ifra.org/press-releases/2014/06/09/world-press-trends-print -and-digital-together-increasing-newspaper-audienc.

5. See www.wptdatabase.org/world-press-trends-2017-facts-and-figures.

6. Ibid.

9 Magazines in the Age of Specialization

1. Greg Dool, "Meredith's *Magnolia Journal* Ups the Ante Again," *Folio*, May 11, 2017, www.foliomag.com/merediths-magnolia-journal-ups -ante-industry-notes.

2. Meredith Corporation, "Meredith to Increase Distribution to 600,000 Copies for Premiere Issue of the *Magnolia Journal*," October 25, 2016, http://meredith.mediaroom.com/index.php?s=2311&item=137020.

3. Sara Guaglione, "*Magnolia Journal* Rakes in 700,000 Subscribers," *MediaPost*, May 10, 2017, www.mediapost.com/publications/article /300854/magnolia-journal-rakes-in-700000-subscribers.html.

4. See Theodore Peterson, *Magazines in the Twentieth Century* (Urbana: University of Illinois Press, 1964), 5.

5. See Richard Ohmann, *Selling Culture: Magazines, Markets, and Class at the Turn of the Century* (New York: Verso, 1996).

6. Peterson, *Magazines*, 5.

7. Rebecca Eisenberg, "Salon Returns to Off-Line Media Roots," SFGate, October 4, 1998, www.sfgate.com/business/article/Salon-returns-to-off -line-media-roots-3066497.php.

8. Generoso Pope, quoted in William H. Taft, *American Magazines for the 1980s* (New York: Hastings House, 1982), 226–227.

9. See S. Elizabeth Bird, *For Enquiring Minds: A Cultural Study of Supermarket Tabloids* (Knoxville: University of Tennessee Press, 1992), 24.

10. "Advertising," Condé Nast, accessed June 5, 2018, http://stag .condenast.com/advertising.

11. See Gloria Steinem, "Sex, Lies and Advertising," *Ms.*, July/August 1990, pp. 18–28.

12. Association of Magazine Media, March 7, 2018, "Magazine Media 360° Brand Audience Report," www.magazine.org/industry-news/press -releases/mpa/magazine-media-360%C2%B0-brand-audience-report -shows-media-mix-has13.

13. Pew Research Center, "News Magazine Overall Circulation," April 27, 2015, www.journalism.org/2015/04/29/news-magazines-fact -sheet-2015/pj_2015-04-29_sotnm_news-magazines_04; "Total Paid, Verified and Analyzed Non-Paid Circulation," Alliance for Audited Media, December 31, 2017, http://abcas3.auditedmedia.com/ecirc /magtitlesearch.asp.

◼ **EXAMINING ETHICS:** The Evolution of Photojournalism, p. 280

1. Carrie Melago, "Ralph Lauren Model Filippa Hamilton: I Was Fired Because I Was Too Fat!" *New York Daily News*, October 14, 2009, http://

www.nydailynews.com/lifestyle/fashion/2009/10/14/2009-10-14 _model_fired_for_being_too_fat.html#ixzz0riJa9skc.

2. Ken Harris, quoted in Jesse Epstein, "Sex, Lies, and Photoshop," *New York Times*, March 8, 2009, http://video.nytimes.com/video/2009/03/09 /opinion/1194838469575/sex-lies-and-photoshop.html.

◼ **GLOBAL VILLAGE:** Cosmopolitan Style Travels the World, p. 286

1. Tess Koman, "'We Can't Publish the Word 'Sex'': What It's Like to Be the Editor of Cosmo Middle East," Cosmopolitan.com, October 20, 2015, www.cosmopolitan.com/career/news/a46331/cosmo-middle-east -brooke-sever-eic-interview.

2. Tess Koman, "What It's Like to Be the Editor of *Cosmo* Chile," Cosmopolitan.com, March 29, 2016, www.cosmopolitan.com/career /news/a55561/cosmo-chile-ignacia-uribe-eic-interview.

3. Sammye Johnson, "Promoting Easy Sex without the Intimacy: *Maxim* and *Cosmopolitan* Cover Lines and Cover Images," in Mary-Lou Galician and Debra L. Merskin, eds., *Critical Thinking about Sex, Love, and Romance in the Mass Media* (Mahwah, N.J.: Erlbaum, 2007), 55–74.

4. Karen S. H. Roggenkamp, "'Dignified Sensationalism': Elizabeth Bisland, *Cosmopolitan*, and Trips around the World," *American Periodicals: A Journal of History, Criticism, and Bibliography* 17, no. 1 (2007): 26–40.

5. John Tebbel and Mary Ellen Zuckerman, *The Magazine in America, 1741–1990* (New York: Oxford University Press, 1991), 116.

◼ **MEDIA LITERACY AND THE CRITICAL PROCESS** Uncovering American Beauty, p. 289

1. Rachel Torgeson, "Kylie Jenner Is RAWRRRR in this Low-Cut, Leopard Print Dress," *Cosmopolitan*, June 6, 2018, www.cosmopolitan.com /style-beauty/fashion/a21201733/kylie-jenner-leopard-dress.

2. Academy for Eating Disorders, "Guidelines for the Fashion Industry," January 10, 2007, https://higherlogicdownload.s3.amazonaws.com /AEDWEB/05656ea0-59c9-4dd4-b832-07a3fea58f4c/UploadedImages /Press_Releases/AED_Guidelines_for_Fashion_Industry.pdf.

3. Academy for Eating Disorders, "Fast Facts on Eating Disorders," accessed June 5, 2018, https://www.aedweb.org/learn/resources /fast-facts.

10 Books and the Power of Print

1. See https://www.publishersweekly.com/pw/by-topic/industry-news /bookselling/article/74418-trade-sales-were-a-bright-spot-in-a-dark -year-for-sales.html.

2. Heid Macdonald, "*NY Times* Ignores 400 Publishing Industry Pros' Pleas to Return Graphic Novel Bestseller Chart," *The Beat*, February 9, 2018, www.comicsbeat.com/ny-times-ignores-400-publishing-industry -pros-pleas-to-return-graphic-novel-bestseller-chart.

3. "Comics and Graphic Novels."

4. Ibid.

5. Michael Cavna, "Rep. John Lewis's National Book Award win is a milestone moment for graphic novels," *Washington Post*, November 17, 2016, www.washingtonpost.com/news/comic-riffs/wp/2016/11/17 /rep-john-lewiss-national-book-award-win-is-a-milestone-moment-for -graphic-novels.

6. Calvin Reid, "Comics Industry Asks *NYT* to Restore Graphic Bestseller Lists," *Publishers Weekly*, February 7, 2018, www.publishersweekly.com /pw/by-topic/industry-news/comics/article/75998-comics-industry -asks-nyt-to-restore-graphic-bestseller-lists.html.

7. Susana Polo, "The *New York Times* Gave Up on Graphic Novels," *Polygon*, January 26, 2017, www.polygon.com/2017/1/26/14401436/new-york-times-graphic-novel-list.

8. Ibid.

9. Olsen, quoted in Reid, "Comics Industry."

10. Book publishing figures from the 2017 *Bowker Annual Library and Book Trade Almanac* (Information Today, Inc.).

11. Elizabeth Eisenstein, *The Printing Press as an Agent of Change* (Cambridge: Cambridge University Press, 1980).

12. See Quentin Reynolds, *The Fiction Factory: From Pulp Row to Quality Street* (New York: Street & Smith/Random House, 1955), 72–74.

13. For a comprehensive historical overview of the publishing industry and the rise of publishing houses, see John A. Tebbel, *A History of Book Publishing in the United States*, 4 vols. (New York: R. R. Bowker, 1972–1981).

14. National Association of College Stores, "Highlights from Student Watch Attitudes & Behaviors toward Course Materials, 2016–17 Report," www.nacs.org/research/studentwatchfindings.aspx.

15. See John P. Dessauer, *Book Publishing: What It Is, What It Does* (New York: R. R. Bowker, 1974), 48.

16. Mid-Continent Public Library, "Based on the Book," accessed June 6, 2018, www.mymcpl.org/books-movies-music/based-book.

17. Jim Milliot, "Trade Sales Were a Bright Spot in a Dark Year for Sales," *Publishers Weekly*, August 14, 2017, www.publishersweekly.com/pw/by-topic/industry-news/bookselling/article/74418-trade-sales-were-a-bright-spot-in-a-dark-year-for-sales.html.

18. Association of American Publishers, "Book Publishing Annual StatShot Survey Reveals Religious Crossover and Inspirational Books Supported Trade Book Growth in 2016," August 1, 2017, http://newsroom.publishers.org/book-publishing-annual-statshot-survey-reveals-religious-crossover-and-inspirational-books-supported-trade-book-growth-in-2016.

19. "*Alice in Wonderland* iPad App Reinvents Reading (Video)," *Huffington Post*, April 14, 2010, www.huffingtonpost.com/2010/04/14/alice-in-wonderland-ipad_n_537122.html.

20. Milliot, "Trade Sales."

21. Chloe Teasley, "Columbus Bookstores Have Independent Spirit," *ColumbusCEO*, May 7, 2018, www.columbusceo.com/business/20180507/columbus-bookstores-have-independent-spirit.

22. David Leonhardt, "Save Barnes & Noble!" *New York Times*, May 6, 2018, www.nytimes.com/2018/05/06/opinion/save-barnes-noble.html.

23. Ryan Raffaelli, quoted in Carmen Nobel, "How Independent Bookstores Have Thrived in Spite of Amazon.com," Harvard Business School, November 20, 2017, https://hbswk.hbs.edu/item/why-independent-bookstores-haved-thrived-in-spite-of-amazon-com.

24. Steve Wasserman, "The Amazon Effect," *Nation*, May 29, 2012, www.thenation.com/article/168125/amazon-effect#.

25. "February 2017 Big, Bad, Wide and International Report: Covering Amazon, Apple, B&N, and Kobo Ebook sales in the US, UK, Canada, Australia, and New Zealand," Author Earnings, February 2017, http://authorearnings.com/report/february-2017. (Figures are rounded by the source.)

26. "January 2018 Report: US Online Book Sales, Q2–Q4 2017," Author Earnings, January 2018, http://authorearnings.com/report/january-2018-report-us-online-book-sales-q2-q4-2017.

27. Kathryn Zickuhr and Lee Rainie, "A Snapshot of Reading in America in 2013," Pew Research Center, January 16, 2014, www.pewinternet.org/2014/01/16/a-snapshot-of-reading-in-america-in-2013.

28. Alvin Kernan, *The Death of Literature* (New Haven, Conn.: Yale University Press, 1990).

29. "How We Will Read: Clay Shirky," interview by Sonia Saraiya, *Findings*, April 5, 2012, http://archive.is/a6qmi.

30. Alan Finder, "The Joys and Hazards of Self-Publishing on the Web," *New York Times*, August 15, 2012, www.nytimes.com/2012/08/16/technology/personaltech/ins-and-outs-of-publishing-your-book-via-the-web.html.

◉ EXAMINING ETHICS: Contemporary Politics Revives Interest in Classic Novels, p. 308

1. Jean Seaton, Tim Crook, and DJ Taylor, "Welcome to Dystopia—George Orwell Experts on Donald Trump," *Guardian*, January 25, 2017, www.theguardian.com/commentisfree/2017/jan/25/george-orwell-donald-trump-kellyanne-conway-1984.

2. John Maher, "Orwell's '1984' Surges After Trump's First Week," *Publishers Weekly*, February 1, 2017, www.publishersweekly.com/pw/by-topic/industry-news/bookselling/article/72667-orwell-s-1984-surges-after-trump-s-first-week.html.

3. Heidi M. Przybyla and Fredreka Schouten, "At 2.6 Million Strong, Women's Marches Crush Expectations," *USA Today*, January 21, 2017, www.usatoday.com/story/news/politics/2017/01/21/womens-march-aims-start-movement-trump-inauguration/96864158.

4. Alexandra Alter, "Uneasy about the Future, Readers Turn to Dystopian Classics," *New York Times*, January 27, 2017, www.nytimes.com/2017/01/27/business/media/dystopian-classics-1984-animal-farm-the-handmaids-tale.html.

5. John Koblin, "How Hulu and 'The Handmaid's Tale' Revived 2 Careers," *New York Times*, April 26, 2017, www.nytimes.com/2017/04/26/business/media/how-hulu-and-the-handmaids-tale-revived-2-careers.html.

◉ GLOBAL VILLAGE Buenos Aires, the World's Bookstore Capital, p. 313

1. Debora Rey, "Bookstore Tourists Should Have One Destination on Their List: Buenos Aires," Associated Press, May 2, 2015, http://skift.com/2015/05/02/bookstore-tourists-should-have-one-destination-on-their-list-buenos-aires.

2. Ibid.

3. Ibid.

4. Catherine Blache, "Why Fixed Book Price Is Essential for Real Competition," International Publishers Association, March 19, 2015, www.internationalpublishers.org/news/blog/entry/why-fixed-book-price-is-essential-for-real-competition.

5. International Publishers Association, "Global Fixed Book Price Report," May 23, 2014, www.internationalpublishers.org/images/reports/2014/fixed-book-price-report-2014.pdf.

6. Blache, "Why Fixed Book Price Is Essential."

7. Matt Chesterton, "Top Bookstores in Buenos Aires," *Travel + Leisure*, August 2014, www.travelandleisure.com/local-experts/buenos-aires/top-bookstores-buenos-aires.

PART 4: THE BUSINESS OF MASS MEDIA

Infographic sources:

www.statista.com/statistics/267805/microsofts-global-revenue-since-2002

www.statista.com/statistics/266206/googles-annual-global-revenue

www.statista.com/statistics/265125/total-net-sales-of-apple-since-2004

www.statista.com/statistics/277229/facebooks-annual-revenue-and-net
-income

www.statista.com/statistics/266282/annual-net-revenue-of-amazoncom

11 Advertising and Commercial Culture

1. Ad Age, *Marketing Fact Pack*, 2018 edition, p. 16.

2. See Emily Steel and Sydney Ember, "Networks Fret as Ad Dollars Flow to Digital Media," *New York Times*, May 10, 2015, www.nytimes .com/2015/05/11/business/media/networks-frets-as-ad-dollars-flow-to -digital-media.html.

3. Ad Age, "Time Spent Using Media," *Marketing Fact Pack*, p. 21.

4. Steel and Ember, "Networks Fret"; Ad Age, "Cost for 30-Second Commercial," *Marketing Fact Pack*, 2018 edition, pp. 18–19.

5. Teresa F. Lindeman, "Product Placement Nation: Advertisers Pushing the Boundaries to Bring in More Bucks," *Pittsburgh Post-Gazette*, May 13, 2011, www.post-gazette.com/pg/11133/1146175-28-0.stm; Aimee Picchi, "Cable Networks Are Speeding Up TV Shows to Cram in Ads," *CBS Money Watch*, February 19, 2015, www.cbsnews.com/news/cable-networks-are -speeding-up-tv-shows-to-cram-in-ads.

6. Caitlin A. Johnson, "Cutting through Advertising Clutter," *CBS Sunday Morning*, September 16, 2006, www.cbsnews.com/stories/2006/09/17 /sunday/main2015684.shtml.

7. For a written and pictorial history of early advertising, see Charles Goodrum and Helen Dalrymple, *Advertising in America: The First 200 Years* (New York: Harry N. Abrams, 1990), 31.

8. Michael Schudson, *Advertising: The Uneasy Persuasion* (New York: Basic Books, 1984), 164.

9. News Media Alliance, "Business Model Evolving, Circulation Revenue Rising," April 14, 2014, printinthemix.com/Fastfacts/Show/849; Ad Age, *Marketing Fact Pack*, 2018 edition.

10. David Gelles, "At Odds, Omnicom and Publicis End Merger," *New York Times*, May 8, 2014, http://dealbook.nytimes.com/2014/05/08/ad-agency -giants-said-to-call-off-35-billion-merger.

11. Natalie Zmuda, "Peterson Milla Hooks Is Ad Age's Comeback Agency of the Year," January 28, 2013, http://adage.com/article/special-report -agency-alist-2013/comeback-agency-year-peterson-milla -hooks/239306. See also PMH website at www.pmhadv.com/about.

12. See TVB, "TV Cost & CPM Trends—Network TV Primetime (M–Su)," accessed September 19, 2014, www.tvb.org/trends/4718/4709.

13. Jordan Robertson, "E-Mail Spam Goes Artisanal," January 19, 2016, www.bloomberg.com/news/articles/2016-01-19/e-mail-spam -goes-artisanal.

14. Bettina Fabos, "The Commercialized Web: Challenges for Libraries and Democracy," *Library Trends* 53, no. 4 (Spring 2005): 519–523.

15. Quentin Hardy, "Google Introduces Products That Will Sharpen Its Ad Focus," *New York Times*, March 15, 2016, www.nytimes.com/2016/03/16 /technology/google-introduces-products-that-will-sharpen-its-ad-focus .html?ref=technology.

16. Jaikumar Vijayan, "Google Introduces Advanced Analysis Capability in Analytics 360," May 18, 2018, www.eweek.com/big-data-and-analytics /google-introduces-advanced-analysis-capability-in-analytics-360.

17. Ad Age, *Marketing Fact Pack*, 2018 edition, p. 16.

18. See www.statista.com/statistics/266206/googles-annual-global -revenue, www.statista.com/statistics/264810/number-of-monthly -active-facebook-users-worldwide, and www.statista.com/statistics /277229/facebooks-annual-revenue-and-net-income.

19. See Ad Age, "Net U.S. Mobile Advertising Revenue by Company," *Marketing Fact Pack*, 2016 edition, p. 16.

20. See www.statista.com/statistics/539477/google-mobile-ad-revenues -worldwide, www.marketing-interactive.com/mobile-advertising -represents-91-of-facebooks-mobile-ad-revenue, and www.statista.com /statistics/255756/twitters-worldwide-mobile-internet-advertising -revenue.

21. "How Media Companies Lost the Advertising Business," *Media Trends*, June 5, 2018, www.axios.com/newsletters/axios-media-trends -432a3456-798e-4b74-a99b-181b48a2a370.html?utm_source=sidebar.

22. Jack Neff, "Unilever to Double Digital Spending This Year," *Advertising Age*, June 25, 2010, http://adage.com/cannes2010/article?article _id=144672.

23. Ad Age, "Time Spent Using Media," *Marketing Fact Pack*, 2016 edition, p. 21; Center for the Digital Future, *Surveying the Digital Future—Year Fifteen*, 2017, www.digitalcenter.org/wp-content/uploads/2013/10/2017 -Digital-Future-Report.pdf.

24. Jon Gibs and Sean Bruich, "NielsenFacebook Report the Value of Social Media Ad Impressions," April 20, 2010, www.nielsen.com/us/en /insights/news/2010/nielsenfacebook-ad-report.html.

25. See Alexandra Ilyashov, "That Dress You Saw All Over Instagram Last Year Might Be a *Really* Expensive Mistake," March 15, 2016, www .refinery29.com/2016/03/106064/lord-and-taylor-ootd-ads-campaign -ftc-settlement.

26. "The Facebook Data Breach Scandal Explained," May 1, 2018, www.techadvisory.org/2018/05/the-facebook-data-breach-scandal -explained.

27. Caitlin Murray, "The Top 25 Highest-Paid Athletes in the World for 2017 Are . . . ," June 7, 2017, https://nypost.com/2017/06/07/the-top -25-highest-paid-athletes-in-the-world-for-2017-are.

28. Leslie Savan, "Op Ad: Sneakers and Nothingness," *Village Voice*, April 2, 1991, p. 43.

29. "2018 BrandZ Top 100 Global Brands," accessed June 12, 2018, www .millwardbrown.com/brandz/top-global-brands.

30. See Mary Kuntz and Joseph Weber, "The New Hucksterism," *BusinessWeek*, July 1, 1999, 79.

31. Schudson, *Advertising*, 210.

32. Eric Pfanner, "Your Brand on TV for a Fee, in Britain," *New York Times*, March 6, 2011, www.nytimes.com/2011/03/07/business/media/07iht -adco.html.

33. Vance Packard, *The Hidden Persuaders* (New York: Basic Books, 1957, 1978), 229.

34. See Eileen Dempsey, "Auld Lang Syne," *Columbus Dispatch*, December 28, 2000, p. 1G; John Reinan, "The End of the Good Old Days," *Minneapolis Star Tribune*, August 31, 2004, p. 1D.

35. See Schudson, *Advertising*, 36–43; Andrew Robertson, *The Lessons of Failure* (London: MacDonald, 1974).

36. Kim Campbell and Kent Davis-Packard, "How Ads Get Kids to Say, I Want It!" *Christian Science Monitor*, September 18, 2000, p. 1.

37. See Jay Mathews, "Channel One: Classroom Coup or a 'Sham'?" *Washington Post*, December 26, 1994, p. A1ff.

38. See Michael F. Jacobson and Laurie Ann Mazur, *Marketing Madness: A Survival Guide for a Consumer Society* (Boulder, Colo.: Westview Press, 1995), 29–31.

39. "Ads Beat News on School TVs," *Pittsburgh Post-Gazette*, March 6, 2006, p. A7.

40. Hilary Waldman, "Study Links Advertising, Youth Drinking," *Hartford Courant*, January 3, 2006, p. A1.

41. Alix Spiegel, "Selling Sickness: How Drug Ads Changed Health Care," National Public Radio, October 13, 2009, www.npr.org/templates/story /story.php?storyid=113675737.

42. ProCon.org, "Should Prescription Drugs Be Advertised Directly to Consumers?" updated March 2014, http://prescriptiondrugs.procon.org/view.answers.php?questionID=001603.

43. Jeffrey Godsick, quoted in T. L. Stanley, "Hollywood Continues Its Fast-Food Binge," *Adweek*, June 6, 2009, www.adweek.com/news/advertising-branding/hollywood-continues-its-fast-food-binge-105907.

44. Douglas J. Wood, "Ad Issues to Watch for in '06," *Advertising Age*, December 19, 2005, p. 10.

45. Associated Press, "Two Ephedra Sellers Fined for False Ads," *Washington Post*, July 2, 2003, p. A7.

46. See Truth Initiative, "Let's Be the Generation to Finish It," www.thetruth.com/about-truth; "Truth Campaign," https://truthinitiative.org/truth%C2%AE-campaign; "Saving Lives through Truth," https://truthinitiative.org/saving-lives-through-truth; "Master Settlement Agreement," https://truthinitiative.org/master-settlement-agreement. All accessed June 15, 2018.

47. See Stephen Ansolabehere and Shanto Iyengar, *Going Negative: How Attack Ads Shrink and Polarize the Electorate* (New York: Free Press, 1996).

48. Center for Responsive Politics, "The Money behind the Elections," accessed June 14, 2013, www.opensecrets.org/bigpicture.

49. See Kate Kaye, "Data-Driven Targeting Creates Huge 2016 Political Ad Shift: Broadcast TV Down 20%, Cable and Digital Way Up," January 3, 2017, http://adage.com/article/media/2016-political-broadcast-tv-spend-20-cable-52/307346.

50. Kantar Media, "Key Sporting Events and Political Ads Increase U.S. Full-Year Advertising Expenditures," March 18, 2015, www.kantarmedia.com/us/newsroom/press-releases/key-sporting-events-and-political-ads-increase-us-fullyear-advertising-expenditures.

☑ **EXAMINING ETHICS** Do Alcohol Ads Encourage Binge Drinking?   p. 347

1. "During Binges, U.S. Adults Have 17 Billion Drinks a Year," March 16, 2018, www.cdc.gov/media/releases/2018/p0316-binge-drinking.html.

2. Amanda Stewart, "Alcohol Ads Have Heavy Impact on Underage Binge Drinking," Design & Trend, January 20, 2015, www.designntrend.com/articles/35740/20150120/alcohol-ads-heavy-impact-underage-binge-drinking.htm. See also FoxNews.com, "Children's Health: TV Alcohol Ad Exposure Linked to Greater Chance of Underage Drinking," January 20, 2015, www.foxnews.com/health/2015/01/20/tv-alcohol-ad-exposure-linked-to-greater-chance-underage-drinking.

3. Stewart, "Alcohol Ads Have Heavy Impact."

4. FoxNews.com, "Children's Health."

☑ **GLOBAL VILLAGE** Smoking Up the Global Market,   p. 352

1. GBD 2015 Tobacco Collaborators, "Smoking Prevalence and Attributable Disease Burden in 195 Countries and Territories, 1990–2015: A Systematic Analysis from the Global Burden of Disease Study 2015," *Lancet*, 389, no. 10082 (May 13, 2017): 1885–1906, www.thelancet.com/journals/lancet/article/PIIS0140-6736(17)30819-X/fulltext?elsca1=tlpr.

2. Cheng Yingqi, "Women Now Main Target of Tobacco Firms," *China Daily*, May 19, 2010, www.chinadaily.com.cn/china/2010-05/19/content_9865347.htm.

3. See Li Hui and Ben Blanchard, "China Tobacco Monopoly Blocks Full Ban on Tobacco," Reuters, September 4, 2014, www.reuters.com/article/2014/09/05/us-china-smoking-idUSKBN0H001N20140905.

4. Cheng, "Women Now Main Target."

5. National Institutes of Health, "Fact Sheet: Global Tobacco Research," October 2010, http://report.nih.gov/nihfactsheets/Pdfs/GlobalTobaccoResearch%28FIC%29.pdf.

⑫ Public Relations and Framing the Message

1. Derek Thompson, "Why NFL Ratings Are Plummeting: A Two-Part Theory," *Atlantic*, February 1, 2018, www.theatlantic.com/business/archive/2018/02/super-bowl-nfl-ratings-decline/551861.

2. Mark Fainaru-Wada and Steve Fainaru, "NFL-NIH Research Partnership Set to End with $16M Unspent," ESPN, July 28, 2017, www.espn.com/espn/otl/story/_/id/20175509/nfl-donation-brain-research-falls-apart-nih-appears-set-move-bulk-30-million-donation.

3. Michael McCann, "Will New CTE Findings Doom the NFL Concussion Settlement?" *Sports Illustrated*, August 15, 2017, www.si.com/nfl/2017/08/15/new-cte-study-effect-nfl-concussion-settlement.

4. "NFL Issues Response to CTE Research Report," NFL, July 26, 2017, www.nfl.com/news/story/0ap3000000822159/article/nfl-issues-response-to-cte-research-report.

5. Louis Bien, "The NFL Is Going to Insulting Lengths to Prove That CTE Isn't a Problem," SB Nation, August 31, 2017, www.sbnation.com/2017/8/31/16233630/nfl-concussion-study-funding-cte-horse-jockeys.

6. "NFL Announces Play Smart. Play Safe., a New Commitment to Improve Player Health and Safety," NFL Communications, September 14, 2016, https://nflcommunications.com/Pages/NFL-Announces-Play-Smart.-Play-Safe.,-a-New-Commitment-to-Improve-Player-Health-and-Safety.aspx.

7. Bien, "NFL Is Going to Insulting Lengths."

8. Jacob Feldman, "Five Former Players Accused of Sexual Harassment in Lawsuit," *Sports Illustrated*, December 13, 2017, www.si.com/nfl/2017/12/13/nfl-network-sexual-harassment-marshall-faulk-themmqb-newsletter.

9. Kevin Draper, "NFL Network Executive Resigns After Reports of Sexually Explicit Tweets," *New York Times*, December 20, 2017, www.nytimes.com/2017/12/20/sports/football/david-eaton-nfl-network-resigns.html.

10. Associated Press, "Saints Ex-Cheerleader Says NFL Team's Policies Discriminate," March 26, 2018, www.apnews.com/152ddd9294044a2d9f5885774371cae0.

11. Matthew J. Culligan and Dolph Greene, *Getting Back to the Basics of Public Relations and Publicity* (New York: Crown, 1982), 100.

12. See Stuart Ewen, *PR! A Social History of Spin* (New York: Basic Books, 1996).

13. Marvin N. Olasky, "The Development of Corporate Public Relations, 1850–1930," *Journalism Monographs* 102 (April 1987): 14.

14. Ivy Lee, quoted in Anthony Fellow, *American Media History* (Boston: Cengage Learning, 2012), 202.

15. Edward Bernays, "The Theory and Practice of Public Relations: A Résumé," in E. L. Bernays, ed., *The Engineering of Consent* (Norman: University of Oklahoma Press, 1955), 3–25.

16. Edward Bernays, *Crystallizing Public Opinion* (New York: Horace Liveright, 1923), 217.

17. Michael Schudson, *Discovering the News: A Social History of American Newspapers* (New York: Basic Books, 1978), 136.

18. Glenn Gray, "Why Public Relations Agencies Are Evolving," *Forbes*, July 21, 2017, www.forbes.com/sites/forbescommunicationscouncil/2017/07/21/why-public-relations-agencies-are-evolving/#3b237c2317f4.

19. "The Real Cost Campaign," FDA, March 30, 2018, www.fda.gov /tobaccoproducts/publichealtheducation/publiceducationcampaigns /therealcostcampaign/default.htm.

20. Center for Responsive Politics, "Lobbying Database," accessed August 26, 2012, http://opensecrets.org/lobby.

21. SourceWatch, "Center for Consumer Freedom," accessed August 20, 2014, www.sourcewatch.org/index.php?title=Center_for_Consumer _Freedom.

22. See One Orlando Alliance, https://oneorlandoalliance.org; Lori Kifer Johnson, "An Orlando Perspective on the 2016 Pulse Shootings," Edelman, June 9, 2017, www.edelman.com/post/orlando-perspective -pulse.

23. David Barstow, "Message Machine: Behind TV Analysis, Pentagon's Hidden Hand," *New York Times*, April 20, 2008, www.nytimes.com /2008/04/20/us/20generals.html.

24. Associated Press, "Open Government Study: Secrecy Up," *Politico*, March 16, 2014, www.politico.com/story/2014/03/open-government -study-secrecy-up-104715.html.

25. "Statement from Starbucks and Attorney Stewart Cohen from Cohen, Placitella & Roth," Starbucks, April 17, 2018, news.starbucks.com /press-releases/statement-from-starbucks-and-attorney-stewart-cohen.

26. Stanley Walker, "Playing the Deep Bassoons," *Harper's*, February 1932, p. 365.

27. Ibid., p. 370.

28. Ivy Lee, *Publicity* (New York: Industries, 1925), 21.

29. Schudson, *Discovering the News*, 136.

30. Ivy Lee, quoted in Ray Eldon Hiebert, *Courtier to the Crowd: The Story of Ivy Lee and the Development of Public Relations* (Ames: Iowa State University Press, 1966), 114.

31. Walter Lippmann, *Public Opinion* (New York: Free Press, 1922, 1949), 221.

32. Christopher R. Martin, *Framed! Labor and the Corporate Media* (Ithaca, N.Y.: Cornell University Press, 2003).

33. *PRWatch*, "About Us," accessed August 26, 2012, www.prwatch.org /cmd.

34. John Stauber, "Corporate PR: A Threat to Journalism?" *Background Briefing: Radio National*, March 30, 1997, www.abc.net.au/radionational /programs/backgroundbriefing/corporate-pr-a-threat-to-journalism /3563876.

35. See Alicia Mundy, "Is the Press Any Match for Powerhouse PR?" in Ray Eldon Hiebert, ed., *Impact of Mass Media* (White Plains, N.Y.: Longman, 1995), 179–188.

36. Dan Rather, interviewed in "Forty Years after Watergate: Carl Bernstein & Dan Rather with CNN's Candy Crowley," *State of the Union with Candy Crowley*, CNN, August 3, 2014, http://cnnpressroom.blogs .cnn.com/2014/08/03/forty-years-after-watergate-carl-bernstein-dan -rather-with-cnns-candy-crowley.

37. Rosanna M. Fiske, "PR Pros: Haven't We Learned Anything about Disclosure?" PRSay, May 11, 2011, http://prsay.prsa.org/index .php/2011/05/11/pr-and-communications-pros-havent-we-learned -anything-about-disclosure.

38. Elizabeth Blair, "Under the Radar, PR's Political Savvy," National Public Radio, May 19, 2011, www.npr.org/2011/05/19/136436263 /under-the-radar-pr-s-political-savvy.

39. Fiske, "PR Pros."

■ **EXAMINING ETHICS** Public Relations and "Alternative Facts," p. 372
1. Jill Abramson, "'Alternative Facts' Are Just Lies, Whatever Kellyanne Conway Claims," *Guardian*, January 24, 2017, www.theguardian.com /commentisfree/2017/jan/23/kellyanne-conway-alternative-facts-lies.

2. Ibid.

3. Jane Dvorak, "PRSA Statement on "Alternative Facts," PRSA, January 24, 2017, www.prsa.org/prsa-statement-alternative-facts.

4. Kimiko de Freytas-Tamura, "George Orwell's '1984' Is Suddenly a Best-Seller," *New York Times*, January 25, 2017, www.nytimes .com/2017/01/25/books/1984-george-orwell-donald-trump.html.

5. Jane Dvorak, Twitter.com, March 22, 2017, https://twitter.com /jkdjane?lang=en.

■ **GLOBAL VILLAGE** Public Relations and Bananas, p. 374
1. Phil Milford, "Dole, Del Monte, Dow Chemical Sued over Banana Pesticide," BloombergBusiness, June 4, 2012, www.bloomberg.com /news/articles/2012-06-04/dole-del-monte-dow-chemical-sued-over -banana-pesticide.

2. Dole Organic Program, "About Us," accessed June 29, 2018, www .doleorganic.com/farms/index.php/about-us.

■ **MEDIA LITERACY AND THE CRITICAL PROCESS** The Invisible Hand of PR, p. 382
1. Stauber, "Corporate PR."

13 **Media Economics and the Global Marketplace**

1. "Netflix's View: Internet Entertainment Is Replacing Linear TV," updated January 22, 2018, https://ir.netflix.com/netflixs-view-internet -tv-replacing-linear-tv.

2. Netflix Form 10-K (2017 Annual Report), January 29, 2018, https://ir .netflix.com/node/29631/html; Netflix, "Overview," https://ir.netflix.com.

3. John Koblin, "Netflix Studied Your Binge-Watching Habit. That Didn't Take Long," *New York Times*, June 8, 2016, www.nytimes.com/2016 /06/09/business/media/netflix-studied-your-binge-watching-habit-it -didnt-take-long.html.

4. "Netflix's View."

5. For this section, the authors are indebted to the ideas and scholarship of Douglas Gomery, a media economist and historian, formerly from the University of Maryland.

6. Douglas Gomery, "The Centrality of Media Economics," in Mark R. Levy and Michael Gurevitch, eds., *Defining Media Studies* (New York: Oxford University Press, 1994), 202.

7. David Rolf, *The Fight for $15: The Right Wage for a Working America* (New York: New Press, 2016).

8. ICNA Council for Social Justice, "Minimum Wage Mythbusters," icnacsj.org/2016/09/minimum-wage-mythbusters.

9. Wesley Morris and James Poniewozik, "Why 'Diverse TV' Matters: It's Better TV. Discuss," *New York Times*, February 10, 2016, www.nytimes .com/2016/02/14/arts/television/smaller-screens-truer-colors.html.

10. Elizabeth Fones-Wolf, *Selling Free Enterprise: The Business Assault on Labor and Liberalism, 1945–60* (Urbana: University of Illinois Press, 1994).

11. David Harvey, *The Condition of Postmodernity: An Enquiry into the Origins of Cultural Change* (Oxford: Basil Blackwell, 1989), 171.

12. Alex S. Jones, "F.C.C. Raised Limits on Total Stations under One Owner," *New York Times*, July 27, 1984, www.nytimes.com/1984/07/27 /business/fcc-raises-limit-on-total-stations-under-one-owner.html.

13. Federal Communications Commission, "Report on Cable Industry Prices," October 12, 2016, https://docs.fcc.gov/public/attachments /DA-16-1166A1.pdf.

14. Tim Arango and Brian Stelter, "Comcast Receives Approval for NBC Universal Merger," *New York Times*, January 11, 2011, www.nytimes .com/2011/01/19/business/media/19comcast.html.

15. Harvey, *Condition of Postmodernity*, 158.

16. Bureau of Labor Statistics, "Union Members Summary," January 19, 2018, www.bls.gov/news.release/union2.nr0.htm.

17. Economic Policy Institute, "The Great Recession," August 17, 2012, http://stateofworkingamerica.org/great-recession.

18. Dave Gilson, "Survival of the Richest," *Mother Jones*, September/October 2014, pp. 32–35.

19. David Gelles, "Want to Make Money Like a C.E.O.? Work for 275 Years," *New York Times*, May 25, 2018, www.nytimes.com/2018/05/25/business/highest-paid-ceos-2017.html.

20. "The Highest-Paid C.E.O.s in 2017," *New York Times*, May 25, 2018, www.nytimes.com/interactive/2018/05/25/business/ceo-pay-2017.html.

21. National Employment Law Project, "Big Business, Corporate Profits, and the Minimum Wage," July 2012, www.nelp.org/wp-content/uploads/2015/03/NELP-Big-Business-Corporate-Profits-Minimum-Wage.pdf.

22. Ibid.

23. Ibid.

24. Antonio Gramsci, *Selections from the Prison Notebooks* (New York: International Publishers, 1971), 12–13.

25. Robert Sher, "Why Half of All M&A Deals Fail, and What You Can Do about It," *Forbes*, March 19, 2012, www.forbes.com/sites/forbesleadershipforum/2012/03/19/why-half-of-all-ma-deals-fail-and-what-you-can-do-about-it.

26. Richard J. Barnet and John Cavanagh, *Global Dreams: Imperial Corporations and the New World Order* (New York: Simon & Schuster, 1994), 131.

27. Ben Bagdikian, *The Media Monopoly*, 6th ed. (Boston: Beacon Press, 2000), 222.

28. Kristal Brent Zook, "Blacks Own Just Ten U.S. Television Stations. Here's Why," *Washington Post*, August 17, 2015, www.washingtonpost.com/posteverything/wp/2015/08/17/blacks-own-just-10-u-s-television-stations-heres-why.

29. Harry First, "Bring Back Antitrust!" *Nation*, June 2, 2008, pp. 7–8.

30. William Paley, quoted in Robert W. McChesney, *Telecommunications, Mass Media, and Democracy: The Battle for Control of U.S. Broadcasting, 1928–1935* (New York: Oxford University Press, 1993), 251.

31. McChesney, *Telecommunications, Mass Media, and Democracy*, 264.

32. Edward Herman, "Democratic Media," *Z Papers* (January–March 1992): 23.

33. Barnet and Cavanagh, *Global Dreams*, 38.

34. Richard J. Barnet and Ronald E. Muller, *Global Reach: The Power of Multinational Corporations* (New York: Simon & Schuster, 1974), 175.

35. See Adam Liptak, "Justices, 5–4, Reject Corporate Spending Limits," *New York Times*, January 22, 2010, www.nytimes.com/2010/01/22/us/politics/22scotus.html.

36. David Sessions, "Chick-fil-A's Place in the Church of Fast Food," *Daily Beast*, July 29, 2012, www.thedailybeast.com/articles/2012/07/29/chick-fil-a-s-place-in-the-church-of-fast-food.html; Michael D. Shear, "Amazon's Founder Pledges $2.5 Million in Support of Same-Sex Marriage," *New York Times*, July 27, 2012, http://thecaucus.blogs.nytimes.com/2012/07/27/amazons-founder-pledges-2-5-million-in-support-of-same-sex-marriage.

37. "Cost of Election," Center for Responsive Politics, accessed June 26, 2018, www.opensecrets.org/overview/cost.php.

38. Pew Research Center's Project for Excellence in Journalism, *State of the News Media 2013*, accessed June 14, 2013, http://stateofthemedia.org/2013/special-reports-landing-page/the-changing-tv-news-landscape.

39. Robert McChesney and John Nichols, "Who'll Unplug Big Media? Stay Tuned," *Nation*, May 29, 2008, www.thenation.com/article/wholl-unplug-big-media-stay-tuned.

40. Center for Responsive Politics, "Lobbying Database," accessed June 26, 2018, www.opensecrets.org/lobby/index.php.

41. Center for Responsive Politics, "2012 Top Donors to Outside Spending Groups," September 1, 2012, www.opensecrets.org/outsidespending/summ.php?cycle=2012&disp=D&type=V.

42. Robert Maguire, "$1.4 Billion and Counting in Spending by Super PACs, Dark Money Groups," Center for Responsive Politics, November 9, 2016, www.opensecrets.org/news/2016/11/1-4-billion-and-counting-in-spending-by-super-pacs-dark-money-groups.

⊡ **EXAMINING ETHICS** Are the Big Digital Companies Too Big?

1. Dylan Byers, "Pacific," May 24, 2018, https://mailchi.mp/cnn/pacific-may-24-2018?e=e6767fbebc.

2. Amanda Lotz, "'Big Tech' Isn't One Big Monopoly—It's 5 Companies All in Different Businesses," *Conversation*, March 23, 2018, https://theconversation.com/big-tech-isnt-one-big-monopoly-its-5-companies-all-in-different-businesses-92791.

3. Ibid.

4. Christopher Mims, "Tech's Titans Tiptoe toward Monopoly; Amazon, Facebook and Google May Be Repeating the History of Steel, Utility, Rail and Telegraph Empires Past—While Apple Appears Vulnerable," *Wall Street Journal*, May 31, 2018, www.wsj.com/articles/techs-titans-tiptoe-toward-monopoly-1527783845.

5. Charles Duhigg, "The Case Against Google," *New York Times Magazine*, February 20, 2018, www.nytimes.com/2018/02/20/magazine/the-case-against-google.html.

⊡ **GLOBAL VILLAGE:** China's Dominant Media Corporations Rival America's, p. 411

1. "2018 BrandZ Top 100 Global Brands," accessed May 29, 2018, www.millwardbrown.com/brandz/top-global-brands/2018.

2. Raymond Zhong, "Worried about Big Tech? Chinese Giants Make America's Look Tame," *New York Times*, May 31, 2018, www.nytimes.com/2018/05/31/technology/china-tencent-alibaba.html.

3. Ibid.

PART 5 OPENER

1. "Facebook and Twitter Are Being Used to Manipulate Public Opinion—Report," *Guardian*, www.theguardian.com/technology/2017/jun/19/social-media-proganda-manipulating-public-opinion-bots-accounts-facebook-twitter.

Infographic source:

https://rsf.org/en/ranking

www.statista.com/statistics/237974/online-advertising-spending-worldwide

14 **The Culture of Journalism: Values, Ethics, and Democracy**

1. Brooke Kroeger, *Nellie Bly: Daredevil, Reporter, Feminist* (New York: Times Books/Random House, 1994).

2. Pulitzer Prizes, "The 2016 Pulitzer Prize Winner in Investigative Reporting," accessed June 29, 2016, www.pulitzer.org/winners/leonora-lapeter-anton-and-anthony-cormier-tampa-bay-times-and-michael-braga-sarasota-herald.

3. Mary Walton, "Investigative Shortfall," *American Journalism Review*, September 2010, www.ajr.org/Article.asp?id=4904.

4. Jason Stverak, "Investigative Journalism Is Alive and Well Outside Mainstream Media," Watchdog.org, January 18, 2013, www.watchdog.org/66865/investigative-journalism-is-alive-and-well-outside-mainstream-media.

5. Neil Postman, "Currents," *Utne Reader*, July/August 1995, p. 35.

6. Reuven Frank, "Memorandum from a Television Newsman," reprinted as Appendix 2 in A. William Bluem, *Documentary in American Television* (New York: Hastings House, 1965), 276.

7. Horace Greeley, quoted in Christopher Lasch, "Journalism, Publicity and the Lost Art of Argument," *Gannett Center Journal* 4, no. 2 (Spring 1990): 2.

8. David Eason, "Telling Stories and Making Sense," *Journal of Popular Culture* 15, no. 2 (Fall 1981): 125.

9. Jon Katz, "AIDS and the Media: Shifting out of Neutral," *Rolling Stone*, May 27, 1993, p. 32.

10. Bill Kovach and Tom Rosenstiel, *The Elements of Journalism* (New York: Three Rivers Press, 2007), 78–112.

11. Herbert Gans, *Deciding What's News* (New York: Pantheon, 1979), 42–48.

12. Ibid.

13. Ibid., 48–51.

14. See Michael Schudson, *Discovering the News: A Social History of American Newspapers* (New York: Basic Books, 1978), 3–11.

15. Dean Baquet and Bill Keller, "When Do We Publish a Secret?" *New York Times*, July 1, 2006, p. A27.

16. Code of Ethics, reprinted in Melvin Mencher, *News Reporting and Writing*, 3rd ed. (Dubuque, Iowa: William C. Brown, 1984), 443–444.

17. Ibid.

18. For reference and guidance on media ethics, see Clifford Christians, Mark Fackler, and Kim Rotzoll, *Media Ethics: Cases and Moral Reasoning*, 4th ed. (White Plains, N.Y.: Longman, 1995); and Thomas H. Bivins, "A Worksheet for Ethics Instruction and Exercises in Reason," *Journalism Educator* (Summer 1993): 4–16.

19. Christians, Fackler, and Rotzoll, *Media Ethics*, 15.

20. See Jimmie Reeves and Richard Campbell, *Cracked Coverage: Television News, the Anti-Cocaine Crusade, and the Reagan Legacy* (Durham, N.C.: Duke University Press, 1994).

21. See David Eason, "On Journalistic Authority: The Janet Cooke Scandal," *Critical Studies in Mass Communication* 3, no. 4 (December 1986): 429–447.

22. Mike Royko, quoted in "News Media: A Searching of Conscience," *Newsweek*, May 4, 1981, p. 53.

23. Don Hewitt, interview conducted by Richard Campbell on *60 Minutes*, CBS News, New York, February 21, 1989.

24. Ina Howard, "Power Sources: On Party, Gender, Race, and Class, TV News Looks to the Most Powerful Groups," *Extra!*, Fairness and Accuracy in Reporting, May 1, 2002, www.fair.org/extra-online/articles/power-sources.

25. The 4th Estate, "Silenced: Gender Gap in the 2012 Election Coverage," accessed September 3, 2012, www.4thestate.net/female-voices-in-media-infographic.

26. See Adrienne LaFrance, "I Analyzed a Year of My Reporting for Gender Bias (Again)," *Atlantic*, February 17, 2016, www.theatlantic.com/technology/archive/2016/02/gender-diversity-journalism/463023.

27. Women's Media Center, *The Status of Women of Color in the U.S. News Media, 2018*, March 2018, www.womensmediacenter.com/assets/site/reports/the-status-of-women-of-color-in-the-u-s-media-2018-full-report/Women-of-Color-Report-FINAL-WEB.pdf.

28. David Carr, "Journalist, Provocateur, Maybe Both," *New York Times*, July 26, 2010, p. B2.

29. William Greider, quoted in Mark Hertsgaard, *On Bended Knee: The Press and the Reagan Presidency* (New York: Farrar, Straus & Giroux, 1988), 78.

30. Bluem, *Documentary in American Television*, 94.

31. See David Carr, "Big News Forges Its Own Path," *New York Times*, June 16, 2013, www.nytimes.com/2013/06/17/business/media/big-news-forges-its-own-path.html.

32. David A. Fahrenthold, "Trump Recorded Having Extremely Lewd Conversation about Women in 2005," October 8, 2016, www.washingtonpost.com/politics/trump-recorded-having-extremely-lewd-conversation-about-women-in-2005/2016/10/07/3b9ce776-8cb4-11e6-bf8a-3d26847eeed4_story.html?utm_term=.22922e95dc18.

33. Based on notes made by the lead author's wife, Dianna Campbell, after a visit to Warsaw and discussions with a number of journalists working for *Gazeta Wyborcza* in 1990.

34. Davis "Buzz" Merritt, *Public Journalism and Public Life: Why Telling the News Is Not Enough* (Hillsdale, N.J.: Lawrence Erlbaum, 1995), 113–114.

35. Lasch, "Journalism, Publicity and the Lost Art of Argument," 1.

36. Jay Rosen, "Forming and Informing the Public," *Kettering Review*, Winter 1992, 69–70.

37. Mike Wendling, "The (Almost) Complete History of 'Fake News,'" January 22, 2018, www.bbc.com/news/blogs-trending-42724320.

38. Katharine Q. Seelye, "Best-Informed Also View Fake News, Study Finds," *New York Times*, April 16, 2007, www.nytimes.com/2007/04/16/business/media/16pew.html.

39. James Agee and Walker Evans, *Let Us Now Praise Famous Men* (Boston: Houghton Mifflin, 1960), xiv.

40. David Broder, quoted in "Squaring with the Reader: A Seminar on Journalism," *Kettering Review* (Winter 1992): 48.

41. Kovach and Rosenstiel, *Elements of Journalism*, 17.

42. See Robert McChesney and John Nichols, *The Death and Life of American Journalism* (New York: Nation Books, 2010), 48.

43. See Pew Research Center, "The Master Character Narratives in Campaign 2012," August 23, 2012, www.journalism.org/2012/08/23/2012-campaign-character-narratives.

44. Alex T. Williams, "The Growing Pay Gap between Journalism and PR," Pew Research Center, August 11, 2014, www.pewresearch.org/fact-tank/2014/08/11/the-growing-pay-gap-between-journalism-and-public-relations.

▣ **GLOBAL VILLAGE** News Bias around the Globe, p. 430

1. Amy Mitchell, Katie Simmons, Katerina Eva Matsa, and Laura Silver, "Publics Globally Want Unbiased News Coverage, but Are Divided on Whether Their News Media Deliver," Pew Research Center, January 11, 2018, www.pewglobal.org/2018/01/11/publics-globally-want-unbiased-news-coverage-but-are-divided-on-whether-their-news-media-deliver.

EXAMINING ETHICS WikiLeaks, Secret Documents, and Good Journalism, p. 449

1. Bill Keller, "The Boy Who Kicked the Hornet's Nest," *New York Times Magazine*, January 30, 2011, pp. 33–34.

2. Ibid., p. 37.

3. Jay Rosen, "The Afghanistan War Logs Released by Wikileaks, the World's First Stateless News Organization," *PressThink*, July 26, 2010, www.pressthink.org/2010/07/the-afghanistan-war-logs-released-by -wikileaks-the-worlds-first-stateless-news-organization.

4. Nikki Usher, "Why WikiLeaks' Latest Document Dump Makes Everyone in Journalism—and the Public—a Winner," Nieman Journalism Lab, December 3, 2010, www.niemanlab.org/2010/12/why-wikileaks -latest-document-dump.

15 Media Effects and Cultural Approaches to Research

1. Rebecca Nicholson, "13 Reasons Why Review—Sex, Drugs and Mixtapes in Netflix's High-School Horror Show," *Guardian*, March 31, 2017, www.theguardian.com/tv-and-radio/2017/mar/31/13-reasons -why-review-sex-drugs-and-mixtapes-in-netflix-high-school-horror-show.

2. Mark Henick, "Why '13 Reasons Why' Is Dangerous," CNN, May 4, 2017, https://edition.cnn.com/2017/05/03/opinions/13-reasons-why -gets-it-wrong-henick-opinion/index.html.

3. Sophie Gilbert, "Did *13 Reasons Why* Spark a Suicide Contagion Effect?" *Atlantic*, August 1, 2017, www.theatlantic.com/entertainment /archive/2017/08/13-reasons-why-demonstrates-cultures-power/535518.

4. Joyce Chen, "Selena Gomez Defends '13 Reasons Why' as Honest Depiction of Teen Suicide," *Rolling Stone*, June 7, 2017, www.rollingstone .com/culture/news/selena-gomez-defends-13-reasons-why-as-honest -w486466.

5. Jon Blistein, "Netflix Adds More Advisory Warnings to '13 Reasons Why,'" *Rolling Stone*, May 2, 2017, www.rollingstone.com/tv/news /netflix-adds-more-advisory-warnings-to-13-reasons-why-w480108.

6. Netflix, *13 Reasons Why*, 2018, www.netflix.com/title/80117470.

7. "Thirteen Reasons Why Talking Points," Suicide Awareness Voices of Education, 2017, https://save.org/13-reasons-why.

8. Alexis de Tocqueville, *Democracy in America* (New York: Modern Library, 1835, 1840, 1945, 1981), 96–97.

9. Steve Fore, "Lost in Translation: The Social Uses of Mass Communications Research," *Afterimage*, no. 20 (April 1993): 10.

10. James Carey, *Communication as Culture: Essays on Media and Society* (Boston: Unwin Hyman, 1989), 75.

11. Daniel Czitrom, *Media and the American Mind: From Morse to McLuhan* (Chapel Hill: University of North Carolina Press, 1982), 122–125.

12. Ibid., 123.

13. Harold Lasswell, *Propaganda Technique in the World War* (New York: Alfred A. Knopf, 1927), 9.

14. Walter Lippmann, *Public Opinion* (New York: Macmillan, 1922), 18.

15. Pew Research Center, "The Age Gap in Religion around the World," June 13, 2018, www.pewforum.org/2018/06/13/the-age-gap-in-religion -around-the-world.

16. Sheldon R. Gawiser and G. Evans Witt, "20 Questions a Journalist Should Ask about Poll Results," 3rd ed., www.ncpp.org/?q=node/4.

17. See W. W. Charters, *Motion Pictures and Youth: A Summary* (New York: Macmillan, 1934); and Garth Jowett, *Film: The Democratic Art* (Boston: Little, Brown, 1976), 220–229.

18. Czitrom, *Media and the American Mind*, 132. See also Harold Lasswell, "The Structure and Function of Communication in Society," in

Lyman Bryson, ed., *The Communication of Ideas* (New York: Harper and Brothers, 1948), 37–51.

19. Wilbur Schramm, Jack Lyle, and Edwin Parker, *Television in the Lives of Our Children* (Stanford, Calif.: Stanford University Press, 1961), 1.

20. See Joseph Klapper, *The Effects of Mass Communication* (New York: Free Press, 1960).

21. For an early overview of uses and gratifications, see Jay Blumler and Elihu Katz, *The Uses of Mass Communication* (Beverly Hills, Calif.: Sage, 1974).

22. See George Gerbner et al., "The Demonstration of Power: Violence Profile No. 10," *Journal of Communication* 29, no. 3 (1979): 177–196.

23. Kaiser Family Foundation, *Sex on TV 4* (Menlo Park, Calif.: Henry C. Kaiser Family Foundation, 2005).

24. Robert P. Snow, *Creating Media Culture* (Beverly Hills, Calif.: Sage, 1983), 47.

25. See Maxwell McCombs and Donald Shaw, "The Agenda-Setting Function of Mass Media," *Public Opinion Quarterly* 36, no. 2 (1972): 176–187.

26. See Nancy Signorielli and Michael Morgan, *Cultivation Analysis: New Directions in Media Effects Research* (Newbury Park, Calif.: Sage, 1990).

27. John Gastil, *Political Communication and Deliberation* (Beverly Hills, Calif.: Sage, 2008), 60.

28. W. Phillips Davison, "The Third-Person Effect in Communication," *Public Opinion Quarterly* 47, no. 1 (1983): 1–15, doi:10.1086/268763.

29. Richard Rhodes, "The Media Violence Myth," 2000, www.abffe.com /myth1.htm.

30. Robert Lynd, *Knowledge for What? The Place of Social Science in American Culture* (Princeton, N.J.: Princeton University Press, 1939), 120.

31. Czitrom, *Media and the American Mind*, 143; and Leo Lowenthal, "Historical Perspectives of Popular Culture," in Bernard Rosenberg and David White, eds., *Mass Culture: The Popular Arts in America* (Glencoe, Ill.: Free Press, 1957), 52.

32. Todd Gitlin, *The Whole World Is Watching* (Berkeley: University of California Press, 1980), 7.

33. Horace Newcomb, *TV: The Most Popular Art* (Garden City, N.Y.: Anchor Books, 1974), 19, 23.

34. See Janice Radway, *Reading the Romance: Women, Patriarchy, and Popular Literature* (Chapel Hill: University of North Carolina Press, 1984).

35. Jürgen Habermas, *The Structural Transformation of the Public Sphere*, trans. Thomas Burger with Frederick Lawrence (Cambridge, Mass.: MIT Press, 1994).

36. Craig Calhoun, ed., *Habermas and the Public Sphere* (Cambridge, Mass.: MIT Press, 1994), 452.

37. James W. Carey, *Communication as Culture* (New York: Routledge, 1989), 23.

38. Venise Berry, "Blackish: Deconstruction and the Changing Nature of Black Identity," www.aejmc.org/home/2017/06/esig-2017-abstracts.

39. James Carey, "Mass Communication Research and Cultural Studies: An American View," in James Curran, Michael Gurevitch, and Janet Woollacott, eds., *Mass Communication and Society* (London: Edward Arnold, 1977), 418, 421.

40. Alan Sokal, quoted in Scott Janny, "Postmodern Gravity Deconstructed, Slyly," *New York Times*, May 18, 1996, p. 1. See also The Editors of *Lingua Franca*, eds., *The Sokal Hoax: The Sham That Shook the Academy* (Lincoln, Neb.: Bison Press, 2000).

MEDIA LITERACY AND THE CRITICAL PROCESS Wedding Media and the Meaning of the Perfect Wedding Day, p. 465

1. Erika Engstrom, *The Bride Factory: Mass Media Portrayals of Women and Weddings* (New York: Peter Lang, 2012).

◘ **GLOBAL VILLAGE** International Media Research, p. 470

1. Luwei Rose Luqiu, "The Cost of Humour: Political Satire on Social Media and Censorship in China," *Global Media and Communication* 13, no. 2 (2017): 123–138, doi.org/10.1177/1742766517704471.

2. Jade Miller, "Global Nollywood: The Nigerian Movie Industry and Alternative Global Networks in Production and Distribution," *Global Media and Communication* 8, no. 2 (2012): 117–133, doi.org/10.1177/1742766512444340.

3. Lucile Davier, "The Paradoxical Invisibility of Translation in the Highly Multilingual Context of News Agencies," *Global Media and Communication* 10, no. 1 (2014): 53–72, doi.org/10.1177/1742766513513196.

4. Ahmed K. Al-Rawi, "Sectarianism and the Arab Spring: Framing the Popular Protests in Bahrain," *Global Media and Communication* 11, no. 1 (2015): 25–42, doi.org/10.1177/1742766515573550.

◘ **EXAMINING ETHICS** Our Masculinity Problem, p. 474

1. Mark Follman, Gavin Aronsen, and Deanna Pan, "A Guide to Mass Shootings in America," *Mother Jones*, July 18, 2016, www.motherjones.com/politics/2012/07/mass-shootings-map; John Wihbey, "Mass Murder, Shooting Sprees and Rampage Violence: Research Roundup," *Journalist's Resource*, October 1, 2015, http://journalistsresource.org/studies/government/criminal-justice/mass-murder-shooting-sprees-and-rampage-violence-research-roundup; and Bonnie Berkowitz, Denise Lu, and Chris Alcantara, "The Terrible Numbers That Grow with Each Mass Shooting," accessed July 2018, www.washingtonpost.com/graphics/2018/national/mass-shootings-in-america.

2. Jackson Katz, "Memo to Media: Manhood, Not Guns or Mental Illness, Should Be Central in Newtown Shooting," *Huffington Post*, updated February 17, 2013, www.huffingtonpost.com/jackson-katz/men-gender-gun-violence_b_2308522.html.

3. Ibid.

4. Rachel Kalish and Michael Kimmel, "Suicide by Mass Murder: Masculinity, Aggrieved Entitlement, and Rampage School Shootings," *Health Sociology Review* 19, no. 4 (2010): 451–464.

5. Dan Barry et al., "'Always Agitated. Always Mad': Omar Mateen, according to Those Who Knew Him," *New York Times*, June 18, 2016, www.nytimes.com/2016/06/19/us/omar-mateen-gunman-orlando-shooting.html.

6. Katz, "Memo to Media."

🔘 16 **Legal Controls and Freedom of Expression**

1. Allan J. Lichtman, "Who Rules America?" *The Hill*, August 12, 2014, http://thehill.com/blogs/pundits-blog/civil-rights/214857-who-rules-america.

2. "Voters Say Money, Media Have Too Much Political Clout," Rasmussen Reports, February 16, 2016, www.rasmussenreports.com/public_content/politics/general_politics/february_2016/voters_say_money_media_have_too_much_political_clout.

3. Center for Responsive Politics, "Cost of Election," OpenSecrets.org, 2018, www.opensecrets.org/overview/cost.php. See also Emily Stewart, "Donald Trump Rode $5 Billion in Free Media to the White House," *The Street*, November 17, 2016, www.thestreet.com/story/13896916/1/donald-trump-rode-5-billion-in-free-media-to-the-white-house.html.

4. Gene Policinski, "Amendment to Undo *Citizens United* Won't Do," First Amendment Center, September 21, 2011, www.firstamendmentcenter.org/amendment-to-undo-citizens-united-wont-do.

5. Lawrence Lessig, "An Open Letter to the Citizens against Citizens United," *Atlantic*, March 23, 2012, www.theatlantic.com/politics/archive/2013/03/an-open-letter-to-the-citizens-against-citizens-united/254902.

6. Committee to Protect Journalists, "1305 Journalists Killed since 1992," accessed June 20, 2018, www.cpj.org/killed.

7. Freedom House, "Freedom of the Press 2017," accessed June 20, 2018, www.freedomhouse.org/report/freedom-press/freedom-press-2017.

8. Fred Siebert, Theodore Peterson, and Wilbur Schramm, *Four Theories of the Press* (Urbana: University of Illinois Press, 1956).

9. See Douglas M. Fraleigh and Joseph S. Tuman, *Freedom of Speech in the Marketplace of Ideas* (New York: St. Martin's Press, 1997), 71–73.

10. Michael Schudson, *The Good Citizen: A History of American Civic Life* (Cambridge, Mass.: Harvard University Press, 1998), 77.

11. See Fraleigh and Tuman, *Freedom of Speech*, 125.

12. Hugo Black, quoted in "*New York Times Company v. U.S.*: 1971," in Edward W. Knappman, ed., *Great American Trials: From Salem Witchcraft to Rodney King* (Detroit: Visible Ink Press, 1994), 609.

13. Robert Warren, quoted in "*U.S. v. The Progressive*: 1979," in Knappman, ed., *Great American Trials*, 684.

14. Lawrence Lessig, "Opening Plenary—Media at a Critical Juncture: Politics, Technology and Culture," National Conference on Media Reform, Minneapolis, Minnesota, June 7, 2008.

15. Glenn Fleishman, "A Landslide of Classic Art Is about to Enter the Public Domain," *Atlantic*, April 8, 2018, www.theatlantic.com/technology/archive/2018/04/copywritten-so-dont-copy-me/557420; and Krista L. Cox, "Will 1923 Finally Arrive in the U.S. Public Domain, or Will Mickey Mouse Stir Up More Mischief?" *Above the Law*, January 25, 2018, https://abovethelaw.com/2018/01/will-1923-finally-arrive-in-the-us-public-domain-or-will-mickey-mouse-stir-up-more-mischief.

16. See Knappman, ed., *Great American Trials*, 517–519.

17. Douglas Gomery, *Movie History: A Survey* (Belmont, Calif.: Wadsworth, 1991), 57.

18. See Eric Barnouw, *Tube of Plenty: The Evolution of American Television*, rev. ed. (New York: Oxford University Press, 1982), 118–130.

19. *Fox Television Stations, Inc., v. FCC*, No. 06-1760 (2nd Cir. 2010).

20. Brooks Boliek, "Sorry, Ms. Jackson: FCC's New Record," *Politico*, September 10, 2014, www.politico.com/story/2014/09/fcc-net-neutrality-record-110818.html.

21. Human Rights Watch, "Become a Blogger for Human Rights," http://archive.li/5e4cl.

22. Herbert J. Gans, *Democracy and the News* (Oxford: Oxford University Press, 2003), ix.

◘ **GLOBAL VILLAGE:** The Challenges of Film Censorship in China, p. 498

1. Clarence Tsui, "China's Film Censorship Paradox: Restricted Content, Unrestricted Access," *South China Morning Post*, March 8, 2017, www.scmp.com/magazines/post-magazine/arts-music/article/2076755/chinas-film-censorship-paradox-restricted-content.

2. Ilaria Maria Sala, "'No Ghosts. No Gay Love Stories. No Nudity': Tales of Film-Making in China," *Guardian*, September 22, 2016, www.theguardian.com/film/2016/sep/22/tales-of-film-making-in-china-hollywood-hong-kong.

3. Patrick Brzeski, "'Ghostbusters' Denied Release in China," *Hollywood Reporter*, July 13, 2016, www.hollywoodreporter.com/news/ghostbusters-denied-release-china-910563.

4. Richard Hartley-Parkinson, "Great Scott! China Ban Films and TV Shows Featuring Time Travel (Just in Case Anyone Wants to Rewrite History)," *Daily Mail*, April 15, 2011, www.dailymail.co.uk/news/article-1376771/Great-Scott-China-bans-time-travel-cinema-TV.html.

5. Sala, "'No Ghosts.'"

6. Ibid.

□ **EXAMINING ETHICS** Is "Sexting" Pornography?   p. 506

1. Richard Wortley and Stephen Smallbone, "Child Pornography on the Internet," U.S. Department of Justice, updated May 2012, www.popcenter .org/problems/pdfs/ChildPorn.pdf.

2. Steven Dettelbach, quoted in Tracy Russo, "'Sexting' Town Hall Meeting Held in Cleveland," *Criminal Justice News*, March 19, 2010, http://criminal-justice-online.blogspot.com/2010/03/sexting.html.

3. Sheri Madigan, Anh Ly, Christina L. Rash, Joris Van Ouytsel, and Jeff R. Temple, "Prevalence of Multiple Forms of Sexting Behavior among Youth: A Systematic Review and Meta-analysis," *JAMA Pediatrics* 172, no. 4 (2018): 327–335, doi:10.1001/jamapediatrics.2017.5314.

4. Sameer Hinduja and Justin W. Patchin, "State Sexting Laws," Cyberbullying Research Center, July 2015, http://cyberbullying.org/state-sexting -laws.pdf.

Extended Case Study Can We Trust Facebook with Our Personal Data?

1. "Stats," Facebook, March 31, 2018, https://newsroom.fb.com /company-info.

2. Marco della Cava, Elizabeth Weise, and Jessica Guynn, "Are Facebook, Google and Amazon Too Big? Why That Question Keeps Coming Up," *USA Today*, September 25, 2017, www.usatoday.com/story /tech/2017/09/25/facebook-google-and-amazon-too-big-question -comes-right-and-left/689879001.

3. Devlin Barrett, Sari Horwitz, and Rosalind S. Helderman, "Russian Troll Farm, 13 Suspects Indicted in 2016 Election Interference," *Washington Post*, February 16, 2018, www.washingtonpost.com/world /national-security/russian-troll-farm-13-suspects-indicted-for -interference-in-us-election/2018/02/16/2504de5e-1342-11e8 -9570-29c9830535e5_story.html; and Leslie Shapiro, "Anatomy of a Russian Facebook Ad," *Washington Post*, November 1, 2017, www.washingtonpost .com/graphics/2017/business/russian-ads-facebook-anatomy.

4. Carole Cadwalladr and Emma Graham-Harrison, "Revealed: 50 Million Facebook Profiles Harvested for Cambridge Analytica in Major Data Breach," *Guardian*, March 17, 2018, www.theguardian.com/news/2018 /mar/17/cambridge-analytica-facebook-influence-us-election.

5. Matthew Rosenberg, Nicholas Confessore, and Carole Cadwalladr, "How Trump Consultants Exploited the Facebook Data of Millions," *New York Times*, March 17, 2018, www.nytimes.com/2018/03/17/us/politics /cambridge-analytica-trump-campaign.html.

6. Sarah Frier, "Facebook Says Data on Most of Its 2 Billion Users Is Vulnerable," *Bloomberg*, April 4, 2018, www.bloomberg.com/news /articles/2018-04-04/facebook-says-data-on-87-million-people-may -have-been-shared.

7. Jonathan Freedland, "Zuckerberg Got Off Lightly. Why Are Politicians So Bad at Asking Questions?" *Guardian*, April 11, 2018, www.theguardian

.com/commentisfree/2018/apr/11/mark-zuckerberg-facebook-congress -senate.

8. Emma Grey Ellis, "Mark Zuckerberg's Testimony Birthed an Oddly Promising Memepocalypse," *Wired*, April 11, 2018, www.wired.com /story/mark-zuckerberg-memepocalypse.

9. Dylan Byers, "Facebook's Problem Is Facebook," CNNTech, May 22, 2018, http://money.cnn.com/2018/05/22/technology/pacific-newsletter /index.html.

10. Ibid.

11. "Facebook Settles FTC Charges That It Deceived Consumers by Failing to Keep Privacy Promises," Federal Trade Commission, November 29, 2011, www.ftc.gov/news-events/press-releases/2011/11/facebook -settles-ftc-charges-it-deceived-consumers-failing-keep.

12. Mark Zuckerberg, "Our Commitment to the Facebook Community," Facebook, November 29, 2011, https://newsroom.fb.com/news/2011/11 /our-commitment-to-the-facebook-community.

13. Reuters, "Facebook Says Technical Flaw Exposed 6 Million Users," *New York Times*, June 21, 2013, www.nytimes.com/2013/06/22/business /facebook-says-technical-flaw-exposed-6-million-users.html.

14. Vindu Goel, "After Uproar, European Regulators Question Facebook on Psychological Testing," *New York Times*, July 2, 2014, https://bits .blogs.nytimes.com/2014/07/02/facebooks-secret-manipulation-of-user -emotions-under-british-inquiry.

15. Mark Scott, "Facebook Ordered to Stop Collecting Data on WhatsApp Users in Germany," *New York Times*, September 27, 2016, www.nytimes .com/2016/09/28/technology/whatsapp-facebook-germany.html.

16. Ibid.

17. Gabriel J. X. Dance, Nicholas Confessore, and Michael LaForgia, "Facebook Gave Device Makers Deep Access to Data on Users and Friends," *New York Times*, June 3, 2018, www.nytimes.com/interactive /2018/06/03/technology/facebook-device-partners-users-friends-data .html.

18. Ime Archibong, "Why We Disagree with the *New York Times*," Facebook, June 3, 2018, https://newsroom.fb.com/news/2018/06 /why-we-disagree-with-the-nyt.

19. Michael LaForgia and Gabriel J. X. Dance, "Facebook Gave Data Access to Chinese Firm Flagged by U.S. Intelligence," *New York Times*, June 5, 2018, www.nytimes.com/2018/06/05/technology/facebook -device-partnerships-china.html.

20. Ibid.

21. Julia Powles, "The G.D.P.R., Europe's New Privacy Law, and the Future of the Global Data Economy," *New Yorker*, May 25, 2018, www.newyorker .com/tech/elements/the-gdpr-europes-new-privacy-law-and-the -future-of-the-global-data-economy.

22. Kevin Roose, "What If a Healthier Facebook Is Just . . . Instagram?" *New York Times*, January 22, 2018, www.nytimes.com/2018/01/22 /technology/facebook-instagram.html.

Glossary

A&R (artist & repertoire) agents talent scouts of the music business who discover, develop, and sometimes manage performers.

access channels in cable television, a tier of nonbroadcast channels dedicated to local education, government, and the public.

acquisitions editors in the book industry, editors who seek out and sign authors to contracts.

action games games emphasizing combat-type situations that ask players to test their reflexes and to punch, slash, shoot, or throw as accurately as possible so as to strategically make their way through a series of levels.

actual malice in libel law, a reckless disregard for the truth, such as when a reporter or an editor knows that a statement is false and prints or airs it anyway.

adult contemporary (AC) one of the oldest and most popular radio music formats, typically featuring a mix of news, talk, oldies, and soft rock.

adventure games games requiring players to interact with individual characters and a sometimes hostile environment in order to solve puzzles.

advergames video games created for purely promotional purposes.

affiliate station a radio or TV station that, though independently owned, signs a contract to be part of a network and receives money to carry the network's programs; in exchange, the network reserves time slots, which it sells to national advertisers.

agenda-setting a media-research argument that says that when the mass media pay attention to particular events or issues, they determine—that is, set the agenda for—the major topics of discussion for individuals and society.

album-oriented rock (AOR) the radio music format that features album cuts from mainstream rock bands.

AM (amplitude modulation) a type of radio and sound transmission that stresses the volume or height of radio waves.

analog in television, standard broadcast signals made of radio waves (replaced by digital standards in 2009).

analog recording a recording that is made by capturing the fluctuations of the original sound waves and storing those signals on records or cassettes as a continuous stream of magnetism—analogous to the actual sound.

analysis the second step in the critical process, it involves discovering significant patterns that emerge from the description stage.

anthology dramas a popular form of early TV programming that brought live dramatic theater to television; influenced by stage plays, anthologies offered new teleplays, casts, directors, writers, and sets from week to week.

arcade an establishment that gathers together multiple coin-operated games.

ARPAnet the original Internet, designed by the U.S. Defense Department's Advanced Research Projects Agency (ARPA).

association principle in advertising, a persuasive technique that associates a product with some cultural value or image that has a positive connotation but may have little connection to the actual product.

astroturf lobbying phony grassroots public affairs campaigns engineered by public relations firms; coined by Texas senator Lloyd Bentsen, it was named after AstroTurf, the artificial-grass athletic field surface.

audience studies cultural studies research that focuses on how people use and interpret cultural content. Also known as reader-response research.

audiotape lightweight magnetized strands of ribbon that make possible sound editing and multiple-track mixing; instrumentals or vocals can be recorded at one location and later mixed onto a master recording in another studio.

authoritarian model a model for journalism and speech that tolerates little public dissent or criticism of government; it holds that the general public needs guidance from an elite and educated ruling class.

avatar a graphic interactive "character" situated within the world of a game, such as *World of Warcraft* or *Second Life*.

bandwagon effect an advertising strategy that uses exaggerated claims that everyone is using a particular product to encourage consumers to not be left behind.

basic cable in cable programming, a tier of channels composed of local broadcast signals, nonbroadcast access channels (for local government, education, and general public use), a few regional PBS stations, and a variety of cable channels downlinked from communication satellites.

Big Five/Little Three from the late 1920s through the late 1940s, the major movie studios that were vertically integrated and that dominated the industry; the Big Five were Paramount, MGM, Warner Brothers, Twentieth Century Fox, and RKO, and the Little Three were those studios that did not own theaters: Columbia, Universal, and United Artists.

Big Six the six major Hollywood studios that currently rule the commercial film business: Warner Brothers, Paramount, 21st Century Fox, Universal, Columbia Pictures, and Disney.

block booking an early tactic of movie studios to control exhibition, involving pressuring theater operators to accept marginal films with no stars in order to get access to films with the most popular stars.

blockbuster the type of big-budget special effects film that typically has a summer or holiday release date, heavy promotion, and lucrative merchandising tie-ins.

block printing a printing technique developed by early Chinese printers that entails hand-carving characters and illustrations into a block of wood, applying ink to the block, and then printing copies on multiple sheets of paper.

blogs sites that contain articles in reverse chronological journal-like form, often with reader comments and links to other articles on the web (from the term *weblog*).

blues originally a kind of black folk music, this emerged as a distinct category of music in the early 1900s; it was influenced by African American spirituals, ballads, and work songs from the rural South, and by urban guitar and vocal solos from the 1930s and 1940s.

book challenge a formal complaint to have a book removed from a public or school library's collection.

boutique agencies in advertising, small regional ad agencies that offer personalized services.

branded content a form of advertising that uses content (for example an article, video, or infographic) to promote a service or a product.

broadband data transmission over a fiber-optic cable—a signaling method that handles a wide range of frequencies.

broadcasting the transmission of radio waves or TV signals to a broad public audience.

browsers information-search services, such as Microsoft's Internet Explorer, Firefox, and Google Chrome, that offer detailed organizational maps to the Internet.

cartridge the early physical form of video games that were played on consoles manufactured by companies like Nintendo, Sega, and Atari.

casual games games that have very simple rules and are usually quick to play, such as *Tetris* or *Angry Birds*.

CATV (community antenna television) an early cable system that originated where mountains or tall buildings blocked TV signals; because of early technical and regulatory limits, CATV contained only twelve channels.

celluloid a transparent and pliable film that can hold a coating of chemicals sensitive to light.

chapter show in television production, any situation comedy or dramatic program whose narrative structure includes self-contained stories that feature a problem, a series of conflicts, and a resolution from week to week (for contrast, see **serial program** and **episodic series**).

cinema verité French term for *truth film*, a documentary style that records fragments of everyday life unobtrusively; it often features a rough, grainy look and shaky, handheld camera work.

citizen journalism a grassroots movement wherein activist amateurs and concerned citizens, not professional journalists, use the Internet and blogs to disseminate news and information.

codex an early type of book in which paper-like sheets were cut and sewed together along an edge, then bound with thin pieces of wood and covered with leather.

collective intelligence the sharing of knowledge and ideas, particularly in the world of gaming.

commercial speech any print or broadcast expression for which a fee is charged to the organization or individual buying time or space in the mass media.

common carrier a communication or transportation business, such as a phone company or a taxi service, that is required by law to offer service on a first-come, first-served basis to whomever can pay the rate; such companies do not get involved in content.

communication the process of creating symbol systems that convey information and meaning (e.g., language, Morse code, film, and computer codes).

Communications Act of 1934 the far-reaching act that established the Federal Communications Commission (FCC) and the federal regulatory structure for U.S. broadcasting.

communist or state model a model for journalism and speech that places control in the hands of an enlightened government, which speaks for ordinary citizens and workers in order to serve the common goals of the state.

compact discs (CDs) playback-only storage discs for music that incorporate pure and very precise digital techniques, thus eliminating noise during recording and editing sessions.

conflict of interest considered unethical, a compromising situation in which a journalist stands to benefit personally from the news report he or she produces.

conflict-oriented journalism found in metropolitan areas, newspapers that define news primarily as events, issues, or experiences that deviate from social norms; journalists see their role as observers who monitor their city's institutions and problems.

consensus narratives cultural products that become popular and command wide attention, providing shared cultural experiences.

consensus-oriented journalism found in small communities, newspapers that promote social and economic harmony by providing community calendars and meeting notices and carrying articles on local schools, social events, town government, property crimes, and zoning issues.

consoles devices people use specifically to play video games.

contemporary hit radio (CHR) originally called *Top 40 radio*, this radio format encompasses everything from hip-hop to children's songs; it appeals to many teens and young adults.

content analysis in social science research, a method for studying and coding media texts and programs.

content communities online communities that exist for the sharing of all types of content, from text to photos and videos.

convergence the first definition involves the technological merging of media content across various platforms (see also **cross platform**). The second definition describes a business model that consolidates various media holdings under one corporate umbrella.

cookies information profiles about a user that are usually automatically accepted by a web browser and stored on the user's own computer hard drive.

copy editors the people in magazine, newspaper, and book publishing who attend to specific problems in writing, such as style, content, and length.

copyright the legal right of authors and producers to own and control the use of their published or unpublished writing, music, and lyrics; TV programs and movies; or graphic art designs.

Corporation for Public Broadcasting (CPB) a private, nonprofit corporation created by Congress in 1967 to funnel federal funds to nonprofit radio and public television.

correlations observed associations between two variables.

country claiming the largest number of radio stations in the United States, this radio format includes such subdivisions as old-time, progressive, country-rock, western swing, and country-gospel.

cover music songs recorded or performed by musicians who did not originally write or perform the music; in the 1950s, some white producers and artists capitalized on popular songs by black artists by "covering" them.

critical process the process whereby a media-literate person or student studying mass communication forms and practices employs the techniques of description, analysis, interpretation, evaluation, and engagement.

cross platform a particular business model that involves a consolidation of various media holdings—such as cable connection, phone service, television transmission, and Internet access—under one corporate umbrella (also known as **convergence**).

cultivation effect in media research, the idea that heavy television viewing leads individuals to perceive reality in ways that are consistent with the portrayals they see on television.

cultural imperialism the phenomenon of American media, fashion, and food dominating the global market and shaping the cultures and identities of other nations.

cultural studies in media research, the approaches that try to understand how the media and culture are tied to the actual patterns of communication used in daily life; these studies focus on how people make meanings, apprehend reality, and order experience through the use of stories and symbols.

culture the symbols of expression that individuals, groups, and societies use to make sense of daily life and to articulate their values; a process that delivers the values of a society through products or other meaning-making forms.

data mining the unethical gathering of data by online purveyors of content and merchandise.

deficit financing in television, the process whereby a TV production company leases its programs to a network for a license fee that is actually less than the cost of production; the company hopes to recoup this loss later in rerun syndication.

demographic editions national magazines whose advertising is tailored to subscribers and readers according to occupation, class, and zip code.

description the first step in the critical process, it involves paying close attention, taking notes, and researching the cultural product to be studied.

design managers publishing industry personnel who work on the look of a book, making decisions about type style, paper, cover design, and layout.

development the process of designing, coding, scoring, and testing a game.

developmental editor in book publishing, the editor who provides authors with feedback, makes suggestions for improvements, and obtains advice from knowledgeable members of the academic community.

digital in television, the type of signals that are transmitted as binary code.

digital communication images, texts, and sounds that use pulses of electric current or flashes of laser light and are converted (or encoded) into electronic signals represented as varied combinations of binary numbers (ones and zeros); these signals are then reassembled (decoded) as a precise reproduction of a TV picture, a magazine article, or a telephone voice.

digital divide the socioeconomic disparity between those who do and those who do not have access to digital technology and media, such as the Internet.

digital recording music recorded and played back by laser beam rather than by needle or magnetic tape.

digital turn a cultural shift away from the traditional consumption of the media industries to a converged digital world; the digital turn began with the emergence of the Internet as a mass medium and continues today.

digital video the production format that is replacing celluloid film and revolutionizing filmmaking because the cameras are more portable and production costs are much less expensive.

dime novels sometimes identified as pulp fiction, these cheaply produced and low-priced novels were popular in the United States beginning in the 1860s.

direct broadcast satellite (DBS) a satellite-based service that for a monthly fee downlinks hundreds of satellite channels and services; DBS began distributing video programming directly to households in 1994.

documentary a movie or TV news genre that documents reality by recording actual characters and settings.

domestic comedy a TV hybrid of the sitcom in which characters and settings are usually more important than complicated situations; it generally features a domestic problem or work issue that characters have to solve.

drive time in radio programming, the periods between 6 and 10 A.M. and 4 and 7 P.M., when people are commuting to and from work or school; these periods constitute the largest listening audiences of the day.

e-book a digital book read on a computer or on an electronic reading device.

e-commerce electronic commerce, or commercial activity, on the web.

electromagnetic waves invisible electronic impulses similar to visible light; electricity, magnetism, light, broadcast signals, and heat are part of such waves, which radiate in space at the speed of light, about 186,000 miles per second.

electronic publishers communication businesses, such as broadcasters or cable TV companies, that are entitled to choose what channels or content to carry.

e-mail electronic mail messages sent over the Internet; developed by computer engineer Ray Tomlinson in 1971.

engagement the fifth step in the critical process, it involves actively working to create a media world that best serves democracy.

Entertainment Software Rating Board (ESRB) a self-regulating organization that assigns ratings to games based on six categories: EC (Early Childhood), E (Everyone), E 10+ (Everyone 10+), T (Teens), M (Mature 17+), and AO (Adults Only 18+).

episodic series a narrative form well suited to television because the main characters appear every week, sets and locales remain the same, and technical crews stay with the program; episodic series feature new adventures each week, but a handful of characters emerge with whom viewers can regularly identify (for contrast, see **chapter show**).

e-publishing Internet-based publishing houses that design and distribute books for comparatively low prices for authors who want to self-publish a title.

ethnocentrism an underlying value held by many U.S. journalists and citizens, it involves judging other countries and cultures according to how they live up to or imitate American practices and ideals.

evaluation the fourth step in the critical process, it involves arriving at a judgment about whether a cultural product is good, bad, or mediocre; this requires subordinating one's personal taste to the critical assessment resulting from the first three stages (description, analysis, and interpretation).

evergreens in TV syndication, popular, lucrative, and enduring network reruns, such as the *Andy Griffith Show* and *I Love Lucy*.

evergreen subscriptions magazine subscriptions that automatically renew on the subscriber's credit card.

experiments in regard to the mass media, research that isolates some aspect of content; suggests a hypothesis; and manipulates variables to discover a particular medium's impact on attitudes, emotions, or behavior.

Fairness Doctrine repealed in 1987, this FCC rule required broadcast stations to both air and engage in controversial-issue programs that affected their communities and, when offering such programming, to provide competing points of view.

famous-person testimonial an advertising strategy that associates a product with the endorsement of a well-known person.

feature syndicates commercial outlets or brokers, such as United Features and Tribune Media Services, that contract with newspapers to provide work from well-known political writers, editorial cartoonists, comic-strip artists, and self-help columnists.

Federal Communications Commission (FCC) an independent U.S. government agency charged with regulating interstate and international communications by radio, television, wire, satellite, cable, and the Internet.

Federal Radio Commission (FRC) a body established in 1927 to oversee radio licenses and negotiate channel problems.

fiber-optic cable thin glass bundles of fiber capable of transmitting along cable wires thousands of messages converted to shooting pulses of light; these bundles of fiber can carry broadcast channels, telephone signals, and a variety of digital codes.

fin-syn (Financial Interest and Syndication Rules) FCC rules that prohibited the major networks from running their own syndication companies or from charging production companies additional fees after shows had completed their prime-time runs; most fin-syn rules were rescinded in the mid-1990s.

first-person shooter (FPS) games that allow players to feel as if they are actually holding a weapon and to feel physically immersed in the drama.

first-run syndication in television, the process whereby new programs are specifically produced for sale in syndication markets rather than for network television.

flack a derogatory term that, in journalism, is sometimes applied to a public relations agent.

FM (frequency modulation) a type of radio and sound transmission that offers static-less reception and greater fidelity and clarity than AM radio by accentuating the pitch or distance between radio waves.

folk music music performed by untrained musicians and passed down through oral traditions; it encompasses a wide range of music, from Appalachian fiddle tunes to the accordion-led zydeco of Louisiana.

folk-rock amplified folk music, often featuring politically overt lyrics; influenced by rock and roll.

format radio the concept of radio stations developing and playing specific styles (or formats) geared to listeners' age, race, or gender; in format radio, management, rather than deejays, controls programming choices.

Fourth Estate the notion that the press operates as an unofficial branch of government, monitoring the legislative, judicial, and executive branches for abuses of power.

fourth screens technologies like smartphones, iPods, iPads, and mobile TV devices, which are forcing major changes in consumer viewing habits and media content creation.

fringe time in television, the time slot either immediately before the evening's prime-time schedule (called *early fringe*) or immediately following the local evening news or the network's late-night talk shows (called *late fringe*).

gag orders legal restrictions prohibiting the press from releasing preliminary information that might prejudice jury selection.

gameplay the way in which a game's rules, rather than its graphics, sound, or narrative style, structure how players interact with it.

gangster rap a style of rap music that depicts the hardships of urban life and sometimes glorifies the violent style of street gangs.

general-interest magazines types of magazines that address a wide variety of topics and are aimed at a broad national audience.

genre a narrative category in which conventions regarding similar characters, scenes, structures, and themes recur in combination.

grunge rock music that takes the spirit of punk and infuses it with more attention to melody.

guilds *or* **clans** in gaming, coordinated, organized team-like groups that can be either small and easygoing or large and demanding.

HD radio a digital technology that enables AM and FM radio broadcasters to multicast two to three additional compressed digital signals within their traditional analog frequency.

hegemony the acceptance of the dominant values in a culture by those who are subordinate to those who hold economic and political power.

herd journalism a situation in which reporters stake out a house or follow a story in such large groups that the entire profession comes under attack for invading people's privacy or exploiting their personal tragedies.

hidden-fear appeal an advertising strategy that plays on a sense of insecurity, trying to persuade consumers that only a specific product can offer relief.

high culture a symbolic expression that has come to mean "good taste"; often supported by wealthy patrons and corporate donors, it is associated with fine art (such as ballet, the symphony, painting, and classical literature), which is available primarily in theaters or museums.

hip-hop music that combines spoken street dialect with cuts (or samples) from older records and bears the influences of social politics, swagger, and confrontational lyrics carried forward from blues, R&B, soul, and rock and roll.

Hollywood Ten the nine screenwriters and one film director subpoenaed by the House Un-American Activities Committee (HUAC) who were sent to prison in the late 1940s for refusing to disclose their memberships or to identify communist sympathizers.

HTML (hypertext markup language) the written code that creates web pages and links; a language all computers can read.

human-interest stories news accounts that focus on the trials and tribulations of the human condition, often featuring ordinary individuals facing extraordinary challenges.

hypodermic-needle model an early model in mass communication research that attempted to explain media effects by arguing that the media figuratively shoot their powerful effects into unsuspecting or weak audiences; sometimes called the *bullet theory* or the *direct effects model*.

hypotheses in social science research, tentative general statements that predict a relationship between a dependent variable and an independent variable.

illuminated manuscripts books from the Middle Ages that featured decorative, colorful designs and illustrations on each page.

indecency an issue related to appropriate broadcast content; the government may punish broadcasters for indecency or profanity after the fact, and over the years a handful of radio stations have had their licenses suspended or denied over indecent programming.

indie rock less commercial rock music, which appeals chiefly to college students and twentysomethings.

indies independent music and film production houses that work outside industry oligopolies; they often produce less mainstream music and film.

individualism an underlying value held by most U.S. journalists and citizens, it favors individual rights and responsibilities above group needs or institutional mandates.

in-game advertisements integrated, often subtle advertisements, such as billboards, logos, or storefronts in a game, that can be either static or dynamic.

instant messaging a web feature that enables users to chat with friends in real time via pop-up windows assigned to each conversation.

intellectual properties in gaming, the stories, characters, personalities, and music that require licensing agreements.

Internet the vast network of telephone and cable lines, wireless connections, and satellite systems designed to link and carry computer information worldwide.

Internet radio online radio stations that either "stream" simulcast versions of on-air radio broadcasts over the web or are created exclusively for the Internet.

Internet service provider (ISP) a company that provides Internet access to homes and businesses for a fee.

interpretation the third step in the critical process, it asks and answers the "What does that mean?" and "So what?" questions about one's findings.

interpretive journalism a type of journalism that involves analyzing and explaining key issues or events and placing them in a broader historical or social context.

interstitials advertisements that pop up in a screen window as a user attempts to access a new web page.

inverted-pyramid style a style of journalism in which news reports begin with the most dramatic or newsworthy information—answering *who*, *what*, *where*, and *when* (and less frequently *why* or *how*) questions at the top of the story—and then trail off with less significant details.

investigative journalism news reports that hunt out and expose corruption, particularly in business and government.

irritation advertising an advertising strategy that tries to create product-name recognition by being annoying or obnoxious.

jazz an improvisational and mostly instrumental musical form that absorbs and integrates a diverse body of musical styles, including African rhythms, blues, big band, and gospel.

joint operating agreement (JOA) in the newspaper industry, an economic arrangement, sanctioned by the government, that permits competing newspapers to operate separate editorial divisions while merging business and production operations.

kinescope before the days of videotape, a 1950s technique for preserving television broadcasts by using a film camera to record a live TV show off a studio monitor.

kinetograph an early movie camera developed by Thomas Edison's assistant in the 1890s.

kinetoscope an early film projection system that served as a kind of peep show in which viewers looked through a hole and saw images moving on a tiny plate.

leased channels in cable television, channels that allow citizens to buy time for producing programs or presenting their own viewpoints.

libel in media law, the defamation of character in written expression.

libertarian model a model for journalism and speech that encourages vigorous government criticism and supports the highest degree of freedom for individual speech and news operations.

limited competition in media economics, a market with many producers and sellers but only a few differentiable products within a particular category; sometimes called *monopolistic competition*.

linotype a technology introduced in the nineteenth century that enabled printers to set type mechanically using a typewriter-style keyboard.

literary journalism news reports that adapt fictional storytelling techniques to nonfictional material; sometimes called *new journalism*.

Little Three See **Big Five/Little Three**.

lobbying in governmental public relations, the process of attempting to influence the voting of lawmakers to support a client's or an organization's best interests.

longitudinal studies a term used for research studies that are conducted over long periods of time and often rely on large government and academic survey databases.

low culture a symbolic expression supposedly aligned with the questionable tastes of the masses, who enjoy the commercial "junk" circulated by the mass media, such as reality television, teen pop music, TV wrestling shows, talk radio, comic books, and monster truck pulls.

low-power FM (LPFM) a new class of noncommercial radio stations approved by the FCC in 2000 to give voice to local groups lacking access to the public airwaves; the 10-watt and 100-watt stations broadcast to a small, community-based area.

magalog a combination of a glossy magazine and retail catalogue that is often used to market goods or services to customers or employees.

magazine a nondaily periodical that comprises a collection of articles, stories, and ads.

manuscript culture a period during the Middle Ages when priests and monks advanced the art of bookmaking.

market research in advertising and public relations agencies, the department that uses social science techniques to assess the behaviors and attitudes of consumers toward particular products before any ads are created.

mass communication the process of designing and delivering cultural messages and stories to diverse audiences through media channels as old as the book and as new as the Internet.

massively multiplayer online role-playing games (MMORPGs) role-playing games set in virtual fantasy worlds that require users to play through an avatar.

mass media the cultural industries—the channels of communication—that produce and distribute songs, novels, news, movies, online computer services, and other cultural products to a large number of people.

media buyers in advertising, the individuals who choose and purchase the types of media that are best suited to carry a client's ads and reach the targeted audience.

media deserts an area that, due to lack of resources, is underserved by the media industries.

media effects research the mainstream tradition in mass communication research, it attempts to understand, explain, and predict the impact—or effects—of the mass media on individuals and society.

media literacy an understanding of the mass communication process through the development of critical-thinking tools—description, analysis, interpretation, evaluation, and engagement—that enable a person to become more engaged as a citizen and more discerning as a consumer of mass media products.

mega-agencies in advertising, large firms or holding companies that are formed by merging several individual agencies and that maintain worldwide regional offices; they provide both advertising and public relations services and operate in-house radio and TV production studios.

megaplexes movie theater facilities with fourteen or more screens.

microprocessors miniature circuits that process and store electronic signals, integrating thousands of electronic components into thin strands of silicon, along which binary codes travel.

minimal-effects model a mass communication research model based on tightly controlled experiments and survey findings; it argues that the mass media have limited effects on audiences, reinforcing existing behaviors and attitudes rather than changing them.

modding the most advanced form of **collective intelligence**; slang for modifying game software or hardware.

modern the term describing a historical era spanning the time from the rise of the Industrial Revolution in the eighteenth and nineteenth centuries to the present; its social values include celebrating the individual, believing in rational order, working efficiently, and rejecting tradition.

monopoly in media economics, an organizational structure that occurs when a single firm dominates production and distribution in a particular industry, either nationally or locally.

Morse code a system of sending electrical impulses from a transmitter through a cable to a reception point; developed by the American inventor Samuel Morse.

movie palaces ornate, lavish single-screen movie theaters that emerged in the 1910s in the United States.

MP3 an advanced type of audio compression that reduces file size, enabling audio to be easily distributed over the Internet and to be digitally transmitted in real time.

muckrakers reporters who used a style of early-twentieth-century investigative journalism that emphasized a willingness to crawl around in society's muck to uncover a story.

multichannel video programming distributors (MVPDs) the cable industry's name for its largest revenue generators, including cable companies and DBS providers.

multiple-system operators (MSOs) large corporations that own numerous cable television systems.

multiplexes contemporary movie theaters that exhibit many movies at the same time on multiple screens.

must-carry rules rules established by the FCC requiring all cable operators to assign channels to and carry all local TV broadcasts on their systems, thereby ensuring that local network affiliates, independent stations (those not carrying network programs), and public television channels would benefit from cable's clearer reception.

myth analysis a strategy for critiquing advertising that provides insights into how ads work on a cultural level; according to this strategy, ads are narratives with stories to tell and social conflicts to resolve.

narrative the structure underlying most media products, it includes two components: the story (what happens to whom) and the discourse (how the story is told).

narrative films movies that tell a story, with dramatic action and conflict emerging mainly from individual characters.

narrowcasting any specialized electronic programming or media channel aimed at a target audience.

National Public Radio (NPR) noncommercial radio established in 1967 by the U.S. Congress to provide an alternative to commercial radio.

net neutrality the principle that every website and every user—whether a multinational corporation or an individual—has the right to the same Internet network speed and access.

network a broadcast process that links, through special phone lines or satellite transmissions, groups of radio or TV stations that share programming produced at a central location.

network era the period in television history, roughly from the mid-1950s to the late 1970s, that refers to the dominance of the Big Three networks—ABC, CBS, and NBC—over programming and prime-time viewing habits; the era began eroding with a decline in viewing and with the development of VCRs, cable, and new TV networks.

news the process of gathering information and making narrative reports—edited by individuals in a news organization—that create selected frames of reference and help the public make sense of prominent people, important events, and unusual happenings in everyday life.

newshole the space left over in a newspaper for news content after all the ads are placed.

newspaper chain a large company that owns several papers throughout the country.

newsreels weekly ten-minute magazine-style compilations of filmed news events from around the world organized in a sequence of short reports; prominent in movie theaters between the 1920s and the 1950s.

news/talk/information the fastest-growing radio format in the 1990s, dominated by news programs and talk shows.

newsworthiness the often unstated criteria that journalists use to determine which events and issues should become news reports, including timeliness, proximity, conflict, prominence, human interest, consequence, usefulness, novelty, and deviance.

nickelodeons the first makeshift movie theaters, which were often converted cigar stores, pawnshops, or restaurants redecorated to mimic vaudeville theaters.

ninjas game players who snatch loot out of turn and then leave a pick-up group, or **PUG**.

noobs game players who are clueless beginners.

O & Os TV stations "owned and operated" by networks.

objective journalism a modern style of journalism that distinguishes factual reports from opinion columns; reporters strive to remain neutral toward the issue or event they cover, searching out competing points of view among the sources for a story.

obscenity expression that is not protected as speech if these three legal tests are all met: (1) the average person, applying contemporary community standards, would find that the material as a whole appeals to prurient interest; (2) the material depicts or describes sexual conduct in a patently offensive way; (3) the material, as a whole, lacks serious literary, artistic, political, or scientific value.

off-network syndication in television, the process whereby older programs that no longer run during prime time are made available for reruns to local stations, cable operators, online services, and foreign markets.

offset lithography a technology that enabled books to be printed from photographic plates rather than metal casts, reducing the cost of color and illustrations and eventually permitting computers to perform typesetting.

oligopoly in media economics, an organizational structure in which a few firms control most of an industry's production and distribution resources.

online fantasy sports games in which players assemble teams and use actual sports results to determine scores in their online games. These games reach a mass audience, have a major social component, and take a managerial perspective on the game.

online piracy the illegal uploading, downloading, or streaming of copyrighted material, such as music or movies.

open-source software noncommercial software shared freely and developed collectively on the Internet.

opinion and fair comment a defense against libel that states that libel applies only to intentional misstatements of factual information rather than to statements of opinion.

opt-in or **opt-out policies** controversial website policies over personal data gathering: *opt-in* means websites must gain explicit permission from online consumers before the site can collect their personal data; *opt-out* means that websites can automatically collect personal data unless the consumer goes to the trouble of filling out a specific form to restrict the practice.

option time a business tactic, now illegal, whereby a radio network in the 1920s and 1930s paid an affiliate station a set fee per hour for an option to control programming and advertising on that station.

Pacifica Foundation a radio broadcasting foundation established in Berkeley, California, by journalist and World War II pacifist Lewis Hill; in 1949, Hill established KPFA, the first nonprofit community radio station.

paperback books books made with relatively cheap paper covers, introduced in the United States (from Europe) in the mid-1800s.

papyrus one of the first substances to hold written language and symbols; produced from plant reeds found along the Nile River.

Paramount decision the 1948 U.S. Supreme Court decision that ended vertical integration in the film industry by forcing the studios to divest themselves of their theaters.

parchment treated animal skin that replaced papyrus as an early pre-paper substance on which to document written language.

partisan press an early dominant style of American journalism distinguished by opinion newspapers, which generally argued one political point of view or pushed the plan of the particular party that subsidized the paper.

pass-along readership the total number of people who come into contact with a single copy of a magazine.

payola the unethical (but not always illegal) practice of record promoters' paying deejays or radio programmers to favor particular songs over others.

pay-per-view (PPV) a cable-television service that allows customers to select a particular movie for a fee, or to pay $25 to $40 for a special onetime event.

paywall an online portal that charges consumers a fee for access to news content.

penny arcade the first thoroughly modern indoor playground, filled with coin-operated games.

penny papers (also *penny press*) refers to newspapers that, because of technological innovations in printing, were able to drop their price to one cent beginning in the 1830s, thereby making papers affordable to the working and emerging middle classes and enabling newspapers to become a genuine mass medium.

phishing an Internet scam that begins with phony e-mail messages that appear to be from an official site and request that customers send their credit card numbers and other personal information to update their account.

photojournalism the use of photos to document events and people's lives.

pinball machine the most prominent mechanical game, in which players score points by manipulating the path of a metal ball on a slanted table sealed within a glass-covered case.

plain-folks pitch an advertising strategy that associates a product with simplicity and the common person.

podcasting a distribution method (coined from *iPod* and *broadcasting*) that enables listeners to download audio program files from the Internet for playback on computers or digital music players.

political advertising the use of ad techniques to promote a candidate's image and persuade the public to adopt a particular viewpoint.

political economy studies an area of academic study that specifically examines interconnections among economic interests, political power, and how that power is used.

pop music popular music that appeals either to a wide cross section of the public or to sizable subdivisions within the larger public based on age, region, or ethnic background; the word *pop* has also been used as a label to distinguish popular music from classical music.

portal an entry point to the Internet, such as a search engine.

postmodern the term describing a contemporary historical era spanning the 1960s to the present; its social values include opposing hierarchy, diversifying and recycling culture, questioning scientific reasoning, and embracing paradox.

premium channels in cable programming, a tier of channels that subscribers can order at an additional monthly fee over their basic cable service; these may include movie channels and interactive services.

press agent the earliest type of public relations practitioner, who seeks to advance a client's image through media exposure.

press releases in public relations, announcements—written in the style of news reports—that give new information about an individual, a company, or an organization, and pitch a story idea to the news media.

prime time in television programming, the hours between 8 and 11 P.M. (or 7 and 10 P.M. in the Midwest), when networks have traditionally drawn their largest audiences and charged their highest advertising rates.

Prime Time Access Rule (PTAR) an FCC regulation that reduced networks' control of prime-time programming to encourage more local news and public affairs programs, often between 6 and 7 P.M.

printing press a fifteenth-century invention whose movable metallic type spawned modern mass communication by creating the first method for mass production; it not only reduced the size and cost of books—making them the first mass medium affordable to less affluent people—but provided the impetus for the Industrial Revolution, assembly-line production, modern capitalism, and the rise of consumer culture.

prior restraint the legal definition of censorship in the United States; it prohibits courts and governments from blocking any publication or speech before it actually occurs.

product placement the advertising practice of strategically placing products in movies, TV shows, comic books, and video games so that the products appear as part of a story's set environment.

professional books technical books that target various occupational groups and are not intended for the general consumer market.

Progressive Era a period of political and social reform that lasted from the 1890s to the 1920s.

progressive rock an alternative music format that developed as a backlash to the popularity of Top 40.

propaganda in advertising and public relations, a communication strategy that tries to manipulate public opinion to gain support for a special issue, program, or policy, such as a nation's war effort.

propaganda analysis the study of propaganda's effectiveness in influencing and mobilizing public opinion.

pseudo-events in public relations, circumstances or events created solely for the purpose of obtaining coverage in the media.

pseudo-polls typically call-in, online, or person-in-the-street nonscientific polls that the news media use to address a "question of the day."

Public Broadcasting Act of 1967 the act by the U.S. Congress that established the Corporation for Public Broadcasting, which oversees the Public Broadcasting Service (PBS) and National Public Radio (NPR).

Public Broadcasting Service (PBS) noncommercial television established in 1967 by the U.S. Congress to provide an alternative to commercial television.

public domain the end of the copyright period for a work, at which point the public may begin to access it for free.

publicity in public relations, the positive and negative messages that spread controlled and uncontrolled information about a person, a corporation, an issue, or a policy in various media.

public journalism a type of journalism, driven by citizen forums, that goes beyond telling the news to embrace a broader mission of improving the quality of public life; also called *civic journalism*.

public relations the total communication strategy conducted by a person, a government, or an organization attempting to reach and persuade its audiences to adopt a point of view.

public service announcements (PSAs) reports or announcements, carried free by radio and TV stations, that promote government programs, educational projects, voluntary agencies, or social reform.

public sphere those areas or arenas in social life—like the town square or coffeehouse—where people come together regularly to discuss social and cultural problems and try to influence politics; the public sphere is distinguished from governmental spheres, where elected officials and other representatives conduct affairs of state.

PUGs in gaming, temporary teams usually assembled by matchmaking programs integrated into a game (short for "pick-up groups").

pulp fiction a term used to describe many late nineteenth-century popular paperbacks and dime novels, which were constructed of cheap machine-made pulp material.

punk rock rock music that challenges the orthodoxy and commercialism of the record business; it is characterized by simple chord structures, catchy melodies, and politically or socially challenging lyrics.

qualified privilege a legal right allowing journalists to report judicial or legislative proceedings even though the public statements being reported may be libelous.

Radio Act of 1912 the first radio legislation passed by Congress; it addressed the problem of amateur radio operators cramming the airwaves.

Radio Act of 1927 the second radio legislation passed by Congress; in an attempt to restore order to the airwaves, the act stated that licensees did not own their channels but could license them if they operated to serve the "public interest, convenience, or necessity."

Radio Corporation of America (RCA) a company developed during World War I that was designed, with government approval, to pool radio patents; the formation of RCA gave the United States almost total control over the emerging mass medium of broadcasting.

radio waves a portion of the electromagnetic wave spectrum that was harnessed so that signals could be sent from a transmission point and obtained at a reception point.

random assignment a social science research method for assigning research subjects; it ensures that every subject has an equal chance of being placed in either the experimental group or the control group.

rating in TV audience measurement, a statistical estimate expressed as a percentage of households tuned to a program in the local or national market being sampled.

regional editions national magazines whose content is tailored to the interests of different geographic areas.

responsible capitalism an underlying value held by many U.S. journalists and citizens, it assumes that businesspeople should compete with one another not primarily to maximize profits but to increase prosperity for all.

retransmission fee the fee that cable providers pay to broadcast networks for the right to carry their channels.

rhythm and blues (R&B) music that merges urban blues with big-band sounds.

right to privacy addresses a person's right to be left alone, without his or her name, image, or daily activities becoming public property.

rockabilly music that mixes bluegrass and country influences with those of black folk music and early amplified blues.

rock and roll music that merges the African American influences of urban blues, gospel, and R&B with the white influences of country, folk, and pop vocals.

role-playing games (RPGs) games that are typically set in a fantasy or sci-fi world in which each player (there can be multiple players in a game) chooses to play as a character that specializes in a particular skill set.

rotation in format radio programming, the practice of playing the most popular or best-selling songs many times throughout the day.

satellite radio pay radio services that deliver various radio formats nationally via satellite.

saturation advertising the strategy of inundating a variety of print and visual media with ads aimed at target audiences.

scientific method a widely used research method that studies phenomena in systematic stages; it includes identifying a research problem, reviewing existing research, developing working hypotheses, determining an appropriate research design, collecting information, analyzing results to see if the hypotheses have been verified, and interpreting the implications of the study.

search engines sites or applications that offer a more automated route to finding content by allowing users to enter key words or queries to locate related web pages.

Section 315 part of the 1934 Communications Act; it mandates that during elections, broadcast stations must provide equal opportunities and response time for qualified political candidates.

selective exposure the phenomenon whereby audiences seek messages and meanings that correspond to their preexisting beliefs and values.

selective retention the phenomenon whereby audiences remember or retain messages and meanings that correspond to their preexisting beliefs and values.

serial program a radio or TV program, such as a soap opera, that features continuing story lines from day to day or week to week (for contrast, see **chapter show**).

share in TV audience measurement, a statistical estimate of the percentage of homes tuned to a certain program compared with those simply using their sets at the time of a sample.

shield laws laws protecting the confidentiality of key interview subjects and reporters' rights not to reveal the sources of controversial information used in news stories.

simulation games games that involve managing resources and planning worlds that are typically based in reality.

situation comedy a type of comedy series that features a recurring cast and set as well as several narrative scenes; each episode establishes a situation, complicates it, develops increasing confusion among its characters, and then resolves the complications.

sketch comedy short television comedy skits that are usually segments of TV variety shows; sometimes known as *vaudeo*, the marriage of vaudeville and video.

slander in law, spoken language that defames a person's character.

slogan in advertising, a catchy phrase that attempts to promote or sell a product by capturing its essence in words.

small-town pastoralism an underlying value held by many U.S. journalists and citizens, it favors the small over the large and the rural over the urban.

snob-appeal approach an advertising strategy that attempts to convince consumers that using a product will enable them to maintain or elevate their social station.

social learning theory a theory within media effects research that suggests a link between the mass media and behavior.

social media digital applications that allow people worldwide to have conversations, share common interests, and generate their own media content online.

social networking sites sites on which users can create content, share ideas, and interact with friends.

social responsibility model a model for journalism and speech in which the press functions as a Fourth Estate, monitoring the three branches of government for abuses of power, and provides information necessary for self-governance.

soul music that mixes gospel, blues, and urban and southern black styles with slower, more emotional, and melancholic lyrics.

sound bite in TV journalism, the equivalent of a quote in print; the part of a news report in which an expert, a celebrity, a victim, or a person on the street is interviewed about some aspect of an event or issue.

space brokers in the days before modern advertising, individuals who purchased space in newspapers and sold it to various merchants.

spam a computer term referring to unsolicited e-mail.

spiral of silence a theory that links the mass media, social psychology, and the formation of public opinion; the theory says that people who hold minority views on controversial issues tend to keep their views silent.

split-run editions editions of national magazines that tailor ads to different geographic areas.

spyware software with secretive codes that enable commercial firms to "spy" on users and gain access to their computers.

stereo the recording of two separate channels or tracks of sound.

storyboard in advertising, a blueprint or roughly drawn comic-strip version of a proposed advertisement.

strategy games games in which perspective is omniscient and the player must survey the entire "world" or playing field and make strategic decisions.

studio system an early film production system that constituted a sort of assembly-line process for moviemaking; major film studios controlled not only actors but also directors, editors, writers, and other employees, all of whom worked under exclusive contracts.

subliminal advertising a 1950s term that refers to hidden or disguised print and visual messages that allegedly register on the subconscious, creating false needs and seducing people into buying products.

subsidiary rights in the book industry, selling the rights to a book for use in other media forms, such as a mass market paperback, a CD-ROM, or the basis for a movie screenplay.

supermarket tabloids newspapers that feature bizarre human-interest stories, gruesome murder tales, violent accident accounts, unexplained phenomena stories, and malicious celebrity gossip.

superstations local independent TV stations, such as WTBS in Atlanta or WGN in Chicago, that have uplinked their signals onto a communication satellite to make themselves available nationwide.

survey research in social science research, a method of collecting and measuring data taken from a group of respondents.

syndication leasing TV stations or cable networks the exclusive right to air TV shows.

synergy in media economics, the promotion and sale of a product (and all its versions) throughout the various subsidiaries of a media conglomerate.

talkies movies with sound, beginning in 1927.

Telecommunications Act of 1996 the sweeping update of telecommunications law that led to a wave of media consolidation.

telegraph invented in the 1840s, it sent electrical impulses through a cable from a transmitter to a reception point, transmitting Morse code.

textbooks books made for the el-hi (elementary through high school) and college markets.

textual analysis in media research, a method for closely and critically examining and interpreting the meanings of culture, including architecture, fashion, books, movies, and TV programs.

third-person effect the theory that people believe others are more affected by media messages than they are themselves.

third screens the computer-type screens on which consumers can view television, movies, music, newspapers, and books.

time shifting the process whereby television viewers record shows and watch them later, when it is convenient for them.

Top 40 format the first radio format, in which stations played the forty most popular hits in a given week, as measured by record sales.

trade books the most visible book industry segment, featuring hardbound and paperback books aimed at general readers and sold at bookstores and other retail outlets.

transistors invented by Bell Laboratories in 1947, these tiny pieces of technology, which receive and amplify radio signals, make portable radios possible.

trolls players who take pleasure in intentionally spoiling a gaming experience for others.

underground press radical newspapers, run on shoestring budgets, that question mainstream political policies and conventional values; the term usually refers to a journalism movement of the 1960s.

university press the segment of the book industry that publishes scholarly books in specialized areas.

urban contemporary one of radio's more popular formats, primarily targeting African American listeners in urban areas with dance, R&B, and hip-hop music.

uses and gratifications model a mass communication research model, usually employing in-depth interviews and survey questionnaires, that argues that people use the media to satisfy various emotional desires or intellectual needs.

Values and Lifestyles (VALS) a market-research strategy that divides consumers into types and measures psychological factors, including how consumers think and feel about products and how they achieve (or do not achieve) the lifestyles to which they aspire.

vellum a handmade paper made from treated animal skin, used to print the Gutenberg Bible.

vertical integration in media economics, the phenomenon of controlling a mass media industry at its three essential levels: production, distribution, and exhibition; the term is most frequently used in reference to the film industry.

video news releases (VNRs) in public relations, the visual counterparts to press releases; they pitch story ideas to the TV news media by mimicking the style of a broadcast news report.

video-on-demand (VOD) cable television technology that enables viewers to instantly order programming, such as movies, to be digitally delivered to their sets.

video subscription services a term referring to cable and video-on-demand providers, introduced to include streaming-only companies like Hulu Plus and Netflix.

viral marketing short videos or other content that marketers hope will quickly gain widespread attention as users share it with friends online or by word of mouth.

vitascope a large-screen movie projection system developed by Thomas Edison.

wiki websites websites that are capable of being edited by any user; the most famous is Wikipedia.

wireless telegraphy the forerunner of radio, it is a form of voiceless point-to-point communication; it preceded the voice and sound transmissions of one-to-many mass communication that became known as broadcasting.

wireless telephony early experiments in wireless voice and music transmissions, which later developed into modern radio.

wire services commercial organizations, such as the Associated Press, that share news stories and information by relaying them around the country and the world, originally via telegraph and now via satellite transmission.

World Wide Web (WWW) a data-linking system for organizing and standardizing information on the Internet; the WWW enables computer-accessed information to associate with—or link to—other information, no matter where it is on the Internet.

yellow journalism a newspaper style or era that peaked in the 1890s, it emphasized high-interest stories, sensational crime news, large headlines, and serious reports that exposed corruption, particularly in business and government.

zines self-published magazines produced on personal computer programs or on the Internet.

Index

AAA Living, 285
AARP (American Association of Retired Persons), 285, 288
AARP Bulletin, 285, 288
AARP The Magazine, 285, 288, 401
ABC (American Broadcasting Company), 8, 12, 139, 168, 192, 327, 328, 370, 402, 408, 440
  Disney and, 394, 397, 401, 402, 403, 408
  news and, 17, 179, 397
"ABC" (Jackson 5), 110
ABC Family, 403
ABC Radio, 147
ABC World News Tonight, 179
Abduction, 211
Abdul, Paula, 335
Abercrombie & Fitch, 398
abolition, 251, 273, 295
abortion, 438, 439
Abramoff, Jack, 375
Abramson, Jill, 247, 372
absolute privilege, 492
absolutist ethics, 431
Absolut Vodka, 351
Academy Awards, 48, 120, 212
access channels, 184
Access Hollywood, 240
accountability, 418, 505
account planners, 337
AC/DC, 145
acquisitions editors, 316
Acta Diurna, 237
action-adventure games, 73
Action for Children's Television (ACT), 350
action games, 73
Action News, 440
Activate, 64
Activision Blizzard, 64, 85, 88
activism, 42, 108, 111, 256
actual malice, 492
Adams, Eddie, 281
Adams, Kohn, 487
Adams, Ryan, 106
Adbusters Media Foundation, 349
Ad Council, 333–334
addiction, gaming, 79
Adele, 95
Adelson, Sheldon, 418
ad impressions, 342
Adorno, T. W., 471

adult contemporary (AC) format, 148
Advanced Research Projects Agency (ARPA), 37
advance money, for authors, 316–317
Advance Publications, 294
adventure games, 73
The Adventures of Huckleberry Finn (Twain), 314
advergames, 78
advertising, 327–359
  alcohol, 347, 351, 352–354
  alternative voices in, 356
  association principle and, 345
  beauty standards and, 351
  book, 317
  children and, 350
  cigarette, 347, 351–352, 367
  cost of, 340
  critical issues in, 349–354
  criticism of, 333–334
  democracy and, 356
  department stores, 332
  digital, 340–343, 421
  digital turn and, 327–328
  electronic gaming and, 78–79
  to female consumers, 333
  forms of, 329
  future of, 357
  health and, 351–354
  history of, 330–334
  influence of, 20
  in 1800s, 330–333
  in schools, 350
  irritation, 344
  magazine, 327, 330
  media organizations and, 390–391
  mobile ads, 50, 250
  as myth and story, 345–346
  newspaper, 237, 239–240, 254, 261–262, 327, 330, 332–333
  online, 192, 340–343
  on smartphones, 342
  paid search, 340–341
  patent medicines, 331–332
  persuasive techniques, 343–348
  placement, 338, 340
  planning, 338, 340
  political, 357
  prescription drugs, 354
  product differentiation and, 331
  product placements, 329, 346, 348

  vs. public relations, 363
  radio, 138, 142, 154
  regulation of, 334, 348–356
  saturation, 338, 340
  slogans, 334
  social change and, 333–334
  social media, 341–343
  spending on, 337
  subliminal, 334
  targeted, 50–51
  television, 187, 192, 292, 327, 328, 329, 340, 350
  visual design and, 334–335
Advertising Age, 285
advertising agencies, 330
  boutique, 335, 336
  global revenue, 336
  mega-agencies, 335–336, 341
  online advertising and, 341
  structure of, 337–340
  types of, 335–337
advertising and sales departments, of magazines, 292
advertising campaigns
  antismoking, 352, 356
  "got milk?," 329
  Miller Lite, 338, 340
  Smokey the Bear, 333–334
advertising industry
  creative development, 338
  current state of, 334–343
Advertising: The Uneasy Persuasion (Schudson), 346
advertorials, 78
advice columns, 241
advocacy journalism, 246
Advocate, 290
Aerosmith, 114
affiliate stations, 179, 189
affirmative action, 252
Afghanistan War, 13, 16
AFL-CIO, 369
Africa, 41, 152, 260, 449
African Americans, 211
  advertising aimed at, 351, 353
  in film industry, 211, 212
  magazines for, 289–290
  media ownership by, 408
  newspapers and, 251–252
  See also Civil Rights movement
Afro-American, 252
Agee, James, 448
agency-model pricing, 319
agenda-setting, 467
aggrieved entitlement, 475

"Ain't That a Shame" (Domino), 108
AirPods, 101
Akira, 78
album-oriented rock (AOR), 145, 148
alcohol advertising, 347, 351, 352–354
Alexa, 47, 48
Alexander, Charles, 275
Alfred Hitchcock Presents, 175
Alibaba, 411
Alice in Wonderland (Carroll), 311, 312
Alice in Wonderland (Disney film), 402
Alice's Wonderland, 402
Alienated American, 251
"All Along the Watchtower" (Dylan), 107
Allen, Gracie, 138
Allen, Paul, 47
Allen, Woody, 176
Alliance for Audited Media, 334
Allrecipes, 284
All the President's Men, 426
All Things Considered, 149
Ally McBeal, 176
Alpert, Phillip, 506
Alphabet, 389
alphabet, 302
Al-Rawi, Ahmed K., 471
alternative ads, 356
"alternative facts," 372
alternative journalism, 256
alternative magazines, 294–295
alternative music, 413
alternative radio, 156–157
Alto's Adventure, 72
Amazon, 11, 12, 44, 46, 47, 48, 59, 221, 311, 313, 319, 325, 388, 389, 391, 392, 406, 407
  advertising revenue, 341
  audiobooks and, 310
  e-books and, 46, 48, 311, 319
  music and, 119, 122
  publishing divisions, 405
  streaming and, 168
  streaming services and, 119
  warehouses, 320
Amazon Appstore, 44, 311
Amazon Createspace, 320
Amazon Fire TV, 44, 221
Amazon Kindle, 46, 48, 311, 319

Amazon Prime, 45, 48, 93, 171, 173, 327, 328
Amazon Publishing, 319
AMC Entertainment, 224
American Bandstand, 108
American beauty ideal, 289, 351
American Booksellers Association (ABA), 305
American culture, 6, 28, 170, 225–226, 406, 413–415
American Dream, 400
American Family Radio, 156
American Graffiti, 210
American Horror Story, 176, 177
American Idol, 348
American Journalism Review, 424
American Legion, 285
American Library Association (ALA), 56, 312
American Magazine, 274
American Rifleman, 285
American Society of Composers, Authors, and Publishers (ASCAP), 102
American Society of News Editors (ASNE), 245
American Spectator, 295
American Tobacco Company, 332, 367
American values, 399–400
America's Got Talent, 13
Amos 'n' Andy, 140–141
AM radio, 143
Amsterdam News, 252
analog recording, 100
analog standard, for television, 164
analysis, 25, 26
Anchorman, 441
Ancient Greece, 14
Anderson Cooper 360, 441
Andreessen, Marc, 40
Andrews McMeel Syndication, 257
Android operating system, 44, 45, 47, 72, 88, 407
Andrus, Ethel Percy, 288
Angelou, Maya, 312
Angels, 109
Angry Birds, 72, 86
animation, 78, 200, 204, 335, 402
anime, 78, 217, 413
Annenberg Inclusion Initiative, 121
Annenberg, Walter, 279–280
anthology dramas, 176–177
anti-paparazzi laws, 494
antislavery magazines, 289
antitrust regulation, 393, 394, 408–412
Anton, Leonara LaPeter, 424

AOL, 40, 47, 266, 394, 396, 408
AOL-Time Warner, 394
Apple, 11, 44, 45, 46, 47, 48, 52–53, 59, 311, 319, 325, 388, 389, 392, 406, 407, 409, 495
Apple HomePod, 47, 48
Apple iCloud, 48
Apple iPad, 44, 45, 70, 311
Apple iPhone, 44, 45, 48, 52–53, 495
Apple iPod, 44, 46, 48
Apple iTunes, 46, 48, 101, 116, 119, 121, 221, 227
Apple Music, 96, 119, 388
Apple Watch, 48
apps, 33, 40, 45
  gaming, 72
  news, 233
App Store, 44, 45, 72, 88
aQuantive, 341
A&R (artist & repertoire) agents, 117
Arab Spring, 41, 42, 247
Arbenz, Jacobo, 374
Arbuckle, Fatty, 499
arcades, 65–66, 67
architecture, 22, 24
archives, digital, 59
Are You My Mother? (Bechdel), 305
Are You the One?, 23
Aristotle, 14, 434
Armstrong, Edwin, 142–143
Armstrong, Louis, 103
Arnold Worldwide, 340
Around the World in Eighty Days (Verne), 241, 287
ARPA, 64
ARPAnet, 37, 38, 39
Arrested Development, 45
art
  classical view of, 14
  fine, 19
Asch, Solomon, 468
Asia, 260, 353
  See also specific countries
Asian American newspapers, 253
Asian Americans, 211, 253, 437
Asian cinema, 216–217
Assange, Julian, 449
assassinations, political, 163, 245, 281, 443
assistant editors, 255
Associated Press (AP), 240, 255, 378
Association of American Publishers (AAP), 305, 312
association principle, 345
Asteroids, 67

Astro Boy, 78
astroturf lobbying, 375–376
Atari, 67, 68
Atari 2600, 67, 68
Atari Flashback series, 67–68
Atkinson, Samuel Coate, 275
The Atlantic, 288
Atlantic Monthly, 288
AT&T, 40, 58, 134, 135, 164, 168, 171, 394, 396, 412
Atwood, Margaret, 308
Audible, 310
audiences
  global, 404
  high culture, 20
  niche, 428
  popular culture, 19
  studies of, 473
audiobooks, 250, 310
Audion, 131
audiotape, 99–100
Audit Bureau of Circulations, 334
Aufderheide, Pat, 479
augmented reality, 76
Australia, 57, 76, 258, 260, 286, 320, 388
authoritarianism, 486
Authors Guild, 312
Author Solutions, 320
The Autobiography of Malcolm X, 312
Avalon, Frankie, 109
avatars, 67, 71
Avett Brothers, 106
Azalea, Iggy, 120

Babbage's, 88
Babylonians, 302
Bacall, Lauren, 501
The Bachelor, 13
Bad Boy Entertainment, 115
Baer, Ralph, 67
Baez, Joan, 111, 254
bagatelle, 66
Bagdikian, Ben, 408
Bahrain, 471
Baidu, 41
Bailey, F. Lee, 495
Baker, Belle, 103
balance, in journalism, 439
BAMtech, 64
banana republics, 374
Bandai Namco, 86
Bandura, Albert, 466
bandwagon effect, 344
banned books, 312, 314, 315
banner ads, 340
Baquet, Dean, 429
Barnes & Noble, 318, 319, 320
Barney & Friends, 180
Barnum, P. T., 364, 373

Barr, Roseanne, 370
Barry, Jack, 167
barter deals, 190
Bartles & Jaymes, 345
basic cable, 169, 171
Batman: Arkham Asylum, 78
Baumgartner, Felix, 373
Beach Boys, 109
Beastie Boys, 115
Beatles, 107, 109, 110, 111
beauty ideal, 289, 351
Bechdel, Alison, 300, 305
Bee, Samantha, 447
Bee Gees, 114
beer ads, 347, 352–354
Bejeweled, 86
Bell, Alexander Graham, 98
Bell, Chichester, 98
Beloved (Morrison), 309
Ben-Hur, 208
Bennett, Chancellor Johnathan, 95
Bennett, James Gordon, 239
Bennett, Jim, 387
Benny, Jack, 138
Bentham, Jeremy, 434
Bergman, Ingmar, 213
Berkley Barb, 254
Berkshire Hathaway, 257, 391
Berle, Milton, 175
Berlin, Irving, 103
Berliner, Emile, 98
Bernays, Edward, 138, 365, 366–368, 374, 399
Berners-Lee, Tim, 39, 46
Bernstein, Carl, 426
Berry, Chuck, 23, 105, 109
Bertelsmann, 315
Best Buy, 119
best-sellers, 309
Better Business Bureau, 334, 354
Better Homes and Gardens, 285, 294
Bewkes, Jeffrey, 396, 398
Beyoncé, 344
Bezos, Jeff, 263, 319, 391, 416
bias, 429, 430
Bible, 24, 307, 312
Bieber, Justin, 118
Big Bang Theory, 161, 328
Big Bopper, 109
Big Brother, 13
Big Brother and the Holding Company, 112
Bigelow, Kathryn, 211, 213
Big Five, 207–208
Big Machine Records, 117
"Big Mac" theory, 20
Big Media, 417
Big Six, 224–225

big tech companies, 392, 405–406, 407, 511
Billboard, 95, 96, 121, 155
Bill of Rights, 487
binary digits, 40
Bing, 41, 47, 340
binge drinking, 347
bin Laden, Osama, 16
Bipartisan Campaign Reform Act, 416
The Birth of a Nation, 208, 209
Biswas-Diener, Robert, 36
bits, 40
Bixby, 47
Black, Hugo, 488
BlackBerry, 44
black cinema, 212
Blackish, 477
The Blacklist, 328
blacklisting, 501
Black Lives Matter, 42, 361
black migration, 104
Black Mirror, 24
Black Panther, 212
Blackwell, Otis, 107
Bleacher Report, 286
Blizzard Entertainment, 85
block booking, 206
Blockbuster, 221, 387–388
blockbusters, 208, 222, 223, 226, 309
block printing, 6, 302–303
bloggers, 343, 376
blogs, 28
Blondie, 113
blues music, 104
Blume, Judy, 312
Blumlein, Alan, 100
Blu-rays, 221
Bly, Nellie, 241, 250, 287, 423–424, 431
Bobo doll experiment, 464, 466
body image, 351
Bogart, Humphrey, 501
"Bohemian Rhapsody" (Queen), 23
Bollea, Terry G., 494
Bollier, David, 59
Bollywood, 214, 216
book challenge, 312, 315
book industry
  alternative voices in, 320
  independent publishers and, 301, 316
  modern, 304–309
  organization and ownership of, 314–320
  structure of, 316–317
  trends and issues in, 309–313
Book Industry Study Group (BISG), 305
books, 6–7, 299–323

audio, 250, 310
banned, 312, 314, 315
best-sellers, 309
block printing and, 302–303
children's, 311
colonial American, 303–304
comics, 299–300, 301, 305
convergence and, 310–311
culture and, 301
democracy and, 320–321
digital gaming and, 78
dime novels, 304
e-books, 46, 48, 311, 312, 319, 321
estimated U.S. revenue, 2016, 306
film and, 309–310
format trends for, 233
future of, 321
graphic novels, 299–300, 305
history of, 301
illuminated manuscripts, 302, 303
manuscript culture and, 302
marketing of, 317
moveable type and, 303
paperback, 304
politics and, 308
preserving and digitizing, 311–312
pricing, 313
printing press and, 303
professional, 306
promotion of, 309–310
pulp fiction, 304
religious, 307
selling, 318–320
television and, 301, 309–310
textbooks, 306–307
trade, 299, 305
types of, 305–309
university press, 309
bookstores, 313, 318–320, 392
book superstores, 318–319
Boone, Daniel, 364
Boone, Pat, 107, 108
Boorstin, Daniel, 373
Borden, 332
Borders, 318, 319
Borgen, 444
Born a Crime (Noah), 309
Born This Way, 13
Boston, 113
Boston Globe, 237, 262, 408
Boston Marathon, 371
Boston News-Letter, 238, 330
bots, 43, 420
Bourke-White, Margaret, 279, 280
boutique agencies, 335, 336
Bowie, David, 105, 113
boxed game/retail model, 87–88

boxing, 14
boxing films, 497, 499
box-office sales, 221, 222
Boy George, 105
Boy's Life, 288
BP, 377
Bradford, Andrew, 274
Brady, Mathew, 275, 276
Braga, Michael, 424
branded content, 292
brand names, 331, 348
brand stretching, 353
BrandZ, 345
Brave New World (Huxley), 22
Breaking Bad, 188, 191, 467
Brennan, William, Jr., 485
bridal industry, 465
Brinkley, David, 178
Britain, 43
British American Tobacco (BAT), 353
British invasion, 109–110
broadband, 40, 57, 58
broadcasting, 132
  deregulation of, 393–394, 395
  regulation of, 501–504
  television, 169
  toll, 135
Broadcasting Corporation of America (BCA), 135
broadcast networks, 182–183, 189, 192–193, 327
  See also specific networks
broadcast news, 244–245
Broder, David, 448
Brokaw, Tom, 178
Broken Bow Records, 117
Brooker, Charlie, 24
Brooks, Mel, 19, 176
Brown, Helen Gurley, 286, 287
Brown, James, 110
Brown, Michael, 42
Brown v. Board of Education, 104
browsers, 39–40
Bruno, 501
Brussels, 43
Buckley, William F., 295
Buckley v. Valeo, 484
Bud Light, 347
Budweiser, 352–353
Buena Vista, 402
Buenos Aires, Argentina, 313
Buffalo Bill, 364
Buffalo News, 257
Buffett, Warren, 257–258, 391
bureau reporters, 255
Burke, James E., 378
Burke, John, 364
Burke, Tarana, 42
Burns, George, 138
Burns, Ken, 499
Burson-Marsteller, 378

Burstyn v. Wilson, 500
Bush, George W., 17, 429
Bush administration, 16, 376
Bushnell, Nolan, 67
business magazines, 285
business strategies, 11–12
Buzzcocks, 113
Bwana Devil, 463
Byers, Dylan, 412
Byrds, 111

The Cabinet of Dr. Caligari, 213
cable companies, 193–194
cable news, 179, 427–428, 442
Cable News Network (CNN), 179
cable television, 8, 59, 165
  access channels, 184
  alternatives, 194
  consolidation in, 194
  cost of, 394
  democracy and, 194–195
  development of, 168–171
  economics of, 187–194
  franchises, 184, 186
  global, 404
  leased channels, 184
  must-carry rules, 183–184
  narrowcasting, 169
  premium channels, 171, 223
  regulation of, 182–187
  role of, 184
  satellite, 171
  services, 169, 171
  syndication and, 189–190
  technology, 168–169
Caesar, Julius, 237
Caesar, Sid, 175
Call Me by Your Name, 218
Call of Duty, 79, 83, 85
Cambridge Analytica, 50, 343, 412
Camel Newsreel Theater, 178
cameras, 202, 280
  in the courtroom, 495–497
campaign financing, 416, 483–484
Campbell, Clive, 114
Campbell, John, 238
Campbell Soup, 331, 355
Campion, Jane, 211
campus newspapers, 259
Canada, 388
Canadian Business, 88
Candy Crush Saga, 70, 85
Canterbury Tales (Chaucer), 303
Cantor, Eddie, 103, 138
Cantor, Jami, 362
Cantril, Hadley, 461, 462
capitalism, 7, 391, 429
Capote, Truman, 245
Captain Underpants (Pilkey), 312

Cara, Alessia, 115, 120
car advertisements, 345, 349
Car and Driver, 294
Carey, James, 457, 476, 477
Carlin, George, 502
Carnation, 332
Carnegie, Andrew, 320, 321, 393
Carnegie Library, 321
Carr, David, 438, 443
Carroll, John, 267
Carson, Rachel, 321
Carter, Jimmy, 393
Cartoon Network, 401
cash deals, 190
Cash Money Records, 117
cassettes, 99–100
casual games, 73
The Casual Vacancy (Rowling), 317
cathode ray tubes (CRTs), 66, 164
Catholic Worker, 256
CATV, 168
cause-effect relationships, 464
CBGB, 113
CBS (Columbia Broadcasting System), 8, 45, 137–138, 168, 192–193, 194, 327, 328
CBS Evening News, 179
CBS Records, 98
The CBS-TV News, 179
CD Baby, 121–122
Celler-Kefauver Act, 393
cell phones, 8, 44, 57
   See also smartphones
celluloid, 202
censorship, 42, 487–489
   books, 312, 314, 315
   Internet, 56
   movie, 497–499
   rock and roll music, 108–109
Center for Consumer Freedom (CCF), 375
Center for Investigative Reporting, 266
Center for Media and Democracy (CMD), 381, 382
Center for Public Integrity, 266
CEO-to-worker wage gap, 398
cereal advertising, 350
Chance the Rapper, 95, 96, 115
Channel One, 350
Chaplin, Charlie, 22, 24, 206
chapter shows, 177
Charles, Ray, 105, 108, 335
Charter Communications, 40, 193
chat systems, in-game, 73
Chaucer, Geoffrey, 303
Chavez, Cesar, 345
Cherokee Phoenix, 253
Cherokee Rose Bud, 253
Chester Cheetah, 78

Chicago Defender, 252
Chick-fil-A, 416
Chieh, Wang, 302–303
Child Online Protection Act, 56
child pornography, 506
children
   advertising and, 350
   media exposure of, 15
children's books, 311
Children's Internet Protection Act, 56
children's magazines, 288
Children's Television Act, 350
Child's Play, 75
China, 42
   cinema in, 217
   film censorship, 498
   first books, 302
   media corporations, 411
   media research in, 470
   smoking in, 352–353
Chiquita Brands, 374
chords, 108
Chrome, 40
chronic traumatic encephalopathy (CTE), 361–362
Chuck E. Cheese, 67
cigarette advertising, 347, 351–352, 367
Cincinnati Enquirer, 243, 257
Cinemark USA, 224
CinemaScope, 221
cinematographs, 203
cinema verité, 215
Cineplex Entertainment, 224
Cinerama, 221
cities, 22
citizen journalism, 264, 444–447
Citizens for Tax Justice, 53
Citizens United case, 416, 483, 484
City Lights Books, 318
Civil Rights movement, 13, 108, 110–111, 251, 252, 281, 443, 491
Civil War, 8, 106, 239, 240, 243, 251, 273, 275, 276, 309, 364
clans, 73
Clapton, Eric, 104
Clarissa; or, The History of a Young Lady (Richardson), 304
Clark, Dick, 107, 108
Clash, 113
classical music, 103
Clayton Antitrust Act, 393
clearance rules, 189
Clear Channel Communications, 102, 152–153, 155
Cleaver, Eldridge, 254
Clerks, 501
click fraud, 51

click-throughs, 342
Clinton, Bill, 13, 247, 394
Clinton, Hillary, 449
closed Internet, 45–46, 47
Cloud Player, 48
cloud services, 47
Club Penguin, 71
CNN (Cable News Network), 9, 16, 264, 404, 428, 442
Coca, Imogene, 175
Coca-Cola, 331, 345, 348
Cochrane, Elizabeth, 423
codex, 302
Cody, William F., 364
Cold War, 218–219, 412, 501
Cole, Nat King, 189
Colgate-Palmolive, 332
collective intelligence, 74–75
college students, advertising aimed at, 353–354
college textbooks, 307
Collier's, 277, 279, 280
Collins, Suzanne, 310
colonial America
   beginning of publishing in, 303–304
   magazines, 274
   newspapers, 238–239, 330
Colony, George, 376
color television, 165
Columbia, 208
Columbia Phonograph Broadcasting System (CPBS), 137
Columbia Phonograph Company, 137
Columbia Pictures, 224, 226
Columbia University, Journalism School, 263
Columbine High School shootings, 82
Combs, Sean "Diddy," 115
Comcast, 40, 58, 193, 226, 389, 394, 396
Comedians in Cars Getting Coffee, 161–162
comedies, 175–176
comics, 299–300, 301, 305
Comics Magazine Association of America, 301
Commercial Alert, 348, 354, 355
commercial culture, 28
commercialism, 78–79, 354–355
commercial press, 238
commercial radio, 145–151
commercial speech, 348–356
Committee on Public Information (CPI), 367
Committee to Defend Martin Luther King, 491
Committee to Protect Journalists (CPJ), 265–266
common carriers, 184

common sense, 399–400
communication
   as culture, 476
   defined, 5
   digital, 8, 40
   electronic, 7–8
   eras in, 6
   oral, 6, 11
   print, 6–7, 11
   written, 6
Communications Decency Act, 56
communism, 486, 501
Communist Party, 42
community antenna television (CATV), 168
community journalism, 264
community relations, 373
compact discs (CDs), 100, 119
compulsory education, 7
computer-based gaming, 70
computer-generated imagery (CGI), 209
computer technology, 281
concussion, 361–362
Condé Nast, 294
Condé Nast Traveler, 287
conflict of interest, 433–434
conflict-oriented journalism, 248
Conrad, Frank, 134, 135
consensus narratives, 228–229
consensus-oriented journalism, 248
consoles, 67–70
consumer choice, 413
consumer control, 413
consumer culture, 7
consumer goods, 332
consumerism, 25, 28, 321, 333
consumer magazines, 285
consumer relations, 373
Consumer Reports, 285, 292
Contact, 368
contemporary hit radio (CHR), 148
content analysis, 464–466
A Contract with God (Eisner), 305
control group, 463
controlled circulations, 293
conventions, gaming, 75
convergence, 6, 10–13, 25, 32
   books and, 310–311
   business strategies for, 11–12
   cross platform, 11
   cultural change and, 12–13
   dual meanings of, 10–11
   impact of, 45–46
   journalism and, 442–443
   magazines and, 283–284
   media industry and, 405–408

mobile media and, 44–47
movies and, 226–227
newspapers and, 261–262
PCs and, 44
radio and, 151–154
sound recording and, 97,
    100–102
television and, 44, 172–173,
    191–192
Conway, Kellyanne, 308, 372
Cook, Fred, 502
Cooke, Janet, 435
cookies, 50–51, 342
Cook's Illustrated, 285, 292
Coolidge, Calvin, 135
Cooper, Anderson, 428, 441
Cooper, Gary, 219
Coopersmith, Tristan, 120
Copeland, Misty, 309
Coppola, Francis Ford, 210
Coppola, Sofia, 211
copy editors, 317
Copyright Act, 489–490
copyright infringement, 489–491
Copyright Royalty Board,
    151–152
cord cutting, 171
Cormier, Anthony, 424
Corporation for Public Broad-
    casting (CPB), 149,
    180, 182
correlations, 464
Cortana, 47
Cosmopolitan, 242, 277, 285,
    286–287, 289, 294
Cosmopolitan en Español, 290
Count Basie, 103
Counterintuitive CEO, 376
Counter-Strike, 64, 75, 88
country music, 105
country radio, 148
Couric, Katie, 179
courtrooms, media in, 495–497
Court TV, 497
cover music, 103, 107–108
Cox, 40, 58
Craft, Christine, 441
Crane, Stephen, 245
Createspace, 320
creative development, 338
credibility, of journalists, 427
Crew Cuts, 108
Crimean War, 280
crime blocks, 440
crises, public relations during,
    377–378
Crisis, 289
critical perspective, 25–28
critical process, 25–28, 54
Crockett, Davy, 364
Cronkite, Walter, 179
crooners, 103

Crosby, Bing, 103
Cross, Katherine, 80
cross platform, 11
The Crown, 188
Crystallizing Public Opinion
    (Bernays), 367
Cullors, Patrisse, 42
cultivation effect, 468
cultural change, 12–13
cultural diversity, 24
cultural imperialism, 406,
    413–415
cultural model, of mass
    communication, 9
cultural narratives, 14–15
cultural studies, 457, 469–477
    conducting research in,
        472–475
    early developments in, 469–472
    evaluating research, 477
    theoretical perspectives,
        475–476
cultural values, of modern
    period, 22–23
culture
    American, 6, 28, 225–226, 406,
        413–415
    books and, 301
    commercial, 28
    communication as, 476
    consumer, 7
    critiquing, 25, 28
    defined, 5–6
    gaming, 79–82
    high, 15, 19, 20, 105
    low, 15, 19–20, 105
    manuscript, 302
    map model of, 20–22
    media, 78
    modern, 23
    movies and, 201
    popular, 19–20, 413–415
    popular media, 14–15
    postmodern, 23–24
    premodern, 23
    radio and, 140–141
    rock and roll music and,
        105–106
    skyscraper model of, 15, 18–20
Cumulus, 155
Cure, 113
Curry, Ann, 440
Curry, Steph, 344
Curtis, Cyrus, 277
Czitrom, Daniel, 457–458,
    460–461

Daddy Yankee, 118
The Daily Show, 446, 447
*The Daily Show with Trevor
    Noah*, 179

Dallas, 12
Dallas Morning News, 262
Daly, John, 179
Dance Dance Revolution, 74
Daniels, Lee, 212
Das Kapital (Marx), 312
data breaches, 343
data journalism, 246
data mining, 50–51
Daughters of the American
    Revolution, 14
Davier, Lucile, 471
da Vinci, Leonardo, 201
Davison, W. Phillips, 468
Day, Benjamin, 239
Day, Dorothy, 256
Daye, Matthew, 303
Daye, Stephen, 303
*A Day in the Life of Marlon
    Bundo* (Oliver), 317
Dayton Daily News, 43
deadheading, 365
Dean, James, 220
The Death of Literature (Kernan),
    321
Death Race, 82
De Beers, 334
deception
    in advertising, 355
    in journalism, 431
deejays, 107, 108, 114
"Deep Throat," 426
Deepwater Horizon oil spill, 377
deficit financing, 188
De Forest, Lee, 131–132, 136
deliberative democracy, 448, 450
Dell, 59
Del Monte, 374
de Martinville, Édouard-Léon
    Scott, 97–98
democracy, 25
    advertising and, 356
    books and, 320–321
    deliberative, 448, 450
    digital gaming and, 89
    digital turn and, 324
    First Amendment and, 507
    free markets and, 412–413
    Internet and, 59
    journalism and, 425, 448–451
    magazines and, 295
    media marketplace and,
        415–417
    media research and, 478–479
    movies and, 228–229
    newspapers and, 265–267
    public relations and, 381–383
    radio and, 157
    social media and, 41–43
    sound recording and, 122
    television and cable and,
        194–195

democratic expression, 420–421
democratic ideals, 20
Democratic-Republican Party,
    487
democratization, 7
demographic editions, 292–293
demographic research,
    369–370
demos, 117
De Palma, Brian, 210
Department of Commerce, 15,
    135
department stores, 331–332
dependent variables, 463
Depp, Johnny, 493
deregulation, 393–394, 395
description, 25, 26
design managers, 317
"Despacito," 118
Destiny, 86
Details, 285
Detroit, 110
Detroit Free Press, 258
Detroit News, 258
Dettelbach, Steven M., 506
developmental editors, 317
Diablo, 85
Diablo 3, 70
dial-up access, 40
Diamond Sutra (Chieh), 302–303
Dick, Kirby, 215
Dickson, William Kennedy, 203
Diddley, Bo, 105
Didion, Joan, 245
Diener, Ed, 36
digital advertising, 340–343, 421
digital archives, 59
digital communication, 8, 40
digital companies, 325, 388, 392,
    405–408, 511
digital divide, 56–57, 59
digital gaming. *See* gaming,
    digital
digital magazines, 284
digital media, time spent on, 328
digital media conglomerates,
    405–407
digital media subscriptions, 93
Digital Millennium Copyright
    Act, 491
digital newspapers, 237,
    246–247, 261–262
digital photography, 281
digital signals, for television,
    164–165
digital sound recording, 100
digital streaming services,
    101–102, 116, 119, 121, 151,
    223, 227, 327, 328, 388,
    394, 404
digital turn, 32–33, 46, 102, 227,
    232, 250, 324, 327–328

digital video, 227–228
dime novels, 304
direct broadcast satellite (DBS), 8, 171, 186, 193–194, 412
directors
 black, 211, 212
 Hollywood, 210–211
 women, 211, 213
DirecTV, 171, 193, 412
dirty words, 502
disassociation, 345
disaster coverage, 435, 436, 467
disaster management, 377–378
disc jockeys, 107, 108
disco, 114
discount rental kiosks, 221, 223
Discover, 287
Discovery Communications, 391
Dish Network, 171, 186, 193, 412
Disney, 71, 189, 192, 224, 225, 226, 389, 401–404, 408, 409
 consolidation and, 394, 396–397
 current state of, 404
 early years of, 401–402
 global expansion of, 402–404
 Sony and, 172
 Star Wars franchise and, 200
 timeline of, 402–403
Disney, Walt, 219, 401, 402
Disney Channel, 403
Disneyland, 402
Disneyland Paris, 403
Disney Publishing Worldwide, 403
distributed networks, 37–38
distribution, television, 189
diversification, 409, 412
diversity, 24
DJ Kool Herc, 114
Doc Martin, 177
Documentary Filmmakers' Statement of Best Practices in Fair Use, 479
documentary films, 214–215
Dole Food Company, 374
domestic spying, 51
Donkey Kong, 67, 68
The Donna Reed Show, 400
Do Not Track legislation, 51
Doom, 70
Doors, 112
Dope, 212
Dorsey, Tommy, 103
Dota 2, 64
DoubleClick, 341
Douglass, Frederick, 251
Downie, Leonard, 263
download speeds, 32
downsizing, 397–398
Downton Abbey, 177

Doyle Dane Bernbach (DDB), 338, 340
Dragnet, 175
Drake, 25, 116
dramas, 176–178
 anthology, 176–177
 episodic series, 177–178
 hybrid, 178
Dreiser, Theodore, 245, 287
Drew, Robert, 215
drive time, 145
Drudge, Matt, 246–247
Drudge Report, 246–247
drug culture, 245
drugs, 111–112
Dualtone Records, 117
Du Bois, W. E. B., 25, 289
Duck Dynasty, 195
dumps, 317
Duncan, David, 281
DuVernay, Ava, 213
DVDs, 8, 172, 221
Dvorak, Jane, 372
DVRs (digital video recorders), 8, 12, 172
Dylan, Bob, 107, 111, 113, 254
Dynasty, 28

earbuds, 101
Earle, Steve, 106
earmarks, 375
earned media, 343
Earth Day, 467
Eason, David, 427
Eastman, George, 202, 280
Eastman Kodak, 202, 331, 332
Easy Rider, 210
eating disorders, 351
Ebony, 289
e-books, 46, 48, 311, 312, 319, 321
Echo, 44, 47, 48
EchoStar, 412
e-cigarettes, 370
The Eclectic Reader, 306
e-commerce, 50
economic divide, 56–57
economics
 of magazines, 291–295
 of media and the Internet, 46
 of movie industry, 221–228
 of newspapers, 239–240
 of radio broadcasting, 154–157
 of television and cable, 187–194
economics, media, 46, 387–419
 analyzing, 389–391
 consolidation and, 389
 democracy and, 415–417
 social issues in, 408–415
Economist, 315
The Eddie Cantor Show, 138
Edelman, 368, 376

Edelman, Daniel J., 368
Edelman, Richard, 368
Edge, 40
Edison, Thomas, 10, 98, 131, 203, 204, 206, 241
editorial departments, of magazines, 291–292
editorial responsibilities, in newspapers, 255
editor in chief, 255, 291
eDonkey, 101
Ed Sullivan Show, 15, 110
education, compulsory, 7
Educational Media Foundation, 156
Edwards, Douglas, 179
Egyptians, 302
Eighth Grade, 215, 218
Eisner, Michael, 397
Eisner, Will, 305
The Elder Scrolls, 75
elections
 1992, 8
 2008, 357
 2012, 357
 2016, 343, 357, 412, 420
 campaign financing, 416, 483–484
 political advertising and, 357
 social media fraud and, 43
electric guitar, 104
electromagnetic spectrum, 130
electromagnetic waves, 130
Electronic Arts (EA), 85–86
Electronic Communications Privacy Act, 494
electronic dance music (EDM), 116
Electronic Entertainment Expo (E3), 75
electronic era, 7–8
electronic gaming. *See* gaming, digital
electronic publishers, 184
Elementary, 6
el-hi textbooks, 306–307
elite magazines, 288
elites, 7
Elle, 294
The Ellen DeGeneres Show, 190
Ellington, Duke, 103
Ellsberg, Daniel, 488
El Misisipi, 252
e-mail, 38, 40, 340
Emancipator, 289
emergence stage, 10
Emerson, Ralph Waldo, 274
Empire, 328
Endeavor, 6
Ender, Erika, 118
engagement, 25, 27

England, 152
Engstrom, Erika, 465
Entertainment Software Association (ESA), 79
Entertainment Software Rating Board (ESRB), 84
Entertainment Weekly, 283, 294
entrepreneurial stage, 10
environmental movement, 110
ephedra, 355
Epicurious, 284
episodic series, 177–178
e-publishing, 320
equal opportunity, 504
e-readers, 46, 48, 311, 319
Eritrea, 57
ESL, 64
Espionage Acts, 489
ESPN, 78
ESPN.go.com, 402
ESPN Radio, 402
ESPN The Magazine, 286, 402
eSports, 63–64
Esquire, 294
Essence, 290
E.T., 348
ethical policies, 434
ethics
 absolutist, 431
 Judeo-Christian, 434
 news media and, 429, 431–435
 PRSA professional, 380
 resolving ethical problems, 434
 situational, 431
 social media, 43
 throwaway, 19
 of war coverage, 16–17
 WikiLeaks and, 449
ethnocentrism, 428–429
Euripides, 14
Europe, 388
 film distribution in, 206
European model of journalism, 444
European Union, 51, 412
evaluation, 25, 27
evangelicals, 307
Evans, Walker, 448
Eve, 351
evergreens, 189
evergreen subscriptions, 293
EverQuest II, 84
evolutionary theory, 24
Excellence in Journalism project, 251
executive compensation, 398
exhibition, film, 206–208
experimental group, 463
experiments, 463–464
expert opinions, 437–438
expletives, 504

expression
  in the media, 501–507
  libel, 491–492
  obscene, 492–493
  seditious, 489
  unprotected forms of, 489–495
  See also free expression
Eyes Wide Shut, 501
Eyewitness News, 440

Fabian, 109
Facebook, 8, 11, 12, 28, 32, 36, 40,
    47, 48, 50, 59, 247, 325, 388,
    389, 392, 406, 407
  advertising revenue, 49, 250,
    341, 342–343
  data breaches, 343
  data privacy and, 511–517
  eSports and, 64
  fraud and elections, 43
  number of users, 45
  privacy violations by, 50
  walled garden of, 45
Facebook Watch, 64
Faces Places, 214
facts, 379, 429
Fairbanks, Douglas, 206, 499
Fair Labor Association (FLA), 53
Fairness and Accuracy in
    Reporting (FAIR), 437
Fairness Doctrine, 133, 146–147,
    505
fair use, 491
fake news, 9, 12, 179, 446–447
Fallows, James, 11–12
Family Circle, 294
Family Guy, 502
family values, 23, 314
Family Video, 172
famous-person testimonials,
    344
Famuyiwa, Rick, 212
Fanning, Shawn, 100
Fantasia, 401
Fantasy Focus, 78
fantasy sports, 71–72, 78
Fantasy Sports Trade Association,
    72
farm magazines, 285
FarmVille, 78
Farnsworth, Philo, 164, 165
Farrow, Ronan, 290
fashion magazines, 289
Fat Boys, 114
Fats Domino, 105, 108
Fax machines, 8
FBI, 495
FCC v. Pacifica Foundation,
    504
Fear of Missing Out (FOMO), 36
feature-length films, 208
feature syndication, 255, 257

Federal Communications Act of
    1934, 108, 146, 184, 501–504
Federal Communications
    Commission (FCC), 27, 146
  7-7-7 Rule, 393–394, 395
  analog standard and, 164
  broadcasting regulation and,
    133, 138, 139, 183–184, 502
  channel assignment by, 165
  fin-syn and, 183
  Internet and, 505
  net neutrality and, 58, 505, 507
Federal Food and Drug Act, 331
Federalist Party, 487
Federal Radio Commission
    (FRC), 50, 138
Federal Trade Commission
    (FTC), 51, 137, 334, 354
  advertising regulation by, 355
  disclosure rules, 343
  "Green Guides," 381
Federer, Roger, 344
Fellini, Federico, 213
Felt, Mark, 426
female consumers, 333
femininity, 105
Feminist Frequency, 81
Fenton, Roger, 280
Fessenden, Reginald, 131–132
FHM, 283
fiber-optic cable, 38–39
Field, Sally, 211
Fifty Shades of Grey (James), 320
fighting games, 73
Fiji Water, 344
file sharing, 100–101, 116
Filkins, Dexter, 245
film, development of, 201–203
film exchange system, 206
film noir genre, 210, 220
films. *See* movies
film studios, 189, 205–211,
    224–226.
    See also Hollywood
Filo, David, 41
financial crisis, 16
Financial Interest and Syndica-
    tion Rules (fin-syn), 183
Financial Times, 315
fine art, 19
Finkel, Michael, 433
Finnegans Wake (Joyce), 21
Firefox, 40
fireside chats, of Roosevelt, 140
First Amendment, 238, 434,
    483–487, 490
  commercial speech and,
    348–349, 350
  democracy and, 507
  digital gaming and, 65, 89
  fake news as attack on, 9
  film and, 497–501

indecency and, 504
Internet and, 505
MPAA and, 501
versus Sixth Amendment,
    495–497
war coverage and, 16
See also free expression
first-person shooter games, 83
first-run syndication, 190
Fitzgerald, F. Scott, 305
fixed book pricing (FBP), 313
Fixer Upper, 271–272
flack, 378
Fleischman, Doris, 367, 368
flexible markets, 397
FM radio, 142–143
Folio, 271
folk music, 110–111
folk-rock, 111
Fonsi, Luis, 118
Food and Drug Administration
    (FDA), 332, 370
Food Marketing Institute, 329
football, 361–362
Ford, Henry, 397, 400
foreign-language movies, 213–214
foreign-language newspapers,
    251
Forever (Blume), 312
format radio, 143–144, 145–148
Fortune, 280, 294
Foster, Jodie, 211
4th Estate study, 437–438
fourth screens, 173
Fox, 327, 328
Fox, William, 205
Foxconn, 52–53, 397
Fox Film Corporation, 205
Fox News, 179, 428, 429, 442
framing research, 472
France, 43, 313, 471
franchises, cable, 184, 186
Francis, Connie, 109
Frankenstein (Shelley), 19
Frankfurt School, 470–472
Franklin, Aretha, 110
Franklin, Benjamin, 238, 239,
    274, 304
Franklin, James, 238
fraud
  elections and, 43
  online, 56
Freed, Alan, 104, 107, 108
freedom of speech, 65, 89,
    348–349, 434.
    See also free expression
Freedom's Journal, 251
free expression, 482–509
  censorship and, 487–489
  cultural and political struggles
    over, 485

First Amendment and,
    486–487
Internet and, 505
in the media, 501–507
libel and, 491–492
origins of, 485–497
unprotected forms of expres-
    sion, 489–495
See also First Amendment
Freeform, 403
Freegate, 42
free markets, 412–413
freemium, 88
Free Press, 415
free press
  First Amendment and,
    486–487
  global, 487
  origins of, 485–497
*Free Speech for Me—but Not for
    Thee* (Hentoff), 314
free-speech movement, 254
free-to-play model, 88
free trade, 400
Freud, Sigmund, 366
Friedkin, William, 210
Fringe, 24
fringe time, 189
Frozen, 211, 401, 403
Fruit Ninja, 72
funk music, 110
Future, 115

gag orders, 495
Gaines, Chip and Joanna,
    271–272, 307
Gallo, 345
Game Boy, 70
Game Informer, 282, 285
Game of Thrones, 45, 188, 310,
    405
gameplay, 72, 73
game publishers, 85–86
#GamerGate, 80–81
GameSpot, 75
gamification, 84
gaming, digital, 63–91
  addiction and, 79
  advertising and, 78–79
  apps, 72
  arcades and, 67
  books and, 78
  business of, 84–89
  communities of play, 72–75
  conventions, 75
  culture of, 79–82
  development of, 65–70
  distribution and, 87–88
  First Amendment and,
    65, 89
  future of, 84
  gaming sites, 75

gaming, digital (*continued*)
  gender and, 79, 80–81
  independent game developers, 88–89
  interactive nature of, 65, 72, 84
  Internet and, 70–72
  marketing and, 87
  media culture and, 78
  misogyny and, 79–82, 83
  modding and, 75
  movies and, 78
  on PCs, 70
  other media and, 78
  ownership and organization of, 85–86
  pay models, 87–88
  portable players, 70
  publishing structure of, 86–87
  regulation of, 82, 84
  television and, 78
  trends and issues in, 78–84
  video game consoles, 67–70
  violence and, 79, 82
  See also video games
gaming, mechanical, 65–66
gaming industry, 82, 84–89
gangster rap, 115–116
Gannett, 258
Gans, Herbert, 428–429
Ganz, 71
Garza, Alicia, 42
gatekeepers, 8–9, 45
Gates, Bill, 47
Gawker, 494
Gaye, Marvin, 113
Gazeta Wyborcza, 444
Gelbart, Larry, 176
gender
  digital gaming and, 80–81
  game addiction and, 79
General Agreement on Tariffs and Trade (GATT), 400
general assignment reporters, 255
General Data Protection Regulation (GDPR), 51
General Electric (GE), 131, 133–135, 137, 192, 193, 226, 394
general-interest magazines
  fall of, 279–283
  rise of, 277–279
General Magazine and Historical Chronicle, 274
Genesis, 145
Genie, 47
genres
  Hollywood, 209–210
  video game, 72, 73, 74
Gerbner, George, 464, 468
Germany, 43, 119, 449
Gershwin, George, 103

Get Out, 218
Gevinson, Tavi, 284
Ghostery, 51
Gibson, Don, 108
Gilligan, Vince, 191
Ginsberg, Allen, 254, 318
The Girl with the Lower Back Tattoo (Schumer), 309
Gitlin, Todd, 472
Gjoni, Eron, 80
Glamour, 286
Glee, 176
global audiences, 404
global cinema, 213–214, 223
global economy, 391–392, 400
globalism, 414–415
global supply chains, 52–53
global warming, 467
Globe, 290
G.L.O.S.S., 113
Gmail, 40
Godey's Ladys Book, 275, 276
Godsick, Jeffrey, 355
Goffin, Gerry, 103
Go-Go's, 113
Golden Age of Hollywood, 13
golden mean, 434
Golden Rule, 434
Goldsmith, Thomas T., 66
Goldwater, Barry, 502
Golf Digest, 286
Golf Magazine, 294
Gomery, Douglas, 497
Gonzales, Emma, 4
Good Housekeeping, 242, 285
Goodman, Benny, 103
Good Morning America, 179, 403, 440
Goodnight Moon, 21
Goodreads, 320
Goodwin, Hannibal, 202
Goodyear, Dana, 174
Google, 48, 263, 325, 340, 342, 388, 389, 392, 406, 407, 409
  advertising, 341, 342
  Chromecast, 46
  control of Internet and, 47, 59
  convergence and, 11–12, 44
  Gmail, 40
  in China, 42
  Project Loon, 57
  search algorithms, 41
Google+, 46, 48
Google AdWords, 342
Google Analytics, 340–341
Google Apps, 48
Google Assistant, 47
Google Books, 312
Google Home, 47
Google News, 12, 252, 491
Google News Lab, 236, 252, 253, 254

Google Play, 44, 45, 48, 72, 88, 119, 221, 320
Gordy, Berry, 110
Gore, Leslie, 109
Gore, Tipper, 122
gospel music, 106
gotcha stories, 439
"Got Milk?" campaign, 329
government regulation
  of advertising, 334, 348–356
  antitrust, 393, 394, 408–412
  of broadcasting, 501–504
  of gaming, 82, 84
  of media, 8
  of media industries, 393–394
  of radio, 133–134
  of television, 182–187
government relations, 375–376
government surveillance, 51
GQ, 294
Grammy Awards, 95, 120–121
gramophones, 98
Gramsci, Antonio, 469
Grandmaster Flash, 114
Grand Theft Auto, 82
Grand Theft Auto V, 88
graphical user interface (GUI), 40
graphic novels, 299–300, 305
graphophones, 98
Grateful Dead, 112
"Great Balls of Fire" (Lewis), 107
Great Depression, 98, 220, 259, 333, 398, 448
The Great Train Robbery, 204
The Great Wall, 214
Greece, 302
Greek philosophy, 6
Greeley, Horace, 427
green marketing, 345
greenwashing, 381
Gremlins, 500
Griffith, D. W., 206, 208
Grokster, 101
grunge music, 113
Guardian, 4, 24, 43, 443
Guardians of the Galaxy, 78
Guatemala, 374
guilds, 73
Guitar Hero, 85
gun control, 3–4, 428
Gutenberg, Johannes, 6, 303
Gutenberg Bible, 303
Guthrie, Arlo, 111
Guthrie, Woody, 111
Guy, Buddy, 104

Habermas, Jürgen, 476
Habitat for Humanity, 373
Hachette, 316
Hadden, Briton, 280
Hale, Sarah Josepha, 275–276
Half-Life, 75

Hallmark Channel, 401
Halo, 69, 85
Hamill, Pete, 320
Hamilton, Alexander, 487
Hamilton, Andrew, 238
Hamilton, Filippa, 281
handheld games, 70
The Handmaid's Tale (Atwood), 308
The Handmaid's Tale (television program), 310
Hannity, Sean, 428
happiness, social media and, 36
Happy Days, 12
happy talk, 441
Hardcore Henry, 228
Hargis, Billy James, 502
HarperCollins, 316
Harper's, 288
Harper's Bazaar en Español, 290
Harper's New Monthly Magazine, 276
Harris, Benjamin, 238
Harris, Ken, 281
Harris-Perry, Melissa, 478
Harry, Debbie, 113
Harry Potter and the Deathly Hallows (Rowling), 305
Harry Potter and the Half-Blood Prince (Rowling), 305
Harry Potter series, 310, 312
Hart, Michael, 310–311
Harvey, David, 397
hashtag activism, 42
Hastings, Reed, 387
Hatfields and McCoys, 177
HathiTrust Digital Library, 312
Hauptmann, Bruno, 495–496
Hawthorne, Nathaniel, 275
Hays, Will, 499
Hays Office, 499
HBO (Home Box Office), 24, 168, 171, 188
HBO Go, 405
HBO Now, 405
HD radio, 151
HDTV, 165
head trauma, NFL and, 361–362
health, advertising and, 351–354
Heard, Amber, 493
Hearst, William Randolph, 241–242, 287, 290, 300
Hearst Corporation, 286, 294
Hearthstone, 64
Hefner, Hugh, 285
hegemony, 398–400
Heinz, 332
Hell's Angels, 112
Hemingway, Ernest, 305
Hendrix, Jimi, 107, 112
Henick, Mark, 456
Hentoff, Nat, 122, 314

Her, 46
herd journalism, 437
Herrold, Charles "Doc," 134
Hertz, Heinrich, 130
Hewitt, Don, 435
HGTV, 271
Hicks, Wilson, 279
hidden-fear appeals, 344
Hidden Folks, 89
The Hidden Persuaders
    (Packard), 349
high culture, 15, 19, 20, 105
high-definition television
    (HDTV), 165
Highlights for Children, 288, 292
high-speed communications
    network (NSFNET), 38, 39
The Hill, 4
Hill+Knowlton, 335, 381
Hillcrest Media, 320
hip-hop, 114–116
Hitchcock, Alfred, 210
Hogan's Alley, 241
Holly, Buddy, 105, 106, 109
Hollywood, 13
    directors, 210–211
    film studios, 224–226
    genres, 209–210
    global market for, 221
    narratives, 208, 209
    race barrier in, 211, 212
    scandals, 499
    style, 209–211
    television and, 220–221
Hollywood studio system,
    204–221
    distribution, 206
    exhibition, 206–208
    golden age of, 208–218
    outside of, 211
    production, 205–206
    transformation of, 218–221
Hollywood Ten, 218–219
Holmes, Oliver Wendell, 489
HoloLens, 47
Holt, Lester, 178
home dubbing, 99
home ownership, 219
HomePod, 47, 48
home video, 172, 223
Hong Kong, film industry in, 217
Hong Kong Disneyland Resort,
    403
Hoover, Herbert, 138
Hopper, Dennis, 210
Horgan, Stephen, 280
Horkheimer, Max, 471
horror films, 210
hot clock, 144
Hotmail, 40
Houghton Mifflin Harcourt, 350
House, Son, 104

House Un-American Activities
    Committee (HUAC),
    218–219, 501
Howl (Ginsberg), 318
Howlin' Wolf, 104
How to Get Away with Murder,
    467
HTML (hypertext markup
    language), 39
Hubbard, Gardiner Greene, 287
Huffington, Ariana, 266
Huffington Post, 266, 396
Hulk Hogan, 494
Hulu, 12, 45, 58, 70, 173, 193, 221,
    227, 327, 328
Hulu Plus, 173
human-interest stories, 239, 426
Hungary, radio in, 153
The Hunger Games (Collins),
    225, 227, 310
The Hunting Ground, 215
Huntley, Chet, 178
Huntley Brinkley Report, 178
Hurricane Maria, 467
The Hurt Locker, 211, 213
Hushmail, 42
Hüsker Dü, 113
Huxley, Aldous, 22
hybrid dramas, 178
Hyman, Mark, 17
Hynde, Chrissie, 113
Hype Machine, 122
hypertext, 39
hypodermic-needle model, 461
hypotheses, 463

I, Frankenstein, 19
IBM, 59
iBook Store, 319
"I Can't Stop Loving You"
    (Gibson), 108
Ice-T, 114
iCloud, 48
identity theft, 56
I.F. Stone's Weekly, 256
Iger, Robert, 200, 398, 404
Iggy Pop, 113
IGN, 75
iHeartMedia, 155–156
iHeartRadio, 121, 156
I Know Why the Caged Bird Sings
    (Angelou), 312
Illinois Central Railroad, 365
illuminated manuscripts, 302,
    303
Il Miracolo, 500
I Love Lucy, 175
The Image (Boorstin), 373
images
    tampering with, 281
    of war, 16–17
IMAX, 209, 224, 227

immigrants, 14
income inequality, 397–398
An Inconvenient Truth, 467
indecent speech, 502, 504
independent bookstores, 313,
    318–319
independent film festivals, 215,
    218
independent films, 215, 218, 228
independent film studios, 225
independent game developers,
    88–89
independent music labels,
    95–96, 116–117, 121–122
independent publishers, 316
independent record labels, 115
Independent Reflector, 274
independent variables, 463
India
    Bollywood, 214, 216
    radio in, 153
*Indiana Jones and the Temple of
    Doom*, 500
Indian Country Today, 253
indie rock, 113–114
indies, 215
individualism, 6, 7, 22, 429
industrialization, 7
Industrial Revolution, 6, 7, 22,
    23, 65, 330, 332, 363
information
    commodification of, 8
    overload, 425
    personal, 51, 511–517
Information Age, 7–8
informational model of
    journalism, 444
information economy, transition
    to, 391–400
infotainment programs, 183
in-game advertisements, 78–79
in-game chat, 73
innovation, attraction of, 21
Instagram, 40, 50, 408
intellectual properties, 87
intellectuals, 478–479
interest films, 214
international radio, 152–153
International Telephone &
    Telegraph (ITT), 394
Internet, 8–10, 37
    access, 40, 56–57
    advertising, 192, 340–343
    censorship, 56
    changing relationship with,
        45–46
    closed, 45–46, 47
    commercialization of, 39–41, 59
    communication policy and,
        505
    content, 56
    cultural change and, 12–13

democracy and, 59
development of, 37–41
digital gaming and, 70–72
economics of, 46, 47–53
fraud on, 56
innovation on, 58–59
journalism and, 440–444
magazines and, 283–284
media convergence and, 44–47
media industry and, 405–408
movies and, 221, 226–227
neutrality of, 58
news, 440–444
newspapers and, 261–262
ownership and control of,
    47–50
privacy, 51
PR messages on, 371
public relations and, 376
radio, 121, 151–153
Semantic Web, 46
sound recording and, 100–102
television and, 172–173
trolls, 43, 72–73, 417
usage, 29
video streaming on, 388
Internet Archive, 59, 312
Internet Explorer, 40
Internet service providers
    (ISPs), 40
interpretation, 25, 26–27
interpretive journalism, 244–245
Interpublic Group, 336
Interstate Commerce Act, 365
interstitials, 340
In These Times, 294, 479
The Invasion from Mars
    (Cantril), 461, 462
inverted-pyramid style, 243–244
investigative journalism, 53,
    235–236, 241, 423–424
Investigative Reporters and
    Editors (IRE), 424
Iowa Center for Public Affairs,
    265
iPad, 44, 45, 70, 311
iPhone, 44, 45, 48, 52–53, 495
iPod, 44, 46, 48
Iraq, 41–42
Iraq war, 13, 16, 17, 266, 486
irritation advertising, 344
ISIS, 16, 41–42
iTunes, 46, 48, 101, 116, 119, 121,
    221, 227
iUniverse, 320
Ivory Soap, 331

J-14, 401
Jackson, Janet, 504
Jackson, Michael, 335
Jagger, Mick, 105, 110
JAMA Pediatrics, 506

James, E. L., 320
James, LeBron, 344
Jan & Dean, 109
Japan, 57, 67, 69, 77, 164, 281, 388
  CDs in, 119
  film industry in, 217
  manga from, 299
Jarrett, Valerie, 370
Jaws, 222, 467
jazz music, 97, 103
The Jazz Singer, 208, 209
Jefferson, Thomas, 487
Jefferson Airplane, 112
Jeffries, Jim, 499
Jenner, Kendall, 373
Jennings, Peter, 179
Jet, 290
Jett, Joan, 113
Jewell, Richard, 434
job losses, 397–398
Jobs, Steve, 46, 48, 52
Joe Camel, 351, 352
John, Elton, 105, 113, 335
Johnson, Jack, 497, 499
Johnson, John H., 289
Johnson, Robert, 103, 104, 109
Johnson & Johnson, 377–378
joint operating agreements
    (JOAs), 258
Jolson, Al, 103, 208, 209
Jones, Grace, 105
Jones, LeRoi, 254
Joplin, Janis, 112
Joplin, Scott, 103
Jordan, 57
journalism, 22, 235–236
  advocacy, 246
  alternative, 256
  alternative models of, 444–447
  attacks on, 246
  balance in, 439
  citizen, 264
  community, 264
  conflict-oriented, 248
  consensus-oriented, 248
  convergence and, 442–443
  cultural values in, 428–429
  culture of, 423–453
  data, 246
  democracy and, 425, 448–451
  ethics and, 429, 431–435
  focusing on the present in,
      435–437
  herd, 437
  in information age, 425–429
  Internet and, 440–444
  interpretive, 244–245
  in TV and Internet age,
      246–247
  inverted-pyramid style,
      243–244
  investigative, 53, 241, 423–424

"just the facts" model, 242,
    243–244
  legacy of print, 435–439
  literary, 245–246
  loss of jobs in, 249, 255
  modern, 242–247
  neutrality of, 427
  new models of, 263–264
  objectivity in, 242–244, 246,
      428
  online, 246–247
  partisanship in, 427–428
  photojournalism, 277, 279,
      280–281
  precision, 246
  public, 444–446, 448
  public relations and, 378–381
  relying on experts in, 437–438
  satiric, 446–447
  scoops in, 436–437
  social responsibility and, 448
  story-driven model, 242
  television and, 440–444
  values in American, 427–429
  yellow, 240–242, 276–277
journalists, 16, 23
  acting as adversaries, 439
  black, 252
  code of ethics, 432
  conflicts of interest and,
      433–434
  credibility of, 427
  deaths of, 265–266, 487
  in Iraq War, 486
  invasion of privacy by, 433
  lost generation of, 450–451
  muckrakers, 23, 276–278, 365,
      366, 507
  use of experts by, 437–438
  women, 423–424
Joyce, James, 21, 493
Judeo-Christian ethics, 434
jukeboxes, 99, 102, 144
The Jungle (Sinclair), 277
Just Dance, 74
"just the facts" model, of
    journalism, 242, 243–244
J. Walter Thompson, 335

Kaiser Family Foundation, 12,
    465
Kaling, Mindy, 317, 327
Kalish, Rachel, 475
Kalman, Maira, 305
Kaltenborn, H. V., 139
Kansas, 113
Kant, Immanuel, 434
Kardashian, Kourtney, 355
Karloff, Boris, 19
Katz, Jackson, 474–475
Katz, Jon, 246
Kazaa, 101

Kazan, Elia, 219
KDKA, 134
Keaton, Buster, 207
Keller, Bill, 429
Kendrick, Anna, 309
Kennedy, Anthony, 416
Kennedy, John F., 281, 443
Kernan, Alvin, 321
Kerouac, Jack, 254
Kesha, 120
Keyes, Evelyn, 501
Kid Rock, 115
Kimmel, Michael, 475
Kindle, 46, 48, 311, 319
Kindle Fire, 48, 311
Kinect, 69, 79, 84
kinescope, 175
kinetographs, 203
kinetoscopes, 203
King, B. B., 104
King, Carole, 103
King, Martin Luther, 443, 492
Kings of Leon, 106
Kipling, Rudyard, 287
Kishi Bashi, 121
Klondike Lite, 355
Knight Ridder, 257, 258
Kobo, 320
Kodak, 280
Koppel, Ted, 17
Korea, 303
Korean War, 245
Kotaku, 75
Ku Klux Klan, 208, 251
Kurosawa, Akira, 213

labor unions, 397
Ladies' Companion, 304
Ladies' Home Journal (LHJ), 277,
    285
Ladies' Magazine, 276
Lady Gaga, 105
LaFrance, Adrienne, 438
Lamar, Kendrick, 115, 120, 121
Lambert, Adam, 105
lampblack, 97
La Opinión, 252
Lasch, Christopher, 444–445
Lassie, 20–21
Lasswell, Harold, 459
Last Week with John Oliver, 24,
    28, 447
Las Vegas shooting, 3
Latina, 290
Latin America, 388
Latin pop music, 118
Lauer, Matt, 174, 440
Lawrence, Jennifer, 354
Lead Belly, 111
The League, 78
League of Legends, 64, 70, 71, 79, 88
The Learning Tree, 212

leased channels, 184
LeBlanc, Adrian Nicole, 245
Lee, Ivy Ledbetter, 365–366, 379,
    393
Lee, Jennifer, 211
The Legend of Zelda, 85
Leiber, Jerry, 103
leisure time, 65
L'Engle, Madeline, 310
Lennox, Annie, 105
Lens, 281
Le Prince, Louis Aime Augustin,
    202
Lessig, Lawrence, 479, 484
Let Us Now Praise Famous Men
    (Agee), 448
Levi Strauss, 331
Lévy, Pierre, 74
Lewinsky, Monica, 13, 247
Lewis, Jerry Lee, 106–107, 109
libel, 238, 491–492
Liberator, 289
libertarianism, 486
Liberty and the News (Lippman),
    457
libraries, 59
Library of Congress, 59
Libya, 41
licensing, digital gaming, 86–87
Lieberman, Joseph, 84
Life, 279, 280–281, 282
Life in Motion (Copeland), 309
The Life of an American Fireman,
    204
Lifetime, 401
Limbaugh, Rush, 147
Limbo, 89
LimeWire, 101
limited competition, 390
limited model, 461–462
Limp Bizkit, 115
Lindbergh, Anne, 496
Lindbergh, Charles, 209, 496
linear model, of mass commu-
    nication, 8–9
linotype, 304
Linux, 58–59
Lionsgate, 225, 227
Lippmann, Walter, 244, 368, 379,
    437, 438, 457, 458
literacy
  media, 4, 25, 26–27, 54
  rates, 7, 22
literary journalism, 245
Lithuania, 43
Little, Brown & Company, 320
Little Caesar, 459
Little Review, 493
Little Richard, 105, 106–107, 108,
    109
Little Three, 207–208
live-tweeting, 13

The Living Desert, 401
Lizzo, 116
LL Cool J, 114
lobbying, 375–376, 393
  astroturf, 375–376
  defined, 375
  total spending on, 375
lobbyists, 365
local papers, 259
longitudinal studies, 464
long lines, 135
long-playing records (LPs),
  98–99
"Long Tall Sally" (Little
  Richard), 108
Lonny, 284
Look, 279, 282, 283
Lord & Taylor, 343
The Lord of the Rings (Tolkien),
  310
Los Angeles Times, 53, 267, 429
Los Del Rio, 118
Lost in Translation, 211
Lotz, Amanda, 392
low culture, 15, 19–20, 105
Lowenthal, Leo, 471
low-power FM (LPFM), 157
low-wage jobs, 398
LSD, 111–112
Lucas, George, 199–200, 210–211,
  226
Lucasfilm, 226
Luce, Henry, 280
Lucky Strike, 367
Lumière, Auguste, 203
Lumière, Louis, 203
Lumino City, 89
Luqiu, Luwei Rose, 470
Lyle, Jack, 462

"Macarena" (Los Del Rio), 118
Macklemore, 96, 122
Macmillan, 316
Macy's, 398
Madden NFL, 71, 86
Maddow, Rachel, 178, 428
Mad Men, 335
Madonna, 335
magalogs, 294
magazine program format, 166
magazines, 7, 271–297
  advertising, 292, 327, 330
  alternative, 294–295
  business or trade, 285
  chains, 294
  children's, 288
  circulation, 276, 277, 293–294
  color, 275
  consumer, 285
  convergence and, 283–284
  defined, 273
  demographic editions, 292–293

departments and duties,
  291–294
development of modern,
  276–284
digital, 284
distribution, 293–294
early history of, 273–276
economics of, 291–295
elite, 288
farm, 285
fashion, 289
first, 273–274
formats, 284
general-interest, 277–283
growth of, 277
illustrated, 276
in colonial America, 274
in democratic society, 295
in nineteenth century, 274–275
men's, 285
minority-targeted, 289–290
national, 275
newsmagazines, 278–279
online fantasy sports, 283–284
regional editions, 292
role of, 273
social reform and, 276–277
Spanish-language, 290
specialization of, 284–291
split-run editions, 292
sports, 286
supermarket tabloids, 290
teen, 288
top 10, 282, 293
travel, 287
women's, 275–276, 282, 285
Magic Lantern, 201
Magnavox, 66, 67, 68
Magnolia Pictures, 227
The Magnolia Story (Gaines), 307
Mailer, Norman, 245
Major League Baseball (MLB), 64
Major League Soccer (MLS), 64
Malaeska: The Indian Wife of the
  White Hunter (Stephens),
  304
malt liquors, 353
managing editor, 255, 291
Manchester by the Sea, 48
manga, 78, 299
The Man in the High Castle, 48
Mann, Estle Ray, 66
Man of Steel, 346
Manson, Charles, 112
Manson, Marilyn, 105
manuscript culture, 6, 302
map model of culture, 20–22
March for Our Lives, 428
Marconi, Guglielmo, 130–131,
  133, 136
Marcus Theatres, 224
Marie Claire, 286

Mario Bros., 68
Mario Kart 8 Deluxe, 78
Marjory Stoneman Douglas
  High School, 3–4, 13, 428,
  474
marketing
  digital games and, 87
  green, 345
  online, 341–342
  viral, 338
Marketing Fact Pack, 328
market research, 337, 460
Markey, Edward, 505
Marlboro, 345
Marlboro Man, 353
Marlon Bundo's Day in the Life of
  the Vice President (Pence),
  317
marriage, same-sex, 22
Marshall, Penny, 211
Martin, Trayvon, 42
marvel, 226
Marvel Entertainment, 404
The Marvelous Mrs. Maisel, 48
Marvel vs. Capcom, 78
Marx, Groucho, 138
Marx, Karl, 312, 469
Mary Tyler Moore Show, 441
masculinity, 105, 474–475
M.A.S.H., 12
Mashable, 12
mass communication
  cultural model of, 9
  defined, 6
  evolution of, 5–9
  linear model of, 8–9
mass consumption, 65
massively multiplayer online
  role-playing games
  (MMORPGs), 71
mass media, 6
  business of, 324–325
  democratic expression and,
  420–421
mass medium stage, 10
mass production, 7, 332, 393
mass shootings, 3–4, 13, 82, 428,
  474–475
Master Settlement Agreement,
  356
Mateen, Omar, 475
Maxim, 285
Maxwell, James, 130
Mayfield, Curtis, 113
MC5, 113
MCA, 172
McCain-Feingold Act, 416
McCarthy, Joseph, 501
McChesney, Robert, 413, 415
McClatchy Company, 257
McClure's Magazine, 277, 366
McDonald's, 355, 398

McGuffey, William Holmes, 306
McLean, Don, 109
McQueen, Steve, 212
Meaning, 9
Meat Inspection Act, 277
mechanical gaming, 65–66
media
  changing relationship
    with, 45
  consolidation, 11, 389, 396,
    402–403, 408–409, 412,
    415–416
  convergence. *see* convergence
  critiquing, 25, 28
  cultural context of, 5–6
  daily consumption by
    platform, 15
  emergence of, 10, 32
  evolution of, 10–13
  gatekeepers, 8–9
  in courtrooms, 495–497
  mobile devices and, 44
  multitasking, 12–13
  responsibilities of, 5
  as watchdogs, 4
  See also specific types
media buyers, 338
media coordination, 338
media culture, 78
media deserts, 259
media economy
  analyzing, 389–391
  democracy and, 415–417
  flexible markets, 397
  hegemony and, 398–400
  social issues in, 408–415
  See also economics, media
media effects research, 457,
  460–469
  agenda-setting and, 467
  conducting, 462–466
  contemporary theories,
    466–469
  cultivation effect and, 468
  early theories, 461–462
  evaluation of, 469
  social learning theory and,
    466–467
  spiral of silence and, 468
  third-person effect and,
    468–469
media industry
  alternative voices in, 413
  business tendencies in,
    397–398
  China, 411
  consolidation in, 11, 394–397,
    415–416
  convergence and, 405–408
  democracy and, 415–417
  deregulation, 393–394, 395
  diversification in, 409, 412

media industry (*continued*)
global, 404
information economy and, 391–400
Internet and, 405–408
mergers and acquisitions, 137, 194, 226, 335, 394, 396, 408, 412, 415–416
ownership in, 394–397
regulation of, 393–394
shifts in, 389
specialization, 400–401
structure of, 390–391
See also specific segments
media kits, 376
media literacy, 4, 25–27, 54
media markets, global, 404
Media Matters, 415
media messages, selective exposure to, 9
The Media Monopoly (Bagdikian), 408
media organizations, 390–391
media reform movement, 416–417
media relations, 371
media research. *See* research, media
medicines, patent, 331–332
Meet the Press, 178
mega-agencies, 335–336, 341
megaplex, 224
Méliès, Georges, 204
Memphis, 105
Men's Health, 285, 294
men's magazines, 285
Meredith Corporation, 294
mergers and acquisitions, 137, 194, 226, 335, 394, 396, 408, 409, 412, 415–416
Merritt, Davis, 444
"The Message" (Grandmaster Flash), 114
#MeToo movement, 42, 120, 174, 288, 361, 362, 440
metropolitan dailies, 248
Meyer, Stephenie, 310
MGM, 207
Miami Herald Publishing Co. v. Tornillo, 502
Miami Herald, 253
microprocessors, 38
Microsoft, 40, 44, 47, 53, 58, 59, 67–70, 85, 325, 341, 388, 389, 392, 406, 407
mid-city movie theaters, 207
Middle Ages, 302
middle class, 7, 239, 243
Middle East, 41, 152
middle-of-the-road (MOR) format, 148

Midwest Living, 294
Midwest Video case, 184
Milano, Alyssa, 42
Mill, John Stuart, 434
Miller, Glenn, 103
Miller, Jade, 471
Miller Lite, 338, 340
Miller v. California, 493
Milton, John, 486
Milton Bradley, 137
Milwaukee Journal Sentinel, 262
Milwaukee Sentinel, 489
The Mindy Project, 327
minimal-effects model, 461–462
minimum wage, 391
miniseries, 177
Minneapolis Star Tribune, 257
MinnPost, 266
minorities
advertising aimed at, 353
in film industry, 211, 212
in newspaper industry, 252
minority-targeted magazines, 289–290
Minutemen, 113
Miracle case, 500
Miracles, 110
misogyny, in digital gaming, 79–82, 83
Mister Rogers' Neighborhood, 180
Miyamoto, Shigeru, 68
mobile advertising, 50, 250
mobile apps, 33, 45
mobile devices, 32, 408
games for, 86
media convergence and, 44
phones, 8, 12, 44, 45, 50, 57, 70, 173, 328
mobile media
convergence and, 44–47
impact of, 45–46
mobile video, 173
modding, 75
Modern Family, 346
modern model of journalism, 444
modern period, 23
cultural values of, 22–23
defined, 22
Modern Times, 22, 24
monopolies, 133–135, 137, 182–183, 390, 394, 396, 429
monopolistic competition, 390
Moonlight, 212
Moonves, Leslie, 398
Morning Edition, 149
morning news shows, 440
Morpheus, 101
Morrison, Jim, 112
Morrison, Toni, 309
Morse code, 129

Mortal Kombat, 84
Mosaic, 40
Mother Jones, 245, 295
Motion Picture Patents Company, 204–205
Motion Picture Producers and Distributors of America (MPPDA), 499
Motion Picture Production Code, 220, 459, 499–500
motion pictures, 97.
See also movies
Motor City, 110
Motown, 110
moveable type, 303
Movie Gallery-Hollywood Video, 221
movie industry
alternative voices in, 227–228
Big Five, 207–208
consolidation in, 225–226
convergence and, 226–227
economics of, 221–228
in India, 214, 216
in Nigeria, 470–471
Little Three, 207–208
self-regulation in, 499–500
vertical integration in, 207, 225–226
See also Hollywood
movie palaces, 207
movies, 8, 13, 14, 199–231
Asian cinema, 216–217
blockbusters, 222, 223, 226
books and, 309–310
censorship, 497–499
costs of, 222
cultural imperialism and, 406
culture and, 201
democracy and, 228–229
digital gaming and, 78
directors, 210–211
distribution, 206
documentary, 214–215
drop in attendance, 219–220
evolution of, 201–203
exhibition of, 206–208
export of American, 229
First Amendment and, 497–501
genres, 209–210
global cinema, 213–214
global market for, 221
Hollywood, 204–221
home entertainment, 221
independent, 215, 218
Internet and, 221, 226–227
Motion Picture Production Code, 499–500
MPAA ratings system, 500–501
narrative, 204
nickelodeons, 204
production of, 205–206

silent era, 208
social and political pressures on, 497, 499
talkies, 208–209
technology, 201–203, 221
television and, 219–221
movie theaters, 204, 206–208, 212, 219–220, 222, 224
MP3s, 100–101
MPAA ratings system, 500–501
Ms., 285
MSNBC, 179, 428, 429, 442
MTV, 23, 335, 404
Muck Rack, 443
muckrakers, 23, 276–277, 278, 365, 366, 507
Muddy Waters, 104, 109
multichannel video programming distributors (MVPDs), 193
multinational corporations, 28
multiplayer online battle arenas (MOBAs), 71, 73
multiplexes, 207, 213, 222
multi-system operators (MSOs), 193
multitasking, 12–13, 45
municipally owned cable systems, 194
The Munsters, 19
Murdoch, Rupert, 134, 258, 281
Murrow, Edward R., 138
music, 95–125
album-oriented rock (AOR), 145
alternative, 413
blues, 104
British invasion, 109–110
censorship and, 108–109
classical, 103
country, 105
cover, 103, 107–108
disco, 114
electronic dance, 116
folk, 110–111
formats, 148
funk, 110
generational differences in, 112
genres, 93
gospel, 106
grunge, 113
hip-hop, 114–116
impact of, 97
in advertising, 335
indie rock, 113–114
jazz, 103
Latin pop, 118
pop, 102–116, 122
progressive rock, 144–145
psychedelic, 111–112
punk rock, 113
rap, 114–116
recorded, 98–99

rhythm and blues, 104
rock, 102, 103–109, 122
rockabilly, 105, 106
sheet, 103
soul, 110
streaming, 101–102, 151
musicals, 210
music industry, 46, 116–119
advisory labels and, 122
A&R agents and, 117
file-sharing and, 100–101, 116
free expression and, 122
independent labels, 95–96, 115,
116, 117, 121–122
Internet and, 100–102
labels, 116–117
profits in, 119, 121
racism in, 105, 107–108, 121
radio and, 102
streaming services and, 119, 121
women in, 120–121
music streaming services, 101,
102, 116, 119, 388, 409, 411
must-carry rules, 183–184
Mutual v. Ohio, 499
Muybridge, Eadweard, 202
Myers, Maddy, 80
Myanmar (Burma), 57
Myspace, 122
Myst, 70
myth analysis, 345–346
My Voice Ohio, 248

Napoleon, 208
Napster, 46, 100–101, 388
narrative films, 204, 208
narratives, 13–15
consensus, 228–229
hegemony and, 399–400
Hollywood, 208, 209
movies and, 204
narrowcasting, 132, 169
Naruto, 78
Nashville, 105
Nation, 294
National Association for the
Advancement of Colored
People (NAACP), 289
National Association of Black
Journalists (NABJ),
251–252
National Association of
Broadcasters (NAB),
146–147, 184, 334, 369
National Basketball Association
(NBA), 64
National Book Award, 300
National Broadcasting Company
(NBC), 136–137
National Cable & Telecommuni-
cations Association
(NCTA), 193

National Center for Super-
computing Applications
(NCSA), 40
National Conference for Media
Reform, 417
National Consumer League, 354
National Dairy Council, 350
National Employment Law
Project, 398
National Enquirer, 290
National Federation for
Decency, 156
National Football League (NFL),
64, 361–362
National Geographic, 287, 294
National Geographic Traveler, 287
National Hockey League
(NHL), 64
National Institutes of Health
(NIH), 362
nationalism, 7
national newspapers, 247
National Public Radio (NPR), 149
National Review, 294, 295
National Rifle Association
(NRA), 4
National Safety Council, 82, 334
National Science Foundation,
38, 39
National Security Agency
(NSA), 51
National Television Systems
Committee (NTSC), 164
nation-states, 7
Native American newspapers,
253–254
Native Americans, 211
Native American Times, 253
natural disasters, 436, 467
NBC (National Broadcasting
Company), 8, 12, 168, 192,
327, 328
NBC Nightly News, 28, 178
NBC Universal, 172, 193, 226,
394
NC-17 rating, 500–501
NCIS, 6
Near v. Minnesota, 487
Negro Digest, 289
Nelson, Ricky, 109
NES Classic Edition, 67
Netflix, 20, 45, 49, 70, 172, 193,
223, 327, 328, 387–388, 389,
404, 405, 406, 407
convergence and, 12
foreign-language shows and,
162
net neutrality and, 58
original shows by, 161–162, 188
streaming and, 173, 191, 227
net neutrality, 58, 417, 505, 507
Netscape, 40

network era, of television, 168
network news, 8, 178–179
networks
broadcast, 182–183, 189,
192–193, 327
radio, 135
network television, 163
neutrality, 427, 439
Newcomb, Horace, 472
New England Courant, 238
new journalism, 245
New Orleans, 103
New Orleans Daily Creole, 251
NewPages, 320
New Pittsburgh Courier, 252
news
bias in, 429, 430
broadcast, 244–245
cable, 179, 427–428, 442
characteristics of, 426–427
defined, 425–426
disaster coverage, 435, 436
"fake," 9, 12, 179, 446–447
morning news shows, 440
network, 8, 178–179
online, 427–428, 440–444
print, 440
promoting publicity and
business as, 379
sound bites, 441
television, 440–444
war coverage, 16–17, 260, 280,
281
news anchors, 441
news apps, 233
News Corp., 134, 225–226, 258,
281, 433
News for Chinese, 253
newshole, 254–255
newsies, 240
newsmagazines, 278–279
news media
coverage of business of, 249
ethics and, 429, 431–435
News of the World, 433
Newspaper Preservation Act,
258
newspapers, 8, 22, 235–269
advertising, 237, 239–240, 254,
261–262, 327, 330, 332–333
African American, 251–252
alternative voices in, 264–265
Asian American, 253
business and ownership of,
247–258
campus, 259
chains, 257
challenges facing, 259–265
circulation, 237, 248, 261
colonial, 238–239, 330
consolidation in, 257–258
convergence and, 261–262

decline in jobs in, 16
declining readership, 236, 259
democracy and, 265–267
digital, 237, 246–247, 261–262
economics of, 239–240
editorial responsibilities, 255
evolution of, 237–242
feature syndicates, 257
foreign-language, 251
joint operating agreements,
258
local, 259
metropolitan dailies, 248
modern journalism and,
242–247
national, 247
Native American, 253–254
news and information from, 4
nondaily, 248
online, 11, 12, 261–262,
427–428
op-ed pages, 245
operations, 254–257
opinion pages, 237
paywalls, 262
penny press era, 239–240, 242
readership across the globe,
260
responsibilities of, 5
role of, 237, 248
Spanish-language, 252–253
targeting of readers by,
251–254
underground press, 254
weekly, 248
wire services, 240, 255, 257
yellow journalism and,
240–242
See also journalism
newspeak, 372
news programs, satiric, 23,
446–447
newsreels, 209, 214
The Newsroom, 444
news/talk/information radio,
146–147
New Super Mario Bros., 68
Newsweek, 278, 408
newsworthiness, 426–427
New York Daily Graphic, 280
New York Dolls, 113
New Yorker, 56, 225, 288
New York Herald, 251
New York Herald Tribune, 378
New York Journal, 241–242
New York Morning Herald, 239
New York Public Library, 312
New York Sun, 239
New York Times, 4, 9, 10, 16, 17,
26–27, 53, 83, 225, 243, 246,
247, 255, 257, 262, 300, 376,
394, 411, 429, 433, 443

New York Times v. Sullivan, 491–492
New York Tribune, 427
New-York Weekly Journal, 238, 239
New York World, 241, 287, 423
New Zealand, 320
Nexus7, 320
niche audiences, 428
niche markets, 191
Nichols, John, 415
Nickelodeon, 401
nickelodeons, 204
Nielsen Corporation, 191, 192
Nigeria, 470–471
Night (Wiesel), 309
Nightline, 17
Night Trap, 84
Nine Inch Nails, 122
1984 (Orwell), 308, 372
ninjas, 72–73
Nintendo, 67, 68–69, 76, 85
Nintendo 3DS, 70
Nintendo Entertainment System (NES), 67, 68
Nintendo Switch, 68–69, 70, 72
Nipkow, Paul, 164
Nirvana, 113
Nixon, Cynthia, 399
Nixon, Richard M., 219, 381, 426, 484
Noah, Trevor, 309, 447
nonprofit news organizations, 264–265
nonprofit radio, 148–149, 150
noobs, 72, 73
Nook, 320
North American Free Trade Agreement (NAFTA), 400
North American Review, 274
North Star, 251
Norway, radio in, 152–153
nostalgia, 21–22, 24
Note to Self, 54–55
Notorious B.I.G., 115
Novak, B. J., 317
novels
  classic, 308
  dime, 304
  graphic, 299–300, 305
N. W. Ayer & Son, 330

O & Os, 189
Oakley, Annie, 364
Obama, Barack, 16, 295, 357, 376, 429
obesity rates, 351
objectivity
  in journalism, 242–244, 246, 428
  in research, 463
obscenity, 492–493, 504

Occupy Wall Street, 42, 247
Oceania, 260
Ochs, Adolph, 243
Ochs, Phil, 111
Oculus VR, 50
Odyssey, 66, 67, 68
Office for iPad, 47
Office Mobile, 47
off-network syndication, 188, 190
offset lithography, 304
offshore profits, 53
Ogilvy & Mather Worldwide, 335, 338
OGN, 64
OK!, 290
Oldsmobile, 349
oligopoly, 116, 205, 219, 390, 393, 409
Oliver, John, 24, 28, 317, 447
Olsen, Charlie, 300
Olympics, 64
Omaha World-Herald, 257
Omnicom Group, 335
On-demand programs, 12
OneDrive, 47
100 Balls, 88
One Orlando Alliance, 376
online advertising, 192
  targeting, 341–342
  trends in, 340–343
online booksellers, 319–320
online fantasy sports, 71–72, 78
online fraud, 56
online journalism, 246–247
online magazines, 283–284
online marketing, 341–342
online newspapers, 11, 12, 261–262, 427–428
online privacy, 51
Ontario Medical Association, 349
op-ed pages, 245
Open Library, 312
open-source software, 58–59
opinion and fair comment, 492
Oprah's Book Club, 309–310
opt-in policies, 51
option time, 138
opt-out policies, 51
Oracle, 59
oral communication, 6, 11
oral storytelling, 301
Orange Is the New Black, 176, 346
Orwell, George, 308, 372
Oswald, Lee Harvey, 281
O: The Oprah Magazine, 285, 294
Outcault, R. F., 241
Outside, 286
outsourcing, 400
Overwatch, 64, 71, 85
OWN, 391

Pacifica Foundation, 149
packaging, 331
Packard, Vance, 349
packet switching, 37
Pac-Man, 67
Pai, Ajit, 58, 505
paid search advertising, 340–341
Paine, Thomas, 274
Paley, William, 138, 166, 412
Palmer, Amanda, 122
Palmer, Volney, 330
Pamela; or, Virtue Rewarded (Richardson), 304
pamphlets, 7
Panavision, 221
Pandora, 101–102, 122, 412
Panera, 398
paper, 6
paperback books, 304
papyrus, 302
paradox, 24
Paramount decision, 219
Paramount Pictures, 205, 206, 207, 224
parchment, 302
Parents Music Resource Center, 122
Parker, Edwin, 462
Parkland, Florida, shooting, 3–4, 13, 428, 474
Parks, Gordon, 212, 279
partisan model of journalism, 444
partisan press, 238–239
partisanship, 427–428
pass-along readership, 279
past, nostalgia for, 21–22, 24
patent medicines, 331–332
Patton, Charley, 104
The Pawnbroker, 500
Payne Fund Studies, 459
payola scandals, 107, 108, 155
pay-per-view (PPV), 171
paywalls, 262
PBS (Public Broadcasting Service), 149, 180–182
Pearson, 315
peer-to-peer (P2P) systems, 101
Pence, Charlotte, 317
Penguin Random House, 315, 316
Penn, William, 331
Pennsylvania Gazette, 238
Pennsylvania Magazine, 274
Penny Arcade, 75
Penny Arcade Expo (PAX), 75
penny arcades, 65–66
penny press, 239–240, 242
Pentagon Papers, 487–488
Pentagon Pundit program, 376
People, 283, 290, 292, 294
People en Español, 290
Pepsi, 373

Perkins, Carl, 105, 106
Perry, Katy, 25
personal computers (PCs), 8, 38
  gaming on, 70
  media convergence and, 44
personal information, privacy of, 51
persuasive techniques
  association principle, 345
  bandwagon effect, 344
  disassociation, 345
  famous-person testimonials, 344
  hidden-fear appeals, 344
  in advertising, 343–348
  irritation advertising, 344
  myth analysis, 345–346
  plain-folks pitch, 344
  product placements, 346, 348
  snob-appeal approach, 344
Peter, Paul, and Mary, 111
Peterson Milla Hooks (PMH), 336
Pew Research Center, 251, 264–265, 416
Pfizer, 354
PG-13 rating, 500
pharmaceutical companies, 354
Philadelphia Inquirer, 257
Philadelphia Zeitung, 251
Philip Morris, 345, 353
Philips, 100
Phillips, Sam, 106
phishing, 56
phonographs, 97, 98, 102, 103
photography, 202, 280
  Civil War, 275
  digital, 281
photojournalism, 277, 279, 280–281
Photoshop, 281
The Piano, 211
Pickett, Wilson, 110
Pickford, Mary, 205–206, 499
Pilkey, Dav, 312
Pillsbury, 332
pinball, 65
pinball machines, 66
Pink, 120, 121
Pink Floyd, 145
Pinocchio, 401
Pittsburgh Courier, 251, 252
Pittsburgh Dispatch, 423
Pixar, 226, 403, 404
Pixel Buds, 101
Pixies, 113
plain-folks pitch, 344
Plants vs. Zombies, 86
platform games, 73
Plato, 6, 14
Playboy, 285

Play Smart, Play Safe initiative, 362
PlayStation, 69
PlayStation Network, 69
PlayStation Plus, 69
PlayStation Portable (PSP), 70
PlayStation Vita, 70
podcasts, 127, 151, 153–154
Pokémon Go, 76–77, 79
Poland, 28, 444
political advertising, 357
political assassinations, 163, 245, 281, 443
political broadcasts, 504
political cartoons, 255
political economy studies, 473–475
political speech, 416
Politico, 263
politics
  classic novels and, 308
  money and, 483–484
  populism in, 23
  pundits and, 442
polls, 459
Polo, Marco, 303
Polo, Susana, 300
Pompeii, 330
Pong, 64, 67
Poor Richard's Almanack, 274
pop charts, 104, 107
Popov, Alexander, 131
popular culture, 19–20
  around the globe, 170
  cultural imperialism and, 413–415
  research on, 472–473
popular media culture, 14–15
popular music, 102–116, 122
  British invasion, 109–110
  impact of, 97
  payola scandals, 108
  progressive rock, 144–145
  reemergence of, 116
  reformations in, 109–116
  rise of, 103
  rock and roll, 103–109
populism, 23
pornography, 56, 506
portable listening, 153–154
portable players, 70
Porter, Cole, 103
Porter, Edwin S., 204
Portlandia, 191
Portnow, Neil, 120, 121
Postal Act of 1879, 276
Postman, Neil, 425
postmodern period, 23–24
Powers, Ann, 120
precision journalism, 246
premium channels, 171, 223

premodern period, 6, 22, 23
prescription drugs, advertising, 354
presidential campaigns, 8, 343.
  See also elections
Presley, Elvis, 14–15, 105, 106, 109, 122
press
  commercial, 238
  freedom of. *see* free press
  partisan, 238–239
  public relations and, 378–381
  underground, 254
  See also journalism; news
press agents, 364–365
press releases, 370–371
Prevention, 294
Primary, 215
Primer, 284
prime time, 166, 182–183, 328, 329, 340
Prime Time Access Rule (PTAR), 182–183
Prince, 105
Principles of Uncertainty (Kalman), 305
print communication, 11
printing press, 6–7, 22, 303
print media, 6–7, 22, 232–233
  See also specific types
print revolution, 6–7
prior restraint, 487–489
privacy
  data breaches, 343
  Facebook and, 511–517
  invasion of, 433
  online, 51
  of personal information, 51, 511–517
  right to, 493–495
Privacy Act of 1974, 494
private research, 462
private sector monopoly, 133–134
Procter & Gamble, 332
product differentiation, 209, 331
production, television, 188–189
production departments, of magazines, 292
product placements, 223–224, 329, 346, 348
product standardization, 209
professional books, 306
profit maximization, 390–391
Progressive, 294
Progressive Era, 22–23
Progressive Grocer, 285
Progressive magazine case, 488–489
progressive rock, 144–145
Project for Excellence in Journalism, 416

Project Gutenberg, 310–311
Project Loon, 57
propaganda, 369, 420
propaganda analysis, 459
proprietary research, 462
ProPublica, 266
Protestant Reformation, 7
protest musicians, 254
PRWatch, 381, 382
pseudo-events, 371, 373
pseudo-polls, 459
psychedelic rock, 111–112
Psycho, 210
psychographic research, 369–370
Public Broadcasting Act of 1967, 149, 180
Public Broadcasting Service (PBS), 149, 180–182
public domain, 490–491
Public Enemy, 114
public good, 391
public intellectuals, 478–479
Publicis Groupe, 336
publicity, 364, 371, 379
publicity stunts, 373
public journalism, 444–446, 448
Publick Occurrences, Both Foreign and Domestick, 238
Public Opinion (Lippmann), 368, 457
public opinion research, 458–459
public radio stations, 133
public relations, 361–385
  vs. advertising, 363
  "alternative facts" and, 372
  alternative voices in, 380–381
  approaches to, 368–369
  bananas and, 374
  big business and, 364–365
  birth of modern, 365–368
  community relations, 373
  consumer relations, 373
  during a crisis, 377–378
  criticism of, 381
  defined, 363, 368
  democracy and, 381–383
  firms, 368–369
  government relations, 375–376
  history of, 363–368
  image of, 380
  impact of, 363
  Internet and, 376
  invisible hand of, 382
  lobbying, 375–376, 393
  media relations and, 371
  messages, 370–371
  NFL and, 361–362
  performance of, 369–376
  practice of, 368–378

press and, 378–381
  pseudo-events, 371, 373
  research in, 369–370
  special events, 371
  Twitter and, 370
  women in, 368
Public Relations Society of America (PRSA), 368, 372, 380
Public Relations Student Society of America (PRSSA), 368
public research, 462
public service announcements (PSAs), 334, 371
public sphere, 476
public television, 180–182
publishing houses, 304–305, 315–316, 320
publishing industry
  beginning of U.S., 303–304
  modern, 304–309
  See also book industry
puffery, 355
PUGs (pick-up groups), 72
Pulitzer, Joseph, 241, 263, 300, 423
Pulitzer Prize, 439
pulp fiction, 304
pundits, 442
punk rock, 113
Pure Food and Drug Act, 277

quadraphonic sound, 100
Quake, 64, 70
Quaker Oats, 331
qualified privilege, 492
Queen, 23, 145
Queen Latifah, 115
Quinn, Zoe, 80, 81
quiz shows, 140, 166, 183
quiz-show scandals, 108, 166–167

race charts, 104, 105, 107
Rachael Ray Every Day, 294
Rachel Maddow Show, 178, 179
racial integration, 104–105
racism, 105, 108, 121, 209, 251
radio, 8, 10, 11, 44, 59, 97, 127–159, 220
  advertising, 138, 142, 154
  alternative, 156–157
  AM, 143
  authority of, 141
  broadcasting, 135
  commercial, 145–151
  convergence and, 151–154
  as cultural mirror, 140–141
  democracy and, 157
  development of, 129–134
  early programming, 139–140
  economics of, 154–157

radio (*continued*)
  evolution of, 134–141
  experimental stations, 144–145
  FM, 142–143
  format, 143–144, 145–148
  golden age of, 139–141
  HD, 151
  international, 152–153
  Internet, 121, 151–153
  interpretive journalism and,
    244–245
  low-power FM, 157
  music formats, 148
  networks, 135
  news/talk/information format,
    146–147
  nonprofit, 148–149, 150
  ownership of, 155–156, 157
  payola scandals, 155
  podcasts, 151, 153–154
  recording industry and, 102
  regulation of, 133–134
  reinvention of, 142–145
  satellite, 150–151
  signal jamming, 152
  specialization, 145–148
  talk, 145, 146–147
  talk shows, 8
  technology, 129–132, 142–143,
    149–150
  television and, 142
  Top 40, 143–144
Radio Act of 1912, 133, 139
Radio Act of 1927, 138–139
Radio Corporation of America
    (RCA), 11, 98–99, 133–137,
    139, 142, 164
Radio Game, 137
radio group, 135
Radiohead, 95, 122
radio stations, 134–135
radio talk shows, 244
radio waves, 130, 143
Radway, Janice, 473
ragtime, 103
railroads, 22, 364–365
Rainey, Ma, 104
Raising Hell (Run-DMC), 114
Ralph Lauren, 377
Ramones, 113
Rampage, 78
Ramsey, Mason, 349
random assignment, 463
Random House, 315, 493
Ranger Rick, 288
rap, 114–116
Rappe, Virginia, 499
"Rapper's Delight" (Sugarhill
    Gang), 114
Rather, Dan, 179
ratings, 191
rational thought, 24

Ray, Johnnie, 104
Ray, Satyajit, 213
RCA. *See* Radio Corporation of
    America (RCA)
RCA-NBC, 394
reader-response research, 473
Reader's Digest, 278, 280, 282, 288
reading trends, 233
Reagan, Ronald, 146, 219, 393
"The Real Cost" campaign, 370
Real Housewives, 13
reality shows, 13, 173
reality TV, 180
Real Simple, 294
Rebel without a Cause, 220
Recording Industry Association
    of America (RIAA), 119
record players, 98
records, 98, 100
Redbox, 221, 223
Red Bull, 373
Red Channels, 501
Red Dead Redemption (RDR), 83
Redding, Otis, 107, 110
*Red Lion Broadcasting Co. v.
    FCC*, 502
Redstone, Sumner, 193
Reed, Lou, 113
Reformer, 289
Regal Entertainment Group,
    224
reggae, 413
regional editions, of magazines,
    292
Reid, Wallace, 499
Reidenberg, Dan, 456
Reiner, Carl, 175
relationships, 36
reliability, in research, 463
religion, 24, 106–107
religious books, 307
R.E.M., 113
REO Speedwagon, 113
reporters, 255.
    See also journalists
Reporters without Borders, 42
Report for America (RFA), 236, 263
The Republic (Plato), 14
Republican Party, 307, 381
research, media, 455–481
  content analysis, 464–466
  cultural approaches to,
    469–477
  democracy and, 478–479
  early methods of, 457–460
  experiments, 463–464
  international, 470–471
  marketing research, 460
  on media effects, 460–469
  propaganda analysis, 459
  public opinion research,
    458–459

social psychology studies,
    459–460
  survey research, 464
Resident Evil, 78
responsible capitalism, 429
retransmission fees, 189
Review, 273
review boards, 497, 499
Revlon, 344
Reynolds, Frank, 179
rhythm and blues (R&B) music,
    104
rhythm games, 73
Richardson, Samuel, 304
Right Media, 341
right to privacy, 493–495
Rihanna, 95
Ring, 290
Riot Games, 64
Ripper Street, 45
R. J. Reynolds, 351
RKO, 207
Roanoke Times, 257
Robert Morris University, 64
Robinson, Max, 179
Robinson, Smokey, 110
rockabilly, 105, 106
rock-and-roll music, 14–15, 102,
    103–109, 122
Rock Band, 74
Rockefeller, John D., 277, 366,
    379, 393
Rocket League, 64
Rodale, 294
role playing games, 73
Rolling Stone, 245, 246
Rolling Stones, 104, 105, 107, 109,
    110, 111
"Roll Over Beethoven" (Berry),
    23, 105
Romans, 302
Ronaldo, Cristiano, 344
Rookie, 284
Roosevelt, Franklin D., 140
Roosevelt, Theodore, 277, 373
Roots, 177
Rose, Charlie, 174
Rosen, Jay, 446
Ross, Diana, 110, 111
Ross, Harold, 288
Rossellini, Roberto, 500
rotation, 144
Roundhay Garden Scene, 202
Rovio, 86
Rowling, J. K., 310, 312, 316–317
Royko, Mike, 435
rugged individualism, 6
Run-DMC, 114
Runner's World, 294
Rushdie, Salman, 312
Russia, election interference by,
    43, 512

Safari, 40
Salem Media Group, 156
Salon, 283, 284
Salt-N-Pepa, 115
same-sex marriage, 22, 458
Samsung, 44
Samsung refrigerator, 46–47
Sanders, Bernie, 505
Sandy Hook school shooting, 3
San Francisco Examiner, 241,
    284
San Jose Mercury News, 257
Santa Barbara, 28
Sapkowski, Andrzej, 78
Sarasota Herald-Tribune, 424
Sarkeesian, Anita, 80–81
Sarnoff, David, 136–137, 142,
    164, 166
The Satanic Verses (Rushdie), 312
satellite radio, 150–151
satellite technology, 168
satellite television, 171, 186,
    193–194, 404, 412
satiric news programs, 23,
    446–447
"Satisfaction" (Rolling Stones),
    107
saturation advertising, 338, 340
Saturday Evening Post, 275,
    277–278, 282
Saturday Night Live (SNL), 28,
    176, 446, 447
Saudi Arabia, 57
Savan, Leslie, 345
Scalia, Antonin, 89
scanning disk, 164
Schenck v. United States, 489
schools, advertising in, 350
school shootings, 3–4, 13, 82,
    428, 474–475
Schorr, Daniel, 438
Schramm, Wilbur, 462
Schudson, Michael, 263, 346,
    379, 487
Schumer, Amy, 309
Schweitzer, Albert, 281
Scientific American, 46, 489
scientific method, 462–463
Scorsese, Martin, 210
Scrappy Little Nobody (Kendrick),
    309
scribes, 302
Scribner's, 305
Scripps, Edward Wyllis, 257
Sea Island, 401
Sean Hannity Show, 179
search engines, 41, 46
Seau, Junior, 361
Section 315, 504
Sedition Act, 487, 489
seditious expression, 489
seditious libel, 238

Seeger, Pete, 111, 254
Sega, 86
Sega Dreamcast, 67, 68
Sega Genesis, 67
segregation, 104
Seierstad, Asne, 245
Seinfeld, 184
Seinfeld, Jerry, 161–162, 184
Selecta, 291
selective exposure, 9, 461
selective retention, 461
self-publishing, 9, 320
Selma, 213
Semantic Web, 46–47
sender-message-receiver
    communication model, 25
sensationalism, 240–242
serial programs, 177–178
A Series of Unfortunate Events
    (Lemony Snicket), 310
Sesame Street, 180, 182
set-top devices, 44
Seven Beauties, 211
7-7-7 Rule, 393–394, 395
Seventeen, 288
Sex and the City, 176
Sex Pistols, 113
sexting, 506
sexual content, 56
Shakespeare, William, 21
Shakur, Tupac, 115
Shanghai Disney Resort, 403
Shangri-Las, 109
share, television, 191
Shark Tank, 13
"Sh-Boom" (Chords), 108
sheet music, 103
Shelley, Mary Wollstonecraft, 19
Sheppard, Sam, 495
Sherlock, 6
Sherman Antitrust Act, 393
shield laws, 495
shooter games, 73
Showgirls, 500–501
signal jamming, 152
silent movies, 14, 208
Silent Spring (Carson), 321
Silly Symphonies, 401
SimCity, 79
Simon, Neil, 175–176
Simon & Schuster, 316
The Simpsons, 21
The Sims Social, 78
simulation games, 73
Sinatra, Frank, 103, 138
Sinclair, Upton, 277
Sinclair Broadcast Group, 17
The Singing Fool, 209
Siouxsie and the Banshees, 113
Siri, 46, 47
Sirius, 150
SiriusXM, 152–153

sitcoms, 175, 176
Sitting Bull, 364
situational ethics, 431
situation comedy, 176
Sixth Amendment, 495–497
60 Minutes, 26–27, 82, 179, 195,
    236, 435
sketch comedy, 175–176
skyscraper model of culture, 15,
    18–20
Slacker, 121
slander, 491
Slate, 283, 284
slogans, 334
Slouching Towards Bethlehem
    (Didion), 245
Slovakia, 43
small-town pastoralism, 429
smartphones, 8, 12, 44, 45, 50,
    57, 70, 173, 328, 342
smart TVs, 221
"Smells Like Teen Spirit"
    (Nirvana), 113
Smith, Bessie, 104
Smith, Jamil, 212
Smith, Patti, 113
Smith, W. Eugene, 280–281
Smith Brothers, 331
Smithsonian, 287
Smithsonian Institution, 59
smokeless tobacco, 370
Smokey the Bear campaign,
    333–334
smoking, 370
Snapchat, 40, 41, 342, 408
Snavely, Andrew, 284
snob-appeal approach, 344
Snowden, Edward, 51, 443
*Snow White and the Seven
    Dwarfs*, 401, 402
social anxiety, 35–36
social apps, 40
social change, 277, 333–334, 507
social issues
    in media economics, 408–415
    journalism and, 439, 445
    magazines and, 245
    movies and, 220
    underground press and, 254
social learning theory, 466–467
social media, 9, 408, 420
    advertising, 341, 342–343
    cultural change and, 12–13
    democracy and, 41–43
    fraud and elections, 43
    magazines and, 292
    news and information from,
        3–4, 8
    public relations and, 376
    social anxiety and, 35–36
    trolls, 43
social movements, 41–42

social psychology studies,
    459–460
social reform, 276–277
social responsibility, 486
Society of Professional Journalists
    (SPK), 431, 432
Socrates, 14
software, open-source, 58–59
Sokal, Alan, 478
Song of Solomon (Morrison), 309
Sonic Youth, 113
Sony, 67, 68, 69, 85, 100, 172, 189,
    226
Sony Music Entertainment, 116
soul music, 110
sound bites, 250, 441
SoundCloud, 122
SoundExchange, 121
sound recording
    analog, 100
    business of, 116–119
    development of, 97–102
    digital, 100
    free expression and, 122
    impact of, 97
    Internet and, 100–102
    magnetic-tape, 99–100
    radio and, 102
    recording sessions, 117
    sales revenue, 99
Sousa, John Philip, 103
South America, 260
South Carolina Gazette, 239
South Korea, 57, 217
Soviet Union, 28, 39
space brokers, 330
Spacewar!, 64, 66
Spacey, Kevin, 174
spam, 340
Spanish-American War, 280
Spanish-language magazines,
    290
Spanish-language newspapers,
    252–253
Spanish-language radio, 148
Spanish-language television,
    180
special events, 371
specialization, 400–401
specialty magazines, 284–291
specialty reporters, 255
Spectrum, 40, 58
Spelunky, 70
Spicer, Sean, 308, 372
spiral of silence, 468
split-run editions, 292
sponsored links, 50
sponsored posts, 343, 376
sponsorship, television, 166
sports, fantasy, 71–72, 78
sports games, 73
Sports Illustrated, 286, 292, 294

sports magazines, 286
Spotify, 101–102, 119, 388, 404,
    412
Spotlight, 235–236
Springsteen, Bruce, 113
spyware, 51
Square Enix, 86
Standard Oil Company, 277, 278,
    366, 393
Stanford Research Institute
    (SRI), 337
Stanford University Artificial
    Intelligence Laboratory, 64
Star, 290
Starbucks, 377
StarCraft, 64, 85
start-up companies, 406, 408
Star Wars, 199–200, 222, 226
Star Wars: Episode VI, 200
Star Wars: Episode VII, 200, 223
Star Wars: The Old Republic,
    86, 88
State Champs, 113
State of Play Games, 89
State of the News Media report,
    259, 264–265
Stauber, John, 382
stealth ads, 355
stealth games, 73
Steam PC platform, 70, 88
Steffens, Lincoln, 277
Steinem, Gloria, 285
Stephens, Ann, 304
Stephenson, Randall, 396
stereo, 100
Stern, Howard, 504
Stewart, Jon, 446
Stockham, Thomas, 100
Stoller, Mike, 103
Stone, Emma, 344
Stone, I. F., 256
Stooges, 113
stories
    comfort of familiar, 20–21
    as foundation of media, 13–14
    in everyday life, 14–15
    See also narratives
storyboards, 338
story-driven model, of journalism,
    242
storytelling, 398–400
    disaster coverage and, 436
    oral, 301
    television and, 181
Stowe, Harriet Beecher, 275, 309,
    321
Stranger Things, 20, 24, 25, 45,
    161, 173, 188
Strategic Business Insights (SBI),
    337
strategy games, 73

streaming music, 101–102, 116, 119, 121, 151, 404
streaming video, 221, 223, 227, 388, 394, 404
Streisand, Barbara, 211
studio system, 205–211
    golden age of, 208–218
    outside of, 211
    transformation of, 218–221
Stverak, Jason, 424
Styx, 113
subeditors, 291–292
subliminal advertising, 334
subscription model, 88
subsidiary rights, 316
suburbs, 219–220
Sugarhill Gang, 114
suicide
    gender and, 475
    media portrayals of, 455–456
Sullivan, Ed, 110
Sullivan, L. B., 491
Summer, Donna, 114
Summit Entertainment, 225
Sun, 493
Sundance Film Festival, 215, 218
Sunday Times of London, 280
SunnyD, 350
Sun Records, 106
Super Bowl ads, 340
Super Mario Bros., 68
Super Mario Odyssey, 69
supermarket tabloids, 290
super PACs, 484
superstations, 169
superstore video chains, 214
Supremes, 110, 111
Surface tablet, 47
survey research, 464
survival games, 73
Sweden, 43, 57
Swift, Taylor, 95, 344
swing bands, 103
Switzerland, 471
syndication, 189–190
synergy, 225, 401, 404
Syria, 41–42, 57
Sza, 114

tablets, 12, 44, 70, 173, 311, 320
Tainter, Charles Summer, 98
talkies, 208–209
Talking Heads, 113
talking heads, 442
talk radio, 8, 145, 146–147
Talladega Nights, 348
Tampa Bay Times, 424
Tangerine, 228
Taobao Marketplace, 411
Tarbell, Ida, 277, 278, 366, 424
Target, 336, 398
targeted advertising, 50–51

Tatler, 274
Taylor, William Desmond, 499
TechAdvisory.org, 343
Technicolor, 221
technology
    advances in, 333
    computer, 281
    film, 201–203, 221
    magazines, 292
    television, 163–165
teen magazines, 288
Teen Mom, 23
Telecommunications Act of 1996, 47, 59, 139, 155–156, 186–187, 189, 394, 395, 502
telegraph, 7–8, 10, 22, 129
telenovela, 413
telephone, 44, 97
telephone group, 135
teleplays, 176
television, 8, 97, 161–197
    #MeToo movement and, 174
    advertising, 187, 192, 292, 327, 328, 329, 340, 350
    affiliate stations, 179, 189
    alternative, 194
    books and, 301, 309–310
    broadcasting, 169
    broadcast networks, 163, 168, 173, 182–183, 192–193
    cable, 59, 165, 168–171, 186
    channels, 165
    color, 165
    commercials, 15
    consolidation in, 194
    consumer culture and, 28
    controlling content on, 165–167
    convergence and, 44, 172–173, 191–192
    democracy and, 59, 194–195
    development of, 163–167
    digital gaming and, 78
    distribution, 189
    economics of, 187–194
    export of American, 170
    frequencies, 165
    future of, 195
    high-definition, 165
    highest-rated series, 192
    Hollywood and, 220–221
    Internet and, 172–173
    journalism and, 440–444
    measuring viewership, 190–192
    most popular shows, 175
    movies and, 219–221
    narrowcasting, 169
    Netflix and, 161–162, 388
    network era, 13, 168
    news, 440–444
    niche markets, 191
    on fourth screens, 173

    on third screens, 172–173
    origins of, 163–165
    photojournalism, 281
    prime time, 166, 182–183, 328, 329, 340
    production, 188–189
    program formats, 166
    public, 180–182
    quiz shows, 166–167
    radio and, 142
    ratings, 191
    reality shows, 13
    regulation of, 182–187
    satellite, 168, 171, 186, 193–194, 404, 412
    sets, 11
    shows, 12
    "smart," 44
    sponsorship, 166
    storytelling and, 181
    syndication, 188, 189–190
    technical standards for, 164–165
    technology, 163–165
    time shifting, 172
    video games and, 67
    viewing, 20
    visual language of, 443–444
    watching, 13
    See also cable television
television programming
    chapter shows, 177
    children's, 180
    comedy, 175–176
    dramas, 176–178
    episodic series, 177–178
    miniseries, 177
    network news, 178–179
    reality shows, 13, 173, 180
    serial programs, 177–178
    sitcoms, 175, 176
    sketch comedy, 175–176
    Spanish-language, 180
    trends, 173–182
television specials, 166
television stations, 165
Telstar, 168
Tencent, 411
The Ten Commandments, 208
Tennessean, 257
tenure, 309
terrorist organizations, 16
Tesla, Nikola, 132
testimonials, 344
Tetris, 67, 72
Texas Instruments, 142
textbooks, 306–307
textual analysis, 472–473
Texture, 293, 294
thaumatrope, 201
theater chains, 224
theme parks, 402

They Are Us (Hamill), 320
third-person effect, 468–469
third screens, 172–173
13 Reasons Why, 455–456
This American Life, 45
This Is Us, 45
Thomas, Lowell, 139
Thompson, Hunter S., 245
Thoreau, Henry David, 274
Thornton, Willie Mae, 105
3-D animation, 335
3-D movies, 221, 463
throwaway ethic, 19
Thug Life (Shakur), 115
Thursday Night Football, 328
Timberlake, Justin, 344
Time, 28, 35, 278–279, 280
Time Inc., 294, 408
time shifting, 172
Time Warner, 40, 394, 396, 408
Time Warner Cable, 194, 292
Timothy, Elizabeth, 238–239
Tin Pan Alley, 103
Tip Top Weekly, 304
Titanic, 133–134, 136
T-Mobile, 412
tobacco, 351–352, 356
Tocqueville, Alexis de, 457
Today Show, 401, 440
Todd, Chuck, 372
Tokyo Disney Resort, 403
Tokyo Game Show, 75
Tolkien, J. R. R., 310
toll broadcasting, 135
Tometi, Opal, 42
Tomlinson, Ray, 38
Top 40 radio, 143–144
Top Chef, 13
Torvalds, Linus, 58
Total Request Live, 116
tough questioning style, 439
Townsquare Media, 156
trade agreements, 400
trade books, 299, 305
trade magazines, 285
trademarks, 331
transistors, 142
Transparent, 48
Travel + Leisure, 287, 294
travel magazines, 287
Treasure Island, 401
Triangle Publications, 280, 281
Tribeca Film Festival, 218
Tribune Content Agency, 257
Tribune Media Services, 257
trolls, 43, 72–73, 417
True Detective, 177
True Story (Finkel), 433
Truffaut, François, 213
Trump, Donald, 9, 58, 247, 295, 308, 370, 372, 399, 425, 428, 443–444, 446–447, 450, 507

Trust, 204–205, 206
trusts, 393
Truth Initiative, 356
truTV, 497
Tucker, Sophie, 103
Tulsa World, 257
Tumblr, 247
TuneCore, 121–122
Tunisia, 41
Turner, Big Joe, 105
Turner, Ike, 110
Turner, Tina, 110
Turner Broadcasting, 394, 408
"Tutti Frutti" (Little Richard), 107, 108
TV Guide, 279–282, 288
TV parental guidelines, 460
TV: The Most Popular Art (Newcomb), 472
Twain, Mark, 245, 274, 314
12-12-12 Rule, 394
12 Years a Slave, 212
Twentieth Century Fox, 189, 205, 207, 225–226
21st Century Fox, 189, 224, 225, 226, 355, 396
Twenty-One, 166, 167
Twilight (Meyer), 310
Twitch, 64, 78, 405
Twitter, 4, 8, 12, 13, 28, 32, 40, 43, 247
   press releases on, 370
Tylenol, 377–378

Ubisoft, 86
Ultimate Ninja Storm Revolution, 69
Ultrasurf, 42
Ulysses (Joyce), 493
Uncharted, 85
Uncle Tom's Cabin (Stowe), 309, 321
underdeveloped countries, 57
underground press, 254
unemployment, 397–398
Unforgivable Blackness, 499
Unilever, 341
union labor, 397
United Artists, 205, 206, 208
United Features, 257
United Fruit, 374
United Independent Broadcasters (UIB), 137
United Kingdom, 43, 57, 76, 81, 258, 313, 320, 382, 406, 449
United Negro College Fund, 334
United Press International (UPI), 255
Universal, 208, 224, 226
Universal Accreditation Board (UAB), 380
Universal Music Group, 116

University of California-Irvine, 64
University of Utah, 64
university press books, 309
Univision, 156, 180
Unsane, 228
Uptown, 351
urban contemporary format, 148
Urbanization, 7
USA PATRIOT Act, 51, 494
USA Today, 45, 246, 247, 257, 262, 511
U.S. Constitution, 486–487.
   See also First Amendment
uses and gratifications model, 462, 463
U.S. Navy Seals, 16
U.S. News & World Report, 278
U.S. Supreme Court, 65, 89, 101, 104, 484
Us Weekly, 290
Utne Reader, 295

vacuum tubes, 131
Valens, Ritchie, 109
validity, in research, 463
Vallée, Rudy, 103
values
   American, 399–400
   family, 23, 314
   in American journalism, 427–429
Values and Lifestyles (VALS) strategy, 337–338, 339
Valve Corporation, 88
Vanderbilt, Cornelius, 393
Van Doren, Charles, 166, 167
Vanidades, 290
Vanity Fair, 288, 294, 334–335
Vann, Robert C., 251
vaudeville, 14, 103
vellum, 303
Velvet Underground, 113
Verizon, 40, 58, 396
Verne, Jules, 241, 287
vertical integration, 205, 207, 225–226, 319
Vevo, 101, 123
VHS, 172
Viacom, 192–193
Victor Talking Machine Company, 11, 98
Victrolas, 98
video
   digital, 227–228
   home, 172, 223
   mobile, 173
videocassette recorders (VCRs), 172, 221
videocassettes, 172
video games
   addiction to, 79

advertising and, 78–79
apps, 72
classic, 67
development of, 86
early, 65, 66–67
genres, 72, 73, 74
home consoles, 44, 67–70
independent, 88–89
Internet and, 70–72
licensing, 86–87
penny arcades and, 65–66
player communities, 72–74
rating system for, 84
television and, 67
tournaments, 63–64
   See also gaming, digital
video game stores, 88
video news releases (VNRs), 371
video-on-demand (VOD), 171, 223
video streaming, 45, 221, 223, 227, 388, 394
video-style ads, 335
video subscription services, 193
Vietnam, 353
Vietnam War, 245, 281
Vietnam War protests, 14, 110
Village Voice, 254
vinyl records, 98, 100, 119
violence
   film, 459, 463–464
   in digital gaming, 79, 82
   in media, 457
   masculinity and, 474–475
viral marketing, 338
Virginia Slims, 351
virtual communities, 72–74
virtual reality, 84
virtual worlds, 71
VistaVision, 221
visual design, 334–335
visual language, 443–444
vitascopes, 203
Vogue, 286, 294, 334–335
The Voice, 13, 173, 191
Voice of San Diego, 266
voice recognition, 47
Volkswagen, 340
Volvo, 355
voter turnout, 4

wage gap, 397–398
wages, 391, 397–398
Wagner-Hatfield Amendment, 148–149
Walk, Charlie, 120
Walker, John Brisben, 287
Walker, Stanley, 378
The Walking Dead, 24, 45
"Walk This Way" (Aerosmith), 114

Wallace, Dewitt, 278
Wallace, Lila Acheson, 278
walled garden, 45–46, 47
Wall Street Journal, 28, 180, 247, 258, 262, 392
Walmart, 119
Walt Disney Company. *See* Disney
Walt Disney World, 402
Walters, Barbara, 179
Walton, Mary, 424
waltz music, 97
War Advertising Council, 333
war coverage, 16–17, 266, 280, 281
Warcraft, 78
Warcraft III, 64
Warhol, Andy, 23
Warner, Jack L., 219
Warner Brothers, 207, 208–209, 219, 224
Warner Communications, 408
Warner Music Group, 116–117
War of the Worlds, 141, 287, 461
Warren, Robert, 488–489
Washington Post, 3, 4, 14, 246, 247, 263, 426, 448
Watchdog.org, 424
Watch Dogs, 86
Watergate scandal, 381, 426, 440, 484
WEAF, 135
Weavers, 111
web advertising, 50–51
web browsers, 39–40
Webcaster Settlement Act, 151–152
Webkinz, 71
websites
   gaming, 75
   opt-in/opt-out policies, 51
WeChat, 411
wedding media, 465
The Week, 278
Weekly Bangla Patrika, 253
weekly newspapers, 248
Weekly Standard, 295
Weinstein, Harvey, 42, 215, 225, 288
Weinstein Company, 225
Wells, H. G., 141, 287, 461
Wertham, Fredric, 301
Wertmüller, Lina, 211
West, Darrell, 4
Western Union, 8
Westinghouse, 134–135, 137
Westworld, 171
Wharton, Edith, 287
WhatsApp, 50
Where the Wild Things Are, 21
The White Album (Didion), 245
"White Christmas" (Berlin), 103

white cover music, 107–108
white flight, 212
White House Communications Office, 373
The Whole Booke of Psalms, 303
Who's Afraid of Virginia Woolf?, 500
Wicker, Tom, 246
Wiesel, Elie, 309
Wii, 68, 84
Wii Fit, 68, 79
Wii Sports, 68
WikiLeaks, 431, 449
Wildmon, Rev. Donald, 156
Williams, Brian, 178
Williamson, Sonny Boy, 104
Wilson, Woodrow, 133, 437
Windows Phone 8, 47
Winfrey, Oprah, 309–310, 391
Wired, 283
wireless earbuds, 101
Wireless Ship Act, 133, 139
wireless telegraphy, 8, 97, 130–131, 133, 136
Wireless Telephone Company, 131
wireless telephony, 131–132
wire services, 240, 255, 257
The Witcher, 78
The Witcher 3: Wild Hunt, 86
Without a Trace, 504

WNBC, 135
Wolfe, Tom, 245
The Wolf of Wall Street, 501
Wolf Warrior II, 216
Woman's Day, 285
Woman's Home Companion, 279
women
    advertising aimed at, 333, 351, 367
    directors, 211, 213
    in music industry, 113, 120–121
    in public relations, 368
    journalists, 423–424
    newspaper owners, 238–239
    stereotypes of, 345
women's magazines, 275–276, 282, 285
Women's March, 308
women's movement, 110, 245, 284
Wonderwall, 283
The Wonder Years, 176
Wood, Natalie, 220
Woodstock, 112
Woodward, Bob, 426
Working class, 7
World Association of Newspapers (WAN), 260
World Journal, 253

World of Warcraft, 70, 71, 74–75, 79, 85, 86, 88
World Trade Organization (WTO), 400
World War I, 133, 367
World War II, 138, 333, 369
World Wide Web, 39–40, 41
Wozniak, Steve, 48
Wreck-It Ralph, 211
A Wrinkle in Time (L'Engle), 310
writers
    book, 316–317
    magazine, 292
Written communication, 6
Wu, Brianna, 80, 81

Xbox, 47, 69–70, 84
Xbox 360, 69
Xbox Live, 69, 73
Xbox One, 69–70
X-Files, 24
Xlibris, 320
XL Recordings, 117
XM, 150
X-Men, 85
X-rating, 500

Yahoo!, 40, 41, 47, 340, 341
Yandex, 41
Yang, Gene Luen, 300

Yang, Jerry, 41
Yeah Yeah Yeahs, 113
yellow journalism, 240–242, 276–277
Yemen, 41
Young Frankenstein, 19
youth, voter turnout by, 4
youth culture, 104, 111–112
Youth's Companion, 288
youth smoking, 370
YouTube, 11, 12, 13, 43, 58, 119, 122, 172–173, 192, 195, 227, 328, 408
YouTube Gaming, 64
You've Got Mail, 318

Zappos, 320
Zaslov, David, 398
Zenger, Anna Maul, 239
Zenger, John Peter, 238
Ziering, Amy, 215
Zimmerman, George, 42
zines, 295
zoetrope, 201–202
Zomorodi, Manoush, 54–55
Zook, Kristal Brent, 408
Zuckerberg, Mark, 45, 50, 412
Zukor, Adolph, 205, 206–207
Zworykin, Vladimir, 164
Zynga, 86, 408

See media in action on LaunchPad

launchpadworks.com

Throughout this book, the text directs you to **LaunchPad for *Media & Culture***, where videos complement the material in the text. Below is a list of all the videos featured in the book, sorted by chapter. For directions on how to access these videos online, please see the instructions on the next page.

Chapter 1: Mass Media and the Cultural Landscape
Is Facebook the Future of News and Journalism?
30 Rock and Corporate Mergers
Agenda Setting and Gatekeeping (see p. 14)
The Simpsons and Soccer
The Media and Democracy

Chapter 2: The Internet, Digital Media, and Media Convergence
Is Snapchat More Like Facebook or Twitter? Neither.
Anonymous and Hacktivism
User-Generated Content

Chapter 3: Digital Gaming and the Media Playground
GameOn: The Mobile Platform for Sports Fans
Anita Sarkeesian and GamerGate
Video Games at the Movies: *Resident Evil* (see p. 78)
Tablets, Technology, and the Classroom

Chapter 4: Sound Recording and Popular Music
How Streaming Services are Saving the Music Industry
Recording Music Today (see p. 100)
Alternative Strategies for Music Marketing (see p. 119)
Touring Onscreen: Katy Perry

Chapter 5: Popular Radio and the Origins of Broadcasting
Radio Is Massively Underutilized Media: Robertson
Going Visual: Video, Radio, and the Web (see p. 149)
Radio: Yesterday, Today, and Tomorrow (see p. 154)
Streaming Music: "Bad Blood"

Chapter 6: Television and Cable: The Power of Visual Culture
Netflix Can't Take Over the World
Television Networks Evolve (see p. 172)
Television Drama: Then and Now (see p. 177)
What Makes Public Television Public? (see p. 183)
Changes in Prime Time
Wired or Wireless: Television Delivery Today

Chapter 7: Movies and the Impact of Images
Why *Black Panther* Could Be a Game Changer for the Film Industry
Race in Hollywood: Tyler Perry
The Theatrical Experience and *The Hobbit*
More Than a Movie: Social Issues and Film (see p. 229)
Technology in *Gravity*

Chapter 8: Newspapers: The Rise and Decline of Modern Journalism
How Print Engages in a Socially Networked World
Investigative Journalism Onscreen: *All the President's Men*
Newspapers and the Internet: Convergence (see p. 247)
Community Voices: Weekly Newspapers (see p. 259)
Newspapers Now: Balancing Citizen Journalism and Investigative Reporting

Chapter 9: Magazines in the Age of Specialization
Essence Magazine Begins a New Chapter
The Power of Photojournalism
Magazine Specialization Today (see p. 285)
Narrowcasting in Magazines (see p. 291)

Chapter 10: Books and the Power of Print
Amazon Bookstore Makes NYC Debut
Based On: Making Books into Movies (see p. 309)
Banned Books Onscreen: *Huck Finn*

Chapter 11: Advertising and Commercial Culture
Why Online Ad Spending May Surpass TV in Six Months
Advertising in the Digital Age
Advertising and Effects on Children (see p. 350)
Product Placement in the Movies: *E.T.*
Blurring the Lines: Marketing Programs across Platforms

Chapter 12: Public Relations and Framing the Message
Uber CEO Kalanick Caught on Video Arguing over Fares
Give and Take: Public Relations and Journalism (see p. 378)
Filling the Holes: Video News Releases
Going Viral: Political Campaigns and Video

Chapter 13: Media Economics and the Global Marketplace
Bibb Says Disney's Iger Is Going to Kill the Cable Industry
Disney's Global Brand (see p. 401)
The Impact of Media Ownership (see p. 412)
The Money behind the Media

Chapter 14: The Culture of Journalism: Values, Ethics, and Democracy
Is Assange the Biggest Threat to Government Secrets?
The Contemporary Journalist: Pundit or Reporter? (see p. 442)
Fake News/Real News with Joe Randazzo of *The Onion*
Journalism Ethics: What News Is Fit to Print?
The Objectivity Myth
Shield Laws and nontraditional Journalists

Chapter 15: Media Effects and Cultural Approaches to Research
Our Social Media Accounts Are Driving Us Crazy
Media Effects Research (see p. 461)
TV Effects: *2 Broke Girls*

Chapter 16: Legal Controls and Freedom of Expression
Reddit CEO Says Net Neutrality Vote Stifles Competition
Stephen Colbert Interviews John Seigenthaler
Bloggers and Legal Rights (see p. 504)
Bullying Converges Online
Freedom of Information